THE CENTENNIAL DIRECTORY OF THE AMERICAN ACADEMY IN ROME

THE CENTENNIAL DIRECTORY OF THE AMERICAN ACADEMY IN ROME

EDITED BY

BENJAMIN G. KOHL
FOR THE SOCIETY OF FELLOWS

WAYNE A. LINKER &
BUFF SUZANNE KAVELMAN
FOR THE AMERICAN ACADEMY IN ROME

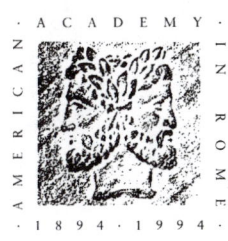

NEW YORK & ROME
1995

Copyright © 1995 American Academy in Rome

American Academy in Rome
7 East 60 Street
New York, NY 10022-1001

Library of Congress Cataloging-in-Publication Data

American Academy in Rome.
    The centennial directory of the American Academy in Rome / edited by Benjamin G. Kohl for the Society of Fellows, Wayne A. Linker & Buff Suzanne Kavelman for the American Academy in Rome.
        p. cm.
    Includes bibliographical references and index.
    ISBN 1-879549-02-6
    1. American Academy in Rome—Directories. 2. Artists--Directories. I. Kohl, Benjamin G. II. Linker, Wayne A. III. Kavelman, Buff Suzanne, 1956- . IV. American Academy in Rome. Society of Fellows. V. Title.
NX21.2.A46A46 1995
700'.92'2—dc20
[B]   95-18310
                                 CIP

ISBN 1-879549-02-6

Printed in the United States of America
5 4 3 2 1

CONTENTS

FOREWORD

WRITING THE FOREWORD to the first Directory of Fellows on the occasion of the 100th anniversary of the American Academy in Rome is a formidable task. The institution has always been quiet and to a certain extent mysterious, so it is a departure to look at it in a larger context, over a longer time, and with a more reflective view of the community.

But observing the Centennial anniversary this year has afforded us many insights that make this possible. First, we feel tremendously blessed to have been launched at the turn of a century when there was optimism, public spiritedness, and ample support for the arts. We feel fortunate to have survived ten unimaginably eventful decades, because in this day and age we could never invent the Academy anew – with its priceless buildings and grounds on the highest point in Rome, its serious but serendipitous history, and its glorious associations.

In fact the most striking fact about our story is that young as we are in the history of the world, we are old indeed in terms of the history of the United States, representing in our one century nearly half the history of the republic.

Thus we cherish most of all the generations of extraordinary people who have been part of the Academy – its Fellows, Residents, Visitors, Directors, Professors-in-Charge, Trustees and staff. They *have* always been the heart of it, and they are the reason this book had to come into being.

The original mission of the Academy was to develop taste, skills, and scholarship in its Fellows. Like any good trip away from home, the experience of being in Rome taught our first Fellows as much about American values as it did about those abroad. Today our small band of artists and scholars gets a similar perspective but also, *de facto,* a more global vision. We are now taking part in a tremendous transition, not only on the Janiculum, but in Italy, in Europe, and on the planet as a whole.

In the late 1800s, going to Rome involved a long sea voyage and took many weeks. Today, we reach Rome in a matter of hours; we are then instantly awash in E-mail, faxes, and contemporary questions.

But the wise still find a place and an experience that have always been the Academy – a center for independent study and advanced research in the fine arts and humanities, a block of time, a measure of peace and quiet, a supportive and stimulating community, a wonderful library, an inexhaustible culture, and a feeling of belonging.

In the words of Gjertrud Schnackenberg, FAAR 84:

"For any artist from anywhere, to have arrived in Rome is to have arrived, at last, at the measure, the calibration, of total artistry, of sublime craftsmanship, of miraculous feats of engineering, vision, and invention. Rome is, necessarily, a summons, and an affirmation of the artist's most personal, overwhelming business, which is that of creating images worthy of being added to that fraction of time known, in Rome, as *aeternitas.*"

So it is the same Rome, but the structure under the Academy has changed as much as life itself has over the last few years. When we started in 1894, the world may have looked steady and promising, but it was not. We have been through two World Wars, the Depression and recessions, the Bauhaus and the Sixties. Now we have currency fluctuations, skyrocketing costs, and disappearing governments.

Although our original founders provided a nest egg large enough to get us through our first seventy-five years, the New York office came into being as costs rose, the Academy slipped somewhat out of view, and fund-raising for a larger endowment became a necessity.

The key to New York now is that it provides a "homeroom" for the Fellows who have returned to the U.S., and, in a variety of ways, it works to fortify the institution abroad. The staff organize the juries and the annual Rome Prize competition, and support a Board of Trustees who increasingly amaze us with their dedication and generosity. New York is also a vessel in which Rome happenings can be repeated – shop talks, book presentations, small exhibits or meetings. But our job is to support and serve Rome, and we are all most rewarded when we are able to see Rome in action.

In Rome, too, the staff have had to change to keep up with the demands of the times. The Director is not just the head intellectual, but also ambassador, mayor, impresario, and community mentor. The Rome staff helps the Director as well as the Fellows: they organize the outings, exhibitions, and concerts, procure the *permessi,* run the library, manage the "hotel," organize and assist with the summer programs, restore and maintain the buildings and grounds, and make it all seem effortless.

In Rome, day-to-day life has changed tremendously in a century. Servants have been replaced by communal laundries, kitchens and darkrooms; we have desk-top publishing, photocopy machines, and a computerized card catalogue in the library. Self reliance is the order of the day. We are reducing the number of steps and expenses required to accomplish our mission and maintaining the necessities so that our artists and scholars can work.

And, on the whole, the place feels the same. Intimacy comes from the smallness of the group, the length of the stays, communal life, and the frequent discovery of common ground. So while the place is not frozen in time, it is still a constant in a wildly changing world.

And the quality of what emerges is remarkable.

The Academy is immensely proud of its alumni, of the work they have aspired to do and have done, of the lives they have led, of what they have made of Rome, and of what they have added to it. We are gratified by the un-selfconscious associations we have been able to afford them by putting them around the dinner table, by packing them together for scholarly walks and trips, and by giving them a key to the library twenty-four hours a day.

And we are determined to continue this gently evolving, beloved, old-fashioned quality-conscious institution. To accomplish this, during our Centenary, we have had five goals: to re-endow the fellowships and the operation of the institution; to restore and renovate the physical plant in Rome, to broaden the Academy's constituency in the United States, to deepen the Academy's relationship with Italy, and to grow beyond our 19th century island into a 21st-century cultural crossroads.

We have made significant progress. The Centennial campaign is nearing its $20 million goal. We have returned the main building in Rome to full use after a painstaking renovation. Last summer, the President of the United States signed a Joint Resolution of Congress honoring the Academy, and the President of Italy presided over the rededication ceremonies in Rome.

But we have a long way to go. We are still fortifying and paying for the fellowships, the library, and the programs, still conserving our rare books, archives, and ancient artifacts.

And to the core community of Fellows, Residents and Visiting Artists and Scholars, members of the Summer School, Summer Seminar, and Summer Program in Italian Archaeology, and the library readers, we have added a handful of new kinds of artists and scholars: last year, for the first time, we introduced, for three months each, three scholars from East-Central Europe. It was also the first year of our regional visiting artists program that draws artists, designers, and composers from targeted geographic areas of the United States.

It has become apparent that this compact group of carefully chosen people is interesting not only to itself but also to the world beyond. Many have been recognized at the highest levels. Our ranks include two winners of the Nobel Prize, four U.S. Poets Laureate, seven winners of the Medal of Arts, thirty Pulitzer Prize winners, nine MacArthur Fellows, one Kennedy Center honoree, seven MacDowell medalists, and countless Guggenheim and Fulbright Fellows.

But the idea of this directory came from the Fellows, whose insatiable curiosity about one another, and pride in this anniversary made it fitting to produce a volume that provided not only each one's vital statistics, but also a sense of each one's callings and achievements.

The project took five years and was a joint venture between the Fellows and the Academy staff. Ben Kohl, FAAR 71, suggested it, Peter Rolland,

FAAR 78, President of the Society of Fellows supported the idea, many Fellows helped with the research, Buff Kavelman supervised it all along, and Emma Scioli worked on it day and night over the last year. The Festschrifts were so cheering they were interspersed as "signatures" among the biographies of their authors. Caroline Bruzelius encouraged us from Rome. Wayne Linker, Jerry Max and William M.V. Kingsland made sure the end result matched up to our most ambitious expectations. Eileen Gardiner and Ronald G. Musto, FAAR 79, both of Italica Press, are our publishers.

No one gets involved with the Academy – whether it be as a Fellow, a Resident, a staff member, or a Trustee – and emerges *indifferent* to it. We all pass through many institutions in life – schools, clubs, churches, colleges – but few are inspired to the kind of loyalty we find for the Academy. It is rare to encounter an "Academy person" who does not put Rome among the top two or three experiences of a lifetime – is it because of the beauty and resources of the place, the quality and variety of the friendships, the depth of Rome, or the time and freedom to work?

The people in this book feel differently than an average group of alumni. At times, the Academy seems like a family, with all the involvements and expectations that entails. At other times, it seems like an institution, with all those traditions and rituals.

Everyone to some extent represents that character in the pages that follow. This is our first edition, and it is full of information, but also imperfections and omissions. We hope it will be issued many times after this, and we look forward to your suggestions and corrections. But most of all, we thank everyone who has been involved in this long labor of love.

Adele Chatfield-Taylor, FAAR 84
President
3 February 1995

■   ■   ■

PREFACE

CONCEIVING THIS PROJECT

THE CONCEPT of a *Centennial Directory* was first bruited a decade ago in the deliberations of the Council of the Society of Fellows under the Presidency of Virginia Bush, FAAR 77. Discussing the question of how best to publicize the enormous achievements of the Academy's Fellows and Residents, it was decided to canvass Fellows and Residents for their resumes and curricula vitae to provide the documentary basis for this achievement. Though the response was good, it was uneven, and the logical next step was to make some sort of systematic inquiry to document the careers of the nearly 1,400 Fellows and Residents, living and dead. The basis for such an inquiry were the names listed in "Directory of Fellows and Residents" published in pamphlet form under the editorship of Virginia Bush in 1984 and updated in 1988. Added to the printed "Directory" were extensive computer files of names, addresses with records of education and employment that had been compiled under Virginia Bush's direction. Thus, by 1988, the American Academy in Rome possessed the instruments to undertake the systematic collection of data for what was to become *The Centennial Directory*.

At this point, the then Secretary of the Society of Fellows, Benjamin G. Kohl, FAAR 71, proposed the creation of a questionnaire which would provide a uniform set of data from all living Fellows and Residents and the format for data collection of the deceased Fellows. The Council of the Society of Fellows, under the leadership of Michael Schwarting, FAAR 70, authorized the exploration of the creation of a questionnaire and the Academy's Trustees and staff confirmed their interest in the project. Benjamin Kohl employed Randolph Cornelius, Associate Professor of Psychology at Vassar, to draw up the questionnaire. The early drafts of the questionnaire went through several permutations, and it was put in final form through the good offices of William Plumb, FAAR 86, of the Plumb Design Group in New York. After exploring several pub-lishing possibilities, the Academy commissioned Italica Press of New York to act as its publishers for this project.

COMPILING THE DIRECTORY

THE TASK IN HAND was no easy one; for not only were nearly 1,000 living Fellows and Residents to be contacted (and sometimes re-found) for this undertaking; but over 300 deceased FAARs and RAARs had also to be identified. Yet, nearly 400 had already responded to the questionnaire with details of their lives, work, and achievements, and the Academy generously opened both its archives and its databases to us to generate lists, compare their various versions, and finally fine tune a definitive roster of those included here. For this work a staff of six people went through files of recent FAARs and RAARs, combed through the Academy's archival materials, researched biographical resources, took copious notes, and provided us with the wealth of material needed to begin.

It soon became clear, however, that much of the material already gathered was quickly growing outdated. For so active a group of creators as the Academy community two or three years was a long time indeed; and the decision was therefore made to launch an entirely new mailing to gather in those questionnaires that had not yet been received and to proceed on a tight but manageable schedule worked out at the Academy offices to bring this book to publication during the Centennial celebration year. Fellows and Residents responded either by completing the questionnaires themselves or by submitting CVs, firm brochures, and other promotional materials. Biographies for Fellows and Residents who did not respond to the questionnaires were compiled at the Academy offices in New York by Emma Scioli and Kate Nitze, working from the Academy's files and standard biographical reference works. Entries for these 185 Fellows and Residents naturally vary in detail with only sketchy information available for nearly thirty Residents; still a considerable effort was made to contact and research all of the missing biographees.

While these responses and compiled entries were being assembled, Italica Press set out to design a database that included all the information on the questionnaire form and that contained more category fields for the in-house use of the Academy staff. The software was off-the-shelf (Filemaker Pro); and the design soon emerged after several meetings with the Academy office to make sure we were all in agreement about what would be entered and in what format.

Italica then began entering the information received: both manually, and by scanning via OCR (optical character recognition) software (Caere's Omnipage) from the questionnaires, then transferring the information into the database using the multi-tasking capacity of the Macintosh workstation. Once all the information from the questionnaires was input to the database, the database itself had to undergo some basic editing for consistency, format, and accessibility.

With the database in proper shape – and coordinated with four others being assembled simultaneously at the Academy and by other researchers – we began doing "dumps" (electronic transfers) from the database to a word-processing program (Microsoft Word 5.2 for the Mac). This raw text was then in the condition to undergo serious copy-editing, for consistency of entry style, types of information contained, its order of presentation, and for basic accuracy. Since many of the questionnaires were becoming dated, and since we were working against a very clear deadline, the decision was made that the biographees themselves would have the main responsibility for editing and updating their biographies.

By the Fall of 1994 the entries spun out of the database were therefore copy-edited and proofread for obvious typos, spelling, and stylistic mistakes. They were then sent off in galley-proof form to the nearly 850 living biographees over a period of about six months. Meanwhile Benjamin Kohl was doing the same for the deceased along with a team of expert scholars, architects, composers, painters, and sculptors who could pick out obvious typo-

graphic and stylistic errors, but who could also recognize research gaps and factual blunders and whose knowledge of their fields guaranteed that no important detail of these lives would be omitted.

The corrected galleys and proofs were then returned to Italica Press, where all the corrections were entered into the electronic Microsoft Word files. Benjamin Kohl explains below the process followed for the deceased; but essentially these were then compiled into various data bases designed at Italica Press and arranged by field of endeavor, which were eventually merged with the main data base of living biographees. Once first galleys were generated using the same methods, they were reviewed by Italica, by Benjamin Kohl, and then by the Academy team of experts within each field.

DECEASED FELLOWS AND RESIDENTS

SOME ONE QUARTER of all the Fellows and Residents (app. 325 out of 1360) whose biographical sketches are included in this *Directory* are deceased. In the early years of the Academy most fellowships were in architecture and classical studies and archaeology, with some awarded for painting and sculpture, and from the early 20s onward in landscape architecture and musical composition. Hence, the majority of the deceased Fellows, who studied at the Academy in the first half of the century, were architects and classicists. They include some giants in these fields, such as the architects John Russell Pope, James Kellum Smith, and Louis Kahn, sculptor Leo Friedlander, and the classicists Lily Ross Taylor, Richmond Lattimore, James H. Oliver, Jr., and Frank E. Brown. And, of course, the *Directory* contains entries on many illustrious deceased Fellows and Residents in other fields, from Aaron Copland in Musical Composition and Philip Guston in Painting to Robert Penn Warren and Mary McCarthy in Literature. But the *Directory* also includes entries on much less famous deceased Fellows in all fields. The documentary evidence available for the careers of these Fellows is sometimes rather thin. With the agreement of the Academy's President Adele Chatfield-Taylor, FAAR 84, and the publishers, Ronald G. Musto, FAAR 79, and Eileen Gardiner of Italica Press, data-entry began from Academy's folders available in the New York office. These typically included applications and subsequent correspondence, augmented by data gathered under Virginia Bush's direction, systematized at Vassar by Allison Scardino, and donated to the Academy's New York archives. All the data in the New York office was entered by Abraham Barretto and Emma Scioli.

When the file for each deceased Fellow and Resident was completed as much as possible from the Academy's own records, the files were copied and shipped to Co-Editor Kohl at Vassar College in Poughkeepsie in the autumn of 1993. There Kohl and his research assistant, Michael Rambadt of the Vassar College Class of 1995, made photocopies of entries on deceased Fellows from a variety of reference works. The identification of potential sources in the public record was made easier by Vassar College Library's copy on CD-ROM of *Gale's Biography and Genealogy Master Index*, which provides source references for over four million persons, indexing 700 biographical dictionaries of all sorts. In the late Spring of 1994 Laura Kohl Ball joined the project to complete the data-entry for hundreds of deceased Fellows and Residents, whose entries were in one way or another still incomplete. It would have been literally impossible to produce this *Directory* without her weeks of patient, careful work in gathering and entering data for the deceased persons listed here.

The data entry done in the late Spring of 1994 was checked and improved by Benjamin Kohl before the disks were dispatched to Italica Press, where Eileen Gardiner and Ronald Musto again checked each entry for accuracy, sometimes adding new information. From December 1994 through March 1995 Benjamin Kohl read three sets of proofs for all the deceased Fellows and Residents, answering many queries from the editors at Italica. In many instances all three editors had been able to augment and improve the entries, especially materials on careers, awards, and publications.

Invaluable for entries on many deceased Academy classicists has been Ward W. Briggs, Jr., *Bio-graphical Dictionary of North American Classicists* (Westport, CT & London: Greenwood Press, 1994), which became available only when the *Directory* was already in proofs. But the some thirty deceased Academy Fellows and Residents given entries in the *Biographical Dictionary* have been cross-listed in our *Directory* to the proper pages in Briggs, which often contain the most complete account of a particular classical scholar.

In the final stages the editors have been helped by area experts: Andrea Olmstead and Brian Mann on Fellows and Residents in Music, Peter Rolland, FAAR 78, for the Landscape Architects, Susan Smyley, FAAR 67, for the Sculptors, George A. Hinds, FAAR 84, for Architects, Kathy Muehlemann, FAAR 88, for Painters, and Laurie Nussdorfer, FAAR 81, of Wesleyan University, retiring Editor of the SOF Newsletter, for a list of recent dates of death of Fellows and Residents. The editors received authoritative help on individual entries from Nicholas Adams, FAAR 88, on Richard Krautheimer, Darby Scott, FAAR 66, for Frank Brown and Lily Ross Taylor, Olympia Lee Falk for Kenneth Sawyer Falk, Joyce P. Gordon for Arthur Ernest Gordon, Ann Ellis Hanson for John Arthur Hanson, Mabel Lang for Richmond Lattimore, J. David Bishop for Doris Taylor Bishop, Virginia Brown, FAAR 68, for E.A. Lowe, Ingrid Edlund-Berry, FAAR 84, for Kyle M. Phillips, Jr., J. Kellum Smith, Jr. for James Kellum Smith, Larissa Bonfante for Ralph Van Deman Magoffin, and Malcolm Bell III, FAAR 70, for Erik Sjöqvist. Most of all, we are indebted to Katherine A. Geffcken, FAAR 55, of Wellesley College for all her work on the careers and publications of the early Fellows in Classics. She has been especially helpful in improving the accuracy of the Historical Lists, and proofreading all the entries on less well-known classicists. At her instance the editors decided to distinguish the designations for those classicists who held fellowships at the American Academy Rome from 1913 onward (FAAR) from the early Fellows of the American School of Classical Studies in Rome (FASCSR). Though the early Fellows in Classical Studies and Christian Archaeology were fully accepted as Fellows of the American Academy after the merger of the two institutions in 1913, historical accuracy still demands that the two sets of Fellows be given their different designations.

A matter of great concern has been to supply the dates of death of all deceased Fellows. Over eighty entries lacked a definite dates of death on the first proofs circulated in December 1994. Benjamin Kohl's culling of national newspapers and the Academy files in New York provided the date of death for a few more entries, and his queries to a number of colleges and universities have provided the date or year of death for over sixty entries. The editors are grateful for information, especially on degrees and dates of death, provided by archivists and alumni officers at Beloit, Brown, Bryn Mawr, Chicago, Columbia, Cornell, Harvard, Haverford, Johns Hopkins, Michigan, Pennsylvania, Princeton, Tufts, Wisconsin, and Yale.

EDITORIAL PROCESS & CONVENTIONS

ALL THE COPY-EDITING had been completed by March 1995. Italica Press was then ready to transfer the type to a page-composition program. The book was composed on PageMaker; and its ability to integrate finely-tuned text with images and a demanding style sheet – and still leave room for a variety of solutions to any number of design and editorial problems – served well during this process.

The *Centennial Directory* that you now read takes advantage of a remarkable and very recent breakthrough in print technology: a printer's ability to take a diskette produced by a publisher in such a program as PageMaker and to turn it into the basic unit of the printing process — a series of printer's plates — far more quickly and accurately than had previously been possible using either hand composition or Linotype and its photographic offshoots.

The technical and editorial process of turning the lives of over 1400 Fellows and Residents of the first century of the American Academy into a useful reference tool was necessarily one of reduction: not only the multidimensional lives and works of so many talented and productive people, but also the very wide differences of style and content among so many fields of endeavor that come together in

Rome at the American Academy. Thus the same format for important works – with only slight modification – that was set out in the original questionnaires was adhered to whether the biographee were a historian of second-century Rome or a performance artist whose works might flash by briefly on the Brooklyn waterfront without permanent record. If we have at times seemed to neglect these differences and to have penciled – and red inked – over nuances we apologize to our biographees but offer as our defense the natural tendency of editors to make all life forms two dimensional and point to the necessities of a vast project of this type and the need to have its information appear as consistently as possible for the present and future user.

Such consistency is apparent in several areas that we use as examples here: the designations of fields of endeavor raised many long-distance eyebrows and elicited many polite questions: "Post-Classical/Humanistic Studies," "Classics/Archaeology," "Design Arts," "History" and finally "History of Art" were among the most frequently raised topics of conversation. The year of fellowship drew a close second, however; but both Fellows and Residents accepted the fact that the Academy has designated as the official fellowship year only their last. Finally, biographees gallantly complied with the somewhat artificial "dozen" rule we were forced to impose on this wealth of material. We therefore ask the indulgence of those who know for a certain fact that they spent more than the one designated as their Academy year; that Academy biographees have produced far more work, had far more exhibitions mounted in their name, received many more awards, and served on far more boards, editorial committees, award juries, and have had many more articles and *Who's Who* entries compiled about them than the baker's dozen we have allowed here.

Apropos of our editorial practices, we should now explain to the reader that the *Directory* also includes two other sorts of entries: Brief Biographies for those members of the Academy community who have been neither Fellows not Residents but whose affiliations and service to the American Academy warrant their inclusion herein; and a third category: one- or two-line listings of non-FAAR or RAAR Charter Members, Trustees, Directors, and Professors-in-Charge, Officers, Staff in both New York and Rome, Affiliated Fellows, Italian Committee Members, and Notable Visitors. These are integrated among the more substantial biographies and provide the name, occupation, and years of such visits or affiliation when known. When the exact years of a visit have not been recorded, we have used the convention of a known range of years indicated by an "m" dash, thus: "1940 — 1945." Known years are indicated by the "n" dash: 1940-45." While the *Directory's* primary goal has been to chronicle the lives and achievements of its Fellows and Residents, it seemed only just that such worthy company be given its due herein.

In the course of planning this *Directory*, the original editors made provision for, and invited all biographees to submit pieces of art, music, written work, and other brief memoirs as tributes to this institution. These "Festschrifts" were submitted by over 200 respondents; and all have been reproduced here and set as close as possible to the entry for the person who created them.

HOW TO USE THIS DIRECTORY

THE FOLLOWING DIRECTORY includes entries on those women and men who have passed through the gates of the American Academy in Rome from its founding in 1894 through the 1994 Fellowship year. All entries are arranged alphabetically, by last name. Full entries provide the following information by topic and then in ascending order by date (most recent last):

NAME (LAST, FIRST, MI) ■ Fellowship or Residence designation and year; other Academy affiliations and years. **Education**: including degree, year, institution. **Other Study**: especially among biographees in the design, visual, and performing arts, naming famous masters under whom they studied; but also for those in the humanities, giving information on non-degree study, with dates if available. **Research/Artistic Interests**: this usually includes a personal statement of the biographee, sometimes a few words, and where the body of work is complex or does not fit into a traditional category, a bit longer. **Career & Employment**: full-time positions listing Institution or Firm, Position & Dates, and then visiting position, and occasional posts. **Memberships & Offices**: includes committees, scholarly and professional societies, and the like, with Institution, Position & Dates. **Fellowships, Honors & Awards**: Granting Institution, Grant Name, Dates. **Publications**: "Article Title," *Journal* 4.1 (Sept. 1900): 000-000; "Article Title in Book or Collection," in *Book Title*, ed. J.H. Doe (New York & London: Publisher, 1900), 00-000; *Book Title* (City: Publisher, 1900); with John Doe, *Book Title*, etc., arranged in ascending chronological order. **Important Works**: here are placed the works of painters, sculptors, designers, architects, composers, and, sometimes, of performance artists. They generally follow the same rules as the above; with the following exceptions: painters and sculptors work are recorded for the most part by the public and private collections housing them, and generally without dates; composers pieces are arranged in the following way: *Title of Work*, instrumentation, Commissioning Institution (Publisher, Recording Label) Date. Architectural and landscape architectural works are recorded by project name, client name, city, state, and date. **Exhibitions/Performances**: here are listed the exhibitions in the visual arts, providing the gallery, city, and date; and sometimes the work of performance artists and designers. **Bio-Bibliography**: this section includes books, exhibition catalogs, dictionary listings, articles, reviews, film, TV, and documentaries *about* Academy biographees. **Home Address. Business Address.**

THIS BOOK ALSO CONTAINS several useful apparatus. The first is a complete list of the abbreviations used in the following entries. By way of caution, our readers will find that many of their most familiar journals and reference works have been rather obviously spelled out (this a necessity in a publication that spans so many other fields of expertise) and that such obvious bodies as the Archaeological Institute of America have emerged from our hands as ArIA, the American Institute of Architects as AIA, the former American Academy of Arts and the American Academy and Institute of Arts & Letters as AAAL. On this score we beg the reader's and biographees' indulgence; but offer the excuse that no one field of study or endeavor has taken precedence in our efforts or attentions.

The second, following the biographies, is a series of lists: rosters of Fellows and Residents arranged by Field and Year, Affiliated Fellows, Notable Visitors, Contributing Institutions, Officers, Trustees, Charter Members, the Italian Committee, Directors and Professors-in-Charge, and the Staff in both New York and Rome.

WHEN THE AMERICAN ACADEMY and the Society of Fellows began this project they set two major goals: first, to compile as complete and accurate a record of the members and achievements of the Academy community as possible; and second, to present this in a worthy volume during the Centennial anniversary year. In accomplishing these goals the editors apologize for any errors of commission or omission but more importantly offer their thanks to the hundreds of individuals and to the institutions who ultimately made it possible.

But despite these efforts and cooperation, we still lack full biographies of several living Fellows and Residents, and a definite date of death for nearly twenty deceased Fellows. Thus, while every effort has been made to ensure the accuracy of each entry, no doubt, gaps and mistakes still remain in a work of this magnitude and scope. This is a beginning, not the end of the enormous task of identifying thousands of American artists, designers, writers, composers and scholars who have spent time at the American Academy in Rome.

Benjamin G. Kohl, FAAR 71
Eileen Gardiner
Ronald G. Musto, FAAR 79
April 9, 1995

■   ■   ■

HISTORICAL INTRODUCTION

THE AMERICAN ACADEMY IN ROME is the foremost American overseas center for independent study and advanced research in the fine arts and the humanities. At its principal site in Rome, the Academy operates a program that has at its core the development of gifted American artists and scholars but that reaches out to an international audience as well. From its New York City office the Academy administers the annual Rome Prize competition to select the Fellows, who are joined in Rome by other distinguished artists and scholars, forming a community of approximately seventy-five residents. In addition, the Academy sponsors exhibitions, concerts, lectures, and symposia that draw audiences to the Rome campus and to the New York headquarters. A first-class research library, a series of summer programs, and projects in archaeology and publishing complement these activities, enabling the Academy to serve more than three thousand people each year.

Originally modeled on the two-centuries-old French Academy at the Villa Medici, the American Academy in Rome was conceived in Chicago at the World's Columbian Exposition of 1893 commemorating the 400th anniversary of Columbus' voyage to America. The planners of the Exposition had erected a temporary building called *the shack* on an island in a man-made lagoon where Chief of Construction Daniel Burnham assembled an elite cadre of the country's most talented architects and artisans to design and build the utopian "White City."

When the Exposition closed the following year, the Rome academy had already become a small but promising reality. One of Burnham's colleagues in Chicago was Charles Follen McKim, of the New York architectural firm of McKim, Mead & White, and together, these two energetic, visionary and determined men, abetted by architect Richard M. Hunt, painters John LaFarge and Francis Millet, and sculptors Augustus Saint-Gaudens and Daniel Chester French – the same artisans with whom they had collaborated in building "the fair to end all fairs" in Chicago – took the initiative to convert talk into action, launching the Academy with funds raised from Chicagoans Cyrus McCormick, Marshall Field, Levi Leiter, Franklin MacVeagh and from their own pockets. The Academy they envisioned concentrated on exposing American students of architecture to the classical archetypes of Roman civilization, but the Academy's activities rapidly swelled to encompass the gamut of the arts and humanities, as well as classical scholarship.

Additional support from philanthropists like J. Pierpont Morgan, Andrew Carnegie, John D. Rockefeller, Jr., William K. Vanderbilt, and Henry Clay Frick enabled the Academy gradually to acquire its eleven-acre site on Rome's highest hill, the Janiculum, remodel and construct buildings providing accommodation, and raise an endowment to fund its programs.

Though chartered by Congress in 1905, the American Academy is the only one among the twenty-four foreign academies in Rome not directly supported by its national government. It relies on the financial support of individuals, foundations, corporations, and other American academic institutions, as well as the National Endowments for the Arts and the Humanities, to provide its $5-million annual program budget. Gifts to the American Academy in Rome are deductible for income and estate-tax purposes to the extent permitted by law.

From the outset the ideal of *community* has been fundamental to the American Academy in Rome. With neither faculty, curriculum, nor student body, Fellows come to Rome to refine and expand independently their own professional, artistic, or scholarly aptitudes, drawing on their colleagues' erudition and experience as well as the inestimable resources of the Italian capital, Europe, and the Mediterranean as a whole. Fellows join Residents, eminent artists and scholars from the United States and other countries invited by the Academy's director and trustees to become part of the Rome community for several months, and other distinguished visiting artists and scholars to form a lively residential, multidisciplinary forum. In summer, the Academy population expands as archaeologists and seminar participants, college students and high-school teachers, visitors and library users are drawn up the Janiculum to take advantage of the institution's programs and resources.

The Academy offers the opportunity to return to the source of our Western humanistic heritage and to engage in a dialogue with Rome's culture. In no other city has history as unfailingly enriched the fabric of daily life. Time spent at the Academy allows residents – stimulated in part by varied walks, talks, tours, and trips, a stream of visitors, and spontaneous table talk – to enter into informed discourse with this past and to draw upon it for their individual explorations.

For a century, the Academy has been a constant force for the enhancement of American culture. In 1994, in honor of the Academy's Centennial, the President of the United States signed a Joint Resolution of Congress in recognition of the Academy's one hundred years of contributions to American intellectual and cultural life. The value of the Academy to teaching, research, scholarship, and artistry is embodied in its legacy of painters and poets, musicians and architects, scholars and sculptors.

Speaking on April 21,1994 at last year's Rome Prize award ceremony at the White House, Hillary Rodham Clinton said:

"With the presentation of the Rome Prize in a few minutes, we will launch the celebration of the 100th birthday of the American Academy in Rome, the institution that has been supporting individual artists and scholars abroad longer than any other entity in United States history. As you can see by the strength of our numbers here today, the Academy is still going strong, and it has long been known to American presidents. By 1905, it had been chartered by Congress for its contributions to the arts and humanities. Its founder, Charles McKim, became a friend of President Theodore Roosevelt while working on one of the earliest restorations of the White House.

McKim's creativity not only shaped designs within this building, but also shaped generations of architects, landscape architects, painters, sculptors, composers, writers, classicists, and scholars.

The Academy's mission has not changed, but the people it is sending to Rome today are as diverse as our nation itself. A hundred years ago, the Rome Prize winners were young, single, white men studying the classics...today they are men and women of all backgrounds and ages, from all over the United States, studying many different subjects. Elite only in their promise, their vision, their imagination and their intellect, they are participants in a larger international community joined together in an ancient city to help enhance the knowledge and progress of modern times.

Now that the Centennial is here, I think I can safely say we are off to a great start for the next hundred years. To those of you whose generous support has helped sustain the Academy and the role it plays in expanding American culture we are grateful."

■ ■ ■

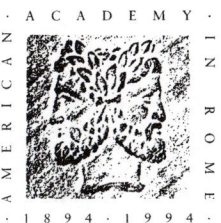

From the Society of Fellows

What more relevant single item could better document the contribution to the arts and scholarship in this country than this *Centennial Directory*. The listing of all those Fellows and Residents who, for the last century since the Academy's founding, have been the constant source of betterment of American culture.

The Society of Fellows first undertook this mammoth project under the leadership of Benjamin Kohl, FAAR 71; and it was brought successfully to its completion with the assistance of the present and past SOF councils and Academy staff. The *Directory* not only provides a link between the past and the present, but it also affords each of us the opportunity to remain in touch with, to relive our past academy experiences, and to venture forward into new and stimulating dialogues and collaborations.

New names will be added annually and sadly some Fellows will pass on to be remembered; this never-ending chain is the legacy of the American Academy in Rome.

To those Fellows who conceived this *Directory*, to those who helped assemble it, and to those who edited it and published it for the American Academy in Rome, we owe our thanks.

Peter Rolland, FAAR 78
President, Society of Fellows

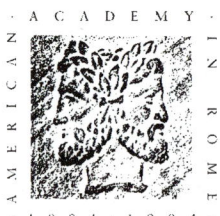

The View from Rome

For all who know and love the American Academy, the reopening of the building on April 5, 1994, after the twenty-two months of restoration, has been almost miraculous. Everything sprang back to life. The lights went on in the building. Fellows filled the rooms, set up their materials in the studios, studies and in the library, and got to work. There was again tea at 4:00 p.m., coffee at 10:00 a.m., long talks at the dinner table, late night pool. In an instant, everything seemed back to normal.

Yet there have also been changes. There are elevators for the Fellows and staff, which make moving in and the delivery of clean laundry much easier. There is a splendid new lecture room in the basement that seats 120 people. We have been wonderfully warm and well bathed as a result of the new electrical, plumbing, and heating systems, which replace the old that was precariously patched and glued together.

But certainly the most dramatic transformation has been the cryptoporticus, the barrel-vaulted halls underneath the cortile arcade which have provided us with a magnificent new space within the Academy building. At the moment, we have installed the Centennial banners there but we are also experimenting with using the space for concerts, inaugurating the idea of having music within the building oriented towards the community and friends, more relaxed in character than the parallel series of musical events that continue at the Villa Aurelia.

We are fortunate in having an especially nice group of Fellows this year, so 1994-95 has been a happy one here at the Academy. The ideal of collaboration between artists, composers, and scholars is flourishing this year; and the walks, talks and trips are all fully subscribed. Indeed, because we have the artists from last year as well as the artists for 1994-95 (as the studios were closed when the building was under renovation) the group in the visual arts is especially large, and wonderfully energetic.

As always, the community here has an organic and ever-changing quality. Not only are some fellowships short-term (the East-Central European Mellon Visiting Scholars, for example, who come for three months each) but also there is the constantly shifting terrain of visitors, residents, friends, and guests. We include in our sense of community many of our library readers, who join us regularly at coffee or tea, as well as our many friends who come to concerts and lectures.   ·

The vitality of the Academy is evident in many ways. The fact that the renewed building works so well now permits us to concentrate on other things: the Fellows above all, the Residents and visitors, and then programs. In Rome the foreign Academies have an especially important role to fill, and I am happy to say that with the assistance of Professor Malcolm Bell, Richard Trythall, Martha Boyden, Pina Pasquantonio and the office staff, we do a wonderful job at contributing an important share.

Caroline Bruzelius, FAAR 86
Director

ABBREVIATIONS

ABBREVIATIONS FREQUENTLY USED IN THIS DIRECTORY

Acad.	Academy
Adj.	Adjunct
Adv.	Advisor, Advisory
Assc.	Associate
Asscs.	Associates
Assn.	Association
Asst.	Assistant
b.	born
BA	Bachelor of Arts
Bd.	Board
Bldg.	Building
BoD	Board of Directors
BoT	Board of Trustees
BS	Bachelor of Science
c.	children
Chair	Chairman, Chairwoman, Chairperson
Chap.	Chapter
Com.	Committee
Comm.	Commission
Contr.	Contributing
contr.	contributor to
d.	died
dec.	deceased, year unknown
Dept.	Department
DFA	Doctor of Fine Arts
Dir.	Director
Dr.	Drive
Ed. Bd.	Editorial Board
Ed.	Editor
Emer.	Emeritus
Exb.	Exhibit, Exhibition
exb. cat.	Exhibition Catalog
Exec.	Executive
Found.	Foundation
Gen.	General
HS	High School
Hon.	Honorary/Honorable
Inst.	Institute, Institution
Instr.	Instructor
Intl.	International
Lect.	Lecturer
Ln.	Lane
m.	married
MA	Master of Arts
MArch	Master of Architecture
Mem.	Member
MFA	Master of Fine Arts
MLArch	Master of Landscape Architecture
MS	Master of Science
Nat.	National
NYC	New York City
Part.	Partner
Pgm.	Program
PhD	Doctor of Philosophy
PO Box	Post Office Box
Pres.	President
Prin.	Principal
Prof.	Professor
rpt.	reprint
Sec.	Secretary
TA	Teaching Assistant
TF	Teaching Fellow
Treas.	Treasurer
Univ.	University
US	United States
VP	Vice President

ABBREVIATIONS OF GROUPS AND ORGANIZATIONS

AAAL	American Academy and Institute of Arts & Letters, New York (combines former American Academy of Arts and Letters and National Institute of Arts & Letters)
AAAS	American Academy of Arts and Sciences
AAR	American Academy in Rome
AAUP	American Association of University Professors
AAUW	American Association of University Women
ACA	American Composers' Alliance
ACLS	American Council of Learned Societies
AHA	American Historical Association
AIA	American Institute of Architects
AIC	Art Institute of Chicago
AILA	American Institute of Landscape Architects
ALNY	Architectural League of New York
ANS	American Numismatic Society
APA	American Philological Association
APS	American Philosophical Society
ArIA	Archaeological Institute of America
ASCAP	American Society of Composers, Authors, and Publishers
ASCSA	American School of Classical Studies, Athens
ASCSR	American School of Classical Studies, Rome
ASID	American Society of Industrial Design
ASL	Art Students' League of New York
ASLA	American Society of Landscape Architects
BMI	Broadcast Music, Inc.
CAA	College Art Association
CAMWS	Classical Association of the Midwest and South
CANE	Classical Association of New England
CASVA	Center for Advanced Study in the Visual Arts, National Gallery of Art, Washington, DC
CRI	Composers Recordings Inc.,
CUNY	City University of New York
FIT	Fashion Institute of Technology
Harvard GSD	Harvard Graduate School of Design
IAS	Institute for Advanced Study (Princeton)
ICCS	Intercollegiate Center for Classical Studies in Rome
IDC	International Design Center, NYC
IFA	Institute of Fine Arts, New York University
MAA	Medieval Academy of America
MAS	Municipal Art Society of New York
MFA	Museum of Fine Arts, Boston, MA
MFA School	Museum of Fine Arts School, Boston, MA
MIT	Massachusetts Institute of Technology
MMA	Metropolitan Museum of Art, NYC
MOMA	Museum of Modern Art, NYC
NAD	National Academy of Design, NYC

NEA	National Endowment for the Arts
NEH	National Endowment for the Humanities
NGA	National Gallery of Art, Washington DC
NIAE	National Institute of Architectural Education
NIAL	National Institute of Arts & Letters
NSS	National Sculpture Society
NYC	New York City
NYFA	New York Foundation for the Arts
NYIT	New York Institute of Technology
NYSCA	New York State Council on the Arts
PAFA	Pennsylvania Academy of Fine Arts
RISD	Rhode Island School of Design
RSA	Renaissance Society of America
SAH	Society of Architectural Historians
SOF	Society of Fellows (AAR)
SSHRCC	Social Sciences and Humanities Research Council of Canada
SUNY	State University of New York
UC	University of California
UCLA	University of California, Los Angeles
UNC	University of North Carolina
VSA	Vergilian Society of America, Cumae, Italy

COMMONLY CITED PUBLICATION TITLES

AJA	*American Journal of Archaeology*
AAR Papers and Monographs	*Papers and Monographs of the American Academy in Rome*
Briggs	Ward Briggs, *A Biographical Dictionary of North American Classicists* (Westport, CT & London: Greenwood Press, 1994)
Memoirs of the AAR	*Memoirs of the American Academy in Rome*
JSAH	*Journal of the Society of Architectural Historians*
The Dictionary of Art	*The Dictionary of Art*, ed. Jane Shoaf Turner, Hugh Brigstocke et al. (London & New York: Macmillan Publishers Ltd., forthcoming)
TAPA	*Transactions of the American Philological Association*
Transactions of the APS	*Transactions of the American Philosophical Society*

■ ■ ■

THE CENTENNIAL
DIRECTORY OF
THE AMERICAN
ACADEMY IN
ROME

A

ABATE, PETER PAUL ■ FAAR Sculpture 51. b. Sept. 21, 1915, Salem, MA. m. Alleyne Abate. c. Alleyne. **Other Studies:** MFA School 1935-39; San Carlos School of Fine Arts, Mexico 1939-40. **Career & Employment:** Peter Abate Summer School of Sculpture, Berkshire Museum, Founder; MFA School, Dept. Head. **Memberships & Offices:** New England Assn. for Contemporary Sculpture, Organizer. **Fellowships, Honors & Awards:** MFA School, Mrs. David Hunt Travelling Scholarship 1939-40; Four Arts Club, Palm Beach, 1st Prize. **Exhibitions/ Performances:** Syracuse Museum of Fine Arts 1954.

ABBATELLI, MAURO ■ AAR – Rome, Maintenance Staff.

ABBEY, EDWIN A. ■ AAR Charter Mem., Mural Painter.

ABBOTT, FRANK FROST ■ AAR Trustee 1911-24, Prof. of Latin.

ABBOTT, SAMUEL A.P. ■ American School of Architecture in Rome, Dir. 1897-1903; AAR Charter Mem.; Lawyer.

ABERCROMBIE, STANLEY ■ FAAR Design Arts 83. b. Feb. 18, 1935, Cedartown, GA. BS 57, Georgia Inst. of Technology; BArch 61, MIT; MArch 67, Columbia Univ. **Career & Employment:** Marcel Breuer & Asscs., Draftsman 1962-65; John Carl Warnecke, Designer 1968-72; *Architecture Plus*, Senior Ed. 1973-74; Harvard GSD, Visiting Lect. 1974-75; *Interiors*, Ed.-in-Chief 1975-77; *Abitare in America*, Ed. 1977; *Architecture*, Senior Ed., Architecture 1978-82; *Interior Design*, Chief Ed. 1983-present., Ed. Dir. & VP 1993-present. **Memberships & Offices:** Union Intl. d'Architecture, Paris, Triennial Honor Awards Jury, US Representative 1974; NEA, Presidential Design Awards, Juror 1988; SAH, Dir. 1988-91; AIA, New York Chap., Dir. 1992-94. **Fellowships, Honors & Awards:** American Soc. of Magazine Editors, Jesse H. Neal Editorial Achievement Award 1974; Loeb Fellow for Advanced Environmental Studies 1974; AIA Fellow 1989; NEA Grant 1989; Inst. of Business Designers, Star Award 1991. **Publications:** *Global Architecture Series* (Japan), text for 4 vols.; *Process: Architecture Series* (Japan), text for 3 vols.; *Ferrocement* (New York: Schocken, 1977 & London: Robert Hale, 1978); *Gwathmey Siegel* (New York: Whitney Library of Design, 1981 & Barcelona: Gustavo Gili, 1982); *Architecture as Art* (New York: Van Nostrand Reinhold, 1984); *A Philosophy of Interior Design* (New York: Harper & Row, 1990); *George Nelson: The Design of Modern Design* (Cambridge, MA: MIT Press, 1994); contr. to many other books; over 600 articles about design published in newspapers and magazines, including *Artforum, House & Garden, JSAH, Horizon, Portfolio, Wall Street Journal, Boston Globe, Independent* (London), *Design* (London), *Architecture & Urbanism* (Tokyo), *Metropolis, Progressive Architecture, Architectural Record*. **Important Works:** Own architectural work (in collaboration with Paul Vieyra) published in *Interior Design, Interiors, Architectural Record, House Beautiful, House Beautiful Building Manual, Process: Architecture*. **Exhibitions/ Performances:** Lectures, Panel Moderating, or Design Juries at: Univ. of Lisbon School of Architecture; Columbia Univ. School of Architecture; Univ. of Chicago, Circle Campus, School of Architecture; UCLA Extension, S. Monica; FIT; Catholic Univ. School of Architecture; North Carolina School of Architecture; Georgia Inst. of Technology School of Architecture; New York School of Interior Design. **Bio-Bibliography:** *Who's Who in America*. **Home Address:** 175 Riverside Dr., NYC 10024. **Business Address:** *Interior Design Magazine*, 249 W. 17th St., NYC 10011.

ABRAMOVITZ, MAX ■ RAAR Architecture 61. b. May 23, 1908, Chicago, IL. m. Anita Brooks. BS, Univ. of Illinois; MA, Columbia Univ. **Other Study:** École des Beaux Arts, Paris. **Career & Employment:** Harrison, Fouilhoux & Abramovitz 1941-45; US Army Corps of Engineers, Lt. Col., World War II; Harrison & Abramovitz 1945-present. **Memberships & Offices:** ALNY; American Soc. of Civil Engineers; Century Assn. Regional Planning Assn., Dir.; Mt. Sinai Hospital & Medical Center, BoT; Legion of Merit; Univ. of Pittsburgh, Consultant Architect; New York Regional Planning Assn., Pres. **Fellowships, Honors & Awards:** École des Beaux Arts, Fellowship; Univ. of Pittsburgh, DFA 1961; Univ. of Illinois Alumni Assn., Award of Achievement 1963; Brandeis Univ., Fellow 1963; AIA, Fellow; American Soc. of Civil Engineers, Life Mem. **Important Works:** Corning Glass Center, Corning, NY 1951; US Steel Bldg., Pittsburgh 1952; ALCOA Bldg., Pittsburgh 1952; US Embassy, Rio de Janeiro 1952; US Embassy, Havana, Cuba 1953; Brandeis Univ., Interfaith Chapels & Rose Art Museum, Waltham, MA 1955; Univ. of Illinois Assembly Hall, Champaign 1963; Phoenix Mutual Life Insurance Bldg., Hartford, CT 1964; Radcliffe-Harvard Hilles Library 1966; Beth Zion Temple, Buffalo, NY 1967; Univ. of Illinois, Krannert Center for the Performing Arts; Univ. of Iowa, Fine Arts Center, Iowa City; Radcliffe-Harvard, Currier Houses; Philharmonic Hall, Lincoln Center for the Performing Arts, NYC; Columbia Univ.: Law School, Library, School of Intl. Affairs; Univ. of Miami, Rosenstiel School of Marine & Atmospheric Science; US Military Acad., Jewish Chapel, West Point, NY; Rockefeller Univ., Scholars Residence, NYC; Steuben Glass Bldg., NYC; Nationwide Insurance Co., Columbus, OH; Owens-Illinois World HQ, Toledo, OH; Rockefeller Center, NYC; Bell Telephone Exb. Bldg., New York World's Fair; Banque Rothschild, Paris; Tour GAN (Groupe des Assurances Nationale), La Defense, Paris; United Nations HQ, NYC; La Guardia Airport, NYC; Central Intelligence Agency, Langley, VA. **Home Address:** 176 Honey Hollow Rd., Pound Ridge, NY 10576.

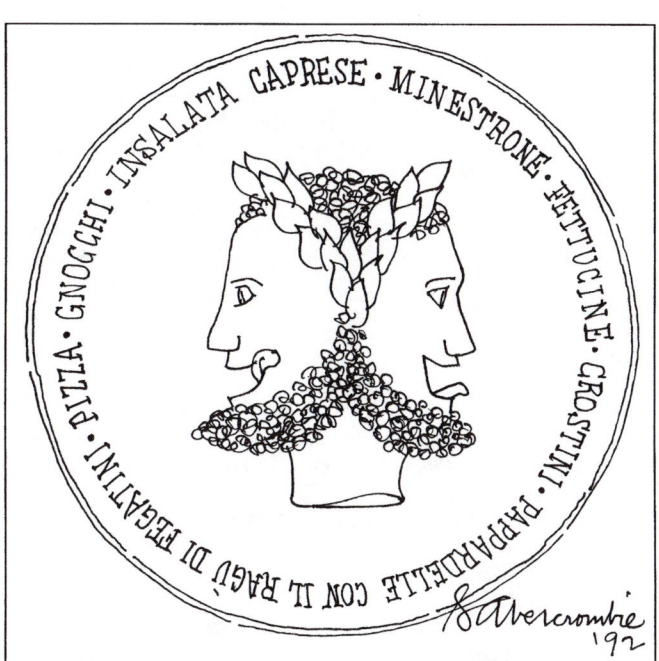

Stanley Abercrombie

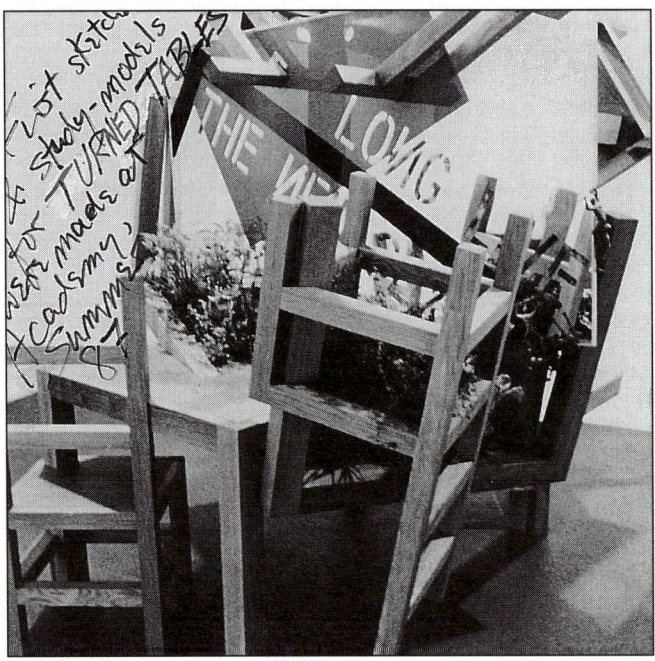

Vito Acconci

ACCONCI, VITO ■ FAAR Sculpture 87. b. Jan. 24, 1940, Bronx, NY. BA 62, College of the Holy Cross; MFA 64, Univ. of Iowa. **Research/Artistic Interests:** Sculpture, public art, essay-writing. **Career & Employment:** Cooper Union 1978, 1986; AIC 1981; San Francisco Art Inst. 1983, 1988; Yale Univ, Visiting Artist 1987-present; Tyler School of Art, Visiting Artist 1990; Bard College, Visiting Artist 1993. **Fellowships, Honors & Awards:** NYSCA 1976; NEA 1976, 1978, 1983; Guggenheim Fellowship 1979; Skowhegan Award 1980. **Publications:** "Notebook on Activity and Performance" (1971); "West, He Said: Notes On Framing," *Vision I* (San Francisco, 1975); *The Art of Performance* (New York: Dutton, 1984); "Notes on Language," in *Perverted by Language,* exb. cat. (Greenvale, NY: C.W. Post, Hillwood Art Gallery, 1986); "Playing with the Word 'Doll'," *The Doll Show,* exb. cat. (Greenvale, NY: C.W. Post, Hillwood Art Gallery, 1986); "Normal Art," *Illuminating Video, Apertu* (1983); "Television, Furniture, & Sculpture" (1984); *Vito Acconci: Domestic Trappings,* exb. cat. (La Jolla: La Jolla Museum, 1987); "Coming Out (Notes on Public Art)," *Vito Acconci,* exb. cat. (New York: MOMA, 1988); "Public Space in a Private Time," *Critical Inquiry* (1990); "Notes on Making Shelter (1988)," *Harvard Architectural Review* (1990); "Frames for Life," *Art + Text* (1991); "Bodies of Land," *Landskab Tiddskrift for Planlaegning* (1992); "Performance after the Fact (1989)," *Documents* (1992). **Important Works:** Centre Pompidou, Paris 1975, 1976, 1991; Whitney Museum, NYC 1976; Museum of Contemporary Art, Los Angeles 1976; Museum of Contemporary Art, Chicago 1977; MOMA 1981, 1991; Coca Cola USA, Atlanta 1987; FRAC, Paris 1991; St. Aubin Park, Detroit 1991; Arvada Art Center 1992. **Exhibitions/Performances:** Documenta, Kassel 1972, 1977, 1982; Kunstmuseum Luzern 1978; Stedelijk Museum, Amsterdam 1978; Museum of Contemporary Art, Chicago 1980; Padiglione d'Arte Contemporanea, Milan 1981; Kunstverein Köln 1981; Univ. of South Florida Art Galleries, Tampa 1986; La Jolla Museum of Contemporary Art 1987; MOMA 1988; Centre d'Art Contemporain, Grenoble 1991; Museo Luigi Pecci, Prato 1992; Osterreicsches Museum für Angewandte Kunst, Vienna 1993. **Bio-Bibliography:** Germano Celant, "Dirty Acconci," *Artforum* (1980); Paul Taylor, "Self as Theatricality:

Samuel Beckett and Vito Acconci," *Art + Text* (1982); Ronald Onorato, *Vito Acconci: Domestic Trappings, exb. cat.* (La Jolla: Museum of Contemporary Art, 1987); Linda Shearer, *Vito Acconci: Public Places,* exb. cat. (New York: MOMA, 1988); Donald Kuspit, "Vito Acconci: The Hunger Artist in the Lonely Crowd," *Artscribe* (1988); Nancy Pricenthal, "Vito Acconci," *Sculpture* (1988); Jeffrey Kipnis, *Vito Acconci: Causes and Effects,* exb. cat. (Prato: Museo Luigi Pecci, 1991); Anthony Vidler, *Vito Acconci,* exb. cat. (Vienna: Osterreisches Museum für Angewandte Kunst, 1993); Kate Linker, *Vito Acconci* (New York: Rizzoli, 1993); *International Who's Who; Who's Who In America.* **Home Address:** 39 Pearl St., Brooklyn, NY 11201. **Business Address:** Barbara Gladstone Gallery, 99 Greene St., NYC 10013.

ACKERMAN, HARRY GREGORY ■ FAAR Painting 34. b. Nov. 12, 1909, Romania. d. June 13, 1988. BFA 30, Yale Univ. **Other Study:** NAD, ASL, Lake Forest Found. of Architecture & Landscape Architecture. **Memberships & Offices:** Grand Central Artists Guild, American Artists Congress. **Fellowships, Honors & Awards:** Louis Comfort Tiffany Found. Fellowship 1930; Suydham Medal; Beaux Arts Inst. Medal. **Exhibitions/ Performances:** NAD, prior to 1935; ASL, prior to 1935. **Bio-Bibliography:** *Who Was Who in American Art.*

ACKERMAN, JAMES S. ■ FAAR History of Art 52, RAAR History of Art 75; AAR Trustee, Trustee Emer. 1967-84. b. Nov. 8, 1919, San Francisco, CA. m. Mildred Rosenbaum, Jill Slosburg. c. Anne, Anthony, Sarah, Jesse. BA 41, Yale Univ.; MA 47, NYU; PhD 52, NYU. **Research/Artistic Interests:** Architectural history, Renaissance art & theory. **Career & Employment:** Yale Univ., Lect. 1946; UC, Asst. Prof. 1952-60; Harvard Univ., Prof. 1961-present, Chair 1963-68, 1982-84, Prof. Emer. 1990; Cambridge Univ., Slade Prof. of Art 1969-70; Columbia Univ., Schapiro Visiting Prof. 1988, Visiting Prof. 1991; IFA, Visiting Prof. 1992. **Memberships & Offices:** *Art Bulletin,* Ed.-in-Chief 1956-60; Harvard Univ. Film Study Center, Co-Founder, Pres. 1967-75; Consiglio Scientifico, Centro Intl. di Studia di Architettura 1969-present; Library of Congress, Council of Scholars 1980-82; NGA, Mellon Lect. 1985; *Annali di Architettura,* Ed. 1992-94. **Fellowships, Honors & Awards:** Fulbright Fellow 1951-52; NGA, 25th Anniversary Medal 1957; Princeton Council on the Humanities, Fellow 1960-61; UC, Centennial Award 1970; NEH Senior Fellow 1974-75; Istituto di Storia dell'Arte Lombarda, Gold Medal 1987; AIA, Inst. Honors 1987; CAA, Distinguished Teaching Award 1991; New York Inst. for the Humanities, Visiting Fellow 1992; Guggenheim Fellow 1992-93; Order of Merit of the Italian Republic, Grand Officer; Honorary Degrees: Kenyon College, Univ. of Maryland, Baltimore, Maryland Inst. of Fine Arts, Massachusetts College of Art, Univ. of Venice. **Publications:** *The Cortile del Belvedere* (Vatican City: Vatican Library, 1954); *The Architecture of Michelangelo* (New York & London: Zwemmer, 1961); with Rhys Carpenter, *Art and Archaeology* (Englewood Cliffs, NJ: Prentice Hall, 1962); *Palladio* (Harmondsworth: Penguin, 1966); *Palladio's Villas* (New York: J.G. Augustin, 1967); *The Villa: Form and Ideology of Country Houses* (Princeton: Princeton Univ. Press & London: Thames & Hudson, 1990); *Distance Points: Studies in Theory and Renaissance Art and Architecture* (Cambridge: MIT Press, 1991); Films: *Looking for Renaissance Rome,* with John Terry & Kathleen Weil-Garris, 1976; *Palladio the Architect and His Influence on America,* with John Terry, 1980; and many articles. **Bio-Bibliography:** *Who's Who in America.* **Home Address:** 12 Coolidge Hill Rd., Cambridge, MA.

ADAIR, WILLIAM B. ■ FAAR Design Arts 92. b. Nov. 5, 1949, Takoma Park, MD. m. Kay Jackson. c. Annie. BA 72, Univ. of Maryland, College Park. **Research/Artistic Interests:** Gilding and carving techniques from various masters over the last twenty years; gold leaf: various methods of application & decorative uses, such as the picture frame; to context of bordering devices as an aesthetic integer in an area that is often ignored. Work now includes developing an archive on frames & the relationship to architecture. The use of photographs, drawings or actual frames is important to this study. **Career & Employment:** Smithsonian Inst., Nat. Portrait Gallery 1972-82; Gold Leaf Studios, Founder & Owner 1982-present. **Memberships & Offices:** American Inst. for Conservation of Historic Works of Art 1973-present; Soc. of Gilders, Founder & Pres. 1985-91; Intl. Inst. for Frame Study, Founder 1992. **Fellowships, Honors & Awards:** Smithsonian Special Merit Award 1974. **Publications:** *The Frame in America 1700-1900: A Survey of Fabrication Techniques and Styles* (Washington, DC: AIA, 1983); *The Regilded Age* (Newark, NJ: Newark Museum, 1990). **Important Works:** Sculpture, "The Spirit of '76," Nat. Museum of American Art, Smithsonian Inst., Washington DC; Restoration of "Republic" by Daniel Chester French, AIC & Chicago Park District; comm. to replicate mirror of Thomas Jefferson, Monticello, Univ. of Virginia; comm. to design frames for Constantine Bermidi Oval Allegories, The White House; comm. to conserve gilded artifacts, Washington Collection, Mt. Vernon; comm. to design and construct frame for "Thomas Jefferson" portrait, Charles Wilson Peale, US State Dept. Collections: restoration, "China Cabin," Nineteenth-Century Social Saloon, Tiburon, Belvedere, San Francisco; Restoration projects & conservation assessments at Hearst Castle, San Simeon; Chicago Historical Soc.; regilding "Pioneer Panel" by Lee Lawrie, Bertram Goodhue & Asscs., Nebraska State Capital, Lincoln; gilding dome, Robert Stern & Assc., Boylston St., Gerald Hines Interests, Boston; Interior Gold Dome, Elie Saarinen, Cranbrook Acad. **Bio-Bibliography:** Alice Leccese Powers, "Young Masters of the Gilder's Art," *Historic Preservation* (Dec. 1984); Glenn Harrell, "Gilt Trip," *HG* (Sept. 1989); Lisa Mason, "Frames of Reference," *Chesapeake Homes & Garden* (Nov.-Dec. 1990); Alice Leccese Powers,

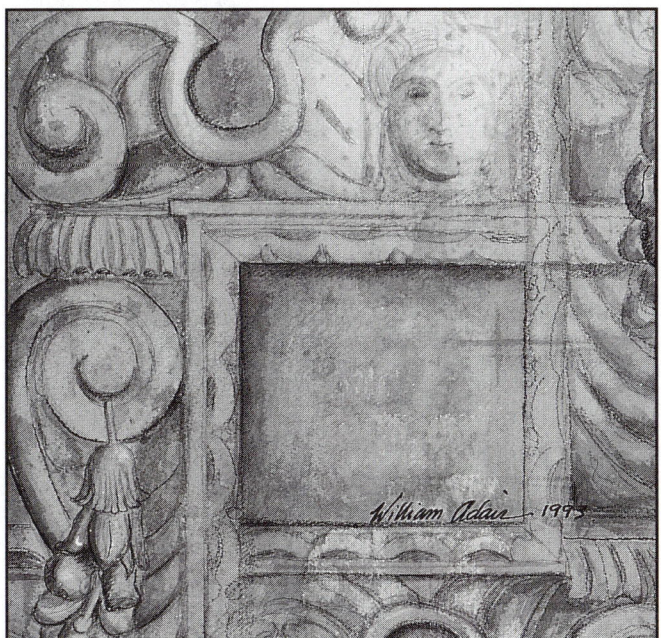

William Adair

"A Sensitive Touch," *Southern Accents* (Feb. 1991); Dan Weeks, "The Framer's Art," *Traditional Home* (June-July 1993). **Business Address:** Gold Leaf Studios, PO Box 50156, Washington, DC 20091.

ADAM, CLAUS ■ RAAR Musical Composition 76. b. Nov. 5, 1917, Sumatra, Indonesia. d. July 4, 1983. m. Eleanor Randolph Bentz. c. Elizabeth Johanna. **Other Studies:** Mozarteum, Salzburg; cello with E. Stoffnegen, D.C. Dounis, Emanuel Feuermann; conducting with Leon Barzin; composition with Stefan Wolpe. **Career & Employment:** Juilliard School 1955-83; Mannes College of Music, Faculty; Philadelphia College for Performing Arts, Faculty; Minneapolis Symphony, Asst. Prin. Cellist 1940-43; WOR, New York, Prin. Cellist 1946-48; New Music String Quartet, Organizer & Cellist 1948-54; Juilliard String Quartet 1955-74. **Fellowships, Honors & Awards:** Ford Found. Grants & Awards; Nat. Found. for the Arts Grants & Awards, Naumberg Found. Grant 1974; NEA Grant 1974; Guggenheim Fellow 1975-76; Paderewski Found. 1976; Friedheim Chamber Music Award 1980. **Important Works:** *Piano Sonata* 1950; *String Trio* 1968; *Song Cycle Herbstgesänge* 1969; *Concerto for Piano & Orchestra* 1973; *String Quartet* 1975; *Concerto Variations for Orchestra* 1976. **Bio-Bibliography:** *Baker's Biographical Dictionary of Musicians; New Grove Dictionary of American Music; Who Was Who in America.*

ADAMS, CHARLES FRANCIS ■ AAR Charter Mem.

ADAMS, EDWARD DEAN ■ AAR Trustee 1911-31, Bank Exec.

ADAMS, FREDERICK B., JR ■ AAR Trustee 1966-71, Museum Dir., Morgan Library.

ADAMS, FREEMAN WILLIAM ■ FAAR Classics/Archaeology 51. b. Aug. 24, 1913, Los Angeles, CA. d. Aug. 24, 1954. BA 37, UCLA; MA 49, Harvard Univ. **Other Study:** Oxford Univ. **Research/Artistic Interests:** Classical philology, ancient history. **Career & Employment:** Hobart College, Lect. 1951-53; Yale Univ., Instr. 1953-54. **Fellowships, Honors & Awards:** Fulbright Scholar 1951. **Publications:** "Observations on the Consular *Fasti* in the Early Empire," *AJA* 55 (1951): 239-41; *"Tabula Imperii Romani," AJA* 58 (1954): 45-51.

ADAMS, GERALD D. ■ FAAR Design Arts 68. b. Jan. 8, 1928, San Francisco, CA. m. Anna Finan. BA 49, UC, Berkeley. **Other Study:** Salzburg Seminar in American Planning Studies; French civilization, Sorbonne, Paris. **Research/Artistic Interests:** French civilization, urban planning, environmental design, historic architecture. **Career & Employment:** *San Francisco Examiner* 1959-present. **Memberships & Offices:** San Francisco Planning & Urban Research Assn. **Fellowships, Honors & Awards:** Soc. of Professional Journalists, Lifetime Achievement Award; Assn. of Catholic Journalists, McQuade Award for Writing 1977; San Francisco Press Club, 1st Prize, Best Daily Story 1978; Associated Press, 1st Prize, Investigative Series 1978; California Newspaper Publishers Assn., 1st Prize for Outstanding Writing 1986; San Francisco Press Club, 1st Prize, George Christopher Award for Investigative Reporting 1986. **Publications:** *The Open Space Explosion* (California Tomorrow, 1970); *A Victory for Urban Esthetics in San Francisco* (Nat. Urban Coalition, 1971); *The Great Oil Spill of San Francisco Bay* (San Francisco: Bank of America, 1972); *The] ault at Warm Springs: A Dam Dream and Earthquake Reality* (San Francisco: Sierra Club, 1974); *Your Money or Your Life: Our Strange Tolerance of Environmental*

Danger (California Tomorrow, 1975); *San Francisco Neighborhood Guide* (San Francisco: San Francisco Examiner, 1980); *Inner Circles: How Money and Politics Shaped the Skyline* (San Francisco: San Francisco Examiner, 1988); *Mission Bay Plan: An Outstanding Planning Process* (American Planning Assn., 1988). **Bio-Bibliography:** Mary Ellen Schoonmaker, "The Real Estate Story," *Columbia Journalism Review* (Jan.-Feb. 1987). **Home Address:** 154 Lombard St., San Francisco, CA 94111.

ADAMS, HERBERT ■ AAR Trustee 1909-45, Architect.

ADAMS, JOHN C. ■ RAAR Musical Composition 88. b. Feb. 15, 1947, Worcester, MA. m. Deborah O'Grady. c. Emily, Sam. BA 69, Harvard College; MA 71, Harvard Univ. **Other Study:** San Francisco Conservatory of Music 1972-82. **Important Works:** *Phrygian Gates,* for piano 1977; *Shaker Loops,* for strings (New Albion Phillips, Virgin) 1978; *Harmonium,* for chorus & orchestra 1981 (ECM); *Grand Pianola Music,* for small orchestra (EMI, Nonesuch) 1983; *Harmonielehre,* for orchestra (EMI, Nonesuch) 1985; *The Chairman Dances,* for orchestra (Nonesuch) 1986; *Nixon in China,* an opera in 3 acts (Nonesuch) 1987; *The Wound-Dresser,* for baritone & orchestra (Nonesuch) 1988; *Fearful Symmetries,* for orchestra (Nonesuch) 1988; *The Death of Klinghoffer,* an opera in 2 acts (Nonesuch) 1991; *El Dorado,* for orchestra 1991; *Chamber Symphony* (Nonesuch) 1993; *Violin Concerto* 1993. Publishers: Assn. Music Publishers, Boosey & Hawkes. **Home Address:** 114 El Camino Real, Berkeley, CA 94705. **Business Address:** Harrison-Pavrott Ltd., 12 Penzance Pl., London W11 4PA, England.

ADAMS, MARK ■ RAAR Painting 63. b. Oct. 27, 1925, White Plains, NY. **Bio-Bibliography:** *Print World Directory, Who's Who in American Art.*

ADAMS, NICHOLAS ■ FAAR History of Art 88. b. Oct. 17, 1947, NYC. c. Robin. BA 70, Cornell Univ.; MA 73, IFA; PhD 78, IFA. **Research/Artistic Interests:** Italian architecture & urbanism. **Career & Employment:** McGill Univ., Visiting Asst. Prof. 1977-78; Lehigh Univ., Asst. Prof.-Prof. 1978-89; Vassar College, Prof. 1989-present; Visiting Prof., School of Architecture, UCLA & Columbia Univ. **Memberships & Offices:** CAA, Monograph Series, Ed. 1989-92; *JSAH,* Assc. Ed. 1992-93, Ed. 1993-96. **Fellowships, Honors & Awards:** NEH Summer Stipend 1980; Center for Italian Studies, Penn-Aquila 1983, 1986; Gladys Krieble Delmas Found. 1989; IAS, Visiting Mem. 1992-93, Mary Conover Mellon Prof. 1994-present. **Publications:** "Architecture for Fish: The Sienese Dam on the Bruna River – Structures and Designs, 1468-ca. 1530," *Technology and Culture* 25 (1984): 768-97; "Military Architecture and Renaissance Art History, or 'Bellezza on the Battlefield'," *Architectura* 14 (1984): 106-18; "The United States Housing Corporation Munitions Worker Suburb in Bethlehem, Pa., (1918) and its Architectural Context," *Pennsylvania Magazine for History and Biography* 108 (1984): 59-86; "The Life and Times of Pietro dell'Abaco, A Renaissance Estimator from Siena (active 1457-1486)," *Zeitschrift für Kunstgeschichte* 48 (1985): 384-95; "The Acquisition of Pienza 1459-1464," *JSAH* 44 (1985): 97-108; with Simon Pepper, *Firearms and Fortifications: Military Architecture and Siege Warfare in Sixteenth-Century Siena* (Chicago: Univ. of Chicago Press, 1986); "Sebastiano Serlio: Military Architect?" in *Sebastiano Serlio,* ed. C. Thoenes (Milan: Electa, 1989), 222-27; "The Construction of Pienza (1459-1464) and the Consequences of *Renovatio*," in *Urban Life in the Renaissance,* ed. R. Weissman (Newark, DE: Univ. of Delaware Press, 1989), 51-79; with Janet Temos, "The Speaking Architecture of E.T. Potter at Lehigh University (1866-

69)," *Res* 22 (1992): 152-71; "L'Architettura militare di Francesco di Giorgio," in *Francesco di Giorgio Architetto* (Milan: Electa, 1993); with Laurie Nussdorfer, "The Italian City 1400-1600," in *Italian Renaissance Architecture from Brunelleschi to Michelangelo* (Milan: Bompiani, 1994), 205-33; *The Architectural Drawings of Antonio da Sangallo the Younger and His Circle,* 3 vols. (Cambridge, MA: MIT Press, 1994); "Il Palazzo Jouffroy a Pienza," *Quaderni dell'Istituto di Storia dell' Architettura* (in press). **Business Address:** Dept. of Art, Vassar College, Poughkeepsie, NY 12601.

ADEL, RAY DEN ■ AAR Classical Soc., Sec. 1994.

AGARD, WALTER ■ AAR Classical Soc., Pres. 1947.

AGNELLI, MARELLA CARACCIOLO ■ AAR Trustee 1989-present, Art Patron. b. Florence, Italy. **Studies:** École des Beaux Arts, Paris; Académie Julian, Paris. **Career & Employment:** Erwin Blumerfeld, Photographer, Asst.; Condé Nast, Ed. & Photographer 1953-present. **Memberships & Offices:** Salk Inst., Intl. BoT; MOMA, Intl. Council; Friends of Palazzo Grassi Com., Venice, BoT; "I 200 del FAI," Fondo Italiano Ambiente, Milan, Pres.; Amici Torinesi Arte Contemporanea, Turin, Pres.; United World Colleges, Nat. Com., VP. **Fellowships, Honors & Awards:** Resources Council, Inc., "Oscar" Product Design Award 1977. **Publications:** *Gardens of the Italian Villas.* **Important Works:** Designs for fabric collections: Abraham Zumsteg, Zurich; Ratti, Italy; Steiner, France; Martex; Marshall Field.

AGNELLI, SUSANNA ■ AAR Visitor 1983-84; AAR Italian Com., Chair 1994-present; Foreign Minister of Italy.

AJOOTIAN, AILEEN ■ Broneer Fellow 1987-88.

ALBERT, STEPHEN JOEL ■ FAAR Musical Composition 67. b. Feb. 6, 1941, NYC. d. Dec. 27, 1992. m. Marilyn Albert. c. Joshua, Katie. BMus 62, Philadelphia Music Acad. **Other Study:** Eastman School of Music, Univ. of Rochester, NY 1958-60; Univ. of Pennsylvania 1963. **Career & Employment:** Philadelphia Acad. of Music 1968-70; Stanford Univ., Lect. 1970-71; Smith College 1974-76; Seattle Symphony, Composer-in-Residence 1985-88; Boston Univ. 1988-90; Juilliard School 1988-92. **Fellowships, Honors & Awards:** BMI, 1st Prize 1961; Bearns Prize 1962; NEA Grants (2); MacDowell Colony Fellowship 1964, 1969; Huntington Hartford Fellowship 1965; Ford Found, CMP Grant 1967-68; Guggenheim Fellowship 1968, 1979; Pulitzer Prize 1985. **Important Works:** *Wolf Time* 1968; *Cathedral Music* 1972; *Voices Within* 1975; *Into Eclipse* 1981; *River Run,* for orchestra 1984; *Flower of the Mountain* 1985; *In Concordiam* 1986; *Anthem and Processionals for Orchestra* 1987; *Songs from the Stone Harp* 1988; *Sun's Heat* 1989; *Cello Concerto* 1989; *Tapioca Pudding for Orchestra* 1990; *Wind Canticle* 1991; *Ecce Pie* 1991; *Symphony No. 2* 1992. **Bio-Bibliography:** David Ewen, *American Composers* (New York: G.P. Putnam's Sons, 1982); *Baker's Biographical Dictionary of Musicians; New Grove Dictionary of American Music; Who's Who in America.*

ALBRIGHT, JOHN J. ■ AAR Charter Mem.

ALBRIGHT, WILLIAM H. ■ RAAR Musical Composition 79. b. Oct. 20, 1944, Gary, IN. m. Pamela Decker. c. John K., Elizabeth M. DMA 70, Univ. of Michigan. **Other Study:** Paris Conservatory. **Research/Artistic Interests:** Composer, performer, recording artist. **Career & Employment:** Univ. of Michigan, Instr. 1970-80; Prof. 1980-present; Chair, Composition Dept.

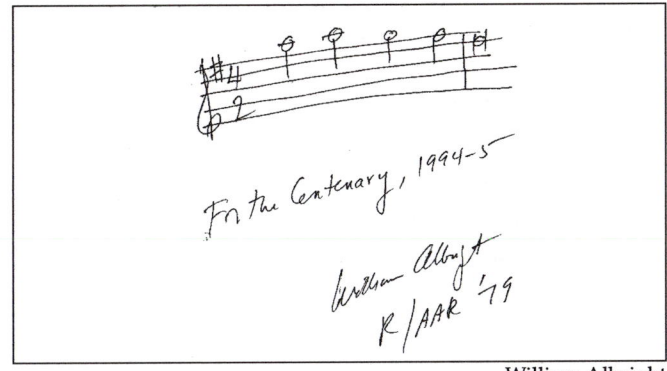

For the Centenary, 1994-5

William Albright

William Albright

1992-present. **Fellowships, Honors & Awards:** ASCAP Awards 1967-present; Queen Marie-José Prize 1968; Fulbright Fellow 1968-69; Guggenheim Fellowship 1976, 1986; American Guild of Organists, Composer of the Year 1993. **Important Works:** Major Publisher: C.F. Peters, NYC; Éditions Jobert, Paris; Major Recording Company: Music Masters, NYC; Gothic Records; Musical Heritage Soc. **Home Address:** 2555 Roseland Dr., Ann Arbor, MI 48103.

ALCHERMES, JOSEPH D. ■ FAAR History of Art 80. b. Aug. 13, 1953, Brooklyn, NY. PhD 89, IFA. **Career & Employment:** Univ. of Minnesota, Asst. Prof. 1988-present; Minnesota Archaeological Research in Western Peloponnesos, Co.-Dir. **Fellowships, Honors & Awards:** McKnight Found. Fellowship 1992; McKnight-Land Grant Prof. 1992-94. **Publications:** with F.A. Cooper, "The Minnesota Morea Project: 1992 Field Report," *Archaeological Reports for 1992-1993* 39 (1993): 26-27, summary in "Chroniques des fouilles et découvertes archéologiques en Grèce en 1992," *Bulletin de Correspondance Hellénique* 117 (1993): 802-4; "*Spolia* in Roman Cities of the Late Empire: Legislative Rationales and Architectural Reuse," *Dumbarton Oaks Papers* 48 (1994): 167-78; "Petrine Politics: Pope Symmachus and the Rotunda of St. Andrew at Old St. Peter's," *Catholic Historical Review* 81 (1995): 1-40; with F.A. Cooper, "Byzantium: The Capital of New Rome," in *The Spiritual and Material Culture of Byzantium* (Univ. Park: Pennsylvania State Univ. Press, forthcoming). **Home Address:** 420 E. 54 St., 27C, NYC 10022.

ALDERMAN, EDWIN A. ■ AAR Charter Mem.

ALDRICH, CHESTER HOLMES ■ AAR Trustee 1925-35, Dir. 1935-40, Architect.

ALDRICH, NELSON W. ■ RAAR Architecture 69. b. Apr. 6, 1911, NYC. d. Sept. 16, 1986. m. Eleanor Tweed, Frances Turner. c. Nelson, Frances D. Maher, Abigail Cheever, Rosalie C. West. BA 34, Harvard Univ.; MArch 38, Harvard Univ.; LLD 62, Emerson College. **Career & Employment:** Harrison & Abramovitz, Designer 1939-40; US Housing Authority, Project Planner 1940-42; Campbell, Aldrich & Nutty, Part. 1947-74; Aldrich, Pounder & Asscs., Pres. 1974-86; Consult. Architect: Dartmouth College, Bradford Jr. College, Philips Exeter Acad. **Memberships & Offices:** AIA; AAAS; Inst. of Contemporary Art, Pres. 1947-60; Boston Arts Festival, Co-Founder & Chair 1952-64; Boston Art Comm., Chair 1955-75; Boston Architecture Center, Dir. 1968-72. **Fellowships, Honors & Awards:** AIA, Fellow; AAAS. **Important Works:** Portsmouth, NH Urban Renewal Project; Tufts Univ. Library; Amherst College: science buildings, two dormitories; Dartmouth Univ., Murdough Center; Univ. of Massachusetts, Amherst: admin-

istration, business school, graduate research buildings. **Bio-Bibliography:** *NY Times*, Obit. (Sept. 20, 1986); *Who Was Who in America*.

ALDRICH, WILL S. ■ Rotch Scholar 1895, American School of Architecture in Rome, Interim Dir. 1896-97.

ALDRICH, WINTHROP ■ AAR Visitor 1959-64, Ambassador.

ALEXANDER, A.H. ■ Sheldon Fellow 1919-20.

ALEXANDER, JAMES W. ■ AAR Charter Mem.

ALEXANDER, JOHN W. ■ AAR Trustee 1914-18, Artist.

ALEXANDER, KATHRYN J. ■ FAAR Musical Composition 89. b. Apr. 18, 1955, Waco, TX. BMus 78, Baylor Univ.; MusM 83, Cleveland Inst. of Music; DMA 88, Eastman School of Music. **Career & Employment:** Cleveland Inst. of Music, Instr.-TA 1980-84; Eastman School of Music, TA 1984-87; Oberlin Conservatory of Music, Visiting Instr. 1987-88. **Fellowships, Honors & Awards:** NEA Fellowship; Ohio State Council of the Arts; Fromm Found. Grant; Koussevitzky Music Found. Fellowship; Brigham Young Univ., Barlow Endowment for Music Composition Comm. 1986; Tulane Univ. & Meet-the-Composer, Residency 1986; Tanglewood Music Center, Claudette Sorel Fellowship 1985.

ALEXANDER, MARGARET AMES ■ AAR Visitor 1970-71, 1994. Historian-Educator. b. May 21, 1916. **Career & Employment:** Univ. of Iowa, Prof. 1962-86; Corpus des Mosaïques de Tunisie, Co-Dir. 1968-present.

ALFANO, MAURIZIO ■ AAR – Rome, Gate Reception.

ALLEN, GEORGE HENRY ■ FASCSR Classics/Archaeology 1902. b. July 28, 1876, Grand Rapids, MI. d. Nov. 20, 1950. m. Wilifred Morris, Ilene Martin. c. George, Edmund. BA 1898, Univ. of Michigan; MA 1899, Univ. of Michigan; PhD 1904. **Other Study:** Univ. of Paris 1902-3; Univ. of Berlin 1911-14. **Career & Employment:** Univ. of Cinncinati, Instr. 1903-6, Assc. Prof. 1906-11; Univ. of Berlin, Bureau of Univ. Travel, Dir. 1911-14; US Army Translator 1917-20; Lafayette College Prof. 1929-47. **Memberships & Offices:** Classical Assn. of Atlantic States; ArIA. **Fellowships, Honors & Awards:** Phi Beta Kappa; Delta Upsilon. **Publications:** *The Roman Cohort* (Cincinnati: Univ. of Cincinnati Press, 1907); ed., *Forum Conche* (Cincinnati: Univ. of Cincinnati Press, 1910); co-author, *The Great War*, 5 vols. (Philadelphia: G. Barrie's Sons, 1921); *The French Revolution* (Philadelphia: G. Barrie's Sons, 1925); articles on archaeology & antiquarian subjects in *AJA*. **Bio-Bibliography:** *Who Was Who in America*.

ALLEN, HUBERT LEE, III ■ FAAR Classics/Archaeology 67; Classical Soc., Pres. 1973, 1974. b. Nov. 11, 1938, St. Louis, MO. m. Marion Allen. c. Lee, Geoffrey. BA 60, Brown Univ.; MA 65, Princeton Univ.; PhD 69, Princeton Univ. **Other Studies:** ASCSA. **Research/Artistic Interests:** Archaeology. **Career & Employment:** Hill School, Pottstown, PA, Faculty 1960-62; Univ. of Illinois c.1971; Illinois-Princeton Archaeological Expedition, Morgantina, Sicily, Dir. **Fellowships, Honors & Awards:** Princeton Univ., Woodrow Wilson Fellow 1963-64, Bayard Henry Fellow 1963-64. **Publications:** "Hieron I" & "Hieron II," in *Encyclopedia Americana*; "The UI Goes to Sicily," *Champaign-Urbana News Gazette* (Apr. 11, 1971).

ALLEN, REGINALD ■ AAR, Acting Dir. 1969-70.

AMATEIS, EDMOND ROMULUS ■ FAAR Sculpture 24. b. Feb. 7, 1897, Rome, Italy. d. May 3, 1981. m. Dorothy F. Amateis. Beaux Arts Inst. of Design, NYC; Academie Julien, Paris. **Career & Employment:** American School of Sculpture 1924-25, 1926-31; Beaux Arts Inst. of Design 1927-29; Columbia Univ. 1937-38; Bennett Junior College 1937-38. **Memberships & Offices:** NIAL; NAD; Century Assn.; NSS, Pres. 1942-44. **Fellowships, Honors & Awards:** ALNY, Henry O. Avery Prize 1929; PAFA, James E. McClese Prize 1933; NSS, Lindsey Sterling Morris Medal, Herbert Adams Memorial Award 1980; Liberty Hyde Bailey Medal 1958. **Publications:** "A Sculptor Speaks His Mind," *Liturgical Arts* 12.1 (Nov. 1943); articles in: *Country Life, Town & Country, Pencil Points.* **Important Works:** Soc. of Medalists, Designer of Medal 1940; US Govt. Medals for Typhus Comm. & Pacific Theater of Operations; sculpture: *Madonna of the Jewel,* Greenville, MS 1922; *Aquatic Water Horses,* Baltimore, War Memorial 1927; *William M. Davidson Memorial,* Pittsburgh 1932; Relief for the Kerckhoff Mausoleum, Los Angeles 1934; Relief for Madison Sq. Post Office, NYC 1937; Reliefs for Philadelphia Post Office & Court House 1938; 3 folklore groups and portrait of A.G. Bell, NY World's Fair 1938; US Commerce Dept. Bldg., Washington, DC. **Bio-Bibliography:** *Sculpture of Edmond Amateis* (Brookgreen, SC: Brookgreen Garden, 1937); *Who Was Who in America; Who Was Who in American Art.*

AMENDOLA, ROBERT ■ FAAR Sculpture 35. b. Apr. 24, 1909, Boston, MA. m. Geraldine R. Lewis. c. Judith, Charles Anthony, Miriam, Caroline, Susan. BA, BFA, Yale Univ. School of Fine Arts. **Other Study:** Massachusetts Normal Art School 1925-30. **Research/Artistic Interests:** Videation in spatial orientation in blindness (perceptual rehabilitation). **Career & Employment:** Chance Vought Aircraft 1942-44; Old Farms Convalescent Hospital, Instr. 1944-47; American Center for Research in Blindness & Rehabilitation, Instr. & Researcher. **Fellowships, Honors & Awards:** Thomas J. Carroll Award for Innovative Leadership in Rehabilitation of the Blind. **Home Address:** 82 Franklin Rd., Hopkinton, MA 01748.

AMES, ANTHONY M. ■ FAAR Architecture 84. b. June 11, 1944, Ogden, UT. m. Ecetra Nippert. c. Huey, Nippy, Louie, Dewey, Daisy. BArch 68, Georgia Tech; MArch 78, Harvard Univ. **Career & Employment:** Univ. of Virginia, Charlottesville, Visiting Assc. Prof. 1981-82, 1983, Shure Prof. 1989; Harvard GSD, Visiting Critic 1982, 1984, 1992; RISD, Visiting Critic 1985; Columbia Univ., Visiting Assc. Prof. 1986, Visiting Prof. 1991; Georgia Tech, Atlanta, Prof. 1989; Princeton Univ., Visiting Prof. 1989; Univ. of Maryland, College Park, Kea Distinguised Prof. 1990; Ohio State Univ., Columbus, Visiting Prof. 1991; Univ. of Nebraska, Hyde Prof. 1993. **Fellowships, Honors & Awards:** *Architectural Record* House Award 1978; AIA, Georgia Assn., Award 1979, 1982, 1984, 1987, 1988, 1989; AIA, South Atlantic Regional Award 1980, 1984, 1986; *AIA Journal* Honor Award Architectural Drawing Competition 1982; AIA, Atlanta Chap., Silver Medal for Excellence 1986; AIA, College of Fellows 1989; *Progressive Architecture* Citation 1982; *Architectural Record,* Interior 1991. **Important Works:** Frank Wilson Hulse IV Guest House & Swimming Pool, Atlanta 1977; Administration & Teaching Facility for Dale Carnegie & Asscs., Atlanta 1979; Chang Residence, Augusta 1980; Frank Wilson Hulse IV Residence, Atlanta 1981; Anthony Ames Garden Pavilion, Atlanta 1982; Administration & Orientation Center for Atlanta Botanical Garden 1984; Branch Library, Fulton County, Alpharetta,

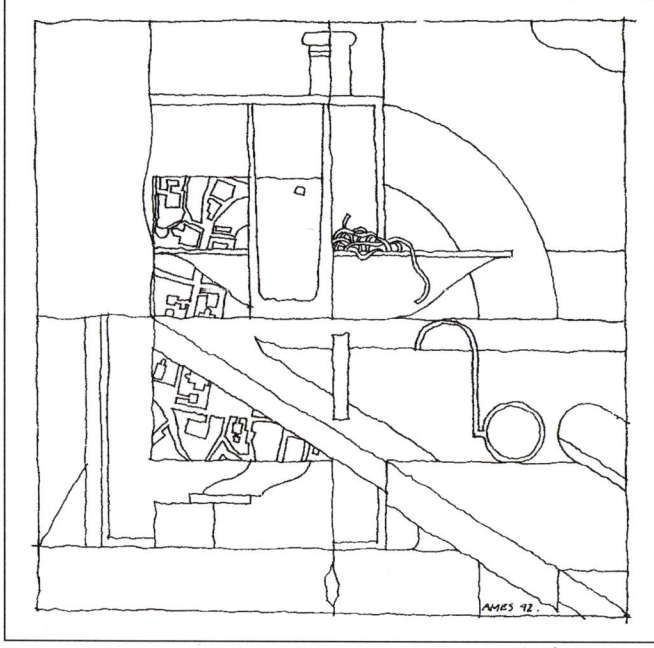

Anthony Ames

GA 1986; Martinelli Residence, Roxbury, CT 1986; Crews Residence, Seaside, FL 1987; Melia-Bryant Renovation, Atlanta 1987. **Exhibitions/Performances:** Nexus Gallery, Atlanta 1980; Peachtree Center, Atlanta 1981, 1982; KIPNIS: Works of Art, Atlanta 1982; Harvard GSD 1982; Univ. of Virginia School of Architecture, Charlottesville 1983, 1989; Ballenford Architectural Books Gallery, Toronto, ONT 1985; RISD 1985; Max Protetch Gallery, NYC 1985; Columbia Univ. School of Architecture & Urban Planning 1986; GA Gallery, Tokyo 1987; Univ. of Texas School of Architecture & Environmental Design, Arlington 1988; Univ. of Arkansas School of Architecture, Fayetteville 1989; Univ. of Alabama Moody Gallery of Art, Tuscaloosa 1989; NAD 1989; Univ. of Maryland School of Architecture, College Park 1990; Univ. of Nebraska, Lincoln 1991. **Bio-Bibliography:** "Project for Villa Chang," *Modulus* (1982): 74-77; *Emerging Voices* (New York: ALNY, 1986), 44-45; *Anthony Ames: Five Houses* (Princeton, NJ: Princeton Architectural Press, 1987); "A Garden Pavilion," *Global Architecture Houses* 21 (Winter 1987): 42-49; "The Emerging Generation in U.S.A.," *Global Architecture Houses Special* 2 (Nov. 1987): 98-103; "Hulse Residence," *Global Architecture Houses* 22 (Dec. 1987): 46-53; "Home at Seaside," *Global Architecture Houses* 27 (Winter 1989): 120-21; "Martinelli Residence," *Global Architecture Houses* 29 (Spring 1990): 126-33; Bill Lacy, *100 Contemporary Architects* (New York: Harry N. Abrams, 1991), 16-17; David Mohney & Keller Easterling, *Seaside* (New York: Princeton Architectural Press, 1991), 192-93; Jude LeBlanc, *18 Houses* (New York: Princeton Architectural Press, 1992), 2-7; Arno Lederer & Jorunn Raanarsdottir, *Wohnen Heute-Housing Today* (Stuttgart & Zurich: Kramer Verlag, 1992), 76-79. **Home Address:** 2608 Habersham Rd., Atlanta, GA 30305. **Business Address:** Anthony Ames Architect, PO Box 54144, Atlanta, GA 30308.

AMICI, PAOLA ■ AAR – Rome, Cashier.

AMISANO, JOSEPH ■ FAAR Architecture 52. b. Jan. 10, 1917, NYC. m. Rosellen Amisano. c. Paul, Tina, Lisa. BA 40, Pratt Inst., NYC. **Research/Artistic Interests:** Affordable housing, (IDEAA), international design for extreme environments, winter cities, polar regions, urban design, city planning. **Career & Employment:** Pratt Architectural Clinic, NYC 1940-41; Harrison, Fouilhoux & Abramovitz, Panama CZ 1941-42; Airport Development Program (ADP) 1943-44, Recife, Brazil 1945-46; Cooper Union, Visiting Faculty 1947; Ketchum Gina & Sharp, NYC 1947-50; Toombs Amisano & Wells 1953-present; Washington Univ., Visiting Faculty 1960; Cornell Univ., Visiting Faculty 1961; Georgia Tech, Visiting Faculty 1977; Southern Tech, Visiting Faculty 1991. **Memberships & Offices:** AIA 1946-present; Design Juror: Virginia Polytechical, Georgia Tech, Southern Tech, Auburn Univ. **Fellowships, Honors & Awards:** Pratt Inst., Design Medal 1940; *Progressive Architecture*, Children's Award 1954, Design Award 1962; AIA Fellow 1960, Award of Merit 1960, 1970, 1973, 1977, Awards for Design Excellence 1962, 1964, 1966, 1968, 1970, Honor Award 1967, 1968, 1976; AIA-American Assn. of School Administrators, Award of Merit 1964, 1967, Exb. Award 1975; AIA, Georgia Chap., Citation for Outstanding Design 1973, Honor Award for Outstanding Design 1973, 1975, 1976, Merit Award 1977, Award for Excellence 1983; AIA Atlanta Chap., Silver Medal 1983, Architect as Artist Award 1991; ALNY, Honorable Mention 1960; Nat. Conference on Church Architecture, Honor Award for Design Excellence 1965, 1966, Award of Merit for Excellence in Religious Architecture 1965; American Inst. of Steel Construction, Award of Excellence 1969; Bell System, Honorable Mention 1973; Architecture in Atlanta, Public Service Prog. 1973, 1974; Prestressed Concrete Inst., Special Recognition 1983; Civil Engineeering Soc., Urban Design Award 1983; Atlanta Urban Design Com., Award of Excellence 1983; Project Awards: Atlanta AIA, Conceptual Design Awards 1984; Atlanta Urban Design Com., Award of Excellence 1984. **Important Works:** Lenox Sq. Regional Shopping Center, Atlanta 1957; Georgia Warm Springs Found., Childrens' Ward 1962; Branch Office, NW Mutual Insurance 1964; Univ. of Georgia, Athens: Pharmacy Lab 1964, Visual Arts Bldg. 1965; John Knox Presbyterian Church, Marietta, GA 1967; Fernbank Science Center, Decatur, GA 1967; Ford Found., A College in the City, NYC 1968; Norfolk Gardens, Norfolk, VA, CBD Study 1971; Harper HS additions, Atlanta 1973; Atlanta Memorial Center 1980;

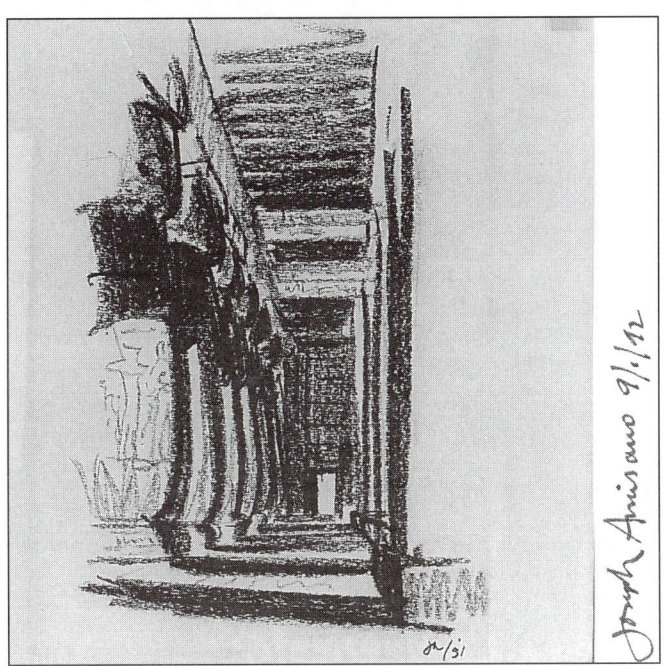

Joseph Amisano

Summit Office Bldg., Atlanta 1980; Atlanta Univ., Woodruff Library 1981; Peachtree Center Subway Station, Atlanta 1983. **Exhibitions/Performances:** numerous solo 1953-77. **Home Address:** 1028 Nawench Dr. NW, Atlanta, GA 30327. **Business Address:** Toombs Amisano & Wells, 1028 Nawench Dr. NE, Atlanta, GA 30327.

AMMERMAN, ALBERT J. ■ FAAR Classics/Archaeology 88. b. July 7, 1942, Detroit, MI. m. Rebecca L. Miller, FAAR 91. c. Richard. BA 64, Univ. of Michigan; PhD 72, Univ. of London. **Research/Artistic Interests:** Archaeology of early Rome; origins of Rome, Athens, & Venice; environmental studies in archaeology; design of archaeological surveys; reconstructing the ancient city. **Career & Employment:** Stanford Univ., Lect. & Senior Research Assc. 1972-77; SUNY Binghamton, Asst. Prof. 1977-83; Univ. of Parma, Italy, Visiting Prof. 1984-92; Colgate Univ., Visiting Prof. 1986-present; Univ. of Trent, Visiting Prof. 1995. **Fellowships, Honors & Awards:** Univ. of Michigan, Hopwood Writing Awards 1964; NEH Fellow 1984; Guggenheim Fellow 1990-91; CASVA, Kress Senior Fellow 1995-96; Grants for Archaeological Research from Consiglio Nazionale di Ricerca, Italy; Delmas Found.; National Geographic Soc.; Nat. Science Found.; SUNY; Wenner-Gren Found. **Publications:** "Surveys and Archaeological Research," *Annual Review of Anthropology* 10:63-88; with L.L. Cavalli-Sforza, *The Neolithic Transition and the Genetics of Populations in Europe* (Princeton: Princeton Univ. Press, 1984); *The Acconia Survey: Neolithic Settlement and the Obsidian Trade* (London: Inst. of Archaeology, Univ. of London, 1985); with G. Shaffer & N. Hartmann, "A Neolithic Household at Piana di Curinga, Italy," *Journal of Field Archaeology* 15 (1988): 121-40; "Old Calabria Revisited," *Antiquity* 62 (1988): 226-33; "Dawn of the Eternal City," *The Sciences* 29.4 (1989): 22-28; "Morfologia ed ambiente dell'area del Foro Romano," *Archeologia Laziale* 10 (1990): 17-20; "On the Origins of the Forum Romanum," *AJA* 94 (1990): 627-45; "Taking Stock of Quantitative Archaeology," *Annual Review of Anthropology* 21 (1992): 231-55; with M. De Min & R. Housley, "New Evidence on the Origins of Venice," *Antiquity* 66 (1992): 913-16; "La morfologia della valle fra Palatino e Velia," *Bollettino di Archeologia* 12 (1993). **Home Address:** 81 Hamilton St., Hamilton, NY 13346.

AMMERMAN, REBECCA MILLER ■ FAAR Classics/Archaeology 91. b. Jan. 30, 1956, Abilene, TX. m. Albert J. Ammerman, FAAR 88. c. Richard. BA 76, Bryn Mawr College; MA 78, Univ. of Michigan; PhD 83, Univ. of Michigan. **Other Study:** ASCS 1975; Middlebury College 1976; Archaeological Field Work: Ubeidiya, Israel; Carthage, Tunisia; Oderza (Treviso), Paestum, & Rome (Crytpa Balbi). **Research/Artistic Interests:** Archaeology of Greek city-states in southern Italy & Sicily; votive use of terracotta figurines in the Greco-Roman world. **Career & Employment:** Colgate Univ., Instr. 1982-83, Asst. Prof. 1984-89, Assc. Prof. 1990-present. **Fellowships, Honors & Awards:** Bryn Mawr College, Nat. Merit Scholar 1972-76; Univ. of Michigan, Rackham Fellowship 1976-77, Rackham Pre-Doctoral Fellowship 1979-80, Dissertation Travel Grant 1980; ArIA, Olivia James Traveling Fellowship 1979-80; Colgate Univ. Research Council Major Grant 1984, 1993, 1994; NEH Fellowship for College Teachers 1987; NSF ILI Grant 1989. **Publications:** "A Late Villanovan Vase from Bologna," in *Italian Iron Age Artifacts in the British Museum: Papers of the Sixth British Museum Classical Colloquium*, ed. J. Swaddling (London: British Museum, 1985), 267-71; "Medma and the Exchange of Votive Terracottas," *Papers in Italian Archaeology* 4, *The Cambridge Conference, British Archaeological Reports* (S.246) (1985):

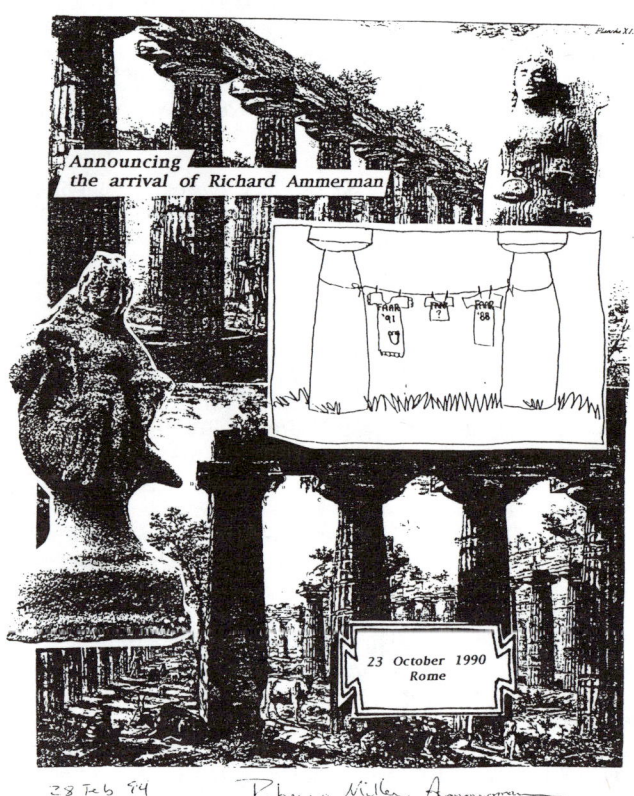

Rebecca Miller Ammerman

5-19; "Στυλιται in Magna Graecia: A Coroplastic Contribution to the History of Columnar Statue Bases," *Rivista di Archeologia* 11 (1987): 25-33; "Terracotte votive: evidenza di culto e contatto culturale in Magna Grecia," *Scienze dell'Antichità* 3-4 (1989-90): 353-62; "The Religious Context of Hellenistic Terracotta Figurines," in *The Coroplast's Art: Greek Terracottas of the Hellenistic World*, ed. J. Uhlenbrock (New Rochelle, NY: Caratzas, 1990), 37-45; "The Naked Standing Goddess: A Group of Archaic Terracotta Figurines from the Sanctuary in the Località Santa Venera at Paestum," *AJA* 95 (1991): 203-30. **Business Address:** Dept. of Classics, Colgate Univ., 13 Oak Dr., Hamilton, NY 13346.

AMMIDON, HOYT ■ AAR Trustee 1962-81, Banker.

AMORE, JOHN ■ FAAR Sculpture 40. b. Feb. 28, 1912, Genoa, Italy. Beaux Arts Inst. of Design, NYC. **Fellowships, Honors & Awards:** Beaux Arts Inst. of Design, Paris Prize 1935; City of New York, Medal of Honor Prize 1948. **Home Address:** 1518 Dorchester Dr., Palm Harbor, FL 34684.

ANDERSON, AMY CHRISTIE ■ FAAR Architecture 81. b. Feb. 27, 1951, Cleveland, OH. BA 73, Wellesley College; MArch 78, Columbia Univ. **Other Studies:** Skowhegan School of Painting & Sculpture 1971. **Fellowships, Honors & Awards:** Columbia Univ., AIA School Medal 1978.

ANDERSON, DAVID ■ FAAR Post-Classical/Humanistic Studies 89. b. Aug. 4, 1952, Fort Benning, GA. m. Teresa Murano. c. David, Maria. BA 73, Univ. of Florida, Gainesville; MA 76, Princeton Univ.; PhD 80, Princeton Univ. **Publications:** "Theban History in Chaucer's *Troilus*," *Studies in the Age of Chaucer* 4 (1982): 109-33; ed., *Pound's Cavalcanti* (Princeton:

Princeton Univ. Press, 1983); "Pound alla ricerca di una lingua per Cavalcanti," *Lettere Italiane* 37 (1985): 24-40; ed., *Sixty Bokes Olde & Newe* (New Chaucer Soc., 1986); *Before the Knight's Tale: Imitation of Classical Epic on Boccaccio's Teseida* (Philadelphia: Univ. of Pennsylvania Press, 1988); "La Cronaca di Fra Paolino di Venezia dalla Corte di Roberto d'Angiò alla Libreria di S. Francesco di Cesena," in *Libraria Domini... Biblioteca Malatestiana*, ed. P. Lucchi (Bologna: Grafis, 1993); "'Dominus Ludovicus' in the Sermons of Jacobus of Viterbo," in *Festschrift S. Wenzel*, ed. R. Newhauser & R. Alford (Binghamton, NY: MRTS, 1994); "The Italian Background to Chaucer's Epic Similes," *Annali d'Italianistica* 12 (1994): 1-24; "Boccaccio's Glosses on Statius," *Studi sul Boccaccio* 22 (1994): 100-275. **Home Address:** 50 Wilhelmstr., Tübingen D-72074, Germany.

ANDERSON, JAMES C., JR ■ FAAR Classics/Archaeology 79; Classical Summer School, Dir. 1992-94; Adv. Council. b. April 15, 1951, Malden, MA. m. Dana L. McCoy. c. Owen, Helena. BA 73, Colorado College; MA 76, UNC, Chapel Hill; PhD 80, UNC, Chapel Hill. **Career & Employment:** Univ. of Georgia, Asst. Prof. 1980-85; Assc. Prof. 1985-92; Prof. 1992-present; ICCS, Mellon Prof.-in-Charge 1993-94. **Memberships & Offices:** CAMWS; Soc. for Promotion of Roman Studies, UK; APA; ArIA, Athens, GA Chap., VP 1984-85, Pres. 1985-86, Sec.-Tres. 1986-88; VSA, Summer Study Dir. 1982, 1985, 1988, BoT 1987-90. **Fellowships, Honors & Awards:** Univ. of Georgia Research Found., Faculty Research Grants 1982, 1983, 1985-87, 1990, 1992; ACLS Grant-in-Aid 1983; NEH Summer Stipend 1983; Univ. of Georgia, Beaver Award for Excellence in Teaching 1988, Outstanding Honors Prof. 1990; NEH Fellowship 1994-95. **Publications:** "Post-Mortem Adventures of the Marble Plan of Rome," *Classical Outlook* 59 (1982): 69-73; "Domitian, the Argiletum and the Temple of Peace," *AJA* 86 (1982): 101-10; "A Topographical Tradition in Fourth-Century Chronicles," *Historia* 32 (1983): 93-105; *Historical Topography of the Imperial Fora*, Collection Latomus 182 (Brussels: Latomus, 1984); "The Date of the Thermae Traianai and the Topography of the Oppius Mons," *AJA* 89 (1985): 499-509; "The Date of the Arch at Orange," *Bonner Jahrbücher* 187 (1987): 159-92; *Roman Brick Stamps: The Thomas Ashby Collection*, Archaeological Monographs of the British School at Rome 3 (London: BSR, 1991); "The Ara Pacis Augustae: Legends, Facts and Flights of Fancy," in *Shapes of City Life in Rome and Pompeii*, ed. M.T. Boatwright & H.B. Evans, (New Rochelle, NY: Caratzas, forthcoming); *Roman Architecture and Society* (Baltimore: Johns Hopkins Univ. Press, forthcoming). **Business Address:** Dept. of Classics, Univ. of Georgia, Athens, GA 30602-6203.

ANDERSON, LENNART ■ FAAR Painting 61. b. Aug. 22, 1928, Detroit, MI. BFA 50, AIC School; MFA 50, Cranbrook Acad. of Art. **Other Studies:** ASL 1954. **Fellowships, Honors & Awards:** Tiffany Award 1957. **Important Works:** Brooklyn Museum. **Exhibitions/Performances:** Tanager Gallery, NYC 1962; Graham Gallery, NYC 1963-72; Bard College 1970; Davis & Langdale Co., NYC 1974-85; Suffolk Community College 1976; Swain School of Design 1982; Darien Library 1984.

ANDERSON, ROSS S. ■ FAAR Design Arts 90. b. Apr. 2, 1951, San Francisco, CA. m. Nina E. Santisi. c. Eva. BA 73, Stanford Univ.; MArch 77, Harvard Univ. **Career & Employment:** Turnbull Asscs. 1977-80; Anderson-Schwartz Architects 1983-present. **Memberships & Offices:** ALNY 1985-present. **Fellowships, Honors & Awards:** *Interiors Magazine*, "40 Under 40" 1987; ALNY, Emerging Voices 1988; *Architectural Record*, Record Houses 1990; Sunset-AIA, Western Home Awards 1991;

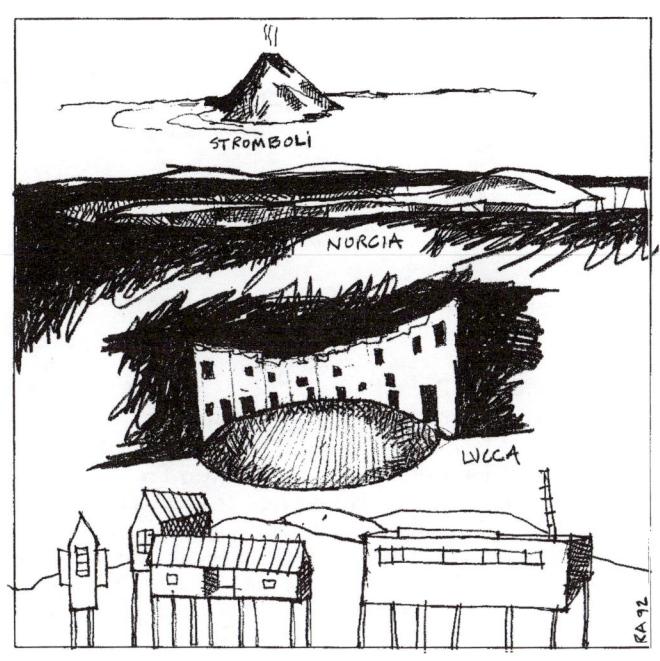

Ross Anderson

Architectural Digest AD 100 1992. **Important Works:** Windham Hill Records, Palo Alto, CA 1987; Rector Gate, Battery Park City, NYC 1987; House in Napa Valley, Rutherford, CA 1988; Reach Networks, NYC 1990; Isaac Mizrahi Offices & Showrooms, NYC 1990. **Exhibitions/Performances:** America Draws, travelling exb., Helsinki, Finland 1980; Skowhegan Competition: Leo Castelli Gallery, Harvard Univ., Yale Univ. 1982; Vermont AIA, Montpelier 1982; Artists Space, NYC 1983, 1984; Storefront for Architecture, NYC 1984, 1986; Protetch Gallery, NYC 1985; Venice Biennale 1985; Harvard GSD 1985; IDC 1986; 40 Under 40: NYC, Chicago, Paris, Tokyo, Los Angeles 1986-87; Baskerville + Watson, NYC 1987; NEOCON, Chicago 1988; New York 6, Video Interviews with Six New York Architects, sponsored by Knoll Intl. & *Metropolitan Home* 1988; American Crafts Museum, NYC 1988; Battery Park City, NYC 1989; MTA Arts for Transit, NYC 1989; Editions Ilene Kurtz, NYC 1989; AIA-SF Gallery, San Francisco 1989, 1992; Columbia Univ., Avery Library 1991; Washington Art Assn., Washington Depot, CT 1992. **Bio-Bibliography:** Sally Woodbridge, "Fine Tuned," *Progressive Architecture* (Sept. 1986): 102-6; Andrew MacNair & Frances Halsband, "40 Under 40," *Interiors Magazine* (Oct. 1986): cover, 1, 7, 149-98; Andrew Bartle & Jonathan Kirchenfeld, "Young Eastern U.S.A. Architecture," *Ottagono* (Fall 1987): 25; Alan Hess, "Windham Hill's Refreshing Offices," *San Jose Mercury News* (Nov. 22, 1987): 3; "Environments," *ID Annual Design Review* (July-Aug. 1988): 65; Aaron Betsky, "The New Primitive," *Metropolitan Home* (Nov. 1989): 169-75; Margaret Gaskie, "High Country," *Architectural Record* (Apr. 1990): 96-99; "Small House-Big View," *A&U* 90.12 (Dec. 1990, no. 243): 40-47; "The AD 100 Architects: A Guide to the World's Foremost Architects," *Architectural Digest* (Aug. 1991): 22-23; "Anderson + Schwartz: Showroom und Baros für Isaac Mizrahi," *Bauwelt* (Feb. 1992): 296-303; "Interior Space: Anderson-Schwartz," *A+U* (Mar. 1992), cover, 60-67; *Who's Who in America* 1992. **Home Address:** 101 Wooster St., NYC 10012. **Business Address:** Anderson-Schwartz Architects, 180 Varick St., NYC 10014.

ANDERSON, WARREN D. ■ AAR World War II Scholar 1942.

ANDERSON, WILLIAM S. ■ FAAR Classics/Archaeology 55; RAAR Classics/Archaeology 72; Classical Soc., Pres. 1963. b. Sept. 16, 1927, Brookline, MA. m. Lorna Bassette, Deirdre Kisich. c. Judith, Blythe, Heather, Meredith, Keith, Eric, Wylie. BA 50, Yale Univ.; BA 52, Cambridge Univ.; PhD 54, Yale Univ. **Research/Artistic Interests:** Latin classical poetry from Plautus to Juvenal. Up to 1970 research focused on Roman satire; since then research & publication on Vergil's *Aeneid*, Ovid's *Metamorphoses*, & the comedies of Plautus. **Career & Employment:** Yale Univ., Instr. 1955-60; UC, Berkeley, Asst. Prof.-Prof. 1960-present. **Memberships & Offices:** *Satire Newsletter*, Ed. Bd. 1962-80; *Vergilius*, Ed. Bd. 1962-present; *Scholia Satirica*, Ed. Bd. 1974-81; APA, BoD 1972-75, Pres. 1977; *California Studies in Classical Antiquity*, Co-Ed. 1978-81. **Fellowships, Honors & Awards:** Yale Univ., Morse Fellowship 1959-60; NEH Senior Fellowship 1972-73; Melbourne Univ., Research Fellowship 1984; Victoria College, Univ. of Toronto, 1st Robson Lect. 1987; Vassar College, Blegen Distinguished Prof. 1989-90. **Publications:** *The Art of the Aeneid* (Englewood Cliffs, NJ: Prentice Hall, 1967); ed., Ovid, *Metamorphoses, Books 6-10: Text and Commentary* (Norman: Univ. of Oklahoma Press, 1972, under auspices of APA); ed. Ovidius, *Metamorphoses, libri xv* (Leipzig: Teubner, 1977) and 5 reprts.; *Studies on Roman Satire* (Princeton: Princeton Univ. Press, 1982); with M.P. Frederick, *Selections from Ovid's Metamorphoses* (New York: Longman, 1988); *Barbarian Play: Plautus's Roman Comedy.* (Toronto: Univ. of Toronto Press, 1993). **Home Address:** 1424 Lincoln St., Berkeley, CA 94702.

Forty-one years of age, a fresh Ph.D. from Yale, I arrived with my new wife and new ambitions for a year at the Academy on the Prix de Rome in Classics. Arthur Hanson, Charles Babcock, and his future wife were completing their first year; Kathie Geffcken started with me. The Director of the Classical School was the incomparable Lily Ross Taylor. What a wonderful period it was for the Academy and Italy in 1954-55. In late May 1955, my first daughter was born at Salvator Mundi. Though obliged to move out, I stayed until August, as Assistant to George Duckworth in one of his great Summer School programs. I have been drawn back five times since.

In 1959-60, I returned on my first faculty fellowship, near the Academy with wife and two children, pursuing Roman satire at the Library. A third daughter was born before Christmas. In 1966-67, as Professor-in-Charge of the Intercollegiate Center for Classical Studies, I lived with five children on Via Ulisse Seni, a block away, and wrote on Vergil. Then, Classicist-in-Residence, on the panoramic top floor of the Villa Chiaraviglio, I became again a part of the Academy family. This time, my project was the manuscripts of Ovid in the Vatican and other libraries of Rome and Italy, as I prepared a Teubner text on the *Metamorphoses*. The 2000th anniversary of Vergil's death brought me back for three months in September 1981. My latest brief visit came over Spring vacation in 1990, when Michael Putnam enlivened the scene. *Omnia haec semper me meminisse iuvat iuvabitque.*

—William S. Anderson

ANDRE, CARL ■ AAR Visitor 1984-85, Sculptor.

ANDRES, GLENN M. ■ FAAR History of Art 69. b. July 15, 1941, Chicago, IL. m. Barbara N. Hann. c. Christopher Andres, Melissa Andres. BArch 64, Cornell Univ.; MFA 67, Princeton Univ.; PhD 71, Princeton Univ. **Research/Artistic Interests:** Italian Renaissance architecture; American architecture. **Career & Employment:** Middlebury College, Prof. 1970-present. **Memberships & Offices:** Soc. for Preservation of New England Antiquities, Vermont Council 1975-81; Sheldon Museum, Middlebury, VT, BoT 1975-85, 1992-present, VP 1979-81; Vermont Adv. Council for Historic Preservation 1986-present. **Fellowships, Honors & Awards:** NEH Summer Stipend 1985; Fulbright Lect., Exeter Univ. 1987-88; Prix Vasari, Paris, to *Art of Florence*, Best Art Book published in France 1989; NEH Summer Inst. on Architectural Theory 1990. **Publications:** "Cardinal Giovanni Ricci: The Builder from Montepulciano," *Il Pensiero italiano del Rinascimento e il tempo nostro: Atti del V Convegno Internazionale del Centro di Studi Umanistici, Montepulciano, 1968* (Florence: Olschki, 1970), 283-312; "The Villa Medici in Rome: The Projects of 1576," *Mitteilungen des Kunsthistorichen Instituts in Florenz* 19.2 (1975): 277-302; *A Walking History of Middlebury* (Middlebury, VT: Addison Press, 1975); *The Villa Medici in Rome* (New York: Garland Publishing, 1976); "Lavius Fillmore and the Federal Style Meeting House," *New England Meeting House and Church 1630-1850: Proceedings of the Dublin Seminar for New England Folklife, 1979* (Boston: Boston Univ. Press, 1980), 30-42; "Middlebury's Marble Fireplaces," *Vermont History* 55.4 (Fall 1987): 197-211; with John M. Hunisak & A. Richard Turner, *The Art of Florence* (New York: Abbeville Press, 1988); *The Medici and the Palazzo Vecchio*, video (New York: Treccani Publishing, 1989); "Nanni di Baccio Bigio et la villa Medicis," in *La Villa Medicis* (Rome: École Français de Rome, 1991), 2:227-56; "Urbanization and Architecture," in *Modern American Culture: An Introduction,* ed. R.M. Gidley (Harlow, UK: Longman, 1993), 189-212; *Hardy Holzman Pfeiffer Associates: Twenty-Five Years,* exb. cat. (Middlebury, VT: Middlebury College Museum of Art, 1992). **Bio-Bibliography:** *Who's Who in American Art.* **Business Address:** Middlebury College, Middlebury, VT 05753.

ANGELL, JAMES B. ■ AAR Charter Mem., Educator.

ANGOTTI, THOMAS ■ FAAR Architecture 90. b. Oct. 21, 1941, Brooklyn, NY. m. Emma Matos-Ramos. c. Antonio, Jacqueline, Aida, Justin. BA 64, Indiana Univ.; MCRP 71, Rutgers Univ.; PhD 73, Rutgers Univ. **Other Study:** Cornell Univ., courses in anthropolgy, Spanish in Peace Corps Training Program. **Research/Artistic Interests:** Urban environment & planning, development & underdevelopment, housing & community development, the politics of planning. **Career & Employment:** Massachusetts Dept. of Community Affairs, Chief Planner 1974-76; Hunter College, CUNY, Asst. Prof. 1976-78; Columbia Univ., Asst. Prof. 1977-81; Consultant, Urban Planning & Community Development 1974-76, 1981-85; NYC Dept. of Housing Preservation Development 1986-88; CUNY, Assc. Prof. 1988-present; NYC Dept. of City Planning, Assc. Planner 1988-94; Pratt Inst., Assc. Prof. 1994-present. **Memberships & Offices:** *Latin American Perspectives,* Participating Ed. 1987-present; *Planners Network,* Ed. 1994-present. **Publications:** "Planning for Regional Waste Water Systems," *Growth and Change* 6.2 (Apr. 1975): 36-42; with Bruce Dale, "Bologna Italy: Urban Socialism in Western Europe," *Social Policy* 7.1 (May-June 1976): 4-11; "Planning and Management of Water Resources in the Ljubljana Regional of Yugoslavia," *Environmental Conservation* 3.3 (Winter 1976): 189-96; *Housing in Italy: Urban Development and Political Change* (New York: Praeger, 1977); "The Housing Question: Engels and After," *Monthly Review* 29.5 (Oct. 1977): 30-51; "A Critical Assessment of Current Approaches to Housing Finance," *The Black Scholar* 11.2 (Nov.-Dec. 1979): 2-12; "The Political Critique of Dependency Theory," *Latin American Perspectives* 8.3-4 (Summer-Fall 1981): 124-37; "Planning the Open-Air Museum and Teaching Urban History: The United States in the World Context," *Museum* 34.3 (1982): 179-88; "The Contributions of José Carlos Mariátegui to Revolutionary Theory," *Latin American Perspectives Issue 49*

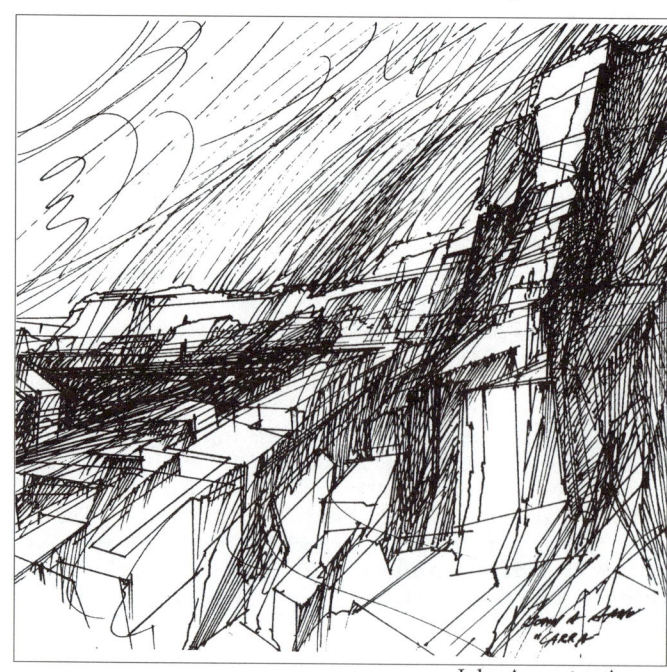

At an American place on the Gianicolo an urbanist gets an overview.

Put down the opera glasses. Là nella piazza troviamo l'urbano.

Thomas Angotti

13.2 (Spring 1986): 33-57; "Housing Strategies: The Limits of Local Actions," *Journal of Housing* 43.5 (Sept.-Oct. 1986): 197-206; "Urbanization in Latin America: Toward a Theoretical Synthesis," *Latin American Perspectives: Issue 53* 14.2 (Spring 1987): 134-56; "The Stalin Period: Opening Up History," *Science & Society* 52.1 (Spring 1988): 5-34; "Unequal Metropolitan Development and Equalization Policies," *Trialog* 26.3 (1990): 5-12; "Il sistema metropolitano degli Stati Uniti: Disuguaglianza e mobilità," *Archivio di Studi Urbani e Regionali* 44-45 (1992): 205-30; *Metropolis 2000: Planning, Poverty and Politics* (New York: Routlege, 1993); over 300 journal & newspaper articles, features, book reviews & technical reports. **Bio-Bibliography:** *International Authors and Writers Who's Who; National Directory of Latin Americanists; Who's Who in the East.* **Home Address:** 808 8th Ave., Apt. 4R, Brooklyn, NY 11215. **Business Address:** Pratt Inst., Graduate Center for Planning & Environment, 200 DeKalb Ave., Brooklyn, NY 11205.

ANNUS, JOHN AUGUSTUS ■ FAAR Painting 60. b. Oct. 25, 1935, Riga, Latvia. m. Edite Zeile. c. Fabiola Annus, Aurelia Annus. BFA 58, Pratt Inst. **Other Study:** NAD with Louis Bouche 1958-59; Accademia degli Belli Arti e Liceo Artistico, Rome 1962-64; Circle in the Square Theater School, NYC 1970-71. **Research/Artistic Interests:** Italian landscape, ancient Ro-

John Augustus Annus

man structures; photographic, multi-media projects: spaces in light. **Career & Employment:** Armstron Circle Theatre CBS, Research Asst. 1958-59; Cine-Centrum, NYC, Co-Founder, Art Dir. 1967-73; N.A.B.E.T. 1973; Feature Film Shadows, Production Designer 1974; Feature Film Looking Up, Production Designer 1976; Linda Yellen Productions, NYC, Production Designer 1975-79. **Memberships & Offices:** NAD, Assc. 1976, Academician 1980; Nat. Soc. of Mural Painters; Nat. Assn. of Broadcast & Television Employees, NYC 1972-79. **Fellowships, Honors & Awards:** Pratt Inst., Soc. of Illustrators Gold Medal 1958; NAD, Albert N. Hallgarten Traveling Grant 1958-59, J. Hallgarten Prize 1964, H.W. Ranger Prize 1965, 1975, S.J. Wallace Truman Prize 1967, Certificate of Merit 1980, 1987; Italian Government Grant Ministero degli Affari Esteri 1961; Mostra Intl. di Arti Figurativi, Roma, Gold Medal 1962. **Important Works:** NAD; Baltimore Museum of Fine Art; Dominican College, Columbus OH; Collection of the Italian Government, Rome. **Exhibitions/Performances:** Vantaggio Gallery Rome 1962, 1971, 1973, 1974; Vendo Nubes Gallery, Chestnut Hill, Philadelphia 1965, 1970, 1976; Skidmore College, Saratoga NY 1975; Pennsylvania Univ. Gallery, Philadelphia 1976; Black Gallery, Taos, NM 1982-84; Toronto Center Art Gallery 1984; Hensley Gallery, Taos, NM 1989; Jakobi Gallery-Paintings & Photographs, Hamburg, Germany 1987; NAD Annuals 1962, 1964, 1965, 1967, 1975, 1977, 1978, 1980, 1987, 1988, 1991, Invitational 1981; Reitner Gallery Riga, Latvia 1992; Museum of Fine Art, Riga, Latvia 1992. **Bio-Bibliography:** *Who's Who in America; Who's Who in American Art; Who's Who in the East.* **Home Address:** Ostmerkstr. 4, Münster 48145, Germany.

ANTONIONI, MICHELANGELO ■ AAR Visitor 1980-81, Film Dir.

APPLEYARD, DONALD ■ RAAR Design Arts 75. b. July 1928, London, England. dec. m. Sheila Fred. c. Rustin, Moana, Bruce, Ian. AA Dipl., Architectural Assn., London; M.C.P., MIT. **Career & Employment:** Architectural & urban design practice in US, England, Italy & Venezuela 1954-61; MIT-Harvard Joint Center for Urban Studies 1961-67; MIT, Asst. Prof. 1961-65, Assc. Prof. 1966-67; UC, Berkeley, Assc. Prof.-Prof. 1967-. **Memberships & Offices:** United Nations, Urban Design Consultant. **Fellowships, Honors & Awards:** Guggenheim Fellow 1974; Fulbright Senior Fellow 1975; Graham Found. Fellow 1980. **Publications:** with Kevin Lynch & John Meyer, *The View from the Road* (Cambridge, MA: MIT Press, 1963); *Planning a Pluralist City: Conflicting Realities in Ciudad Guayama* (Cambridge, MA: MIT Press, 1976); ed., *The Conservation of European Cities* (Cambridge, MA: MIT Press, 1979); *Livable Streets* (Berkeley: UC Press, 1980); with D.T. Smith, *Improving the Residential Street Environment* (Washington, DC: US Dept. of Transportation, 1980).

AQUILINO, DONALD ■ FAAR Painting 60, Art Liaison 1979-81. b. June 11, 1930, NYC. m. Ellen L. Davis. AA 49, Wesley Junior College, Dover, DE; BA 51, American Univ.; MA 57, American Univ. **Career & Employment:** American Univ. 1954-55; RISD, European Honors Program 1966, 1975-78; Temple Univ. Abroad-Tyler School of Art 1968-69; Dartmouth College, Artist-in-Residence 1975, Visiting Prof. 1985-86. **Fellowships, Honors & Awards:** American Univ., Clendenon Fellowship 1951; Via Margutta Annual, Bronze Medal 1959; David H. Zell Memorial Award 1964; *Progressive Architecture* Design Awards, Citation 1965; Acireale, Sicily, Premio Intl., 2d Prize 1968. **Exhibitions/Performances, Solo:** Gloria Luria Gallery, Miami 1969; Dartmouth College, Hanover, NH 1975, 1985; RISD 1975;

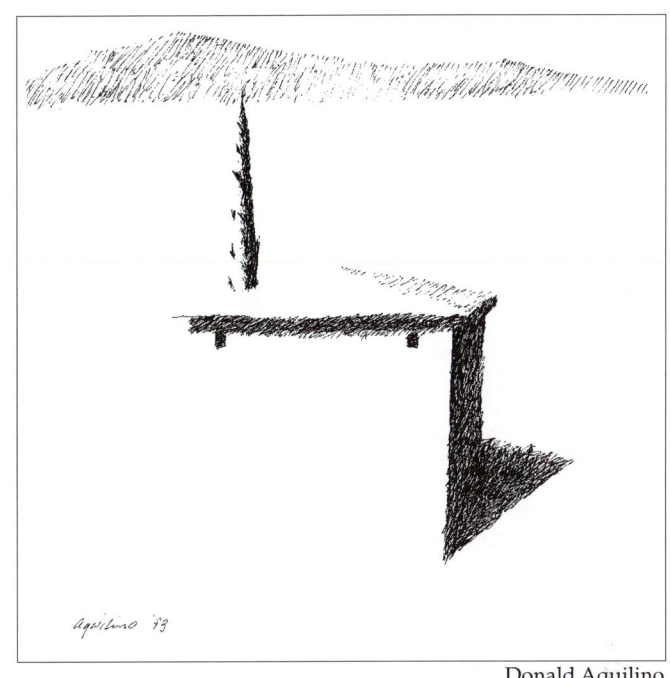
Donald Aquilino

Selected Group: Forsythe Gallery, Ann Arbor, MI 1962; Flint Art Inst., Flint, MI 1962; Allan Stone Gallery, NYC 1980; AAAL Annual Award Exb. 1985; Berta Walker Gallery, Provincetown, MA 1992. **Home Address:** 95 Sutherland Rd., Brookline, MA 02146. **Business Address:** Irving Gallery, 332 Worth Ave., Palm Beach, FL 33480.

ARBASINO, ALBERTO ■ AAR Visitor 1981-82, Writer.

ARGAN, GIULIO CARLO ■ AAR Visitor 1976-77, Mayor of Rome.

ARMANI, GIORGIO ■ AAR Italian Com. 1994, Fashion Designer.

ARMBRUST, ALAN ■ Chicago Architectural Club, Burnham Prize 1988-89.

ARMOUR, ALLISON V. ■ AAR Trustee 1911-14.

ARMOUR, GEO. ALLISON ■ AAR Trustee 1914-20.

ARMSTRONG, ERIC ■ FAAR Landscape Arch 61. b. Feb. 1, 1922, Indianapolis, IN. BS 48, UC, Berkeley. **Career & Employment:** Village Gallery, Bandon, Owner. **Home Address:** PO Box 926 Bandon, OR 97411.

ARMSTRONG, HENRY HERBERT ■ FASCSR 03; Carnegie Inst., Research Assc. at ASCSR 1909-10. b. Dec. 24, 1879, Waterloo, IN. d. Nov. 15, 1935. BA 01, Univ. of Michigan; MA 02, Univ. of Michigan; PhD 05, Univ. of Michigan. **Career & Employment:** Juniata College, Prof. 1905-6; Whitworth College, Tacoma WA, Prof. 1906-8; Yankton College, SD, Prof. 1908-9; Princeton Univ., Faculty 1910-11; Oberlin College, Faculty 1911-14; Drury College, Springfield, MO, Prof. 1914-19; Beloit College, Prof. 1918-35. **Publications:** "Autobiographical Elements in Latin Inscriptions," in *Latin Philology*, ed. Clarence L. Meader (New York: Macmillan, 1910), 215-85; "Inscriptions from Privernum," *AJA* 14 (1910): 318-23; "Privernum," *AJA* 15 (1911):

44-59, 170-94, 386-402; "Topographical Studies at Setia," *AJA* 19 (1915): 34-56; "Essentials in the Development of a Teacher," *Bulletin. Wisconsin Assn. Modern Language Teachers* 13 (Nov. 1919). **Bio-Bibliography:** Univ. of Michigan Archives.

ARMSTRONG, JAMES I. ■ FAAR Classics/Archaeology 56. b. April 20, 1919, Princeton, NJ. m. Carol Aymar. c. Carol, James, Jr., Elizabeth. BA 41, Princeton Univ.; MA 47, Princeton Univ.; PhD 49, Princeton Univ. **Research/Artistic Interests:** Homeric poems, Greek history & literature. **Career & Employment:** Princeton Univ., Instr. 1947-48, Asst. & Assc. Prof. 1952-63, Graduate School, Asst. & Assc. Dean 1958-62; Indiana Univ., Instr. 1949-50; Middlebury College, Pres. 1963-75; Westbrook College, Pres. 1986-87. **Memberships & Offices:** Vermont Higher Education Council, Pres. 1964-65; New England Colleges Fund, Pres. 1966-67; American Council on Education, Com. on Plans & Objectives 1965-67; Princeton Univ., BoT 1968-72; Shelburne Museum, BoT 1973-85. **Fellowships, Honors & Awards:** Phi Beta Kappa 1941; Woodrow Wilson Fellow 1946-47; Hon. LLD, Princeton Univ. 1967; Hon. LHD, Bates College 1967; Hon. Litt.D., Grinnell College 1967; Hon. Litt.D., Norwich Univ. 1977; Hon. Litt.D., Middlebury College 1977. **Publications:** "The Arming Motif in the Iliad," *American Journal of Philology* 79 (1958): 337-54; "The Marriage Song in the *Odyssey*," *TAPA* 89 (1958): 38-43; Introduction to *The Odyssey*, trans. S.H. Butcher & A. Lang (New York: Dodd, Mead, 1959); trans. of John Phillips, *Responsio*, in *The Complete Prose Works of Milton* 4.2 (New Haven: Yale Univ. Press, 1966); *Artes Liberales: A Selection of Addresses* (Middlebury, VT: Middlebury College, 1973). **Bio-Bibliography:** *Who's Who in America.* **Home Address:** 80 Lyme Rd., Apt. 1017, Hanover, NH 03755.

ARNALDI, GIROLAMO ■ Italian Fulbright Fellow 1955-56.

ARNHEIM, RUDOLF ■ RAAR History of Art 78. b. July 15, 1904, Berlin, Germany. m. Mary Arnheim. c. Margaret Nettinga. PhD 28, Univ. of Berlin. **Research/Artistic Interests:** Psychology of art. **Career & Employment:** Sarah Lawrence College 1943-68; Harvard Univ. 1968-74; Univ. of Michigan, Ann Arbor 1974-84. **Memberships & Offices:** American Psychological Assn., Division 10 (Psychology of Art), Pres. 1957, 1965, 1971; American Soc. for Aesthetics, Pres. 1959, 1979; AAAS. **Fellowships, Honors & Awards:** Guggenheim Fellow 1942-43; Fulbright Lect., Ochanomizu Univ., Tokyo. **Publications:** *Art and Visual Perception* (Berkeley & Los Angeles: UC Press, 1954); *Visual Thinking* (Berkeley & Los Angeles: UC Press, 1969); *The Dynamics of Architectural Form* (Berkeley & Los Angeles: UC Press, 1977); *The Power of the Center* (Berkeley & Los Angeles: UC Press, 1988); *To the Rescue of Art* (Berkeley & Los Angeles: UC Press, 1992). **Home Address:** 1200 Earhart Rd., No. 537, Ann Arbor, MI 48105.

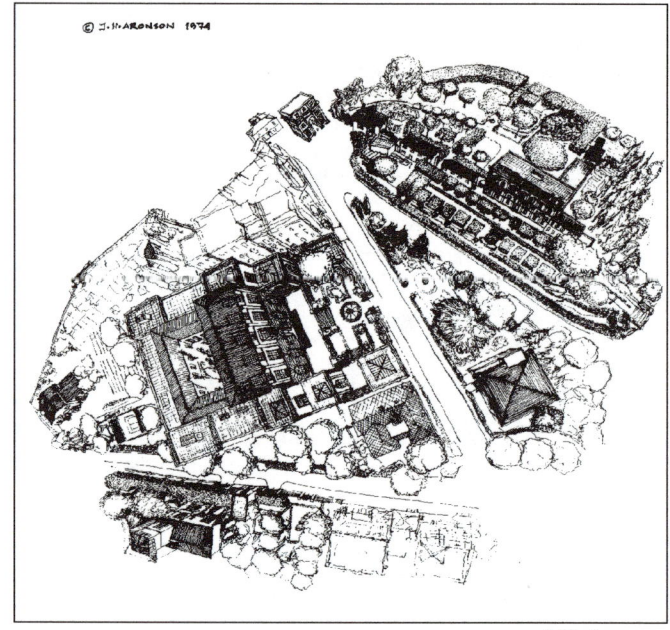

J.H. Aronson

ARONSON, J.H. ■ FAAR Design Arts 74. b. Feb. 7, 1937, NYC. Cornell Univ. School of Architecture 1955-58; Columbia Univ., Avery School of Architecture 1959-61. **Research/Artistic Interests:** Urban evolution & the problem of depiction; aerial photography, mapping from the "primitive eye." **Career & Employment:** Independent graphic designer & printmaker; Victor Gruen Asscs. 1961-63; J.H. Aronson, Publisher, Pres. 1984-present; MIT, Visiting Scholar 1995. **Memberships & Offices:** Community Planning Board No. 6, NYC; SAH; Vernacular Architecture Forum; Soc. of Panoramic Photographers; City & Country School, NYC, BoD, Treas., Sec., Chair 1982-88; Catskill Center for Conservation & Development; Catskill Forest Owners' Assn. **Fellowships, Honors & Awards:** Guggenheim Fellowship 1975-76; Graham Found. Grant 1981. **Important Works:** Public Collections: New York Public Library; Avery Library, Columbia Univ.; MMA; Galleria degli Uffizi; ARCO Found. **Home Address:** Townsend Hollow Rd., PO Box 302, Highmount, NY 12441.

ARROWSMITH, WILLIAM AYRES ■ FAAR Classics/Archaeology 57. b. Apr. 13, 1924, South Orange, NJ. d. Feb. 20, 1991. m. Jean Reiser. c. Beth, Nancy. BA 47, Princeton Univ.; BA 51, Oxford Univ.; MA 58, Oxford Univ.; PhD 54, Princeton Univ. **Career & Employment:** Princeton Univ., Instr. 1951-53; Wesleyan Univ. 1953-54; UC, Riverside 1954-56; Univ. of Texas 1959-70, Chair 1965-66; Visiting Prof.: MIT 1970-71, Boston Univ.

My months at the Academy in the Spring of 1978 renewed my love for Italy and allowed me to spend time with my old Italian friends, Paolo Milano, Fedele D'Amico, and Pietro Ingrao. My daily trips down the hill on the crowded bus greatly refreshed my image of the Baroque buildings, and in my little office on the top floor of the Academy, with its windows open to the blackbird, which on top of the poplar tree supplied melody to my writing, I wrote in English and thought in Italian.

Rudolf Arnheim

Ann Arbor, Michigan
August 1992

Rudolf Arnheim

1971-77, Yale Univ. 1976-77; Johns Hopkins Univ., Prof. 1977-81; Emory Univ., Prof. 1982-86; Boston Univ., Prof. 1986-1991. **Memberships & Offices:** *Chimera*, Founding Ed. 1942-44; PEN; Kirkland College, Academic Adv. Council 1967-70; York College, Council for Academic Development 1967-69; Nat. Professions Found.; American Assn. for Higher Education, Eastern Regional Bd.; American Assn. of Colleges, Com. on Liberal Studies 1972-73; Nat. Book Awards 1967-72; Acad. of Literary Studies; Intl. Council for the Future of the Univ.; Columbia Univ., Intl. Council Translation Center 1975. **Fellowships, Honors & Awards:** Woodrow Wilson Found. Fellowship 1947-48; Rhodes Scholar, Oxford Univ. 1954; Guggenheim Fellowship 1957-58; Univ. of Texas, Bromberg Award for Excellence in Teaching 1959, Morris L. Ernst Award for Excellence in Teaching 1962; Longview Award in Criticism 1960; Phi Beta Kappa Visiting Scholar 1964-65; Piper Prof., Outstanding Academic Achievement 1966; Loyola Univ., Hon. LLD 1968; St. Michaels College, Hon. LHD; Harbison Award for Distinguished Teaching 1971; Landon Translation Prize 1986; Shestack Poetry Prize 1987; Intl. Montale Prize 1990. **Publications:** trans., *The Satyricon of Petronius* (Ann Arbor: Univ. of Michigan Press, 1959); *Cyclops, Bacchae, Heracles, Orestes* and *Hercuba*, in *The Complete Greek Tragedies*, ed. David Grene & Richmond Lattimore (Chicago: Univ. of Chicago Press, 1960); trans. with an introduction, *The Birds of Aristophanes* (Ann Arbor: Univ. of Michigan Press, 1961); ed. with Roger Shattuck, *The Craft and Context of Translation* (Austin: Univ. of Texas Press, 1961); trans. with an introduction, *The Clouds of Aristophanes* (Ann Arbor: Univ. of Michigan Press, 1962); ed., *Image of Italy* (Austin: Univ. of Texas Press, 1961); ed., *Six Modern Italian Novellas* (New York: Pocket Books, 1964); trans. with D.S. Carne Ross, Cesare Pavese, *Dialogues with Leuco* (Ann Arbor: Univ. of Michigan Press, 1965); trans., Eugenio Montale, *The Storm and Other Things* (New York: Norton, 1985); trans., Eugenio Montale, *The Occasions* (New York: Norton, 1987). **Bio-Bibliography:** *Blue Book: Leaders of the English Speaking World*; *Briggs*, 21-23; *Contemporary Authors*, *Dictionary of International Biography*, *Directory of American Scholars*, *International Who's Who in Community Service*, *International Who's Who in Poetry*, *Midcentury Authors*, *Poets and Writers*, *Who's Who in America*, *Who's Who in the American Theatre*, *Who's Who in the Northeast*, *Who's Who in the World*, *Writers and Artists Yearbook*.

ASH, PERCY ■ Univ. of Pennsylvania Fellow, American School of Architecture 1895; Stewardson Memorial Scholar 1911-12, 1913. Architect. b. Nov. 5, 1865. d. July 19, 1933. **Career & Employment:** George Washington Univ., Prof., Architecture Dean 1903-10; Univ. of Illinois, Prof. 1913-18; private architectural practice, Philadelphia 1918-33. **Important Works:** Federal Buildings at the 1904 Louisiana Purchase Exposition.

ASHTON, SIR LEIGH ■ AAR Visitor 1943-51, Victoria & Albert Museum, Dir.

ASKEW, HENRY ESS ■ FAAR Classics/Archaeology 32. b. Aug. 23, 1906, Kansas City, MO. d. June 7, 1985. BA 28, Harvard Univ. **Other Study:** ASCSA, Fellow 1928-30. **Career & Employment:** Manufacturer, Eden, NY 1935-80. **Publications:** "Portrait of Caracalla in Corinth," *AJA* 35 (1931): 442-47; contr., *Corinth: Architecture*, ed. R. Stillwell et al. (Cambridge, MA: Harvard Univ. Press for ASCSA, 1941).

AUCHINCLOSS, LILY ■ AAR Trustee 1983-present. **Memberships & Offices:** MOMA, BoT, Architecture Com., Chair; Intl. Council, Sec.; Cooper Union, BoT; Orpheus Chamber Orchestra, BoT; Morgan Library, Fellow; van Ameringen Found., VP.

AVERY, HARRY ■ AAR Trustee 1974-77, Trustee Emer.

AVERY, WILLIAM T. ■ FAAR Classics/Archaeology 39. b. Sept. 9, 1912, East Cleveland, OH. d. Mar. 20, 1985. m. Frances Elizabeth Jordan c. Frances, Elizabeth, Avery Hardy. BA 34, Western Reserve Univ.; MA 35, Western Reserve Univ.; PhD 37, Western Reserve Univ. **Research/Artistic Interests:** Latin literature, textual criticism of Greek & Latin authors. **Career & Employment:** Fenn College, Instr. 1940-42; US Army Air Force 1942-45; Dickinson College, Assc. Prof. 1946-48; Louisiana State Univ., Prof. 1948-55; Univ. of Maryland, Prof. & Chair 1955-78; Univ. of Maryland, Prof. 1978-82. **Memberships & Offices:** APA; Dante Soc. of America; Classical Assn. of Atlantic States; Sigma Chi; Eta Sigma Phi; Phi Eta Sigma. **Publications:** "The *Adoratio Purpurae* and the Importance of the Imperial Purple in the Fourth Century of the Christian Era," *Memoirs of the AAR* 17 (1940): 66-80; "*Mentem mortalia tangunt*," *Classical Philology* 48 (1953): 19-20; "*Corvus albus*," *Classical Journal* 50 (1955): 257-58; "Augustus and the *Aeneid*," *Classical Journal* 52 (1957): 225-29; "The Onomatopoeia of *Aeneid* III, 699-715," *Classical Journal* 54 (1959): 350-52; "The *Vita* of Tibullus," *Classical Philology* 55 (1960): 24-27; "The Year of Tibullus' Death," *Classical Journal* 55 (1960): 205-9; "*Culex 174, un emendamento*," *Rivista di filologia e di istruzione classica* 38 (1960): 165-69; "A Crux in Aulus Gellius, *Noctes Atticae* 1.15.1," *Traditio* 17 (1961): 427-32; "Tibullus' Death Again," *Classical Journal* 56 (1961): 229-33; "*Patiens pulvis atque solis*," *Classical Philology* 61 (1966): 176-79; "Ovid, *Ars amatoria* 1.114: An Emendation," *Classical Philology* 69 (1974): 279-80. **Bio-Bibliography:** *Directory of American Scholars*; *Who Was Who in America*.

AVESANI, RINO ■ Italian Fulbright Fellow 1959-60.

AYERS, RICHARD W. ■ FAAR Architecture 38. b. Nov. 23, 1910, Jefferson, GA. d. 1995. m. Vaughan Benz. c. Richard Allan, Allan Winston, Claire Vaughan. BFA 32, Yale Univ.; MFA 34, Yale Univ. **Other Study:** Piedmont College, Demorest, GA 28. **Career & Employment:** Buckler Fenhagen Meyer & Ayers, Architects, Part. 1946-55; Meyer Ayers Saint, Architects, Pres. 1955-86; Ayers Saint Gross, Architects, Chair. 1986-91. **Memberships & Offices:** State of Maryland, Bd. of Architecture Review 1947-55, 1963-75; Baltimore Art Com. 1955-68, 1980-88; Baltimore Museum of Art, Bldg. Com., Chair. 1955-60; Baltimore Bldg. Congress, BoT 1956-58; Fulbright Fellowship Selection Com. 1959-62; Com. on the Nat. Capitol 1963-64. **Fellowships, Honors & Awards:** Yale Univ., Garland Fellow 1933-34; AIA Fellow 1968; NAD Assc. 1969. **Important Works:** Johns Hopkins Univ.: Shriver Hall 1954, Newton H. White Athletic Center 1965, Milton S. Eisenhower Library 1965, Physics & Astronomy Bldg. 1989; Social Security Buildings, Woodlawn, MD: HQ Bldg. 1961, Annex 1962, HQ Extension 1963, Adm. & Warehouse 1970, Adm. Bldg. Annex 1971, Computer Bldg. 1975; Maryland Historical Soc. 1967; Loyola College & College of Notre Dame Library 1971; Walters Art Gallery Addition, Baltimore 1971; State of Maryland, Central Laboratory & Office Bldg. 1974; Goucher College Athletic Facility 1986; George Washington Univ., Communications Bldg., Washington, DC 1988; Univ. of Delaware Laboratory Bldg. 1989; Univ. of Virginia Student Union 1991; Univ. of Maryland: Wye Research & Education Center 1991, Health Sciences Bldg. 1993. **Bio-Bibliography:** *Who's Who in America*. **Home Address:** 105 Cotswold Rd., Baltimore, MD 21210. **Business Address:** Ayers Saint Gross, 222 St. Paul Pl., Baltimore, MD 21202-2091.

AYRES, LARRY M. ■ FAAR History of Art 84. b. Nov. 15, 1939, Lewistown, PA. BA 64, Dartmouth College; B.Litt. 66, New College, Oxford Univ.; PhD 70, Harvard Univ. **Research/ Artistic Interests:** History of the book in the Middle Ages, pictorial arts of the Middle Ages, medieval book production & manuscript illumination, medieval art in Rome. **Career & Employment:** UC, Santa Barbara, Asst. Prof. 1970-74, Assc. Prof. 1974-79, Prof. 1979-present, Chair 1976-79, 1980-83, 1986-87. **Memberships & Offices:** Intl. Center of Medieval Art, BoD 1976-82; Società di Storia della Miniatura 1986. **Fellowships, Honors & Awards:** NEH Fellowship 1972, Grant 1988; ACLS Grant 1973; Alexander von Humboldt Stiftung Fellowship 1979-80, 1986, 1993; APS Grant 1981, 1982. **Publications:** "Parisian Bibles in the Berlin Staatsbibliothek," *Pantheon: Internationale Zeitschrift für Kunst* 40 (1982): 5-13; "A Fragment of a Romanesque Bible in Vienna (Oesterreichische Nationalbibliothek Cod. Ser. nov. 4236) and its Salzburg Affiliations," *Zeitschrift für Kunstgeschichte* 45 (1982): 130-44; "Collaborative Enterprise in Romanesque Manuscript Illumination and the Artists of the Winchester Bible," *Transactions of the British Archaeological Association* 6 (1983): 20-35; "The Bible of Henry IV and an Italian Romanesque Pandect in Florence," *Studien zur mittelalterlichen Kunst: Festschrift Florentine Mütherich* (Munich, 1985), 157-66; "An Italianate Episode in Romanesque Bible Illumination at Weingarten Abbey," *Gesta* 24 (1985): 121-28; "An Italian Romanesque Manuscript of Gregory the Great's *Moralia in Job*," *Florilegium in Honorem Carl Nordenfalk Octogenarii Contextum: Festschrift Carl Nordenfalk* (Stockholm, 1987), 31-46; "An Italian Romanesque Manuscript of Hrabanus Maurus' *De Laudibus Sanctae Crucis* and the Gregorian Reform," *Dumbarton Oaks Papers: Studies on Art and Archaeology in Honor of Ernst Kitzinger* 41 (1987): 13-27; "Gregorian Reform and Artistic Renewal in Manuscript Illumination: The 'bibbia atlantica' as an International Artistic Denomination," *Studi Gregoriani* 14 (1991): 145-52; "A Classicizing Byzantine Style and Manuscript Illumination at St. Peter's Basilica in the Eleventh Century," *Hülle und Fülle: Festschrift für Tilmann Buddensieg* (Bonn, 1993), 3-12; "The Italian Giant Bibles: Aspects of their Touronian Ancestry and Early History," *The Early Medieval Bible* (Cambridge, 1994), 125-54; "Bibbie italiane e bibbie francesi: il tredicesimo secolo," in *Presenze del Gotico Europeo in Italia* (Naples, 1994); "An Early Christian Legacy in Italian Romanesque Miniature Painting," *Weiner Jahrbuch für Kunstgeschichte* 46 (1993-4): 17-24. **Home Address:** 4042 Primavera Rd., No. 9, Santa Barbara, CA 93110. **Business Address:** Dept. of History of Art & Architecture, UC, Santa Barbara, CA 93106.

AYRES, LOUIS ■ AAR Trustee 1929-44, Architect.

■ ■ ■

B

BAADE, ERIC C. ■ FAAR Classics/Archaeology 57, Cosa Excavation Staff Mem. 53-57, AAR Summer School, Asst. Dir. 1956. b. Feb. 1, 1928, Fort Wayne, IN. m. Isobel J.W. Milne. c. Anne Baade. BA 49, Yale Univ.; PhD 56, Yale Univ. **Other Study:** AAR Summer School 1950. **Career & Employment:** Brooks School, Master-Chair, Classics 1949-51, 1964-73, 1975-90; Yale Univ., Instr.-Asst. Prof. 1957-1961; Trinity College (Hartford), Instr. 1958; Phillips Acad. (Andover), Master 1961-64; Columbia Univ. Summer School, Asst. Prof. 1972; St. Stephen's School (Rome), Chair, Classics 1973-75; Center for Mediterranean Studies (Rome), Asst. Prof. 1974-75. US Army, Corporal 1951-53; Barbizon Light of New England, Theatrical Consultant 1979-85; *New England Entertainment Digest*, Ed. Staff 1980-85; *Brooks Bulletin*, Ed. 1980-89. **Fellowships, Honors & Awards:** Yale Univ., Davenport College, Fellow 1958. **Publications:** with Allan G. Gillingham, *The Mostellaria of Plautus*. (Andover, MA: Phillips Acad., 1964); with Allan G. Gillingham, *Plautus for Production*. (Andover, MA: Phillips Acad., 1965); with Allan G. Gillingham, *Plautus for Reading and Production* (Glenview, IL: Scott Foresman, 1965); *Seneca's Tragedies* (New York: Macmillan, 1966); with Charles Jenney Jr. & Rogers V. Scudder, *First Year Latin* (Boston: Allyn & Bacon, 1968); with Charles Jenney Jr. & Rogers V. Scudder, *Second Year Latin* (Boston: Allyn & Bacon, 1968); with Allan G. Gillingham, *An Ovid Reader* (Columbus, OH: Charles E. Merrill, 1969); *First Year Latin* (New York: Prentice Hall, 1990); with Thomas K. Burgess, Rogers V. Scudder, David Coffin, *Second Year Latin* (New York: Prentice Hall, 1990). **Home Address:** 20 Main St., No. 12, Rockport, MA 01966-1542.

BABCOCK, CHARLES L. ■ FAAR Classics/Archaeology 55; RAAR Classics/Archaeology 86; AAR Trustee 1981-83, Trustee Emer.; Classical Soc., Pres. 1957; Dir. of Summer Session 1966; Acting Mellon Prof.-in-Charge, School of Classical Studies 1988-89; Adv. Council, School of Classical Studies, Chair 1991-94; Friends of Library, Former Chair. b. May 26, 1924, Whittier, CA. m. Mary A. Taylor, FAAR 54. c. Robert S., Jennie R. Chapman, Jonathan T. BA 48, UC, Berkeley; MA 49, UC, Berkeley; PhD 53, UC, Berkeley. **Research/Artistic Interests:** Principal areas of research have been in Latin literature (particularly in Horace and other Augustans and Tacitus), Latin epigraphy, and in various aspects of Roman civilization. I have also been concerned as an administrator with broader areas of the Humanities. **Career & Employment:** Cornell Univ., Instr. 1955-57; Univ. of Pennsylvania, Asst.-Assc. Prof. 1957-66, Asst. Dean 1960-62, Vice Dean 1962-64, Acting Dean 1964; Ohio State Univ., Prof. 1966-92, Chair 1966-68, 1980-88, Dean, College of Humanities 1968-70; Prof. Emer. 1992-present. **Memberships & Offices:** APA, Dir. 1968-72 & numerous committees; CAMWS, Exec. Com. 1970-74, Pres. 1977-78; VSA, BoT 1967-70, VP 1971-75, Pres. 1975-76; ICCS, Prof.-in-Charge 1974, Managing Com. Chair 1975-82; Advanced Placement Pgm., Com. of Examiners in Latin 1967-72, Chair 1972-74; Assn. of Depts. of Foreign Languages, Exec. Com. 1984-86, Pres. 1986. **Fellowships, Honors & Awards:** UC, Phi Beta Kappa 1948; Fulbright Scholar 1953-55; Univ. of Pennsylvania, Outstanding Faculty Award, Friars Senior Soc. 1963; Ohio State Univ., Alfred Wright Award 1968, Alumni Distinguished Teaching Award 1982, Exemplary Faculty Award (1st) College of Humanities 1989; CAMWS, Ovatio Award of Merit 1982. **Publications:** "The Study of Latin Inscriptions," *Classical World* 52 (1959): 237-44; "The Role of Faunus in Horace, *Carmina* 1.4," *TAPA* 92 (1961): 13-19; "An

Inscription of Trajan Decius from Cosa," *American Journal of Philology* 83 (1962): 147-58; "Dio and Plutarch in the *damnatio* of Antony," *Classical Philology* 57 (1962): 30-32; "The Early Career of Fulvia," *American Journal of Philology* 86 (1965): 1-32; "*Si certus intrarit dolor*: A Reconsideration of Horace's Fifteenth Epode," *American Journal of Philology* 87 (1966): 400-419; "Horace *Carm*. 1.32 and the Dedication of the Temple of Apollo Palatinus," *Classical Philology* 62 (1967): 189-92; "The Classics and the New Humanist," in *The Eternal Fountain*, ed. M.P.O. Morford (Columbus: Ohio State Univ. Press, 1972), 3-27; "*Omne militabitur bellum*: The language of commitment in *Epode* I," *Classical Journal* 70 (1974): 78-93; "Horace, *Epodes* 13: Some Comments on Language & Meaning," *Wege der Worte, Festscrift for Wolfgang Fleischauer* (Cologne: Bohlau, 1978), 107-18; "*Recreatio* and *Consilium* in the Pierian Cave," *Classical Journal* 75 (1979): 1-9; with J.T. Davis, et al., *Aspects of Roman Civilization* (Columbus, OH, 1980); "*Carmina operosa*: Critical Approaches to the *Odes* of Horace 1945-75," *Aufsteig und Niedergang der Römische Welt II*, 31,3 (Berlin: de Gruyter, 1981), 1560-1611; "*Sola...multis e matribus*: A Comment on Vergil's Trojan Women," *The Two Worlds of the Poet: New Perspectives on Vergil*, ed. R.M. Wilhelm and H. Jones (Detroit, MI: Wayne State Univ. Press, 1992), 39-50. **Bio-Bibliography:** *Who's Who in America*. **Home Address:** 973 Lynbrook Rd., Columbus, OH 43235-3307. **Business Address:** Dept. of Classics, Ohio State Univ., 414 Univ. Hall, 230 N. Oval Mall, Columbus, OH 43210.

BABCOCK, MARY TAYLOR ■ FAAR Classics/Archaeology 54; Classical Soc., Sec 1958. b. Mar. 8, 1929, Highland Park, NJ. m. Charles L. Babcock, FAAR 55. c. Robert S., Jennie R. (Chapman), Jonathan T. BA 50, Mt. Holyoke College; MA 51, Bryn Mawr College. **Career & Employment:** Northfield School for Girls, Teacher 1954-55; Wells College, Visiting Instr. 1956-57; Baldwin School, Teacher 1957-59; Girl Scouts of America, Troop Leader 1971-78. **Memberships & Offices:** Seal of Ohio, BoD; Mt. Holyoke College: Alumnae Admissions Rep., Regional Admissions Co-Ordinator 1977-91; Indian Hills Residence Assn., BoT, Pool Manager; Columbus Public Schools, "I Know I Can" Program, Adv. **Fellowships, Honors & Awards:** Fulbright Fellowship 1953-54; Columbus Public Schools, Golden Ruler Award 1994. **Home Address:** 973 Lynbrook Rd., Columbus, OH 43235-3307.

BACE, ED ■ Michigan Fellow 78. Archaeologist, Banker.

BACON, EDMUND N. ■ AAR Trustee 1967-76, Trustee Emer., Architect-Urban Planner.

BACON, HELEN H. ■ RAAR Classics/Archaeology 69; Barnard Representative to Adv. Council 70-89. b. Mar. 9, 1919, Berkeley, CA. BA 40, Bryn Mawr College; PhD 55, Bryn Mawr College. **Other Study:** UC, Berkeley 1940-41; Radcliffe College 1941-42; ASCSA 1952-53. **Research/Artistic Interests:** Apart from one fairly technical book and one translation with poet Anthony Hecht of a tragedy of Aeschylus, my main research interests have appeared in a series of literary critical essays. These explore form and meaning in my specialty, Greek tragedy, and in a fairly wide range of Greek and Latin literary texts, both in terms of the artistic traditions of the cultures in which they were produced and in relation to the more general artistic traditions in which all literatures exist. A rewarding extension of this interest has been a group of articles on the widespread presence in Robert Frost's poems of themes, devices and veiled echoes of Greek and Roman literature. **Career & Employment:** USNR-WVS, Ensign-Full Lieutenent 1942-45;

Bryn Mawr, Instr. 1946-49; Smith College, Instr.-Assc. Prof. 1953-61; Barnard College, Assc. Prof.-Prof. 1961-89, Prof. Emer. 1989-present; Breadloaf School of English, Faculty Summers 1966, 1968, 1973, 1975; Vassar College, Distinguished Visiting Research Prof. 1979; Harvard Univ., Visiting Prof. 1983; NIH Consultant on Latin Translation 1974-85; APA 1946-present, Dir. 1976-79, 1983-86, 2nd VP, 1st VP, Pres. 1983-85; ASCSA, Managing Com., Barnard Rep. 1962-89, Exec. Com. 1987-91; Nat. Phi Beta Kappa, Nominating Com. 1976-82, Sibley Award Com. 1981-83; Columbia Univ., Soc. of Fellows in Humanities, Senior Fellow 1977-present. **Fellowships, Honors & Awards:** ASCSA Student Fellowship, Fulbright 1952-53, Visiting Research Fellow 1984-85; AAUW, Founders Fellow 1963-64; Barnard College, Hon. Phi Beta Kappa 1966; Middlebury College, Hon. Litt.D. 1970. **Publications:** *Barbarians in Greek Tragedy* (New Haven: Yale Univ. Press, 1961); with Anthony Hecht, *Aeschylus' Seven Against Thebes*, verse trans. with intro. & notes (New York: Oxford Univ. Press, 1973); "Socrates Crowned," *Virginia Quarterly Review* 35 (1959): 415-30; "The Shield of Eteocles," *Arion* 3 (1964): 27-38; "For Girls: From 'Birches' to 'Wild Grapes,'" *Yale Review* (Autumn 1977): 13-29; "The Contemporary Reader and Robert Frost: The Heavenly Guest of 'One More Brevity' and *Aeneid* 8," *St. John's Review* (Summer 1981): 3-10; "Aeschylus and Early Tragedy," in *Ancient Authors: Greece and Rome*, ed. T.V. Luce (New York: Scribners, 1983), 99-155. "The *Aeneid* as a Drama of Election," *TAPA* 116 (1986): 305-34; "The Poetry of Phaedo," in *Cabinet of the Muses*, ed. Mark Griffith & Donald Mastronarde (Atlanta: Scholars Press, 1990), 147-62; "The Chorus in Greek Life and Drama," *Arion* (forthcoming). **Bio-Bibliography:** *Who's Who in America; Who's Who Among American Scholars*. **Home Address:** Box 169, Williamsburg, MA 01096.

BADGELEY, CLARENCE DALE ■ FAAR Architecture 29. b. Feb. 21, 1899, Warren County, OH. d. Aug. 27, 1990. m. Elizabeth Gilman. BA 23, Ohio State Univ.; BA 25, Columbia Univ.; MArch 32, Columbia Univ. **Career & Employment:** Badgeley & Woods, Part. 1934-42; Military service 1942-46; Badgeley & Bradbury, Part. 1946-48; C. Dale Badgeley, Pres. 1949-70. **Memberships & Offices:** AIA; NY State Assn. of Architects, Dir. 1946-48; Brunner Scholar Com. **Fellowships, Honors & Awards:** Soc. of Beaux Arts Architects, Medal 1924-25; Columbia Univ., Alumni Assn. of School of Architecture, Medal of Honor 1925; NY State Assn. of Architects, Merit Award 1947; Ohio State Univ., School of Engineering & Dept. of Architecture, Distinguished Alumnus Award 1984. **Publications:** "The Capitolium at Ostia," *Memoirs of the AAR* 7 (1928): 221-23. **Important Works:** Shell Co., Office Bldg., Venezuela 1946; Shell Co., Mavesa Plant, Caracas 1948; Eighth Church of Christ Scientist, NYC 1951; with Charles D. Faulkner, Cornell Univ., Animal Husbandry Bldg. 1958; with James C. Mackenzie, Edificio Phelps Condominium, Caracas 1969; with Josa Puig, Camoflage Projects in East US during WWII. **Exhibitions/Performances:** School of Architecture, Ohio State Univ., Columbus 1983. **Bio-Bibliography:** *American Architects Directory*.

BADONI PARISE, FRANCA ■ Italian Fulbright Fellow 1966-67.

BAER, MORLEY ■ FAAR Design Arts 80. b. Apr. 5, 1916, Toledo, OH. m. Frances Manney Baer. c. Joshua. BA 35, Univ. of Michigan; MA 36, Univ. of Michigan. **Other Study:** I came to Carmel, California in 1976 hopefully to study photography with Edward Weston (I had been using a camera since 1939 in the Midwest). Weston could not take me on as a student but a number of years were spent in studying his work and his per-

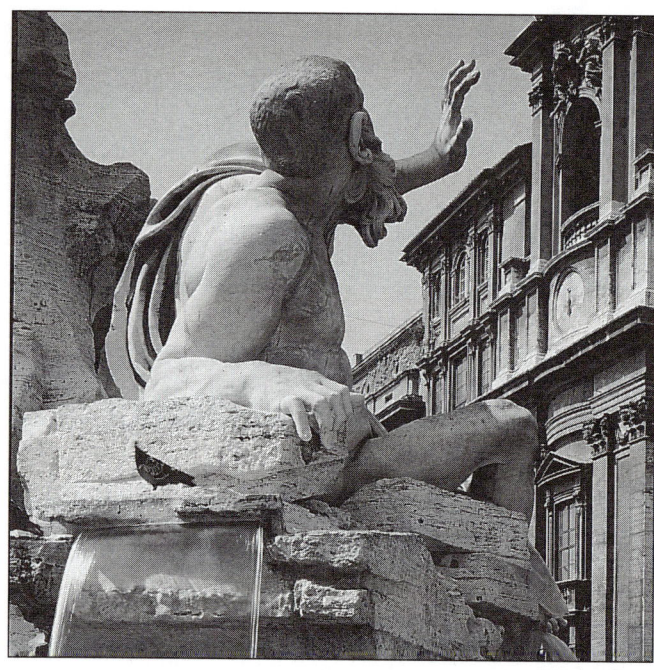

Morley Baer

son. His life and work became the base for my own work. **Research/Artistic Interests:** As a self-employed, free-lance photographer, I have concentrated for over forty years now on architecture and the landscape mainly in the areas of the West Coast. Assignments on architectural material have come from many of San Francisco's most prestigious architectural firms – Skidmore, Owings & Merrill; Wurster, Bernardi & Emmons; Milono, Rockwise, Campbell & Wong, etc. Work on the land has usually been self-directed. **Memberships & Offices:** Friends of Photography, BoT 1965-91; American Soc. of Media Photographers, Mem. 1965-present. **Fellowships, Honors & Awards:** AIA, Medal of Honor for Architectural Photography 1965. **Publications:** *Here Today,* text by Roger Olmsted & T.H. Watkins (San Francisco: Chronicle Books, 1968); *Adobes in the Sun,* text by Augusta Fink (San Francisco: Chronicle Books, 1972); *California Design, 1910,* ed. Timothy Anderson, Eudorah Moor, and Robert Winter (Salt Lake City: Gibbs-Smith, 1974); *Bay Area Houses,* ed. Sally Woodbridge, intro. by David Gebhardt (New York: Oxford Univ. Press, 1976); *Painted Ladies,* text by Elizabeth Pomada (New York: E.P. Dutton, 1978); *Room and Time Enough,* lines by Mary Austin, intro. by Augusta Fink (Flagstaff, AZ: Northland Press, 1979); *Charles Moore,* text by Gerald Allen (New York: Whitney Library of Design, 1980); *The Wilder Shore,* text by David Rains Wallace, foreword for Wallace Stegner (San Francisco: Sierra Club Books, 1984); *Light Years,* text by Jim Jordan (Carmel, CA: Photography West Graphics, 1988). **Important Works:** Many photographs are in the collections of various national museums such as the De Young, the San Francisco Museum of Art, the Amon Carter Museum, the State of New Mexico Museum, and the Monterey Peninsula Museum of Art; Crocker Museum, Sacramento; Santa Barbara Museum of Art; architectural work has appeared in many magazines, such as *Architectural Record, Progressive Architecture, Architectural Forum, House & Garden,* and *House Beautiful.* Photographs of both kinds are in the hands of many individual collectors. **Exhibitions/Performances:** Solo: De Young Museum, San Francisco 1962, 1968; Oakland Museum 1963; Friends of Photography Gallery, Carmel 1986; Monterey Peninsula Museum of Art 1989; Vision Gallery, San Francisco

1994; Crocker Museum, Sacramento 1994. **Bio-Bibliography:** Jim Jordan, *Light Years* (Carmel, CA: Photography West Graphics, 1988); Owen Edwards, "Bare Essentials," *American Photographer* (1988); Joseph A. Dickerson, "California Dreamer," *Pro-Photo* (1991). **Home Address:** PO Box 222537, Carmel CA 93922.

BAERNSTEIN, P. RENEE ■ FAAR Post-Classical/Humanistic Studies 91. b. June 18, 1963, Bar Harbor, ME. BA 85, Cornell Univ.; PhD 93, Harvard Univ. **Research/Artistic Interests:** Social & cultural history of Renaissance Italy, Protestant and Catholic Reformations, history of women. **Fellowships, Honors & Awards:** Fulbright Fellowship 1988-89; Whiting Fellowship, 1991-92. **Publications:** "Riforma monastica e disciplinamento sociale nell'opera di Carlo Borromeo," in *Lombardia Spagnola, Lombardia Borromaica,* ed G. Signorotto & P. Pissavino (forthcoming). **Home Address:** 126 Lowell St., No. 3, Somerville MA 02143.

BAETJER, EDWARD BRUCE ■ FAAR Landscape Architecture 54. b. July 24, 1917, Chattalonee, MD. d. Mar. 6, 1975. BArch 40, Princeton Univ.; MFA 48, Princeton Univ.; MLA 52, Harvard GSD. **Career & Employment:** Private practice, landscape architecture, Pikesville, MD 1955-75; Alexander S. Cochran, Architect, Baltimore 1948-49.

BAGG, ROBERT E. ■ FAAR Literature 58. b. Sept. 21, 1935, Orange, NJ. m. Sarah R. Bagg. c. Theodore, Christopher, Jonathan, Melissa, Hazzard. BA 57, Amherst College; MA 61, Univ. of Connecticut, Storrs; PhD 65, Univ. of Connecticut,

ROME 1980

(December 17th at the American Academy)

The Rome below our windows this December night
is not the same eternal field of prizes to be won
as lay before us in the sixties, Old Buddies:
Amabile and Garrett, Starbuck and Scully:
Maderna's fountains, which Wilbur raised to their Christian heights
again, those "clear, high cavorting heads"
are turned waterfountain low these days,
except when the Queen of England comes to town.
And Garrett—that standing lover in Tarquinia you found
"so hugely gifted, whether by nature or by art"
no longer has the experts' blessing
to fill the tomb's long dark night with joy—
they say he's there to outrage and divert
a god's jealous gaze from his tombmates: our souls
never more vulnerable than in death.
Rome's sunny markets, great domes, satyrs and martyrs
whose thought and impulse well
imperiously to their eyes;
lovers, mad traffic, skittish aristocrats
whose speech dances from one language to the next
like feeding sparrows—all of that is still there,
but often at gunpoint, and so worth preserving
someone will want it soon to explode.

Robert Bagg

Robert E. Bagg

Storrs. **Other Study:** Study of Greek & Latin with John Andrew Moore & Thomas Gould 1959-65. **Research/Artistic Interests:** Translation for stage and publication of Greek drama; poetry, novel writing, essays on Greek and Latin literature. **Career & Employment:** Univ. of Washington, Instr. 1963-65; Univ. of Massachusetts, Asst. Prof. 1965-70, Assc. Prof. 1970-75, Prof. 1975-present, Chair. 1986-92; Smith College, Lect. 1968; Univ. of Texas (Austin), Visiting Assc. Prof. 1971. **Memberships & Offices:** MLA, Mem. 1965-present; *Massachusetts Review,* Poetry Ed. 1970-75; Univ. of Massachusetts Press, Poetry Bd.

1969-86; Chair 1972-75, 1982-86. **Fellowships, Honors & Awards:** Nat. Book Awards, Finalist 1962; Ingram Merrill Found. Grant 1962, 1963, 1964, 1974; NEA Grant 1974; Guggenheim Fellowship 1980-81. **Publications:** *Madonna of the Cello* (Middletown, CT: Weslyan Univ. Press, 1961); "Love, Ceremony and Daydream in Sappho's Lyrics," *Arion* 3.3 (1964): 44-82; "Some Versions of Lyric Impasse in Shakespeare and Catullus," *Arion* 3.4 (1965): 64-95; "The Rise of Lady Lazarus." *Mosaic* 3.2 (1969): 9-36; "Translating the Abyss," *Arion* 8.1 (1969): 51-65; "The Electromagnet and the Shred of Platinum," *Arion* 8.3 (1969): 407-29; "The Loneliness of the Long Distance Runner," in *Frames of Reference: Essays on the Rhetoric of Film*, ed. Walz, Harrington, Di Marco (Dubuque: Kendall-Hunt, 1972), 59-68; *The Scrawny Sonnets and Other Narratives: Poems* (Urbana: Illinois Univ. Press, 1973); trans. and ed., Euripides, *Hippolytos* (Oxford & New York: Oxford Univ. Press, 1978); *Body Blows: Poems New and Selected* (Amherst: Univ. of Massachusetts Press, 1982); trans. & ed., Sophocles, *Oedipus the King* (Amherst: Univ. of Massachusetts Press, 1982); "Tongues of Fire: Translating Ancient Greek into Modern American," *Boston Review* 7.1 (1982): 15-17; "Merlin and Faust in Two Post-War Poems," in *Merlin Versus Faust: Contending Archetypes in Western Culture*, ed. Charlotte Spivack (Lewiston, NY: Edwin Mellen Press, 1992), 189-98. **Exhibitions/Performances:** Productions of translations: of Euripides, *The Cyclops*: Amherst College 1957, 1958, 1963, Yale 1958; Euripides, *Hippolytos*: Greece 1974; Cambridge Univ. 1974; Toronto 1974; Wesleyan Univ. 1975; Univ. of Illinois 1977; Northwestern Univ. 1980; Alexandria, VA 1990; Colby, KA 1994; Euripides, *The Bakkhai*: Univ. of Utah 1978; Univ. of Massachusetts 1978; Groton 1979; Univ. of Manitoba 1979; Yale Drama 1980; Smith College 1981; SUNY, Albany 1982; Hampshire College 1985, 1993; Bloomington, IN 1987; Harvard-Radcliff 1987; UNC, Greensboro 1988; Boston 1988; Univ. of San Diego 1990; Univ. of Colorado 1990; Univ. of Michigan, Ypsilanti 1991; Univ. of Pennsylvania 1992; Wesleyan Univ. 1992; Bloomsburg, PA 1992; North Carolina School of Arts 1993; Venice, CA 1993; Herbert Lehman College, NYC 1994; Cleveland, OH 1995; Sophocles, *Oedipus the King*: Univ. of Utah 1980; Nashville 1983; Univ. of Manitoba 1985; *Women of Trachis*: Univ. of Massachuesetts 1992. **Bio-Bibliography:** *Who's Who in America*. **Home Address:** 181 Linseed Rd., Hatfield, MA 01038.

BAILEN, ELIOT ■ Sheldon Fellow 1926-27.

BAILEY, JACK L. ■ FAAR Painting 72. b. Aug. 8, 1927, Detroit, MI. m. Katherine Bailey. BS 54, Wayne State Univ.; MA 55, Wayne State Univ. **Career & Employment:** Wayne State Univ., Assc. Prof. 1955-71; CBS Nat. TV 1967. **Exhibitions/Per-**

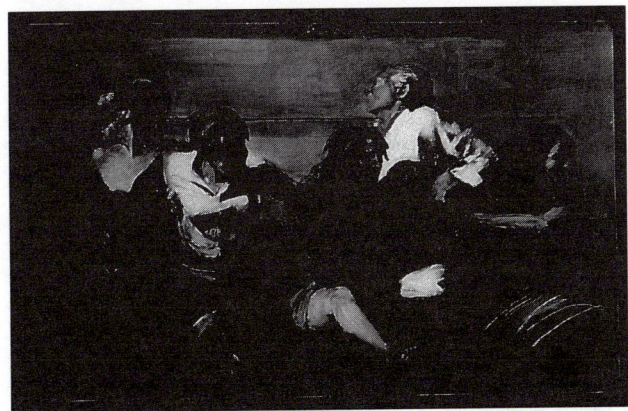

Jack L. Bailey

formances: RISD 1972; Tyler School of Art 1972; Pace Gallery, Milan 1973; Milanart Gallery, Bologna 1973; Intl. Exb., Basel 1973; Gallery Paralle, Geneva 1975; Macler Gallery, Sarasota 1980; Museum Retrospective, Melbourne, FL 1983; Retrospective, Michigan Gallery, Detroit 1986. **Home Address:** 4211 Old Bradenton Rd., Sarasota, FL 34234.

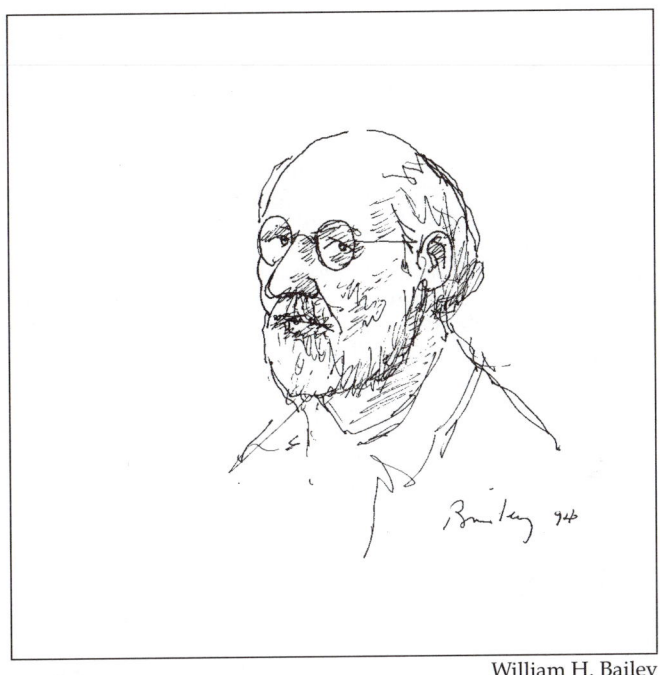

William H. Bailey

BAILEY, WILLIAM ■ RAAR Painting 76. b. Nov. 17, 1930, Council Bluffs, IA. m. Sandra S. Bailey. c. Ford, Hamilton, Alix, Brook. BFA 55, Yale Univ. School of Art; MFA 57, Yale Univ. School of Art. **Other Study:** Univ. of Kansas 1948-51. **Research/Artistic Interests:** I am a painter. My work is figurative. **Career & Employment:** Yale School of Art, Instr. 1957-61, Asst. Prof. 1961-62, Prof. 1969-79, Kingman Brewster Prof. 1979-present; Indiana Univ., Asst. Prof. 1962-65, Prof. 1965-68. **Memberships & Offices:** CAA, BoD 1983-87; Louis Comfort Tiffany Found., BoT 1970-present; Yaddo, Mem. of Corp. 1985-present; Nat. Council on the Arts, Mem. 1992-present. **Fellowships, Honors & Awards:** Yale Univ., Alice Kimball Fellowship 1955, Award for Distinguished Artistic Achievement 1985; Guggenheim Fellowship 1965; Ingram Merrill Fellowship 1979; AAAL 1986; Hon. Doctorates: Univ. of Utah 1987, Adelphi Univ. 1993, Accademia Nazionale San Luca 1991, Accademia di Belle Arti 1992. **Exhibitions/Performances:** Solo: Robert Schoelkopf Gallery, NYC 1979, 1982, 1986, 1991; Fendrick Gallery, Washington, DC 1979; Galleria Il Gabbiano, Rome 1980, 1985, 1993; Meadows School of Art, Southern Methodist Univ., Dallas 1983; Univ. of Utah, Salt Lake 1984; Museum of Contemporary Art, Wright State Univ., Dayton 1987; FIAC Paris Grand Palais, Paris 1987; John Berggruen Gallery, San Francisco 1988; RISD Museum, Providence 1988; Fairfield Univ., Fairfield, CT 1989; Donald Morris Gallery, Birmingham, MI 1991; André Emmerich, NYC 1992, 1994. **Bio-Bibliography:** Andrew Forge, *Disegni e Tempere di William Bailey* (Milan: Olivetti, 1987); Mark Strand, *William Bailey* (New York: Harry N. Abrams, 1987); Giuliano Briganti & John Hollander, *William Bailey* (New York: Rizzoli, 1991); *Who's Who in America, Who's Who in American Art*. **Home Address:** 33 Island View Ave., Branford, CT 06405. **Business Address:** André Emmerich Gallery, 41 E. 57 St., NYC 10022.

BAKEMA, JACOB BEREND ■ RAAR Architecture 69. b. Mar. 8, 1914, Groningen, Netherlands. d. Feb. 20, 1981. m. Silina Th. van Borssum Waalkes. c. Brita, Erika, Nils. Dip. Arch. 41, Acad. of Architecture, Technical Univ., Delft, Netherlands. **Career & Employment:** Office of Cor van Eesteren, Amsterdam 1937-41; Office of van Tijen & Maaskant 1941; Rotterdam Municipal Housing Dept. 1945; Architectengemeenschap van den Broek en Bakema, Rotterdam 1948-1981; Technical Univ., Delft, Netherlands, Prof. 1963-80; Staaliche Hochschule für Bildende Kunste, Hamburg, Germany, Prof. 1965-80; Visiting Prof.: Intl. Summer Acad., Salzburg, Austria 1965-69, 1973-75; Columbia Univ. 1970-71; Cornell Univ. 1972. **Memberships & Offices:** Architectura et Amicitia, Amsterdam, BoD 1965-67; Congrès Intl. d'Architecture Moderne 1947-81; Akademie der Kunste, Berlin 1971-81; Honorary Mem.: AIA; Zentral Vereinigung Architekten Osterreichs; Bund Deutscher Architekten, Germany; Assn. of Scottish Architects; Suomen Arkkitehtiliitto, Finland; Orange-Nassau Order, Nertherlands, Officer 1958; Order of Nederlandse Neeuw, Knight 1971; Order of La Couronne, Belgium; *Forum* (Hilversum, Netherlands), Co-Ed. 1954-69. **Fellowships, Honors & Awards:** Intl. Assn. of Art Critics, Dutch Critics Prize 1972; Camillo Sitteprize, Austria 1977; Honorary Cross, Salzburg, Austria 1978. **Publications:** *Towards an Architecture for Society* (1963); *Van Stoeh tot Stadt* (Zeist: W. de Haan, 1964); *Stadtbauliche Architektur* (Salzburg, 1965); *L.C. van der Vligt* (Amsterdam: Meulan Koff, 1968); contr., *Team Ten Primer,* ed. Alison Smithson (London: Academy Editions, 1968); *Thoughts about Architecture,* ed. Marianne Gray (London: Academy Editions, 1981); contr., *Architektur der Zukunft, Zukunft der Architektur* (Stuttgart: K. Kramer, 1982); and numerous articles. **Important Works:** Approximately a hundred works; last works include: de Grave Home for the Retarded, Gorinchem, Netherlands 1971-73; Erasmus College Secondary School, Zoetermeer, Netherlands 1971-76; Zeckendorf House, Bahamas 1973; Sunter Town Plan Project, Djakarta, Indonesia 1973; Kurhaus District Redevelopment, Supervising Architects, Scheveningen, Netherlands 1973; Barre Molen Windmill Restoration, Zoeterwoude, Netherlands 1973; City Center Plan for Eindhoven 1974; World Trade Centre, Rotterdam 1974; Kaatstraat Renovation, Utrecht, Netherlands 1974; Weerdjes District Renovation, Arnhem, Netherlands 1975. **Exhibitions/Performances:** Boymens Museum, Rotterdam 1963, toured the Netherlands, Germany, Austria & Italy; Stedelijk Museum, Amsterdam 1965, toured the Netherlands, Austria & the US; Samen Bouwen, Town Hall, Schoonhoven, Netherlands 1972, toured Austria & Germany; Progette Opere, Castello Nuovo, Naples 1974, toured Italy. **Bio-Bibliography:** *Contemporary Architects; CIAM 1959 in Otterlo* (1959); J. Joedicke, *Architektur und Stadtebau das Werk van den Broek und Bakema* (Stuttgart: K. Kramer, 1963); *Bouwen voor een open Samenleving,* exb. cat. (Rotterdam: Van Beuningen, 1963); *van den Broek-Bakema,* ed. C. Gubitosi & A. Izzo, exb. cat., Naples 1974 (Rome: Officina, 1976); *Architecture-Urbanism: Architectengemeenschap van der Broek en Bakema* (Stuttgart: K. Kramer, 1976).

BAKER, WALTER C. ■ AAR Trustee 1950-71, Bank Exec.

BALDINI, ALESSANDRA ■ Italian Fulbright Fellow 1979-80.

BALDWIN, GORDON C. ■ FAAR Design Arts 78. b. Feb. 20, 1939, Cleveland, OH. BA 60, Amherst College. **Other Study:** Harvard Law School 1960-63; Harvard GSD 1963-69. **Research/ Artistic Interests:** 19th-century photography. **Career & Employment:** J. Paul Getty Museum, Dept. of Photographs, Registration Asst. 1984-85, Curatorial Asst. 1985-87, Study-Room Supervisor 1987-90, Asst. Curator 1990-present. **Memberships & Offices:** CAA Mem. 1992-present; European Soc. for the History of Photography, Mem. 1991-present. **Fellowships, Honors & Awards:** Wurlitzer Found., Residence Grant 1975-76; Briarcombe Found., Residence Grant 1982. **Publications:** *Looking at Photographs: A Guide to Technical Terms* (Malibu & London: J. Paul Getty Museum-British Museum, 1991). **Important Works:** Drawings in the collections of the Achenbach Found., California Palace of the Legion of Honor, San Francisco; Amherst College; Helene Wurlitzer Found., Taos, NM. **Exhibitions/Performances:** Solo: Rex Evans Gallery, Los Angeles 1969; Shepherd Gallery, NYC 1974; California Palace of the Legion of Honor 1976. **Home Address:** 7652 Sunset Blvd., No. 105, Los Angeles, CA 90046.

BALDWIN, GREGORY S. ■ FAAR Architecture 71. b. Dec. 21, 1940, Portland, OR. m. Joan Lamb. c. Benjamin, Sera. BA 62, Harvard Univ.; BArch-MArch 66, Harvard Univ.; MAUD 67, Harvard Univ. **Career & Employment:** Environmental Disciplines, Part. 1973-78; Zimmer, Gunsul Frasca, Part. 1979-present. **Memberships & Offices:** *Progressive Architecture,* Juror 1992; Harvard GSD Alumni/ae Council, Pres. **Fellowships, Honors & Awards:** Fulbright Fellowship 1969 (declined); Marshall Prize 1969 (declined); AIA, Fellow, Honor Award 1978, Firm Award 1991, Urban Design Award 1991; *Progressive Architecture* Award 1969, 1984, 1986; AIA/American Assn. of School Administrators 1979; American Planning Assn. Honor Award 1982. **Important Works:** Multnomah Athletic Club, Portland 1972, 1994; Portland Downtown Plan 1972-94; Portland Transit Mall 1977, 1994; Federal Courthouse, Portland 1982; Oregon Health Services Univ. Master Plan 1984-94; Banfield & West Side Light Rail Corridors, Portland 1987-94; Embarcadero, San Francisco 1988-91; Central Platte Valley Plan & Infrastructure, Denver 1985-94; Bank of America Tower, Portland 1988; Union Station Redevelopment, Seattle, 1988; Alsea Bay Bridge, OR 1990; Pacific Lutheran Univ., Concert Hall & Music Center, Tacoma 1994; Pacific Medical Center, Seattle 1994; River District Plan & Infrastructure, Portland 1992-94; Washington State Univ., Campus Plan & Bldgs., Vancouver 1993-present. **Home Address:** 693 Terrace Dr., Lake Oswego, OR 97034. **Business Address:** Zimmer, Gunsul Frasca Partnership, 320 S.W. Oak, Suite 500, Portland, OR 97204.

BALDWIN, HENRY DEFOREST ■ AAR Trustee 1931-40; Lawyer.

BALDWIN, HENRY DEFOREST ■ AAR Trustee 1969-78, Trustee Emer.; Lawyer.

BALDWIN, MARTHA R. ■ FAAR Post-Classical/Humanistic Studies 88. b. Sept. 13, 1950, Jacksonville, FL. m. Benjamin W. Guy III. c. William, Sarah. BA 73, Smith College; MA 75, Univ. of Chicago; PhD 87, Univ. of Chicago. **Research/Artistic Interests:** Science & its cultural context in the 17th & 18th centuries. **Career & Employment:** Harvard Univ., TA 1992-present. **Fellowships, Honors & Awards:** Harvard Univ., Post-Doctoral Fellow 1990-92. **Publications:** "Magnetism in the Anti-Copernican Polemic," *Journal for the History of Astronomy* 16 (1985): 155-74; "Pious Ambition: The Patronage of Jesuit Scientific Books in the Seventeenth Century," in *Jesuit Science,* ed. Mordechai Feingold (Princeton: Princeton Univ. Press, forthcoming); "Toads and Plague: Amulet Therapy in the Seventeenth Century," *Bulletin of the History of Medicine* (Forthcoming). **Home Address:** PO Box 92, Westport Point, MA 02791. **Business Address:** Harvard Univ., Science Center 235, Cambridge, MA 02138.

BALDWIN, PHILLIP R. ■ FAAR Design Arts 94. b. June 24, 1959, Colorado Springs, CO. c. Ravenna. BA 81, Gustavus Adolphus College, St. Paul; MFA 87, Yale Univ. **Research/Artistic Interests:** Drawing, model making, watercolor, stage architecture, urban planning. **Career & Employment:** Freelance Design 1987-present; Bard College 1989-93; Smith College 1993-present. **Important Works:** Scenic Design: Lucille Lortell Theater, NYC 1985; Yale Repertory Theater, New Haven 1986; Lincoln Center, NYC 1986, 1990; Home for Contemporary Theater & Art, NYC 1988; Women's Project 1988; Playmakers Repertory, Chapel Hill 1988; Kaufman Theater, NYC 1988, 1989, 1991; Apple Corps Theater, NYC 1989; The Kitchen, NYC 1989; Circle Rep Lab, NYC 1989, 1990; Long Island Stage 1989-91; Bard College 1989-present; RAAP Arts Center, NYC 1990; Cucaracha Theater, NYC 1990; Skylight Opera 1991; Rockland Opera 1992; Minetta Lane Theater, NYC 1992; Smith College 1993-present. **Home Address:** 147 Vernon, Northampton, MA 01060; 100 Manhattan Ave., Union City, NJ.

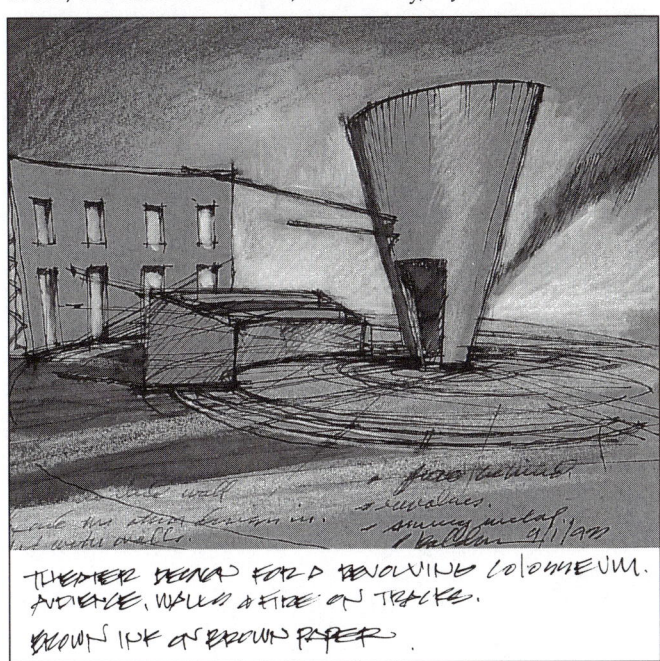

Phillip R. Baldwin

BALDWIN, SHERMAN ■ AAR Trustee 1946-63, Lawyer.

BALET, MARC IRA ■ FAAR Architecture 75. b. Apr. 13, 1948, Waterbury, CT. BFA 71, RISD; BArch 72, RISD. **Career & Employment:** *Vogue Patterns* 1977; *Interview Magazine*, Art Dir. 1977-; *Fame*, Creative Dir. 1988-. **Exhibitions/Performances:** Whitney Museum, NYC; Inst. of Contemporary Arts, London 1972; Group: RISD 1970, 1971.

BALIS, JOSEPH F. ■ Chicago Architectural Club, Burnham Prize 1939-40.

BALL, LARRY F. ■ FAAR History of Art 89. b. May 7, 1956, St. Paul, MN. BA 78, Oberlin College; PhD 87, Univ. of Virginia. **Other Study:** Univ. of Washington, Seattle, Classics, Art History 1978-79; ASCSA, Reg. Mem. 1982-83; RISD, Summer School Archaeological Drafting Course 1984. **Career & Employment:** Radford Univ., Lect. 1987-88; American Univ., Adj. Prof. 1990-91; Univ. of Wisconsin, Asst. Prof 1991-present. **Memberships & Offices:** AIA 1980-present; CAA 1988-present; SAH

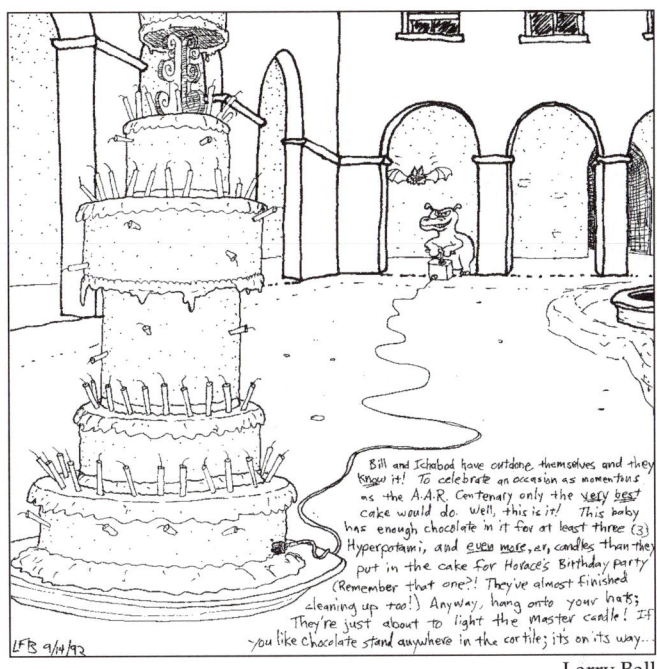

Larry Ball

1993-present. **Fellowships, Honors & Awards:** Univ. of Virginia, Davidge, Aunspaugh & DuPont Fellowship 1982-83; Samuel H. Kress Travel Fellowship 1986-87; Andrew W. Mellon Fellow 1988-89; UWSP-UPDC Development Grant 1992-93. **Publications:** "A Reappraisal of Nero's Domus Aurea," *JRA*, suppl. 11 (1994). **Home Address:** 3825 Robert Pl., No. 8, Stevens Point, WI 54481. **Business Address:** Dept. of Art & Design, FAC B116, Univ. of Wisconsin-Stevens Point, Stevens Point, WI 54881.

BALLOU, SUSAN HELEN ■ FASCSR 06; Collegiate Alumnae Fellow, ASCSR, Assc. 1901-02; ASCSR Student 1903-04. b. Sept. 28, 1868, Dubuque, Iowa. d. June 1940. BA 1897, Univ. of Chicago; PhD 11. **Other Study:** Univ. of Chicago 1897-1901, Göttingen 1910, Giessen 1910-11. **Research/Artistic Interests:** Manuscripts of the *Scriptores Historiae Augustae*. **Career & Employment:** Univ. of Chicago, Assc. 1900-1907, Instr. 1907-15; Michigan Western State Normal School, Kalamazoo, Latin Dept., Head 1915-17; Univ. of Wisconsin, Instr. 1917-20; Bryn Mawr College, Assc. Prof. 1921-30. **Publications:** "The Manuscripts of the *Historia Augusta*," *Classical Philology* 3 (1908): 273-77; *De Clausulis a Flavio Vopsico Syracusio Scriptore Historiae Augustae adhibitis* (Weimar: Wagner, 1912); *The Manuscript Tradition of the Historia Augusta* (Leipzig: Tuebner, 1914); "The Clausula and the Higher Criticism," *TAPA* 46 (1915): 157-71; "The Carriere of the Higher Roman Officials in Egypt in the Second Century," *TAPA* 52 (1921); ed., Latin text, *Scriptores Historiae Augustae*, vol. 1 (London: Loeb, 1922). **Bio-Bibliography:** *De Clausulis*, 105-6; Bryn Mawr College Archives.

BALTHUS ■ AAR Visitor 1943-51, Artist.

BANEVER, GILBERT ■ FAAR Painting 36. b. June 8, 1913, New Haven, CT. m. Sadye M. Shepatin. c. Carol, Robert. BFA 34, Yale Univ., School of Fine Arts. **Other Study:** Fresco painting with Feruccio Ferazzi (Rome). **Career & Employment:** Freelance painter 1937-present; Memphis Acad. of Arts, Dir. & Instr. 1938-43; General Electric Co., Industrial Designer 1944-46; MGM Studios, Matte Shot Artist 1945-46; Gilbert Banever & Assc., Package Design Consultants 1947-59; Whitney School of Art, New Haven, Instr. 1951-52; New Haven Board & Carton Co., Design Dir. 1959-64; Soltz & Banever, Mgr. 1964-68; Paier College of Art, Hamden, CT, Instr.-Prof. 1969-82. **Home Address:** 567A Pequot Ln., Stratford, CT 06497.

BARBER, SAMUEL ■ FAAR Musical Composition 37, RAAR Musical Composition 47. b. Mar. 9, 1910, West Chester, PA. d. Jan. 23, 1981. BMus 32, Curtis Inst. of Music; MusD 45, Curtis Inst. **Other Studies:** Studied under Isabel Vengerova, Emilio de Gogorza, Rosario Scalero. **Career & Employment:** Curtis Inst., Faculty 1939-42; ASCAP, Dir. 1969-81; NIAL. **Memberships & Offices:** AAAL 1958. **Fellowships, Honors & Awards:** Guggenheim Fellowship 1945, 1947, 1949; NY Music Critics Award 1946; Pulitzer Prize for Music 1958, 1963; Harvard Univ., Hon. DFA 1959; Gold Medal for Music 1976. **Important Works:** *Overture to the School of Scandal,* for orchestra 1933; *Music for a Scene from Shelley,* for orchestra 1933; *Symphony No. 1,* in one movement 1935; *Adagio for Strings,* arranged from *String Quartet No. 2* 1936; *Violin Concerto* 1939; *Symphony No. 2* 1944; *Excursions,* for solo piano 1945; *The Serpent Heart,* a ballet 1946; *Knoxville, Summer of 1915,* for voice & orchestra 1948; Piano Sonata, 1949; *Prayers for Kierkegaard,* for soprano, orchestra & chorus 1954; *A Hand of Bridge,* an opera 1958; *Vanessa* 1958; *Piano Concerto* 1962; *Anthony and Cleopatra,* an opera, Metropolitan Opera at Lincoln Center Opening Comm. 1966. **Bio-Bibliography:** Nathan Broder, *Samuel Barber* (New York: G. Schirmer, 1956); *Who Was Who, Baker's Biographical Dictionary of Musicians;* D. Hennessee, *Samuel Barber: A Bio-bibliography* (Westport, CT: Greenwood, 1985); J. Kreiling, *The Songs of Samuel Barber* (Ann Arbor: Univ. of Michigan, 1987); Barbara Heyman, *Samuel Barber: The Composer and his Music* (New York: Oxford Univ. Press, 1992).

BARBIERI, GUIDO ■ Italian Fulbright Fellow 1960-61.

BARGMANN, JULIE ■ FAAR Landscape Architecture 90, Design Arts Jury, Mem. 1993. BFA 80, Carnegie-Mellon Univ.; MLA 87, Harvard GSD. **Career & Employment:** Michael VanValkenburgh Asscs., Assc. & Project Landscape Architect 1985-87, 1990-92; Carr, Lynch, Hack and Sandell Asscs., Landscape Designer 1988; Landscape Architecture Consultant 1992-present; Univ. of Minnesota, Asst. Prof. 1992-present. **Memberships & Offices:** Univ. of Minnesota, Public Arts on Campus Com.; Weisman Art Museum, Design Arts Bd. **Fellowships, Honors & Awards:** Univ. of Minnesota Graduate School, Grant-in-Aid of Artistry, Scholarship, & Research 1992-93; Graduate School Faculty Summer Research Fellowship 1993; McKnight Arts and Humanities Fellowship 1993; Design Center for American Urban Landscape 1993; Graham Found. Grant for Advanced Study in the Fine Arts 1990; Harvard GSD, Jacob Weidenman Prize in Design 1987. **Important Works:** SEI Corp. Landscape, Oaks, PA; Sahara West Library and Museum, Las Vegas; Coolidge Point, Manchester-by-the-Sea, MA; Graves Warehouse Garden, Princeton; Janesville Public Library, Janesville, WI; Riverside South Park, NYC; Mill Race Park, Columbus, IN; Hudson River Park, Battery Park City, NYC. **Home-Studio Address:** 1900 Colfax Ave. S., Minneapolis, MN 55403.

BARINGER, RICHARD E. ■ FAAR Architecture 53. b. Dec. 3, 1921, Elkhart, IN. d. Jan. 26, 1980. BA 48, Inst. of Design; BArch 50, Harvard GSD; MArch 51, Harvard GSD. **Memberships & Offices:** AIA, Virgin Islands Chap., Pres. 1975. **Career & Employment:** Southwestern Univ., TX 1941-42; USAAF, Captain 1942-45; Illinois Inst. of Techology, Assc. Prof. 1954;

Inst. of Design (Chicago), Assc. Prof. 1956-60; Columbia Univ., Asst. Prof. 1962-63; Kencliff Asscs., Adv. Art Dir. 1946-47; Acad. of Applied Art, Chicago, Instr. 1947-48; Inst. of Contemporary Art, Boston, Design Research 1949-51; PACE Asscs., Chicago, Designer 1951-53; George Fred Keck, William Keck, Architects, Chief Designer 1953-55; Pvt. practice architecture: Chicago 1955-61 & NYC 1961-67. **Fellowships, Honors & Awards:** Northern Indiana Annual Art Exb., 1st Prize 1939; Southern MI & Vicinity Annual Art Exb., 2nd Prize 1942; Chicago Tribune "Better Rooms" Competition, 4th Prize 1947, 1948, 1949; Harvard Univ., Edward H. Kendall Scholarship 1950-51; Sheldon Fellow 1951-53; *Progressive Architecture* Award 1957; *Architectural Record* Award 1958; AIA Award 1959, Fellow. **Exhibitions/Performances:** Solo: Margaret Brown Gallery, Boston 1949; MIT 1951; Bertha Schaefer Gallery, NYC 1962, 1963, 1964; Columbia Univ. 1963; Nelson Taylor Gallery, NYC 1963; Dwan Gallery, NYC 1967; Notre Dame Univ. 1968. Group: California Palace of Legion of Honor 1949; Inst. of Contemporary Arts, Boston 1951; Arts Club, Chicago 1961; Washington Gallery of Modern Art 1963; Albright Museum, Buffalo, NY 1964; MOMA 1965. **Bio-Bibliography:** *Who Was Who in America.*

BARLETTA, BARBARA A. ■ FAAR Classics/Archaeology 90, Adv. Council, Mem. 1983-present. b. Aug. 6, 1952, Carmel, CA. BA 74, UC, Santa Barbara; MA 77, Bryn Mawr College; PhD 81, Bryn Mawr College. **Other Study:** Univ. of Bergen, Norway 1972-73; ASCSA, Reg. Mem. 1977-78, Assc. Mem. 1980. **Research/Artistic Interests:** Greek art, especially architecture and its interconnections throughout the Greek world, including the colonies of southern Italy & Sicily. **Career & Employment:** Tulane Univ., Visiting Asst. Prof. 1981-82; Univ. of Missouri, Columbia, Visiting Asst. Prof. 1982-83; Univ. of Florida, Asst. Prof. 1983-88, Assc. Prof. 1988-present. **Memberships & Offices:** ArIA 1975-present; CAA 1981-present. **Fellowships, Honors & Awards:** NEH Fellowship 1989-90 (declined). **Publications:** *Ionic Influence in Archaic Sicily: The Monumental Art.* Studies in Mediterranean Archaeology (Göteborg: Paul Aströms Förlag, 1983); "An Ionic Porch at Gela," *Mitteilungen des deutschen archäologischen Instituts, Römische Abteilung* 92 (1985): 9-17; "The Draped Kouros Type and the Workshop of the Syracuse Youth," *AJA* 91 (1987): 233-46; "An 'Ionian Sea' Style in Archaic Doric Architecture," *AJA* 94 (1990): 45-72; "Some Ionic Archtectural Elements from Selinus in the Getty Museum," *Studia Varia from the J. Paul Getty Museum* 1 (1993): 55-62. **Business Address:** Dept. of Art, Univ. of Florida, 302 FAC, Gainesville, FL 32611.

BARLOW, CLAUDE W. ■ FAAR Classics/Archaeology 38. b. Aug. 2, 1907, Stafford, CT. d. Jan. 1976. BA 28, Amherst College; MA 30, Indiana Univ.; PhD 35, Yale Univ. **Career & Employment:** Indiana Univ., Instr. 1930-31; Yale Univ., Instr. 1934-35; Mt. Holyoke, Instr. 1938-42; US Air Force 1942-45; Univ. of Tennessee Asst. Prof. 1947; Clark Univ. Asst. Prof. 1947-52, Assc. Prof. 1952-61, Prof. 1961-72. **Memberships & Offices:** APA; ArIa; MAA; NECA, Sec.-Tres. 1953-63, Pres. 1968-69. **Fellowships, Honors & Awards:** Phi Beta Kappa; Guggenheim Fellow 1945-46. **Publications:** "A Sixteenth-Century Epitome of Seneca, *De Ira,*" *TAPA* 68 (1937): 26-42; ed., Pseudo-Seneca, *Epistolae Senecae ad Paulum et Pauli ad Senecam,* AAR Papers & Monographs 10 (Rome: AAR, 1938); ed., Saint Martin of Braga, *Opera Omnia,* AAR Papers & Monographs 12 (New Haven: Yale Univ. Press, 1950); trans., *The Iberian Fathers,* 2 vols. (Washington, DC: Catholic Univ. Press, 1969). **Bio-Bibliography:** *Contemporary Authors.*

BARNES, EDWARD LARRABEE ■ RAAR Architecture 67, 78, AAR Trustee 63-78, 1st VP 1973, 1st Vice-Chair 1975. b. Apr. 22, 1915, Chicago, IL. m. Mary Cross. c. John, Cecil. BS 38, Harvard College; MArch 42, Harvard Univ. **Career & Employment:** Edward Larrabee Barnes, Architect, Prin. 1949-79; Edward Larrabee Barnes Asscs., Prin. 1980-88; Edward Larrabee Barnes-John M. Y. Lee & Partners, Prin. 1989-present; Pratt Inst. Design Critic and Lect. 1954-59; Yale Univ. Design Critic and Lect. 1957-64. **Memberships & Offices:** Municipal Art Soc. of New York, Dir. 1960, Treasurer 1961; MIT, Visiting Com. 1965-68; Westchester Council of the Arts 1967-71; NAD, Assc. 1969, Academician 1974; Urban Design Council of the City of New York 1972-76; MOMA, BoT 1975-present; Westchester Planning Bd. 1976-88; AAAS Fellow 1978; Harvard GSD, Visiting Com. 1978-present; Harvard Univ., Graduate GSD, Eliot Noyes Critic 1979; Univ. of Virginia, Thomas Jefferson Prof. in Architecture 1980; Haystack Mountain School of Arts and Crafts, Hon. BoT 1980; Trust for Public Land, Adv. Council 1984-91; AAAL, Mem. 1991. **Fellowships, Honors & Awards:** Sheldon Traveling Fellowship 1941-42; NIAL, A.W. Brunner Prize 1959; Yale Univ. Award for Distinction in the Arts 1959; ALNY, Silver Medal 1960, Citation in Landscape Architecture 1965; AIA, Northern California & East Bay Chaps., Merit Award 1963; US Federal Housing Administration, 1st Honor Award 1963; US Urban Renewal Administration, 1st Honor Award 1964 (2); AIA, Fellow 1966; AIA New York Chap. Medal of Honor 1971; AIA Collaborative Achievement Award 1972; AIA Honor Award 1972, 1977, 1986, Finn Award 1980, Westchester-Mid-Hudson Chap., 1st Honor Award for Recognition of Architectural Excellence 1990; ASLA, Merit Award 1972, 1978; Boston Soc. of Architects, Harleston Parker Medal 1972; City Club of New York, Albert S. Bard Award for Excellence in Architecture & Urban Design 1978, 1985; Intl. Union of Bricklayers & Allied Craftsmen, Louis Sullivan Award for Architecture 1979; Bldg. Stone Inst. Tucker Award, Citation for Design Excellence 1979, 1985; Chicago Horticultural Soc., Hutchinson Medal 1979; Municipal Art Soc. Bronze Plaque 1979; New York Landmarks Conservancy Chair's Certificate for Excellence 1980; Connecticut Soc. of Architects, Honor Award 1980; Univ. of Virginia, Thomas Jefferson Medal in Architecture 1981; Mayor of the City of New York, Award of Honor for Art and Culture 1982; New Mexico Soc. of Architects, Honor Award 1983; RISD, Hon. DFA 1983; New York State Assc. of Architects, Excellence in Design Award 1984; Amherst College, Hon. DHL 1984; City Club of New York, Intl. Masonry Inst., New England Chap., 1st Award for Design Excellence 1986; New York Soc. of Architects, Sidney L. Strauss Award 1986; Harvard Univ. 350th Anniversary Medal 1986; Interfaith Forum on Religion, Art & Architecture, Honor Award 1989; Harvard GSD, Alumni Lifetime Achievement Award 1993. **Publications:** "Defense Housing," *Task* 2 (1941); "The Design Process," *Perspecta* 5 (1959); "Furnishings, Unity and Space," *Architectural Record* (1960); "Control of Graphics is Essential to Good Shopping Center Design," *Architectural Record* (June 1962); "Remarks on Continuity and Change," *Perspecta* 9-10 (1965); "Church Architecture: The Real Questions," *The World* (Sept.-Oct. 1989). **Important Works:** Straus House, Pound Ridge, NY 1957; Haystack Mountain School of Arts and Crafts, Deer Isle, ME 1961; St. Paul's School Dormitories, Concord, NH 1962 and 1970; Christian Theological Seminary, Indianapolis 1962-87; Walker Art Center, Minneapolis 1971; Heckscher House, North East Harbor, ME 1974; IBM World HQ, Mt. Pleasant, NY 1974; Dallas Museum of Art 1983; IBM, 590 Madison Ave., NYC 1983; 599 Lexington Ave, NYC 1983; Minneapolis Sculpture Garden 1988; Federal Judiciary Bldg., Washington, DC 1992. **Exhibitions/**

Performances: Katonah Museum of Art, NY 1970, 1987; MOMA 1971, 1979; Sarah Scaife Gallery Pittsburgh, PA 1974; Neuberger Museum, Purchase, NY 1981; Whitney Museum, NYC 1982; Nat. Bldg. Museum, Washington, DC 1989. **Bio-Bibliography:** *The Ideal Theatre: Eight Concepts* (New York, 1962); Paul Heyer, *Architects on Architecture* (New York, 1966); Barbaralee Diamonstein, *American Architecture Now* (New York, 1979); Arthur Drexler, *Transformations in Modern Architecture* (New York, 1979); Barbaralee Diamonstein, *Inside New York's Art World* (New York, 1979); *Contemporary Architects* (New York: St. Martin's Press, 1980); Helen Searing, *New American Art Museums*, exb. cat. (New York, 1982); Paul Venable Turner, *Campus: An American Planning Tradition* (Cambridge: MIT Press, 1984); "Edward Larrabee Barnes" *Space Design* (July 1985); *Dictionary of Art* (New York: Macmillan, 1986); *Encyclopedia of Architecture* (New York: John Wiley & Sons, 1987); *Edward Larrabee Barnes Museum Designs*, exb. cat. (Katonah, NY: Katonah Museum of Art, 1987); Peter Blake, *Edward Larrabee Barnes, Architect* (New York: Rizzoli, 1994); *International Directory of Architects & Architecture; International Who's Who; Who's Who in America*. **Home Address:** 205 Wood Rd., Mt. Kisco, NY 10594.

BARNES, SUSAN J. ■ FAAR History of Art 82; SOF Council 1988-92. b. Sept. 28, 1948, Houston, TX. BA 70, Rice Univ.; MA 80, IFA; PhD 86, IFA. **Research/Artistic Interests:** 17th-century painting & sculpture, 20th-century painting. **Career & Employment:** CASVA, Acting Asst. Dean-Asst. Dean 1984-87; North Carolina Museum of Art, Chief Curator 1987-89; Dallas Museum of Art, Senior Curator of Western Art 1989-92; Deputy Dir., Collections & Exbs., Chief Curator 1992-94; Menil Found., VP, Chief Operating Officer 1994-present. **Memberships & Offices:** CAA, BoD, Nominating Com. 1990; NEA, Internships & Museum Training Programs Panel 1990; Texas Comm. for the Arts 1990-92; CAA, DTOAH Award Com., Chair 1991-94. **Fellowships, Honors & Awards:** Goldwater Summer Fellowship 1980; Robert Lehman Research Fellow 1980-81; Fulbright Fellowship 1981-82 (declined); David E. Finley Fellow, NGA 1981-84. **Publications:** "The Decoration of the Church of the Hospital of Charity at Illescas," *Studies in the History of Art* 11 (1982); co-ed. & contr., "Cultural Differentiation and Cultural Identity in the Arts," *Studies in the History of Art* 27 (1989); *The Rothko Chapel: An Act of Faith* (Austin: Univ. of Texas Press, 1989); *Anthony Van Dyck*, exb. cat. (Washington, DC: NGA, 1990); ed., with Arthur Wheelock, "Van Dyck 350," *Studies in the History of Art* 46 (1994). **Home Address:** 1219 Bartlett, Houston, TX 77006.

BARNETT, JONATHAN ■ AAR Visitor 1955-59, Yale, Clare Exchange Student.

BARNEY, CHARLES T. ■ AAR Charter Mem., Investment Banker.

BARR, ALFRED HAMILTON, JR ■ AAR Visitor 1943-55; Art Historian, Museum Dir. b. Jan. 28, 1902. d. Aug. 15, 1981. **Career & Employment:** MOMA, Dir. 1929-43. **Memberships & Offices:** CAA, Dir. 1943-48. **Fellowships, Honors & Awards:** NIAL, Distinguished Service to the Arts Award 1968. **Important Works:** as co-ed, *Art in America in Modern Times* (1936); as co-author, *Twentieth Century Italian Art* (1949); *Matisse: His Art and His Public* (1951); *Masters of Modern Art* (1954); plus 31 exb. cats.

BARRETTO, ABRAHAM ■ AAR – New York, Receptionist, Administrative Asst.

BARSCH, WULF E. ■ FAAR Painting 76. b. Aug. 27, 1943, Reudnitz, Bohemia. m. Sandra Kellee. c. Buck, James, Aram, Joseph. BFA 68, Werkunstschule, Hanover, Germany; MA 70, Brigham Young Univ.; MFA 71, Brigham Young Univ. **Other Study:** Staatliche Hochschule für Bildende Künste, Hamburg, Germany 1962-63. **Career & Employment:** Brigham Young Univ., Prof. 1972-present. **Memberships & Offices:** Wyoming Council on the Arts, Juror 1985. **Fellowships, Honors & Awards:** CCAC, World Print Competition, San Francisco Museum of Art 1973; WSTAF, Santa Fe, NM, Western States Printmaking Award 1980, Painting Award 1983; Karl G. Maeser Found., Research & Creative Award 1985. **Important Works:** Library of Congress, Washington, DC; Museu de Arte Moderna, Rio de Janeiro, Brazil; Museum of Art, Univ. of New Mexico, Albuquerque; Tamarind Inst., Albuquerque; Museum of Fine Art, Salt Lake City; Museum of Arts and Crafts, Oakland, CA; Museum of Art, Univ. of Houston; Brooklyn Museum, NYC; Permanent Collection, Brigham Young Univ., Provo, UT; Museum of Church History & Art, Salt Lake City; Nora Eccles Harrison Museum of Art, Logan, UT; Museum of Art, McAlester College, St. Paul, MN; Springville Museum of Art, Springville, UT; Delta Airlines, Salt Lake City; Compac Computer, Long Island, NY; US Embassy, El Salvador; Shell Oil, Houston; Bank South, Inc., Atlanta; Philip Arensberg Collection, Albany, NY; Alembitz, Fine & Callney, Atlanta; Univ. of Illinois, Springfield; State Senate, Hamburg, Germany; Frederick R. Weissman Found., Los Angeles; Orem, UT City Collection; Atlantic Richfield Oil Company, Permanent Collection, Houston; M-Bank, Houston; Transco, Houston; AMACO, Denver; American Express, Salt Lake City; Reinhard Kraft, Hanover, Germany; John Kirsky, Houston; Sidney Schlinker Corp., Houston. **Exhibitions/Performances:** NO HO Gallery, Stamford, CT 1988; River Center Gallery, Memphis, TN 1988; Trinity Gallery, Atlanta 1989, 1991; Liza Kurtz Gallery, Memphis, TN 1989; Art Space, Atlanta 1989; Dolores Chase Fine Arts, Salt Lake City 1989, 1991; Sylvia Schmidt Gallery, New Orleans 1991; Elaine Horwitcz Galleries, Scottsdale, AZ 1991; Gremillion & Co., Houston 1991; Strecker Gallery, Manhattan, KS 1991. **Bio-Bibliography:** *Folio Seventy-Three*, exb. cat. (San Francisco: Museum of Modern Art, 1973); "Wulf Barsch, Making the Invisible Visible"; Judith McConkie, "The Shadows of Pyramids," *Art Space* (Fall 1984); Katherine Nelson, "Wulf Barsch: The Spirit in Paint," *Utah Holiday* (Fall 1984); George Dibble, "Works by Wulf Barsch Possess Mystique of His Inner Thoughts," *Deseret News*; Frederic Koeppel, "Barsch Explores Ambitious Item," *Memphis News* (Mar. 20, 1988); Jeff Metcalf & Mark Taylor, "Wulf Barsch, Man and Shadow," *Salt Lake City Magazine* (June 1990); *Selected Works*, exb. cat. (Houston, TX: Gremillion & Co.); *Dictionary of International Biography; Encyclopedia of Mormonism; Men of Achievement; Outstanding Young Man of America; Who's Who in American Art; Who's Who in Society; Who's Who in the West.* **Home Address:** PO Box 1359, Boulder, UT 84716. **Business Address:** Gremillion & Co., Fine Arts, Inc., 2501 Sunset Blvd., Houston, TX 77005.

BARTHELME, DONALD ■ AAR Visitor 1988-89, Writer.

BARTHOLOMEW, REGINALD ■ AAR Visitor 1994, US Ambassador to Italy.

BARTHOLOMEW, RICHARD W. ■ FAAR Architecture 72. b. Sept. 28, 1941, Bristol, PA. m. Julia Moore Converse. c. Alexander Converse, Denis Converse, Andrew Bartholomew. BA 63, Univ. of Pennsylvania; MArch 65, Univ. of Pennsylvania. **Other Study:** Cambridge Univ. 1965-67. **Career & Employ-**

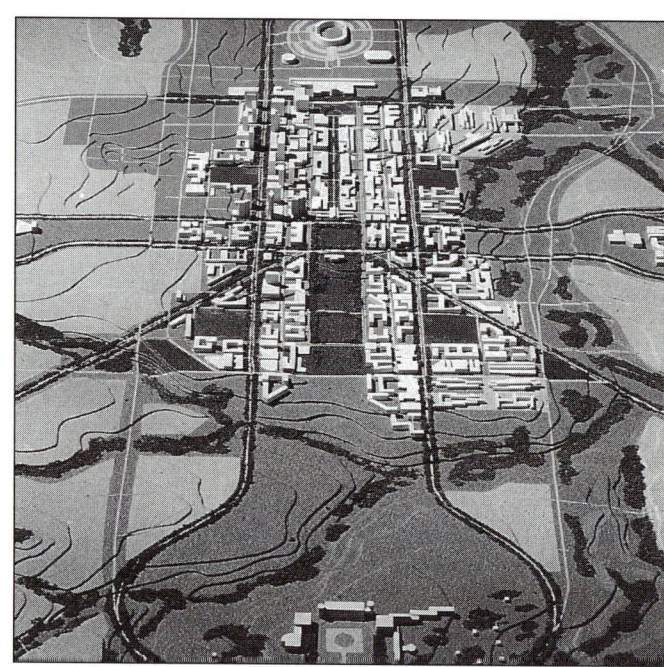

Richard W. Bartholomew

ment: David A. Crane & Assc. 1967-71; Geddes Brecher Qualls Cunningham 1972-73; Brown & Goldfarb 1973-74; Univ. of Pennsylvania, Lect. 1974-92; Drexel Univ., Lect. 1975-76; Kling Partnership 1975-78; Wallace McHarg Roberts & Todd 1978-80; Wallace Roberts & Todd, Project Dir. 1980-81, Senior Assc. 1981-85, Part. 1986-present. **Memberships & Offices:** AIA 1981-present; American Inst. for Certified Planners; Inst. for Urban Design, Fellow; The Waterfront Center, Bd. of Adv. 1991-93. **Fellowships, Honors & Awards:** Univ. of Pennsylvania: Alpha Rho Chi Medal 1965, Charles Merrick Gay Prize 1965, Thouron Fellowship 1965-67; Fulbright Scholarship 1965 (declined). **Important Works:** Radisson, NY, New Community Master Plan 1968; Abuja, Nigeria, Master Plan 1979; Hershey Foods, Corp. Administrative Center, Hershey, PA 1980; Orlando, FL, Growth Management Plan: Downtown Plan, Centroplex Master Plan, Downtown Streetscape Design Guidelines 1981; Liberty Place Master Plan, Philadelphia 1983; New Government Centers Master Plan, US Virgin Islands 1983; duPont Centre Master Plan, Orlando, FL 1984; Lincoln Harbor Master Plan, Weehawken, NJ 1987; Univ. of Connecticut Master Plan, Storrs 1987; Southern Gateway Master Plan, Richmond, VA 1992; New Orleans 2000 Riverfront Master Plan 1992; Southeast Federal Center Design Guidelines, Washington, DC 1994. **Business Address:** Wallace Roberts & Todd, 260 S. Broad St., Philadelphia, PA 19102.

BARTMAN, ELIZABETH ■ FAAR History of Art 83; SOF, Common Council 1991-92, Treas. 1992-present. b. Jan. 30, 1953, Saratoga Springs, NY. m. Andrew P. Solomon. c. Daria. BA 75, Brown Univ.; PhD 84, Columbia Univ. **Other Study:** ICCS, ASCSA. **Research/Artistic Interests:** Roman art. **Career & Employment:** Univ. of Pennsylvania, Lect. 1984-86, Asst Prof. 1986-90; MMA, Lect. 1990-present. **Memberships & Offices:** ArIA, Sec. of Philadelphia Soc. 1988-89, Governing Bd. of New York Soc. 1992-present. **Fellowships, Honors & Awards:** MMA, Jane and Morgan Whitney Fellowship 1991-92; Kress Triangulation Fellow 1981-83; NEH Summer Seminar 1994. **Publications:** *Ancient Sculptural Copies in Miniature* (Leiden: E. J. Brill, 1992). **Home Address:** 15 W. 81 St., Apt. 5A, NYC 10024.

BARTOLI, CECILIA ■ AAR Visitor 1990-91, Classical Singer.

BASS, MERCEDES TAVACOLI ■ AAR Trustee 1991-present. b. Teheran, Iran. Dipl., École Superieure de Commerce, Neuchatel. **Memberships & Offices:** Modern Art Museum, Ft. Worth, President's Circle; Van Cliburn Found., Exec. Comm.; Ft. Worth Symphony Assn., Exec. Comm.; American Friends of Covent Garden, BoT; Carnegie Hall Corp., BoT; Lincoln Center, Chairman's Council for the Performing Arts; MMA, Chairman's Council; Metropolitan Opera, BoT; MOMA, Chairman's Council; Music Asscs. of Aspen, Adv. Board; NGA, Collectors Comm.

BASSANI, GIORGIO ■ AAR Visitor 1980-81, Writer.

BASSETT, EDWARD CHARLES ■ RAAR Architecture 70. b. 1921. **Bio-Bibliography:** *Who's Who in America.*

BASSETT, LESLIE R. ■ FAAR Musical Composition 63. b. Jan. 22, 1923, Hanford, CA. m. Anita D. Bassett. c. Wendy L., Bratton, Noel L. Bassett. BA 47, Fresno State College; MusM 49, Univ. of Michigan; A.MusD 56, Univ. of Michigan. **Other Study:** École Normale de Musique, Paris 1950-51; private student of Ross Lee Finney, Arthur Honnegger, Nadia Boulanger, Roberto Gerhard and (electronic music) Mario Davidovsky. **Research/Artistic Interests:** Music composition. **Career & Employment:** Univ. of Michigan 1952-91, Albert A. Stanley Distinguished Univ. Prof. of Music. **Memberships & Offices:** AAAL 1981-present; Michigan Soc. of Fellows 1977-81; ACA, Nat. Bd. 1982-present. **Fellowships, Honors & Awards:** Fulbright Fellowship 1950-51; Soc. for the Publication of American Music Fellowship 1960; NIAL Fellowship 1964; Nat. Found. for the Arts & Humanities Fellowship 1966; Pulitzer Prize 1966; Guggenheim Fellowship 1973, 1980; Naumberg Recording Award 1974; California State Univ., Distinguished Alumnus 1978; Michigan Council for the Arts, Distinguished Artist Award 1981; Univ. of Michigan, Music Alumni Assn., Citation of Merit 1980; Univ. of Michigan, Henry Russel Lect. 1984.

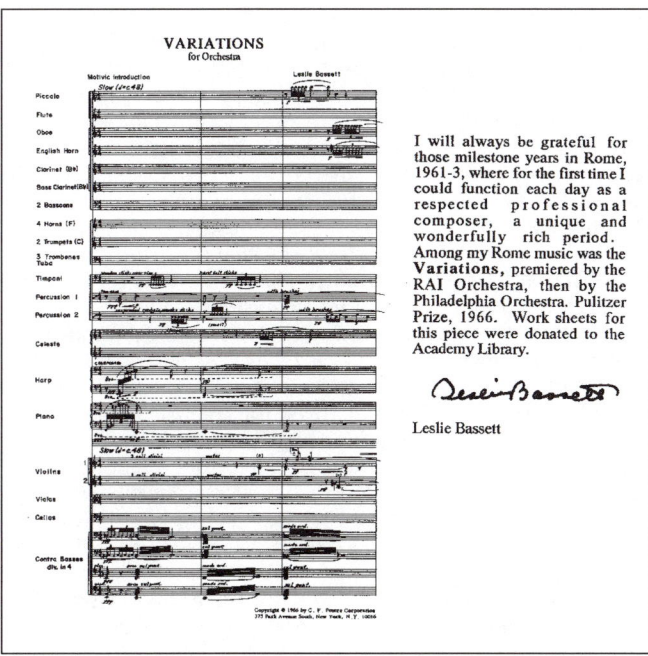

I will always be grateful for those milestone years in Rome, 1961-3, where for the first time I could function each day as a respected professional composer, a unique and wonderfully rich period. Among my Rome music was the **Variations**, premiered by the RAI Orchestra, then by the Philadelphia Orchestra. Pulitzer Prize, 1966. Work sheets for this piece were donated to the Academy Library.

Leslie Bassett

Leslie R. Bassett

Important Works: *Five Pieces for String Quartet* 1957; *Variations for Orchestra* (CRI) 1963; *Collect* 1969; *Celebration in Praise of Earth* 1970; *Sextet for Piano and Strings* (CRI) 1971; *Echoes from an Invisible World* (CRI) 1975; *Concerto for Two Pianos and Orchestra* 1976; *Sounds, Shapes and Symbols* 1977; *Fourth String Quartet* 1978; *A Ring of Emeralds* 1979; *Trio for Violin, Clarinet and Piano* (Leonardo) 1980; *Liturgies* 1980; *Concerto Lirico* 1983; *Preludes* 1984; *Colors and Contours* 1984; *From a Source Evolving* (Opus One) 1985; *Fantasy for Clarinet and Wind Ensemble* 1986; *Dialogues* 1988; *Pierrot Songs* 1988; *Illuminations* (Opus One) 1989; *Concerto for Orchestra* 1991. Recordings on CRI, Crystal Records, Desto, Golden Crest, Leonardo Records, New World Records, Opus One. Publishers: primarily C.F. Peters; also Merion Music, Highgate Press, Robert King (Alphonse Leduc), World Library, Philharmonia, Alfred, Musica Rara, Roseanne. **Home Address:** 1618 Harbal, Ann Arbor, MI 48105. **Business Address:** School of Music, Univ. of Michigan, Ann Arbor, MI 48109.

BASTEDO, PHILIP ■ AAR Trustee 1978-87, Lawyer.

BASTIANICH, LIDIA ■ AAR Visitor 1991-92, Restauranteur & Chef.

BATCHELDER, RALPH JOHNSON ■ Rotch Scholar 1914.

BATES, DAVID SNOW ■ FAAR Musical Composition 75. b. June 21, 1936, Massillon, OH. d. Nov. 6, 1974. m. Susan Bates. BMus 58, Univ. of Michigan; MusM 60, Univ. of Michigan; MusD 72, Univ. of Michigan. **Career & Employment:** California State Univ., Fresno, Asst. Prof.; Electronic Music Studio, Dir. **Fellowships, Honors & Awards:** BMI Student Composers' Award, 1st Prize 1959; Univ. of Michigan, John Reed Memorial Award 1970, Teaching Fellowship 1959-60, 1962-63, 1970-71; Ford Found. Contemporary Music Project Fellowships, San Antonio, TX 1966-67, Denver 1967-68; Pennsylvania Fine Arts Program for the Artistically Gifted, Composer in Residence 1968. **Important Works:** *Fantasy for Violin and Piano* 1958; *Solo Violin Sonata* 1961. **Bio-Bibliography:** *Contemporary American Composers.*

BAYER, HERBERT ■ RAAR Architecture 78. b. Apr. 5, 1900, Haag, Austria. d. Sept. 30, 1985. m. Joella Bayer. c. Julia. **Studies:** The Bauhaus 1925. **Research/Artistic Interests:** Painting, photography, design, architecture. **Career & Employment:** The Bauhaus, Master of Workshop for printing & advertising 1925-28; Freelance Studio in Berlin 1928-38; Container Corp. of American, Advertising Designer 1945; Design Consutant for Aspen, CO as cultural center & ski resort 1940s; Atlantic Richfield Co, Consultant 1966-85. **Fellowships, Honors & Awards:** Ambassador's Award, London 1968; American Inst. of Graphic Arts, Gold Medal 1970; Albert Stifter Preis, Austria 1971; RISD, Athena Award 1984; Royal Acad. of Fine Arts, Netherlands, Hon. Fellow; Art Dirs. Club Hall of Fame. **Publications:** ed., with Walter Gropius & Isle Gropius, *Bauhaus, 1919-28* (New York: MMA, 1938); ed., *World Geographic Atlas* (New York: Oxford Univ. Press, 1953); *Herbert Bayer Book of Drawings* (Chicago: P. Theobald, 1961); contr., *Books for Our Time*, ed. Marshall Lee (1951); *Herbert Bayer: Painter, Designer, Architect* (New York: Rinehart, 1967); contr., *Great Ideas of Western Man* (Chicago, 1968); *Herbert Bayer: Visual Concept Total* (New York: Rinehart, 1975). **Important Works:** MOMA, exb. on the Bauhaus 1938; Earth Sculpture, Marble Garden 1955; Anderson Park, Aspen CO 1973; Double Ascensio, Los Angeles 1972; Aspen Inst. of Humanistic Studies; represented in museum collections throughout Europe & US. **Exhibitions/Perfor-**

mances: Solo: New York, Berlin, Paris, London, San Francisco & other major cities; Retrospectives: Nürnberg, Munich, Zurich, Amsterdam, Brussels, Berlin. **Bio-Bibliography:** Alexander Borner, *The Way Beyond Art: The Work of Herbert Bayer* (New York: Wittenborn, Schultz, 1947); *Herbert Bayer: From Type to Landscape,* exb. cat. (Hanover, NH: Dartmouth College, 1977); Arthur A. Cohen, *Herbert Bayer: The Complete Work* (Cambridge, MA: MIT Press, 1984); *NY Times,* Obit. (Oct. 1, 1985); *Oxford Dictionary of Art* (Oxford: Oxford Univ. Press, 1988); *Who Was Who in America.*

BAZANT, JAN ■ Mellon East-Central European Visiting Scholar 1994.

BEASER, ROBERT H. ■ FAAR Musical Composition 78; AAR Trustee 1993-present. b. May 29, 1954, Boston, MA. m. Catherine S. Banat. c. Adam , Julia. BA 76, Yale College; MM 77, Yale School of Music; MMA 81, Yale School of Music; DMA 86, Yale School of Music. **Other Study:** Private studies with Arnold Franchetti at Hartt School of Music; Goffredo Petrassi in Rome. **Career & Employment:** Musical Elements, Co-Music Dir., Conductor 1978-90; American Composers Orchestra, Composer-in-Residence 1988-93, Artistic Adv. 1993-present; Juilliard School, Prof., Chair 1993-present. **Memberships & Offices:** Phi Beta Kappa 1976-present; BMI 1977-present; Century Assn. 1991-present; *Contemporary Music Review,* Issue Ed. 1992; American Composers Orchestra, BoD 1993-present; MacDowell Colony, BoD 1993-present. **Fellowships, Honors & Awards:** Tanglewood Fellowship 1976; Fulbright Fellowship 1977; AAAL, Charles Ives Scholarship 1978; NEA Fellowship 1978; ASCAP Award 1979; Nonesuch Comm. Award 1982; Guggenheim Fellowship 1983; AAAL, Goddard Lieberson Fellowship 1986; Grammy Nomination 1986. **Important Works:** *Symphony,* for soprano & orchestra 1976-77; *Shadow & Light,* for woodwind quintet 1978, 1980; *The Seven Deadly Sins,* for baritone & piano (Albany Records) 1979; *Notes on a Southern Sky,* for solo guitar, Eliot Fisk-NEA Comm. (EMI-Electrola) 1980; *Variations,* for flute & piano, Concert Artists Guild Comm. (Musicmasters) 1981-82; *The Seven Deadly Sins,* for baritone &

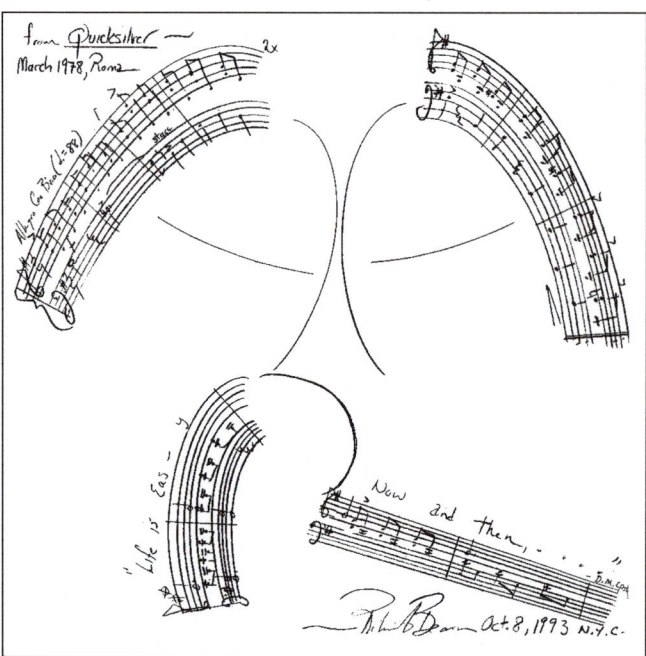

Robert H. Beaser

orchestra, New York Philharmonic/Horizons '84 Festival Comm. (London-Argo) 1984; *Mountain Songs,* for flute & guitar, Paula Robison & Eliot Fisk Comm. (Musicmasters) 1984-85; *Songs from "The Occasions,"* for tenor & chamber ensemble, St. Louis Symphony-Nonesuch Comm. 1985; *Song of the Bells,* for flute & orchestra, Paula Robison & Ransom Wilson-NEA Consortium Comm. (New World Records) 1987; *Concerto for Piano and Orchestra,* Pamela Mia Paul & St. Louis Symphony Comm. (London-Argo) 1989-90; *Double Chorus,* for orchestra, Chicago Symphony Comm. 1990-91; *Chorale Variations,* for orchestra, American Composers Orchestra Comm. (London-Argo) 1992; *The Heavenly Feast,* for soprano & orchestra, Baltimore Symphony Orchestra-Dawn Upshaw Comm. 1994. **Home Address:** 333 W. End Ave., 9C, NYC 10023. **Business Address:** European American Music Corp., PO Box 850, Valley Forge, PA 19482.

BEASLEY, ELLEN ■ FAAR Design Arts 89. Sept. 4, 1940, E. St. Louis, IL. BA 62, Univ. of Wisconsin; MA 64, Univ. of Delaware. **Other Study:** Drury College (Springfield, MO) 1958-60; Seminar for Historical Administrators, Colonial Williamsburg, 1964; UNESCO and ICOMOS, US Rep. to first intl. exchange program on preservation & rehabilitation of historic districts 1978. **Career & Employment:** Winterthur Museum, Curatorial Asst. 1964-65; Nat. Trust for Historic Preservation, Assc. Curator 1965-70; Preservation Consultant, Nashville 1970-73; Univ. of Texas, Visiting Lect. 1976, 1977; Preservation Planning Consultant, Galveston 1973-88; Preservationist-Writer, Houston 1989-present. **Memberships & Offices:** Intl. Council on Monuments and Sites, US Com., Exec. Com. & BoT 1980-89; US-ICOMOS, Historic Towns Com. 1990-94; Houston Archaeological & Historical Comm. 1993-95. **Fellowships, Honors & Awards:** Nat. Trust for Historic Preservation, Research Grant 1977-78; NEA Grant 1977-78; Harvard GSD, Loeb Fellowship 1983-84; Graham Found. for Advanced Studies in Fine Arts, Research Grant 1985-86; NEA Fellowship 1986-87. **Publications:** *Made in Tennessee: An Exhibition of Early Arts and Crafts* (Nashville: Tennessee Fine Arts Center, 1971); "The End of the Rainbow," *Historic Preservation* (Jan.-Mar. 1972): 18-23; *Festival USA, Galveston Bicentennial Pilot Project Report* (Galveston, TX: American Revolution Bicentennial Comm.-Texas Comm. on the Arts & Humanities, 1974 & 1976); "Impressions of Gulf Coast Architecture," in *The Cultural Legacy of the Gulf Coast 1870-1940,* Proceedings of the Sixth Annual Gulf Coast History & Humanities Conference (Pensacola: Gulf Coast History & Humanities Conference, 1976), 93-102; "New Construction in Residential Historic Districts," in *Old and New Architecture: Design Relationships* (Washington, DC: Preservation Press, 1980), 229-56; *Design Development: Infill Housing Compatible with Historic Neighborhoods* (Washington, DC: Nat. Trust for Historic Preservation 1988); *Factory-Built Housing: Finding a Home in Historic Neighborhoods* (Washington, DC: Nat. Trust for Historic Preservation, 1989); *Reviewing New Construction Projects in Historic Areas: Procedures for Local Preservation Commissions* (Boston: NE Regional Office, Nat. Trust for Historic Preservation, 1986; rev. ed., Washington, DC: Nat. Trust for Historic Preservation, 1992); "The Corner Store of Galveston: A Family's Residence, A Neighborhood's Parlor," *Center: A Journal for Architecture in America* (1993): 62-71; "Reviewing New Design in Historic Districts," in *Design Review: Challenging Urban Aesthetic Control* (New York: Chapman & Hall, 1994), 20-30; *The Alleys and Back Buildings of Galveston* (Houston: Rice Univ. Press, 1995). **Exhibitions/Performances:** Tennessee Fine Arts Center, Nashville 1971; The Octagon, AIA, Washington, DC 1975; Galveston Arts Center, TX 1975; Harvard GSD 1984; Houston Intl. Festi-

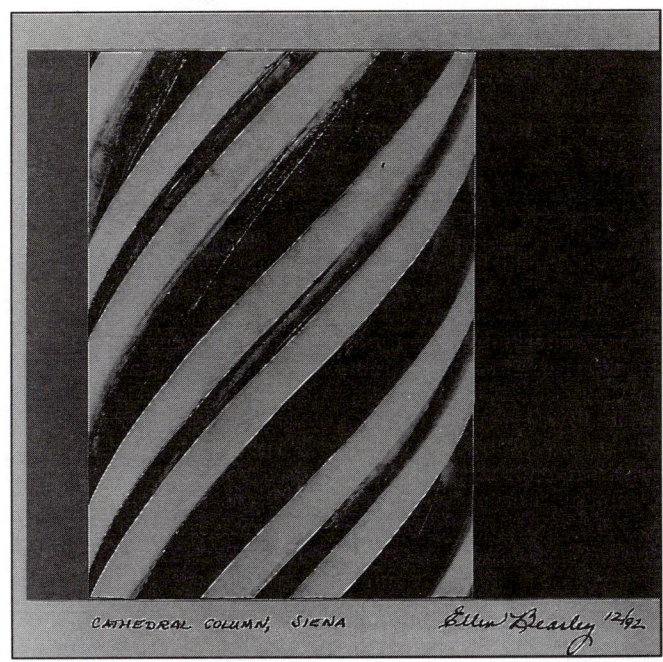

CATHEDRAL COLUMN, SIENA   Ellen Beasley 12/92

Ellen Beasley

val 1994. **Home Address:** 7326 Staffordshire, Apt. 3, Houston, TX 77030.

BECK, DUNBAR DYSON ■ FAAR Painting 30. b. Sept. 16, 1902, Delaware, OH. d. Feb. 23, 1986. BFA 26, Yale School of Fine Arts. **Other Studies:** Northwestern Univ., Ohio Wesleyan Univ. **Research/Artistic Interests:** Decorating; mural painting. **Memberships & Offices:** Pennslyvania Acad. of the Fine Arts. **Important Works:** Decorated the East Room of the White House, Washington, DC; altar, church paintings in NYC, Philadelphia, St. Paul, MN, Sacramento; US Post Office, Danvers, MA; KMJ Radio Station, Fresno, CA, Designer 1951. **Exhibitions/Performances:** Decorators Club Gallery, Hadlyme, CT. **Bio-Bibliography:** *Who Was Who in American Art.*

BECK, GEORGE W. ■ American School of Architecture in Rome, Dir. 1906-9.

BEEBE, DWIGHT S. ■ AAR Trustee 1932-63, Corp. Exec.

BEESON, JACK ■ FAAR Musical Composition 50; RAAR Musical Composition 66; SOF, Pres. 1963-64; AAR Trustee 1975-87, Trustee Emer. b. July 15, 1921, Muncie, IN. m. Nora B. Sigerist. c. Miranda Beeson, Christopher. BMus 42, Eastman School of Music, Univ. of Rochester; MusM 43, Eastman School of Music, Univ. of Rochester. **Other Study:** Eastman School of Music, Univ. of Rochester; Columbia Univ., graduate seminars (musicology) with Paul Henry Lang 1945-47; private study (composition) with Béla Bartók 1944-45; private coaching (conducting) with Rudolph Thomas 1945-48. **Career & Employment:** Columbia Univ., Asst. in Music to MacDowell Prof. of Music 1945-88 and intermittently thereafter; Juilliard School, Lect. 1961-63; Columbia Univ., Music Dept., Acting Chair 1964, 1976, Chair 1968-72; Columbia Univ., Music Division, Acting Chair, three terms. **Memberships & Offices:** Composers' Forum, Bd. of Governors 1950-75, Vice-Chair 1959-62, 1968-75, Chair 1962-68, Adv. Bd. 1975-present; ACA, Bd. of Governors 1954-59; Alice M. Ditson Fund of Columbia Univ., Adv. Com.

1960-present, Acting Sec. 1961-62, Sec. and Officer-in-Charge 1962-88; Found. Music Adv. Com. 1961-1986; Pulitzer Prize, Adv. for the Pulitzer Prize in Music 1962-present; ASCAP 1959-present, BoD 1991-present; American Music Center, Adv. Council 1964-66; BoD 1967-76; CRI, BoD 1967-80, VP 1967-75, Co-acting Pres. 1975-6, Hon. BoT 1980-present; ISCM-League of Composers, BoD 1969-72; Meet the Composer, Adv. Bd. 1976-present; NEA, Composers Policy Panel 1979-80, Opera-Musical Theater Panel 1986-91; AAAL, BoD & Treas. 1980-83, 1989-92, VP for Music, 1984-87; Center for Contemporary Opera, Adv. Council 1982-present. **Fellowships, Honors & Awards:** City of Rochester, Lillian Fairchild Award 1944; Fulbright Fellow 1949-50; Special Mention, La Scala Intl. Opera Competition, for *Jonah* 1951; Guggenheim Fellowship 1958-59; Annual ASCAP Awards 1959-present; AAAL, Marc Blitzstein Award for the Musical Theatre 1968, Election 1976; Rockefeller Found., Bellagio Center Residency 1976; Nat. Arts Club, Gold Medal for Music 1976; Columbia Univ., Soc. of Older Graduates, Great Teacher's Award 1979; Meet the Composer, Grants 1979-present; Univ. of Rochester, Eastman School of Music, Alumni Achievement Award 1985; Phi Beta Kappa 1988. **Important Works:** *Jonah*, opera 1950; *Hello Out There*, opera (CRI/BCD) 1954; *The Sweet Bye and Bye*, opera (Desto/CRI) 1956; *Symphony in A* (CRI) 1959; *Transformations* 1959; *Lizzie Borden*, opera, Ford Found. Comm. for NYC Opera (CRI) 1965; *My Heart's in the Highlands*, opera, NET Opera Comm. 1969; *Captain Jinks of the Horse Marines*, opera, NEA & Ford Found. Recording Comm. (RCA/Desto) 1975; *Dr. Heidegger's Fountain of Youth*, opera, Nat. Arts Club Comm. (CRI) 1978; *Cyrano*, opera 1990; various chamber works, about 75 vocal works & about 75 choral works, including *Knots* (GSS); *Magicke Pieces* (GSS); *Epitaphs*. **Bio-Bibliography:** There are discussions of the operas in numerous volumes, including Quaintance Eaton, *Opera Production*, 2 vols. (1961-74); Andrew Drummond, *American Opera Librettos* (New York: Scarecrow Press, 1973); *Music Educators Journal* 66.2 (Oct. 1979); Janet Seitzer, "The Solo Piano Works of Jack Beeson" (PhD Diss., Baltimore, MD: Johns Hopkins Univ.); *Jack Beeson*, television documentary, WGBH, Boston for NET 1967; *Opera Monthly* 7.1; entries in Anderson, Baker, Ewen, Grove's, Thomson, *Who's Who*, *Who's Who in the East*, *Who's Who in Music*, Vinton, & other such reference works. **Home Address:** 404 Riverside Dr., NYC 10025.

BEGLEY, WAYNE EDISON ■ FAAR Painting 61. b. Dec. 29, 1937, Kenvir, KY. m. Jane Woody Begley. c. Benjamin. BA 58, Univ. of Louisville. **Other Studies:** Louisville Art Center 1952-54; State Univ. of Iowa from 1958. **Research/Artistic Interests:** Abstract painting; Indian philosophy & Indian art. **Career & Employment:** Rice Univ., Andrew W. Mellon Prof. 1985; Univ. of Iowa, Prof. **Memberships & Offices:** CAA. **Fellowships, Honors & Awards:** State Univ. of Iowa, Woodrow Wilson Fellowship 1958-59; Univ. of Louisville & State Univ. of Iowa, various prizes in student art shows. **Exhibitions/Performances:** Arts in Louisville House Gallery, Louisville, KY 1959; Frame House Gallery, Louisville, KY 1962; Univ. of Kentucky Art Gallery 1962; Guild Gallery, Iowa City 1962. **Bio-Bibliography:** "Abstract Art," *The Courier-Journal Magazine* (Oct. 1, 1961).

BELL, JANIS C. ■ FAAR History of Art 90. b. Sept. 13, 1950, Philadelphia, PA. c. Lisa. BA 71, Univ. of Pennsylvania; MA 1974, Boston Univ.; PhD 83, Brown Univ. **Research/Artistic Interests:** Italian Renaissance & Baroque painting, art theory, color theory & practice. **Career & Employment:** Kenyon College, Asst. Prof. 1982-88, Assc. Prof. 1988-present. **Memberships**

& Offices: ATSAH, Founder & Pres. 1991-present; CAA 1982-present; Women's Caucus for the Arts 1982-90; Midwest Art History Soc. 1983-present. **Fellowships, Honors & Awards:** Fulbright Fellowship 1978-79; NEH Summer Stipend 1984; ACLS Post-Doctoral Research Grant 1984; I Tatti Fellowship 1989-90; NEH Summer Seminar 1992. **Publications:** as Janis Clearfield, "Cosimo de Medici's Tomb in San Lorenzo," *Rutgers Art Review* 2 (1981): 13-30; "The Life and Works of Fra Matteo Zaccolini," *Regnum Dei* 41.111 (1985): 227-58; "Cassiano dal Pozzo's Copy of the Zaccolini Manuscripts," *Journal of the Warburg and Courtauld Institutes* 51 (1988): 103-25; "Zaccolini and Leonardo's MS. A," *Il collezionismo dei leonardeschi a Milano e la Madonna Litta*, ed. M.T. Fiorio and P.C. Marani (Milan: Electa, 1991), 183-93; "Color Perspective c. 1492," *Achademia Leonardi Vinci* 5 (1992); "Some Seventeenth-Century Appraisals of Caravaggio's Coloring," *Artibus et Historiae* 14.27 (1993); "Aristotle as a Source for Leonardo's Theory of Colour Perspective after 1500," *Journal of the Warburg & Courtauld Institutes* 56 (1993): 100-118; "Light and Color in Caravaggio's Supper at Emmaus," *Artibus et Historiae* 15.29 (1994); "Zaccolini's Theory of Color Perspective," *Art Bulletin* 75 (Mar. 1993): 91-112; *Raphael's School of Athens* in Masterpiece in Context Series, ed. Marcia Hall (Cambridge: Cambridge Univ. Press, 1995); "Pietro Accolti," "Alberti Family Tree," "Alessandro Alberti," "Cherubino Alberti," "Giovanni Alberti," "Gian Galeazzo Arconati," "Chiaroscuro," "Light," "Tenebrism," "Marcello Venusti," "Matteo Zaccolini," co-authored with Martin Kemp "Perspective," sections on non-linear perspective: color, acuity, light and shadow for *The Dictionary of Art*; "Revisioning Raphael as a 'Scientific Painter,'" in *Reframing the Renaissance*, ed. Claire Farago (New Haven: Yale Univ. Press, 1995). **Business Address:** Bailey House, Kenyon College, Gambier, OH 43214.

BELL, LARRY THOMAS ■ FAAR Musical Composition 83. b. Jan. 17, 1952, Wilson, NC. m. Andrea L. Olmstead. BMus 74, Appalachian State Univ., Boone NC; MusM 77, Juilliard School; DMA 82, Juilliard School. **Other Study:** East Carolina Univ. (Greenville) 1970-73. **Career & Employment:** Juilliard School, Pre-College Div. Instr. (solfège & theory) 1979-84; Boston Conservatory, Faculty (composition) 1980-present; New England Conservatory of Music 1992-present. **Memberships & Offices:** Pi Kappa Lambda 1973; Sigma Alpha Iota, Nat. Arts Assoc 1987; ACA, Exec. Officer 1989-93; BMI, composer, publisher, juror 1980-present. **Fellowships, Honors & Awards:** Juilliard School, Gretchaninoff Prize 1976; AAAL Charles Ives Award 1977; MacDowell Colony Fellow 1981; Guggenheim Fellow 1981-82; Meet the Composer Grant 1984, 1987, 1989; Rockefeller Found. in Bellagio, Resident 1985; Virginia Center for the Creative Arts, Fellow 1987, 1988, 1993, 1994; Bennington College, Composer in Residence 1992. **Publications:** "Some Remarks on the New Tonality," *Contemporary Music Review* (1992). **Important Works:** *String Quartet No. 1* 1973; *The Idea of Order at Key West*, for soprano, violin, string orch. & percussion 1979-81; *String Quartet No. 2* 1982; *Fantasia on an Imaginary Hymn*, for cello & viola, Joel Krosnick Comm. 1983; *Sacred Symphonies* for orchestra, Verio Piroddi Comm. 1985; *River of Ponds* for cello & piano, Joel Krosnick Comm. 1986; *A Sacred Harp*, Ellen Ritscher Comm. 1986; *The Black Cat* for narrator, cello & piano, Eric Bartlett Comm. 1987; *Piano Quartet*, Boston Conservatory 125th Anniversary Comm. 1991; *Concerto for Oboe and Five Instruments,* Speculum Musicae Comm. 1988; *Piano Concerto*, Gerard Schwarz Comm. for Music Today 1989; *Late Night Thoughts on Listening to Mahler's Ninth Symphony* (based on a text by Lewis Thomas) for narrator-violinist & piano, Joanna Jenner Comm.

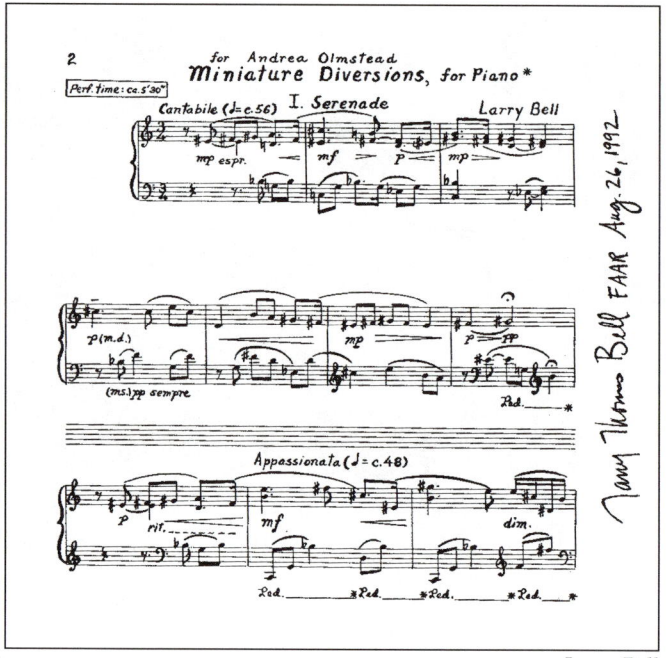

Larry Bell

1991; *Sacred Symphonies,* Seattle Symphony 1987, Radio Bratislava Symphony Orchestra (Vienna Modern Masters) 1992; *Idumea Symphony* 1993. **Business Address:** New England Conservatory of Music, 290 Huntington Ave., Boston, MA 02115.

BELL, MALCOLM, III ■ FAAR Classics/Archaeology 70, RAAR Classics/Archaeology 89, Classical Soc., Pres. 1979-80; Mellon Prof.-in-Charge, School of Classical Studies 1991-92, 1993-present. b. June 1, 1941, Savannah, GA. m. Ruth Marshall. c. Raphael Austin, Margaret Cornelia. BA 63, Princeton Univ.; PhD 72, Princeton Univ. **Research/Artistic Interests:** Greek art, the western Greeks, topography of the Janiculum. **Career & Employment:** Univ. of Virginia, Prof. 1971-present; Morgantina Excavations, Field Dir. 1980-present. **Memberships & Offices:** ArIA. **Fellowships, Honors & Awards:** Fulbright Fellowship 1968; NEH Fellowship 1975-76; Guggenheim Fellowship 1989-90. **Publications:** *Morgantina Studies* I, *The Terracottas* (Princeton: Princeton Univ. Press, 1982); "Some Sikeliote Tanagras," *OpusRom* 12 (1972): 85-95; "Stylobate and Roof in the Olympieion at Akragas," *AJA* 84 (1980): 359-72; "Recenti scavi nell'agora di Morgantina," *Kokalos* 30-31 (1984-85): 501-20; "Excavations at Morgantina 1980-85, Preliminary Report XII," *AJA* 92 (1988): 313-42; "Observations on Western Greek Stoas," *Eius Virtutis Studiosi, Classical and Postclassical Studies in Honor of Frank Edward Brown*, Studies in the History of Art 43, ed. Ann R. Scott & Russell T. Scott (Washington, DC: NGA, 1993), 327-43; "An Imperial Flour Mill on the Janiculum," in *L'Italie méridonale et le ravitaillement en blé de Rome* (Naples: Collections Centre Jean Bèrard II, 1994), 73-87; "Orpheus and Eurydike in the Underworld," *Greek East, Latin West: Essays in Honor of Kurt Weitzman*, ed. Christopher Moss (Princeton: Princeton Univ. Press, 1994); "The Motya Charioteer and Pindar's Isthmian 2," *Memoirs of the AAR* (forthcoming). **Home Address:** 433 N. 1st St., Charlottesville, VA 22902.

BELL, RICHARD C. ■ FAAR Landscape Architecture 53, RAAR Landscape Architecture 75. b. Apr. 10, 1928, Elizabeth City, NC. m. Mary Jo H. Bell. c. Sharon Elizabeth, Richard C.

Jr., Cassandra Lynn. BS 50, North Carolina State Univ., Raleigh. **Other Study:** Apprentice to Simonds & Simonds, Pittsburgh 1950-51; Frederic B. Stresau, Ft. Lauderdale 1953-54. **Career & Employment:** Godwin & Bell, Part. 1955-61; Richard C. Bell Assc. 1961-72; Bell Design Group 1972-89; Bell-Glazener Design Group 1989-present. **Fellowships, Honors & Awards:** ASLA Award of Merit 1960, 1963, 1967; Brochure Award Design, Small Office Category 1976; ASLA, NC Chap., Honor Award 1978, 1980, 1985, 1986, 1989, 1993. **Publications:** "Landscape Architecture," *North Carolina Architect,* special issue (1971); "The North Carolina Land-Use Congress," *North Carolina Architect,* special issue (1973); "What Has Happened to Our Downtowns?" *North Carolina Architect,* special issue (1975); "Toward Barrier-Free Thinking Designers," *North Carolina Architect* (1977); *Energy Efficient Design* (1980); with Dennis M. Glazener & Sharon E. Bell, White Paper to North Carolina Government, *Curriculum for North Carolina Community Colleges: Landscape Design and Nursery Operation for Energy Conservation* (1982). **Important Works:** 82nd Airborne NCO Club, Fayetteville, NC 1960, Southeastern Flower & Garden Show, Raleigh, NC 1963; Sir Walter Chevrolet Display, Raleigh, NC 1964; Office Environment for Design, Raleigh, NC 1967; I-40 Welcome Center, NC-TN 1978; Pullen Park, Raleigh, NC 1980; Bicentennial Plaza, Raleigh, NC 1985; Meredith College Amphitheater, Raleigh, NC 1985; Peace College, Raleigh, NC 1986; Moore Sq. Station, Raleigh, NC 1989; Protagonist Painter Blvd., E.I.S. Western Corridor Location, Greensboro, NC 1993. **Home Address:** 5011 Carteret Dr., Raleigh, NC 27612. **Business Address:** Bell-Glazener Design Group, 8408-C Glenwood Ave., Raleigh, NC 27612.

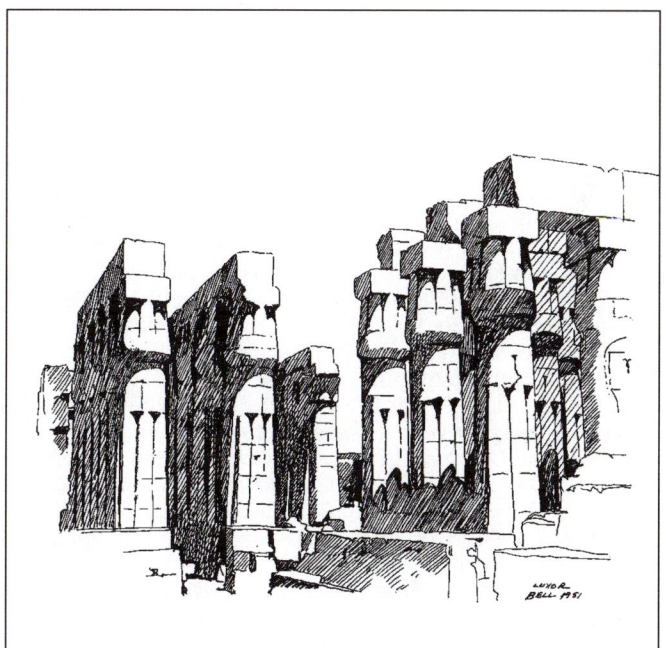

Richard C. Bell

BELLUSCHI, PIETRO ■ RAAR Architecture 54. b. Aug. 18, 1899, Ancona, Italy. d. Feb. 14, 1994. m. Helen Hemmila, Marjorie Bruckner. c. Peter, Anthony. Dott. Ing. 23, Univ. of Rome; CE 24, Cornell Univ. **Career & Employment:** A.E. Doyle, Architect 1925-27; A.E. Doyle & Asscs., Chief Designer 1927-42; Pietro Belluschi, Architect 1943-51; MIT, School of Architecture & Planning, Dean 1951-65; Private Practice, Boston 1951-73; Private Practice, Portland 1973-91. **Memberships & Offices:** Nat. Fine Arts Com.; Adv. to US State Dept. on Foreign Buildings Operations; Portland Art Museum, BoD, BoT 1935-48, Pres. 1937-38; AIA, Fellow 1948; NIAL; AAAS. **Fellowships, Honors & Awards:** AIA, 1st Award 1953, 1955, Gold Medal 1972; NEA, Nat. Medal of Arts 1991. **Publications:** "The Spirit of the New Architecture," *Architectural Record* (Oct. 1953); "The Meaning of Regionalism in Architecture," *Architectural Record* (Dec. 1955). **Important Works:** Portland Art Museum, Portland, OR 1932, 1943; Equitable Bldg., Portland, OR 1947; First Presbyterian Church, Cottage Grove, OR 1949; Portsmouth Abbey, Portsmouth, RI 1953-91 (church and monastery, science bldg., administration bldg., library, classroom bldg., boys' dormitory, girls' dormitory, skating rink, dining hall, infirmary, all in assoc. with other architects); Church of the Redeemer, Baltimore 1956, in assoc. with Rogers & Taliaferro; Bank of America, World HQ, San Francisco 1970, consultant to Wurster Bernardi & Emmons and SOM; St. Mary's Cathedral, San Francisco 1971, with McSweeney Ryan & Lee and Pier Luigi Nervi; Juilliard School of Music at Lincoln Center for the Performing Arts, NYC, with Eduardo Catalano & Helge Westermann; Univ. of Portland Chapel, Portland, OR 1989, with Yost Grube Hall; and many residences in Pacific Northwest. **Bio-Bibliography:** Jo Stubblebine, ed., *The Northwest Architecture of Pietro Belluschi* (New York: F.W. Dodge, 1953); Meredith L. Clausen, *Spiritual Space: The Religious Architecture of Pietro Belluschi* (Univ. of Washington Press, 1992); C. Gubitosi & A. Izzo, *Pietro Belluschi: Edifice e Progetti 1932-73* (Rome: Officina Edizioni, 1973); Meredith L. Clausen, "Pietro Belluschi," in *Encyclopedia of Architecture,* ed. Joseph Wilkes, vol. 1. (New York: John Wiley, 1988), 441-48; Meredith L. Clausen, *Pietro Belluschi: Modern American Architect* (Cambridge, MA: MIT Press, 1994); *Who's Who in America.*

BENARIO, HERBERT W. ■ AAR Classical Soc., Pres. 1965.

BENARIO, JANICE M. ■ AAR Classical Soc., Pres. 1969.

BENDER, RICHARD ■ RAAR Architecture 80. b. Jan. 9, 1930, NYC. m. Sue Rosenreid. c. Michael, David. BCE 51, City College, CUNY; MS 52, MIT; MArch 56, Harvard GSD. **Other Study:** Worked with Walter Gropius 1950-53; with Jose Sert & Paul Lester Weiner 1959-65. **Research/ Artistic Interests:** Design & research in urban & community planning, housing, urban infrastructure through the Urban Construction Laboratory, College of Environmental Design, UC, Berkeley, Dir. **Career & Employment:** Columbia Univ., Lect. 1958-61; Cooper Union, Asst. Prof. 1961-68; Town Planning Asscs., Part. 1963-70; UC, Prof. 1968-present, Dean 1976-88; Richard Bender, Arch., Part. 1968-present; Univ. of Tokyo, Visiting Chair in Urban Design 1989-93. **Publications:** *A Crack in the Rearview Mirror: Views of Industrialized Building* (New York: Van Nostrand Reinhold, 1973); in Spanish as *Una Vision de la Construccion Industrializada* (Barcelona: Editorial Gustavo Gili, 1976); "A Framework for Industrialization," in *The Form of Housing,* Sam Davis, ed. (New York: Van Nostrand Reinhold, 1977), 173-89; with John Parman, "The Question of Style in Research," in *Architectural Research,* ed. James C. Snyder (New York: Dowden, Hutchinson & Ross, 1984), 51-64; with John Parman, "Systems Building," in *Encyclopedia of Building Technology* (New York: Prentice Hall, 1986), 269-71; "Housing in the Third Millenium," in *A Global Strategy for Housing in the Third Millenium* (London: Royal Soc., 1992), 179-85. **Important Works:** Getty Center, Brentwood, CA Planning & Design Consultant; UC, Berkeley, Master Plan 1979-88; The "GC-5," Consortium, Shimizu, Kajima Taisei, Tekenaka, Construction Companies, Tokyo,

Consultant for Urban Design 1988-present; Établissment Public d'Améagement (EPA) de Cergy-Pontoise et Paris, Consultant for Urban Design 1992-present; Architectural Review Panel for the San Francisco Downtown Plan, Chair 1985-92; San Francisco Dept. of Planning & Planning Comm., Consultant 1985-92; San Francisco Museum of Modern Art, Planning & Design Adv. 1986-90; UC, San Diego, Master Plan 1987-89; EDAW, San Francisco, Achitecture-Urban Design Consultant 1987-present; Skidmore, Owing & Merrill, San Francisco, Architecture-Urban Design Consultant 1987-present; UC, Davis, Master Plan 1990-present; UC, Santa Cruz, Master Plan 1992-present. **Home Address:** 804 Santa Barbara Rd., Berkeley, CA 94707.

BENEŠ, MIROSLAVA ■ FAAR History of Art 84. m. Mirka Beneš. BA 74, Princeton Univ.; MA 76, Yale Univ.; PhD 89, Yale Univ. **Career & Employment:** MIT, Adj. Prof. 1987; Harvard GSD, Asst. Prof. 1988-94, Assc. Prof. 1994-present. **Fellowships, Honors & Awards:** Gladys Krieble Delmas Grant 1978; Centro Internazionale di Studi di Architettura "Andrea Palladio" Annual Seminar Scholarship 1978; Dumbarton Oaks Junior Fellowship 1978-79; AAUW Fellowship 1979-80; SAH, Rosann S. Berry Annual Meeting Scholarship 1984; Harvard Univ., William F. Milton Fund Award 1990; NEH, Travel to Collections Grant 1990; Harvard Univ., Thomas Temple Hoopes Prize 1990; NEH Summer Stipend 1991; Council of Educators in Landscape Architecture, Award of Distinction for Excellence in Teaching 1991; J.P. Getty Post-Doctoral Fellowship 1991-92; Samuel H. Kress Found. Publication Fellowship 1991-92. **Publications:** "La Villa Imperiale di Pesaro rivisitata," *Verde M(arche) (Giornale di Architettura, Ancona)* 1 (1984); "Historiography of the Public Garden and Public Park in Modern Europe," preface to Franco Panzini, *Per piaceri del Popolo. L'evoluzione del giardino pubblico in Europa dalle origini al XX secolo* (Bologna-Milan: Zanichelli, 1993), ix-xiii; "Inventing a Modern Sculpture Garden in 1939 at the Museum of Modern Art, New York," *Landscape Journal* 13.1 (1994): 1-20; *The Papal Villa of Innocent X Pamphili in Baroque Rome (1644-70): Rus in Urbe and the Roman Contribution to the European Garden and Park* (New York, forthcoming); entries on 17th-century Roman art and patronage for *The Dictionary of Art*; "The Representation of the Roman Campagna in the Park of the Villa Borghese in Rome, 1606-1630," *JSAH* (forthcoming). **Business Address:** Dept. of Landscape Architecture, Gund Hall 409, Harvard GSD, 48 Quincy St., Cambridge, MA 01238.

BERENSON, BERNARD ■ AAR Visitor 1939-40. Scholar, Art Historian, Author. b. June 26, 1865. d. Oct. 6, 1959. **Publications:** *Venetian Painting in America: The Fifteenth Century* (1916); *Italian Pictures of the Renaissance* (1932); *Piero della Francesca* (1954); *Arch of Constantine* (1954). Bequeathed his home, Villa i Tatti near Florence, to Harvard Univ.

BERGMAN, ROBERT P. ■ FAAR History of Art 80. b. May 17, 1945, Bayonne, NJ. m. Marcelle Bergman. c. Maggie. BA 66, Rutgers Univ.; MFA 69, Princeton Univ.; PhD 72, Princeton Univ. **Research/Artistic Interests:** Medieval art and architecture, particularly Italian. **Career & Employment:** Univ. of Rochester, Asst. Prof. 1972-76; Princeton Univ., Asst. Prof., Dir. of Undergraduate Programs 1972-76; Harvard Univ., Assc. Prof., Dir. of Graduate Programs 1976-81; Walters Art Gallery, Baltimore, Dir. 1981-93; Johns Hopkins Univ., Adj. Prof. 1981-93; Cleveland Museum of Art, Dir. 1993-present; Case Western Reserve Univ., Adj. Prof. 1993-present. **Memberships & Offices:** Assn. of Art Museum Directors, Pres. 1992-93, 1st VP 1991-92, BoT 1991-present; American Arts Alliance, BoD

1988-present, Treas. 1991-92, Chair 1992-93; American Assn. of Museums, 1992 Annual Meeting, Gen. Chair, Accreditation Comm., Senior Examiner 1986-89, 1991, 1994; Museum Assessment Program, Consultant 1986-89; AAM-ICOM, BoD 1992-95; Intl. Center for Medieval Art, BoD 1982-85, 1993-97, Bd. of Adv. 1989-92; Princeton Univ., Dept. of Art & Archaeology, Adv. Council 1991-93; US Nat. Com. for Byzantine Studies; *Cultura e Territorio* (series), Amalfi, Gen. Ed. with M. Bignardi 1989-present. **Fellowships, Honors & Awards:** Phi Beta Kappa 1966; NDEA Fellow 1966-69; Fulbright Fellow 1969-70; Dumbarton Oaks Junior Fellow 1970-71; Princeton Univ. Com. on Research in the Humanities and Social Sciences, Summer Grants 1973-75; Harvard Graduate Soc. Fund, Grants, 1977-80; NEA Summer Stipend 1978; CAA, Millard Meiss Fund 1979; John Simon Guggenheim Found., Fellow 1981-82 (declined). **Publications:** "Portraits of the Evangelists in Greek Manuscripts," in *Illuminated Greek Manuscripts from American Collections*, ed. G. Vikan, (Princeton: Princeton Univ. Press, 1973), 44-49; "The Four Gospels" (fragment), Ibid., 152-53; "The Four Gospels," Ibid., 180-83; "A School of Romanesque Ivory Carving in Amalfi," *Metropolitan Museum Journal* 9 (1974): 163-86; "Amalfi nascosta," *Notizario del Centro di Cultura e Storia Amalfitana* 3 (1977): 12-15; "Varieties of Romanesque Sculpture," *Apollo* 107 (1978): 370-76; "Amalfi Sommersa: Myth or Reality?" *The Salerno Ivories: Ars Sacra From Medieval Amalfi* (Cambridge, MA: Harvard Univ. Press, 1980); "Amalfi 'Sommersa': Myth or Reality," *Archivio storico per le provincie napoletane* 39 (1981): 23-30; "The Walters Gallery: Its Sumptuous Ivories," *Sculpture Review* 33 (1984): 16-24; "Amalfi medievale: La struttura urbana e le forme dell'economia e della società," in *Atti del Congresso Internazionale di Studi Amalfitani* (Amalfi: Centro di Cultura Storia Amalfitana, 1986), 95-111; "Leo of Ostia," in *Dictionary of the Middle Ages*, ed. J. Strayer et al., vol. 7 (New York: Scribner's, 1986), 547; "The Frescoes of Santa Maria Annunciata, Minuto (Amalfi)," *Dumbarton Oaks Papers* 42 (1987): 71-83; "Applaud a Grand Exhibition, Assess Serious Scholarship: A Plea for Scholarly Review of Art Exhibitions," *Humanities* 10 (1989): 10-14; "Gli affreschi della Santissima Annunziata di Minuto," *Rassegna del Centro di Cultura e Storia Amalfitana* 9 (1989): 155-56; "Museum Director's Journal," *Museum News* (Sept. 1990): 94-95; "The Earliest Eleousa: A Coptic Ivory in the Walters Art Gallery," *Journal of the Walters Art Gallery* 48 (1990): 37-56; "Byzantine Influence and Private Patronage in a Newly-Discovered Medieval Church in Amalfi: S. Michele Arcangelo in Pogerola," *JSAH* 50 (1991): 421-45; "Developing a Disaster Plan: The Director's Perspective," in *Emergency Preparedness and Response* (Washington, DC: Nat. Inst. for the Conservation of Cultural Property, 1991), 17-19; with A. Cerenza, *Santa Maria de Olearia: Architettura e affreschi* (Amalfi: Centro di Cultura e Storia Amalfitana, 1994); "Amalfi," in *Enciclopedia dell' Arte Medievale*, vol. 1 (Rome, forthcoming). **Bio-Bibliography:** *Who's Who in America, Who's Who in American Art, Who's Who in the East, Who's Who in Maryland.* **Business Address:** Cleveland Museum of Art, 11150 E. Blvd., Cleveland, OH 44106.

BERGMANN, BETTINA A. ■ FAAR Classics/Archaeology 82. b. Jan. 8, 1952, San Rafael, CA. m. Michael T. Davis. c. Alexander. BA 73, UC, Berkeley; MA 76, Institut für Archäologie, Bochum, Germany; PhD 86, Columbia Univ. **Research/Artistic Interests:** Ancient wall painting, gardens, villas. **Career & Employment:** Mt. Holyke College, Asst. Prof. 1985-94, Assc. Prof. 1995-present; Harvard Univ., Visiting Asst. Prof 1989-91. **Fellowships, Honors & Awards:** Rotary Intl. Found. Fellowship 1974-75; ANS Summer Grant 1977; Columbia Univ.,

President's Fellowship 1977-78, 1978-79; Samuel H. Kress Fellowship 1979-80; Milton J. Lewine Travel Grant 1980; Mt. Holyoke College, Faculty Grant 1986, 1988, 1993; Dumbarton Oaks Summer Fellowship 1988; J. Paul Getty Postdoctoral Fellowship 1988-89. **Publications:** "Exploring the Grove: Pastoral Space on Roman Walls," *Studies in the History of Art* 36 (1992): 21-46; "Painted Perspectives of a Villa Visit," in *Roman Art in the Private Sphere*, ed. Elaine Gazda (Ann Arbor: Univ. of Michigan Press, 1991), 49-70; "The Roman House as Memory Theater," *Art Bulletin* 76 (1994): 225-56; "Pliny the Elder," in *The Dictionary of Art*; "The Pregnant Moment: Tragic Wives in the Roman Interior," in *Sexuality in Ancient Art: Near East, Egypt, Greece and Italy*, ed. Natalie Boymel Kampen (New York: Cambridge Univ. Press, forthcoming); *Sacred Groves and Sunlit Shores: The Roman Art of Landscape* (Princeton: Princeton Univ. Press, forthcoming). **Home Address:** 233 Mosier St., South Hadley, MA 01075. **Business Address:** Art Dept., Mt. Holyoke College, South Hadley, MA 01075.

BERIO, LUCIANO ■ AAR Italian Com. 1994, Composer.

BERMAN, BERTRAM ■ FAAR Classics/Archaeology 49, Cosa Archeological Project, Staff Photographer. b. Jan. 24, 1924, Cincinnati, OH. m. Kathryn Lewis. c. Elizabeth, Jessica, Ann Bucher. BA 47, Univ. of Cincinnati; MA 48, Univ. of Cincinnati. **Other Study:** History of art, medieval, Renaissance & contemporary periods; archaeological studies, Pompei under Prof. Tatiana Warscher. **Career & Employment:** Telecommuniations & Show Business 1951-71: Proctor & Gamble & Universal Studios, Exec. Producer; CBS, VP for Daytime & Late Night; Producer and-or writer of numerous network TV shows; N. Kentucky Univ., Prof.; Univ. of Cincinnati, College of Medicine, Educational Resources, Research Prof.; Hopewell Farms, Founder & Pres. 1980-present (Hopewell Farms has been acclaimed as one of the country's leading growers of herbs & flowers); Hopewell Design Studio 1990-present (a leading design firm – decorative accessories – in the field of visual merchandising & display, serving a number of the country's principal department & specialty stores. **Memberships & Offices:** Save the Museum Com., Los Angeles, Founding Mem., Dir. of Public Relations; Contemporary Art Soc., Los Angeles, BoD; Municipal Art Soc., NYC, BoD; Community Cable Access Resource Group, Cincinnati, Founder. **Fellowships, Honors & Awards:** Phi Beta Kappa; Fulbright Fellowship 1950; Taft Teaching Fellowship. **Home Address:** 225 Berman Rd., Manchester, OH 45144. **Business Address:** Hopewell Farms, 301 Pearl St., Manchester, OH 45144.

BERMAN, EUGENE ■ RAAR Painting 59. b. Nov. 4, 1899, St. Petersburg, Russia. d. Dec. 14, 1972. m. Ona Munson. **Other Studies:** Private study with P. S. Naumoff, S. Grusenberg 1915-18; Academie Ranson, Paris, with Edouard Vuillard, Maurice Denis, Pierre Bonnard, Felix Vallaton 1920-22; with Emilio Terry 1920. **Memberships & Offices:** NIAL. **Fellowships, Honors & Awards:** Guggenheim Fellow 1947, 1949. **Important Works:** Leader of Neo-Romantic movement since Paris 1925 Exb. Ballet & opera design. Collections: MMA; MOMA; Fogg Art Museum, Cambridge, MA; Baltimore Museum of Art; MFA; Cincinnati Art Museum; Denver Art Museum; Graphische Sammlung Albertine; Hartford Wadsworth Atheneum; Univ. of Illinois; State Univ. of Iowa; Los Angeles County Museum of Art; Philadelphia Museum of Art; Paris Moderne; Phillips Gallery, Washington, DC; St. Louis City Museum; Santa Barbara Museum of Art; Smith College; Tate Gallery; Vassar College; Venice Contemporaneo; Washington Univ.; commissions

(murals): Hartford Music Festival 1936; L'Opera de Quatre Sous, Paris 1936; Wright Ludington 1938; Jown Yeon 1951; Icare, NYC 1939; Concerto Barocco, NYC 1951. **Exhibitions/Performances:** Solo: Galerie Granoff, Paris 1927; Gallerie de l'Étoile, Paris 1928; Galerie Bonjean, Paris 1929; Balzac Gallery, NYC 1929; Galerie des Quatre Chemins, Paris 1929; Julien Levy Galleries, NYC 1932, 1933, 1935, 1936, 1937, 1939, 1941, 1943, 1946, 1947; Zwemmer Gallery, London 1935; Renoir & Lolle, Paris 1937; Galerie Montaigne, Paris 1939; Couvoisier Gallery, San Francisco 1941; MOMA 1945; Princeton Univ. 1947; Kraushaar Galleries 1948, 1949, 1954, 1960; Hanover Gallery 1949; M. Knoedler, NYC 1949, Paris 1965; Richard Larcada Gallery 1967, 1970, 1972, 1973; Maxwell Galleries, San Francisco 1970; Retrospective: Inst. of Modern Art, Boston c.1941; Spoleto 1973; Univ. of Texas, Austin 1975. **Bio-Bibliography:** *Paintings by Eugene Berman*, exb. cat. (New York: M. Knoedler, 1960); *The Graphic Work of Eugene Berman* (New York: C.M. Potter, 1971); *Eugene Berman: A Retrospective Exhibit*, exb. cat. (Spoleto, 1973); *Dictionary of Contemporary American Artists; Who Was Who in America.*

BERNIER, ROSAMOND ■ AAR Visitor 1981-82. Art Historian, Lecturer. Frequent lecturer at the MMA. Lectured on "Art and the Garden," at the AAR in celebration of the announcement of the winners of the 1991-92 Rome Prize.

BERNOUDY, WILLIAM ■ AAR Visitor 1984-85, Architect; in memory of her husband, Gertrude Bernoudy created the endowed residency in architecture at the Academy.

BERNSTEIN, LEONARD ■ AAR Visitor 1943-51. Composer, Pianist, Conductor. b. Sept. 25, 1918. d. Oct. 14, 1990. **Career & Employment:** New York Philharmonic, Co-conductor 1958-69; conductor of major orchestras in US & Europe 1946-90. **Fellowships, Honors & Awards:** Lifetime Achievement Grammy Award 1985; AAAL, Gold Medal 1985; Royal Philharmonic Soc., Gold Medal 1987; Govt. of Japan, Praemium Imperiale Award for lifetime achievement 1990. **Important Works:** *Symphony No. 2, The Age of Anxiety* 1949; *Trouble in Tahiti* 1952; *Candide* 1956; *West Side Story* 1957; *Divertimento for Orchestra* 1980.

BERWIND, EDWARD J. ■ AAR Charter Mem., Industrialist.

BIANCHERI, BORIS ■ AAR Italian Com. 1994.

BIDDLE, GEORGE ■ RAAR Painting 52. b. Jan. 24, 1885, Philadelphia. d. Nov. 6, 1973. m. Anne Coleman, Jane Belo, Helene Sardeau. c. Michael John. BA 08, Harvard Univ.; LLB 11, Harvard Univ. **Other Studies:** Academie Julian, Paris 1911. **Career & Employment:** Columbia Univ.; UC; Colorado Springs Fine Arts Center. **Memberships & Offices:** American Soc. of Painters, Sculptors, & Graveurs; NIAL; Nat. Soc. of Mural Painters, Pres. 1935; Mural Artists Guild, Pres. 1937-38; Nat. Soc. of Arts & Letters, VP 1962. **Fellowships, Honors & Awards:** Yaddo, Fellowship; MacDowell Colony, Fellowship 1956; Huntington Hartford Found. Fellowship 1954; Brandeis Univ. Purchase Prize. **Publications:** *Green Island* (New York: Coward-McCann, 1930); *American Artist's Story* (Boston: Little Brown, 1936); *Artist at War* (New York: Viking, 1944); *George Biddle's War Drawings* (New York: Hyperion Press, 1944); *The Yes and No of Contemporary Art* (Cambridge, MA: Harvard Univ. Press, 1957); *Indian Impressions* (New York: Orion Press, 1960); *Tahitian Journal* (Minneapolis: Univ. of Minnesota Press, 1968). **Important Works:** Commissions (murals): US Justice Dept.,

Washington, DC; Supreme Court Bldg, Mexico City; Nat. Library, Rio de Janeiro; Collections: Berlin Nat. Museum; Corcoran Gallery, Washington, DC; MMA; Mexico City Nat. Museum; NGA; Chrysler Museum, Norfolk; Modern, Tokyo; Whitney Museum, NYC; Butler, Youngstown. **Exhibitions/Performances:** Solo: Milch Gallery 1919, then more than 100 in US, Japan, India; retrospective: PAFA 1947. **Bio-Bibliography:** M. Pennigar, *The Graphic Art of George Biddle, with Catalogue Raisonné* (Washington, DC: Corcoran Gallery, 1979); *Dictionary of Contemporary American Artists; Who Was Who in America*.

BIEG, H.K. ■ NIAE, John Dinkeloo Traveling Fellow 1926-27.

BIEHLE, FREDERICK C. ■ FAAR Architecture 87. b. Mar. 19, 1955, Cleveland, OH. BSArch 77, Univ. of Virginia; MArch 82, Harvard Univ. **Other Study:** Central London Polytechnic 1976. **Research/Artistic Interests:** Archeology as a catalyst to architectural invention. **Career & Employment:** Biehle Demaret Studio, Part. 1986-present; RISD, Rome, Critic 1987; Univ. of Notre Dame, Rome, Adj. Asst. Prof. 1988; Ohio State Univ., Adj. Asst. Prof. 1989; Columbia Univ., Adj. Asst. Prof. 1989-present; Pratt Inst., Adj. Asst. Prof. 1993-present. **Memberships & Offices:** ALNY Competition, Urban Center, NYC., Juror 1986. **Fellowships, Honors & Awards:** ALNY Competition, Young Architects Competition Winner 1985. **Publications:** "Constructions from the Roman Forum," *Places: Journal of Environmental Design* 5.1 (1988): 46-50; "A Competition for a Gate," *Harvard Architectural Review* 5 (1986); "Abstract Expression," *Interiors* (Nov. 1986): 150-56; "Building Their Reputations," *Interview Magazine* (Oct. 1985): 87-88; "Young American Educators in Architecture," *SPACE, Arts & Architecture, Environment* (Nov. 1994): 66-70. **Exhibitions/Performances:** Urban Center Gallery, NYC 1985, 1986; Ohio State Univ. Gallery, Columbus 1989; Grand Central Station, NYC 1988-89; *Progressive Architecture* Travelling Show, Washington, DC 1992-94; Tribeca 148 Gallery, NYC 1994. **Business Address:** 40 Hudson St., NYC 10013.

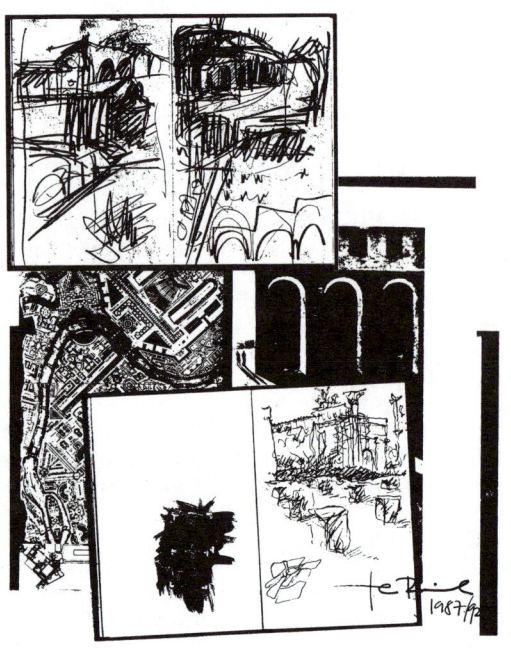

Frederick C. Biehle

BILARDELLO, VINCENZO ■ Italian Fulbright Fellow 1968-69.

BILLANOVICH, MARIA PIA ■ Italian Fulbright Fellow 1963-64.

BILLINGTON, JAMES ■ AAR Visitor 1988-89, Library of Congress.

BINKS, RONALD C. ■ FAAR Painting 60. b. Oct. 20, 1934, Oak Parl, IL. m. Lawsanna Henderson. c. Justin L., Livia J. BFA 56, RISD; MFA 60, Yale School of Art. **Other Study:** George Eastman House, Rochester 1954; Cumminton School of the Arts, Cummington 1955; Hochschule für Bildende Künste, Berlin 1958; private study with Minor White, photography. **Research/Artistic Interests:** Painting, drawing, photography. **Career & Employment:** RISD, Instr.-Asst. Prof 1962-76; Univ. of Texas at San Antonio, Prof. 1976-present. **Memberships & Offices:** Nat. Council of Art Administrators, Bd. 1981-82, Chair of Bd. 1982-83; *Photographer's Forum*, Ed. Bd. Adv. 1980-present; Nat. Assn. of Schools of Art & Design 1976-83; CAA 1968-86. **Fellowships, Honors & Awards:** Nat. Merit Scholarshp 1952; Flaherty Found. Award 1955; Fulbright-Hays Grant, Inst. for Intl. Education 1956-58. **Important Works:** Amon Carter Museum, Ft. Worth; Museum of West Texas, Lubbock; San Antonio Museum of Art; Yale Univ.; Univ. of Texas, San Antonio; Del Mar College, Corpus Christi, TX. **Exhibitions/Performances:** Berlin, Rome, NYC, Chicago, Boston, Naples, Mexico City, Quinto (Peru) and others. **Bio-Bibliography:** *American Photographers; Who's Who in American Art; Who's Who in Southwestern Art*. **Home Address:** PO Box 404, Helotes, TX 78023. **Business Address:** Univ. of Texas at San Antonio, San Antonio, TX 78249.

BIRKERTS, GUNNAR ■ RAAR Architecture 76. b. Jan. 17, 1925, Riga, Latvia. m. Sylvia Zvirbulis. c. Sven Peter, Andra Sylvia, Erik Gunnar. Architekt 49, Technische Hochschule, Stuttgart, Germany. **Research/Artistic Interests:** Subterranean urban systems. **Career & Employment:** Perkins & Will, Chicago, Designer 1950-51; Eero Saarinen & Asscs., Designer 1951-55; Minoru Yamasaki & Asscs., Prin., Chief Designer 1956-59; Birkerts & Straub, Part. 1959-62; Gunnar Birkerts and Asscs., Inc., Pres. 1962-present; Univ. of Michigan, Prof. 1961-90; Univ. of Michigan, Prof. Emer. 1990-present. **Fellowships, Honors & Awards:** Intl. Furniture Competition, Cantu, Italy, 1st Prize 1955; Tau Sigma Delta, Gold Medal in Architecture 1971; Graham Found. Fellow 1971; Latvian Architects Assn., USA, Fellow 1971; AIA, Fellow 1990; Latvian Architects Assn., Latvia, Fellow 1991; Latvian Acad. of Sciences, Elected Mem. 1991; AIA, Detroit, Gold Medal 1975; Michigan Soc. of Architects, Gold Medal 1980; AAAL, Arnold W. Brunner Memorial Prize in Architecture 1981; Univ. of Illinois, Lawrence J. Plym Distinguished Prof. in Architecture 1982; Univ. of Michigan, Thomas S. Monaghan Architect-in-Residence Prof. in Architecture 1984; Assn. for Advancement of Baltic Studies, Honored for Outstanding Achievement 1986; Arts Found. of Michigan, Michigan Arts Award 1988; Assn. of Collegiate Schools of Architecture, Distinguished Prof. 1990; Riga Technical Univ., Hon. Doctorate 1990; Univ. of Oklahoma, Bruce Alonzo Goff Prof. 1990. **Important Works:** Lincoln Elementary School, Columbus, IN; Federal Reserve Bank of Minneapolis; IBM Corporate Computer Center, Sterling Forest, NY; Corning Museum of Glass, Corning, NY; Univ. of Michigan, Ann Arbor, Law Library Addition; Univ. of Iowa, College of Law Bldg.; Cornell Univ., Uris Library Addition; US Embassy, Caracas, Venezuela; Sports Center, Venice, Italy; Novoli, Multi-Use Center, Flo-

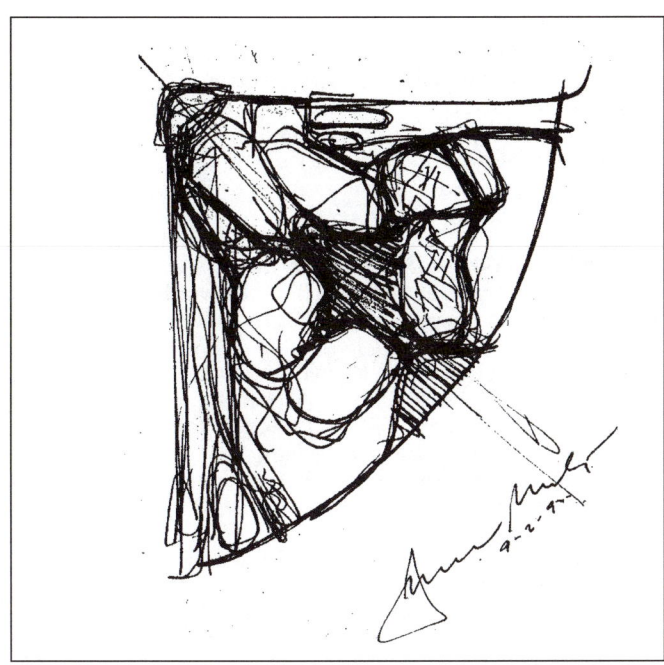

Gunnar Birkerts

rence, Italy; Nat. Library, Riga, Latvia; Library, Kemper Museum of Contemporary Art & Design of Kansas City Art Inst., MO. **Exhibitions/Performances:** Cantu, Italy 1954; Akron Inst. of Art, OH 1954; Bienniale, São Paulo, Brazil 1962; AAAL 1981; Univ. of Michigan, Ann Arbor 1981, 1988, 1990; Univ. of Illinois at Urbana-Champaign 1983; Kingswood, Cranbrook Educational Community, Bloomfield Hills, MI 1983; Saginaw Art Museum, MI 1985; Triennale, Milan, Italy 1986; Nat. Center for the Study of Frank Lloyd Wright, Ann Arbor, MI 1988; St. Peter's Church, Riga, Latvia 1989; Nat. Bldg. Museum, Washington, DC 1990. **Bio-Bibliography:** William Marlin, "The Long Baltic Current," *Inland Architect* (Nov. 1980): 6-17; Yukio Futagawa, ed., *GA Architect 2; Gunnar Birkerts and Asscs.* (Tokyo: A.D.A. Edita, 1982); Gunnar Birkerts, *Buildings, Projects and Thoughts: 1960-1985* (Ann Arbor: Univ. of Michigan, College of Architecture & Urban Planning, 1985); Robert Benson, "Gunnar Birkerts and the Domino Theory," *Inland Architect*, (Jan.-Feb. 1986): 20-27, and "An Interview with Gunnar Birkerts," pp. 28-33; Ann Lee Morgan & Colin Naylor, ed., *Contemporary Architects*, 2d ed. (St. James Press, 1987), 99-100; Kay Kaiser, *The Architecture of Gunnar Birkerts* (Florence: Centro Di, & Washington, DC: AIA, 1989); Joseph A. Wilkes & Robert T. Packard, ed., *Encyclopedia of Architecture: Design, Engineering and Construction* (New York: John Wiley & Sons, 1988), 448-51; Gunnar Birkerts, *Process and Expression in Architectural Form* (Norman: Univ. of Oklahoma Press, 1994); Robert T. Packard & Balthazar Korab, eds., *Encyclopedia of American Architecture* (New York: McGraw-Hill, 1994), 44-45; *International Who's Who; Who's Who in America; Who's Who in Technology Today.* **Home Address:** 1830 Tahquamenon Ct., Bloomfield Hills, MI 48302.

BIRMELIN, ROBERT A. ■ FAAR Painting 64. b. Nov. 7, 1933, Newark, NJ. m. Blair Tillisch. c. Lucas, Nicholas. Certif. 54, Cooper Union Arts School; BFA 56, Yale Univ. School of Art; MFA 60, Yale Univ. School of Art. **Other Study:** Slade School, Univ. of London 1960-61. **Research/Artistic Interests:** Perception of figures in action, contemporary New York, the movement and psychology of crowds on the street. **Career & Employment:** Yale Norfolk Summer Art School 1960; Skowhegan

School of Painting and Sculpture 1967; Queens College of CUNY, Asst., Assc., Prof. 1964-present. **Memberships & Offices:** NAD, Assc. 1987. **Fellowships, Honors & Awards:** Fulbright for study in the UK 1960-61; PAFA, Henry G. Schiedt Memorial Prize for Painting 1962; NIAL 1968; AAAL, Childe Hassam Fund Purchase Awards 1971, 1976, 1980; Louis Comfort Tiffany Found. 1973; NEA 1976, 1982, 1989; New Jersey Council for the Arts 1980, 1988; NAD, Carnegie Prize for Painting 1987. **Important Works:** Public Collections: Bowdoin College Museum of Art, Brunswick, ME; Denver Art Museum; Hirshhorn Museum, Washington, DC; Museum of Contemporary Art, Nagoaka, Japan; MMA; MOMA; Nat. Museum of American Art, Smithsonian Inst., Washington, DC; Neuberger Museum, SUNY, Purchase; Santa Barbara Art Museum; Sara Roby Found., NYC; Sheldon Swope Art Gallery, Terre Haute, IN; Univ. of Texas Art Museum, Michener Found., Austin; Worcester, MA Art Museum. **Exhibitions/Performances:** Stable Gallery, NYC 1960, 1964, 1967; Alpha Gallery, Boston 1968, 1971, 1973; Terry Dintenfass, NYC 1970, 1972, 1975; Bowdoin College Art Museum, Brunswick, ME 1980; Odyssia Gallery, NYC 1980, 1981; Galerie Claude Bernard, Paris 1981; Fendrick Gallery, Washington, DC 1982, 1985; Montclair Museum of Art, Montclair, NJ 1984; Sherry French Gallery, NYC 1984, 1986; Claude Bernard Gallery, NYC 1988, 1990; Galerie Mara, Buenos Aires 1990; Morris Museum, Morristown, NJ 1991; Contemporary Realists Gallery, San Francisco 1994; Public Commisions: mural painting, "Paterson" for the Federal Bldg. in Paterson, NJ 1992. **Bio-Bibliography:** John Lynch, "Robert Birmelin," *Art New England* (June, 1980); Gerard Haggerty, "Movies as Modern Muse," *Journal of the Los Angeles Museum of Contemporary Art* (Summer 1982); John Yau, "How We Live: Paintings by Robert Birmelin, Eric Fischl and Ed Paschke," *Art Forum* (Apr. 1983); John Yau, "Disrupted Narratives, Recent Paintings of Robert Birmelin," *Arts* (Mar. 1984); "Robert Birmelin," *Arts New Jersey* (Winter 1989-90); Laurie Hurwitz, "Contemporary Masters: Robert Birmelin," *American Artist* (Apr. 1990); Robert Berlind, "From the Corner of the Mind's Eye," *Art in America* (Mar. 1991); Margaret Tsuda, "A Closer Look at Urban Blur," *Christian Science Monitor* (Aug. 17, 1991): 9; Marge Keyishian, "Mural Honors Paterson's Rich History," *New York Times* (Nov. 17, 1991); *Who's Who in American Art.* **Home Address:** 176 Highwood Ave., Leonia, NJ 07605.

BISCARDI, CHESTER ■ FAAR Musical Composition 77; Adv. Bd. & Music Jury 1979-80. b. Oct. 19, 1948, Kenosha, WI. BA 70, Univ. of Wisconsin, Madison; MA 72, Univ. of Wisconsin, Madison; MM 74, Univ. of Wisconsin, Madison; MMA & DMA 76 & 80, Yale Univ. **Other Study:** Composers Conference, study with Mario Davidovsky, Johnson State College, VT 1974, 1975; Conducting with Jaques Monid 1979-80. **Career & Employment:** Sarah Lawrence College, Faculty 1977-present, Chair 1987-present; Composer in Residence: Univ. of Wisconsin, Madison 1985. **Memberships & Offices:** ACA, Com. Mem. 1978-85, Bd. of Governors 1983-86; Ed Di Lello Dance Group, BoD 1980-85; American Music Center; American Symphony Orchestra League, Composer Rep. 1981-85; BMI, Judge 1982; Guild of Composers, BoD 1982-85; Musical Elements, Adv. Bd. 1986; New York Youth Symphony, Adv. Com. 1986, 1992; Concerts Atlantique-Global Music Network, Bd. of Adv. & Jury 1986-present; MacDowell Colony, Composers Admissions Panel 1986-90, 1992; Chamber Music Conference & Composers Forum of the East 1990; Inst. of Intl. Education, Nat. Screening Com., Composition, Fulbright & Foreign Grants 1990-present; CRI, Ed. Com. 1990-present; Century Club, Music Com. 1991-present; Cygnus Ensemble, BoD 1991-present. **Fel-**

lowships, Honors & Awards: AAAL, Charles Ives Scholarship 1975-76; Wisconsin Arts Bd.-NEA-Univ. of Wisconsin Grant 1976; Brookline Library Music Assn. Prize 1977; League ISCM Nat. Composers Compositions Winner 1985, Hon. Men. 1978 & 1979, Finalist 1987; Andrew Mellon Found. Grant 1979; Guggenheim Found. Fellowship 1979-80; American Music Center Grant 1980; ACA Recording Award 1981, Hon. Men. 1979; NEA Grants 1977-78, 1980-81; MacDowell Fellowships 1981, 1984, 1992; Meet the Composer Grants 1981-87; Jerome Found. Grant 1982; Martha Baird Rockefeller Fund for Music Grant 1982; CAPS Fellowship 1983; Virgil Thomson Found. Grant 1988; Japan Found. Professional Fellowship 1989-90; Paul Revere Award, Music Publishers Assn. 1990; New York Found.

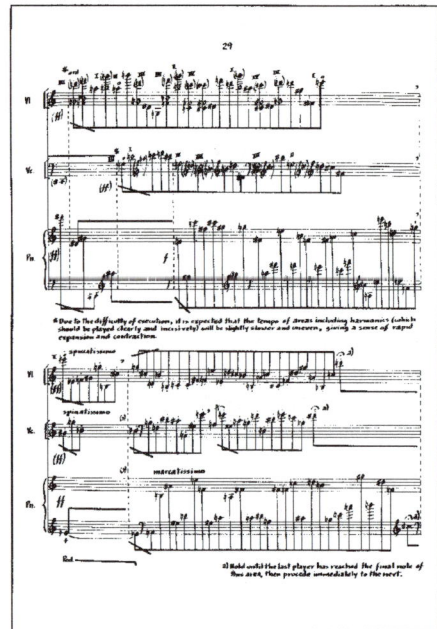

Chester Biscardi

for the Arts Fellowship 1990; Rockefeller Found., Bellagio Center Resident 1993. **Important Works,** Selected, recent: *They Had Ceased to Talk,* for violin, viola, horn in F & piano 1975; *Tenzone,* for 2 flutes & piano 1975; *Trio,* for violin, violoncello & piano, Cambium Trio-Wisconsin Arts Bd.-NEA Comm. 1976; *At the Still Point,* for orchestra 1977; *Mestiere,* for piano, Tulane Univ. Festival of Piano Music Comm.-Mellon Found. Comm. 1979; *Trasumanar,* for 12 percussionists & piano 1980; *Di Vivere,* for clarinet & piano with flute, violin & cello 1981; *Piano Concerto,* for piano & orchestra 1983; *Incitation to Desire,* a tango, for piano 1984; *Tight Rope,* an opera, Univ. of Wisconsin Comm. 1985; *Piano Sonata,* Anthony de Mare Comm. 1986; *Traverso,* for flute & piano, Nat. Flute Assn. Comm. 1987; *The Gift of Life,* for soprano & piano 1990-93. Music publishers, unless noted: Merion Music Inc.-Theodore Presser Co., C.F. Peters Co., & American Composers Edition; Recordings: CRI, Intim Musik (Sweden), New Albion. **Bio-Bibliography:** *Contemporary American Composers; Dictionary of International Biography; International Who's Who in Music; New Grove Dictionary of Music; Who's Who in America; Who's Who in American Education; Who's Who in American Music.* **Home Address:** 542 Ave. of the Americas, 4R, NYC 10011. **Business Address:** Sarah Lawrence C¡ollege, Bronxville, NY 10708.

BISHOP, DORIS TAYLOR ■ FAAR Classics/Archaeology 49; AAR Cosa Excavation Team 1948, 1949, 1951, 1953. b. Oct. 11, 1917, Pendleton, IN. d. July 29, 1969. m. J. David Bishop. BA 39, Indiana Univ.; MA 45, Indiana Univ.; PhD 55, Bryn Mawr College. **Other Study:** Excavation experience: William L. Bryant Found. Excavation at Alcudia, Majorca 1958, 1959, 1960; Princeton Univ. Excavation at Morgantina, Sicily 1958, 1960. **Career & Employment:** Rockford College, Instr. 1949-50; Western Reserve Univ., Instr. 1950-52; Smith College, Instr. 1953-55; Wheaton College, Asst. Prof. 1955-60, Assc. Prof 1960-64, Prof. 1964-69, Chair 1955-68; Tufts Summer Latin Workshop 1966, 1968. **Memberships & Offices:** ArIA; American Soc. of Papyrology; APA; NECA; AAUP. **Fellowships, Honors & Awards:** Phi Beta Kappa; Indiana Univ. Fellowship 1939; Bryn Mawr College Fellowship 1945-47; AAUW, Fellow 1952-53; Guggenheim Fellow 1959-60; APA Grant 1963-64; Carnegie Inst. Grant 1965. **Publications:** "Cosa: Black-glaze Pottery," *Memoirs of the AAR* 25 (1957): 66-193; ed. & completed, Marion E. Blake, *Roman Construction in Italy from Nerva through the Antonines,* Memoirs of the APS 96 (Philadelphia: APS, 1972). **Bio-Bibliography:** *Who's Who of American Women.*

BISHOP, WILLIAM WARNER ■ FASCSR 1898. b. July 20, 1871, Hannibal, MO. d. Feb. 19, 1955. m. Finie Murfree Burton. c. William. BA 1892, Univ. of Michigan; MA 1893, Univ. of Michigan. **Career & Employment:** Missouri Wesleyan College, Prof. 1893-94; Garret Bibl. Inst., Asst. Librarian 1895-98; Poly Inst. of Brooklyn, Librarian & Instr. 1899-1902; Princeton Univ., Head Cataloguer 1902-4; Library of Congress, Reference Librarian 1904-7, Supt. of Reading Room 1907-15; Univ. of Michigan, Librarian 1915-41. **Memberships & Offices:** Carnegie Corp., Adv. Group on College Libraries, Chair 1928-34, Adv. Group on Junior College Libraries, Chair 1935-37, Adv. Group on Academic Libraries, Chair 1939-43; Intl. Federation Library Assn., Pres. 1931-36; American Library Assn., Pres. 1921-23, BoD Chair 1936-38. **Fellowships, Honors & Awards:** Univ. of Michigan, Phi Beta Kappa 1892; Library Assn. of Great Britain and Argentina, Hon. Fellow 1941; Litt.D: Miami Univ. 1926, NYU 1927, Columbia Univ. 1930, Nat. Univ. of Ireland 1937, Catholic Univ. 1939; LLD: Oberlin College 1928, Univ. of Western Ontario 1932, Ohio Wesleyan 1937. **Publications:** *Practical Handbook of Modern Library Cataloguing* (Baltimore: Williams & Wilkins, 1924); *The Backs of the Books* (1925); *Carnegie Corporation and College Libraries 1929-1938* (New York: Carnegie Corp., 1938); *Checklist of American Copies of S.T.C. Books,* 2d ed. (Ann Arbor: Univ. of Michigan Press, 1944); contributor of numerous articles to library publications. **Bio-Bibliography:** *Who Was Who in America.*

BLACKALL, ROBERT MURRAY ■ Rotch Scholar 1920.

BLAKE, MARION ELIZABETH ■ FAAR Classics/Archaeology 25; AAR Summer Session 1924. b. Mar. 23, 1892, New Britain, CT. d. Sept. 1, 1961. BA 13, Mt. Holyoke College; MA 18, Cornell Univ.; PhD 21, Cornell Univ. **Research/Artistic Interests:** Roman mosaics; Roman buildings of the Republic and Early Empire; Roman construction from prehistoric times to the Empire. **Career & Employment:** Wethersfield, CT, HS Teacher 1913-17; Illinois College, Instr. 1921-22; Converse College, Asst. Prof. 1922-23, Assc. Prof. 1923-27; Mt. Holyoke College, Assc. Prof. 1929-35; Sweet Briar College, Assc. Prof. 1935-36; Winthrop College, Assc. Prof. 1936-37; Carnegie Inst. of Washington, Research Assc. 1938-47. **Memberships & Offices:** ArIA, APA. **Fellowships, Honors & Awards:** Guggenheim Fellow 1927-29, 1953-54; ACLS, Summer Grants-in-Aid 1933, 1935, 1937; APS, Grant-In-Aid 1948-49; Fulbright Grant 1949-50; Western College, Hon. LittD 1954. **Publications:** "The Pavements of the Roman Buildings of the Republic and Early Empire," *Memoirs of the AAR* 8 (1930): 9-159; *Ancient Roman Construction in Italy from the Prehistoric Period to Augustus* (Washington, DC: Carnegie Inst., 1947); *Roman Construction in Italy from Tiberius through the Flavians* (Washington, DC: Carnegie Inst., 1959); ed. & completed by Doris Taylor Bishop, *Roman Construction in Italy from Nerva through the Antonines,* Memoirs of the APS 96 (Philadelphia: APS, 1973). **Bio-Bibliography:** *Directory of American Scholars.*

BLANCHARD, JEFFREY ■ FAAR History of Art 78. b. Feb. 22, 1951, Sacramento, CA. BA 73, Stanford Univ.; MPhil 77, Yale Univ. **Other Study:** Univ. of Florence 1974. **Career & Employment:** Univ. of Notre Dame, Rome, Prof. 1980-present; Cornell in Rome, Prof. 1988-present, Interim Dir. 1993-present. **Fellowships, Honors & Awards:** Stanford Univ., Phi Beta Kappa 1972; Fulbright-Hays Grant 1973-74; Samuel H. Kress Travel Grant 1976. **Publications:** "Theater," in *Jacques Collot: Prints and Related Drawings* (Washington, DC: NGA, 1975); "Il revival delle strisce: Episodi di gusto architettonico da Street a Stirling," in *Il Bianco e il Verde: Architettura policroma fra storia e restauro* (Florence: Univ. of Florence, 1991). **Home Address:** Via Giulia 23A, Rome 00186 Italy. **Business Address:** Cornell in Rome College of Architecture, Art & Planning, Palazzo Massimo alle Colonne, Corso Vittoria Emanuele II, 141 Rome 00186.

BLANK, FRANCES G. ■ FAAR Classics/Archaeology 40. b. Oct. 4, 1913, Indianapolis, IN. BA 34, Indiana Univ.; MA 37, Indiana Univ. **Other Study:** Bryn Mawr College 1937-38, 1940-41; self-study and language study in the US Defense Dept. 1942-77. **Home Address:** 2706 8th St. S., Apt. 263-C, Arlington VA 22204.

BLASHFIELD, EDWIN HOWLAND ■ AAR Charter Mem., Trustee 1912-29, Artist. b. Dec. 15, 1848. d. Oct. 12, 1936. **Memberships & Offices:** NIAL, Pres. 1915-16. **Fellowships, Honors & Awards:** NIAL, Gold Medal 1923. His decorative paintings appear on the walls and ceilings of many buildings across the country.

BLAUSTEIN, AL H. ■ FAAR Painting 57. b. Jan. 23, 1924, NYC. m. Lotte Heilbraun. c. Marc. Cooper Union, NYC. **Research/Artistic Interests:** Portraits: painting in oil and drawing in ink. **Career & Employment:** Drawing assignment, LIFE and British Overseas Food Corp., East Africa 1948-49; Albright Art School, Buffalo 1949-52; Fresco Mural, South Solon Meeting House, Maine 1953; Yale-Norfolk Summer School 1954-59, 1961-66; Pratt Inst. 1959-present; Yale Univ. 1959-62; Pratt Graphic Center 1964-69; College for Art Studies Abroad, Paris 1967; Skowhegan School of Painting 1969-70; *Fortune* Magazine Assignment 1970. **Fellowships, Honors & Awards:** Guggenheim Fellowships 1958, 1961; AAAL Grant 1958; PAFA, Eyre Medal for Graphics 1959; *Art USA* Graphics Prize 1959; Butler Inst., Hon. Mention 1959, 1st Prize in oils 1961; Virginia Museum of Art, Drawing Prize 1961; Soc. of American Graphic Artists, 1st Prize 1962; Audubon Artists, Medal of Honor 1962, Painting Prize 1974; Ford Found. Artist-in-Residence Fellowship 1965; Childe Hassam Purchase Fund 1969; Bayonne Landscape Prize 1972; Ball State Drawing Prize 1974; Nat. Acad. Figure Painting Prize 1990. **Important Works,** Public collections: Whitney Museum, NYC; Library of Congress; MMA; PAFA; Butler Art Inst.; MFA; AIC; Wadsworth Atheneum; Syracuse Univ.; Albany Art Inst.; Norfolk Museum; Everhart Museum; Brooklyn Museum; Univ. of North Dakota; Washington

Univ.; Univ. of Massachusetts; Sara Roby Found., NYC. **Exhibitions/Performances:** Nordness Gallery 1959, 1961, 1963; Univ. of Nebraska 1961; Philadelphia Art Alliance 1962; Laeubli Gallery, Zurich 1962; Philadelphia Print Club 1964; Franklin Siden Gallery, Detroit 1965; Albany Art Inst. 1965; Randolph-Macon College 1967; Troup Gallery, Dallas 1968; Terry Dintenfass Gallery 1969, 1972; Univ. of Missouri 1983; Sumers Gallery 1982, 1992; Washington Art Assn. 1992; Pratt Inst., NYC 1993. **Home Address:** 141 E. 17th St., NYC 10003.

BLAZIS, ROBERT ANTHONY ■ FAAR Post-Classical/Humanistic Studies 65. b. Aug. 7, 1934, Nanticoke, PA. BA 57, Yale Univ.; MS 63, Bridgeport Univ.; MA 63, Stanford Univ. **Career & Employment:** Yale Univ., Stirling Memorial Library, Librarian. **Fellowships, Honors & Awards:** Yale Univ., Charles H. Pine Scholarship 1952-53, 1955-57.

BLEGEN, CARL WILLIAM ■ AAR Visitor 1951-55, Archaeologist. b. Jan. 27, 1887. d. Aug. 24, 1971. **Career & Employment:** Univ. of Cincinnati, Faculty 1927-57; ASCSA, Dir. 1948-49. **Fellowships, Honors & Awards:** ArIA, Gold Medal 1965.

BLISS, ANNA CAMPBELL ■ FAAR Design Arts 84. b. July 10, 1925, Morristown, NJ. m. Robert L. Bliss. BA 46, Wellesley College; MArch 50, Harvard GSD. **Other Study:** Art & Color Studies: Gyorgy Kepes, MIT; Josef Albers, Malcolm Myers, Richard Haas, Cameron Booth & Bernard Arnest at Univ. of Minnesota & Minneapolis College of Art; Computer & General Studies, Univ. of Utah; Study-Travel: Europe, Mexico, South America, Orient, Middle East & Africa. **Research/Artistic Interests:** I explore the area between art and architecture in a variety of media, most recently with the help of the computer. Color and light were the focus for my early art and research, leading to a significant body of painting, printing, lectures and publications. Color also provided a bridge with architecture and my fascination with the forms and perceptions of many cultures. Growing impatient with boundaries, I began to explore new media and the creative potential of the computer for expanding our range of vision. **Career & Employment:** Artist, Consultant to Architects & Industry; Bliss & Campbell, Architects & Consultants, Part. 1956-present; Visiting Lect. on Color & Art: Univ. of Utah, California Polytechnic State Univ., San Luis Obispo 1970-75, Utah State Univ. 1975, Syracuse Univ. 1976, Univ. of Maryland 1976, UCLA 1977, Kuwait Univ. 1978, Yale Univ. 1979, Clemson Univ. 1979, Ohio State Univ. 1980, Univ. of Virginia 1982. **Memberships & Offices:** Utah Museum of Fine Arts, Adv. Bd. 1972-present; Inter-Soc. Color Council, Delegation Chair 1976-84, BoD 1983-86, Co-Chair Annual Meeting 1989; ASID Nat. & Regional Conferences, Seminars 1974-91; Salt Lake City Art Design Bd. 1979-84; NEA Jury for Artists' Grants 1980; Contemporary Arts Group, Founder & Pres. 1984-86; Conference Chair, 1985-91. **Fellowships, Honors & Awards:** Celanese Interior Design Competition & Exb., Regional Winner 1961; Graham Found. for Advanced Studies in the Fine Arts Fellowship 1980; ASID Presidential Citation 1981; Utah & Regional Painting & Printing Exbs., Purchase Awards 1988-94; *Computer World* Smithsonian Award, Nominee & Finalist 1991. **Publications:** Guest Ed., "Children's Furniture," *Design Quarterly* 57 (1963); "Ambivalent Color," *Utah Architect* (Summer 1967); "Color/Light/Module," *Screen Prints* (Aug 1973); "Color Selection as a Design Decision," *AIA Journal* 67.12 (1978): 60-65; "Art, Color, Architecture," *AIA Journal* 71.2 (Feb 1982): 48-55; "Color for the Hospital Environment," *The Designer* (Nov 1982): 26, 55; "New Technologies of Art: Where Art and Science Meet," *Leonardo* 19.4 (1986): 311-16; "Mixed

Media Studies in Tactility: An Alternate to Computer Art," *Leonardo*, Supplement (1988): 117; "Talking About Color: Art and Visual Measure," *Color Research and Application* 13.6 (Dec. 1988): 345; "Art Criticism?" *Salt Lake Art Center* (Spring 1991): 1-2; "Mathematics for the Garden of the Mind," *Leonardo* 26.1 (1993). **Important Works:** *Passages,* Salt Lake City Airport Competition 1978-80; *Windows,* Data Processing Center, Utah State Capitol 1989-90; *Color-Light-Module:* Collections of: MMA; Utah Museum of Fine Arts, Salt Lake City; Marriott Library, Salt Lake City; Univ. of Minnesota Museum, Minneapolis; Paintings, prints or selections in the following collections: AIC; Salt Lake Art Center; Springville Museum of Salt Lake County; Utah State Collection; Major Corporate Collections: Atlantic Richfield, Los Angeles; Amoco, Chicago; 3M, Minneapolis; Prudential Insurance, IN; AT&T, San Francisco; Utah Innovation Center, Salt Lake City; Consulting Projects (Color, Design): Conoco Oil Co.; International Paper Co.; Peerless Electric Co.; Walker Art Center, FFKR Architects, Salt Lake City; St. Thomas More Catholic Church, UT; Stillwater Clinic, MN. **Exhibitions/Performances:** Solo: Lowe Art Gallery, Syracuse, NY 1976; Source Gallery, San Francisco 1977; Univ. Gallery of Fine Art, Ohio State Univ. 1980; Focus Gallery, San Diego Museum of Art 1981; Salt Lake Art Center 1983; American Assn. for the Advancement of Science, Washington, DC 1991, Group: Stuttgart Design Center, Germany; Graham Found., Chicago 1983; Intl. Color-Design Competition 1980-81, 1986-87; Kansas City Art Inst. 1988; *Computer World,* Smithsonian Awards Exb., Nat. Bldg. Museum, Washington, DC; Salt Lake Art Center 1989; Utah Arts Council Visual Artist Fellowship Exb., Salt Lake Art Center 1992. **Bio-Bibliography:** "Bliss and Campbell Architects," *Northwest Architect* 27.2 (1963): 19-25; "Record Houses of 1963," *Architectural Record* 133.6 (May 1963): 118-21; "Record Houses of 1964," *Architectural Record* 135.6 (May 1964): 84-87; Barbara Groseclose, "Color in the Art of Anna Camphell Bliss," *Dialogue* (Mar.-Apr. 1980); George Dibble, "Anna Campbell Bliss Explores Uncharted Territory," *Salt Lake Tribune* (Mar. 25, 1990); "Windows: Computer-based Mural," *Scientific American* (Sept. 1991): 62-63; *American Women Artists, Past and Present; International Who's Who of Professional and Business Women; Who's Who of American Women; Who's Who of Interior Design; Who's Who in the West; Who's Who in the World.* **Home Address:** 27 Univ. Street, Salt Lake City, UT 84102. **Business Address:** Bliss & Campbell, Architects & Consultants, 27 Univ. St., Salt Lake City, UT 84102.

BLOCH, HERBERT ■ RAAR Classics/Archaeology 87; School of Classical Studies, Prof.-in-Charge 1957-59. b. Aug. 18, 1911, Berlin, Germany. m. Clarissa Coolidge Holland (d. Aug. 16, 1958); Ellen Cohen (d. May 9, 1987). c. Anne Coolidge, Mary Alice. Dott. Lett. 35, Univ. of Rome; Diploma 37, Scuola de Perfezionamento, Univ. of Rome. **Other Study:** Univ. of Berlin. **Research/Artistic Interests:** Greek historiography, Roman history, Latin epigraphy, Roman archaeology (esp. Roman architecture), medieval Latin literature, the survival of the Classics in the Middle Ages, topography of ancient and medieval Rome, Monte Cassino, Greek & Latin literature. **Career & Employment:** Ostia Excavations, Staff 1938-39; Harvard Univ., Instr.-Asst. Prof. 1941-47; Assc. Prof. 1947-53; Prof. 1953-73; Pope Prof. 1973-82; Pope Prof. Emer. 1982-present. **Memberships & Offices:** AAAS, Fellow 1950; Phi Beta Kappa, Hon. Mem. 1956; Pontificia Accademia Romana di Archeologia, Corresponding Mem. 1958; Istituto di Studi Romani, Corresponding Mem. 1958; APS 1958; ArIA, BoT 1959-62; APA, Dir. 1959-64, 1966-70, VP 1966-68, Pres. 1968-

69; Deutsches Archäologisches Inst., Corresponding Mem. 1956, Ordentliches Mitglied 1960; MAA, Fellow 1974, Pres. of the Fellows 1990-93; Zentraldirektion of the *Monumenta Germaniae Historica,* Corresponding Mem. 1980; Finnish Acad. of Science & Letters, Foreign Mem. 1984; Pontificia Accademia Romana di Archeologia, Hon. Mem. 1990. **Fellowships, Honors & Awards:** Harvard Univ., Clark Fellow 1948; Fulbright Award & Guggenheim Fellow 1950-51; IAS 1953-54; Dumbarton Oaks, Bd. of Scholars 1953-59; Walter Channing Cabot Fellow in the Faculty of Arts & Sciences 1961-62; Harvard Univ. Press, Bd. of Syndics 1961-65; Loeb Classical Library, BoT 1964-73; Harvard Univ., Soc. of Fellows, Senior Fellow 1964-79; Faculty Council of the Faculty of Arts & Sciences 1970-73; NEH Fellow 1976-77; Praemium Urbis, Rome 1987; MAA, Haskins Medal 1988; Univ. of Cassino, LLD, Honoris Causa 1989. **Publications:** "I bolli laterizi e la storia edilizia romana: Contributi all' archeologia e alla storia romana," *Bullettino della comm. archeol. com.* 64 (1936): 141-225, 65 (1937): 83-191, 66 (1938): 61-221, 71 (1943-45): aggiunta, 1-20; as book under same name (Rome: Comune di Roma, 1948, 2d ed., Rome: Bretschneider, 1968); "Studies in the Historical Literature of the Fourth Century B.C.," *Athenian Studies Presented to W.S. Ferguson,* Harvard Studies in Classical Philology, Suppl. 1 (Cambridge, MA: Harvard Univ. Press, 1940), 303-76; "A New Document of the Last Pagan Revival in the West, 393-394 A.D." *Harvard Theological Review* 38 (1945): 199-244; "Monte Cassino, Byzantium, and the West in the Earlier Middle Ages," *Dumbarton Oaks Papers* 3 (1946): 163-224; *Supplement to Vol. 15.1 of the* Corpus Inscriptionum Latinarum, *Including Complete Indices to the Roman Brickstamps* (Cambridge, MA: Harvard Univ. Press, 1949; 2d ed. Rome: Bretschneider, 1967); "Ostia: Iscrizioni rinvenute tra il 1930 e il 1939," *Notizie degli Scavi di Antichità* (Accademia dei Lincei) 78 (1953): 239-306; ed., Felix Jacoby, *Abhandlungen zur griechischen Geschichtsschreibung* (Leiden: E.J. Brill, 1956); "Der Autor der *Graphia aureae urbis Romae,*" *Deutsches Archiv für Erforschung des Mittelalters* 40 (1984): 55-175 (to be published as a book by the *Monumenta Germaniae Historica*); *Monte Cassino in the Middle Ages,* 3 vols. (Rome: Edizioni di Storia e Letteratura & Cambridge, MA: Harvard Univ. Press, 1986); "Un romanzo agiografico del XII secolo: Gli scritti su Atina di Pietro Diacono di Montecassino," *Conferenze dell'Unione Internazionale degli Istituti di Archeologia, Storia e Storia dell'Arte in Roma* 8 (1991); *The Atina Dossier of Peter the Deacon of Monte Cassino: A Hagiographical Romance of the Twelfth Century* (Vatican City: Studi e Testi, forthcoming). **Bio-Bibliography:** Arnold Esch, "Herbert Bloch," in *Conferenze dell'Unione Internazionale degli Istituti di Archeologia, Storia, e Storia dell'Arte in Roma* 8 (1991): 7-13; Francis Newton, "Review of *Monte Cassino in the Middle Ages,*" *Speculum* 64 (1989): 663-70. **Home Address:** 524 Pleasant St., Belmont, MA 02178.

BLOSSER, NICHOLAS D. ■ FAAR Painting 85. b. Nov. 1, 1958, Columbiana, OH. m. Melinda A. Taylor. c. Greta, Peter. BFA 80, Ohio State Univ.; MFA 82, Ohio State Univ. **Other Study:** Mount Vernon Nazarene College 1976-78. **Research/Artistic Interests:** Out-of-doors-landscape paintings with an equal measure of imagination-memory – these are small paintings done in egg tempera on wood panels surrounded by handworked frames also painted in egg-tempera. **Career & Employment:** Mount Vernon Nazarene College., Instr. 1985-89; Miligan College, Asst. Prof. 1991-present. **Fellowships, Honors & Awards:** NEA Fellowship 1987, 1991. **Exhibitions/Performances:** Solo: Houghton College Art Gallery, Houghton, NY 1986; Olin Gallery, Kenyon College, Gambier, OH 1987;

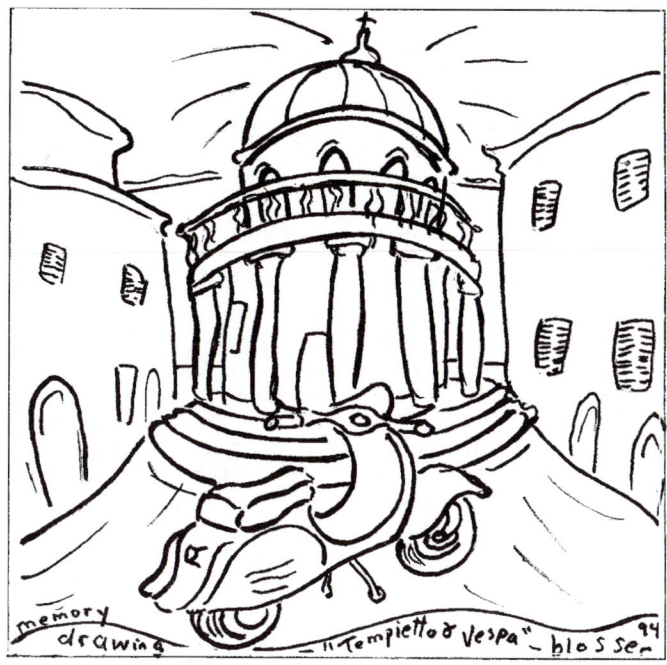

Nicholas D. Blosser

Univ. of Akron Art Gallery, OH 1988; Bowling Green State Univ., OH 1989; Spaces Gallery, Cleveland 1989; Milligan College Student Center, Milligan College, TN 1992; Jamison-Thomas Gallery, Portland, OR 1992, 1993, 1994; Mount Vernon Nazarene College Art Gallery, Mt. Vernon, OH 1993; Group: Jamison-Thomas Gallery, Portland, OR 1990; Montgomery Museum of Art, AL 1992; Moody Gallery, Univ. of Alabama, Tuscaloosa 1993. **Bio-Bibliography:** *Who's Who in American Art.* **Home Address:** 402 Holly St., Johnson City, TN 37604.

BLOUKE, PIERRE ■ Chicago Architectural Club, Burnham Prize 1919-20.

BLUME, PETER ■ RAAR Painting 57, RAAR 62, 74; AAR Trustee 1959-74. b. Oct. 27, 1906, Smorgon, Russia. d. Nov. 30, 1992. m. Grace Douglas. **Fellowships, Honors & Awards:** Carnegie Intl. Exb., Pittsburgh, 1st Prize 1934. **Exhibitions/Performances:** Julian Levy Galleries, NYC 1937.

BOATWRIGHT, MARY T. ■ Michigan Fellow 78; AAR Adv. Council, Sec.-Treas. 88-92. b. Apr. 16, 1952, Norfolk, VA. m. Paul J. Feldblum. c. Joseph Feldblum, Samuel Feldblum. BA 73, Stanford Univ.; MA 76, Univ. of Michigan; PhD 80, Univ. of Michigan. **Other Study:** Università per Stranieri, Perugia (Etruscology) 1975. **Research/Artistic Interests:** Roman history (social, architectural, cultural, political), Latin historiography. **Career & Employment:** ICCS, Graduate Asst. 1976-77; Duke Univ., A.W. Mellon Asst. Prof. 1979-82, Asst. Prof. 1982-85, Assc. Prof. 1985-present; ICCS, A.W. Mellon Prof.-in-Charge 1992-93. **Business Address:** Dept of Classical Studies, Duke Univ., Durham, NC 27706.

BOBER, PHYLLIS PRAY ■ NEH Summer Seminar, Co-Dir. 1990, Art Historian.

BOCANEGRA, SUZANNE H. ■ FAAR Sculpture 91. b. Feb. 14, 1957, Houston, TX. m. David Lang. c. Isaac Lang. BFA 79,

Univ. of Texas, Austin; MFA 84, San Francisco Art Inst. **Career & Employment:** Middlebury College, Visiting Asst. Prof. 1988-present. **Fellowships, Honors & Awards:** Dallas Women's Club Fine Arts Scholarship 1979; Univ. of Texas Merit Grant 1979; Ford Found. Grants 1977, 1978, 1979; Glassell School of Art Scholarship 1980, 1981; Pollock-Krasner Found. Grant 1988, 1990; Yaddo Residency 1989; New York Found. for the Arts Fellowship 1989, 1992, 1993; Middlebury College, Faculty Research Grant 1990, 1991, 1992; Mid-Atlantic Arts Council Grant 1993; Marie Walsh Sharpe Arts Found. Studio Grant 1993; NEA Fellowship 1993. **Important Works:** Public Collections: Mills College Art Gallery, Oakland; Prudential Life Insurance Co.; Champion Intl. Corp., CT; Knoll Intl., NYC. **Exhibitions/Performances:** Solo: 3221 Gallery, Houston 1982; Christian A. Johnson Memorial Gallery, Middlebury College 1988; Women's Studio Workshop, Rosendale, NY 1990; Victoria Munroe Gallery, NYC 1990; Victoria Munroe Fine Art, NYC 1992; SKEP, NYC 1992; California Center for the Arts, Escondido 1993; Queens Museum Bulova Center 1993; Freedman Gallery, Albright College, Reading, PA 1993. **Home Address:** 66 Greene St., NYC 10012.

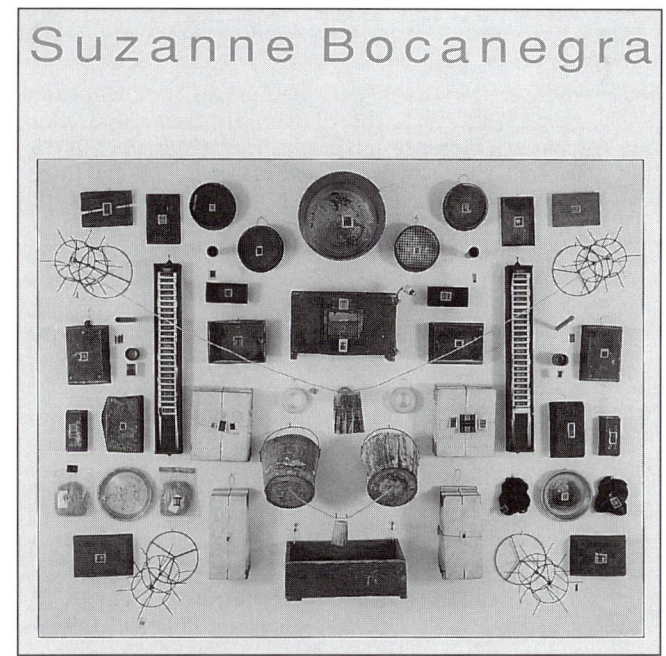

Suzanne H. Bocanegra

BOCCI PACINI, PIERA ■ Italian Fulbright Fellow 1956-57.

BOCHKOR, STEPHEN FREDERICK ■ FAAR Landscape Architecture 57. b. Mar. 6, 1928, Cleveland, OH. m. Monique Bochkor. BS 51, NYS College of Forestry. **Other Studies:** Harvard GSD. **Career & Employment:** US Air Force 1951-53; Boston Planning Comm. 1954; Univ. of Oregon, Faculty 1961-.

BOCHNER, MEL ■ RAAR Visual Arts 92. b. Aug. 23, 1940, Pittsburgh, PA. m. Lizbeth Marano. c. Francesca, Piera. BFA 62, Carnegie Inst. of Technology. **Fellowships, Honors & Awards:** Guggenheim Fellowship 1972; NEA Grant 1974, 1982; Creative Arts Public Service Grant 1978; AAAL Grant 1990. **Publications:** "Primary Structures," *ARTS Magazine* 40.8 (June 1966); with Robert Smithson, "The Domain of the Great Bear," *Art Voices* 5.4 (Fall 1966); "Serial Art (Systems: Solipsism)," *Arts*

Magazine 41.8 (Summer 1967); "Alfaville, Godard's Apocalypse," *Arts Magazine* 42.7 (May 1968); "Excerpts from Speculation (1967-70)," *Art Forum* 8.9 (May 1970); *Misunderstandings (A Theory of Photography)* (New York: Multiples, Inc., 1970); *Primer* (Milan: Flash Art Edizioni, 1973); *11 Excerpts* (Paris: Edition Sonnabend, 1971); "Bochner on Malevich, an Interview," *Art Forum* 12.10 (June 1974). **Important Works:** MOMA; Whitney Museum, NYC; MMA; AIC; Baltimore Museum of Art; Philadelphia Museum of Art; MFA; Detroit Inst. of Art; Albright-Knox, Buffalo; Fogg Art Museum, Cambridge, MA; Tate Gallery, London; Centre George Pompidou, Paris. **Exhibitions/Performances:** Solo: School of Visual Arts, NYC 1966, Heiner Friedrich Gallery, Munich 1969; MOMA 1971; Sonnabend Gallery, NYC 1972, 1989; Sonnabend Gallery, Paris 1973; Baltimore Museum of Art 1976; Abbaye de Senanque, Gordes, France 1982; Kunstmuseum, Luzern 1986; David Nolan Gallery, NYC 1988; Galleria Primo Piano, Rome 1990; SteinGladstone, NYC 1991; Gallery 360, Tokyo 1993. **Bio-Bibliography:** Bruce Boice, *Mel Bochner: Axiom of Indifference: 1971-73* (New York: Sonnabend Gallery, 1974); Brenda Richardson, *Mel Bochner: Number & Shape*, exb. cat. (Baltimore: Baltimore Museum of Art, 1976); Robert Pincus-Witten, *Postminimalism* (New York: Out of London Press, 1977); Kathy Halbreich, *Mel Bochner-Richard Serra* (Cambridge: MIT, 1980); Olle Granath, *Flyktpunkter-Vanishing Points* (Stockholm: Moderna Museet, 1984), 61-74; Elaine King & Charles Stuckey, *Mel Bochner: 1973-85*, exb. cat. (Pittsburgh: Carnegie Mellon Univ. Art Gallery, 1985); Joseph Jacobs, *This is Not a Photograph: Twenty Years of Large-Scale Photography, 1966-86*, exb. cat. (John & Mable Ringling Museum of Art Found., 1987); Benjamin Buchloh, *L'Art Conceptual, une perspective* (Paris: Musée d'Art Moderne de la Ville de Paris, 1989-90), 126-29; Carolyn Christov-Bakargiev, *Mel Bochner (Fontana's Light: Omaggio a Lucio Fontana)* (Milan: Studio Casoli, 1991); Thomas Dreher, *Konceptuelle Kunst in Amerika und England zwischen 1963 und 1976* (Frankfurt-M: Peter Lang, 1992), 227-56; James Meyer, "Bochner's Measurement Series," in *Kontext Kunst* (Cologne: Dumont Buchverlag, 1994), 128-33. **Home Address:** 108 Franklin St., NYC 10013. **Business Address:** Sonnabend Gallery, 420 Broadway, NYC 10013.

BODEL, JOHN P. ■ FAAR Classics/Archaeology 83; AAR Summer Session, Asst. Dir. 1983; NEH Summer Seminar for College Teachers, Dir. 1991, 1995. b. Jan. 25, 1957, Sharon, CT. m. Helen U. Wright. c. Michael Bodel, Anne Bodel. BA 78, Princeton Univ.; MA 79, Univ. of Michigan; PhD 84, Univ. of Michigan. **Research/Artistic Interests:** Latin epigraphy, Roman history, Latin literature. **Career & Employment:** Harvard Univ., Asst Prof.-Assc. Prof. 1984-92; Brown Univ., Visiting Assc. Prof. 1992-93; Rutgers Univ., Assc. Prof. 1993-present. **Fellowships, Honors & Awards:** NEH, Senior Research Fellowship 1993. **Publications:** *Roman Brick Stamps in the Kelsey Museum* (Ann Arbor: Univ. of Michigan Press, 1983); *Graveyards and Groves: A Study of the* Lex Lucerina, *American Journal of Ancient History* 11 (1994). **Home Address:** 22 Partridge St., Watertown, MA 02172. **Business Address:** Dept. of Classics, Rutgers Univ., New Brunswick, NJ 08903.

BODNAR, JAMES L. ■ FAAR Architecture 80. b. June 25, 1951, South Bend, IN. m. Anne D. Bodnar. c. Katharine. Certif. 72, École des Beaux Arts, Fountainbleau; BArch 74, Catholic Univ.; MArch 79, Yale Univ. **Career & Employment:** I.M. Pei & Partners, Designer 1978; Skidmore Owings & Merrill, Assc. Part. 1980-90; Harvard Univ., Guest Critic 1991; Univ. of Texas, Guest Critic 1992; James Bodnar, Architect 1991-present. **Memberships & Offices:** AIA; Royal Inst. of British Architects. **Fellowships, Honors & Awards:** Steedman Traveling Fellowship, Washington Univ. 1979; AIA School Medal, Yale Univ. 1979. **Home Address:** 333 E. 49th St., Apt. 10M, NYC 10017. **Business Address:** James Bodnar, Architect, 611 Broadway, Suite 201, NYC 10012.

BOETHIUS, AXEL ■ AAR Visitor 1939-40, Independent Scholar & Writer, Goteborg, Sweden.

BOGHOSIAN, VARUJAN Y. ■ RAAR Sculpture 67, 75; AAR Trustee 1974-76, Trustee Emer. b. June 26, 1926, New Britain, CT. m. Marilyn H. Boghosian. c. Heidi. BFA 57, Yale Univ.; MFA 59, Yale Univ. **Career & Employment:** Univ. of Florida, Gainsville 1958-59; Cooper Union 1959-64; Brown Univ. 1964-68; Dartmouth College 1968-present. **Memberships & Offices:** MacDowell Colony, BoT, Co-Chair & Chair 1980-present; Harvard Univ. Overseers Com. on Visual & Environmental Design, Chair 1988-present; AAAL, Fellow 1986. **Fellowships, Honors & Awards:** Fulbright Grant 1953; Howard Found. Fellowship 1966; NIAL Award 1972; Guggenheim Fellowship 1985; St. Botolph Club Found. Award 1991. **Important Works:** Museum Collections: Addison Gallery of American Art, Phillips Acad., Andover, MA; Albright-Knox Art Gallery, Buffalo, NY; Brooklyn Museum, NYC; Currier Gallery of Art, Manchester, NH; Hood Museum of Art, Hanover, NH; Herbert F. Johnson Museum of Art, Cornell Univ., Ithaca, NY; Indianapolis Museum of Art; Museum of Art, RISD; MOMA; Newark Museum; Neuberger Museum, Purchase, NY; Whitney Museum, NYC. **Exhibitions/Performances:** Solo: Swetzoff Gallery, Boston 1950-65; Stable Gallery, NYC 1963-66; Hopkins Center, Dartmouth College, Hanover, NH 1968; Currier Gallery of Art, Manchester, NH 1968; Cordier & Ekstrom, NYC 1969-88; Arts Club of Chicago 1970; Alpha Gallery, Boston 1972; Long Point Gallery, Provincetown, MA 1978-88; Philadelphia College of Art 1980; Center Gallery, Bucknell Univ., Lewisburg, PA 1987; Aldrich Museum of Contemporary Art, Ridgefield, CT 1988; Hood Museum of Art, Hanover, NH 1989; Claude Bernard Gallery, NYC 1991; Brown Univ. 1992. **Bio-Bibliography:** Emily Genauer, "Varujan Boghosian," *New York Herald Tribune* (1963); John Canady, "Found Objects Put to Imaginative Use," *New York Times* (1965); Dore Ashton, "Portrait of the Artist as Litterateur," *Studio International* (1965); "The Myth Maker," *Time* (1970); Alexandra Anderson, "Architectural Collages of Varujan Boghosian," *Art World* (1974); John Russell, "A Beauty that Refuses to Flinch," *New York Times* (1977); John Russell, "A Builder with Grand Designs," *New York Times* (1979); John Loughery, "Varujan Boghosian," *Arts* (1986); Carl Little, "Varujan Boghosian at Cordier & Ekstrom," *Art in America* (1988). **Home Address:** 1 Read Rd., Hanover, NH 03755.

BOGNER, WALTER F. ■ Rotch Scholar 1925.

BOIME, ALBERT ■ FAAR History of Art 80. b. Mar. 17, 1933, St. Louis, MO. m. Myra Boime. BA 61, UCLA; PhD 68, Columbia Univ. **Career & Employment:** Columbia Univ., Instr. 1966-67; SUNY, Stony Brook, Asst.-Assc. Prof. 1967-72; SUNY, Binghamton, Prof. 1972-78; Williams College, Visiting Prof. 1978; UCLA, Prof. 1980s. **Fellowships, Honors & Awards:** ACLS Fellowship 1970-71; UC, Santa Barbara, College of Creative Studies, Art Historian-in-Residence 1973; Arthur Kingsley Porter Prize 1973; Guggenheim Fellowship 1974-75, 1984; Millard Meiss Grant 1986. **Publications:** "Georges Rouault and the Academic Curriculum," *Art Journal* (Fall 1969); *The Acad-*

emy and French Painting in the Nineteenth Century (London: Phaidon Press, 1971); "The Teaching Reforms of 1863 and the Origins of Modernisme in France," *Art Quarterly* (Autumn 1977); *A Social History of Modern Art*, 2 vols. (Chicago: Univ. of Chicago Press, 1987, 1990); *The Art of Exclusion: Representing Blacks in the Nineteenth Century* (Washington, DC: Smithsonian Institution Press, 1990); *The Magisterial Gaze: Manifest Destiny and American Landscape Painting* (Washington, DC: Smithsonian Institution Press, 1991).

BOLT, THOMAS ■ FAAR Literature 94. b. Nov. 21, 1959, Washington, DC. m. Sophie Forrester. BA 82, Univ. of Virginia. **Research/Artistic Interests:** Poetry, fiction writing, painting, drawing, printmaking, printing & graphic arts, computer graphics. **Career & Employment:** *Bomb: A Quarterly*, Contr. Ed. 1990-present. **Fellowships, Honors & Awards:** Yale Younger Poets Award 1988; Ingram-Merrill Found. Fellowship 1991; Acad. of American Poets, Peter I.B. Lavan Younger Poets Award 1993. **Publications:** *Out of the Woods*, Yale Younger Poets Series 84 (New Haven: Yale Univ. Press, 1989); "Dark Ice," *Bomb* (Fall 1993): 88-95. **Important Works:** *Land*, Limited ed., hand printed on intaglio & letterpress of poems & etchings, 1982: in Rare Book collections of Library of Congress & Univ. of Virginia Library. **Exhibitions/Performances:** Sherry French Gallery, NYC 1986; Poetry Center of the 92nd St. Y, NYC 1990; Alliance Stage, NYC 1995. **Bio-Bibliography:** *Who's Who in America.* **Home Address:** 110 Suffolk St., 6B, NYC 10002.

BONFANTE, LARISSA ■ AAR Classical Soc., Pres. 1983-84; NEA Summer Seminar, Dir. 88; Jury Mem. 91-93; Friend of the Library. b. Mar. 27, 1932, Naples, Italy. m. Leo Raditsa. c. Alexandra, Sebastian. BA 54, Barnard College; MA 57, Univ. of Cincinnati; PhD 66, Columbia Univ. **Other Study:** Radcliffe College (Cambridge) 1949-50; Istituto di Archeologia, Univ. of Rome 1951. **Research/Artistic Interests:** Etruscan studies, early Roman art & civilization, ancient dress & nudity. **Career & Employment:** NYU, Instr.-Prof 1963-present, Chair 1982-90. **Home Address:** 50 Morningside Dr., NYC 10025. **Business Address:** Classics Dept., NYU, 25 Waverly Place, Rm. 704, NYC 10003.

BONFIOLI PANCIERA, MARA ■ Italian Fulbright Fellow 1958-59.

BONITO, VIRGINIA A. ■ FAAR History of Art 80. b. Aug. 19, 1947, NYC. BA 69, Fordham Univ.; MA 72, Queens College of CUNY; PhD 83, IFA. **Research/Artistic Interests:** Italian Renaissance art, 1300-1600, including aspects of architecture, sculpture & painting; conservation philosophies & methodologies, techniques of restoration of paintings, sculpture & architecture. **Career & Employment:** Queensborough Community College, NYC, Adj. Lect. 1973-77; Queens College, NYC, Adj. Lect. 1974-78, 1981; Yale Univ., Lect. 1981-83, Asst. Prof. 1983-88; New School for Social Research, NYC, Lect. 1988; MMA, Lect. 1988, 1989; Vazquez & Bonito, Inc., NYC, Part. 1989-90; Virginia Anne Bonito Fine Arts, Inc., NYC, Prin. 1990-present. **Publications:** "The Saint Anne Altar in Sant'Agostino, Rome: A New Discovery," *Burlington Magazine* (May 1980): 268-75; "The Saint Anne Altar in Sant'Agostino, Rome: Restoration and Interpretation," *Burlington Magazine* (Dec. 1980): 805-11; "Some Technical Observations on Raphael's Isaiah and the Accademia San Luca Putto," *Source: Notes in the History of Art* 3.4 (1984): 60-80; contr., *The Dictionary of Art*; contr., *Encyclopedia of the Renaissance* (Market House Books, 1987). **Home Address:** 154 Waterview St., W. Northport, NY 11768.

BOORSTIN, DANIEL J. ■ AAR Visitor 1986-87, Educator, Author, Librarian. b. Oct. 1, 1914. **Career & Employment:** Univ. of Chicago, Prof. 1956-69; Library of Congress, Librarian 1975-87, Librarian Emer. 1987-. **Fellowships, Honors & Awards:** Pulitzer Prize 1974; Nat. Book Award 1989; NEH, Charles Frankel Prize 1989. **Publications:** *The Americans: The Colonial Experience* (1958); *The National Experience* (1965); *The Democratic Experience* (1973); *The Discoverers* (1983); *The Creators* (1992).

BOOTON, J.F. ■ Stewardson Memorial Scholar 1924-25, 1925-26.

BOREN, HENRY C. ■ RAAR History of Art 68. b. 1921. **Bio-Bibliography:** *Contemporary Authors, Directory of American Scholars.*

BORING, WILLIAM ALCIPHRON ■ AAR Charter Mem., Trustee 1906-37. Architect, b. Sept. 9, 1859. d. May 5, 1937. **Career & Employment:** Architect, Los Angeles 1883-86; Architect, NYC 1891-. **Memberships & Offices:** Soc. of Beaux Arts Architects in America, Pres.; ALNY, Pres. **Important Works:** Univ. of Southern California, Los Angeles; US Immigration Station, Ellis Island.

BORLETTI, ILARIA ■ AAR Italian Com. 1994-present.

BOSWORTH, THOMAS L. ■ FAAR Architecture 81. b. June 15, 1930, Oberlin, OH. m. Elaine Rost Pedigo. c. Thomas Bosworth, Nathaniel Bosworth, Robert Pedigo, Kevin Pedigo. BA 52, Oberlin College; MA 54, Oberlin College; MArch 60, Yale Univ. **Other Study:** Princeton Univ. Graduate School 1952-53; Harvard Univ. Graduate School 1956. **Research/Artistic Interests:** Architectural design, use of natural light, integration with landscape, & regionalism. **Career & Employment:** Eero Saarinen & Asscs., Designer 1960-64; Yale Univ., Asst. 1962-65; Yale Univ., Visiting Lect. 1965-66; RISD, Asst. Prof. 1964-66, Assc. Prof. & Dept. Head 1966-68; Univ. of Washington, Prof. 1968-present, Chair 1968-72; Pilchuck Glass School, Dir. 1977-80; Thomas L. Bosworth, Architect, Prin. 1965-68 (RI), 1972-present (WA). **Memberships & Offices:** AIA, Honor Awards Juror: Gulf States 1965, New England 1968, Seattle 1970, Nat. 1984, Georgia 1988, Ohio 1992, Washington 1994; Environmental & Policy Development Comm., King County, WA, Chair 1970-77; Pilchuck Glass School, Stanwood, WA, BoT 1980-91; Northwest Inst. for Architecture & Urban Studies in Italy, BoT 1983-91, Pres. 1983-85; Monday Club, Seattle, WA 1990-present, Pres. 1992-93. **Fellowships, Honors & Awards:** Oberlin College, Graduated with honors 1952; Yale Univ. Graduated with honors 1960; Yale Univ., Winchester Traveling Fellowship 1960; Yale Univ., Esra Stiles College, Fellow 1963-80, Assc. Fellow 1980-present; Tau Sigma Delta Nat. Hon. Soc. 1980-present; Japan-US Consortium in Education, Travel Grant to Japan 1982; Kobe Univ., Japan, Masuda Research Fellowship 1990; AIA & American Wood Council, 12 Architectural Design Awards: 1973-92. **Publications:** "Sophomore Architectural Design," *RISD Bulletin* (Sept. 1965); "The Pilchuck Buildings," *Craft Horizons* (Apr. 1979); with Grant Hildebrand, "The Last Cottage of Wright's Como Orchard Complex," *JSAH* (Dec. 1982); "Cows in a Field," *Journal of Architecture and Building Science*, Architectural Inst. of Japan, Tokyo, Japan (June 1984); "Its All in the Mind: The Where, What, When & How of Architecture," *Arcade: The Northwest Journal for Architecture + Design* (Feb.-Mar. 1990); "A Pilchuck Retrospective: The Building of a School," *Journal of The Monday Club* (Mar. 1990). **Important Works:** Pilchuck Glass School, Campus plans & 15 buildings, Stanwood, WA 1973-86; Ensminger-Kellam House, Pasadina,

MD 1984; Le Resche-Von Korff House, Seattle, WA 1985; Ragen House, San Juan Island, WA 1986; Frankland House, Bainbridge Island, WA 1987; Edward Bosworth House, Ridgeway, CO 1987; Overlake School, Campus plans, 2 buildings & 2 alterations, Redmond, WA 1985-90; Tobin House, Gig Harbor, WA 1990; Broudy House, Decatur Island, WA 1991; Clark House, Vashon Island, WA 1991; Lundeen Park Bldgs. (design only) Lake Stevens, WA 1991; Mohi House, San Juan Island, WA 1992; Meyer House, Stuart Island, WA 1992; Rabel House, Whidby Island, WA 1992; Evenden House, Teanaway Valley, WA 1992; Ruckelshaus Hause, San Juan Island 1994. **Exhibitions/ Performances:** Yale Univ. School of Architecture 1977; Univ. of Washington, Gould Hall 1985-88, 1991-92, 1994; Intl. Show of photography, Univ. of Washington Faculty, Meany Hall 1989-90. **Bio-Bibliography:** Charles Dunshire, "Little Known Giant: King County's 134-man Environmental Development Commission," *Seattle Post Intelligencer* (July 1973); Richard Campbell, "The Extraordinary Pilchuck Glass Center," *Seattle Post Intelligencer* (Oct. 1977); Jim Murphy, "Timber and Glass," *Progressive Architecture* (cover) (June 1981); Toshio Nakamura, ed., "The Pilchuck School," *A+U Tokyo* (June 1982); Mary Beth Jordan, "Prairie Style Hits the Beach," *Metropolitan Home* (July 1988); Humphrey & Albert, *American Design: The Northwest* (cover & chap.) (New York: Bantam 1989); Carol A. Crotta, "Capturing Light in the Classic Style," *Home Magazine* (Mar. 1991); Beatrice Le Guenedal, "Au Large de Vancouver le Style Country," *Elle Decoration* (cover) Paris (May 1991); Beatrice Le Guenedal, "Aux Sources du Natural," *Elle Decoration*, Paris (May 1992); Tao Siu Tip, ed., "In the USA Country Style," *Elle Decoration* (cover) Hong Kong (Summer 1992); Dominique Mailliard, "Sobre un Mar de Hierea," *Elle Decoration* (cover) (Sept 1992); *Who's Who in America*. **Home Address** (and office): 4532 E. Laurel Drive NE, Seattle, WA 98105.

BOTTOMLEY, WILLIAM LAWRENCE ■ McKim Scholar 1911-12, 1913, Architect. b. Feb. 24, 1883. d. Feb. 1, 1951. McKim Scholarship to the Academy 1906-9. **Career & Employment:** Hewitt & Bottomley, Architects 1912-19. **Honors & Awards:** ALNY, Medal of Honor 1934. **Important Works:** Turtle Bay Gardens, NYC.

BOUCHÉ, LOUIS ■ RAAR Painting 61; AAR Trustee 1958-63. b. March 18, 1896, NYC. d. 1969. Academie Colarossi; Academie la Grande Chaumiere; Academie des Beaux-Arts, Paris 1910-15, with Jules Bernard, Frank V. DuMond, Bernard Baudin; ASL 1915-16. **Career & Employment:** ASL, NAD. **Fellowships, Honors & Awards:** NAD, Saltus Gold Medal 1915; Guggenheim Fellow 1933; PAFA, Carol H. Beck Gold Medal 1944; MMA, Artists for Victory, 3d Prize 1944; NAD, Adolph & Clara Obrig Prize 1951, Benjamin Altman Prize 1955, 1962. **Important Works:** Commissions (murals): US Interior Dept. Bldg, US Justice Dept. Bldg, Washington, DC; US Post Office, Ellenville, NY; Radio City Music Hall, NYC; Pennsylvania Railroad, Bar Lounge Cars; Eisenhower Center, Abilene, KS. Collections: AAAL; Britannica; Cincinnati Art Museum; Columbus Art Museum; Cranbrook Museum; Des Moines; Fort Dodhe, Banden; Lehigh Univ.; Los Angeles County Art Museum; MMA; Univ of Nebraska; New Britain; Univ. of Oklahoma; PAFA; Philadelphia Museum of Art; Whitney Museum, NYC; Wichita Art Museum; Worcester Art Museum; Phillips Gallery, Washington, DC; US State Dept. **Exhibitions/Performances:** Solo: Kraushaar Galleries, NYC 1936-64; Retrospective: Temple Univ.; Group Shows: Independents, NYC 1917; Daniel Gallery, NYC 1918-31; Carnegie 1937, 1939; NAD; PAFA 1941, 1942, 1945; Cincinnati Art Museum 1948. **Bio-Bibliogra-**

phy: *Dictionary of Contemporary American Artists; Oxford Companion to Twentieth-Century Art; Who Was Who in American Art.*

BOVIE, SMITH PALMER ■ FAAR Classics/Archaeology 49, Summer Session, Dir. 1960-62; Classical Soc., Pres. 1962. b. Dec. 24, 1917, Gallipolis, OH. m. Maria E.F. Feiler. c. Claudia, Sharon, Eric. BA 40, Princeton Univ.; MA 48, Columbia Univ.; PhD 52, Columbia Univ. **Career & Employment:** Columbia College & Barnard College, Asst. Prof. 1948-58; Indiana Univ. 1958-62; Rutgers Univ. 1962-86. **Memberships & Offices:** Columbia Univ., Adv. to John Hay Fellows 1955-57; Phi Beta Kappa, Gauss Com. 1968-71, Chair 1971. **Publications:** "The Imagery of Ascent-Descent in Virgil's Georgics," *American Journal of Philology* 77 (Oct. 1956): 337-38; trans., *The Georgics of Virgil* (Chicago: Univ. of Chicago Press, 1956); "Classical Allusions," *Classical Weekly* 52 (Oct. 1958): 1-2; trans., *The Satires and Epistles of Horace* (Chicago: Univ. of Chicago Press, 1958); "Current Literary Criticism and the Classics," *Classical Journal* 55 (Nov. 1959): 74; "Translation as a Form of Criticism," in *The Craft and Context of Translation* (Austin: Univ of Texas Press, 1961); trans., *The Menaechmi of Plautus* (Chicago: Chandler, 1962), rpt. in *Roman Drama,* ed. Robert Corrigan (New York: Dell, 1966); ed., *Bulfinch's Mythology* 2 vols. (New York: New American Library, 1962); "Manus: Virgil's Portraiture of Human Hands," *The Minnesota Review* (Summer 1964): 513-20; "Didactic Poetry," in *Princeton Encyclopedia of Poetry and Poetics* (Princeton: Princeton Univ. Press, 1965, 1974); trans., *Cicero: Nine Orations and the "Dream of Scipio"* (New York: New American Library, 1967); "Highet and the Classical Tradition," *Arion* (Spring 1967): 98-115; "The Amphitryon Theme from Plautus to Pinter," *The Minnesota Review* (Fall 1967): 304-13; "The Insider (An Essay)," *The Minnesota Review* (Spring 1968): 63-67; trans., *Five Roman Comedies* (New York: Dutton, 1970); trans., *Epigrams of Martial* (New York: New American Library, 1970); trans., *Lucretius: De Rerum Natura* (New York: New American Library, 1974); trans., *The Complete Comedies of Terence* (New Brunswick: Rutgers Univ. Press, 1974); "Martial: Complete Translations," *Modern Language Notes* (1975): 800-808; ed., with David Slavitt, *The Complete Roman Drama in Translation* (Baltimore & London: Johns Hopkins Univ. Press, 1994). **Home Address:** 35 Franklin St., PO Box 2147, East Millstone, NJ 08875.

BOWEN, ELIZABETH D. ■ RAAR Literature 60. b. June 7, 1899, Dublin, Ireland. d. Feb. 22, 1973. m. Alan Charles Cameron. Trinity College, Dublin 1919. **Fellowships, Honors & Awards:** AAAL; Order of British Empire, Cmdr.; Irish Acad. of Letters; Hon. DLitt: Trinity College, Dublin 1949, Oxford Univ. 1954; Royal Soc. of Literature, Companion of Literature 1965; James Tait Black Memorial Prize 1970. **Publications:** *Encounters: Early Stories* (London: Sidgwick & Jackson, 1924); *Ann Lee's* (New York: Dial Press, 1926); *The Hotel* (New York: Dial Press, 1928); *The Last September* (New York: Dial Press, 1929); *Joining Charles* (London: Jonathan Cape, 1929); *Friends & Relations* (New York: Dial Press, 1931); *To The North* (New York: Knopf, 1932); *The Cat Jumps, and Other Stories* (New York: Dial Press, 1934); *The House in Paris* (New York: Knopf, 1935); *The Death of the Heart* (New York: Knopf, 1938); *Look at All Those Roses* (New York: Knopf, 1941); *Bowen's Court* (New York: Knopf, 1942); *Seven Winters* (New York: Knopf, 1943); *The Demon Lover* (New York: Knopf, 1945); *The Heat of the Day* (New York: Knopf, 1945); *Collected Impressions* (New York: Knopf, 1950); *Shelbourne Hotel* (New York: Knopf, 1951); *A World of Love* (New York: Knopf, 1955); *A Time in Rome* (New York: Knopf, 1960); *W.W. Heath* (New York: Knopf, 1961); *Afterthoughts: Pieces about Writing* (London: Longmans, 1962); *A Day* *in the Dark* (New York: Knopf, 1965); *Eva Trout; or, Changing Scenes* (New York: Knopf, 1968); *Collected Stories* (New York: Knopf, 1981). **Bio-Bibliography:** E.J. Kenney, *Elizabeth Bowen* (Lewisburg, PA; Bucknell Univ. Press, 1974); Victoria Glendinning, *Elizabeth Bowen* (New York: Knopf, 1978); J.M. Sellery & W.O. Harris, *Elizabeth Bowen: A Bibliography* (Austin: Humanities Center, Univ. of Texas, 1981); *Articles on Women Writers* (1986); Patricia Craig, *Elizabeth Bowen* (New York: Penguin, 1986); Phyllis Lassner, *Elizabeth Bowen* (Savage, MD: Barnes & Noble, 1989); *Dictionary of National Biography*; *Dictionary of Irish Biography*; *International Authors and Writers Who's Who.*

BOWEN, WILLIAM ■ AAR Visitor 1989-90, Mellon Found., Pres.

BOWER, PHILIP ■ Pulitzer Fellow 1924-25.

BOWERSOCK, GLEN W. ■ AAR Visitor 1955-59, Rhodes Scholar.

BOYCE, ALINE ABAECHERLI ■ FAAR Classics/Archaeology 35. b. Aug. 22, 1905, Cleveland, OH. m. George K. Boyce. BA 27, Univ. of Cincinnati; MA 28, Bryn Mawr College; PhD 32, Bryn Mawr College. **Other Studies:** Univ. of Chicago 1925. **Research/Artistic Interests:** Archaeology, excavation at Ostia. **Career & Employment:** Univ. of Cincinnati, TF 1932-33. **Publications:** "Ancient Ostia," *Scientific American* (Feb. 1942).

BOYCE, GEORGE KENNETH ■ FAAR Classics/Archaeology 35; AAR Librarian 1939-41. b. May 12, 1906, Clifton, NY. m. Aline Abaecherli, FAAR. BA 27, Cornell Univ.; MA 28, Cornell Univ.; PhD 33, Yale Univ. **Research/Artistic Interests:** Ancient history. **Career & Employment:** Univ. of Michigan, Morgan Library, Librarian 1941-. **Publications:** "Preface," *Memoirs of the AAR* 14 (New York: AAR, 1937).

BOYDEN, MARTHA ■ AAR – Rome, Visual Arts Liaison.

BOYHAN, MATTHEW WILLIAM ■ FAAR Painting 38. b. Feb. 29, 1916, Newport News, VA. Vesper George School of Art; MFA School. **Career & Employment:** Harvard Univ., Instr.; MFA School, Instr.; Vesper George School of Art, Teacher. **Important Works:** Mural work at Tufts Univ.; Kresge Bldg. at Harvard Business School. **Exhibitions/Performances:** Ferargil Galleries, NYC 1945; Botolph Center, Boston 1959. **Bio-Bibliography:** *Who Was Who in American Art.*

BOYNTON, LOUIS H. ■ Rotch Scholar 1896.

BOZA, DANIEL ■ FAAR Painting 35. b. Jan. 6, 1911, Cleveland, OH. d. June 21, 1967. m. Gertrude Boza. Cleveland School of Art. **Research/Artistic Interests:** Copying the works of masters for display. **Career & Employment:** Southern Illinois Univ., Vocational Instr., Faculty Chair; School of Fine Arts, Washington Univ., St. Louis, Instr.; Division of Engineering, Niagra Falls, NY, Technical Publications Supervisor. **Fellowships, Honors & Awards:** World's Fair New York, Prize 1939. **Important Works:** Developer of porcelain enamel. **Exhibitions/Performances:** Sunset Memorial Park, Cleveland 1941. **Bio-Bibliography:** *Who Was Who in American Art.*

BRADEMAS, JOHN ■ AAR Visitor 1980-81, Educator.

BRADFORD, FRANCIS SCOTT ■ FAAR Painting 27; AAR Trustee 1937-47. b. Aug. 17, 1898, Appleton, WI. d. Oct. 2, 1961. m. Thelma Sylvia Saxe. AFD 32, Lawrence College; Cumming School of Art; Chicago Acad. of Fine Arts; NAD; Fontainbleu School of Painting. **Research/Artistic Interests:** murals, mosaics. **Career & Employment:** NAD, Instr. 1932-37, Cooper Union; Yale School of Fine Arts; WWI, 2d Lieut. 1917-28, Battalion Adjutant 1918-19; WWII, Capt., Chemical Warfare Service 1942-44. **Memberships & Offices:** ALNY, 1st VP 1958-; Nat. Soc. of Mural Painters; NAD; Century Assn. **Fellowships, Honors & Awards:** NAD, Mooney Traveling Fellowship 1923; Army Commendation Medal 1947; ALNY, Silver Medal 1958; Samuel Breese Morse, Gold Medal 1961. **Important Works:** illus., "The Basic Thing for which We Fight" by Robert N. Wilkin, *NY Times Magazine*, (Oct. 29, 1944); Memorial Chapel, 8th & 9th Airforce, Cambridge, England, Mosaic ceiling & apse; Nat. Shrine of the Immaculate Conception, Washington, DC, Mosaic Tympana; Pennsylvania Railroad Room, Sheraton Hotel, Philadelphia; Milwaukee County Court House, Panels; New York World's Fair 1939, murals; Appleton County Court House, WI, frescoes; Lever Bros. Co., Cambridge, MA, murals; Morristown Trust Co., Morristown, NJ, panel; designed & rebuilt residences of Mr. & Mrs. Roger W. Straus, Jr., and Geoffrey N. Hellman, NYC. **Exhibitions/Performances:** Century Club, NYC; ALNY; NAD; New Haven Paint & Clay Club; Pennsylvania Acad. of Design; Sharon Gallery of CT. **Bio-Bibliography:** *Who Was Who in American Art.*

BRADFORD, LINDSAY ■ AAR Trustee 1951-59, Corp. Exec.

BRADLEY, DENIS J.M. ■ FAAR Post-Classical/Humanistic Studies 72. b. Jan. 1, 1943, Detroit, MI. BA 63, Assumption Univ., Windsor, Ont.; MA 64, Univ. of Chicago; PhD 71, Univ. of Toronto. **Career & Employment:** Univ. of Toronto, Scarborough College, Lect. 1966-67; York Univ., Lect. 1967-68; Duquesne Univ., Instr. 1970-71; Georgetown Univ., Asst. Prof. 1972-76, Assc. Prof. 1976-present. **Fellowships, Honors & Awards:** Woodrow Wilson Fellowship 1963-64; Canada Council, Fellow 1967-69; ACLS Grant-in-Aid 1975, 1983; Georgetown Univ. Faculty Fellowship 1977, 1981, 1985, 1991. **Publications:** "The Transformation of the Stoic Ethic in Clement of Alexandria," *Augustinianum* 14 (1974): 41-66; "Transcendental Critique and Realist Metaphysics," *The Thomist* 39.4 (1975): 631-67; "Rahner's Spirit in the World: Aquinas or Hegel?" *The Thomist* 41.2 (1977): 167-99; "Religious Faith and the Mediation of Being: The Hegelian Dilemma in Rahner's Hearers of the Word," *The Modern Schoolman* 55 (1978): 127-46; "Aristotelian Science and the Science of Thomistic Theology," *Heythrop Journal* 22.2 (1981): 162-72; "Thomistic Theology and the Hegelian Critique ot Religious Imagination," *New Scholasticism* 59 (1985): 60-78; "Philosophy and Theology, Western: To Mid-12th Century," *Dictionary of the Middle Ages*, vol. 9 (New York: Charles Scribner's Sons, 1987), cols. 582-90; "Philosophical Pluralism and 'The Internal Evolution of Thomism': Some Realist Animadversions," in *Thomistic Papers VI*, ed. John F.X. Knasas (Houston: Center for Thomistic Studies, 1994), 195-228; *Aquinas on the Twofold Human Good: Reason and Human Happiness in Aquinas's Moral Science* (forthcoming). **Home Address:** 1718 Hoban Rd. NW, Washington, DC 20007.

BRAGINTON, MARY ■ AAR Classical Soc., Pres. 1942.

BRANDT, JOSEPH GRANGER ■ FAAR Classics/Archaeology 12. b. Dec. 30, 1880, Allen Grove, WI. d. Oct. 28, 1933. m. Frances Reynolds Irving. c. Mary Elizabeth; Helen Charis;

Miriam Frances; Joseph Granger, Jr. BA, Lawrence College; PhB 03, Lawrence College; PhD 11, Univ. of Wisconsin. **Career & Employment:** Univ. of Wisconsin, Instr. 1912-13, Assc. Prof. 1913-15; Univ. of Kansas, Assc. Prof. 1916-21, College of Liberal Arts and Sciences, Dean 1921-33. **Memberships & Offices:** Carnegie Research Assn. 1911-12. **Bio-Bibliography:** *Who Was Who in America.*

BRANDT, KATHLEEN WEIL-GARRIS ■ RAAR History of Art 76, 82; AAR Fellowship Juries 1977-82; Friends of the Library, BoD 1988-present. b. England. BA 56, Vassar College; MA 58, Harvard Univ.-Radcliffe; PhD 65, Harvard Univ. **Other Study:** Univ. of Bonn, Germany 1956-57; Sculpture with Rhys Caparn 1948-52. **Research/Artistic Interests:** Italian Renaissance art & architecture, history of techniques, of criticism & of conservation. **Career & Employment:** Vassar College, teaching practice of sculpture 1952-56; Wadsworth Atheneum, Hartford, CT, Curatorial Asst. 1956; Harvard Univ., TF, Tutor, Dept. Asst. 1958-60; NYU, College of Arts & Science 1963-present; IFA 1966-present, Prof. 1973-present. **Memberships & Offices:** Com. to Rescue Italian Art 1967; Friends of the Vassar Art Gallery, BoD 1974-83; *Art Bulletin*, Ed. Bd. 1975-77, Ed.-in-Chief 1977-81, *Art Bulletin* Com. 1981-93; Harvard Univ., Visiting Prof. 1980; Vatican Museums, Consultant for Renaissance Art 1987-present; *Revue d'Art Canadienne*, Intl. Adv. Bd. 1988-93; *Renaissance Quarterly*, Ed. Bd. 1992-present; IFA-MMA, joint program in museum training: liaison and supervision 1967-68, 1988; Phi Beta Kappa, NYU Chap., VP 1972-76; CAA, Nat. Program Chair., annual meetings, NYC 1973, 1978, BoD 1973-74, 1977-81; Millard Meiss Publication Fund Com. 1981-86; Women's Caucus for Art, BoD 1973-77; RSA Jury 1977; ACLS Jury 1977; Comité Intl. d'histoire de l'art 1977-80; New York Acad. of Sciences, Fellow 1978-present; evaluator of graduate programs in the US & Canada; juries for various institutions & foundations; CASVA, Bd. of Adv. 1992-95, Chair 1995. Other service: J. Paul Getty Center, Consultant to photo archive 1984; Kress Found., Conservator's group visit to the Sistine Ceiling: art Historian Mem. 1987; CAA, RSA, SAH, Italian Art Soc., Instituto per la storia dell'arte lombarda, Women's Caucus for Art, Metropolitan Soc. for the History of Science, Columbia Univ. Renaissance Seminar. **Fellowships, Honors & Awards:** American Acad. of Poets, 1st Prize 1955; Phi Beta Kappa 1955; Fulbright Fellow 1956-57; Harvard Univ., Samuel Fels Found. Fellow 1960-61; Outstanding Young Women of America 1967; Lindback Found. Award for Distinguished Teaching 1967; NEH Younger Fellow 1968-69; Samuel H. Kress Found. Fellow 1971; NYU Graduate School of Arts & Science Fellow 1971, Research Fund 1979; NEH Senior Fellow 1975-76; ACLS Grant 1975-76, Travel Grant 1979; Gugggenheim Fellow 1976-77; IAS, Visitor 1976-77; NEH Basic Research Grant 1981-84; CASVA, Visiting Senior Fellow 1985; Alexander von Humboldt Found., German Federal Republic, Research Prize 1985; Gerda Henkel Fellow, Bibliotheca Hertziana, Max-Planck Inst., Rome 1987; IFA, Mellon Faculty Development Research Grant 1989; NYU, Golden Dozen Award for Distinguished Teaching 1993; Intl. Woman of the Year 1993; Decoration Officer, Order of Merit of the Italian Republic 1993. **Publications:** with Donald Posner, "More on the Bob Jones University Collection of Religious Art," *Art Journal* 26 (1966-67): 144-53; with Charles Seymour and others, *The Italian Heritage* (Providence, RI, 1967); "Notes on Santa Maria dell'Anima," *Storia dell'Arte* 2 (1970): 121-38; "Raphael's Transfiguration and the Legacy of Leonardo," *Art Quarterly* 25 (1972): 342-74; "Cloister, Court and City Square," *Gesta* 12 (1973): 123-32; "Comments on the Medici Chapel and Pontormo's Lunette at Poggio a Caiano," *Burlington Magazine*

115 (1973): 641-49; "Alcuni progetti per piazze e facciate di Bramante e di Antonio da Sangallo il Giovane," *Studi Bramanteschi: Atti del Congresso internazionale (1970)* (Rome, 1974), 313-38; *Leonardo and Central Italian Art: 1515-1550* (New York: NYU Press, 1974); *The Santa Casa di Loreto: Problems in Cinquecento Sculpture* (New York: Garland Press, 1977); with John D'Amico, "The Renaissance Cardinal's Ideal Palace: A Chapter from Cortesi's 'De Cardinalatu'," in *Studies in Italian Art and Architecture*, ed. H. Millon (Rome, 1979; published separately in Rome: Edizione del Elefante, 1980); "Bandinelli and Michelangelo: A Problem of Artistic Identity," in *Art, the Ape of Nature: Studies in Honor of H.W. Janson* (New York, 1981), 223-51; "'Were this Clay but Marble': A Reassessment of Emilian Terracotta Group Sculpture," in *Le arti a Bologna e in Emilia dal XVI al XVII secolo: Atti del Congresso Internazionale di Storia dell'Arte* (Bologna: *CIHA*, 1983), 61-80; "On Pedestals: Michelangelo's David, Bandinelli's Hercules and Cacus, and the Sculpture of the Piazza della Signoria," *Römisches Jahrbuch für Kunstgeschichte* (1984): 372-415; "Cosmological Patterns in the Chigi Chapel," *Raffaello a Roma: Atti del Convegno Raffaellesco. Bibliotheca Hertziana-Vatican, 1983* (Rome, 1986), 127-58; "Michelangelo's Pietà for the Cappella del Re di Francia," *Il se rendit en Italie: Études offertes à André Chastel* (Paris & Rome, 1987), 77-119; "International Symposium on Conservation of Wall Paintings," *Burlington Magazine* 129 (Oct. 1987): 753-55; "Twenty-five Questions about Michelangelo's Sistine Ceiling," *Apollo* (Dec. 1987): 392-400; "The Self-Created Bandinelli," in *World Art: Themes of Unity in Diversity: Acts of the XXVI International Congress of the History of Art* (University Park: Pennsylvania State Univ. Press, 1988); with Richard Krautheimer, Introduction to James S. Ackerman, *Distance Points: Essays in Theory and Renaissance Art and Architecture* (Cambridge, MA: MIT Press, l991), ix-xxi; "La morte d'Raffaello e la 'Trasfigurazione,'" in *Raffaello e L'Europa: Atti del IV Corso Internazionale di Alta Cultura (1983)* (Rome, Istituto Poligrafico...dello Stato, 1992), 179-87; "The Nurse of Settignano: Michelangelo's Beginnings as a Sculptor," in *The Genius of the Sculptor in Michelangelo's Work*, exb. cat. (Montreal: Museum of Fine Art, 1992), 21-43; "Mrs. Gardner's Renaissance: Her Portrait by John Singer Sargent," in *Imaging the Self in Renaissance Italy* (Boston: Isabella Stewart Gardner Museum, 1992), 10-30; "Michelangelo's Early Projects for the Sistine Ceiling: Practical Considerations and Artistic Consequences," in *Michelangelo Drawings: Studies in the History of Art 33, Symposium Papers XVII*, ed. Craig Hugh Smyth (Washington, DC: NGA, 1993), 57-88; "The Grime of the Centuries is a Pigment of the Imagination: the Cleaning of Michelangelo's Sistine Ceiling," *Palimpsest: Editorial Theory in the Humanities* (Ann Arbor: Univ. of Michigan Press, 1993), 257-69; "The Relation of Sculpture and Architecture in the Renaissance and a Painting by Piero di Cosimo," in *Italian Architecture from Brunelleschi to Michelangelo*, exb. cat. (Venice: Palazzo Grassi & traveling, 1994), 75-100; "Michelangelo's Changing Colors on the Sistine Ceiling," in *Michelangelo Pittore: Acts of the 1990 Vatican International Conference and the Report of the Sistine Conservation Project; Michelangelo and the Sistine Chapel* (Novara: De Agostini), and English Edition (3 vols.) Gen. Ed., forthcoming. **Television and Film:** "The Age of Michelangelo" (course for college credit), CBS-TV, Sunrise Semester 1965-66; "Dossiers de l'Ecran," Special two-hour birthday feature on Michelangelo, Antenne 2, Paris 1975; Film with James Ackerman, "Looking for Renaissance Rome," RAI, Rome 1975-76; "Omaggio a Raffaello," RAI, Rome 1983; 2 radio broadcasts on the Raphael Year 1983; "The Borgias," Interviews with Edward Newman, Art & Entertainment Network, NYC 1985; Consultant, film by Amalie Rothschild on Richard Haas, 1985-

87; series consultant, participant, "Art of the Western World," WNET-Channel 13, NYC 1986-89; consultant, participant, "Nova," on the conservation and restoration of the Sistine Ceiling, WGBH, Boston 1987-88 (Emmy Award 1989); with Juan Downey, "Michelangelo's Medici Chapel," MMA & Getty Found. Program on Film: treatment grant 1989; consultant, participant, program on Michelangelo, RAI 1990; consultant, participant for Italian Renaissance segment, "Art of the Western World," TVSouth, England 1990-91; consultant, participant, "Michelangelo," TV2, London 1992; consultant, participant, "The Sexuality of Michelangelo," BBC, London 1993; "Unsolved Mysteries," "Leonardo's Mona Lisa," Los Angeles 1993; "The Isabella Stewart Gardner Museum," BBC, London 1993. **Bio-Bibliography:** *Dictionary of International Biography, Directory of American Scholars, Directory of Distinguished Americans, International Scholars Directory, International Who's Who of Professional Women, International Who's Who of Women, Notable American Women, Who's Who in America, Who's Who in American Art, Who's Who in Science and Engineering, Who's Who in the Americas 2000, Who's Who in the East, Who's Who in the World, Who's Who of American Women, World Who's Who of Women.* **Home Address:** 37 Washington Sq. W., NYC 10011. **Business Address:** IFA, 1 E. 78 St., NYC 10011.

BRAUNSCHWEIGER, ROBERT W. ■ FAAR Design Arts 74. b. Sept. 18, 1937, Newark, NJ. m. Louise Yardley. c. Jennifer Braunschweiger. BArch 61, Univ. of Washington, Seattle. **Other Study:** Japan Found., Landscape Architecture 1959. **Career & Employment:** Columbia Univ., Office of Univ. Planning, Dir. 1962-69; William L. Pereira Asscs., Exec. Planner 1969-72; Albert C. Martin & Asscs., Prin. Planner 1972-73, Dir. of Planning 1974-80, Prin. in Charge 1980-86, Gen Mgr. 1986-present. **Important Works:** Planning Projects: EDS Center, Dallas; Metro Pointe, Costa Mesa, CA; City View: A "New-Town in-Town," NYC; Ranch of San Juan Capistrano, CA; West Bank of the Port of Los Angeles; Joaquin Ranch, Riverside, CA; Master Plan for El Pueblo de Los Angeles; Master Plan for Four Campuses for the Univ. of Missouri; Master Plan for Columbia Univ.; Significant Buildings: IBM Corp., Tucson; Exxon Administration Bldg., Baytown, TX; Hydril Technology Center, Houston; Metro Pointe, Costa Mesa, CA; Brinderson Plaza, Irvine, CA; Bixby Old Ranch Office Park, Seal Beach, CA; Parker Hannifin Manufacturing Facility, Irvine, CA; Restoration of Los Angeles City Hall. **Home Address:** 1933 Laguna St., San Francisco, CA 94115. **Business Address:** Albert C. Martin & Asscs., 811 W. 7th St., Los Angeles, CA 90017.

BRECK, GEORGE WILLIAM ■ FAAR Painting 99; American School of Fine Arts in Rome, Dir. 1906-9. b. Sept. 1, 1863, Washington, DC. d. Nov. 22, 1920. ASL. **Fellowships, Honors & Awards:** MMA, Lazarus Scholarship 1897-1902; St. Louis Exposition, Silver Medal 1904. **Important Works:** Univ. of Virginia, mural decorations; Public Library, Watertown, NY, mural decorations; St. Paul's Church (PE), Rome, mosaics; Whitelaw Reid Residence, NYC, decorations. **Bio-Bibliography:** *National Cyclopedia of American Biography; Who Was Who in America.*

BREITENBACH, T.E. ■ FAAR Painting 73. b. July 29, 1951, Queens, NY. m. Debra A. Breitenbach. c. Travis, Tuesday. **Study:** Univ. of Notre Dame; self-taught. **Research/Artistic Interests:** I found my friendships with artists Peter Blume & John Hanseggar to be of great importance in the early formation of my career. The humor & color of our language (proverbs, idioms, jargon) especially when painted literally. The construction of a castle studio in the Helderberg Mts. (17 years so far),

writing, typography, blacksmithing, film, music composition, & computers. **Career & Employment:** Self-employed 1972-present; Castle Arts, Distributor 1983-present; Perfect Litttle Company, Licensing Agent 1988-present. **Memberships & Offices:** Guilderland League of Arts, BoD 1979-82; Empire State College, Tutor 1979. **Fellowships, Honors & Awards:** Creative Artist Public Service Comm. of New York State, Fellowship 1978. **Important Works,** Selected: Proverbidioms; Proverbidioms "EATS" II; Cathchpenny; Sporttease; Shakespearience. **Exhibitions/ Performances:** Schenectady Museum 1974, 1978; Center Galleries 1977, 1981-82, 1984-86, 1991-92; Woods-Gerry Gallery, RISD 1978; SUNY, Oneida 1978; R.C.C.A., Troy, NY 1980, 1990; Artworks Gallery, Saratoga, NY 1980; Snite Museum of Art, Univ. of Notre Dame 1980; NY State Museum 1981; FIT 1981; Art Expo New York 1981, 1990; Springfield Museum of Art, Utah 1989; Soc. of Illustrators, NYC 1989. **Bio-Bibliography:** Lyon Todd Show, WMHT 1973; "Proverbidioms" filler piece, Public Televisio 1978; News feature, NBC 1980; "T.E. Breitenbach: Keeping Imagination Alive," Documentary for Public Television 1983; Feature, "PM Magazine," CBS 1983; Theresa Pickrell, "T.E. Breitenbach's Grumparar's New Creatures," Workshops for teachers of the gifted (Oak Ridge, TN 1991); Douglas Lenat, "Cyc: A Midterm Report," *Artificial Intelligence Magazine* (1990). **Home Address:** PO Box 538, Altamont, NY 12009.

BRENDEL, OTTO J. ■ FAAR Classics/Archaeology 51. b. Oct. 10, 1901, Nuremberg, Germany. d. Oct. 8, 1973. m. Maria Weigert. c. Cornelia. PhD 28, Univ. of Heidelberg. **Research/ Artistic Interests:** Etruscan, Greek & Roman art, sculpture & portraiture; connection of art with history of religion, philosophy & political history; symbolism of art. **Career & Employment:** German Archaeological Inst., Berlin, Central Office, Asst. 1928-29; Archaeological Inst., Erlangen Univ., Bavaria, Asst. Prof. 1931-37; German Archaeological Inst. in Rome, 1st Asst. 1932-36; Washington Univ., Visiting Asst. Prof. 1939-41; Indiana Univ., Prof. 1941-56; Columbia Univ., Prof. 1956-73. **Memberships & Offices:** ArIA, CAA, RSA. **Fellowships, Honors & Awards:** German Archaeological Inst., Traveling Fellowship 1929-30; Fulbright Fellowship 1950. **Publications:** "Spätägyptischer Porträtkopf in den Berliner Museen," *Die Antike* 9 (1933): 130-41; "Dionysiaca," *Romanische Mitteilungen* 48 (1933): 153-81; "Der Schild des Achilles," *Die Antike* 12 (1936): 272-88; "The Corbridge Lanx," *Journal of Roman Studies* 31 (1941): 100-127; "Three Archaic Bronze Discs from Italy," *AJA* 47 (1943): 194-208; "Prolegomena to a Book on Roman Art," *Memoirs of the AAR* 21 (1953): 8-77; "Borrowings from Ancient Art in Titian," *Art Bulletin* 37 (1955): 113-25; "The Classical Style in Modern Art," in *From Sophocles to Picasso: The Present-Day Vitality of the Classical Tradition,* ed. W.J. Oates (Bloomington: Indiana Univ. Press, 1962), 69-118; "Der grosse Fries in der Villa dei Misteri," *Jahrbuch des Deutschen Archäologischen Instituts* 81 (1966): 206-60; "The Scope and Temperament of Erotic Art in the Greco-Roman World," in *Studies in Erotic Art,* ed. T. Bowie et al. (New York: Basics Books, 1970), 3-107; *Etruscan Art* (New York: Penguin, 1977); *Symbolism of the Sphere* (Leiden: Brill, 1977); *Prolegomena to the Study of Roman Art* (New Haven: Yale Univ. Press, 1979); *The Visible Idea: The Interpretation of Classical Art* (Washington, DC: Decatur House, 1980). **Bio-Bibliography:** *In Memoriam Otto J. Brendel,* ed. L. Bonfante et al. (Mainz: von Zabern, 1976), xii-xiv; *Who Was Who in America.*

BRENNAN, T. COREY ■ FAAR Classics/Archaeology 88. b. Nov. 24, 1959, Scranton, PA. m. Antonia C. Fried. BA 81, Univ. of Pennsylvania; MA 83, Oxford Univ.; MA 85, Harvard

Univ.; PhD 90, Harvard Univ. **Research/Artistic Interests:** Greek & Roman history; historiography. **Career & Employment:** Bryn Mawr College, Asst. Prof. 1990-present. **Memberships & Offices:** ANS, Assc. Mem. 1992-present. **Fellowships, Honors & Awards:** NEH Fellowship 1994-95. **Publications:** "C. Aurelius Cotta, Praetor Iterum (CIL I² 610)," *Athenaeum 67* (1989): 467-87; "Sulla's Career in the Nineties: Some Reconsiderations," *Chiron* 22 (1992): 103-58. **Business Address:** Dept. of Latin, Bryn Mawr College, Bryn Mawr, PA 19010.

BRENTANO, ROBERT ■ RAAR Classics/Archaeology 79; NEH Summer Seminar Dir. 1983. b. 1926. m. Carroll Brentano. **Career & Employment:** UC, Berkeley, Prof. **Fellowships, Honors & Awards:** MAA, Haskins Medal; Catholic Historical Assn., John Gillmarry Shea Award. **Publications:** *Rome before Avignon* (New York: Basic Books, 1974); *Two Churches: England and Italy in the Thirteenth Century* (Berkeley: UC Press, 1988); *A New World in a Small Place: Church and Religion in the Diocese of Rieti, 1188-1378* (Berkeley: UC Press, 1994); numerous articles & reviews.

BRESNICK, MARTIN I. ■ FAAR Musical Composition 76. b. Nov. 13, 1946, NYC. m. Anna Broell. c. Johanna Bresnick. BA 67, Univ. of Hartford; MA 68, Stanford Univ.; DMA 72, Stanford Univ. **Other Study:** Akademie für Musik, Vienna 1969. **Career & Employment:** San Francisco Conservatory of Music, Instr. 1971-72; Stanford Univ, Lect. 1972-75; Yale Univ., Asst. Prof. 1976-81; Yale School of Music, Prof. 1981-present; Amherst College, Valentine Visiting Prof. 1993; Adelaide Univ., Australia, Composer-in-Residence 1993. **Memberships & Offices:** *New Observations*, Ed. Bd. 1990-present, Guest Ed. 1991; ASCAP; Minnesota Composers Forum; Connecticut Composers Inc. **Fellowships, Honors & Awards:** Fulbright Fellowship 1969-70; NEA Composers Grant 1974, 1979, 1990; Premio Ancona, 1st Prize 1980; Yale Univ., Morse Fellowship 1980-81; Composers Inc., 1st Prize 1985, 1989; Friedheim Awards, Semi-Finalist 1987; Koussevitzky Comm. 1988; Fromm Found. Comm. 1993. **Publications:** "Cage's Unexpected Offspring: Context, Periodicity and Space," *Mosaic* (Autumn 1974); "Harmonielehre," *Journal of Music Theory* (Spring 1979); "New Music," in *How Music Works*, ed. Keith Spence (New York: Macmillan, 1981); "A Good Place to Start," *Yale School of Music Alumni Magazine* (1986); "We, Rhinocerus," *New Observations* (1991); "Convention and the Hermetic in Schumann's Frauenliebe und Leben," in *Leonard Ratner Festschrift* (New York: Pendragon Press, 1992). **Important Works:** Symphonic Ensembles: *Ocean of Storms* 1970; *Wir Weben, Wir Weben* 1978; *One* 1986; *Little Suite* 1987; *Pontoosuc* 1989; *Angelus Novus* 1991; *Falling* 1994. Large Chamber Ensembles: *Introit* 1969; *Musica* 1972; *B.'s Garlands* (CRI) 1973; *Ants* 1976; *Wir Weben, Wir Weben* (CRI) 1978; *Der Signal* 1982; *Bread & Salt* 1984; *Opere della Musica Povera* (many versions) 1990-

present; *Tucket* 1990; *Follow Your Leader* 1991; *Pigs & Fishes* 1991. Small Chamber Ensembles: *Trio* 1966; *String Quartet No. 1* 1968; *Conspiracies* (CRI) 1979; *High Art* 1983; *String Quartet No. 2 "Bucephalus"* (CRI) 1984; *Tent of Miracles* 1984; *Just Time* (New World Records, Artifact Music) 1985; *Trio* (CRI) 1988; *String Quartet No. 3* (CRI) 1992. Choral Works: *Where is the Way* 1970; *Three Choral Songs* 1985-88. Solo Compositions: *Theme and Variations* 1964; *Four Short Piano Pieces* 1964, 1968; *3 Intermezzi* (CRI) 1971; *Bag O' Tells* 1984; *Lady Neil's Dumpe* (CRC) 1987. Published by Bote & Bock, Musik- und Bühnenverlag, Berlin and CommonMuse Music Publishers, New Haven. Recording companies: CRI, CRC, New World, Artifact Music. **Bio-Bibliography:** *Baker's Bibliographical Dictionary of Music and Musicians; Grove's Dictionary; International Who's Who in Music.* **Business Address:** Yale School of Music, 96 Wall St., New Haven, CT 06520.

BREWSTER, E.H. ■ AAR Classical Soc., Pres. 1941.

BREWSTER, WALTER S. ■ AAR Trustee 1928-39, Bank Exec.

BRICKBAUER, CHARLES G. ■ FAAR Architecture 57. b. Apr. 11, 1930, Plymouth, WI. BArch 54, Yale Univ. **Other Study:** Univ. of Wisconsin 1948-49; Univ. of Hawaii 1949-50. **Career & Employment:** Philip C. Johnson, Architect 1954-55; Harrison & Abramovitz, Architects 1958-62; Designers Partnership, Rome, Part. 1962-63; Peterson & Brickbauer, Inc., Part. 1963-present. **Memberships & Offices:** *Perspecta,* Yale Architecture Journal, Founder & Ed. 1952-55. **Fellowships, Honors & Awards:** AIA Awards 1966, 1972, 1976, 1991, 1992; US Transportation Dept., Design for Transportation Award 1981. **Important Works:** Mercantile Bank & Trust Bldg., Baltimore 1967; Blue Cross of Maryland, Towson 1976; Baltimore-Washington Intl. Airport Terminal 1980; Fidelty & Guaranty Life Insurance Co. HQ Bldg., Baltimore 1990. **Exhibitions/Performances:** US State Dept., Traveling Exb. 1973; MOMA 1979; Maryland Historical Soc. 1992. **Bio-Bibliography:** Herbert Lieberman, *Award-Winning Architecture* (Philadelphia: Artists/USA, 1973), 153; G.E. Kidder-Smith, *Architecture in America* (New York: American Heritage, 1976), 243-45; Arthur Drexler, *Transformations in Modern Architecture* (New York: MOMA, 1979), 83; *Who's Who in America.* **Home Address:** 217 W. Lanvale St., Baltimore, MD 21217. **Business Address:** Peterson & Brickbauer, Inc., 823 E. Baltimore St., Baltimore, MD 20210.

BRIDGE, JOHN ■ Sheldon Fellow 1921-22, 1922-23.

BRIEF, TODD ■ FAAR Musical Composition 82. b. 1953, NYC. BM 76, New England Conservatory of Music; MM 78, New England Conservatory of Music; MA 81, Harvard Univ.; PhD 83, Harvard Univ. **Other Study:** Antioch College, 1971-72; Darmstadter Ferienkurse für Neue Musik 1972; Univ. of Chicago 1973; Tanglewood Music Center 1976. **Career & Employment:** Harvard Univ., TF 1980-81; Private Instr. 1980-89; Darmstadt Univ., Lect. 1986, 1988; NYU, Asst. Prof. 1988-present; Guildhall School of Music, London, Guest Lect. 1991. **Fellowships, Honors & Awards:** AAAL Goddard Lieberson Award 1982-90; Yaddo Residency Fellowship 1982-91; DAAD Fellowship 1984; City of Stuttgart, Forderungspreis 1984; "Young Generation in Europe" Prize, Cologne 1985; Virginia Center for the Creative Arts Fellowships 1985-88; New Music Consort Competition, 1st Prize 1986; MacDowell Colony Fellowships 1986-89; NEA Fellowships 1987, 1991, 1994; Bartók Prize 1989; New York Found. for the Arts Fellowship 1989; Schubert Club Comm. Grant 1989; IBM-Nicholson Fellowship

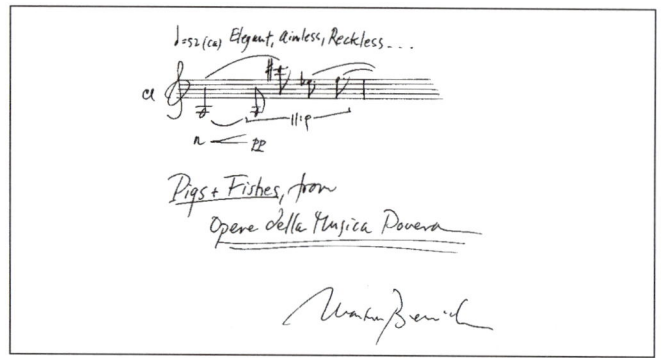

Martin I. Bresnick

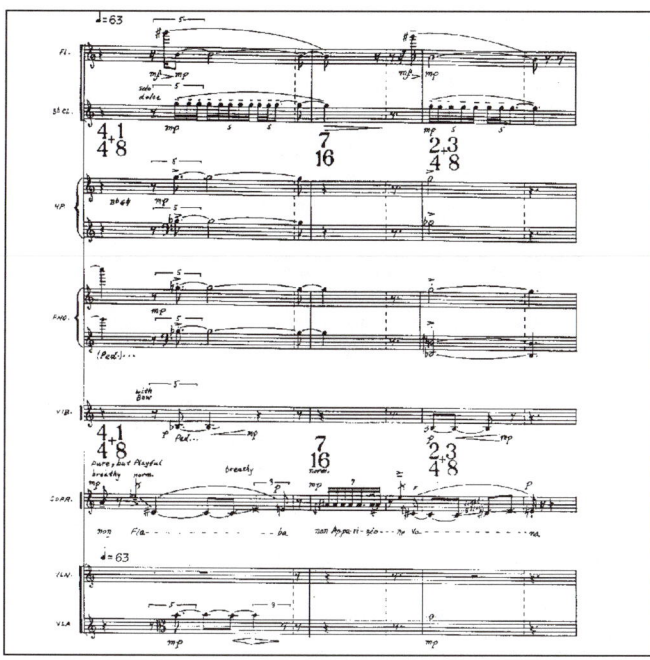

Todd Brief

to the Djerassi Found. 1989; Fulbright- Chester-Schirmer Fellowship to the UK 1991-92; Spectri Sonori Composition Prize 1992. **Important Works:** *Fantasy,* for violin & piano (Albany Records) 1976; *Cantares,* for soprano & large orchestra (text by P. Neruda) (CRI) 1976-79, rev. 1982; *Moments,* for harp (CRI) 1979; *Concert Étude,* for piano (CRI) 1980; *Canto,* for flute (CRI) 1983; *Slow Lament,* for soprano & piano (text by Pablo Neruda) 1984; *Nightsong,* for piano 1985; *Idols* 1986-87; *Jeweled Light* (texts by Pavese & Luzi) 1988; *Water Image,* for piano 1989; *Ceremonial Song,* for six female voices (text by R.M. Rilke) 1992; *Light Shadows* 1993; *Concerto for violin and orchestra* 1995. **Home Address:** 33 Sherwood Pl., Greenwich, CT 06830.

BRIGGS, CECIL CLAIR ■ FAAR Architecture 31. b. Apr. 10, 1904, Waukee, IA. m. Frances Elizabeth Briggs. BA 25, Simpson College; BArch 28, Columbia Univ. **Other Studies:** Cummings School of Art, Des Moines; NAD. **Career & Employment:** Pratt Inst., Prof.-Dept. Head; Columbia Univ., Asst. Prof.; Consultant-Lect.: Cornell Univ., GA Tech., NY School of Applied Design, Univ. of Pennsylvania; Consultant Designer for Congoleum-Nairn Co., Emerson Drug Co., Gleitzman Corp., Proctor & Gamble, Pelee Door and US Gypsum & Co. **Memberships & Offices:** AIA. **Fellowships, Honors & Awards:** Museum of City of NY, Winning Design; Awards for General Electric Co., Chicago Bridge & Iron Works; Smithsonian Inst., Nat. Competition Hon. Mention. **Publications:** "The 'Pantheon' of Ostia (and Its Immediate Surroundings)," *Memoirs of the AAR* 8 (1930): 161-69. **Important Works:** US Gov. Demountable Housing Projects, Demountable Dormitories for NY Central Railroad.

BRILLIANT, RICHARD ■ FAAR Classics/Archaeology 62. b. Nov. 20, 1929, Boston, MA. m. Eleanor Luria. c. Stephanie, Livia, Franca, Myron. BA 51, Yale Univ.; LLB 54, Harvard Law School; MA 56, Yale Univ.; PhD 60, Yale Univ. **Research/Artistic Interests:** Greek & Roman art, history & theory of art history. **Career & Employment:** Univ. of Pennsylvania, Asst. Prof., Prof. & Chair 1962-70; Columbia Univ., Prof. 1970-present, Anna S. Garbedian Prof. 1990-present; Univ. of Pittsburgh, Vis-

iting Mellon Prof. 1971; Scuola Normale Superiore, Pisa, Visiting Prof. 1974, 1980, 1988. **Memberships & Offices:** *Art Bulletin,* Ed. Designate 1990-91, Ed.-in-Chief 1991-94; German Archaeological Inst., Berlin, Corresponding Mem. 1974-present; ASCSA, Managing Com. 1974-present. **Fellowships, Honors & Awards:** Fulbright Fellowship 1957-59; Guggenheim Fellowship 1967-68; NEH Senior Fellow 1972-73; Univ. of Pennsylvania, Lindback Found. Award for Distinguished Teaching 1969; Soc. of Columbia Graduates, Columbia Univ., Great Teacher Award 1990. **Publications:** *Gesture and Rank in Roman Art,* Memoirs of Connecticut Academy of Arts and Sciences 14 (New Haven, 1963); "The Arch of Septimus Severus in the Roman Forum," *Memoirs of the AAR* 29 (1967); "Studia dell'Arte e Sociologia," *La Critica Sociologica* 5 (1968): 77-88; "Temporal Aspects in Late Roman Art," *L'Arte* 10 (1970): 64-87; "On Portraits," *Zeitschrift für Ästhetik und allgemeine Kunstwissenschaft* 16 (1971): 11-21; *Roman Art from the Republic to Constantine* (London: Phaidon, 1974); *Pompeii: A.D. 79: The Treasure of Rediscovery* (Kent: Volair, 1979); "I Piedistalli del Giardino di Boboli: 'Spolia in Se,' 'Spolia in Re'," *Prospettiva* 31 (1982): 1-17; "Una Statua Ritratta del Territorio di Tarquinia," *Bollettino d'Arte* 26 (1984): 1-12; *Visual Narratives* (Ithaca: Cornell Univ. Press, 1984); "Intellectual Giants: A Classical Topos and The School of Athens," *Source* 3 (1984): 1-12; "The Bayeux Tapestry: A Stripped Narrative for Their Eyes and Ears," *Word & Image* 7.2 (1991): 98-126; *Portraiture* (London: Reakton Press & Cambridge, MA: Harvard Univ. Press, 1991); *Commentaries on Roman Art* (London: Pindar, 1994). **Bio-Bibliography:** *Who's Who in America, Who's Who in American Art.* **Home Address:** 10 Wayside Ln., Scarsdale, NY 10583. **Business Address:** Dept. of Art History, Columbia Univ., NYC 10027.

BRINKERHOFF, DERICKSEN M. ■ FAAR Classics/Archaeology 61. b. Oct. 4, 1921, Philadelphia, PA. m. Mary Weston Brinkerhoff. c. Derick, Elizabeth, Jonathan, Caroline. BA 43, Williams College; MA 46, Yale Univ.; PhD 58, Harvard Univ. **Other Study:** Universität Zürich 1947-48. **Career & Employment:** Brown Univ., Instr. 1952-54; RISD, Assc. Dean, Div. of Liberal Arts 1952-59; Penn State Univ., Assc. Prof. 1961-62;

March 26, 1993

Happy birthday and best wishes for 100s more to the Academy, now approaching 100, that has stood in loco parentis for 100s. Already its first fellow, John Russell Pope, 1895, wrote, "We were a particularly congenial and happy family." my first acquaintance with the Academy dated from 1949, when my wife and I visited the building now being refurbished for its centenary. Laurance Roberts, who welcomed us warmly, a decade later interviewed me in Boston and then welcomed me to Rome as a fellow in classical studies, along with my wife and four children. As the Academy founders intended, association with representatives of many disciplines provided intellectual stimulus. My memories are of joyous immersion in professional activity and warm personal cameraderie. When the six of us left Rome after two years in 1961, the occasional difficulties were submerged by a richly nurturing experience. Certainly for me, I cannot recall another period in my life to date of such far reaching significance. To quote Pope again, "I still look back on Rome as the cream of it all."

Dericksen Brinkerhoff

Dericksen M. Brinkerhoff

Temple Univ., Tyler School of Art, Assc. Prof. 1962-65; UC, Riverside, Prof. 1965-92, Prof. Emer. 1991-present. **Fellowships, Honors & Awards:** ANS Seminar Prize 1952; Belgian-American Educational Found., Summer Fellow 1959; NEH Summer Seminar, Participant 1988. **Publications:** Sculpture section in *Ptolemais: City of the Libyan Pentapolis*, ed. Carl H. Kraeling (Chicago: Oriental Inst., 1962), 177-207; "New Examples of the Hellenistic Statue Group, 'The Invitation to the Dance,' and Their Significance," *AJA* 69 (1965): 25-37; *A Collection of Sculpture in Classical and Early Christian Antioch*, CAA Monograph 22 (New York: NYU Press, 1970); "Figures of Venus, Creative and Derivative," *Studies Presented to George M.A. Hanfmann*, ed. David G. Mitten, John G. Pedley & Jane A. Scott (Cambridge, MA, 1971), 9-16; *Hellenistic Statues of Aphrodite* (New York: Garland, 1978); "Hypotheses on the History of the Crouching Aphrodite Type in Antiquity," *J.P. Getty Museum Journal* 6-7 (1978-79): 83-96. **Bio-Bibliography:** *Who's Who in America.* **Home Address:** 4985 Chicago Ave., Riverside, CA 92507-5859. **Business Address:** Dept. of History of Art 011, UC, Riverside, CA 92521.

BROCKIE, ARTHUR H. ■ Stewardson Memorial Scholar 1911-12, 1913.

BRODKEY, HAROLD ■ FAAR Literature 61. b. Oct. 25, 1930, Alton, IL. m. Ellen Schwamm. Harvard Univ. **Career & Employment:** Columbia Univ., Prof.; Univ. of Michigan, Poet-in-Residence. **Memberships & Offices:** International PEN. **Fellowships, Honors & Awards:** Brandeis Univ., Creative Arts Award 1974; Magazine Award 1974; Bavarian Acad. of Fine Arts 1974; O. Henry Short Story Prize 1975, 1976; AAAS 1977; Guggenheim Fellow 1978; Yale Univ., Hon. DHL 1978; AAAL 1979. **Publications:** *First Love and Other Sorrows* (Dial Press, 1957); *Selected Poems* (New York: Penguin, Harper & Row, 1974); *Avedon: Photos 1947-77* (New York: Farrar, Straus & Giroux, 1978); *A Part of Speech* (New York: Farrar, Straus & Giroux, 1980); *Stories in an Almost Classical Mode* (New York: Knopf: 1988); *The Runaway Soul* (New York: Farrar, Straus & Giroux, 1991); *Profane Friendship* (London: Jonathan Cape, 1994); contr., *American Poetry Review, Antaeus, Discovery, Esquire, New American Review, New York Review of Books, New Yorker, Partisan Review.* **Bio-Bibliography:** David Remnick, "Remembrance of Harold Brodkey: U.S.'s Unpublished 'Proust'?," *International Herald Tribune* (Mar. 1-2, 1986).

BRODSKY, JOSEPH A. ■ RAAR Literature 81. b. May 24, 1940, St. Petersburg, USSR. **Research/Artistic Interests:** Poetry. **Career & Employment:** Univ. of Michigan; Columbia Univ.; Mt. Holyoke, Prof. **Fellowships, Honors & Awards:** Guggenheim Fellowship 1976; Premio Mondello 1979; John D. & Catherine T. MacArthur Award 1981; Nobel Prize for Literature 1987; Nat. Book Critics Circle Award 1987; Doctor in Honoris Causa, Oxford Univ. 1991; Poet Laureate of US, Library of Congress 1991-92. **Publications:** *Ostanovka v pustyne* (Chekov, 1970, reissued, Ann Arbor: Ardis, 1989); *Konets prekrasnoy epokhi* (Ann Arbor: Ardis, 1977); *Chast Rechi* (Ann Arbor: Ardis, 1977); *A Part of Speech* (New York: Farrar, Straus & Giroux, 1980); *Novye Stansy k Avguste* (Ann Arbor: Ardis, 1983); *Mramor* (Ann Arbor: Ardis, 1984); *Uraniia* (Ann Arbor: Ardis, 1984); *Less than One* (New York: Farrar, Straus & Giroux, 1986); *To Urania* (New York: Farrar, Straus & Giroux, 1988); *Marbles* (New York: Farrar, Straus & Giroux, 1989); *Chast Rechi: Izbrannie Stichi 1962-1989* (Moscow: Khudozhestvennaia Literatura, 1990). Plays: *Marbles* (New York); *Democracy!* (London, Frankfurt, Washington, DC). **Bio-Bibliography:** Czeslaw

```
Lean over.  I'll whisper something to you: I am
grateful for everything: for the chicken cartilage
and for the chirr of scissors already cutting
out the void for me--for it is your hem.
Doesn't matter if it's pitch black, doesn't matter if
it holds nothing: no ovals, no limbs to count.
The more invisible something is,
the more certain it's been around,
and the more obviously it's everywhere.  You
were the first to whom all this happened, were you?
For a nail holding something one would divide by two--
were it not for remainders--there is no gentler quarry.
I was in Rome.  I was flooded by light.  The way
a splinter can only dream about.
Golden coins on the retina are to stay--
enough to last one through the whole blackout.


                              from
                              "Roman Elegies"
                              Joseph Brodsky
                              1981
```

Joseph A. Brodsky

Milosz, "A Struggle against Suffocation," *New York Review of Books* (Aug. 14, 1980); Richard Howard, review of *Less Than One*, Boston Globe (June 8, 1986); Derek Walcott, "Magic Industry," *New York Review of Books* (Nov. 24, 1988); Lev Loseff & Valentina Polukhina, eds., *Brodsky's Poetics and Aesthetics* (London: Macmillan, 1990); *Razmerom Podlenneka* [essays on J.B.] (Talinn, 1991); David Bethea, "Exile, Elergy, and Auden....," *PMLA* (Mar. 1992); David Bethea, *Joseph Brodsky and the Creation of Exile* (Princeton: Princeton Univ. Press, 1994). **Business Address:** Dept. of English, Mt. Holyoke College, S. Hadley, MA 01075.

BRONFMAN, EDGAR M., JR ■ AAR Trustee 1987-91, Trustee Emer.; Corp. Exec.

BROOKE, STEVEN ■ FAAR Design Arts 91. b. Aug. 17, 1944, Urbana, IL. BA 65, Univ. of Michigan; MS 75, Inst. for Molecular & Cellular Evolution, Univ. of Miami. m. Suzanne Martinson. c. Miles. **Research/Artistic Interests:** History of architectural depiction, systems of pictorial composition. Medium: large-format photography. **Career & Employment:** Inst. for Molecular & Cellular Evolution, Univ. of Miami, Research Assc. 1968-78; Steven Brooke Studios, Prin. 1979-present; Univ. of Miami, Adj. Prof. 1991-present. **Memberships & Offices:** Miami Design Preservation League, BoT 1989-present; Seaside Inst., BoT 1991-present; Miami Museum of Science; Exb. Dir. 1979. **Fellowships, Honors & Awards:** AIA Photographer of the Year, Florida Assc. 1980, 1982, 1983; AIA, Nat. Inst. Honor Award 1987; Art Deco Socs. of America, Distinguished Achievement Award 1987; Historical Museum of Southern Florida, Distinguished Achievement Award 1987; City of Miami Beach, Distinguished Achievement Award 1987; Graham Found. Grant 1994. **Publications:** *Vizcaya Museum and Gardens* (Miami: Martori Publications, 1984); with Barbara Capitman, *Deco Delights* (New York: E.P. Dutton, 1988); with Laura Cerwinske, *Miami* (New York: C.N. Potter; 1990); *Views of Rome* (New York: Rizzoli, 1995); *Seaside* (Gretna: Pelican, 1995); contr. to: *Architectural Digest, Architectural Record, Architecture, Historic Preservation, Progressive Architecture, Smithsonian.* **Exhibitions/Per-**

formances: Mt. Holyoke Museum of Art; Buell Center, Columbia Univ.; Tampa Museum of Science & Industry; Michael C. Carlos Museum, Atlanta; Cummer Museum, Jacksonville; Santa Barbara Museum of Art; Vizcaya Museum 1983; Miami Intl. Airport; Permanent Exb.; Art Deco in Miami; San Francisco Intl. Airport 1988-90; Bass Museum, Permanent Collection. **Home Address:** 7910 SW 54 Court, Miami, FL 33142.

BROOKINGS, ROBERT S. ■ AAR Charter Mem.

BROOKS, H. TURNER ■ FAAR Architecture 84. Apr. 12, 1943, NYC. m. Pebble Brooks. c. Abigail, Benjamin, Rosemary. BA 65, Yale Univ.; MArch 70, Yale School of Architecture. **Career & Employment:** Private Practice 1972-; Carnegie Mellon Univ. 1980; Yale Univ., Design Studio 1981, 1982. **Fellowships, Honors & Awards:** Skowhegan School of Art Competition, Finalist 1982. **Exhibitions/Performances:** Urban Center, NYC 1987. **Bio-Bibliography:** "Turner Brooks," *Architectural Digest* (Aug. 1991).

BROOKS, JAMES D. ■ RAAR Painting 63. b. 1902. d. Mar. 10, 1992. m. Charlotte Brooks. **Bio-Bibliography:** *NY Times,* Obit. (Mar. 12, 1992); *Current Biography.*

BROOKS, ROBERT A. ■ AAR World War II Scholar 1941.

BROOKS, VAN WYCK ■ RAAR Literature 56. b. Feb. 16, 1886, Plainfield, NJ. d. May 2, 1963. m. Elenor K. Stimpson, Gladys Rice. c. Charles, Oliver. BA 08, Harvard Univ. **Career & Employment:** Stanford Univ., Instr. 1911-13; Century Co. Publications, Ed. 1915-18; *The Freeman,* Assc. Ed. 1920-24. **Memberships & Offices:** AAAS, Royal Soc. of Literature, AAAL, APS, Soc., Phi Beta Kappa. **Publications:** *The Wine of the Puritans* (London: Sisley's, 1909); *The World of H.G. Wells* (New York: M. Kennedy, 1915); *America's Coming of Age* (New York: Huebsch, 1915); *Letters and Leadership* (New York: Huebsch, 1918); *The Ordeal of Mark Twain* (New York: Dutton, 1920); *The Pilgrimage of Henry James* (New York: Dutton, 1925); *The Life of Emerson* (New York: Dutton, 1932); *The Flowering of New England, 1815-1865* (New York: Dutton, 1936); *New England Indian Summer, 1865-1915* (New York: Dutton, 1940); *The Times of Melville and Whitman* (New York: Dutton, 1947); *The Confident Years, 1885-1915* (New York: Dutton, 1952); *The Writer in America* (New York: Dutton, 1953); *Scenes and Portraits: Memories of Childhood and Growth* (New York: Dutton, 1954); *Days of the Phoenix: The 1920s I Remember* (New York: Dutton, 1957); *The Dream of Arcadia: American Writers and Artists in Italy* (New York: Dutton, 1958); *Howells: His Life and World* (New York: Dutton, 1959); *From the Shadow of the Mountain: My Post-Meridian Years* (New York: Dutton, 1961). **Bio-Bibliography:** W. Wasserstrom, *The Legacy of Van Wyck Brooks* (Carbondale: Southern Illinois Univ. Press, 1971); James Hooper, *Van Wyck Brooks: In Search of American Culture* (Amherst: Univ. of Massachusetts Press, 1977); Raymond Nelson, *Van Wyck Brooks: A Writer's Life* (New York: Dutton, 1981); *Who Was Who in America.*

BROUGHTON, THOMAS ROBERT SHANNON ■ RAAR Classics/Archaeology 60, 61; School of Classical Studies, Prof.-in-Charge 59-61. b. Feb. 17, 1900, Corbetton, ONT., Canada. d. Sept. 17, 1993. m. Annie Leigh. c. Thomas, Margaret. BA 21, Victoria College, Univ. of Toronto; MA 22, Univ. of Toronto; PhD 28, Johns Hopkins Univ. **Other Study:** Univ. of Chicago 1922, 1923, 1925. **Research/Artistic Interests:** Classical Greek & Latin authors, Roman history & institutions. **Career & Employment:** Amherst College, Instr. 1926-27; Bryn Mawr College, Asst.-Assc. Prof. 1928-37, Prof. 1937-65; Johns Hopkins Univ., Visiting Prof. 1938-40; UNC, Paddison Prof. 1965-70, Paddison Prof. Emer. 1970-present. **Memberships & Offices:** APA, Ed. 1941-44, Dir. 1945-48, 2d VP 1949-50, 1st VP 1950-53, Pres. 1954; Intl. Fed. of Societies for Classical Studies, VP 1959-69. **Fellowships, Honors & Awards:** Guggenheim Fellow 1945-46; Fulbright Research Grant in Italy 1951-52; APA, Goodwin Award of Merit 1953; APS Mem. 1955; AAAS, Fellow; Soc. for Promotion of Roman Studies, Hon. Mem.; British Acad., Corresponding Fellow; Deutches Inst. für Archäologie, Corresponding Mem.; Hon. LLD: Johns Hopkins Univ. 1968, Univ. of Toronto 1971, UNC, Chapel Hill 1974. **Publications:** *The Romanization of Africa Proconsularia* (Baltimore: Johns Hopkins Univ. Press, 1929); "Roman Asia Minor," in *An Economic Survey of Ancient Rome,* ed. Tenney Frank (Baltimore: Johns Hopkins Univ. Press, 1938), 4:499-950; *The Magistrates of the Roman Republic,* Vol. I: *509 BC-100 BC,* Vol. II: *99 BC-31 BC* (Philadelphia: APA, 1951-52); Vol. III: *Supplement,* (Philadelphia: APA, 1986); "Candidates Defeated in Roman Elections: Some Ancient Roman 'Also-Rans'," *Transactions of the APS* 81.4 (1991). **Bio-Bibliography:** Briggs, 64-66.

BROWN, ANDREA CLARK ■ FAAR Architecture 80. b. Aug. 10, 1953, Oswego, NY. m. Leonard P. Reina. BA 75, Bryn Mawr College; MArch 78, Univ. of Virginia, Grad. School of Architecture. **Research/Artistic Interests:** Television presentation of house renovation in Naples, FL for nationally televised "Home Again with Bob Vila." **Career & Employment:** Dept. of Community Development, Charlottesville, VA, Intern Planner 1974; Patton, Harris, Rust & Guy, Planners, Surveyors, & Engineers, Intern Architect 1976; John Farmer, Architect, Intern Architect 1977-78; Mitchell-Giurgola Architects, Project Team 1978-79; Pomeroy-Lebdusca Architects, Project Designer 1980-81; Design Collaborative Architects, Project Manager 1981-83; Catholic Univ., Foreign Studies Program in Rome, Italy, Visiting Prof. 1982, 1983; Harvard Univ., Visiting Critic 1983; Eisenman-Robertson Architects, Project Team 1983-85; Syracuse Univ. School of Architecture, Asst. Prof. 1985-86; Andrea Clark Brown, AIA, Architect, Prin. 1986-present; Univ. of Virginia, Graduate Studio, Lect. 1990; Univ. of Minnesota, School of Architecture, Cass Gilbert Prof. 1992. **Memberships & Offices:** Texas Soc. of Architects; Architectural & Urban League, NYC 1978-present; Nat. Council of Architectural Registration Bd., Certified Mem.; Univ. of Miami School of Architecture, Visiting Critic 1986-87; Univ. of Illinois, Chicago Circle, School of Architecture, Visiting Critic 1988; AIA Annual Honor Awards, Jury Mem. 1989, Florida SW Chap., Chap. Sec. 1990, Nat. Com. on Design 1990-present; Stewardson Fellowship Award Philadelphia, Jury Mem. 1990; Collier Leadership of Naples, FL, Class Mem. 1991; Florida Concrete &Products Assn., Jury Mem. 1992. **Fellowships, Honors & Awards:** Bryn Mawr College, Preceptorship Grant 1974; AIA Florida SW Chap., Honor Award 1987, Award of Excellence 1989, 1991, Merit Award 1991. **Publications:** 'Observations on the Herman Wiemer Winery," *UKZ Architects;* "Werk, Bauen & Wohnen (Apr. 1986): 2; "In Caesura: The First Year of Eisenman Seminars at Harvard," *Three Years of Eisenman Seminars at the GSD,* exb. cat. (Cambridge, MA: Harvard GSD, 1986); "Observations on the Schine Center," *100% Rag* 4.4 (May 1986). **Important Works:** Brown Residence, Naples, FL 1985-86; Gardella Residence, Naples, FL 1987-88; Goodland Marina, Retail, Restaurant & Administrative Offices, Goodland, FL 1989-90; Soft Art Professional Office Bldg., Naples, FL 1990-91; interior design, Church of St. John the Evangelist, Naples, FL 1990-92; Owen Residence, Naples, FL 1991; Mango Bay Condominium,

Naples, FL 1991; Bob Vila Cottage, Naples, FL 1991; Old Naples Shopping Area, Master Plan & Design Implementation of Street Improvements 1992; Fidelity Brokerage, Branch Office, Northern Trust Bldg., Naples, FL 1992; Kirsten Design's Boutique at Waterside Shops, Pelican Bay, Naples, FL 1992; Crabby Lady's Crabhouse Restaurant, Goodland, FL 1992; Petras Residence, Naples, FL 1992; Carroll Residence, Naples, FL 1992; Schultzel Residence, Naples, FL 1992; St. Ann Catholic Church, Naples, FL 1993-94. **Exhibitions/ Performances:** Young-Hoffman Gallery, Chicago, & NAD, "Late Entries for the Chicago Tribune Bldg. 1980; Cooper Union & Traveling 1981; Chicago Architectural Center 1982, 1990; Univ. of Virginia, Charlottesville 1984; Syracuse Univ., School of Architecture, Faculty Exb. 1986; Edison College Art Gallery, Fort Myers, FL 1988; AIA Exb. by Women in Architecture, NYC and Traveling 1988; Lee County Alliance of the Arts, Fort Myers, FL 1989; Florida Center for Contemporary Art, Tampa 1991. **Bio-Bibliography:** Stanley Tigerman, *Late Entries to the Chicago Tribune Competition*, Vol 2 (1981); Tod Williams & Richard Scofidio, *Window, Room, Furniture*, exb. cat. (New York: Copper Union, 1981); Andrea O. Dean, "Women in Architecture, Profiles...and Issues," *AIA Journal* (1982); "Window, Room, Furniture, Exhibitions," *S.D. 8304* 233 (1983); Wendy McMullen, "A Woman's Place," *Home and Condo* (1986); Jinny Dean, "Decidedly Different," *Gulfshore Life* 17.6 (1987); Pamela Humphrey, "Pelican Bay: Perfect Locale for a Showcase Home," *Home and Condo* (1987); Royce Haiman, "Architect at Work: Andrea Brown," *Florida Real Estate* 2.1 (1988); Andrea Meyer, "Nouveau Naples," *South Florida Home and Garden* (1988); Leigh Mitchell, "Architect in Naples, Brown Renovates," *Home and Condo* (1988); Lori Capullo, "Casa del Sol, Historical Beginnings Combine with Contemporary Endings," *Florida Home & Garden* (1990); Karen Salmon, "Women in Architecture: On the Boards," *Architecture* (1991); Roberta Klein, "The Designs of Florida," *Florida Real Estate* 5.1 (1991); Renee Garrison, "Where Interior Meets Exterior: A House without Bounds," *Florida Architect* (1992). **Home Address:** 316 Third Ave. N., Naples, FL 33940. **Business Address:** Andrea Clark Brown, AIA, Architect, 316 Third Ave. N., Naples, FL 33940.

BROWN, DENISE SCOTT ■ AAR Visitor 1981-82, Architect.

BROWN, DONALD FREDERICK ■ FAAR Classics/Archaeology 41. b. Oct. 30, 1909, NYC. m. Marguerite L. Brown. BA 32, NYU; MA 36, NYU. **Career & Employment:** NYU, Univ. Fellow 1937-38. **Publications:** *Temples of Rome as Coin Types*, Numismatic Notes & Monographs 90 (New York: ANS, 1940).

BROWN, DONALD FREEMAN ■ FAAR Classics/Archaeology 53. b. Nov. 26, 1908, Holyoke, MA. m. Linda Brown. c. Linda. BA 30, Harvard Univ.; MA 35, Harvard Univ. **Research/ Artistic Interests:** Archaeology: excavation of Greek city of Sybaris. **Career & Employment:** Northeastern Univ. & Calvin Coolidge College, Instr. 1936-42. **Fellowships, Honors & Awards:** Fulbright Award 1949-50; Viking Fund, Fellowship 1949; Harvard Univ., Thaw Travelling Fellowship 1948-49.

BROWN, EARLE ■ RAAR Musical Composition 87. **Memberships & Offices:** 39th Annual BMI Student Composer Awards, Juror 1991.

BROWN, FRANK EDWARD ■ FAAR Classics/Archaeology 33; RAAR Classics/Archaeology 54, 55; AAR Trustee 1954-63, School of Classical Studies, Prof.-in-Charge 1947-52, Andrew W. Mellon Prof.-in-Charge 1963-76; AAR, Dir. 1965-69, Acting Dir. 1973-74; AAR, Medal of Merit 1976; NEH Summer

Seminar Leader 1980. b. May 24, 1908, LaGrange, IL. d. Feb. 28, 1988. m. Jaquelin Goddard. BA 29, Carleton College; PhD 38, Yale Univ. **Research/Artistic Interests:** Archaeology, Cosa, Dura-Europos, Regia in the Roman Forum. **Career & Employment:** Yale Univ. in Dura-Europos, Asst. & Dir. 1932-37; Yale Univ., Research Asst.-Instr.-Asst. Prof. 1938-42; OWI, Syria & Lebanon, General Representative 1942-45; Republic of Syria, Dir. General of Antiquities 1945-47; Yale Univ., Thatcher Prof. 1952-63, Jonathan Edwards College, Master, 1953-56. **Memberships & Offices:** APA; AHA; ArIA; American Oriental Soc.; SAH; American School of Oriental Research; Intl. Assn. for Classical Archaeology, VP; Intl. Federation of Societies of Classical Studies, VP; Intl. Union of the Institutes of Archaeology, History, & the History of Art in Rome, Pres. 1966-67; Istituto di Studi Etruschi ed Italici, Florence. **Fellowships, Honors & Awards:** Yale Univ., Kellogg Fellowship 1930-31; Pontificia Accademia Romana di Archeologia 1967; Carleton College, Hon. LLD 1968; "Cultore di Roma," Gold Medal 1983; Accademia Nazionale dei Lincei, Foreign Fellow. **Publications:** "Violation of Sepulture in Palestine," *American Journal of Philology* 52 (1931): 1-29; ed. with E.H. Sturtevant, *T. Macci Plauti Pseudolus* (New Haven: Yale Univ. Press, 1932); "The Regia," *Memoirs of the AAR* 12 (1935): 67-88; co-ed. & contr., *The Excavations at Dura-Europos. Preliminary Report of the Seventh and Eighth Seasons of Work*, vols. 7-8 (New Haven: Yale Univ. Press, 1939); *The Excavations at Dura-Europos, Final Reports*, 5 vols. (New Haven: Yale Univ. Press, 1945-69, Los Angeles, 1977); co-ed. & contr., *Fasti Archaeologici*, vols. 1-5 (Florence: Sansoni, 1946-50); "Cosa I: History and Topography," *Memoirs of the AAR* 20 (1951): 5-133; with Emeline Richardson & Lawrence Richardson, jr, *Cosa II: The Temple of Arx*, Memoirs of the AAR 26 (New York and Rome: AAR, 1960); *Roman Architecture* (New York: Braziller, 1961); *Cosa: The Making of a Roman Town* (Ann Arbor: Univ. of Michigan Press, 1980); "La protostoria della Regia," *Rendiconti della Pontificia Accademia Romana di Archeologia* 47 (1974-75): 15-36; "Of Hut and Houses," in *In Memoriam Otto J. Brendel*, ed. L. Bonfante et al. (Mainz: von Zabern, 1976), 5-12; with Emeline Richardson & Lawrence Richardson, jr, *Cosa III: The Buildings of the Forum: Colony, Municipium and Village*, Memoirs of the AAR 37 (New York & Rome: Pennsylvania State Univ. Press for AAR, 1993). **Important Works:** Excavations at Dura-Europos; Excavations of the Latin Colony of Cosa; construction & equipping of the site museum, the Nat. Museum of Cosa 1981-87; Supervision of field work & the preparation of publications of Cosa in the *Memoirs of the American Academy in Rome*; Excavation of the Regia in the Roman Forum. **Bio-Bibliography:** *Eius virtutis studiosi: Classical and Postclassical Studies in Memory of Frank Edward Brown*, ed. Russell T. Scott & Ann Reynolds Scott (Washington, DC: NGA, 1993); Russell T. Scott, "Memoir," *AJA* 92 (1988): 577-79; *Contemporary Authors; Directory of American Scholars; Who Was Who in America*.

BROWN, GLENN ■ AAR Charter Mem.

BROWN, J. CARTER ■ AAR Trustee 1973-present. **Studies:** Harvard Univ., École du Louvre, IFA. **Career & Employment:** NGA, Dir. 1969-93, Dir. Emer. 1993-present. **Memberships & Offices:** Comm. of Fine Arts, Washington, DC, Chair; Ovation, Inc., Chair.; American Federation of Arts, BoT; John F. Kennedy Center for the Performing Arts, BoT; Nat. Geographic Soc., BoT; World Monuments Fund, BoT; Brown Univ., BoT; Com. for the Preservation of the White House; Federal Council on the Arts & Humanities. **Fellowships, Honors & Awards:** Nat. Medal of Arts, plus honors from the governments of France, Norway,

Egypt, Portugal, Austria, The Netherlands, Italy, Spain, Sweden & Great Britain.

BROWN, JOHN MASON ■ AAR Visitor 1959-64, Writer.

BROWN, PATRICIA FORTINI ■ FAAR History of Art 90. b. Nov. 16, 1936, Oakland, CA. Walter K. Winslow (companion). c. Paul Meyer, John Jeffrey Meyer. BA 59, UC, Berkeley; MA 78, UC, Berkeley; PhD 83, UC, Berkeley. **Other Study:** Brigham Young Univ. 1954-57. **Research/ Artistic Interests:** Art & culture of Venice in the Middle Ages & the Renaissance. **Career & Employment:** Mills College, Lect. 1983; Princeton Univ., Asst. Prof. 1983-89, Assc. Prof. 1989-present. **Memberships & Offices:** CAA 1978-present; RSA, Adv. Council, Rep. Discipline of Visual Arts 1988-90, 1994-96. **Fellowships, Honors & Awards:** Fulbright-Hays Grant to Italy 1980-81; Social Science Research Council & ACLS, Intl. Doctoral Research Fellowship 1980-82; Gladys Krieble Delmas Found., Grant for Research in Venice 1982; Guggenheim Fellowship 1989; Premio "Salotto Veneto 89," 2d Prize, to *Venetian Narrative Painting in the Age of Carpaccio* 1989; Princeton Univ., Andrew W. Mellon Prof. 1991-94; Museo Italo-Americano, San Francisco, Italian American Woman of the Year 1992. **Publications:** "Painting and History in Renaissance Venice," *Art History* 7 (1984): 263-94; "Honor and Necessity: The Dynamics of Patronage in the Confraternities of Renaissance Venice," *Studi veneziani*, n.s. 14 (1987): 179-212; *Venetian Narrative Painting in the Age of Carpaccio* (New Haven & London: Yale Univ. Press, 1988); "The Ritual Conception of History in Venetian Renaissance Art," in *World Art: Themes of Unity in Diversity. Acts of the XXVIth International Congress of the History of Art*, ed. Irving Lavin (University Park & London: Pennsylvania State Univ. Press, 1989), 599-602; "Measured Friendship, Calculated Pomp: The Ceremonial Welcomes of the Venetian Republic," in *All the World's a Stage: Art and Pageantry in the Renaissance and Early Baroque*, Papers in Art History 6 (University Park: Pennsylvania State University Press, 1990), 136-86; "The Self-Definition of the Venetian Republic," in *City-States in Classical Antiquity and Medieval Italy, Athens and Rome, Florence and Venice*, ed. A. Molho, K. Raaflaub, & J. Emlen (Stuttgart: Steiner Verlag, 1991), 511-48; *La pittura nell'età di Carpaccio: I grandi cicli narrativi* (Venice: Abrizzi Editori, 1992); "The Antiquarianism of Jacopo Bellini," *Artibus et Historiae* 26 (1992): 65-84; "Sant' Agostino nello studio di Carpaccio: un ritratto nel ritretto?" in *Bessarione e l'Umanenimo*, ed. Gionfrancesco Fiaccadori (Naples: Istituto Italiano per gli Studi Filosofici-Biblioteca Nazionale Marciana, 1994), 303-19; "Committenza e arte di stato," in *Storia di Venezia, 3. Formazione dello stato patrizio*, ed. G. Arnaldi, A. Tenenti & G. Cracco (Rome: Istituto della Enciclopedia Italiana, Fondazione Giorgio Cini, Treccani Editore: in press); "Le Scuole," in *Storia di Venezia, 4. Venezia Rinascimentale*, ed. A. Tenenti & U. Tucci (Rome: Istituto della Enciclopedia Italiana, Fondazione Giorgio Cini, Treccani Editore: in press); "*Renovatio* or *Conciliatio*? How Renaissances Happened in Venice," in *Rereadings in the Renaissance*, ed. Alison Brown (Oxford & New York: Oxford Univ. Press, in press); *Venice and Antiquity: The Venetian Sense of the Past* (New Haven: Yale Univ. Press, forthcoming); *Venice: The Art of a Renaissance Republic* (London: Calman & King, forthcoming). **Bio-Bibliography:** *Princeton Alumni Weekly* (Oct. 27, 1993): 5; *Contemporary Authors; ; Who's Who in American Education; Who's Who of American Women; Who's Who in the East; Who's Who in Humanities; Who's Who in New Jersey; World's Who's Who of Women*. **Home Address:** 54 Humbert St., Princeton, NJ 08542.

BROWN, THEODORE L. ■ FAAR Architecture 88. b. July 20, 1956, Trenton, NJ. m. Anne Munly. BArch 78, Univ. of Virginia; MArch 81, Princeton Univ. **Career & Employment:** Michael Graves Architect, Assc. 1980-85; Princeton School of Architecture, Assc. Prof. 1984, 1985; Oregon School of Design, Prof. 1985, 1986; Syracuse Univ. in Florence, School of Architecture Program, Dir. 1990. **Fellowships, Honors & Awards:** Princeton Univ., AIA Student Medal 1981; NEA Grant 1987; Graham Found. Grant 1987.

BROWN, VIRGINIA ■ FAAR Classics/Archaeology 68, AAR Adv. Council 1978-present; Publications Com. 1981-90; Post-Classical and Humanistic Jury 1984. m. James Hankins, FAAR 82. BA 62, Manhattanville College of the Sacred Heart; MA 64, UNC, Chapel Hill; PhD 69, Harvard Univ. **Other Study:** Dipl., Scuola Vaticana di Paleografia e Diplomatica, Vatican City 1966-68. **Research/Artistic Interests:** Transmission of classical texts in the Middle Ages & Renaissance; Beneventan script; liturgy & culture of medieval southern Italy & Dalmatia; Renaissance liturgy. **Career & Employment:** Salem College, Winston-Salem, NC, Lect. 1964; Newton College of the Sacred Heart, Lect. 1965-66; Research Asst. to E.A. Lowe, IAS 1968-70; Pontifical Inst. of Mediaeval Studies, Toronto, Junior Fellow 1970-74, Senior Fellow 1974-present; Univ. of Toronto, Asst. Prof. 1970-75, Prof. 1975-present. Other Positions: St. Hilda's College, Oxford, Distinguished Visiting Fellow 1980; Centro Universitario Europeo per i Beni Culturali, Ravello, Montecassino, Rome, Faculty 1989; UCLA, Distinguished Visiting Prof. 1992; Università degli Studi di Venezia, Distinguished Visiting Prof. 1993. **Memberships & Offices:** APA; American Assn. for Neo-Latin Studies; Amici di Capua; Canadian Classical Assn.; Henry Bradshaw Soc.; Intl. Soc. of Neo-Latin Studies; Società Napoletana di Storia Patria; RSA, Councillor 1978-81; *Mediaeval Studies*, Ed. 1974-88; MAA Councillor 1976-79, Haskins Medal Com. 1979-81, Nominating Com. 1992-93; Hill Monastic Manuscript Library, Adv. Bd. 1978-85; *Catalogus translationum et commentariorum*, Ed. Bd. 1977-79, Exec. Com. 1979-present, Sec. & Ed. 1985-present; NEH, Research Tools & Grants Panel 1984; *Journal of the History of Ideas*, Ed. Bd. 1986-present; Comité Intl. de paléographie 1986-present; Cambridge Studies in Palaeography & Codicology, Ed. Bd. 1989-present; *International Journal of the Classical Tradition*, Ed. Bd. 1992-present. **Fellowships, Honors & Awards:** Canada Council, Research Grants 1971, 1972, 1974, 1978, Fellowship 1975-76, Publication Grant for Mediaeval Studies 1977-79; Guggenheim Fellowship 1975-76; Harvard Univ. Center for Renaissance Studies, Villa I Tatti, Florence, Fellowship 1975-76; APS Research Grant 1979; St. Hilda's College, Oxford, Distinguished Visiting Fellowship 1980; Nuffield Found. Research Grant 1980; SSHRCC: Publication Grants 1980-88, Fellowships 1981-82, Research Grants 1981, 1984, 1986-94; ACLS Fellowship 1981-82; NEH Research Tools Grant 1982-86, Summer Stipend 1992; Comité d'honneur, Cinquantenaire de l'Institut de Recherche et d'Histoire des Textes, Paris 1987; Arbeo-Gesellschaft, Munich 1989-present; Accademia degli Agghiacciati Sulmona, Mem. & Corres. 1991-present. **Publications:** *The Textual Transmission of Caesar's Civil War* (Leiden: Brill, 1972); "Gaius Julius Caesar," *Catalogus translationum et commentariorum*, ed. F.E. Cranz & P.O. Kristeller, vol. 3 (Washington, DC: Catholic Univ. of America Press, 1976), 87-139; "A Second New List of Beneventan Manuscripts (I)," *Mediaeval Studies* 40 (1978): 239-89; ed., E. A. Lowe, *The Beneventan Script*, 2d ed., 2 vols. (Rome: Catholic Univ. of America Press, 1980); "Marcus Porcius Cato," *Catalogus translationum et commentariorum*, ed. F.E. Cranz & P.O. Kristeller, vol. 4 (Washington, DC: Catholic Univ. of America Press, 1980), 223-47; "Marcus Terentius Varro" ibid., 451-500;

"Portraits of Julius Caesar in Latin Manuscripts of the Commentaries," *Viator* 12 (1981): 319-53; "The Survival of Beneventan Script: Sixteenth-Century Liturgical Codices from Benedictine Monasteries in Naples," in *Monastica: Scritti raccolti in memoria del XV centenario della nascita di S. Benedetto (480-1980)*, vol. 1 (Montecassino: Badia di Montecassino, 1982), 237-355; "A New Beneventan Calendar from Naples: The Lost "Kalendarium Tutinianum" Rediscovered," *Mediaeval Studies* 46 (1984): 385-449; "A Second New List of Beneventan Manuscripts (II)," *Mediaeval Studies* 50 (1988): 584-625; "Boccaccio in Naples: The Beneventan Liturgical Palimpsest of the Laurentian Autographs (MSS. 29.8 and 33.31)," *Italia medioevale e umanistica* 34 (1991): 41-127; ed.-in-chief, with F.E. Cranz & P.O. Kristeller, *Catalogus translationum et commentariorum*, 8 (Washington, DC: Catholic Univ. of America Press, forthcoming). **Business Address:** Pontifical Inst. of Medieval Studies, 59 Queen's Park Cresent E., Toronto, ONT M5S 2C4, Canada.

BROWNELL, HERBERT ■ AAR Visitor 1959-64, Lawyer.

BRUCIA, MARGARET A. ■ FAAR Post-Classical/Humanistic Studies 92; SOF, Council Mem. b. Oct. 18, 1948, NYC. m. James E. Campbell. c. Angela Campbell, Benedict Campbell. BA 70, Manhattanville College; MA 74, Long Island Univ., Greenvale, NY; MA-PhD 90, Fordham Univ. **Other Study:** AAR & VSA Summer School 1973; ASCSA 1975; RSA Paleography Workshop 1977. **Career & Employment:** Friends Acad., Locust Valley, NY 1971-78; Port Jefferson HS & Middle School 1978-present. **Memberships & Offices:** *Classical Outlook*, Assc. Ed.; Suffolk Classical Soc., Pres 1984-present. Educational Testing Service & College Bd., Consultant 1983-present; New York State Bureau of Foreign Languages, Consultant 1985-present. **Fellowships, Honors & Awards:** Fulbright-Hays Fellowship 1973; RSA Grant 1979; NEH Fellowship 1993. **Publications:** *Teacher's Guide to AP Courses in Latin* (New York: College Board, 1986, 1995); "An Analysis of Student Performance on the Multiple-Choice Section of the AP Latin Exam," *Classical Outlook* 69 (1992): 1-7; "The Rome Prize from a Secondary School Teacher's Perspective," *Classical Outlook* 70 (1993): 45-46. **Home Address:** 115 Greenlawn Rd., Huntington, NY 11743.

BRUDER, WILLIAM P. ■ FAAR Architecture 87. b. Aug. 28 1946, Milwaukee, WI. m. J. Simon. BFA 69, Univ. of Wisconsin. **Career & Employment:** Apprenticeships: William P. Wenzler, Michael P. Johnson, Paolo Soleri, Gunnar Birkerts, Florence & Walling, Michael & Kemper Goodwin. **Fellowships, Honors & Awards:** American Plywood Assc. Design Competition, 1st Honor Award 1977; *Architectural Record*, Award of Excellence for Design 1977, 1993; American Concrete Inst., Arizona Chap., Special Award 1979; Arizona Passive Solar Design Competition, 1st Place Award 1981; American Car Wash Assn., Car Wash Beautiful Competition, Grand Nat. Award 1987; Phoenix Home & Garden-AIA Homes of the Year Competition, Honor Award 1988; Metal Construction Assn. Merit Awards Program, Honor Award 1989; Scholarship Honor Award 1991; Domino's 30 Award 1990; Valley Forward Assn., Crescordia Award 1993; Excellence in Masonry Awards, Gold Trowel Award 1993. **Important Works:** J.L. Bammerlin Credit Union, Phoenix 1974; Bruder Studio, New River, AZ 1975, 1978; Rotharmel Studio, Glendale, AZ 1976; Mesquite Branch Public Library, Phoenix 1979; PDSD-Gym Auditorium, Phoenix 1981; Rosenbaum Residence, Cave Creek, AZ 1981; Weiss Residence, Paradise Valley, AZ 1985; Arizona Historical Museum Comp. 1985; Weiss Guys Car Wash, Chandler, AZ 1986; NAU Honors College, Flagstaff, AZ 1986; Cholla Library Expansion, Phoenix 1986;

IMCOR Office Expansion, Phoenix 1988; Mulvihill Gravemarker, Cave Creek, AZ 1989; Theuer Residence, Ahwatukee, AZ 1989; Phoenix Central Library 1990; Hill-Sheppard Residence, Phoenix 1990; Kett Residence, Prescott, AZ 1991; Temple Kol Ami, Phoenix 1992; Teton County Library, Jackson, WY 1993; Cox Residence, Cave Creek, AZ 1993; Deer Valley Rock Art Museum 1994; Horne Residence, Beverly, MA 1994. **Exhibitions/Performances:** Fine Arts Center, Tempe, AZ 1983; Southern California Inst. of Architecture, Santa Monica 1984; Graham Found. for Advanced Studies in the Fine Arts, Chicago 1985. **Home Address:** 1314 W. Circle Mountain Rd., New River, AZ 85027. **Business Address:** William P. Bruder-Architect, Ltd., 1314 W. Circle Mountain Rd., New River, AZ 85027.

BRUZELIUS, CAROLINE A. ■ FAAR History of Art 86, RAAR History of Art 89, Juror, 1990, 1991; *Memoirs of the AAR*, Ed. Bd.; AAR Dir. 94-present. b. Apr. 18, 1949, Stockholm, Sweden. c. Anders Wallace. BA 71, Wellesley College; MA 74, Yale Univ.; PhD 77, Yale Univ. **Research/Artistic Interests:** Architectural history specializing in French & Italian Gothic architecture; I have also begun to do research on the architecture of medieval convents, with a special focus on the Clarissan houses of southern Italy; medieval sculpture. **Career & Employment:** Dickinson College, Asst. Prof. 1977-79; Duke Univ., Andrew W. Mellon Asst. Prof. 1981-87, Assc. Prof. 1987-91, Prof. 1991-present, Chair 1989-93. **Memberships & Offices:** SAH, Dir. 1991-94; CASVA, Bd. of Adv. 1991-93; Center for Medieval & Renaissance Studies, Duke Univ., Ed. Bd., Monograph Series. **Fellowships, Honors & Awards:** NEH Grant 1979-80, Summer Research Grant 1984; Mellon Fellowship, Harvard Univ., 1980-81; ACLS Grant-in-Aid 1983; Duke Univ. Alumni Distinguished Teaching Award 1985; Fulbright-Hays Grant for Research in Italy 1985-86; Samuel H. Kress Senior Fellow, CASVA 1988. **Publications:** *Cistercian High Gothic: The Abbey Church of Longpont and the Architecture of the Cistercians in the Early Thirteenth Century*, Analecta Cisterciensia vol. 25 (1979): 3-204; French edition: *L'Apogée de l'art gothique: L'Eglise abbatiale de Longpont et l'architecture cistercienne au début du XIIIe siècle*, trans. Marie-Françoise Brunet (Citeaux, Commentarii cistercienses, 1990); *The Thirteenth-Century Church at Saint-Denis* (New Haven: Yale Univ. Press, 1985); "The Construction of Notre-Dame in Paris," *Art Bulletin* 69 (1987): 540-69; "The Abbey of St.-Denis and the Politics of Restoration," *Crit* (American Inst. of Architecture) (Apr. 1987): 31-37; "The Second Campaign of Saint-Urbain in Troyes," *Speculum* 62 (1987): 635-40; ed. & contr., *The Brummer Collection of Medieval Art* (Durham: Duke Univ. Press, 1991); "*Ad modum franciae:* Charles of Anjou's Gothic Architecture in the Kingdom of Sicily," *JSAH* 50 (1991): 402-20; "Art, Architecture, and Urbanism in Naples," in Enrico Bacco, Cesare d'Engenio Caracciolo and others, *Naples: An Early Guide*, ed. & trans. Eileen Gardiner (New York: Italica Press, 1991), lxv-lxxix; "Hearing is Believing: Clarissan Architecture 1212-1340," with Connie Berman, introduction to an issue on medieval convents, *Gesta* (Dec. 1992): 73-75; "Il coro di San Lorenzo e la ricezione dell'arte gotica nella Napoli angioina," *Presenze del Gotico Europeo in Italia*, ed. V. Pace (Naples: Electa, 1994), 265-77; "L'Abbaye cistercienne de Longpont," in *Congrès archéologique 1995* (Departement de l'Aisne, forthcoming). **Bio-Bibliography:** *Who's Who in America; Who's Who of American Women.* **Business Address:** American Academy in Rome, Via Angelo Masina 5, 00153 Rome, Italy.

BRYAN, WALTER REID ■ FAAR Classics/Archaeology 22. b. May 6, 1886, Hillsdale, MI. d. Sept. 18, 1966. PhD 20, Univ. of Wisconsin. **Research/Artistic Interests:** Prehistoric & Roman archaeology, Italic hut urns and hut-urn cemeteries. **Career & Employment:** Columbia Univ. **Publications:** "The Conventions of the Chorus in Greek Drama," *University of Wisconsin Studies in Language and Literature* 15, Classical Studies 2 (1922); *Italic Hut Urns and Hut-Urn Cemeteries,* AAR Papers and Monographs 4 (New York & Rome: AAR, 1925); *An Outline for a Home Study Course in Elementary Latin* (New York: Columbia Univ. Press, 1929).

BUCCI, ANTONELLA ■ AAR – Rome, Assc. Librarian

BUCHANAN, MARVIN HARRY ■ FAAR Architecture 76. b. Apr. 13, 1940, Kern County, CA. m. An Ra Hong. BArch 65, UC, Berkeley; MArch 66, Yale Univ. **Career & Employment:** Charles W. Moore Asscs., Assc. 1965-71; Moore, Lyndon, Turnbull, Assc. 1970; UC, Berkeley, Lect. 1971-75; Desmond Muirhead Inc., Designer 1972; Behn-Buchanan, Part. 1972-73; Architects Associated, Designer 1974-75. **Fellowships, Honors & Awards:** UC, Eisner Prize 1963; HUD Award 1969; *Progressive Architecture,* 1st Honor Award 1970, Citation 1970. **Publications:** "New Hope for Scotland, Maryland," *Architectural Forum,* (Oct. 1966); "Pop Scene for Profs," *Architectural Forum* (Mar. 1969).

BUCHANAN, ROBERT THOMAS ■ FAAR Landscape Architecture 59. b. Jan. 25, 1932, Jackson, MI. m. Odiee Buchanan. c. Isabel Ludovica. BS 55, Univ. of Michigan; MLArch 56, Harvard Univ. **Career & Employment:** US Interior Dept., Nat. Park Service, Asst. 1954; Sasaki & Novak, Design & Construction 1956; UC, Berkeley, Prof. 1959-62. **Fellowships, Honors & Awards:** ASLA Certificate of Merit 1955. **Exhibitions/Performances:** Cambridge Art Assn., MA 1956; Busch Reisinger Museum, Cambridge 1956; Jordan Marsh Annual, Boston 1957; UC, Berkeley Art Festival 1961; Pomeroy & Triangle Galleries, San Francisco; Solo: Galleria Scorpio, Rome 1964.

BUCHER, GREGORY S. ■ FAAR Classics/Archaeology 96. b. July 5, 1963, Burbank, CA. BS 86, BA 87, UC, San Diego; CPhil 91; Brown Univ. **Research/Artistic Interests:** Late Roman Republican history, Greek paleography, ancient methods of keeping records. **Fellowships, Honors & Awards:** NEH Dissertation Fellowship (declined) 1993-94; ASCSA, Oscar Broneer Fellow 1993-94. **Publications:** "The *annales maximi* in the Light of Roman Methods of Keeping Records," *American Journal of Ancient History* (forthcoming). **Home Address:** 3751 Del Mar Ave., San Diego, CA 92106.

BUHRING, HERMAN C. ■ Stewardson Memorial Fellow 1911-12, 1913.

BULLARD, JAMES EDWARD ■ FAAR Post-Classical/Humanistic Studies 75. b. May 10, 1943, Marietta, GA. m. Melissa Meriam Bullard, FAAR 84. BA 65, Princeton Univ.; MDiv 68, Duke Divinity School. **Other Studies:** Stanford Univ. 1968-69, 1971-. **Research/Artistic Interests:** Reformation history. **Fellowships, Honors & Awards:** Dempster Graduate Award 1971-72; Stanford Univ., California State Fellowship 1972-73.

BULLARD, MELISSA M. ■ FAAR Post-Classical/Humanistic Studies 84. b. Mar. 12, 1946, Berkeley, CA. m. James E. Bullard, FAAR 75. c. Edward L. BA 67, Duke Univ.; MA 69, Cornell Univ.; PhD 77, Cornell Univ. **Research/Artistic Interests:** 15th- & 16th-century Italian history. **Career & Employment:** UNC, Chapel Hill, Asst. Prof. 1977-81, Assc. Prof. 1981-

89, Prof. 1989-present. **Memberships & Offices:** RSA, Council Rep. for History 1989-94; Harvard Univ., Villa I Tatti, Adv. Council 1993-present. **Fellowships, Honors & Awards:** Harvard Univ., Villa I Tatti Fellow 1980-81; NEH Fellowship 1980-81; Rockefeller Found., Bellagio Study Center Fellow 1981; Guggenheim Fellowship 1987-88; UNC, Pogue Faculty Fellowship 1988, Inst. for the Arts & Humanities 1993. **Publications:** "*Mercatores Florentini Romanam Curiam Sequentes* in the Early Sixteenth Century," *Journal of Medieval and Renaissance Studies* 6 (1976): 51-71; "Marriage Politics and the Family in Renaissance Florence: The Strozzi-Medici Alliance of 1508," *American Historical Review* 84.3 (June, 1979): 688-87; *Filippo Strozzi and the Medici: Favor and Finance in Sixteenth-Century Florence and Rome* (Cambridge & New York: Cambridge Univ. Press, 1980); "Grain Supply and Urban Unrest in Renaissance Rome: The Crisis of 1533-1534," *Rome in the Renaissance: The City and the Myth,* ed. P.A. Ramsey (Binghamton, NY: Center for Medieval and Early Renaissance Studies, 1983), 279-92; "Farming Spiritual Revenues: Innocent VIII's Appalto of 1486," *Renaissance Studies in Honor of Craig Hugh Smyth,* ed. Andrew Morrogh et al. (Florence: Giunti-Barbera, 1985), 2:238-51; "The Magnificent Lorenzo de' Medici: Between Myth and History," *Politics and Culture in Early Modern Europe: Essays in Honour of Helmut G. Koenigsberger,* ed. M. Jacob & P. Mack (Cambridge: Cambridge Univ. Press, 1987), 25-58; "The Inward Zodiac: A Development in Ficino's Thought on Astrology," *Renaissance Quarterly* 43.4 (1990): 687-708; "Marsilio Ficino and the Medici: the Inner Dimensions of Patronage," *Christianity and the Renaissance. Environments of Religious Imagination in the Quattrocento,* ed. Timothy Verdon & John Henderson (Syracuse, NY: Syracuse Univ. Press, 1990), 467-92; "Filippo Strozzi, il Giovane, l'uomo e le sue lettere," *Palazzo Strozzi Meta Millennio 1489-1989,* ed. Daniela Lamberini (Rome, 1991), 30-37; "Raising Capital and Funding the Pope's Debt," in *Renaissance Society and Culture: Essays in Honor of Eugene F. Rice, Jr.,* ed. J. Monfasani & R.G. Musto (New York: Italica Press, 1991), 23-32; "Middle Managers and Middlemen in Renaissance Banking," *Travail et les travailleurs a la fin de Moyen Age,* ed. C. Dolan (Quebec, 1991), 271-90; ed., *Lettere di Lorenzo de' Medici,* IX (Istituto Nazionale di Studi sul Rinascimento); "In Pursuit of *honore et utile:* Lorenzo de' Medici and Rome," *Lorenzo il Magnifico e il suo mondo,* ed. Giancarlo Garfagnini, (Florence, 1994); "Lorenzo de' Medici and Patterns of Diplomatic Discourse in the Late Fifteenth Century," in vol ed. by Nicholas Mann (London: Warburg Inst., forthcoming); "Lorenzo de' Medici: Anxiety, Image Making, and Political Reality in the Renaissance," *Lorenzo de' Medici Studi,* ed. Giancarlo Garfagnini (Florence), 1-40. **Home Address:** 510 North. St., Chapel Hill, NC 27514. **Business Address:** History Dept., Hamilton Hall, CB No. 3195, UNC, Chapel Hill, NC, 27599.

BULLITT, WILLIAM C. ■ AAR Visitor 1939-40, US Ambassador to France.

BUNKLEY, BRIT ■ FAAR Sculpture 86. b. Apr. 3, 1955, NYC. m. Andrea Gardner. c. Noah. BFA 77, Minneapolis College of Art & Design; MFA 84, Hunter College. **Other Study:** Macalester College, St. Paul, MN 1973-75. **Career & Employment:** Self-employed sculptor & commercial photographer; RISD in Rome, Visiting Artist 1986; Dorland Mountain Community, Temecula, CA, Artist-in-Residence 1987; Blue Mountain Center, NY, Artist-in-Residence 1989; Univ. of SW Louisiana, Lafayette, Visiting Artist 1989. **Fellowships, Honors & Awards:** NEA Fellowship 1980-81; Creative Artist's Program Service, Artist's Fellowship 1983; NYSCA Grant 1984-85. **Pub-**

lications: "Smyth Spirit," *Stroll Magazine* (Fall 1987). **Exhibitions/Performances:** Kathrine Nash Gallery, Minneapolis 1979; Ward's Island, NYC 1981, 1982; Central Park Gallery Annex, NYC 1982; Cadman Plaza, Brooklyn, NY 1982; Harborside Industrial Center, Brooklyn, NY 1983; City Gallery, NYC 1983; Islip Art Museum, East Islip, NY 1984; "Gate Mask," installed at Franklin & Center Streets Park, NYC 1984; Katz Gallery, NYC 1985; Newhouse Gallery, Snug Harbor, NY 1987; Metropolitan Museum and Art Center, Coral Gables, FL 1988; Kenneth Myers Park, Coconut Grove, FL 1988; Michael Lintas Worldwide, NYC 1989; 55 Mercer St. Gallery, NYC 1990; Robischon Gallery, Denver 1991; Denver Art Museum 1991; Minnesota History Center Comm., St. Paul 1992; L.I.R.R. train station, NYC MTA Comm., Bayshore, NY 1992; Shepherd Hall Comm., City College, CUNY 1995. **Bio-Bibliography:** Alan Wallach, "C.A.P.S. Sculptors," *Arts Magazine* (Dec. 1983); Michael Brenson, "Sculpture Goes Outdoors for the Summer," *New York Times* (July 13, 1984); Helen Harrison, "The Working of the Artist's Mind," *New York Times* (Sept. 23, 1984); "How a Work Comes into Being," *Newsday* (Oct. 8, 1984); Michael Brenson, "City as Sculpture Garden: Seeing the New and Daring," *New York Times* (July 17, 1987); Mary Ann Esquivel, , "Sculpture Competing for Display," *Miami Herald* (Feb. 11, 1988); "Proposals for Art in History Center," *Twin Cities Star-Tribune* (May 11, 1988); Public Art Fund, Inc., *Anniversary Edition Catalog, 1977-87*; "Making History Come Alive," *Minneapolis Star Tribune* (Apr. 19, 1992). **Home Address:** 201 Front St., Brooklyn, NY 11201.

BUOTTA, MARIO ■ AAR Visitor 1984-85, Architect.

BURCHFIELD, CHARLES E. ■ AAR Trustee 1952-55, Artist.

BURCK, RICHARD C. ■ FAAR Landscape Architecture 82. b. Jan. 7, 1952, Trenton, NJ. m. Alice E. Hecht. c. Samuel. BS 74, Michigan State Univ.; MLA 85, Harvard GSD. **Other Study:** Cranbrook Acad. of Art 1977-78. **Career & Employment:** Prote Krause Assc. 1974-77; Sasaki Asscs. 1978-81; Carol R. Johnson & Asscs. 1982-83; Richard Burck & Asscs., Prin. 1985-88; Burck Ryan Asscs. Inc., Prin. 1989-present. **Memberships & Offices:** ASLA, Nat. Assn. of Olmsted Parks, BoT, Reservations, Fort Point Channel Citizens Adv. Com. **Fellowships, Honors & Awards:** ASLA, Merit Award 1983; Presidential Award for Design Excellence 1988; Boston Soc. of Landscape Architects, Merit Award 1989; AIA Washington Chap., Award for Excellence 1993, Boston Chap. Urban Design Award 1994. **Publications:** *Olmsted Park Historic Landscape Report*, ed. Cynthia Ziatzevsky (Boston: Olmsted Historic Landscape Preservation Pgm., Dept. of Environmental Management, 1986); *Jamaica Pond and the Arborway*, ed. Cynthia Ziatzevsky (Boston: Olmsted Historic Landscape Preservation Pgm., Dept. of Environmental Management, 1987). **Important Works:** with Sasaki Asscs. Team, Pennsylvania Avenue Redesign, Washington, DC 1981; River Park Housing Development, Middletown, CT 1990; Chancellors Rock Farm Master Plan, VA 1991, Cabin Landscape 1992, Pool Complex 1993. **Exhibitions/Performances:** Vietnam Veteran's Memorial Competition, Washington, DC 1981; Harvard GSD 1985; Women's Rights Nat. Historic Park, Seneca Falls, NY 1987, & Competition Exhibitions 1988; Hermann Park Competition & Exb., Dallas 1992, 1993. **Home Address:** 3 Forest St., Lexington, MA 02173. **Business Address:** Burck Ryan Asscs., Inc., 125 Walnut St., Watertown, MA 02172.

BURDEN, WILLIAM ■ AAR Visitor 1951-55, MOMA, Pres.; Diplomat.

BURESH, TOM ■ NIAE, John Dinkeloo Traveling Fellow 1986-87.

BURGALETA, MARIA EUGENIA ■ FAAR Painting 75. b. Dec. 20, 1952, NYC. BFA 73, Cooper Union.

BURGESS, ANTHONY ■ AAR Visitor 1981-82, Writer.

BURKE, PAUL FREDERIC, JR ■ FAAR Classics/Archaeology 80. b. Feb. 11, 1944, Arlington, MA. m. Barbara Johnson. c. Sarah Burke. BA 65, Stanford Univ.; PhD 71, Stanford Univ. **Other Study:** Bowdoin College 1961-63; ICCS 1966. **Research/Artistic Interests:** Classical mythology & religion, art & archaeology, Judaism & Christianity in the ancient world, Homer. **Career & Employment:** McMaster Univ., Asst. Prof. 1971-75; VSA, Managing Dir., Classical Summer School in Campania & Rome 1974, 1977; Boston Univ., Visiting Asst. Prof. 1975-76; Inst. of Nautical Archaeology, Summer Field School 1976; Clark Univ., Asst. Prof. 1976-79, Assc. Prof. 1979-present, Chair, Dept. of Foreign Languages & Literatures 1981-83; Clark European Center in Luxembourg 1988, 1989, 1992. **Memberships & Offices:** APA 1971-present, Chair, Com. on Awards for Excellence in Teaching 1985; VSA, BoT 1977-83. **Fellowships, Honors & Awards:** Stanford Univ., Edwin J. Doyle Memorial Fellowship 1969-70; APA Award for Excellence in Teaching 1979; NEH Grants 1978, 1981, 1986, Fellowship 1979-80; Clark Univ.: Research Fund Stipend 1979, Grant from the Higgins School for the Humanities 1990, Grant from the Clark European Center in Luxembourg 1990, 1993. **Publications:** "The Role of Mezentius in the *Aeneid*," *Classical Journal* 69 (1974): 202-9; "Mezentius and the First-Fruits," *Vergilius* 20 (1974): 28-29; "Virgil's Amata," *Vergilius* 22 (1976): 24-29; "*Drances Infensus*: A Study in Vergilian Character Portrayal," *Transactions of the APS* 108 (1978): 15-20; "Roman Rites for the Dead and *Aeneid* 6," *Classical Journal* 74 (1979): 220-28; "Charisma and Ecclesiastical Authority in the Cult of the Saints," in *Mélanges for Professor Julien Ries*, ed. C.M. Ternes (Luxembourg: Grand Duchy of Luxembourg, 1993); ed. with C.M. Ternes, *Roman Religion in Gallia Belgica and the Germaniae* (Luxembourg, 1994); "Malaria in the Greco-Roman World," in *Aufstieg und Niedergang der Römischen Welt*, II, 37.3 (1995); "Hera," "Hermes," and "Ares," articles for the *Perseus Project CD-ROM*; author-photographer of "Classical Forms in the Homes of New England," filmstrip & tape cassette program distributed to secondary schools by Pompeiana, Inc. **Business Address:** Dept. of Foreign Languages, Clark Univ., Worcester, MA 01610.

BURNETT, ANNE PIPPIN ■ FAAR Classics/Archaeology 59. b. Oct. 10, 1925, Salt Lake City, UT. m. Virgil M. Burnett. c. Maud, Melissa. BA 46, Swarthmore College; MA 47, Columbia Univ.; PhD 53, UC, Berkeley. **Research/Artistic Interests:** Greek poetry, Greek tragedy, Greek religion. **Career & Employment:** Vassar College, Instr. 1957-58; Univ. of Chicago, Asst. Prof. 1961-66, Assc. Prof. 1967-69, Prof. 1970-92. **Memberships & Offices:** *Classical Philology*, Ed. Bd. 1961-92, Ed. 1970-71; Center for Hellenic Studies, Search Com. 1984-85, Senior Fellow 1986-91. **Fellowships, Honors & Awards:** AAUW Fellowship 1956-57; APS Grant 1960; ACLS Grant 1962, Fellowship 1968-69; Wesleyan Center for Humanities, Fellowship 1973; Guggenheim Fellowship 1981-82. **Publications:** "Helena," in *Euripides, Wege der Forschung* 89, ed. E.R. Schwinge (Darmstadt, 1968), 392-416; "Admetus" in *Euripides*, ed. E. Segal (Englewood Cliffs, NJ: Prentice-Hall, 1968), 51-89, rprnt. in *Oxford Readings in Greek Tragedy* (Oxford: Oxford Univ. Press, 1983); Euripides, *Ion* (Englewood Cliffs, NJ: Prentice-Hall, 1970); *Catastrophe*

Survived: Euripides' Plays of Mixed Reversal (Oxford: Clarendon Press, 1971); *Three Archaic Poets* (London: Duckworth & Cambridge, MA: Harvard 1983); *The Art of Bacchylides: Martin Classical Lectures* (Cambridge, MA: Harvard 1985); "The Scrutiny of Song: Pindar and Politics" *Critical Inquiry* 13 (1987): 434-49, rpt. in *Poetry and Politics* ed. R. von Hallberg (1988); "Early Greek Lyric: One Voice and Many," *Ars Lyrica* (1988): 13-28; "Jocasta in the West: The Lille Stesichorus," *Classical Antiquity* 7 (1988): 107-54; "Performing Pindar's Odes," *Classical Philology* 84 (1989): 283-93; "Signals from the Unconscious in Early Greek Poetry," *Classical Philology* 86 (1991); *Revenge in Attic and Later Tragedy: Sather Lectures* (Berkeley, CA & London: Univ. of California Press, forthcoming). **Home Address:** 51 Avon St., Stratford, ONT N5A 5N5, Canada. **Business Address:** Dept. of Classics, Univ. of Chicago, Chicago, IL 60637.

BURNHAM, CHAS LEROY PEARL ■ Rotch Scholar 1906.

BURNHAM, DANIEL HUDSON ■ AAR Co-founder & Charter Mem. Architect. b. Sept. 4, 1846. d. June 1, 1912. **Career & Employment:** Burnham & Root, Senior Mem. 1872-91; Chicago Exposition, Chief Architect 1890-93; D.H. Burnham & Co., Prin. 1891-1912. **Memberships & Offices:** AIA, Pres. 1894. **Important Works:** World's Columbia Exposition, Chicago; Flatiron Building, NYC; Union Station, Washington, DC. In 1917, Mr. Burnham's daughter gave the Academy $25,000 for the Daniel Burnham Fund in Architecture.

BUSH, PRESCOTT S. ■ AAR Visitor 1959-64, US Senator.

BUSH, VIRGINIA L. ■ FAAR History of Art 77; AAR Trustee 1984-88, Trustee Emer., SOF, Sec.-Tres. 1980-84, Pres. 1984-88. b. Mar. 2, 1938, Philadelphia PA. m. Paul Suttman, FAAR 68. BA 59, Wellesley College; MA 63, Columbia Univ.; PhD 67, Columbia Univ. **Other Study:** NYU, Graduate School of Business 1981-83. **Research/Artistic Interests:** Art history, particularly Italian Renaissance. **Career & Employment:** City College of CUNY, Instr. 1967-70; Rutgers Univ., Douglas College, Asst. Prof. 1970-77, Acting Chair 1974-76, Graduate Faculty of Arts & Sciences, Asst. Prof. 1971-77; Union College, Assc. Prof. 1977-80, Chair 1977-80; Estate of Paul Suttman, Executrix. **Fellowships, Honors & Awards:** Columbia Univ., Special Tuition Scholarship & New York State Scholar Incentive Award 1965-67; Rutgers Univ. Research Council Grants 1972-73, 1975-76, 1976-77; APS Research Grant 1976; Union College Humanities Faculty Development Grants 1978, 1979. **Publications:** *Colossal Sculpture of the Cinquecento* (New York: Garland Publishing, 1976); "Notes on the New Installation of Cinquecento Sculpture at the Bargello," *Burlington Magazine* 119 (May 1977): 367-71; "Leonardo da Vinci's Sforza Monument and Cinquecento Sculpture," *Arte Lombarda* 50 (1978): 47-68; "The Sources of Giotto's *Meeting at the Golden Gate* and the Meaning of the Dark-Veiled Woman," *Bollettino del Museo Civico di Padova* 61 (1978): 7-29; "Bandinelli's *Hercules and Cacus* and Florentine Traditions," in *Studies in the History of Art, Memoirs of the AAR* (Rome: AAR, 1980), 163-206; "Giovanni Bologna's *Mars*" ("The Stalwart Pose: An Alternative Convention in Renaissance Figure Style"), Recorded in 1979 for BBC Radio, Open Univ., Italian Art 1480-1580; "Exploring Art: Forms and Ideas in Western Art: A Five-Part Video (New York: Thomas S. Klise, 1992); "The Political Contexts of the Sforza Horse," in *Leonardo de Vinci's Sforza Monument Horse*, ed. Diane Cole Ahl (Lehigh, PA: Lehigh Univ. Press, 1995). **Home Address:** 3 Camps Flat Rd., S. Kent, CT 06785.

BUTLER, HOWARD CROSBY ■ FASCSR Classics/Archaeology 98. b. Mar. 7, 1872, Croton Falls, NY. d. Aug. 15, 1922. BA 1892, Princeton Univ.; MA 1893, Princeton Univ. **Research/Artistic Interests:** Archaeology. **Career & Employment:** Archaeological Expeditions, Sardis 1899-1900, 1904-5, 1909; Princeton Univ. Prof. 1905-22. **Memberships & Offices:** ArIA, Honorary Mem.; AAAL. **Fellowships, Honors & Awards:** Princeton Univ., Classical Studies Fellow 1893, 1897; Drexel Gold Medalist 1910. **Publications:** *Scotland's Ruined Abbeys* (New York: Century, 1900); *The Story of Athens* (New York: Century, 1902); *Architecture and the Arts* (New York: Century, 1903); *The Temple of Artemis, Sardis*, ed. W.H. Buckler & C.M. Reed, Publications of the American Soc. for the Excavation of Sardis 2 (Leiden: Brill, 1925); *Early Churches in Syria, Fourth to Seventh Centuries*, ed. E. Baldwin Smith (Princeton: Princeton Univ. Press, 1929). **Bio-Bibliography:** *Who Was Who in America*.

BUTLER, NICHOLAS MURRAY ■ AAR Charter Mem., AAR Trustee 1911-18, Educator, Philanthropist.

BYRD, DALE CLAUDE ■ FAAR Architecture 51. b. Dec. 20, 1920, Anadarko, OK. BS 44, Univ. of Oklahoma; MArch 45, Harvard Univ. **Research/Artistic Interests:** Romanesque & Gothic architecture. **Career & Employment:** Ketchum, Gina, & Sharp, Architects 1944-45; Marcel Breuer Architect 1945-46; Skidmore, Owings, & Merrill, Architects 1946-47, 1948-50; Private Practice, El Reno, OK 1950-70s. **Fellowships, Honors & Awards:** Rotch Travelling Scholarship 1947-48.

■ ■ ■

C

CADWALADER, JOHN L. ■ AAR Charter Mem.; Lawyer; US State Dept., Asst. Sec.

CAGE, JOHN ■ AAR Visitor 1943 — 1951. Composer. b. Sept. 5, 1912. d. Aug. 12, 1992. **Career & Employment:** Merce Cunningham & Dance Co., Musical Dir. 1944-66. **Important Works:** *The Seasons* 1947; *Suite for Toy Piano* 1960; *Renga with Apartment House 1776* for orchestra, four quartets & eight soloists 1989; *101* 1989.

CAIN, WALKER OSCAR ■ FAAR Architecture 48; AAR World War II Prize 1941; AAR Trustee 1952-84, Chair, BoT 1974-81; SOF, Sec. 1950-51. b. Apr. 14, 1915, Cleveland, OH. d. June 1, 1993. m. Abby Cain. c. Susan Berry. Diplome 37, École des Beaux Arts, Fontainbleau; BArch 38, Western Reserve Univ.; MFA 40, Princeton Univ. **Career & Employment:** McKim, Mead & White, Asscs.; Steinmann & Cain, Architects, Part. 1961-67; Cain, Farrell & Bell, Architects 1967-80. **Memberships & Offices:** Beaux-Arts Inst. of Design, Education Com. 1949-51, BoT 1951, Com. on Scholarships, Chair 1951; AIA, NY Chap. Com. of Awards 1951; ALNY, Exec. Com. & House Com. 1951; Taconic State Park Comm., NY; East Hudson Parkway Authority; American Arbitration Assn.; Garrison's Landing Assn., BoD, Hon. Chair. **Fellowships, Honors & Awards:** AIA Book Award 1938; Emerson Prize, 1st Medal 1938; Cleveland Museum of Art, Charles Schweinfurth Scholar; Princeton Univ., Palmer Fellowship 1938-40; Robert Perry Rogers Prize 1939; Union College, Hon. Degree. **Important Works:** Union College, Science Center & other buildings; Princeton Univ., various buildings, including Jadwin Gym & Field House; Bowdoin College, Library;

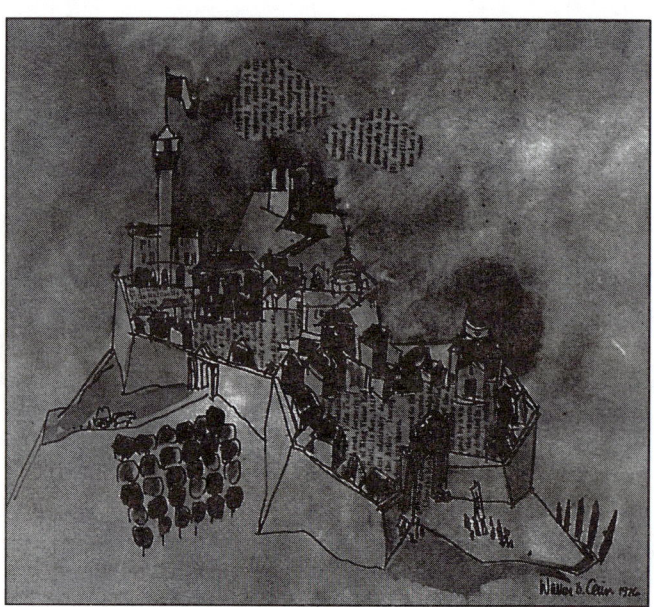

Walker Oscar Cain

American Univ. in Beirut, Lebanon, Library; St. Vartan Armenian Cathedral, NYC; Schenectady Museum; ME State Cultural Bldg., Augusta; Museum of History & Technology, Smithsonian Inst.; Woods Hole Oceanographic Inst.; Lawrenceville School, Dining Facility; Vassar College, Dining Facility. **Bio-Bibliography:** *Directory of American Architects.*

CALDWELL, JOSEPH K. ■ FAAR Literature 80. b. Oct. 2, 1928, Milwaukee, WI. **Studies:** Marquette Univ., Columbia Univ., Yale School of Drama. **Fellowships, Honors & Awards:** Arts of the Theatre Found. Award; Yale Univ., John Golden Fellowship 1956-58, American Broadcasting Company Fellowship 1965-66. **Publications:** *In Such Dark Places* (New York: Farrar, Straus & Giroux, 1978); *The Deer at the River* (Boston: Little, Brown & Co., 1984); Plays: *The Cockeyed Kite; The Downtown Holyland; Jack Fallon, Fare Thee Well.*

CALIFANO, JOSEPH A., JR ■ AAR Visitor 1980-81, Statesman, US Health, Education & Welfare Dept., Sec.

CALIN, MARIUS MIHAIL ■ NIAE, John Dinkeloo Traveling Fellow 1991-92.

CALISHER, HORTENSE ■ AAR Visitor 1951 — 1955, Writer.

CALLAHAN, JOHN F. ■ AAR Visitor. b. May 13, 1912, Chicago, IL. BA 33, Loyola Univ.; MA 34, Loyola Univ.; PhD 40, Univ. of Chicago. **Research/Artistic Interests:** Classsical philology, ancient philosophy. **Career & Employment:** Univ. of Chicago, TF 1936-37; Loyola Univ., Chicago, Instr. 1937-40; Harvard Univ., Visiting Instr. 1940-41; Loyola Univ., Chicago, Asst. Prof. 1941-43; US Navy 1943-46; Georgetown Univ., Assc. Prof., Prof., Prof. Emer. 1946-present; Harvard Univ., Dumbarton Oaks, Project Dir. 1977-86. **Home Address:** 3 Pooks Hill Rd., Bethesda, MD 20814.

CALVESI, MAURIZIO ■ Italian Fulbright Fellow 1964-65.

CALVINO, ITALO ■ AAR Visitor 1981-82, Writer.

CAMDEN, HARRY POOLE ■ FAAR Sculpture 27. b. Mar. 10, 1900, Parkersburg, WV. d. July 29, 1943. m. Helen Trefts. c. Susan, John, Juliette. BFA 24, Yale Univ. **Other Studies:** Carnegie Inst. of Technology. **Career & Employment:** Univ. of Oregon, Prof. 1927-29; Cornell Univ., Prof. 1929-37; US Air Force, Capt. 1941-43. **Memberships & Offices:** Nat. Sculpture Soc., VP; Iroquis Assn. Art Schools, Western NY. **Fellowships, Honors & Awards:** $10,000 Prize for "Government", a statue of a female figure adorning the facade of the Federal Bldg., NY. **Important Works:** Memorials at Cornell Univ.; Leaburg Power Plant, Eugene, OR; Statues at Federal Bldg., NYC; World's Fair, NY 1939; US Post Office, Clarks Summit, PA. **Bio-Bibliography:** *Who Was Who in American Art.*

CAMP, DONALD ■ Philadelphia Regional Visiting Artist 1994.

CAMPANA, AUGUSTO ■ Italian Fulbright Fellow 1955-56.

CAMPBELL, MALCOLM ■ AAR Visitor 1989-90, Scholar.

CAMPBELL, ROBERT ■ AAR Visitor 1992-93, Critic.

CAMPUS, LUCREZIA ■ Italian Fulbright Fellow 1977-78.

CANFIELD, CASS ■ AAR Visitor 1959 — 1964, Publisher.

CANIER, CAREN R. ■ FAAR Painting 78. b. Mar. 25, 1953, NYC. m. Langdon C. Quin. c. Dino, Adrian. BFA 74, Cornell Univ.; MFA 76, Boston Univ. **Research/Artistic Interests:** Painting. **Career & Employment:** Rensselaer Polytechnic, Assc. Prof. 1978-present. **Fellowships, Honors & Awards:** Artists for En-

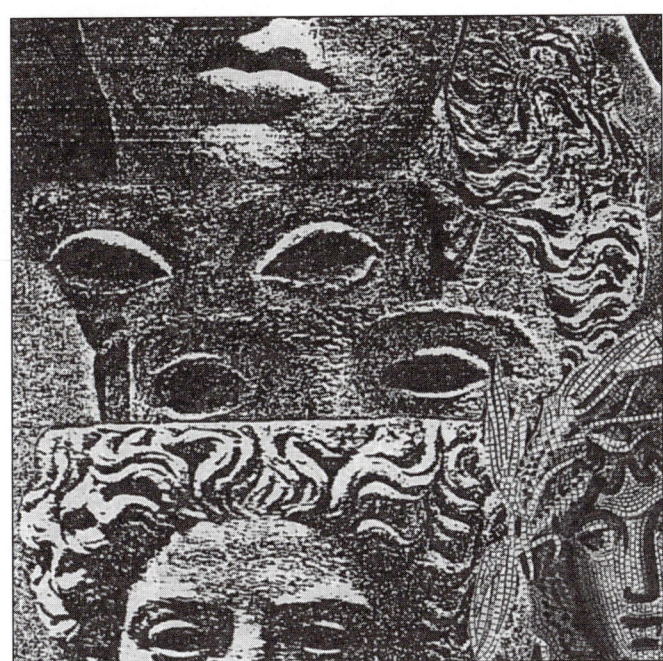
Caren R. Canier

vironment Found., Delaware Watergap, Artist-in-Residence 1977; Mohawk-Hudson Regional Exb., 1st Prize 1979; New York State CAPS Grant 1980; New York Found. for the Arts Fellowship 1985, 1990; Ingram Merrill Found. Grant 1986; Rensselaer Polytechnic Inst., Beer Trust Minigrant 1989; Pollock-Krasner Found. Grant 1990. **Important Works:** Collections: Chemical Bank, NYC; SUNY, Albany; Glenn Janss Collection, Sun Valley, ID; Texas Commerce Bankshares; Amerada-Hess, TX; Herbert F. Johnson Museum of Art, Ithaca, NY; Union Bank, Pacific Bell, AT&T, Chicago. **Exhibitions/Performances:** Solo: Rensselaer Polytechnic Inst., School of Architecture 1979; Albany Acad., Albany, NY 1984; Robert Schoelkopf Gallery, NYC 1985, 1991. **Bio-Bibliography:** Jeanne Mackin, "Caren Canier: Recreating the Familiar," *American Artist* 48.507 (Oct. 1984): 53-59; Ken Johnson, "Caren Canier," *Arts Magazine* 59.8 (Apr. 1985): 2; Lawrence Campbell, "Caren Canier at Schoelkopf," *Art in America* 73.7 (July 1985): 137-38; *In Praise of Women Artists* (Bo-Tree Publications, 1988); "Back Cover" *Menniger Perspectives* 19.2 (1988): 32; Sharon Gill & Cathy Kimball, "An American in Rome," *New Jersey Center for Visual Arts* (1994): 3-5. **Home Address:** 468 McChesney Ave. Ext., Troy, NY 12180.

CAPECHI, GABRIELLA ■ Italian Fulbright Fellow 1972-73.

CAPONEGRO, MARY ■ FAAR Literature 92. b. Nov. 11, 1956, Brooklyn, NY. BA 78, Bard College; MA 83, Brown Univ. **Career & Employment:** Brown Univ., Adj. Instr. 1983-86; RISD, Instr. 1987-89; Hobart & William Smith College, Asst. Prof. 1989-present. **Fellowships, Honors & Awards:** Bard College, Milton Moore Lockwood Prize 1978; Brown Univ., Peter Kaplan Memorial Fellowship 1981; Rhode Island Fellowship in Literature 1987; Pushcart Prize, Special Mention 1988-89; General Electric Found. Award for Younger Writers 1988. **Publications:** *Addressing the Negative* (New York: Text Magazine, 1981); *Tales from the Next Village* (Providence: Lost Roads, 1985); *The Star Cafe* (New York: Scribner's, 1990; paper ed. New York: Norton, 1991); *The Change* (Kaldewey Press, 1992); stories in *Sulfur* 1; *Mississippi Review* 34-35; *Brown Journal of the Arts* (1984), *Conjunctions* 7, 10, 14, 17, 21; *Tyuonyi* 1, 4; *Notiz* (1988); *Fiction In-*

ternational (1987-88). **Home Address:** 64 Cortland St., Geneva, NY 14456. **Business Address:** Georges Borchardt Literary Agency, NYC.

CAPONERA, CIRO ■ AAR – Rome, Grounds Staff.

CAPPEL, CARMEN BAMBACH ■ FAAR History of Art 94. b. Nov. 3, 1959, Santiago, Chile. m. Steven Trent Cappel. BA 81, Yale Univ.; MA 83, Yale Univ.; PhD 88, Yale Univ. **Research/Artistic Interests:** Italian art & architecture, 1300-1600, especially workshop practice & design theory. **Career & Employment:** Fordham Univ., Asst. Prof. 1989-95; MMA 1995-present. **Memberships & Offices:** CAA 1984-present; Drawing Soc. 1989-present; RSA 1990-present; SAH 1992-present. **Fellowships, Honors & Awards:** Yale Univ., Mark Deitz Memorial Prize 1981, Alumni & Univ. Fellowships 1983-87, Council of Western European Studies Grant 1984, Kress Fellowship 1985-86; NEH Grant 1985, 1989; MMA, Andrew Mellon Fellowship 1990-91; APS Grant 1992; Fordham Univ., Faculty Fellowship 1992, Faculty Research Grant 1993. **Publications:** "Connecticut's Historic Theaters," *Connecticut Preservation News* (Autumn 1983): 1-8; "A Note on Michelangelo's Cartoon for the Sistine Ceiling: Haman," *Art Bulletin* 65 (Dec. 1983): 661-65; "Michelangelo's Cartoon for the Crucifixion of St. Peter Reconsidered," *Master Drawings* 25 (Summer 1987): 131-42; "Francesco Solimena," & entries on paintings by Giordano, Solimena, & De Matteis, in *A Taste for Angels: Neapolitan Painting in North America, 1650-1750*, ed. George Hersey & Judith Colton, exb. cat. (New Haven: Yale Univ. Art Gallery, 1987), 147-50, 153-56, 163-83, 185-93, 197-202, 207-10, 237-42; "The Uffizi's Sixteenth-Century Drawings in Detroit and Some Tuscan Drawings in Philadelphia," *Master Drawings* 28 (Summer 1990): 197-221; "Pounced Drawings in the Codex Atlanticus," *Achademia Leonardi-Vinci: Journal of Leonardo Studies and Bibliography of Vinciana* 3 (1990): 129-31; "Leonardo, Tagliente, and Dürer: 'la scienza del far di groppi'," *Achademia Leonardi-Vinci: Journal of Leonardo Studies and Bibliography of Vinciana* 4 (1991): 72-98; "Foreshortened Letters," *Achademia Leonardi-Vinci: Journal of Leonardo Studies and Bibliography of Vinciana* 4 (1991): 99-106; with Lucy Whitaker, "Lost Designs of Knots and Interlaces," *Achademia Leonardi-Vinci: Journal of Leonardo Studies and Bibliography of Vinciana* 4 (1991): 107-10; "A Substitute Cartoon for Raphael's Disputa," *Master Drawings* 30 (Spring 1992): 9-30; "Piero della Francesca, the Study of Perspective, and the Development of the Cartoon in the Quattrocento," *Atti del Congresso Internazionale di Studi su Piero della Francesca*, ed. Marisa Dalai Emiliani (Florence: Marsilio Editore, 1994), 87-102; "On 'la testa proporzionalmente degradata': Luca Signorelli, Leonardo, and Piero della Francesca's *De Prospectiva Pingendi*," in *Disegno: Drawing at the Time of Lorenzo il Magnifico*, Villa Spelman Colloquium Series 4, ed. Elizabeth Cropper (Bologna: Nuova Alfa Editoriale, 1994), 17-43; "Problemi di tecnica nei cartoni di Michelangelo per la Cappella Sistina," *Atti del Convegno Internazionale di Studi Michelangelo: La Cappella Sistina*, ed. Kathleen Weil-Garris Brandt (Rome: Agostini, 1994), 96-115; English ed., "Problems of Technique in Michelangelo's Cartoons for the Sistine Chapel," (Harvey Miller Publishers, forthcoming); "Pouncing" & "Modello," *The Dictionary of Art*; *The Cartoons of the Italian Renaissance Artists: Workshop Practice and Design Theory, 1300-1600* (New York: Cambridge Univ. Press, 1995). **Home Address:** 215 W. 95 St., Apt. 11-F, NYC 10025-6356. **Business Address:** Dept. of Prints & Drawings, MMA.

CARANDINI, ANDREA ■ Italian Fulbright Fellow 1964-65, Archaeologist.

CARBONI, MARIO ■ AAR – Rome, Housekeeping Staff.

CARDOZA, ANTHONY L. ■ FAAR Post-Classical/Humanistic Studies 77. m. Catherine M. Mardikes. c. Michael. BA 69, UC, Davis; MA 72, Princeton Univ.; PhD 75, Princeton Univ. **Career & Employment:** Princeton Univ., Instr. 1974-76; Loyola Univ., Asst. Prof. 1977-83, Assc. Prof. 1983-93, Prof. 1993-present. **Fellowships, Honors & Awards:** Princeton Univ. Fellowship 1970-74; Soc. of Italian Historical Studies, Best Unpublished Manuscript Award 1975, Howard R. Marraro Prize 1983; *Choice*, Outstanding Academic Publication 1983; Loyola Univ., Summer Research Grant 1984, Travel Grant 1984, 1987, 1988, 1989, Summer Stipend 1992; Columbia Univ., Seminar on Italian History, Assc. Fellow 1985-present. **Publications:** "Agrarians and Industrialists: The Evolution of an Alliance in the Po Delta, 1896-1914," in *Gramsci and Italy's Passive Revolution: Essays on the Origins of Fascism in Italy,* ed. John Davis (Croom Helm, 1979), 172-213; articles on "Fasci di Combattimento," "Squadristi," "Ras," & "The March on Rome," in *An Historical Dictionary of Fascist Italy* (Westport, CT: Greenwood Press, 1982); *Agrarian Elites and Italian Fascism: The Province of Bologna 1901-1926* (Princeton: Princeton Univ. Press, 1983); "The Enduring Appeal of Aristocracy: Ennoblement in Liberal Italy (1861-1914)," in *Les noblesses européenes au XIX siècle* (Rome: École française de Rome, 1988), 595-605; "An Officer and a Gentleman: The Piedmontese Nobility and Military in Liberal Italy," in *Esercito e città dall'Unità agli anni trenta,* Deputazione di Storia Patria per l'Umbria (Perugia: Panetto & Petrelli, 1989), 1:185-200; "The Piedmontese Nobility: 1815-1915," *Bollettino di informazione del gruppo di studio sulla Borghesie del XIX secolo* 7 (July 1989): 2-3; "Tra casta e classe, clubs maschili dell'elite torinese, 1840-1914," *Quaderni Storici* 26.2 (Aug. 1991): 357-82; "Landownership and the Crisis of Agrarian Power: Bologna, 1901-1930," in *Landownership and Power in Modern Europe,* ed. Martin Blinkhorn & Ralph Gibson (San Francisco: Harper-Collins, 1991), 181-99; "L'Associazione Agraria Subalpina e rapporti tra nobiltà e borghesia in Piemonte preunitario," in *Fra studio, politica ed economia: La Società agraria dalle origini all'età Giolittiana,* ed. Roberto Finzi (Bologna, 1992), 215-31; "The Long Goodbye: The Landed Aristocracy in Northwestern Italy, 1880-1930," *European History Quarterly* 23.3 (July 1993): 323-59; "Le aristocrazie agrarie piemontesi: I modelli di riproduzione," in *Annali dell'Istituto Giangiacomo Feltrinelli,* ed. P. D'Attorre & A. De Bernardi (Milan: Feltrinelli, 1994), 65-87; "Il circolo del Whist" in *Storia illustrata di Torino,* vol. 10, ed. Valerio Castronovo (Turin, 1995); "Elites of Wealth in Nineteenth-Century Turin (1862-1912)," in *Storia e Società* (forthcoming). **Business Address:** Dept. of History, Loyola Univ., 6525 N. Sheridan Rd., Chicago, IL 60626.

CAREY, FRED M. ■ Sheldon Fellow 1923-24, AAR Classical Soc., Pres. 1943.

CARISSIMI, RENZO ■ AAR – Rome, Gate Reception.

CARL, PETER WILLIAM ■ FAAR Architecture 75. b. Feb. 4, 1946, Plainfield, NJ. m. Elsa Carl. c. Emily Carl. BA 68, Princeton Univ.; MArch 74, Princeton Univ. **Career & Employment:** Princeton Univ., TA 1971-74; Robert Geddes Architect 1971; Michael Graves Architect 1972, 1973.

CARLHIAN, JEAN PAUL ■ RAAR Architecture 75. b. Nov. 7, 1919, Paris, France. m. Elizabeth M. Carlhian. c. Penelope, Isabelle, Judith, Sophie. BL 36, Univ. of Paris; M. City Planning 47, Harvard GSD; Architecte Diplomé par le Gouvernement 48, École Nationale Superieure des Beaux Arts, Paris. **Research/Artistic Interests:** The influence of the teaching of the École des Beaux Arts upon American architects & architecture, 1886-1936. **Career & Employment:** Harvard GSD, Instr., Asst. Prof. 1948-55; Harrison & Abramovitz Architects, Designer 1949; Coolidge Shepley Bulfinch & Abbott Designer 1949-52; Yale Univ. School of Architecture, Visiting Critic 1958-61; Shepley Bulfinch Richardson & Abbott, Designer 1952-58, Assc. 1958-62, Part. 1963-72, VP-Prin. 1972-89, Consulting Prin. 1990-present. **Memberships & Offices:** Royal Comm. on Teaching Architecture in the Province of Quebec 1963-64; Boston Landmarks Comm. 1969-76; Boston, Back Bay Architectural Comm. 1966-79; AIA Com. on Design, Chair 1969, Inst. Honors Jury Chair 1976, Honorary Members Jury Chair 1989; Royal Soc. of the Arts, London 1980; Academie d'Architecture, Paris 1981; NAD, Assc. Mem. 1981; French-American Com. for the Restoration of the Statue of Liberty 1983-85. **Fellowships, Honors & Awards:** Harvard GSD, Wheelwright Fellow 1947; AIA: Fellow 1973, Firm Award 1973, New England Regional Council Honor Award 1976, Nat. Honor Award 1977, Design Project Fellowship 1978-79, Edward C. Kemper Award 1989; NEA Design Fellow 1976-77; Chevalier de l'Ordre des Arts et des Lettres 1990; US General Services Administration Design Honor Award 1990. **Publications:** "Charles Garnier," in *Encyclopedia Britannica*; "Charles Allerton Coolidge," in *Dictionary of American Biography;* articles in professional magazines. **Important Works:** Harvard Univ.: Quincy House 1958, Leverett House 1960, Baker Hall & McCollum Center 1968, Mather House 1970; Middlebury College, Christian A. Johnson Music & Arts Center 1968; Brown Univ., Grad. Center 1969, Bio-Medical Center 1970; Vassar College Center 1977; Museum of Our Natural Heritage 1976; Univ. of Vermont, Billings Center; Smithsonian Inst.: Quadrangle, Nat. Museum of African Art, Sackler Museum, S. Dillon Ripley Center 1987; General Electric Co., Management Development Inst. 1987; Cornell Univ., Law School Addition 1989; Andover Companies, Office HQ 1989; Smith College, Anne T. & Robert M. Bass Hall 1991. **Bio-Bibliography:** *Who's Who in America.* **Home Address:** 219 Heath's Bridge Rd., Concord, MA 01742. **Business Address:** Shepley Bulfinch Richardson & Abbott, 40 Broad St., Boston, MA 02109.

CARLTON, NEWCOMB ■ AAR Trustee 1929-38, Corp. Exec.

CARNEGIE, ANDREW ■ AAR Charter Mem., Philanthropist. b. Nov. 25, 1835. d. Aug. 11, 1919. **Career & Employment:** Carnegie Steel Co., Principal Owner. Gave libraries to cities & towns across America; was a financial supporter of the Academy during its early years.

CARONE, NICHOLAS ■ AAR World War II Prize 1941.

CARPENTER, KENNETH EARL ■ FAAR Architecture 15. b. January 13, 1884, Attleboro, MA. dec. RISD, MIT. **Research/Artistic Interests:** Vatican courtyards, temple of Mars Ultor, Rome, interior study of Piccolomini library, Siena. **Career & Employment:** Peabody & Stearns; Codman & Despradelle, Boston; Stone, Carpenter & Willson, Providence. **Fellowships, Honors & Awards:** MIT, Rotch Prize 1909; RISD, AIA Prize.

CARPENTER, RHYS ■ AAR School of Classical Studies, Prof.-in-Charge 1939-40.

CARR, STEPHEN M. ■ RAAR Design Arts 75. b. July 16, 1935, Portland, OR. m. Louise J. Elving. c. James, Julia. BArch

59, Stanford Univ.; MArch 61, MIT. **Other Study:** MIT, postgraduate studies in City Planning & Urban Design 1961-62, 1963-64. **Research/Artistic Interests:** Historic, photographic & plan documentation of major public spaces in central Rome. Analysis of daily & weekly variations in contemporary use of these spaces. Image study of central Rome with three generations of Romans living in center, 19th-century suburbs & periphery. Continuing research interests in perception, use & social significance of public space, often in collaboration with environmental psychologists & other social scientists. Interest in democratic design processes leading to participatory work with various social groups & in various contexts from neighborhood planning to central-city urban design. Current interest in influence of environmental movement on public perceptions of cities & on environmental design. Now undertaking two-volume work on theory of democratic environmental design: the process & the product. **Career & Employment:** John R. Myer, Project Architect 1960-62; Ashley-Myer-Smith, Project Architect & Assc. 1965-69; Arrowstreet, Prin. 1969-77; Carr, Lynch Asscs., Pres. 1977-86; Carr, Lynch, Hack & Sandell, Inc., Pres. 1986-present. **Memberships & Offices:** US Presidential Design Awards, Juror 1984; Massachusetts Governor's Design Awards, Juror 1987. **Fellowships, Honors & Awards:** Fulbright Fellow 1962-63; US Dept. of Housing & Urban Development Design Award 1970; Intl. Competition of Making the City More Meaningful, Milan, Italy, 1st Prize 1972; Graham Found. Grant 1976; Guggenheim Fellowship 1974-75; Florida Planners Assc., 1st Award 1985; NEA Grant 1985; Massachusetts Governor's Design Award 1987; Boston Soc. of Architects, Award for Excellence in Urban Design 1988; AIA, Citation for Excellence in Urban Design 1990; Open Intl. Idea Competition, 1st Prize 1991. **Publications:** "The City of the Mind," in *Environment for Man*, ed. William R. Ewald, Jr. (Bloomington: Indiana Univ. Press, 1967, rpt. Germany, Italy, Japan & Cuba); with Kevin Lynch, "Where Learning Happens," *Daedalus* 97 (Fall 1968); with Dale Schessler, "The City as a Trip," *Environment & Behavior* 1 (Fall 1969); *City Signs and Lights* (Cambridge, MA: MIT Press, 1972); with Curt Lamb & others at Arrowstreet, "Another Side of Architecture," *Progressive Architecture* (Dec. 1976); with Stephen Tilly, "Streets for People," *Progressive Architecture* (Dec. 1976); with Kevin Lynch, *Open Space, Freedom and Control* (New York: Cooper Hewitt Museum, 1979); *Public Space* (New York & Cambridge: Cambridge Univ. Press, 1992). **Important Works:** Public Spaces: Church St. Marketplace Pedestrian Mall, Burlington, VT 1980-82; Lowell Heritage State Park Entrance Plazas, Lowell, MA 1981-84; Hudson River Park & North Esplanade, Battery Park City, NYC 1987-92; Large-Scale Urban Landscapes: Rio Salado Plan, Salt River, Phoenix, Tempe & Mesa, AZ 1982-83; Tennessee Riverpark Plan for 20 Miles of Tennessee River, Chattanooga 1984-87; Hudson River Esplanade Park, NYC 1987-90; New Charles River Basin: Urban Design & Park System, Boston 1991-present; Perth, Australia, Central Waterfront 1991-present; Urban Designs-Plans: Signs-Lights-Boston, a National Policy Study, Boston 1962; Boston Waterfront Renewal Plan 1962; Arts District Plan, Dallas 1977; Detroit Near East Riverfront Development Plan 1982; Downtown Urban Design Plan, St. Petersburg, FL 1983-84; Downtown Roanoke, VA "Design '85" Plan 1985-86; Prudential Center Redevelopment Plan, Boston 1987-90. **Exhibitions/Performances:** Demonstration Information Center; Boston 1968-70. **Home Address:** 36 Cottage St., Cambridge, MA 02139. **Business Address:** Carr, Lynch, Hack & Sandell, Inc., 1385 Cambridge St., Cambridge, MA 02139.

CARRÉRE, JOHN M. ■ AAR Trustee 1911-12, Architect.

CARRION, ANIBAL ■ AAR – New York, Finance Asst.

CARROLL, EUGENE A. ■ FAAR History of Art 61. b. June 17, 1930, St. Louis, MO. BA 52, Harris Teachers College, St. Louis; MA 58, Harvard Univ.; PhD 64, Harvard Univ. **Career & Employment:** St. Louis Public Schools, Teacher 1952-53; Washington Univ., St. Louis, Grad. Asst. 1953-54; Wellesley College, Instr. 1961-64; Williams College, Visiting Asst. Prof. 1964-65; Vassar College, Asst. Prof. 1965-68, Assc. Prof. 1968-74, Prof. 1974-present, Chair 1980-83. **Fellowships, Honors & Awards:** Fulbright Scholarship 1954-55; Harvard Univ., Bacon Scholarship 1955-57; Lehman Scholarship 1957-58; Sheldon Fellowship 1958-59; Fulbright Travel Grant 1968-69; Vassar College Felowship 1968-69; IAS 1983. **Publications:** "Some Drawings by Rosso Fiorentino," *Burlington Magazine* 103 (1961): 446-54; "Drawings by Rosso Fiorentino in the British Museum," *Burlington Magazine* 108 (1966): 168-80; "Lappoli, Alfani, Vasari, and Rosso Fiorentino," *Art Bulletin* 49 (1967): 297-304; "Some Drawings by Salviati Formerly Attributed to Rosso Fiorentino," *Master Drawings* 9.1 (1971): 15-37; "Fontainebleau: Fruit of a Royal Commitment," *Art News* 72.5 (May, 1973): 72-75; "Rosso in France," *Actes du Colloque Internationale sur l'Art de Fontainebleau* (Paris, 1975), 17-28; *The Drawings of Rosso Fiorentino* (New York: Garland, 1976); "A Drawing by Rosso Fiorentino of Judith and Holofernes," *Los Angeles County Museum Art Bulletin* 24 (1978): 24-49; *Rosso Fiorentino: Drawings, Prints and Decorative Arts* (Washington, DC: NGA, 1987); *The Print Images of Rosso Fiorentino* (Los Angeles: Grunwald Center for Graphic Arts, UCLA, 1989). **Business Address:** Vassar College, PO Box 307, Poughkeepsie, NY 12601.

CARROZZA, VINCENT A. ■ AAR Trustee 1983-88, Real Estate.

CARSON, JO ANNE ■ FAAR Painting 83. b. 1953, NYC. BA 76, Univ. of Illinois, Chicago; MFA 79, Univ. of Chicago. **Career & Employment:** SUNY, Albany, Assc. Prof. 1985-present; Temple Univ., Tyler School of Art, Rome, Visiting Asst. Prof. 1988; visiting artist & critic, various schools 1981-93. **Fellowships, Honors & Awards:** NEA Fellowship 1982; Illinois Arts Council Individual Artists' Fellowship 1983; Awards in the Visual Arts (4) 1985. **Important Works:** Fort Worth Art Museum, TX; Joslyn Art Museum, Omaha, NE; Museum of Contemporary Art, Chicago; Frederick Weisman, Los Angeles. **Exhibitions/Performances:** Solo: Moming Gallery, Chicago 1981; Nancy Lurie Gallery, Chicago 1981; N.A.M.E. Gallery, Chicago 1982; Fort Worth Art Museum, TX 1982; Museum of Contemporary Art, Chicago 1985; Dart Gallery, Chicago, 1986; Ruth Siegel Gallery, NYC 1987, 1990; Eve Mannes Gallery, Atlanta 1988; Sylvia Schmidt Gallery, New Orleans 1992, 1994. **Home Address:** 131 Chrystie St., NYC 10002.

CARTER, EDWARD C., II ■ AAR Visitor 1978. b. Jan. 10, 1928 Rochester, NY. m. Louise D. Carter. BA 54, Univ. of Pennsylvania; MA 56, Univ. of Pennsylvania; PhD 62, Bryn Mawr College. **Career & Employment:** Univ. of Pennsylvania, Phillips Acad., & Univ. of Delaware, Instr. 1958-1964; St. Stephen's School, Rome, History Dept., Chair 1965-69; Catholic Univ. of America, Assc. Prof. 1969-77, Prof. 1977-80; Johns Hopkins Univ., Dept. of History, Fellow 1969-81, Visiting Prof. 1980-81; *The Papers of Benjamin Henry Latrobe*, Ed.-in-Chief 1970-present; APS, Librarian 1980-present; Univ. of Pennsylvania, Adj. Prof. of History & the History & Sociology of Science 1980-present. **Home Address:** 15 S. Valley Forge Rd., Wayne, PA 19087. **Business Address:** APS, 105 S. Fifth St., Philadelphia, PA 19106.

CARTER, ELLIOTT ■ FAAR Musical Composition 53, RAAR Musical Composition 68, AAR Trustee 1968-84, Trustee Emer. 1984-present, AAR Medal of Honor 1990. b. Dec. 11, 1908, NYC. m. Helen Front-Jones. BA 30, Harvard College; MA 32, Harvard Univ.; DrMus 35, École Normale, Paris. **Other Study:** Paris, with Gustav Holst, Nadia Boulanger 1932-35. **Career & Employment:** George Ballanchine Ballet Caravan, Music Dir. 1937-39; St. John's College, Annapolis, Prof. of Greek & Maths 1940-42; Columbia Univ., Prof. of Music 1948-50; Yale Univ., Prof. of Music 1960-61; Juilliard School of Music, Prof. 1965-88. **Fellowships, Honors & Awards:** NIAL 1956; New York Critics' Circle Award 1960, 1961; Pulitzer Prize 1960, 1971; UNESCO 1st Prize 1960; Sibelius Medal, Harriet Cohen Found., London 1961; AAAS 1962; Princeton Univ., DrMus 1967; City of Florence, Premio delle Muse 1969; Harvard Univ., DrMus 1970; Yale Univ., DrMus 1970; NIAL Gold Medal for Music 1971; AAAL 1971, Akad. der Kunste, Berlin 1971; Handel Medallion, NYC 1978; City of Los Angeles, Elliott Carter Day, 27 Apr. 1979; Ernst Von Siemens Prize, Munich 1981; MusD Cantab. 1983; MacDowell Colony, Gold Medal 1983; Nat. Medal of Arts, USA 1985; French Government, Commandeur dans l'Ordre des Arts et des Lettres 1987; Accademia di Santa Cecilia 1989; Govt. of Italy, Order of Merit, Commendatore 1991. **Publications:** *The Writings of Elliott Carter* (Bloomington: Univ. of Indiana Press, 1977). **Important Works:** *Pocahontas*, a ballet 1939; *First Symphony* 1942-43; *Holiday Overture* 1944; *Piano Sonata* 1946; *The Minotaur*, a ballet 1946-47; *Sonata for Cello & Piano* 1948; *Eight Etudes & A Fantasy*, for woodwind quartet 1949; *First String Quartet* 1950-51; *Sonata for Flute Oboe, Cello & Harpsichord* 1952; *Variations for Orchestra* 1953; *Second String Quartet* 1960; *Double Concerto for Harpsichord & Piano* 1961; *Piano Concerto* 1967; *Concerto for Orchestra* 1970; *Third String Quartet* 1971; *Duo for Violin & Piano* 1973-74; *Brass Quintet* 1974; *A Mirror on which to Dwell*, song cycle 1976; *A Symphony of Three Orchestras* 1977; *Syringa* 1979; *Night Fantasies*, for piano 1980; *In Sleep in Thunder* 1982; *Triple Duo* 1983; *Penthode* 1985; *Fourth String Quartet* 1986; *Oboe Concerto*, Heinz Holliger Comm. 1988; *Three Occasions for Orchestra* 1989; *Violin Concerto* 1990; *Quintet for Piano & Winds* 1991; *Trilogy for Oboe & Harp* 1992; *Partita*, for orchestra 1994; *Adagio Tenebroso*, for orchestra 1995; Publishers: Associated Music Publishers (G. Schirmer); Boosey & Hawkes; Recordings: Sony, Virgin, Nonesuch, Erato, DGG, Bridge, New World, CRI, Music & Arts, etc. **Bio-Bibliography:** David Schiff, *The Music of Elliott Carter* (London & New York: Eulenburg Books, Da Capo Press, 1983); "Elliott Carter," Documentary, London Weekend TV & Netherlands Broadcasting 1985; *Who's Who in America*. **Business Address:** Boosey & Hawkes, 24 E. 21 St., NYC 10010.

CARTER, JESSE BENEDICT ■ ASCSR, Dir. 1907-13, AAR, Dir. 1913-17. AAR Dir. until his death in 1917, when he was serving the American Red Cross on the Italian front. His widow gave the AAR library his working library of 1,050 classical volumes.

CARTER, JOSEPH COLEMAN ■ FAAR Classics/Archaeology 71. b. Dec. 23, 1941, NYC. m. Daniela Bini. c. Joseph, Laura, Leo. BA 63, Amherst College; PhD 71, Princeton Univ. **Other Study:** ASCSA 1964-65; Univ. of London, Inst. of Classical Studies 1979-80. **Research/Artistic Interests:** Sculpture of Priene & Asia Minor in the British Museum; art & architecture of Magna Graecia; archaeological excavation, survey & interdisciplinary research in Greek colonial southern Italy; Greek colonies on the Black Sea. **Career & Employment:** Univ. of Texas at Austin, Asst. Prof. 1971-76, Assc. Prof. 1976-83, Prof. 1983-present, Centennial Prof. of Classical Archaeology 1985-present; Excavations in Southern Italy, Dir. 1974-present; Inst. of Classical Archaeology, Dir. 1978-present; Excavations at Chersonesos on the Black Sea, Dir. **Memberships & Offices:** Soc. of Antiquaries of London, Fellow 1984; ArIA; Istituto per la storia e l'archeologia della Magna Grecia, Socio Ordinario; Soc. for the Promotion of Hellenic Studies; Società Magna Grecia, Socio; Soc. for the Promotion of Roman Studies. **Fellowships, Honors & Awards:** Amherst Memorial Fellow 1963-64; Princeton Univ. Fellowships 1963-65; ASCSA, J.W. White Fellow 1964-65; Fulbright Fellow 1967-68, 1968-69; NEH Younger Humanist Award 1973-74, Fellowship 1988-89; ACLS Research Grant 1979; Guggenheim Fellowship 1994-95. **Publications:** *The Sculpture of Taras*. Transactions of the APS n.s. 65.7 (Philadelphia: APS 1975); *The Sculpture of the Sanctuary of Athena Polias at Priene* (London: Soc. of Antiquaries & British Museum, 1983); "Sicily and Magna Grecia," *Cambridge Ancient History* 7 (Cambridge: Cambridge Univ. Press, 1984), 71-80; "The Date of the Relief Sculpture from the Altar of Athena at Priene," in *Studi in onore di Achille Adriani* (Rome: Bretschneider, 1984), 227-43; "Population and Agriculture: Magna Grecia in the Fourth Century B.C.," in *Papers in Italian Archaeology 4.1, The Human Landscape,* ed. C. Malone & S. Stoddard (London: British Archaeological Reports, Int. Ser. 243, 1985), 281-312; "Metaponto and Croton," *Archaeological Field Survey in Britain and Abroad,* (London: Soc. of Antiquaries, Occasional Paper 4, 1985), 146-57; "Between the Bradano and Basento: Archaeology of the Rural Landscape of Metaponto," in *Earth Patterns: Essays in Landscape Architecture,* ed. W. Kelso (Charlottesville, 1990); "Metapontum, Land, Wealth and Population," in *Greek Colonists and Native Populations,* ed. J.P. Descouedres (Oxford; Clarendon, 1990), 405-41; "Pytheos," *Akten des XIII internationalen Kongresses für klassicsche Archäologie, Berlin, 1988* (Mainz-am-Rhein: Philipp von Zabern, 1990), 129-36; with M. Henneberg & R. Henneberg, "Health in Colonial Metaponto," *National Geographic Research and Exploration* 8.4 (1992): 446-59; contr., *Eius Virtutis Studiosi: Classical and Postclassical Studies in Memory of Frank Edward Brown (1908-1988),* ed. Russell T. Scott, Jr. & Ann R. Scott (Washington, DC: NGA, 1993); "Sanctuaries in the Chora of Metaponto," in *Placing the Gods,* ed. S.E. Alcock & R. Osborne (Oxford: Clarendon, 1994), 159-98. **Exhibitions/Performances:** "Ancient Crossroads: The Rural Population of Classical Italy," traveling 1977-79: Michener Galleries, Austin; Museum of Fine Arts, Houston; Art Museum of South Texas, Corpus Christi; Anthropological Museum, Vancouver. **Home Address:** 2205 W. 11 St., Austin, TX 78703. **Business Address:** Dept. of Classics, Univ. of Texas, Austin, TX 78712.

CARUSO, IDA ■ Italian Fulbright Fellow 1975-76.

CASANI, MARCO ■ AAR – Rome, Grounds Staff.

CASANOVA, ALDO J. ■ FAAR Sculpture 61, RAAR Sculpture 75, Sculpture Juror 1964, 1974. b. Feb. 8, 1929, San Francisco, CA. m. Judith Boice. c. Anabelle, Aviva, Liana. BA 50, San Francisco State Univ.; MA 51, San Francisco State Univ.; PhD 57, Ohio State Univ. **Research/Artistic Interests:** Sculptor, working primarily in bronze, monumental abstract as well as intimate figurative. **Career & Employment:** San Francisco State Univ., Instr. 1951-53; Antioch College, Asst. Prof. 1956-58; Temple Univ., Tyler School, Assc. Prof. 1961-64; Tyler School in Rome 1968-70; Scripps College, Assc. Prof. 1966-68, Prof. 1970-present; Skowhegan School of Painting & Sculpture 1973, 1974; SUNY, Albany, Visiting Prof. 1980-81. **Memberships & Offices:** Pittsburgh Art League, Sculpture Juror 1962; Da Vinci

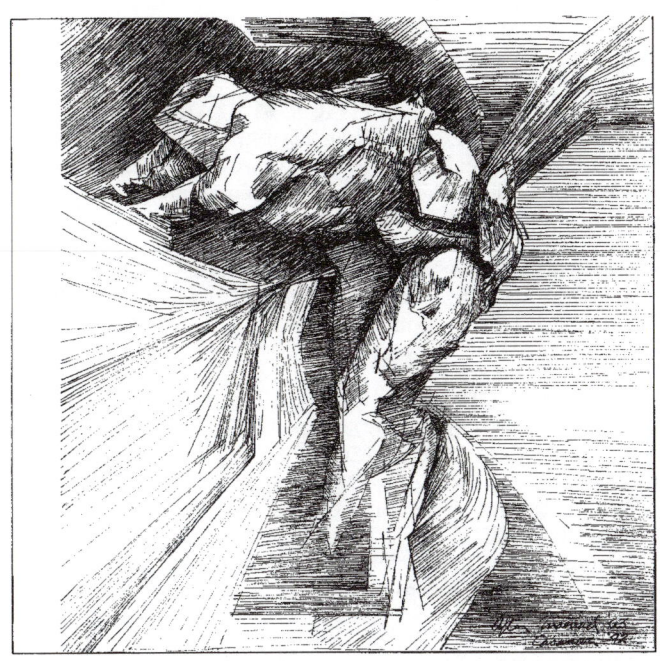

Aldo J. Casanova

Art Alliance, Philadelphia, Sculpture Juror 1963; Louis Comfort Tiffany Grant, Jury 1972; Laguna Beach Museum Annual, Sculpture Juror 1977. **Fellowships, Honors & Awards:** Louis Comfort Tiffany Found., Purchase Award 1970; NAD, Elected 1992. **Important Works:** *Great Owl I,* San Francisco Museum of Art 1963; *Earth Form,* Stanford Research Inst. 1966; *Artemis of Ephesus,* Franklin Murphy Sculpture Garden, UCLA 1967; *Instant,* Tiffany Purchase Award to Whitney Museum 1969; *Mushroom,* Hirshhorn Collection 1970; *Juncture,* Scripps College, 1973; *Halcyon,* Johnson Museum, Cornell Univ. 1975; *Halcyon,* Colby College Museum of Art 1975; *Lunar,* Cal Tech 1975; *Mushroom II,* Rancho Santa Ana Botanical Gardens, Claremont, CA 1975; *Juncture,* Smalley Sculpture Garden, Univ. of Judaism, Los Angeles 1981; *Sunshaft,* Corporate acquisition, San Francisco 1982; *Gaia, De Chirico's Cue,* NAD. **Exhibitions/Performances:** Solo: Esther-Robles Gallery, Los Angeles 1967; Santa Barbara Art Museum 1967; Cal Tech 1972; Carl Schlosberg Fine Arts, Sherman Oaks, CA 1977; SUNY 1980; Pasadena City College 1992. **Bio-Bibliography:** *Art News* (1965); *Art in America; Dictionary of Modern Sculpture* (Milan: Carandente, 1967); Anthony Padovano, *The Process of Sculpture* (New York: Doubleday, 1981), 234, 246; Jonathan Block & Jerry Leisure, *Understanding Three-Dimensions* (New York: Prentice Hall, 1987), 96, 97; Leonora Langley, *Antiques and Fine Art: Hugh Hefner's Fine Art Collection* (1987), 37; *Dictionary of Contemporary European Art; International Directory of the Arts; Who's Who in America; Who's Who in American Art.* **Home Address:** 818 E. Endicott, Claremont, CA 91711. **Business Address:** Carl Schlosberg Fine Arts, 15447 Valley Vista Blvd., Sherman Oaks, CA 91403.

CASARTELLI NOVELLI, SILVANA ■ Italian Fulbright Fellow 1957-58.

CASBARIAN, JOHN J. ■ FAAR Architecture 86. b. Dec. 17, 1946, Alexandria, Egypt. m. Natalye L. Appel. c. Claudia. BA 69, Rice Univ.; MFA 71, California Inst. of the Arts; BArch 72, Rice Univ. **Other Study:** American Univ. of Beirut 1964-65. **Career & Employment:** Taft Architects, Part. 1972-present; Rice Univ., School of Architecture, Prof. 1973-present, Dir. 1993-

present. **Fellowships, Honors & Awards:** with partners, AIA Honor Awards 1981, 1982, 1983, local & state chapters over 50 honor awards since 1975, Fellow 1991; Venice Biennale 1980; Yale Univ., Davenport Chair Prof. 1984; Graham Found. Fellowship 1985-86. **Important Works:** Hendley Bldg., Galveston 1977-79; Municipal Control Bldg., Quail Valley 1978-79; YWCA Masterson Branch & Office Bldg., Houston 1979-81; Talbot House, Nevis 1980-81; River Crest Country Club, Fort Worth 1981-84; Water Resources Bldg., The Woodlands 1982-85; Corpus Christi City Hall 1984-88; Hope Elementary School, TX 1986-88; Olson House, Nevis 1987-88; Rothwell House, Houston 1988-93; Lycée Technique Bernard Palissy, Saintes, France 1990-94; Penn-Plax Assembly Plant, Saintes, France 1991; Rice School, Houston 1991-94; Tribune & Educational Bldg., Sogndal, Norway 1992-94. **Bio-Bibliography:** Charles Jencks, ed., *Post Modern Classicism* (London: Academy Editions, 1980); Venice Biennale, *Architecture 1980: The Presence of the Past* (New York: Rizzoli, 1980); Charles Jencks, *Architecture Today* (New York: Abrams, 1982); E. McCoy & B. Goldstein, *Guide to U.S. Architecture: 1940-1980* (Santa Monica: A + A Press, 1982); Paolo Portoghesi, *After Modern Architecture* (New York: Rizzoli, 1982); Charles Jencks, *Abstract Representation* (London: Academy Editions, 1983); Robert Jensen & Patricia Conway, *Ornamentalism* (New York: Potter, 1983); *101 Contemporary Architects in the World* (Tokyo: Kajima Publishers, 1985); Architectural League, *Emerging Voices: A New Generation of Architects in America* (New York: Princeton Architectural Press, 1986); Charles Jencks, *Post Modernism* (New York: Rizzoli, 1987); Stanley Tigerman, ed., *The Chicago Tapes* (New York: Rizzoli, 1987); Robert A.M. Stern, *Post-Modern Classicism* (New York Rizzoli, 1988); Sylvia Hart Wright, *Sourcebook of Contemporary North American Architecture* (New York: Van Nostrand, 1989); Roberto Masiero, *Neoclassico* (Venice: Marsilio Editori, 1990); Stephen Fox, ed., *Houston Architectural Guide* (Houston: Houston AIA-Herring Press, 1990); *Architecture Address Book* (New York: Rizzoli, 1992); Sydney LeBlanc, *20th Century American Architecture* (New York: Whitney Library of Design, 1993); Ben E. Graves, *School Ways* (New York: McGraw Hill, 1993). **Home Address:** 2346 Dunstan Rd., Houston, TX 77005. **Business Address:** Taft Architects, 807 Peden, Houston, TX 77006.

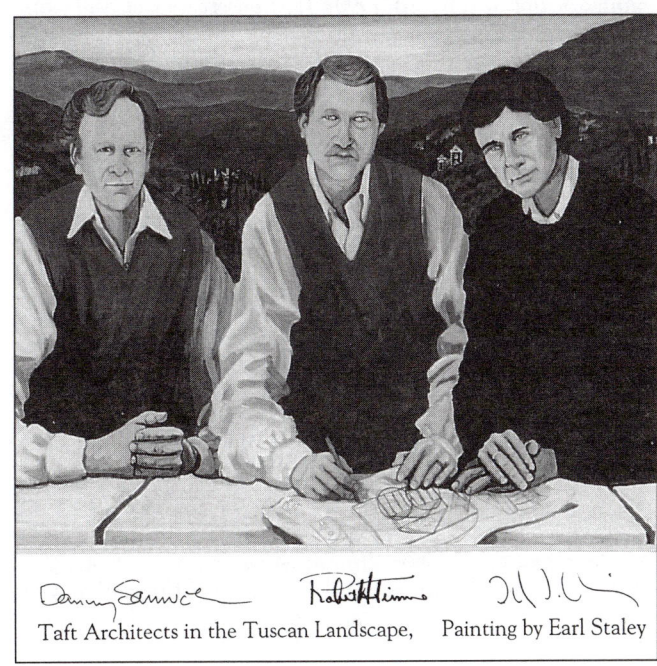

Taft Architects in the Tuscan Landscape, Painting by Earl Staley

CASEY, JOHN D. ■ RAAR Literature 91. b. Jan. 18, 1939, Worcester, MA. m. Rosamond P. Casey. c. Maud, Eleanor, Clare, Julia. BA 62, Harvard Univ.; LLB 65, Harvard Univ.; MFA 68, Univ. of Iowa. **Other Study:** Outward Bound, Hurricane Island, ME 1969, 1977. **Career & Employment:** Univ. of Virginia, Prof. 1972-92. **Fellowships, Honors & Awards:** Guggenheim Fellow 1979-80; NEA Fellow 1983; National Book Award 1989; Strauss Living Fellow, AAAL 1993-97. **Publications:** *An American Romance* (New York: Atheneum, 1977; Pocketbooks, 1987; Atheneum, 1987; Avon, 1990); *Testimony & Demeanor* (New York: Knopf, 1979; Avon, 1990); *Spartina* (New York: Knopf, 1989; Avon, 1990); stories, essays & reviews in *The New Yorker, Sports Illustrated, Harper's, Esquire, Ploughshares, Shenendoah, New York Times Magazine, New York Times Book Review,* etc. **Bio-Bibliography:** *Who's Who in America.* **Home Address:** 1326 Rugby Rd., Charlottesville, VA 22903. **Business Address:** Michael Carlisle, William Morris Agency, 1350 6th Ave., NYC 10019.

CASKEY, JILL E. ■ FAAR History of Art 93. b. Apr. 13, 1964, Rockford, IL. BA 86, Bryn Mawr College; MA 89, Yale Univ.; PhD 94, Yale Univ. **Research/Artistic Interests:** Medieval art & architecture, southern Italy. **Fellowships, Honors & Awards:** Fulbright Grant 1990-91. **Publications:** "Una fonte cinquecentesca per la storia dell'arte medievale ad Amalfi," *Rassegna del Centro di Cultura e storia amalfitana* 12 (1992): 71-81. **Home Address:** 3435 Yuma St., NW, No. 304, Washington, DC 20008.

CASSON, LIONEL ■ AAR Trustee 1979-84, Trustee Emer.; School of Classical Studies, Andrew W. Mellon Prof.-in-Charge 1981-82; NEH Summer Seminar Dir. 1978.

CASTAGNOLI, FERDINANDO ■ Italian Fulbright Fellow 1951-52.

CATHER, SHARON L. ■ FAAR History of Art 82. b. Aug. 5, 1947, Berkeley, CA. BA 68, UC, Santa Barbara; MA 80, Princeton Univ. **Career & Employment:** Courtauld Inst. of Art, Univ. of London, Lect. 1985-present. **Publications:** *Drawings by Gianlorenzo Bernini* (Princeton: Princeton Univ. Press, 1981); with D. Park & P. Williamson, *Early Medieval Wall Painting and Painted Sculpture* (Oxford, 1990); *The Conservation of Wall Paintings* (Los Angeles: Getty Conservation Inst., 1991). **Business Address:** Courtauld Inst. of Art, Univ. of London, Somerset House, Strand, London WC2R 0RN, England.

CAVE, ELMORE ■ AAR World War II Prize 1942.

CECERE, GAETANO ■ FAAR Sculpture 23. b. Nov. 26, 1894, NYC. d. Jan. 1985. NAD; Beaux Arts Inst., NYC. **Research/Artistic Interests:** Relief, medal design. **Career & Employment:** Mary Washington College, Assc. Prof.; NAD, Faculty 1940-70. **Memberships & Offices:** NAD 1938-85; NSS. **Fellowships, Honors & Awards:** NAD, Leon Forst Award, Barnett Prize 1924; PAFA Prize 1930; NSS, Lindsey Morris Memorial Prize 1935. **Important Works:** War memorials in Plainfield, Clifton & Princeton, NJ; Pediment group, Stambaugh Auditorium, Youngstown, OH; Medals: US Army, Columbia Broadcasting System, Soc. of Medalists, AAR; Permanent Collection: MMA; ANS; Brookgreen Gardens, SC; Norton Gallery, West Palm Beach. **Exhibitions/Performances:** ALNY 1924-33; NSS 1924-36; NAD 1924-46; PAFA 1924-46; AIC 1924-27; Grand Central Art Galleries, NYC 1930; Whitney Museum, NYC 1934; MMA 1936; St. Louis Art Museum 1942-46. **Bio-Bibliography:** *Mary Washington College, Sculpture, Drawings, and Pastels of Gaetano*

Cecere, exb. cat. (Fredericksburg, VA: Mary Washington College, 1963); *Who Was Who in American Art.*

CELENZA, CHRISTOPHER S. ■ FAAR Post-Classical/Humanistic Studies 94. b. Aug. 20, 1967, Cleveland, OH. BA 88, SUNY, Albany; MA 89, SUNY, Albany. **Fellowships, Honors & Awards:** Duke Univ., Medieval-Renaissance Fellow 1989-92; Fulbright Fellow 1992-93; Univ. of Hamburg, Graduierten Kolleg-Textüberlieferung 1994-96. **Publications:** "Renaissance Humanism and the New Testament: Lorenzo Valla's Annotations to the Vulgate," *Journal of Medieval and Renaissance Studies* 21 (1994): 33-52. **Home Address:** 261 London Rd., Staten Island, NY 10306.

CERASI, VINCENT CHARLES ■ FAAR Landscape Architecture 50; AAR Trustee 1972-76. b. Feb. 15, 1912, Italy. d. Mar. 20, 1987. m. Judith Cerasi. c. Gary, Debbie Campbell. BLA 36, Cornell Univ. **Career & Employment:** WWII, Major, Coast Artillery, Anti-Aircraft Mobile; Clarke & Rapuano, Landscape Architects, NYC 1947-55; Independent Landscape Architect, Katonah-White Plains 1956-87. **Memberships & Offices:** ASLA; ALNY. **Fellowships, Honors & Awards:** Fulbright Fellowship.

CERBU, THOMAS ■ FAAR Post-Classical/Humanistic Studies 83. b. Feb. 26, 1955, Issy-les-Moulineaux, France. BA 76, Stanford Univ.; PhD 86, Harvard Univ. **Research/Artistic Interests:** Renaissance, Byzantium, history of scholarship. **Career & Employment:** Harvard Univ., Lect. 1986-89; Univ. of Georgia, Asst. Prof. 1989-present. **Home Address:** 155 Morton Ave., Athens, GA 30605.

CHABANNE, HENRI EMILE ■ FAAR Landscape Architecture 34. b. Aug. 10, 1906, Madison, CT. d. July 28, 1944. BLA 31, Univ. of Pennsylvania. **Career & Employment:** Taconic State Park Comm., Poughkeepsie, NY 1931-32; US Army, Lieutenant 1942-44. **Fellowships, Honors & Awards:** Garden Club of America, Fellowship in Landscape Architecture.

CHAFEE, JUDITH ■ FAAR Architecture 77. BA 54, Bennington College; BArch-MArch 60, Yale Univ. **Career & Employment:** Office of Paul M. Rudolph, New Haven 1960-61; Architects' Collaborative, Cambridge, MA 1962-63; Eero Saarinen & Asscs., Hamden, CT 1963-65 Edward Larrabee Barnes, Connecticut Office 1965-69; Judith Chafee, Architect, Hamden, CT 1966-69; Judith Chafee, Architect, Tucson 1969-present; Univ. of Arizona, College of Architecture, Tucson, Visiting Critic 1973-76; Univ. of Texas, College of Architecture, Austin, Guest Architect, Critic to Advanced Students 1976; MIT, Dept. of Architecture, Distinguished Visitor's Studio, Visiting Prof., Advanced Studio 1986, 1988; Washington Univ., St. Louis, MO, School of Architecture, Visiting Prof., Advanced Design Studio 1988; Univ. of Arizona, Tucson, College of Architecture, Adj. Prof. 1977-present. **Memberships & Offices:** Nat. Trust for Historic Preservation; Habitat for Humanity; Nature Conservancy; Museum of Northern Arizona; Tucson Mountain Assn.; Old Fort Lowell Neighborhood Assn.; El Presidio Neighborhood Assn. **Fellowships, Honors & Awards:** Yale Univ. Fellowship Award for Hospital Design 1959; *Architectural Record* Award of Excellence for House Design 1970; Burlington House Award 1975; *Architectural Record* Award of Excellence for Design 1975; AIA Housing Award, 1st Honor 1978; American Concrete Inst. Award 1978, 1984; Tucson-Pima County Historical Comm. Award 1978; *Architectural Record* Record Houses of 1979, Award of Excellence 1979; AIA Fellow 1983; Nature Conservancy Recognition for Architectural Services 1986; Univ. of Arizona, Mortar Board Citation Award 1988. **Bio-Bibliography:** *Who's Who in America.* **Home Address:** 317 N. Court Ave., Tuscon, AZ 85701.

CHALFIN, PAUL ■ FAAR Painting 09. b. Nov. 2, 1874, NYC. d. Feb. 16, 1959. **Other Studies:** Harvard Univ., NAD, ASL. **Career & Employment:** Art advisor to James Deering, Miami FL; Painter, NYC; Architect, private practice NYC; MFA, Curator of Japanese Art. **Memberships & Offices:** ALNY 1911; American Inst. of Decorators, Hon. Mem. **Fellowships, Honors & Awards:** AIA Citation; MMA, Lazarus Scholarship 1905. **Important Works:** Vizcaya, estate of James Deering, now Dade County Art Museum. **Bio-Bibliography:** *NY Times,* Obit. (Feb. 16, 1959); *Who Was Who in American Art.*

CHAMBERLIN, FRANK TOLLES ■ FAAR Painting 11. b. Mar. 10, 1873, San Francisco, CA. d. July 24, 1961. m. Katherine Beecher Stetson. c. Dorothy Stetson, Walter Stetson. **Other Studies:** Hannan Business College, Hartford, CT; ASL. **Career & Employment:** William Wheeler Smith, Architect, NYC; Beaux Arts Inst. of Design, NYC, Teacher; Otis Art Inst., CA, Teacher; Chouinard Art Inst., CA, Co-Founder-Instr.; Univ. Southern California, School of Architecture, Teacher; Jepson Art Inst., CA, Teacher. **Memberships & Offices:** Beaux Arts Inst. of Design, Honorary Life Mem.; Bookworkers Guild, NYC; California Art Club; California Watercolor Soc.; Pasadena Soc. of Artists; Artists of the Southwest. **Fellowships, Honors & Awards:** Intl. Mural Competition, Los Angeles Museum, Honorable Mention; ALNY Prize 1920. **Important Works:** McKinley Junior HS, Pasadena, CA, Library Mural 1942; New Rochelle Public Library; Peabody Inst., Baltimore. **Exhibitions/Performances:** ALNY 1913, 1914, 1920; NAD; PAFA; AIC; Panama-Pacific Exposition 1915; Palace Legion of Honor, San Francisco Museum of Art 1924-46; Pasadena Art Inst. 1934; Found. of Western Arts 1935-40; California Watercolor Soc., Scripps College, Claremont, CA 1937; Golden Gate Exposition, San Francisco 1939; California Art Club; Soc. for Sanity in Art 1940; Retrospective Exb., Pasadena Art Museum 1955. **Bio-Bibliography:** *Who Was Who in American Art.*

CHAMPLIN, EDWARD ■ RAAR Classics/Archaeology 94. b. June 3, 1948, NYC. **Career & Employment:** Princeton Univ., Prof. **Bio-Bibliography:** *Who's Who in America.*

CHANDLER, FRANCIS WARD ■ AAR Trustee 05, Architect.

CHAPIN, DONALD ■ AAR Trustee.

CHATFIELD-TAYLOR, ADELE ■ FAAR Design Arts 84, AAR Pres. 1988-present. b. Jan. 29, 1945, Washington, DC. m. John Guare. BA 66, Manhattanville College, Purchase; MS 73, Columbia Univ. **Other Study:** Harvard GSD, Loeb Fellow 1978-79; Acad. for Educational Development 1982-83. **Career & Employment:** Edward R. Luters & Asscs., Draftsman 1965-66; Robert S. Yale, Draftsman 1966; Historic America Bldgs. Survey, Architectural Historian 1967; Urban Deadline Architects, Co-Founder & Dir. 1968-73; NYC Landmarks Preservation Comm., Landmarks Preservation Specialist 1973-74, Asst. to Chair 1974-79; New York Landmarks Preservation Found., Exec. Dir. 1980-84; Columbia Univ., Graduate School of Architecture & Planning, Adj. Asst. Prof. 1976-84; NEA, Design Arts Program, Dir. 1984-88. **Memberships & Offices:** Nat. Com. on US-China Relations 1982-present; Mayors Inst. for City Design,

Design Arts Pgm., Founder 1985-present; Statue of Liberty-Ellis Island Centennial Comm., Historic Preservation Adv. Panel 1986-88; Getty Grant Pgm., Architectural Conservation Grant, Adv. Com. 1988-92; Law & the Arts, Adv. Com. 1988-present; Jefferson Restoration Adv. Bd., Mem. & Vice-Chair 1989-present; Comm. of Fine Arts 1989-94; Nat. Bldg. Museum, BoT 1989-present; Architectural Com.-Adv. Bd.: Yale Univ. 1990-95, Univ. of Virginia 1990-95, Princeton Univ. 1990-94; Architectural History Found., Dir. 1991-94; Harvard GSD, Visiting Com. **Publications:** "Historic Districts," *Progressive Architecture* (1981); "Introduction," Mike Lipske, *Places as Art* (Washington, DC: Publishing Center for Cultural Resources, NEA, 1985); "Prospect, Advancing Design," *Landscape Architecture Magazine* (Spring 1985): 172; "Historic Preservation and the Mayor," in *MICD Handbook* (Washington, DC: Mayors Inst. for City Design, NEA, 1985); "Richard Serra and the Crisis of Public Art," *Architecture and Abstraction, Pratt Journal of Architecture* 1 (1985); "The Design Arts as a Laboratory," *Places* 6.5 (Sept.-

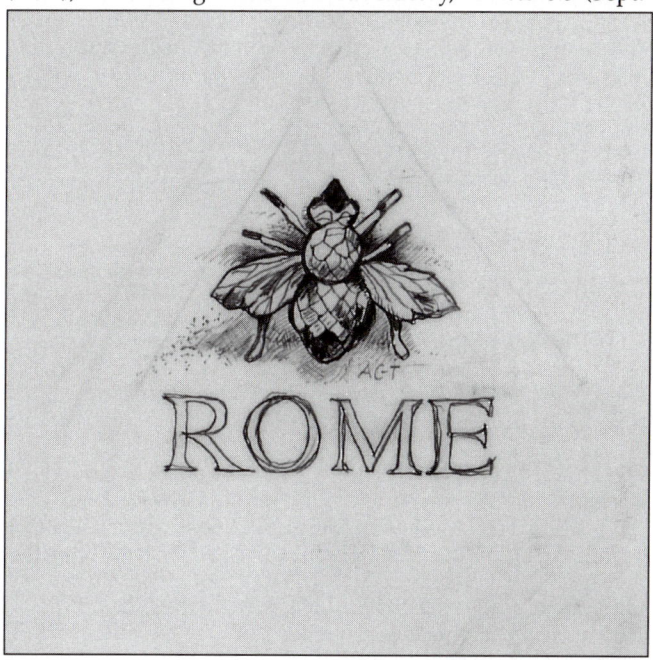

Adele Chatfield-Taylor

Oct. 1986): 3; "Architectural Art: Affirming the Design Relationship: A Discourse," (New York: American Craft Museum, 1988); "The Mayor's Institute on City Design," *Places* 5.4; "From Ruskin to Rouse," *Heritage Canada;* "The Essence of Design: the Work of Two Talented Amateurs," in *Architecture: A Place for Women,* Ellen Perry Berkeley, ed., & Matilda McQuaid, assc. ed. (Washington, DC: Smithsonian Inst. Press, 1988); "Design: An Agenda for the 90s," *Interiors Magazine* (Spring 1990); "Consider Aesthetics & Economics," *Preservation Forum* 3.4 (Winter 1990): 6. **Bio-Bibliography:** *Who's Who of American Women.* **Home Address:** 51 Fifth Ave., NYC 10003. **Business Address:** American Academy in Rome, 7 E. 60 St., NYC 10022.

CHATHAM, WALTER F. ■ FAAR Design Arts 89. b. Jan. 7, 1952, Washington, DC. m. Mary B. Adams. c. William, Alexander, Roma. BArch 78, Univ. of Maryland, College Park. **Other Study:** Philadelphia College of Art (painting) 1972; Inst. for Architecture & Urban Studies (post-graduate) 1978-79. **Career & Employment:** Peter D. Eisenman, FAIA 1978-79; Arquitectonica, Miami 1979-81; Bulter Rogers Basket 1983; Jaquelin Taylor Robertson, FAIA 1981-82. **Fellowships, Hon-**

ors & Awards: AIA, New York Chapter, Distinguished Architecture Award 1988, 1990, 1992; AIA, Distinguished Architecture Award 1991. Home Address: 55 Crosby St., NYC 10012.

CHEEVER, JOHN ■ AAR Visitor 1959 — 1964, Writer. b. May 27, 1912. d. June 18, 1982. Honors & Awards: National Book Award 1958; Pulitzer Prize 1979. Selected Publications: The Wapshot Chronicle (1957); The Wapshot Scandal (1964); Bullet Park (1969); Falconer (1977); The Stories of John Cheever (1978).

CHEILIK, SAUL MICHAEL ■ FAAR Classics/Archaeology 64. b. Oct. 31, 1937, NYC. d. Oct. 26, 1990. BA 59, City College, CUNY; MA 62, Johns Hopkins Univ.; PhD 65, Johns Hopkins Univ. Research/Artistic Interests: Ancient history, Roman & Greek archaeology; ancient intellectual development; US architecture. Career & Employment: Lehman College, CUNY, Assc. Prof. 1965-90; Bronx Inst. for Regional & Community History Studies, Co-Dir. 1988-90. Memberships & Offices: AHA; ArIA. Fellowships, Honors & Awards: ANS, Summer Fellowship 1966; APS Grant 1966; Hunter College, Grant. Publications: "A Roman Terracotta Savings Bank," AJA 67 (1963): 70-71; "Numismatic and Pictorial Landscapes," Greek, Roman and Byzantine Studies 6 (1965): 215-25; Ancient History (New York: Barnes & Noble, 1968); Western Civilization, vol. 1 (New York: Barnes & Noble, 1971); "The Bronx Apartment House," Profile (1977); "Public Buildings in the Bronx," Profile (1980). Bio-Bibliography: Directory of American Scholars.

CHERLI, RITA ■ AAR – Rome, Housekeeping Staff.

CHERMAYEFF, SERGE ■ AAR Visitor 1955 — 1959, Architect. Career & Employment: Harvard GSD, Prof. 1953-62; Yale Univ., Prof. 1962-71. Important Works: Walter Horn House, Richmond, CA; British Railways Office, Rockefeller Center, NYC.

CHESNUT, GLENN F. ■ FAAR Classics/Archaeology 79. b. June 28, 1939, Springfield, OH. BS 60, Univ. of Louisville; BD 64, Southern Methodist Univ.; PhD 68, Oxford Univ. Research/Artistic Interests: Roman stoicism. Career & Employment: Univ. of Virginia, Acting Asst. Prof. 1968-70; Indiana Univ., Lect.-Prof. 1971-77; Boston Univ., Visiting Prof. 1984-86. Fellowships, Honors & Awards: Fulbright Grant 1965-67; Dempster Fellowship 1966-67; Rockefeller Doctoral Fellowship 1967-68.

CHILDS, DAVID M. ■ AAR Trustee 1987-present. Studies: Yale Univ. Career & Employment: Pennsylvania Ave. Comm., Washington, DC; Skidmore, Owings & Merrill, Washington, DC, Dir. 1971-84; Skidmore, Owings & Merrill, NYC, Design Part. 1984-present. Memberships & Offices: Nat. Capital Planning Comm., Chair 1965-81; Municipal Arts Soc., BoT; ALNY, BoT; New York City Partnership, BoT. Fellowships, Honors & Awards: AIA, Fellow. Important Works: Worldwide Plaza, NYC; Riverside South, NYC, Master Plan; Stuyvesant School Bridge, NYC; Federal Courthouse, Charleston, WV; US Embassy, Ottawa; NYMEX Bldg, Battery Park City, NYC; State Office Bldg., San Francisco.

CHILLMAN, JAMES HENRY ■ FAAR Architecture 22. b. Dec. 24, 1891, Philadelphia, PA. d. May 13, 1972. m. Dorothy Dawes. c. Helen, Dawes. BS 13, Univ. of Pennsylvania; MS 14, Univ. of Pennsylvania. Other Studies: PAFA 1915-16. Research/Artistic Interests: Hadrian's Villa; Church of Redentore, Venice; Villa Mondragone, Frascati; museum administration. Career & Employment: Univ. of Pennsylvania, Instr. 1914-16; Rice Univ., Prof. 1916-70; Museum of Fine Arts, Houston, Dir. 1924-53. Memberships & Offices: AIA. Fellowships, Honors & Awards: Burnham Fellowship 1919. Publications: "The Casino of the Semicircular Arcades at the Tiburtine Villa of the Emperor Hadrian," Memoirs of the AAR 4 (1924): 103-20; "Giotto and the Modern Age," Rice Institute Pamphlet 35.3 (1948): 46-63; "Art is Fun," Rice Institute Pamphlet 42.1 (1955): 26-53. Bio-Bibliography: Artist of the American West (1981); Who Was Who in America.

CHUBB, ETHEL LEIGH ■ FAAR Classics/Archaeology 21. b. June 12, 1882, Toronto, Canada. d. Mar. 13, 1980. BA 06, Univ. of Toronto; MA 09, Univ. of Toronto; PhD 20, Univ. of Pennsylvania. Research/Artistic Interests: Epigraphy, numismatics. Career & Employment: Girls' HS, Philadelphia, Teacher 1922-47. Fellowships, Honors & Awards: Carter Memorial Fellowship.

CHURCH, THOMAS DOLLIVER ■ RAAR Landscape Architecture 60; Sheldon Fellow 1926-27. b. Apr. 27, 1902, Boston, MA. d. Aug. 30, 1978. m. Elizabeth Roberts. c. Judith, Belinda. BA 23, UC, Berkeley; MS 26, Harvard Graduate School of Landscape Architecture. Career & Employment: Ohio State Univ., Asst. Prof. 1927-29; UC, Berkeley, Asst. Prof. 1929-30; Pasatiempo Estates, Santa Cruz, Landscape Architect 1930-32; Thomas D. Church & Asscs., Prin. 1933-78; Consultant Landscape Architect: Stanford Univ. 1957-77; UC, Berkeley & Santa Cruz 1959-77. Fellowships, Honors & Awards: AIA, Fine Arts Medal 1951; Garden Club of America, Oakleigh Thorne Medal 1969; ASLA, Honor Award 1971, Gold Medal 1976; American Horticultural Soc. Citation for Outstanding Contributions 1974.; American Inst. of Interior Designers, Hon. Fellow 1970; AAAS, Fellow 1978. Publications: Gardens Are for People (New York: Reinhold, 1955); Your Private World: A Study of Intimate Gardens (San Francisco, 1969). Important Works: Approximately 2,000 private gardens through the US, 1930-77; landscape designer: War Memorial Opera House Garden Court, San Francisco 1935; Park Merced, San Francisco 1941-50; GM Research Center, Detroit 1945; El Panama Hotel, Panama City 1946; Des Moines Art Center 1946; Stanford Medical Center 1958; Stuart Pharmaceutical Co., Pasadena 1958; UC, Berkeley, Master Plan 1961; Sunset Magazine Gardens, Menlo Park, CA 1963; UC, Santa Cruz, Master Plan 1961; Strybing Arboretum Home Demonstration Gardens, Golden Gate Park, San Francisco 1963; Harvey Mudd College, Claremont, Master Plan 1963; Caterpillar Tractor Co., Peoria 1964; Stanford Univ., Master Plan 1965; Scripps College, Claremont, Master Plan 1969. Bio-Bibliography: Mary Vance, Thomas D. Church, Landscape Architect (Monticello, IL, 1980); Pam-Anela Messenger, Bibliography: Thomas Dolliver Church (Monticello, IL, 1981).

CIAMPAGLIA, CARLO A. ■ FAAR Painting 23. b. Mar. 8, 1891, Roccoraso, Italy. d. Dec. 1975. m. Rosalie. NAD. Research/Artistic Interests: Mural painting. Career & Employment: Traphagen School of Fashion, NYC, Teacher c.1944. Memberships & Offices: NAD, Assc. Mem.; Art Alliance. Publications: Contributor to architectural magazines, newspapers & Encyclopedia Britannica. Important Works: Murals: Cranbrook Acad. of Art; Slovak Girls Acad., Danville, PA; Masonic Temple, Scranton, PA; Fairmont Mausoleum, Newark, NJ; Court House, Sunbury, PA. Exhibitions/Performances: Texas Centennial Expo 1936; World's Fair, NYC 1939; NAD. Bio-Bibliography: Who Was Who in American Art.

CIANFROCCA, ALFREDO ■ AAR – Rome, Housekeeping Staff.

CIAPPONI, ANGELA LUCIA ■ Italian Fulbright Fellow 1960-61.

CIARDI, JOHN ■ FAAR Literature 57. b. June 24, 1916, Boston, MA. d. Mar. 30, 1986. m. Myra Judith Hostetter. c. Myra, John L., Benn A. BA 38, Tufts Univ.; MA 39, Univ. of Michigan. **Research/Artistic Interests:** Italian literature, poetry, writing for children. **Career & Employment:** Harvard Univ., Instr.-Asst. Prof. 1946-53; Rutgers Univ., Lect.-Assc. Prof. 1953-61; Breadloaf Writers Conference, Dir.-Lect. for 30 years; *The Saturday Review*, Poetry Ed. 1956-72. **Memberships & Offices:** NIAL, Pres.; AAAS, Fellow; Nat. College English Assn., Dir. 1955-57, Pres. 1958-59; North East College English Assn., Pres. **Fellowships, Honors & Awards:** *Poetry Magazine*, Oscar Blumenthal Prize 1943; Eunice Tietjens Award 1945; Levinson Prize 1946; New England Poetry Club, Golden Rose Trophy 1948; Ford Found. Grant 1952-53; Harriet Monroe Memorial Award 1955; Nat. Council of Teachers of English, Award for Excellence 1982; plus many honorary degrees. **Publications:** *Homeward to America* (New York: Holt, 1940); *Other Skies* (Boston: Atlantic Monthly Press, 1947); *From Time to Time* (Boston: Twayne, 1951); trans., Dante's *Divine Comedy* (1954); *How Does A Poem Mean?* (Boston: Houghton Mifflin, 1960); *In the Stoneworks* (New Brunswick, NJ: Rutgers Univ. Press, 1961); *An Alphabestiary* (New York: Lippincott, 1964); *Lives of X: Poems* (New Brunswick, NJ: Rutgers Univ. Press, 1971); *The Little That Is All* (New Brunswick, NJ: Rutgers Univ. Press, 1974); *A Browser's Dictionary* (New York: Harper, 1980); *Good Words to You: An All-New Dictionary and Native's Guide to the Unknown American Languages* (New York: Harper & Row, 1987); *Languages* (New York: Harper & Row, 1987); *Selected Letters of John Ciardi* (Fayetteville: Univ. of Arkansas Press, 1991); Children's titles: *The Reason for the Pelican* (1959); *I Met a Man* (1961); *The Wish-Tree* (1962); *Fast and Slow: Poems for Advanced Children and Beginning Parents* (1975). **Bio-Bibliography:** W. White, *John Ciardi: A Bibliography* (Detroit: Wayne State Univ. Press, 1959); *The Achievements of John Ciardi: A Comprehensive Selection of His Poems with a Critical Introduction* (New York: Scott, Foresman, 1969); *Contemporary Authors*.

CIMORONI, GIOVANNI ■ AAR – Rome, Maintenance Superintendent.

CINI, WALTER T. ■ AAR Asst. Dir. 1973-82. b. Mar. 5, 1916, NYC. m. Stéphane Jeaucour. c. Carol, Mark, Peter. **Studies:** Sorbonne, Paris; Univ. of Florence; Univ. of Rome; Univ. of Munich for Fine Arts & Humanities 1935-39. **Career & Employment:** US Military Serv., Office of Strategic Services X-2, SA 1942-47; US State Dept., 1st Sec. 1947-73; Nat. Historical Intel. Museum, Exec. Dir. 1984-88. **Home Address:** 7001 Meadow Ln., Chevy Chase, MD 20815.

CIUCCI, GIORGIO ■ AAR Visitor 1982-83, Architectural Historian.

CIVITELLO, JOHN PATRICK ■ FAAR Painting 70. b. Aug. 17, 1939, Paterson, NJ. BA 61, Paterson State College; MA 62, NYU. **Research/Artistic Interests:** Humanism. **Career & Employment:** College of Insurance, Boston, Teacher; Montclair State College, Assc. Prof.; Great Falls Historic District, Patterson, NJ, Art Project Dir. **Memberships & Offices:** Found. for the Community Artists of NY. **Fellowships, Honors & Awards:** Governor of NJ, Purchase Award of the NJ State Museum, Trenton; Hassam Purchase Award 1971; Creative Artists Public Service Grant 1972; AAAL 1976. **Important Works:** Collections: Nat. Museum of American Art, Smithsonian Inst.; Monterey Peninsula Museum of Art; 3M Corp., St. Paul, MN; NBC-TV, NYC; Lloyd's Bank, California; Computer Science Corp., Los Angeles. **Exhibitions/Performances:** A.M. Sachs Gallery, NYC 1972, 1974, 1975; Arts Club of Chicago 1974; Group Shows: Philbrook Art Center, Tulsa, OK; 30th Biennial of American Art, Corcoran Gallery, Washington, DC 1967; NJ State Museum; Sewall Art Gallery, Houston; Dayton Art Inst., OH. **Bio-Bibliography:** E. Bilardello, "Pittori Americani a Roma," *Margutta: Periodico d' Arte Contemporanea* (Rome 1970); *Who's Who in American Art*.

CLARK, ANTHONY MORRIS ■ RAAR History of Art 77. b. Oct. 12, 1923, Philadelphia, PA. d. Nov. 22, 1976. BS 45, Harvard Univ. **Other Studies:** Student painter in Europe & NYC 1945-54. **Research/Artistic Interests:** 18th-century paintings in Rome; Roman baroque & neoclassical art. **Career & Employment:** Harvard Univ., Salzburg Seminar, Faculty Asst. 1950; RISD, Museum of Art, Conservation Asst. 1953, *Museum Notes*, Section Ed.-Ed. 1955-59; Byzantine Inst., Istanbul, Field Worker 1954; Minneapolis Inst. of Arts, Curator 1961-63, Dir. 1963-73; MMA, European Paintings, Chair 1973-75; NYU, Adj. Prof. 1975-76. **Memberships & Offices:** IRS, Art Advisory Panel; NEA, Sub-Panel for Conservation; Socio Benemerito, Amici dei Musei di Roma; ArIA; ICOM; American Assn. of Museums; CAA, Dir. 1970-73; Intermuseum Conservation Assn., Pres. 1966-67, 1970-73; American Federation of Arts; English Speaking Union; Drawing Society; *Art Quarterly*, Consultative Com.; *Eighteenth Century Studies*, Ed. Bd. **Fellowships, Honors & Awards:** NGA, David E. Finley Fellowship 1959-61; Order of Royal North Star, Sweden; Order of Merit, Italy. **Publications:** *The Age of Canova*, exb. cat. (Providence, RI: RISD Museum of Art, 1957); *Pompeo Battoni: A Complete Catalogue of his Works* (New York: NYU Press, 1985); *Studies in Roman 18th Century Painting* (Washington, DC: Decatur House, 1981). **Exhibitions/Performances:** Philadelphia Art Alliance 1948; RISD 1954. **Bio-Bibliography:** *Who Was Who in America*.

CLARK, CHARLES UPSON ■ FACSR 01; AAR School of Classical Studies, Prof.-in-Charge 1916-19. b. Jan. 14, 1875, Springfield, MA. d. Sept. 29, 1960. m. Annie White Fray. c. Mrs. John F. Gunther. BA 1897, Yale Univ.; PhD 03. **Other Study:** Univ. of Munich, Grenoble, Paris 1898-1901. **Research/Artistic Interests:** Ammianus Marcellinus, Rumania, Spanish exploration in America. **Career & Employment:** Yale Univ., Asst. Prof. 1904-16; Massawippi Summer School, Hartley, QUE, Prin. 1908-28; Rumania, Lect. 1927, 1930, 1935-37, 1940; Smithsonian Inst. 1929-31, 1936, 1939-41; City College, CUNY, Prof. 1932-40. **Memberships & Offices:** MAA; Royal Historical Soc.; Romanian Acad.; Spanish-American Acad., Cadiz. **Fellowships, Honors & Awards:** American Geographical Soc., Fellow; Commander, Crown of Italy. **Publications:** ed. with L. Traube & G. Feraeo, Ammianus Marcellinus, *Rerum gestarum libri*, 2 vols. (Berlin, 1910-15); *Greater Roumania* (New York: Dodd, Mead & Co., 1922); *Second-Year Latin* (Chicago: Mentzer, Rush, 1924); *Medieval and Late Latin Selections* (Chicago: Mentzer, Rush, 1925); *Bessarabia, Russia and Roumania on the Black Sea* (New York: Dodd, Mead & Co., 1927); ed. & trans., *Voyageurs, robes noires et coureurs de bois: Stories from the French Exploration of North America* (New York: Columbia Univ. Press, 1934); *Racial Aspects of Roumaina's Case* (New York: Caxton Press, 1941); trans., A. Vazquez de Espinosa, *Compendium and Description of the West Indies* (Washington, DC: Smithsonian Inst., 1942); ed., A. Vazquez de Espinosa, *Compendio y descripción de los Indios* *ocidentales* (Washington, DC: Smithsonian Inst., 1948); "Itinerary of Spanish America in 1612-21 by Vazquez de Espinosa," *Smithsonian* 10 (1948). **Important Works:** Discovery of the Badianus Aztec herbal of 1552. **Bio-Bibliography:** *NY Times*, Obit. (Sept. 30, 1960); *Speculum* 36 (1961): 536; *American Authors and Books* (New York: Crown, 1972); Briggs, 97-98; *Who Was Who among North American Authors, 1921-39; Who Was Who in America.*

CLARK, CHAS CAMERON ■ Rotch Scholar 1912.

CLARK, JOSEPH H. ■ McKim Scholar 1911-12, Columbia Scholar 1913.

CLARKE, GILMORE D. ■ AAR Trustee 1931-63, Landscape Architect.

CLAUSEN, WENDELL V. ■ FAAR Classics/Archaeology 53. b. Apr. 2, 1923, Coquille, OR. m. Corinne Slice, Margaret Woodman. c. John, Raymond, Thomas. BA 45, Univ. of Washington, Seattle; PhD 48, Univ. of Chicago. **Research/Artistic Interests:** Greek & Latin literature. **Career & Employment:** Amherst College, Instr.-Assc. Prof. 1948-59; Harvard Univ., Prof. 1959-82, Victor S. Thomas Prof. 1982-88, Prof. of Comparative Literature 1984-present, Pope Prof. 1988-present; Univ. College, London, Visiting Prof. 1971; UC, Berkeley, Sather Prof. 1982; Villa I Tatti, Visiting Prof. 1989. **Memberships & Offices:** *American Journal of Philology,* Assc. Ed. 1976-81. **Fellowships, Honors & Awards:** Phi Beta Kappa 1945; ACLS Fellow 1962-63; Cambridge Univ., Fellow Commoner, Peterhouse 1962-present; AAAS, Fellow 1963-present. **Publications:** *A. Persi Flacci Saturae* (Oxford: Clarendon, 1956); *A. Persi Flacci et D. Iuni Iuuenalis Saturae* (Oxford: Clarendon, 1959); with others, *Appendix Vergiliana* (Oxford: Clarendon, 1966); assc. ed. & contr., *Cambridge History of Latin Literature* (Cambridge: Cambridge Univ. Press, 1982); *Virgil's Aeneid and the Tradition of Hellenistic Poetry* (Berkeley: UC Press, 1987); *A Commentary on Virgil's Eclogues* (Oxford: Clarendon, 1994). **Bio-Bibliography:** *Who's Who in America.* **Home Address:** 8 Kenway St., Cambridge, MA 02138. **Business Address:** Dept. of Classics, 319 Boylston Hall, Harvard Univ., Cambridge, MA 02138.

CLELAND, EMILY LEONARD WADSWORTH ■ FAAR Classics/Archaeology 21. b. July 20, 1892, Pittsburgh, PA. d. 1979. BA 15, Smith College; MA 16, Columbia Univ. **Research/Artistic Interests:** Technique & motives in Roman stucco relief. **Career & Employment:** Illinois College, Instr. 1922-24; Independent Scholar, Williamstown, MA 1925-40; US War Dept., Military Intelligence Division, Clerk. **Publications:** "Stucco Reliefs of the First and Second Centuries Still Extant in Rome," *Memoris of the AAR* 4 (1924): 9-102.

CLEMONS, WALTER, JR ■ FAAR Literature 62. b. Nov. 14, 1929, Houston, TX. d. July 6, 1994. BA 51, Princeton Univ.; BA 53, Magdalen College, Oxford Univ. **Career & Employment:** McGraw-Hill, Ed. 1966-68; *New York Times Book Review,* Ed. 1968-71; *Newsweek,* Ed., Book Critic, Senior Writer 1971-82, 1983-88; *Vanity Fair,* Ed.-Writer 1982, 1983. **Fellowships, Honors & Awards:** Rhodes Scholarship 1953; Univ. of Illinois, Benjamin Franklin Magazine Award 1957; Princeton Univ., Hodder Fellow 1959-60; Texas Inst. of Letters, Jesse Jones Award 1960. **Publications:** *The Dark Roots of the Rose* (1957); *The Poison Tree and Other Stories* (Boston: Houghton Mifflin, 1959); *A Separate Peace: A Critical Commentary* (American RDM Corp., 1965); *The Credibility of Harper Lee's Southern Vision* (American RDM Corp.,

1965); *Graham Greene's* The Power and the Glory: *A Critical Commentary* (American RDM Corp., 1966); Tristram Shandy: *Chapter Notes and Criticism* (American RDM Corp., 1966).

CLINTON, HILLARY RODHAM ■ AAR Visitor 1994, US First Lady.

CLINTON, JACQUELYN C. ■ FAAR Classics/Archaeology 69. b. Aug. 11, 1938, Chicago, IL. m. Kevin M. Clinton. c. Alexandra, Gregory. BA 60, Mt. Holyoke College; MA 64, Columbia Univ.; PhD 70, Columbia Univ. **Other Study:** ASCSA, Summer Session 1967. **Research/Artistic Interests:** Greek & Roman art & archaeology. **Career & Employment:** MMA, Cataloger 1960-62; Univ. of Missouri, Instr. 1969-70; Syracuse Univ., Asst. Prof. 1970-71; Ithaca College, Asst. Prof. 1971-82; Wells College, Asst. Prof. 1989-93; Hobart & William Smith Colleges, Asst. Prof. 1993-94. **Memberships & Offices:** ArIA, Fingerlakes Soc., Sec.-Treas. 1976-78, 1992-94, VP 1988-90; CAA. **Fellowships, Honors & Awards:** NEH Fellowship 1981; APS Summer Research Grants 1972, 1982. **Publications:** *A Late Antique Shrine of Liber Pater at Cosa,* Études Préliminaire aux Religions orientales dans l'Empire Romain 64 (Leiden: E.J. Brill, 1977); "A Hellenistic Torso at Cosa," in *Eius Virtutis Studiosi: Classical and Post-Classical Studies in Memory of Frank Edward Brown,* ed., Russell T. Scott Jr. & Ann R. Scott, Studies in the History of Art 43 (Washington, DC: NGA, 1993), 257-78. **Home Address:** 633 Ringwood Rd., RR 2, Ithaca, NY 14850.

CLOGAN, PAUL M. ■ FAAR Post-Classical/Humanistic Studies 67. b. July 9, 1933, Boston, MA. c. Michael, Margaret, Patrick. BA 56, Boston College; MA 57, Boston College; PhD 61, Univ. of Illinois. **Research/Artistic Interests:** Medieval & Renaissance studies, in particular medieval English literature. **Career & Employment:** Duke Univ., Asst. Prof. 1961-65; Case Western Reserve Univ., Assc. Prof. 1965-72; Univ. of N. Texas, Denton, Prof. 1972-present. **Memberships & Offices:** MLA, Exec. Com., Program Com., Delegate Assembly; MAA, Nominating Com., John Nicholas Brown Prize Com.; Inst. of Intl. Education, Natl. Screening Com.; Comm. on Colleges of Southern Assn. of Colleges & Schools, Institutional Self-Study; Intl. Assn. of Univ. Professors of English; Medieval & Renaissance Soc., Ed., *Medievalia et Humanistica.* **Fellowships, Honors & Awards:** Duke Univ. Endowment Grant 1962; ACLS Research Fellowships 1962-64, 1988; Fulbright-Hays Postdoctoral Senior Research Fellowship 1965-66, Senior Research Grant 1978; Bollingen Found., Research Grant 1966-67; NEH Research Fellowships 1969-70, 1986, 1990; Univ. of N. Texas: Faculty Research Grant 1972-82, Faculty Development Grant 1989. **Publications:** *The Medieval Achilleid of Statius* (Leiden: E.J. Brill, 1968); *Social Dimensions in Medieval & Renaissance Studies,* Medievalia et Humanistica, n.s. 3 (1972); *Medieval and Renaissance Spirituality,* Medievalia et Humanistica, n.s. 4 (1973); *Medieval Historiography,* Medievalia et Humanistica, n.s. 5 (1974); *Medieval Hagiography and Romance,* Medievalia et Humanistica, n.s. 6 (1975); *Medieval Poetics,* Medievalia et Humanistica, n.s. 7 (1976); *Transformation and Continuity,* Medievalia et Humanistica, n.s. 8 (1977); *Byzantine and Western Studies,* Medievalia et Humanistica, n.s. 12 (1984); *Fourteenth and Fifteenth Centuries,* Medievalia et Humanistica, n.s. 14 (1986); *The Early Renaissance,* Medievalia et Humanistica, n.s. 15 (1987); *Literary Theory,* Medievalia et Humanistica, n.s.16 (1988); *Spectrum,* Medievalia et Humanistica, n.s. 18 (1991); *Renaissance and Discovery,* Medievalia et Humanistica, n.s. 19 (1993); *Breaching Boundaries,* Medievalia et Humanistica, n.s. 20 (1994). **Bio-Bibliography:** *Dictionary of International Biogra-*

phy, Directory of American Scholars, International Directory of Medievalists, International Who's Who in Education, Personalities of the South, Repertoire of Neo-Latinists, Who's Who in America, Who's Who in American Education, Who's Who in the Midwest, Who's Who in the South and Southwest, **Home Address:** 3704 Granada Trail, Denton, TX 76205. **Business Address:** Dept. of English, Univ. of N. Texas, Denton, TX 76203.

CLOSE, CHUCK ■ AAR Trustee 1993-present. b. Monroe, WA. **Studies:** Univ. of Washington, Seattle; Yale Univ. School of Art & Architecture; Akademie der Bildenden Kunste, Vienna. **Career & Employment:** Univ. of Massachusetts, Amherst; School of Visual Arts, NYC; NYU; Yale Summer School of Music & Art. **Fellowships, Honors & Awards:** Intl. Center of Photography, Infinity Award 1990; Acad.-Inst. Art Award 1991; Skowhegan Arts Medal 1991. **Important Works:** Collections: major museums worldwide. **Exhibitions/Performances:** Solo: MOMA; Museum of Contemporary Art, Chicago; Los Angeles County Museum of Art; San Francisco Museum of Art; Musée National d'Art Moderne, Pompidou Centre, Paris; Univ. Art Museum, UC, Berkeley; Contemporary Arts Museum, Houston; Retrospective, Walker Arts Center, traveled to Museum of Contemporary Art, Chicago, St. Louis Art Museum, Whitney Museum, NYC 1980-81.

CLURMAN, HAROLD ■ AAR Visitor 1971-72, Writer, Theater Dir., Critic.

COATES, EDWARD H. ■ AAR Charter Mem; PAFA, Pres.

COATES, ROBERT ■ AAR Visitor 1959 — 1964, Writer, Critic.

COBB, HENRY N. ■ RAAR Architecture 92, AAR Trustee 1968-90, Trustee Emer. 1990-present. b. Apr. 8, 1926, Boston, MA. m. Joan Spaulding. c. Sara Quincy, Emma Trow, Pamela Codman. BA 47, Harvard College; MArch 49, Harvard GSD. **Career & Employment:** Hugh Stubbins, Architect 1949-50; Webb & Knapp, Inc., 1950-55; I.M. Pei & Partners-Pei Cobb Freed & Partners, Founding Part. 1955-present; Yale Univ., Visiting Prof. 1973, 1975, 1978; Harvard GSD, Prof. 1980-85, Architecture Dept., Chair 1980-85. **Memberships & Offices:** AIA Fellow; AAAL, BoD, VP for Art 1993-present; AAAS, Fellow; NAD, Academician; Cooper Union School of Art & Architecture, Adv. Council 1967-71; ALNY, Exec. Com. 1968-71, 1975-80, 1988-94; Harvard GSD Assn., Pres. 1969-71; AIA Com. on Design, Chair 1971; AIA Honor Awards Jury, Chair 1972, 1987; Brearley School, BoT 1975-80; Inst. for Architecture & Urban Studies, BoT 1982-85; NEA, Design Arts Program, Chair, Overview Panel 1984-88; Princeton Univ., Adv. Council of the School of Architecture 1985-present; Presidential Design Awards, Chair, Jury for Architecture & Interior Design 1988; Chicago Inst. for Architecture & Urbanism, BoT 1989-94. **Fellowships, Honors & Awards:** AAAL, Arnold W. Brunner Memorial Prize 1977; AIA, New York Chap., Medal of Honor 1982, Illinois Council, Chicago Architecture Award 1985; Bowdoin College DFA 1985; Swiss Federal Inst. of Technology, Doctor Honoris Causa in Technical Sciences 1990; New York Soc. of Architects, Lifetime Achievement Award 1992. **Important Works:** Place Ville Marie, Montreal 1962; SUNY, Fredonia 1969; John Hancock Tower, Boston 1976; 16th St. Transitway Mall, Denver 1982; Johnson & Johnson World HQ, New Brunswick, NJ 1983; ARCO Tower, Dallas 1983; Portland Museum of Art, ME 1983; Pitney Bowes World HQ, Stamford, CT 1985; Commerce Sq., Philadelphia 1987; Anderson Graduate School of Management, UCLA 1995; American Assn. for the Advance-

ment of Science HQ, Washington, DC 1997; US Courthouse, Boston 1998. **Bio-Bibliography:** *Who's Who in America.* **Business Address:** Pei Cobb Freed & Partners, 600 Madison Ave., NYC 10022.

COCOZZA, LUIGI ■ AAR – Rome, Grounds Staff.

COHEN, LEWIS C. ■ FAAR Sculpture 70. b. Apr. 19, 1936, Minneapolis, MN. m. Adrianne Cohen. c. Julia, Aaron. Dipl. 62, MFA School; MFA 76, Claremont Graduate School. **Other Study:** Harvard Medical School, Anatomy 1956; Private study with Hyman Bloom 1957-58; École des Arts Décoratifs, Paris 1962-63; École des Beaux Arts, Paris, studio with Jean Coutier 1962-63. **Career & Employment:** Boston Univ., Instr. 1964-67; Scripps College, Asst. Prof. 1974-75; California State Univ., Long Beach, Lect. 1972-87; College of William & Mary, Assc. Prof. 1987-present. **Fellowships, Honors & Awards:** MFA School, Traveling Fellowship 1962; Nat. Gallery of Design, Assc. Mem. 1990, Academician 1991. **Important Works:** Hirshhorn Museum, Smithsonian Inst., Washington DC; Boston Public Library; NAD; College of William & Mary, Williamsburg, VA; Harvey Mudd College, Claremont, CA; British Royal Collection. **Exhibitions/Performances:** Solo: Eltingen Gallery, Laguna Beach College of Art 1978; Long Beach Jewish Community Center 1983; Four Oaks Gallery, Pasadena, CA 1985; Twentieth Century Gallery, Williamsburg, VA 1988; Martin Sumers Gallery, NYC 1991. **Home Address:** 9 Sussex Ct., Williamsburg, VA 23188. **Business Address:** Dept. of Art & Art History, College of William & Mary, Williamsburg, VA 23185.

COHEN, THOMAS V. ■ FAAR Post-Classical/Humanistic Studies 92. b. Dec. 12, 1942, Norfolk, VA. m. Elizabeth Storr. c. William, Julia. BA 64, Univ. of Michigan; MA 65, Harvard Univ.; PhD 74, Harvard Univ. **Research/Artistic Interests:** Cultural anthropology of Renaissance Rome. **Career & Employment:** York Univ., North York, Canada, 1969-present. **Publications:** "Why the Jesuits Joined," *Canadian Historical Papers* (1974): 237-58; with R.C. Hoffmann, "*El Tratadico e la Pesca:* The Little Treatise on Fishing by Fernando Basurto from his *Dialogue*," *American Fly Fisherman* 2.3 (1984): 8-13; "Diversità nell' Esperienza Religiosa tra i primi Gesuiti," *Annali Accademici Canadesi* 1 (1986): 7-25; "Sociologie de la Croyance: Les Jésuites au Portugal et en Espagne," in *Les Jésuites parmi les Hommes,* ed. G. Demerson et al. (Clermont-Ferrand: Faculté des Lettres et Sciences Humaines de l'Université, 1987), 21-34; "The Case of the Mysterious Coil of Rope: Street Life and Jewish Persona in Rome in the Middle of the Sixteenth Century," *Sixteenth Century Journal* 19.2 (1988): 209-21; with E.S. Cohen, "Camilla the Go-Between: The Politics of Gender in a Roman Household (1559)," *Continuity and Change* 4.1 (1989): 53-77; "A Long Day in Monte Rotondo: The Politics of Jeopardy in a Village Rising (1558)," *Comparative Studies in Society and History* 33 (1991): 639-68; "A Note on Fra Pelagio, a Hermit-Prophet in Rome," in *Prophetic Rome in the High Renaissance Period,* ed. Marjorie Reeves (Oxford: Clarendon Press, 1992), 231-37; "The Lay Liturgy of Affront in Sixteenth-Century Rome," *Journal of Social History* 25 (1992): 857-77; "Agostino Bonamore and the Secret Pigeon (1559)," in *Essays of Life Writing,* ed. Marlene Kadar (Toronto: Univ. of Toronto Press, 1992), 94-112; trans., Irene Polverini Fosi, "Justice and Its Image: Political Propaganda and Judicial Reality in the Pontificate of Sixtus V," *Sixteenth Century Journal* 24.1 (1993): 75-96; with E.S. Cohen, *Words and Deeds in Renaissance Rome: Trials before the Pope's Magistrates* (Toronto: Univ. of Toronto Press, 1993). **Business Address:** History Dept., York Univ., 4700 Kelle St., N. York, ONT M3J 1P3, Canada.

COLANTUONO, ANTHONY D. ■ FAAR History of Art 85. b. May 5, 1958, Somerville, NJ. m. Margaret N. Burri. BA 80, Rutgers Univ.; MA 82, Johns Hopkins Univ.; PhD 87, Johns Hopkins Univ. **Research/Artistic Interests:** European painting, sculpture & architecture of the 16th & 17th centuries, especially problems of interpretation & theory, historical method, etc. **Career & Employment:** Kenyon College, Visiting Asst. Prof. 1986-88; Wake Forest Univ., Visiting Asst. Prof. 1988-89; Vanderbilt Univ., Asst. Prof.-Mellon Fellow 1989-90; Univ. of Maryland, College Park, Asst. Prof. 1990-present. **Fellowships, Honors & Awards:** Kress Fellowship 1983-85; NEH Summer Stipend 1990. **Publications:** "Titian's Tender Infants: On the Imitation of Venetian Painting in Baroque Rome," *I Tatti Studies* 3 (1989): 207-34; *"Dies Alcyoniae*: The Invention of Bellini's Feast of the Gods," *Art Bulletin* 73 (1991): 237-56. **Home Address:** 3423 Univ. Pl., Baltimore, MD 21218. **Business Address:** Art History Dept., Univ. of Maryland, College Park, MD 20742.

COLBURN, GUY BLANDIN ■ FASCSR 10. b. Aug 29, 1882, Townshend VT. d. Aug. 7, 1968. m. Caroline H. Smedley. c. Guy B., Jr. BA 04, Brown Univ; MA 05, Univ. of Wisconsin; PhD 08, Univ. of Wisconsin. **Career & Employment:** Iowa College, Acting Prof. 1908-9; Swarthmore College, Instr. 1910-12; Univ. of Missouri, Asst Prof. 1913-17; Princeton Univ., Instr. 1920-22; Fresno State College, Prof. 1922-52, Prof. Emer. 1952-68. **Memberships & Offices:** APA; MLA; Assn. of Teachers of Spanish, Sec.-Treas. 1934-38. **Publications:** "Civita Lavinia, the Site of Ancient Lanuvium," *AJA* 18 (1914): 18-31, 185-98, 363-80; "Juvenal I.111," *Classical Philology* 9 (1914): 177-79. **Bio-Bibliography:** Brown Univ. Archives, *Directory of American Scholars.*

COLONNA, GIOVANNI ■ Italian Fulbright Fellow 1962-63.

COLQUHOUN, ALAN H. ■ RAAR Architecture 85. b. June 27, 1921. A.A. Dipl. 49. **Other Study:** Architectural Assn., Edinburgh College of Art 1939-42. **Career & Employment:** Edinburgh College of Art, Architectural Assn., Tutor 1957-64; Colquhoun & Miller, Architects 1961-85; Princeton Univ., Visiting Lect. 1966, 1968, 1970, 1978-81, Prof. 1981-91, Prof. Emer. 1991-present; Cornell Univ., Visiting Lect. 1968, 1971; Polytechnic of Central London, Senior Lect. 1974-76, Prin. Lect. 1976-78; L'École Polytechnique Federale de Lausanne, Visiting Prof. 1977; Univ. of Virginia, Visiting Prof. 1980; Colquhoun, Miller & Partners, Architects 1985-88; Alan Colquhoun, Architect 1988-present. **Memberships & Offices:** Univ. College, Dublin, School of Architecture, External Examiner 1978-79; Kingston Polytechnic, School of Architecture, External Examiner 1979-80; Competition for Civic Centre in Kitchener, ONT, Jury 1989; MIT, School of Architecture, Adv. Com. 1990-present; Aga Khan "Think Tank," Geneva, Switzerland 1991; Harvard Univ., Norton Lectures, Selection Com. 1991-present; PA Awards, Jury 1992; Univ. of Florida, School of Architecture, Adv. Com. 1992-present; Waterfront Competition, San Francisco, Jury 1993. **Fellowships, Honors & Awards:** CAYC Award for Best Architectural Critic 1984. **Publications:** *Ensayos* (Barcelona: Gustavo Gili, 1978); *Essays in Architecture: Modern Architecture and Historical Change* (Cambridge, MA: MIT Press, 1981); *Receuil d'Essais Critique: Architecture Moderne et Changement Historique* (Brussels: Mardaga, 1985); *Modernity and the Classical Tradition: Architectural Essays 1980-87* (Cambridge, MA: MIT Press, 1989); *Architettura Moderna e Storia* (Bari: Laterza, 1989); "Kolmenlaista Historicismia," in *Modernismi-Historismi. Ajankohta* 1 (Helsikni: Abacus, 1989); *Mimari Elestiri Yazilari* (Komitesi, Turkey, 1990); "Conversation with Richard Serra," in *Carnegie International* (New York: Rizzoli, 1991); "The Concept of Regionalism," *Werk,*

Bauen & Wohnen (Mar. 1993); "The 19th-Century Railroad Station: Aspects of Design and Reception," in *Territorial Myths* (Princeton: Princeton Architectural Press, 1994). **Business Address:** School of Architecture, Princeton Univ., Princeton, NJ 08544.

COMFORT, HOWARD ■ FAAR Classics/Archaeology 29. b. June 4, 1904, Haverford, PA. d. Sept. 20, 1993. m. Elizabeth Comfort. c. Wistar, Laura Kesel. BA 24, Haverford College; MA 27, Princeton Univ.; PhD 32, Princeton Univ. **Other Studies:** Univ. of Pennsylvania 1926. **Research/Artistic Interests:** Latin philology, Roman pottery, cricket. **Career & Employment:** Haverford School, Teacher 1924-26; Hamilton College, Instr. 1929-30; Haverford College, Asst. Prof.-Prof.-Chair. 1932-69, Emer. Prof. 1969-93; American Friends Com., Rome, Directing Officer 1940; US Embassy in Rome, Cultural Attaché 1950-51; American Legation, Bern 1951-52. **Memberships & Offices:** Deutsches Archäologisches Inst., Corresponding Mem. 1936-93; APA, Sec.-Treas. 1946-49, 2d VP 1960-61, 1st VP 1961-62, Pres. 1962-63; ArIA; Accademia Petrarca Lettere, Arti e Scienze, Corresponding Mem.; Rei Cretariae Romanae Fautores, Pres. 1957-71, Hon. Pres. 1971-93; Religious Society of Friends (Quakers), Haverford Monthly Meeting; Meeting on Worship and Ministry of Philadelphia Yearly Meeting, Clerk 1958-60; Fédération Internationale des Associations d'Études Classiques, Delegate 1963-68. **Fellowships, Honors & Awards:** Society of Antiquaries of London, Fellow; IAS 1956, 1960; APS Travel Grant 1961. **Publications:** "De Collectione praecipue epigraphica vasculorum arretinorum apud Accademiam Americanam conservata," *Memoirs of the AAR* 7 (1928): 177-219; "Arretine Signatures Found in the Excavations in the Theatre District of Corinth," *AJA* 33 (1929): 484-501; "Date of Pausanias, Book II," *AJA* 35 (1931): 310-18; "Preliminary Studies of Late Italian Sigillata," *AJA* 40 (1936): 437-51; "Terra Sigillata," in *Paulys Real-Encyclopädie der classichen Alterumswissenschaft,* suppl. 7 (Stuttgart, 1940), 1295-1352; "Terra Sigillata from Minturnae," 47 (1943): 313-30; "Imported Pottery and Glass from Timba," in *Archaeological Discoveries in South Arabia,* ed. R.L. Bowen, et al. (Baltimore: Johns Hopkins Press, 1958), 199-212; ed., *Oxe's Corpus Vasorum Arretinorum: A Catalogue of the Signatures, Shapes and Chronology of Italian Sigillata* (Bonn: Habelt, 1968); with others, *Terra Sigillata: La ceramica a rilievo ellenistica e romana* (Rome, 1968); "Notes on Roman Ceramic Archaeology," *Rei Cretariae Fautorum Acta,* Suppl. 4 (1979). **Bio-Bibliography:** "Memoir," *AJA* 98 (1994): 561-62; *APA Newsletter* 17.1 (Feb. 1994): 22-23; *Directory of American Scholars, Who's Who in America.*

COMMAGER, HENRY STEELE ■ AAR Visitor 1955 — 1959, Harvard Fellowship, Historian.

COMSTOCK, FRANCIS F.A. ■ RAAR Architecture 58, 60.

CONARROE, JOEL ■ AAR Visitor 1988-89, Guggenheim Found., Pres.

CONELLI, MARIA ANN ■ FAAR History of Art 88. b. Nov. 1, 1957, Brooklyn, NY. m. Kim J. Hartswick. BA 80, Brooklyn College, CUNY; MA 83, IFA; PhD 92, Columbia Univ. **Career & Employment:** MMA, Dept. of Ed., Instr. 1981-84; Parsons School of Design, Summer Paris Program, Instr. 1984-present, Dept. of Architecture & Environmental Design, Faculty 1983-91; Cooper-Hewitt Nat. Design Museum, Masters Program, Chair 1991-present. **Memberships & Offices:** CAA 1981-present; SAH 1981-present; Parsons School of Design, Council of Chairs 1991-present. **Fellowships, Honors & Awards:** MMA, Graduate Asst. 1981; NYU, TA 1982; Columbia Univ. Research

Asst. 1984-84, Fellowship 1986-89, Howard Hibbard Fellowship 1986-87. **Publications:** "Santa Maria dei Gesuiti and Sacred Theater," *Daidolos* 29 (Sept. 1988): 72-77; with Thomas Willette, "The Tribune Vault of the Gesu Nuovo in Naples," in *Ricerche sul '600 napoletano. Milan, Oct. 1989*, (Milan, 1989), 169-213. **Home Address:** 4682 Kell Ln., Alexandria, VA 22311. **Business Address:** Cooper-Hewitt Nat. Design Museum, 2 E. 91st St., NYC 10128.

CONFORTI, MICHAEL ■ FAAR History of Art 76. b. Apr. 3, 1945, Bradford, MS. m. Licia Peterson. c. Peter, Julia. BA 68, Trinity College, Hartford; MA 73, Harvard Univ.; PhD 77, Harvard Univ. **Other Study:** UC, Berkeley, Museum Management Inst. 1985. **Research/Artistic Interests:** 17th- & 18th-century sculpture; architecture & interiors of 19th & 20th century; decorative arts; history of museums & institutional & private collecting practices. **Career & Employment:** Sotheby & Co., London, Cataloger 1968-69; Sotheby Parke Bernet, NYC, Dir. of Training Program, Cataloguer 1969-71; MMA, Intern 1975; Victoria & Albert Museum, London, Intern 1975; Fine Arts Museums of San Francisco, Curator 1977-80; Minneapolis Inst. of Arts, Chief Curator & Bell Memorial Curator 1980-94, Interim Dir. of Art 1987-88; Sterling & Francine Clark Art Inst., Williamstown, MA, Dir. 1994-present; Williams College, Adj. Prof. 1994-present. **Memberships & Offices:** Midwest Art History Soc., BoD 1981-83; American Federation for the Arts, Exb. Adv. Com. 1985-89; SAH, BoD 1986-89; J. Paul Getty Trust, Publications Adv. Com. 1987-90; J. Paul Getty Museum, Visiting Com. 1989-present. **Fellowships, Honors & Awards:** Harvard Univ., Kingsbury Fellow 1971-74; NEA, Museum Fellowship 1974-75; Bush Found. Fellowship 1985; Robert C. Smith Award, Most Distinguished Article in Decorative Arts 1987; J. Paul Getty Museum, Guest Scholar 1988; Order of the Polar Star, 1st Class, Sweden 1988; Charles F. Montgomery Prize 1989; CASVA, Andrew Mellon Visiting Scholar 1992-93. **Publications:** "Pierre Legros and the Role of Sculptors as Designers in Late Baroque Rome," *Burlington Magazine* (Aug. 1977); "Planning the Lateran Apostles, *Memoirs of the AAR* (Rome: AAR, 1980); "Orientalism on the Upper Mississippi: The Work of John S. Bradstreet, 1874-1914," *Bulletin of the Minneapolis Institute of Arts* (1986); "Hoving's Legacy Reconsidered," *Art in America* (June 1986); "The Swedish Imperial Experience and its Artistic Legacy," in *Sweden: A Royal Treasury, 1550-1700*, ed. M. Conforti & Guy Walton, exb. cat. (1988); "The Transfer and Adaptation of European Culture in North America," in *The American Craftsman and the European Tradition, 1620-1820*, ed. M. Conforti & Francis Puig, exb. cat. (1989); "Deaccessioning in American Museums: Some Thoughts for England," *Apollo* (Sept. 1989); "Expanding the Canon (of Art Collecting in American Museums)," *Museum News* (Oct. 1989); "The Decorator and the Antique Room: The Collecting of European Decorative Arts in the United States from the 1890s to the 1990s," *Burlington Magazine* (1992); "History Value and the 1990s Art Museum," *Papers of the XXVII International Kongress für Kunstgeschichte, Berlin, 15-20 July, 1992*; also published in *Journal of Museum Management and Curatorship* 12.3 (Sept. 1993); "Introduction: Art and Life on the Upper Mississippi, 1890-1915," & "Bradstreet's Craftshouse: Retailing in the Arts and Crafts Style," *Minnesota 1900: Art and Life on the Upper Mississippi, 1890-1915*, ed. Michael Conforti, exb. cat. (Minneapolis: Inst. of Arts, 1994); "The Wideners and the Decorative Arts," Introduction, *Catalogue of European Furniture, Ceramics and Tapestries* (Washington, DC: NGA, in press). **Bio-Bibliography:** *Who's Who in America, Who's Who in American Art.* **Home Address:** 1382 Main St., Williamstown, MA 01267.

CONGDON, DENNIS E. ■ FAAR Painting 84. b. Aug. 31, 1953. m. Susan Lichtman. c. Rosa Elinor. BFA 75, RISD; MFA 79, Yale Univ. **Career & Employment:** AIC School of Art, Instr. 1979-80; Tyler School of Art, Instr. 1980-82; San Francisco Art Inst., Instr. 1989; RISD, Assc. Prof. 1984-present, Dept. Head 1991-present. **Fellowships, Honors & Awards:** Ford Found. Grant 1978; Yale Univ., Phelps Berdan Memorial Scholarship 1979. **Exhibitions/Performances:** MoMing Art Gallery, Chicago 1980; Moore College of Art, Philadelphia 1981; Fleisher Art Memorial, Philadelphia 1981; College of William & Mary, Williamsburg, VA 1983; Rose Art Museum, Waltham, MA 1983; Bannister Gallery, Rhode Island College, Providence 1986; Ruth Siegel Ltd., NYC 1987; AAAL 1988; Hartell Gallery, Cornell Univ. 1990; Wheeler Gallery, Providence 1992; 55 Mercer Gallery, NYC 1993; RISD Museum of Art 1994. **Bio-Bibliography:** Robert Taylor, "Six Boston Painters at Brandeis," *Boston Globe* (Mar. 27, 1983); Christopher Swan, "Boston Arts," *Christian Science Monitor* (Apr. 21, 1983); Bill Van Siclen, "Roaming the Garden with a Neo-Cubist," *Providence Journal-Bulletin* (Dec. 12, 1986). **Home Address:** 93 Fairview Ave., Rehoboth, MA 02769. **Business Address:** RISD, 2 College St., Providence, RI 02903.

CONLIN, DIANE ATNALLY ■ FAAR Classics/Archaeology 91. b. Dec. 27, 1963, Gainesville, FL. m. Michael T. Conlin. c. Kevin Michael. BA 85, SUNY, Stony Brook; MA 88, Univ. of Michigan; PhD 93, Univ. of Michigan. **Other Study:** Archaeological Field Work, Tel Anafa, Israel. **Career & Employment:** Univ. of Michigan, Visiting Asst. Prof. 1994-95. **Memberships & Offices:** ArIA. **Fellowships, Honors & Awards:** Phi Beta Kappa 1985; Univ. of Michigan, Rackham Travel Grant 1990, Rackham Fellowship 1991-92; Samuel H. Kress Fellowship 1990-91. **Publications:** "The Reconstruction of Antonia Minor on the Ara Pacis," *Journal of Roman Archaeology* 5 (1992): 209-15; *The Artists of the Ara Pacis and the Process of Hellenization in Roman Relief Sculpture* (Chapel Hill: UNC Press, forthcoming). **Home Address:** 32541 Benson Dr., Westland, MI 48185.

CONNORS, JOSEPH J. ■ RAAR History of Art 87, AAR Dir. 1988-92. b. Feb. 5, 1945, NYC. m. Françoise Moison. c. Geneviève, Thomas. BA 66, Boston College; MA 68, Cambridge Univ.; PhD 78, Harvard Univ. **Research/Artistic Interests:** History of Italian architecture, 1400-1750. **Career & Employment:** Univ. of Chicago, Instr. 1975-79; Columbia Univ., Assc. Prof. 1980-present. **Memberships & Offices:** Fulbright Comm. for Italy 1988-92; Accademia di San Luca, Cultore 1993-present; Beirat, Biblioteca Hertziana 1994-present; Centro Palladio, Vicenza 1994-present. **Fellowships, Honors & Awards:** Marshall Scholarship 1966-68; NGA, Chester Dale Fellowship 1973; Guggenheim Fellowship 1986. **Publications:** *Borromini and the Roman Oratory: Style and Society* (New York & Cambridge, MA: MIT Press & Architectural History Found., 1980; Italian trans., Turin: Einaudi, 1989); *The Robie House of Frank Lloyd Wright* (Chicago: Univ. of Chicago Press, 1984); with Louise Rice, *Specchio di Roma barocca: Una guida inedita del xvii secolo* (Rome: Edizioni dell'Elefante, 1991); "Alliance and Enmity in Roman Baroque Urbanism," *Römanisches Jahrbuch der Bibliotheca Hertziana* 25 (1989): 207-94; "Ars Tornandi: Baroque Architecture and the Lathe," *Journal of the Warburg and Courtauld Institutes* 53 (1990): 217-36; "Virtuoso Architecture in Cassiano's Rome," *Quaderni Puteani* 3 (1992): 23-40. **Home Address:** 445 Riverside Dr., NYC 10027. **Business Address:** Art History Dept., Columbia Univ., NYC 10027.

CONSAGRA, SOPHIE CHANDLER ■ AAR Dir. 1980-84, Pres. 1984-88, Vice Chair-Special Projects 1988-90. b. Apr. 28,

1927, Radnor, PA. c. Maria, Pierluigi, Francesca, George. BA 49, Smith College; MA 52, Newnham College, Cambridge Univ. **Other Study:** Univ. of Geneva 1947-48. **Career & Employment:** Delaware, Div. of Historical & Cultural Affairs, Historic Site Surveyor 1971-72; Delaware State Arts Council, Exec. Dir. 1972-77; NYSCA, Visual Arts & Architecture, Dir. 1977-80. **Fellowships, Honors & Awards:** Smith College Medal 1986. **Home Address:** 955 Lexington Ave., NYC 10021.

CONSTANT, CAROLINE B. ■ FAAR Architecture 79. b. Sept. 23, 1944, Bryn Mawr, PA. c. Alison. MArch 76, Princeton Univ. **Other Study:** Vassar College 1962-65. **Career & Employment:** Univ. of Maryland, Asst. Prof. 1979-82; Univ. of Miami, Visiting Critic 1982; Harvard Univ., Visiting Critic 1983-84, Asst. Prof. 1984-88, Assc. Prof 1988-92; Rice Univ., Visiting Critic 1989; Univ. of Florida, Assc. Prof. 1992-present. **Memberships & Offices:** SAH; Friends of the Swedish Architecture Museum. **Fellowships, Honors & Awards:** Princeton Univ., AIA Medal 1976; Florida AIA, Unbuilt Architecture Award 1984; Delmas Scholar, Gladys Krieble Delmas Found. 1984-85; ALNY Young Architects Award 1985; Graham Found. Grant 1989; Fulbright Award 1989-91; Swedish Bldg. Council Research Grant 1991; American-Swedish Found. Research Grant 1991; Peter & Birgitta Celsing Found. Research Fellow 1991; Harvard Univ., William F. Milton Research Grant 1992. **Publications:** "Mannerist Architecture," & "Map Guide: 16th-Century Rome," *Architectural Design* 49.3-4 (1979): 19-26; *The Palladio Guide* (Princeton: Princeton Architectural Press, 1985); "The Stockholm Public Library: Architecture between Nature and the City," *Arquitectura* 70.280 (Sept.-Oct. 1989): 54-67; "The Barcelona Pavilion as Landscape Garden: Modernity and the Picturesque," *AA Files* 20 (Fall 1990): 46-54; "Le Corbusier and the Landscape of Chandigarh," in *Denatured Visions: Landscape and Culture in the Twentieth Century,* ed. Stuart Wrede & William Howard Adams (New York: MOMA, 1991), 79-93; *The Woodland Cemetery: Toward a Spiritual Landscape* (Stockholm: Byggförlaget, 1994); "E.1027: the Non-heroic Modernism of Eileen Gray," *JSAH* 53.4 (1994): 265-79; with Claes Dymling & Wilfried Wang, *Architect Sigurd Lewerentz: Photos and Drawings,* ed. Claes Dymling (Stockholm: Byggförlaget, 1995); "Eileen Gray: Architecture and the Politics of Leisure,"in *Form: Modernism and History. Festschrift for Eduard Sekler,* ed. Alexander Von Hoffman (Cambridge, MA: Harvard GSD, forthcoming); *The Non-Heroic Modernism: The Architecture of Eileen Gray* (New York: Princeton Architectural Press, forthcoming). **Important Works:** with Cameron Roberts (project), Seaside Fire Station, Seaside, FL 1983-85; with Kim Tanzer, Center for Women's Studies & Gender Research (project), Univ. of Florida 1993-94. **Exhibitions/ Performances:** Group: New Jersey Soc. of Architects, Trenton 1976; Inst. for Architecture and Urban Studies 1977; Univ. of Maryland 1982; A.I.R. Gallery, NYC 1984; ALNY 1985; Princeton Univ. School of Architecture 1988; NAD 1988; Women's Study Center, Univ. of Florida 1992. **Bio-Bibliography:** *Detail: The Special Task,* exb. cat. (New York: A.I.R. Gallery, 1984); "An Ideal Vacation House," *New England Monthly* 2.6 (June 1985): 54; David Mohney & Keller Esterling, *Seaside* (Princeton: Princeton Architectural Press, 1991), 136-37; *Who's Who in the East.* **Home Address:** 1500 NW 16th Ave., No. 265, Gainesville, FL 32605.

CONWILL, HOUSTON ■ FAAR Sculpture 85. b. 1947. m. Kinshasa Holman. **Bio-Bibliography:** *Afro-American Artists; Who's Who in American Art.*

COOK, LINDA J. ■ FAAR Landscape Architecture 89. b. May 15, 1957, Richmond, VA. BS 79, Univ. of Delaware, Newark; MLA 83, Cornell Univ. **Research/Artistic Interests:** History of Italian gardens, European cemetery design, photography (silver & non-silver). **Career & Employment:** S.W.A Group, Designer 1984-86; City of Boston, Sen. Landscape Architect 1986-88; Harvard Univ., Visiting Faculty 1990-91; Univ. of Minnesota, H.W.S. Cleveland Prof. 1991-92; Radcliffe College, Faculty 1986-present; RISD, Faculty 1993. **Fellowships, Honors & Awards:** with Elizabeth Dean & Michael Stasi, Vietnam Veterans Design Competition, Meritorious Award 1981; Cornell Univ., A. Henry Detweiller Scholarship 1981, Robert James Eidlitz Traveling Fellowship 1983; ASLA, Certificate of Honor 1983; Massachusetts Artists Found. Fellowship 1986; Graham Found. Grant 1990; Hubbard Educational Trust Grant 1991. **Publications:** "The Italian Way of Death," *Landscape Architecture* (Feb. 1991); *Italian Gardens Guide* (New York: Princeton Architectural Press, 1995). **Important Works:** with S.W.A Group, 9-90 Crossing, Framingham, MA 1985; with S.W.A Group, Andover Companies Corp. HQ, Andover, MA 1986; with S.W.A Group, Milwin Farm, Ocean Township, NJ 1986; Raphael Hernandez Park, Roxbury, MA 1988; "The Chapel Project: A Journey into Art, Architecture, and Performance," Boston City Hall 1988; Boston Center for Adult Education Garden, Courtyard 1992. **Exhibitions/ Performances:** Massachusetts Artists Found., Boston Architectural Center 1986; Boston City Hall 1988; Memphis Botanic Garden 1992. **Bio-Bibliography:** "Artists Fellowships," *Art New England* (1986); Anthony Aziz, "Boston City Hall and Plaza, The Chapel Project," *Art New England* (July 1988); *Who's Who of American Women.* **Home Address:** 87 Bristol St., No. 1A, Cambridge, MA 02139.

COOKE, HEREWARD LESTER ■ FAAR History of Art 54. b. February 16, 1916, Princeton, NJ. d. Oct. 5, 1973. m. Elizabeth Miles. BA 37, Oxford Univ.; MFA 46, Princeton Univ.; PhD 56, Princeton Univ. **Other Studies:** ASL; Yale School of Fine Arts 1939-40; Sorbonne, Paris. **Research/Artistic Interests:** 18th-century drawing: French & Italian. **Career & Employment:** Freelance Artist 1937-41; US Army Air Corps, Combat Intelligence Specialist 1942-46; NASA, Art Adv., South Vietnam Combat Artist; Princeton Univ., Instr. 1947-51; Corcoran Gallery of Art, Instr. 1957-58; NGA, Curator of Painting 1962-73. **Memberships & Offices:** CAA. **Fellowships, Honors & Awards:** American Beaux Arts Competition, 1st Prize, Mural Painting 1939; US Bronze Star & Air Medal; Fulbright Fellowship; Italian Government, "Cavaliere all'Ordine del Merito della Repubblica" 1963. **Publications:** with H. Hazard, *Atlas of Islamic History* (Princeton: Princeton Univ. Press, 1951); with Anthony Blunt, *Roman Drawings of the XVII and XVIII Centuries at Windsor Castle* (London: Phaidon, 1960); intro., *An Artist's Panorama* (Washington, DC: St. Alban's School, 1962); *Painting Lessons from the Great Masters* (Washington, DC: Batsford, 1967); *The National Gallery of Art in Washington* (Munich: Knorr & Horth Verlag, 1971); *Fletcher Martin* (New York: Abrams, 1977). **Exhibitions/Performances:** Franz Bader Gallery, Washington, DC 1958. **Bio-Bibliography:** *Contemporary Authors.*

COOLIDGE, CHARLES A. ■ AAR Trustee 1917-20, Brigadier-General.

COOLIDGE, CLARK ■ RAAR Literature 85. b. 1939. **Bio-Bibliography:** *Contemporary Authors, Contemporary Poets, International Who's Who in Poetry, Writers Directory.*

COOLIDGE, FREDERIC SHURTLEFF ■ FAAR Architecture 48. b. Apr. 13, 1918, Washington, DC. d. Jan. 1994. m. Anne Coolidge. BS 40, Harvard Univ.; BArch 46, Harvard Univ.

COOLIDGE, THOMAS JEFFERSON ■ AAR Charter Mem.

COOPER, KATE ■ FAAR Classics/Archaeology 91. b. Oct. 10, 1960, Washington, DC. m. Conrad Leyser. BA 82, Wesleyan Univ.; MTS 86, Harvard Divinity School; PhD 93, Princeton Univ. **Research/Artistic Interests:** The social & religious history of the later Roman Empire, with a special emphasis on the problems of the rise of Christianity & the construction of gender within the Christian & polytheist traditions. **Career & Employment:** Barnard College, Columbia Univ., Asst. Prof. 1992-95; Univ. of Manchester, UK, Lect. 1995-present. **Fellowships, Honors & Awards:** Woodrow Wilson Found., Charlotte Newcombe Fellowship 1991. **Publications:** "Insinuations of Womanly Influence: An Aspect of the Christianization of the Later Roman Aristocracy," *Journal of Roman Studies* 82 (1992): 113-27. **Business Address:** Dept. of Religions, Univ. of Manchester, Manchester, M13 9PL, UK.

COOPER, MICHAEL J. ■ FAAR Sculpture 80. b. Oct. 13, 1943, Richmond, CA. m. Gayle V. Cooper. BA 66, San Jose State Univ.; MA 68, San Jose State Univ.; MFA 69, UC, Berkeley. **Other Study:** with Fletcher Benton. **Research/Artistic Interests:** Combination of materials & processes: wood, machined aluminum & steel, fabricating, welding, painting. **Career & Employment:** J.L. Brandt & Asscs., Los Altos, CA, Graphic Designer 1966-67; San Jose State College, Graduate Asst. 1966-68; Sacramento, Graphic Designer 1967; Steven Jacobs Design Asscs., Palo Alto, Illustrator 1967-68; Graphic Center West; UC, Berkeley, Instr. 1969; Foothill College, Los Altos, CA, Instr. 1969-76; De Anza College, Cupertino, CA, Instr. 1977. **Fellowships, Honors & Awards:** San Jose State College, Graduate Research Grant 1966, Associated Student Body Scholarship 1967-68; UC, Berkeley, Eisner Prize for Sculpture 1969; Foothill College Innovations Com. Grant 1972, Professional Development Grant 1974; Soc. for the Encouragement of Contemporary Art Award 1977; NEA, Craftsmen's Fellowship Grant 1978; Crafts Council of Australia, Fellowship 1979. **Important Works:** Public Collections: Oakland Museum, CA; Objects USA, Collection of Contemporary American Objects; Johnson Wax Collection, NYC; Metromedia Collection, Los Angeles; Student Union, San Jose State Univ., CA; Queensland State Art Gallery, Brisbane, Australia; Queen Victoria Museum & Art Gallery, Lauceston, Tasmania, Australia; Darwin College of Advanced Education, Darwin, Australia; Art Gallery of Western Australia, Perth. **Exhibitions/Performances:** Solo: San Jose State College 1968; Arleigh Gallery, San Francisco 1968; Esther Robles Gallery, Los Angeles 1969; Oregon College of Education, Monmouth 1969; Boehm Gallery, Palomar College, San Marcos, CA 1976; San Francisco Museum of Modern Art 1977; Redding Museum, Redding, CA 1978; Union Gallery, San Jose State Univ. 1978; Central Oregon Community College, Bend 1978; Queensland Museum; Kelvin Grove, College of Advanced Education, Queensland State Art Gallery; Inst. of Modern Art, Brisbane 1979; Fremantle Art Gallery, Fremantle, Western Australia 1979; Caulfield Art Center, Melbourne 1979; Crafts Council of Australia Gallery, Sydney 1979; Art Gallery of Western Australia, Perth 1982. **Home Address:** 11547 Green Valley Rd., Sebastopol, CA 95472.

COPLAND, AARON ■ RAAR Musical Composition 51. b. Nov. 14, 1900, Brooklyn, NY. d. Dec. 2, 1990. **Study:** with Victor Wittgenstein, Clarence Adler, Rubin Goldmark; with Nadia Boulanger, Fontainebleau School of Music, France 1920-24. **Career & Employment:** American Festival of Contemporary Music at Yaddo, First Dir.; New School for Social Research, Guest Lect. 1927-37; Harvard Univ. 1935, 1944; Berkshire Music Center, Chair 1940-65; Boston Symphony, Guest Conductor 1960s. **Memberships & Offices:** League of Composers-I.S.C.M., Co-chair; Koussevitzky Music Found., VP; Edward MacDowell Assn., Pres.; Walter M. Naumburg Music Found., Dir.; American Music Center, Dir.; ACA, Pres.; NIAL; ASCAP; Hon. Mem.: Accademia Nazionale di Santa Cecilia in Rome, Royal Acad. of Music, Royal Soc. of Arts in London. **Fellowships, Honors & Awards:** Guggenheim Fellowship; Pulitzer Prize 1945; New York Music Critics' Circle Award 1945, 1947; Acad. Award 1950; AAAL, Gold Medal 1956; Brandeis Univ., Creative Arts Medal 1960; Edward MacDowell Medal 1961; NAACC, Henry Hadley Medal 1964; Presidential Medal of Freedom 1964; many honorary degrees from universities including Princeton, Harvard, and Oberlin; American Symphony Orchestra League, Gold Baton Award 1978; Kennedy Center Achievement Award 1979; Congressional Gold Medal 1986. **Publications:** *What to Listen for in Music* (New York, 1939; 2d ed. 1957); *Music and Imagination* (Cambridge, MA, 1952); *Copland on Music* (New York, 1960); *The New Music 1900-1960* (New York, 1968); with V. Perlis, *Copland*, 2 vols. (New York, 1984, 1989). **Important Works:** *Music for Theater* 1925; *Symphony* 1925; *Short Symphony* 1933; *The Second Hurricane* 1936; *El Salon Mexico* 1936; *Billy the Kid*, a ballet 1938; *An Outdoor Overture* 1938; *Of Mice and Men*, film score 1939; *Quiet City*, suite for English horn, trumpet & strings 1939; *Our Town*, film score 1940; *Fanfare for the Common Man*, for brass & percussion 1942; *Rodeo*, a ballet 1942; *Lincoln Portrait*, for speaker & orchestra 1942; *Appalachian Spring*, a ballet 1944; *Third Symphony* 1946; *The Heiress*, film score 1948; *The Tender Land*, an opera 1954; *Dance Panels* 1962. Recordings: Columbia. **Bio-Bibliography:** Arthur Bergen, *Aaron Copland* (New York, 1953); Julia Smith, *Aaron Copland: His Work and Contribution to American Music* (1955); *Aaron Copland: A Complete Catalogue of his Works* (1960); *Tempo* (Winter 1970-71); Vivian Perlis, *Copland*, 2 vols. (New York: St. Martin's, 1984, 1989); J. Skowronski, *Aaron Copland: A Bio-Bibliography* (Westport, CT: Greenwood, 1985); N. Butterworth, *The Music of Aaron Copland* (New York: Toccata Press, 1985); William W. Austin, *The New Grove Twentieth-Century American Masters* (New York, 1987); John Rockwell, "Why Aaron Copland and Music Are Synonymous," *NY Times* (Dec. 4, 1990); *Baker's Biographical Dictionary of Musicians*.

CORNWELL, DEAN ■ AAR Trustee 1958-60, Artist.

CORTISSOZ, ROYAL ■ AAR Trustee 1921-47, Writer, Editor, Critic, Art Historian.

COTEL, MORRIS M. ■ FAAR Musical Composition 68. b. Feb. 20, 1943, Baltimore, MD. m. Aliya Cheskis. c. Orli, Sivan. BMus 64, Juilliard School; MS 65, Juilliard School. **Other Study:** Hebrew Univ., Jerusalem. **Career & Employment:** Rubin Acad. of Music, Jerusalem 1970-72; Peabody Conservatory of Music 1972-present. **Memberships & Offices:** Artists' Task Force for Soviet Jewry, Baltimore, Organizer 1976; New York Musicians' Com. for Soviet Jewry, NYC, Coordinator 1977. **Fellowships, Honors & Awards:** Juilliard School, TF 1964-66; ASCAP Annual Awards 1975-present; NEA Composer Grant 1975; Intl. Arnold Schoenberg Piano Competition, 2d Prize 1975; Israel Nat. Council for Culture & the Arts, Intl. Competition Winner 1978; Memorial Found. for Jewish Culture Award 1985. **Im-**

portant Works: *Symphonic Pentad* for orchestra 1964; *Concerto for Piano & Orchestra* 1968; *Variations on a Theme by Haydn* 1973; *Tehom,* for 3 pianos 1974; *Harmony of the World,* for string orchestra 1975; *Piano Sonata* (Grenadilla) 1976; *The Fire & the Mountains,* for chorus, children's chorus, soloists & percussion (Grenadilla) 1977; *August 12, 1952: The Night of the Murdered Poets,* for narrator & chamber ensemble (Grenadilla) 1978; *Yetsira,* for 2 microtonal pianos 1978-79; *Dreyfus,* an opera in 2 acts 1980-83; *Haftarah,* for solo piano 1986; *Deronda,* an opera in 3 acts 1985-89. All published by Midbar Music Press, ASCAP. **Home Address:** 639 West End Ave., NYC 10025.

COTTLE, MARK H. ■ NIAE, John Dinkeloo Traveling Fellows 1991-92.

COURTRIGHT, NICOLA ■ FAAR History of Art 83. b. Jan. 10, 1954. m. David A. Levine, FAAR 78. c. Anna Tione Levine, Luisa Cecilie Levine. BA 76, Oberlin College; MA 78, Yale Univ.; PhD 90, IFA. **Other Study:** Univ. of Würzburg, Germany 1976-77. **Career & Employment:** Univ. of Delaware, Visiting Instr. 1986; Connecticut College, Visiting Instr. 1986-87; Princeton Univ., Lect. 1987-88; Amherst College, Visiting Asst. Prof. 1989-90, Asst. Prof. 1990-present. **Fellowships, Honors & Awards:** Fulbright-Hays Grant 1976-77; MMA, Theodore Rousseau Fellowship 1980-81; IFA, Council of Friends Fellowship 1981-82, Theodore Rousseau & Florence Waterbury Fellowship 1983-84; Amherst College, Trustee Faculty Fellowship 1994-95; ACLS, Post-Doctoral Grant 1994-95. **Publications:** entries for *Drawings by Gianlorenzo Bernini from the Museum der bildenden Künste, Leipzig,* ed. Irving Lavin et al. (Princeton: Princeton Univ. Press, 1981): 72-77, 78-85, 108-19, 136-48, 200-18, 241-47; "The Vatican Tower of the Winds and the Architectural Legacy of the Counter Reformation," in *IL 60: Essays Honoring Irving Lavin on his Sixtieth Birthday,* ed. Marilyn A. Lavin (New York: Italica Press, 1990), 117-44; *Northern Travelers to Sixteenth-Century Italy: Drawings from New England Collections,* exb. cat. (Amherst, MA: Mead Art Museum, 1990); "Observations on the Origins of Rembrandt's Drawing Style," in *Artistic Exchange: Acts of the XXVIII International Congress of the History of Art, Berlin, 15-20 July 1992,* ed. Thomas W. Gaehtgens (Berlin: Akademie Verlag, 1993), 607-20; "Matthew and Paul Bril," *The Dictionary of Art.* **Home Address:** 11 Blake Field, Amherst, MA 01002. **Business Address:** Dept. of Fine Arts, Amherst College, Amherst, MA 01002.

COUSINS, MORISON S. ■ FAAR Design Arts 85. b. Apr. 10, 1934, NYC. c. Michele, Elizabeth, BID 55, Pratt Inst. **Career & Employment:** Intl. Harvester, Designer 1955-58; US Army, Pvt. Security 1956-58; Schwartz-Wyssing, Designer 1960-62; Cousins Design, Founder-Part. 1963-90; Tupperware, Design VP 1990-present. **Memberships & Offices:** Industrial Designers Soc. of America. **Important Works:** Space-Tel Telephone: MOMA; Staatliches Museum für Angewadte Kunst, Munich; Museum Boymans van Beuningen, Rotterdam; Museum für Kunst & Gewerbe, Hamburg; Virginia Museum of Fine Arts, Richmond. Gillette Promax Hairdryer: MOMA, Staatliches Museum für Angewadte Kunst, Munich; Museum Boymans van Beuningen, Rotterdam. Privecode Telephone Access Controller: MOMA; Staatliches Museum für Angewadte Kunst, Munich; Museum für Kunst & Gewerbe, Hamburg; Virginia Museum of Fine Arts, Richmond. Maxim Convection Oven: Museum Boymans van Beuningen, Rotterdam. Capt. Kelley Fire Extinguisher, Gillette: Museum für Kunst & Gewerbe, Hamburg. Tupperware: Brooklyn Museum of Art, NYC; Nat. Design Museum, Smithsonian Inst., NYC; Victoria & Albert

Museum, London; Philadelphia Museum of Art; Musée des Arts Décoratifs de Montreal; MMA. **Exhibitions/Performances:** Hayden Gallery, MIT 1984; Katonah Gallery, Katonah, NY 1984; Denver Museum of Art 1985; Whitney Museum, NYC 1985; Design Museum, London 1992. **Home Address:** 241 W. Lake Sue Ave., Winter Park, FL 32789. **Business Address:** Tupperware, PO Box 2353, Orlando, FL 32802.

COWLES, RUSSELL ■ FAAR Painting 20. b. Oct. 7, 1887, Algona, IA. d. Feb. 20, 1979. m. Nancy Cardozo Egleson. BA 09, Dartmouth College. **Other Studies:** ASL; NAD. **Fellowships, Honors & Awards:** AIC, Norman Wait Harris Silver Medal 1926; Denver Art Museum, Yetter Prize 1936; Hon. DFA: Grinnell College 1945, Dartmouth College 1951, Cornell Univ. 1958. **Important Works:** Permanent Collections: Phillips Andover; Britannica; Dartmouth College; Denver Art Museum; Des Moines; Los Angeles County Museum; Minneapolis Inst.; New Britain Museum; PAFA; Santa Barbara Museum of Art; Witchita Art Museum. **Exhibitions/Performances:** Solo: Ferargil Gallery, NYC 1935; Los Angeles County Museum of Art 1937; Kraushaar's, NYC 1939, 1941, 1944, 1946, 1948, 1950, 1954, 1959; Dalzell Hatfield Gallery 1936, 1939, 1943; Dayton Art Inst. (3-person) 1942; Dartmouth College 1943, 1963; Des Moines 1955; Dalzell Hatfield Galleries, Los Angeles 1959, 1975; Minneapolis Inst. of Arts 1966, Group Shows: ALNY; AIC; California Palace; Wichita Art Museum; Corcoran Art Gallery. **Bio-Bibliography:** "Artist Defies All Traditions," *New York Sun* (Jan. 25, 1935); Ernest J. Watson, "Russell Cowles," *American Artist* (Nov. 1945); *Russell Cowles: Recent Paintings,* exb. cat. (Los Angeles, 1959); *Dictionary of Contemporary American Artists.*

COWLEY, MALCOLM ■ RAAR Literature 58. b. Aug. 25, 1898, Belsano, PA. d. Mar. 27, 1989. m. Marguerite Frances Baird, Muriel Maurer. c. Robert William. BA 20, Harvard Univ.; Dipl. 22, Université de Montpellier. **Career & Employment:** *The New Republic,* Literary Ed. 1929-40; Viking Press, Literary Adv. 1948-80; Visiting Prof.: Univ. of Washington 1950; Stanford Univ. 1956, 1959, 1960-61, 1965; Univ. of Michigan 1957 UC 1962; Cornell Univ. 1964; Hollins College 1968, 1970; Univ. of Minnesota 1971; Univ. of Warwick 1973. **Memberships & Offices:** American Writers Congress 1935; League of American Writers; Yaddo Corp., Dir.; Sherman, CT, Zoning Bd., Chair; NIAL, Pres. 1956-59, 1962-65; AAAL, Chancellor 1967-76; Club des Bibliophages; Phi Beta Kappa; Century Assn. **Fellowships, Honors & Awards:** Levinson Prize 1928; Harriet Monroe Memorial Prize 1939; NIAL Grant 1946; NEA Grant 1967; Signet Soc. Medal 1976; Litt. D.: Franklin & Marshall College 1961, Colby College 1962, Univ. of Warwick 1975, Univ. of New Haven 1976, Monmouth College 1978. **Publications:** *Blue Juanita* (New York: Jonathan Cape, 1929); *Exile's Return* (New York: Norton, 1934); *The Dry Season* (Norwalk, CT: New Directions, 1941); ed., *The Portable Hemingway* (New York: Viking, 1944); ed., *The Portable Faulkner* (New York: Viking, 1946); ed., *The Portable Hawthorne* (New York: Viking, 1948); *The Literary Situation* (New York: Viking, 1954); with D.P. Mannix, *Black Cargoes: A History of the Atlantic Slave Trade 1518-1865* (New York: Viking, 1962); *The Faulkner-Cowley File* (New York: Viking, 1966); *Blue Juanita: Collected Poems* (New York: Viking, 1968); *Think Back on Us: A Contemporary Chronicle of the 1930s* (Cardondale: Southern Illinois Univ., 1969); *A Many-Windowed House: Collected Essays on American Writers and American Writing* (New York: Viking, 1970); *The Lesson of the Masters* (New York: Viking, 1971); *A Second Flowering: Works and Days of the Lost Generation* (New York: Viking, 1973); *And I Worked at the Writer's Trade* (New York: Viking, 1978); *The Dream of the Golden Moun-*

tains (New York: Viking, 1980); *Remembering the 1930s* (New York: Viking, 1980); *The View from Eighty* (New York: Viking, 1980); *The Selected Correspondence of Kenneth Burke and Malcolm Crowley* (New York: Viking, 1988). **Bio-Bibliography:** Diane U. Eisenberg, *Malcolm Cowley: A Checklist of His Writings, 1915-1973* (Carbondale: Southern Illinois Univ. Press, 1975); *Current Biography Yearbook* (1989); *Cyclopedia of World Authors II* (1989); *Major Twentieth-Century Writers* (1991); *Contemporary Authors; Dictionary of Literary Biography.*

COX, ALLYN ■ FAAR Painting 20; AAR Trustee 1954-63. b. June 5, 1896, NYC. d. Sept. 26, 1982. m. Ethel H. Potter. NAD 1911-16; ASL 1915-16; Studied under father, Kenyon Cox. **Research/Artistic Interests:** Mural painting. **Memberships & Offices:** Nat. Soc. of Mural Painters, Honorary Pres.; NYC Art Comm., Pres.; American Artists Professional League, VP; ALNY; Fine Arts Federation of NY; Municipal Art Soc. **Fellowships, Honors & Awards:** Los Angeles County Art Museum, Medal 1926; Artists Professional League, Medal 1945; ALNY, Gold Medal of Honor 1954. **Important Works:** Clark Memorial Library, Los Angeles 1924-27; Univ. of Virginia, Law Bldg. 1930-34; S.S. "America" 1940; Guaranty Trust Co., NYC 1946; George Washington Masonic Memorial, Alexandria, VA 1948-56; Rotunda, Capitol Bldg., Washington, DC 1952; Great Experiment Hall, Capitol Bldg., Washington, DC 1973-82; Gen. U.S. Grant Memorial, NYC; Princeton Museum. **Exhibitions/Performances:** Los Angeles Museum of Art 1926; NAD. **Bio-Bibliography:** *The Murals of Allyn Cox in the U.S. Capitol* (Washington, DC, 1986); *American Painters, Sculpters and Engravers; The American Story in Art: Who Was Who in American Art.*

COX, DONALD M. ■ AAR Trustee 1983-present. b. WV. BS, Virginia Polytechnic Inst. **Career & Employment:** Exxon Corp., Dir. & Sen. VP until 1985; Teagle Found. Chair & Dir.; Polytechnic Univ. of New York, Dir.; Emigrant Savings Bank, Dir. **Memberships & Offices:** American Federation of Arts, BoT; Bluefield College, VA, BoT; Pilgrims of the United States.

COX, GARDNER ■ RAAR Painting 61; AAR Trustee 1963-75. b. Jan. 2, 1906, Holyoke, MA. d. Jan. 14, 1988. m. Phyllis Moyra Byrne. c. Benjamin, Katherine Gilbert Abbot, James Byrne, Phyllis Byrne. ASL 1924; Harvard Univ. 1924-27; MFA School 1928-32; MIT 1929-31. **Career & Employment:** MFA School 1954-55. **Memberships & Offices:** Blanche Coleman Award Jury 1964-81; Boston Arts Festival, Exec. Com. 1959-67; Massachusetts Fine Arts Comm. 1965-88; Saint-Gaudens Memorial, BoT 1959-88; AAAS; NIAL; NAD, Academician. **Fellowships, Honors & Awards:** AIC, M.V. Kohnstamm Prize 1949; Norman Wait Harris Bronze Medal 1951; Tufts Univ., D.F.A. Posthumous 1988. **Important Works:** Permanent collections: MFA; Fogg Museum, Harvard; Addison Gallery, Andover, MA; Wadsworth Atheneum, Hartford; Yale Univ.; Wellesley College; Wabash College; MIT; Mt. Holyoke College; Boston Athenaeum; Santa Barbara Art Museum; Middlebury College; Nat. Portrait Gallery; Brandeis Univ.; Princeton Univ.; Clark Inst., Williamstown; US Depts. of State, Army, Defense, Transportation, FAA; Boston State House. **Exhibitions/Performances:** Carnegie Inst. 1941; Virginia Museum of Fine Arts 1946, 1948; AIC 1948, 1949, 1951; MMA 1950; Univ. of Illinois 1950-51; Inst. of Contemporary Art, Boston 1953; Solo: Farnsworth Museum, Rockland, ME 1956; Newport Art Assn., RI 1966; Corcoran Gallery, Washington, DC 1975; Boston Athenaeum 1981. **Bio-Bibliography:** *Portraits and Paintings by Gardner Cox,* exb. cat. (Rockland, ME: Farnsworth Art Museum, 1956); *Portraits by Gardner Cox,* exb. cat. (Washington, DC:

Corcoran Gallery of Art, 1975); *NY Times,* Obit. (Jan. 16, 1988); *Gardner Cox: In Memoriam, 1906-1988,* exb. cat. (Boston: St. Botolph Club, 1988); *Who Was Who in America; Who Was Who in American Art.*

COYNE, JOHN ■ NIAE, John Dinkeloo Traveling Fellow 1988-89.

CRACCO, LELIA RUGGINI ■ Italian Fulbright Fellow 1956-57.

CRAWFORD, CALEB ■ NIAE, John Dinkeloo Traveling Fellow 1990-91.

CRAWFORD, JANE W. ■ FAAR Classics/Archaeology 82, AAR Adv. Council 1993-present. b. Oct. 11, 1945, Huntington, WV. m. Bernard D. Frischer. c. Katherine. BA 68, Boston Univ.; MA 74, 76, UCLA; PhD 81, UCLA. **Research/Artistic Interests:** Greek & Roman literature, rhetoric, Roman history. **Career & Employment:** Loyola Marymount Univ., Asst. Prof. 1984-88, Assc. Prof. 1988-93, Prof. 1993-present; Chair 1985-present; Humanities Pgm., Dir. 1991-present. **Memberships & Offices:** California Classical Assn. 1980-present; VSA 1988-present; APA 1980-present; Com. for Excellence in Teaching 1990-present, Chair 1992-93. **Fellowships, Honors & Awards:** IAS, Fellow 1988-89; APA, Award for Excellence in Teaching 1989. **Publications:** *M. Tullius Cicero: The Lost and Unpublished Speeches* (Göttingen: Vendenhoeck & Ruprecht, 1984); "Cicero's Influence on Vergil," *Enciclopedia Vergiliana* (Rome: Enciclopedia Vergiliana, 1986), 1:774-76; "The Prosopography of the Hermosopids and the Motives of Their Accusers," *Favonius* 2 (1988): 1-18; *M. Tullius Cicero: The Fragmentary Speeches. An Edition with Commentary* (Atlanta: APA Monographs, 1994). **Home Address:** 3441 Butler Ave., Los Angeles, CA 90066. **Business Address:** Dept. of Classics, Loyola Marymount Univ., 7101 W. 80 St., Los Angeles, CA 90045.

CRAWFORD, JOHN RAYMOND ■ FAAR Classics/Archaeology 14. b. July 4, 1886, Chicago, IL. d. April 15 1929. m. Pauline Avery. c. William, John. BA 06, Allegheny College; MA 08, Harvard Univ.; PhD 16, Harvard Univ. **Other Studies:** Univ. of Munich 1908-9. **Career & Employment:** Upper Louisiana Univ., Acting Prof. 1906-7; Harvard Univ., Asst. 1911-12; Columbia Univ., Instr. 1912-17, Asst. Prof. 1917-19; US Army 2d Lt. 1918; Lafayette College, Prof., Dept. Head 1919-29. **Publications:** *Lest We Forget* (London, 1897); "Capita desecta and Marble Coiffures," *Memoirs of the AAR* 1 (1918): 103-19; "Child Portrait of Drusus Junior in the Ara Pacis," *AJA* 26 (1922): 307-15; *Greek Tales for Tiny Tots* (Bloomington, IL: Public School Publishing Co., 1929). **Bio-Bibliography:** *Who Was Who in America.*

CREA, ENZO ■ AAR Visitor 1983-84, Publisher.

CREAGHAN, JOHN SYLVESTER, SJ ■ FAAR Classics/Archaeology 48; Adv. Council. b. Dec. 8, 1913, Baltimore, MD. d. June 3, 1960. BA 36, Woodstock College; MA 38, Fordham Univ.; MA 47, Princeton Univ.; PhD 51, Princeton Univ. **Research/Artistic Interests:** Early Christian epitaphs in Athens, Latin Christian inscriptions, Early Christian religious ideas. **Career & Employment:** Georgetown Univ., Faculty 1938-41, 1948-52; Woodstock College, Faculty 1941-43; Bellarmine Novitiate, Faculty 1952-54; Loyola Seminary, Shrub Oak, NY, Faculty 1954-60. **Publications:** with A.E. Raubitschek, "Early Christian Epitaphs from Athens," *Hesperia* 16 (1947): 1-54 (rpt., Woodstock, MD: Theological Studies, 1947). **Bio-Bibliography:** *NY Times,* Obit. (June 4, 1960).

CRILE, SUSAN ■ RAAR Painting 90. Aug. 12, 1942, Cleveland, OH. m. Joseph S. Murphy. BA 65, Bennington College. **Research/Artistic Interests:** Painting: oil, works on paper: pastel, charcoal, oil stick, prints: lithograph, etching, woodcut, screen print. **Career & Employment:** Princeton Univ. 1973-76; Sarah Lawrence College 1976-79; School of Visual Arts, NYC 1976-82; Barnard College 1983-86; Hunter College, CUNY, Prof. 1983-present. **Memberships & Offices:** Rep. to Hungary & Portugal for the Intl. Communications Agency 1981; Yaddo, Saratoga Springs, NY 1985; NEA, Visual Arts Panel, Painting 1987; NEA Overview Policy Panel for the Visual Arts 1987; Yaddo, BoD 1991. **Fellowships, Honors & Awards:** Yaddo Grants 1970, 1972, 1975, 1978; Ingram Merrill Grant 1972; MacDowell Colony Grant 1982; NEA Fellowship 1982, 1989. **Important Works:** Public Collections: MMA; Hirshhorn Museum, Washington, DC; Phillips Collection, Washington, DC; Guggenheim Museum, NYC; Cleveland Museum of Art; Brooklyn Museum; Albright-Knox Art Gallery, Buffalo, NY; Museum of Art, Carnegie Inst., Pittsburgh; Portland Museum of Art, ME; Mt. Holyoke College Art Museum; Weatherspoon Gallery, Greensboro, NC; Grey Art Gallery & Study Center, NYU; Bowdoin College Museum of Art, Brunswick, ME; Museum of Art, Carnegie Inst., Pittsburgh; Arizona State Univ. Art Museum, Tempe; Denver Museum of Art. **Exhibitions/Performances:** Museum Exhibitions: Phillips Collection, Washington, DC 1975; St. Louis Museum of Art 1994. Solo: Kornblee Gallery, NYC 1971, 1972, 1973; Fischbach Gallery, NYC 1974, 1975, 1977; Brooke Alexander Gallery, NYC 1975; New Gallery, Cleveland, OH 1977; Center Gallery, Bucknell Univ., Lewisburg, PA 1978; Droll-Kolbert Gallery, NYC 1978, 1980; Nina Freudenheim Gallery, Buffalo, NY 1980, 1984; Ivory Kimpton Gallery, San Francisco 1981, 1984, 1988; Janie C. Lee Gallery, Houston 1982; Van Straaten Gallery, Chicago 1983; Lincoln Center Gallery, NYC 1983; Cleveland Center for Contemporary Art 1984; Graham Modern, NYC 1985, 1987, 1988, 1990; Adams-Middleton Gallery, Dallas 1986; Gloria Luria, Bay Harbor Island, FL 1987, 1988; Univ. Art Museum, California State Univ., Long Beach 1994; Blaffer Gallery, Univ. of Houston 1994. **Home Address:** 168 W. 86th St., NYC 10024. **Business Address:** Hunter College, 695 Park Ave., NYC 10021.

CRISCUOLO, LUCIA ■ Italian Fulbright Fellow 1978-79.

CROWLEY, ROGER A. ■ FAAR Architecture 85. b. Jan. 6, 1955, Oakridge, TN. BFA 77, RISD; BArch 78, RISD; MArch 83, Princeton Univ. **Career & Employment:** Charles G. Hilgenhurst & Asscs., Draftsman-Designer 1978-80; Michael Graves Architect, Designer 1981-82; Kohn, Pedersen & Fox, Asscs., Designer 1983-. **Fellowships, Honors & Awards:** RISD, Herbert & Claiborne Pell Gold Medal 1977; RISD, AIA School Medal & Certificate of Merit 1978; *Progressive Architecture* Intl. Furniture Competition, Award with Michael Graves 1982, 1st Award 1983.

CROWNINSHIELD, FREDERIC ■ American School of Architecture in Rome, Dir. 1909-12; AAR Trustee 1912; Artist.

CRUZ, TEDDY ■ FAAR Architecture 92. b. Mar. 31, 1962, Guatemala City, Guatemala. c. Alexandra. BArch 87, California Polytechnic State Univ, San Luis Obispo. **Other Study:** Universidad Rafael Landivar, Guatemala, architecture 1979-82; Architecture under Gianni Pettena & Cristiano Toraldo de Francia, Florence. **Research/Artistic Interests:** Latin American architectural studies-research, the role of drawing & painting in the design process. **Career & Employment:** PAPA-Pacific Asscs. Planners Architects, Designer 1984-89; Rob Wellington Quigley, Architect, Project Designer 1989-94; San Diego New School of Architecture, Design Instr. 1992-present; SCI-ARC-Southern California Inst. of Architecture, Latin American Design Studio, Los Angeles-Mexico City, Design Instr. 1993-present; OdA-Oficina de Arquitectura, Prin. 1993-present. **Memberships & Offices:** Social Movements in Art/Smart, Artist-in-Residence; UC, San Diego "Urban Futures" Design Charrette, Design Mem. 1993; Citizen's Coordinate for Century 3 Com. 1993-present; SCI-ARC L.A.-L.A. Program Seminar Lect., Guatemala, Mexico, Peru 1994. **Fellowships, Honors & Awards:** AIA San Diego Chap., Annual Design Awards 1986, 1989, 1993, Honor Award 1994, *Progressive Architecture* Award 1986. **Important Works:** with Joaquin Garcia, Garcia Residence 1981; Coronado Residence, Coronado, CA 1988; Fallbrook Residence, San Diego 1989; with Rob Quigley, FAIA, Capistrano Beach Glass House 1990; with Rob Quigley FAIA, Capistrano Residence 1991; "Six Drawings on Paper," Xerox Corp. Public Art Collection 1991; Las Gradas Residence, Tijuana, Mexico 1991; Six Row Houses, Tijuana, Mexico 1993; Zimeri Residence, Guatemala City, Guatemala 1994. **Exhibitions/Performances:** "San Diego Young Architects," San Diego 1988; Simayspace, San Diego 1990; Gallery of Functional Art, Los Angeles 1990; Temple Univ. Gallery, Rome 1992; Atheneum, La Jolla, CA 1994. **Bio-Bibliography:** "Home Sweet Home," *Progressive Architecture* (Jan. 1986); "'Urban Architextures,' Cities Reformulated in California," *Visions Art Quarterly* (Winter 1990); "Rob Quigley: Capistrano Beach Glass House," *Project 1990 GA Houses* 28; Dirk Sutro, "Cruz's Winning Style," *Los Angeles Times* (May 9, 1991), E1 & E13; Ralph Resling," Lessons from Rome, An Interview with Teddy Cruz," *Cartouche* (1992); Kay Kaiser, "Architect Goes to the Wall for Inspiration," *San Diego Union* (Nov. 21, 1993); Ann Jarmusch, "Tijuana House Wins Top Prize in Architecture," *San Diego Union* (June 26, 1994); Ann Jarmusch, "Taking Concept of Home to New Level," *San Diego Union* (Aug. 14, 1994). **Home Address:** 710 13 St., Suite 312, San Diego, CA 92101. **Business Address:** Oficina de Arquitectura, 710 13 St., Suite 312, San Diego, CA 92101.

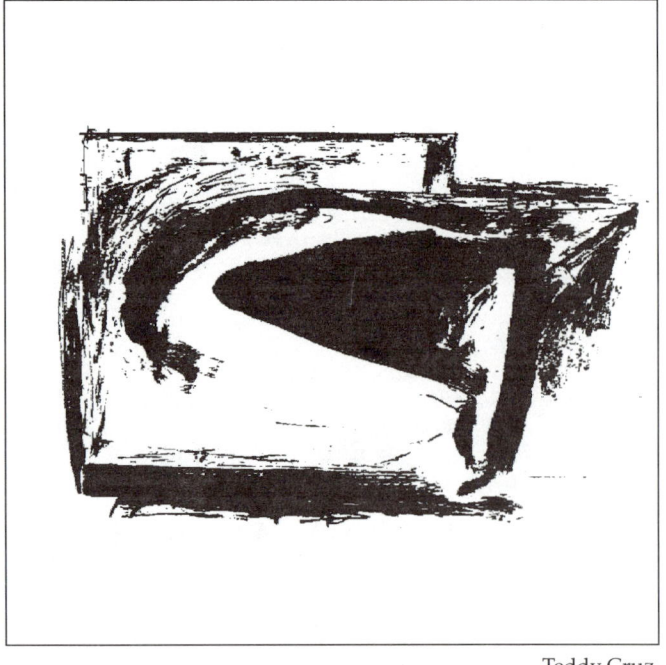

Teddy Cruz

CULLEY, THOMAS, SJ ■ FAAR Post-Classical/Humanistic Studies 67. b. Feb. 4, 1928, Holdenville, OK. BMus 54, Loyola Univ.; MA 59, Harvard Univ.; PhD 65, Harvard Univ. **Career & Employment:** Weston College, Faculty c.1966.

CULLMAN, DOROTHY ■ AAR Trustee 1991-present. **Memberships & Offices:** New York Public Library, BoT, Exec. Comm.; Library for the Performing Arts Com., Co-Chair; Research Libraries, Corp. Com.; New York Shakespeare Festival, BoT; Film Soc. of Lincoln Center, Chair, VP; MOMA, Intl. Council; Human Rights Watch. **Important Works:** Public Television, 3 films.

CULP, RUSSELL R. ■ FAAR Design Arts 80. b. Dec. 23, 1946, Chicago, IL. m. Barbara J. Bradley. c. Woodrow Yeong Hwan, Cecilia Min Young. BArch 70, Univ. of Illinois. **Career & Employment:** George Sexton Asscs., Senior Designer, Project Manager 1982-91; State Hermitage Museum, St. Petersburg & Pushkin State Museum, Moscow, independent consultant to private collector 1992-93; Freer Gallery of Art, Senior Designer, Project Manager 1991-93. **Fellowships, Honors & Awards:** Illinois Arts Council Grants 1970-79. **Important Works:** Museum exhibition & light design at: Freer Gallery of Art, George Ortiz Collection, Cincinnati Art Museum, John & Mable Ringling Museum of Art, Sainsbury Centre for the Visual Arts, AIC, MMA, Memphis Convention Center, Virginia Museum of Fine Arts, Yale Univ. Art Gallery, Kuwait Nat. Museum, Detroit Inst. of Arts. **Home Address:** 3620 Porter St. NW, Washington, DC 20016. **Business Address:** Smithsonian Inst., Freer Gallery, 1150 Independence Ave., Washington, DC 20560.

CUMMER, WELLINGTON WILLSON ■ FAAR Architecture 77. b. Nov. 1, 1938, Jacksonville, FL. m. Sarah Virginia Boll. c. Clementine, Charles. BA 61, Yale Univ.; MA 68, Univ. of Pennsylvania; PhD 70, Univ. of Pennsylvania. **Other Studies:** ASCSA 1968-70. **Career & Employment:** American Research Inst., Ankara Dir. & Fellow 1970-72; Cornell Univ., Asst. Prof. c.1976; Summer Field School, Rome Faculty 1982; RISD, Faculty; Summer Field School, Rome 1984. **Memberships & Offices:** American Inst. of Nautical Archaeology, BoD; ArIA, Finger Lakes Soc., Pres. 1973-74. **Publications:** with Elizabeth Schofield, *Keos III, Ayia Irini, House A* (von Zabern, 1984).

CUOMO, MATILDA ■ AAR Visitor 1989-90, Wife of Governor of New York.

CURRAN, BRIAN ■ FAAR History of Art 94. m. Mary Juszynski. BFA 79, Massachusetts College of Art; MA 89, Univ. of Massachusetts, Amherst; MA 92, Princeton Univ. **Career & Employment:** MFA, Curatorial Consultant & Dept. Asst. 1984-90; Univ. of Massachusetts, Amherst, Instr. 1988-90; Museum of Fine Arts, Springfield, MA, Instr. 1990; Princeton Univ., Instr. 1992-93. **Memberships & Offices:** CAA, RSA, ArIA. **Fellowships, Honors & Awards:** Princeton Univ.: Program for Italian Studies Summer Research Grant 1992, Mellon Found. Dissertation Seminar Grant 1993; Samuel H. Kress Found., Inst. Fellowship at the Bibliotheca Hertziana, Rome 1993-95. **Publications:** "Les incrustations en ivoire," & 20 catalog entries, in *Kerma, royaume de Nubie: L'antiquité africaine au temps des pharaons*, ed. Charles Bonnet, exb. cat. (Geneva, 1990); with Anthony Grafton, "A 15th-Century Site Report on the Vatican Obelisk," *Journal of the Warburg and Courtauld Institutes* (forthcoming). **Business Address:** Dept. of Art & Archaeology, McCormick Hall, Princeton Univ., Princeton, NJ 08544.

CURRIER, ALBERT DEAN ■ AAR Charter Mem., Lawyer.

CURRIER, CHARLES AMOS ■ FAAR Landscape Architecture 48. b. Aug. 1912, Meriden, CT. d. Sept. 4, 1980. m. Doris Currier. BEd, Boston Univ.; MLA, Harvard GSD. **Career & Employment:** Charles A. Currier & Asscs. 1939-80. **Fellowships, Honors & Awards:** Charles Elliot Traveling Fellowship 1939.

CURRIER, SEBASTIAN ■ FAAR Musical Composition 94. b. Mar. 16, 1959, Huntingdon, PA. m. Emma Tahmizian. MM 81, Manhattan School of Music; MM 89, Juilliard School of Music; DMA 92, Juilliard School of Music. **Other Study:** With George Perle & Milton Babbitt. **Career & Employment: Juilliard School, Faculty;** Fontana Concert Soc., Composer-in-Residence 1992; Bowdoin Summer Music Festival, Composer-in-Residence 1992-present; California State Univ., Festival of New Music, Sacramento, Composer-in-Residence 1993. **Fellowships, Honors & Awards:** Delius Composition Competition, 1st Prize 1986; Tanglewood Fellowhip 1987; AAAL, Charles Ives Scholarship 1987, Charles Ives Award 1993; ASCAP Grant 1988; Theodore Presser Award 1989; Barlow Endowment Comm. 1990; NEA Fellowship 1991; Kennedy Center, Friedheim Award 1991; MacDowell Resident 1991; Yaddo Resident 1991; Guggenheim Fellowship 1992; Koussevitzky Comm. 1994. **Important Works:** *Assertions-Reflections*, for solo guitar 1988; *Clockwork*, for violin & piano 1989; *Vocalissimus*, for voice & ensemble, Barlow Endowment Comm. 1991; *Time's Hand*, for orchestra 1991; *Theo's Sketchbook*, for piano 1992; *Entanglement*, for violin & piano, Pro Musicis Found. Comm. 1992; *Aftersong*, for violin & piano 1993; *Uncertainties*, for viola & piano 1993. **Home Address:** 442 W. 57 St., Apt. 6K, NYC 10019.

CURRIER, STEPHEN ■ AAR Trustee 1967, Art Patron.

CURRY, JAMES JOSEPH MARK ■ FAAR Classics/Archaeology 63. b. Oct. 3, 1936, Lawrence, MA. m. Kay Curry. c. Elizabeth, Mary Jane. BA 58, Columbia College; MA 60, Cornell Univ.; PhD 62, Cornell Univ. **Career & Employment:** Univ. of Pittsburgh.

CURTIS, CHARLES DENSMORE ■ FAAR Classics/Archaeology 15; Lect., Assc. Prof. 1915-25; Publications of AAR, Ed. 1915-25; AAR Museum, Curator 1915-25. b. Oct. 16, 1875, Augusta, ME. d. June 7, 1925. BA 1900, Pomona College; MA 01, Univ. of Colorado. **Other Study:** ASCSR 1905-6; Columbia Univ. 1907-9. **Research/Artistic Interests:** Triumphal arches, ancient jewelry; Tripoli & Sardis. **Career & Employment:** Expeditions for the excavation of Cyrene Tripoli 1910-11; Sardis 1920-25. **Fellowships, Honors & Awards:** Pontificia Accademia Romana di Archeologia, Fellow; Union Club, Rome. **Publications:** "Coins from Asia Minor," *AJA* 11 (1907): 194-95; trans., Ettore Pais, *Ancient Italy* (Chicago: Univ. of Chicago Press, 1908); "Roman Monumental Arches," *Supplementary Papers of ASCSR* 2 (1908): 26-83; trans. E. Pais et al. "The Differences between Sand and Pozzolana," *Journal of Roman Studies* 3 (1913): 197-203; "An Early Graeco-Etruscan Fibula," *Journal of Roman Studies* 5 (1914): 17-25; "Ancient Granulated Jewelry of the Seventh Century B.C. and Earlier," *Memoirs of the AAR* 1 (1917): 63-85; "The Bernardini Tomb," *Memoirs of the AAR* 3 (1919): 9-90; "Recent Archaeological Discoveries in Rome and at Veii," *Art and Archeology* 9 (1920): 271-77; "Sappho and the 'Leucadian Leap,'" *AJA* 24 (1920): 146-50; "The Barberini Tomb," *Memoirs of the AAR* 5 (1925): 9-52; *Jewelry and Gold Work: Sardis*, Publications of the American Society for the Excavation of Sardis 13 (Rome, 1925). **Bio-Bibliography:** A.W. Van Buren, "Memoir," *AJA* 30 (1926): 99-100; *Who Was Who in America*.

CUTLER, ANTHONY ■ RAAR History of Art 92. b. Feb. 18, 1934, London, England. m. Aalo A. Cutler. c. Andrew, Lisa. BA 55, Trinity College, Cambridge; MA 60, Trinity College, Cambridge; PhD 63, Emory Univ. **Other Study:** Istituto di Studi Storici, Naples 1955-56; Belgrade Nat. Univ., Yugoslavia 1962-63. **Career & Employment:** Morehouse College, Instr. 1960-63; Emory Univ., Asst. Prof. 1963-67; ANS, Visiting Lect. 1968; Pennsylvania State Univ., Assc. Prof. 1967-74, Prof. 1974-87, Research Prof. 1987-present; UC, Berkeley, Visiting Assc. Prof. 1969. **Memberships & Offices:** *Choice*, Consultant on Byzantine history & art history 1967-present; ArIA, Inst. Lect. 1967-69, 1971-72, 1982, 1984; Pennsylvania State Univ. Press, Consultant on Byzantine art & archaeology 1969-present; ArIA, Delegate to XIV Intl. Congress of Byzantine Studies, Bucharest, Roumania 1971; NEH, Div. of Research Grants, Consultant, Fellowships, Public Programs 1973-74, 1976-77, 1980, 1985-86; *Art Bulletin*, Reader 1973-present; Byzantine Studies Conference, Governing Bd. 1976, Program Chair 1977, VP 1978; US Nat. Com. for Byzantine Studies 1977-present, Adv. Bd. for XVII Intl. Congress 1986; Dumbarton Oaks Alumni Assn., VP 1979-88, Pres. 1989-91; XVI Intl. Congress, Vienna 1981; *The Oxford Dictionary of Byzantium*, Art History Ed. 1984-90; J. Paul Getty Trust, Consultant 1986-present; Central Pennsylvania Soc., Pres. 1989-91; *Byzantinische Zeitschrift, Word and Image*, Ed. Bd. 1992-present. **Fellowships, Honors & Awards:** Trinity College, Cambridge, Open Scholarship 1952; Inst. of Historical Studies, Rockefeller Postgraduate Fellow, Naples, Italy 1956-57; British Council Fellow in Belgrade, Yugoslavia 1962; ANS, Grant-in-Aid 1963; Southeastern Inst. of Medieval & Renaissance Studies, Duke Univ. Fellow 1966; Pennsylvania State Univ., Research Fellow, Inst. for the Arts & Humanistic Studies 1967, 1974, 1975, 1977, 1981, 1985, Life Fellow 1985-present; ACLS Grant-in-Aid 1969, Publication Subsidy 1974, Travel Grants 1975, 1977, Grant-in-Aid 1981; ASCSA, Gennadeion Fellow 1970-71; Dumbarton Oaks Fellow 1975-76, 1982-83, 1990; CAA, Millard Meiss Fund, Publication Subsidy 1980; Corpus Christi College, Cambridge, Senior Research Fellow 1983; NEH Research Programs Grants 1984-85, 1986-87, 1988-90, Travel to Collections Grants 1984, 1992; APS, Research Grant 1984; Deutscher Akademischer Austauschdienst, Study Visit Grant 1987; Pennsylvania State Univ., Faculty Scholar Medal 1988, Alumni Teaching Award 1988; Univ. of Wisconsin, Inst. for Research in the Humanities, Madison, Brittingham Prof. 1988; Soc. of Antiquaries, London, Fellow 1988; IAS 1989; Intl. Research & Exchanges Bd., Research Grant 1991; American Publishers Assn., Hawkins Prize 1992. **Publications:** *The Aristocratic Psalters in Byzantium*, Bibliothèque des Cahiers Archéologiques 13 (Paris: Picard, 1984); "Under the Sign of the Deesis: On the Question of Representativeness in Medieval Art & Literature," *Dumbarton Oaks Papers* 41 (1987): 145-54 "Un triptyque byzantin en ivoire: La Nativité du Louvre, Étude comparée," *Revue du Louvre* 38 (1988): 21-28; with N. Oikonomides, "An Imperial Byzantine Casket and its Fate at a Humanist's Hands," *Art Bulletin* 70 (1988): 77-87; "The Disputà Plate in the J. Paul Getty Museum and its Cinquecento Context," *J. Paul Getty Museum Journal* 18 (1990): 5-32; ed., with A.P. Kazhdan et al. *The Oxford Dictionary of Byzantium*, 3 vols. (New York: Oxford Univ. Press, 1991); ed., with S.C. Franklin, *Homo Byzantinus: Essays in Honor of Alexander Kazhdan*, Dumbarton Oaks Papers 46 (Washington, DC: Dumbarton Oaks, 1992); "*Pas Oikos Israel*: Ezekiel and the Politics of Resurrection in Tenth-Century Byzantium," *Dumbarton Oaks Papers* 46 (1992): 47-58; "Five Lessons in Late Roman Ivory," *Journal of Roman Archaeology* 6 (1993): 167-92; *The Hand of the Master: Craftsmanship, Ivory, and Society in Byzantium* (Princeton: Princeton Univ. Press, 1994). **Business Address:** Dept. of Art History 225, Arts II, Pennsylvania State Univ., Univ. Park, PA 16802.

CUTLER, PHOEBE ■ FAAR Landscape Architecture 89. b. Jan. 18, 1947, Boston, MA. m. Desmond F. Smith. c. Bayard Martensen. BA 69, Harvard Univ.; MLA 73, UC, Berkeley. **Research/Artistic Interests:** The influence of the Italian garden on the US. **Publications:** "On Recognizing a WPA Rose Garden or a CCC Privy," *Landscape* (Winter 1977); "How the WPA Transformed San Francisco," *Landscape Architecture* (Jan. 1979); *The Public Landscape of the New Deal* (New Haven: Yale Univ. Press, 1986); "Two Oases in San Francisco," *Horticulture* (Oct. 1986); "Church's Cozy Clutter," *Garden Design* (Fall 1987); "State Parks," in *American Landscape Architecture: Designers and Places*, ed. William H. Tischler (Washington, DC: Nat. Trust for Historic Preservation, 1988); "Street Trees are Stars in Beverly Hills," *Landscape Architecture* (July, 1988); "Gardening in the First Quintile," *Landscape Architecture* (June 1991): 52-54; "Introduction," *America in Bloom: Great Public Gardens Open to the Public* (New York: Rizzoli 1991); "New Angles in Berkeley, *Garden Design* (May-June 1992); "Thomas Church," *The Dictionary of Art*; *Caprarola in America: The Italian Garden in New England and New York* (work in progress). **Home Address:** 445 Clipper St., San Francisco, CA 94114.

CZARNOWSKI, THOMAS V. ■ FAAR Architecture 67. b. May 28, 1943, Bennington, VT. BA 64, Princeton Univ.; MFA 66, Princeton Univ. **Other Study:** Cambridge Univ. School of Architecture. **Career & Employment:** Univ. of Virginia, Asst. Prof. 1968-70; Inst. for Architecture & Urban Studies, Research Assc. 1970-71; MOMA, Consultant 1971-72; Edward L. Barnes Asscs., Assc. 1972-86; Emilio Ambasz & Asscs., VP 1986-88; Fox & Fowle Architects, Assc. Part. 1988-present. **Home Address:** 24 E. 71st St., NYC 10021.

■ ■ ■

D

D'ABOVILLE, BENEDETTA CRAVERI ■ AAR Italian Com. 1994-present.

D'ACCONE, FRANK ANTHONY ■ FAAR Post-Classical/ Humanistic Studies 64. b. June 13, 1931, Somerville, MA. BMus 52, Boston Univ.; MMus 53, Boston Univ.; MA 55, Harvard Univ.; PhD 60, Harvard Univ. **Career & Employment:** SUNY Buffalo, Asst. Prof. 1960-62; UCLA.

D'ACIERNO, PELLEGRINO A. ■ FAAR Post-Classical/ Humanistic Studies 89. b. Sept. 12, 1943, Weehawken, NJ. BA 65, Columbia College; MA 67, Columbia Univ.; PhD 73, Columbia Univ. **Research/Artistic Interests:** Research: Italian studies, Italian philosophical & theoretical culture; 20th-century Italian culture; comparative literature, modernism, postmodernism, the avant-garde; critical theory-cultural studies; cinema, history & theory; interdisciplinary studies, architecture & cinema, the metropolis. Creative Writing: poetry, screenwriting. **Career & Employment:** Columbia Univ., Asst. Prof. 1973-81; Barnard College, Asst. Prof. 1981-82; Hofstra Univ., Assc. Prof.-Prof. 1983-94. Visiting Appointments: Cornell Univ. 1984; NYU 1985, 1988; Southern California Inst. of Architecture 1990-93; Columbia Univ. 1993, 1995. **Memberships & Offices:** Columbia Univ., Lionel Trilling Prize Jury 1978; Center for Intl. Scholarly Exchange, Assc. Dir. 1980-82; Italian American Writiers Assn. 1991-present; American Entertainment Group, Dir. 1993-present. **Fellowships, Honors & Awards:** Fulbright Fellowship 1966-67; Columbia Univ.: Thomas S. Da Ponte Fellowship 1968-69, Chamberlain Fellowship 1978-79, Council for Research in the Humanities Grant 1979; Harvard Univ., Villa I Tatti Fellowship 1979-80; Guggenheim Fellowship 1995. **Publications:** ed. & English trans., with R. Connolly, M. Tafuri, *The Sphere and the Labyrinth: Avant-Gardes and Architecture from Piranesi to the 1970s* (Cambridge, MA: MIT Press, 1987); *F.T. Marinetti and the Freedom of Poetry*, European Writers Series 9: *The Twentieth Century* (New York: Scribner's, 1989);

co-ed. with Karin Barnaby, *C.G. Jung and the Humanities: Toward a Hermeneutics of Culture* (Princeton: Princeton Univ. Press, 1989); "The Manifesto as Text," in *Comparative Literary History as Discourse: Festschrift in Honor of Anna Balakian* (Bern, 1991); *Prospero's Books: The Traveling of Italian Culture* (Hempstead, NY: Hofstra Museum Publications, 1992); ed., *A Critical History of the Italian-American Cultural Experience*, vol. 1 of *The Encyclopedia of New Ethnic American Literature and Art*, ed. George Leonard (New York: Garland, 1994); "Cinema Paradiso: The Representation and Self-Representation of the Italian-American in Cinema," in *The Encyclopedia of New Ethnic American Literature and Art* (New York: Garland, 1994); "ROMA/AMOR: Rome and its Cinematic Double, from Neorealism to Postmodernism," in *Rome as a Generating Image in American Architecture*, ed. Robin Middleton & Neil Levine (New York: Rizzoli, forthcoming); *The Adventures of the Avant-Garde: From Dandyism to Postmodernism* (Westport, CT: Greenwood-Praeger, forthcoming). **Home Address:** 118 E. Maple St., Teaneck, NJ 07666. **Business Address:** Dept. of Comparative Literature, Hofstra Univ., Hempstead, NY 11550.

DAHILL, THOMAS H., JR ■ FAAR Painting 57. b. June 22, 1925, Cambridge, MA. BS 49, Tufts College. **Other Studies:** MFA School 1949-54; Harvard Summer School, Fogg Museum 1952; Skowhegan School of Painting & Sculpture 1953. **Research/Artistic Interests:** Mural painting. **Career & Employment:** Tufts College, Faculty 1954-55; MFA School, Faculty 1954-55. **Fellowships, Honors & Awards:** Max Beckman Geselshaft, Murnau, Germany, Resident 1956. **Exhibitions/Performances:** Downtown Gallery, NYC 1956; Grover Cronin Gallery, Waltham, MA 1957; ALNY 1958; Carl Siembab Gallery 1959; St. Botolph Club, Boston 1990; Emerson College 1991.

DALEY, ROYSTON TUTTLE ■ FAAR Architecture 62. b. Jan. 12, 1929, Boston, MA. m. Lillian Mary Stuart Tod. BA 51, Williams College; BArch 56, Harvard GSD. **Career & Employment:** Alfred T. Granger Asscs. 1952-53; Kelly & Gruzen 1954; Shepley, Bullfinch, Richardson & Abbott 1954-59; Edwin T. Steffian 1959-. **Fellowships, Honors & Awards:** *Progressive Architecture*, Design Award 1960.

DALLAPICCOLA, LUIGI ■ AAR Visitor 1971-72, Composer.

DALTAS, SPERO ■ FAAR Architecture 51; AAR Trustee 1968-92; AAR Trustee Emer. 1993-present; Patron; Friends of the AAR Library, Life Mem.; School of Fine Arts, Plant & Planning Com., Co-Chair 1989-91; Juries: Architecture Chair 1981, 1984, 1986; Design Arts 1983, 1987. b. Mar. 13, 1920, St. Paul, MN. c. Florence Adong. BArch 43, Univ. of Minnesota; MArch 48, MIT. **Other Study:** Aalto Studio with Alvar Aalto, Louis Kahn, Eero Saarinen. **Career & Employment:** US Navy Gunnery & Torpedo Officer 1943-46; Northwest Airlines, Airport & Terminal Planner 1946-47; Carl Koch & Asscs., Designer 1948-49; Royal Acad. of Art, Visiting Prof. 1951; Eero Saarinen & Asscs., Campus Planner-Designer 1951-56; Amman & Whitney, Masterplanning Consultant 1956-57; Brown, Daltas & Asscs., Design Prin. 1957-present; Spero Daltas & Asscs., Design Prin. 1958-present. **Memberships & Offices:** AIA 1981-present; Nat. Trust for Historic Preservation 1980-present; Friends of the Public Garden, Boston 1982-present; AIA, Rocky Mountain Region, Juror 1983; Rotch Found., Juror 1988. **Fellowships, Honors & Awards:** MIT, Chamberlain Prize 1948; Mies, Saarinen, Harrison, Hudnut, Hidden Talent Competition Award 1949; Fulbright Fellowship 1951; Australian Parliament House Competition Award 1979; Milwaukee Lakefront Intl. Competition,

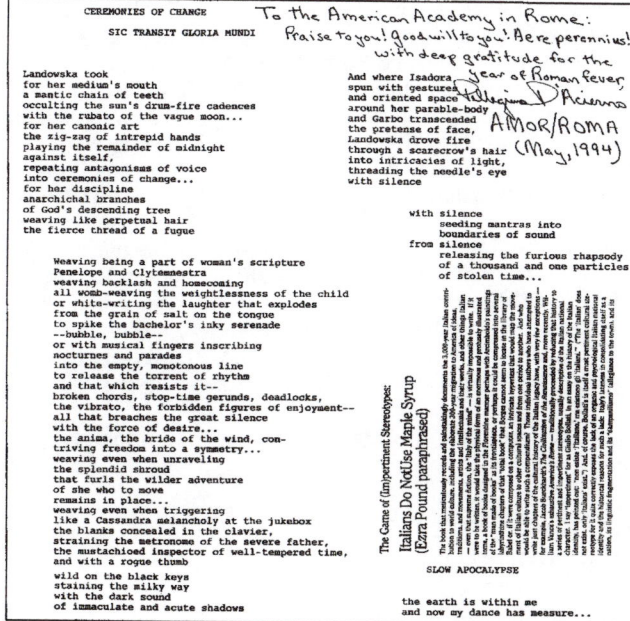

Pellegrino A. D'Acierno

1st Prize 1980; Nat. Center for Science & Technology, Saudi Arabia, 1st Prize 1981. **Publications:** *Climate, Culture, Crafts – Burma: The Determinants of a Regional Architecture* (Rangoon: Rangoon Univ. Press, 1963). **Important Works:** Civic Action Pgm., Iran 1962; Istanbul Office Tower & Shopping Arcade, Teheran, Iran 1962; Rajshahi Univ., Bangladesh, Master Plan & Central Library 1964; Primary Teacher Training College Pgm., Uganda 1969; New Arts College, Rangoon Univ., Master Plan & Comprehensive Design 1962-70; SUNY, Farmingdale, Master Plan & Comprehensive Design 1964-70; Universidad de las Americas, Puebla, & Mexico City, Mexico 1966-85; Exec. Office Bldg. for HRH Prince Sultan, Minister of Defense & Aviation 1985; Bank HQ, Saudi Arabian Monetary Agency 1976-85; King Khalid City & Airport Master Plan, Saudi Arabia 1985; Saudi Arabian Nat. Center for Science & Technology, Master Plan 1986; World Trade Center Complex, Jeddah, Saudi Arabia 1989; Markaz Al Mahmal, Jeddah, Saudi Arabia; US Embassy Complex, Singapore. **Exhibitions/ Performances:** Royal Acad. of Art, Copenhagen 1951, 1984; AIA, Upper Midwest Region 1954; Rocky Mountain Region-Univ. of Arizona 1954; Rangoon Univ. 1963; Ministry of Education, Kampala, Uganda 1968; Univ. of Minnesota, Minneapolis 1980; Biennale di Venezia 1982; MIT 1990. **Home Address:** Via Gregoriana 12, Rome 00187, Italy. **Business Address:** Spero Daltas & Asscs., Via Gregoriana 12, Rome, Italy 00187.

DALY, STEPHEN J. ■ FAAR Sculpture 75. b. July 4, 1942, Governor's Island, NY. m. Sharon J. Daly. c. Sabina. BA 64, San Jose State Univ.; MFA 67, Cranbrook Acad. of Art. **Research/ Artistic Interests:** Abstract figuration in cast metal. **Career & Employment:** Univ. of Minnesota, Minneapolis, Asst. Prof. 1967-69; Humboldt State Univ., Asst. Prof. 1969-75, Assc. Prof. 1975-79; Univ. of Texas, San Antonio, Asst. Prof. 1979-81; Univ. of Texas, Austin, Asst. Prof. 1981-86, Assc. Prof. 1986-92, Full Prof. 1992-present. **Memberships & Offices:** Texas Comm. on the Arts, Panelist 1980-82; Univ. of Texas, Austin, Coordinator, 4th Texas Sculpture Symposium 1983; San Antonio Art Inst., Curator 1983; Blue Star Art Space, San Antonio, BoD 1989-92. **Fellowships, Honors & Awards:** Reinhart Fellowship in Sculpture 1974-75; Louis Comfort Tiffany Award in Sculpture 1977-78; Univ. of Texas, Austin: Excellence in Teaching Award 1984, Grace Hill Milam Centennial Fellowship 1984-85, 1990-91, Foxworth Centennial Fellowship 1988-89, Case Prof. of the Year, Nominee 1989. **Important Works:** Public Collections: Western Washington State College, Bellingham; Art Center, Jackson, MS; Shasta College, Redding, CA; Oakland Art Museum; Sheinbaum Found., NYC; Texas A & M Univ., College Station; Bank of San Antonio; Library at Univ. of Texas, El Paso; Triton Museum, Santa Clara; McNay Museum, San Antonio. **Exhibitions/ Performances:** Solo: William Campbell Contemporary Art, Ft. Worth 1986-91, 1993; McNay Art Museum, San Antonio 1988; Hooks-Epstein Gallery, Houston 1991; Beasley-Daly-Hooks-Epstein Gallery 1993; Grounds for Sculpture, Hamilton, NJ 1994-95. **Bio-Bibliography:** *Men of Achievement; New York Art Review; Notable Americans; Personalities of the South; Personalities of the World; Who's Who in American Art; Who's Who in Education; Who's Who in Society; Who's Who in the South; Who's Who in the Southwest.* **Home Address:** 421 Mission St., San Antonio, TX 78210. **Business Address:** Dept. of Art & Art History, Univ. of Texas, Austin, TX 78712.

D'AMBRA, EVE ■ FAAR History of Art 86. b. Oct. 6, 1956, NYC. m. Franc D. Palaia. BA 78, Univ. of Arizona; MA 81, UCLA; PhD 87, Yale Univ. **Research/Artistic Interests:** Roman imperial sculpture & social history. **Career & Employment:** Rutgers Univ., Newark 1987-88, Rutgers Univ., New Brunswick 1988; Boston Univ., Visiting Asst. Prof. 1989; Univ. of Rhode Island, Asst. Prof 1989-90; Vassar College, Asst. Prof. 1990-present. **Memberships & Offices:** ArIA 1983-present; CAA 1986-present. **Fellowships, Honors & Awards:** Yale Univ. Fellowship 1982-86; Fulbright Fellowship (declined) 1984; Samuel Kress Found. Fellowship 1984-86; NEH Travel to Collections Grant 1991. **Publications:** "A Myth for a Smith: A Meleager Sarcophagus from a Tomb in Ostia," *AJA* 92 (1988): 85-100; "The Cult of Virtues and the Funerary Relief of Ulpia Epigone," *Latomus* 48 (1989): 392-400; "Pudicitia in the Frieze of the Forum Transitorium," *Römanische Mitteilungen* 98 (1991): 243-48; *Private Lives, Imperial Virtues: The Frieze of the Forum Transitorium in Rome* (Princeton: Princeton Univ. Press, 1993); ed., *Roman Art in Context* (New York: Prentice Hall, 1993). **Home Address:** 371 Fourth St., Jersey City, NJ 07302. **Business Address:** Art Dept., Vassar College, Poughkeepsie, NY 12601.

D'AMICO, JOHN FRANCIS ■ FAAR Post-Classical/Humanistic Studies 76, RAAR Classics/Archaeology 88. b. Feb. 15, 1947, Philadelphia, PA. d. Dec. 9, 1987. BA 69, St. Joseph's College; MA 70, Univ. of Rochester; PhD 77, Univ. of Rochester. **Other Studies:** Latin Paleography Seminar, MAA, Harvard Univ. 1972; Univ. of Pennsylvania 1980-81. **Research/Artistic Interests:** Humanism as a cultural movement, Latin paleography, the Roman Curia; Renaissance humanism; Rome in the Renaissance. **Career & Employment:** Univ. of Rochester, Instr. 1977-78; Univ of Illinois, Cavagna Collection, Asst. Bibliographer 1979-80; George Mason Univ., Asst. Prof.-Prof. 1981-87. **Fellowships, Honors & Awards:** Univ. of Rochester, NDEA Fellowship 1970-73; Center for Reformation Research, 11th Inst. for Reformation Research, Fellow 1973; Harvard Univ., Villa I Tatti, Univ. Fellow 1978-79; Univ. of Pennsylvania, Mellon Post-Doctoral Fellow 1980-81; Stanford Univ. Humanities Center, Fellow 1985-86; American Catholic Historical Assn., Howard R. Marraro Prize 1984. **Publications:** "The Library of St. Victor of Marseilles and the Rochester Catalogue of 1374," *University of Rochester Library Bulletin* 28.3 (1974): 2-23, with P.A. Gunther, "A Humanist Response to Marin Luther: Raffaele Maffei's *Apologeticus*," *Sixteenth Century Journal* 6 (1975): 37-56; with Kathleen Weil-Garris, "The Renaissance Cardinal's Ideal Palace: A Chapter from Cortesi's *De Cardinalatu*," in *Studies in Italian Art and Architecture*, ed H.A.Millon, Memoirs of the AAR 35 (Rome: Elefante, 1979): 45-123; *Renaissance Humanism in Papal Rome: Humanists and Churchmen on the Eve of the Reformation* (Baltimore: Johns Hopkins Univ. Press, 1983); *Theory and Practice in Renaissance Textual Criticism: Beatus Rhenanus between Conjecture and History* ((Berkeley: Univ. of California Press, 1988); contr., *Contemporaries of Erasmus,* 3 vols. (Toronto: Univ. of Toronto Press, 1985-87); *Roman and German Humanism, 1450-1550, Collected Studies,* ed. Paul F. Grendler (London: Variorum, 1993). **Bio-Bibliography:** *Catholic Historical Review* 74 (1988): 364-65; Paul F. Grendler, Preface to D'Amico, *Roman and German Humanism, 1450-1550* (1993), vii-xii, with bibliography of his writings; *Contemporary Authors.*

D'AMICO, MASOLINO ■ AAR Italian Com. 1994-present, Writer.

DAMROSCH, WALTER ■ AAR Trustee 1928-43; Musician, Conductor; AAAL, Pres.

D'ANNA, GIOVANNI ■ Italian Fulbright Fellow 1955-56; Univ. of Rome, Prof.

DARDANELLO, GIUSEPPE ■ Italian Fulbright Fellow 1991-92.

DARDEN, DOUGLAS ■ FAAR Architecture 89. b. Oct. 20, 1951, Denver, CO. BA 74, Univ. of Colorado; MArch 83, Harvard GSD. **Other Studies:** Parsons School of Design 1977-78. **Career & Employment:** Catholic Univ., Lect. 1984; Columbia Univ., Adj. Asst. Prof. 1984-87; New Jersey Inst. of Technology, Visiting Lect. 1987; Univ. of Colorado. **Fellowships, Honors & Awards:** ALNY, 4th Young Architects' Forum Award 1985; New Jersey Council on the Arts, Fellowship 1985-86; Art Matters, Inc., Project Grant 1987. **Publications:** "From Here to Eternity," Artists Space exb. cat. (June 1986); "Spaces Left Behind," *Appearances* (Dec. 1987); "Condemned Buildings," *A + U* (Apr. 1988); "Tropes and Trapts," *University of Tennessee Journal of Architecture* (Apr. 1988). **Exhibitions/Performances:** Rhona Hoffman Gallery, Chicago 1984; M.A.P. Gallery, Baltimore 1984; Storefront for Art & Architecture, NYC 1985; Max Protetch Gallery, NYC 1985; Artists Space, NYC 1986; Nat. Inst. for Architectural Education, NYC, 1993.

D'ARMS, JOHN H. ■ RAAR Classics/Archaeology 72, 84; Prof.-in-Charge, Summer School 1971-73; Prof.-in-Charge 1977-80, Dir. 1977-80; AAR Trustee 1973-76, 1981-93, Trustee Emer. 1993. b. Nov. 27, 1934, Poughkeepsie, NY. m. Teresa Waugh. c. Helena, Justin. BA 56, Princeton Univ.; BA 59, New College, Oxford Univ.; PhD 65, Harvard Univ. **Research/Artistic Interests:** Roman social, cultural, & economic history; Roman historiography; Latin epigraphy; Roman art, architecture & archaeology; Latin prose & poetry. **Career & Employment:** Tufts Univ., Tufts Classical Year in Cumae, Naples, Italy, Dir. & Instr. 1962-63; Harvard Univ., TF 1963-65; VSA, Classical Summer School in Cumae, Italy, Asst. Dir. 1965, Dir. 1969; ICCS, Asst. Prof. 1967-68; Univ. of Michigan, Asst. Prof.-Prof. 1965-72, Chair 1972-75, 1976-77, 1980-85, Horace H. Rackham School of Graduate Studies, Dean 1985-present; Prof. of History 1986-present; Vice Provost for Academic Affairs 1990-present. **Memberships & Offices:** VSA 1962-present, BoT 1966-70; APA 1963-present, BoD 1977-80; ArIA 1966-present; Soc. for the Promotion of Roman Studies, England 1967-present; CAMWS 1969-present, VP 1976-77; Columbia Univ. Seminar on Classical Civilization 1973-83; *Puteoli: Studi di Storia Antica*, Ed. Com. 1976-present; Intl. Assn. for Classical Archaeology, Exec. Com. 1977-80. **Fellowships, Honors & Awards:** Honorary Woodrow Wilson Fellow 1956; Harvard Univ., Moors Scholar & Howard Fellow 1959-61; Fulbright Fellowship 1961-62; Univ. of Michigan: Horace H. Rackham School of Graduate Studies, Faculty Summer Research Fellowship 1966, Phi Beta Kappa Annual Lect. 1971, Distinguished Faculty Achievement Award 1982, G.F. Else Prof. 1983-present; ACLS Fellowship 1971-72; Guggenheim Fellow 1975-76; IAS, School of Historical Studies, Visiting Mem. 1975-76; German Archaeological Inst., Rome, Corresponding Mem. 1980-present; AAAS, Fellow 1992-present; Nat. Council on the Humanities, Pres. Clinton Appointment 1994-2001. **Publications:** *Romans on the Bay of Naples: A Social and Cultural Study of the Villas and their Owners from 150 B.C. to A.D. 400* (Cambridge, MA: Harvard Univ. Press, 1970); co-ed. with J.W. Eadie, *Ancient and Modern: Essays in Honor of Gerald F. Eise* (Ann Arbor, MI: Center for Coordination of Ancient & Modern Studies, 1977); co-ed. with E.C. Kopff, *Roman Seaborne Commerce: Studies in Archaeology and History*, Memoirs of the AAR 36 (Rome: AAR, 1980); *Commerce and Social Standing in Ancient Rome* (Cambridge, MA: Harvard Univ. Press, 1981); "Pompeii, A.D. 79 in American Cities," in *La regione sotterrrata dal Vesuvio: studi e prospettive*, Acts of the Intl. Congress, Naples, 1979 (Naples, 1982), 89-97; "Upper-Class Roman Attitudes towards *Viri Municipales* and Towns in the Early Empire," *Athenaeum* 62 (1984): 440-67; "Control, Companionship, and *Clientela*: Some Social Functions of the Roman Communal Meal," *Echos du Monde Classique (Classical Views)* n.s. 3 (1984): 327-48; "Notes on Multiple Municipal Magistracies in Julio-Claudian Italy," Festschrift for J.F. Gilliam, *Bulletin of the American Society of Papryologists* 21.1-4 (1984): 49-54; "*Puteolana Analecta:* Inscriptions in the Kelsey Museum," *Puteoli* 9-10 (1985-86): 74-78; "Pompeii and Rome in the Augustan Age and Beyond: The Eminence of the gens Holconia," in *Studies in Honor of W. Jashemski* (1989), 51-68; "Communications in the Roman Empire," *International Encyclopedia of Communications* (Philadelphia, 1989), 473-81; "The Roman *convivium* and the Idea of Equality," in *Sympotica: A Symposium on the* Symposium, ed. O. Murray (Oxford: Clarendon Press, 1990), 308-20; "The Social and Economic History of Italy from the Augustan Age through the Time of Cassiodorus," in *Europäische Wirtschafts und Sozialgeschichte in der römischen Kaiserzeit*, ed. F. Vittinghoff (Stuttgart, 1990), 375-426; "Slaves at Roman Convivia," in *Dining in a Classical Context*, ed. W.J. Slater (Ann Arbor: Univ. of Michigan Press, 1991), 171-83. **Business Address:** Office of the Dean of the Graduate School, Rackham Bldg., Univ. of Michigan, 915 E. Washington St., Ann Arbor, MI 48109.

D'ASSIA, ENRICO ■ AAR Visitor 1983-84, Set Designer, Painter.

DAVIDSON, BERNICE F. ■ RAAR History of Art 83. b. Apr. 17, 1927, NYC. BA 49, Wellesley College; PhD 54, Radcliffe College, Harvard Univ. **Career & Employment:** Harvard Univ., Brown Univ., IFA, part-time teaching at various dates; RISD Museum, Chief Curator 1956-60; Frick Collection, Research Asst. 1954-56, Research Curator 1966-present. **Memberships & Offices:** CAA, BoD 1974-78; Women's Caucus for Art, Nat. Adv. Bd. 1974-78; Columbia Univ., Dept. of Art, Adv. Council, 1975-present. **Fellowships, Honors & Awards:** ACLS 1960, 1979; AAUW 1961. **Publications:** "Drawings by Perino del Vaga for the Palazzo Doria, Genoa," *Art Bulletin* 41 (1959): 315-26; "Early Drawings by Perino del Vaga," *Master Drawings* 13 (1963): 3-16; *Mostra di disegni di Perino del Vaga e la sue cerchia*, exb. cat. (Florence: Uffizi, 1966); "Daniele da Volterra and the Orsini Chapel," *Burlington Magazine* 109 (1967): 553-61; comp., *The Frick Collection: An Illustrated Calatogue*, vols. 1-2 (New York: Frick Collection, 1968); "The Decoration of the Sala Regia under Pope Paul III," *Art Bulletin* 58 (1979): 397-423; "Pope Paul III's Additions to Raphael's Logge: His Impresse on the Logge," *Art Bulletin* 61 (1979): 385-404; "The Landscapes of the Vatican Logge from the Reign of Pope Julius III," *Art Bulletin* 65 (1983): 587-602; "Pius IV and Raphael's Logge," *Art Bulletin* 66 (1984): 382-89; *Raphael's Bible: A Study of the Vatican Logge*, CAA Monograph (State College: Pennsylvania State Univ. Press, 1985); "The *Furti di Giove* Tapestries Designed by Perino del Vaga for Andrea Doria," *Art Bulletin* 70 (1988): 424-50; "The *Navigation d'Enea* Tapestries Designed by Perino del Vaga for Andrea Doria," *Art Bulletin* 72 (1990): 35-50. **Home Address:** 333 E. 68th St., NYC 10021. **Business Address:** Frick Collection, 1 E. 70th St., NYC 10021.

DAVIDSON, GEORGE ■ FAAR Painting 16. b. May 10, 1889, Russia. d. June 15, 1965. m. Elsie Davidson. **Other Studies:** NAD; with F.C. Jones; Douglas Volk. **Research/Artistic Interests:** Landscape drawings. **Career & Employment:** Cooper Union Art School, Teacher. **Memberships & Offices:** NAD, Assc. 1936; Nat. Soc. of Mural Painters. **Fellowships, Honors & Awards:** ALNY, Medal of Honor 1926. **Important Works:**

Collections: Nebraska Art Assn., Lincoln; Addison Gallery, Andover College; Mattatuck Historical Soc., Waterbury, CT. **Exhibitions/Performances:** ALNY; Barnard College; Buffalo Savings Bank; Addison Gallery of American Art; NAD; Sterling Library, Yale. **Bio-Bibliography:** *Who Was Who in America, Who Was Who in American Art.*

DAVIS, HARRY A. ■ FAAR Painting 41. b. May 21, 1914, Hillsboro, IN. m. Lois I. Peterson. c. Joanna (dec.), Mark. BFA 38, Herron School of Art of Indiana-Purdue Univ., Indianapolis. **Other Study:** Skowhegan Art School, ME 1951. **Research/Artistic Interests:** As a combat-artist with the 5th Army in Italy (1942-46), I recorded battle sites & army life on the front in ink, casein, & oil painting – these works are located in the Pentagon. From 1946 to 1960, I concentrated on figure composition about Midwestern life in oils, pastels, watercolors, & drawing media. After 1960, I became interested in painting the disappearing landmarks of the Midwest. I developed a textural technique of underpainting in acrylics against which I build forms & shapes in dark & light values, using strong patterns of sunlight & shadow whenever possible. For accuracy, I first photograph the site. While primarily planned for strong composition & mood, these paintings also have historical value. In addition, I painted a series of life-sized figures of "Youth of the 60s." These reflected the hippy movement with which I became familiar at the art school where I taught. **Career & Employment:** Beloit College, Artist-in-Residence 1941-42; Herron School of Art, Instr. 1946-67, Assc. Prof. 1967-70, Prof. 1970-83, Prof. Emer. 1983; Univ. of Missouri, Guest Artist 1981; Evansville Museum of Arts, Artist-in-Residence 1981; Indianapolis Art League, Instr. 1983-90. **Memberships & Offices:** Indiana Artists Club 1946-present, Pres. 1955-56; The Portfolio, Indianapolis 1963-present, Pres. 1971-72; Indiana Acad., Indianapolis 1972-present; Brown County, IN, Artists Guild 1979-present, Pres. 1987-89; Watercolor USA Honor Soc., Missouri Charter Mem. 1987-present. **Fellowships, Honors & Awards:** Hoosier Salon Annual Exb., Indianapolis, 33 awards 1947-94, including Best of Show 1967, 1970, 1974, 1976, 1979-80, 1988-89, 1994; Mainstreams Intl. Exb., Marietta, OH, Merit Award 1968, 1970-74, Purchase Award 1971; Purdue Univ., Old Masters Program 1971; Indiana Arts Comm. & I.U.P.U.I. Bicentennial Com., Matching Grants for Bicentennial Traveling Show 1976; Butler Inst., Youngstown, OH, Mid-Year Show: Purchase Award 1961, 1978, Merit Award 1978; Watercolor USA Competition, Springfield Museum of Art, MO 1965-68, 1970, 1972-73, 1976, 1992, Missouri Sesquicentennial Prize 1971; Realism '74, Nat. Competition, Owensboro, KY, 1st Prize; Bluegrass Exb., Louisville, KY, Top Award 1975; "500" Festival, Indianapolis, 10 awards 1966-78, including Best of Show 1966, 1970, 1973. **Important Works:** Indianapolis Museum of Art; Greater Lafayette, IN, Museum of Art; Doane College, NE; Springfield, MO, Art Museum; Butler Inst. of American Art, Youngstown, OH; Evansville, IN, Museum of Arts & Science; Indiana Museum of Medical History & Indiana State Museum, Indianapolis; Peoples Bank, Brazil, IN; Purdue Univ.; Marietta College; Carroll Reece Museum, Johnson City, TN. **Exhibitions/Performances:** Richmond, VA, Bi-annual Exb. 1938, 1949; Indiana Artists Exb., Indianapolis Museum of Art 1946, 1954, 1958-59, 1961, 1964-65, 1977; PAFA 1947, 1949; Corcoran Bi-Annual, Washington, DC 1947; Chautauqua Nat. Competition, NY 1959-71; Ball State Nat. Drawing & Small Sculpture Show 1960, 1962, 1965-66, 1968, 1972; Mid-States Exb., Evansville Museum of Science 1968-70, 1976, 1982; Indianapolis Sesquicentennial Exb. 1971; Anderson Fine Arts Center, IN 1971, 1973, 1975, 1982; Bluegrass Exb., Louisville, KY 1975; US Bicentennial Travelling Exb. 1976; Western Assn. of Art Museums Travelling Show 1979-81; Chateau de Tours, France 1987; Nat. Wa-

tercolor Invitational Exb., Parkland College, IL 1989; Herron Gallery, Indianapolis 1989. **Bio-Bibliography:** *International Who's Who in Arts and Antiques; Who's Who in American Art; Who's Who in American Education; Who's Who in the Midwest.* **Home Address:** 6315 Washington Blvd., Indianapolis, IN 46220.

DAVIS, ROBERT S. ■ FAAR Architecture 91; Com. for Centennial Events, Dir. Search Com. b. Nov. 10, 1943, Birmingham, AL. m. Daryl R. Davis. c. Micah. BA 65, Antioch College; MBA 67, Harvard Graduate School of Business. **Career & Employment:** Antioch College, Assc. Dir. of Development, Assc. Dir. of Admissions 1968-71; Housing Corp. of America, Project Manager 1971-72; Kanter Corp., VP 1972-73; Serendipity in the Grove, Pres. & Prin. 1973-74; Davis Development Corp., Pres. & Prin. 1974-78; Seaside Community Development Corp., Pres. & Prin. 1979-present. **Memberships & Offices:** 1000 Friends of Florida, BoD 1988-present; Elms Com. 1992; Seaside Inst., Bd. of Governors 1992-present; Antioch College, BoT 1993; South Walton Conservation & Development Trust, BoT 1993. **Fellowships, Honors & Awards:** South Florida AIA Award 1983; *Progressive Architecture* Citation for Town Plan 1984; Florida Governor's Design Award 1986; *Builder*, Builder's Choice Grand Award 1986, Honor Award 1988; *Progresive Architecture*, Citation for Hybrid Bldg. 1987; Florida AIA, Citation for Excellence in Urban Design 1988; Aurora Grand Award, SE Builders' Conf. 1988; *Time* Design of Decade 1990; AIA Honor Award 1991. **Bio-Bibliography:** *Princeton Journal* (1985); *Lotus* (1986); *Wall Street Journal* (July 1986); *Baumeister* (Sept. 1986); *Atlantic* (Mar. 1988); *Travel & Leisure* (Mar. 1988); *Architectural Record* (Apr. 1989); *NBC Nightly News* (Oct. 1990); *Travel & Leisure* (Aug. 1990); *Time* (Jan. 1990); Mahoney & Easterling, *Seaside: Making a Town in America* (1991); *Smithsonian* (Jan. 1991); *Architectur und Wohnen* (Apr.-May 1992); Peter Katz, *The New Urbanism* (1994). **Home Address:** PO Box 4730, Santa Rosa Beach, FL 32459. **Business Address:** Seaside Community Development Corp., PO Box 4730, Santa Rosa Beach, FL 32459.

DAVIS, THOMAS K. ■ NIAE-John Dinkeloo Traveling Fellow 1983-84. b. Aug. 4, 1953, San Francisco, CA. m. Marleen Kay. c. Stephen Mabon, Robert Jackson. BArch 77, Cornell Univ.; MArch 83, Cornell Univ. **Research/Artistic Interests:** Architecture & urban design. **Career & Employment:** Moore & Salsbury Architects 1977-78; Desmond & Lord Architects 1978-80; John Carl Warnecke & Asscs. 1980-81; Syracuse Univ., Asst. Prof. 1984-89, Assc. Prof. 1989-94; Univ. of Tennessee, Knoxville, Assc. Prof. 1994-present. **Home Address:** 1935 Cherokee Blvd., Knoxville, TN 37919. **Business Address:** Univ. of Tennessee School of Architecture, 1715 Volunteer Blvd., Knoxville, TN 37996.

DAVISON, JEAN M. ■ RAAR Classics/Archaeology 82, School of Classical Studies Adv. Council 1976-present. b. Apr. 19, 1922, Glens Falls, NY. BA 44, Univ. of Vermont; MA 50, Yale Univ.; PhD 57, Yale Univ. **Other Study:** Middlebury Language Schools (Summer), German 1949, Italian 1971; ANS, Graduate Seminar, Summer 1952; Università per Stranieri, Perugia, Diploma in Etruscology & Italic Antiquities, 1960; Archaeological Excavations: Petra, Jordan 1961; Hagios Stephanos, Greece 1963; Hebron, Jordan 1965; Diocletian's Palace, Split 1969; Ortu Comidu, Sardinia 1977; House of Vestal Virgins, Roman Forum 1989. **Research/Artistic Interests:** Influence of Near East on Greece & Italy, 8th-6th Centuries BCE; Greeks in Sardinia; Vitruvius: Resinant vases in Greek & Roman theaters. **Career & Employment:** US Dept of War, Cryptanalyst 1944-45; US State Dept., Foreign Service Clerk, US Embassy, Athens & American Legation, Vienna 1945-49; Univ. of Vermont, Instr. 1955-57, Asst. Prof. 1957-63, Assc. Prof. 1963-69, Prof. 1969-92, Lyman-Roberts

Prof. 1972-92, Emer. 1992-present; ASCSA, Visiting Prof. 1974-75. **Memberships & Offices:** ASCSA, Managing Com. 1965-present; Exec. Com. 1973-77; Com. for Summer Session 1983-87, Chair 1983-84. **Fellowships, Honors & Awards:** Phi Beta Kappa, Alpha of Vermont 1944; ANS Summer Grant 1952; Fulbright Award, ASCSA 1954-55; APS Research Grant 1967-68; Yale Univ., NEH Summer Seminar 1978; Harvard Univ., NEH Summer Seminar 1985. **Publications:** *Attic Geometric Workshops,* Yale Classical Studies 16 (New Haven: Yale Univ. Press, 1961); *Seven Italic Tomb-Groups from Narce* (Perugia: Università per Stranieri & Rome: Univ. of Rome 1972); "The Oikoumene in Ferment: A Cross-Cultural Study of the Sixth Century," in *Scripture in Context: Essays on the Comparative Method,* Pittsburgh Theological Monographs 34 (Pittsburgh: Univ. of Pittsburgh Press, 1980), 197-219; "Greeks in Sardinia: The Confrontation of the Archaeological Evidence and Literary Testimonia," in *Studies in Sardinian Archaeology,* ed. Miriam S. Balmuth & Robert J. Rowland (Ann Arbor: Univ. of Michigan Press, 1983), 67-82; "Greek Presence in Sardinia: Myth and Speculation," in *Studies in Sardinian Archaeology,* ed. Miriam S. Balmuth (Ann Arbor: Univ. of Michigan Press, 1986), 186-200; "Egyptian Influence on the Greek Legend of Io," *Discussions in Egyptology,* Special no. 1 (Oxford, 1989): 61-79; "The Greeks and the Periphery," in *Myth and the Polis,* ed. Dora Pozzi & John Wickersham (Ithaca, NY: Cornell Univ. Press, 1991), 49-63; "Greeks in Sardinia: Myth and Reality," in *Sardinia in the Mediterranean: A Footprint in the Sea. Studies in Sardinian Archaeology Presented to Miriam S. Balmuth,* ed. Robert H. Tyket & Tamsey K. Andrews (Sheffield: Sheffield Academic Press, 1992), 284-93. **Bio-Bibliography:** Elaine K. Harrington, "Listening to the Ancients," *University of Vermont Quarterly* (Winter 1992): 43-45; *Who's Who* in several categories. **Home Address:** 71 W. Williams St., No. 6, Burlington, VT 05401. **Business Address:** Dept. of Classics, Univ. of Vermont, 481 Main St., Burlington VT 05405.

DAWSON, STUART O. ■ RAAR Landscape Architecture 76. b. Apr. 27, 1935, Urbana, IL. m. Ellen Washington. c. Mark O., Emilie S., Julie D. Orsatti. BFA 57, Univ. of Illinois; MLA 58, Harvard Univ. **Career & Employment:** Sasaki Asscs., Prin. Designer & Part. 1962-present; Harvard GSD, Design Critic 1989-present. **Memberships & Offices:** ASLA, Fellow 1987. **Important Works:** Deere & Co. Corp. HQ, Moline, IL 1962-present; Urban Designer-Landscape Architect: Market Sq. & Historic Waterfront, Newburyport, MA 1972; Christian Science Center, Boston 1975; Boston Waterfront Park 1976; Indianapolis Art Museum 1978; Baxter-Travenol Labs. Corp. HQ, Deerfield, IL 1978; Hercules Office Bldg. & Park-Atrium, Wilmington, DE 1979; Toledo Waterfront, Owens-Illinois Plaza 1979; Dallas Arts District Master Plan & "Street-Scape" 1980; TRW Nat. HQ, Cleveland 1982; Highland Park, IL, Improvements 1983; Frito-Lay Corp. HQ, Plano, TX 1984; MacDonalds Corp. HQ, Oak Brook, IL 1984; Smithsonian Inst., Enid Haupt Garden, Washington, DC 1985; Charleston, SC, Waterfront Park 1990; Fountain Plaza, Buffalo, NY 1991; Rice Univ. Master Plan, Houston 1992; Kansas City, MO, Waterfront Park 1992; Memorial Court at Purdue Univ., West Lafayette, IN 1992; White River State Park, Indianapolis 1994; Wheeling Heritage Park, WV 1994. **Exhibitions/Performances:** Sasaki Retrospective, Grand Hall, Harvard GSD 1982. **Bio-Bibliography:** *Who's Who in America.* **Business Address:** Sasaki Asscs., Inc., 64 Pleasant St., Watertown, MA 02172.

DAWSON, THOMAS LAUGHEAD, JR ■ FAAR Architecture 52. b. Dec. 1, 1922, Kansas City, MO. BArch 49, Yale Univ. **Other Studies:** Univ. of Kansas, School of Engineering 1940-42; Univ. of Michigan, USAAF Electronics Studies 1944-45; École des Beaux Arts, Fontainebleau 1947. **Career & Employment:** Edward

D. Stone, Architect, Architectural Designer 1949-50; Joseph B. Platt, & Asscs., Project Designer 1950; Arabian American Oil Co., Rome, Architect 1952-54; J. Walter Thompson Co., Review Board Sec. 1955-62. **Fellowships, Honors & Awards:** Univ. of Kansas, Alice B. Chittenden Memorial Prize 1942; Yale Univ., Annie G.K. Garland Memorial Fellow 1947; Fulbright Fellow 1950. **Important Works:** "The French Hill," Los Angeles, Restoration. **Bio-Bibliography:** *Architectural Digest* (Spring 1966).

DAY, FRANK MILES ■ AAR Charter Mem., Trustee 1911-18, Architect.

DAY, JOHN ■ FAAR Classics/Archaeology 27. b. Feb. 25, 1902, Brink Haven, OH. d. Dec. 27, 1961. m. Ernestine Billingham. BA 21, Ohio State Univ.; PhD 25, Johns Hopkins Univ. **Other Studies:** ASCSA 1925-26. **Research/Artistic Interests:** Classical literature & history, papyrology. **Career & Employment:** Hamilton College, Assc. Prof. 1927-29; Barnard College, Instr.-Prof. 1931-61; Columbia Univ., Papyrus Collection, Curator 1954-61. **Memberships & Offices:** ASCSA, Managing Com.; APA, Managing Com. **Fellowships, Honors & Awards:** Yale Univ., Sterling Fellow 1929-31; Italian Government, Medal of Merit 1948. **Publications:** "Phalerum and the Phaleric Wall," *TAPA* 59 (1928): 164-78; "Agriculture in the Life of Pompeii," *Yale Classical Studies* 3 (1932): 165-208; *An Economic History of Athens under Roman Domination* (New York: Columbia Univ. Press, 1942); ed. with C.W. Keyes, *Tax Documents from Theadelphia; Papyri of the Second Century A.D.* (New York: Columbia Univ. Press, 1956). **Bio-Bibliography:** *NY Times,* Obit. (Dec. 29, 1961); Briggs, 128-29.

DE ALBA, ROBERTO ■ NIAE, John Dinkeloo Traveling Fellow 1989-90.

DEAM, ARTHUR FRANCIS ■ FAAR Architecture 26. b. Oct. 1, 1895, Springfield, OH. dec. m. Thyra C. Sodenberg. c. Edward Lee, Martha Severt, Norman Arthur. BArch 21, Ohio State Univ.; BArch, Columbia Univ. **Research/Artistic Interests:** Temple of Fortune, Rome; Santa Croce, Florence; Piazza Campidoglio, Rome. **Career & Employment:** Architectural Draftsman, NYC 1919-20; H.D. Smith, Columbus, OH, Draftsman 1920-21; Helmet & Corbett, Designer 1922-23; N. Max Dunning, Chicago, Designer 1926; D.H. Burnham & Co., Chicago, Designer 1926-30; Armour Inst. of Technology, Asst. Prof. 1928-29; Univ. of Illinois, Prof. 1930-45; Univ. of Pennsylvania, Prof. 1945-60, Chair 1945-50. **Memberships & Offices:** Summer School of Painting, Sagatuck MI, Pres. BoD; Architectural Sketch Club of Chicago; Philadelphia Art Alliance; Alpha Rho Chi; Pi Kappa Alpha. **Fellowships, Honors & Awards:** AIA, Fellow. **Bio-Bibliography:** *Who Was Who in America.*

DEAN, ANDREA O. ■ FAAR Design Arts 80. b. June 8, 1935, Berlin, Germany. m. Grant S. Shotwell. c. Joanna Cohen, Nathaniel Cohen, Lisa Cohen. BA 57, Columbia Univ. **Other Study:** Painting & drawing at MFA School & Univ. of Massashusetts, Amherst. **Career & Employment:** *The Art Scene,* Assc. Ed. 1970; *DC Gazette,* Assc. Ed. 1970-73; *Washington Post & Washington Star,* Freelance Writer 1971-74; *Washingtonian,* Feature Writer & Contr. Ed. 1971-73; *Women's Work,* Founder & Ed. 1974-75; *Architecture Magazine,* Exec. Ed. 1975-89; *Historic Preservation,* Ed.-at-Large 1991-present. **Memberships & Offices:** Intl. Com. of Architectural Critics 1984-present. **Fellowships, Honors & Awards:** Australia Arts Council, Traveling Grant 1984. **Publications:** *Bruno Zevi: On Modern Architecture* (New York: Rizzoli, 1983); "Introduction," in *American Architecture of the 1980s* (Washington, DC: AIA Press, 1990). **Bio-Bibliography:** *Who's Who* *in the East.* **Home Address:** 3929 Huntington St. NW, Washington, DC 20015.

DEAN, JEFFREY J. ■ FAAR Post-Classical/Humanistic Studies 81. b. Mar. 31, 1954, Alexandria, VA. BA 76, Swarthmore College; PhD 84, Univ. of Chicago. **Career & Employment:** Univ. of Chicago, Lect. **Fellowships, Honors & Awards:** Mrs. Giles Whiting Found. Fellowship.

DEAN, KATHRYN A. ■ FAAR Architecture 87. b. June 24, 1957, Grand Forks, ND. m. Charles A. Wolf. c. Carolyn. BArch 81, North Dakota State Univ., Fargo; MArch 83, Univ. of Oregon, Eugene. **Career & Employment:** Kohn Pedersen Fox 1984-86, 1989-91; Dean-Wolf Architects 1987-88, 1991-present; Columbia Univ. 1991-present; Univ. of Florida, Distinguished Visiting Prof. 1992. **Memberships & Offices:** AIA. **Publications:** "A Quiet Place Apart," *Architecture* (Oct. 1989): 79; "Peeled Perimeter Library," *Progressive Architecture* (July 1993): 98. **Important Works:** "Inside Outside Studio," Hansen Studio, San Mateo, CA 1988; "Peeled Perimeter Library," Forer Residence, Bronxville, NY 1992; "Spiral House," Greenberg Residence, North Castle, NY. **Home Address:** 40 Hudson St., 6th Fl., NYC 10013.

DE ANGELIS DE VITA, GABRIELLE ■ Italian Fulbright Fellow 1968-69.

DE BENEDICTIS, ALBERTO ■ AAR Trustee 1991-present. b. 1952, Rome, Italy. **Studies:** School of Economics, Univ. of Rome; School of Foreign Service, Georgetown Univ. **Career & Employment:** World Bank, Italian Exec. Dir. Office, Washington, DC, Economist 1977-81; Finmeccanica, NYC 1981-83; North American representative 1983-89, Sen. VP 1989-95, Dir. of Strategic Planning 1995-present.

DE DAEHN, COLONEL PETER ■ AAR Librarian 1948-61; Acting Librarian 1938-39, 1940-48.

DE FOREST, ROBERT W. ■ AAR Trustee 1909-31, Lawyer.

DE FUCCIO, ROBERT ■ FAAR Design Arts 76. b. Apr. 12,

Robert De Fuccio

1936, Brooklyn, NY. m. Sally A. Fors. c. Elise Di Corato, Simonee Marhefka, Katherine De Fuccio. BS 58, SUNY, Oswego. **Other Study:** Rochester Inst. of Technology 1958-59. **Research/Artistic Interests:** Furniture design, design engineering & product development. **Career & Employment:** Knoll Intl. 1960-71; private consulting 1971-present; Philadelphia College of Art, Adj. Prof. 1971-84. **Fellowships, Honors & Awards:** 18th Annual Industrial Design Review selects furniture designs 1971; 22nd Annual Industrial Design Review selects "Triangle Chair" 1975; Inst. of Business Designer's Gold Award for Chairs 1975; *Design Michigan* selects "Triangle Chair" 1977; *Interior Design Magazine*, Significant Furniture Designs for Past 50 Years for "Triangle Chair" 1982. **Home Address:** PO Box 68, Spinnerstown, PA 18968.

DE GRASSI, DONATELLA ■ Italian Fulbright Fellow 1986-87.

DE GRAZIA, DIANE M. ■ RAAR History of Art 91. b. July 20, 1943, Lincoln, NB. BA 65, Smith College; MA 67, Indiana Univ., Bloomington; PhD 72, Princeton Univ. **Research/Artistic Interests:** 16th- through 18th-century Italian paintings & drawings. **Career & Employment:** Indiana Univ. Art Museum, Registrar 1967-68; AIC, Research Asst. 1970; Denver Art Museum, Curator of European Art 1972-73; NGA, Contract Curator 1973-74, Curator of Italian Drawings 1974-89, Curator of Southern Baroque Painting 1989-present; Univ. of Pittsburgh, Visiting Andrew Mellon Prof. 1987; Case Western Reserve Univ., Florence Stone Mather Distinguished Visiting Prof. 1993; Smith College, Ruth & Clarence Kennedy Prof. 1994. **Memberships & Offices:** Print Council of America, CAA, ICOM. **Fellowships, Honors & Awards:** NDEA Fellowship 1968-71; Art Library Soc., Publication Award for *Carracci* catalogue 1980; Princeton Univ., Ione M. Spears Travel Grant 1980; NEA Museum Profesional Grant 1981; Gladys Krieble Delmas Grant 1981-82; J. Paul Getty Museum, Visiting Scholar 1986; CASVA Curatorial Fellow 1986. **Publications:** *Prints and Related Drawings by the Carracci Family: A Catalogue Raisonné* (Washington & Bloomington: NGA & Indiana Univ. Press, 1979); *Le Stampe dei Carracci* (Bologna: Nuova Alfa, 1984); *Correggio and His Legacy: Sixteenth-Century Emilian Drawings,* exb. cat. (Washington, DC: NGA, & Parma: Galleria Nazionale, 1984); *Bertoia, Mirola and the Farnese Court* (Bologna: Nuova Alfa, 1991); with Eric Garberson, *The Collections of the National Gallery of Art Systematic Catalogue: Italian Prints of the Seventeenth and Eighteenth Centuries* (Washington, DC: NGA, 1995); also numerous articles & published lectures. **Business Address:** NGA, Washington, DC 20565.

DE GRAZIA, VICTORIA ■ FAAR Post-Classical/Humanistic Studies 78, Council of Fellows 1981-85. b. Nov. 16, 1948, Chicago, IL. m. Leonardo Paggi. c. Livia Paggi. BA 68, Smith College; PhD 76, Columbia Univ. **Other Study:** Univ. of Florence, Italy 1965, 1969. **Research/Artistic Interests:** 20th-century Italian history & culture; culture & politics in Europe. **Career & Employment:** Lehman College, Asst. Prof. 1974-76; Rutgers Univ., Prof. 1976-93; Columbia Univ., Prof. 1993-present. **Memberships & Offices:** Soc. for Italian Historical Studies, Nat. Adv. Com.; Social Science Research Council, Joint Com. on Western Europe 1982-88; Council for European Studies, Nat. Adv. Com. 1981-85; *Journal of Modern History,* Ed. Bd. 1981-84; *Radical History Review,* Founding Ed. 1976-91; Rutgers Center for Historical Analysis, Proj. Dir. 1991-93. **Fellowships, Honors & Awards:** Soc. of Italian Historical Studies, Prize for Best Unpublished Manuscript 1976; Columbia Univ., Stephen B. Clough Dissertation Prize 1976; ACLS Fellowship 1981-82;

Shelby Dullum Davis Center Fellowship 1987; European Univ., Jean Monnet Fellowship 1989-90; German Marshall Fund of the US Fellowship 1989-90; *Journal of Modern History,* Chester Highy Prize 1990; AHA, Joan Kelly Memorial Prize for Best Book on Women 1992. **Publications:** *The Culture of Consent: Mass Organization of Leisure in Fascist Italy* (Cambridge: Cambridge Univ. Press, 1981; Italian ed., Bari & Rome: Laterza, 1981); "Mass Culture as Sovereignty: The American Challenge to European Cinemas," *Journal of Modern History* 61 (Mar. 1989): 53-87; "The Arts of Purchase: How U.S. Advertising Subverted the European Poster," in *Remaking History,* ed. Barbara Kruger & Phil Moviani (Seattle: Bay Press, 1989), 221-57; with L. Paggi, "Story of an Ordinary Massacre: Civitella, June 29, 1944," *Carduso Review of Law and Letters* 3.1 (Jan. 1992): 1-45; *How Fascism Ruled Women, Italy 1922-45* (Berkeley: UC Press, 1992; Italian ed., Venice: Marsilio, 1993). **Home Address:** 207 W. 106th St., Apt. 11D, NYC 10025. **Business Address:** Dept. of History, Columbia Univ., NYC 10027.

DEGRUMMOND, NANCY T. ■ AAR Classical Soc., Pres. 1987, 1988.

DE LA CROIX, HORST ■ FAAR History of Art 63. b. Nov. 26, 1915, Berlin, Germany. d. Feb. 22, 1992. BA 39, UC, Berkeley; MA 55, UC, Berkeley; PhD 58, UC, Berkeley. **Career & Employment:** San Jose State College, Prof. 1960-90. **Publications:** "Military Architecture and the Radical City Plan in 16th-Century Italy," *Art Bulletin* 42 (1960): 263-90; "The Literature on Fortification in Renaissance Italy," *Technology and Culture* 4 (1963): 30-50; "Palmanova: A Study in 16th-Century Urbanism," *Saggi e memorie di storia dell'arte* 5 (1967): 23-41, 175-79; *Military Considerations in City Planning: Fortifications,* Planning and Cities 1 (New York: George Braziller, 1972).

DEL CHIARO, MARIO A. ■ FAAR Classics/Archaeology 60. b. Apr. 22, 1925, San Francisco, CA. m. Christina E. Del Chiaro. c. Kari, Marco, Paola. BA 50, UC, Berkeley; MA 51, UC, Berkeley; PhD 55, UC, Berkeley. **Other Study:** Archaeological expeditions: Morgantina, San Giovenale, Trebisnjica, Rome, Cosa, Salona, Split, Ghiaccio Forte, Scansano. **Career & Employment:** UC, Santa Barbara, Asst. Prof.-Prof. 1956-present. **Fellowships, Honors & Awards:** UC, Berkeley, Fellowship 1951; John Wesley Brittan Traveling Fellowship 1952-53; MMA, Fellowship 1953-54; ANS Summer Seminar Grantee 1954; Phi Beta Kappa (Alpha of California) 1955; APS Grant 1957; UC Humanities Inst., Senior Faculty Fellowship 1967-68; Istituto di Studi Etruschi ed Italici, Florence, Corresponding Mem. 1968-present; UCLA, Inst. of Archaeology, Faculty 1975-present; NEH Grant 1977; Explorers Club 1979-present; Deutsches Archaologisches Institut, Berlin, Corresponding Mem. 1981-present; Istituto Archeologico Germanico, Rome, Corresponding Mem. 1981-present; European Acad. of Sciences & Art, Salzburg, Austria, Honorary Mem. 1983; Order of Merit of the Italian Republic, Cavaliere Ufficiale 1990-present. **Publications:** "The Genucilia Group: A Class of Etruscan Red-Figured Plates," *University of California Publications in Classical Archaeology* 3.4 (1957): 243-72; *The Etruscan Funnel Group: A Tarquinian Red-Figured Fabric* (Florence, 1974); *Etruscan Red-Figured Vase-Painting at Caere* (Berkeley: UC Press, 1974); *Classical Art at the Santa Barbara Museum of Art: Sculpture* (Santa Barbara: Museum of Art, 1984); ed., *Corinthiaca: Studies in Honor of Darrell A. Amyx* (New York: Columbia Univ. Press, 1986); plus numerous articles. **Bio-Bibliography:** *Who's Who in America; Who's Who in American Art.* **Business Address:** Dept. of Art History, UC, Santa Barbara, CA 93106.

DEL DRAGO, GIOVANNI ■ Longtime friend and frequent visitor to the Academy. Resides in Bolsena, Italy and has entertained groups from the Academy on the Isola Bisentina on Lago di Bolsena.

DE LIMA, SIGRID ■ FAAR Literature 54. b. Dec. 4, 1921, NYC. m. Stephen Greene. c. Alison. BA 42, Columbia Univ.; BS 44, Columbia Univ. **Career & Employment:** Free-lance journalist 1946-48; United Press, Financial Writer 1946-48. **Publications:** *Captain's Beach* (New York: Scribners, 1950); *The Swift Cloud* (New York: Scribners, 1952); *Carnival by the Sea* (New York: Scribners, 1954); *Praise a Fine Day* (New York: Random House, 1959); *Oriane* (New York: Harcourt Brace, 1968). **Bio-Bibliography:** Charles Poore, "Books of the Times," *NY Times* (Mar. 6, 1954 & June 25, 1959); Edmund Fuller, "Off-Season Shambles," *Saturday Review* (Mar. 13, 1954); Gertrude Buckman, "Overblown Fantasia," *NY Times* (Mar. 7, 1954).

DELL'OSPEDALE, CHRISTOPH ■ AAR – Rome, Maintenance Staff.

DEL TREDICI, DAVID ■ RAAR Musical Composition 85. b. Mar. 16, 1937, Cloverdale, CA. BA 59, UC, Berkeley; MFA 64, Princeton Univ. **Other Study:** Piano with Bernhard Abramowitsch & Robert Helps; Composition with Seymour Shifrin, Roger Sessions, Earl Kim. **Career & Employment:** Harvard Univ., Faculty 1968-72; Buffalo Univ. 1973; Boston Univ. 1973-84; CUNY 1984-86, Distinguished Prof. 1986-present; Juilliard School of Music, Faculty 1993-present. **Memberships & Offices:** BoD: Yaddo, MacDowell Colony, Aaron Copland Fund for Music; ASCAP; AANIAL. **Fellowships, Honors & Awards:** Phi Beta Kappa; Comms. from Fromm Found., Koussevitzky Found., San Francisco Symphony, Chicago Symphony, Philadelphia Orchestra, St. Louis Symphony, Concertgebouw Orchestra, NY Philharmonic; Kimber Award 1955; Woodrow Wilson Fellow 1959; Hertz Award 1962; Guggenheim Fellow 1966; NAAL Award 1968; Naumberg Recording Award 1972; Brandeis Univ., Creative Arts Award 1973; NEA Grant 1973, 1974; Creative Artists Pub. Service Grant 1975; Pulitzer Prize 1980; Friedheim Award 1982. **Important Works:** Instrumental: *String Trio, Soliloquy, Fantasy Pieces, Virtuoso Alice, Scherzo, Acrostic Song;* settings of James Joyce include: *Six Songs on Texts of James Joyce, I Hear an Army, Night Conjure-Verse, Syzygy;* settings of Lewis Carroll include *Pop-Pourri, An Alice Symphony (Illustrated Alice, In Wonderland, The Lobster Quadrille), Adventures Underground, Vintage Alice, Final Alice, Child Alice (In Memory of a Summer Day, Quaint Events, Happy Voices, All in the Golden Afternoon), Haddocks Eyes;* orchestral: *The Last Gospel, March to Tonality, Happy Voices, Tattoo, Steps.* **Exhibitions/ Performances:** Recital & symphony pianist; appeared with symphony orchs., including San Francisco Symphony; Composer-in-residence Tanglewood Music Festival 1964-65, 1985; Marlboro Music Festival 1966-67, Aspen Music Festival 1975, 1984; Rockefeller Found. at Bellagio, Italy 1983; NY Philharmonic 1988-90. **Bio-Bibliography:** *Who's Who in America.* **Home Address:** 7 Forest Rd., Sag Harbor, NY 11963.

DE MAIO, SALVATORE ■ FAAR Painting 33. b. Feb. 22, 1908, New Haven, CT. d. Feb. 10, 1960. m. Clelia De Maio. c. Letitia; Vanna; Salvatore, Jr. BFA, Yale School of Fine Arts. **Other Studies:** Lake Forest School. **Career & Employment:** Connecticut Telephone & Electric Div., Chief Production Illustrator; Weathervane Restaurant, Hamden CT. **Important Works:** Murals, New Haven Public Library, Hamden HS, Governor's Foot Guard Army. **Exhibitions/Performances:**

Gallery of Fine Arts, Yale Univ. **Bio-Bibliography:** *NY Times,* Obit. (Feb. 11, 1960).

DEMPSEY, CHARLES G. ■ FAAR History of Art 65. b. Mar. 11, 1937, Providence, RI. m. M. Elizabeth Cropper. BA 59, Swarthmore College; MFA 62, Princeton Univ.; PhD 63, Princeton Univ. **Research/Artistic Interests:** Renaissance & Baroque Italian art. **Career & Employment:** Bryn Mawr College, Asst. Prof.-Prof. 1965-80, Chair 1975-80; Johns Hopkins Univ., Prof. 1980-present, Chair 1989-present; Visiting Appointments: Johns Hopkins Univ. 1971-73, Univ. of Melbourne 1977, Folger Inst. 1977, Princeton Univ. 1985. **Memberships & Offices:** CASVA, Bd. of Adv. 1986-88; US Com. for History of Art 1985-present; Fellowship Coms.: NEH, CASVA. **Fellowships, Honors & Awards:** ACLS 1969-70; Villa I Tatti Fellowship 1973-74; NEH Fellow 1978-79; IAS, Visiting Mem. 1989-90. **Publications:** *Annibale Carracci and the Beginning of Baroque Style,* Villa I Tatti Monographs 3 (Glückstadt, 1977); "Some Observations on the Education of Artists in Florence and Bologna," *Art Bulletin* 62 (1980): 552-69; "Annibal Carrache au Palais Farnèse," in *Le Palais Farnèse* (Rome: École Française de Rome, 1981), 269-311; "Mythic Inventions in Counter-Reformation Painting, in *Rome in the Renaissance,* ed. P.A. Ramsey (Binghamton: SUNY Press, 1982), 55-75; "Malvasia and the Problem of the Early Raphael and Bologna," *Studies in the History of Art* 17 (1986): 237-51; "The Carracci Reform of Painting," in *The Age of Carreggio and the Carracci* (Bologna, Washington & New York, 1986), 237-54; with Elizabeth Cropper, "The State of Research in Italian Painting of the Seventeenth Century," *Art Bulletin* 69 (1987): 494-509; "The Greek Style and the Prehistory of Neoclassicism," in *Pietro Testa 1612-1560,* ed. E. Cropper (Philadelphia, 1988), 37-65; "Renaissaance Hieroglyphic Studies and Gentile Bellini's St. Mark Preaching in Alexandria," in *Hermeticism and the Renaissance* (Washington, DC, 1988), 342-65; "Introduction" to *Gli scritti dei Carracci,* Villa Spelman Colloquia 2, ed. Giovanna Perini (Bologna, 1990); "Gli studi sui Carracci: Lo statto della questione," *Arte a Bologna* 1 (1990): 21-31; *The Portrayal of Love: Botticelli's Primavera and Humanist Culture at the Time of Lorenzo the Magnificent* (Princeton: Princeton Univ. Press, 1992). **Bio-Bibliography:** *Who's Who in America.* **Home Address:** 3906 St. Paul St., Baltimore, MD 21218. **Business Address:** Dept. of History of Art, Johns Hopkins Univ., Baltimore, MD 21218.

DENISON, WILLIAM KENDALL ■ FASCSR 96. b. May 17, 1867, Irasburgh, VT. d. Aug. 23, 1963. BA 1891, Tufts College; MA 1892, Harvard Univ.; MA 1893, Tufts College. **Career & Employment:** Tufts Univ., Asst. Prof. 1897-99, Prof. 1899-1938, Prof. Emer. 1938-63. **Memberships & Offices:** APA, ArIA, CANE. **Bio-Bibliography:** *Directory of American Scholars;* Tufts Univ. Archives.

DENNISON, WALTER ■ FASCSR 1897; AAR Annual Prof. 1908-9. Aug. 9, 1869, Saline, MI. d. Mar. 18. 1917. m. Anna L. Green. BA 1893, Univ. of Michigan; MA 1894, Univ. of Michigan; PhD 1897, Univ. of Michigan. **Other Studies:** Univ. of Bonn 1894-95. **Research/Artistic Interests:** Latin & Oscan epigraphy, Roman history. **Career & Employment:** Univ. of Michigan, Instr. 1897-99; Oberlin College, Prof. 1899-1902; Univ. of Michigan, Jr. Prof. 1902-10; Swarthmore College Prof. 1910-17. **Memberships & Offices:** *Classical World,* Assc. Ed. 1913-17; Classical Soc. of Atlantic States, Pres. 1915-16. **Publications:** with. John C. Rolfe, *A Junior Latin Book* (Boston: Allyn & Bacon, 1898); *Vergil's Aeneid: Books 1-6* (New York: American Book Co., 1902); ed., Livy, *Book I and Selections from Books II-X* (New York:

Macmillan, 1908); with C.R. Morey, *Studies in East Christian and Roman Art* (New York: Macmillan, 1918); *A Treasure of the Late Roman Period* (New York: Macmillan, 1918); Mario Torelli & Martha Baldwin, *Latin Inscriptions in the Kelsey Museum: The Dennison Collection* (Ann Arbor: Univ. of Michigan, 1979). **Bio-Bibliography:** Briggs, 132-33; *Dictionary of American Biography;* Dennison File, Bentley Historical Library, Univ. of Michigan; *Who Was Who in America.*

DENNY, WILLIAM DOUGLAS ■ FAAR Musical Composition 41. b. July 2, 1910, Seattle, WA. d. Sept. 2, 1980. m. Jeanne Denny. BA 31, UC; MA 33 UC, Berkeley. **Other Studies:** UC, Berkeley with Modeste Alloo, Albert Elkus, Edward G. Stricklen & Randall Thompson; fugue, composition & orchestration with Paul Dukas in Paris. **Career & Employment:** Harvard Univ. 1941-42; Vassar College 1942-44; UC, Berkeley, Prof. 1945-78. **Fellowships, Honors & Awards:** George Ladd Prix de Paris, UC 1933-35; Fromm Found. Award 1953. **Important Works:** *Incidental Music for "A Horace Festival"* 1935; *Suite for Small Orchestra* 1934-36; *Concertino for Orchestra* 1937; Orchestration of the piano part of "Tarantella" by Randall Thompson; *Three Movements of a Symphony in A* 1938; 3 *String Quartets* 1938, 1952, 1955; *Symphony No. 1,* CBS Radio 1939; *Sinfonietta for Strings,* NBC Radio 1940; *Suite for Chamber Orchestra* 1940; *Most Glorious Lord of Life,* a cantata 1943; *Viola Sonata* 1943-44; *Overture for Strings* 1945; *Praeludium* 1946; *Motets* (3) 1946-47; *Symphony No. 2* 1949; *Symphony No. 3* 1955-57; *Partita for Organ* 1958; *Trio for Strings* 1965. **Bio-Bibliography:** *Baker's Biographical Dictionary of Musicians; New Grove Dictionary of American Music.*

DE PACE, JOSEPH A. ■ FAAR Architecture 85. b. Feb. 3, 1954, NYC. BArch 78, City College School of Architecture; MArch 82, Harvard GSD. **Career & Employment:** Walker Group, Inc., Job Captain 1978-80; Perkins & Will Architects, Job Captain 1980; Rothzeid Kaiserman Thomson & Bee, P.C., Job Captain 1982-84; Lance Jay Brown Architecture & Urban Design, Project Architect 1985-89; City College School of Architecture, Adj. Prof. 1987-present; Joseph De Pace, Architecture + Public Art, Prin. 1989-present. **Fellowships, Honors & Awards:** New York Soc. of Architects, Del Gaudio Award for Excellence in Design 1978; Art Comm. of City of New York, Award for Excellence in Design 1991; Congressional Citation, Award for Excellence in Design 1993. **Important Works:** Indira Ghandi Nat. Cultural Centre Competition 1986; Clemson Univ. Performing Arts Center Competition 1989; Sculpture Center Studios, Masterplan & Penthouse Renovation, NYC 1989; Red Ink, Office Interior, NYC 1990; "Rivers," Langston Hughes Memorial & Burial, Schomburg Center, NYC 1990; Evanston Public Library Competition 1991; "Du Sable's Journey," Harold Washington Library, Chicago 1991; Ziegler Residence, Addition, Scarsdale, NY 1992; "Revelations," Martin Luther King Memorial, Yerba Buena Gardens, San Francisco 1993; "Stations," Markers for the Underground Railroad Sites, Niagara, NY 1993; "The Freedom Ring" Amphitheater, Community College of Philadelphia 1994; "The New Ring Shout," African Burial Ground Memorial NYC 1994. **Exhibitions/Performances:** MOMA Project Series 1989; Spoleto Festival, Charleston, SC 1991; Brooklyn Museum 1992. **Bio-Bibliography:** Elizabeth Heeken Bartels, "Spectacle Island," *Landscape Architecture* (Jan.-Feb. 1984): 87-90; Aldo Rossi et al., *Progetto di Venezia: Terzo Mostra Internazionale di Architettura* (Milan: Electa, 1985), 134; Moshe Safdie, *The Harvard Jerusalem Studio* (Cambridge, MA: MIT Press, 1986), 93, 108-9; "Precedent and Invention," *Harvard Architecture Review* 5 (New York: Rizzoli 1986): 28-29; Razia

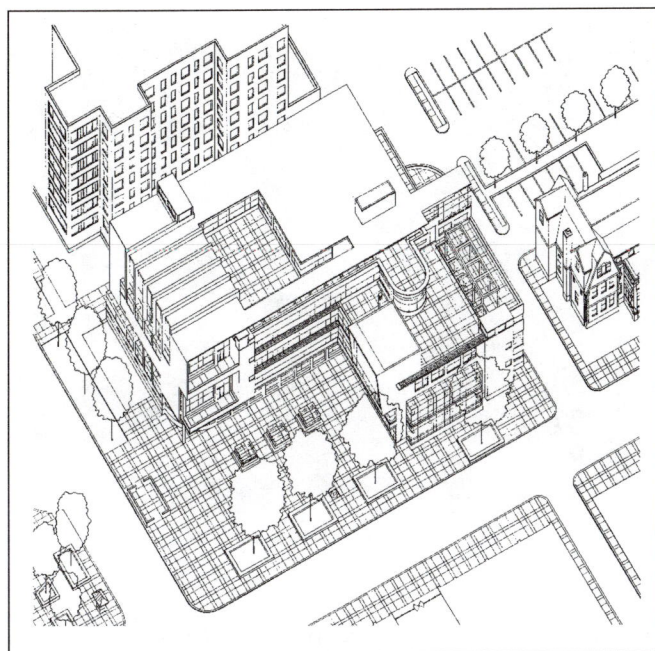

Joseph A. De Pace

Grover, ed., *Concepts and Responses* (Chidambaram, Ahmedabad, India: Mapin Publishing, 1992), 160-61; Mary Jane Jacob, *Places with a Past: New Site-Specific Art at Charleston's Spoleto Festival* (New York: Rizzoli, 1992), 146-51; Catherine Ingraham, "Tom, Dick, (Jane) and Harry," *Progressive Architecture* (Feb. 1992): 70-71; Parul Kapur, "Mythologies," *New Yorker* (Feb. 3, 1992): 12; Susan Snodgrass, "All Here Come Together to Mix and Contend...," *New Art Examiner* (Apr. 1992): 18-23; Alan Temco, "After 3 Decades, Yerba Buena Center Is a Winner," *San Francisco Chronicle* (Oct. 12, 1993): 1, 15; Heidi Landecker, "Community Garden," *Architecture* (Feb. 1994): 54-57; Leonard W. Boasberg, "In a Perfect Circle, Art Shows Ideal of Freedom," *Philadelphia Inquirer* (Nov. 12, 1994): B1. **Business Address:** Joseph De Pace, Architecture + Public Art, 147 W. 22nd St., 10S, NYC 10011.

DE ROSSI, GIOVANNI MARIA ■ Italian Fulbright Fellow 1968-69.

DEVRIES, PETER B. ■ FAAR Painting 67. b. Apr. 2, 1942, Paterson, NJ. m. Judith A. Schumaker. BFA 64, RISD; MFA 69, Maryland Inst., College of Art. **Research/Artistic Interests:** Landscapes, still lifes, figure studies, portraits. I use oil paint, watercolors, pastels. **Career & Employment:** Cambridge School of Weston, MA, Faculty 1969-73; Drawing, Printmaking. Since I have painted independently, I am presently a men's clothing salesman & am pursuing my artwork in my spare time. **Fellowships, Honors & Awards:** Carnegie Found. Grant 1964. **Important Works:** Adler, Pollack & Sheehan, Providence, RI; Mr. & Mrs. John Schleyer, Warwick, RI. **Exhibitions/Performances:** Solo & two-person: Gaugler Salon, Saddle River, NJ 1965; The Gallery, Bloomingdale's, NYC 1972; Rhode Island Hospital, Providence 1980; with Paula Martiesian, Leonore Gray Gallery, Providence 1986. Group: RISD 1974; Art Assn. of Newport, RI 1975; Silvermine Guild of Artists, New Canaan, CT 1975, 1977; Jury Show, Bristol, RI Art Museum 1975; Any Art Gallery, Providence, RI 1979; Gallery One, School One, Providence, RI 1984. **Home Address:** 15 Bradburn St., Rochester, NY 14619.

DE WITT, NORMAN WENTWORTH ■ FASCSR 04. b. Sept. 18, 1876, Tweedside, ONT. d. Sept. 20, 1958. m. Katherine Ida Johnston. c. Norman Johnston DeWitt. BA 1899, Victoria College, Univ. of Toronto; PhD 06, Univ. of Chicago. **Other Study:** Univ. of Jena. **Career & Employment:** Lincoln College, IL, Prof.; Washington Univ., Instr. 1905-7; Miami Univ., OH, Prof. 1907-8; Victoria College, Univ. of Toronto, Prof. 1908-45, Dean of Arts 1924-28; Cornell Univ., Acting Prof. 1928-29. **Memberships & Offices:** Royal Acad. of Mantua, Corresponding Fellow; Royal Soc. of Canada, Fellow, Pres. 1925; APA, Pres. 1946-47. **Publications:** "The Arrow of Alcestes," *American Journal of Philology* 41 (1920): 369-78; "Virgil at Naples," *Classical Philology* 16 (1921): 338-44; *Virgil's Biographia Litteraria* (Toronto: Victoria College Press, 1923); *A Brief World History* (Toronto: Macmillan, 1927); trans., with Norman Johnston De Witt, Demosthenes, *Funeral Speech, Erotic Essay and Letters*, Loeb Classical Library (Cambridge MA: Harvard Univ. Press, 1949); *Epicurus and his Philosophy* (Minneapolis: Univ. of Minnesota Press, 1954); *St. Paul and Epicurus* (Minneapolis: Univ. of Minnesota Press, 1954). **Bio-Bibliography:** *NY Times*, Obit. (Sept. 22, 1958); *Toronto Globe and Mail*, Obit. (Sept. 22, 1958); *Phoenix* 12 (1958): 139-40; Briggs, 136-37.

D'HARNANCOURT, RENE ■ AAR Visitor 1951-55, MOMA, Dir.

DIAMOND, DAVID ■ AAR World War II Prize 42, RAAR Musical Composition 72. b. 1915, Rochester, NY. Eastman School of Music with Bernard Rogers; Cleveland Inst. with Andre de Ribaupierre. **Other Study:** privately with Roger Sessions, Nadia Boulanger, & Hermann Scherchen. **Career & Employment:** Manhattan School of Music, Prof. & Chair; Juilliard School Faculty 1973-present. **Fellowships, Honors & Awards:** Guggenheim Fellowships 1938, 1942, 1958; Univ. of Rome, Fulbright Prof.; SUNY, Buffalo, Slee Prof. 1961, 1963; NIAL, Elected Mem. 1966; Paderewski Prize; Ernest Bloch Award; League of Composers Comm.; Koussevitzky Found. Comm.; Rockefeller Found. Comm.; Fromm Found. Comm.; Soc. for Publication of American Music Award; Ballet Guild Award; NIAL Award; ASCAP Stravinsky Award; Library of Congress, Rheta Sosland Chamber Music Prize; McKim Fund Comm. 1980; Second William Schuman Life Achievement Award 1985; MacDowell Assn., Gold Medals; AANIAL Letters for Lifetime Achievement 1991. **Important Works:** *Symphonies* 1-11; *Sinfonia Concertante*; *Psalm for Orchestra*; *Choral Symphony*; *Music for Shakespeare's Romeo and Juliet*; 3 *Concerti for violin and orchestra*; *Concerto for Cello and Orchestra*; *Concertino for Piano and Orchestra*; *Concerto for String Quartet*; ten *String Quartets*; chamber music works; 75 *Songs*; numerous *Song Cycles* for voice & piano; choral a capella music; music for films & theater. Publisher: Peer-Southern, G. Schirmer, Theodore Presser. Recordings: Delos. **Bio-Bibliography:** Victoria Kimberling, *Diamond: A Bio-Bibliography* (Scarecrow); *David Diamond: Festschrift for His Eightieth Birthday* (Pendragon Press, 1985); *International Who's Who; Who's Who in America; Who's Who in Music; Who's Who in the World*. **Home Address:** 249 Edgerton St., Rochester, MA 14607.

DICKISON, SHEILA K. ■ b. Nov. 14, 1942, Walkerton, ONT., Canada. BA 64, Univ. of Toronto; MA 66, Bryn Mawr College; PhD 72, Bryn Mawr College. **Other Study:** ANS Summer Program 1966; Univ. of Perugia, Etruscology 1968; Pontifical Inst. of Early Christian Archaeology, Rome 1974-75. **Research/Artistic Interests:** Roman historiography, ancient social history, history of women, Latin pedagogy. **Career & Employment:**

Univ. of Florida, Assc. Prof. 1976-present, Assc. Dean of College of Liberal Arts & Sciences 1989-present. **Home Address:** 3000 NW 66 Terrace, Gainesville, FL 32606. **Business Address:** Classics Dept., Univ. of Florida, Gainesville, FL 32611.

DIESENDRUCK, TAMAR ■ FAAR Musical Composition 84. b. Aug. 3, 1946, Tel-Aviv, Israel. m. Eric H. Moe. BA 68, Brandeis Univ.; MA 79, UC, Berkeley; PhD 83, UC, Berkeley. **Other Study:** Instrumental instruction from childhood on piano & violin, cello as an adult. **Research/Artistic Interests:** Music composition. Have composed for solo instruments, small & large ensembles, vocal music, orchestral music; majority of compositions are chamber music. **Career & Employment:** UC, Berkeley, Lect. 1981-83; San Francisco Conservatory, Instr. 1984-85; San Francisco State Univ., Lect. 1986; NYU, Assc. Prof. 1987-88; Univ. of Wisconsin, Madison, Lect. 1992; Univ. of Pittsburgh, Visiting Asst. Prof. 1993-present. **Fellowships, Honors & Awards:** Resident Composer, American Dance Festival 1979; UC, Nicolo di Lorenzo Prize 1980; Koussevitzky Found.-Library of Congress Comm. 1987; Mellon Found. Post-Doctoral Fellowship 1987; Wellesley Composers Conf., Fellow 1989; Pennsylvania Council on the Arts Fellowship 1991, 1993; Wellesley Composers' Conference Fellowship 1993; American Women Composers, Recording Grant 1993. **Important Works:** *The Palm at the End of the Mind,* for contralto & 8 instruments, poem by Wallace Stevens 1984; *Quartet,* for clarinet-bass clarinet, violin, cello, piano 1984; *The Second Coming,* for baritone & orchestra, poem by W.B. Yeats 1986; *Etudes,* for solo violin 1987; *Such Stuff,* String Quartet No. 1, Koussevitzky Found.-Library of Congress Comm. 1988; *Sound Resoning in the Tower of Babel,* No. 1 in *Theater of the Ear,* for solo piano, for Eric Moe 1990; *Coming to Terms in the Tower of Babel,* No. 2 in *Theater of the Ear,* for cello & piano, NYSCA Comm. for the Washington Sq. Contemporary Music Series 1990; *On That Day,* No. 3 in *Theater of the Ear,* for violin, cello, piano, Stony Brook Chamber Ensemble Comm. 1991; *String Quartet No. 2,* No. 4 in *Theater of the Ear* 1992; *The What of the How,* for solo viola 1992; *How/Feel,* for 14 players, No. 5 in *Theater of the Ear* 1993; *A Spire Ring,* for brass quintet 1994; *Being as How,* for 7 players 1995. **Bio-Bibliography:** *American Composers; Contemporary Music Review;* Eric Moe, *The Emerging Generation: Beyond Right and Wrong Ways to Write Music: Tsontakis, Rosenblum and Diesendruck.* **Home Address:** 418 Stratton Ln., Pittsburgh, PA 15206.

DIETERLEN, CHARLES T.E. ■ McKim Fellow 1913.

DIETSCH, C. (CLARENCE) PERCIVAL ■ FAAR Sculpture 09. b. May 23, 1881, NYC. d. 1961. **Memberships & Offices:** New York School of Art; NSS 1910; ALNY 1911; Soc. Four Arts, Palm Beach. **Fellowships, Honors & Awards:** Peabody Inst., Rinehart Scholarship; P.-P. Expo Prize 1915; Soc. Four Arts Prize 1938. **Important Works:** Peabody Inst., Baltimore; Rice Inst., Houston; Lighthouse for the Blind, NYC; Besso Library, Rome; Soc. Four Arts; War Memorial, Deep River, CT. **Exhibitions/Performances:** PAFA 1907; NAD; Norton Gallery; P.-P. Expo 1915; Florida Federal Artists; Soc. Four Arts 1938. **Bio-Bibliography:** *Who Was Who in America, Who Was Who in American Art.*

DILLARD, ANNIE ■ AAR Visitor 1982-83, Writer.

DILLER, ELIZABETH ■ NIAE, John Dinkeloo Traveling Fellow 1980-81.

DI MAIO, JUDITH ■ FAAR Architecture 78; SOF Council 1982-85, VP 1986-87; Juror 1990. b. Providence, RI. BA 72,

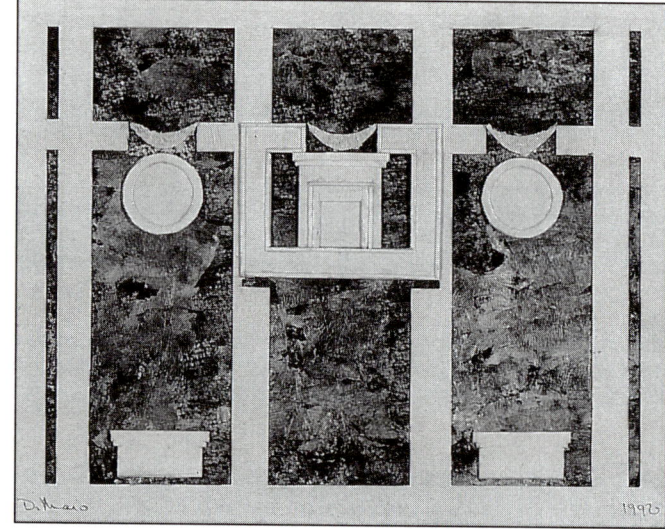
Judith Di Maio

Bennington College; BArch 75, Cornell Univ.; MArch 76, Harvard Univ. **Research/Artistic Interests:** Ancient Roman nymphaea; collage drawings of invented Roman walls or facades inspired by ancient Roman walls & 16th-century Italian facades. **Career & Employment:** Harry M. Weese & Assc. 1972; Univ. of Kentucky, Asst. Prof. 1976-81; Kohn Pederson Fox Assc. P.C., Sen. Designer 1981-87; Univ. of Notre Dame, Rome, Assc. Visiting Prof. 1984-85; Judith Di Maio, Architect, Prin. 1987-present; Univ. of Illinois, Chicago, Visiting Prof. 1987; Yale Univ., Critic 1988-present, Undergraduate Major in Architecture, Dir. 1994-present; Columbia Univ., Adj. Assc. Prof. 1993; Visiting Critic: Univ. of Pennsylvania 1984, RISD 1985, Rice Univ. 1986, Columbia Univ. 1987. **Memberships & Offices:** Nat. Inst. of Architectural Education, BoT; Bennington College, BoT 1972-74. **Fellowships, Honors & Awards:** Bennington College Grant 1969; Birch Burdette Long Competition, Hon. Mention 1975; Harvard Univ., Alexander Phillips Bequest 1979; Univ. of Kentucky Grant 1979; Fulbright-Hays Scholar 1979. **Important Works:** Administration Bldg. Entryways, Bennington College 1972; Friedlander Garden, Sacramento 1983-84; Convention Center Site Tower, NYC 1987-90; Davis Residence, NYC 1989; with William Palmore, Biblioteca Alexandrina, Egypt Project 1989; 1200 New York Ave., Washington, DC 1990-92; West Colonnade Pavilion, Seaside, FL 1992-present; Healy-DeLeon Barn, White Creek, NY 1993-present; Segal Residence Addition, Architectural Facade, Rye, NY 1994. **Exhibitions/Performances:** Cooper Union, NYC 1975; Walker Art Center, Minneapolis 1977; Usdan Gallery, Bennington College 1978; "Roma Interrota," Markets of Trajan, Rome & Cooper Hewitt Museum, NYC 1978-79; "Tribune Tower: Late Entries Competition," New Haven, Dallas-Ft. Worth, Chicago 1980-82; Ann Plumb Gallery, NYC 1988; Woods-Gerry Gallery, Providence 1988; Yale Univ. 1991. **Bio-Bibliography:** *Quadrille* (Feb. 1994). **Home Address:** 17 W. 67 St., NYC 10023. **Business Address:** Judith Di Maio Architect, Judith Di Maio Studio, 17 W. 67 St., NYC 10023.

DINNERSTEIN, SIMON A. ■ FAAR Painting 78. b. Feb. 16, 1943, Brooklyn, NY. m. Renée Sudler. c. Simone. BA 65, City College, CUNY. **Other Study:** Brooklyn Museum Art School 1964-67; Hochschule für Bildende Kunst, Kassel, Germany 1971. **Research/Artistic Interests:** Painting, drawing, graphics, wide range of figurative work. **Career & Employment:** New School for Social Research 1975-89; New York City Technical

College 1979-present; Pratt Inst., Visiting Prof. 1986-87; Calhoun School, NYC, Artist-in-Residence 1988, 1989; US Information Service, Barcelona & Madrid, Lect. 1979; Palmer Museum of Art, Pennsylvania State Univ., Univ. Park 1984; St. Paul's School, NH 1992; Nassau Community College, NYC 1993. **Fellowships, Honors & Awards:** Brooklyn Museum Art School Scholarship 1964-67; Fulbright Fellowship, Germany 1970-71; Minnesota Museum of Art, Purchase Award 1968, 1975; NAD, Edwin Austin Abbey Fellowship, Hon. Mention 1975, Cannon Prize 1988, Elected Mem. 1992-present; Louis Comfort Tiffany Grant 1976; E.D. Found. Grant 1977, 1978; Ingram Merrill Award 1978-79; AAAL, Childe Hassam Purchase Award 1976, 1977, 1978; MacDowell Colony Fellowship 1969, 1979; NYFA Fellowship 1987; Artists Space Grant 1983, 1985, 1987. **Publications:** "Looking at One's Own Artwork," *American Artist* (Apr. 1986): 68-71, 98, 100, 101. **Important Works:** Public Collections: Minnesota Museum of Art; Stephens, Inc., Little Rock, AR; Palmer Museum of Art, Pennsylvania State Univ., Univ. Park; Museum of Art & Archaeology, Univ. of Missouri, Columbia; Muncie, Williams, Proctor Inst., Utica, NY; Art Gallery, Univ. of Maryland, College Park; Paul, Weiss, Rifkind, Wharton & Garrison, NYC; Martin Luther King Labor Center, NYC; Nat. Museum of American Art, Smithsonian Inst.; Vinson & Elkins, Dallas; Curtis, Mallet-Prevost, Colt & Mosle, NYC; NAD. **Exhibitions/Performances:** Solo: Inst. of Intl. Ed., UN Plaza, NYC 1976-77, 1979; New School for Social Research, NYC 1981, 1993; Gallery 1199, Martin Luther King Labor Center, NYC 1985; Pratt Inst., Brooklyn, NY 1987; Staempfli Gallery, NYC 1975, 1979, 1988; St. Paul's School, NH 1991; NJ Center for Visual Arts 1994. **Bio-Bibliography:** John Russell, "In Dinnerstein's Painting, an Echo Chamber," *NY Times* (Feb. 25, 1975): 21; Michel André, "Simon Dinnerstein," *Art News* 74.3 (Mar. 1975): 112-14; Theodore F. Wolff, "The Kind Word for Such Art is Conservative," *Christian Science Monitor* (Apr. 25, 1988), 21; Shirley Romaine, "Interviews: Simon Dinnerstein," *Art Scene on Long Island*, CableVision, Cable 44 & 20, Aug. 22-23 & Nov. 13, 1989; Albert Boime, Intro., & Thomas M. Messer, *The Art of Simon Dinnerstein* (Little Rock: Univ. of Arkansas Press, 1990); Doug Turetsky, "Simon Dinnerstein: Artist in the

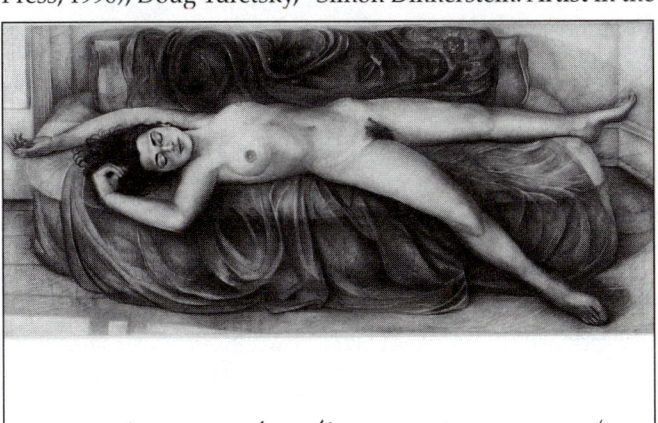

With thanks for such a rich and rewarding stay in Rome (9-'76 to 1-'79)!
Simon Dinnerstein

Simon Dinnerstein. A, 1992, conté crayon, colored pencil, pastel, 24 1/4 x 63 3/8"

Simon A. Dinnerstein

Round," *Brooklyn Affairs* 2.3 (Apr. 1985): 6-7; Richard Merkins, "Essential Realities: Simon Dinnerstein Draws the Essence of Art from the Commonplace," *Concord Monitor* (Feb. 25, 1991): Arts 1, 3; *Who's Who; Who's Who in American Art; Who's Who in American Education; Who's Who in the East.* **Home Address:** 415 First St., Brooklyn, NY 11215.

DINSMOOR, WILLIAM B. ■ AAR Trustee 1932-58, Acting Dir. 1944, Classicist.

DIRSMITH, RON ■ FAAR Architecture 60. b. Feb. 27, 1932, Chicago, IL. m. Suzanne Roe. c. Timothy Patrick, Colleen Roe, Brian Sean. BS 54, Univ. of Illinois, Chicago & Champaign; MArch 56, Univ. of Illinois, Champaign. **Research/Artistic Interests:** For over 33 years The Dirsmith Group been a tightly knit association of architects, interior designers, specialty engineers, artisans, sculptors, landscape planners & lighting environmentalists, in what we call, "the Renaissance Tradition of Versatility." Currently we are most interested in the historical development of the human species from the time of the cave paintings at Les Eyzies & the Dordogne Valley. **Career & Employment:** Perkins & Will, Architects & Engineers 1954-62; Ron Dirsmith, Architect, then The Dirsmith Goup, Inc., Intl. Architects 1962-present. **Memberships & Offices:** North Shore Unitarian Church, BoT; School District 107, BoT; Legacy Found, BoT. I have been a visiting lecturer, juror, officer & mem. of a number of institutions over the past 35 years, as well as a mem. & honorary mem. of a variety of societies. **Fellowships, Honors & Awards:** Chicago Chamber of Commerce & Industry, Illinois-Indiana Masonry Council, Chicago Chapter AIA, Ville Giardini, Il Bagno, *North Shore Magazine*, Pioneer Press, & a variety of professional societies. Univ. of Illinois, Nathan Ricker Prize in Architecture. **Important Works:** North Shore Unitarian Church, Deerfield, IL; Congregation Kam/Isaiah Israel, Chapel Sanctuary & Gardens, Chicago; Hope Unitarian Church, Tulsa; Dirsmith Group Corp. Offices, Highland Park, IL; Fox Environments, Hybernia, Highland Park, IL; Hideaway, Casa de Campo, La Romana, Dominican Republic; Preserve, Highland Park, IL; Romantic Retreat, Boca West, Boca Raton, FL; Corporate & Private Fantasy Land, Playboy Mansion West; Delos Co., Vernon Hills, IL; Hotel il San Pietro, Positano, Italy; Richard E. Byrd Acad., Cabrini Green, Chicago; Creative Human Environment, Sacred Spaces Secret Places, Travelling Exb. **Bio-Bibliography:** Gordon Gould, "He Blueprints Better Schools," *Chicago Tribune Magazine* (Feb. 8, 1959); Gordon Gould, "Bubble House: Last Word in Modern Living," *Chicago Tribune Magazine* (Jan. 13, 1963); Don Schwartz, "An Architect and His Curves," *Chicago Sun Times* (Mar. 13, 1967); Dorothy Andries, "Unitarian New Church: An Architectural Departure with Links to the Past," *Lerner Life* (July 17, 1968); Betty Karger, "Past, Present, Future Bright for Designer," *Waukegan News Sun* (Mar. 15, 1969); Rosemary Sazanoff, "They Want the Best Too," *Lerner Life* (Jan. 27, 1972); Ruth Deitel, "Bringing Sun into an Urban Canyon," *Chicago Daily News* (Nov. 21, 1975); Gilberto Oneto, "Acqua in Salotto," & "Giardino di Simboli," *Ville Giardini* (Oct. 1982); Gilberto Oneto, "Il Giardino di Playboy," *Ville Giardini* (Mar. 1983); Dorothy Andries, "Winning Team," *Pioneer Press Quarterly* (Autumn 1983); Mariaclara Goldschmidt, "Ispirato dalla natura," *Il Bagno* (July 1984); Grazia Gamberoni, "Residenza Privata," *Il Bagno* (July 1984); Pier Giuseppe Torrani, "Zoo-Paesaggio," *Ville Giardini* (May 1985); Gilberto Oneto, "Un Gioco ben Fatto," *Ville Giardini* (Mar. 1988); Luisa Basso, "A Return to Nature," *Ville Giardini* (Apr. 1990); Gilberto Oneto, "Una Fetta di Paradiso," *Ville Giardini* (May 1990); Valli Herman, "Hef's Haven," *Chicago Tribune* (Sept. 22,

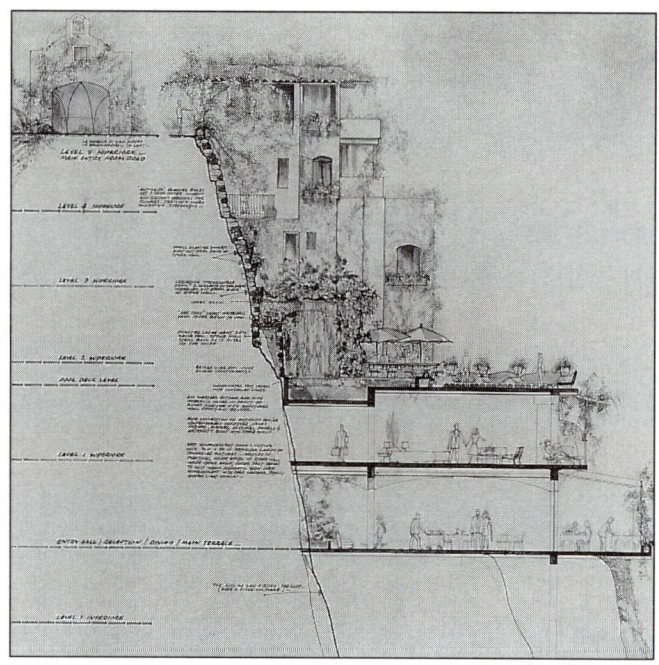

Ron Dirsmith

1991); Vittoria Morganti, "Alla Ricerca dello Zen," *Il Bagno* (May 1992). **Home Address:** 318 Maple Ave., Highland, IL 60035. **Business Address:** The Dirsmith Group, Intl. Architects, 318 Maple Ave., Highland Park, IL 60035.

DI VITA, ANTONINO ■ Italian Fulbright Fellow 1962-63.

DODGE, ROBERT G. ■ FAAR Sculpture 76. b. Aug. 14, 1939, Boston, MA. m. Gwendolyn Kerber. Sarah-Elsie, Jason, Benjamin. BA 63, Univ. of Pennsylvania; BFA 65, Univ. of Pennsylvania; MFA 66, Univ. of Pennsylvania. **Other Study:** Colloborative work with woodworker-craftsman Mark Sfirri, 1987-present. **Career & Employment:** Bucks County Community

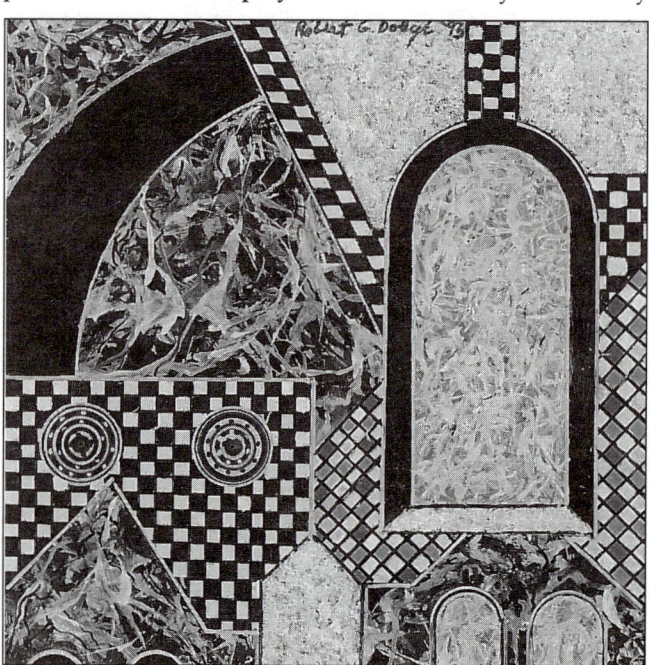

Robert G. Dodge

College, Prof. 1967-present. **Important Works:** Public Collections: Blue Cross-Blue Shield, Philadelphia; Bulgari Jewelers, NYC; CIT, Livingstone, NJ; Equitable Corp., NYC; DuPont Corp., Wilmington, DE; Ethicon, Somerville, NJ; IBM Corp., NYC; Janssen Pharmaceutica, Washington's Crossing, NY; Johnson & Higgins, Princeton, NJ; Merck, Sharp & Dohme; Squibb Corp. **Exhibitions/Performances:** Recent: PAFA 1991; James A. Michener Art Museum, Doylestown, PA 1991, 1992; New York School of Interior Design 1991; Sansar Gallery, Washington, DC 1992; Rabbet Gallery, New Brunswick, NJ 1992; Parsons School of Art, NYC 1992; Langman Gallery, Willow Grove, PA 1993; Trenton City Museum 1993; Jasuta Gallery, Philadelphia 1994; Gallery 500, Elkins Park, PA 1994. **Home Address:** 445 Durham Rd., Newtown, PA 18940.

DODGE, WILLIAM E. ■ AAR Charter Mem., Industrialist.

DORAZIO, PIETRO ■ AAR Visitor 1985-86, Artist.

DOUGHERTY, JOANNA ■ FAAR Landscape Architecture 86. b. June 5, 1952, Washington, DC. BFA 74, RISD; BLArch 75, RISD; MLArch 84, Cornell Univ. **Career & Employment:** TAC, Benjamin Thompson Asscs., Landscape Architect 1977-80; Univ. of Virginia, Asst. Prof. 1984-; Boston Architectural Center, Instr. 1984.

DOUGLAS, WILLIAM ■ FAAR Architecture 28. b. Apr. 11, 1896, New London, CT. d. June 18, 1964. BA 18, Yale Univ.; BFA 23, Yale Univ. **Other Studies:** École des Beaux Arts, Paris. **Research/Artistic Interests:** Santo Spirito; San Miniato, Chapel of Portuguese Cardinal. **Career & Employment:** Orr & Del Grella, Architects, New Haven 1924; Lyman Allyn Museum, New London, CT, Dir. 1944-46; Independent Scholar, Sorrento, Italy 1947-62. **Fellowships, Honors & Awards:** Beaux Arts Inst. of Design Prize.

DOWNEY, SUSAN B. ■ FAAR Classics/Archaeology 65, Classical Jury 1975, 1976. b. Dec. 22, 1938, Kansas City, MO. BA 60, Bryn Mawr College; MA 61, Yale Univ.; PhD 63, Yale Univ. **Research/Artistic Interests:** Near East in the Greco-Roman period. **Career & Employment:** UCLA, Asst. Prof. 1965-72, Assc. Prof. 1972-78, Prof. 1978-present, Chair 1990-93. **Memberships & Offices:** *Classical Antiquity*, Ed. Bd. 1980-92. **Fellowships, Honors & Awards:** AAUW Fellow 1968-69; APS Grants 1966, 1969, 1975, 1978, 1989; ACLS Grant-in-Aid 1978-79; German Archaeological Inst. Fellow 1989, Corresponding Mem. 1994. **Publications:** "Cult Banks from Hatra," *Berytus* 16 (1966): 97-109; "Possible Ancient Prototypes for the Cyprus Plates," *Greek, Roman, and Byzantine Studies* 8 (1967): 309-13; "The Jewelry of Hercules at Hatra," *AJA* 72 (1968): 211-17; *The Excavations at Dura-Europos: Final Report* III, Part I, fasc. 1: *The Heracles Sculpture* (New Haven, Dura-Europos Publications, 1969); "A Preliminary Corpus of the Standards of Hatra," *Sumer* 26 (1970): 195-225; "Temples à escaliers: The Dura Evidence," *California Studies in Classical Antiquity* 9 (1976): 21-39; *The Stone and Plaster Sculpture: Excavations at Dura-Europos*, Monumenta Archaeologica 5 (Los Angeles: Inst. of Archaeology, UC, 1977); "Syrian Images of Mithras Tauroctonos," *Acta Iranica: Textes et Memoires* 4, *Études mithraiques* (1978): 135-49; "Two Buildings at Dura-Europos and the Early History of the Iran," *Mesopotamia* 20 (1985): 111-29; "The Citadel Palace at Dura-Europos," *Syria* 63.1-2 (1986): 27-37; "A Stele from Hierapolis-Bambyce," Deutsches Archäologisches Institut, Abteilung Baghdad, *Mitteilungen* 17 (1986): 301-98; *Mesopotamian Religious Architecture: Alexander through the Parthians* (Princeton: Princeton Univ.

Press, 1988); "Archival Archaeology: Frank Brown's Notes on the Citadel Palace," *Syria* 69 (1992); "The Palace of the Dux Ripae at Dura-Europos and 'Palatial' Architecture in Late Antiquity," in *Eius Virtutis Studiosi: Classical and Post-Classical Studies in Memory of Frank Edward Brown*, ed. Ann R. Scott & Russell T. Scott, Studies in the History of Art 43 (Washington, DC: NGA, 1993), 183-98; *Architectural Terracottas from the Regia* (Ann Arbor: Univ. of Michigan Press, forthcoming). **Business Address:** Dept. of Art History, UCLA, 405 Hilgard Ave., Los Angeles, CA 90024-1417.

DRABKIN, MIRIAM FRIEDMAN ■ FAAR Classics/Archaeology 40. b. Feb. 14, 1915, NYC. m. Israel E. Drabkin. c. Susan, William. BA 35, Hunter College, CUNY; MA 36, Cornell Univ.; PhD 38, Cornell Univ. **Other Study:** Vatican Library, Diploma in Palaeography 1940. **Research/Artistic Interests:** Latin Palaeography, history of Greek & medieval medicine. **Career & Employment:** UN Printing Div. 1949-51; City College, CUNY & Graduate Div., Lect.-Prof. 1951-85. **Memberships & Offices:** *Journal of the History of Medicine and Allied Sciences*, Asst. Ed. 1946-48; History of Science Soc. 1965-present, Exec Com. 1955, Metropolitan NY Sect. Nominating Com. 1955-65; New York Classical Club, Pres. 1967-68; Phi Beta Kappa, City College, Pres. & various other offices. **Fellowships, Honors & Awards:** Phi Beta Kappa 1935; Eta Sigma Phi 1935; Phi Kappa Phi 1938; Cornell Univ., Graduate Scholarships & Fellowships 1935-38. **Publications:** articles in *Bulletin of the History of Medicine* 1942; articles & translations in *Journal of History of Medicine and Allied Sciences* 1947-48; ed. with Israel E. Drabkin, Caelius Aurelianus, *Gynaecia* (Baltimore: Johns Hopkins Univ Press, 1951); ed. of vol. 2, with Ludwig Edelstein, Henry E. Sigerist, *History of Medicine* (Oxford & New York: Oxford Univ. Press, 1960); ed. with Stillman Drake, *Mechanics in Sixteenth-Century Italy* (Madison: Univ. of Wisconsin Press, 1969). **Bio-Bibliography:** *Guide to the History of Science* (Philadelphia, 1986); *American Philosophical Association, Proceedings and Addresses* (Newark, DE, 1990); *Directory of Women in the History of Science, Technology and Medicine* (Clemson, SC: 1991); *Directory of College and University Classicists in the United States and Canada* (1992). **Home Address:** 1027 Garrison Ave., Teaneck, NJ 07666.

DRAEGERT, JOE ■ FAAR Painting 79. b. Mar. 28, 1945, Chariton, IL. m. Colette Tanaka. BFA 68, Kansas City Art Inst.; MFA 70, UC, Davis. **Career & Employment:** Shasta College, Redding CA, Instr. 1970-81; UC, Davis, Asst. Prof. 1983; UC, Berkeley, Guest Lect. 1987. **Fellowships, Honors & Awards:** Kansas City Art Inst., Fellowship 1964-68; Yale Summer School of Art & Music Fellowship 1967. **Important Works:** Redding Art Museum; Nelson Atkins Gallery, Kansas City, MO; E.B. Crocker Museum, Sacramento, CA; UC, Davis; Oakland Museum; John F. Kennedy Univ., Orinda, CA; San Francisco Museum of Modern Art; People's Republic of China; Denver Art Museum; City of Sunnyvale. **Exhibitions/Performances:** Solo: Jewish Museum, Kansas City 1968; Davis Art Center 1969; Artist's Contemporary Gallery, Sacramento 1971; Hank Baum Gallery, San Francisco 1973, 1975, 1976, 1978; Redding, CA Art Museum 1976, 1985; Texas Christian Univ., Ft. Worth 1979; Bechtel Intl. Center, Stanford, CA 1981; Chowning Gallery, San Francisco 1981, 1982, 1983, 1984, 1985; Univ. of the Pacific, Stockton 1985; Shasta College, Redding, CA 1985; Sacramento City College 1985; Erickson & Elins Gallery, San Francisco 1986, 1987, 1990, 1991; Van Stavern Fine Art, San Francisco 1987, 1988; Sunnyvale Creative Arts Center 1988; 44 Montgomery, San Francisco 1988; Campeau Bldg., San Francisco 1988; & numer-

ous group shows. **Home Address:** 2 Broadmoor, San Anselmo, CA 94960. **Business Address:** Erickson & Elins Gallery, 345 Sutter St., San Francisco, CA 94108.

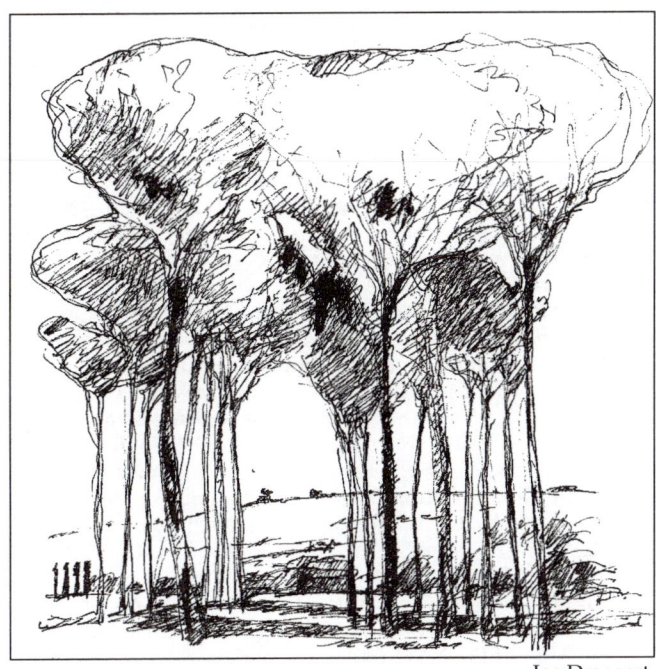

Joe Draegert

DRAPER, WILLIAM F. ■ AAR Charter Mem.; US Congressman, Ambassador to Italy.

DREWS, ROBERT H. ■ RAAR Classics/Archaeology 81. b. Mar. 26, 1936, Beaver Dam, WI. m. Phoebe B. Drews. c. Elizabeth, Richard. BA 56, Northwestern College, Watertown, WI; MA 57, Univ. of Missouri, Columbia; PhD 60, Johns Hopkins Univ. **Career & Employment:** Duke Univ., Instr. 1960-61; Vanderbilt Univ., Asst. Prof. 1961-64, Assc. Prof. 1964-73, Prof. 1973-present. **Memberships & Offices:** APA, ArIA, Soc. for the Promotion of Hellenic Studies, Assn. of Ancient Historians. **Fellowships, Honors & Awards:** Center for Hellenic Studies Fellowship 1966-67; ACLS Fellowship 1973-74; Guggenheim Fellowship 1980-81. **Publications:** *The Greek Accounts of Eastern History* (Cambridge, MA & Washington, DC: Harvard Univ. Press & Center for Hellenic Studies, 1973); *Basileus: The Evidence for Kingship in Geometric Greece* (New Haven: Yale Univ. Press, 1983); *In Search of the Shroud of Turin* (Totowa, NJ: Rowman & Allenheld, 1984); *The Coming of the Greeks: Indo-European Conquests in the Aegean and the Near East* (Princeton: Princeton Univ. Press, 1988); *The End of the Bronze Age: Changes in Warfare and the Catastrophe ca. 1200 BC* (Princeton: Princeton Univ. Press, 1993). **Home Address:** 136 Cheek Rd., Nashville, TN 37205.

DRIES, LINDA DAUW ■ FAAR Sculpture 69. b. Jan. 14, 1943, Moline, IL. m. Danny Dries. BFA 65, Minneapolis School of Art; MFA 67, Pratt Inst.

DRON, EDWARD EMIL ■ FAAR Sculpture 70. b. July 15, 1938, NYC. BA 61, UC, Santa Barbara; MFA 65, Claremont Graduate School. **Career & Employment:** Acad. of Art College, San Francisco, Faculty 1990; UC, Santa Barbara, Faculty 1971-.

DRUCKMAN, JACOB ■ RAAR Musical Composition 82, AAR Trustee 1984-90, Trustee Emer. 1990-present. b. June 26, 1928, Philadelphia, PA. m. Muriel Topaz. c. Karen Jeanneret, Daniel Druckman. BS 54, Juilliard School; MS 56, Juilliard School. **Other Study:** École Normale de Musique, Paris 1954-55; Tanglewood, with Aaron Copland, Summers 1949, 1950. **Career & Employment:** Juilliard School, Faculty 1956-72; Brooklyn College, Prof. 1972-76; Yale Univ. School of Music, Prof. 1976-present; New York Philharmonic, Composer-in-Residence 1982-86. **Memberships & Offices:** AAAL 1978-present; Koussevitzky Music Found., Pres. 1972-present; Aaron Copland Fund for Music, Pres. 1992-present. **Fellowships, Honors & Awards:** Guggenheim Fellowship 1957, 1968; Pulitzer Prize 1972; Brandeis Univ. Creative Arts Comm. Citation 1975; Phi Beta Kappa Visiting Scholar 1987-88. **Important Works:** *Windows,* for orchestra (CRI) 1972; *Lamia,* for soprano & orchestra (Louisville First Edition Records) 1974-75; *Viola Concerto,* for orchestra 1978; *Prism,* for orchestra (New World Records) 1980; *Vox Humana,* for voices & orchestra 1982-83; *Aureole,* for orchestra (New World Records) 1986; *Brangle,* for orchestra 1989; *Nor Spell nor Charm,* for chamber orchestra (Deutsche Grammophon) 1990; *Summer Lightning,* for orchestra 1991; *Seraphic Games,* for orchestra 1992; *Come Round,* for sextet 1992; *Counterpoise,* for soprano & orchestra 1994. All published by Boosey & Hawkes, except *Windows* (MCA). **Bio-Bibliography:** *New Grove Dictionary of American Music; Who's Who in America.* **Business Address:** Boosey & Hawkes Publishers, 24 E. 21 St., NYC 10010.

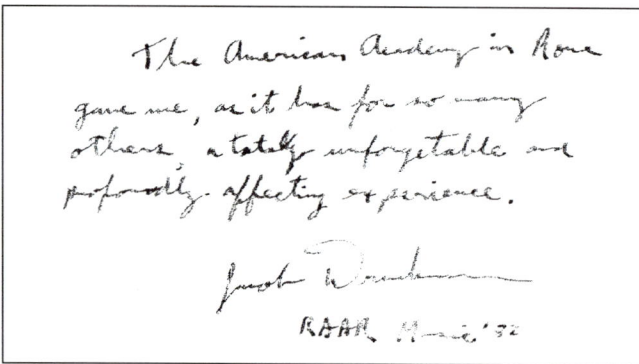

Jacob Druckman

DRUMLEVITCH, SEYMOUR ■ FAAR Painting 52, RAAR Painting 66. b. July 9, 1923, NYC. dec. Cert. 46, Cooper Union. **Other Studies:** NYA Silk Screen Workshop 1941-42; New School for Social Research 1941-42. **Career & Employment:** Albright School, Buffalo, NY, Instr. **Fellowships, Honors & Awards:** Joseph Hirshhorn Fellowship 1946-47; Western New York Show, Prize 1948, 1949, 1953; Courtland County Fair, 4th Place 1948. **Exhibitions/Performances:** MOMA 1950; Martha Jackson Gallery 1953; Museum of Modern Art, Rome, Italy; Buscaglia-Castellani Art Gallery, Niagara Falls, NY 1979; Albright-Knox Gallery, Buffalo, NY 1988. **Bio-Bibliography:** "American Federation of the Arts: Forty Artists under Forty," *The Federation* (1962); R. Huntington, *Seymour Drumlevitch,* exb. cat. (Buffalo, NY: Albright-Knox Gallery, 1988).

DUBOIS, MARGARET HOUSTON ■ FAAR Classics/Archaeology 72. b. June 14, 1938, Wheeling, WV. BS 64, Columbia Univ.; MA 66, Columbia Univ.

DUCKWORTH, GEORGE E. ■ AAR Trustee 1948-59, Classicist.

DUFFY, JOSEPH M., JR ■ AAR World War II Scholar 1945.

DUGAN, ALAN ■ FAAR Literature 63. **Fellowships, Honors & Awards:** Pulitzer Prize; Nat. Book Award 1962. *Poems; Poems 2* (New Haven: Yale Univ. Press, 1963).

DUHRING, H. LOUIS ■ Stewardson Memorial Scholar 1911-12, 1913.

DUNCAN, P.M. ■ Winchester Fellow 1925-26.

DURBE, DARIO ■ Italian Fulbright Fellow 1968-69.

D'URSO, ALESSANDRO ■ AAR Italian Com. 1994-present.

D'URSO, JOSEPH P. ■ FAAR Design Arts 88. b. Apr. 8, 1943, Newark, NJ. BFA 65, Pratt Inst.; MAD 66, Manchester Polytechnic. **Career & Employment:** D'Urso Design, Prin. 1966-present; Pratt Inst., Instr. 1967-81; Parsons School of Design 1981-82; New York School of Interior Design 1992. **Fellowships, Honors & Awards:** Royal College of Art, London 1966; *Interior Design,* Design Hall of Fame 1988; Pratt Alumni Award 1992. **Important Works:** Furniture Collection, Knoll Intl.; Calvin Klein Showrooms (4); Esprit Stores, Los Angeles, Washington, DC; I Club, Hong Kong. **Bio-Bibliography:** *Joe D'Urso,* Design Quarterly 12 (Minneapolis: Walker Arts Center & Cambridge, MA: MIT Press, 1984); *Architectural Digest; Architectural Record; Architectural Review; House & Garden; Interior Design; Vogue; Who's Who in America.* **Home Address:** PO Box 1154, Water Mill, NY 11976.

DVOŘÁK, ROBERT (RAFFAELLO) REGIS ■ FAAR Design Arts 72. b. Oct. 24, 1938, Madison, WI. m. Linda J. Dvorak. c. Michael, David. BArch 61, Univ. of Illinois; MArch 67, UC, Berkeley. **Other Study:** Univ. of Oregon 1967-76; with Paul Pei Jen Hau, Chinese brush painting 1978-82; Canada Community College, printmaking 1982. **Research/Artistic Interests:** Original graphics, woodcut & etching; painting: watercolor & oriental ink & watercolor acrylic; experimental filmmaking. **Career & Employment:** Max O. Urbahn & Asscs., NYC, Designer 1961-63; Urbahn, Roberts, Seeley & Moran, Designer 1962-63; Architects Collaborative in Rome, Designer 1963-64; Gen. Design & Asscs., Tokyo, Designer 1965; John J. Flad & Asscs., NYC, Designer 1966; Univ. of Oregon, Prof. 1966-70, 1972-76; UC, Instr. 1980-present; extensions & community colleges in California & Hawaii. **Memberships & Offices:** Nat. Speakers Assn. 1987-present; American Soc. for the Advancement of Chinese Art, Pres. 1985; World Business Acad. 1990-present. **Fellowships, Honors & Awards:** Film Award, Journées Intles. du Cinema d'Animation Festival, France 1971; Best Short Film, Bellevue Film Festival 1974; Artist in Residence: Belmont, CA School District 1984-85, Redwood City, CA School District 1985-92, California Arts Council 1989-90, Yosemite Nat. Park annually. **Publications:** *The Pocket Drawing Book-Pad* (Montara, CA: Inkwell Press, 1986); *Drawing without Fear* (Palo Alto, CA: Dale Seymour, 1987); *The Pathfinders' Guide to Creative Power* (Menlo Park, CA: Inkwell Press, 1987); *Productivity at the Workstation* (Menlo Park, CA: Crisp Publications, 1990); *Experiential Drawing* (Menlo Park, CA: Crisp Publications, 1991); *The Magic of Drawing* (Montara, CA: Inkwell Press, 1993). **Important Works:** Public Collections: Bank of America, San Francisco; Brooklyn Museum, NYC; Carnegie Inst., Pittsburgh; Del Monte Corp.,

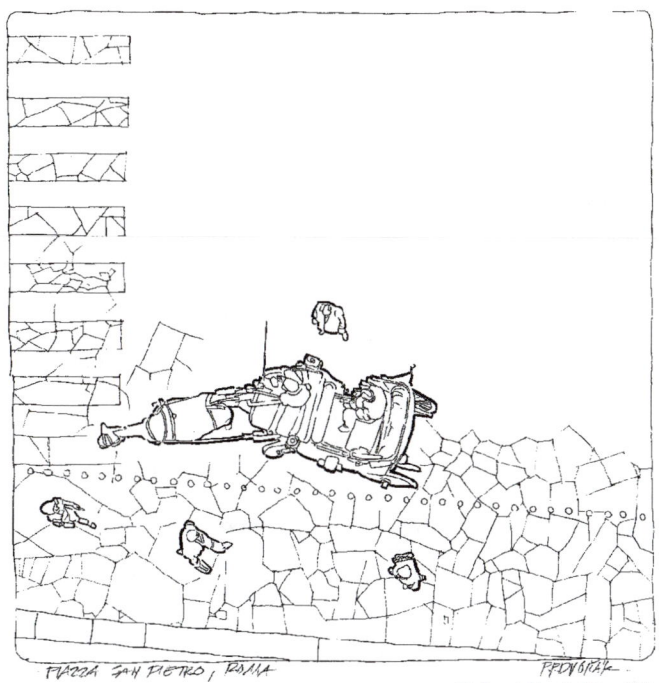

PIAZZA SAN PIETRO, ROMA
RRDVORAK

Robert Regis Dvořák

San Francisco; MMA; MOMA; OMI of California; Smithsonian Inst., Washington DC; Syracuse Univ., NY; Walker Art Center. **Exhibitions/Performances:** Fran-Nell Gallery of Art, Tokyo 1965; Univ. of Wisconsin, Wisconsin Center, Madison 1966; Original Print Gallery, Portland, OR 1979; Bank of America HQ, Concourse Gallery, San Francisco 1980; Bridge Gallery, San Francisco 1981; Bank of America HQ, Plaza Gallery, San Francisco 1982; Long Beach Art Museum 1982; Stanford Univ. Intl. Center 1983; North Point Gallery, San Francisco 1984; Seipp Gallery, Palo Alto 1986; Metro Contemporary Gallery, Foster City, CA 1989; Nut Tree, Vacaville, CA 1990. Film Programs: Contemporary Crafts Gallery, Portland, OR 1970; Reid Hall, Paris 1971; US Information Service, Malta 1971; Malta College of Arts, Sciences & Technology, Malta 1971; Univ. of Oregon, Eugene 1973; Pacific Cinemateque, Vancouver, BC 1974; California Polytechnic State Univ., San Luis Obispo 1974, 1975; Portland, OR Art Museum 1975; Channel J Cable TV, NYC 1977; San Francisco Art Inst. 1981; Solo Film Exbs. (10). **Home Address:** 624 Ruisseau Français Ave., Half Moon Bay, CA 94019. **Business Address:** Inkwell Press, PO Box 370371, Montara, CA 94037.

DWYER, CHARLES M. ■ FAAR Painting 79. b. Newport, RI. m. Kathleen Svoboda. c. Michael. BFA 70, RISD; MFA 72, Boston Univ. **Other Study:** Skowhegan School of Painting & Sculpture. **Career & Employment:** Town of Bristol, RI, Artist-in-Residence 1976; South County Museum, North Kingston, RI, Dir. of Development 1977; RISD, Instr. 1979-83, Summer Sessions, Instr. 1980-present; Wesleyan Univ., Middletown, CT, Graduate Liberal Studies Program, Instr. 1983, 1987-88; Univ. of Michigan, Ann Arbor, School of Art, Asst. Prof. 1983-88; Univ. of Massachusetts, Dartmouth, Art Dept., Instr. 1991. **Fellowships, Honors & Awards:** Skowhegan School Purchase Award 1969; Falmouth Artists' Guild, 1st Guild Prize 1973; Newport Art Museum, Natale Bayard Brown Prize 1973; Providence Art Club, Florence B. Kane Prize 1975; Massachusetts Council on the Arts & Humanities Grant 1976; Rhode Island State Council on the Arts Comm.; NEA Grant 1981; Univ. of Michigan,

Rackham Faculty Grant for Research & Artistic Activities 1984-85; Rackham Faculty Research Grant 1986. **Important Works:** Public Collections: Shearson Lehman Brothers, NYC; Rhode Island Hospital, Dept. of Psychiatry; Hospital Trust Bank, Providence, RI; Town of Bristol & Town of Narragansett, RI. **Exhibitions/Performances:** Solo: Woods-Gerry Gallery, RISD 1974; Falmouth, MA Artists' Guild 1974; Brockton, MA Art Center-Fuller Memorial Museum 1974; Newport, RI Art Museum 1974, 1982; Robley Gallery, Roslyn, NY 1977; Wesleyan Univ., CT 1983; Forsythe-DeGraaf Gallery, Ann Arbor, MI 1984; Allied Corp., World HQ, Southfield, MI 1985; DeBlois Street Gallery, Newport, RI 1987; Albion College, Albion, MI 1987; Spring Bull Gallery, RI 1991, 1992. **Home Address:** 80 Connection St., Newport, RI 02840. **Business Address:** Robley Gallery, Roslyn, NY.

DYSON, STEPHEN ■ AAR Classical Soc., Pres. 1971, 1972.

■ ■ ■

E

EAMES, CHARLES ■ AAR Visitor 1976-77, Designer, b. 1907. d. 1978. **Fellowships, Honors & Awards:** MOMA, Organic Design in Home Furnishing, 1st Prize 1940.

EAMES, WILLIAM S. ■ AAR Charter Mem., Architect.

EARNSHAW, ALBERT F. ■ FASCSR 1896-97. b. Aug. 1, 1870, Sheffield, England. d. Dec. 7, 1936. m. Lucille H. Fenn. BA 1892, Princeton Univ.; Graduate 1896, Union Theological Seminary. **Other Study:** Harvard Univ. 1931. **Career & Employment:** Congregational Minister; Pastor, Phillips, ME 1897-1901; Asst. Pastor, High St. Church, Portland, ME 1901-4; Pastor: Chelmsford, MA; Mystic, CT; Portland, ME. **Fellowships, Honors & Awards:** Phi Beta Kappa. **Bio-Bibliography:** *NY Times*, Obit. (Dec. 8, 1936); *Princeton Herald*, Obit. (Dec. 11, 1936); Princeton Univ. Archives.

EATON, FREDERICK ■ AAR Visitor 1959 — 1964, US Ambassador.

EATON, JOHN ■ FAAR Musical Composition 62, RAAR Musical Composition 75. b. Mar. 30, 1935, Bryn Mawr, PA. m. Nelda Nelson. c. Estela, Julian. BA 57, Princeton Univ.; MFA 59, Princeton Univ. **Career & Employment:** Univ. of Chicago, Prof. **Memberships & Offices:** UNESCO Intl. Rostrum of Composers 1970. **Fellowships, Honors & Awards:** Guggenheim Fellowship 1962, 1965; NIAL Citation 1972; Peabody Award 1973; Ohio State Award 1973; Nat. Inst. of Music Theater, Nat. Music Theater Award 1988; MacArthur Found. Fellowship 1990; Comm.s: Fromm Found., Koussevitzky Found., Corp. for Public Broadcasting. **Publications:** articles in *Kenyon Review*, *Musicological Journal, Musical Courier, Semiotica.* **Important Works:** *The Lion & Androcles*, opera 1973; *The Cry of Clytaemnestra*, opera 1980; *The Tempest*, opera 1985; *The Reverend Jim Jones*, opera, NEA Comm. 1986; *Peer Gynt*, opera 1991; *Let's Get this Show on the Road*, opera 1993; *Songs of Desperation & Comfort; Myshkin*, opera, Corp. for Public Broadcasting Comm. Recordings on CRI, Indiana Univ. Press, (American) Decca, & Turnabout. Works published by Shawnee Press & G. Schirmer. **Home Address:** 125 N. Roosevelt, Bloomington, IN 47408.

EBERHARD, DENNIS J. ■ FAAR Musical Composition 79. b. Dec. 9, 1943, Cleveland, OH. BMus 67, Kent State Univ.; MusM 69, Univ. of Illinois; DMA 73, Univ. of Illinois. **Career & Employment:** Univ. of Illinois, Lect. 1972-73; Western Illinois Univ., Asst. Prof. 1976-77; Univ. of Nebraska, Visiting Prof. 1980; Cleveland State Univ., Lect. 1983-87, Prof. 1993-present.; Oberlin Conservatory of Music, Assc. Prof. 1991. **Fellowships, Honors & Awards:** BMI Young Composers Award 1968; Fulbright-Polish Government Grant 1973-75; NEA Grant 1977, 1987; Guest Composer on the XIX & XXII Intl. Festivals of Contemporary Music, "Warsaw Autumn" 1975, 1978; Intl. Gaudeamus Composers' Competition, 3d Prize & participant in the Gaudeamus Music Week, the Netherlands 1977; American Music Center, Composer Grant 1978, 1982; Kate Neil Kinley Memorial Fellowship 1978; MacDowell Colony Residencies 1980, 1988, 1989; Bascom Little Fund Grant 1982; Martha Baird Rockefeller Grant 1982; Cleveland Arts Prize 1984; Ohio Arts Council Grant 1986, 1989, 1991; *Northern Ohio Live Magazine*, Award of Achievement in Classical Music 1990; Kent State Univ., Distinguished Alumnus Award 1993. **Important Works:** *Morphos*, Champaign HS Comm. (Margun Music) 1973; *Ikona*,

Polish Radio, Warsaw, Comm. 1975; *Marginals*, Warsaw Trombone Quartet Comm. (Margun Music) 1975; *Visions of the Moon*, New Consort, Champaign, IL, Comm. 1977; *Ephrata*, Percussao Agora & the Sao Paolo, Brazil, State Symphony Orchestra Comm. 1980; *De Profundis*, Univ. of Nebraska Singers, Lincoln, Comm. 1980; *Epodie*, Reconnaissance Contemporary Music Ensemble Comm. 1982; *Especially...,* Alice Giles Comm. (C.F. Peters) 1983; *Voix Celestes*, Cleveland Chamber Symphony Comm. 1983; *Night Tides*, Ohio Chamber Orchestra, Cleveland, Comm. 1983; *Let the Heavens Be Glad*, Euclid Ave. Congregational Church Comm. 1986; *Endgame*, Cleveland Octet Comm. (Margun Music) 1987; *To the End of Dream Time*, NEA for Alice Giles 1987; *The Bells of Elsinore*, Cleveland Orchestra Comm. (Margun Music) 1988; *Berceuse*, Cleveland Chamber Symphony Comm. (Margun Music) 1989; *O Sing a New Song to God*, American Guild of Organists Comm. 1989; *Encontros* (Cadenzas & Interludes), PAND Cleveland 1990; *Suite, Oac*, Kim Cook Comm. 1992; *The Bird of Four Hundred Voices*, Cleveland Chamber Symphony Comm. 1992; *For the Musicians of the Queen*, Cincinnati Symphony Orchestra Comm. 1993; *Songs for Grieving Children*, Comm. 1995. **Home Address:** 2555 Kemper Rd., Apt. 311, Shaker Heights, OH 44120.

EDEL, LEON ■ AAR Visitor 1983-84, Biographer, Educator. b. Sept. 9, 1907. **Career & Employment:** Univ. of Hawaii, Prof. 1971-78, Prof. Emer. 1978-. **Honors & Awards:** Pulitzer Prize, 1963; Nat. Book Award 1963. **Selected Publications:** *The Life of Henry James*, 5 vols. (1953-1972).

EDGELL, GEORGE HAROLD ■ FASCSR 12; Prof. 1919-20. b. Mar. 4 1887, St. Louis, MO. d. June 29, 1954. m. Jean Walters Delano. c. George, Delano, Henry. BA 09, Harvard Univ.; PhD 13, Harvard Univ. **Career & Employment:** Harvard Univ., Asst. 1909-10, Instr. 1912-14, Asst. Prof. 1914-22; Assc. Prof. 1922-25; Prof. 1925-35; Interallied Comm. for Propaganda, Italian General Staff 1918; MFA, Dean of Architecture 1925-35, Curator of Paintings 1934-38, Dir. 1935-54. **Memberships & Offices:** Boston Art Comm. 1925-50; MA State Art Comm., Chair 1941-51; MFA, BoT 1927-50; American Assn. of Museums, Pres. 1949-51; US Comm. for UNESCO; ArIA. **Fellowships, Honors & Awards:** Phi Beta Kappa, Harvard Chap., Pres. 1940-42; AAAS, Fellow; Harvard Univ., Hon. DFA, 1948; Chevalier of the Legion of Honor. **Publications:** "Architectural Backgrounds in the Series of 'Scenes from the Life of San Bernardino' at Perugia," *AJA* 17 (1913): 223-41; *The American Architecture of Today* (New York: Scribner's, 1928); *A History of Sienese Painting* (New York: Dial, 1932); with Fiske Kimball, *A History of Architecture* (New York: Harper, 1946); *The Bee Hunter* (Cambridge, MA: Harvard Univ. Press, 1949); *French Painters in the Museum of Fine Arts: Corot to Utrillo* (Boston: MFA, 1949). **Bio-Bibliography:** "Memoir," *AJA* 59 (1955): 65; *Who Was Who in America.*

EDLUND-BERRY, INGRID E.M. ■ FAAR Classics/Archaeology 84; AAR Classical Soc., Treas.; SOF, Adv. Council; AAR Classical Jury 1986-87; Friends of the Library. b. Sept. 18, 1942, Lund, Sweden. m. John L. Berry. c. Dana Elena Edlund Berry, Robert John Edlund Berry. FM 65, Univ. of Lund; FL 69, Univ. of Lund; MA 69, Bryn Mawr College; PhD 71, Bryn Mawr College. **Other Study:** Bryn Mawr College Excavations in Tuscany at Poggio Civitate, Murlo 1967-71; Univ. of Texas Excavations at Metaponto 1977-81; Univ. of Virginia & Princeton Univ. Excavations at Morgantina 1985-present. **Research/Artistic Interests:** Etruscan & Roman archaeology. **Career & Employment:** ICCS, TA 1971-72, Asst. Prof. 1977-78; Univ. of

Georgia, Visiting Asst. Prof. 1973-78, Studies Abroad in Classics 1975, 1976; Univ. of Minnesota, Visiting Prof. 1982; Univ. of Texas at Austin, Asst. Prof. 1978-87, Assc. Prof. 1987-present **Memberships & Offices:** APA; ArIA, Athens Soc., VP 1976-77; ArIA, Austin Soc., Pres. 1979-81; ArIA, Lecture Program Comm. 1989-92; Assn. of Ancient Historians; CAMWS; Friends of Medelhavsmuseet, Stockholm; Friends of the Swedish Inst. in Athens; Friends of the Swedish Inst. in Rome; Georgia Classical Assn.; Swedish Archaeological Soc.; Texas Classical Assn.; Junior Classical League, Offices Examiner 1974-77; Etruscan Found., Adv. Bd. 1991-present; Texas Swedish Cultural Found., BoT 1988-present. **Fellowships, Honors & Awards:** ACLS, Grant-in-Aid 1975, Travel Grant 1982, Fellowship 1987; APS, Grant-in-Aid 1977, Grant 1988; Univ. of Texas, Research Grant 1979, 1980, 1982, 1985, 1986, 1990, 1994, Faculty Research Assignment 1983-84, 1987, Special Research Grant 1989, 1991, 1992, 1993; Alexander von Humboldt-Stiftung, Research Fellowship 1983-84; Fondazione Famiglia Rausing, Research Grant, Swedish Inst. of Classical Archaeology in Rome 1983, 1985, 1992. **Publications:** *The Iron Age and Etruscan Vases in the Olcott Collection at Columbia University, New York,* Transactions of the APS (Philadelphia: APS, 1980); with Anna Marguerite McCann & Claire Richter Sherman, "Gisela Marie Augusta Richter (1882-1972): Scholar of Classical Art and Museum Archaeologist," in *Women as Interpreters of the Visual Arts, 1820-1979,* ed. Claire Richter Sherman & Adele M. Holcomb (Westport, CT: Greenwood Press, 1981), 275-300; "Università del Texas: Scavi nella zona di Metaponto, 1979," *Bollettino d'Arte* 39-40 (1986): 119-22; *The Gods and the Place: Location and Function of Sanctuaries in the Countryside of Etruria and Magna Graecia (700-400 B.C.)* (Stockholm: Acta Instituti Romani Regni Sueciae, 1987); "*Mens Sana in Corpore Sano*: Healing Cults as a Political Factor in Etruscan Religion," *Acta Universitatis Upsaliensis, Boreas* 15 (1987): 51-56; "The Sacred Geography of Southern Italy in Lycophron's *Alexandra,*" *Opuscula Romana* 16.2 (1987): 43-49; "Four Terracotta Heads from Poggio Civitate (Murlo): Towards a Definition of the 'Murlo Style'," *Opuscula Romana* 17.3 (1989): 21-32; *The Seated and Standing Statue Akroteria from Poggio Civitate (Murlo)* (Rome: Bretschneider, 1992); "The Central Sanctuary at Morgantina (Sicily): Problems of Interpretation and Chronology," in *Scienze dell'Antichità: Storia, Archeologia, Antropologia* 3-4 (1989-90), ed. Paolo Matthiae (Rome: Università degli Studi di Roma. Dipartimento di Scienze Storiche, 1992), 327-38; with Kyle M. Phillips, Jr. "Poggio Civitate (Murlo) 1966-1987: An Annotated Bibliography of Primary and Secondary Publications," in *In the Hills of Tuscany,* ed. Karen B. Vellucci (Philadelphia: Univ. of Pennsylvania Museum, 1993); "Ritual Destruction of Cities and Sanctuaries: The 'Un-founding' of the Archaic Monumental Building at Poggio Civitate (Murlo)," in *Murlo and the Etruscans,* ed. Richard D. De Puma & J. Penny Small (Madison: Univ. of Wisconsin Press, 1994), 16-28; "Etruscans at Work and Play: Evidence for an Etruscan Calendar," *Kotinos: Festschrift für Erika Simon* (Mainz/Rhein, 1992), 330-38. **Business Address:** Dept. of Classics, Univ. of Texas, Austin, TX 78712.

EDMONDSON, FREDERICK WILLIAM, JR ■ FAAR Landscape Architecture 48. b. June 13, 1914, Pittsburgh, PA. m. Margaret McAneny Loud. BLArch 38, Cornell Univ. **Career & Employment:** US Marine Corps, Lieut., WW II. **Fellowships, Honors & Awards:** Cornell Univ., Sands Medal 1937, Charles Beckwith Brown Medal 1938.

EDWARDS, GEORGE H. ■ FAAR Musical Composition 75, Music Jury 1989. b. May 11, 1943, Boston, MA. m. Rachel C. Hadas. c. Jonathan. BA 65, Oberlin College; MFA 67, Princeton Univ. **Career & Employment:** New England Conservatory of Music, Faculty 1968-76; MIT, Lect. 1971; Columbia Univ., Asst. Prof. 1976-85, Assc. Prof. 1986-93, Prof. 1993-present. **Memberships & Offices:** ACA; Assn. for the Promotion of New Music; BMI; Asst. to Luciano Berio, music for a production of Sophocles' *Philoctetes,* Teatro di Roma 1975; League of Composers-ISCM 1976-78, 1986-present, Program Com. 1987-89; Composers Guild for Performance 1976-82, Pres. 1980-82; CRI 1977-93, Sec. 1979-84; Alice M. Ditson Fund of Columbia Univ., Adv. Com. 1988-present, Sec. 1988-present. Juries: Harvard Univ., Fromm Music Found. 1992; ACA Recording Award; Washington Square Contemporary Music Competition; Joseph M. Bearns Prize; Rapoport Prize; Columbia Univ. Music Press; Wellesley College, Composers Conference 1986; Univ. of the South, Sewanee Summer Music Festival, Guest Composer 1992; Ensemble 21, BoD 1993-present. **Fellowships, Honors & Awards:** Woodrow Wilson Fellowship 1965; Koussevitzky Composition Prize 1967; Composers Quartet Prize 1970; Naumburg Recording Award 1974; Koussevitzky Music Found. Award 1981; ISCM Nat. Competition Winner 1983; Guggenheim Fellowship 1985, 1990; Fromm Found. Comm. 1991; MacDowell Colony Residence 1976, 1986, 1987, 1992. **Publications:** "The Nonsense of an Ending: Closure in Haydn's String Quartets," *Musical Quarterly* 75.3 (Fall 1991): 227-54; "Music and Postmodernism," *Partisan Review* 58.4 (1991): 693-706; "Involuntary Affinities: New Music and Performance in the Twentieth Century," *Southwest Review* (Fall, 1990): 424-43; "A 'Conversation' about New Music," *Threepenny Review* (Mar. 1990): 31-32; "The Pleasure of its Being Over: a View of Contemporary Music," *Partisan Review* 57.3 (1990): 414-22. **Important Works:** *String Quartet* (CRI) 1971; *Kreuz und Quer* (CRI) 1975; *Exchange-Misere* (CRI) 1976; *Veined Variety* (Opus One) 1981; *String Quartet No. 2,* 1982; *Moneta's Mourn,* for orchestra, Koussevitzky Music Found. Comm. 1983; *Suave Mari Magno,* for solo piano 1984; *Five Etudes,* for solo piano 1985; *A Mirth but Open'd,* for soprano & piano 1986; *Trio,* for violin, horn, & piano 1987; *Heraclitean Fire,* for string quartet & string orchestra 1987; *Parallel Convergences,* for 11 players, Speculum Musicae Comm. 1988; *Concerto for Piano & Orchestra* 1990; *Plus ça Change...,* for 7 players 1992; *The Resurrection of the Wheat,* for soprano & piano 1993. Publisher: all works ACA. **Home Address:** 838 West End Ave., Apt. 3A, NYC 10025. **Business Address:** Dept. of Music, Columbia Univ., NYC 10027.

EDWINN, EDWIN ■ G.I. Resident 1945-47, Singer.

EGBERT, JAMES C. ■ AAR Trustee 1911-45, Classicist.

EINAUDI, KARIN ■ AAR – Rome, *Fototeca Unione,* Dir.

EINSTEIN, LEWIS ■ US Diplomat. b. March 15, 1877. d. 1949. Served in several embassies 1903-30. **Honors & Awards:** Columbia Univ., Medal of Excellence 1934. **Selected Publications:** *American Foreign Policy by a Diplomatist* (1909); *Roosevelt, His Mind in Action* (1930); *Historical Change* (1946). AAR Donor, bequeathed rare book collection to the library.

EISEMAN, FERDINAND ■ Chicago Architectural Club, Burnham Prize 1924-25, 1925-26.

EISENBERG, MARVIN ■ AAR Visitor 1977-78, Art Historian.

EISENMAN, PETER ■ AAR Visitor 1975-76, Architect.

EKIZIAN, MICHELLE L. ■ FAAR Musical Composition 89, SOF Council 1989-present, VP in Music 1994-present. b. Nov. 21, 1956, Bronxville, NY. BMus 77, Manhattan School of Music; MusM 78, Manhattan School of Music; DMA 88, Columbia Univ. **Other Study:** Composition studies with Chou Wen-chung, Mario Davidovsky, Nicolas Flagello, & Vladimir Ussachevsky. **Research/Artistic Interests:** Symphonic, operatic & chamber works incorporating metaphorical structurings concerning exile, journey & stability, along with recastings of traditional, spiritual folk melodies drawn from an Armenian heritage; multi-layered music that crosses the boundaries between Western European-influenced concert music & folk-spiritual song of all times & people. **Career & Employment:** Columbia Univ., TA 1983-87. **Memberships & Offices:** Nat. Assc. of Composers USA, BoD 1979-87; BMI 1980-present; ACA 1980-present; American Music Center 1980-present; College Music Soc. 1988-present. **Fellowships, Honors & Awards:** Guggenheim Fellowship 1987; NEA Composers Fellowship 1987; ACA Recording Award 1987; Jerome Found. Grant 1988; Louisville Orchestra Composition Prize 1990; Harvard Univ., Fromm Found. Fellowship 1991; Brigham Young Univ., Barlow Fellowship 1991; Meet the Composer-Readers Digest Consortium Comm. 1992; Mary Flagler Cary Charitable Trust Grant 1992; Women's Philharmonic-Nat. Composers Resource Center, Lili Boulanger Award 1992; NYFA Fellowship 1994. **Important Works:** *Akhtamar*, for two violins, piano & percussion (Schirmer) 1982; *The Exiled Heart*, for orchestra (Schirmer) 1982; *Midnight Voices*, concerto for oboe & orchestra 1983; *Birthday Chords*, a variation on *Happy Birthday* for orchestra 1983; *Octoéchos*, for double string quartet with soprano at epilogue 1986; *Morning of Light*, for orchestra with mezzo-soprano at epilogue 1987; *Beyond the Reach of Wind & Fire*, for orchestra with mezzo-soprano at epilogue 1989; *The Crane*, double concerto for clarinet, conga drums & ensemble 1990; *David of Sassoun*, chamber opera for soprano, mezza-soprano, tenor, baritone & ensemble 1992; *Saber Dances*, for orchestra 1992; *Symphony No. 1: When Light Divided*, for orchestra with baritone & mezzo-soprano 1994; *Ceremonies of Change*, concerto for piano with string orchestra 1994. All published by ACA, ex-

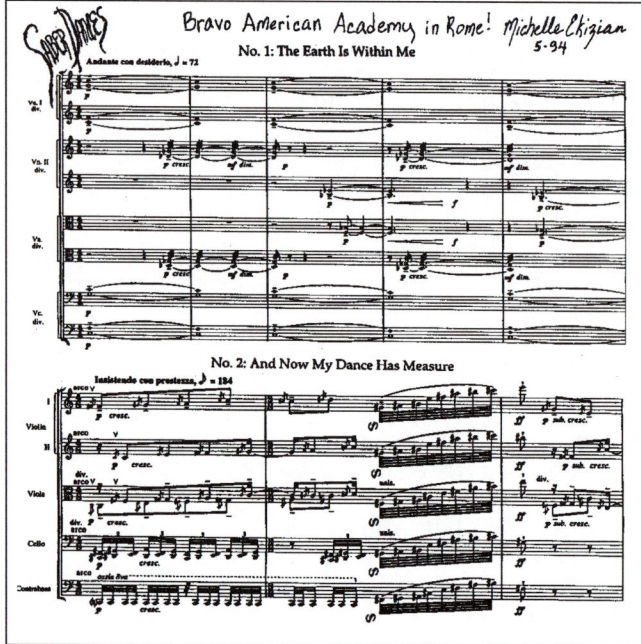

Michelle L. Ekizian

cept where indicated. Recording: *Music of Michele Ekizian*, Group for Contemporary Music (New World Records). **Bio-Bibliography:** *Grove Dictionary of Music, Women in Music.* **Home Address:** 8 Prince Willow Ln., Mamaroneck, NY 10543. **Business Address:** ACA, 170 W. 74th St., NYC 10023.

ELDER, ELDON ■ AAR Visitor 1959 — 1964, Set Designer.

ELDER, FRANK RAY ■ FASCSR 12. b. Apr. 3, 1885, Albia, IA. d. Feb. 3, 1962. m. Frances Lanphere. c. James, Stanley, William, Robert. BA 06, Monmouth College; DD 06, Monmouth College; Litt. B 08, Princeton Univ.; MA 11, Princeton Theological Seminary. **Research/Artistic Interests:** Church history & early Christian archaeology. **Career & Employment:** United Presbyterian Church, Ordained Minister; Pastor, Hanover IL 1913-16; Pastor, Chicago IL 1916-18; Pastor, Wilkinsburg PA 1918-28; Covenant First Presbyterian, Cincinnati 1928-50. **Publications:** Contributor to various religious journals. **Bio-Bibliography:** *Who Was Who in America.*

ELIOT, CHARLES W. ■ AAR Charter Mem., Educator.

ELLETT, THOMAS H. ■ Cresson Fellow 1911-12, 1913, Architect.

ELLIOTT, OSBORN ■ AAR Visitor 1959 — 1964; Columbia Univ., Dean of Journalism.

ELLIS, MARGARET HOLBEN ■ FAAR Conservation 94. b. Apr. 6, 1952, Philadelphia, PA. m. Michael M. Ellis. c. Ethan, Alexander. BA 75, Barnard College; MA-Dipl. 79, IFA. **Other Study:** Moravian College 1970-72. **Research/Artistic Interests:** Materials of 20th-century art. **Career & Employment:** MMA, Asst.-Assc. Conservator 1976-87; Consulting Conservator 1987-present; IFA, Conservation Center, Chair & Assc. Prof. 1987-present. **Memberships & Offices:** American Inst. for Conservation of Historic & Artistic Works, Assc. 1976-81, Professional Assn. 1982-85, BoD 1985-88, Fellow 1986-present; Intl. Inst. for Conservation of Historic & Artistic Works, Assc. 1976-86, Fellow 1987-present; Inst. of Paper Conservation Assc. 1976-present; Nat. Inst. for the Conservation of Cultural Property, Voting Mem. 1987-present; Bd. of Overseers of Harvard College, Com. to Visit the Art Museums, Appointed Mem. 1992-98; Harvard Univ. Art Museums Collections Com., Appointed Mem. 1992-97; Art Table 1993-present. **Publications:** "The Precarious Life of Drawings," *Art News* 84.10 (1985): 81-85; *The Care of Prints and Drawings* (Nashville, TN: American Assn. for State & Local History, 1987); "Works of Art on Paper," in *Caring for Your Collections*, Nat. Com. to Save America's Cultural Collections (New York: Abrams, 1992), 40-51. **Home Address:** 21 E. 87 St., NYC 10128. **Business Address:** Conservation Center, IFA, 14 E. 78 St., NYC 10021.

ELLIS, RICHARD H. ■ FAAR Sculpture 65. b. Jan. 8, 1938, Vernal, UT. m. Jocelyn R. Ellis. c. Vanessa, Allegra. MFA 63, Otis Art Inst., Los Angeles. **Career & Employment:** City of Los Angeles, Cultural Affairs Dept., Art Center Dir. 1988-present. **Important Works:** Collections: Savings of America, Marion, OH 1987; Home Savings of America, San Marino, CA 1987; Hilton Hawaiian Village, Honolulu, HI 1987; City of Fremont, CA, Central Park 1988; Ronald McDonald House, Orange, CA 1989; Acad. of Television Arts & Sciences, N. Hollywood, CA 1990, 1993; American Red Cross, Westwood, CA 1990; Academy Venture, N. Hollywood, CA 1991; Acad. of Television Arts & Sciences, N. Hollywood, CA 1992; "Paladion," San Diego, CA 1992; City of Santa Fe Springs, CA 1992 "Casablanca Pro-

```
                    LA PIETRA SANTA
             RICHARD H. ELLIS  FAAR 63-64


      Take this chip in your hand
      and its weight
      and remember it's source in the mountain
      beneath trattorias where wine glass prisms
      have spangled the sunlight on tables al-fresco
      for patient ages of rowdy diners
      under olive trees with roots in the rocks
      by streams flowing to the quarries to wash cutting cables
      releasing the blocks to be sliced like rude bread
      by row-saws exposing the veins of earth's body.

      In your hand is a shining
      that has been in the mountain
      long past remembering.

      This flake on your tongue is the host
      where roots for the vine's blood
      drink holy communion.

      In this hammer by your ear
      is the striking of the ringing stone
      that echos from Cro-Magnon caves
      and rings through Michelangelo

      Hug the block
      full body
      as it were your mother.
```

Richard H. Ellis

ductions" West Hollywood, CA 1993; Scripps College, Clairmont, CA, Millard Sheets School of Art 1993. **Exhibitions/Performances:** Galleria Margutta, Rome 1964; Long Beach City College Gallery, CA 1967; Orlando Gallery, Encino, CA 1967, 1968; Downey Art Museum, Downey, CA 1969; Whittier Art Assn., CA 1970; Ceejee Gallery, Los Angeles 1973, 1974; Zachary Waller Gallery, Los Angeles 1975, 1976, 1978; Loyola Marymount Univ. Gallery, Los Angeles 1977, 1978; Alison Holmes Gallery, Lake Arrowhead, CA 1981; Plaza Pasadena, Pasadena 1981; City of S. Pasadena Invitational 1986, 1987, 1988; Mission West Gallery, S. Pasadena 1988. **Home Address:** 1422 Stratford Ave., S. Pasadena, CA 91030. **Business Address:** Richard H. Ellis, Sculpture, 1015 Mission St., S. Pasadena, CA 91030.

ELLISON, RALPH WALDO ■ FAAR Literature 57. b. Mar. 1, 1914, Oklahoma City, OK. d. Apr. 16, 1994. m. Fanny McConnell. **Other Studies:** Tuskegee Inst. 1933-36. **Career & Employment:** Salzburg Seminar, Lect. 1942; *Negro Quarterly*, Ed. 1942; US Merchant Marine, WW II; Bard College, Instr. 1958-61; Univ. of Chicago, Alexander White Visiting Prof. 1961; Rutgers Univ., Visiting Prof. 1962-64; UCLA, Ewing Lect. 1964; Library of Congress, Gertrude Clark Whittall Lect. 1964; Yale Univ., Visiting Fellow 1964-. **Memberships & Offices:** PEN; Authors' Guild; AAAL; Century Assn. **Fellowships, Honors & Awards:** Rosenwald Grant 1945; Nat. Newspaper Publishers Award 1953; Nat. Book Award 1953; Russwurm Award 1953; Tuskegee Inst., Hon. DHL PhD 1963; City College of CUNY, Langston Hughes Medallion 1984; Nat. Medal of Arts 1985. **Publications:** contr., *Cross Section* (Fischer, 1944); *Invisible Man* (New York: Random House, 1953); contr., *A New Southern Harvest* (New York: Bantam, 1957); contr., *The Living Novel* (New York: Macmillan, 1957); contr., *Best Short Stories of WW II* (New York: Viking, 1957); contr., *I Have Seen War* (New York: Hill & Wang, 1960); contr., *The Angry Black Lancer* (1962); contr., *Soon One Morning* (New York: Knopf, 1963); *Shadow and Act* (New York: Random House, 1964). **Bio-Bibliography:** Mark Busby, *Ralph Ellison* (Boston: Twayne, 1991); Edith Schir, *Visible Ellison* (1993); David Remnick, "Visible Man," *The New Yorker* (Mar. 14, 1994).

ELWELL, (GEORGE) HERBERT ■ FAAR Musical Composition 27. b. May 10, 1898, Minneapolis, MN. d. Apr. 17, 1974. Univ. of Minnesota 1916-19; Studied composition with Ernest Bloch, NYC 1919-21; with Nadia Boulanger at American Conservatory, Fontainebleau 1921-24. **Career & Employment:** Cleveland Inst., Dept. Head 1928-45; *Cleveland Plain Dealer*, Music Critic 1932-64; Cleveland Inst. Symphony Orchestra, Asst. Dir. & Conductor. **Memberships & Offices:** Yaddo Festival, Chair 1952; Yaddo Corp. **Fellowships, Honors & Awards:** Eastman School Publication Contest 1927; Juilliard Publication Contest 1943; Paderewski Prize 1945; Western Reserve Univ., Hon. Doctorate 1946; Ohioana Library Assn., Medal 1947; Cleveland Arts Prize 1961; NIAL Award 1969. **Important Works:** *Concert Suite*, for violin and orchestra; *Ode*; Quintet, for strings and piano, 1925; *The Happy Hypocrite*, ballet 1927; *Introduction and Allegro*, for orchestra 1942; *String Quartet* 1944; *Blue Symphony*, for voice & string quartet 1944; *Lincoln: Requiem Aeternam*, for baritone, chorus & orchestra 1946; *The Forever Young*, for voice & orchestra 1953; *Pastorale*, for voice and orchestra 1954; *Suite*, for violin & orchestra 1957. **Bio-Bibliography:** F. Koch, "Herbert Elwell and his Music," *Bulletin of the National Association of Teachers* (Dec. 30, 1971); *Baker's Biographical Dictionary of Musicians*; *New Grove Dictionary of American Music*; *Who Was Who in America*.

ELY, THEODORE N. ■ AAR Charter Mem., Trustee 1911-16, Railroad Exec.

EMERSON, JON S. ■ FAAR Landscape Architecture 67. b. Sept. 2, 1935, San Francisco, CA. AA 57, UC, Berkeley; BLA 60, UC, Berkeley; MLA 62, Harvard Univ. **Career & Employment:** Royston, Hanamoto, Mayes & Assc., Designer 1961; Sasaki, Dawson, DeMay & Asscs., Sen. Designer-Project Manager 1962-65; Unicorn Studio, Prin. 1967-83; Louisiana State Univ., Prof. 1967-present; Emerson, Ribes & Asscs., Prin.-Part. 1983-89; Jon Emerson & Asscs., Prin. 1989-present. **Fellowships, Honors & Awards:** ASLA, State of Louisiana Design Awards program: Design Award of Honor (4), Design Award of Merit (8). **Important Works:** Country Club of Louisiana, Baton Rouge; Pennington Biomedical Research Center, Baton Rouge; Fourth Avenue Office Complex, Lake Charles, LA; Twelfth St. Development, Baton Rouge; Transit Information Referral Systems, Downtown Development District, Baton Rouge; Baton Riverfront Development, Baton Rouge; Jean Lafitte Nat. Park, New Orleans; plus over 100 residential projects. **Home Address:** 4645 Bluebell Dr., Baton Rouge, LA 70808. **Business Address:** Jon Emerson & Asscs., Inc., 601 St. Joseph St., Baton Rouge, LA 70802.

EPSTEIN, DANIEL M. ■ FAAR Literature 78. b. Oct. 25, 1948, Washington, DC. c. Johanna Ruth, Benjamin Robert. BA 70, Kenyon College. **Research/Artistic Interests:** Poetry, biography, playwriting. **Fellowships, Honors & Awards:** Woodrow Wilson Fellowship 1971; Danforth Found. Fellowship 1971; NEA Fellowship 1975; *Virginia Quarterly Review*, Emily Clark Balch Award 1981; Guggenheim Fellowship 1982. **Publications:** *No Vacancies in Hell, Poems* (New York: Liveright, 1973); *The Follies, Poems* (New York: Overlook-Viking, 1977); *Young Men's Gold, Poems* (New York: Overlook-Viking, 1978); *The Book of Fortune, Poems* (New York: Overlook-Viking, 1982); *Star of Wonder, Essays & Stories* (New York: Overlook-Viking, 1986); *Spirit, Poems* (New York: Overlook-Viking, 1987); *Love's Compass, Essays* (New York: Addison Wesley, 1990); *Sister Aimee: Biography of Aimee Semple McPherson* (New York: Harcourt Brace Jovanovich, 1993); *The Boy in the Well, Poems* (New York: Overlook-Viking, 1995); Plays: *Jenny and the Phoenix* at the Theatre Project, Baltimore 1977; *The Midnight Visitor* at St. Peter's Church, Off-Broadway, NYC 1981. **Bio-Bibliography:** *Who's Who.* **Home Address:** 218 E. University Pkwy., Baltimore, MD 21218. **Business Address:** Donadio-Ashworth, 231 W. 22 St., NYC 10011.

ERB, DONALD J. ■ RAAR Musical Composition 92. b. Jan. 17, 1927, Youngstown, OH. m. Lucille I. Hyman. c. Christine M. Hoell, Matthew T. Erb, Stephanie Erb Hanket, Janet Erb Carroll. BS 50, Kent State Univ.; MusM 53, Cleveland Inst. of Music; MusD 64, Indiana Univ. **Other Study:** Private study with Nadia Boulanger, Paris 1952-53. **Career & Employment:** Bowling Green State Univ., Asst. Prof. 1964-65; Indiana Univ., Visiting Prof. 1975-76, Prof. 1981-84; Cleveland Inst. of Music, Composer-in-Residence 1966-81, Prof. 1987-present; Southern Methodist Univ., Algur H. Meadows Prof. 1981-84; Visiting Prof.: Roosevelt Univ. 1966, California State, Los Angeles 1977, Peabody Conservatory 1979, Univ. of Melbourne 1984, Univ. of Wollongong 1992. **Memberships & Offices:** Ohio Arts Council, Performance Arts Adv. Panel, Chair 1971-73; Cleveland Area Arts Council, Bd. 1972-77; NEA Panel 1973-77, Chair 1977-79; American Music Center, Bd. 1979-82, Pres. 1982-86; BMI Student Awards BoD 1985-present; ACA, League-ISCM Nat. Adv. Bd. 1986-present. **Fellowships, Honors & Awards:** Bakersfield Ford Found., Composer-in-Residence 1962; Guggenheim Fellow 1965; Nat. Council on the Arts & NEA 1967, 1980, 1984, 1991; Dallas Symphony, Rockefeller Found. Composer-in-Residence 1968; Naumburg Found., Recording Award 1974; Rockefeller Found., Bellagio Study & Conference Center 1980, 1989; AAAL Award 1985; St. Louis Symphony, Meet the Composer, Composer-in-Residence 1988-91. **Publications:** "Orchestration," in *Encyclopedia Britannica.* **Important Works:** *Symphony of Overtures* (Turnabout) 1964; *Reconnaissance,* for violin, string bass, piano, percussion, 2 electronic performance setups (Nonesuch) 1967; *The Seventh Trumpet,* for orchestra (Turnabout) 1969; *Concerto for Violoncello & Orchestra* (New World) 1975; *Concerto for Trombone and Orchestra* (Koss) 1976; *Concerto for Brass & Orchestra* (New World) 1986; *Three Poems for Violin & Piano* 1987; *Symphony for Winds,* for high school or college wind ensemble

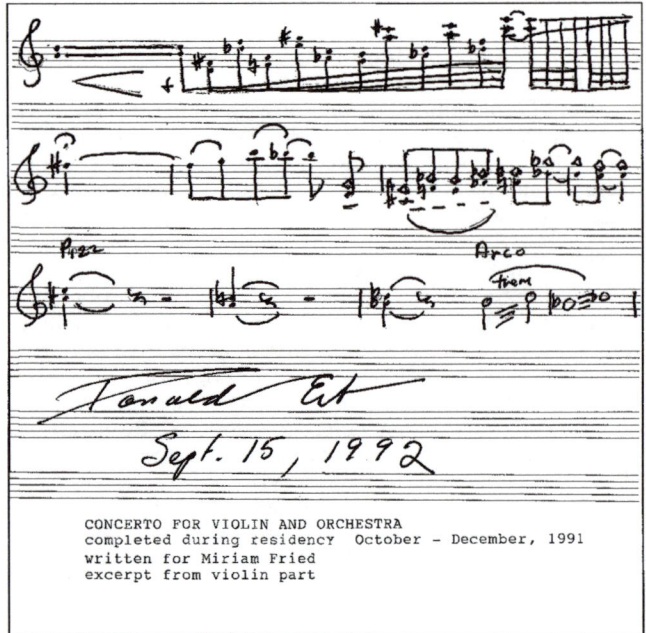

CONCERTO FOR VIOLIN AND ORCHESTRA
completed during residency October - December, 1991
written for Miriam Fried
excerpt from violin part

Donald J. Erb

or band (New World) 1989; *String Quartet No. 2* (Albany Records) 1989; *Drawing Down the Moon,* for piccolo & percussion (New World) 1991; *Ritual Observances* (New World) 1991; *Evensong* 1993. **Bio-Bibliography:** Elliot Schwartz & Daniel Godfrey, *Music Since 1945* (New York: Schirmer, 1992); *Baker's Dictionary of Music; New Grove Dictionary of Music and Musicians; Who's Who in America.* **Home Address:** 4073 Bluestone Rd., Cleveland Heights, OH 44121. **Business Address:** Cleveland Inst. of Music, 11021 East Blvd., Cleveland, OH 44106.

ERMAN, GERALDINE ■ FAAR Sculpture 91. b. Oct. 5, 1953, Detroit, MI. m. Paul J. Perilli. BFA 75, Wayne State Univ.; MFA 78, Cranbrook Acad. of Art. **Career & Employment:** Univ. of Massachusetts, Boston, Instr. 1980-85, Asst. Prof. 1986-87; RISD, Instr. 1986-87; Bard College, Visiting Asst. Prof. 1988-92; MIT, Visiting Lect. 1993-94. **Fellowships, Honors & Awards:** Massachusetts Artists' Found. Fellowship 1985, 1988; NEA Fellowship 1986; Pollock-Krasner Found. 1988; Louis Comfort Tiffany Award 1989-90; Guggenheim Fellowship 1994-95. **Exhibitions/Performances:** Inst. of Contemporary Art, Boston 1984, (group exb.) 1991; Harvard GSD 1987; P.S. 1, Long Island City, NYC 1988; Petrosino Park: Temporary Outdoor Installation, spons. by Lower Manhattan Cultural Council 1989; Kingsboro College Gallery, Brooklyn, NY 1989; Rotunda Gallery, Brooklyn, NY 1990 (group exb.); Bard College, Faculty Exb. 1990; Boston Center for the Arts, 1990; Sally Hawkins Gallery, NYC (group exb.) 1992; Sculpture Center, NYC 1992; Watson Gallery, Wheaton College (solo) 1993; Snug Harbor Cultural Center, Staten Island, NYC 1993. **Home Address:** 91 Java St., Brooklyn, NY 11222.

ETLIN, RICHARD A. ■ FAAR Post-Classical/Humanistic Studies 81. b. Feb. 28, 1947, NYC. c. David, Marc. BA 69, Princeton Univ.; MArch 72, Princeton Univ.; MA 73, Princeton Univ.; PhD 78, Princeton Univ. **Career & Employment:** Univ. of Kentucky, College of Architecture 1975-81; Univ. of Maryland, School of Architecture 1981-present. **Memberships & Offices:** Fulbright Scholar Awards in Architecture & City Planning, Council for Intl. Exchange of Scholars, Washington, DC, Discipline Screening Com. Chair 1985-88; *Design Action,* Founding & Exec. Ed. 1982-84; Univ. of Maryland, Dir. & Teacher, Summer Humanities Inst. 1986-88; Cambridge Univ. Press, *Modern Architecture & Cultural Identity,* Series Ed. 1994-present. **Fellowships, Honors & Awards:** Pre-Dissertation Summer Research Grant, Council for European Studies 1971; Fulbright-Hays Fellowship 1973; Dumbarton Oaks-Harvard Univ., Center for Studies in Landscape Architecture, Fellow 1979-80; NEA, Project Fellowship, Design Arts Program 1979-80; Fulbright-Hays Junior Research Fellowship for Italy 1980-81; NEH Post-Doctoral Fellowship 1980-81; Guggenheim Fellow 1985-86; "Most Outstanding Book in Architecture & Urban Planning for 1991," Assn. of American Publishers; Univ. of Maryland, College Park, Distinguished Teacher-Scholar 1990-91; AIA, Intl. Architecture Book Award 1992; SAH, Alice Davis Hitchcock Award 1992; CASVA, Paul Mellon Senior Fellow 1992-93. **Publications:** "Architecture and the Festival of Federation, Paris, 1790," *Architectural History* 18 (1975): 23-42; "L'Air dans l'urbanisme des Lumières," *Dix-huitième siècle* 9 (1977): 123-34; "Landscapes of Eternity: Funerary Architecture and the Cemetery, 1793-1881," *Oppositions* 8 (1977): 14-31; "'Les Dedans,' Jacques-François Blondel and the System of the Home," *Gazette des Beaux-Arts* 91 (Apr. 1978): 137-47; "Grandeur et décadence d'un modèle: L'Église Sainte-Geneviève et les changements de valeur esthétique au XVIIIe siècle," *Les Cahiers de la Recherche Architecturale* (Oct. 1980): 26-37; "Italian Rationalism" (cover story), *Progressive Architecture* (July 1983):

86-94; *The Architecture of Death: The Transformation of the Cemetery in Eighteenth-Century Paris* (Cambridge, MA: MIT, 1984, paper ed., 1987); A Paradoxical Avant-Garde: Le Corbusier's Villas of the 1920s," *Architectural Review* 181 (Jan. 1987): 21-32; "Le Corbusier, Choisy, and French Hellenism: The Search for a New Architecture," *Art Bulletin* 69 (June 1987): 264-78; *Modernism in Italian Architecture, 1890-1940* (Cambridge, MA: MIT, 1991); ed. & contr., *Nationalism in the Visual Arts,* Studies in the History of Art 29 (Washington, DC: NGA, 1991); *Frank Lloyd Wright and Le Corbusier: The Romantic Legacy* (Manchester: Manchester Univ. Press, 1994); *Symbolic Space: French Enlightenment Architecture and Its Legacy* (Chicago: Univ. of Chicago Press, 1994); *In Defense of Humanism: Value in the Arts and Letters* (New York & Cambridge: Cambridge Univ. Press, forthcoming). **Bio-Bibliography:** *Who's Who in the East.* **Business Address:** School of Architecture, Univ. of Maryland, College Park, MD 20742.

EVANS, ELIZABETH CORNELIA ■ FAAR Classics/Archaeology 32; AAR Classical Soc., Pres. 1950. b. Mar. 19, 1905, North Hampton, NH. d. Apr. 25, 1977. BA 26, Radcliffe College; MA 27, Radcliffe College; PhD 30, Radcliffe College. **Research/Artistic Interests:** Latin Paleography & Epigraphy, local cults of Sabine territory, Roman religion. **Career & Employment:** Wheaton College, Instr. 1932-36, Asst. Prof. 1936-39, Assc. Prof. 1939-42; Vassar College, Assc. Prof. 1942-53; Connecticut College, Prof. 1953-63; Dept. Chair 1953-70, Henry B. Plant Prof. 1963-70; Prof. Emer. 1970-77. **Memberships & Offices:** APA, MAA, NECA. **Fellowships, Honors & Awards:** AAUW Fellowship 1960; Shirley Farr Fellow; APS Grant 1960-61. **Publications:** "Descriptions of Personal Appearance in Roman History and Biography," *Harvard Studies in Classical Philology* 46 (1935): 43-84; *The Cults of the Sabine Territory,* AAR Papers & Monographs 11 (New York & Rome: AAR, 1939); "The Study of Physiognomy in the Second Century A.D.," *TAPA* 74 (1941): 96-108; "Galen the Physician as Physiognomist," *TAPA* 76 (1945): 287-98; "A Stoic Aspect of Senecan Drama: Portraiture," *TAPA* 81 (1959): 169-84; *Physiognomics in the Ancient World,* Transactions of the APS 59.5 (Philadelphia: APS, 1969). **Bio-Bibliography:** *Directory of American Scholars; Who's Who in America;* Briggs, 164-65.

EVANS, HARRY B. ■ FAAR Classics/Archaeology 73, RAAR Classics/Archaeology 91, AAR Summer Session, Asst. Prof. 1973-74, Prof. 1983-85. b. Mar. 27, 1942, Scranton, PA. BA 64, Yale Univ.; PhD 73, UNC, Chapel Hill. **Career & Employment:** Wayne State Univ., Asst. Prof. 1973-76, 1977-78; ICCS, Rome, Asst. Prof. 1976-77, Prof.-in-Charge 1978-79; Rutgers Univ., Asst. Prof. 1979-82; Fordham Univ., Assc. Prof. 1982-93, Prof. 1993-present; Chair 1983-86, 1993-present. **Memberships & Offices:** *Classical Journal,* Ed. 1982-86; APA, Sec.-Treas. 1985-90; ICCS, Rome, Managing Com., Chair 1993-present; New York Classical Club, Custodian of Funds 1991-present. **Fellowships, Honors & Awards:** Phi Beta Kappa 1963; UNC Fellowship 1969-71; Woodrow Wilson Dissertation Fellowship 1971-72; Wayne State Univ., Faculty Research Award 1974; ACLS Grant-in-Aid 1975; NEH Summer Seminar Award 1977; Rutgers Univ., Faculty Research Award 1980; Fordham Univ., Faculty Fellowship 1991. **Publications:** co-author, "A Thirteenth-Century Manuscript of Honorius of Autun's *De Cognitione Verae Vitae,*" *Manuscripta* 16 (1972): 112-19; "Winter and Warfare in Ovid's Tomis (Tr. 3.10)," *Classical Journal* 70.3 (1975): 1-9; "Ovid's Apology for *Ex Ponto* 1-3," *Hermes* 104 (1976): 103-12; "Horace, Satire 2.7: Saturnalia and Satire," *Classical Journal* 73 (1978): 307-12; "The Romulean Gates of the Pa-

latine," *AJA* 84 (1980): 93-96; "Agrippa's Water Plan," *AJA* 86 (1982): 401-11; "Nero's Arcus Caelimontani," *AJA* 87 (1983): 392-99; *Publica Carmina: Ovid's Books from Exile* (Lincoln: Univ. of Nebraska Press, 1983); "Rome's Aqueduct System," in *The Ancient City: Its Concept and Expression,* ed. K.V. Hartigan (Lexington, MA: Ginn, 1983), 228-36; "Water Distribution: *Quorsum et Cui Bono,*" *Future Currents in Aqueduct Studies,* ed. A. Trevor Hodge (Leeds: Francis Cairns, 1991), 21-27; "*In Tiburtium Usum:* Special Arrangements in the Roman Water System," *AJA* 97 (1993): 447-55; *Water Distribution in Ancient Rome: The Evidence of Frontinus* (Ann Arbor: Univ. of Michigan Press, forthcoming); co-ed. with Mary T. Boatwright, *Shapes of City Life in Rome and Pompeii* (New Rochelle, NY: Caratzas, forthcoming). **Home Address:** 754 Bronx River Rd., No. B65, Bronxville, NY 10708. **Business Address:** Classics Dept., Fordham Univ., 441 E. Fordham Rd., Bronx, NY 10458.

EVANS, J.L. ■ Stewardson Memorial Fellow 1925-26.

EVANS, ROBERT WARD ■ FAAR Architecture 73. b. June 9, 1946, Cleveland, OH. m. Carol Chapman. BA 71, Rice Univ.; BArch 71, Rice Univ. **Career & Employment:** Muchow Asscs., Designer 1969-70; CRS Asscs., Designer 1970-72; Gruzen & Partners, Sen. Designer 1973-78; Kohn Pedersen Fox Asscs., Prin. 1978-92; Evans Heintges Architects, Prin. 1992-present. **Fellowships, Honors & Awards:** Vietnam Veterans Memorial Competition, Hon. Mention 1981; AIA, NYC and NY Chap., Distinguished Architecture Award 1985; Brick in Architecture Award 1989, 1993; Architectural Firm of the Year, to Kohn Pedersen Fox Asscs. 1990; Hermann Park Competition, Hon. Mention 1992; Embarcadero Waterfront Competition, 1st Prize 1993. **Important Works:** Recreation Center, Shahan Shahr, Iran 1977; ABC Television Studios 23-24, NYC 1984; CNG Tower, Pittsburgh 1987; US Intl. Trade Comm. HQ, Washington, DC 1987; Capital Cities/ABC Inc. HQ, NYC 1989; Tobishima Corp. HQ, Tokyo 1990; Irvine Center Parcel Nine, Irvine, CA 1991; Lake Robbins Plaza, The Woodlands, TX 1991; Ameritrust Center, Cleveland 1991; Office of the Comptroller of the Currency, One Independence Sq., Washington, DC 1991; NASA HQ, Two Independence Sq., Washington, DC 1992; Stride Rite Corp. HQ, Lexington, MA 1995. **Exhibitions/Performances:** Columbus Circle Competition, New York Cultural Center 1981; Vietnam Veterans Memorial Competition, AIA Traveling Exb. 1981-82; ALNY-NAD Traveling Exb. 1988-92; Nat. Building Museum, Washington, DC 1989, 1990; AIA Convention, Houston 1990; ALNY 1992; Staatsrat, Berlin 1993; Columbia Univ. School of Architecture 1993; Rice Univ. School of Architecture 1993; Goethe House, NYC 1993; Bay Front Gallery, San Francisco 1993. **Business Address:** Evans Heintges Architects, 122 Hudson St., NYC 10013.

EVERETT, HERBERT EDWARD ■ FAAR Classics/Archaeology 06. Feb. 16 1863, Worcester, MA. d. Dec. 10 1932. m. Catherine Arms Childs. c. Jane Hamlin, Catherine Arms. Harvard Univ. **Other Studies:** MFA School, Julian Acad. **Research/Artistic Interests:** Painting, Italian Renaissance art. **Career & Employment:** Univ. of Pennsylvania, Prof. 1892-1929; Cornell Univ., Lect. 1900-1901; Smith College, Lect.-Prof. 1900-1905. **Fellowships, Honors & Awards:** Univ. of Pennsylvania, Hon. Doc. of Aesthetic Arts 1921. **Publications:** *Cyclopedia of Drawing* (Chicago, 1905); *Freehand and Perspective Drawing* (Chicago: American Technical Soc., 1909). **Bio-Bibliography:** *National Cyclopedia of American Biography, Who Was Who in America.*

EVERETT, RICHARD, JR ■ Winchester Fellow 1926-27.

F

FAHY, EVERETT P., JR ■ AAR Visitor 1959 — 1964. Art Historian, Museum Dir. **Career & Employment:** Fogg Art Museum, Harvard Univ., Dir. **Selected Publications:** *Metropolitan Flowers* (New York: MMA, 1982).

FAIRBANKS, FRANK PERLEY ■ FAAR Painting 12; AAR Fine Arts School, Prof. 1919, Dir. 1922-32; Alumni Assn., Pres. 1926. b. July 17, 1875, Boston, MA. d. Aug. 8, 1939. m. Sophie Grace Griswold François. c. David, Barbara Fite. Lowell School of Design; MIT; Gowles Art School; MFA School. **Research/ Artistic Interests:** Portraits & interiors. **Career & Employment:** Paris & Wiley 1932-39; Red Cross, Italy, Captain, WWI. **Memberships & Offices:** Union Club, Rome; ALNY 1913; Nat. Soc. of Mural Painters. **Important Works:** Murals: Public Library, St. Paul, MN; US Supreme Court Bldg., Washington, DC; Controller's Rooms, Municipal Bldg., NYC; Univ. of Cincinnati; Memorial Apse, Tivoli-on-Hudson; Scottish Rite Temple, Washington, DC. **Exhibitions/Performances:** Paris Salon, London Acad. **Bio-Bibliography:** *Who Was Who in American Art.*

FALDI, ITALO ■ AAR Visitor 1977-78, Galleria Nazionale d'Arte Moderna, Dir.

FALK, KENNETH SAWYER ■ FAAR Classics/Archaeology 53. b. May 12, 1925, Hillsdale, MI. d. July 11, 1992. m. Olympia Lee Barbieri. c. Aurelia Renata. BA 49, Harvard Univ.; PhD 61, Harvard Univ. **Research/Artistic Interests:** Classical philology, Latin poetry, recreating vase replicas from Attic red-figure period & Berlin painter. **Memberships & Offices:** APS, Phi Beta Kappa. **Career & Employment:** Univ. of Knoxville, Faculty 1956-58; Hampden-Sydney College, Asst. Prof. 1958-65; Louisiana State Univ., Assc. Prof. 1965-86, Classical Languages, Dir. 1965-86.

FANCELLI, PAOLO ■ Italian Fulbright Fellow 1976-77.

FANE, LAWRENCE ■ FAAR Sculpture 63. b. Sept. 10, 1933, Kansas City, MO. m. Diana Piper Gilmore. c. Dimitri, Anthea. BA 55, Harvard Univ. **Other Study:** MFA School 56; Student & Asst. of sculptor George Demetrios. **Research/Artistic Interests:** Sculpture, primarily in steel & wood, often polychromed. The imagery now refers to the landscape in relation to the human body. **Career & Employment:** RISD, Instr. 1963-66; Queens College, CUNY, Prof. 1966-present. **Fellowships, Honors & Awards:** Ingram Merrill Found. Fellowship 1972-73, 1984; US Dept. of Housing & Urban Development Grant 1973; CUNY Research Found. 1982, 1986. **Important Works:** Commissions & Public Collections: Brooklyn Museum; De Cordova Museum, Lincoln, MA; Outdoor Sculpture for Trent Univ., Peterborough, ONT; Corcoran Gallery of Art, Washington, DC; Union of American Hebrew Congregations, NYC; Museum of Contemporary American Art, Udine, Italy; Museum of the Univ. of Massachusetts, Amherst; Weatherspoon Gallery, UNC; Museum of the Univ. of Texas, Austin; Outdoor Sculpture for Nichol Home, Milwaukee, WI; Fountain for Villa San Lorenzo, Assisi, Italy; Secker & Warburg, Ltd., London; Pyramid Companies, Syracuse, NY; Museum of Art & Archeology, Univ. of Missouri, Columbia; William Benton Museum, Univ. of Connecticut, Storrs; NYC Board of Education. **Exhibitions/Performances:** Solo: Zabriskie Gallery, NYC 1969; Marilyn Pearl Gallery, NYC 1976, 1978, 1982, 1985; Bard College, Annandale-on-Hudson, NY 1977; Duke Univ., Durham, NC 1977; Spazio Oolp, Turin, Italy 1980; Washington Art Assn., Washington, CT 1983;

Bill Bace Gallery, NYC 1991, 1993, 1995; School of Design, State Univ. of North Carolina 1993; plus numerous group shows. **Business Address:** 10 Beach St., NYC 10013.

FANT, J. CLAYTON ■ FAAR Classics/Archaeology 92. b. May 28, 1947, NYC. BA 69, Williams College; PhD 76, Univ. of Michigan. **Other Study:** ICCS, Rome 1968. **Research/Artistic Interests:** Roman social & economic history; Roman archaeology & architectural history, Greek & Roman historiography. **Career & Employment:** Wellesley College, Instr. & Asst. Prof. 1974-79; St. Stephen's School, Rome, Instr. 1979-81; Tyler School of Art, Temple Univ., Rome, Lect. 1980-81, 1983; Univ of Michigan, Visiting Asst. Prof. 1981-83; Univ. of Akron, Asst. Prof. 1984-89, Assc. Prof. 1989-present. **Fellowships, Honors & Awards:** NEH Stipend 1985, 1993; Univ. of Akron, Faculty Fellowship 1985, 1988, Research Grant 1986, Faculty Achievement Award 1991; Kress Found. Grant 1986; APS Grant 1986; ACLS Grant 1986, 1988. **Publications:** "The Choleric Roman Official of Philostratus, *Vitae Sophistarum* p. 512: L. Verginius Rufus," *Historia* 30 (1980): 240-47; ed., *Ancient Marble Quarrying and Trade*, British Archaeological Reports, International Series 453 (Oxford: British Archaeological Reports, 1988); "IRT 794b and the Building History of the Hadrianic Baths at Leptis Magna," *Zeitschrift für Papyrologie und Epigraphik* 75 (1988): 291-94; *Cavum Antrum Phrygiae: The Organization und Operations of the Roman Imperial Marble Quarries at Docimium*, British Archaeological Reports, International Series 482 (Oxford: British Archaeological Reports, 1989); "Poikiloi Lithoi: the Anomalous Economics of the Roman Imperial Marble Quarry at Teos," in *The Greek Renaissance in the Roman Empire*, Papers from the Xth British Museum Classical Colloquium, *Bulletin of the Institute of Classical Studies (BICS)* suppl. 55 (1989): 206-18; "Ideology, Gift and Trade: A Distribution Model for the Roman Imperial Marbles," in *The Inscribed Economy: Production and Distribution in the Roman Empire in the Light of* Instrumentum Domesticum, ed. William V. Harris & S. Panciera, *Journal of Roman Archaeology* supp. 6 (1993): 145-70. **Home Address:** 62 Kuder Ave., Akron, OH 44303. **Business Address:** Dept. of Classics, Univ. of Akron, Akron, OH 44325-1910.

FARRAND, MAX ■ AAR Trustee 1939-43, Educator.

FAULKNER, BARRY ■ FAAR Painting 10; AAR Trustee 1922-44, various committees; Outstanding Service Medal 1960. b. July 12, 1881, Keene, NH. d. Oct. 27, 1966. Harvard Univ.; ASL; under Abbott H. Thayer. **Research/Artistic Interests:** Mural painting. **Career & Employment:** US Army Engineers, France, 1st Lieut., WWI; NAD, Instr. **Memberships & Offices:** AAAL, NIAL, NAD, Soc. of Mural Painters; Century Assn. **Fellowships, Honors & Awards:** ALNY Medal 1914. **Important Works:** Murals: Nat. Archives Bldg., Washington, DC; RCA Bldg., Rockefeller Center, NYC; John Hancock Bldg., Boston; Senate Chamber, State House, Concord, NH; State Capitol, Salem, OR; Cunard Bldg., NYC; Eastman School of Music, Rochester; Library, Univ. of Illinois; Phillips Acad., Andover; Radio City Music Hall, NYC; Archives Bldg., Washington, DC; American War Cemeteries, Thiaucourt & Suresnes, France; Metropolitan Life Insurance Co., Ottawa; Bushnell Memorial, Hartford, CT. **Exhibitions/Performances:** ALNY 1914. **Bio-Bibliography:** *Barry Faulkner, Sketches from an Artist's Life* (Dublin, NH: W.L. Bauhan, 1973); *National Cyclopedia of American Biography; Who Was Who in American Art.*

FAUSTOFERRI, AMALIA ■ Italian Fulbright Fellow 85-86. b. June 12, 1957, Campobasso, Italy. m. Wilfred A. Geominy. c.

Sebastian. Th. 76, Liceo Classico "M. Pagano," Campobasso; Degree 81, Facoltà di Lettere & Filosofia, Università di Perugia; Diploma 86, Scuola di Perfezionamento in Discipline Archeologiche, Urbino. **Other Study:** Bryn Mawr, Massentia, Rome 1982-83; Munich 1984-85; Archaeological excavations: St. Blaise, France; Baz Hill, Scotland; Fregelee; Campo Mazino & M. Pallano, Italy. **Research/Artistic Interests:** Research in Laconian art & iconography; interest in archaic pottery from Samnium area. **Career & Employment:** Soprintendenza Archeologica dell'Abruzzo, Chieti 1992-present. **Home Address:** Via Gramsci 11, 86100 Campobasso, Italy.

FAVARO, JAMES B. ■ FAAR Architecture 86. b. Aug. 17, 1956, Vallejo, CA. BSEngr 78, Stanford Univ.; MArch 82, Harvard Univ. **Research/Artistic Interests:** Building, drawing, writing. **Fellowships, Honors & Awards:** Stanford Univ., Phi Beta Kappa 1977; Graham Found. Grant 1991. **Important Works:** Yerkovich Production Studio 1989-91; Austin Residence 1991-present; Crowell Residence 1994-95. **Exhibitions/Performances:** Barnsdall Gallery, Los Angeles 1991. **Home Address:** 912 1/2 S. Mansfield, Los Angeles, CA 90036. **Business Address:** Steve Johnson & James Favaro, 3304 Airport Ave., Santa Monica, CA 90405.

FAVRO, DIANE ■ Fulbright Fellow 79-80. b. Nov. 30, 1950, Ventura, CA. m. Fikret Yegul. BA 73, San Jose State Univ.; MA 76, UC, Santa Barbara; PhD 84 UC, Berkeley. **Career & Employment:** UC, Santa Barbara, TA 1974-76; UC, Berkeley, TA 1978-81; San Francisco State College, Lect. 1980; Florida A & M Univ., School of Architecture, Asst. Prof. 1982-84; UCLA, Graduate Dept. of Architecture & Urban Design, Assc. Prof. 1984-present. **Home Address:** 2825 Puesta del Sol, Santa Barbara, CA 93105.

FAYER, CARLA ■ Italian Fulbright Fellow 1965-66.

FEARS, JESSE RUFUS ■ FAAR Classics/Archaeology 71. b. Mar. 7, 1945, Atlanta, GA. m. Charlene Fears. BA 66, Emory Univ.; MA 67, Harvard Univ. **Other Studies:** Kiel Univ., Germany 1963-64. **Career & Employment:** Harvard Univ., TF 1968-69; Boston Univ. **Fellowships, Honors & Awards:** Harvard Univ., Woodrow Wilson Fellow 1966-67, Danforth Fellow 1966-68.

FEATHER, MORRIS ■ Appleton Fellow 1913.

FEDERICI, FRANCESCO ■ AAR – Rome, Grounds Staff.

FEHL, PHILIPP ■ RAAR History of Art 67, Adv. Council 1982-90. b. May 9, 1920, Vienna, Austria. m. Maria Raina. c. Katherine, Caroline. BA 47, Stanford Univ.; MA 48, Stanford Univ.; PhD 63, Univ. of Chicago. **Other Study:** AIC School 1940-42. **Research/Artistic Interests:** History of the Classsical tradition in art; painter & printmaker. **Career & Employment:** Univ. of Chicago, Lect. 1951-54; Instr. in Home Study 1951-63; Univ. of Nebraska, Asst. Prof., Assc. Prof., Prof. 1954-63; UNC, Chapel Hill, Prof. 1963-69; Univ. of Illinois, Urbana-Champaign, Prof. 1969-90, Prof. Emer. 1990-present; Cicognara Project, Univ. of Illinois & Vatican Library, Ed.-in-Chief 1987-present. **Memberships & Offices:** *Art Bulletin*, Ed. for book reviews 1965-68; CAA, BoD 1967-71; *Gazette des Beaux Arts*, Adv. Council 1975-present; Intl. Survey of Jewish Monuments, Adv. Council, Dir. 1977-present; Leopoldo Cicognara Program at the Univ. of Illinois Library, Dir. 1987-present. **Fellowships, Honors & Awards:** Brussels Art Seminar, Belgian American Ed. Found. 1952; Warburg Inst., Research Fellow 1952-53; Univ. of Chicago,

Com. on Social Thought, Assc. 1963-present; NEH Fellow 1977-78; Univ. of Illinois, Center for Advanced Study, Resident Assc. 1988-present; Ateneo Veneto, Corresponding Mem. 1988-present; Brannschweigische Wissenschaftliche Gesellschaft, Corresponding Mem. 1992-present. **Publications:** ed. & trans., *A Course in Drawing by Denis Diderot and Nicolas Corduin* (Chicago: Univ. of Chicago Press, 1954); "The Rocks on the Parthenon Frieze," *Journal of the Warburg & Courtauld Institutes* 34 (1961): 325-54; "Michelangelo's Crucifixion of St. Peter," *Art Bulletin* 53 (1971): 326-43; *The Classical Monument* (New York: NYU Press, 1972); "The Ghosts of Nuremberg," *Atlantic Monthly* 229.3 (1972): 70-80; "Vasari's Extirpation of the Huguenots: The Challenge of Pity and Fear," *Gazette des Beaux Arts* 81 (1974): 257-83; "Poetry and the Entry of the Fine Arts into England," in *The Age of Milton* (Manchester: Univ. of Manchester Press, 1980), 273-306; ed. with Maria Raina Fehl & Keith Aldrich, *Franciscus Junius: The Literature of Classical Art* (Berkeley: UC Press, 1992); "Dürer's Literal Presence in his Pictures," in *Der Künstler über sich in seinem Werk*, ed. M. Winner (Weinheim: Acta Humaniora, 1992), 191-244; ed. *Albrecht Dürer's Small Passion and its Latin Text* (Champaign-Urbana: Univ. of Illinois Press, 1993); "Raphael as a Historian: Poetry and Historical Accuracy in the Sala di Costantino," *Artibus et Historia* (1993); "Leopoldo Cicognara und die Erfindung der modernen Kunstgeschichte," *Der Kunsthistoriker* (Vienna, 1993). **Important Works:** Books of Drawings: *The Bird*, serigraph & pen & ink (Urbana: Finial Press, 1970); ed. Wilfried Skreiner, *Capricci* (Graz: Neue Galerie, 1971); *Birds of a Feather*, intro. by Mauurice Cope (Urbana: Univ. of Illinois Press, 1991); drawings reproduced in: *Carolina Quarterly* (Winter 1966); *Voyages* 4 (1971, 1973-74); *North Carolina Museum of Arts Bulletin* 12.4 (1975); *Archaeological News* 4 (1975); works in Public Collections: *Capricci*, Neue Galerie, Graz; North Carolina Museum of Art, Raleigh; Kraunert Art Museum, Univ. of Illinois, Champaign; *Artibus et Historiae*, Vienna. **Exhibitions/Performances:** Solo: Neue Galerie am Joanneum, Graz 1971; Roberts Gallery, London 1971; Galerie im Stock, Vienna 1973; Folger Shakespeare Library, Washington, DC 1973; College of William & Mary, Williamsburg, VA 1977; Kenyon College, Gam-

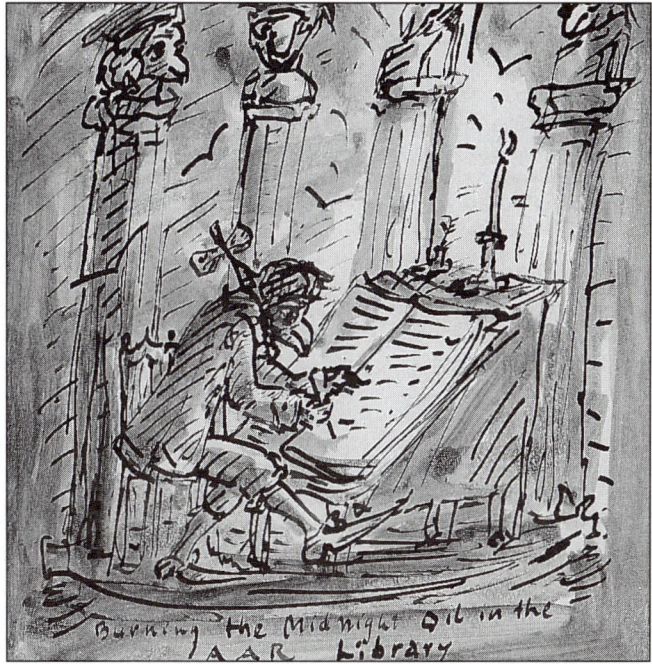

Philipp Fehl

bier, OH 1979; Mt. Holyoke College, South Hadley, MA 1979; Società Dante Alighieri, Venice 1980-81; Tel Aviv Univ., Dept. of Art 1982; Herzog August Bibliothek, Wolfenbüttel 1982; Univ. of Virginia Art Museum, Charlottesville 1986; "Retrospective," Krannert Museum of Art, Univ. of Illinois 1991; Central European Univ., Prague 1993. **Bio-Bibliography:** *Dictionary of International Biography; Directory of American Scholars; International Authors and Writers Who's Who; Who's Who in American Art; Who's Who in Austria; Who's Who in Europe; Who's Who in Society; Writers Directory.* **Home Address:** 710 W. Indiana, Urbana, IL 61801. **Business Address:** The Cicognara Project, Vatican Libray, Vatican City.

FEIGENBAUM, GAIL ■ FAAR History of Art 80. b. May 14, 1951, Providence, RI. m. William Tronzo, FAAR 79. c. Phoebe Marguerite Tronzo, FAAR 79. BA 72, Oberlin College; MA 75, Oberlin College; MFA 77, Princeton Univ.; PhD 84, Princeton Univ. **Career & Employment:** Oberlin College, Allen Memorial Art Museum, Asst. to the Curator 1973-74; Princeton Univ., TF 1976-77, Lect. 1980-81; Research Asst. to Prof. John R. Martin 1977-78; Research Asst. to Prof. Rensselaer W. Lee 1981-82; NGA, Education Dept., Staff Lect. 1982-83, Dept. of Public Programs, Coordinator of Special Exhibitions Projects 1983-85, Coordinator of Academic Programs 1987-89, Curator of Academic Programs 1990-94; Georgetown Univ., Professorial Lect. 1988; CASVA, Acting Assc. Dean 1994-present. **Memberships & Offices:** Inter-Museum Task Force on Pluralism 1990-present; *Studi di Storia dell'arte,* Ed. Bd. 1991-present; CAA, Com. on Cultural Diversity 1993-present; Maryland State Council for the Arts, Visual Arts Panel 1994-present. **Fellowships, Honors & Awards:** Oberlin College, Kress Found. Fellowship 1974-75, Henry J. Haskell Fellowship, Alumni Award 1978-79; Princeton Univ., Dept. of Art & Archaeology, Fellowship 1975-78; Woodland Found. Fellowship, Honorary Award 1977-78; Spears Grant 1981, Com. on Research in the Humanities, Research Assistance Grant 1981; J. Paul Getty Postdoctoral Fellowship 1986-87; Johns Hopkins Univ., Visiting Scholar 1986-91; CASVA, Ailsa Mellon Bruce Curatorial Fellow 1987, 1990-91; NEH Travel to Collections Grant 1988; NEH Summer Stipend 1991; ACLS Grant-in-Aid 1991. **Publications:** with John R. Martin, *Van Dyck as Religious Artist* (Princeton: Princeton Univ. Press, 1979); "Lodovico Carracci's Saint Raymond of Peñaforte: A Copy *in situ*," *Paragone* 429 (Nov. 1985): 96-99; "Lodovico Carracci's Kiss of Judas," *The Record of the Art Museum at Princeton* 48.1 (1989): 2-17; "The Early History of Lodovico Carracci's Annunciation Altarpiece," *Burlington Magazine* 132 (Sept. 1990): 616-22; "Drawing and Collaboration in the Carracci Academy," in *IL 60: Essays Honoring Irving Lavin on his 60th Birthday,* ed. Marilyn A. Lavin (New York, Italica Press, 1990), 145-66; "When the Subject Was Art: The Carracci as Copyists," in *Il luogo ed il ruolo della città di Bologna tra Europa Continentale e Mediterranea,* Atti del Colloquio C.I.H.A. (Bologna: Nuova Alfa, 1992), 297-312; "Practice in the Carracci Academy," in *The Artist's Workshop,* Studies in the History of Art 38 (Washington, DC: NGA, 1993), 58-76; *Lodovico Carracci, 1555-1619: A Retrospective,* exb. cat. (Italian ed., Bologna: Pinacoteca Nazionale, 1993; English ed., Fort Worth: Kimbell Art Museum, 1993). **Home Address:** 332 Suffolk Rd., Baltimore, MD 21218. **Business Address:** NGA, Washington, DC 20565.

FELDHERR, ANDREW M. ■ FAAR Classics/Archaeology 90. b. Oct. 28, 1963, Edmonton, Canada. m. Deborah Steiner. BA 85, Princeton Univ.; MA 87, UC, Berkeley. **Career & Employment:** Dartmouth College. **Fellowships, Honors & Awards:** Princeton Univ., Mellon Fellow 1985; Salutatorian 1985.

FELLOWS, WILLIAM K. ■ McKim Scholar 1911-12, 1913.

FELTUS, ALAN E. ■ FAAR Painting 72. b. May 1, 1943, Washington, DC. m. Lani H. Irwin. c. Tobias, Joseph. BFA 66, Cooper Union; MFA 68, Yale Univ. School of Art & Architecture. **Other Study:** Tyler School of Fine Arts, Temple Univ. 1961-62. **Research/Artistic Interests:** Oil painting. **Career & Employment:** Dayton Art Inst. 1968-70; American Univ. (Washington) 1972-84. **Fellowships, Honors & Awards:** Louis Comfort Tiffany Found. Grant 1980; NEA Grant 1981; Pollack-Krasner Found. Grant 1992; NAD 1994. **Publications:** "Inside the Painter's Mind," *Artist's Magazine* (Jan. 1992): 38-43; "Living and Working in Italy," *American Artist* (Aug. 1992): 54-57. **Important Works:** Nat. Museum of American Art, Washington, DC; Hirshhorn Museum & Sculpture Garden, Washington, DC; Bayly Museum, Charlottesville, VA; Lobby of AMA HQ, 999 E. St., NW, Washington DC; Dayton Art Inst.; New Jersey State Museum; Springfield, MA Museum; Wichita Art Museum; California Palace of the Legion of Honor, San Francisco. **Exhibitions/ Performances:** Solo: Jacob's Ladder Gallery, Washington, DC 1973; Northern Virginia Community College, Annandale 1976; Forum Gallery, NYC 1976, 1980, 1983, 1985, 1987, 1991, 1994; Wichita Art Museum 1987; Simms Fine Arts, New Orleans 1988; Louis Newman Galleries, Beverly Hills 1992; Ann Nathan Gallery, Chicago 1994. **Bio-Bibliography:** Jim Brodey, review in *Arts Magazine* (Apr. 1977); Jill Wechsler, "Alan Feltus:The Mystery in Painting," *American Artist* (Apr. 1980); "The Lonely Art of American Realism," *Life Magazine* (Oct. 1980); David Tannous, review in *Art in America* (Oct. 1980); Valerie Brooks, "Alan Feltus," *MD Magazine* (July 1983); Edward Lucie-Smith, *American Art Now* (New York: Morrow, 1985), 106-7; Charles Jencks, *The New Classicism in Art and Architecture* (London: Academy Editions, 1987), 171-73; Howard Dalee Spencer, *Alan Feltus, Recent Work,* exb. cat. (Wichita Art Museum, 1987); Howard Dalee Spencer, "Alan Feltus in Italy," *American Arts Quarterly* (Winter 1992); Maureen Mullarkey, review in *Arts Magazine* (Jan. 1992). **Home Address:** Porziano 68, 06081 Assisi PG, Italy.

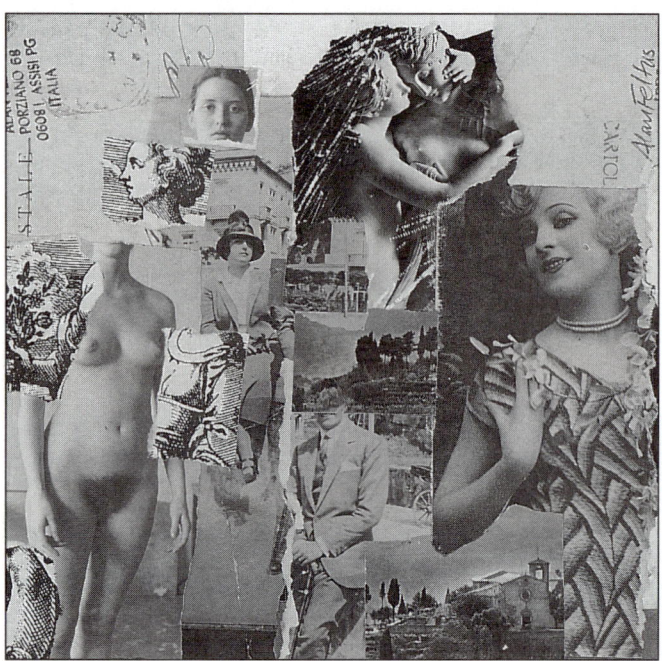

Alan E. Feltus

FENTON, W.H. ■ Cresson Fellow 1911-12, 1913.

FENTRESS, ELIZABETH ■ AAR Visitor 1990-present, Archaeologist.

FENWICK, MILLICENT ■ AAR Visitor 1983-84, US Ambassador to the UN.

FERLINGHETTI, LAWRENCE ■ AAR Visitor 1984-85, Poet, Publisher.

FERRARO, RICHARD J. ■ FAAR Post-Classical/Humanistic Studies 79. b. Jan. 22, 1951, NYC. BA 72, Cornell Univ.; MA 75, Univ. of Wisconsin. **Career & Employment:** Emory Univ. **Fellowships, Honors & Awards:** Fulbright-Hays Fellowship 1977-78; Univ. of Wisconsin, NRS Fellowships 1974-75, 1976-77.

FIELD, ARTHUR M. ■ FAAR Post-Classical/Humanistic Studies 80. b. Aug. 3, 1948, Charleston, SC. BA 70, Duke Univ.; MA 71, Univ. of Chicago; PhD 80, Univ. of Michigan. **Career & Employment:** Hunter College, Adj. Asst. Prof. 1985-87; Princeton Univ., Lect. 1987-89; Indiana Univ., Assc. Prof. 1989-present. **Memberships & Offices:** RSA, Adv. Council 1991-93. **Fellowships, Honors & Awards:** Villa I Tatti, Fellow 1983-84, Visiting Scholar 1993-94; Fulbright Fellow 1983-84; ACLS Fellowship 1983-84, 1992-93; Princeton Univ. Research Grant 1988; *Journal of History of Ideas*, Morris D. Forkosch Prize, Hon. Mention 1988; Indiana Univ., Grant in-Aid 1990-91, Faculty Fellowship 1990, 1991; Guggenheim Fellowship 1993-94. **Publications:** "A Manuscript of Cristoforo Landino's First Lectures on Virgil, 1462-63," *Renaissance Quarterly* 31 (1978): 17-20; "An Inaugural Oration by Cristoforo Landino in Praise of Virgil," *Rinascimento* ser. 2, 21 (1981): 235-45; "The Studium Florentinum Controversy, 1455," *History of Universities* 3 (1983): 31-59; "Cristoforo Landino's First Lectures on Dante," *Renaissance Quarterly* 39 (1986): 16-48; "John Argyropoulos and the 'Secret Teachings' of Plato," in *Supplementum Festivum: Studies in Honor of Paul Oskar Kristeller*, ed. J. Hankins, John Monfasani & Frederick Purnell, Jr. (Binghamton, NY: MARTS, 1987), 299-326; *The Origins of the Platonic Academy of Florence* (Princeton: Princeton Univ. Press, 1988). **Home Address:** 1012 E. 2 St., Bloomington, IN 47401. **Business Address:** Dept. of History, Indiana Univ., Bloomington, IN 47405.

FIELD, EDWARD ■ FAAR Literature 82. b. June 7, 1924, Brooklyn, NY. NYU 1946-48. **Career & Employment:** Eckerd College, Poet-in-Residence 1971; Sarah Lawrence College 1973. **Memberships & Offices:** Alfred Chester Soc. *Newsletter*, Ed. 1987-present. **Fellowships, Honors & Awards:** Lamont Award, American Acad. of Poets 1963; Guggenheim Fellowship 1963; Poetry Soc. of America, Shelley Memorial Award 1974. **Publications:** *Stand Up, Friend, With Me* (New York: Grove Press, 1963); *Variety Photoplays* (New York: Grove Press, 1967); trans., *Eskimo Songs and Stories* (New York: Delacorte Press, 1973); *A Full Heart* (Sheep Meadow Press, 1977); *Stars In My Eyes* (Sheep Meadow Press, 1978); ed., *A Geography of Poets* (New York: Bantam Books, 1979); *The Lost, Dancing* (Watershed Tapes, 1984); *New and Selected Poems* (Sheep Meadow Press, 1987); ed., *Head of a Sad Angel, Stories by Alfred Chester* (Los Angeles: Black Sparrow, 1990); ed., *Looking for Genet: Literary Essays by Alfred Chester* (Los Angeles: Black Sparrow, 1992); ed., *A New Geography of Poets* (Univ. of Arkansas Press, 1992); *Counting Myself Lucky, New and Selected Poems* (Los Angeles: Black Sparrow, 1992). **Bio-Bibliography:** Richard Howard, *Alone with America*

After Cavafy

An old man in tears before The Muse:
In my whole lfe, he complains,
I have only written a few
slim books of poetry,
and gotten little attention for them.
I even see it in your pitiless eyes:
Why didn't I do more?

Perhaps they were too slim, too few.
But how to explain?
If I didn't try hard enough,
I don't even know why,
but always, other things
seemed to be more important.
Tell me, have I wasted my life,
as well as my talents?

Thus replies the statue:
Wipe your tears, old man.
You have taken a step
on the difficult ladder of poetry,
and even getting to the first rung
is an accomplishment the gods all praise.
Feel good about that, with my blessings,
for on this path
there is on failure.

~ Edward Field

Edward Field

(New York, 1969); Dennis Lynch, *Contemporary Poets* (1991). **Home Address:** 463 West St., A323, NYC 10014.

FIELD, MARSHALL ■ AAR Charter Mem., Businessman & Philanthropist.

FILSON, RONALD C. ■ FAAR Architecture 70; SOF, Council Membr. 1988-90. b. Dec. 11, 1946, Chardon, OH. m. Susan V. Saward. c. Timothy, Lily. BArch 70, Yale Univ. School of Art & Architecture. **Career & Employment:** Atelier d'Études et de Restauration de la Vallé du M'Zab 1971-73; UCLA, Grad. School of Architecture & Urban Planning, Asst. Prof.-Asst. Dean 1973-1980; Tulane Univ., School of Architecture, Dean 1980-92, Prof. 1980-present; Eskew Filson, Architects, Part. 1985-present. **Memberships & Offices:** AIA 1975-present, Pres. 1994; American Collegiate Schools of Architecture 1975-present; Contemporary Arts Center, Dir. 1981-85; Arts Council of New Orleans, Dir. 1986-present, Pres. 1989-92; Inst. of Urban Design, Fellow 1989-present; Yale Alumni Assn. of Louisiana 1984-present, Treas. 1989-present, Pres. 1992-present. **Fellowships, Honors & Awards:** NIAE, Education Merit Award 1968; *Progressive Architecture*, Design Citations, 1969, 1976; AIA, Southern California, Design Citation 1979; Cubo de Plata, Biennale de Buenos Aires 1979; Mission Hill Artists Housing Competition (M.A.F.), First Place 1987; AIA, New Orleans Chap., Honor Award 1987, 1994, Louisiana Chap., Honor Award of Excellence 1994, Gulf States Chap., Honor Award 1988; Omicron Delta Kappa 1991; DAAD, Berlin Research Grant 1992; Tulane Univ. Inaugural Richardson Medal 1992. **Publications:** "The Piazza d'Italia," *Architectura* (Madrid, Apr. 1979); contr., *Learning from Las Vegas*, ed. Venturi, Scott Brown & Izenour (Cambridge, MA: MIT Press, 1982); ed., *A China Journal* (Spokane: People-to-People, 1983); "Metaphor & Ritual: The Whitehead Garden," *Arts & Architecture* 1.4 (Feb. 1983); *Six City Sites: A Critical Overview*, exb. cat. (New Orleans: Preservation Resource Center, 1983); "A Youthful Tribute," & "Remembrances of the Piazza d'Italia and a Look at Ethnicity," in *Places*, ed. Donlyn Lyndon (Cambridge, MA: MIT Press, 1984); "Architectural Education & Practice," *Architectural Record* (New

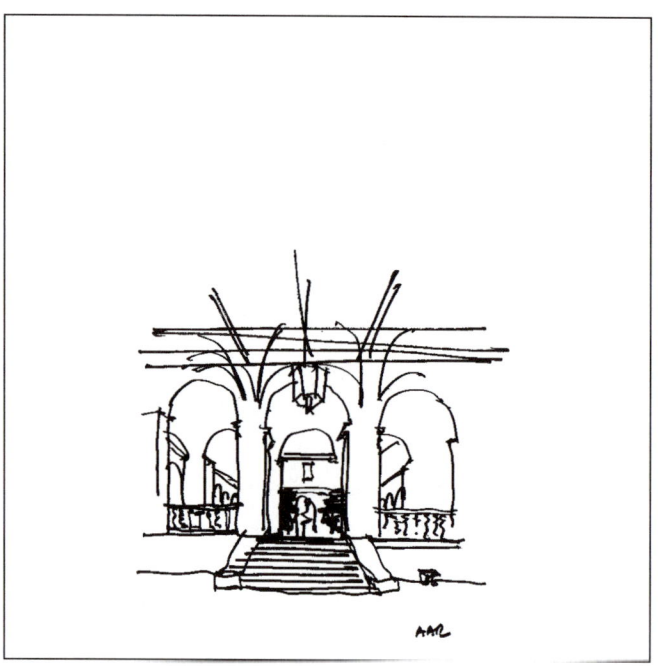

Ronald C. Filson

York: McGraw-Hill, 1985), 26-28; "Tall Buildings: A Plea," in *High Rise Buildings: Recent Progress*, ed. Howard Beedle (Lehigh, PA: Lehigh Univ. Press, 1986); ed., *Who Designs America?* (Washington, DC: ACSA Press 1988); "Foreword," in Abbye A. Gorin, *Conversations with Samuel Wilson, Jr.* (New Orleans: Louisiana Landmarks Soc., 1991), xi-xix; "Authenticity," in *Vision 1991* (New Orleans: New Orleans Realtors Assn., 1991). **Important Works:** with C.W. Moore, Eola Hotel, Natchez, MS 1977; King's Rd. Housing, Los Angeles 1978; with C.W. Moore, The Piazza d'Italia, New Orleans 1978; Comprehensive Masterplan, Tulane Univ., New Orleans 1982; Tower of New Orleans Project 1983; Lee House, Metarie, LA 1983; Environmental Education Center, Barataria, LA 1990; Town & Retail Center, Kentlands, Gaithersburg, MD, Project 1990; Forsythe Park, Monroe, LA 1990; Canal Place, New Orleans, modifications 1990-present; Sealab Aquarium, Dauphin Island, AL 1991; NPS Environmental Education Center 1993; Pincus House 1994. **Exhibitions/ Performances:** PS 1, NYC 1982; Krewe of Klones 1983; Centro de Arte y Comunicacion, Buenos Aires 1983; Southeast Architectural Archives, New Orleans 1983; Biennale di Venezia 1985; Biennale, Buenos Aires 1987; ALNY 1988. **Bio-Bibliography:** "Some Young and Perhaps, Post-Modern Los Angeles Architects," *A & U* (Apr. 1978); C. & P. Donnadieu, H. & J.M. Didillon, *Habiter le Desert, Les Maisons Mozabites* (Liège: Mardabe, 1978); *Charles Moore & Co.* (Tokyo: Global Architecture Press, 1981); "The Shelton House," *Architectural Digest* (Mar. 1980): 84-90; Tod Marder, ed. *The Critical Edge: Controversy in Recent American Architecture* (Cambridge, MA: MIT Press, 1985); "Il Ponte della Accademia," *Terza Mostra Internazionale di Architectura* (Naples: Electa, 1986); "Young American Architects," *Space Design* (Tokyo), 82-108; *Who's Who in the South & Southwest*. **Business Address:** Eskew Filson Architects, 1008 N. Peters St., New Orleans, LA 701116.

FINLEY, A(UGUSTUS) CLEMENS ■ FAAR Painting 28. b. April 7, 1900, Harding, WV. dec. NAD; Beaux Arts Inst., Paris. **Career & Employment:** WPA, Federal Art Project, Artist. **Important Works:** US Post Offices: Brooklyn, Kensington Station, Buffalo. **Bio-Bibliography:** *Who Was Who in American Art*.

FINLEY, DAVID E. ■ AAR Visitor 1943 — 1951; NGA, Dir.

FINNEY, ROSS LEE ■ RAAR Musical Composition 60. b. Dec. 23, 1906, Wells, MN. m. Gretchen L. (dec.). c. Ross L., Henry C. BA 27, Carleton College. **Other Study:** Student of Nadia Boulanger, Roger Session & Alban Berg. **Publications:** *Profile of a Lifetime* (New York: C.F. Peters, 1992). **Bio-Bibliography:** Frederic Goossen, *Thinking About Music: The Collected Writings of Ross Lee Finney* (Tuscaloosa: Univ. of Alabama Press, 1984); Gretchen Finney, *Facts and Memories* (New York: C.F. Peters, 1990); *Who's Who in America*. **Home Address:** 2015 Geddes Ave., Ann Arbor, MI 48104.

FISHER, LOREN RUSSELL ■ FAAR Painting 42. b. Mar. 16, 1913, Needham, IN. m. Gertrude Huntress. c. Mishell. **Study:** John Herron Art School, Indianapolis. **Research/Artistic Interests:** Mural painting. **Career & Employment:** US Army, WWII; Independent Artist, FL. **Important Works:** Mural: US Post Office, Anchorage, AK.

FITCH, CLEO RICKMAN ■ AAR Visitor, Artist, Scholar. Active in Cosa excavations. **Publications:** co-author, *Cosa: The Lamps*.

FITCH, JAMES MARSTON ■ AAR Visitor 1975-76. Architectural Preservationist, Architectural Historian.

FIZDALE, ARTHUR ■ AAR Visitor 1951 — 1955, Pianist.

FLACCAVENTO, GIORGIO ■ Italian Fulbright 1963-64.

FLOEGEL, ALFRED ERNST ■ FAAR Painting 25. b. Sept. 4, 1894, Leipzig, Germany. d. Aug. 27, 1976. m. Marianne Hourihan. **Study:** Art Trade School, Germany; NAD; NY School of Industrial Art; Beaux Arts Inst.; C.C. Curran, F.C. Jones & I.G. Olinsky. **Research/Artistic Interests:** Architectural design, interior design for churches & theaters. **Memberships & Offices:** Rochester Steuben Soc., ALNY, Soc. of Mural Painters. **Important Works:** Design of a cockpit for supersonic aircraft; "Floegelgram," architectural sketch with 3-dimensional perspective. **Bio-Bibliography:** *Who Was Who in American Art*.

FLORY, MARLEEN BOUDREAU ■ FAAR Classics/Archaeology 86. b. Jan. 2, 1944. m. Stewart Flory. BA 65, Mt. Holyoke College; PhD 75, Yale Univ. **Career & Employment:** Salem College, Asst. Prof. 1977-78; Mt. Holyoke College, Asst. Prof. 1976-77; Gustavus Adolphus College, Asst.-Assc. Prof. 1978-.

FONTENROSE, JOSEPH ■ FAAR Classics/Archaeology 52; Classical Soc., Pres. 1955. b. June 17, 1903, Sutter Creek, CA. d. July 7, 1986. m. Marie Holmes. c. Jane Burnett, Robert, Anne Mujadeddy. BA 25, UC, Berkeley; MA 28, UC; PhD 33, UC. **Research/Artistic Interests:** Classical mythology, relationship between art & mythology; English & American literature, Native American lore. **Career & Employment:** Cornell Univ., Instr. 1931-33; Univ. of Oregon, Asst. Prof. 1934; UC, Berkeley, Instr.-Asst. Prof.-Assc. Prof. 1937-55, Prof. 1955-70, Chair 1962-66; Brandeis Univ., Visiting Prof. 1971. **Memberships & Offices:** APA; Philological Assn. of Pacific Coast, Pres. 1973-74; ArIA; American Folkore Soc.; California Folklore Soc.; Fabian Soc. of London; MLA; Sierra Club; American Federation of Teachers. **Fellowships, Honors & Awards:** ASCSA & ACLS, Fellow 1935-36; Yale Univ., Sterling Fellow 1936-37; Guggenheim Fellowship 1958-59; Dickens Fellow. **Publications:** *Python: A Study of Delphic Myth and its Origins* (Berkeley: UC Press, 1959); *The*

Cult and Myth of Pyrros at Delphi (Berkeley: UC Press, 1960); *John Steinbeck: An Introduction and Interpretation* (New York: Holt, Rinehart & Winston, 1963); *The Ritual Theory of Myth* (Berkeley: UC Press, 1966); *The Delphic Oracle: Its Responses and Interpretations* (Berkeley: UC Press, 1981); *Steinbeck's Unhappy Valley: A Study of the Pastures of Heaven* (Berkeley: UC Press, 1981); *Orion: The Myth of the Hunter and the Huntress* (Berkeley: UC Press, 1981); *Didyma: Apollo's Oracle, Cult, and Companions* (Berkeley: UC Press, 1988); *Classics at Berkeley: The First Century, 1869-1970* (Berkeley: UC Press, 1982); plus over 25 articles in various journals. **Bio-Bibliography:** Kenneth Burke, "Myth, Poetry and Philosophy," *Journal of American Folklore* 73 (1960): 283-306; *Steinbeck Quarterly*, Special Number in Honor of Joseph Fontenrose 6.2 (Spring 1973); *Who Was Who in America.*

FORGE, ANDREW ■ RAAR Painting 85, AAR Trustee 1983-89, Trustee Emer. b. 1923, Hastingleigh, Kent, England. Camberwell School of Art, with William Coldstream, Kenneth Martin & Victor Pasmore 1947-49. **Career & Employment:** Slade School, Univ. College, London 1950-64; Goldsmith's College, London Univ., Dept. of Fine Art, Head 1964-70; Univ. of Reading, Lect. 1971-72; Cooper Union, Visiting Prof. 1973-74; New York Studio School, Assc. Dean 1974-75; Visitor 1975-present; Yale Univ. School of Art, Prof. 1975-94, Dean 1975-83. **Memberships & Offices:** Nat. Council Diplomas in Art & Design, Fine Arts Panel 1962-72, Council 1964-72; UK, Ministry of Education, Joint Working Party 1968-70; UK, Gulbenkian Com. 1969-71; Tate Gallery, BoT 1964-74, Chair, Exhibitions Com., Chair, Conservation Com. 1972-74; National Gallery, BoT 1966-71; London Group, Pres. 1966-72; *Studio International*, Ed. Bd. 1966-72; Greater London Arts, Chair, Visual Arts Panel 1969-71; NAD, Assc. 1992. **Fellowships, Honors & Awards:** Guggenheim Fellowship 1980; Merrill Found. Award 1985; AAAIL, Painting Prize 1990. **Publications:** *Klee* (London: Faber & Faber 1953); *Vermeer* (London: Faber & Faber 1954); *Soutine* (Hamlyn, 1964); *Rauschenberg* (New York: Abrams, 1970); *Art/Nature* (London: Royal Inst. of Philosophy 1973); *Monet at Giverny* (Miller, Mathews, Dunbar 1973); "Painting and the Whole Self," *Artforum* (1975); *Monet* (New York: Abrams, 1983); with Robert Gordon, *The Last Flowers of Monet* (New York: Abrams, 1986); with Robert Gordon, *Degas* (New York: Abrams, 1987); numerous articles & reviews in *The Times (London), The New Statesman, The Listener, The Spectator, Times Literary Supplement, Art International, Art News, Artforum, Palleten, Spirone, l'Art Vivant, Art & Literature*. **Important Works:** Public Collections: Tate Gallery, Arts Council of Great Britain, UK Ministry of Works, Corcoran Museum, Yale Art Gallery, Yale British Art Center, NAD; Corporate Collections: Reuters, Aetna, Southern New England Telephone, General Electric. **Exhibitions/Performances:** Agnews Gallery, London 1953; Artists Intl. Assn. Gallery, London 1963; City Art Gallery, Bristol, England 1964; New York Studio School Gallery 1978, Ten-year retrospective 1989; Mona Berman Gallery, New Haven, CT 1983, 1985; Underwood Gallery, Rome 1985; Ruggiero Gallery, NYC 1989, 1991; Robert Morrison Gallery, NYC 1993, 1994; Broadcasts for the BBC Third Program, 1953-1973, interviews with Francis Bacon, Anthony Caro, Naum Gabo, Kenneth Martin, Graham Sutherland, Kokoshka, Morton Feldman, Jean Renoir, Roland Penrose, William Tucker; Contributions to *The Critics, Picture of the Month, Looking at Pictures;* Devised & edited radio documentaries *Art in the Thirties, Art and Architecture.* **Home Address:** 22 Shinar Mountain Rd., Washington Depot, CT 06794.

FORMAN, STEVEN ■ NIAE, John Dinkeloo Traveling Fellow 78. b. Nov. 27, 1954, NYC. m. Sandra-Lisa Schwartz. c. Jus-

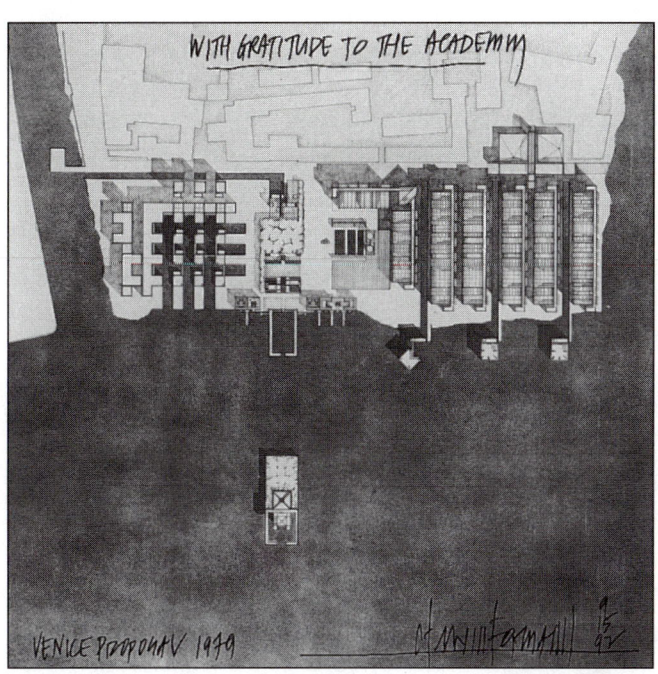

WITH GRATITUDE TO THE ACADEMY

VENICE PROPOSAL 1979

Steven Forman

tin, Ian. BArch 77, Cooper Union; MArch 79, Cornell Univ. **Other Study:** Asst. to the Architect John Hejduk in 1976 for submissions to Venice Biennale. **Research/Artistic Interests:** Advanced study in architectural drawing & architectural photography. **Career & Employment:** John Hejduk Architect, Asst. 1976-77; Richard Meier & Partners, Architects, Assc. 1979-82; Gwathmey Siegel & Asscs., Architects, Project Architect 1982-86; Steven Forman Architect, Prin. 1986-present. **Home Address:** 353 E. 83rd St., NYC 10028. **Business Address:** Steven Forman Architect, 353 E. 83rd St., Studio 17H, NYC 10028.

FORNI, GIOVANNI ■ Italian Fulbright Fellow 1959-60.

FORTE, BETTIE LUCILLE ■ FAAR Classics/Archaeology 60. b. Apr. 7, 1933, Columbus, GA. BA 55, Agnes Scott College; MA 56, Bryn Mawr College. **Bio-Bibliography:** *Directory of American Scholars.*

FORTNER, JACK R. ■ FAAR Musical Composition 68. b. July 2, 1935, Grand Rapids, MI. m. Phyllis Perry. c. Lydia. BMus 59, Aquinas College; MusM 65, Univ. of Michigan; MusD 68, Univ. of Michigan. **Career & Employment:** Grand Rapids, MI, Symphony, Asst. Conductor 1964-65; Univ. of Michigan, Instr. 1965-70; Contemporary Directions Ensemble, Univ. of Michigan, Conductor 1966-70; Sinfonia Chamber Orchestra, Grand Rapids, MI, Music Dir. 1968-69; California State Univ., Fresno, Prof. 1970-present, Orchestra Conductor 1972-present, Dept. Chair 1985-86, 1990-present, Coordinator of String & Orchestral Studies 1986-present; Merced, CA, Symphony, Music Dir. 1971-77; Orpheus, Fresno, CA, Artistic Dir. 1978-present; Dance Spectrum, San Francisco, Conductor 1979. **Memberships & Offices:** Conductors Guild, Soc. of Composers, American Music Center, Pacific Contemporary Music Center, Univ. Music Executives of California, Nat. Assn. of Schools of Music. **Fellowships, Honors & Awards:** Fondation Royaumont Intl. Composition Prize 1965; Martha Baird Rockefeller Found. Grants 1967, 1969; NEH Grant 1969; NEA Commissioning Grant 1975. **Important Works:** *Variations for Orchestra* 1964; *Burleske for Two Chamber Orchestras* (Editions Jobert) 1965; *Cantilenae for Flute*

& *Piano* (Elkan Vogel) 1965; *S pr ING*, 4 songs on e.e. cummings poems (Editions Jobert, Jeune Musique) 1966; *Quadri* (Editions Jobert, Vienna Modern Masters) 1967; *Quartet, 4 Pieces for String Quartet* (Editions Jobert) 1967; *June dawns, July noons, August evenings* (Elkan Vogel) 1969; *De Plus en Plus* (Elkan Vogel) 1971; *Flow Chart 1: Aprés Jonas 5:5* (Elkan Vogel) 1974; *Found Objects* 1985; *Prelude to an Opera: The House of Atreus* (Vienna Modern Masters) 1988; *Pas de Quatre for String Quartet* 1989; *Trois Gymnopédies* for clarinet, bassoon, piano 1990; *Declamations, Commentaries, & Ritornellos-Concertpiece for Cello, Concertante & Orchestra* 1992; *Symphonies* (Vienna Modern Masters) 1992; *Sonnets* 1994. **Home Address:** 6358 N. Benedict, Fresno, CA 93711.

FOSS, LUKAS ■ FAAR Musical Composition 52, RAAR Musical Composition 78. b. Aug. 15, 1922, Berlin, Germany. m. Cornelia Brendel. c. Christopher, Eliza. **Important Works:** *Ode* (Koss) 1944, rev. 1958; *The Prarie* (Vox) 1944; *Song of Songs* (Koss, Columbia, CRI, Sony) 1946; *String Quartet No. 1* (Columbia); *Capriccio* (RCA, Music Arts) 1946; *Parable of Death* (Columbia) 1952; *Psalms* (CRI, Pro Arte) 1956; *Time Cycle* (Columbia, Epic, CRS, Wergo) 1960; *Echoi* (Wergo, Epic, Columbia) 1963; *Fragments of Archilochos* (Wergo) 1965; *Baroque Variations* (Nonesuch) 1967; *GEOD* (Candide-Vox) 1969; *Curriculum Vitae,* for accordian (CRI) 1977; *Music for Six* (CRI) 1977-78; *Thirteen Ways of Looking at a Blackbird* (CRI) 1978; *Round a Common Center* (Pro Arte) 1979; *Night Music for John Lennon* (Gramavision) 1981; *Solo Observed* (Gramavision) 1982; *Renaissance Concerto,* for flute & orchestra (New World Records) 1985; *Tashi* (RCA) 1986; *With Music Strong* (Koss) 1988; *Three Early Pieces,* for flute & piano (Nonesuch); *Oboe Concerto* (Crystal); *Jumping Frogs,* an opera (Lyrichord); *Piano Concerto No. 2* (Decca, Varèse, Sarabande); *Behold, I Build an House* (CRI, Vox, Chesky); *Studies in Improvisation* (RCA); *Phorion* (Columbia, Deutsche Grammophon); *Non-Improvisation* (Wergo); *Paradigm* (Deutsche Grammophon, Vox); *Three Airs for Frank O'Hara* (Vox); *Cave of the Winds* (Vox); *Ni Bruit, Ni Vitesse* (Vox); *String Quartet No. 3* (CRI); *Measure for Measure* (Gramavision); *Orpheus & Euridice* (New World Records); *Salomon Rossi Suite* (New World Records); *Solo* (CRI); *Three Pieces for Violin & Piano* (Gasparo); *The Curriculum Vitae*

One of my favorite compositions composed at the American Academy is Quintet for orchestra, originally a Brass Quintet: "The Rocks on the mountains begin to shout". A 5 note chord dominates the composition. It is endlessly repeated, varied, permutated, transposed and inverted. It invades the entire piece via persistent, pulsating, echoing and crisscrossing quarter notes. Toward the end there is an explosion which liberates us from the domination of the five note chord. All this can be explained and analysed. But I cannot explain why this chord which dominates through repetition, variation, permutation, transposition and inversion of persistent, pulsating, echoing and crisscrossing quarternotes lingers like a wound until "the rocks begin to shout". Nor do I know what it is that rocks shout perhaps Charles Ives does. perhaps rocks cry "help" because we do not see that we are in danger; or perhaps, they merely shout a reminder of what every work of art tries to tell us -- that we must change our lives

Lukas Foss

Lukas Foss

Tango (Music/Arts); *Saxophone Quartet* (MCA Classics). **Bio-Bibliography:** *Lukas Foss, A Bio-Bibliography* (Westport, CT: Greenwood Press) **Home Address:** 1140 Fifth Ave., NYC 10128.

FOSTER, MARK M. ■ FAAR Architecture 84. m. Kathie Stafford. c. Emily Steen Foster, Evan Winfield Foster. BArch 79, Univ. of Oregon; RISD 1977-78. **Career & Employment:** Griggs Lee Ruff Ankrom, P.C. 1979-80; SRG Partnership, P.C. 1985-89; Oregon School of Design, Adj. Prof. 1987-88; Mark M. Foster, Architect 1989-90; Zimmer Gunsul Frasca Partnership 1980-83, Assc. Part. 1990-present. **Memberships & Offices:** American Youth Hostels, Oregon Council BoD 1987-present, VP 1987-88, VP of Hostel Development 1990-93. **Fellowships, Honors & Awards:** James H. Steedman Traveling Fellowship 1983-84. **Important Works:** Nat. Inst. of Biologicals, NOIDA, India; Portland Intl. Airport, Terminal Expansion North; Washington State Univ., Vancouver Campus Master Plan; Washington State Univ., Vancouver Campus: Laboratory, Library & Student Services Bldgs.; Tri-Met Westside Light Rail Transit Corridor: Washington Park Station, Sunset Transit Center Station, Portland; Waterfront Village Master Plan, Seattle; Private Residence, Woodlands, TX; Johnson Residence, Portland, OR; Speckman Residence, Salem, OR; Hook-Foster Cabin, Neskowin, OR; Conrath Residence, Gresham, OR. **Home Address:** 4735 SE 31 St., Portland, OR 97202. **Business Address:** Zimmer Gunsul Frasca Partnership, 320 SW Oak, Suite 500, Portland, OR 97204.

FOWLER-MAGERL, LINDA ■ FAAR Post-Classical/Humanistic Studies 65. b. Sept. 12, 1939, Cleveland, OH. m. Arnulf M. Magerl. c. Emerenz. BA 60, Western Reserve Univ.; MA 62, Univ. of Wisconsin; PhD 70, Univ. of Wisconsin. **Research/Artistic Interests:** Medieval legal history. **Career & Employment:** Univ. of Nebraska 1969-72; Max Planck Inst. für Europäische Rechtsgeschichte 1973-75; Univ. of Regensburg 1975-85. **Publications:** as Fowler, "*Recusatio iudicis* in Civilian and Canonist Thought," *Studia Gratiana* 15 (1972): 717-85; "Innocent Uselessness in Civilian and Canonist Thought," *Zeitschrift für Rechtsgeschichte Kan. Abt.* 58 (1972): 107-65; "Forms of Arbitration," *Proceedings of the Fourth International Congress of Medieval Canon Law, Toronto 21-25 August 1972, Monumenta Iuris Canonici C/5* (Vatican, 1976), 133-47; as Fowler-Magerl: "Vier französische und spanische Kanonessammlungen," in *Aspekte europäischer Rechtsgeschichte: Festgabe für Helmut Coing zum 70. Geburstag,* ed. C. Bergenfeld et al., Ius Commune Sonderhefte 17 (Frankfurt-am-Main: Klostermann, 1983), 123-46; *Ordo iudiciorum vel ordo iudiciarius, Begriff und Literaturgattung,* Ius Commune Sonderhefte 19 (Frankfurt-am-Main: Klostermann, 1984); *Ordines iudiciarii und Libelli de ordine iudiciorum,* Typologie des Sources du Moyen Age Occidental 63 (Turnhout: Brepols, 1994). **Home Address:** Bergstr. 7, Piesenkofen D-93083, Germany.

FRAMPTON, KENNETH ■ AAR Visitor 1985-86, Architect.

FRANCIS, ROBERT ■ FAAR Literature 58. b. 1901. d. 1987. **Bio-Bibliography:** *NY Times,* Obit. (July 16, 1987); *Contemporary Authors; Who Was Who in America.*

FRANCIS, WILLIAM C. ■ Columbia Fellow 1911, McKim Fellow 1913.

FRANK, ERIC MARSHALL ■ FAAR History of Art 82. b. Nov. 13, 1952, NYC. m. Penni Montalbano. c. Adam, Daniel. BA 74, Dartmouth College; MA 77, Syracuse Univ.; PhD, IFA. **Career & Employment:** UC, Berkeley, Faculty 1984-87; Occidental College, Prof. 1987-. **Fellowships, Honors & Awards:** Dartmouth College Library Prize 1974; Syracuse Univ., Florence Fellow 1975; Robert Lehman Research Fellow 1977-79; RSA Summer Fellow 1978. **Publications:** contr., *Source* (1990); contr., *Andrea Verrocchio and Late Quattrocentro Sculpture* (1990).

FRANK, ISABELLE S. ■ FAAR History of Art 87. b. May 2, 1959, Minneapolis, MN. m. Mark Lilla, FAAR 87. BA 80, Princeton Univ.; MA 84, Harvard Univ.; PhD 91, Harvard Univ. **Research/Artistic Interests:** Italian Renaissance painting, focused on a 15th-century painter, Melozzo da Forli, who painted mostly in Rome. Papal history & the development of Rome in the Renaissanc; figural foreshortening in Renaissance theory & practice. **Career & Employment:** CASVA, Asst. Curator 1991-92; Bard Grad. Center in the Decorative Arts, Asst. Prof. 1993-present. **Home Address:** 25 Union Sq. W., PH-L, NYC 10003. **Business Address:** CASVA, Washington, DC 20565.

FRANK, RICHARD I. ■ FAAR Classics/Archaeology 64. b. March 7, 1932, Philadelphia, PA. m. Anne Frank. c. Jonathan, Benjamin, Siena. BA 53, UCLA; MA 57, UCLA; PhD 65, UC, Berkeley. **Other Study:** German in Monterey, CA, Army Language School 1953-54. **Research/Artistic Interests:** Roman Empire, Renaissance humanism. **Career & Employment:** Reed College, Asst. Prof. 1964-66; UC, Irvine, Assc. Prof. 1966-present. **Fellowships, Honors & Awards:** ACLS Fellow 1972-73. **Publications:** *Scholae Palatinae* (Rome: AAR, 1969); trans., *Agrarian Sociology of Ancient Civilization* (London: NLB, 1976). **Home Address:** 625 Glomstad Ln., Laguna Beach, CA 92651. **Business Address:** Dept. of History, UC, Irvine, CA 92717.

FRANK, TENNEY ■ AAR School of Classical Studies, Prof.-in-Charge 1922-25.

FRANKLIN, CARMELA VIRCILLO ■ FAAR Post-Classical/Humanistic Studies 85. b. Oct. 29, 1949, S. Caterina Albanese, Italy. m. R.W. Franklin. c. Corinna, Beatrice. BA 71, Radcliffe College; PhD 77, Harvard Univ. **Career & Employment:** St. John's Univ., Asst. Prof. 1977-83; Assc. Prof. 1983-90; Dept. Chair 1988-92; Prof. 1990-present; Carleton College. Visiting Assc. Prof. 1987; Hill Monastic Manuscript Library, Interim Dir. 1992-94; Columbia Univ., Assc. Prof. 1994-present. **Memberships & Offices:** MAA, Nominating Com. 1987-89. **Fellowships, Honors & Awards:** ACLS Fellowship 1984-85 (declined); St. John's Univ., Burlington-Northern Faculty Achievement Award 1990; NEH Fellowship 1990-91, Travel to Collections Grant 1992; National Humanities Center, Fellowship 1991-92. **Publications:** with Ivan Havener, OSB & J. Alcuin Francis, OSB, *Early Medieval Rules: The Rule of the Fathers and the* Regula Orientalis (Collegeville: Liturgical Press, 1982); with Paul Meyvaert, "Has Bede's Version of the *Passio S. Anastasii* Come Down to Us in BHL 408?" *Analecta Bollandiana* 100 (1982): 373-400; "Ein unbekannte Fassung der *Annales Casinenses*," *Deutsches Archiv für Erforschung des Mittelalters* 43.2 (1987): 81-109; "On the Authorship of the *Inventio et Miracula S. Secundini*," *Analecta Bollandiana* 106 (1988): 323-32; *The Ecclesiae Atinatis Historia of Marcantonio Palombo*, 2 vols. (Rome: Studi e Testi, 1992); "The Restored Life and Miracles of Dominic of Sora by Alberic of Monte Cassino," *Mediaeval Studies* 55 (1993): 285-347; "Theodore of Tarsus and the *Passio S. Anastasii* (BHL 410b)," in *Archbishop Theodore, 690-1990*, ed. M. Lapidge (Cambridge: Cambridge Univ. Press, 1995). **Business Address:** Classics Dept., Columbia Univ., NYC 10027.

FRANKLIN, GILBERT A. ■ FAAR Sculpture 49; RAAR Sculpture 66; Juror; AAR Trustee 1973-79, Trustee Emer. b. June 6, 1919, Birmingham, England. m. Joyce Gertrude Swirsky. c. Nina Berson. BFA 41, RISD. **Other Study:** studied in Mexico on alumni fellowship for 6 mos. in 1942; studied painting with John R. Frazier, summers of 1939-41; studied stone carving with John Howard Benson, John Stevens Shop, Newport, RI; worked with Waldemar Raemisch, studio asst. for 4 years. **Research/Artistic Interests:** Bronze casting, flexible mould forming, painting. **Career & Employment:** San Jose State College, Instr. 1944-45; RISD, Asst. Prof. 1942-44; Assc. Prof. 1945-53; Sculpture Dept., Head 1953-60; Division of Fine Arts, Chair 1960-75; European Honors Program, Rome, Italy, Dir.; Division of Fine Arts & Design, Dean 1975-84; Visiting Faculty: Harvard Univ. 1951-52; Yale Univ. 1952-53; Univ. of Pennsylvania 1975-76; Danforth Distinguished Prof. 1982-84. **Memberships & Offices:** Boston Univ., Bd. of Overseers, Fine Arts 1960s; Univ. of Pennsylvania Graduate School of Fine Arts, Bd. of Overseers, Assc. Trustee 1976-82; Fulbright Comm., Sculpture Com. Juror, Chair; Harvard Univ. Visiting Com., Overseers Visual Studies 1988-94; Saint-Gaudens Memorial, BoT 1992. **Fellowships, Honors & Awards:** RISD, Alumni Fellowship 1941, Traveling Fellowship, Mexico 1942; Grand Prize Boston Fine Arts Festival 1958; Providence Art Club Medal for Excellence in the Arts 1975; H.M. Danforth Chair in Fine Arts 1982; NAD, Nat. Academician 1991. **Important Works:** Public Commissions: Harvey Trust, Providence; Frazier Memorial, Providence; Metcalf Memorial; Providence College 1976; Harry S. Truman Memorial, Independence, MO 1976; Design for Governors Award for Excellence in the Arts, Rhode Island 1976; McGrath Memorial, RI Capitol 1977; Design for Medal, RI Arts Council 1977; Design for Truman Award 1977; Fountain Piece, Hallmark Collection, Kansas City; Gannett Bldg., Washington, DC; Collections: Museum of Art, Providence; MFA; Miami Univ., Miami, OH; Walter P. Chrysler Collection; Boston Safe Deposit & Trust Co., Boston; G.A.F.A. Collection, Baltimore; Corcoran Gallery, Washington, DC; Hopkins Center, Dartmouth; UNC; Vassar College; Currier Gallery, Manchester, NH; Providence Art Club. **Exhibitions/Performances:** Solo: Providence Art Club 1941, 1955, 1965, 1978, 1986; San Jose State College 1945; Rhode Island League for Art 1953, 1956, 1958; Kanegis Gallery, Boston 1959, 1960, 1961, 1963, 1964, 1966, 1968, 1969; Michael Walls Gallery, San Francisco 1967; Tirca-Karlis Gallery 1973-74; Univ.

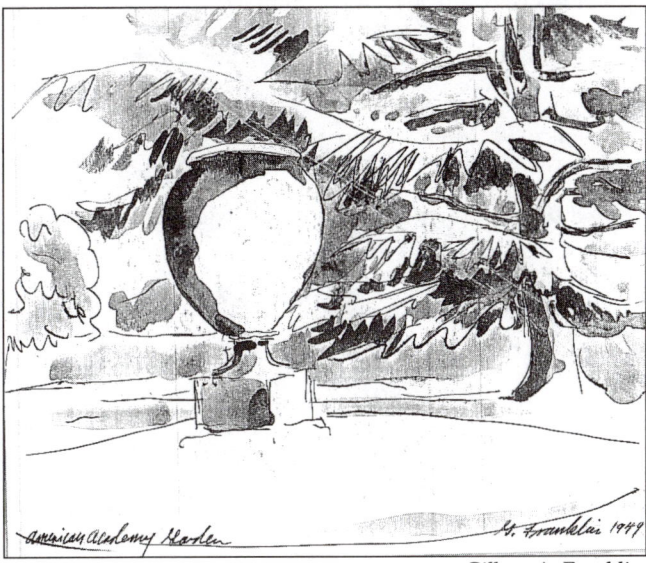

Gilbert A. Franklin

of Connecticut 1975; Dartmouth College 1975; Long Point Gallery, Provincetown 1981, 1992, 1993, 1994; Maryland Cultural Center, Retrospective Exb. 1982; RISD, Museum of Fine Art 1983. **Bio-Bibliography:** *Who's Who in America; Who's Who in Art.* **Home Address:** PO Box 171, S. Wellfleet, MA 02663.

FRANKLIN, JAMES L., JR ■ FAAR Classics/Archaeology 75; Adv. Council to School of Classical Studies, Sec. 1976-87, Pres. 1988-91. b. July 19, 1947, Dayton, OH. BA 69, Denison Univ.; MA 70, Queen's Univ., Ontario; PhD 75, Duke Univ. **Research/Artistic Interests:** Latin Literature, Pompeian studies, Roman archaeology. **Career & Employment:** Barnard College, Asst. Prof. 1975-76; Wellesley College, Asst. Prof. 1976-77; Univ. of Michigan, Visiting Asst. Prof. 1977-80; Indiana Univ., Asst. Prof. 1981-84, Assc. Prof. 1984-92, Prof. 1992-present, Honors Division 1986-90, Supervisor of teaching in elementary Latin program 1981-86; ICCS, A.W. Mellon Prof.-in-Charge 1994-95. **Memberships & Offices:** Michigan Classical Conference, Exec. Com. 1979-80; Council for Intl. Exchange of Scholars, Adv. Screening Com., Classics, Fulbright Senior Scholar Awards 1982-85; APA, Elected Mem., Com. on Education 1985-89; ArIA, Associazione Internazionale Amici di Pompei; CAMS, Exec. Com. 1988-92; VSA, BoT 1992-94; ICCS, Rome, Elected Mem., Managing Com. 1989-94. **Fellowships, Honors & Awards:** NEH Fellowship 1980-81. **Publications:** "Notes on Pompeian Prosopography: *Programmatum Scriptores,*" *Cronache Pompeiane* 4 (1978): 54-74; "Notes on Pompeian Prosopography: Two Non-Existent Ancients and the DD. Lucretii Valentes," *La Parola del Passato* 34 (1979): 405-14; *Pompeii: The Electoral Programmata Campaigns and Politics, A.D. 71-79,* AAR Papers and Monographs 28 (Rome: AAR, 1980); "Games and a Lupanar: Prosopography of a Neighborhood in Ancient Pompeii," *Classical Journal* 81 (1985-86): 319-28; "Pantomimists at Pompeii: Actius Anicetus and his Troupe" in *American Journal of Philology* 108 (1987) 95-107; *Pompeii: The "Casa del Marinaio" and Its History,* Monografie della Soprintendenza Archeologica di Pompei 3 (Naples: SAP, 1990); "Literacy and the Parietal Inscriptions of Ancient Pompeii," in *Literacy in the Roman World,* ed. J. Humphrey, *Journal of Roman Archaeology* supp. vol. 3 (Ann Arbor: JRA, 1991): 77-98. **Business Address:** Dept. of Classical Studies, Indiana Univ., Bloomington, IN 47405.

FRASER, GEORGE ■ FAAR Architecture 28. b. Sept. 17, 1895, St. Paul, MN. d. Oct. 4, 1966. BArch 19, Univ. of Minnesota; MArch 21, Cornell Univ. **Research/Artistic Interests:** Collegiate architecture, Baths of Septius Magna. **Career & Employment:** Fraser Asscs., Founder c.1960-66; Jackson, Robertson & Adams, Providence, RI. **Memberships & Offices:** Hope Club, Providence Art Club. **Important Works:** Providence County Court House & State House Annex; architect for various buildings at Cornell Univ. & others at the Univ. of Rhode Island; Classroom Bldg., RISD.

FRASER, JAMES EARLE ■ AAR Trustee 1931-52, Sculptor.

FRASER, LEON ■ AAR Trustee 1938-44, Bank Exec.

FRAZER, ALFRED KNOX ■ FAAR Classics/Archaeology 61, RAAR Classics/Archaeology & History of Art 87. b. May 23, 1928, Birmingham, AL. d. May 28, 1994. m. Margaret English. c. Martha, Zoe, Andrew. BArch 49, Alabama Polytechnic Inst.; MA 57, IFA; PhD 64, IFA. **Career & Employment:** US Army 1949-52; Architectural Design, NYC 1952-57; Vassar College, Asst. Prof. 1957-58, 1962-66; Columbia Univ., Assc.

Prof.-Prof. 1966-94, Dept. Chair 1972-78. **Memberships & Offices:** CASVA, Bd. of Adv. 1983-94; SAH, Dir. 1965-72, NY Chap., Dir 1967-69; CAA, Dir. 1974-77. **Fellowships, Honors & Awards:** Tatiana Warsher Memorial Prize 1961, APS Grant 1965. **Publications:** contr., *Key Monuments of the History of Architecture,* ed. Henry A. Millon (New York: Abrams, 1965); "The Iconography of the Emperor Maxentius' Buildings in Via Appia," *Art Bulletin* 48 (1966): 385-92; "The Porch of the Tor de' Schiavi at Rome," *AJA* 73 (1969): 45-48; "Modes of European Courtyard Design before the Medieval Cloister," *Gesta* 12 (1973): 1-12; "Numismatic Sources for Michelangelo's First Design for the Tomb of Julius II," *Art Bulletin* 57 (1975): 53-57; "From Column to Wall: The Peribolos of the Mausoleum of Maxentius," *In Memoriam Otto J. Brendel,* ed. L. Bonfante et al. (Mainz: von Zabern, 1976), 185-90; "Macedonia and Samothrace: The Architectural Late Bloomer," *Studies in the History of Art* 16 (1981): 190-203; *The Propylon of Ptolemy II,* Samothrace 10, 2 vols. (Princeton: Princeton Univ. Press, 1990); "The Roman Villa and the Pastoral Ideal," *Studies in the History of Art* 26 (1992): 48-61; "The Imperial Fora: Their Dimensional Link," in *Eius Virtutis Studiosi: Classical and Postclassical Studies in Memory of Frank Edward Brown (1908-1988),* ed. Russell T. Scott & Ann R. Scott (Washington DC: NGA, 1993), 411-20. **Important Works:** Curator, "Age of Spirituality: Late Antique and Early Christian Art, Third to Seventh Century," MMA 1977. **Bio-Bibliography:** Estelle Gilson, "The Vatican Collections, Margaret and Alfred Frazer Help Bring the World's Oldest Museum to the New World," *Columbia* (Feb. 1983); *NY Times,* Obit. (May 28, 1994); *Directory of American Scholars; Who's Who in America.*

FRAZER, MARGARET ■ RAAR History of Art 87. b. 1940. **Bio-Bibliography:** Estelle Gilson, "The Vatican Collections, Margaret and Alfred Frazer Help Bring the Worlds' Oldest Museum to the New World," *Columbia* (Feb. 1983); *Who's Who in America; Who's Who in American Art; Who's Who in the East.*

FREEMAN, ANN ■ FAAR Post-Classical/Humanistic Studies 58. b. June 30, 1926, Springfield, MA. m. Paul Meyvaert. c. Jenny. BA 48, Wellesley College; PhD 56, Harvard Univ. **Career & Employment:** Wellesley College, Lect. 1951; Chatham College, Asst. Prof. 1958-64, Assc. Prof. 1964-68; Univ. of Pittsburgh, Visiting Assc. Prof. 1965; Duke Univ., Lect. 1968; North Carolina Central Univ., Visiting Prof. 1969-71; Brandeis Univ., Visiting Prof. 1974-75. **Memberships & Offices:** Phi Beta Kappa 1947-present; MAA 1948-present; *Monumenta Germaniae Historica,* Mitarbeiterin 1975-present. **Fellowships, Honors & Awards:** ACLS, Grant-in-Aid 1963-64, 1966; APS, Travel Grant 1963, Research Grant 1965; NEH, Research Grant 1980-82; Wellesley College, Stevens Fellowship 1980-82; *Monumenta Germaniae Historica,* Korrespondierend Mitglied 1995. **Publications:** trans., 6 sermons, in *No Uncertain Sound; Sermons that Shaped the Pulpit Tradition,* ed Ray C. Petry (Philadelphia: Westminster Press, 1949), 96-102, 104-8, 199-204, 218-23, 289-94; "Theodulf of Orleans and the *Libri Carolini,*" *Speculum* 32 (1957): 663-705; "Further Studies in the *Libri Carolini,* I: Palaeographical Problems in Vaticanus Latinus 7207, & II: Patristic Exegesis, Mozarabic Antiphons, and the *Vetus Latina,*" *Speculum* 40 (1965): 203-8; "Further Studies in the *Libri Carolini,* III: The Marginal Notes in Vaticanus Latinus 7207," *Speculum* 46 (1971): 597-612; "Theodulf of Orleans" and "The *Libri Carolini,*" in *New Catholic Encyclopedia* (Washington, DC: Catholic Univ. Press, 1967); "Carolingian Orthodoxy and the Fate of the *Libri Carolini,*" *Viator* 16 (1985): 65-108; "Theodulf of Orleans and the Psalm Citations of the *Libri Carolini,*" *Revue Benedictine* 97 (1987): 195-224; "Additions and Corrections to the *Libri Carolini*: Links with Alcuin and the Adoptionist Controversy," in Scire Litteras: *Festschrift for Bernhard Bischoff*, ed. S. Kramer & M. Bernhard (Munich: Bayerische Akademie der Wissenschaften, 1988), 159-69; "Theodulf of Orleans: A Visigoth at Charlemagne's Court," *L'Europe Heritière de l'Espagne Visigothique*, Paris CNRS Colloquium, 1990 (Madrid: Casa de Valázquez, 1992), 185-94; "Scripture and Images in the *Libri Carolini*," in *Testo e Immagine nell'Alto Medioevo*, Settimana di Studio Centro Italiano di Studi sull'Alto Medioevo 41 (Spoleto: CISAM, 1994), 1:163-88; ed., *Opus Caroli regis contra synodum (Libri Carolini), Monumenta Germaniae Historica*, Concilia Suppl. 2 (Hanover: Hahnsche, 1995); contr., *The Dictionary or Art*; contr., *Lexikon des Mittelalters* (Munich: Artemis & Winkler, forthcoming). **Home Address:** 8 Hawthorne Pk., Cambridge, MA 02138.

FREER, CHARLES L. ■ AAR Charter Mem., Investor, Art Collector.

FREIBERG, JACK ■ FAAR History of Art 77. b. May 31, 1948, NYC. BA 72, Hunter College; MA 74, IFA; PhD 88, IFA. **Career & Employment:** Hunter College, Instr. 1977-78; NYU, Instr. 1979; ICCS, Rome, Lect.-Asst. Prof. 1980-89; Univ. of Notre Dame, Rome, Asst. Prof. 1989-90; Rensselaer Polytechnic Inst., Asst. Prof. 1990; Syracuse Univ., Florence, Asst. Prof. 1990; Duke Univ., Visiting Asst. Prof. 1991-92; Florida State Univ., Asst. Prof. 1992-present. **Fellowships, Honors & Awards:** Samuel H. Kress Found. Fellow 1976-77, 1978-79; MMA, Chester Dale Fellow 1980-81, Mellon Fellow 1981-82; APS Grant 1991; Florida State Univ. Grant 1993, 1994. **Publications:** "Clement VIII, the Lateran, and Christian Concord," in *IL 60: Essays Honoring Irving Lavin on His Sixtieth Birthday*, ed. Mailyn Aronberg Lavin (New York: Italica Press, 1990), 167-90; "The Lateran Patronage of Gregory XIII and the Holy Year 1575," *Zeitschrift für Kunstgeschichte* 57 (1991): 66-87; "Paul V, Alexander VII, and a Fountain by Nicolò Cordier Rediscovered," *Burlington Magazine* 133 (1991): 833-43; "In the Sign of the Cross: The Image of Constantine in the Art of Counter-Reformation Rome," in *Studies in the History of Art* 48, ed. Marilyn Aronberg Lavin (Washington, DC: NGA, 1995); *The Lateran in 1600: Christian Concord in Counter-Reformation Rome* (Cambridge: Cambridge Univ. Press, 1995). **Business Address:** Florida State Univ., Tallahassee, FL 32306.

FRENCH, DANIEL CHESTER ■ AAR Incorporator, Trustee 1911-32, Sculptor. b. April 20, 1850. d. Oct. 7, 1931. **Memberships & Offices:** Nat. Comm. on Fine Arts, Chair 1912-15; MMA, BoT. **Important Works:** bronze doors, Boston Public Library; statue of Abraham Lincoln, Lincoln Memorial, Washington; Statue of Alma Mater, Columbia Univ., NYC.

FRENCH, W.M.R. ■ AAR Charter Mem.; AIC, Dir.

FRICK, HENRY CLAY ■ AAR Founder, Trustee 1911-19, Manufacturer. b. Dec. 19, 1849. d. Dec. 2, 1919. **Career & Employment:** Carnegie Bros., Chair. 1889-92; H.C. Frick Coke Co., Pres. & Chair 1897-1919. Capitalist in coal and steel, art collector.

FRIEDBERG, M. PAUL ■ RAAR Landscape Architecture 84, AAR Trustee, Trustee Emer. b. 1931, NYC. m. Ester Louise Hidary, Dorit Shalar. c. Mark, Jeffrey. BS 54, Cornell Univ. **Career & Employment:** US Army, 1st Lieut. 1954-56; Columbia Univ. 1971; New School for Social Research 1971; Pratt Inst. 1971; M. Paul Friedberg & Partners, Founding Part. 1958-present; CCNY, Urban Landscape Pgm., Founder & Dir. 1971-91, Prof. Emer. 1991; Visiting Lect.: Harvard Univ. 1966, 1990;

Univ. of Pennsylvania 1967; Syracuse Univ. 1967; & others. **Memberships & Offices:** Inst. of Urban Design, Adv.; Int. Design Conference, Aspen, Adv.; American Inst. of Planners 1964-present; CLARB; Cornell Univ. School of Architecture, Adv. Bd; ASLA 1964-present, ALNY 1964-present. **Fellowships, Honors & Awards:** ASLA, Fellow 1979; AIA Medal 1980; Ball State Univ., Hon. Doctor of Law 1983; Design Awards from: ASLA; American Assn. of Nurserymen; New York Assn. of Architects; HUD; Municipal Arts Society of New York; *Progessive Architecture; Industrial Design*; Building Stone Inst. **Publications:** *Playground for City Children* (Assn. for Childhood Education Intl., 1969); *Creative Play Areas* (Niedermeyer-Martin, 1970); *Play ard Interplay* (New York: Macmillian, 1970); "Is This Utopia?" in *The Social Impact of Urban Design* (Chicago: Univ. of Chicago Center for Policy Study, 1975); *Handcrafted Playgrounds* (New York: Random House, 1988); "The Place: An American View," *Arredo Urbano* 25 (1988); "Collaboration," *Arredo Urbano* 27-28 (1988); "Random Thoughts on Stone," *Building Stone Magazine* (1989); *Process: Architecture* 82 (Process Architecture, 1989); *Sourcebook of Contemporary North American Architecture* (New York: Van Nostrand Reinhold, 1990). **Important Works:** Robert Clement State Park, Worcester, MA, Galleria; US Pavilion at World's Fair in Osaka, Japan; Moscow Trade Center; Winter Garden Project at Niagara Falls; City Hall Fountain, NYC; Peavy Plaza & Honeywell Plaza, Minneapolis; Malls: in Madison, WI; Grand Rapids, MI; Minneapolis, MN; Pershing Park, Wasington, DC; Transpotomac Canal Center, Alexandria, VA; Battery City Park-World Financial Center, NYC. **Business Address:** M. Paul Friedberg & Partners, 41 E. 11 St., 3rd. Fl., NYC 10003.

FRIEDLANDER, LEO ■ FAAR Sculpture 16. b. Jul. 6, 1890, NYC. d. Oct. 24, 1966. m. Rhoda Lichter. c. Gordon. ASL; École des Beaux Arts, Brussels & Paris; NAD. **Memberships & Offices:** NSS, Pres. 1954-57; ALNY, VP 1950s; NIAL; NAD. **Fellowships, Honors & Awards:** NAD, Helen Foster Barnett Prize 1918, 1924; Sesquicenntenial Expo, Philadelphia Medal of Honor 1926; ALNY, Gold Medal 1933; NSS, Medal of Honor 1951; Herbert Adams Memorial Medal 1955. **Publications:** "The New Architecture and the Master Sculptor," *The Architectural Forum* 46.1 (Jan. 1927); and many essays in *Architectural Forum* and other journals. **Important Works:** Washington Memorial Arch, Valley Forge, PA 1912; "Memory" War Memorial, Richmond, VA 1930; Sculptures: New York World's Fair 1939-40; Arlington Memorial Bridge; American Military Cemetery, Hamm, Luxembourg; Eastman School of Music, Rochester; Masonic Temple, Detroit; MMA; Nashville Federal Courthouse 1950; Nat. Chamber of Commerce, Washington, DC; Oregon State Capitol, Salem; *Pioneer Woman*, State College of Women, Denton, TX; *Roger Williams*, Columbia Terrace, Providence, RI; Sculptured Clock, House of Representatives, Washington, DC; Univ. of Michigan Museum, Ann Arbor; Cranbrook Church, MI; Chapel, UC, Berkeley. **Exhibitions/Performances:** NAD 1918, 1924; AIC 1920; Sesquicentennial Expo, Philadelphia 1926; ALNY 1933; Hudson River Museum, Westchester, NY 1984; Graphicstudio, Tampa, FL 1991-92. **Bio-Bibliography:** : Joel Rosenkranz, *Sculpture on a Grand Scale: Works from the Studio of Leo Friedlander*, exb. cat. (Yonkers, NY: Hudson River Museum of Westchester, 1984); *Who Was Who in American Art*.

FRIEDMAN, DAVID H. ■ FAAR History of Art 89. b. Aug. 15, 1943, Allentown, PA. m. Ann R. Gabhart. BA 66, Brandeis Univ.; PhD 73, Harvard Univ. **Other Study:** Univ. of Munich, Fine Arts Seminar 1965-66. **Career & Employment:** Univ. of Pennsylvania, Visiting Lect. 1973, Asst. Prof. 1973-78; MIT, Asst.

Prof. 1978-81, Assc. Prof. 1981-present. **Memberships & Offices:** SAH, 1st VP, Urban History Chap. 1981-83; BoD 1991-94; CAA. **Fellowships, Honors & Awards:** German Govt. Exchange Fellowship 1965; Harvard Univ. Fellowship 1966-67; NDEA Title IV Fellowship 1967-69; Villa I Tatti, Florence, Fellow 1969-71, Assc. 1976, Guest Scholar 1988; Univ. of Pennsylvania Faculty Fellowship 1974; ACLS Fellowship 1976-77; NEH Stipend 1983, 1992; IAS 1985; SAH, Hitchcock Award 1989. **Publications:** "The Burial Chapel of Filippo Strozzi in Santa Maria Novella in Florence," *L'Arte* 3.9 (1970): 109-31; "Le 'terre nuove' fiorentine," *Archeologia Medioevale* 1 (1974): 231-47; "The Porta a Faenza and the Last Circle of Walls of the City of Florence," in *Essays Presented to Myron P. Gilmore*, ed. G. Ramakus & S. Bertelli (Florence: La Nuova Italia Editrice, 1978), 179-92; "The Modern Medieval City: Public Space in Florentine Founded Towns," *Modulus* 17 (1984): 142-53; *Florentine New Towns: Urban Design in the Late Middle Ages* (New York, Architectural History Found., 1989); "Florentine New Towns," *Architectural Design* 59.5-6 (1989): 82-88; "Il palazzo e la città: facciate fiorentine tra xiv e xv secolo," in *Il palazzo dal rinascimento a oggi*, ed. S. Valtieri (Rome: Gangemi Editore, 1989), 101-12; "Palaces and the Street in Late Medieval and Renaissance Italy," in *Urban Landscape: International Perspectives*, ed. J. Whitehand & P. Larkin (London: Routledge, 1992), 69-113. **Home Address:** 76 Prince St., Jamaica Plain, MA 02130. **Business Address:** MIT, Rm. 10-303, 66 Massachusetts Ave., Cambridge, MA 02139.

FRIEND, A.M., JR ■ AAR Trustee 1947-56, Classicist.

FRIER, BRUCE W. ■ FAAR Classics/Archaeology 68, AAR Trustee 1987-89, Trustee Emer. b. Aug. 31, 1943, Chicago, IL. BA 64, Trinity College, Hartford; PhD 70, Princeton Univ. **Career & Employment:** Bryn Mawr College, Lect. 1968-69; Univ. of Michigan, Asst. Prof. 1969-75, Assc. Prof. 1975-83, Prof. 1983-present. **Memberships & Offices:** APA, Ed. Bd. for Monographs 1979-82, Publications Com. 1986-89. **Fellowships, Honors & Awards:** ACLS Fellow 1972-73; NEH Fellow 1976-77, 1992-93; IAS 1983, 1992-93; APA, Goodwin Award of Merit 1983; Clare Hall, Cambridge Univ., Visiting Fellow 1984-85. **Publications:** "The Rental Market of Early Imperial Rome," *Journal of Roman Studies* 67 (1977): 27-37; "Law, Technology, and Social Change," *Savigny Zeitschrift* 96 (1979): 204-28; *Libri Annales Pontificum Maximorum: The Origins of the Annalistic Tradition* (Rome & New York: AAR, 1979); *Landlords and Tenants in Imperial Rome* (Princeton: Princeton Univ. Press, 1980); "Roman Life Expectancy: Ulpian's Evidence," *Harvard Studies in Classical Philology* 86 (1982): 213-51; "Roman Law and the Wine Trade," *Savigny Zeitschrift* 100 (1983): 258-95; *The Rise of the Roman Jurists: Studies in Cicero's Pro Caecina* (Princeton: Princeton Univ. Press, 1985); *A Casebook on the Roman Law of Delict* (Scholar's Press, 1989); with Roger Bagnall, *The Demography of Roman Egypt* (Cambridge, MA: Cambridge Univ. Press, 1994); "Law, Economics, and Disasters down on the Farm," *Bolletino dell'Istituto di Diritto Romano* (forthcoming); "The Demography of the Early Roman Empire," in *Cambridge Ancient History* 11 (forthcoming). **Home Address:** 2142 Overlook Ct., Ann Arbor, MI 48103. **Business Address:** Law School or Dept. of Classical Studies, Univ. of Michigan, Ann Arbor, MI 48109.

FRISCHER, BERNARD D. ■ FAAR Classics/Archaeology 76. b. May 23, 1949, Cleveland, OH. m. Jane W. Crawford. c. Katherine. BA 71, Wesleyan Univ.; PhD 75, Univ. of Heidelberg. **Research/Artistic Interests:** Greek & Roman literature, philosophy & art. **Career & Employment:** UCLA, Asst. Prof.

1976-80, Assc. Prof. 1980-91, Prof. 1991-present, Chair 1984-88; UC, Padua Study Center, Dir. 1988-90. **Memberships & Offices:** APA 1971-present, California Classical Assn. 1976-present, VP 1993-present; ArIA 1976-present; VSA 1985-present, American Assn. for Neo-Latin Studies 1991-present. **Fellowships, Honors & Awards:** Nat. Merit Semi-Finalist 1967; Phi Beta Kappa 1970; Woodrow Wilson Fellowship 1971; Michigan SOF, Junior Fellow 1971-74; ACLS Fellowship 1981-82; Univ. of Bologna, Visiting Prof. 1993; Univ. of Pennsylvania, Visiting Prof. 1994. **Publications:** "*Concordia Discors* and Characterization in Euripides' Hippolytos," *Greek, Roman and Byzantine Studies* 11 (1970): 85-100; At Tu Aureus Esto: *Eine Interpretation von Virgils 7. Ekloge* (Bonn: Rudolf Habelt, 1975); *The Sculpted Word: Epicureanism and Philosophical Recruitment in Ancient Greece* (Berkeley & Los Angeles: UC Press, 1982); "Monumenta et Arae Honoris Virtutisque Causa: Evidence of Memorials for Roman Civic Heroes," *Bulletino della Commissione Archeologica di Roma* 88 (1982-83): 51-86; "Horace and the Monuments: A New Interpretation of the Archytas Ode (c. 1.28)," *Harvard Studies in Classical Philology* 88 (1984): 71-102; *Shifting Paradigms: New Approaches to Horace's Ars Poetica*, APA Monograph Series 27 (Atlanta, 1991). **Bio-Bibliography:** *Who's Who in the West*. **Home Address:** 3441 Butler Ave., Los Angeles, CA 90066.

FROHNE, VINCENT S. ■ FAAR Musical Composition 66. b. Oct. 26, 1936, La Porte, IN. m. Joan E. Ruebush. c. Andrea E., Theodora M., Ellhaum. BMus 58, De Pauw Univ.; MusM 59, Univ. of Rochester, Eastman School of Music; PhD 63, Univ. of Rochester, Eastman School of Music; Cert. 61, Goethe Inst., Luneburg. **Other Study:** Aspen School of Music with Darius Milhaud 1957; Tanglewood School of Music with Leon Kirchner 1959; Hochschule für Musik, Berlin, Zwischenprüfung certificate, with Boris Blacher 1960, 1962, 1966; Hochschule für Bildenekunst, Berlin 1962. **Research/Artistic Interests:** Use of augmented 6th chords in 20th-century Russian composers; use & history of "Polar" harmony; Doppler harmonic effects; regions of a polychord; psychological limits of tempo & timbre; multiple series with step dynamics; general critique of the avant garde, 1955-1972; basic problems in computer & electronic music; use of universal principles as a critical tool of all art. **Career & Employment:** Berlin Volkshochschulen, Dozent 1967-70; Kammermusik des 20. Jahrhunderts, Chamber-concert series, Dir. 1968-70; Schiller College, Berlin Music Program, Dir.-Founder-Prof. 1970-74; Univ. of Tulsa, Assc. Prof. 1975-78; Tulsa Junior College 1979; Western Illinois Univ., Guest Prof. 1979-80; St. Paul R.C. Church, Macomb, IL, Organist 1984-present; Carl Sandburg College, Galesburg, IL, Lect. 1988. **Memberships & Offices:** GEMA, Ausserordentlich Mem. 1968-present; Phi Mu Alpha, Life Mem., Past Pres. Lambda Chapter, Pi Kappa Lambda 1957-present; Music Teachers Nat. Assn. 1977; Macomb Philosophy Club, Pres. 1987-88; American Guild of Organists. **Fellowships, Honors & Awards:** Eastman School of Music, Benjamin Award 1959; Fulbright Grant 1960; Koussevitzky Comm., Library of Congress 1965; Guggenheim Fellow 1966; Rockefeller Orchestra Prize, Rockefeller Found. & Univ. of Washington 1967. **Important Works:** *Piano Sonata* 1960; *Three Pieces for Orchestra* 1960; *Ordine II*, for orchestra 1963; *Quartet for Horn & String Trio* 1963; *Adam's Chains*, for soprano & orchestra 1964; *Sonata for Cello Solo* 1965; *String Quartet* 1966; *Pendulum*, for flute & piano 1968; *The Sacred Songs of William Blake*, for narrator, soprano & orchestra 1969-72; *Marchen*, for piano & tape, organ & tape 1972; *My Spectre*, for a capella chorus 1976; *Carol for Choir, Organ & Celeste-bells* 1976; *Movements for Brass, In Memoriam I. Stravinsky* 1979-80; *The Mighty Power,* cantata for SATB, childrens' choir (SA), bells & organ 1982; *Verlust,* for piano 1983; *Wind Trio,* for alto sax, horn & bassoon 1985; *Fanfare,* for brass 1986; *Concerto for Flute & Orchestra (Pendulum II)* 1988-89; *Sonata for Violin & Piano* 1993. **Bio-Bibliography:** W. Becker, *Philharmonischen Blättern* 4 (Berlin, 1968-69); Bote & Bock, *Tagebuch* 28 (Berlin-Wiesbaden, 1969); *Contemporary American Composers* (Boston: G.K. Hall, 1979); *American Keyboard Artists; Dictionary of Contemporary Music; Dictionary of International Biography; International Who's Who in Music; Men of Achievement; Who's Who in American Education; Who's Who in Entertainment;* radio discussions, e.g., BBC. **Home Address:** 12965 E. 900 St., Macomb, IL 61455.

FRUDAKIS, EVANGELOS ■ FAAR Sculpture 52. b. May 13, 1921, Rains, UT. m. Gerd H. Frudakis. c. Anthony, Jennifer. Cert. 49, PAFA. **Other Study:** Studio asst. to Jo Davidson & Paul Manship, Beaux Arts Inst. of Design, NYC 1940-41. **Research/Artistic Interests:** Figurative sculpture in bronze & marble. **Career & Employment:** PAFA, Instr. 1969, Lect. 1976; Nat. Acad. School of Fine Arts, Instr. 1969-76; Frudakis Acad. of Fine Arts, Founder 1976-90. **Memberships & Offices:** NAD, Academician; NSS, Fellow, Council Mem.; Allied Artists of America. **Fellowships, Honors & Awards:** PAFA, Cresson Traveling Scholar 1947, Henry Scheidt Memorial Scholar 1949; Louis Comfort Tiffany Scholarship 1949; Eben Demarest Trust Fund (Pittsburgh) 1949-50; NAD, Watrous Gold Medal 1968, Dessie Greer Prize for Best Portrait 1970, Artists Fund Prize 1975, 1977, 1990, Gold Medal 1984; NSS, Richards Prize for Best Portrait 1972, Gold Medal 1972, Herbert Adams Award for Outstanding Contribution to American Sculpture 1976, Meiselman Prize 1981. **Important Works:** John F. Kennedy Memorial, Atlantic City, NJ; Nashua, NH; Guaymas, Mexico 1964; Icarus & Daedalus Fountain, Little Rock, AR 1966; Fishing Bear Fountain, Philadelphia Zoological Gardens 1980; The Signer, Independence Nat. Historic Park, Philadelphia 1982; Naiad Fountain, Philadelphia Civic Center 1982; Welcome Fountain, Rittenhouse Hotel, Philadelphia 1989; Minute Man, Nat. Guard Bldg., Washington, DC 1991. **Exhibitions/Performances:** NAD Annuals 1948-present; NSS Annuals; Atlantic City Art Center 1956, 1961; Woodmere Art Museum, Chestnut Hill, PA 1957; Philadelphia Art Alliance 1958; Briarcliff College 1974; Grand Central Gallery, NYC 1992. **Bio-Bibliography:** *Who's Who in America; Who's Who in American Art; Who's Who in the World.* **Home Address:** 312 Valley Dr., Kerrville, TX 78028.

FRUHAN, CATHERINE E. ■ FAAR History of Art 89. b. Nov. 6, 1948, Lakewood, OH. BA 70, Connecticut College; MA 74, Univ. of Michigan; PhD 86, Univ. of Michigan. **Other Studies:** Univ. of Florence 1970-71. **Career & Employment:** College of Wooster, Instr.-Asst. Prof. 1980-84; DePauw Univ., Asst. Prof. 1984-. **Fellowships, Honors & Awards:** Lyman Allyn Museum Award 1970; Samuel H. Kress Found. Grant for Dissertation Research 1976; Connecticut College, Phi Beta Kappa Award 1976; Univ. of Michigan, Distinguished Dissertation Award 1986; NEH Summer Inst. 1987.

FRY, SHERRY EDMUNDSON ■ FAAR Sculpture 11. b. Sept. 29, 1879, Creston, IA. dec. AIC; Juliens Acad. & Beaux Arts Acad., Paris; studied with Frederick MacMonnies, Barries, Verlet, & Lorado Taft. **Career & Employment:** US Army, WWI. **Memberships & Offices:** NSS 1908; ALNY 1911; NAD 1931. **Fellowships, Honors & Awards:** Paris Salon, Hon. Mention 1906, Gold Medal 1907; Panama P. I. Exposition, San Francisco, Silver Medal 1915; NAD, Gold Medal 1917; AIC, Prize 1921,

Gold Medal 1922. **Important Works:** Fountains: Staten Island, NY; Toledo Museum of Art; Mt. Kisco NY; Worcester, MA; Frick House, NYC; Statues: Univ. of Vermont; Pediment, Clark Mausoleum, Los Angeles. **Bio-Bibliography:** *Who Was Who in America, Who Was Who in American Art.*

FULFORD, ERIC R. ■ FAAR Landscape Architecture 91. b. July 16, 1951, Atlanta, GA. m. Ann F. Reed. c. Ian. BS 73, Oregon State Univ.; MLA 77, Univ. of Illinois; Dipl. 78, Univ. of Edinburgh. **Career & Employment:** Dalton-Morgan & Partners Architects 1978; *Historic American Engineering Record,* US Interior Dept., Lockport, IL 1979; Indiana State Planning Services Agency 1979-81; McGuire & Shook Corp. 1981-82; James Architects & Engineers 1983-85; Browning Day Mullins Dierdorf 1985-87; Rundell Ernstberger & Asscs. 1988-94. **Memberships & Offices:** ASLA, Roster for Visiting Evaluators. **Fellowships, Honors & Awards:** ASLA, Indiana Chap. Merit Award 1988, 1994, Honor Award 1988, 1994, Tennessee Chap., Excellence in Development 1993; City of Indianapolis, Monumental Award 1988, Honor Award 1989, 1992, Merit Award 1992; Indiana Soc. of Architects, Merit Award 1990; Masonry Inst. & Masonry Contractors of Indiana, Excellence in Masonry Award 1988, 1989; AIA, Indiana Chap., Merit Award 1991, Middle Tennessee Chap., Excellence in Landscape Architecture Award 1992, Excellence in Development 1993; Building Stone Inst., Tucker Award 1992; Consulting Engineers of Indiana, Honor Award 1993; Nat. Terrazzo & Mosaic Assn., Honor Award 1993. **Publications:** *Farmville Appearance Handbook: Guidelines for Physical Rehabilitation and Restoration* (Charlotte, NC: Dalton-Morgan, Architects 1978); *Lockport Illinois: An HCRS Project Report* (Washington, DC: US Dept. of the Interior, 1979); *Indiana's Shoreline: A Recreation Guide* (Indianapolis: State Planning Services Agency 1980); *Lake Michigan Shoreline Program* (Indianapolis: State Planning Services Agency 1980); *Small Town Revitalization Series* (Indianapolis: State Planning Services Agency 1981); "A Temple through Time: A Landscape Architect's Visual History of a Roman Sanctuary Spanning 1,800 Years," *Archaeology* (Sept.-Oct. 1994). **Important Works:** Alexandrian Free Public Library, Mt. Vernon, IN 1985; Mu-

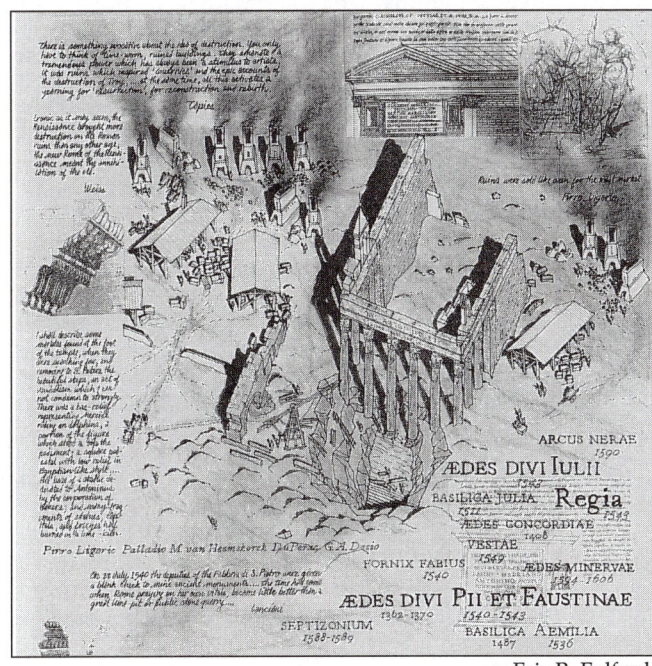

Eric R. Fulford

seum-on-a-Bridge, Project, Indianapolis 1985; Lower Central Canal, Indianapolis 1985; Pan American Plaza, Indianapolis 1986; Eiteljorg Museum of the American Indian & Western Art: Indianapolis 1987; Indiana Govt. Center, Indianapolis 1988-89; Murfreesboro Civic Gardens & Plaza, Murfreesboro, TN 1990; St. Vincent Hospital & Health Care Facility, Project, Indianapolis 1991; Employee Health Services Courtyard, Indianapolis 1992; Museum Indiana Project, Indianapolis 1993; Middle Fork Gardens Project, Indianapolis 1993; Tri-State Univ. Master Plan, Angola, IN 1993. **Bio-Bibliography:** Steve Mannheimer, "Proposed Mall Has Beauty Battling Thrift," *Indianapolis Star* (Apr. 8, 1990); Susan Wampler, "Roman Holiday," *Indianapolis Business Journal* (Apr. 5, 1991); Steve Mannheimer, "Turn a New Leaf," *Indianapolis Star* (Sept. 29, 1991); William Thompson, "Portfolios," *Landscape Architecture* (May 1993); Steve Mannheimer, "The Case for Saving the Silos," *Indianapolis Star* (May 16, 1993); Robert Riley & Brenda Brown, "Most Influential Landscapes, *Landscape Journal* (Fall 1993); Susan Neville, "Making Amber Waves," *Arts Indiana* (Jan. 1994); Michael Leccese, "Tilting at Grain Mills," *Landscape Architecture* (Apr. 1994); Patrick Baggatta, "Inter-rupted History," *Landscape Architecture* (Dec. 1994). **Home Address:** 685 Middle Dr., Woodruff Pl., Indianapolis, IN 46201. **Business Address:** Rundell Ernstberger Circler Tower Bldg., Suite 1429, 55 Monument Circle, Indianapolis, IN 46204.

FULLER, (RICHARD) BUCKMINSTER ■ AAR Visitor 1969-70, Designer, Geometrician. b. July 12, 1895. d. July 1, 1983. **Career & Employment:** Dymaxion Dwelling Machine Corp., Chair & Chief Engineer 1944-46; Fuller Research Found., Chair 1946-54; Southern Illinois Univ., Prof. 1959-75. **Honors & Awards:** Nat. Architectural Soc., Gold Medal Scarab 1958; 47 honorary doctorates from N. American universities 1954-80. **Important Works:** Inventor-discoverer of geodesic structures.

FUNG, HSIN-MING ■ FAAR Design Arts 92. b. May 29, 1953, Hanoi, Vietnam. m. Craig E. Hodgetts. BA 77, California State Univ., Dominguez Hills; MA 80, UCLA. **Other Study:** Oxford College, Oxford, OH 1971-73; Miami Univ., Oxford, OH 1973-74. **Career & Employment:** Charles Kober & Asscs. 1980-84; Hodgetts & Fung Design Asscs., Co-founder & Prin. 1984-present; California State Polytechnic Univ., Lect. 1985-86, Asst. Prof. 1986-90, Assc. Prof. 1990-present; Yale Univ. Saarinen Prof. 1995; Visiting critic & lect. at numerous colleges & universities. **Memberships & Offices:** Assn. of Collegiate Schools of Architecture, Design Project Jury 1989; Los Angeles Forum for Architecture & Urban Design, BoD 1991-93, Pres. 1994; Architectural Design Support Council, MOCA; Urban Design Adv. Coalition 1994. **Fellowships, Honors & Awards:** *Progressive Architecture* Citation 1984; AIA, Los Angeles Chap., Special Citation 1990, Bi-Annual Library Award 1993, Merit Award 1993, C.C. Merit Award 1993; *Architectural Record*, Interiors Award 1990; Graham Found. Grant 1992; Interior Illuminating Engineers Soc. Award 1993. **Important Works:** Franklin-La Brea Housing 1988; Near Things: Five Shrines 1988; Arts Park L.A., Los Angeles 1989; Blueprints for Modern Living, Los Angeles 1989; Visionary San Francisco 1990; Viso Residence, Hollywood 1990; Hemdale Film Corp. Facility 1990; UCLA Gateway, Westwood Village 1991; Click Talent Agency, Los Angeles 1992; UCLA Towell Library 1992; Craft & Folk Art Museum; MASH, Las Vegas. **Exhibitions/Performances:** G. A. Gallery, Tokyo 1987; Nat. Museum of Fine Arts, Buenos Aires 1987; Pacific Design Center, Los Angeles 1988; World Financial Center, NYC 1988; Artspace Gallery, Woodland Hills, CA 1989; Museum of Contemporary Arts, Los Angeles 1989;

San Francisco Museum of Modern Art 1990; Functional Art Gallery, Los Angeles 1990; Bryce Bannatyne Gallery, Los Angeles 1991; Leo Castelli-Gagosian Gallery, NYC 1992; Los Angeles City Hall 1993. **Bio-Bibliography:** "The Emerging Generation, U.S.A., *Global Architecture Houses*, Special No. 2:22-27; "Creative Trends, Wood Pulse, NY," *Axis* (Summer 1980): 12; "The Ephemerality of a Cinematic Architecture," *Architectural Review* (Dec. 1987): 59-60; "Utopia in the Suburbs," *Art in America* (Mar. 1990): 184-93; "Change in Scene," *Architectural Record* (Sept. 1990): 104-9; "Craig Hodgetts and Ming Fung, You Send Me," *Terrazzo* 4 (1990): 93-108; "Al Borde del Abismo, Residencia Viso, Hollywood,' *Monografias de Arquitectura y Vivienda* 32 (1991): 34-37; "Arts Park, Los Angeles," *L'Arca* (Sept. 1991): 40-45; "Under the Big Top," *Architectural Record* (Mar. 1993): 94-101; "Panem et Circenses," *Architecture and Urbanism* (May 1993): 9-31; "Casting Castle," *Architectural Record* (Oct. 1993): 92-95; "The I.D. Forty, Contemporary Solutions," *International Design Magazine* (Jan.-Feb. 1994): 49. **Business Address:** Hodgetts & Fung Design Asscs., 1748 Berkeley St., Santa Monica, CA 90404.

■   ■   ■

G

GABBA, EMILIO ■ Italian Fulbright Fellow 1954-55.

GACH, JAY ANTHONY ■ FAAR Musical Composition 83. b. Mar. 9, 1953, NYC. m. Ellen C. Zaehringer. PhD 82, SUNY, Stony Brook. **Research/Artistic Interests:** Computer-assisted music notation & MIDI programs, orchestration models, folk music, film music. **Career & Employment:** Independent composer. **Fellowships, Honors & Awards:** St. Paul Chamber Orchestra, American Composers Competition Winner 1985; Brooklyn Philharmonic, Frederick P. Rose 1st Prize 1988; London College of Music, Fellow 1993. **Important Works:** *Front Lines,* for large orchestra, Astral Found. of New York & Philadelphia Comm. 1985; *Il Ponentino* 1985; *Violin Duets* (16) (Presser, Merion Music) 1986; *Chants for Orchestra* 1988; *Schemes, Circuses & Roundabouts,* Fromm Found. Comm. 1992; *The Hurlers,* film music 1993; *Tattoo,* Nat. Italian Youth Orchestra Comm. 1993; *A "London" Sonata,* 3d British Contemporary Piano Competition Comm. 1994. **Bio-Bibliography:** *Strings Magazine* (July-Aug. 1991). **Home Address:** 133 Lauderdale Tower, Barbican, London EC2Y 8BY, England.

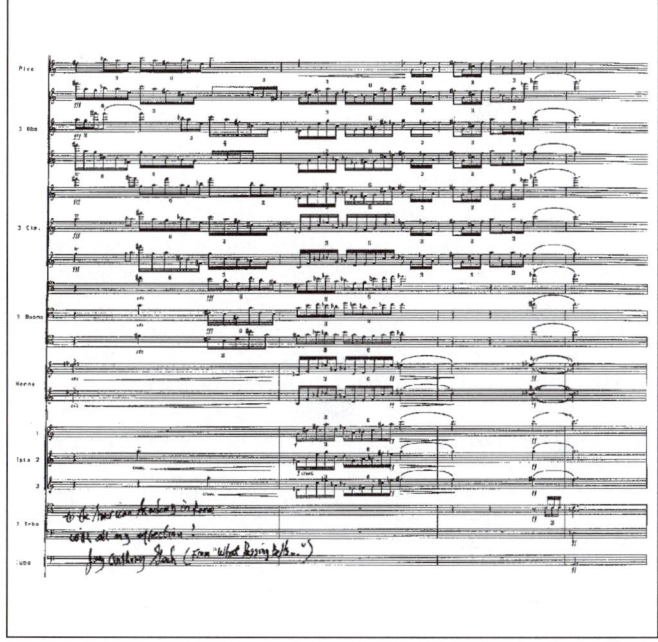

Jay Anthony Gach

GAEHDE, JOACHIM ERNEST ■ FAAR History of Art 57. b. Apr. 4, 1921, Dresden, Germany. MA 55, IFA. **Other Studies:** Univ. of Munich 1946-49. **Research/Artistic Interests:** Wall decoration in churches & palaces from the Carolingian period. **Career & Employment:** Brandeis Univ., Prof.; ANS, Medieval Numismatics Summer Seminar, Lect. 1954, 1955. **Fellowships, Honors & Awards:** ANS Fellowship 1952; Dumbarton Oaks, Junior Fellowship 1953-54; IFA Fellowship 1954-56.

GAGE, LYMAN J. ■ AAR Charter Mem.; Bank Exec.; US Treasury Dept., Sec.

GAISSER, JULIA HAIG ■ NEH Summer Seminar Dir. 1990.

GALASSO, GIUSEPPE ■ AAR Italian Com. 1994-present.

GALINSKY, KARL ■ RAAR Classics/Archaeology 73; School of Classical Studies, Adv. Council, Chair 1982-85; Classical Jury 1970-72. b. Feb. 7, 1942, Strasbourg, Alsace. m. Harriet E. Harris. c. Robert, John. BA 63, Bowdoin College; PhD 66, Princeton Univ. **Research/Artistic Interests:** Roman cvilization. **Career & Employment:** Princeton Univ., Instr. 1965-66; Univ. of Texas, Austin, Asst. Prof. 1966-68, Assc. Prof. 1968-72, Prof. 1972-present, Chair 1974-90, Centennial Prof. 1984-present; Tulane Univ., Visiting Mellon Prof. 1995. **Memberships & Offices:** VSA, BoT, VP 1972-77; NEH, Juror-Panelist 1976-present; CAMWS, Pres. 1980-81; APA, Dir. 1980-83; Mellon Fellowships in the Humanities, Regional Chair 1982-90; MLA, Assn. of Depts. of Foreign Languages, Pres. 1983. **Fellowships, Honors & Awards:** ACLS Fellow 1968-69; Univ. of Texas Teaching Excellence Award 1970, 1976; Guggenheim Fellow 1972-73; Fulbright Research Award 1972-73; APA Teaching Excellence Award 1979; Humboldt Found. Research Award 1993; NEH Fellowship 1993-94. **Publications:** *Aeneas, Sicily and Rome* (Princeton: Princeton Univ. Press, 1969); *Albii Tibulli Carmina* (Leiden: Brill, 1971); *The Herakles Theme* (Oxford: Blackwell, 1972); *Ovid's Metamorphoses* (Oxford: Blackwell, 1975); *Classical and Modern Interactions: Post-Modern Architecture, Multiculturalism, Decline and Other Issues* (Austin: Univ. of Texas Press, 1992); *The Interpretation of Roman Poetry: Empiricism or Hermeneutics* (Frankfurt & New York: Peter Lang, 1992); *Augustan Culture* (Princeton: Princeton Univ. Press, forthcoming). **Bio-Bibliography:** K. Pierce, "Summer with Horace and Virgil," *Time* (Aug. 15, 1983): 39; P. Monaghan, "Classicists Debate Strategies for Survival," *Chronicle of Higher Education* (Jan. 6, 1993); J. Griffin, "Ancient Hearts on Fire," *New York Review of Books* (June 24, 1993); *Who's Who in America.* **Home Address:** 4508 Edgemont Dr., Austin, TX 78731. **Business Address:** Dept. of Classics, Univ. of Texas, Austin, TX 78712.

GAMEL ORLANDI, MARY-KAY ■ FAAR Classics/Archaeology 69. b. Sept. 15, 1942, Springfield, MA. m. Giuseppe Orlandi. BA 63, Smith College; MA 64, Harvard Univ.; PhD 72, UC, Berkeley. **Career & Employment:** Boston Univ., Asst. Prof. 1969-73; UC, Santa Cruz, Assoc. Prof. **Memberships & Offices:** APA; Philological Assn. of Pacific Coast, Exec. Com. 1976-79; California Classical Assn., Pres. 1977-78. **Fellowships, Honors & Awards:** UC, Berkeley, Fellowship 1964-66; NEH Summer Stipend 1976. **Publications:** *Classics and Comparative Literature: A Study Guide;* "Ovid True and False in Renaissance Poetry," *Pacific Coast Philology* 13. **Bio-Bibliography:** *People* (Oct. 1975).

GANS, HERBERT J. ■ AAR Visitor 1970-71, Sociologist, Educator. b. May 7, 1927. **Career & Employment:** Univ. of Pennsylvania, Lect.-Assc. Prof. 1953-64; Columbia Univ., Prof. 1971-, Robert S. Lynd Prof. of Sociology 1985-. **Memberships & Offices:** Adv. Ed., *Urban Life* (now *Journal of Contemporary Ethnography*) 1971-. **Selected Publications:** as co-author, *The Urban Villagers* (1962); *Deciding What's News* (1979); *People, Plans and Policies* (1991).

GARDNER, MILDRED MCCONNELL ■ FAAR Classics/Archaeology 28. b. 1896. d. Dec. 11, 1942. m. Edward Markham Gardner. BA 20, Ripon College; MA 23, Univ. of Wisconsin. **Research/Artistic Interests:** Latin, Italian, French, Roman archaeology. **Career & Employment:** Winthrop College, Dept. Head 1925-26; Westover School, Middlebury, CT 1929-32; Independent Scholar, CA 1932-42. **Fellowships, Honors & Awards:** Univ. of Wisconsin, Teaching Fellowship.

GARDNER, RICHARD ■ AAR Visitor 1959 — 1964, US Ambassador to Italy.

GARNSEY, ELMER ELLSWORTH ■ AAR Charter Mem., Mural Painter.

> NIGHT MUSIC: ROME
>
> When the great grey European dark
> falls upon this city like a spell,
> the streetlights haloed, old people
> huddled in doorways, eyes alert,
> and my heart sags in its net of veins
> like a rock in a sling (for History
> is a giant here, stretches and straddles
> the dark continent) and I walk home
> and would go on tiptoes if I could,
> so as not to break anything,
> not to kiss dust from anybody's lips
> or change anything from stone to flesh,
>
> then always I see the lovers,
> the Roman lovers on the sidewalk,
> leaning together, he whispering
> and she listening, laughing, so close
> they make one perfect shadow.
> O Noah's pairs of all creation
> couldn't please me more! I hurl
> my heart into the deepest night
> and hear the astounded giant fall.
> And I rejoice. I fumble for my keys
> to open doors. I kiss my wife
> and hold my children hostage in my arms.
>
> George Garrett

George P. Garrett

GARRETT, GEORGE P. ■ FAAR Literature 59. b. June 11, 1929, Orlando, FL. m. Susan P. Jackson. c. William Palmer, George Gorham, Rosalie Alice. BA 52, Princeton Univ.; MA 57, Princeton Univ.; PhD 85, Princeton Univ. **Other Study:** Screen plays for three produced films: *The Young Lovers, The Playground, Frankenstein Meets the Space Monster*. **Research/Artistic Interests:** Fiction, poetry, film, criticism, Elizabethan history. **Career & Employment:** Wesleyan Univ., Asst. Prof. 1957-60; Univ. of Virginia, Assc. Prof. 1962-67, Prof. 1984-present; Hollins College, Prof. 1967-71; Univ. of South Carolina, Prof. 1971-74; Princeton Univ. Senior Fellow 1974-78; Univ. of Michigan, Prof. 1978-79, 1983-84. **Memberships & Offices:** *Transatlantic Review*, Poetry Ed. 1958-71; *Hollins Critic*, Co-ed. 1965-71; Associated Writing Programs, Pres. 1971-74; Fellowship of Southern Writers, Vice-Chancellor 1988-present; *Texas Review*, Fiction ed. 1986-present. **Fellowships, Honors & Awards:** *Sewanee Review*, Poetry Fellowship 1958; AAAL Fellowship 1958-59; Ford Found. Drama Grant 1960-61; NEA Grant 1966; Guggenheim Fellowship 1974; AAAL, Award in Literature 1985; Ingersoll Found., T.S. Eliot Award 1989; PEN-Malamud Award for Short Fiction 1990; Hollins College Medal 1992. **Publications:** *The Reverend Ghost* (New York: Scribner's, 1957); *King of the Mountain* (New York: Scribner's, 1958); *The Sleeping Gypsy and Other Poems* (Austin: Univ. of Texas Press, 1959); *The Finished Man* (New York: Scribner's, 1959); *Abraham's Knife and Other Poems* (Chapel Hill: UNC Press, 1961); *In the Briar Patch* (Austin: Univ. of Texas Press, 1961); *Which Ones Are the Enemy?* (Boston: Little Brown, 1961); *Sir Slob and the Princess: A Play for Children* (New York: Samuel French, 1962); *Cold Ground Was My Bed Last Night* (Columbia: Univ. of Missouri Press, 1964); *Do Lord. Remember Me*

(New York: Doubleday, 1965); *For a Bitter Season: New and Selected Poems* (Columbia: Univ. of Missouri Press, 1967); *A Wreath For Garibaldi and Other Stories* (London: Rupert Hart-Davis, 1969); *Death of the Fox* (New York: Doubleday, 1971); *The Magic Striptease* (New York: Doubleday, 1973); *Welcome to the Medicine Show* (Winston-Salem: Palaemon Press, 1978); *Luck's Shining Child* (Winston-Salem, Palaemon Press, 1981); *Enchanted Ground* (York, ME: Old Gaol Museum, 1982); *The Succession: A Novel of Elizabeth & James* (New York: Doubleday, 1983); *The Collected Poems of George Garrett* (Fayetteville: Univ. of Arkansas Press, 1984); *James Jones: A Biography* (San Diego: Harcourt Brace, 1984); *An Evening Performance* (New York: Doubleday, 1985); *Poison Pen* (Winston-Salem: Stuart Wright, 1986); *Understanding Mary Lee Settle* (Columbia: Univ. of South Carolina Press, 1988); *Entered from the Sun* (New York: Doubleday, 1990); *The Sorrows of Fat City* (Columbia, SC: Univ. of South Carolina Press, 1992); *Whistling in the Dark* (New York: Harcourt Brace Jovanovich, 1992). **Bio-Bibliography:** Stuart Wright, *George Garrett: A Bibliography, 1947-88* (Huntsville: Texas Review Press, 1989); R.H.W. Dillard, *Understanding George Garrett* (Columbia: Univ. of South Carolina Press, 1988); *Contemporary Literary Criticism; Contemporary Poets; Contemporary Novelists; Dictionary of Literary Biography; Who's Who in America; Who's Who in the World; Who's Who in Writers, Editors and Poets*. **Home Address:** 1845 Wayside Pl., Charlottesville, VA 22903.

GASPERINI, LIDIO ■ Italian Fulbright Fellow 1959-60.

GAVIN, FRANK ■ G.I. Resident 1945-47, Singer.

GAZDA, ELAINE K. ■ AAR Trustee, 1994-present; Adv. Council to Com. on School of Classical Studies 1975-present; Classical Studies Juror 1982-83; Classical Soc. 1974-present, Pres. 1989-90, Exec. Com.; Com. on the Constitution 1992-present; Excavation Team for Harbor of Cosa 1971-87; NEH Summer Seminar Leader 1994. b. Apr. 27, 1943, Scranton, PA. m. James H. McIntosh. c. Karina McIntosh. BA 64, Marietta College; MA 66, Univ. of Pennsylvania; PhD 71, Harvard Univ. **Research/Artistic Interests:** Roman art & archaeology with emphasis on Roman sculpture, painting, & building techniques; Etruscan art & archaeology, Hellenistic sculpture; Egyptian art of the Graeco-Roman period. **Career & Employment:** Univ. of Southern California, Asst. Prof. 1971-74; Univ. of Michigan, Asst. Prof & Asst. Curator 1974-78, Assc. Prof & Assc. Curator 1978-88, Prof. & Curator 1988-present; Kelsey Museum, Assc. Dir. 1981-86, Dir. 1986-present. **Business Address:** Kelsey Museum of Archaeology, Univ. of Michigan, Ann Arbor, MI 48109.

GEBHARD, ELIZABETH R. ■ AAR Visitor 1980-81, Classicist, Archaeologist, Educator. **Career & Employment:** Univ. of Illinois, Prof. Established the Oscar Broneer Fellowship, supported by funds from the Luther I. Replogle Found., which enables Fellows of the Academy or of the ASCSA to spend an additional year at the other institution.

GEFFCKEN, KATHERINE A. ■ FAAR Classics/Archaeology 55; School of Classical Studies Adv. Council 1966-present; Sec. 1976, 1979; Exec Com. 1980-82; Chair of Nominating Com. 1982, Adv. Council Rep. on AAR BoT 1992-95; Classical Jury 1971-73; Classical Soc., VP 1968-69; Pres. 1970; SOF, VP 1973-79; Summer Session, Dir. 1980-82, 1991. b. July 24, 1927, Atlanta, GA. BA 49, Agnes Scott College; MA 52, Bryn Mawr College; PhD 62, Bryn Mawr College. **Research/Artistic Interests:** Classical comedy, oratory, Latinity, topography; American scholars in Italy, particularly women scholars & the American experience in Italy; numismatics, especially Roman coinage; the 1849 Revolution in Italy; topography of the Janiculum. **Career & Employment:** Kemper Hall, Kenosha, WI, Faculty 1949-51; Bryn Mawr College, Asst. Dean 1955-58, 1959-61, 1962-63; Wellesley College, Lect. 1963-64, Asst. Prof. 1964-69, Assc. Prof. 1969-75, Prof. 1975-present, Chair for 4 terms. **Memberships & Offices:** ICCS, Prof.-in-Charge 1977-78; Agnes Scott College, BoT 1975-present; VSA, BoT 1977-80, Pres. 1985-87, Exec. Com. 1983-89; APA, Dir. 1979-81; *Classical Journal*, New England Ed. 1968-76; referee for several scholarly journals over the years, also referee for other granting agencies like NEH. **Fellowships, Honors & Awards:** Fulbright Fellowship to Italy 1954-55. **Publications:** *Comedy in the* Pro Caelio, *with an Appendix on the* In Clodium et Curionem (Leiden: Brill, 1973); "June 3, 1849 and Angelo Masina," *Newsletter of the Classical Society of the AAR* (1988): 7-9; "June 29-30, 1849, Morosini, and Casino Malvasia," *Newsletter of the Classical Society of the AAR* (1989): 15-18; "June 26, 1849, Anita Garibaldi and the Villa Spada," *Newsletter of the Classical Society of the AAR* (1990): 15-18; "Days before the Janiculum: The Early Classical School 1895-1914," *Newsletter of the Classical Society of the AAR* (1991); contr. to Karin Einaudi, *Esther B. Van Deman: Images from the Archive of an American Archaeologist in Italy at the Turn of the Century* (Rome: AAR, 1991); "Who Were the Fratelli Bonnet?" *Newsletter of the Classical Society of the AAR* (1993): 15-17. **Business Address:** Depts. of Greek & Latin, Wellesley College, 106 Central St., Wellesley, MA 02181.

GEHL, PAUL FRANCIS ■ FAAR Post-Classical/Humanistic Studies 78. b. Sept. 24, 1949, West Bend, WI. BA 71, John Carroll Univ.; MA 72, Univ. of Chicago; PhD 76, Univ. of Chicago. **Career & Employment:** Newberry Library, John M. Wing Found., Custodian 1988-present. **Fellowships, Honors & Awards:** Univ. of Chicago, Special Humanities Fellowship 1971-74.

GEHRY, FRANK O. ■ AAR Trustee 1990-94, Trustee Emer.; Architect.

GELDMAN, STEPHEN S. ■ FAAR Painting 80. b. Apr. 27, 1945, Fullerton, CA. m. Judith Dancoff. BFA 70, California State Univ.; MFA 74, UC, Irvine. **Exhibitions/Performances:** Fine Arts Museum of San Francisco 1977; Space Gallery, Los Angeles 1977, 1978; Lester Gallery, Inverness, CA 1978.

GELLER, MATTHEW ■ FAAR Painting 92. b. Sept. 28, 1954, NYC. m. Andrea Callard. c. Callard Luke. BA 76, Connecticut College; MFA 78, Univ. of Delaware. **Career & Employment:** LINE Assn., Co-Dir. 1981-83; NYSCA, TV-Media Panel, Panelist 1985-87, Co-Chair 1986-88; Inst. for Art & Urban Resources, Video Curator 1986-88. **Fellowships, Honors & Awards:** FIVF Donor Advised Fund, NEA, Jerome Found., NY Media Alliance, Corp. for Public Broadcasting, NYFA, WNET-WGBH (PBS)-"New Television," NYSCA, Beard's Fund, LINE Asscs., ZBS Media; Nat. Education Film & Video Festival, Houston Film Festival, Sinking Creek Film Festival, Humboldt Film Festival, Philadelphia Film Festival, Chicago Film Festival, Video Culture Intl. Festival, San Mateo Film Festival, Columbus Film & Video Festival, Marin County Film Festival, Atlanta Film & Video Festival, Wadsworth Video Festival, US Film & Video Festival. **Publications:** *1983 Engagements* (Works Press, 1982); *From Receiver to Remote Control: The TV Set, New Museum* (1990); *The Television Set* (1991). **Exhibitions/Performances:** San Francisco Museum of Art & 6 other cities 1980; Museum del Barrio 1982; Jack Tilton Gallery 1983; 911, Seattle 1985; Home Box Office 1986; Queens Museum 1986; The New Museum,

NYC 1986, 1990; Franklin Furnace, NYC 1990; Art Gallery of Hamilton 1990. **Bio-Bibliography:** George Mannes, "Box Populi," *Video Review* (1990).

GELSTHARP, ALFRED, JR. ■ FAAR Classics/Archaeology 33. b. Oct. 20, 1906, Manchester, England. d. 1971. BA 28, Amherst College; MA 29, Princeton Univ. **Research/Artistic Interests:** Early development of the Roman theater, Latin historiography, Roman epigraphy, religion of ancient Rome, German, French. **Career & Employment:** Christ School, Arden, NC, Faculty 1933-35; Hillsdale College, Assc. Prof 1935-36; Independent Scholar, Springfield, MA. **Fellowships, Honors & Awards:** Princeton Univ., Page Fellowship 1929-30, Proctor Fellowship 1930-31.

GENDEL, MILTON ■ AAR Visitor 1980-81, European Correspondent for *ArtNews*.

GENTNER, PHILIP J. ■ FASCSR 07. b. Sept. 9, 1871, Wilkesbarre, PA. d. Oct. 20, 1941. BA 1898, Harvard Univ.; MA 1899, Harvard Univ. **Career & Employment:** Indiana 1899-1900; Harvard Univ. Asst. 1900-1902; Univ. of Wisconsin, Instr. 1904-5; Art Dealer, Florence, 1910-41. **Publications:** ed., *Pope: The Iliad of Homer. Books I, VI, XXII and XXIV* (Boston: H. Sanborn, 1899). **Bio-Bibliography:** Harvard Univ. Archives.

GHIRADO, DIANE Y. ■ FAAR History of Art 87. b. July 14, 1950, Missoula, MT. m. Ferruccio Trabalzi. c. Rachel Van Cleave, Christopher Van Cleave. BA 73, San Jose State Univ.; MA 76, Stanford Univ.; PhD 82, Stanford Univ. **Research/Artistic Interests:** 20th-century Italian architecture, especially the Fascist period; contemporary architecture. **Career & Employment:** Stanford Univ., Lect. 1979-83; Texas A & M Univ., Asst. Prof. 1983-84; Univ. of Southern California, Prof. 1984-present. **Memberships & Offices:** *Journal of Architectural Education*, Ed. 1987-94; Assn. of Collegiate Schools of Architecture, VP 1993-94, Pres. 1994-95. **Fellowships, Honors & Awards:** Danforth Found. Fellowship 1974-78; Fulbright Fellowship 1976-77. **Publications:** "Italian Architects and Fascist Politics: The Rationalist's Role in Regime Building," *JSAH* 39 (May 1980): 109-27; "Politics of a Masterpiece: The Vicenda of the Facade Decoration, The Casa del Fascio, Como," *Art Bulletin* 62 (Sept. 1980): 466-78; "New Deal, New City," *Modulus* 16 (1983): 16-29; with Kurt Forster, "Modelli delle Città di Nuova Fondazione in Età Fascista," in Cesare de Seta, ed., *Annali di Storia d'Italia* 8 (1985): 627-74; "Architecture and Theater: The Street in Fascist Italy," in *Event Arts and Art Events*, ed. S. Foster (Ann Arbor: Univ. of Michigan Research Press, 1987), 175-99; *Building New Communities: New Deal America and Fascist Italy* (Princeton: Princeton Univ. Press, 1989); "Deceit of Post-Modern Architecture," in *After the Future*, ed. G. Shapiro (Albany: SUNY Press, 1990), 231-52; "City and Theater: The Rhetoric of Fascist Architecture," *Stanford Italian Review* 61 (1990): 165-94; "Politik und Architektur im Faschistischen Italien," in *Giuseppe Terragni 1904-43: Moderne und Faschismus in Italien*, ed. S. Germer & A. Preiss (Munich: Klinkhardt & Biermann, 1991), 39-55; "From Reality to Myth: Italian Fascist Architecture in Rome," *Modulus* 21 (1991): 10-33; "Theater of Shadows," in *Aldo Rossi 1980-1990*, ed. M. Adjmi (New York: Princeton Architectural Press, 1991), 10-15; ed., *Out of Site: A Social Criticism of Architecture* (Seattle: Bay Press, 1991); "Architects, Exhibitions and the Politics of Culture in Fascist Italy," *Journal of Architectural Education* 45 (1992): 67-75; *Mark Mack* (Wasmuth Verlag, 1994); *Architecture after Modernism* (London: Thames & Hudson, 1995). **Home Address:** 1223 Wilshire Blvd., No. 500, Santa Monica,

CA 90403. **Business Address:** School of Architecture, Watt 203, Univ. of Southern California, Los Angeles, CA 90089.

GIANNINI, VITTORIO ■ FAAR Musical Composition 36. b. Oct. 19, 1903, Philadelphia, PA. d. Nov. 28, 1966. m. Lucia Avella, Joan Adler. Royal Conservatory of Milan, Italy 1913-17; with Hans Letz & Rubin Goldmark at Juilliard Graduate School 1925-31. **Career & Employment:** Juilliard School of Music, Faculty 1939-64; Manhattan School of Music 1941-56; Curtis Inst. of Music 1956; North Carolina School of the Arts, Winston-Salem, Founding Com., Pres. 1964-66. **Memberships & Offices:** ASCAP, Dir. **Fellowships, Honors & Awards:** American Musical Found. Prize; Juilliard School of Music, Fellowship (2); Intl. Inst. for Arts & Letters, Fellow. **Important Works:** *Lucieda*, an opera 1934; *In Memoriam, Theodore Roosevelt*, a symphony 1935; *The Scarlet Letter*, an opera 1938; *Beauty and the Beast*, an opera, CBS Comm. 1938; *Blennerhasset*, an opera, CBS Comm. 1939; *The Taming of the Shrew*, an opera 1953; *Canticle of the Martyrs*, choral work, Moravian Church Comm. 1957; *The Medead*, for soprano & orchestra 1960; *The Harvest*, an opera 1961; *Rehearsal Call*, opera buffa 1962; *Psalm 130*, concerto for double bass & orchestra 1963; *The Servant of Two Masters*, an opera 1967; plus numerous songs, miscellaneous orchestral works, and film scores. **Bio-Bibliography:** *Baker's Biographical Dictionary of Musicians, New Grove Dictionary of American Music, Who Was Who in America.*

GIBBES, CATHERINE SPOTSWOOD ■ FAAR Classics/Archaeology 76; Summer School 1973. b. Oct. 28, 1950, Albemarle County, VA. BA 72, Randolph-Macon Woman's College; MA 73, Bryn Mawr College; PhD 78, Bryn Mawr College; ALM 82, Middlebury College. **Other Study:** Hebrew College, Brookline, MA, Certificate 1991; Goethe Inst., Boston, German; Longy School of Music, Cambridge, MA; Museum of Science Library, Boston. **Research/Artistic Interests:** Artificial intelligence, linguistics, international trade. **Career & Employment:** MIT, Research Librarian-Lect. 1980-83; Postdoctoral researcher, editor, translator, consultant 1983-present; Hebrew College, Brookline, MA, Library 1988-present. **Memberships & Offices:** American Inst. for Biosocial Research, Ed. Bd. of Journal 1981-82; Intl. Jewish Vegetarian Soc., Life Mem. **Fellowships, Honors & Awards:** Phi Beta Kappa, Delta of Virginia 1972; Bryn Mawr College Scholar & Fellow 1972-75; ANS, Dissertation Fellowship 1976; Harvard Univ., Visiting Postdoc. Fellowship 1978. **Home Address:** 1622 Rose Hill Dr., Charlottesville, VA 22903. **Business Address:** Hebrew College, 43 Hawes St., Brookline, MA 02146.

GIBBS, (THEODORE) HARRISON ■ FAAR Sculpture 38. b. Sept. 24, 1908, Rosemont, PA. d. Dec. 26, 1944. m. Maurine Montgomery. c. Ramona. PAFA; Cranbrook Acad. of Art. **Career & Employment:** Cornell Univ., Instr. 1938-41; US Army 1943-44. **Fellowships, Honors & Awards:** Stimson Prize 1933; Cresson Foreign Traveling Scholarship 1934; PAFA, Posthumous 1945. **Important Works:** Sculpture: US Post Office, Dundalk, MD. **Bio-Bibliography:** *Who Was Who in American Art.*

GIEDION, SIGFRIED ■ RAAR History of Art 66. b. Apr. 14, 1893, Longran, Switzerland. d. Apr. 1968. m. Carola Welcher. c. Verena, Andreas. PhD 22, Univ. of Munich. **Career & Employment:** Harvard Univ., Charles Eliot Norton Prof. 1938-39; Federal Inst. of Tech., Switzerland, Prof. 1947-58; NGA, Mellow Lect. 1957. **Publications:** *Spatbarocker und romantischer Klassizismus* (Munich: F. Bruckmann, 1922); *Walter Gropius* (Paris, 1931); *Space, Time and Architecture: The Growth of a New*

Tradition (Cambridge, MA: Harvard Univ. Press, 1941); *Mechanization Takes Command* (New York: Oxford Univ. Press, 1948); *Walter Gropius: Work and Teamwork* (London: Architectural Press, 1954); *Architecture, You and Me: The Diary of a Development* (Cambridge, MA: Harvard Univ. Press, 1958); *The Eternal Present: The Beginnings of Art*, 2 vols. (New York: Pantheon, 1962); *Beginnings of Art* (1962); *Architecture and the Phenomena of Transition* (Cambridge, MA: Harvard Univ. Press, 1971); *The Beginning of Architecture* (Princeton: Princeton Univ. Press, 1981). **Bio-Bibliography:** *Homage to Giedion* (Basel: Birkhauser, 1971); S. Georgiadis, *Sigfried Giedion: An Intellectual Biography* (Edinburgh: Edinburgh Univ. Press, 1992); *Who Was Who in America.*

GILBERT, CASS ■ AAR Charter Mem., Trustee 1911-19, Architect.

GILDER, RICHARD WATSON ■ AAR Charter Mem., Trustee, Editor.

GILL, KATHERINE J. ■ FAAR Post-Classical/Humanistic Studies 88. m. David Gillerman, FAAR 88. c. Roland. MA 83, Harvard Divinity School; PhD 94, Princeton Univ. **Other Study:** Gregorian Univ., Rome, Schola Superior Litterarum Latinarum 1982-84; Scuola de Paleografia, Diplomatica e Archivistica, Vatican City 1982-84; Harvard Univ. 1990-91. **Career & Employment:** Vatican Archives Project, Project Historian 1989-94; Yale Univ. Divinity School, Asst. Prof. 1992-94. **Fellowships, Honors & Awards:** Andrew W. Mellon Fellowship 1987; Woodrow Wilson Research Grant 1987; Social Science Research Council & ACLS Fellowship 1987-89. **Publications:** "Open Monasteries for Women in Late Medieval and Early Modern Italy: Two Roman Examples," in *The Crannied Wall: Women, Religion and the Arts in Early Modern Europe*, ed. Craig Monson (Ann Arbor: Univ. of Michigan Press, 1992); "*Scandala*: Controversies Concerning Clausura and Women's Religious Communities in Late Medieval Italy," in *Christendom and its Discontents: Exclusion, Persecution & Rebellion 1000-1500*, ed. Scott Waugh & Peter Diehl (New York: Cambridge Univ. Press, forthcoming); "Women & the Production of Religious Texts in the Vernacular," in *Creative Women in Medieval and Early Modern Italy*, ed. John Coakley & Ann Matter (Philadelphia: Univ. of Pennsylvania Press, forthcoming). **Home Address:** PO Box 2340, New Haven, CT 06520. **Business Address:** Yale Divinity School, 409 Prospect St., New Haven, CT 06511.

GILLERMAN, DAVID M. ■ FAAR History of Art 88. b. Aug. 24, 1953, Newton, MA. m. Katherine J. Gill, FAAR 88. c. Roland. BA 76, Sarah Lawrence College; PhD 87, IFA. **Research/Artistic Interests:** History of Italian art & architecture, 13th-16th centuries. **Career & Employment:** Loyola Univ. of Chicago, Rome, Instr. 1983; New Jersey Inst. of Technology 1985-87; Providence College, Asst. Prof. 1989-95. **Fellowships, Honors & Awards:** IFA, Robert H. Lehman Fellow 1979-82, Benjamin Sonnenberg Fellow 1982-83, Bernard Berenson Fellow 1983-84; NGA, Chester Dale Fellowship 1984-85; J. Paul Getty Fellowship 1988-89; SAH, Founders Award 1989. **Publications:** "La facciata: introduzione al rapporto tra scultura e architettura," in *Il Duomo di Orvieto*, ed. Lucio Ricetti (Rome & Bari: Laterza, 1988); "S. Fortunato in Todi: Why the Hall Church?," *JSAH* 48 (1989): 158-171; "S. Domenico in Orvieto: the Date of Construction," *Saggi in onore di Renato Bonelli*, 2 vols., ed. Corrado Bozzoni, Giovanni Carbonara, Garbriella Villetti, *Quaderni dell'Istituto di Storia dell'Architettura* 15-20 (Rome: ISA, 1992), 1:181-86; "The Evolution of the Design of Orvieto Cathedral," *JSAH* 53 (1994): 300-21. **Home Address:** PO Box 2340, New Haven, CT 06520.

GILLESPIE, GREGORY J. ■ FAAR Painting 67. b. Nov. 29, 1936, Elizabeth, NJ. m. Peggy Gillespie. c. Vincent, Lydia, Julianna. BFA 62, San Francisco Art Inst.; MFA 62, San Francisco Art Inst. **Other Study:** Cooper Union, NYC 1954-60. **Fellowships, Honors & Awards:** Fulbright Grant; Chester Dale Fellowship 1963, 1965, 1966; Louis Comfort Tuffany Found. Grant 1967. **Important Works:** Public collections: Arkansas Art Center, Little Rock; Bowdoin College Museum of Art, Brunswick, ME; Creative Arts Center, West Virginia Univ., Morgantown; Georgia Museum of Art, Athens; Hirshhorn Museum & Sculpture Garden, Washington, DC; MMA; Nat. Museum of American Art, Washington, DC; Nebraska Art. Assn., Woods Memorial Collection, Lincoln; New Jersey State Museum, Trenton; Palmer Museum of Art, Pennsylvania State Univ., University Park; San Diego Museum of Contemporary Art; Sara Roby Found. Collection, NYC; Virginia Mueum of Fine Arts, Richmond; Weatherspoon Art Gallery, UNC, Greensboro; Whitney Museum, NYC; Wichita Art Museum. **Exhibitions/Performances:** Solo: Forum Gallery, NYC 1966, 1968, 1970, 1972, 1973, 1976, 1977, 1979, 1982, 1984, 1986, 1989, 1991, 1992, 1993-94; Georgia Museum of Art, Athens 1970; Alpha Gallery, Boston 1971, 1974, 1982, 1986; Smith College Museum of Art, Northampton, MA 1971; Galleria il Fante di Spade, Rome & Milan 1974; Retrospective, Hirshhorn Museum & Sculpture Garden, Washington, DC 1977; Berggruen Gallery, San Francisco 1983; J. & M. Muscarelle Museum, College of William & Mary, Williamsburg, VA 1983; Duke Univ. Art Museum, Durham, NC 1986; Atrium Gallery, Univ. of Connecticut, Storrs 1986; J. Rosenthal Fine Arts, Chicago 1988; Cooper Union, NYC 1989; Nielsen Gallery, Boston 1990, 1992; Harcourts Modern & Contemporary, San Francisco 1992; plus numerous two-person & group exhibits 1961-present. **Bio-Bibliography:** numerous exb. cats. **Home Address:** 715 Federal St., Belchertown, MA 01007.

GILLETTE, FRANK ■ RAAR Sculpture 85.

GILLIARD, FRANK D. ■ FAAR Post-Classical/Humanistic Studies 65. b. Feb. 12, 1937, Jacksonville, FL. BA 57, Univ. of Flordia, Gainesville; MA 61, UC, Berkeley; PhD 66, UC, Berkeley. **Research/Artistic Interests:** Roman Empire, early Christianity. **Career & Employment:** California State Univ., Hayward, Prof. 1966-present. **Publications:** "Notes on the Coinage of Julian the Apostate," *Journal of Roman Studies* 54 (1964): 135-41; "Theodoret, *historia ecclesiastica* 4.9.5," *Byzantinische Zeitschrift* 63 (1970): 283-84; "Teleological Development in the *Athenaion Politeia*," *Historia* 20 (1971): 430-35; "The Birth Date of Julian the Apostate," *California Studies in Classical Antiquity* 4 (1971): 147-51; "Chaucer's Attitude Toward Astrology," *Journal of the Warburg Institute* 36 (1973): 365-66; "The Apostolicity of Gallic Churches," *Harvard Theological Review* 68 (1975): 17-33; "The Senators of Sixth-Century Gaul," *Speculum* 54 (1979): 685-97; "Senatorial Bishops in the Fourth Century," *Harvard Theological Review* 77 (1984): 153-75; "The Problem of the Antisemitic Comma between 1 Thessalonians 2:14 and 15," *New Testament Studies* (1989): 481-502; "More Silent Reading in Antiquity: *Non omne verbum sonabat*," *Journal of Biblical Literature* 112 (1993): 689-94; "Paul and the Killing of the Prophets in 1 Thess. 2:15," *Novum Testamentum* 36 (1994): 259-70. **Home Address:** 2652 Shasta Rd., Berkeley, CA 94708.

GILMAN, DANIEL COIT ■ AAR Charter Mem.; Carnegie Inst., Pres.; Johns Hopkins Univ., Pres.

GINSBURG, JUDITH R. ■ FAAR Classics/Archaeology 76; Classical Juror 1991-93, Adv. Council 1980-present. b. Oct. 18, 1944, Omaha, NE. BA 66, UC, Berkeley; MA 67, UC, Berkeley; PhD 77, UC, Berkeley. **Research/Artistic Interests:** Roman social history, representations of women in classical antiquity. **Career & Employment:** UC, Berkeley, Acting Instr. 1973-74; Cornell Univ., Asst. Prof. 1976-83, Assc. Prof. 1984-present; Univ. of Maryland, Visiting Assc. Prof. 1991. **Memberships & Offices:** APA, Chair of Com. on Status of Women & Minority Groups 1985-87, Com. on Professional Ethics 1987-89, Com. on Professional Matters 1991-93. **Fellowships, Honors & Awards:** AAUW Fellowship 1984-85. **Publications:** *Tradition and Theme in the Annals of Tacitus* (New York: Arno Press, 1981; rpt. ed. Salem, NH: Ayer Co., 1984); "Nero's Consular Policy," *American Journal of Ancient History* 6 (1982): 51-68; "Speech and Allusion in Tacitus, *Annals* 3.49-51 and 14.48-48," *American Journal of Philology* 107 (1986): 525-41; "*In maiores certamina:* Past and Present in the *Annals*," in *Tacitus and the Tacitean Tradition,* ed. T.J. Luce and A.J. Woodman (Princeton: Princeton Univ. Press, 1993), 86-103. **Business Address:** Dept. of Classics, Cornell Univ., Ithaca, NY 14853.

GINZEL, ANDREW H. ■ FAAR Visual Arts 94. b. July 14, 1954, Chicago, IL. m. Kristin A. Jones, FAAR 94. Bennington College 1972-74; SUNY 1978-81. **Other Study:** My education is based primarily on experience during the years 1973-83 assisting established sculptors in New York, throughout the United States & Europe. In addition, I have taken extensive research trips to Asia, North Africa, India & Asia Minor. **Research/Artistic Interests:** I work in collaboration with Kristin Jones. Our work evolves from a fascination of dynamic opposites. We are concerned with the definition & interrelationships of polarities. We attempt to build seductive, contemplative work which challenges perception while endowed with a sense of reverence for the larger mysteries. Working with a range of evocative elements that propose concurrent realities, we attempt to present the drama & the extreme fragility of equilibrium. Both empirical & intuitive elements bring into question the tangibility of time. **Career & Employment:** Oxbow Summer School of Art, Saugatuck, MI 1976-82; Cooper Union, Lect. 1982-86; School of Visual Arts 1985-present; numerous visiting positions. **Fellowships, Honors & Awards:** Artists Grant, Artists Space, NYC 1985; NYSCA Award 1986; NEA Fellowship 1986; The Bessie, New York Dance & Performance Award 1986; Yaddo, Fellowship 1987; NYFA Fellowship 1987; Mass. Council on the Arts & Humanities, New Works Program Grant 1988; Art Comm. of the City of New York, Award for Excellence in Design 1989; NEA Grant 1989, 1991, Scholarship 1994; MacDowell Colony Fellowship 1989, 1991, 1993; Indo-American Fellowship, Council for Intl. Exchange of Scholars 1990; Louis Comfort Tiffany Found. Award 1991; American Center Paris, Cité Intl. des Arts, Residency 1993-94; Pollock-Krasner Found 1994. **Important Works:** *Moribus (Cruxis)*, Museo d'Arte Contemporanea Permanent Collection Comm., Prato 1988; *Analemma*, Wadsworth Atheneum, Hartford, CT 1988; *Field and Figures*, for Merce Cunningham Dance Co., NYC 1989; *Mnemonics*, Battery Park City, NYC 1989-92; *Atol*, Univ. Art Museum, UC, Santa Barbara 1990; *Principia*, Oregon Convention Center, Portland 1990; *Diaxiom*, Commerce Sq. One, I.M. Pei & Partners, Philadelphia 1991; *Plethora*, 7th Triennale, India, USIS, New Dehli 1991; *Soundings*, Pennsylvania Convention Center, Philadelphia 1994; Permanent Collections: Brooklyn Museum; Centro per l'Arte Contemporanea Luigi Pecci, Prato, Italy; Kunsthalle Basel; Wadsworth Atheneum. **Bio-Bibliography:** Douglas C. McGill, "Art People: Collaborators Depict Nature,"

NY Times (Nov. 21, 1986): C33; *Tyiptych* (New York: New Museum of Contemporary Art, 1987); Margot Crutchfield, *Installations*, exb. cat. (Richmond: Virginia Museum of Fine Arts, 1987); Andrea Miller-Keller, *Matrix 99*, exb. cat. (Hartford, CT: Wadsworth Atheneum 1988); Pam Lambert, "Art: The World According to Jones-Ginzel," *Wall Street Journal* (June 15, 1989): 11A; Dmitri L. Coromilas, "Kristin Jones + Andrew Ginzel: *Antithesis*," *Tehni/Art* 1.1 (Nov. 28, 1989): 14-15, 38-39; Jim Jenkins & Dave Quick, *Motion-Motion Kinetic Art* (Salt Lake City: Gibbs Smith Publishers, 1989), 54-57; Thomas Kellein & Patricia C. Phillips, *Antithesis*, exb. cat. (Basel: Kunsthalle Basel, 1989); Thomas Kellein, "Jones + Ginzel: Künstler-paare," *Kunstforum International* (Mar.-Apr. 1990): 178-80; Phyllis I. Freeman, *New Art* (New York: Abrams, 1990), 97; "Plethora: A Project for Artforum," *Artforum* 29.9 (May 1991), 128; Andy Lansett, "Public Art," Nat. Public Radio, Weekend Edition (Sept. 1992). **Home Address:** 289 Bleecker St., NYC 10014.

GIORDANO, JEANNE M. ■ FAAR Design Arts 87. b. Sept. 21, 1947, Philadelphia, PA. BA 69, Rosemont College. **Other Study:** Harvard GSD 1979-80; Salzburg Seminars in Planning & Design 1980. **Research/Artistic Interests:** The use of public space internationally & public buildings, such as markets & train stations. **Career & Employment:** City of Philadelphia, City Planner 1970-75; Salem, OR, Dir. of Development 1975-79; Carley Group, Philadelphia Office, Dir. 1981-84; Rouse & Asscs., Project Dir. 1984-86; Private Consultant, Design & Development 1988; New York City MTA, Grand Central Terminal Development Office, Dir. 1989-present. **Memberships & Offices:** Found. for Architecture, Philadelphia, BoT 1982-86; Philadelphia Festival of New Plays, Found. for Architecture, BoD 1983-86; American Theatre Festival, BoD 1985-86; Philadelphia Chamber of Commerce, Arts & Cultural Council, BoD 1985-86; ALNY; Municipal Arts Council; Harvard GSD, Alumni Council. **Fellowships, Honors & Awards:** NEA Grant 1979; Harvard GSD, Loeb Fellow 1980. **Business Address:** 341 Madison Ave., NYC 10017.

GITHENS, A. M. ■ Stewardson Memorial Scholar 1911-12, 1913.

GIULIANI, FULVIO CAIROLI ■ Italian Fulbright Fellow 1967-68.

GIURGOLA, ROMALDO ■ RAAR Architecture 78; AAR Trustee 1978-89, Trustee Emer. 1990-present; Com. on School of Fine Arts 1978; Nominating Com. 1980; Com. on Plant & Planning 1980-88. b. Sept. 2, 1920, Rome, Italy. m. Adelaide F. Bercivenga. c. Paola. Laurea in Arch. 48, Univ. of Rome; MSArch 51, Columbia Univ. **Career & Employment:** Giurgola & Dallolio, Rome, Italy, Part. 1948-50; Mitchell-Giurgola Architects, Philadelphia, Part. 1958-88; Mitchell-Giurgola Architects, NYC, Part. 1958-91; Mitchell-Giurgola & Thorp Architects, Canberra, Australia, Part. 1980-present; Cornell Univ., Asst. Prof. 1952-54; Univ. of Pennsylvania, Prof. 1954-67; Columbia Univ., Dept. of Architecture, Chair 1967-72, Ware Prof. 1972-91. **Memberships & Offices:** AIA Fellow 1975-present; AAAL 1977-present; Accademia Nazionale di San Luca, Rome 1980-present; Royal Australian Inst. of Architects, Fellow 1983-present. **Fellowships, Honors & Awards:** NIAL, Arnold Brunner Award in Architecture 1966; AIA Gold Medal 1982; Univ. of Virginia, Thomas Jefferson Medal in Architecture 1987; Royal Australian Inst. of Architects, Gold Medal 1988; Assn. of Collegiate Schools of Architecture, Distinguished Prof. Award 1988; Commonwealth of Australia, Hon. Officer (AO) in the Order of Australia 1989. **Publications:** "Architecture in

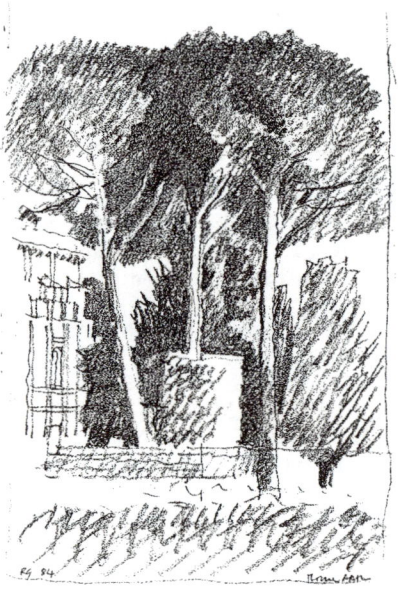

Romaldo Giurgola

Change," *Journal of Architectural Education* 17 (Nov.-Dec. 1962): 104-6; "Reflections on Buildings and the City: The Realism of the Partial Vision," *Perspecta* 9-10 (1965): 107-30; "A Propos de Louis Kahn," *L'Architecture d'Aujourd'hui* (Feb.-Mar. 1969): 4-5; " Discreet Charm of the Bourgeoisie," *Architectural Forum* (May 1973): 56-57; with Jaimini Mehta, *Louis I. Kahn* (Zurich: Verlag für Architektur & Boulder: Westview Press, 1975); *Roma Interrotta* (Rome: Incontri Internationali d'Arte, 1979), 118-28; "Utzon, Jørn," in *Contemporary Architects* (New York: St. Martin's Press, 1980), 829-31; "Notes on Architecture and Morality," *Precis* 2 (1980): 51-52; "Notes on Buildings and Their Parts," *Harvard Architectural Review* (Spring 1981): 172-75; with Pamille Berg, "Kahn, Louis I.," *Macmillan Encyclopedia of Architects* (New York: Macmillan), 2:537-46; "Reflections on the Order of the City and the Order of the Land," *Architect (Melbourne)* (Dec. 1983): 8-9; with Ehrman B. Mitchell, *Mitchell/Giurgola Architects* (New York: Rizzoli, 1983). **Important Works:** Wright Brothers Memorial Visitor Center, Nat. Park Service, Kill Devil Hills, NC 1960; AIA Nat. HQ, Washington, DC, project 1965; United Fund HQ, Philadelphia 1975; Liberty Bell Pavilion, Philadelphia 1975; Tredyffrin Public Library, Tredyffrin Township, Strafford, PA 1976; Sherman Fairchild Center for the Life Sciences, Columbia Univ. 1977; Wainwright State Office Complex, St. Louis 1981; AB Volvo Corp. HQ, Gothenburg, Sweden 1984; Parliament House, Canberra, Australia 1988; St. Thomas Aquinas Parish Church, Canberra, Australia 1989; IBM Advanced Business Inst., Palisades, NY 1990; IBM Westlake Park Phase I, Office-Parking Complex, Solana, TX 1990. **Exhibitions/Performances:** "200 Years of American Architectural Drawing," American Federation of Arts, travelling exb. 1977-78; Drawing Center, NYC 1977; "Roma Interrotta," Markets of Trajan, Rome, Italy 1978; Walker Art Center, Minneapolis 1980; "Parliament House Competition, Canberra, Australia," ALNY 1980; Max Protetch Gallery, NYC 1981; Whitney Museum, NYC 1982; Temple Hoyne Buell Center, Columbia Univ. 1983; "Honor and Intimacy: Architectural Drawings 1907-1983," AIA travelling exb. 1984-85; Meyerson Hall Galleries, Univ. of Pennsylvania 1991. **Bio-Bibliography:** Lamia Doumato, *The Firm of Mitchell/Giurgola 1958* (Monticello,

IL, 1980); Robert B. Harmon, "The Architecture of Reality in the Work of Romaldo Giurgola: A Selected Bibliography," in Ehrman B. Mitchell & Romaldo Giurgola, *Mitchell/Giurgola Architects* (New York: Rizzoli, 1983), 261-67; *Contemporary Architects*; *International Dictionary of Architects and Architecture*. **Home Address:** 23/9 Jardine St., Kinsgton, ACT 2604, Australia.

GLANDRA, ELENA ■ Italian Fulbright Fellow 1989-90.

GLASS, DOROTHY F. ■ FAAR History of Art 86. BA 64, Vassar College; PhD 68, Johns Hopkins Univ. **Career & Employment:** Johns Hopkins Univ., Junior Instr. 1965-66; Queen's Univ., Ontario, Lect. 1966; Boston Univ., Asst. Prof. 1969-74; SUNY, Buffalo, Assc. Prof. 1974-81, Prof. 1981-present; Visiting Prof.: Brown Univ. 1974; Univ. of Puget Sound 1991. **Memberships & Offices:** American Friends of the Vatican Library; CAA; Dumbarton Oaks Alumni Assn.; Friends of the Gallery, Vassar College; Hagiography Soc.; Intl. Center of Medieval Art, *Newsletter*, Ed.; MAA, Councillor; Medieval Club of New York. **Fellowships, Honors & Awards:** Johns Hopkins Univ. Fellowship 1964-65, Gilman Fellowship 1965-66, Faculty of Philosophy Fellowship 1965-66; Matthew Vassar Fellowship for Prospective College Teachers 1964-65; Vassar College, Mary Wardle Squier Townsend Fellowship 1967-68; Samuel H. Kress Found. Travelling Fellowship 1966-68; Dumbarton Oaks Center for Byzantine Studies Junior Fellowship 1968-69; ACLS Grant 1970, Fellowship 1979-80; APS Grant-in-Aid 1971, 1988; Boston Univ. Grant-in-Aid 1971; M. Aylwin Cotton Fellowship 1973; SUNY, Buffalo, UAC/JAC Grant-in-Aid 1976-77, Chancellor's Award for Excellence in Teaching 1977, Women's Caucus Award for Outstanding Achievement 1979, Julian Park Fund 1980; SUNY Research Found. Fellowship 1979-80; NEH Post-Doctoral Fellowship 1985-86; Fulbright Fellowship 1989-90; MMA & The Cloisters, Jane & Morgan Whitney Senior Research Fellow 1991-93. **Publications:** "The Archivolt Sculpture at Sessa Aurunca," *Art Bulletin* 52 (1970): 119-31; "Romanesque Sculpture in Campania and Sicily: a Problem of Method," *Art Bulletin* 56 (1974): 315-24; "Sicily and Campania: The Twelfth-Century Renaissance," *ACTA* 2 (1975): 131-46; "Jonah in Campania: a Late Antique Revival," *Commentari* 27 (1976): 179-93; *Studies on Cosmatesque Pavements* (Oxford: British Archaeological Reports, 1980); "Wiligelmo and his School at the Cathedral of Modena: a Problem of Method," in *Problemi di Metodo: Condizioni di Esistenza di una Storia dell'Arte*, ed. Lajas Vayer, Atti del XXIV Congresso Internazionale di Storia dell'Arte 10 (Bologna: CISA, 1982), 159-66; "'In Principio': The Creation in the Middle Ages," in *Approaches to Nature in the Middle Ages*, ed. L.D. Roberts (Binghamton: MRTS, 1982), 67-104; *Italian Romanesque Sculpture: an Annotated Bibliography* (Boston: G.K. Hall, 1983); "Pseudo-Augustine, Prophets and Pulpits in Campania," *Dumbarton Oaks Papers, Studies in Art and Archaeology in Honor of Ernst Kitzinger on His Seventy-Fifth Birthday* 41 (1987): 215-26; *Romanesque Sculpture in Campania: Patrons, Programs and Style* (College Park: Penn State Univ. Press, 1991); "The Archivolts from Alife," in *The Brummer Collection of Medieval Art, Duke University Museum of Art*, ed. Caroline Bruzelius (Durham & London: Duke Univ. Press, 1991), 74-95; "Romanesque Sculpture in Campania," in *The Dictionary of Art*. **Home Address:** 11 Riverside Dr., NYC 10023. **Business Address:** Dept. of Art History, SUNY, Buffalo, 606 Clemens Hall, Box 604640, Buffalo, NY 14260.

GLEASON, KATHRYN L. ■ FAAR Classics/Archaeology 87. b. June 7, 1957, Chicago, IL. BS 79, Cornell Univ.; MLA 83, Harvard GSD; D.Phil. 91, Oxford Univ. **Other Study:** Archaeological field work at Gritille & Sardis, Turkey; Carthage & Thurburbo Maius, Tunisia; Masada, Jericho & Caesarea Maritima, Israel; Rome; Great Bedwyn, England. **Research/Artistic Interests:** Archaeology of ancient Roman gardens & designed land; the role of archaeology in contemporary design. **Career & Employment:** Univ. of Pennsylvania, Asst. Prof. 1988-present, Excavations at Caesarea, Israel, Dir. 1990-present; Univ. Museum, Philadelphia, Consulting Scholar 1990-93. **Memberships & Offices:** ArIA; US/ICOMOS; Cornell Landscape Architecture Alumni Council, Pres. 1991-94; Cornell Univ., College of Architecture, Art & Planning, Visiting Com. 1991-present. **Fellowships, Honors & Awards:** Fulbright Scholarship 1983-85; NEH Fellowship, Albright Inst., Jerusalem 1995-96. **Publications:** "Tourism and Archaeology," *Council of Educators in Landscape Architecture Forum* 1.2 (Summer 1982): 7-10; "The Archaeology of Gardens," *The Herbarist* 51 (1985): 5-14; "Uncovering Herod's Seaside Palace," *Biblical Archaeology Review* 19.3 (May-June 1993): 50-57; "Garden Excavations at the Herodian Winter Palace in Jericho, 1985-87," *Bulletin of the Anglo-Israel Archaeological Society* 7 (1987-88): 21-40; "The Garden Portico of Pompey the Great," *Expedition* 32.2 (1990): 3-13; "Porticus Pompeiana: A New Perspective on the First Public Park in Ancient Rome," *Journal of Garden History* 14.1 (1993): 13-27; with Naomi F. Miller, *The Archaeology of Garden and Field* (Philadelphia: Univ. of Pennsylvania Press, 1994); "The Late Roman Agricultural Landscape," in *The Roman Villa at Castle Copse, Wilts*, ed. Eric Hostetter, (Bloomington: Indiana Univ. Press, forthcoming). **Business Address:** Dept. of Landscape Architecture, Univ. of Pennsylvania, 119 Meyerson Hall, Philadelphia, PA 19104.

GOHEEN, ROBERT F. ■ FAAR Classics/Archaeology 53; AAR Trustee 1952-53, Trustee Emer. b. Aug. 15, 1919, Vengurla, India. m. Margaret S. Goheen. c. Anne, Gertrude, Stephen, Megan, Elizabeth, Charles. BA 40, Princeton Univ.; MA 47, Princeton Univ.; PhD 48, Princeton Univ. **Career & Employment:** Princeton Univ., Instr.-Asst. Prof. 1948-57, Pres. 1957-72, Pres. Emer. 1972-present, Senior Fellow in Public & Intl. Affairs 1980-present; Council on Foundations, Chair & CEO 1972-77; US Ambassador to India 1977-80; Mellon Fellowships in the Humanities, Dir. 1981-92. **Memberships & Offices:** Phi Beta Kappa 1939-present; AAAS 1975-present; Assn. of Asian Studies 1980-present; APS 1984-present; Nat. Humanities Center, BoT 1983-present; Bharatiya Vidya Bhavan, USA 1982-present. **Fellowships, Honors & Awards:** Princeton Univ., Woodrow Wilson Award 1978, James Madison Award 1990; Hon. degrees from 26 colleges & universities. **Publications:** *The Imagery of Sophocles' Antigone* (Princeton: Princeton Univ. Press, 1949); *The Human Nature of a University* (Princeton: Princeton Univ. Press, 1971); "Problems of Proliferation: The U.S. & the Third World," *World Politics* 35.2 (Jan. 1983): 194-215. **Home Address:** 1 Orchard Circle, Princeton, NJ 08540.

GOLD, ROBERT ■ AAR Visitor 1951 — 1955, Pianist.

GOLDBERG, ARTHUR ■ AAR Visitor 1959 — 1964, US Supreme Court Justice.

GOLDER, ROBERT MORRIS ■ FAAR Architecture 63. b. Oct. 2, 1931, Philadelphia, PA. m. Poppy Wolff. BArch 60, Univ. of Pennsylvania. **Fellowships, Honors & Awards:** Univ. of Pennsylvania, Throphius Parsons Chandler Fellowship 1960-61. **Bio-Bibliography:** Rita Reif, "A Couple Hired Each Other and Turned Disaster into a Home," *NY Times* (Nov. 7, 1970).

GOLDIN, LEON H. ■ FAAR Painting 58. b. Jan. 16, 1923, Chicago, IL. m. Meta Goldin. c. Joshua, Daniel. BFA 48, AIC School; MFA 50, Univ. of Iowa. **Career & Employment:** California College of Arts & Crafts, Instr.-Assc. Prof. 1950-52, 1954-55; Cooper Union, Adj. Prof. 1960-64; Columbia Univ. School of the Arts, Instr.-Prof. 1962-92. **Fellowships, Honors & Awards:** NAD, Tiffany Found. Grant 1951; Fulbright Fellowship, Paris 1952-53; Guggenheim Fellowship 1959; Ford Found. Fellowship 1960; PAFA, Jennie Sensan Gold Medal 1966; NEA Grant 1967, 1980; NIAL Grant for Painting 1968; NYSCA, CAPS Grant 1980. **Important Works:** Addison Gallery of American Art; Baltimore Museum of Art; Brooklyn Museum; Cincinnati Museum of Art; St. Louis Museum; Everson Museum; LA County Museum; Munson Williams Proctor Inst.; Smithsonian Inst.; Oakland Art Museum; PAFA; Portland, ME Art Museum; Santa Barbara Museum; J.B. Speed Museum, Louisville; California Palace of the Legion of Honor; Worcester Museum; Univ. of Colorado; Univ. of Southern California. **Exhibitions/Performances:** Solo: Oakland Museum 1955; Felix Landau Gallery, Los Angeles 1956, 1957, 1960; Galleria L'Attico, Rome 1958; Kraushaar Galleries, NYC 1960-64, 1968-72, 1984, 1988, 1990, 1993; Univ. of Houston 1981; participated in group exhibitions since 1948 in such institutions as: MOMA, MMA, Corcoran Gallery, New School, Carnegie Inst., Smithsonian Inst., Brooklyn Museum, LA County Museum, San Francisco Museum, AIC, PAFA, Cincinnati Museum, Univ. of Illinois. **Bio-Bibliography:** *Who's Who in America, Who's Who in American Art.* **Home Address:** 438 W. 116th St., Apt. 32, NYC 10027. **Business Address:** Kraushaar Galleries, 724 Fifth Ave., NYC 10019.

GOLDMAN, NORMA WYNICK ■ AAR Classical Soc., Pres. 1992-94; School of Classical Studies; Archaeologist, Educator. **Career & Employment:** Wayne State Univ., Adj. Prof. **Selected Publications:** as co-author, *Cosa: The Lamps.*

GOLDSMITH, BARBARA ■ AAR Trustee 1994-present. **Career & Employment:** *New York Magazine,* Founding & Contr. Ed.; *Harper's Bazaar,* Sen. Ed.; *NY Times,* Writer; *The New Yorker,* Writer. **Memberships & Offices:** New York Public Library, BoT; Nat. Library of Medicine, Preservation & Access Comm., Permanent Paper Task Force; PEN, Permanent Paper Com.; Nat. Dance Inst., Dir.; New York Soc. Library, BoT; Authors League; Authors Guild of America; Poets & Writers; Nat. Book Awards Found. **Fellowships, Honors & Awards:** New York Public Library Literary Lions, Permanent Paper Citation; *LMP* Publishers Award; Hon. DLitt; Hon DHL. **Publications:** *Johnson v. Johnson; Little Gloria...Happy at Last; The Straw Man.* Preservation Laboratories at NYU & New York Public Library, Donor; Goldsmith Center for Learning Disabilities, Kennedy Center, Albert Einstein College of Medicine, Founder; PEN Freedom to Write Award, Donor.

GOODFELLOW, CHARLOTTE ELIZABETH ■ FAAR Classics/Archaeology 48. b. Aug. 25, 1908, Coatesville, PA. d. Nov. 9, 1965. BA 29, Mt. Holyoke College; MA 31, Bryn Mawr College; PhD 35, Bryn Mawr College. **Other Studies:** AAR & Univ. of Munich 1931-32. **Research/Artistic Interests:** Ancient history, Roman citizenship, mythology. **Career & Employment:** Wilson College, Instr. 1933-39; Wellesley College, Asst. Prof. 1939-48, Assc. Prof. 1948-60, Prof. 1960-65. **Memberships & Offices:** APA, ArIA, MAA, CANE. **Publications:** *Roman Citizenship: A Study of Its Territorial and Numerical Expansion* (Lancaster, PA: Lancaster Press, 1935). **Bio-Bibliography:** *Who's Who of American Women;* Wellesley College Archives.

GORDAN, PHYLLIS W.G. ■ AAR Trustee 1971-83, Renaissance Scholar. Endowed a Rome Prize Fellowship in Classical Studies. **Publications:** *Two Renaissance Book Hunters: The Letters of Poggius Bracciolini to Nicolaus De Niccolis* (New York: Columbia Univ. Press, 1974).

GORDIMER, NADINE ■ RAAR Literature 84. b. Nov. 20, 1923, Springs, South Africa. m. Reinhold Cassirer. c. Oriane Taramasco, Hugo Cassirer. **Study:** Literature through libraries. **Research/Artistic Interests:** World literature, African literature. **Career & Employment:** Life-long self-employed as writer. **Memberships & Offices:** Intl. PEN, VP. **Fellowships, Honors & Awards:** Brooker Prize; MLA Award; AAAS, Hon. Mention; AAAL, Hon. Mention; Nobel Prize in Literature 1991; & numerous other awards. **Publications:** Eleven novels, eight story collections & two essay collections, including: *The Essential Gesture* (essays), *Burger's Daughter, A Sport of Nature, My Son's Story, None to Accompany Me* (novels), *Jump* (story collection). **Bio-Bibliography:** all major biographical & literary reference works. **Home Address:** 7 Frere Rd., Parktown West, Johannesburg 2193, South Africa. **Business Address:** Russell & Volkening, 50 West 29th St., NYC 10001.

GORDON, ARTHUR ERNEST ■ FAAR Classics/Archaeology 24, RAAR Classics/Archaeology 49; Classical Soc., Pres. 1951. b. Oct. 7, 1902, Marlborough, MA. d. May 11, 1989. m. Maddalena Belloni, Joyce Stiefbold. c. Paola Zinnecker. BA 23, Dartmouth College; PhD 29, Johns Hopkins Univ. **Research/Artistic Interests:** Latin paleography & epigraphy. **Career & Employment:** Dartmouth College, Instr. 1925-27; Johns Hopkins Univ., Faculty 1927-28; Univ. of Vermont, Assc. Prof. 1929-30; UC, Berkeley, Prof. 1930-70. **Memberships & Offices:** APA; ArIA; Philological Assn. of the Pacific Coast, Pres. 1952; California Classical Assn.; Société des Études Latines, Paris; Soc. for the Promotion of Roman Studies, London. **Fellowships, Honors & Awards:** Johns Hopkins Univ., Johnston Scholar 1928-29; Guggenheim Fellowship & Research Scholarship 1955-56; Fulbright Research Scholarship 1955-56; NEH, Senior Fellowship 1972-73, Grant 1986. **Publications:** co-author: *Album of Dated Latin Inscriptions Part I-IV* (Berkeley: UC Press, 1958-1965); *The Letter Names of the Latin Alphabet,* California Classical Studies 9 (Berkeley: UC Press, 1973); *The Inscribed Fibula Praenestina: Problems of Authenticity,* California Classical Studies 16 (Berkeley: UC Press, 1975); with J. Gordon, *Contributions to the Paleography of Latin Inscriptions* (Berkeley: UC Press, 1977); *Illustrated Introduction to Latin Epigraphy* (Berkeley: UC Press, 1983). **Bio-Bibliography:** Briggs, 226-28; *Directory of American Scholars; Who's Who in America; Who Was Who in America; Who's Who in the World.*

GORDON, B. ■ Cresson Fellow 1919-20.

GORLIN, ALEXANDER C. ■ FAAR Architecture 84. b. June 25, 1955, NYC. m. Debra Solomon. BArch 78, Cooper Union School of Architecture; MArch 80, Yale School of Architecture. **Career & Employment:** Richard Meier Architect 1974; I.M. Pei & Partners 1979-81; Kohn Pederson Fox 1985-86; Yale School of Architecture, Critic & Lect. 1981-91; Alexander C. Gorlin, Architect 1987-present. **Fellowships, Honors & Awards:** Cooper Union, AIA School Medal 1978, Alfred Kazan Award 1978; New York Soc. of Architects Award 1978; Carroll L. V. Meeks Memorial Award 1980. **Publications:** "An Analysis of the Governor's Palace at Chandigarh," *Opposition* 19/20 (Apr. 1980): 159-83; "Le Corbusier and Surrealism," *Perspecta* 18 (June 1980): 50-65; "Introduction," in *Le Corbusier Sketchbook* 4 (1981)

1-10; "The Cleaning of the Sistine Chapel," *Interior Design* (Oct. 1984): 236-41; "The Restoration of the Roman Forum," *Progressive Architecture* (Nov. 1984): 110-13; "The Shops of Ancient Rome," *Interior Design* (Feb. 1985): 226-31; "The Domus Aurea, The Golden House of Nero," *Princeton Architecture Journal* (Apr. 1985): 6-21; "Biblical Imagery in the Work of Louis Kahn," *Architecture + Urbanism* (May 1985): 80-92; "Geometry and Nature in the Work of Louis Kahn," *Architecture + Urbanism* (Apr. 1988): 50-57; "Frank Lloyd Wright and the Italian Villa," *Architecture + Urbanism* (Nov. 1990): 32-51; "Frank Lloyd Wright's Furniture," *Architecture + Urbanism* (Oct. 1992): 3-11. **Important Works:** Mirabella-Cahan House, Bedford, NY 1987; Villa Jovis, Jupiter, FL 1988; Villa Viare, East Hampton, NY 1989; Adrienne Vittadini House, Watermill, NY 1989; Colonial Life Insurance HQ, Kingston, NY 1990; S.I. Newhouse Apt., NYC 1991; Lisa de Kooning House, East Hampton, NY 1992; Alexander Liberman Apartment, NYC 1992; Leake Townhouse, Seaside, FL 1992; Stern House, Shelter Island, NY 1993; Gorlin Townhouse, Seaside, FL 1994; Battery Park City, Design Guidelines for the N. Residential Neighborhood, NYC 1994. **Exhibitions/Performances:** Cooper Union, NYC 1981; Spreebogen Urban Design Ideas Competition Exb., Berlin 1992; Goethe House, NYC 1993. **Bio-Bibliography:** "Country House, Bedford, NY," *Metropolitan Home* (Feb. 1988): 84-85; "Villa Santa Guglielmo," *Architectural Digest* (Feb. 1990): 164-69; "A Grand House Sticks out Its Tongue," *NY Times* (Aug. 31, 1990): C1, 6; "Villa Jovis," *Architectural Digest* (Feb. 1991): 86-90; "Three Villas," *Architecture + Urbanism* (July 1991): 3-28; "The AD 100 Architects," *Architectural Digest* (Aug. 1991): 100-101; "Introducing New Forms to Seaside, FL," *Architectural Digest* (Dec. 1993): 38-46; "Apartment in United Nations Plaza," *Interior Design* (Sept. 1993): 166-78; House in New Jersey, House in Seaside FL, *Global Architecture* 41 (Apr. 1994): 60-65. **Home Address:** 143 Greene St., NYC 10012. **Business Address:** Alexander C. Gorlin, Architect, 380 Lafayette St., NYC 10003.

GORSKI, GILBERT ■ Chicago Architectural Club, Burnham Prize 1987-88.

GOTOFF, HAROLD C. ■ FAAR Classics/Archaeology 59. b. Apr. 19, 1936, NYC. m. Margot Jacobson. c. Leila, Daniel. BA 56, Amherst College; BA 58, Cornell Univ.; BA 62, Peterhouse College, Cambridge; PhD 65, Harvard Univ. **Research/Artistic Interests:** Classical philology. **Career & Employment:** UNC, Instr. 1965-66; Harvard Univ., Asst. Prof. 1966-73; Univ. of Massachusetts, Assc. Prof. 1973-77; Univ. of Illinois, Assc. Prof.-Prof. 1977-86; Princeton Univ., Visiting Prof. 1982, 1983; Univ. of Cincinnati, 1986-present. **Fellowships, Honors & Awards:** NEH Grant 1984-85. **Publications:** "On the Fourth Eclogue of Virgil," *Philologus* 111 (1967): 66-79; *The Textual Tradition of Lucan in the Ninth Century* (Cambridge: Cambridge Univ. Press, 1971); "Tibullus: Nunc levis est tractanda Venus," *Harvard Studies in Classical Philology* 78 (1974): 231-51; *Cicero's Elegant Style* (Urbana: Univ. of Illinois Press, 1979); "Thrasymachus of Calchedon and Ciceronian Style," *Classical Philology* 75 (1980): 297-311; "Cicero vs. Ciceronianism in the *Ciceronianus*," *Illinois Classical Studies* 5 (1980): 163-73; "Cicero's Style for Relating Memorable Sayings," *Illinois Classical Studies* 6 (1981): 294-316; "Stylistic Criticism in Erasmus' *Ciceronianus*," *Illinois Classical Studies* 7 (1982): 359-70; "A Response to W.V. Clausen, On Virgil's *Eclogues*," *Colloquy* 43 (1982): 31-34; "Towards a Practical Criticism of Caesar's Prose Style," *Illinois Classical Studies* 9.1 (1984): 1-18; "The Transformation of Mezentius," *TAPA* 114 (1984): 1-28; "The Difficulty of the Ascent from Avernus," *Classical Philology* 80 (1985): 35-40; "Cicero's Analysis of the Pros-

ecution Speeches in the *Pro Caelio:* An Exercise in Practical Criticism," *Classical Philology* 81 (1986): 122-32; ed. & trans. *Cicero's Caesarian Speeches* (Chapel Hill: UNC Press, 1993); "Ciceronian Oratory: The Art of Illusion," *Harvard Studies in Classical Philology* 95 (1993): 289-313. **Home Address:** 340 Thrall St., Cincinnati, OH 45220.

GOTTLEIB, BEATRICE ■ AAR World War II Scholar 1945.

GOULD, ALBERT ■ AAR World War II Prize 1942.

GRAFTON, ANTHONY ■ AAR Visitor 1990-91, Historian.

GRAUSMAN, PHILIP ■ FAAR Sculpture 65. b. July 16, 1935, NYC. BA 57, Syracuse Univ.; MFA 59, Cranbrook Acad. of Art. **Other Study:** Skowhegan School of Painting & Sculpture 1956, 1957; ASL, with Jose de Creeft 1959. **Career & Employment:** Cooper Union, Instr. 1965-67; Pratt Inst., Instr. 1965-69; Dartmouth College, Artist-in-Residence 1972; Skowhegan School of Painting & Sculpture, Instr. 1973; Yale Univ., Visiting Prof. 1973-76, Critic 1974-present; Vermont Studio Center, Instr. 1992. **Fellowships, Honors & Awards:** ALNY, Special Hon. Mention 1957; Huntington Hartford Fellowship 1958; Audobon Artists, Gold Medal 1958; Louis Comfort Tiffany Found. Grant 1959; NIAL Grant 1961; PAFA, Alfred G.B. Steel Memorial Prize 1962; Ford Found. Purchase Award 1962; Silvermine Guild, Solon H. Borgliem Award 1980, Albert Jacobson Mem. Award, 1st Prize 1984; NAD, Dessie Greer Prize 1981, Gold Medal 1988, Elected Mem. 1992, Cert. of Merit 1993. **Important Works:** Akron Art Museum; Art Museum of South Texas, Corpus Christi; Baltimore Museum of Art; Rose Art Museum, Brandeis Univ.; Brooklyn Museum; Columbus Art Museum; Herbert F. Johnson Museum of Art, Cornell Univ.; Dartmouth College; De Cordova Museum of Art, Lincoln, MA; Hebrew Union College, Jerusalem; MMA; Louis B. Mayer Found., Los Angeles; Munson Williams Proctor Inst., Utica, NY; Museum of Contemporary Art, Udine, Italy; Nat. Portrait Gallery, Washington, DC; Newark Museum; Pennsylvania State Univ.; Neuberger Museum, SUNY, Purchase; Univ. of Connecticut, Storrs; Univ. of Massachusetts, Amherst; Univ. of Michigan; Univ. of New Hampshire, Durham; Vassar College; Wadsworth Atheneum, Hartford; Williams College; Worcester Art Museum; Yale Univ. Art Museum. **Exhibitions/ Performances:** Selected Solo: Borgenicht Gallery, NYC 1966, 1974, 1979; Alpha Gallery, Boston 1968, 1975; Dartmouth College, 1972; Univ. of Connecticut 1976; Pennsylvania State Univ. 1977; Univ. of New Hampshire 1977; Image Gallery, Stockbridge, MA 1978; Washington Art Assn. Washington Depot, CT 1978, 1981; Robert Schoelkopf Gallery, NYC 1983, 1987; Mattatuck Museum, Waterbury, CT 1988; Wichita Museum of Art 1988; Babcock Galleries, NYC 1993. **Bio-Bibliography:** Allan I. Ludwig, "Philip Grausman," *Arts Magazine* (Nov. 1974); Vivien Raynor, "Portraiture Revisited," *NY Times* (July 16, 1978): 34C; Tom Cole, "Philip Grausman," *Arts Magazine* (Oct. 1979); Hilton Kramer, "Art," *NY Times* (Oct. 5, 1979); Blair Birmelin, "Philip Grausman," *Arts Magazine* (Nov. 1983); Ruth Bass, "Philip Grausman," *Art News* 83.1 (Jan. 1984); Vivien Raynor, "From Farm, Field and Zoo, Animals in Artistic Limelight," *NY Times* (July 29, 1984); Hoffman, "Grausman Unravels Unique Vision," *New Milford Times* (Oct. 4, 1984): 1, 3; Lois Tarlow, "Alternative Space," *Art New England* (Feb. 1986); Michael Brenson, "Philip Grausman," *NY Times* (Nov. 20, 1987); Vivien Raynor, "Sculpture in Metals from Aluminum to Zinc, at the Mattatuck," *NY Times* (June 19, 1988): 34C; Lynn Kari Petrich, "Philip Grausman," *American Artist Magazine* (Sept. 1988). **Home Address:** PO Box 1249, Washington, CT 06793-0249.

GRAVES, MICHAEL ■ FAAR Architecture 60; RAAR Architecture 79; AAR Trustee 1981-93, Trustee Emer. b. July 9, 1934, Indianapolis, IN. c. Sarah Browning, Adam Daimhin, Anne Gilbert, Liza Gilbert. BSArch 58, Univ. of Cincinnati; MArch 59, Harvard GSD. **Career & Employment:** Schirmer Prof. of Architecture, Princeton Univ. 1962-present; Michael Graves, Architect, Prin. 1964-present. **Fellowships, Honors & Awards:** *Progressive Architecture* Design Awards 1970, 1976, 1977, 1978 (2), 1979, 1980 (3), 1983, 1988, 1989 (2); AIA, Nat. Honor Awards 1975, 1979, 1982, 1983, 1985, 1987 (2), 1990, 1992, Mid-Florida Chap., Design Award 1988, Eastern Ohio Chap., Design Award 1989, Fellow; New Jersey Soc. of Architects Awards 1967, 1973, 1974, 1975 (2), 1976 (2), 1977, 1978 (4), 1980 (3), 1981 (2), 1982, 1983 (3), 1984, 1985 (2), 1987 (6), 1988, 1989 (2), 1990 (3), 1991 (6), 1992 (3), 1994 (3); AAAL Arnold W. Brunner Memorial Prize in Architecture 1980, Inducted as Mem. of Inst. 1991; Resources Council Commendations 1980, 1982; *Interiors Magazine* Awards 1981 (2), 1986 (2); Univ. of Cincinnati, Hon. Doctorate 1982; New Jersey Soc. of Architects, Special Recognition Honor Award 1982; *Progressive Architecture* Furniture Design Awards 1982, 1983; Inst. of Business Designers 1982 (2), 1990; Henry Hering Memorial Medal 1986; Indiana Arts Award 1983; Euster Award, Miami, FL 1983; Boston Univ., Silver Spoon Award 1984, Hon. Doctorate 1984; Young Women of the Arts, Atlanta, Honored Artist 1985; Savannah College of Art, Hon. Doctorate 1986; American Acad. of Achievement, Gold Plate Award 1986; *International Design* Awards 1989 (2), 1990; American Federation of Arts, Award of Excellence, Graphic Design 1990; New Jersey Business & Industry Assn. 1990; Downtown New Jersey Excellence Award for Downtown Development 1990; RISD, Hon. Doctorate 1990; *Metropolitan Home* Magazine Design 100 Award 1990; Inducted into the *Interior Design* Hall of Fame 1991; New Jersey Governor's Pride Award, Walt Whitman Creative Arts Award 1991; New Jersey Inst. of Technology, Hon. Doctorate 1991; *Print* Magazine Award 1993; Chicago Atheneum, Louis H. Sullivan Award 1994; Rutgers Univ., Hon. Doctorate 1994. **Important Works:** Portland Bldg., Portland, OR 1980; Environmental Education Center, Liberty State Park, Jersey City 1981; Humana Bldg., Louisville, KY 1982; Newark Museum 1982; San Juan Capistrano Library 1982; Emory Univ., Art Museum Renovation, Atlanta 1982; Riverbend Music Center, Cincinnati 1983; Clos Pegase Winery & Residence, Napa Valley, CA 1984; Whitney Museum, NYC 1985; Sotheby's Apt. Tower, NYC 1985; Phoenix Municipal Government Center 1985; Disney Co. Corp. HQ, Burbank, CA 1986; Crown American Corp. Office Bldg., Johnstown, PA 1986; Historical Center for Industry & Labor, Youngstown, OH 1986; Aventine Mixed Use Development, La Jolla, CA 1986; Shiseido Health Club, Tokyo 1986; Walt Disney World Dolphin & Walt Disney World Swan Hotels, FL 1987; Univ. of Virginia Arts & Sciences Bldg., Charlottesville 1987; Yokohama Portside District Condominium Tower, Yokohama, Japan 1987; 15 Stores & Galleries for Lenox, various locations 1987-90; Metropolis Master Plan & Phase One Office Bldg., Los Angeles 1988; 10 Peachtree Plaza Office Bldg., Atlanta 1988; Momochi District Apt. Bldg., Fukuoka, Japan 1988; Hotel New York, Euro Disneyland, France 1989; Federal Triangle Development Site Competition, Washington, DC 1989; Detroit Inst. of Arts 1990; Univ. of Cincinnati, Science & Engineering Bldg. 1990; Clark County Library & Theater, Las Vegas 1990; Fukuoka Hotel & Office Project, Fukuoka, Japan 1990; Denver Central Library 1990; Emory Univ. Art Museum Addition, Atlanta 1990; Indianapolis Art Center 1990; Exhibition: "Birth of Democracy," Nat. Archives, Washington, DC 1991; Richard Stockton State College Arts & Sciences Bldg., Pomona, NJ 1991; Makuhari Intl. Market, Japan 1991; NTT Corp. HQ Interiors, Tokyo 1991; Pittsburgh Cultural Trust, Theater, & Office Bldg. 1992; Thomson Consumer Electronics HQ & Technology Center, Indianapolis 1992; Delaware River Port Authority Office Bldg., Camden, NJ 1992; Nat. Westminster Bank, renovations & new designs, New York & New Jersey 1992; Astridplein Hotel, Antwerp, Belgium 1992; Federal Courthouse, Trenton, NJ 1992; Exhibition: "Rome Reborn," Library of Congress, Washington, DC 1993; Taiwan Pre-History Museum, Taipei 1993; Archdiocesan Center, Newark 1993; Intl. Finance Corp. HQ, Washington, DC 1993; Bayou Place Theater, Houston 1993; Woodlands Theaters, Woodlands, TX 1993; Bancroft/Jefferson Condominiums, Miami 1994; Delaware River Port Authority, Camden, NJ 1994; Saint Martin's College Library, Lacey, WA 1994. **Bio-Bibliography:** *Michael Graves* (Academy Editions, 1979); *Michael Graves: Buildings and Projects 1966-1981* (New York: Rizzoli, 1981); *Michael Graves: Buildings and Projects 1982-89* (New York: Princeton Architectural Press, 1990); *Michael Graves: Design Monograph* (Ernst & Sohn, 1994); *Michael Graves: Buildings and Projects 1990-94* (New York: Rizzoli, 1995); *Who's Who in America*; *Who's Who in Education*; *Who's Who in Interior Design*. **Business Address:** Michael Graves Architect, 341 Nassau St., Princeton, NJ 08540.

GRAVES, NANCY ■ RAAR Painting 79. b. Dec. 23, 1940, Pittsfield, MA. BA 61, Vassar College; BFA-MFA 64, Yale Univ. School of Art & Architecture. **Fellowships, Honors & Awards:** Fulbright-Hayes Grant in Painting 1965; Vassar College Fellowship 1972; Paris Biennale Grant 1971; NEA Grant 1972; CAPS Grant 1974; Skowhegan Medal for Drawings-Graphics 1980; Yale Arts Award for Distinguished Artistic Achievement 1985; Vassar College Distinguished Visitor Award 1986; PAFA, Award of American Art 1987; Skidmore College, Hon. Degree 1989; AAAL 1990; Univ. of Maryland, Hon. DFA 1992; Yale Univ., Hon. DFA 1992. **Important Works:** 6 films 1970-75; Set & costume design for Trisha Brown's *Lateral Pass*; Public Collections: Akron Art Museum; Albright-Knox Gallery, Buffalo; Allen Mem. Art Gallery, Oberlin; Art Museum of South Texas, Corpus Christi; Berkshire Museum, Pittsfield, MA; Birmingham Museum of Art; Brooklyn Museum; Brooks Mem. Art Gallery, Memphis; AIC; Corcoran Gallery of Art, Washington, DC; Des Moines Art Center; Ft. Worth Art Museum; Hirshhorn Museum & Sculpture Gallery, Washington, DC; La Jolla Museum of Contemporary Art; Los Angeles County Museum of Art; Ludwig Museum, Cologne; MMA; Museum of Contemporary Art, Chicago; Museum of Fine Arts, Dallas; MFA; MOMA; Museum of Modern Art, Vienna; NGA; Nat. Gallery of Canada, Ottawa; Nelson-Atkins Museum of Art, Kansas City; Neuberger Museum, Purchase, NY; Neue Galerie im Alten Kurhaus, Aachen; PAFA; St. Louis Art Museum; Guggenheim Museum, NYC; Univ. Art Museum, Berkeley; Vassar Art Gallery, Poughkeepsie; Walker Art Center, Minneapolis; Weatherspoon Art Gallery, UNC, Greensboro; Whitney Museum, NYC. **Exhibitions/Performances:** Recent Solo: Knoedler, NYC 1980, 1981, 1982, 1983, 1985, 1986, 1988, 1989, 1991, 1992, 1993; Knoedler, Zurich 1982; Knoedler, London 1987, 1989; Albright-Knox Art Gallery, Buffalo 1980 travelled to Akron Art Inst.; Contemporary Arts Museum, Houston; Brooks Memorial Art Gallery, Memphis; Neuberger Museum, SUNY, Purchase; Des Moines Art Center; Walker Art Center, Minneapolis; Richard Gray Gallery, Chicago 1981, 1986; Gloria Lauria Gallery, Bar Harbor Islands, FL 1983; Janie C. Lee Gallery, Houston 1983, 1984; Greenberg Gallery, St. Louis 1985; Vassar College Art Gallery 1986, travelled to Berkshire Museum, Pittsfield, David Winton Bell Gallery, Brown Univ.; Retrospective at Fort Worth Art Museum, Hirshhorn Museum & Sculpture Garden, Fort

Worth Museum, Santa Barbara Art Museum, & Brooklyn Museum 1987-88; Associated American Artists, NYC 1988; Heland Wetterling Gallery, Stockholm 1988, Gothenburg 1990; Gallery Mukai, Tokyo 1988; Linda Cathcart Gallery, Santa Monica 1989; Gerald Peters Gallery, Santa Fe & Dallas 1990; Locks Gallery, Philadelphia 1991; Meredith Long Gallery, Houston 1991; Irving Galeries, Palm Beach 1992; Margulies Taplin Gallery, Boca Raton, FL 1993; Fine Arts Gallery, Baltimore 1993, travelled to Lamont Gallery, Phillips Exeter Acad., Exeter, NH 1993; Massachusetts College of Art, Boston 1993; Chrysler Museum Norfolk, VA 1994; Jacksonville Art Museum, FL 1994; Brenan Univ. Gallery, Gainesville, GA 1995. **Bio-Bibliography:** Lucy R. Lippard, "Distancing: The Films of Nancy Graves," in *From the Center: Feminist Essays on Women's Art* (New York: Dutton, 1976), 280-90; Linda Cathcart, *Nancy Graves: A Survey 1969-1980* (Buffalo, NY: Albright-Knox Gallery, 1980); Estella Lauter, *Women as Mythmakers: Poetry and Visual Art by Twentieth-Century Women* (1984), 158-63; Debra Bricker Balken, *Nancy Graves: Painting, Sculpture, Drawing 1980-85* (Poughkeepsie, NY: Vassar College Art Gallery, 1986); E.A. Carmean, Jr., Linda L. Cathcart, Robert Highes & Michael Shapiro, *The Sculpture of Nancy Graves: A Catalogue Raisonné* (New York: Hudson Hills Press, 1987); Jan Greenberg & Sandra Jordan, *The Sculptor's Eye* (New York: Delacorte Press, 1993); E.A. Carmean, Jr., Robert Morgan & David Yager, *Nancy Graves: Recent Works* (Baltimore: Univ. of Maryland, 1993); Charlotte Streiger Rubinstein, *American Women Sculptors: A History of Women Working in Three Dimensions* (Boston: G.K. Hall), 453-56; plus hundreds of articles, reviews, interviews. **Business Address:** M. Knoedler, 19 E. 70th St., NYC 10021.

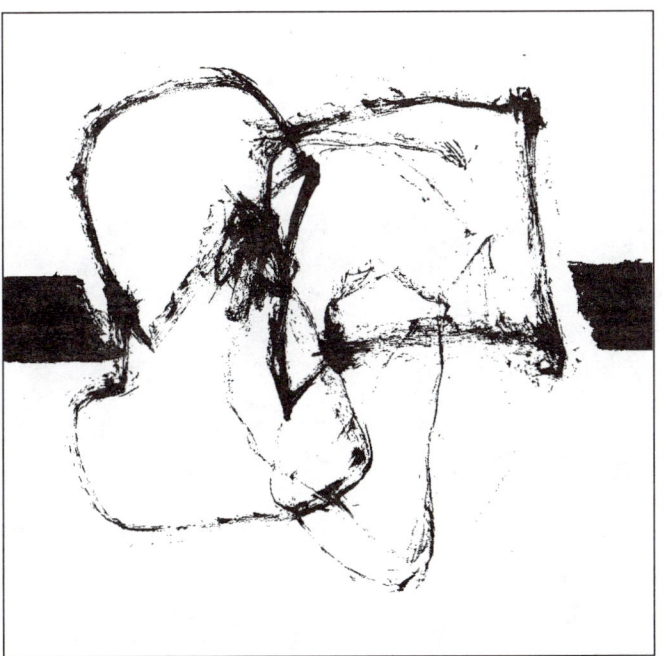

Cleve Gray

GRAY, CLEVE ■ RAAR Painting 80. b. 1918, NYC. m. Francine du Plessix, RAAR 80. Princeton Univ. 1936-40. **Other Study:** With André Lhote & Jacques Villon in Paris 1945-46. **Career & Employment:** US Army 1943-46; *Art in America*, Contr. Ed. 1960-67. **Important Works:** Selected Public Collections: MFA; Brooklyn Museum; Columbus Museum of Art; Corcoran Gallery, Washington, DC; Guggenheim Museum, NYC; Honolulu Acad.

of the Arts; Jewish Museum, NYC; MMA; Minnesota Museum of Art, St. Paul; Museum of Fine Arts, Houston; Nat. Museum of American Art, Washington, DC; Newark Museum; Oklahoma City Art Center; Phillips Collection, Washington, DC; Tennessee Botanical Gardens & Fine Arts Center, Nashville; Wadsworth Atheneum, Hartford, CT; Whitney Museum, NYC; Commissions: Neuberger Museum, SUNY, Purchase; Outdoor at the the Station, Union Station, Hartford, CT. **Exhibitions/Performances:** Selected Solo: Jacques Seligmann Gallery 1947, 1949, 1950, 1952, 1954, 1957, 1959; Whitney Museum Annual, NYC 1947, 1960, 1961, 1963, 1964, 1965; MMA 1947, 1950; Toledo Museum of Art 1947; AIC 1948, 1949; Corcoran Gallery, Washington, DC 1949, 1955, 1961, 1963; Brooklyn Museum 1951, 1987; Wadsworth Atheneum, Hartford, CT 1960, 1983; Betty Parsons Gallery, NYC 1970, 1972, 1974, 1976, 1977, 1979, 1981, 1982, 1983; Guggenheim Museum, NYC 1977; Cathedral of St. John the Divine, NYC 1978, 1990; Armstrong Gallery, NYC 1984, 1986, 1987. **Bio-Bibliography:** *Who's Who in America; Who's Who in American Art.* **Home Address:** 102 Melius Rd., Warren, CT 06754.

GRAY, DAVID ■ AAR Visitor 1939-40, Minister to Irish Free State.

GRAY, FRANCINE DU PLESSIX ■ RAAR Literature 80. b. Sept. 25, 1930, Warsaw, Poland. m. Cleve Gray, RAAR 80. c. Thaddeus Ives, Luke Alexander. BA, Barnard College. **Research/Artistic Interests:** Women's studies, 18th & 19th century French studies. **Career & Employment:** United Press Intl., Writer 1952-54; *Elle* Magazine 1954-56; *Art in America*, book ed. 1961-64; Teaching appointments: CUNY, Yale Univ., Co-

```
ODE TO A LIBRARY

        It is cold and dark here, at the library in Rome where I am
reading Homer. The window adjoining my long oak table looks out
on a stretch of the Aurelian wall, a bank of flowering almond
trees; by the wall a large white plaster statue of Jesus Christ
stretches out its arms in a pleading, come-hither gesture. I am
surrounded here by earnest maidens who spend years decoding the
inscriptions of one Roman catacomb, by robed, ageing priests
deciphering the symbolism of Medieval candelabra, by merry
scholars classifying the strata of a burial mound in some part of
Tuscany. This is the sixth January in a row that I sit in the
same seat, at the same library of the American Academy in Rome. I
travel here yearly to escape the harshest weeks of the New
England winter, to feast on mosaics, ruins, Caravaggio, Bernini,
Gregorian chants, the lives of the saints, concerts of Baroque
music held in vault-cold Borromini churches. I return yearly to
this palimpsest of history to satisfy my passion for memorials,
archaic traditions, shrines, to rewind the fragile threads
between past and present. And in this blessed library I also
recapture a lost youth by doing what I then did best, what I
would happily spend a lifetime doing--read and study in
labyrinths of dusty mellow books, inhaling a fragrant immortality
from their pages.
        As I loaf in my winter haven inviting my soul to Virgil and
Homer, staring at the white plaster Christ, the almond trees in
February bloom beneath the ancient Roman wall, I am filled with a
gratitude to the past akin to a sense of the holy. In this
library I have come to understand that scholarship, like Homeric
honor, might be concerned with the nurture, deciphering,
celebration of the dead....

(Francine du Plessix Gray, journal excerpt, 1987)
```

Francine du Plessix Gray

lumbia Univ., Princeton Univ. **Fellowships, Honors & Awards:** Nat. Catholic Book Award 1970; Guggenheim Fellowship 1991-92; Hon. Doctorates: Oberlin College, CUNY, etc.; French Govt. Chevalier de l'Ordre des Arts et des Lettres; AAAL. **Publications:** *Divine Disobedience: Profiles in Catholic Radicalism* (1970); *Hawaii: The Sugar-Coated Fortress* (1972); *Lovers & Tyrants* (1976); *World Without End* (1981); *October Blood* (1985); *Adam and Eve* *and the City* (1987); *Soviet Women: Walking the Tightrope* (1990); *Rage and Fire: A Life of Louise Colet* (1994). **Bio-Bibliography:** *Contemporary Authors; Contemporary Authors Autobiography; Who's Who in America.* **Home Address:** 102 Melius Rd., Warren, CT 06754. **Business Address:** Georges Borchardt, 136 E. 57 St., NYC 10022.

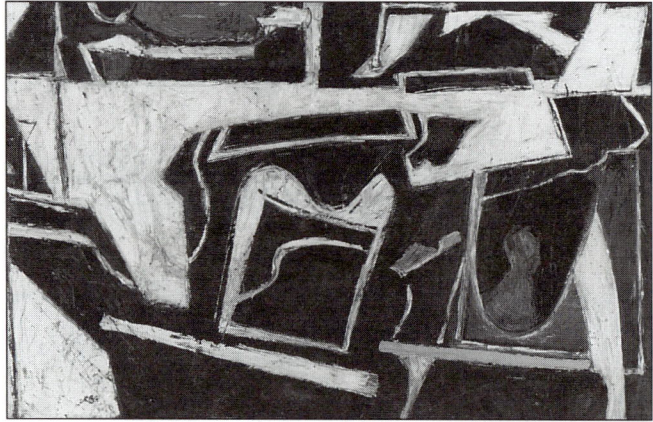

Robert Berkeley Green

GREEN, ROBERT BERKELEY ■ FAAR Painting 38. b. July 28, 1909, Pittsburgh, PA. m. Miriam S. Green. c. Robert B. Green, J. Bryant Green. BA 31, Carnegie Mellon Univ.; BFA 35, Yale Univ. **Other Study:** Studied fresco painting with Ferruccio Ferrazzi, who was Director of the Acad. of Fine Arts in Rome, 1936. **Career & Employment:** Yale Univ. School of Fine Arts, Instr. 1934-35; Univ. of Kansas, Asst. Prof. 1946-50, Assc. Prof. 1950-57, Prof. 1957-79, Prof. Emer. 1979-present. **Memberships & Offices:** Univ. of Kansas Graduate School, Graduate Representative for the Dept. of Painting 1977-79. **Fellowships, Honors & Awards:** American Watercolor Soc., Goetz Award 1980; State of Kansas, Governor's Artist 1981-82; Univ. of Kansas School of Law, Painting Comm. 1983; Hallmark Permanent Collection 1985; Kansas Watercolor Soc., Rickerby Award 1987. **Exhibitions/Performances:** Recent Solo: Broadway Gallery, Seattle 1984; Kellas Gallery, Lawrence, KS 1985, 1986; Traveling Show, Kansas Arts Comm. 1991-92, 1992-93; Union Hill Arts Gallery, Kansas City, MO 1992; Invited by the Gulbenkian, Lisbon, Portugal 1993; Group: Special Invitational Exb., Nelson Art Museum, Kansas City, MO 1982; Three-Person Show, Nelson Art Museum, Kansas City, MO 1983; Mulvane Art Museum 1985; Kansas Watercolor Soc., Wichita Art Museum 1985; Kansas Watercolor Soc. 1987; American Legacy Gallery, Kansas City, MO 1988; Kellas Gallery, Lawrence, KS 1988, 1990; Hutchinson Art Museum, KS 1989; Invitational Retrospective Exb., Lawrence Art Center, KS 1991; Univ. of Kansas, Dept. of Art, Faculty Show 1991. **Home Address:** 1031 Sunset Dr., Lawrence, KS 66044.

GREENE, CHESTER CARR, JR. ■ FAAR Classics/Archaeology 34. Oct. 16, 1908, Providence, RI. d. June 11, 1941. BA 29, Brown Univ.; PhD 35, Princeton Univ. **Research/Artistic Interests:** Political theory of Cicero & St. Augustine, Classical epics. **Career & Employment:** Cornell Univ., Instr. 1934-41. **Fellowships, Honors & Awards:** Princeton Univ., Proctor Fellowship 1931-32. **Publications:** "Cicero's Political Ideal and the Question of the Moderator," *TAPA* 65 (1934): xxxi-xxxii.

GREENE, JEROME D. ■ AAR Trustee 1920-39, Found. Exec.

GREENE, STEPHEN ■ FAAR Painting 54. b. Sept. 19, 1917, NYC. m. Sigrid De Lima. c. Alison. BFA 42, State Univ. of Iowa; MA 45, State Univ. of Iowa. **Other Study:** Studies at Iowa with Philip Guston; NAD & ASL 1935-38. **Career & Employment:** Indiana Univ., Instr. 1945-46; Washington Univ., Instr. 1946-47; Princeton Univ., Artist-in-Residence 1956-59; Columbia Univ., Asst. Prof. 1961-68; Tyler School of Art, Temple Univ., Prof. 1968-85; ASL, Instr. 1959-65, 1985-present. **Memberships & Offices:** Tiffany Found., BoT 1966-91. **Fellowships, Honors & Awards:** Virginia Museum of Fine Arts, Purchase Prize Biennial of American Painting 1946; Palace of Legion of Honor, San Francisco, 1st Prize 1947; Corcoran Museum Copper Medal & William A. Grant Prize 1965; NYC Council of Arts & Letters Grant 1966; NIAL Award 1967; NAD Andrew Carnegie Award 1970. **Publications:** "A Case in Point," *Art in America* 49 (1961): 84-85; "The Tragic Sense," in *From Sophocles to Picasso* (Bloomington: Indiana Univ. Press, 1962); "Sensibility of the Sixties," *Art in America* 55 (Jan.-Feb. 1967): 46; "Aspects of Reality in My Paintings," *Leonardo* 6 (1973). **Important Works:** AIC, Brooklyn Museum, Carnegie Art Museum, Corcoran Gallery of Art, Detroit Inst. of Arts, Fogg Art Museum, Guggenheim Museum, High Museum of Art, Hirshhorn Museum & Sculpture Garden, Kalamazoo Inst. of Arts, MMA, MOMA, Nelson-Atkins Museum, Newark Museum, Norton Simon Museum of Art, St. Louis Art Museum, San Francisco Museum of Modern Art, Tate Gallery, Neuberger Museum, Virginia Museum of Fine Arts, Wadsworth Atheneum, Whitney Museum, NYC, Yale Univ. Art Gallery, Princeton Univ. Art Museum, & others. **Exhibitions/Performances:** Solo: Durlacher Bros., NYC 1947-54; Grace Borgenicht, NYC 1954-59; Staempfli Gallery, NYC 1961-69; Wm. Zierler Gallery, NYC 1971-76; Marilyn Pearl Gallery, NYC 1977-89; also solo shows in Rome, Los Angeles, Detroit & Boston; Retrospective Exhibitions: Corcoran Gallery & travelling 1963-64; Akron Art Inst. 1978; St. Louis Art Museum 1989; numerous group exhibitions in USA & abroad. **Bio-Bibliography:** "Stephen Greene," in *The New Decade: 35 American Painters and Sculptors* (New York: Whitney Museum, 1955), 36-38; Dore Ashton, "Exhibition at Staempfli," *Art International* (June-Aug. 1961); Barbara Rose, "Stephen Greene: A Retrospec-

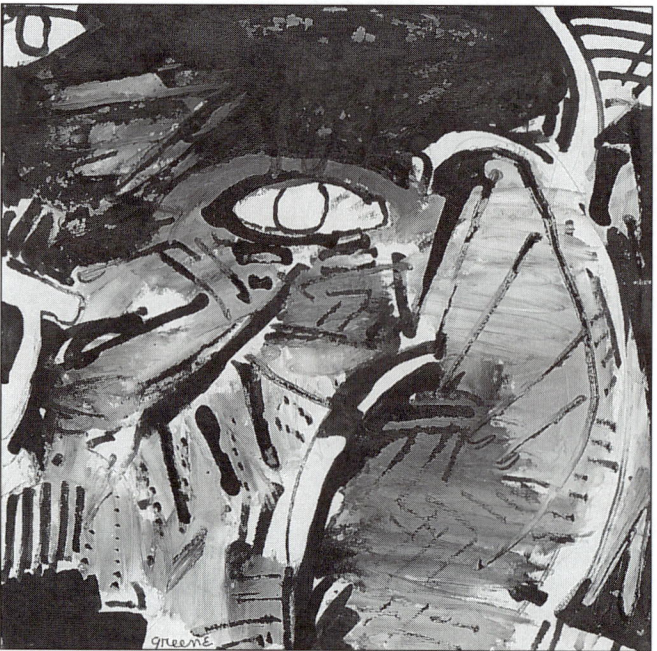

Stephen Greene

tive Exhibition," *Art International* (Apr. 25, 1963); Brian O'Dougherty, "Stephen Greene Perfectionist," *N.Y. Times* (May 16, 1964); "Historicism and Respect for Tradition," *The Studio* (June 1966); Michael Fried, "The Goals of Stephen Greene," *Arts* (May 1963); Karen Wilkin, "Stephen Greene," *Art International* (Feb. 1973); Martica Sawin, "Stephen Greene: Recent Paintings," *Arts* (Oct. 1975); April Kingsley, "Diebenkorn & Greene," *Soho News* (Jan. 1977); John Yau, "Luminous Shrouds: The Recent Paintings of Stephen Greene," *Arts* (1983); also articles on the work in *Life* & *Time* magazines; *Who's Who in American Art; Who's Who in America; Who's Who in the World.* **Home Address:** 407 Storms Rd., Valley Cottage, NY 10989.

GREENE, W.C. ■ AAR Classical Soc., Pres. 1944.

GREENWOLD, MARK A. ■ FAAR Painting 88. b. Oct. 19, 1942, Cleveland, OH. m. Martha Jaremko. c. Simon, Anya. BFA 66, Cleveland Inst. of Art.; MFA 69, Indiana Univ. **Other Study:** Carnegie Inst. of Technology 1961. **Fellowships, Honors & Awards:** NEA Grant 1985-86; NYFA Fellowship 1987, 1994; Louis Comfort Tiffany Found. Award 1991; AAAL, Acad. in Art Award 1993. **Important Works:** Cleveland Museum of Art; Indiana Univ. Museum of Art, Bloomington; MMA. **Exhibitions/Performances:** Solo: Phyllis Kind Gallery, NYC 1976, 1986, 1993; "Art and the Law," 14th Annual Exb. 1989-90, travels for one year. Selected Group: Chrysler Museum, Norfolk, VA 1981; Florida Intl. Univ. Museum 1988; De Cordova Museum & Sculpure Park, Lincoln, MA 1992; Drawing Center, NYC 1993; AAAL, NYC 1993; Exit Art/The First World, NYC 1994. **Bio-Bibliography:** Christopher Finch, *Twentieth-Century Watercolors* (New York: Abbeville, 1988), 288-89; John L. Ward, *American Realist Painting 1945-1980* (Ann Arbor: UMI Research Press, 1989), 225-29. **Home Address:** 17 Elsmere Ave., Delmar, NY 12054. **Business Address:** Phyllis Kind Gallery, 136 Greene St., NYC 10012.

GREGORY, JOHN CLEMENTS ■ FAAR Sculpture 15; AAR Trustee 1925-42. b. May 17, 1879, London, England. d. Feb. 21, 1958. m. Katharine Van Rensselaer Crosby. c. John Delafield. **Other Study:** ASL 1900-1903; École des Beaux Arts, Paris, 1904-6; studied with George Grey Barnard & Anton Mercie. **Career & Employment:** Columbia Univ., Instr. 1916-25; Beaux Arts Inst. of Design, NYC, Dir. of Sculpture; US Navy, Naval Construction, Camouflage Sect., Asst. Inspector 1918; Private Practive, NYC 1925-50. **Memberships & Offices:** NSS, Pres. 1934-39; AIA, Honorary Mem.; NIAL; Beaux Arts Inst. of Design; NYC Art Comm. **Fellowships, Honors & Awards:** ALNY, Medal of Honor 1921; Concord Art Assn., Medal of Honor 1926; PAFA, George D. Widener Memorial Gold Medal 1933. **Important Works:** Folger Shakespeare Library, Washington, DC; American War Memorial Cemetery, Suresnes, France; Huntington Mausoleum, San Marino, CA; Statue of Gen. Anthony Wayne, Philadelphia Museum of Fine Arts; Beveridge Monument, Indianapolis; MMA; Corcoran Gallery of Art, Washington, DC. **Exhibitions/Performances:** Whitney Museum, NYC; NSS; ALNY 1921; AIC 1921; Concord Art Assn. 1926; PAFA 1933. **Bio-Bibliography:** *National Cyclopedia of American Biography; Who Was Who in America; Who Was Who in American Art.*

GRESHAM, JAMES A. ■ FAAR Architecture 56. b. June 20, 1928, Indianapolis, IN. m. Florence C. Gresham. c. Ann Marie. BArch 53, Univ. of Oklahoma, Norman. **Career & Employment:** Univ. of Arizona, College of Architecture, Prof. 1962-71; Gresham Hockings Architects, Part. 1968-75; James Gresham & Asscs., Part. 1975-80; Gresham-Larson Asscs., Part. 1980-85; NBBJ, Prin. 1985-

present. **Memberships & Offices:** AIA, Southern Arizona Chap., Pres. 1971; AIA, Arizona Soc. of Architects, Pres. 1972, 1974; AIA, Com. on Design 1973-74, 2000 Program 1988-present; Patronato San Xavier, Pres. 1988-present. **Fellowships, Honors & Awards:** Guggenheim Grant 1965; AIA Design Awards 1970, 1978, 1979, 1980, 1981, 1982, 1985 (2), 1987 (2), 1988 (3), 1990 (2), 1991, 1992 (3); AIA Fellowship 1981; Tucson Tomorrow Leadership Award 1986; Pima County, AZ, Leadership Award 1988; Univ. of Arizona, College of Business & Public Admin., Distinguished Citizen 1991. **Publications:** "Structure and the Future of Architecture," *Arizona Architect* (May/June 1967): 12-15; "San Felice," *Arizona Architect* (Mar.-Apr. 1969): 22-25; "Too Little, Too Late?" *Arizona Architect* (Aug.-Sept. 1974): 11-13; "Casas Adobes Post Office and Residence," *Architecture + Urbanism* (Nov. 1981): 98-101; "Fresh, Inspiring, School Architecture," *School Administrator* (June 1988); "Canyon View School," *Architecture* (Jan. 1991): 62-63; "Di Miguel Elementary School," *Progressive Architecture* (July 1991); "Catalina High: Another Casualty of Our Throwaway Culture," *Arizona Daily Star* (Feb. 16, 1992): F3. **Important Works:** Gresham Residence, Tucson 1970; Navajo County Government Center, Holbrook, AZ 1976; Greenlee County Correctional Facility, Clifton, AZ 1979; Tortolita Junior HS, Tucson 1984; Mountain View HS, Tucson 1986; Canyon View Elementary School, Tucson 1988; St. Gregory HS Multi-Purpose Bldg., Tucson 1988; Di Miguel Elementary School, Flagstaff 1989; Mountain View Residence Hall, Northern Arizona Univ., Flagstaff 1990; Arizona State Dept. of Economic Security Bldg., Phoenix 1991; Arizona Health Sciences Center Library, Tucson 1992; C.E. Rose Elementary School, Tucson 1992; Arizona State Office Bldg., Tucson 1992. **Bio-Bibliography:** Lawrence W. Cheek, "Designing Buildings that Worship the Sunlight," *Tucson Citizen* (Sept. 10, 1975); Walt Nett, "Local Architect Finds Happiness with Big Firm," *Arizona Daily Star* (June 18, 1990): D9; *Who's Who in America.* **Business Address:** 620 N. Country Club Rd., Tuscon, AZ 85716.

GRIEB, DONALD L. ■ AAR World War II Prize 1941.

GRIFFIN, BRAND N. ■ FAAR Architecture 74. b. Aug. 17, 1947, Medford, OR. m. Susan M. Weatherford. c. Lauren, Keely, Cara, Natalie. BArch 70, Washington State Univ., Pullman; MFA 71, California Inst. of Arts, Valencia; MArch 72, Rice Univ. **Other Study:** Private pilot; Scuba; Space suit: certified in NASA's neutral buoyancy simulator, 50 hrs. space station testing. **Research/Artistic Interests:** Large-scale systems integration, spacecraft design, human performance in space. **Career & Employment:** Tulane Univ., Asst. Prof. 1974-77; Rice Univ., Visiting Prof. 1978-79; Univ. of Washington, Lect. 1979-83; Intl. Space Univ., Co-Chair, System Architecture Dept. 1988, 1991, 1993; Boeing Co., Preliminary Design Mgr., Advanced Civil Space Systems 1981-93; Griffin Design 1994-present. **Memberships & Offices:** American Inst. of Aeronautics & Astronautics, Sen. Mem.; Intl. Space Univ., Founder's Assc., Charter Mem. 1988; Boeing Executive Focal Pgm., Intl. Space Univ. College of Teachers. **Fellowships, Honors & Awards:** Rice Univ., Darden Medal 1972; NASA-American Soc. of Engineering Education Fellowships 1977, 1978, 1979; American Inst. of Aeronautics & Astronautics Award 1993; Boeing Co., Exec. on Loan, Intl. Space Univ. 1993. **Publications:** *Cities in the Sky* (Houston: Rice Univ.-NASA, 1972); *The Influence of Zero-G and Acceleration on the Human Factors of Spacecraft Design* (Houston: NASA, 1978); *The Space Operations Center Habitable Service Center* (Seattle: Boeing Co., 1982); *Zero-G Simulation Verifies EVA Servicing for Space Station Modules* (Washington, DC: AIAA, 1986); "Lunar Landing Vehicle," *Aviation Week and Space Technology* (Jan. 18, 1988): covers; *A Space Suit for Lunar Construc-*

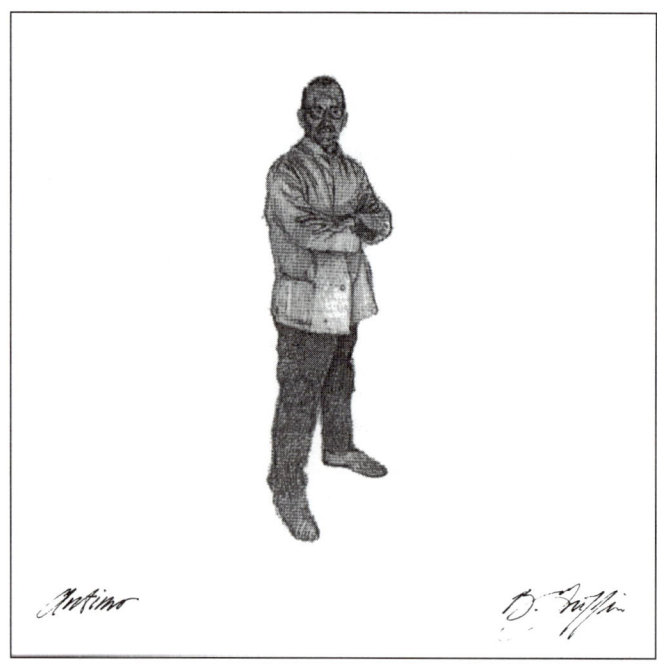

Brand N. Griffin

tion and Exploration (Washington, DC: AIAA, 1990); consulting ed., *Spacefarers: Voyage Through the Universe* (New York: Time-Life Books, 1990); "Engineering, Construction, and Operations in Space," in *An Infrastructure for Early Lunar Development*, ed. S.W. Johnson & J.P. Wetzel (New York: ASCE, 1990); consulting ed., *Starbound: Voyage Through the Universe* (New York: Time-Life Books, 1991); *A Mobile Habitat for Early Lunar Exploration* (Paris: Intl. Aeronautical Fed., 1991); with P. Hudson, *Smart Suits for Space Exploration* (Washington, DC: AIAA, 1991); with D. Thrasher & B. Wallace, Boeing Co., *A Pressurized Rover for Early Lunar Exploration* (Washington, DC: AIAA, 1992); "Command-Control Pressure Suit," *Aviation Week and Space Technology* (Apr. 12, 1993): covers; ed. & contr., *Space Systems Architecture, Core Curriculum* (Strausbourg: Intl. Space Univ., 1993). **Important Works:** Space: Command-Control Pressure Space Suit; Space Station Configurations, Boeing's lead designer; Space Station Testing (weightless simulation in space suit); Meteoroid-Debris Shield & Body Mounted Radiator Test Repair Procedures for EVA in the Earth's shadow; Manned Autonomous Work Station, One-person spacecraft designed for weightless operation; Lunar Utility Vehicle Spacecraft designed for surface-to-surface operations; Lunar Landing Vehicle Spacecraft designed for a surface-to-orbit operations; Lunar Rovers Daylight Rover for medium range surface operations; Rover 1st for quick return & early telescience; Lunar Base; Mars lander; Zero-G Design Guide. Architecture: P.T. Stanley addition, Tacoma, WA 1980; Janice Neimi Law Office remodel, Seattle, WA 1982. **Exhibitions/Performances:** Trajan's Market, Rome, Italy 1979; Erica Williams-Anne Johnson Gallery, Seattle 1980; Smithsonian Inst., Nat. Air & Space Museum, Washington, DC 1992; IBM Gallery, NYC, & Smithsonian's Nat. Air & Space Museum, Washington, DC 1992; US Astronaut Hall of Fame, Kennedy Space Center, FL 1992; Huntsville Museum of Art, Huntsville, AL 1992-93. **Bio-Bibliography:** Joel Davis, "Boeing's 'A-Team' Has Designs on the Future," *Washington* 1.3 (Nov.-Dec. 1984); Jerome Richard, "The Dream Team," *Final Frontier* (Nov.-Dec. 1989). **Home Address:** 11321 Dellcrest Dr. SE, Hunstville, AL 35803.

GRIFFIN, MARGARET ■ NIAE, John Dinkeloo Traveling Fellow 1988-89.

GRIMM, RICHARD EUGENE ■ FAAR Classics/Archaeology 56; AAR Classical Soc., Pres. 1968. b. Aug. 31, 1926, Urbana, IL. BA 49, Indiana Univ.; MA 51, Indiana Univ.; PhD 59, Princeton Univ. **Career & Employment:** UC, Davis, Assc. Prof.; Univ. of Oregon, Asst. Prof. 1958-60. **Memberships & Offices:** Philological Assn. of Pacific Coast; APA; California Classical Assn. Northern Region, Pres. **Fellowships, Honors & Awards:** Fulbright Travel Grant 1951-52, 1966-67.

GRISWOLD, A. WHITNEY ■ AAR Visitor 1959-64, Yale Univ., Pres.

GRISWOLD, RALPH ESTY ■ FAAR Landscape Architecture 23. b. Aug. 23, 1894, Warren, OH. d. June 23, 1981. m. Dorothy Griswold. c. Romola. BLA 16, Cornell Univ.; MLD 17, Cornell Univ. **Other Studies:** Bellevue Art Training Center, Paris. **Research/Artistic Interests:** Restoration, upper garden of the Villa Caparola; topography, Villa Catena; Williamsburg, 18th-century gardens. **Career & Employment:** US Army, Camouflage Section, WWI; A.D. Taylor, Cleveland 1923-27; Nicolet & Griswold, Pittsburgh, Landscape Architect 1927-30; Ralph E. Griswold & Asscs., Pittsburgh 1930-64; Griswold, Winters, Swain & Mullin, Inc. Landscape Architects, Part. 1964-81. **Memberships & Offices:** AIA; NAD; Pittsburgh Architectural Club. **Fellowships, Honors & Awards:** Garden Club of Amercia, Sarah Gildersleeve Fife Award, Gold Medal; Royal Order of George I, King of Hellenes, Gold Cross; ASLA, Pennsylvania-Delaware Chap., Distinguished Service Award; AIA, Hon. Mem., Allied Professions Award; Dumbarton Oaks Research Library & Collections, Research Fellow. **Publications:** "Landscape Development of the Athenian Agora," *Landscape Architecture* 44 (1954): 121-26; "Our Parks Sparked Our Renaissance," *Carnegie Magazine* (Feb. 1964); *Thomas Jefferson, Landscape Architect* (Charlottesville: Univ. of Virginia Press, 1978); with Fredrick Deveton Nichols, *Opportunities in Landscape Architecture* (Lincolnwood, IL: VGM Careers Horizon, 1979). **Important Works:** Commissions include: Longue Vue; Fox Chapel; Rolling Rock Country Club; Buhl Found.; Chatham Villiage Housing; Aluminium Co. American Laboratory; Cyrus McCormick; Lessing Rosenwald; Mrs. Max Ascoli; Edgar Kaufman; Consultant: Pittsburgh Housing Authority; Federal Housing Authority; Univ. of Pittsburgh; Westminster College; Georgia Warm Springs Found.; Pennsylvania College for Women; R.B. Mellon Estate; Jones Laughlin Steel Corp.; Landscape Architect: American Military Cemetery, Anzio, Italy; Agora, Athens, ASCSA. **Bio-Bibliography:** *Who's Who in America.*

GROSE, DAVID FREDERICK ■ FAAR Classics/Archaeology 74; Classical Jury 1990-94. BA 66, St. Olaf College; PhD 75, Harvard Univ. **Other Study:** Univ. of Durham & Newcastle-upon-Tyne 1966-67. **Career & Employment:** Univ. of Missouri, Asst. Prof. 1975-76; Toledo Museum of Art, Curator 1976-77; Univ. of Massachusetts, Amherst, Chair & Prof. 1977-present; Smith College Museum of Art, Acting Dir. 1986-87. **Memberships & Offices:** Phi Beta Kappa, United Chapters, Gen. Council 1985-present; 15th Annual Byzantine Studies Conference, Co-organizer 1989; Massachusetts Annual Latin Workshops, Organizer 1993-present; Old Sturbridge Village Museum, Overseer; & numerous academic & professional committees. **Fellowships, Honors & Awards:** Fulbright-Hays Fellowship 1966-67; Harvard-Ford Found. Fellowship 1968-73; ANS Grant 1969;

NEA Summer Fellowship 1976; ACLS Grant-in-Aid 1980-81, Senior Fellowship 1983-84; Corning Museum of Glass, Juliette & Leonard Rakow Intl. Prize 1984; Commonwealth of Massachusetts, Joseph P. Healey Grant 1986; NEH Fellowship 1990-91; Univ. of Pennsylvania, NEA Exb. Grant 1994, 1995; Soc. of Antiquaries of London, Fellow 1991-present. **Publications:** *Early Ancient Glass: The Core-Formed, Rod-Formed and Cast Vessels & Objects from Late Bronze Age to Early Roman Times* (New York: Hudson Hills-Toledo Museum of Art, 1989); with Charles Chetham & Ann H. Sievers, *Guide to the Collections* (Northampton, MA: Smith College Museum of Art, 1986); *Tel Anafa (Upper Galilee): The Hellenistic, Roman and Islamic Glass*, The Excavations at Tel Anafa 2 (Ann Arbor: JRA Supplement, 1994); *The Hellenistic, Roman, and Medieval Glass from Cosa*, Memoirs of the American Academy in Rome (Rome: AAR, forthcoming); *Morgantina: The Pre-Hellenistic, Hellenistic, Roman, and Medieval Glass*, Morgantina Studies (Princeton: Princeton Univ. Press, forthcoming); plus numerous articles & contributions to edited collections. **Business Address:** Dept. of Classics, Herter Hall 539, Univ. of Massachusetts, Amherst, MA 01003.

GROSSI, OLINDO ■ FAAR Architecture 36; SOF, Pres. b. July 17, 1909, NYC. m. Martha Seymour. c. Susan, John, Thomas. BA 30, Columbia Univ.; BArch 32, Columbia Univ.; MSArch 33, Columbia Univ. **Other Study:** Univ. of Paris 1930. **Career & Employment:** Bard College, Assc. in Arch. & Fine Arts 1939-42; Pratt Inst., School of Architecture, Chair & Dean 1945-69; Columbia Univ., Instr. 1946; NYIT, Dean 1971-82, Adj. Prof. 1982; campus consultant for LIU, NYU, C.W. Post; Industry consultant for Monsanto, Chemstrand, American Plywood; consultant to NYC Planning Comm., Downtown Brooklyn Civic Center Study 1962; consultant on tropical architecture & architectural education to the Asia Found., Southeast Asia 1965-1966. **Memberships & Offices:** ALNY, Pres. 1957-58; AIA, NY Chap., Exec. Com. 1961-63; Nat. Assn. of Collegiate Schools of Architecture, Pres. 1961-63; ACSA, Pres. 1961-63; Goals for Nassau County, Chair; New York Chiropractic College, Old Brookville, Assc. Architect. **Fellowships, Honors & Awards:** Carnegie Scholarship to Paris 1930; Brunner Scholarship 1949; NY State Convention, 1st Prize 1949; AIA Grant 1949, 1969; AIA Emer. Fellow; Sidney L. Strauss Memorial Award, NY State Assn. of Architects 1954; ALNY, 1st Prize 1969. **Publications:** Published articles on education, architecture, & planning; designs of residences, stores, campuses in professional architectural press & newspapers, including *AIA Journal, Architectural Forum, Architec-*

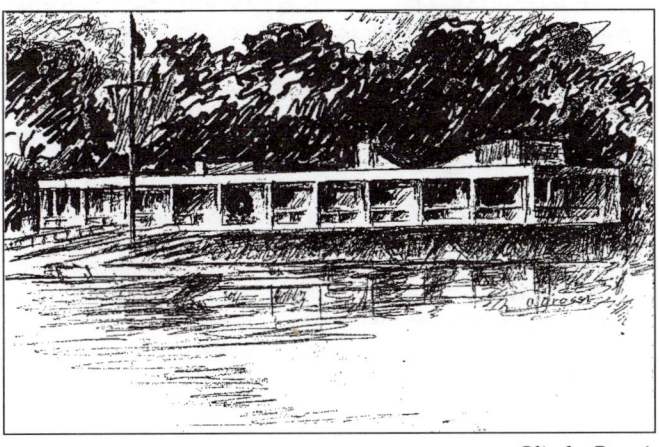

Olindo Grossi

tural Record, Architettura, Empire State Architect, House and Home, Interiors, Jersey Architect, Living for Young Homemakers, Memoirs of the American Academy in Rome, Modern Steel Construction, Progressive Architecture. **Important Works:** Residences: Sands Point, NY 5; Connecticut 5; New Jersey 5; & others; Regional education building in Africa; housing in Re-Union City, Israel; medical campus on Long Island, academic building & anatomy lab; housing, the Minimal Apartment, Cluster Design, Flexible Partitions, design of houses oriented to the sun. **Exhibitions/Performances:** Archaeology studies in Permanent Exhibit at library of NY Inst. of Technology, Old Westbury, including "Forum of Julius Caesar," measured drawings of St. Peter in Tuscania, Italy. **Bio-Bibliography:** *Who's Who in America.* **Home Address:** 234 Manhasset Ave., Manhasset, NY 11030.

GROVES, THOMAS D. ■ FAAR Classics/Archaeology 84; Broneer Fellow 1983-84. b. Sept. 18, 1954, Passaic, NJ. m. Deirdre J. Larkin. BA 76, Cornell Univ.; MA 78, Univ. of Illinois; MA 82, Princeton Univ. **Other Study:** ASCSA 1981-82. **Research/Artistic Interests:** Late antique studies, numismatics. **Career & Employment:** Rutgers Univ., Visiting Prof. 1985; D'Arcy Masius Benton & Bowles, Asst. Dir. of Business Development 1986-91; Anderson & Lembke, Dir. of Account Planning 1991-92; J. Walter Thompson, Senior VP, Dir. of Strategic Planning 1992-present. **Memberships & Offices:** ArIA 1974-present; ANS 1976-present; Advertising Research Found. 1987-present. **Fellowships, Honors & Awards:** ASCSA, John Williams White Fellow 1981. **Publications:** with Kenan Erim, T. Buttrey & R. Ross Holloway, *Morgantina Studies II: The Coins* (Princeton: Princeton Univ. Press, 1989). **Home Address:** 720 Ft. Washington Ave., Apt. 2F, NYC 10040. **Business Address:** J. Walter Thompson, 466 Lexington Ave., NYC 10017.

GRUBER, SAMUEL D. ■ FAAR History of Art 87. m. Judith Meagan. BA 77, Princeton Univ.; MA 84, Columbia Univ.; PhD 93, Columbia Univ. **Other Study:** Cornell Summer Session, Rome 1981; archaeological field work: Yorktown, VA; Assunpink Creek, NJ; 64 Pearl St., NYC; Rimon, Israel; Tuscania, Gubbio, Cremona & San Vicenzo al Volturno, Italy; Temple Univ., Rome 1984-86. **Career & Employment:** Jewish Heritage Council, World Monuments Fund, Dir. 1989-present; Syracuse Univ., Adj. Prof. 1994. **Memberships & Offices:** Hebrew Univ., Assn. for Gravestone Studies, Center for Jewish Art; CAA; Intl. Center for Medieval Art; Intl. Survey of Jewish Monuments; MAA; Municipal Art Soc., NYC; Nat. Trust for Historic Preservation; Partners for Sacred Places; RSA; SAH; Vernacular Architecture Forum; Practical Cats Theater Co., BoD; Morningside Heights Residents Com., Co-chair Landmarks Com.; Com. on Historic & Cultural Landmarks. **Fellowships, Honors & Awards:** Athens College, Greece, Fellowship 1977-78; Columbia Univ., Travel Grants 1981, 1985, Preceptorship 1987-89; Univ. of Pennsylvania & Univ. of Aquila, Research Grant 1985; Kress Fellowship, declined 1986. **Publications:** cat. entries, *Gardens and Ghettos, the Art of Jewish Life in Italy*, ed. V. Mann (Berkeley: UC Press, 1989); *The Future of Jewish Monuments*, exb. cat. (New York: Hebrew Union College, 1990); "Ordering the Urban Environment: City Statutes & City Planning in Medieval Todi, Italy," in *Ideas of Order in the Middle Ages*, ed. Warren Ginsberg (ACTA, 1990); "Private Initiatives in Preservation," *The Cracow Symposium on the Cultural Heritage of the CSCE Participating States, Commission on Security and Cooperation in Europe* (Washington, DC, 1991), 9-23; "Survey of Jewish Cemeteries in Poland Yields Results," *Avotaynu* 8.4 (Winter 1992); "Preservation Update: USA," *Judaica News* 3.4 (Fall 1992):

3-4; "Urbanism, Western Medieval," in *Scribner's Dictionary of the Middle Ages* (New York: Scribner's), 12:320-31; contr., *San Vincenzo al Volturno 1: The 1980-1986 Excavations*, Archaeological Monographs of the British School at Rome 7, ed. Richard Hodges (London: BSR, 1993); "The Synagogues of Eastern Europe," *Metropolis Magazine* (June 1993); co-author, *Survey of Historic Jewish Sites in Poland* (New York: World Monuments Fund, 1994). **Home Address:** 126 Circle Rd., Syracuse, NY 13210.

GRUEN, ERICH S. ■ RAAR Classics/Archaeology 90. b. May 7, 1935, Vienna, Austria. m. Joan B. Gruen. c. Bonnie, Keith, Jason. BA 57, Columbia Univ.; MA 60, Oxford Univ.; PhD 64, Harvard Univ. **Research/Artistic Interests:** Greek & Roman history. **Career & Employment:** Harvard Univ., Instr. 1964-66; UC, Berkeley, Asst. Prof.-Prof. 1966-present. **Fellowships, Honors & Awards:** Rhodes Scholarship 1957; Guggenheim Fellowship 1969, 1989; IAS 1973; NEH Grant 1984, 1995; Univ. of Cincinnati, Semple Classical Lect. 1985; AAAS Fellow 1986; UC, Distinguished Faculty Award 1987; AHA, James Breasted Prize 1988; Cornell Univ., Townsend Classical Lect. 1991. **Publications:** *Roman Politics and the Criminal Courts, 149-78 BC* (Cambridge, MA: Harvard Univ. Press, 1968); *The Image of Rome* (Englewood Cliffs, NJ: Prentice-Hall, 1969); *Imperialism in the Roman Republic* (New York: Holt, Rinehart & Winston, 1970); *The Roman Republic* (Washington, DC: AHA, 1972); *The Last Generation of the Roman Republic* (Berkeley: UC Press, 1974); *The Hellenistic World and the Coming of Rome*, 2 vols. (Berkeley: UC Press, 1984); *Studies in Greek Culture and Roman Policy* (Leiden: Brill, 1990); *Culture and National Identity in Republican Rome* (Ithaca: Cornell Univ. Press, 1992). **Home Address:** 1045 Mariposa Ave., Berkeley, CA 94707.

GUAITOLI, MARCELLO ■ Italian Fulbright Fellow 1972-73.

GUALANDI, MARIA LETIZIA ■ Italian Fulbright Fellow 1979-80.

GUALDO, LUCIA ROSA ■ Italian Fulbright Fellow 1956-57.

GUGGENHEIM, PEGGY ■ AAR Visitor 1959-64; Peggy Guggenheim Museum, Founder.

GUGLER, ERIC ■ Columbia Scholar 1911-14; AAR Trustee 1938-67, Architect.

GULIAS, JOHN ■ FAAR Sculpture 49. b. May 4, 1917, Shamokin, PA. **Study:** Leonardo Da Vinci Art School, NYC. **Career & Employment:** Independent Artist, Bronx, NY.

GURAN, MICHAEL ■ FAAR Architecture 71. b. Aug. 4, 1940. c. Helen, Alexander, Peter. BA 62, Univ. of Pennsylvania; MArch 64, Univ. of Pennsylvania. **Career & Employment:** Visiting Lect.: MIT 1973-75, Massachusetts College of Art 1973-75, Univ. of Southern California 1977-78; Univ. of Oregon, Asst. Prof. 1967-70; Moshe Safdie Asscs., Senior Designer 1979-94. **Fellowships, Honors & Awards:** Warren Powers Laird Memorial Prize 1962; NEA Fellowship 1970. **Important Works:** Musée Nat. de la Civilisation, Quebec 1981; Canadian Museum of Man, Hull 1983; Nat. Gallery of Canada, Ottawa 1983-84; Supreme Court of Israel, Jerusalem 1986; Toronto Ballet Opera House 1988-90; Vancouver Theater 1992-93; Design of the Shandin Community Center, Navajo reservation (Two Grey Hills area) 1992-94. **Exhibitions/Performances:** Shows have included sculpture spanning the main rotunda at MIT & electronically amplified

sculpture at the Palazzo Orsini Taverna, Rome; an annual installation in Davis Sq., Somerville, MA is performed with children. **Home Address:** 1 Fitchburg St., Somerville, MA 02143. **Business Address:** Harbor Studios, 1 Fitchburg St., B 150, Somerville, MA 02143.

GUSSOW, ALAN ■ FAAR Painting 55, RAAR Painting 87. b. May 8, 1931, Bronx, NY. m. Joan Dye. c. Adam, Seth. BA 52, Middlebury College; Cooper Union 1952-53. **Other Study:** Atelier 17, apprentice, graphic arts print shop, NYC 1952-53. **Research/Artistic Interests:** Through a series of actions – making art, organizing collective projects, teaching & lecturing, promoting ceremonies & rituals, writing essays, & directing workshops – I work to redefine the function of art in our time & to direct us toward a fuller appreciation of the Earth as our home. To promote an ecological viewpoint, I encourage others to know which systems they depend upon, and, as well, which systems depend upon them. Since the Earth is an experiential abstraction, I promote activities that are intended to bring people into intimate contact with the worlds that surround them, all the while asserting the importance of a sense of place. **Career & Employment:** Parsons School of Design, Instr. & Chair 1956-68; Sarah Lawrence College, Instr. 1959; Ohio State Univ., Visiting Artist 1974; Rockland Community College 1974; UC, Santa Cruz, Senior Lect. 1975, Visiting Prof. 1982, 1991, 1992, Regents Prof. 1990; Pace Univ., Adj. Assc. Prof. 1977; Bard College, Fellow 1978; Western State College of Colorado, Visiting Artist 1978; New York Studio School, Instr. 1978, 1982; UC, Berkeley, Visiting Lect. 1982; Queens College, CUNY, Summer Landscape Program, Instr. 1983; Iowa State Univ., Univ. Scholar & Artist-in-Residence 1984; Portland, OR State Univ. 1984; Middlebury College, Visiting Prof. 1986; College of the Atlantic, Visiting Lect. 1989; Beloit College, Visiting Critic & Lect. 1990. **Memberships & Offices:** Friends of the Earth, BoD 1974-94; Learning Alliance, Pres.-Chair, BoD 1989-91; Other Economic Summit, Chair BoD 1989-90; Seventh Generation, Burlington, VT, Bd. of Adv.; Rockland County, NY, Art in Public Places Com., Beautification Comm; Conway School of Landscape Design, Adv. Bd.; Edward Hopper Landmark Preservation Found., Nyack NY, BoT; Delaware Water Gap, Artists for Environment Found., 1st Chair, BoD. **Fellowships, Honors & Awards:** Cape Cod Nat. Seashore, Artist-in-Residence 1968; Hudson River Valley under Creative Art Public Service Program, Artist-in-Residence 1971; AAAL Award 1977; Thorpe-Intermedia Gallery, Sparkill, NY, Artist-in-Residence 1989. **Publications:** *A Sense of Place: The Artist and the American Land*, intro. by Richard Wilbur, forward by David Brower (San Francisco: Saturday Review Press & Friends of the Earth, 1972); "The Ecological Viewpoint: Nature as Source, not Scene," *The Structurist* (1976): 132-37; "Let's Put the Land into Landscapes," *NY Times* (Mar. 14, 1976): 1, 29; "In the Matter of Scenic Beauty," *Landscape* 21.3 (1978): 26-35; "Re-defining Art in a Nuclear Age," *Social Policy* (1983): 33-36; "Images from My Garden," *Country Journal* (May 1983); "Moving Toward the Center of Life," *In Context* (Spring 1984): 6-10; "A Land We Know but Have not Valued: Visions of New Beauty in the Hudson River Valley," intro. to *The New Response: Contemporary Painters of the Hudson River*, exb. cat. (Albany: Albany Inst. of History & Art, 1985), 9-14; "Land Places for Peace," *New American Land Magazine* (Nov.-Dec. 1987): 46-48; Untitled essay, in *The Emerging Landscape of Peace* (New York: Architects & Planners for Social Responsibility, 1987), 60-65; "Landscape Architect as Designer or Shaman?" in *Places for Peace, Working Papers*, ed. Karl Linn & Carl Anthony (Boston: World Congress of the Intl. Federation of

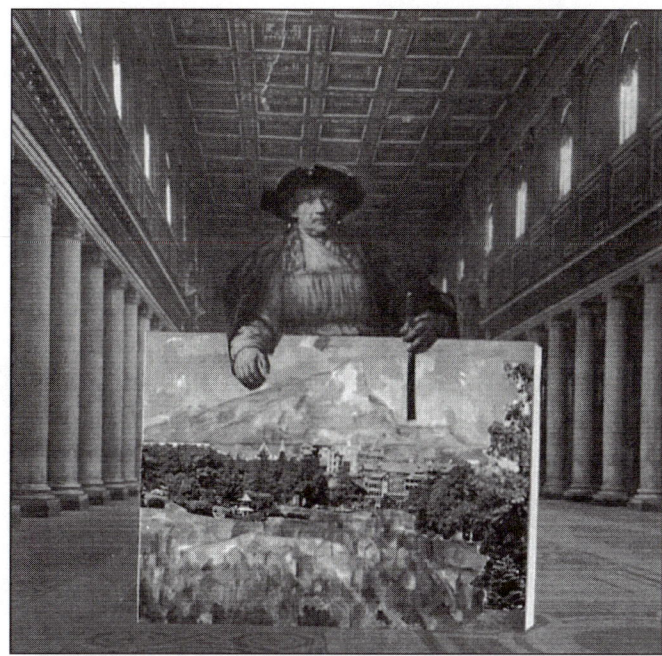

Alan Gussow

Landscape Architects, 1988), 50-53; *Art and Ecology in the City*, Proceedings of the First Intl. Conference on the Ecological City (Berkeley, CA: Urban Ecology, 1990); *The Artist as Native: Reinventing Regionalism*, intro. by John Driscoll (San Francisco, Pomegranate Art Books, 1993). **Important Works:** Public Collections: Arnot Art Museum, Elmira, NY; Bowdoin College Museum of Art, Brunswick, ME; Guild Hall, Easthampton, NY; Montgomery Museum of Fine Art, AL; Portland Museum of Art, ME; Sheldon Memorial Art Gallery, Lincoln, NE; Corcoran Gallery of Art, Washington, DC; Wichita Museum of Fine Art, KS; Virginia Museum of Fine Art, Richmond; Middlebury College, VT; UC, Santa Cruz; Green Gulch Farm, Zen Center, Sausalito, CA; Nat. Museum, Udine, Italy. **Exhibitions/Performances:** Solo: Middlebury College Arts Festival, VT 1961; Washington Co. Museum of Fine Arts, Hagerstown, MD 1961; Peridot Gallery, NYC 1962, 1963, 1964, 1966, 1967, 1969, 1970, 1972; Market Fair Gallery, Nyack, NY 1964; Kendall Gallery, Wellfleet, MA 1971; Portland Museum of Art, ME 1971; Lowe Gallery, Syracuse Univ., NY 1972; Joe de Mers Gallery, Hilton Head Island, SC 1972, 1973, 1978; Jacob's Ladder Gallery, Washington, DC 1974; Canessa Gallery, San Francisco 1975; Arnot Art Museum, Elmira, NY 1975; Sesnon Art Gallery, UC, Santa Cruz 1976; Frost Gully Gallery, Portland, ME 1976; Greenburgh Nature Center, Scarsdale, NY 1977; Washburn Gallery, NYC 1977, 1980; Retrospective, Rockland Center for the Arts, West Nyack, NY 1978; Inst. of Contemporary Art of the Virginia Museum, Richmond 1979; Art Center at Hargate, St. Paul's School, Concord, NH 1979; William Sawyer Gallery, San Francisco 1980; UC, Santa Cruz 1980, 1981; Hull Gallery, Washington, DC 1980, 1983; Hopper House, Nyack, NY 1983; Deutsch Gallery, NYC 1984; Gallery 181, College of Design, Iowa State Univ., Ames 1984; Univ. of Maine, Orono 1986; Blue Hill Cultural Center, Pearl River, NY 1987; Thorpe-Intermedia Gallery, Sparkill, NY 1989; Piermont Flywheel Gallery, Piermont, NY 1994; List Gallery, Swarthmore College 1994. **Bio-Bibliography:** *Dictionary of Contemporary American Artists; Who's Who in America, Who's Who in American Art.* **Home Address:** 563 Piermont Ave., Piermont, NY 10968.

GUSTON, PHILIP ■ FAAR Painting 49, RAAR Painting 71; AAR Trustee 1969-76. b. June 27, 1913, Montreal, Canada. d. June 7, 1980. m. Musa McKim. c. Musa Jane Guston Mayer. **Study:** Otis Art Inst. 1930. **Career & Employment:** WPA Mural Painter 1935-40; Univ. of Iowa, Teacher 1941-45; Washington Univ., St. Louis, 1945-46; NYU, Adj. Prof. 1951-58; Pratt Inst., Faculty 1953-58; Independent Painter, Woodstock, NY 1967-80; Boston Univ., Univ. Prof. 1975-77. **Memberships & Offices:** Nat. Soc. of Mural Painters; Mural Artist Guild; American Artist Congress, NIAL; AAAS. **Fellowships, Honors & Awards:** NY World's Fair, 1st Prize 1939; Virginia Museum of Fine Arts, 5th Biennial, John Barton Bayne Medal & Purchase 1946; PAFA, Pennell Memorial Medal 1947; NAD, Altman Prize 1947; Guggenheim Fellowship 1947, 1968; Flora Mayer Witkowsky Prize 1959; Ford Found. Grant 1959. **Important Works:** Collections: Tate Gallery, London; Guggenheim Museum, NYC; MOMA; Phillips Collection, Washington, DC; MMA; Whitney Museum, NYC; Albright-Knox Gallery, Buffalo; Cleveland Museum of Art; AIC; Los Angeles County Museum; City Art Museum, St. Louis; Worcester Art Museum; Virginia Museum of Fine Arts, Richmond. Works: Univ. of Michoacan, Mexico; Los Angeles Sanitorium, Duarte, CA; WPA Bldg.; St. Louis Art Museum; Washington Univ.; Virginia Museum of Fine Art; Wesleyan Univ.; Univ. of Iowa; Queensbridge Housing Project, NY; US Post Office, Commerce, GA; Forestry Bldg., Laconia, NH; Social Security Bldg., Washington, DC; President Lines: "SS Monroe," "SS Van Buren," "SS Jackson." **Exhibitions/Performances:** Whitney Museum, NYC 1938-45; World's Fair NY 1939; MOMA 1940; ALNY 1940; Carnegie Inst. 1941-44, 1945; American Federation of Art 1942; AIC 1942-45; Corcoran Gallery of Art, Washington, DC 1943-44; PAFA 1944-45; Midtown Gallery, NYC 1945; Critic's Choice, Honorary Show 1945; Virginia Museum of Fine Arts 1946; MFA 1946; Retrospectives: 5th Biennal, Sao Paolo, 1959; 30th Biennale, Venice 1960; Guggenheim Museum, NYC 1962; San Francisco Museum of Art 1980, traveled to Brussels, London & Los Angeles; MOMA 1988. **Bio-Bibliography:** Dore Ashton, *Yes But...A Critical Study of Philip Guston* (New York: Viking Press, 1976); *Philip Guston*, exb. cat. (New York: George Braziller 1980); "Philip Guston: "It's a Strange Thing to Be Immersed in the Culture of Painting," *Art News* (Sept. 1980); "Gust, Gusto, Guston," *Art Forum* (Oct. 1980); Robert Storr, *Philip Guston*, Modern Masters Series 11 (New York: Abbeville Press, 1986); Musa G. Mayer, "My Father, Philip Guston," *NY Times Magazine* (Aug. 7, 1988); *Who Was Who in American Art.*

GUTMAN, ROBERT ■ AAR Visitor 1989-90.

■   ■   ■

H

HAAG, ED C. ■ FAAR Landscape Architecture 79. b. Dec. 6, 1946, Sacramento, CA. m. Renee L. Haag. c. Allison, Olivia. BS 69, California Polytechnic; MLA 78, Univ. of Pennsylvania. **Research/Artistic Interests:** Steel sculpture. **Career & Employment:** Kenneth Anderson Asscs., Designer 1969-70; Johnson Leffingwell & Asscs., Designer 1970-73; Lawrence Halprin &

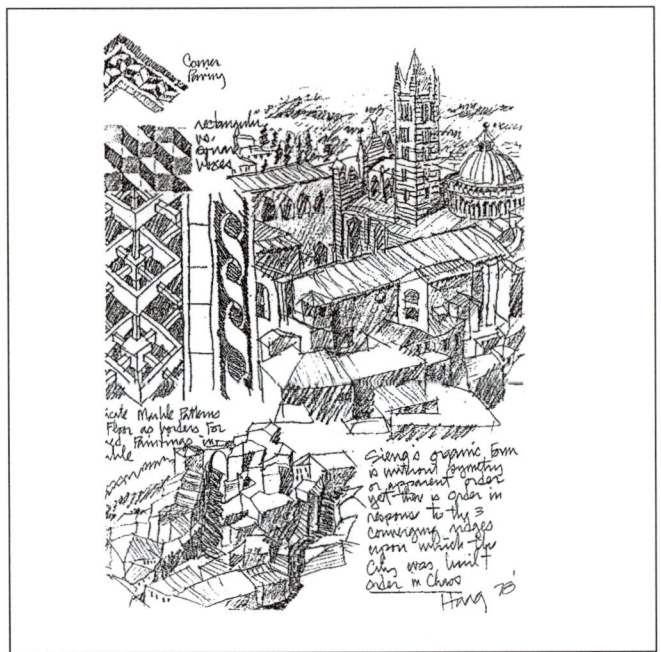

Ed Haag

Asscs., Designer 1974-76; Wallace Mcharg Roberts & Todd, Designer 1977; Hanna Olin, Ltd. 1978. **Memberships & Offices:** ASLA. **Important Works:** Colorado River Edge Study for Colorado Div. of Highways, Glenwood Springs 1977; Cook Residence 1981; Concord Corner, with Stuart Nelson, Entry to City of Concord 1986; Gerson Bakar Residence, Napa, CA 1988; *People Fence,* Topiary Steel Figures for Hyatt Hotel, Sacramento 1989; Old Sacramento Waterfront State Park 1989; Southern Pacific Railyard Master Plan, Landscape 1991; Kubic's Aquatic Garden, *Lincoln Log,* Graveland Holland 1993; Old Sacramento Vest Pocket Park 1993; *Man's Best Friends,* with Peter Van Venberge, Topiary & Ceramics Sculpture for Sacramento Arts Comm. 1993; D.O. Mills Rooftop Garden 1993; *Ribbons of Steel,* Granite & Stainless Steel Sculpture for LRT Station, Sacramento 1994. **Home Address:** 4323 G St., Sacramento, CA 95819. **Business Address:** Renee Lee, 4323 G St., Sacramento, CA 95819.

HADLEY, ARTHUR T. ■ AAR Charter Mem.; Educator; Yale Univ., Pres.

HADZI, DIMITRI ■ RAAR Sculpture 74. b. Mar. 21, 1921, NYC. m. Martha Leeb, FAAR 54; Cynthia Hoyle. c. Christina Hadzi, Stephen Hadzi. Cert. 50, Cooper Union. **Other Study:** Polytechnic Inst., Athens 1950-51; Belle Arti, Rome 1952-53; Museo Artistico Industriale, Rome 1953-54; Asst. in the studio of sculptors: Milton Hebald, John Hohvanis, Berta Margolis. **Research/Artistic Interests:** Sculpture, printmaking, painting, lapidary. **Career & Employment:** Harvard Univ., Prof. 1975-89, Prof. Emeritus 1989-present. **Memberships & Offices:**

AAAL, Awards Com., Juror 1988-91, Chair. 1991-92. **Fellowships, Honors & Awards:** Fulbright Fellow 1950; Guggenheim Fellowship 1957; Louis Comfort Tiffany Award 1962; NIAL Grant 1962; Harvard Univ., Hon. MA 1977; AAAS Fellow 1978; Whiting Teaching Travel Grant 1982; AAAL Fellow 1983; Asian Cultural Council Travel Grant to Japan 1984; Lawrence Univ., Hon. DFA 1987; Cooper Union, Saint-Gaudens Award 1989. **Publications:** illust., Anthony Hecht, *Venetian Vespers* (Boston: Godine, 1984); illus., Seamus Heaney, *Keeping Going, Poems* (Concord, NH: Ewert, 1994). **Important Works:** Collections: Guggenheim Museum, NYC; Hirshhorn Museum, Washington, DC; Hakone Outdoor Sculpture Museum, Tokyo; MIT; Phillips Collection, Washington, DC; Yale Univ. Art Gallery; Whitney Museum, NYC; MOMA; Avery Fisher Hall, Lincoln Center, NYC; Owens-Illinois Co., Toledo, OH; Hugo Black Federal Courthouse, Birmingham, AL; Harvard Sq., Cambridge, MA; Copley Place, Boston; Federal Office Bldg., Portland, OR; Commissions: Bronze Doors, St. Paul's Church, Rome. **Exhibitions/ Performances:** Seiferheld Gallery, NYC 1959; Galeria Schneider, Rome 1958, 1960; Felix Landau Gallery, Los Angeles 1960; Galerie Van de Loo, Munich 1961; Stephen Radich Gallery, NYC 1961, 1962; Hayden Gallery, Cambridge, MA 1963; Hopkins Center, Dartmouth College, Hanover, NH 1969; Alpha Gallery, Boston 1971, 1977; Richard Gray Gallery, Chicago 1972; Jodi Scully Gallery, Los Angeles 1973; Galleria dell'Obelisco, Rome 1974; Mekler Gallery, Los Angeles 1977, 1981, 1982; Gruenebaum Gallery, NYC 1978, 1984; Fogg Art Museum, Cambridge, MA 1984; Richard Gray Gallery, Chicago 1987; Martin Sumers Gallery, NYC 1988; Rikugien Gallery, Tokyo 1989; Kouros Gallery, NYC 1989, 1995; Sert Gallery, Carpenter Center, Harvard Univ. 1989; Smith Anderson Gallery, Palo Alto, CA 1990; St. Luke's Gallery, Washington, DC 1990; Newman Galleries, Beverly Hills 1990, 1991; Levinson-Kane Gallery, Boston 1991; Art Museum, Duxbury, MA 1991; Gremillion Gallery, Houston 1992. **Bio-Bibliography:** A. Elsen, "Sculpture with a Memory," *Art News* 9 (1978); J. Masheck, "Dimitri Hadzi's Omphalos for Harvard Sq.," *Arts Magazine* (May 1986); G. Norland, *Dimitri Hadzi,* exb. cat. (Cambridge, MA: Harvard Univ., 1989); T.E. Stebbins, *The Lure of Italy,* exb. cat. (Boston: MFA, 1992); *Who's Who in America, Who's Who in American Art.* **Home Address:** 7 Ellery Sq., Cambridge, MA 02138. **Business Address:** Studio Hadzi, 111 Charles St., Cambridge, MA 02141.

HADZI, MARTHA LEEB ■ FAAR Classics/Archaeology 54. b. Dec. 24, 1919, Short Hills, NJ. c. Cristina, Stephen. BA 41, Vassar College; MA 50, IFA; PhD 56, Yale Univ. **Other Study:** Belgian American Educational Found. 1949; NEH Summer Inst. 1983. **Research/Artistic Interests:** Sojourner Truth, Sears-Robuck pre-fabs. **Career & Employment:** MMA, Docent 1941-42; Vassar College, Visiting Asst. Prof. 1943-44; Bennett Junior College, Instr. 1944-45; Smith College, Instr. 1946-50; Wellesley College, Instr. 1972; Mt. Holyoke College, Asst. Prof.-Assc. Prof.-Prof. 1972-85. **Memberships & Offices:** *Art in America,* Ed. Staff 1961-63; AIA, Western MA, Sec. 1983-84, VP 1984-89. **Fellowships, Honors & Awards:** Fulbright Grant 1950-52; APS Research Grant 1979; Mt. Holyoke College Faculty Grant 1979. **Publications:** contr., *Samothrace,* ed. Karl Lehmann & Phyllis Williams Lehmann, vol. 3, *The Hieron* (Princeton: Princeton Univ. Press. 1969), 256-58; vol. 4.1, "The Altar Court" (New York: Bollingen Found., 1962), 169-74; vol. 5, "The Temenos" (Princeton: Princeton Univ. Press, 1982), 172-220, 233-52, 304-12; *Transformations in Hellenistic Art,* exb. cat. (Northampton, MA: Mt. Holyoke Art Museum, 1983.) **Home Address:** 159 Glendale Rd., Amherst, MA 01002.

HAECKL, ANNE E. ■ FAAR Classics/Archaeology 78; AAR Classical Summer School, Asst. Dir. 1978. b. Jan. 3, 1951, Cincinnati, OH. BA 73, College of Wooster, OH; MA 77, Univ. of Michigan. **Other Study:** Archaeological field work: Tell Gezer, Israel; Carthage, Tunisia; El-Lejjun & Umm-el-Jimal, Jordan. **Career & Employment:** Univ. of Colorado, Instr. 1979-84; Archaeological Field School in Carthage, Assc. Dir. 1982, 1983, 1990, 1992-94. **Fellowships, Honors & Awards:** College of Wooster, Scholarship 1971-73; Eta Sigma Phi 1972-73; Phi Beta Kappa 1973, Frank Hewitt Cowles Memorial Prize 1973; Univ. of Michigan Fellowships 1974-79, 1986-89. **Publications:** "Head of the Deified Vespasian," and "Head of an Old Man," in *Roman Portraiture: Ancient and Modern Revivals*, ed. E.K. Gazda (Ann Arbor: Univ. of Michigan Press, 1977), 16-17, 30-31; ed. & contr., *The Gods of Egypt in the Graeco-Roman Period* (Ann Arbor: Univ. of Michigan Press, 1977), 1-117; "The *Principia* of El-Lejjun," in *The Roman Frontier in Jordan: Interim Report on the Limes Arabicus Project, 1980-1985*, ed. S.T. Parker, BAR Intl. Series 340.1 (1987): 203-60; co-ed. with Elaine K. Gazda, *Roman Art in the Private Sphere: Essays on the Art of the Domus, Villa and Insula* (Ann Arbor: Univ. of Michigan Press, 1991); with Naomi J. Norman, "The Yasmina Necropolis at Carthage, 1992," *Journal of Roman Archaeology* 6 (1993): 238-50; with Elaine K. Gazda, "Roman Portraiture: Reflections on the Question of Context," *Journal of Roman Archaeology* 6 (1993): 289-302. **Home Address:** 324 S. Ashley, Apt. 5, Ann Arbor, MI 48104. **Business Address:** Braithwaite Consultants, Inc., 3928 Varsity Dr., Ann Arbor, MI 48018.

HAHN, WALTER HUMPHREY ■ FAAR Painting 57. b. Sept. 17, 1927, Milwaukee, WI. m. Maude Hahn. c. Kim. BAE 51, AIC School. **Fellowships, Honors & Awards:** AIC Pauline Palmer Purchase Prize 1951. **Exhibitions/Performances:** G Gallery, NYC 1957, 1958-59.

HAIEFF, ALEXEI ■ FAAR Musical Composition 49, RAAR Musical Composition 53, 58. b. Aug. 25, 1914, Biagoveschensk, Siberia. d. Mar. 1, 1994. m. Shiela Haieff. **Studies:** Juilliard Grad. School with Rubin Goldmark & Frederick Jacobi 1934-38; with Nadia Boulanger 1938-39. **Career & Employment:** Carnegie Inst. of Technology, Visiting Andrew Mellon Prof. 1962-63; SUNY, Buffalo, Visiting Slee Prof., 1962, 1964-65; Brandeis Univ., Visiting Prof. 1965-66; Univ. of Utah, Composer-in-Residence 1967-70. **Fellowships, Honors & Awards:** Lili Boulanger, 1st Award 1942; AAAL Medal 1945; Guggenheim Fellowship 1946, 1949; NYC Music Critics' Award 1952. **Important Works:** *Symphonies* 1942, 1958, 1961; *Divertimento for Small Orchestra* 1944; *Sonata for Two Pianos* 1945; *Violin Concerto* 1948; *Piano Concerto* 1949-50; *String Quartet No. 1* 1951; *Eclogue*, for harp & string orchestra 1953; *Ballet in E* 1955; *Saints' Wheel*, variations for piano 1960; *Sonata for Cello* 1963; *Slavonic Liturgical Chants for Holy & Easter Weeks*, for a cappella chorus 1969; *Caligula*, for baritone & orchestra 1971; *Rhapsodies*, for guitar & harpsichord 1980. **Bio-Bibliography:** *Baker's Biographical Dictionary of American Musicians, New Grove Dictionary of American Music.*

HAIGHT, ELIZABETH ■ AAR Classical Soc., Pres. 1939.

HALE, WILLIAM GARDNER ■ ASCSR, Dir. 1895-96.

HALPERIN, DAVID MARTIN ■ FAAR Classics/Archaeology 77. b. Apr. 2, 1952, Chicago, IL. BA 73, Oberlin College. **Other Studies:** Stanford Univ. c.1978-79. **Career & Employment:** MIT, Prof. **Fellowships, Honors & Awards:** Oberlin College, Florence A. Frew Prize 1972; Stanford Univ. Fellow 1973-78.

HAMILL, ALFRED E. ■ AAR Trustee 1928-39, Bank Exec.

HAMILTON, LORENZO ■ Winchester Fellow 1920-21, 1921-22.

HAMILTON, ROBERT G. ■ RAAR Painting 74. b. Oct. 1, 1916, Seneca Falls, NY. m. Nancy D. Hamilton. c. Scott, Victoria. BFA 47, RISD. **Other Study:** ASL 1940. **Career & Employment:** RISD, Prof. 1948-81. **Fellowships, Honors & Awards:** Boston Arts Festival, 1st, 2d, 3d Prizes 1956, 1958, 1959. **Important Works:** Public Collections: MIT; Brown Univ; DeCordova Museum, Lincoln, MA; Brandeis Univ.; Univ. of Massachusetts; Tougaloo College, Univ. of Tennessee, Knoxville; Farnsworth Museum, Rockland, ME. **Exhibitions/Performances:** Solo: Kanegis Gallery, Boston 1957, 1959, 1960, 1961, 1962; Cambridge Art Assn. 1958; Inst. of Contemporary Art, Boston 1958, 1962, 1964, 1967; Carnegie Intl. Exb. 1959; Univ. of Illinois Nat. Exb. 1959, 1960; Cornell Univ. 1960; DeCordova Museum, Lincoln, MA 1961, 1963, 1964; Alpha Gallery, Boston 1966, 1968, 1969; Lily Iselin Gallery, Providence 1982; Virginia Lynch Gallery 1986; Icon Gallery, Brunswick, ME 1990; Frick Gallery, Belfast, ME 1994. **Home Address:** PO Box 158, Port Clyde, ME 04855.

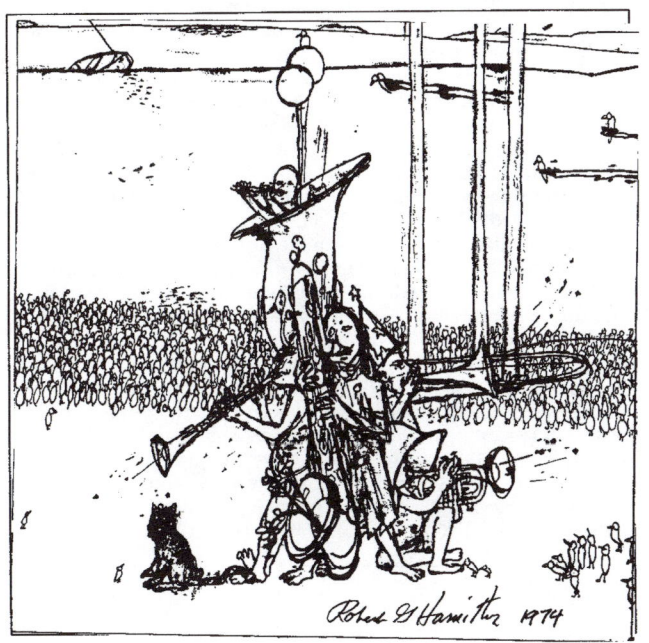

Robert G. Hamilton

HAMMOND, FREDERICK F. ■ FAAR Post-Classical/Humanistic Studies 66. b. Aug. 7, 1937, Binghamton, NY. BA 58, Yale Univ.; Cert. Russian 60, Yale Univ.; PhD 65, Yale Univ. **Research/Artistic Interests:** 17th-century Italian music & culture. **Career & Employment:** Univ. of Chicago, Instr. 1962-65; Queens College, CUNY, Asst. Prof. 1966-68; UCLA, Asst. Prof.-Prof. 1968-93; Bard College, Irma Brandeis Prof. 1989-present. **Memberships & Offices:** Clarion Music Society, Assc. Music Dir. 1973-present; E. Nakamichi Festival, Dir. 1986-present. **Fellowships, Honors & Awards:** Yale Univ., Carnegie Fellow 1958-59; Cavaliere al merito della Reppublica, Italian Government 1986. **Publications:** *Girolamo Frescobaldi* (Cambridge: Harvard Univ. Press, 1983); *Frescobaldi: A Guide to Research* (New York: Garland, 1988); *Music and Spectacle in Baroque Rome* (New Haven: Yale Univ. Press, 1994). **Exhibitions/Performances:** Solo recitals in the US, France, Italy, including Anno Europeo della Musica, Festival di Monreale, Smithsonian Inst., Villa I Tatti. **Bio-Bibliography:** *Baker's Biographical Dictionary.* **Business Address:** Bard College, Annandale-on-Hudson, NY 12504.

HAMMOND, MASON ■ RAAR Classics/Archaeology 52, 63; School of Classical Studies, Prof.-in-Charge 1937-39, 1955-57; Summer School; AAR Trustee 1941-76, Trustee Emer. b. Feb. 14, 1903, Boston, MA. m. Florence Hohior Pierson. c. Florence, Anstiss, Elizabeth. BA 25, Harvard Univ.; BA 30, Oxford Univ. **Other Study:** As a teacher of classics (Latin & Roman history) life has been pretty steadily study. **Career & Employment:** Harvard Univ., Instr.-Pope Prof. 1928-73; Pope Prof. Emer. 1973-present. **Fellowships, Honors & Awards:** Rhodes Scholar, 1925-28; French Legion of Honor, Italian, Dutch. **Bio-Bibliography:** *Harvard Fiftieth Class Report for Class of 1925.* **Home Address:** 153 Brattle St., Cambridge, MA 02138. **Business Address:** Harvard Univ., Dept. of Classics, Cambridge, MA 02138.

> IN 1937-38 UNDER CHESTER ALDRICH and his sister, Miss Amy Aldrich, the Academy community was then smaller and closely knit. As I recall there were no married fellows; and in Mussolini's Rome the foreign academies were more turned in on themselves, though we never, that I recall, had any direct interference by the Fascists. The Fellows were generally younger than they now are, and Miss Amy served as a surrogate mother when necessary. A great friend of the Academy was a retired Italian Air Force general called Helbig, the son of a distinguished director of the German Institute and a Russian mother. He lived in the basement of the Villa Lante (now the Finnish Academy) at the middle of the Janiculum and rented the upper floor to an American girls' school. Helbig used to organize Sunday walks in the country for American Ambassador and Mrs. William Phillips and their daughter, Beatrice, and for the Aldriches and us. He led these with German discipline and Italian appreciation of scenery and monuments.
>
> During the Second World War, the Director of the Swedish Institute, Prof. Sjöqvist, took care of the Academy; and the Library was kept open for scholars, among whom the most regular in attendance was Prof. Van Buren, who had been a Fellow of the Classical School in 1906. When, after Italy surrendered in World War II, Prof. Henry Rowell, then of the U.S. Military Monuments, Fine Arts, and Archives unit, entered Rome and went up to the Academy, Prof. Van Buren lifted his head from his work, said "Hello Henry," and continued what he was doing. He survived into the 1950s.

Mason Hammond

HAMMONS, DAVID ■ FAAR Sculpture 90. b. 1943, Springfield, IL. 65, Los Angeles Trade Technical City College; 68, Chouinard Art Inst., Los Angeles; 72, Otis Art Inst., Parsons School of Design, Los Angeles. **Fellowships, Honors & Awards:** NEA 1982; NYSCA 1982; Guggenheim Fellowship 1983-84; Art Matters, NYFA 1987; Tiffany Grant 1990; MacArthur Award 1991; DAAD Berlin 1992. **Important Works:** Abstract Crashing, Studio Museum of Harlem, NYC 1978; Evening Glow, Central Park, NYC 1979; Blizzard Ball Sale, Cooper Square, NYC 1983; Higher Goals, Harlem, NYC 1986; Doll Shoe Salesman, Astor Place, NYC 1986. **Exhibitions/Performances:** Solo: Brockman Gallery, Los Angeles 1971; Fine Arts Gallery, Los Angeles 1974; Just Above Midtown, NYC 1975, 1976, 1986; Neighborhood Art Center, Atlanta 1977; New Museum of Contemporary Art, NYC 1980; Exit Art, NYC 1989; Jack Tilton Gallery, NYC 1990; Retrospective: Inst. of Contemporary Art-P.S. 1, Long Island City, NY 1990, traveling to Inst. of Contemporary Art, Philadelphia & San Diego Museum of Contemporary Art, La Jolla 1991; Williams College Art Center,

Williamstown, MA 1993, traveling to San Francisco Museum of Modern Art 1993; Illinois State Museum, Springfield 1993; & numerous group shows. **Bio-Bibliography:** *Rousing the Rubble,* exb. cat. (Cambridge: MIT Press, 1991); *Coming Home,* exb. cat. (Illinois State Museum, 1993). **Home Address:** c/o A.C. Hudgins, 94 Grand Ave., Englewood, NJ 07631. **Business Address:** Jack Tilton Gallery, 49 Greene St., NYC 10013.

HAMPTON, MARK ■ AAR Trustee 1990-present. BA, De Pauw Univ.; MA, IFA. **Memberships & Offices:** American Soc. of Interior Designers. **Fellowships, Honors & Awards:** Interior Design Hall of Fame; Morgan Library, Fellow. **Important Works:** Blair House, Washington, DC, Restoration; Governor's Mansion, Albany, NY, Restoration; Gracie Mansion, NYC, Restoration; Villa Aurelia, Rome, Restoration; White House, Washington, DC, Oval Office & Reception Rooms of West Wing Restoration. **Publications:** *Mark Hampton on Decorating* (New York: Random House, 1989); *Legendary Decorators of the Twentieth Century* (New York: Doubleday, 1992); articles in *Vogue, The World of Interiors, Architectural Digest, NY Times, Vanity Fair* & *Harper's Bazaar.*

HANCOCK, WALKER K. ■ FAAR Sculpture 28, RAAR Sculpture 57, 63; AAR Exec. Com.; AAR Trustee 1956-74, Trustee Emer. b. June 28, 1901, St. Louis, MO. c. Saima E. Natti, Deane French. DFA 19, Washington Univ., School of Fine Arts; LHD, UC, Berkeley. **Other Study:** Yale Divinity School; PAFA 1920-24; Studio of Charles Grafly. **Career & Employment:** PAFA 1929-61. **Memberships & Offices:** NAD, Academician; NSS, Fellow; Royal Soc. of Arts, Benjamin Franklin Fellow. **Fellowships, Honors & Awards:** PAFA, Widener Gold Medal 1925, Gold Medal of Honor 1953; NAD, Anonymous Prize for Sculpture 1949; ALNY, Silver Medal 1955; NSS, Medal of Honor 1981; NEA, Nat. Medal of Arts 1989; Saint-Gaudens Medal 1992. **Important Works:** St. Louis Soldiers Memorial; Pennsylvania Railroad War Memorial, Philadelphia; Founders' Memorial, Bell Telephone Co. of Canada, Montreal; *John Paul Jones,* Fairmont Park, Philadelphia; Field Service Memorial, Blérancourt, France; *Gethsemane Group,* Topsfield, MA & Trappist, KY; *Gen. Douglas MacArthur,* US Military Acad., West Point, NY; *James Madison,* Library of Congress, Washington, DC; *Air,* Civic Center, Philadelphia; *Abraham Lincoln,* Nat. Cathedral, Washington, DC; *George Bush,* US Capitol, Washington, DC; Flight Memorial, US Military Acad., West Point, NY. **Bio-Bibliography:** *Who's Who in America.* **Home Address:** Box 7133, Lanesville, Gloucester, MA 01930.

HANES, JAMES ■ FAAR Painting 53. m. Teresa Butini. c. Paul, Nicole, Jamie. **Fellowships, Honors & Awards:** PAFA, Toppan Prize for Composition 1949, Lambert Purchase Prize 1950; Louis Comfort Tiffany Found. 1st Award 1950; NAD, Allied Artists of America Exb., Gold Medal 1950, Maynard Portrait Prize 1962, Annual Exb. Purchase Award 1964, Salmagundi Prize 1964, Annual Exb. Portrait Prize 1974. **Important Works:** PAFA; Univ. of Tampa; Yale Univ.; NAD; La Salle College, Philadelphia; Germantown Friends School, Philadelphia; Randall Thompson Collection, Harvard Univ. **Exhibitions/Performances:** Group: PAFA Annual 1949, 1951, 1955, 1960; Palazzo Venezia, Rome 1951; Palazzo dell' Esposizione, Rome 1953; NIAL 1955; Philadelphia Museum of Art, Regional Exb. 1956, 1961, 1962; Solo: Univ. of Pittsburgh 1972; E.I. Du Pont Co., Wilmington, DE 1975; PAFA, Peale House Galleries 1979; Goldsmith Garden Center, Memphis 1980; Berks Gallery, Reading, PA 1983; Palazzo Papale, Orvieto, Italy 1985. **Bio-Bibliography:** Valerio Mariani, "Un Pittore Americano," *IDEA* (Aug.

16, 1953); *Dictionary of International Biography; Who's Who in American Art.* **Home Address:** 415 W. Stafford St., Philadelphia, PA 19144.

HANKINS, JAMES ■ FAAR Post-Classical/Humanistic Studies 82. b. Jan. 31, 1955, Philadelphia, PA. m. Virginia Brown, FAAR 68. BA 77, Duke Univ.; MA 78, Columbia Univ.; MPhil 80, Columbia Univ.; PhD 84, Columbia Univ. **Career & Employment:** Columbia Univ., Instr. 1982-83, Lect. 1983-85; Harvard Univ., Asst. Prof. 1985-89, Assc. Prof. 1989-91, Prof. 1992-present; Villa I Tatti, Visiting Prof. 1992. **Fellowships, Honors & Awards:** Fulbright Scholarship 1980-81; Columbia Univ., Soc. of Fellows in the Humanities 1983-85; Villa I Tatti Fellow 1988-89; ACLS Fellow 1988-89; *Journal of the History of Ideas,* Morris D. Forkosch Prize 1990; Guggenheim Fellow 1992. **Publications:** trans. & ed., with Gordon Griffiths & David Thompson, *The Humanism of Leonardo Bruni: Selected Texts* (Binghamton, NY: MRTS, 1987); ed., with J. Monfasani & F. Purnell, Jr., *Supplementum Festivum: Studies in Honor of Paul Oskar Kristeller* (Binghamton, NY: MRTS, 1987); *Plato in the Italian Renaissance,* 2 vols. (Leiden: E.J. Brill, 1990); "The Latin Poetry of Leonardo Bruni," *Humanistica Lovaniensia* 39 (1990): 1-39; "Cosimo de'Medici and the 'Platonic Academy'," *Journal of the Warburg and Courtauld Institutes* 53 (1990): 144-62; "The Humanist, the Banker, and the Condottiere: An Unpublished Letter of Cosimo and Lorenzo de' Medici Written by Leonardo Bruni," in *Renaissance Society and Culture: Essays in Honor of Eugene F. Rice, Jr.,* ed. J. Monfasani & R.G. Musto (New York: Italica Press, 1991), 59-70; "Bruni Manuscripts in North America: A Handlist," in *Per il Censimento dei codici dell' Epistolario di Leonardo Bruni, Nuovi Studi storici* 10 (Rome: Istituto Storico Italiano per il Medio Evo, 1991), 55-90; "The Myth of the Platonic Academy of Florence," *Renaissance Quarterly* 44.3 (1991): 429-75; "Cosimo de' Medici as a Patron of Humanistic Literature," in *Cosimo 'il Vecchio' de' Medici, 1389-1989: Essays in Commemoration of the 600th Anniversary of Cosimo de' Medici's Birth,* ed. F. Ames-Lewis (Oxford: Clarendon Press, 1993), 69-94; "The Popes and Humanism," in *Rome Reborn: The Vatican Library and Renaissance Culture,* ed. Anthony Grafton, exb. cat. (Washington, DC: Library of Congress, 1993), 46-85; "Lorenzo de' Medici as a Patron of Philosophy," *Rinascimento* n.s. 34 (1994): 1-38; "Renaissance Crusaders: Humanist Crusade Literature in the Age of Mehmed II," *Dunbarton Oaks Papers* 48 (1994): in press; *Repertorium Brunianum: A Critical Bibliography of the Writings of Leonardo Bruni,* vol. 1 (Rome: Istituto Storico per il Medio Evo, in press); "Remarks on the Textual Tradition of Leonardo Bruni's *Epistulae familiares,*" in *Miscellanea di studi umanistici in onore di Gian Vito Resta,* ed. V. Fera & G. Ferraù (Messina: Facoltà di lettere e filosofia, Università di Messina, in press). **Home Address:** 993 Memorial Drive, No. 603, Cambridge, MA 02138. **Business Address:** Dept. of History, Harvard Univ., Cambridge, MA 02138.

HANNA, ROBERT MITCHELL ■ FAAR Landscape Architecture 76. b. May 21, 1935, Deming, NM. m. Beverly Briggs. c. Robert Mitchell, Jr. BArch 59, Univ. of Washington, Seattle; MLA 67, Harvard Univ. **Career & Employment:** Richard Haag Asscs. 1963-66; Boston Redevelopment Authority, Urban Design Architect 1967-69; Univ. of Pennsylvania, Adj. Prof. 1969-present; Hanna-Olin, Ltd., Prin. 1976-present; Found. for Architecture, Philadelphia, BoT 1992-present; Harvard GSD, Alumni Council 1993-present. **Fellowships, Honors & Awards:** Univ. of Pennsylvania, Hon. MArch 1978. **Publications:** with J. Wampler & S.I. Rifaat, *Environmental Design Program* (Boston: BRA Publication, 1967); with Walter Issard & Chas. W.

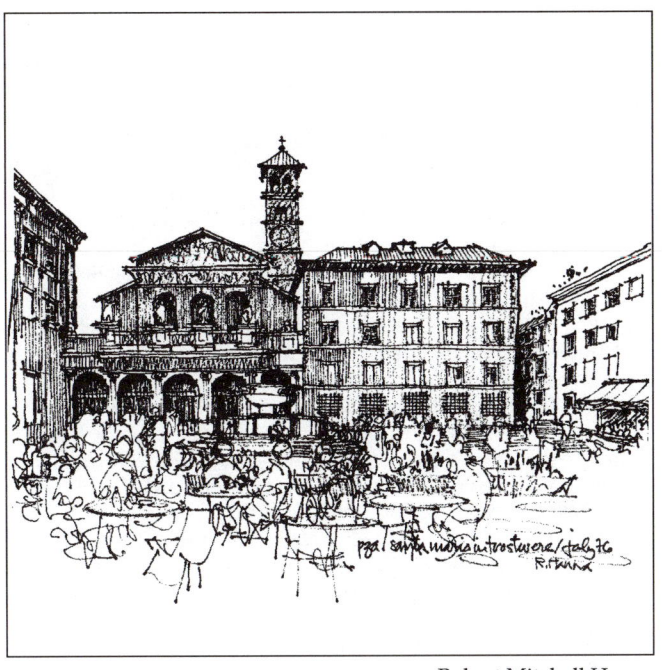

Robert Mitchell Hanna

Harris, "A Quantitative Approach to the Analysis of Visual Environmental Attribute," *Study of Continental Shelf Resources* (Boston: Harvard Univ., Dept. of Landscape Architecture Research Office, 1967); with S. Higenhurst & S. Diamond, *Downtown Design and Development* (Boston: Boston Redevelopment Authority, 1969); with J. Wampler, C.Y. Lee, J. Kriken, *Boston Expo-New Community, Proposal for the 1976 Bicentennial* (Boston: BRA Publication, 1969); with Laurie D. Olin & A.T. Lager, *Assessment and Long Range Planning for the Li-Wu River Gorge: Toroko National Park* (PRC, 1986); with Laurie D. Olin, Peter Shepheard, & others, *Landscape Architecture Master Plan for the University of Pennsylvania* (Philadelphia: Univ. of Pennsylvania, 1977); with Univ. of Pennsylvania City Planning Comm., *Open Space and Public Facilities Framework for Tioga-Nicetown* (Philadelphia: Citizens of Tioga-Nicetown, 1977). **Important Works:** Battery Park City, NYC, Master Plan 1980, & Phases I & II with Cooper Eckstut 1981-present; Carnegie Center Office Park, Princeton, Master Plan with Stubbins Assc. & Phase II & IV Development 1982-present; Commerce Sq., Phases I & II, Philadelphia 1984-92; Ellis Island Nat. Museum of Immigration, NYC 1985-1993; Westlake Sq., Seattle 1989; Univ. of Washington, Student Union & Library Green & Grieg Memorial Grove 1989; 20-Year Strategic Plan for Downtown Los Angeles, with E. Moule, S. Polyzoides, et al. 1992; Univ. of Pennsylvania, Shearson Lehman Quadrangle & Class of '62 Walk 1992; US Holocaust Memorial Museum, Washington, with Pei Cobb Freed 1993; Cleveland Public Library, Eastman Garden, Cleveland, current; Univ. of Washington Branch Campus, Tacoma, Master Plan & Phase I Development, with Moore Ruble Yuddel, current; Univ. of Pennsylvania, Revlon Student Center with Kohn, Pedersen, Fox, current; with R. Dickson, S. Woodland, Urban Design Plan for Canberra, Australia for Nat. Capitol Planning Authority. **Exhibitions/Performances:** Denver Museum of Art 1979; Whitney Museum, NYC 1982; ASLA, Nat. Design Awards, Washington 1982, Phoenix 1984, Seattle 1988; Inst. of Contemporary Art, Philadelphia 1986; Harvard GSD 1987; Urban Center, NYC 1987; Univ. of Virginia School of Architecture 1989, Lancaster School of Art & Design 1992. **Bio-Bibliography:** *AIA Journal, Architectural Record, Architec-*

ture, Chinese Architect, Landscape Architecture, Places, Progressive Architecture, Urban Design International. **Home Address:** 324 S. 21 St., Philadelphia, PA 19103.

HANSON, ANNE C. ■ RAAR History of Art 74. b. Dec. 12, 1921. BFA 43, Univ. of Southern California; MA 51, UNC; PhD 62, Bryn Mawr College. **Other Study:** Skidmore College 1939-40; ASL 1944-45. **Career & Employment:** Wagner College, Lect. 1949-50; Miss Fine's School, Princeton, NJ, Art Teacher 1952-55; Univ. of Buffalo, Albright Art School, Instr. 1955-58; Cornell Univ., Visiting Assc. Prof. 1963; Swarthmore College, Asst. Prof. 1963-64; Bryn Mawr College, Asst. Prof. 1964-68; MOMA, Dir., Intl. Study Center 1968-69, Consultant 1969-70; NYU, Adj. Assc. Prof. 1969-70; Yale Univ., Visiting Lect. 1969-70, Prof. 1970-78, Chair 1974-78, John Hay Whitney Prof. 1978-92; Yale Univ. Art Gallery, Acting Dir. 1985-87; Williams College, Clark Visiting Prof. 1990; CASVA, Samuel H. Kress Prof. 1992-93. **Memberships & Offices:** CAA 1968-91, Monograph Ed. 1968-71, *Art Bulletin* Com. 1968-90, Publications Com. 1968-77, Ed. Bd. 1971-77, *Art Journal,* co-ed. 1979-83, Program Chair, Annual Conference 1969, BoD 1969-73, 1979-83, Executive Com. 1971-72, Pres. 1972-74, Art History Com. 1975-77, Distinguished Teacher of Art History Prize Com. 1975-76, 1991, Long Range Planning Com. 1987-90; Council on Museums & Education in the Visual Arts 1973-77; Council of Intl. Exchange of Scholars, Screening Com. 1975-78; Wadsworth Athenaeum, Hartford, Elector 1975-81; Comité Intl. de l'histoire de l'art, Nat. Mem. 1975-92; Millard Meiss Publication Fund Com. 1976-80; Yale Univ. Press Governing Bd. 1977-91; Swann Found. for Caricature & Cartoon, Adv. Bd. 1980-present; Yale Center for British Art, Adv. Bd. 1985-87; Hill-Stead Museum, Farmington, Bd. of Governors 1988-92, VP 1991-92. **Fellowships, Honors & Awards:** ACLS, Summer Grant 1963, Fellowship 1983-84; NEH Fellowship 1967-68; Yale Univ., Griswald Faculty Research Awards 1974, 1975; Charles Rufus Morey Award for Scholarship in the History of Art 1977; IAS 1983; UNC, Distinguished Alumna Award 1989; CAA, Distinguished Teacher of Art History Award 1990. **Publications:** "A Group of Marine Paintings by Manet," *Art Bulletin* 44 (1962): 332-36; *Jacopo della Quercia's Fonte Gaia* (Oxford: Clarendon Press, 1965); *Edouard Manet: 1832-1883,* exb. cat. (Philadelphia: Museum of Art, 1966); "Notes on Manet Literature," *Art Bulletin* 48 (1966): 432-38; "Manet's Subject Matter and a Source of Popular Imagery," *Museum Studies of the Art Institute of Chicago* 111 (1968): 63-80; "Popular Imagery in the Work of Edouard Manet," in *French Nineteenth Century Painting and Literature,* ed. Ulrich Finke (Manchester: Univ. of Manchester, 1972), 133-65; "The Literature of Art: Engraved Work by Manet," *Burlington Magazine* 114 (July 1972): 481-83; *Manet and the Modern Tradition* (London & New Haven: Yale Univ. Press, 1977); "Jacopo della Quercia fra classico e rinascimento: Alcuni pensieri sui motivi de Ercole e Adamo," in *Atti del Convegno su Jacopo della Quercia fra Gotico e Rinascimento* (Siena: Centro Di, 1977), 119-30; "Manet's *Les Gitanos* and the Cut Canvas," *Burlington Magazine* 112 (Mar. 1978): 158-66; "The Tale of Two Manets," *Art in America* 67.8 (Dec. 1979): 58-68; "The Human Eye, A Dimension of Cubism," in *Art the Ape of Nature: Essays in Honor of H.W. Janson,* ed. Moshe Barasch & Lucy Sandler (New York: Harry Abrams & Prentice Hall, 1981): 739-48; "Edward Hopper: American Meaning and French Craft," *Art Journal* 41.2 (1981): 142-54; "Manet's Pictorial Language," in *Manet, 1832-83,* exb. cat. (New York: MMA & Paris: Musée D'Orsay, 1983), 22-28; *The Futurist Imagination* (New Haven: Yale Univ. Art Gallery, 1983); "Portrait of Soffici and Conclusion: Two Drawings by Carlo Carra," *Yale University Art Gallery Bulletin* (1987): 70-77. **Bio-Bibliog-**

raphy: *Directory of American Scholars; Who's Who in America; Who's Who in American Art; Who's Who of American Women.* **Home Address:** 28 Lincoln St., New Haven, CT 06511. **Business Address:** Dept. of History of Art, Yale Univ., PO Box 208272, Yale Station, New Haven, CT 06520.

HANSON, HOWARD HAROLD ■ FAAR Musical Composition 24. b. Oct. 28, 1896, Wahoo, NE. d. Feb. 26, 1981. m. Margaret Elizabeth Nelson. BA 16, Northwestern Univ. **Other Studies:** Luther College, Wahoo, NE; Inst. of Musical Art 1914-15; piano with James Friskin. **Career & Employment:** College of the Pacific, Music School, Instr.-Dean 1916-19; Eastman School of Music, Univ. of Rochester, Dir. 1924-64. **Memberships & Offices:** Nat. Music Council; Boston Music Soc.; ASCAP; Hon. Mem.: Pi Kappa Lambda, Phi Mu Alpha; Century Assn.; NYSCA, Concert Advancement Panel; APS; Newcomen Soc.; Phi Beta Kappa; NIAL 1935; AAAL 1979. **Fellowships, Honors & Awards:** Hon. MusD: Syracuse Univ., American Conservatory of Music, New England Conservatory; Juilliard Scholarship; Royal Acad. of Music, Sweden 1938; Pulitzer Prize 1944; George Foster Peabody Award 1946; Huntington Hartford Found. Award 1959. **Publications:** *Harmonic Materials of Modern Music: Resources of the Tempered Scale* (New York: Appleton-Century-Crofts, 1960). **Important Works:** *Scandinavian Suite,* for piano 1919; *California Forest Suite,* a ballet with solo voices, chorus & orchestra 1920; *Before the Dawn,* symphonic poem 1920; *North and West,* for chorus & orchestra 1923; *Nordic Symphony* 1922; *Lux Aeterna,* symphonic poem 1923; *Lament for Beowulf,* for chorus & orchestra 1925; *Romantic Symphony,* Koussevitzky-Boston Symphony Orchestra Comm. 1930; *Merry Mount,* an opera 1933; *The Requiem,* 4th symphony 1943; *Symphonia Sacra,* 5th symphony 1954; *The Mystic Trumpeter,* for narrator, chorus & orchestra 1969; *Sea Symphony,* 7th symphony with chorus 1977. **Bio-Bibliography:** Ruth Wantanabe, *Music of Howard Hanson* (Rochester, NY, 1966); H. Gleason & W. Becker, "Howard Hanson," *Twentieth-Century American Composers* (Bloomington: Indiana Univ. Press, 1981); James E. Perone, *Howard Hanson: A Bio-Bibliography* (Westport, CT: Greenwood Press, 1993); *Baker's Biographical of Musicians; New Grove Dictionary of American Music; Who Was Who in America.*

HANSON, JOHN ARTHUR ■ FAAR Classics/Archaeology 55, RAAR Classics/Archaeology 71; Classical Soc., Pres. 1964; AAR Summer School, Dir. 1968, 1969, 1970. b. March 5, 1931, Charleston, WV. d. Mar. 28, 1985. m. Ann Ellis. c. Mary Elizabeth. BA 51, Univ. of Michigan; MA 53, Princeton Univ.; PhD. 56, Princeton Univ. **Research/Artistic Interests:** Roman topography, Roman theaters, epigraphy, architecture, ancient Mediterranean civilization. **Career & Employment:** Univ. of Michigan, Instr.-Asst. Prof. 1955-64; Princeton Univ., Assc. Prof. 1964-73, Prof. 1973-85. **Memberships & Offices:** APA, Ed. 1965-70, Dir. 1972-75, Ed. Bd., Chair 1973-74. **Fellowships, Honors & Awards:** Princeton Univ., Woodrow Wilson Fellowship 1951-52, Page Fellowship 1952-53; Fulbright Grant 1953-54; Princeton Council for Humanities, Hodder Fellowship 1958-59. **Publications:** *Roman Theater-Temples* (Princeton: Princeton Univ. Press, 1959); "Plautus as a Source Book for Roman Religion" *TAPA* 90 (1959): 48-101; contr., *Roman Drama* (London: Routledge, 1965); ed. & trans., Apuleius, *Metamorphoses,* 2 vols. (Cambridge, MA: Loeb Classical Library, 1987). **Bio-Bibliography:** Briggs, 256-57; *Directory of Amercian Scholars.*

HARADA, HIGO HUGO ■ FAAR Musical Composition 60. b. Dec. 7, 1927, Hanford, CA. dec. m. Noriko Harada. BMus

53, Cleveland Inst. of Music; MusM 55, Cleveland Inst. of Music. **Other Studies:** Composition with Marcel Dick. **Career & Employment:** *Sun Papers*, Music Columnist; UC, Santa Barbara; San Jose State College, Music Dept., Asst. Chair. **Fellowships, Honors & Awards:** Cleveland Inst. of Music Scholarship 1951-52; BMI, Composition Award 1953; Woolley Scholarship 1956-57; Los Angeles Philharmonic Orchestra Composition Competition, Hon. Mention 1955. **Important Works:** *Sketch,* for piano; *Elegy,* for orchestra 1954; *Do,* 1956; *Sketch,* for solo piano 1956. **Bio-Bibliography:** *Contemporary American Composers.*

HARBISON, JOHN H. ■ RAAR Musical Composition 81; AAR Trustee 1991-93, Trustee Emer. b. Dec. 20, 1938, Orange, NJ. m. Rose Mary Pedersen. BA 60, Harvard College; MFA 63, Princeton Univ. **Other Study:** Tanglewood 1959; Hochschule für Musik, Berlin 1961. **Career & Employment:** Reed College, Rockefeller Composer-in-Residence 1968-69; MIT, Prof. 1969-present; Pittsburgh Symphony, Composer-in-Residence 1983-85; Los Angeles Philharmonic, Composer-in-Residence 1986-88; St. Paul Chamber Orchestra, Creative Chair 1990-92. **Memberships & Offices:** Koussevitzky Found., BoD 1986-present;

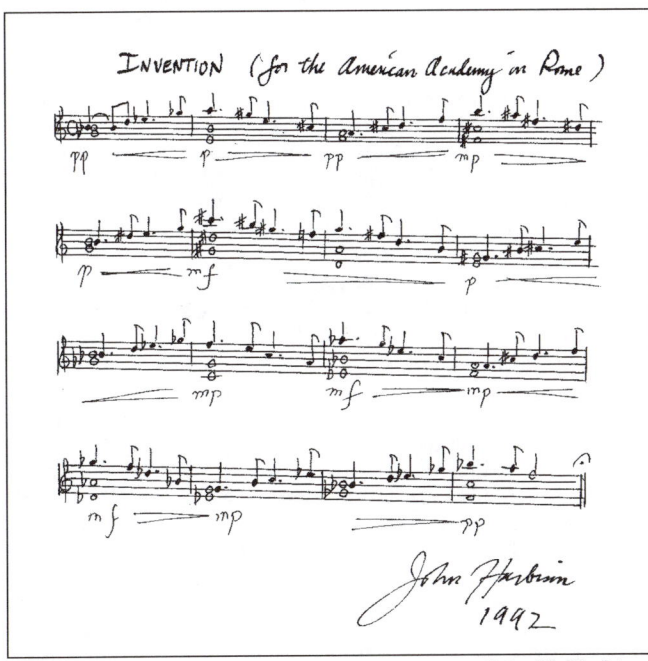

John H. Harbison

Copland Fund, BoD 1992-present. **Fellowships, Honors & Awards:** Harvard Univ. Junior Fellowship 1963-68; Guggenheim Fellowship 1977; Kennedy Center, Friedheim Award 1980; Pulitzer Prize 1987; MacArthur Fellowship 1989. **Publications:** "Roger Sessions," in *New Grove Dictionary of American Music* (New York: Grove, 1984); *Six Tanglewood Talks* (Perspectives in New Music, 1985). **Important Works:** *Five Songs of Experience,* for solists, chorus & chamber ensemble (CRI) 1971; *Winter's Tale,* opera in two acts 1974; *Violin Concerto* 1980; *Motetti di Montale,* for mezzo soprano & piano 1980; *Variations,* for clarinet, violin & piano 1982; *The Flight into Egypt,* for solists, chorus & orchestra (New World) 1985; *Symphony No. 2* 1987; *String Quartet No. 2* (Harmonia Mundi) 1987; *Concerto for Double Bass Choir & Orchestra* (New World) 1988; *Words from Paterson,* for baritone 1988; *Between Two Worlds,* for soprano & four players 1991; *Three City Blocks,* for large wind ensemble 1992. Other

recordings on Nonesuch, New World, Koch. **Home Address:** 449 Franklin St., Cambridge, MA 02139. **Business Address:** Music Dept., MIT, Cambridge, MA 02139.

HARDIN, ADLAI S. ■ RAAR Sculpture 62. b. Sept. 23, 1901, Minneapolis, MN. d. Oct. 1989. m. Carol Moore. c. Adlai S., Jr.; Carol H. Kimball. BA 23, Princeton Univ. **Other Studies:** AIC. **Research/Artistic Interests:** Wood & bronze sculpture. **Career & Employment:** William Esty Co., VP 1932-59. **Memberships & Offices:** NAD; NSS, Pres. 1957-59; Century Assn.; Lyme Acad. of Fine Arts, CT. **Fellowships, Honors & Awards:** ALNY, Henry O. Avery Award; NSS, Ecclesiastical Competition, Lindsey Morris Prize, Herbert Adams Memorial Medal; Mrs. Louis Bennett Prize; Hudson Valley Art Assn., Anna Hyatt Huntington Award; Saltus Gold Medal; Daniel Chester French Gold Medal; NAD Gold Medal; Numismatic Art Assn., Numismatic Art Award. **Important Works:** Murals: Interchurch Center, NYC; Seaman's Bank for Savings, NYC; First Congregational Church, Old Lyme, CT; permanent collections: PAFA; New Britain Museum of American Art; Brookgreen Gardens, SC; IBM Collection of Sculpture of the Western Hemisphere; McMaster Divinity College, McMaster Univ.; Aid Assn. for Lutherans, Appleton, WI; St. Ann's Episcopal Church, Old Lyme, CT. **Bio-Bibliography:** *Who Was Who in American Art.*

HARDING, CHARLES B. ■ AAR Trustee 1951-77, Investment Banker.

HARDY, HUGH & TIZIANA ■ AAR Visitors 1992-93, Architects.

HARMON, AUSTIN MORRIS ■ FASCSR 07. b. Sept. 28, 1878, Brockport, NY. d. June 29, 1950. BA 1902, Williams College; MA 1903, Yale Univ.; PhD 1908, Yale Univ. **Other Study:** Göttingen 1903-4. **Career & Employment:** Princeton Univ., Instr. 1907-16; Yale Univ,. Prof. 1916-23, Hillhouse Prof. 1923-34, Lampson Prof. 1934-45. **Memberships & Offices:** *Yale Classical Studies,* Ed. 1928-42; CANE, Pres. 1932-35; APA, Pres. 1939. **Fellowships, Honors & Awards:** AAAS, Fellow; Williams College LHD 1927. **Publications:** "The *Clausulae* in Ammianus Marcellinus," *Transactions of the Connecticut Academy of Arts and Sciences* 16 (1911): 117-245; "Protesilaudamia Laevi," *American Journal of Philology* 33 (1912): 185-94; trans., Lucian of Samosata, *Works,* 5 vols. (Cambridge, MA: Loeb Classical Library, 1913-36); with Esther V. Hansen, "Greek Vases in the Museum of the American Academy in Rome," *Memoirs of the AAR* 10 (1932): 103-27; "The Scene of the *Persians* of Aeschylus," *TAPA* 63 (1932): 7-19; "Egyptian Property Returns," *Yale Classical Studies* 4 (1934): 135-230. **Bio-Bibliography:** *NY Times,* Obit. (June 30, 1950); Briggs, 261-62; *Who Was Who in America.*

HARNEY, PAUL ■ NIAE, John Dinkeloo Traveling Fellow 1989-90.

HARRIMAN, RAYMOND DAVIS ■ FAAR Classics/Archaeology 16. b. June 6, 1888, Grinnell, IA. d. May 31, 1972. m. Mary Ruth Martin. c. John, Joan. BA 1909, Grinnell College; MA 14, Univ. of Wisconsin; PhD 15, Univ. of Wisconsin. **Research/Artistic Interests:** The spread of Latin in Egypt under the Roman Empire. **Career & Employment:** Muscatine HS, IA, Faculty 1909-12; Univ. of Wisconsin Fellow in Latin 1913-14, Asst. Prof. 1914-15; Univ. of Utah, Instr. 1917-22, Asst. Prof. 1922-28, Assc. Prof.-Acting Dean of Men 1926-28; Univ. of Chicago, Visiting Assc. Prof. 1927; Stanford Univ., Assc. Prof. 1928-34, Prof. 1934-53, Exec. Dept. Head 1937-53; School of Letters,

Chair 1940-42; School of Humanities, Chair 1941-42; Acting Dean 1947-48; Emer. Prof. 1953-72; Univ. of Washington, Visiting Prof. 1953-54. **Memberships & Offices:** APA, Philological Assn., Pacific Coast, Pres. 1945; Classical Assn., Pacific Coast, Pres. 1931; AAUP. **Fellowships, Honors & Awards:** Phi Beta Kappa; Grinnell College, LHD 1959. **Publications:** "Suggestions for Americanization Teachers," *Bulletin of the University of Utah* 10.16 (1920). **Bio-Bibliography:** *Who Was Who in America.*

HARRINGTON, KARL ■ AAR Classical Soc., Pres. 1946.

HARRIS, DAVID T. ■ AAR Trustee 1967-80, Banker.

HARRIS, PRITCHETT ALLEN ■ FAAR Sculpture 61. b. Sept. 29, 1924, St. Louis, MO. d. Dec. 1970. m. Jean Campbell Harris. c. Thomas Harmon, Tad. **Other Studies:** Washington & Jefferson; PAFA. **Research/Artistic Interests:** Bronze casting. **Career & Employment:** PAFA, Instr. 1965-70; Philadelphia College of Art, Faculty 1961-65. **Fellowships, Honors & Awards:** Cresson Travelling Scholarship 1950; Tiffany Found. Grant 1951; PAFA, Fellowship Gold Medal 1952; St. Louis Art Museum, Lewis Award 1957; NAD, Helen Foster Barnett Prize 1957, Samuel Finley Breese Award 1963; Da Vinci Art Alliance, Philadelphia, Da Vinci Gold Medal 1958, 1962. **Important Works:** Commissions: Lincoln & Grant Portraits, Washington, DC; Nat. Guard Assn., Truman Portrait 1966; Sculpture Figures, American Zinc Co. Bldg., St. Louis; Matteo della Corte Portrait, Cortile of Honor, Pompeii 1965. **Exhibitions/Performances:** Philadelphia Art Alliance 1965; Vendo Nubes Gallery, Philadelphia 1967; Provident Nat. Bank, Philadelphia 1971-72.

HARRIS, WILLIAM V. ■ RAAR Classics/Archaeology 79, 83; Adv. Council 1976-present. b. Sept. 13, 1938, Nottingham, England. c. Neil. BA 61, Oxford Univ.; MA 64, Oxford Univ.; D. Phil. 68, Oxford Univ. **Research/Artistic Interests:** Greek & Roman history. **Career & Employment:** Columbia Univ., Instr.-Prof. 1965-present, Chair 1988-94. **Memberships & Offices:** Istituto di Studi Etruschi ed Italici, Foreign Mem. 1973-present; Columbia Studies in the Classical Tradition, Ed. Bd., Ed. 1973-present; IAS 1970-71, 1978. **Fellowships, Honors & Awards:** ACLS Research Fellow 1970-71; Corpus Christi College, Oxford, Visiting Research Fellow 1975; NEH Senior Research Fellow 1978; Guggenheim Fellowship 1982-83; All Souls College, Visiting Fellow 1983; Soc. of Antiquaries, London, Fellow 1984-present; Finnish Soc. of Sciences, Foreign Mem. 1988-present; Academia Europaea, Foreign Mem. 1994-present. **Publications:** "On War and Greed in the Second Century B.C.," *American Historical Review* 76 (1971): 1371-85; *Rome in Etruria and Umbria* (Oxford: Clarendon Press, 1971); *War and Imperialism in Republican Rome, 327-70 B.C.* (Oxford: Clarendon Press, 1979, rpt. 1985); "Towards a Study of the Roman Slave Trade," *Memoirs of the AAR* 36 (1980): 117-40; "Roman Terracotta Lamps: The Organisation of an Industry," *Journal of Roman Studies* 70 (1980): 126-45; ed., *The Imperialism of Mid-Republican Rome,* Papers & Monographs of the American Academy in Rome (Rome: AAR, 1984); ed., with R.S. Bagnall, *Studies in Roman Law in Memory of A. Arthur Schiller* (Leiden: Brill, 1986); "The Roman Father's Power of Life and Death," in *Studies in Roman Law in Memory of A. Arthur Schiller,* ed. R.S. Bagnall & W.V. Harris (Leiden: Brill, 1986), 81-95; "The Expansion of the Roman Empire in the West," in *Cambridge Ancient History* 8, 2d ed. (Cambridge: Cambridge Univ. Press, 1989), 107-62; *Ancient Literacy* (Cambridge, MA: Harvard Univ. Press, 1989); "Invisible Cities: the Beginnings of Etruscan Urbanization," in *Atti del Secondo*

Congresso Internazionale Etrusco (Rome, 1989), 1:375-92; "Why Did the Codex Supplant the Book-Roll?" in *Renaissance Society and Culture: Essays in Honor of Eugene F. Rice, Jr.,* ed. J. Monfasani & R.G. Musto (New York: Italica Press, 1991), 71-85; ed., *The Inscribed Economy: Production and Distribution in the Roman Empire in the Light of* instrumentum domesticum, Suppl. vol. 6 of *Journal of Roman Archaeology* (Ann Arbor: JRA, 1993). **Bio-Bibliography:** *Who's Who in America.* **Home Address:** 456 Riverside Dr., Apt. 9B, NYC 10027. **Business Address:** History Dept., Columbia Univ., NYC 10027.

HARRISON, CHARLES C. ■ AAR Charter Mem., Educator.

HARRISON, FAIRFAX ■ AAR Trustee 1921-24, Railroad Pres.

HARRISON, WALLACE KIRKMAN ■ Rotch Scholar 1922; AAR Trustee 1959-64; Architect. b. Sept. 28, 1895. d. Dec. 2, 1981. **Honors & Awards:** AIA, Gold Medal 1967. **Important Works:** Metropolitan Opera House, Lincoln Center, NYC; Museum of Science, NYC; United Nations Building, NYC; co-architect of Rockefeller Center, NYC.

HARSH, PHILIP ■ AAR Classical Soc., Pres. 1953.

HART, WILLIAM B., JR ■ AAR Trustee 1995-present. **Career & Employment:** Found. for the Nat. Capital Region, Pres.; Dunfey Group, Pres; Nat. Trust for Historic Preservation, New England Field Office, Dir., Adv. Services Office, Dir.; Historic Harrisville, Inc., Pres.; New Hampshire Charitable Found., Pres. **Memberships & Offices:** Nat. Trust for Historic Preservation, BoT; Currier Gallery of Art, BoT; Working Assets Management Co., Chair; First NH Banks, Inc., Dir.

HARTKE, STEPHEN P. ■ FAAR Musical Composition 92. b. July 6, 1952, Orange, NJ. m. Lisa Stidham. BA 73, Yale Univ.; MA 76, Univ. of Pennsylvania; PhD 82, UC, Santa Barbara. **Career & Employment:** Carl Fischer, Educational Dir. 1980; UC, Santa Barbara, Visiting Prof. 1981-83, 1985-87; Universidade de São Paulo, Fulbright Prof. 1984-85; Los Angeles Chamber Orchestra, Composer-in-Residence 1988-92; UC, Assc. Prof. 1987-present. **Memberships & Offices:** Assn. of California Symphony Orchestras, Curator of New Music Exb. 1991. **Fellowships, Honors & Awards:** ASCAP Grant 1982; Kennedy Center, Friedheim Award 1985; Chamber Music America Comm. Grant 1987; Louisville Orchestra Prize 1987; NEA Consortium Comm. Grant 1988; Composer-in-Residence Grants 1989, 1990, 1991; Burlington Northern Found. Faculty Achievement Award 1990; Koussevitzky Music Found. Comm. Grant. 1992; AAAL, Acad. Award 1993; Fromm Found. Comm. Grant 1994. **Important Works:** *Caione,* for solo violin, (Orion Master Recordings) 1980; *Iglesia Abandonada,* for soprano & violin (Orion Master Recordings) 1982; *Alvorada,* for string orchestra, Pasadena Chamber Orchestra Comm. 1983; *Oh Them Rats is Mean in My Kitchen,* for violin duo (New World Records) 1985; *Maltese Cat Blues,* for orchestra (New World Records) 1986; *Pacific Rim,* for orchestra, NEA-Los Angeles Chamber Orchestra & St. Paul Chamber Orchestra-Hudson Valley Philharmonic Comm. 1988; *The King of the Sun,* for violin, cello & piano, Los Angeles Piano Quartet Comm. (New World Records) 1988; *Night Rubrics,* for solo cello 1990; *Symphony No. 2,* for orchestra, Los Angeles Chamber Orchestra Comm. 1990; *Wir Kuessen Ihnen Tausendmal die Haende,* for chamber ensemble, Los Angeles Chamber Orchestra Comm. (CRI) 1991; *Concerto for Violin & Orchestra,* Koussevitzky Found.-Albany Symhony Comm. 1992. Music published by Norruth Music, St. Louis. **Bio-Bib-**

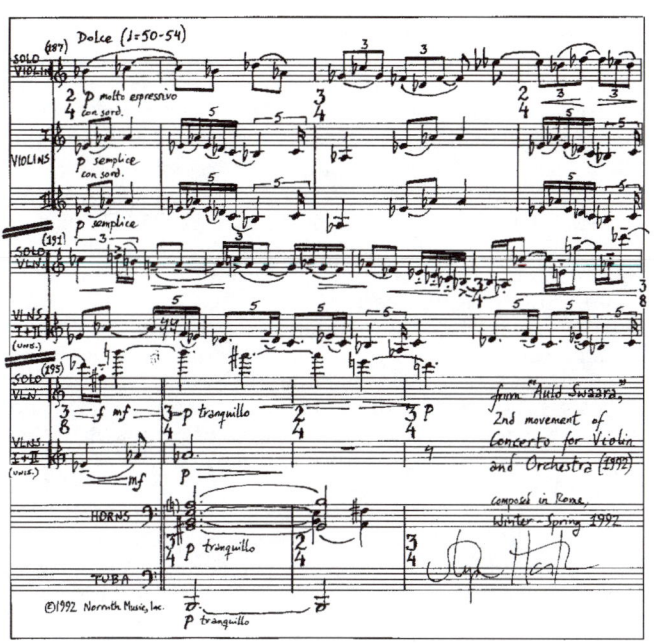

Stephen P. Hartke

liography: *International Who's Who in Music; Who's Who in America*. **Home Address:** 624 W. Milford St., Glendale, CA 91203. **Business Address:** Norruth Music Inc., MMB Music, Inc., 3526 Washington Ave., St. Louis, MO 63103.

HARTMAN, GEORGE E. ■ FAAR Architecture 78. b. May 7, 1936, Fort Hancock, NJ. m. Ann Burdick. c. Sarah, Joshua. BA 57, Princeton Univ.; MFA 60, Princeton Univ. **Career & Employment:** Keyes Lethbridge & Condoo 1960-64; Hartman-Cox Architects, 1964-present. **Memberships & Offices:** AIA, Washington Chap., Pres. 1975; Cosmos Club, Washington, DC, Pres. 1985; Com. of Fine Arts, Washington, DC 1990-94; US Dept. of State, Architectural Review Bd. 1991-94. **Fellowships, Honors & Awards:** AIA, Nat. Honor Award 1970, 1971, 1981, 1983, 1989, 1994; Fellow 1975, Firm Award 1988, Intl. Sullivan Award 1972, plus 75 regional & local awards. **Publications:** with A.E. Washburn, "Contemporary Architecture," *Aspen Institute Quarterly* 4.2 (Spring 1992). **Important Works:** Mt. Vernon College Chapel 1969; Euram Bldg. 1971; Nat. Permanent Bldg. 1977; Immanuel Presbyterian Church 1978; US Chancery, Kuala Lampur, Malaysia 1979; 1001 Pennsylvania Ave. 1979; Folger Shakespeare Library Additions 1982; Chrysler Museum 1984; Dumbarton Oaks Additions 1984; Market Sq. 1990; Franklin Sq. 1990; Georgetown Univ. Law Library 1991. **Bio-Bibliography:** *Who's Who in America*. **Business Address:** Hartman-Cox Architects, 1074 Thos. Jefferson St., Washington, DC 20007.

HARTSHORNE, RICHARD GARDNER, JR ■ FAAR Architecture 39. b. August 12, 1912, Wakefield, MA. d. Jan. 15, 1949. BArch 37, Yale Univ. **Other Studies:** Bowdoin College 1931-33. **Research/Artistic Interests:** Restoration of the theater at Tusculum. **Career & Employment:** US Army 1942-45; Hutchins & French, Boston 1945-48.

HARVEY, BUNNY ■ FAAR Painting 76. b. Mar. 18, 1946, NYC. m. Frank Muhly, Jr. c. Nicolas Muhly. BFA 67, RISD; MFA 72, RISD. **Other Study:** Stamperia 2RC, Rome 1966-67. **Career & Employment:** Wellesley College, Prof. 1976-present; Harvard

Univ., Visiting Prof. 1991-92. **Fellowships, Honors & Awards:** Rhode Island State Council on the Arts, Individual Artist Grant 1976. **Important Works:** Graham Gund Collection, American Nat. Can Co., Fuller Museum of Art, Roy Neuberger Collection, Miami Dade Jr. College Museum, RISD Museum of Art, Finch Group, Rhode Island Hospital. **Exhibitions/Performances:** Selected Solo: Terry Dintenfass, NYC 1979; Wellesley College Museum 1980; Newport Art Museum 1982; Augustus Saint-Gaudens Nat. Historic Site, Cornish, NH 1984; Randall Beck Gallery, Boston 1987, 1989; Brockton Art Museum 1987; Berry-Hill Galleries, NYC 1990, 1992, 1994; RISD Museum of Art 1993; Selected Group: Soviet Artists' Union Gallery, Moscow 1988; Newport Art Museum 1988; Wellesley College Museum 1990; RISD 1990; Jan Weiss Gallery, NYC 1991; Chrysler Museum, Norfolk 1992. **Home Address:** 5 Catalpa Rd., Providence, RI 02906. **Business Address:** Berry-Hill Galleries, 11 E. 70th St., NYC 10021.

HARVEY, CHARLES ■ FAAR Sculpture 10. dec.

HARZ, ELEANOR ■ AAR World War II Scholar 1942.

HASKELL, FRANCIS ■ RAAR History of Art 90. b. Apr. 7, 1928. m. Larissa Salmina. **Study:** Eton College, King's College, Cambridge. **Career & Employment:** Cambridge Univ., Fellow of King's College 1954-67, Librarian of the Fine Arts Faculty 1962-67; Oxford Univ., Prof. 1967-present. **Memberships & Offices:** British Acad., Fellow 1971-present; Wallace Collection, BoT 1976-present; AAAS, Foreign Hon. Mem. 1979-present; Accademia Pontaniana, Naples, Corresponding Mem. 1982-present; King's College, Hon. Fellow 1986; Ateneo Veneto, Corresponding Mem. 1986-present; Accademia Clementina of Bologna, Hon. Mem. 1990-present;. Freie Universitat Berlin, Hon. Fellow 1993-present; APS Fellow 1994. **Fellowships, Honors & Awards:** British Acad., Serena Medal for Italian Studies 1985; Officier de l'Ordre des Arts et des Lettres 1990. **Publications:** *Painters & Patrons* (London & New York: Chatto & Windus, 1963; 2d ed., Yale Univ. Press); *Rediscoveries in Art* (London & Ithaca: Cornell Univ. Press, 1976); *L'Arte e il linguaggio della politica* (Florence: S.P.E.S., 1978); with Nicholas Penny, *Taste and the Antique* (London & New Haven: Yale Univ. Press, 1981); *Past and Present in Art and Taste* (London & New Haven: Yale Univ. Press, 1987); *The Painful Birth of the Art Book* (London: Thames & Hudson, 1987); *History and its Images* (London & New Haven: Yale Univ. Press, 1993). **Bio-Bibliography:** *Who's Who*. **Business Address:** Dept. of the History of Art, Univ. of Oxford, 25 Beaumont St., Oxford, OX1 2PG, England.

HASTINGS, THOMAS ■ AAR Charter Mem., Architect.

HAUB, CHRISTIAN DE SUREMAIN ■ FAAR Painting 84. Feb. 22, 1952, Miami, FL. BA 76, Princeton Univ. **Exhibitions/Performances:** Solo: Anne Plumb Gallery, NYC 1987, 1989, 1990; Group: Hal Bromm Gallery, NYC 1980; William Patterson College, Wayne, NJ 1982; Gloria Luria Gallery, Bay Harbor Islands, FL 1983; Louis K. Meisel Gallery, NYC 1985; Condeso Lawler Gallery, NYC 1985; Max Protetch Gallery, NYC after 1989.

HAUS, STEPHEN C. ■ FAAR Landscape Architecture 79. b. Jan. 7, 1955, Brookline, MA. BFA 77, RISD. **Other Study:** Nakane Garden Research Inst. 1981-82. **Career & Employment:** Oklahoma City Zoo, Landscape Architect for Africana 1980-81; Haus Asscs., Prin. 1983-present. **Memberships & Offices:** ASLA 1986-present, Hawaii Chap., Environment & Policy

Com., Chair 1992; American Assn. of Zoological Parks & Aquariums, Assc. Mem. 1981-present. **Fellowships, Honors & Awards:** Henry Luce Scholar 1981-82; People to People, Citizen Ambassador to China 1988, Citizen Ambassador to Vietnam 1992. **Publications:** "Zoosounds: To the Return of the Tall Grass Prairie," *Oklahoma Zoological Society Journal* 16.4 (Aug. 1980); "Zoosounds: A Walk through Africana," *Oklahoma Zoological Society Journal* 16.5 (Oct. 1980); "Zoosounds: Ecozoo," *Oklahoma Zoological Society Journal* 17.4 (Aug. 1981). **Important Works:** Henry Moore Sculpture Reserve, Columbia Univ., Harriman Campus, David Finn Found. 1977-78; Africana Masterplan, Oklahoma City Zoo 1980-82; Mapes Garden, Lyon Arboretum, HI 1983; Outrigger Canoe Club Gardens, HI 1986-94; Kahala Hilton Hotel Masterplan, Honolulu 1986-87; Commander-in-Chief of the Pacific, Entry Courtyard Gardens, HI 1987; Royal Hawaiian, Princess Kaaiulani, Moana Hotels, Waikiki 1987-89; Ian Fleming Estate, Jamaica 1990; Pacific Club Courtyard Garden 1990; Young Garden, Lyon Arboretum, HI 1992; Waipio Valley Environmental Center Masterplan, Honolulu 1992; Strawberry Hill Masterplan, Jamaica 1994; Pink Sands Masterplan, Bahamas 1995; Young Island Masterplan, St. Vincent 1995; Lupita Manda Residence, Java, Indonesia 1995. **Home & Business Address:** 1519 One'ele Pl., Honolulu, HI 96822.

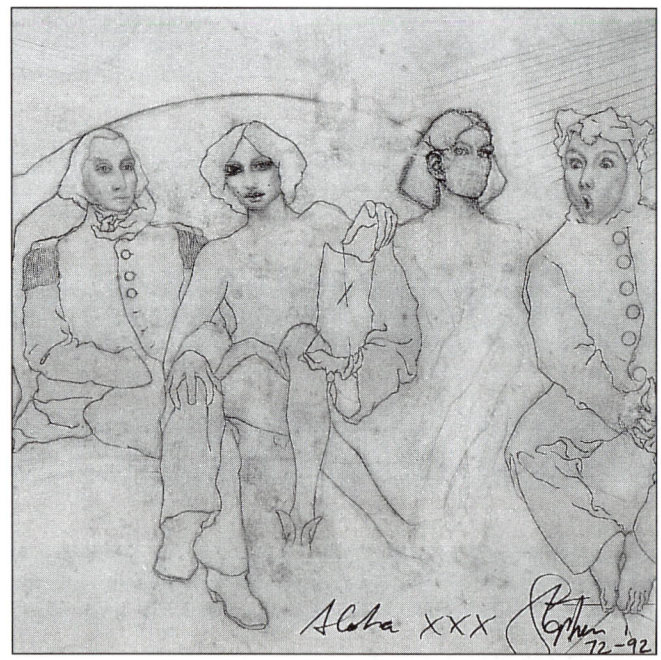

Stephen C. Haus

HAWKINS, DALE HARPER ■ FAAR Landscape Architecture 52. b. Nov. 1, 1901, Seward County, NE. BSLA 33, Iowa State College. **Other Studies:** MIT 1941. **Career & Employment:** Oklahoma State Landscape Architect 1938-39; Tennessee State Planning Comm., Nashville, Community Planner 1940-42; US Naval Base, Puerto Rico, Asst. Site Planner 1942-43; US Naval Reserve, Commissioned Officer 1943-46; American Graves Registration Command, Paris, Landscape Architect 1946-48; Nashville TN Housing Authority, Dir. of Planning 1949-50; Nat. Park Service: OK, TN, CA, DC, Landscape Architect. **Publications:** "Capitol Hill Development, Nashville, TN," *Landscape Architecture* (Apr. 1950).

HAYES, BARTLETT H., JR ■ RAAR History of Art 65; AAR Dir. 1970-73. b. Aug. 5, 1904, Andover, MA. d. Feb. 14, 1988.

BA 26, Harvard Univ. **Career & Employment:** Phillips Acad., Instr. 1933-69, Addison Gallery of American Art, Dir. 1940-69; Honolulu Acad. of Fine Arts, Adv.-Lect. 1969-70. **Memberships & Offices:** American Federation of Arts, BoT 1940-70; MFA, BoT 1951-72; Boston Arts Festival, BoT 1954-65; Old Sturbridge Village, BoT 1951-70; Print Council of America, BoT 1957-63; Amon Carter Museum of Western Art, Ft. Worth, BoT 1968-76; Saint-Gaudens Memorial, Cornish, NH, BoT 1973-88; MIT, Com. on Study of Arts, Chair 1952-53, 1969-70; Smithsonian Inst., Art Com.; Research Prog., "Education Through Vision" 1963-69; American Studies Seminar, Salzburg, Austria, Faculty 1960, 1971; Nat. Humanities Center, Faculty 1969-70; IRS, Art Adv. Panel 1970-74. **Fellowships, Honors & Awards:** Guggenheim Fellow 1955-56; Fulbright Research Grant 1955-56; AAAS, Fellow. **Publications:** with Mary C. Rathbun, *Layman's Guide to Modern Art: Painting for a Scientific Age* (New York: Oxford Univ. Press, 1949); *The Naked Truth and Personal Vision: A Discussion about the Length of the Artistic Road* (Andover, MA, 1955); *The American Line: 100 Years of Drawing* (Andover, MA, 1959); *American Drawings* (New York: Shorewood Publishers, 1965); ed., with Sara T. Weeks, *Search for the Real, and Other Essays* (Cambridge, MA: MIT Press, 1967); *Art and Nature* (New York: Holt, 1973); *Up from the Ground* (New York: Holt, 1973); *Tradition Becomes Innovation: Modern Religious Architecture in America* (New York: Pilgrim Press, 1983). **Bio-Bibliography:** *NY Times*, Obit. (Feb. 16, 1988); *Contemporary Authors*; *Directory of American Scholars*.

HAYS, WILLIAM C. ■ Stewardson Memorial Scholar 1911-12, 1913.

HAZZARD, SHIRLEY ■ AAR Visitor 1981-82, Writer.

HEALY, BRIAN ■ NIAE, John Dinkeloo Traveling Fellow 1982-83.

HEBALD, MILTON ELTING. ■ FAAR Sculpture 59. b. May 24, 1917, NYC. m. Cecille Rosner. c. Margo Hebald-Heymann Embry. **Other Study:** ASL 1927-28; NAD 1931-32; Beaux Arts Inst. of Design, NYC 1933-35. **Other Study:** Technical Studies: anatomy, dissection at Flower Hospital, ceramics, foundry. **Career & Employment:** Cooper Union, Teacher 1947-55; Brooklyn Museum Art School 1947-54; Univ. of Minnesota, Visiting Prof. 1949; Univ. of Long Beach, Visiting Prof. 1968, 1971. **Memberships & Offices:** Sculptors Guild 1937-92. **Fellowships, Honors & Awards:** Social Security Bldg., Washington, DC, Competition, Runner-Up 1940; East Bronx Hospital, Facade Competition, 1st Prize & Comm. 1951. **Important Works:** *Family Group*, Albert Einstein Hospital, Bronx 1953; Stairwell, Isla Verde Airport, PR 1954; AAAL, A. Macleish Bust 1957; Zodiac Screen, Kennedy Airport, Pan Am Bldg. 1959; *Galaxy*, Seattle World's Fair 1962; Wm. Hays Ackland Memorial, UNC, Chapel Hill 1962; *Amant*, Johnsons Wax Center, Racine, WI 1964; James Joyce Monument, Funtern Fredhof, Zurich 1966; Tower Museum, Dublin 1967; Richard Tucker Monument, Tucker Sq., NYC 1970; *Dancing Family*, Jewish Community Center, Washington, DC 1970; C.V. Starr, Heroic Portrait, Tokyo 1974; *Tempest*, Delacorte Theater, Central Park, NYC 1975; Shakespeare Monument, Aschenhaug Verlag, Oslo 1975; Noah Fountain, Wustum Museum, Racine, WI 1975; TWA Bldg., Los Angeles 1981; Hyde Collection, Lake George, NY 1986; Olympiad & Handstand, YMCA Park, Los Angeles 1986; Children's Zoo, Ft. Wayne, IN 1988; Dellora Cultural Center, St. Charles, IL 1989; *Romeo & Juliet*, Delacorte Theater, Central Park, NYC. **Exhibitions/Performances:** Solo: Notre Dame, IN 1955; Kover

Gallery, Chicago 1966, 1970; Nordness Gallery, NYC; Group: Whitney Museum NYC 1937-58; Sculptors Guild 1937-92; MOMA 1938, 1941, 1950; PAFA 1946-50; 3d Sculpture Intl., Fairmont Park Museum, Philadelphia 1949; Premio Fiorine, Florence 1965; Sterling Library, Yale Univ. 1965; 6th Biennale, Rome 1968; Harmon-Meek Gallery, Naples, FL 1971-92; London Arts 1973. **Bio-Bibliography:** Arthur Moyer, "Hebald on Joyce," *Art Scene* (1968); *Studies in Drawings from the Cecille & Milton Hebald Collection* (Los Angeles: Grunwald Graphic Arts Found, UCLA, 1970); Frank Getlein, *Milton Hebald* (New York: Viking Press, 1971); Frank Getlein, "Sculptor of Everyday Life," *In Dialogue* 5 (1972); *Printworld Directory of Contemporary Prints; Who's Who in America; Who's Who in American Art.* **Home Address:** Traversa Quarto del Lago, 13 Bracciano 00062. **Business Address:** Harmon Meek Gallery, 386 Broad Ave. S., Naples, FL 33940.

HECHT, ANTHONY E. ■ FAAR Literature 51, RAAR Literature 69; AAR Trustee 1983-91, Trustee Emer. b. Jan. 16, 1923, NYC. m. Helen d'Alessandro. c. Jason, Adam, Evan Alexander. BA 44, Bard College; MA 50, Columbia Univ. **Other Study:** With John Crowe Ransom, Kenyon College 1946; Alan Tate, NYU 1947; William Empson, F.O. Mattiessen, Kenyon School of English 1948; Austin Warren, Univ. of Iowa 1949. **Career & Employment:** Kenyon College, Instr. 1947; Bard College, Instr. 1952-54, Assc. Prof.-Prof. 1961-67; Smith College, Asst. Prof. 1956-59; Univ. of Rochester, Deane Prof. 1967-85; Harvard Univ. Visiting Prof. 1973; Yale Univ., Visiting Prof. 1977; Georgetown Univ., Univ. Prof. 1985-93, Prof. Emer. 1993. **Memberships & Offices:** Pulitzer Poetry Jury 1973, Chair 1975; Bollingen Poetry Prize Jury; Copernicus Prize Jury; Nobel Prize in Literature, Consultant 1976-85; Nat. Book Awards Jury 1978; Richard Rodgers Production Award Jury 1983-89. **Fellowships, Honors & Awards:** Guggenheim Fellowship 1954, 1959; Ford Found. Fellow 1960; Rockefeller Found. Fellow 1967; Pulitzer Prize 1967; Acad. of American Poets, Hon. Fellow 1969, Chancellor 1971-95; Yale Univ., Bollingen Prize 1983; Eugenio-Montale Award 1984; Ruth Lilly Prize for Poetry 1988. **Publications:** *A Summoning of Stones: Poems* (New York: Macmillan, 1954); with John Hollander,

Jiggery Pokery (New York: Atheneum, 1967); *The Hard Hours* (New York: Atheneum & London: Oxford Univ. Press, 1967); trans., with Helen Bacon, *Seven Against Thebes* (New York: Oxford Univ. Press, 1973); *Millions of Strange Shadows* (New York: Atheneum & London: Oxford Univ. Press, 1979); *The Venetian Vespers* (New York: Atheneum & London: Oxford Univ. Press, 1979); *Obbligati: Essays in Criticism* (New York: Atheneum, 1986); ed., *The Essential Herbert* (New York: Ecco Press, 1987); *Collected Earlier Poems* (New York: Knopf & Oxford: Oxford Univ. Press, 1990); *The Transparent Man* (New York: Knopf & Oxford: Oxford Univ. Press, 1990); *The Hidden Law: A Study of the Poetry of W.H. Auden* (Cambridge, MA: Harvard Univ. Press, 1993); *The Presumptions of Death,* illus. Leonard Baskin (Northampton: Gehenna Press, 1995); *On the Laws of the Poetic Art: The Andrew Mellon Lectures for 1992* (Princeton: Princeton Univ. Press, forthcoming). **Bio-Bibliography:** Peter Steele, *Expatriates: Reflections on Modern Poetry* (Melbourne: Melboune Univ. Press, 1975); J.D. McClatchy, "Interview," *Paris Review* (Fall 1988): 160-205; Norman German, *Anthony Hecht* (New York: Peter Lang, 1989); Sydney Lea, *The Burdens of Formality: Essays on the Poetry of Anthony Hecht* (Athens & London: Univ. of Georgia Press, 1989); Willard Spiegelman, *The Didactic Muse* (Princeton: Princeton Univ. Press, 1989); Wyatt Prunty, *"Fallen from the Symboled World"* (New York & Oxford: Oxford Univ. Press, 1990); Henry Taylor, *Compulsory Figures* (Baton Rouge & London: Louisiana State Univ. Press, 1992); *Who's Who.* **Home Address:** 4256 Nebraska Ave. NW, Washington, DC 20016.

HECHT, ROBERT E., JR ■ FAAR Classics/Archaeology 49. b. June 3, 1919, Baltimore, MD. m. Elizabeth Chase. c. Daphne, Andrea, Donatella. BA 41, Haverford College. **Career & Employment:** Fine Arts Dealer. **Publications:** "A Head of Polyphemus," *Memoirs of the AAR* 24 (1956): 137-45; "Some Greek Imperial Coins in the Museum of Fine Arts, Boston," *Numismatic Chronicle* (1964): 159-68. **Home Address:** 15 Boulevard de Latour Maubourg, Paris 75007, France.

HEDBERG, BETTY NYE ■ AAR World War II Scholar 1943.

HEDREEN, GUY M. ■ FAAR Classics/Archaeology 94. b. Dec. 12, 1958, Dallas, TX. m. Elizabeth P. McGowan. BA 81, Pomona College; MA 83, Bryn Mawr College; PhD 81, Bryn Mawr College. **Other Study:** ASCSA 1984-86. **Career & Employment:** Franklin & Marshall College, Visiting Asst. Prof. 1988-89; Middlebury College, Asst. Prof. 1989-90; Williams College, Asst. Prof. 1990-present. **Fellowships, Honors & Awards:** ASCSA 1985-86; Whiting Found. Fellowship 1987-88. **Publications:** "The Cult of Achilles in the Euxine," *Hesperia* 60 (1991): 313-30; *Silens in Attic Black-Figure Vase-Painting: Myth and Performance* (Ann Arbor: Univ. of Michigan Press, 1992); "Silens, Nymphs, and Maenads," *Journal of Hellenic Studies* 114 (1994): 47-69. **Business Address:** Dept. of Art, Williams College, Williamstown, MA 01267.

HEIBGES, URSULA M. ■ FAAR Classics/Archaeology 66. b. Dec. 17, 1928, Paderborn, Germany. BA 54, Catholic Univ. of America; MA 55, Columbia Univ.; PhD 62, Bryn Mawr College. **Research/Artistic Interests:** The musical element in the comedy of Plautus; the relationship between language & music, especially in regard to accentuation in Latin & Greek. **Career & Employment:** Shipley School, Latin Teacher 1955-57; Middlebury College, Instr.-Asst. Prof.-Assc. Prof. 1961-90; Indiana Univ., Visiting Prof. 1970-71. **Memberships & Offices:** APA 1961-present; NECA 1961-present. **Fellowships, Honors**

```
           This is Italian. Here
       Is cause for the undiminished bounce
Of sex, cause for the lark, the animal spirit
To rise, aerated, but not beyond our reach, to spread
Friction upon the air, cause to sing loud for the bed
Of jonquils, the linen bed, and establsihed merit
Of love, and grandly to pronounce
           Pleasure without peer.

       Goddess, be with me now;
Commend my music to the woods.
There is no garden to the practiced guze
Half so erotic: here the sixteenth century thew
Rose to its last perfection, this being chiefly due
To the provocative role the water plays.
Tumble and jump, the fountains' moods
       Teach the world how....


       Gratefully,
```

Anthony E. Hecht

& Awards: Woodrow Wilson Fellowship 1954-55; NEA Fellowship 1967-68; AAUW Fellowship 1978-79. **Publications:** "Cicero, A Hypocrite in Religion?" *American Journal of Philology* 90.3 (July 1969); "Religion and Rhetoric in Cicero's Speeches," *Latomus: Revue d'Études Latines* 28.4 (Oct.-Dec. 1969). **Home Address:** 10 1/2 Weybridge St., Middlebury, VT 05753.

Ursula M. Heibges

HEIMBAUGH, JOHN D. ■ FAAR Architecture 70. b. Nov. 24, 1942, Chicago, IL. m. Lois E. Swanson. c. Brook J., Kristin L. BS 64, Washington Univ.; BArch 66, Washington Univ. **Career & Employment:** Heimbaugh Capital Development Corp., Pres. 1990-present. **Important Works:** Developer: Chinatown Sq., Chicago; Printing House Row, Chicago. **Home Address:** 2450 Pioneer Dr., Evanston, IL 60201.

HEINEMAN, JOHN ■ FAAR Musical Composition 69. b. Jan. 21, 1939, Queens, NY. BS 62, Columbia Univ. **Other Studies:** Mannes College of Music, NYC 1956-59; Acad. of Santa Cecilia, Rome 1964-66. **Fellowships, Honors & Awards:** Inst. of Intl. Education, Grant-in-Aid 1965-66; Italian Government Scholarship 1965-66. **Important Works:** *Three Movements,* for clarinet & flute 1958; *Largo and Moderato,* for brass quartet 1959; *Piece,* for snare & sax 1960; *Three Songs,* for baritone & piano 1962; *Songs* for soprano & 2 clarinets 1963; *Views,* for vibraphone & 4 winds 1964; *Continuum,* for 13 players 1964; *Sospesi per Quattro Strumenti* 1965; *Per Coro a Capella* 1965; *You Are in Danger* 1968; *The Melting Pot* 1968.

HEINKE, JAMES LAWRENCE ■ FAAR Musical Composition 72. b. Aug. 20, 1945, Cedar Rapids, IA. m. Sandra Heinke. BMus 67, Oberlin College; MFA 70, Brandeis Univ.; DMA 76, Stanford Univ. **Fellowships, Honors & Awards:** NDEA Fellowship 1967; NEA Composers Grants 1973, 1978.

HEISKELL, ANDREW ■ AAR Trustee 1990-present, Exec. Com. Chair 1990-present. b. Naples, Italy. **Studies:** Harvard Graduate School of Business. **Career & Employment:** *New York Herald Tribune; Life,* Science & Medical Ed.; Time, Inc., CEO &

Chair until 1980. **Memberships & Offices:** New York Public Library, Chair Emer. 1981-90; President's Comm. on the Arts & Humanities 1982-90; Nat. Urban Coalition, BoD, Founding Mem.; New York Urban Coalition, BoD, Founding Mem.; Harvard College, Board of Overseers, Fellow, Pres.; Bryant Park Restoration Corp., Chair; Brookings Inst., Hon. Trustee; Inst. for Intl. Education, BoT; People for the American Way, Dir.; Enterprise Found., Dir.; Vivian Beaumont Theater, Lincoln Center, Vice Chair; Graduate School & Univ. Center, CUNY, Bd. of Visitors. **Fellowships, Honors & Awards:** Harvard Univ., Hon. Doctor of Law; Magazine Publishers Assn., Publisher of the Year 1982; Publishing Hall of Fame 1986; New York Public Library, Andrew Heiskell Library for the Blind & Physically Handicapped 1991.

HELD, AL ■ RAAR Painting 81; AAR Trustee 1982-88, Trustee Emer. b. Oct. 12, 1928, Brooklyn, NY. c. Mara Held. **Other Study:** ASL, Academie de la Grande Chaumière, Paris. **Career & Employment:** Yale Univ. 1962-80. **Fellowships, Honors & Awards:** Guggenheim Fellowship 1966; Brandeis Univ., Jack I. & Lillian L. Poses Creative Arts Award 1983; AAAL Fellow 1984. **Important Works:** Akron Art Inst.; Kunstmuseum, Basel; Albright-Knox Gallery, Buffalo; Dallas Museum of Fine Arts; Guggenheim Museum, NYC; MMA; MOMA; Whitney Museum, NYC; San Francisco Museum of Art; Stattsgalerie, Stuttgart; Smithsonian Inst., Hirshhorn Gallery, Washington, DC; Empire State Plaza, Albany; Tower East, Cleveland; Dallas Southland Center; Mid-Atlantic Program Center, Philadelphia; Kunsthaus, Zurich; Yale Univ. Art Gallery; Fogg Art Museum, Harvard Univ.; High Museum of Art, Atlanta; Delaware Museum of Art, Wilmington; Cleveland Museum of Art; St. Louis Art Museum. **Exhibitions/Performances:** Galerie Huit, Paris 1952; Poindexter Gallery, NYC 1959-60, 1961, 1962; Galerie Renée Ziegler, Zurich 1964; Stedelik Museum, Amsterdam 1966; André Emmerich Gallery, NYC, annually 1966-68, 1970, 1972-92; San Francisco Museum of Art 1968; Donald Morris Gallery, Detroit 1971, 1974, 1977, 1983, 1988; Whitney Museum, NYC 1974; Adler Castillo, Caracas, Venezuela 1975; Annely Juda Fine Art, London 1977; Boston Inst. of Contemporary Art 1978; Krannert Art Museum 1993; and numerous others. **Bio-Bibliography:** Robert Pincus-Witten, *Systemic Painting* (1966); Hilton Kramer, *Assimilation of Modern Movements* (1967); Harold Rosenberg, *The Art World* (1967); *New Yorker* (Aug. 26, 1967); Barbara Rose, *American Painting: The Twentieth Century* (1969); Daniel M. Mendelowtiz, *A History of American Art* (New York: Holt, Rinehart & Winston, 1970): Barbara Rose, "Long Distance Runner," *New York Magazine* (Apr. 5, 1972); Dore Ashton, *Modern American Painting* (New York: Mentor-UNESCO, 1970); Irving Sandler, *The New York School: The Painters and Sculptors of the Fifties* (New York: Harper & Row, 1978); Matthew Biagell, *Dictionary of American Art* (New York: Harper & Row, 1979); Harold Osborne, ed., *The Oxford Companion to Twentieth-Century Art* (New York: Oxford Univ. Press, 1981); Irving Sandler, *Al Held* (New York: Hudson Hills Press, 1984); Richard Armstrong, *Al Held* (New York: Rizzoli, 1991). **Business Address:** André Emmerich Gallery, 41 E. 57th St., NYC 10022.

HELFER, WALTER ■ FAAR Musical Composition 28. b. Sept. 30, 1896, Lawrence, MA. d. Apr. 16, 1959. BA 20, Harvard Univ.; MA, Columbia Univ. **Other Studies:** With Caussade in Paris; Respighi in Rome 1925-28. **Career & Employment:** Hunter College, Prof. 1929-50. **Fellowships, Honors & Awards:** New England Conservatory, Endicott Prize; Paderewski Prize 1939. **Important Works:** *How Long O Jehovah; Fantasy of Children's Tunes,* for orchestra 1935; *Symphony on Canadian Airs* 1937;

Concertino, for piano & chamber orchestra 1947; *Soliloquy*, for cello & piano 1947; *String Quartet; String Trio; Elegaic Sonata*, for piano 1931; *In modo giocoso; Water Idyll*, for orchestra. **Bio-Bibliography:** *Baker's Biographical Dictionary of American Musicians, Contemporary American Composers.*

HELIKER, JOHN EDWARD ■ FAAR Painting 49. b. Jan. 17, 1909, Yonkers, NY. **Other Studies:** ASL 1928-30. **Career & Employment:** Parsons School of Design, Instr.; New York Studio School, Instr.; ASL, Instr.; Columbia Univ., Instr. **Memberships & Offices:** Connecticut Acad. of Fine Arts, 56th Annual Exhibition Juror 1965. **Fellowships, Honors & Awards:** Corcoran Biennial Gold Medal 1941; Guggenheim Fellowship 1951; NIAL Prize 1957; Ford Found. Purchase Award 1959, 1961; Colby College, Hon. DFA 1966; Childe Hassam Fund Purchase Award 1967. **Important Works:** Collections: Hudson River Museum 1970. **Exhibitions/Performances:** Kraushaar Galleries, NYC 1948, 1951, 1954, 1957, 1983. **Bio-Bibliography:** Jed Perl, "John Heliker: Scenes From Memory," *American Artist* (Apr. 1980).

HELLERMANN, WILLIAM D. ■ FAAR Musical Composition 74. b. July 15, 1939, Milwaukee, WI. m. Bettina L. Broer. c. Elspeth, Django. BSME 62, Univ. of Wisconsin; MA 69, Columbia Univ.; DMA 76, Columbia Univ. **Other Study:** Private study with Stefan Wolpe 1963-65. **Career & Employment:** *Calendar for New Music*, Ed. 1980-present; SoundArt Found., Pres. 1982-present. **Memberships & Offices:** ACA 1969-present; Columbia County Council of the Arts, Bd. Mem. 1993-94. **Fellowships, Honors & Awards:** Tanglewood Fellowship 1967; Dartmouth 1st Intl. Electronic Music Competition Prize 1968; Gaudeamus Festival 1970, 1972; American Music Center Composer Assistance Award 1970, 1975; Alte Kirche Boswil Found. Prize 1972; Martha Baird Rockefeller Award 1975, Grant 1980; Creative Artists Public Service Grant 1976, 1978; Center for the Creative & Performing Arts, Buffalo, Composer-in-Residence 1977; NEA Fellowship 1977, 1979, Grant 1991; Gallery Assn. of New York Grant 1978; NYSCA Grant 1983, 1984, 1985, 1988, 1989, 1990; Rensselaer County Council on the Arts Grant 1992. **Important Works:** *Time & Again*, for symphony orchestra 1969; *Passages 13 – The Fire*, for trumpet & tape 1971; *Part Sequences 1, for an Open Space*, for four musicians, four actors, four dancers, & four sets 1972; *Row Music (Tip of the Iceberg)*, for solo piano 1973; *Long Island Sound*, for four instruments 1974; *"But, The Moon…,"* for guitar & 13 instruments 1975; *Squeek*, for solist 1977; *"anyway…,'* for symphony orchestra 1977; *Tremble*, for solo guitar 1978; *Still Lives*, sculptural performance pieces 1984; *Post/Pone*, for guitar 1990; *Blood on the Dining Room Floor*, vocal score for theater 1991; *Hoist by Your Own Retard*, for clarinet, marimba, accordian, piano 1993. Recordings: Turnabout, Edipan Records, CRI, Nonesuch Records. **Bio-Bibliography:** *New Grove Dictionary of Music and Musicians.* **Home Address:** PO Box 850, Philmont, NY 12565.

HELLMAN, LILLIAN ■ AAR Visitor 1951-55, Playwright.

HELPRIN, MARK ■ FAAR Literature 83. b. 1947, NYC. m. Lisa Helprin. **Other Studies:** Harvard Univ. Center for Middle Eastern Studies. **Career & Employment:** British Merchant Navy, Israeli Infantry, Israeli Air Force. **Publications:** *The Dove of the East and Other Stories* (1975); *Refiner's Fire: The Life and Adventures of Marshall Pearl, A Foundling* (New York: Delta, 1977); *Ellis Island and Other Stories* (New York: Delacorte Press, 1981); *Winter's Tale* (New York: Harcourt Brace Jovanovich, 1983); *Retelling of Swan Lake* (Boston: Houghton Mifflin, 1988);

A Soldier of the Great War (New York: Harcourt Brace Jovanovich, 1991). **Bio-Bibliography:** Helen Dudar, "Inflating This Fall's Lit Biz Balloon," *Wall Street Journal* (Oct. 1983); Paul Alexander, "Big Books, Tall Tales," *NY Times Magazine* (Apr. 28, 1991).

HENDERSON, JACK ■ FAAR Painting 65. b. Mar. 12, 1931, Kenosha, WI. BFA 52, Kansas City Art Inst. & School of Design; MFA 52, Kansas City Art Inst. & School of Design. **Other Studies:** École des Beaux Arts, France 1952-53; ASL 1955-58. **Research/Artistic Interests:** Mural painting. **Career & Employment:** Pratt Inst., Faculty; Moore College of Art, Faculty. **Memberships & Offices:** Nat. Soc. of Mural Painters. **Fellowships, Honors & Awards:** Fulbright Fellowship 1952-53; Pulitzer Traveling Scholarship 1955; American Watercolor Soc., James A. Goldsmith Purchase Prize 1959; Emily Lowe Award 1959; NAD, Thomas B. Clarke Prize 1967. **Exhibitions/Performances:** Solo: Everhart Museum, Scranton, PA 1956; Palm Beach Galleries, FL 1962; NAD 1968; Group: ACA Gallery, NYC; Ward Eggleston Gallery, NYC; Duveen-Graham Galleries, NYC; Addison Gallery of American Art; PAFA Annuals; Nat. Arts Club; American Watercolor Soc. Annuals; Audubon Artists.

HENDRICK, L.M., JR ■ Appleton Fellow 1919-20.

HENDRICKSON, GEORGE L. ■ AAR School of Classical Studies, Prof.-in-Charge 1913-14, 1919-20.

HENNESSEY, JAMES J. ■ FAAR Painting 64. b. Oct. 25, 1936, Chicago, IL. m. Pamela A. Potter. c. James D., Mary M. BFA 58, Illinois Wesleyan Univ.; MFA 60, Univ. of Colorado. **Other Study:** Yale Univ., Norfolk Summer Session 1959. **Career & Employment:** Univ. of Illinois, Champaign-Urbana 1960-65; Maryland Inst., College of Art, Baltimore 1965-present; Italian Program, Sorrento, Summers 1991, 1992, Co-Dir. 1991-95. **Fellowships, Honors & Awards:** Yale Univ., Norfolk Summer Session, Fellow 1959; Univ. of Illinois, Faculty Research Grant 1962; Louis Comfort Tiffany Found. Grant 1967; Union of Independent Colleges of Art, Faculty Research Grant 1969; Mary-

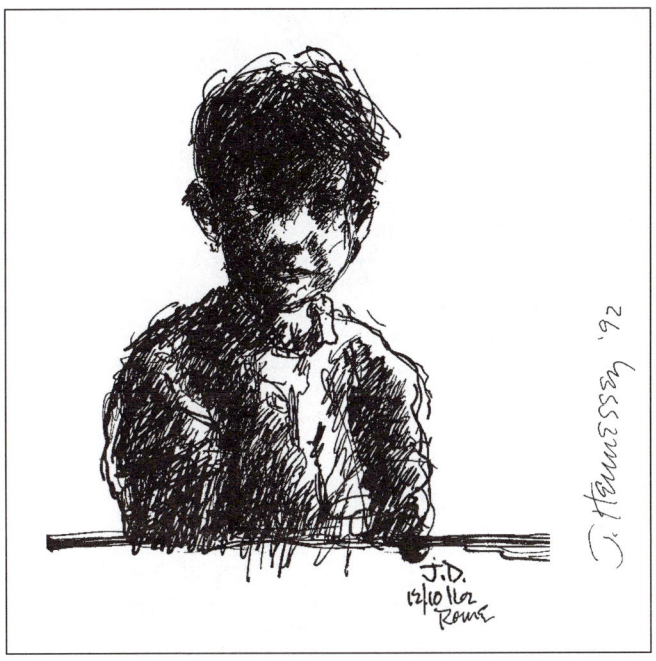

James H. Hennessey

land Inst., Excellence in Teaching Award 1982; Mellon Found., Works in Progress Grant 1985. **Important Works:** Univ. of Masssachusetts; Univ. of Colorado; Citibank, NYC; Commerce Bancshares, Kansas City, MO; American Telephone & Telegraph, Chicago; Nat. Brewing Co., Baltimore; Broventure Co., Baltimore. **Exhibitions/Performances:** Solo: USIS Gallery, Milan 1964; Boris Mirski Gallery, Boston 1965, 1967; Alpha Gallery, Boston 1984; Marilyn Pearl Gallery, NYC 1987, 1988, 1989, 1991; Group: MOMA 1962; NAD Annual Exb. 1986; S. Giovanni Val d'Arno, Impruneta, Cortona 1986; Indiana Univ. 1987. **Bio-Bibliography:** John Canaday, "Welcome Windup," *NY Times* (May 27, 1962); Robert Taylor, "James J. Hennessey's Debut Introduces a Rare Style," *Boston Sunday Herald* (Jan. 19, 1965); Paul Bernard, "Double Decker of Excellence," *City Paper* (Baltimore, Dec. 17, 1978); Craig Hankin, "Jim Hennessey, Figuratively Speaking He's One of the Best," *Baltimore News American* (Nov. 30, 1979); Richard Martin, *Artoday-Arteoggi* (Florence, 1986); "James Hennessey's Works on Exhibit at Midtown Gallery," *Irish Echo* (May 27, 1989); John Dorsey, "Faculty Puts Sabbatical to Good Use," *Baltimore Sun* (Aug. 29, 1991); Mike Giuliano, "Hot for Teacher," *City Paper* (Baltimore, Nov. 5, 1993). **Home Address:** 3934 Ednor Rd., Baltimore, MD 21218.

HENRY, BARKLIE MCKEE ■ AAR Trustee 1960-66, Banker, Corp. Exec.

HENRY, MARGARET R. ■ Classical Assn. b. Mar. 7, 1939, Montclair, NJ. m. Clyde W. Henry. c. Andrew. BA 61, Mt. Holyoke College; MA 66, San Francsico State Univ.; PhD 84, UC, Berkeley. **Career & Employment:** Univ. of Hartford, Instr. 1969-70; San Francisco State Univ., Lect. 1971-73, 1977-78, 1987-95. **Home Address:** 109 Kensington Rd., Kensington, CA 94707.

HERMANN, ELIZABETH DEAN ■ FAAR Landscape Architecture 87. b. Mar. 30, 1956, Framingham, MA. m. Heinrich G. Hermann. BS 77, Univ. of Vermont; MLA 83, Cornell Univ. **Other Study:** Harvard Univ. 1990-present. **Research/Artistic Interests:** History of architecture & urbanism in the Islamic world from the Middle Ages to the present; cross-cultural exchange between the Islamic world & the West; issues of multiculturalism & critical regionalism in contemporary design; dissertation focus: the urban development of Granada, Spain in the 14th century. **Career & Employment:** Sasaki Asscs., Landscape Architect 1984-90; Radcliffe College Seminars, Instr. 1988-93; RISD, Instr. 1994-95; Harvard GSD, Instr. 1995. **Fellowships, Honors & Awards:** Cornell Univ., Council for the Creative & Performing Arts Grant 1981; Pi Alpha Xi 1983; Harvard Univ., Penny White Award 1993; Aga Khan Program for Islamic Architecture Grant 1993; Real Colegio Complutense Universidad de Madrid, Research Grant 1993. **Exhibitions/Performances:** Herbert F. Johnson Museum, Cornell Univ. 1983; Nat. Peace Garden Competition Exb., Washington, DC 1989; New York Flower Show 1990; Radcliffe College 1992, 1993, 1995. **Home Address:** 36 Highland Ave., No. 45, Cambridge, MA 02139.

HERMS, GEORGE ■ FAAR Sculpture 83. b. July 5, 1935, Woodland, CA. m. Gaylyn Grace, Pixie Weir. c. Wilder, Aeryl, Nalota, Lily Belle. **Career & Employment:** UC, Irvine, Lect. 1976; UCLA, Lect. 1980-81, 1987-90; UC, San Diego, Lect. 1985; Otis Parsons, Los Angeles, 1987, 1994; Santa Monica College of Design, Arts & Architecture, Lect. 1991-95. **Fellowships, Honors & Awards:** Servant of Holy Beauty Award 1962; NEA Fellowship 1968, 1977, 1984; California State Univ., Fullerton, Visiting Artist 1977-79; Univ. of Denver, Artist-in-Residence

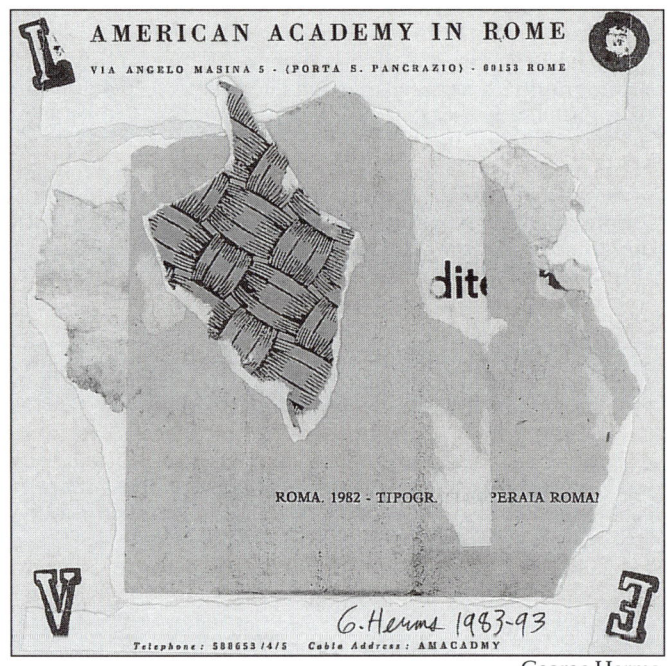
George Herms

1981; Guggenheim Fellowship 1983-84; Pollock Krasner Found. Grant 1987; Pico Seagate Competition, Finalist 1989; Robbins Found. 1991. **Important Works:** *Clock Tower Monument to Unknown,* MacArthur Park, Los Angeles 1987; *Moon Dial,* Beverly Hills 1988; *Portals to Poetry,* Citicorp Plaza, Los Angeles 1989. **Exhibitions/Performances:** Solo: Hermosa Beach, CA 1957; Semina Gallery, Larkspur, CA 1960; Batman Gallery, San Francisco 1961; Stryke Gallery, NYC 1965; California State Univ., Los Angeles 1972; Memorial Union Art Gallery, UC, Davis 1973; Manitoba Museum of Find Art, San Francisco 1977; Newport Harbor Art Museum, Newport Beach, CA 1979; L.A. Louver Gallery, Venice, CA 1982, 1989; Art Gallery, California State Univ., Fullerton 1984; Municipal Art Gallery, Los Angeles 1992; plus numerous group exhibitions. **Home Address:** 1001 E. First St., No. 12, Los Angeles, CA 90012.

HERRIMAN, WILLIAM H. ■ AAR Charter Mem., Painter, Art Collector.

HERRMANN, ARIEL H. ■ AAR Trustee 1979, Trustee Emer.; Classicist.

HERSEY, JOHN RICHARD ■ RAAR Literature 70. b. June 17, 1914, Tientsin, China. d. Mar. 24, 1993. m. Barbara Day Adams Kaufman. c. Brook, Martin, John Jr., Baird, Ann. BA 36, Yale Univ. **Other Studies:** Clare College, Cambridge Univ., Fellow 1936-37. **Career & Employment:** Private Secretary to Sinclair Lewis 1937; *Time Magazine,* Ed. & Correspondent 1937-45; *Life Magazine,* Ed. & Correspondent 1945-46; Self-employed Writer 1946-65; Yale Univ., Master Pierson College, Lect. 1965-70, Visiting Prof., Adj. Prof. 1971-84; Self-employed Writer 1984-92. **Memberships & Offices:** Authors League of America, VP 1949-55, Pres. 1975-80; NIAL; Council Authors Guild 1946; AAAL 1953, Sec. 1962-76, Chancellor 1981-84. **Fellowships, Honors & Awards:** Mellon Fellowship 1936-37; Pulitzer Prize 1945; Washington Jefferson College, LLD 1946; Yale Univ., Hon. MA 1947; Dropsie College, DHLitt.; New School for Social Research, LHD 1950; Sidney Hillman Found. Award 1951; Yale Univ., Howland Medal 1952; Wesleyan Univ., DLitt. 1957; Clare

College, Hon. Fellowship 1967; Hon. Degrees: Clarkson College 1982; Syracuse Univ. 1983; Yale Univ. 1984; William & Mary College 1987; Albertus Magnus College 1988. **Publications:** *Men on Bataan* (New York: Knopf, 1942); *Into the Valley* (New York: Sundial, 1943); *A Bell for Adano* (New York: Knopf, 1944); *Hiroshima* (New York: Knopf, 1946); *The Wall* (New York: Knopf, 1950); *The Marmot Drive* (New York: Knopf, 1953); *A Single Pebble* (New York: Knopf, 1956); *The War Lover* (New York: Knopf, 1959); *Here to Stay* (London: H. Hamilton, 1963); *White Lotus* (New York: Knopf, 1965); *Too Far to Walk* (New York: Knopf, 1966); *Under the Eye of the Storm* (New York: Knopf, 1967); *The Algiers Motel Incident* (New York: Knopf, 1968); *Letter to the Alumni* (New York: Knopf, 1970); *My Petition for More Space* (New York: Knopf, 1974); *The President* (New York: Knopf, 1975); *Aspects of the Presidency* (New Haven: Ticknor & Fields, 1980); *The Call* (New York: Knopf, 1985); *Fling and Other Stories* (New York: Knopf, 1990); *Key West Stories* (New York: Knopf, 1994). **Bio-Bibliography:** David Sanders, *John Hersey* (Boston: Twayne, 1967); Nancy L. Huse, *The Survival Tales of John Hersey* (Troy, NY: Whitston, 1983): David Sanders, *John Hersey Revisited* (Boston: Twayne, 1990); *International Who's Who*.

HEWLETT, JAMES MONROE ■ AAR Trustee 1932-34; AAR, Dir. 1932-34; Architect.

HIBBARD, HOWARD ■ FAAR History of Art 58. b. May 23, 1928, Madison, WI. d. Oct. 29, 1984. m. Shirley Griffith. c. Claire Fletcher, Susan, Carla. BA 49, Univ. of Wisconsin; MA 52, Univ. of Wisconsin; PhD 58, Harvard Univ. **Other Studies:** Columbia Univ. 1952-53. **Research/Artistic Interests:** Italian art of the 16th & 17th centuries, Martino Lunghi, Flaminio Ponzio, Palazzo Borghese, religious architecture. **Career & Employment:** Columbia Univ., Prof.-Chair 1959-84; Oxford Univ., Slade Prof. 1976-77. **Memberships & Offices:** CAA, RSA, SAH, AAUP, Assn. of Art Historians. **Fellowships, Honors & Awards:** Harvard Univ., John Thornton Kirkland Travelling Fellow 1956; ACLS Fellow 1962; Guggenheim Fellow 1965, 1972; NEH Fellow 1967, 1979-80; Oxford Univ., Hon. MA 1977. **Publications:** "Palazzo Borghese Studies," *Burlington Magazine* 100 (1958): 204-12, 252-53; "Early History of Sant'Andrea della Valle," *Art Bulletin* 43 (1961): 289-318; *The Architecture of the Palazzo Borghese,* Memoirs of the AAR 27 (New York: AAR, 1962); "Scipione Borghese's Garden Palace on the Quirinal," *JSAH* 23 (1964): 163-92; *Bernini* (Baltimore: Pelican, 1965); *Bernini e il Barocco* (Rome: Fabbri, 1966); ed. with others, *Essays in the History of Architecture Presented to Rudolf Wittkower* (London: Phaidon, 1967); "Di alcune licenze rilasciate dai Maestri di Strade per opere di edificazione a Roma," *Bollettino d'Arte* 52 (1967): 99-117; *Masterpieces of Western Sculpture* (New York: Harper & Row, 1968); *Carlo Maderno and Roman Architecture 1580-1630* (London: Zwemmer, 1972); *Poussin: The Holy Family on the Steps* (New York: Viking, 1974); *The Metropolitan Museum of Art* (New York: Harper & Row, 1980); "Caravaggio's Two St. Matthews," *Römisches Jahrbuch für Kunstgeschichte* 20 (1983): 181-91; *Caravaggio* (New York: Harper & Row, 1983); *Michelangelo,* 2d ed. (New York: Harper & Row, 1985). **Bio-Bibliography:** *Contemporary Authors; Directory of American Scholars; Who Was Who in America; Who Was Who in American Art;* "Obituary," *Art in America* 72 (1984): 198; I. Lavin, "Obituary," *Burlington Magazine* 127 (1985): 305.

HIGGINBOTHAM, JAMES A. ■ FAAR Classics/Archaeology 89. b. Apr. 24, 1958, Columbia, OH. m. Janice A. Jaffe. c. Susannah. BS 81, Univ. of Michigan; MA 86, Univ. of Michigan; PhD 91, Univ. of Michigan. **Other Study:** Univ. of Michi-

gan excavations at Tel Anafa, Israel, Summers 1980, 1981, 1986; Univ. of Michigan & Univ. of Perugia excavations at Paestum, Italy, Summers 1982-86; ASCSA excavations at Kauousi, Crete, Summer 1988; AAR excavations of Atrium Vestae, Roman Forum, Rome, Summer 1989; Univ. of Michigan-Bowdoin College Excavations, Paestum, Italy 1992-present. **Research/Artistic Interests:** The material culture & archaeology of the Roman Empire. **Career & Employment:** Bowdoin College, Asst. Prof. 1990-91, 1994-present; Carleton College, Asst. Prof. 1991-92; Georgetown Univ., Asst. Prof. 1992-94. **Fellowships, Honors & Awards:** Fulbright-Hayes Research Grant in Italy 1988-89; Oscar Broneer Fellowship in Classical Archaeology 1989. **Publications:** "The Piscina," in *The Sanctuary at Sancta Venera at Paestum,* 1, ed. J.G. Pedley & M. Torelli (Rome: Bretschneider, 1993): 121-47. **Home Address:** 6 South St., Brunswick, ME 04011. **Business Address:** Dept. of Classics, Bowdoin College, Brunswick, ME 04011.

HIGGINSON, HENRY LEE ■ AAR Founder, AAR Trustee 1905-9, Banker. b. Nov. 18, 1834. d. Nov. 15, 1919. **Career & Employment:** Lee, Higginson & Co., Part. 1868-. **Memberships & Offices:** New Boston Music Hall, Pres. Gave $100,000 Founders gift in the name of Harvard College.

HIGHET, GILBERT ■ AAR Trustee 1960-65, Classicist.

HIJUELOS, OSCAR ■ FAAR Literature 86. b. Aug. 24, 1951, NYC. BA, City College of CUNY; MA 76, City College of CUNY. **Fellowships, Honors & Awards:** UN Inst. of Education, Cintas Found. Grant 1978; New York Creative Artists Programs Service Grant 1980; Ingram Merrill Found. Grant 1982; NEA Fellowship 1987; Pulitzer Prize for Fiction 1990. **Publications:** *Our House in the Last World* (New York: Persea Books, 1983); *The Mambo Kings Play Songs of Love* (New York: Farrar, Straus & Giroux, 1989). **Bio-Bibliography:** Manuel Mendoza, "Book: A Tale about Author's Culture," *Milwaukee Journal* (Apr. 25, 1991).

HILDERBRAND, GARY R. ■ FAAR Landscape Architecture 94. b. Aug. 21, 1956. Wappinger Falls, NY. BS 78, SUNY, College of Environmental Science & Forestry, Syracuse; BLA 79, SUNY, College of Environmental Science & Forestry, Syracuse; MLA 85, Harvard GSD. **Career & Employment:** Architects Collaborative 1979-83; Morgan Wheelock, Inc. 1984; Sasaki Asscs. 1985-91; Harvard GSD, Instr. 1985, Prin. Instr. for Special Programs 1987-89, Visiting Critic 1988-89, 1990-91, Lect. & Critic 1991-93, Asst. Prof. 1993-present; Gary M. Hilderbrand, Landscape Architect 1991-present. **Memberships & Offices:** ASLA, Boston Soc. of Landscape Architects; Historic Massachusetts Inc., BoD. **Fellowships, Honors & Awards:** ASLA, Cert. of Honor 1979, 1985; Harvard Univ., Charles Eliot Traveling Fellowship 1985; NEA Fellowship (declined) 1985. **Important Works:** Four Monument Sq., Charlestown, MA 1983; Moreau-Weinreb Garden, MA 1989; Memorial Grove, Jacob's Pillow Dance Festival, Becket, MA 1992-93; with Burck Ryan Asscs., Groton School Landscape Plan, Groton, MA 1993-94; with Burck Ryan Asscs., Sedgwick Gardens at Long Hill, Master Plan, Beverly, MA 1993-95; Page Farm, Weigel Residence, Lincoln, MA. **Home Address:** 11 Spruce St. Watertown, MA 02172.

HILLES, SUSAN MORSE ■ AAR Trustee 1973-79.

HINDEMITH, PAUL ■ AAR Visitor 1943 — 1951, Composer.

HINDS, GEORGE A. ■ FAAR Architecture 84. b. June 8, 1922, Malone, NY. c. Mark, Christopher, Gregory, Sarah. BArch

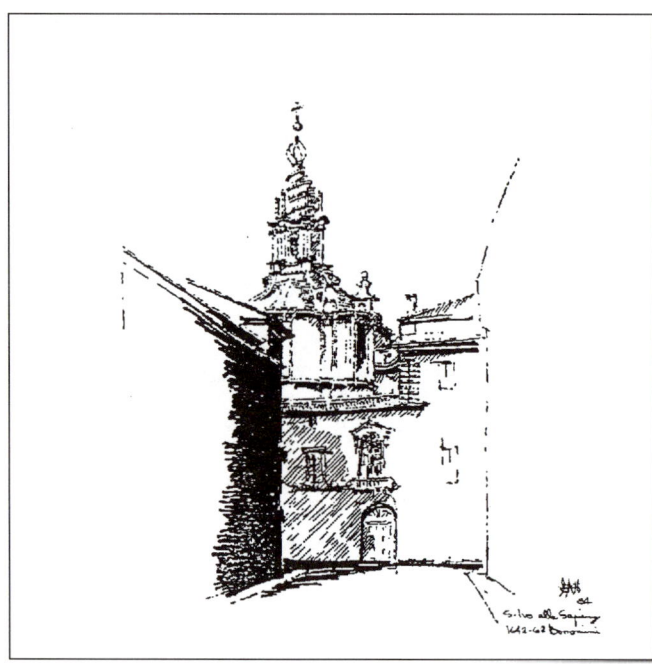

George A. Hinds

49, Yale Univ.; MCity Planning 53, Yale Univ. **Career & Employment:** Smith, Hegner & Moore, Designer 1949; Stockholm Planning Comm., Designer 1951-52; Greenetown Asscs., Consultant 1958-59; Philadelphia Redevelopment Authority, Plan Designer 1953-58, Prin. Planner 1956-58, Acting Dir. of Planning 1958; HSW Ltd., Hinds & Schroeder, George A. Hinds & Asscs., Lenders Architectural, Ltd., Prin. 1963-present; Institut Teknology Bandung, Indonesia, Assc. Prof. 1960-63; Univ. of Illinois, Prof. 1963-87, Prof. Emer 1987. **Memberships & Offices:** AIA; American Inst. of Certified Planners; Evanston Zoning Bd. 1966-76, Planning Comm. 1976-78. **Fellowships, Honors & Awards:** *Progressive Architecture* Design Award 1960; Great Cities Project, Ford Found. Design Award 1966; Illinois Assn. of School Boards, Design Award 1974; Chicago Metropolitan Masonry Council, Design Award 1978; AIA, Chicago Chap., Distinguished Bldg. Award 1978, Distinguished Interior Architectural Award 1981. **Publications:** with James Ward, "Heart of the City," in volume ed. by J. Tyrwhitt, J.L. Sert, & E.N. Rogers (New York: Pellegrini & Cudahy, 1952), 146-47; "Lessons in Regionalism from Indonesia," *AIA Journal* (Feb. 1965): 31-36; "From Asylums to Homes for Children," *AIA Journal* (Aug. 1971): 17-21; "Comments on the Work of Harry Weese," in *Process, Architecture* 11 (Tokyo: Process Architecture, 1979), 152-53; "Sketching, Memory and History," in *Threshold III*, ed. Jack Naughton (New York: Rizzoli, 1985), 52-59; "Studying Architecture Abroad," *Inland Architect* (Mar.-Apr. 1985): 11-12; with Richard Solomon, "Putting River North to the Test," *Inland Architect* (May-June 1987): 21-25; "A New Home for the Bears: A Political Football," *Inland Architect* (Jan.-Feb. 1988): 68-74; "Awash and Awaiting: What Next for Navy Pier?," *Inland Architect* (May-June 1988): 10-14; "Biblioteca Post Urbanistica," *Chicago AIA Focus* (Aug. 1988): 10-12. **Important Works:** Univ. of Chicago Dormitories; Lawrence Hall School of Boys; Mary Bartleme School for Girls; Nat. College of Chiropractic Medicine, Student Center; Jenner & Block Center, Illinois Inst. for Continuing Legal Education. **Exhibitions/Performances:** AIC, Burnham Gallery 1981, 1982, 1983, 1984, 1985; Musée-Galarie de la Seita, Paris 1983; Museum of Science & Industry, Chicago 1985. **Home Address:** 155 N. Harbor Dr., Apt. 1004, Chicago, IL 60602.

HIRONS, FREDERIC CHARLES ■ Rotch Scholar 1904.

HIRSCH, EDWARD ■ FAAR Literature 88. b. Jan. 20, 1950, Chicago, IL. m. Janet Landay. c. Gabriel. BA 72, Grinnell College; PhD 79, Univ. of Pennsylvania. **Career & Employment:** Wayne State Univ., Asst. Prof. 1978-82, Assc. Prof. 1982-85; Univ. of Houston, Assc. Prof. 1985-88, Prof. 1988-present. **Fellowships, Honors & Awards:** Delmore Schwartz Memorial Award 1985; Guggenheim Fellowship 1986-87; Nat. Book Critics Circle Award 1987. **Publications:** *For the Sleepwalkers* (New York: Knopf, 1981); *Wild Gratitude* (New York: Knopf, 1986); *The Night Parade* (New York: Knopf, 1989); *Earthly Measures* (New York: Knopf, 1994); ed., *Transforming Vision: Writers on Art* (Bullfinch, 1994). **Business Address:** Dept. of English, Univ. of Houston, Houston, TX 77204.

HITCHCOCK, HENRY RUSSELL ■ AAR Visitor 1959 — 1964, Architectural Historian.

HOAK, WARREN ■ Stewardson Memorial Scholar 1926-27.

HOFER, PHILIP ■ RAAR History of Art 57. b. Mar. 14, 1898, Cinncinati, OH. d. Nov. 9, 1984. m. Frances L. Heckscher. c. Myron Arms. BA 21, Harvard Univ.; MA 29, Harvard Univ. **Career & Employment:** W.II. Warner Co., Assc. 1922-27, Asst. to Pres. 1922-26; Philip Hofer & Co., Part. 1924-27; New York Public Library, Spencer Collection, Adv. 1929-34; Pierpont Morgan Library, Asst. Dir. 1934-37; Harvard Library, Dept. of Printing & Graphic Arts, Founder & Curator 1938-67, Emer. 1968-84; Harvard Business School, Asst. Dean 1942-44, Harvard Univ., Fogg Art Museum, Sec. 1952-64. **Memberships & Offices:** Corning Glass Museum, BoT Emer.; MFA, BoT 1943-71, BoT Emer. 1971-84; Massachusetts Historical Soc., BoT; Museum of China Trade, Adv. Bd.; Princeton Art Museum, Adv. Comm. 1970-84; Harvard Univ., Boston Athenaeum, Overseer; ASCA, Overseer; Signet Soc. **Fellowships, Honors & Awards:** Soc. of Antiquaries, London, Fellow; Order of St. John of Jerusalem, Assc. Officer; Peabody Museum, Salem MA, Hon. Curator; Gutenberg Museum, Germany, Hon. Mem.; Bates College, DFA 1962; Harvard Univ., LHD 1967. **Publications:** contr., *Fragonard Drawings for Ariosto* (New York: Pantheon, 1945); *Baroque Book Illustration* (Cambridge, MA: Harvard Univ. Press, 1951); *Eighteenth-Century Book Illustrations* (Los Angeles: William Andrews Clark Memorial Library, 1956); *John Howard Renson and His Work 1901-1956* (New York: Typophiles, 1957); *Edward Lear as a Landscape Draftsman* (Cambridge, MA: Harvard Univ. Press, 1967); *Approaches to Drawing* (New York, 1963); *Edward Lear's Flora Nonsensica* (Cambridge, MA: Harvard College Library, 1963). **Bio-Bibliography:** D.P. Becker, *Drawings for Book Collections, The Hofer Collection,* exb. cat. (Cambridge, MA: Houghton Library, Harvard Univ., 1980); *Who Was Who in America.*

HOFFMAN, JAMES JOSEPH ■ FAAR Painting 56. b. Nov. 4, 1925, Racine, WI. d. Sept. 14, 1959. BFA 48, Univ. of Illinois. **Other Studies:** ASL; Brooklyn Museum of Fine Arts. **Career & Employment:** Middlebury College, Instr. 1957. **Fellowships, Honors & Awards:** Guggenheim Fellowship 1959; Univ. of Illinois, Kate Neil Memorial Fellowship 1948-49. **Exhibitions/Performances:** Wustum Museum of Fine Arts 1960.

HOFFMAN, MARTHA W. ■ FAAR Classics/Archaeology 53. b. Nov. 8, 1922, Newton, MA. m. William A. Lewis. c. James Lewis, John Lewis. BA 43, UC, Berkeley; MA 49, Bryn Mawr College; PhD 51, Bryn Mawr College. **Research/Artistic Inter-**

ests: Roman history. **Career & Employment:** Red Bluff Union HS, Teacher 1944-45; Piedmont HS, Teacher 1945-48; Univ. of Illinois, Asst. Prof. 1953-56; Rockhurst College, Assc. Prof. 1963-82. **Memberships & Offices:** APA 1951-present. **Fellowships, Honors & Awards:** Bryn Mawr College Fellowship 1949-51; Fulbright Fellowship 1951-53; Phi Beta Kappa. **Publications:** "The Official Priests of Rome under the Julio-Claudians: A Study of the Nobility from 44 BC to 68 AD," *AAR Papers & Monographs* 16 (Rome: AAR, 1955); "Power and Passion: The Orchid in Literature," *Orchid Biology: Reviews and Perspectives* 5 (1990): 207-49. **Home Address:** 716 W. 109th Ter., Kansas City, MO 64114.

HOFFMAN, RICHARD J. ■ FAAR Classics/Archaeology 72. b. Mar. 23, 1943, Los Angeles, CA. BA 65, UC, Berkeley; MA 67, UC, Berkeley; PhD 72, UC, Berkeley. **Other Study:** Roman Law with David Daube, UC, Berkeley 1975-76; with Michael Jameson, Stanford Univ. 1983. **Research/Artistic Interests:** Greek & Roman political, legal & social history. **Career & Employment:** San Francisco State Univ., Prof. 1972-present; UC, Berkeley, Visiting Prof. 1981, 1983, 1986. **Memberships & Offices:** AHA, Assn. of Ancient Historians, California Classics Assn. **Fellowships, Honors & Awards:** ACLS Fellowship 1975-76; San Francisco State Univ., President's Professional Development Grant 1979, Meritorious Performance Award 1987, Professional Research & Development Award 1988-89; NEA Summer Fellowship 1983. **Publications:** "Perdikkas and the Outbreak of the Peloponnesian War," *Greek, Roman, and Byzantine Studies* 16 (1975): 359-77; "Epigraphic Notes on IG I2 71," *California Studies in Classical Antiquity* 8 (1976): 89-104; "Civil Law Procedures in the Provinces of the Late Roman Republic," *Irish Jurist* 11 (1977): 355-74; "Classics in the Courts of the United States, 1790-1800," *American Journal of Legal History* 22 (1978): 55-84; "Vices, Gods, and Virtues: Cosmology as a Mediating Factor in Attitudes Towards Male Homosexuality," *Journal of Homosexuality* 9 (1983-84): 27-44; "Ritual License and the Cult of Dionysus," *Athenaeum* 67 (1989): 91-115. **Business Address:** Dept. of History, San Francisco State Univ., 1600 Holloway, San Francsico, CA.

```
Super flumina caerulea
    illic grassati sumus et risimus
    cum recordaremur facini nostri.

In platanis in medio eius
    et ad locos communes irriguos
    sedimus ac disseruimus de Xysto.

In civitate omnium gnara
    et nihil reticetur:

Urbem, urbem, cole,
    et in ista luce vive!

                Romae
            a. d. v Kal. Mai.
```

Richard J. Hoffman

HOFFMANN, HERBERT ■ FAAR Classics/Archaeology 58. b. Apr. 3, 1930, Luckenwalde, Germany. m. Phyllis Hoffmann. c. Andrea. BA 51, Harvard Univ.; MA 52, Harvard Univ.; PhD 59, Harvard Univ. **Career & Employment:** MMA, Curatorial Asst. 1959; Museum für Kunst und Gewerbe, Hamburg, Curator 1960-73; King's College, Cambridge, Visiting Fellow, 1977; Sorbonne, Visiting Prof. 1978; Univ. of Hamburg, Prof. 1979; Univ. of Hamburg, Privatdozent; Gestalt-Psychotherapist, Private Practice 1980-. **Fellowships, Honors & Awards:** Guggenheim Fellow 1965, 1973; Univ. of Hamburg, D.Habil. 1973; British Council, Fellow 1975; Royal Anthropological Inst., Fellow.

HOLDEN, JAMES NEWHALL ■ Rotch Scholar 1917.

HOLLAND, LOUISE ELIZABETH WHETENHALL ADAMS ■ FAAR Classics/Archaeology 23, RAAR Classics/Archaeology 60. b. July 3, 1893, Brooklyn, NY. m. Leicester B. Holland. c. Barbara Adams Holland; Marian Holland McAllister; Lawrence Rozier Holland. d. June 21, 1990. BA 14, Barnard College; MA 15, Columbia Univ.; PhD 20, Bryn Mawr College. **Research/Artistic Interests:** Civilization of the Faliscans, Roman writers of the Golden Age, commerce of Latium, early Iron Age. **Career & Employment:** Smith College, Instr.-Asst. Prof. 1918-23, 1957-64; Vassar College, Asst. Prof. 1925-27; Bryn Mawr College, Visiting Prof. 1928-55; Miami Univ., Instr. 1951-52. **Memberships & Offices:** APA, ArIA. **Fellowships, Honors & Awards:** Bryn Mawr College, Travelling Fellowship 1917-18; Guggenheim Fellowship 1949; Bryn Mawr College, Lucy Martin Donnelly Fellowship 1964; APA, Book of the Year 1965; Smith College, LittD 1965; Barnard College, Distinguished Alumnae Award 1978. **Publications:** *A Study of the Commerce of Latium from the Early Iron Age through the Sixth Century*, Smith College Classical Studies 11 (1921); *The Faliscans in Prehistoric Times*, AAR Papers & Monographs (New York: AAR, 1925); "Qui Terminum Exarasset," *AJA* 37 (1933): 549-54; "Herodotus I,94: A Phocaean Version of an Etruscan Tale," *AJA* 41 (1937): 377-82; "The Shrine of the Lares Compitales," *TAPA* 68 (1937): 428-41; "Forerunners and Rivals of the Primitive Roman Bridge," *TAPA* 80 (1949): 281-319; "Septimonitum or Saeptimonium?" *TAPA* 84 (1953): 16-34; "The Purpose of the Warrior Image from Capestrano," *AJA* 60 (1956): 243-47; *Janus and the Bridge*, AAR Papers & Monographs 21 (New York: AAR, 1961); *Lucretius and the Transpadanes* (Princeton: Princeton Univ. Press, 1979). **Bio-Bibliography:** *Who's Who of American Women*; Briggs, 287-89.

HOLLANDER, LORIN ■ AAR Visitor 1973-74, Pianist. b. July 19, 1944. **Fellowships, Honors & Awards:** Carnegie Hall, NYC, Debut 1956; Youngest Artist of Great Artist Series 1956.

HOLLINGSWORTH, STANLEY WALKER ■ FAAR Musical Composition 58. b. Aug. 27, 1924, Berkeley, CA. BMus 53, Curtis Inst. **Career & Employment:** Curtis Inst., Instr.; San Jose State College, Instr. **Fellowships, Honors & Awards:** NBC Opera Theatre Comm. 1955; San Jose State College Comm. 1957.

HOLLOWAY, BENJAMIN ■ AAR Trustee 1987-92, Trustee Emer.; Corporate Exec, Real Estate.

HOLLOWAY, R. ROSS ■ FAAR Classics/Archaeology 60, RAAR Classics/Archaeology 70, 92. b. Aug. 15, 1934, Newton, MA. m. Nancy June Degenhart. c. Anne Lovelace, Suzanna Porter. BA 56, Amherst College; MA 57, Univ. of Pennsylvania; MA 60, Princeton Univ.; PhD 60, Princeton Univ. **Other Study:** Archaeological field work: Morgantina. **Research/Artistic Interests:** Italian prehistory, ancient numismatics, ancient Greek art. **Career & Employment:** Princeton Univ., Visiting Asst. Prof. 1963; UNC, Asst. Prof. 1963-64; Brown Univ., Asst. Prof. 1964-67, Assc. Prof. 1967-69, Prof. 1970-present, Elisha

Benjamin Andrews Prof. 1989-present; Center for Old World Archaeology & Art, Dir. 1978-87, 1994; Archaeological Field Work, Excavation Dir.: Athens 1965, Satrianum 1966-67, Buccino 1968-74, Trentinara 1977, La Muculufa 1981-87, Ustica 1989-present. **Memberships & Offices:** RISD Museum of Art, Hon. Consulting Curator 1971-present; Intl. Center for Numismatic Studies, Naples, Pres. 1980-86; Assn. for Field Archaeology, Co-Founder, Pres. 1976-78; Ed. Bds.: *Journal of Field Archaeology* 1974-95, *AJA* 1985-94, *Archaeologia Transaltantica*, Co-Ed. 1981-present. **Fellowships, Honors & Awards:** APS Grant 1962; ACLS Fellowship 1969; NEA Grants 1972, 1982, 1983, 1984, Fellowship 1977; Amherst College, LHD 1976. **Publications:** *The Thirteen-Months Coinage of Hieronymos of Syracuse*, Antike Münzen und Geschnittene Steine 3 (Berlin: De Gruyten, 1969); *Satrianum: The Archaeological Investigations Conducted by Brown University in 1966 and 1967* (Providence: Brown Univ. Press, 1970); *Buccino: The Eneolithic Necropolis of San Antonio and Other Prehistoric Discoveries Made by Brown University in 1968 and 1969* (Rome: De Luca, 1973); *A View of Greek Art* (Providence: Brown Univ. Press, 1973); with N.P. Nabers, S.S. Lukesh, et al., "Buccino: The Early Bronze Age Village of Tufariello," *Journal of Field Archaeology* 2 (1975): 11-81; *Influences and Styles in the Late Archaic and Early Classical Greek Sculpture of Sicily and Magna Graecia* (Louvain: Catholic Univ. & Inst. of Archaeology & Art History Monographs, 1975); *Art and Coinage in Magna Graecia* (Bellinzona: Edizioni Arte e Moneta, 1978); *Italy and the Aegean: 3000-700 BC*, Archaeologia Transatlantica 1 (Providence, RI: Center for Old World Archaeology & Art, Brown Univ. & Louvain: Centre d'archéologie greque, Catholic Univ. of Louvain, 1982); with G.K. Jenkins, *The Coinage of Terina* (Bellinzona: Edizioni Arte e Moneta, 1982); ed. with T. Hackens & N.D. Holloway, *Crossroads of the Mediterranean*, Archaeologia Transatlantica 2 (Providence, RI: Center for Old World Archaeology & Art, Brown Univ. & Louvain: Centre d'archéologie greque, Catholic Univ. of Louvain, 1984); with T.V. Buttrey, K.T. Erim, & T. Groves, *Morgantina Studies II, The Coins* (Princeton: Princeton Univ. Press, 1989); *The Archaeology of Ancient Sicily* (London: Routledge, 1991); with M.S. Joukowsky, J. Léon & S.S. Lukesh, *La Muculufa, the Early Bronze Age Sanctuary: The Early Bronze Age Village (Excavations of 1982 and 1983)*, Archaeologia Transatlantica (Louvain: Dept. d'archéologie et d'histoire de l'art, Catholic Univ. of Louvain, 1992), also in *Revue des Archéologues et Historiens d'Art de Louvain* 23 (1990): 11-65; *The Archaeology of Early Rome and Latium* (London: Routledge, 1994). **Bio-Bibliography:** *International Who's Who, Who's Who in America.* **Business Address:** PO Box 1837, Providence, RI 02912.

HOLMES, FRANK B. ■ FAAR Painting 75. b. Dec. 20, 1938, Detroit, MI. m. Jill Mackie. BFA 62, Pratt Inst.; MFA 72, Ohio Univ. **Other Study:** Univ. of New Mexico, Albuquerque 1956-58. **Career & Employment:** Parsons School of Design, Instr. 1963-68; NYIT, Instr. 1968-70; Ohio Univ., Guest Lect. 1972-73; C.W. Post Center, Long Island Univ., Assc. Prof. 1976-79. **Fellowships, Honors & Awards:** Ingram Merrill Found. Award 1977. **Important Works:** Collections: Dayton Art Inst.; Robertson Center for the Arts & Sciences, Binghamton, NY; Capricorn Gallery, Bethesda, MD; Ohio Univ. School or Art, Athens; American Express Intl., NYC; Owens-Corning Collection, Toledo, OH. **Exhibitions/ Performances:** Solo: Dayton Art Inst. 1972; Myrna Citron Gallery, NYC 1979; Monique Knowlton Gallery, NYC 1979, 1980; TLK Gallery, Costa Mesa, CA 1983; Gallerie Tamenaga, NYC 1991, 1993; Selected Group: Grand Palais, Paris 1980; AAAL 1980; Newport Harbor Art Museum, Newport Beach, CA 1981; Butler Inst., Youngstown,

OH 1987; Sherry French Gallery, NYC 1989; Nat. Acad. of Sciences , Washington, DC 1989. **Bio-Bibliography:** Arthur Wright, "Long Moments: The Paintings of Frank Holmes," *American Art Review* 4.6 (1978): 120-31. **Home Address:** 24 Grove St., Narrowsburg, NY 12764.

HOOD, RAYMOND MATHEWSON ■ AAR Special Student 1912-13, Architect. b. Mar. 29, 1881. d. Aug. 14, 1934. **Career & Employment:** Architectural practice, NYC 1914-. **Important Works:** *Chicago Tribune* Tower; American Radiator Bldg.; the McGraw Hill Bldg., NYC.

HOOD, WALTER K. ■ FAAR Painting 55. b. Aug. 19, 1928, Catawba County, NC. m. Elizabeth K. Welch. c. David. BFA 57, Univ. of Pennsylvania; MFA 61, Univ. of Hawaii; PhD 66, Northwestern Univ. **Other Study:** Antioch College, Yellow Springs, OH; work & study in the stained-glass studio of Robert Metcalf, Yellow Springs, OH 1948-49; PAFA 1949-53; private studies & work in mosaic with Italian mosaicist, Giuli Giovannetti, Rome 1954; fresco studies with Jean Charlot, Honolulu 1961. **Research/Artistic Interests:** Mural painting & mosaic, fresco, egg tempera; portrait & landscape painting with egg tempera, oil, watercolor, sumi; the art life of American mural painter, war artist, & writer George Harding; the flora of Oahu's mountain trails. **Career & Employment:** Catawba College, Prof. & Dept. Chair 1971-90. **Memberships & Offices:** Nat. Soc. of Mural Painters 1956-present. **Fellowships, Honors & Awards:** PAFA, Cresson European Travelling Award 1952, J. Henry Schiedt Foreign Traveling Award 1953; Northwestern Univ. Fellowship 1962, 1963. **Publications:** (publisher in all cases: Salisbury, NC: Walter Hood), *Seventeen Hundred Syllables* (1983); *Images in Ink* (1983); *Pictures Cast in Words* (1984); *Estival Imaginings* (1985); *Gossamer Days* (1986); *Thoughts in Monochrome* (1987); *Springtide Cadences* (1988); *Permutations* (1989); *Echoes Black & White* (1990); *Dreams upon the Hither Shore* (1991); *Lightning in the Valley* (1991). **Important Works:** *Christ's Life, Death & Resurrrection*, St. Peter's Church, Glenside, PA 1958; *Portrait of Dr. T. Foard*, Foard School, Catawba County, NC n.d.; *Sorting Totora*, PAFA,

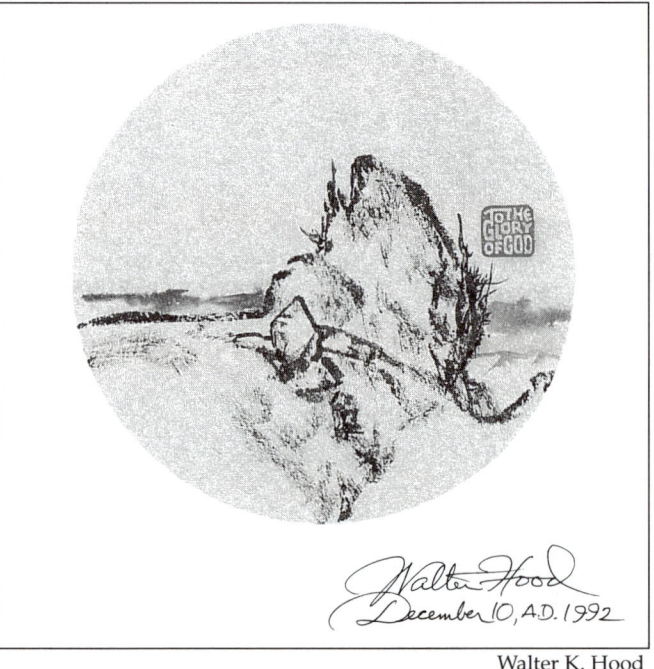

Walter K. Hood

Permanent Collection 1950s; *Portrait of Dr. Theodore Leonard*, Corriher-Linn-Black Library, Salisbury, NC c.1982; Historical Mural, Salisbury Mall, Salisbury, NC 1990. **Exhibitions/Performances:** Solo: La Fontanella Gallery, Rome 1955; ALNY 1956; Hilton Head Island 1967; Atlanta Fine Arts Gallery 1967; Group: American Artists Professional League, Nat. Exb., NYC 1974, 1975, 1976; Nat. Soc. of Painters in Casein & Acrylic, Nat. Exb., NYC 1976, 1977, 1978. **Bio-Bibliography:** *Who's Who in American Art, Who's Who in the South & Southwest*. **Home Address:** 2508 West Innes St., Salisbury, NC 28144.

HOOD, WILLIAM EATHERLEY, JR ■ FAAR History of Art 74. b. Apr. 20, 1940, Birmingham, AL. BFA 65, Univ. of Georgia; MA 67, Univ. of Georgia; PhD 77, IFA. **Career & Employment:** Oberlin College, Prof. 1974-present, Chair 1987-91. **Memberships & Offices:** CAA, *Art Bulletin*, Ed. Bd.; MAA; RSA; Asia Soc. of America, Gay & Lesbian Caucus. **Fellowships, Honors & Awards:** Phi Beta Kappa; IFA, Bernard Berenson Prize 1971; Oberlin College Grants 1977-79, 1983, 1986, 1987, 1989, 1993; NEH Fellowship 1981-82, Grant 1990; Harvard Univ., I Tatti Fellowship 1984-86, I Tatti Visiting Prof. 1989-90; ACLS Grant 1986. **Publications:** with Charles Hope, "Titian's Vatican Altarpiece and the Pictures Underneath," *Art Bulletin* 59 (1977): 534-53; "The Narrative Mode in Titian's Presentation of the Virgin," in *Studies in Italian Art History*, ed. H. Millon (Rome: AAR, 1980), 125-62; "Ciro Ferri's *Pensiero* for the Altarpiece of the Blessed Stansilaus Kostka in Sant' Andrea al Quirinale," *Allen Memorial Art Museum Bulletin* 36 (1980): 26-49; "The Sacro Monte of Varallo and Popular Religion in the Renaissance," in *Monasticism and the Arts*, ed. T. Verdon (Syracuse: Syracuse Univ. Press, 1984), 291-311; "St Dominic's Manners of Praying: Gestures in Fra Angelico's Cell Frescoes at San Marco," *Art Bulletin* 78 (1986): 195-205; "In Defense of Art History: A Response to Ridgeway," *Art Bulletin* 78 (1986): 480-81; "The State of Research in Italian Renaissance Art," *Art Bulletin* 79 (1987): 174-86; "Fra Angelico at San Marco: Art & the Liturgy of Cloistered Life," in *Christianity and the Renaissance*, ed. T. Verdon & J. Henderson (Syracuse: Syracuse Univ. Press, 1990), 109-31; *Fra Angelico at San Marco* (New Haven & London: Yale Univ. Press, 1993); "Creating Memory: Monumental Painting and Cultural Definition," *Cultural Definition and the Renaissance*, ed. A. Brown (Oxford: Oxford Univ. Press, 1994). **Home Address:** 257 W. College St., Oberlin, OH 44074. **Business Address:** Dept. of Art, Oberlin College, Oberlin, OH 44074.

HOOPER, ROBERT T. ■ FAAR Painting 79. b. Apr. 28, 1952, Detroit, MI. m. Julia D. Laupmanis. c. John, Katharine. BFA 74, Pratt Inst.; MFA 77, Yale Univ. School of Art & Architecture. **Research/Artistic Interests:** Painting. **Career & Employment:** Indiana Univ. 1981-82; Univ. of New Hampshire 1985-89; Brandeis Univ. 1989-90; Wellesley College 1991-92. **Fellowships, Honors & Awards:** Pollock-Krasner Found. Grant 1990. **Exhibitions/Performances:** Solo: Madeleine Carter, Boston 1981, 1985, 1988; Treat Gallery, Bates College 1982; Genovese Gallery, Boston 1991, 1992, 1993; Selected Group: Rose Museum, Boston 1985, 1992; Genovese Gallery, Boston 1988. **Bio-Bibliography:** *St. Louis Post-Dispatch* (Apr. 15, 1983); *Art New England* (Jan. 3, 1985); *Boston Herald* (Apr. 7, 1985); *Boston Globe* (Apr. 7, 1985, June 11, 1992, Apr. 21, 1994); *South End News* (June 18, 1992, May 5, 1994); *Ardent Gestures*, exb. cat. (Waltham, MA: Rose Art Museum). **Home Address:** 21287 W. Cliffside Dr., Kildeer, IL 60047. **Business Address:** Genovese Gallery, 535 Albany St., Boston, MA.

HOOVER, HENRY ■ Sheldon Fellow 1926-27.

HOOVER, IRA W. ■ Stewardson Memorial Scholar 1911-12, 1913.

HOPKINS, ALDEN ■ FAAR Landscape Architecture 36. b. Dec. 11, 1905, Chepachet, RI. d. Sept. 16, 1960. BS 28, Univ. of Rhode Island; MLA 34, Harvard GSD. **Other Studies:** Univ. of Massachusetts. **Research/Artistic Interests:** Restoration, colonial Virginia. **Career & Employment:** Landscape Architect, Private Practice 1938-41; Colonial Williamsburg, Resident Landscape Architect 1941-60; US Navy, Lieut. Commander, WWII. **Memberships & Offices:** ASLA, SAH, Nat. Trust for Historic Preservation. **Fellowships, Honors & Awards:** US Marine Corps, Bronze Star; Garden Club of America, Sarah Gildersleeve Fife Award 1955; ASLA, Fellow 1958. **Publications:** "An Okinawan Farm Group: Memoranda from an Ex-Naval Officer's Handbook," *Landscape Architecture* (Jan. 1947); "Early Gardens in Maryland and Virginia," *Garden Club of America Bulletin* (Sept. 1950); "The Period Garden at the White House of the Confederacy, Richmond," *Richmond Times-Dispatch* (Jan. 8, 1956); "Hollies for Topiary," *American Horticultural Journal* (Jan. 1957); "The Woodlawn Garden Restoration," *Garden Club of Virginia Journal* (Sept.-Oct. 1960); "Old Fashioned Roses of Woodlawn," *Garden Club of Virginia Journal* (Nov.-Dec. 1960). **Important Works:** Extensive restoration of gardens in Colonial Williamsburg; Restoration of Thomas Jefferson's Monticello; Restoration at the Univ. of Virginia; Landscape Architect on many public and historical projects in Maryland, Delaware, Rhode Island, Washington, DC, North Carolina, New York & Virginia. **Exhibitions/Performances:** San Francisco Museum of Art c.1936. **Bio-Bibliography:** *National Cyclopedia of American Biography*.

HOPKINS, HENRY ■ AAR Visitor 1992-93.

HOPPNER, PETER ■ FAAR Design Arts 77. b. Sept. 6, 1937, Albany, NY. m. Joyce Hoppner. BA 59, Trinity College; BArch 62, Rensselaer Polytechnic Inst.; MArch 64, Yale Univ., School of Architecture. **Career & Employment:** Paul Rudolph, Architect, Job Captain-Draftsman 1964-70; Private Practice, 1970-.

HORNS, MILLER ■ FAAR Design Arts 90. b. Nov. 8, 1948, Birmingham, AL. BFA 86, Cleveland Inst. of Art. **Other Study:** Univ. of Akron 1975-81. **Research/Artistic Interests:** Electrostatics & thermal color transfer. **Career & Employment:** Independent artist 1986-92. **Memberships & Offices:** Univ. of Akron, Fine Arts & Women's Studies Juror 1987. **Fellowships, Honors & Awards:** Ohio Rehabilitation Services Comm., Arts Expressions Artist with Disabilities, Honorable Mentions (2) 1988; *Parade Magazine*, American Women Photo Contest Finalist 1988; NEA Grant 1989-90; Hoyt Inst. of Fine Arts, Distinguished Merit Award 1991; Ohio Arts Council, Professional Development Grant 1992. **Exhibitions/Performances:** Solo: William Busta Gallery, Cleveland 1991; Nat. City Bank, Cleveland 1991; Group: Hoyt Inst., New Castle, PA 1991; Martin Luther King Center, Columbus, OH 1991; Butler Inst., Youngstown 1991; Charles Mayer Studio, Akron 1991, 1992; William Busta Gallery, Cleveland 1991; Great Northern Corp., Porter Center Art Gallery, Cleveland 1992; North Branch Library, Akron 1992; Traveling Exchange Exb., Univ. of Akron & Xiaman Univ., South China 1992-93. **Bio-Bibliography:** Neil Gabay, "Miller Horns/Electrostatics," *Dialoge Magazine* (1982): 17; Helen Gullinan, "Juke Box Saturday Night," *Cleveland Plain Dealer Friday Magazine* (1988): 8; K. Kisner, "Miller Horns,"

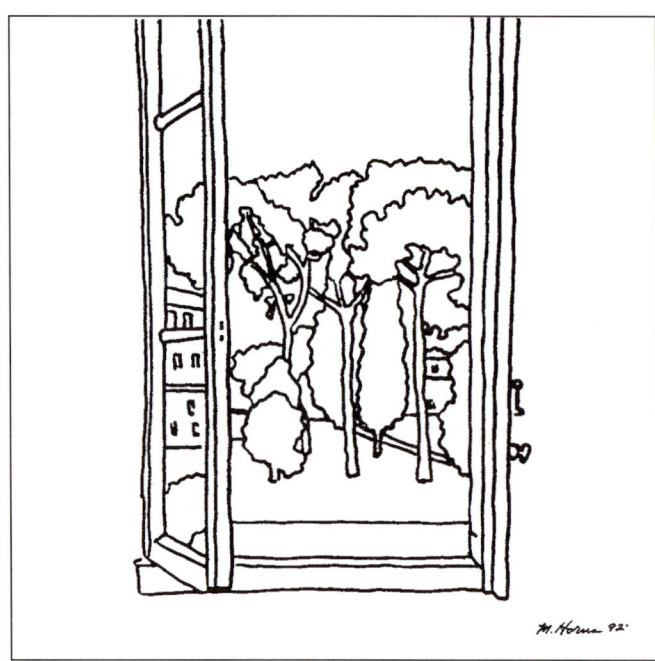

Miller Horns

Northern Ohio Live Magazine (1989): 47; Rhonda Kiefer, "Miller Horns Art," *West Side Leader* (1988); Luigi Gavazzi, "Miller Horns Xeroart dall'Ohio," *Doc. Ufficio Milan* (1990): 9, 52-55; Dorothy Shinn, "Interview with Artist," *Akron Beacon Journal* (1990): D6; Faith Whitcumb, "Unique Visions," *Cleveland Plain Dealer* (1991); Helen Gullinan, "Image Rome/Roma," *Cleveland Plain Dealer* (1991): 19; Beth Chico, "Miller Horns/Busta Gallery," *Dialoge Magazine* (1991): 14-15. **Home Address:** 25 West Tallmadge Ave., No. 4, Akron, OH 44310.

HORNSBY, ROGER A. ■ RAAR Classics/Archaeology 83; AAR Trustee 1990-92, Trustee Emer.; Classical School, Jury 1986, 1987, 1991; Adv. Council, 1972-present, Sec. 1975-77, Pres. 1977-79. b. Aug. 8, 1926, Nye, WI. m. Jessie L. Gillesie. BA 49, Adelbert College, Western Reserve Univ.; MA 51, Princeton Univ.; PhD 52, Princeton Univ. **Research/Artistic Interests:** Classical philosophy, Latin poetry, Roman numismatics, topography of Rome. **Career & Employment:** Univ. of Iowa, Instr.-Prof. 1954-91; Chair 1966-81; Trinity College, Hartford, Visiting Prof. 1967; UCLA, Visiting Prof. 1976; Mount Mary College, Milwaukee, Visiting Prof. 1980. **Memberships & Offices:** ArIA 1952-present, Iowa Chap., Sec. 1961-62, Pres. 1967-68, 1984-85; APA 1952-present, Dir. 1973-76, Textbook Series Ed. 1976-81, Advanced Placement Latin, Chief Reader 1965-69; CAMWS 1952-present, Pres. 1968-69; ASCSA, Managing Com. 1968-90; ANS 1976-present, 2d VP 1984-present; ACLS Delegate 1984-present; VSA, BoT 1990-92. **Fellowships, Honors & Awards:** ANS Scholar 1951, 1952; Univ. of Iowa, Research Prof. 1960, 1970, Univ. Prof. 1983; Fulbright Comm. Travel Grant 1970-71; ACLS Senior Fellow 1970-71. **Publications:** *Reading Latin Poetry* (Oklahoma City: Oklahoma Univ. Press, 1967); *Patterns of Action in the* Aeneid (Iowa City: Univ. of Iowa Press, 1970); "The Armor of the Slain," *Philological Quarterly* 45 (1966): 347-59; "Maior Nascitur Ordo," in *Mnemai: Classical Studies in Memory of Karl H. Hulley*, ed. H.D. Evien (Missoula: Scholars Press, 1984). **Bio-Bibliography:** *Directory of American Scholars, Who's Who in America*. **Home Address:** 201 1st Ave. N, Apt. 306, Iowa City, IA 52245.

HOSTETTER, ERIC R. ■ FAAR Classics/Archaeology 83; Palatine East Excavations, Dir. 1988-present. b. Nov. 16, 1948, Fayetteville, AR. m. Maryline G. Parca. c. Maïté, Isaure, Loïc. BA 71, UC, Santa Cruz; MA 75, Harvard Univ.; PhD 79, Harvard Univ. **Other Study:** Univ. of Lund, Sweden 1969-70; Archaeological Field Work: Castle Copse, Wiltshire; Villa d'Agosta, Giglio, Giannuatri & Monte Argentario; Sardis, Turkey; Palatine East, Rome. **Research/Artistic Interests:** Etruscan, Roman & Lydian art & archaeology. **Career & Employment:** Univ. of Michigan, Visiting Asst. Prof. 1979-80; Indiana Univ., Asst.-Assc. Prof. 1980-90; Castle Copse Excavations, Dir. 1983-present; Univ. of Illinois, Urbana-Champaign, Assc. Prof. 1991-present. **Fellowships, Honors & Awards:** Indiana Univ. Grant 1982, 1984, 1989, Fellowship 1988; ACLS Grant 1982; Harvard Univ., Getty Postdoctoral Fellow 1985-86, Arnold O. Beckman Research Award 1991, 1992; Univ. of Illinois, Center for Advanced Study, Assc. Fellow 1993. **Publications:** *Bronzes from Spina I: The Classical Figures* (Mainz: Philipp von Zabern, 1986); *Lydian Architectural Terracottas: A Study in Tile Replication, Display and Technique,* Illinois Classical Studies Supplemental Monograph Series 5 (Atlanta, 1994); with T.N. Howe, "The Romano-British Villa of Castle Copse," *Archeology* 39.5 (1986): 36-43; with T.N. Howe & J. Kenfield, "Preliminary Report on Excavations of the Late Roman Villa at Castle Copse, Great Bedwyn, 1986," *Wiltshire Archaeological & Natural History Magazine* 81 (1987): 62-56; "A Weary Herakles at Harvard," *Harvard Studies in Classical Philology* 91 (1987): 367-79; with T.N. Howe & R. Brandt, "Palatine Excavations of the Late Roman Buildings," *Bollettino di Archeologia* 3 (1990): 89-91; "A Bronze Banqueting Service from Tomb 58 C Valle Pega," in *Dionysos: Mito e Mistero. Atti del Convegno Internazionale, Comacchio 3-5 Nov. 1989,* ed. F. Berti (Comacchio, 1991), 89-106; with T.N. Howe, R. Brandt, A. St. Clair & T. Peña, "Complesso tardo romano sul versante NE del Palatino (1990)," *Bollettino di Archeologia* 9 (Fall 1993): 47-56; with T.N. Howe, R. Brandt, A. St. Clair, T. Peña, M. Parca, K. Gleason, N. Miller, "A Late Roman Complex on the NE Slope of the Palatine Hill," *Journal of Roman Archaeology,* Supp. 11 (1994): 131-82; with C.W. Beck & D.R. Stewart, "A Bronze Situla from Tomb 128, Valle Trebba: Chemical Evidence for Resinated Wine at Spina," *Studi Etruschi* 59 (1995); with T.N. Howe, R. Brandt, A. St. Clair, M. Parca & T. Peña, "Complesso tardo romano sul versante NE del Palatino (1991)," *Bollettino di Archeologia* (forthcoming); ed., with T.N. Howe, *The Roman Villa at Castle Copse, Great Bedwyn* (W. Lafayette: Indiana Univ. Press, forthcoming). **Home Address:** 708 W. Indiana Ave., Urbana, IL 61801.

HOUCK, LESTER CLARENCE ■ FAAR Classics/Archaeology 39. b. Aug. 8, 1911, Port Huron, MI. d. Apr. 8, 1980. BA 33, Univ. of Michigan; MA 34, Univ. of Michigan; PhD 37, Univ. of Michigan. **Research/Artistic Interests:** Classical philology. **Career & Employment:** Univ. of Texas, Austin, Prof. 1941-47; US Government Service, Washington, DC 1947-51, 1955-64, Overseas 1952-55, 1964-70. **Fellowships, Honors & Awards:** Univ. of Michigan, Simon Mandelbaum Scholar, Buhl Classical Fellow.

HOUGH, WILLIAM J.H. ■ FAAR Architecture 17. b. July 19, 1888, Ambler, PA. d. June 23, 1969. m. Mae Shoemaker. c. Charles, William J.H. Jr. BArch 11, Univ. of Pennsylvania; MArch 13, Univ. of Pennsylvania. **Research/Artistic Interests:** Palace of the Caesars on the Palatine, Pantheon, Temple of Neptune, bridge design. **Career & Employment:** American Red Cross, WWI; Paul P. Cret, Architect c.1920-45; Harbeson, Hough, Livingston & Larson, Part. 1945-67. **Memberships &**

Offices: AIA, Philadelphia Art Alliance, PAFA, Ambler Borough Council, Ambler School Bd. **Fellowships, Honors & Awards:** AIA, Fellow. **Important Works:** Walt Whitman Bridge, Philadelphia; Benjamin Franklin Bridge, Philadelphia. **Bio-Bibliography:** *Who Was Who in America.*

HOUGHTON, ARTHUR A., JR ■ AAR Trustee 1954-60; Book Collector; Steuben Glass, Pres.

HOUSTON, GEORGE W. ■ FAAR Classics/Archaeology 69; School of Classical Studies Summer Session, Dir. 1977-79; Classical Soc., Sec.-Treas. 1974-77. b. Nov. 15, 1941, NYC. m. Jean Verlaney. c. Kerr, Michael. BA 63, Haverford College; PhD 71, UNC. **Research/Artistic Interests:** Latin epigraphy, Roman technology, Roman historiography. **Career & Employment:** UNC, Instr. 1969-71, Asst. Prof. 1971-77, Assc. Prof. 1977-93, Prof. 1993-present; Univ. of Bologna, Visiting Prof. 1982. **Memberships & Offices:** VSA, Classical Study Tours Dir. 1972, 1976, 1982, Pres. 1979-80; *Classical Journal,* Ed. Bd. 1983-91; Carolina Summer: Arts & Sciences for Academically Gifted HS Students, Dir. 1987-89. **Fellowships, Honors & Awards:** Fulbright Grant 1967-68; UNC, Kenan Leave 1978-79, Bowman & Gordon Gray Prof. 1986-88; APS Research Grant 1982; Inst. for the Arts & Humanities, Chapel Hill, Lurcy Research Leave 1989. **Publications:** "M. Plancius Varus and the Events of A.D. 69-70," *Transactions of the APS* 103 (1972): 167-80; Θρονος, Διφρος, and Odysseus' Change from Beggar to Avenger," *Classical Philology* 70 (1975): 212-14; "The Duration of the Censorship of Vespasian and Titus," *Emerita* 44 (1976): 397-402; "Vespasian's Adlection of Men *in Senatum*," *American Journal of Philology* 98 (1977): 35-63; "Nonius Flaccus: A New Equestrian Career from Firmum Picenum," *Classical Philology* 72 (1977): 232-38; "The Administration of Italian Seaports during the First Three Centuries of the Roman Empire," *Memoirs of the AAR* 36 (1980): 157-71; "Tiberius on Capri," *Greece and Rome* 32 (1985): 179-96; "Lucian's *Navigium* and the Dimensions of the Isis," *American Journal of Philology* 108 (1987): 444-50; "A Revisionary Note on Ammianus Marcellinus 14.6.18: When Did the Public Libraries of Ancient Rome Close?" *Library Quarterly* 58 (1988): 258-64; "Ports in Perspective: Some Comparative Materials on Roman Merchant Ships and Ports," *AJA* 92 (1988): 553-64; "The State of the Art: Current Work in the Technology of Ancient Rome," *Classical Journal* 85 (1989): 63-80; "The Altar from Rome with Inscriptions to Sol and Malakbel," *Syria* 67 (1990): 189-93. **Home Address:** 704 Tinkerbell Rd., Chapel Hill, NC 27514. **Business Address:** Dept. of Classics, CB 3145, UNC, Chapel Hill, NC 27599.

HOWE, GEORGE ■ RAAR Architecture 47-50; AAR Trustee 1950-55. b. June 17, 1886, Worcester, MA. d. Apr. 16, 1955. m. Maritje Patterson. c. Anne, Helen West. BArch 1907, Harvard Univ. **Other Studies:** École des Beaux Arts 1908-12. **Career & Employment:** Furness, Evans & Co. 1914-16; Mellor, Meigs & Howe, Part. 1916-1928; Private Practice 1928-29; Howe & Lescaze, Part. 1929-34; Private Practice 1935-40; Kahn & Stonorov, Part. 1942-43; Ferderal Works Agency, Public Bldgs. Administration, Supervising Architect 1942-44, Deputy Commissioner for Design & Construction 1944-45; Private Practice 1945-48; Part. with Robert Montgomery 1949-55; Yale Univ., Faculty 1950-54. **Fellowships, Honors & Awards:** AIA, Gold Medal 1922, 1939; AIA, Fellow. **Publications:** *The Work of Mellor, Meigs, and Howe* (New York, 1923); with William Lescaze, *A Modern Museum* (Springdale, CT, 1930); "Functional Aesthetics and the Social Ideal," *Pencil Points* (Apr. 1932); "New York World's Fair," *Architectural Forum* (July 1940); "A Lesson from the Jefferson Memorial Competition," *AIA Journal* (Mar. 1951);

"Old Cities and New Frontiers," *AIA Journal* (Jan. 1952). **Important Works:** Philadelphia Saving Fund Society Bldg. 1931; Emigrant Savings Bank & Office Bldg., NYC 1931; with Louis I. Kahn & Oscar Stonorov, Carver Court Housing, Coatesville, PA 1941; with Louis I. Kahn & Oscar Stonorov, Pennypack Housing, Philadelphia 1942; with Louis I. Kahn & Oscar Stonorov, Lincoln Rd. Housing, Coatesville, PA 1943; with Louis I. Kahn & Oscar Stonorov, Lily Ponds Housing, Washington, DC 1943; Evening & Sunday Bulletin Bldg., Philadelphia 1954-55. **Exhibitions/Performances:** Modern Architecture Intl. Exhibition, MOMA 1932; Collections: Avery Library, Columbia Univ.; Athenaeum Architectural Archives, Philadelphia. **Bio-Bibliography:** Helen West Howe, *George Howe, Architect, 1886-1955* (Philadelphia: W. Nunn Co., 1973); Robert A.M. Stern, *George Howe* (New Haven: Yale Univ. Press, 1975); Sandra L. Tatman, "A Study of the Work of Mellor, Meigs & Howe," (PhD Diss., Univ. of Oregon, 1977).

HOWELLS, CARL ■ Stewardson Memorial Scholar 1913.

HRABAK, MICHAEL SCOTT ■ FAAR Sculpture 74. b. June 6, 1946, Chicago, IL. dec. BFA 68, Univ. of Arizona; MFA 71, Indiana Univ. **Research/Artistic Interests:** The function of sculpture in structuring exterior space. **Career & Employment:** Indiana Univ., Instr. 1970-71; Murray State Univ., Asst. Prof. 1971-72. **Exhibitions/Performances:** Swihart Gallery, Tucson, 1968; Indiana Univ. 1969, 1970, 1971; Murray State Univ. 1972.

HUBBARD, HENRY V. ■ AAR Trustee 1934-44.

HUBBELL, E.L. ■ Plym Fellow 1923-24.

HUBBELL, HARRY MORTIMER ■ RAAR Classics/Archaeology 51. b. Aug. 30, 1881, Belvue, KS. d. Feb. 24, 1971. m. Alice P. Clark, Mary Williard Bird. c. Henry. BA 02, Yale Univ.; MA 05, Yale Univ.; PhD 13, Yale Univ. **Career & Employment:** Waterville HS, Asst. Principal 1902-3; Pingry School, Master 1904-7; Pennington School, Dean 1907-10; Yale Univ., Instr. 1911-14, Asst. Prof. 1914-24, Assc. Prof. 1924-27, Prof. 1927-34, Talcott Prof. 1934-50, Prof. Emer. 1950-71; UC, Berkley, Visiting Prof. 1950. **Memberships & Offices:** APA; CANE, Pres. 1932-33; *Yale Classical Studies,* Ed. 1948-61. **Publications:** *The Influence of Isocrates on Cicero* (New Haven: Yale Univ. Press, 1913); "Isocrates and the Epicurians," *Classical Philology* 11 (1916): 405-18; trans., *The Rhetorica of Philidemus* (New Haven: Connecticut Acad. of Arts & Sciences, 1920); "Chrysostom and Rhetoric," *Classical Philology* 19 (1924): 261-76; "Ptolemy's Zoo," *Classical Journal* 31 (1935-36): 68-76; trans., Cicero, *Brutus and Orator* (Cambridge, MA: Loeb Classical Library, 1939); trans., Cicero, *De Inventione, De optima genere oratorum, Topica* (Cambridge, MA: Loeb Classical Library, 1949); ed., J.M. Davison, *Attic Geometric Workshops* (New Haven: Yale Univ. Press, 1961); "A Christian Liturgy from Egypt, P.488 Yale, Sixth C.," *Yale Classical Studies* 19 (1966): 171-86. **Bio-Bibliography:** *NY Times,* Obit. (Feb. 26, 1971); C.M. Dawson, "Memoir," *Yale Classical Studies* 22 (1972): vii-viii; Briggs, 295-96; *Contemporary Authors; Who Was Who in America.*

HUEMER, CHRISTINA ■ AAR Librarian, 1992-present.

HUGHES, DIANE OWEN ■ RAAR Post-Classical/Humanistic Studies 92. b. 1941. **Bio-Bibliography:** *Directory of American Scholars.*

HUGHES, ROBERT ■ AAR Visitor 1988-89, Writer, Critic.

HUMSTONE, ELIZABETH ■ FAAR Design Arts 86. b. Apr. 13, 1948, Glen Ridge, NJ. m. Reginald Gignoux. c. Christopher. BA 70, Wheaton College; MA 73, Harvard GSD. **Career & Employment:** Anthony Adams, AIA, Staff Planner 1973; Terrence J. Boyle, Landscape Architect, Staff Planner 1973-74; Agency of Development & Community Affairs, Land Use Specialist 1974-76; State Planner, State Planning Office 1976-78; Elizabeth Humstone, Planning Consultant 1978-.

HUNENKO, ALEXANDER I. ■ FAAR Sculpture 68. b. Mar. 5, 1937, Romanivka, Ukraine. m. Maria Pshenychna. c. Olena, Oksana. BFA 61, Minneapolis College of Art; MFA 63, Yale Univ. School of Art. **Other Study:** Skowhegan School of Painting & Sculpture, Summer 1959, 1960. **Research/Artistic Interests:** Develop international relations-perspective via the visual arts. **Career & Employment:** US Information Agency, Arts Specialist 1963-64; Univ. of Hartford, Instr. 1969-72; Skidmore College, Asst. Prof. 1972-75; Hunenko Arts Atelier 1975-present; Visual Arts Intl., Consulting Dir. 1975-present; also many artist-in-residences, visiting professorships, etc. **Fellowships, Honors & Awards:** Yale Univ., Woodrow Wilson Fellowship 1961-63, Alice Kimball English Traveling Fellowship 1963-64, Fulbright Grant 1966-67, Davenport Fellowship 1986-present. **Important Works:** *Winter 1963*, Yale Univ. Art Gallery; *Choatanes*, Choate Rosemary Hall-Paul Mellon Arts Center, Wallingford, CT; *Bohunha*, Univ. of New Haven; *Ikkaanune*, Southern Connecticut State Univ. Gallery, New Haven; *Hadunca*, Univ. of Northern Colorado, Greeley; *Orange & Bethany*, Amity Regional Schools, CT; *Bornba*, Ukrainian Inst. of Modern Art, Chicago; *Kinetz*, Walker Art Center, Minneapolis; Minneapolis Inst. of Arts; & numerous private collections. **Exhibitions/Performances:** Solo: Carlton College Art Gallery, Northfield, MN 1966; Skidmore College Art Gallery 1973; Southern Connecticut State Univ. Art Gallery, New Haven 1972; Ukranian Inst. of Modern Art, Chicago 1974, 1984; Paul Mellon Arts Center-Gallery, Wallingford, CT 1980, 1993; Yale Univ., Davenport Studio 56 Gallery 1988. **Bio-Bibliography:** Numerous newspaper & journal articles. **Home Address:** 9 Cleveland Rd., New Haven, CT 06515-2708. **Business Address:** Visual Arts Intl., 9 Cleveland Rd., New Haven, CT 06515.

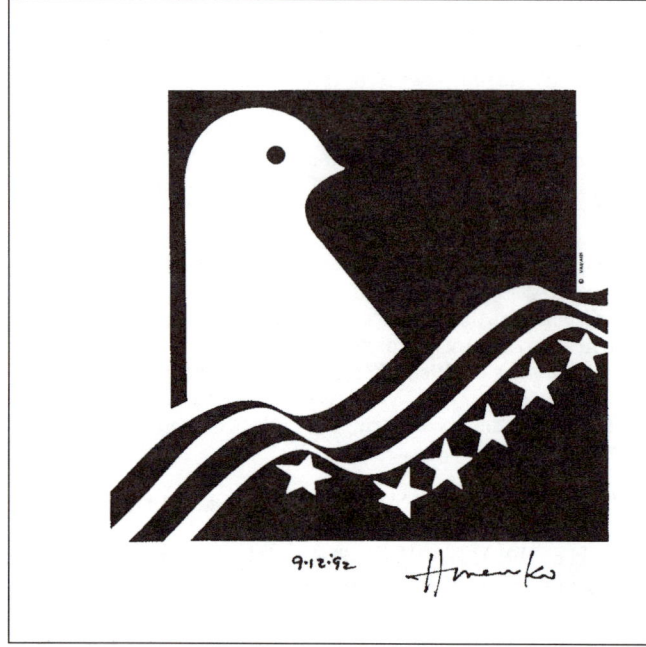

Alexander I. Hunenko

HUNT, RICHARD ■ AAR Trustee 1978-79, Trustee Emer.; Sculptor.

HUNT, RICHARD MORRIS ■ Organizer & temporary AAR Chair appointed by Charles F. McKim; Architect. d. 1895.

HUNT, SUSAN G. ■ FAAR History of Art 84. BA 77, Wellesley College; MPhil 79, Warburg Inst., Univ. of London; PhD 82, IFA. **Career & Employment:** Simon & Schuster, Asst. Ed. 1984-85, Assc. Ed. 1985-86, Project Mgr.-Ed. 1986-88, Ed. 1988-90, Sen. Acquisitions Ed. 1990-93. **Memberships & Offices:** Friends for the Preservation of Czech Culture, Inc., Dir. of Projects 1992-94. **Fellowships, Honors & Awards:** Wellesley College, Summa cum Laude, Phi Beta Kappa, Stecher Scholarship 1974, Trustee Scholar 1977, Shaw Mem. Scholarship 1977-79; IFA, Francis Waterbury Fellowship 1981-82. **Home Address:** 150 W. 55 St., Apt. 3E, NYC 10019.

HUNTER, JAMES M. ■ RAAR Architecture 63. b. April 19, 1908, Omaha, NE. d. Sept. 11, 1983. m. Madelyn J. Engleman. c. John David, Janet Diane Hunter Powers. BArch 36, Univ. of Illinois. **Other Studies:** Architectural Engineering, Iowa State Univ. 1927-31. **Research/Artistic Interests:** Solar design. **Career & Employment:** James M. Hunter & Asscs. 1945-78; American Window Glass Co., Consultant; George Lof Residence, Denver, Designer 1950s; G.H. Huntington, AIA, Designer 1936; Univ. of Colorado, Head Draftsman 1940; Planner-Architect: Colorado State Univ.; Ft. Lewis College; Tarkio College, MO; Regis College, Denver; US Navy, Lieut., WWII. **Memberships & Offices:** Assn. for Applied Solar Energy, Adv. Bd.; Assn. for Applied Solar Energy, Professional Adv.; AIA, 2d VP 1960-61, Rocky Mountain Region, Dir.; Colorado Soc. of Architects, Pres.; Colorado Bd. of Examiners of Architects, Pres. **Fellowships, Honors & Awards:** AIA, Merit Award 1955, Regional Awards 1954-58, 1960, 1962, 1965, 1967; ALNY Award 1954, 1955. **Bio-Bibliography:** *Who Was Who in America*.

HUSSEL, ELIZABETH ■ AAR World War II Scholar 1944.

HUTCHINSON, CHARLES L. ■ AAR Charter Mem., Bank Exec.

HUZAR, ELEANOR G. ■ AAR Visitor. b. June 15, 1922, St. Paul, MN. m. Bruce I. Granger. BA 43, Univ. of Minnesota; MA 45, Cornell Univ.; PhD 48, Cornell Univ. **Career & Employment:** Stanford Univ., Instr. 1948-50; Univ. of Illinois, Asst. Prof. 1951-55; Southeast Missouri Univ., Assc. Prof. 1955-59; Carleton College, Assc. Prof. 1959-60; Michigan State Univ., Prof. 1960-90, Emer. 1990-present. **Home Address:** 1375 Burcham Dr., East Lansing, MI 48823.

HYLA, LEE J. ■ FAAR Musical Composition 91. b. Aug. 31, 1952, Niagara Falls, NY. BMus 75, New England Conservatory of Music; MA 78 SUNY, Stony Brook. **Career & Employment:** New England Conservatory, Prof 1992-present. **Fellowships, Honors & Awards:** Tanglewood Fellowship 1974; NEH Youth Grant 1978; MacDowell Colony Residency (8) 1979-91; New Jersey State Council for the Arts Grant 1980; Guggenheim Fellowship 1985; Wellesley Composers Conference Fellowship 1986; AAAL, Goddard Lieberson Fellowship 1987; NEA Fellowship 1986, 1989; NYFA Fellowship 1985, 1991; Chamber Music Soc. of Lincoln Center, Elise Stoeger Prize 1992. **Important Works:** *Amnesia*, for six instruments 1979; *Pre-Amnesia*, for alto saxophone (Opus One Records) 1979; *String Trio* (CRI) 1981; *In Double Light*, for viola, bass clarinet, piano & percussion 1983; *Pre-Pulse Suspended*, for twelve instruments

1984; *String Quartet #2* 1985; *Mythic Birds of Saugerties,* for bass clarinet 1985; *The Dream of Innocent III* (CRI) 1987; *Concerto for Violin & Chamber Orchestra* 1987; *Anhinga,* for amateur chamber ensemble 1987; *Concerto for Bass Clarinet & Chamber Orchestra* 1988; *String Quartet #3* 1989; *Amnesia Variance,* for clarinet, violin, viola, cello, piano & hammered dulcimer 1989; *Ciao, Manhattan,* for viola, flute, cello & piano 1990; *Amnesia Breaks,* for woodwind quintet 1990; *Concerto for Piano & Chamber Orchestra # 2* 1991; *We Speak Etruscan,* for bass clarinet & baritone sax 1992; *Howl,* for string quartet & narrator 1993; *Quartet,* for bassoon & string trio 1993. **Home Address:** 10 Thacher St., Boston, MA 02113.

HYLAND, JOHN W., JR ■ AAR Trustee 1978-present, BoT, Chair 1981-94; Chair Emer. **Studies:** Williams College, Harvard Graduate School of Business. **Career & Employment:** Morgan Stanley & Co., Part. & Managing Dir.; Warburg Paribas Becker, Inc., Vice Chair; Paine Webber-Young & Rubicam Ventures, Vice Chair; Rho Management Co., Managing Dir.; McFarland Dewey & Co., Managing Dir. **Memberships & Offices:** Columbia Univ., BoT; Teachers College, BoT; CAA, BoT; Sterling & Francine Clark Inst., BoT; Nat. Bldg. Museum, Washington, DC, BoT; Century Assn.

■　■　■

I

IANZITI, GARY J. ■ FAAR Post-Classical/Humanistic Studies 87. b. Feb. 25, 1947, Napa, CA. m. Jeanne C. Rolin. BA 69, Univ. of San Francisco; MA 73, UNC; PhD 77, UNC; Dott. 87, Scuola Normale Superiore, Pisa. **Research/Artistic Interests:** Italian Renaissance studies (1350-1550), including culture, politics & society. **Career & Employment:** Univ. of Wollongong, Lect. 1979-83, Senior Lect. 1984-present; Università di Trieste, Prof. e Contratto 1988-91; Queensland Univ. of Technology, Assc. Prof. **Fellowships, Honors & Awards:** Fulbright Fellowship 1976-77; NEH Fellow, Villa I Tatti, Harvard Univ. 1981-82; Andrew Mellon Fellowship 1986-87. **Publications:** "From Flavio Biondo to Lodrisio Crivelli," *Rinascimento* 20 (1980): 3-39; "A Humanist Historian and His Documents," *Renaissance Quarterly* 34 (1981): 491-516; "The First Edition of Giovanni Simonetta's *De rebus gestis,*" *Bibliothèque d'humanisme et Renaissance* 44 (1982): 137-47; "Storiografia come propaganda," *Società e storia* 22 (1983): 909-18; "Patronage and the Production of History," in *Patronage, Art and Society* (Oxford: Oxford Univ. Press, 1987), 299-311; *Humanistic Historiography under the Sforzas* (Oxford: Oxford Univ. Press, 1988); "The Rise of Sforza Historiography," in *Florence and Milan* (Florence: La Nuova Italia, 1989), 79-94; "Storiografia e contemporaneità," *Rinascimento* 30 (1990): 3-28; "Humanism's New Science," *I Tatti Studies* 4 (1991): 59-88. **Bio-Bibliography:** *Who's Who in the World.* **Business Address:** Queensland Univ. of Technology, Beamns Rd., Carseldine, Brisbane QLD, Australia.

ILIESCU, SANDA D. ■ FAAR Architecture 95. b. Apr. 18, 1959, Bucharest, Romania. BSE 82, Princeton Univ.; MA 86, Princeton Univ. **Other Study:** Columbia Univ 1982-83. **Research/Artistic Interests:** Painting, mixed media, acrylics, water media. **Career & Employment:** Geddes, Brecher, Qualls, Cunningham, Designer 1986-88; Hillier Group, Architect 1990-91; Princeton Univ., Lect. 1989-90; UNC, Charlotte, Asst. Prof.

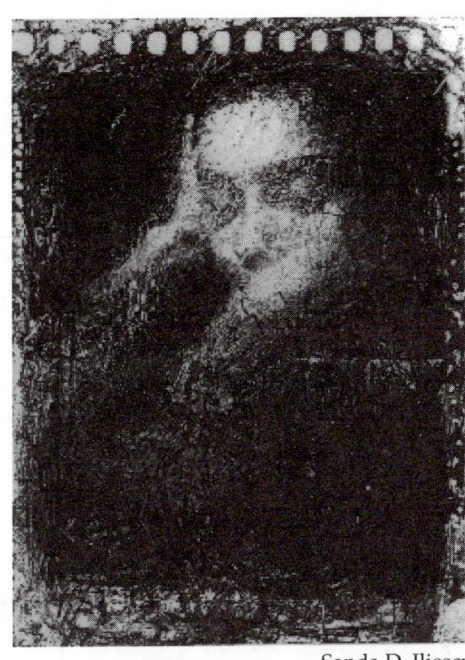
Sanda D. Iliescu

1992-present. **Memberships & Offices:** *Now This,* Poetry & Arts Journal, Ed. & Designer 1992. **Fellowships, Honors & Awards:** Princeton Univ., Carmichael Prize 1982; Royal Soc. of Arts, Silver Medal 1982; AIA Medal 1986; New Jersey State Council of the Arts Grant 1991; UNC, Charlotte, Grant 1994. **Important Works:** Public Collections: Johnson & Johnson Corporate Art Collection, New Brunswick, NJ; Jansen Pharmaceutica, Titusville, NJ. **Exhibitions/Performances:** Solo: W.P.A. Gallery, Princeton 1993; UNC, Charlotte 1994; Group: Norbert Considine Gallery, Princeton 1989; Artworks, Trenton 1991; Mercer County Community College, NJ 1991; Gallery at Bristol-Myers Squibb, Princeton 1991; Prallsville Mills Gallery, Stockton, NJ 1992; W.P.A. Gallery, Princeton 1992, 1994. **Business Address:** College of Architecture, UNC, Charlotte, NC 28223.

IMBRIE, ANDREW W. ■ FAAR Musical Composition 49, RAAR Musical Composition 68. b. Apr. 6, 1921, NYC. m. Barbara Cushing. c. Andrew Philip, John Haller (dec.). BA 42, Princeton Univ.; MA 47, UC, Berkeley. **Other Study:** With Nadia Boulanger 1937; Roger Sessions 1937-47; piano with Robert Casadesus 1941; piano & composition with Leo Ornstein until 1942. **Research/Artistic Interests:** Musical composition, orchestral, chamber, choral, vocal, solo, opera. **Career & Employment:** UC, Berkeley, Prof. 1949-91, Hemmings Chambers Chair 1989-91, Faculty Research Lect. 1990-91; Brandeis Univ., Jacob Ziskind Visiting Prof. 1982; Sandpoint Summer Festival, Composer-in-Residence 1989-92; Tanglewood, Composer-in-Residence 1991; Univ. of Alabama, Endowed Chair 1992; San Francisco Conservatory of Music, Faculty 1967-present; Univ. of Chicago & Northwestern Univ., Visiting Prof. 1994; NYU, Visiting Prof. 1995. **Memberships & Offices:** AAAL 1969-present; AAAS 1980-present; Koussevitzky Found., BoD; San Francisco Symphony, Bd. of Governors 1982-91. **Fellowships, Honors & Awards:** NY Music Critics' Award 1944; Columbia Univ., Alice M. Ditson Award 1947; NIAL Grant 1950; Boston Symphony, Merit Award 1955; Guggenheim Fellowship 1953-54, 1959-60; Brandeis Univ., Creative Arts Award 1957; Hinrichsen Award 1971; UC, Berkeley, Berkeley Citation 1991. **Important Works:** *Violin Concerto,* Koussevitzky Found. Comm.

1954; *Symphony No. 1*, San Francisco Symphony Comm. 1965; *Symphony No. 3*, 1970; *Angle of Repose*, an opera, San Francisco Opera Comm. 1976; *Short Story*, for piano solo, Claudia Stevens Comm. (C.F. Peters) 1982; *Pilgrimage*, for flute, cello, violin, vc., pf., percussion, Collage Ensemble of Boston Comm. (C.F. Peters) 1983; *Requiem, In Memoriam John Imbrie*, for soprano, mixed chorus, orchestra, San Francisco Symphony Comm. 1984; *Dream Sequence*, for flute, oboe, cello, violin viola, vc., pf., percussion, Frank Taplin Comm. (C.F. Peters) 1986; *String Quartet No. 5*, Pro Arte Quartet Comm. (GM) 1987; *Trio No. 2*, for violin, vc., pf., *Readers Digest*-Meet the Composer-Chamber Music America Comm. 1989; *Piano Concerto No. 3*, for orchestra, percussion (2), solo piano, strings, Riverside Orchestra of New York Comm. 1993; *Adam*, cantata for soprano, mixed chorus & orchestra, Cantata Singers of Boston Comm. 1994. **Bio-Bibliography:** *New Grove Dictionary of American Music, New Grove Dictionary of Music & Musicians, Who's Who in America*. **Home Address:** 2625 Rose St., Berkeley, CA 94708.

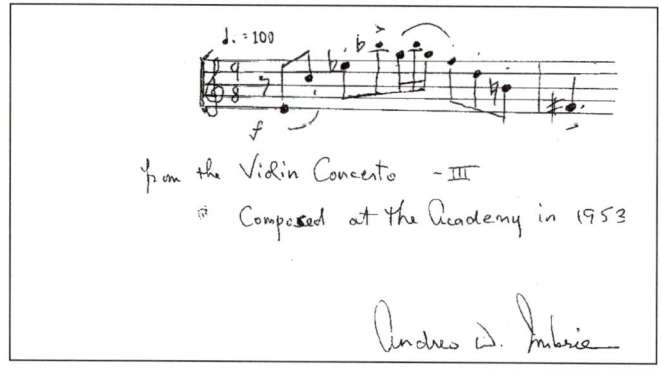

Andrew W. Imbrie

IMPERATORI, PAOLO ■ AAR – Rome, Library Asst.

IMPERATORI, ULDERICO ■ AAR – Rome, Dir. of Administration.

IMPERIALE, ALICIA A. ■ NIAE, John Dinkeloo Traveling Fellow 1987-88. b. Jan. 29, 1962, Brooklyn, NY. m. Quintilio Polilli. BArch 86, Pratt Inst. **Other Study:** Hunter College. **Research/Artistic Interests:** The relationship between music & architecture in Renaissance Italy; contemporary architectural design; architectural competitions; architectural design education. **Career & Employment:** Joseph Giovannini & Asscs., Architects 1989; James Stewart Polshek & Partners, Staff Architect 1989-90; Alicia A. Imperiale, Architect, Prin. 1991-present; City College, CUNY, Adj. Asst. Prof 1992-93; Pratt Inst., Visiting Asst. Prof. 1993-present; Columbia Univ. & Barnard College, Adj. Asst. Prof. 1994-present. **Home Address:** 109 6th Ave., Brooklyn, NY 11217.

INCE, KAMRAN ■ FAAR Musical Composition 88. b. May 6, 1960, Glendire, Montana. m. Övül Inana. Oberlin College; DMA 87, Eastman School of Music. **Other Study:** With Joseph Schwantner, Christopher Rouse & David Burge. **Career & Employment:** Univ. of Michigan, Visiting Asst. Prof. 1990-92; California Symphony, San Francisco, Composer-in-Residence 1991-93; Univ. of Memphis, Asst.-Assc. Prof. 1992-present. **Fellowships, Honors & Awards:** Guggenheim Fellowship 1987-88; Lili Boulanger Prize 1988; Brooklyn Phiharmonic Rose Prize 1988; Commissions from Minnesota Orchestra, Meet-the-Composer, ASCAP, *Readers Digest*-Pew Charitable Trust, Ford

Found., Koussevitzky Found., Fromm Found., Jerome Found. **Important Works:** *Before Infrared* 1986; *Waves of Talya*, Koussevitzky Comm. 1987; *Ebullient Shadows*, Minnesota Orchestra Comm. 1987; *Hammer Music*, Fromm Found. Comm. 1990; *Fantasie of a Sudden Turtle*, Michigan Arts Council Comm. 1990; *Night Panage*, Readers Digest Comm. 1992; *Plexus*, a ballet, Houston Ballet. Comm. 1992; *Domes*, California Symphony Comm. 1993; *Symphony No. 2: Fall of Constantinople*, Albany Symphony Comm. 1994; *Tracing*, Paul Gmeinder Comm. 1994; *Arches*, Present Music Comm. 1994; *Symphony No. 3*, Albany Symphony Orchestra Comm. 1995; Recordings: chamber music CD, recorded by Present Music, on Northeastern; Publisher: European American Music. **Home Address:** 4934 Bradfield Run, Memphis, TN 38125. **Business Address:** Music Dept., Univ. of Memphis., Memphis, TN 38152.

INCH, HERBERT REYNOLDS ■ FAAR Musical Composition 34. b. Nov. 25, 1904, Missoula, MT. d. Apr. 14, 1988. m. Miriam Hirschenbaum. c. Margaret Arnold. BMus 25, Univ. of Rochester; MusM 28, Univ. of Rochester; BA 31, Eastman School of Music, Univ. of Rochester; MusD 43, Univ. of Rochester. **Other Studies:** State Univ. of Montana with Josephine Swenson & A.H. Weisberg, 2 years; Eastman School of Music with Howard Hanson. **Career & Employment:** New York Public Library, Music Division, Reference Asst. 1935-38; Hunter College, Prof. 1937-65, Prof. Emer. 1965-88. **Fellowships, Honors & Awards:** Ernest Bloch Award 1945. **Important Works:** *Variations on a Modal Theme* 1927; *Three Pieces for Small Orchestra* 1930; *Piano Quintet* 1930; *Symphony* 1932; *Mediterranean Sketches*, for string quartet 1933; *3 Piano Sonatas* 1935, 1946, 1966; *Piano Concerto* 1940; *Answers to a Questionnaire*, for orchestra 1942; *Three Conversations* for string quartet 1944; *Return to Zion* 1945; *Northwest Overture* 1947; *3 Symphoniettas* 1948, 1950, 1955; *Piano Trio* 1963. **Bio-Bibliography:** D. Ewen, *American Composers Today* (New York, 1949); *Baker's Biographical Dictionary of Musicians; New Grove Dictionary of American Music*.

ISELIN, LEWIS ■ AAR Trustee 1966-73.

ISRAEL, FRANKLIN D. ■ FAAR Architecture 75; AAR Trustee 1990-95. b. Dec. 2, 1945, NYC. BA 67, Univ. of Pennsylvania; MArch 71, Columbia Univ. **Other Study:** Yale Univ., Graduate School of Art & Architecture 1967-68. **Career & Employment:** Bower & Fradley, Model Builder 1967; Gruzen & Partners, Model Builder-Draftsman 1968-69; Mitchell, Giurgola, Model Builder 1969; Urban Design Group, Asst. Designer 1968-70; Giovanni Pasanella Asscs., Project Architect & Designer 1971-73; Franklin D. Israel 1973-75; Notre Dame Univ., Rome, Adj. Asst. Prof. 1974-75; Saratoga Asscs., Assc. Architect 1974-75; Llewelyn-Davies, Weeks, Forestier-Walker & Bor, Sen. Architect 1975-77; Frank Israel & Renz Kuper Design Collaborative 1977-79; UCLA, Assc. Prof. 1977-present; Franklin D. Israel Design 1979-82; Israel-Johnson 1982-84; Franklin D. Israel Design Asscs. 1984-present; Visiting Design Critic: Univ. of Idaho 1980, Harvard Univ. 1989. **Memberships & Offices:** ALNY, BoT 1972-75; *Controspazio*, Contr. Ed. 1975, American Correspondent 1974-76; Los Angeles Forum for Architecture & Urban Design, Founder 1987. **Fellowships, Honors & Awards:** Columbia Univ., William Kinney Fellow 1970, Lucilee Snyster Memorial Award 1971; AIA Gold Medal 1971; AAAL Architecture Award 1993. **Important Works:** Propaganda Films, Hollywood 1988; Bright & Asscs., Venice, CA 1990; Hague House, Netherlands 1991; Baldwin Apts., Venice, CA 1991; Limelight Productions, Hollywood 1991; Virgin Records, Beverly Hills, CA 1991; Weisman Pavilion, Los Angeles 1991;

Offices for Tisch-Avnet Financial, Culver City, CA 1991; Bunka Shutter, Tokyo 1992; plus numerous residences. **Exhibitions/ Performances:** La Jolla Museum of Art 1982; UCLA, Pentagon House 1983, Perloff Hall 1987; Architectural Assn., London 1983; Getty Center, Santa Monica 1990-91, 1991; 65 Thompson St. Gallery, NYC 1992; Denver Art Museum 1992; Pacific Design Center, Los Angeles 1992; Chicago Athenaeum 1992; Santa Monica Museum of Art 1993; LIMN Gallery, San Francisco 1993. **Bio-Bibliography:** *Franklin D. Israel: Buildings & Projects* (New York: Rizzoli, 1992); "Hague House, Baldwin Studio, Drager House," *GA Project* 37 (May 1993); "Franklin D. Israel," *GA Houses* 36 (1994); *Franklin D. Israel,* Architectural Monographs 34 (London: Academy Editions, 1994); "The Triumph of L.A.'s Avante Garde Architecture," *L.A. Times Magazine* (May 1994); Herbert Muschamp, "An Art Center Grown from Fragments," *NY Times* (Aug. 28, 1994); "Israel on Israel," *Elle Decor* (Sept. 1994). **Business Address:** 254 S. Robertson Blvd., Beverly Hills, CA 90211.

IVERSEN, ERLING F. ■ FAAR Architecture 40. b. Aug. 25, 1910, Brooklyn, NY. d. Nov. 5, 1990. m. Violet S. Hamilton. c. Ann Parke, Margaret Iversen Lubbock, Susan McHale. BArch 36, NYU. **Other Study:** Pratt Inst. School of Architecture 1931-34; Princeton Univ. Graduate College 1936-37; study of camouflage in Italy, Germany, Scandinavia 1937-39. **Research/Artistic Interests:** Designed, imported & sold marble products from Italy and Belgium, such as luxury cigarette boxes, trays, lamps, etc. **Career & Employment:** Self-employed as designer & manufacturer of camouflage for aircraft factories on Long Island, NY 1940-42; York & Sawyer, Architects, Designer-Draftsman 1945-50; B.C. Bauman, AIA, Chief Designer & Project Manager 1952-55; F.P. Weidermsum, Asscs. Valley Stream, NY 1955-70; Frederick R. Harris, Inc., Boston, Designer & Resident Chief Inspector 1970-72; Collaborated with Robert Adams McKelvey, AIA 1973-84; Self-employed, Designer of residences, adviser & designer for Greenwich Architectural Conservancy 1984-90. **Fellowships, Honors & Awards:** Soc. of Beaux Arts, Paris Prize Competition, 1st Prize Medal 1935, 1936, 1937.

IZENOUR, GEORGE ■ AAR Visitor 1976-77, Yale Univ., Theater Theoretician & Educator.

■ ■ ■

J

JACKSON, J.B. ■ RAAR Landscape Architecture 83.

JACOB, DAVID J. ■ FAAR Architecture 58, RAAR Architecture 70. b. July 8, 1928, Detroit, MI. m. Marian R. Jacob. c. Mia, Dana, Erin, Sera, Moria. BArch 51, Syracuse Univ.; MArch 53, Cranbrook Acad. of Art. **Career & Employment:** Eero Saarinen, Architects, Assc. 1956, 1958-61; Kevin Roche, John Dinkeloo, Architects, Assc. 1965-82. **Fellowships, Honors & Awards:** Graham Found. Fellowship 1962, 1974; Found. for Environmental Design Fellowship 1969; Guggenheim Fellowship 1970. **Important Works:** "A Dwelling for a Family of Five," Model, Collection of the MOMA. **Home Address:** 31 School St., Stony Creek, CT 06405.

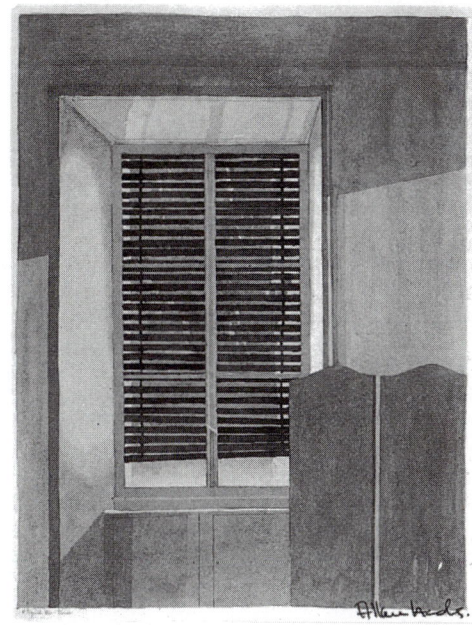

Allan B. Jacobs

JACOBS, ALLAN B. ■ FAAR Architecture 86. b. Dec. 29, 1928, Cleveland, OH. c. Amy, Matthew, Janet. BArch 52, Miami Univ., Oxford; MCP 54, Univ. of Pennsylvania. **Other Study:** University College, London 1954-55. **Research/Artistic Interests:** Urban design; painting: watercolor & oils. **Career & Employment:** PGH Regional Planning Assn., Asst. Dir. 1955-63; Ford Found., Senior Planner, Calcutta 1963-65; Univ. of Pennsylvania, Assc. Prof. 1963-67; San Francisco City Planning Dept., Dir. 1967-75; UC, Berkeley, Prof. 1975-present, Chair., Dept. of City Planning twice. **Fellowships, Honors & Awards:** Guggenheim Found. Fellowship 1981-82 & many more. **Publications:** *Making City Planning Work* (Chicago: American Planning Assn., 1978); *Looking at Cities* (Cambridge: Harvard Univ. Press, 1985); & too many articles to list. **Important Works:** San Francisco Urban Design Plan 1972. **Exhibitions/Performances:** De Young Museum 1974-75; watercolor shows 1987, 1992, etc. **Home Address:** 200 Beacon St., San Francisco, CA 94131. **Business Address:** UC, Berkeley, CA 74720.

JACOBS, HARRY ALLEN ■ McKim Scholar 1911-12, 1913.

JAFFE, STEPHEN ■ FAAR Musical Composition 81; Music Jury 1986-87. b. Dec. 30, 1954, Washington, DC. m. Mindy Oshrain, MD. c. Anna Aliza Jaffe, Elana Felice Jaffe. BA 77, Univ. of Pennsylvania; MA 78, Univ. of Pennsylvania. **Other Study:** Piano with Marc Durand, Paul Larson, Dwight Peltzer for eleven years; with A.F. Marescotti in composition, at Conservatoire de Musique, Geneva 1972; with Frederic Tillis, Univ. of Massachusetts 1973; Tanglewood, composition 1979. **Career & Employment:** Composers Conference 1977, 1978; Moravian College, Assc. 1978; Swarthmore College, Instr. 1979-80, Lect. 1986; Duke Univ., Asst. Prof. 1982-88, Assc. Prof. 1988-present. **Memberships & Offices:** BMI; MacDowell Colony Fellow; American Music Center. **Fellowships, Honors & Awards:** Conservatoire de Genève, Premier Medaille d'Harmonie 1972; BMI Awards to Student Composers 1975; Joseph H. Bearns Prize, 1st Prize 1976; Composers Forum, NYC 1978; Tanglewood, Crofts Fellowship 1979; NEA Fellowship 1981; Guggenheim Fellowship 1984-85; Brandeis Univ. Creative Arts Citation 1989; North Carolina Arts Council, Artist Fellowship 1991; Kennedy Center, Friedheim Award 1991; AAAL Prize 1993. **Publications:** "Conversation between SJ and JS on the New Tonality," *Contemporary Music Review* 6.2 (1992): 27-38. **Important Works:** *Four Images,* for orchestra 1983; *A Nonesuch Serenade,* Nonesuch Comm. Award 1984; *The Rhythm of the Running Plough,* for chamber orchestra (Bridge Records) 1985/88; *The Rhythm of the Running Plough,* for alto flute, doubles on piccolo, flute, violin, cello, percussion, New York New Music Ensemble Comm. 1985; *Autumnal,* for Orchestra, New Hampshire Symphony Comm. 1986; *Four Songs with Ensemble,* Appalachian Summer & North Carolina Arts Council, for the Broyhill Ensemble Comm. (Bridge Records) 1988; *Three Figures and a Ground,* for flute & piano, NEA Consortium Comm. (Neuma) 1988; *Double Sonata,* for 2 pianos, Naumburg Found. Comm. (Bridge Records) 1989; *Fort Juniper Songs,* for soprano, mezzo-soprano & piano, Terry Rhodes & Ellen Williams Comm. (Albany Records) 1989; *Pedal Point,* for baritone, 3 violas, 4 cellos, harp, timpani 1989/93; *First Quartet,* for string quartet, Ciompi Quartet Comm. (Albany Records) 1991; *Triptych,* for piano & woodwind quintet, Hexagon & Raleigh Chamber Music Soc. Comm. 1993; *Chamber Concerto (Singing Figures),* for oboe, keyboard (2), violin, viola & cello, Orchestra of St. Luke's Comm. 1995. All published by Theodore Presser Co. **Bio-Bibliography:** Daniel Webster, "New Jersey Symphony Premiers a Work by Stephen Jaffe," *Philadelphia Inquirer* (Mar. 28, 1988); Dean Olsher, "Fighting the Muzak of the Mind," *North Carolina Independent* (June 15, 1988): 9; Old Romantics-New Romantics," North Carolina Public Television (Dec. 1988); Will Crutchfied, "Two Commissioned Works and a Bit of Tapping," *New York Times* (June 28, 1989); David Perkins, "Red Hot and a Little Romantic," *Raleigh News & Observer* (Jan. 9, 1992): H1-7; Katie Moser, "Modern Music Man," *Duke Alumni Magazine* (July-Aug. 1992): 49-51; Tim Page, "Exciting New Modern Sounds at Tanglewood," *Newsday* (July 29, 1992): 55-58; Ellen Williams, "Contemporary Music, Tailor Made: Fort Juniper Songs of Stephen Jaffe," *Nat. Assn. of Teachers of Singing Journal* 50.3 (1994): 13-16. **Business Address:** Dept. of Music, Duke Univ., Durham, NC 27708; also Theodore Presser Co., Presser Pl., Bryn Mawr, PA 19010.

JAMES, ELLERY S. ■ AAR Trustee 1929-32.

JAMES, FRANK DEXTER ■ FAAR Landscape Architecture 68. b. Sept. 27, 1931, Seattle, WA. BArch 61, Univ. of Washington; MLArch 65, Harvard GSD. **Career & Employment:** John Graham Co., Architects-Engineers, Design Draughtsman 1960-61; Richard Haag Asscs., Inc. Landscape Architects, Assc. 1961-65; Sasaki Associates, Inc., Senior Assc.-Lead Project Designer 1965-66, 1972-83; Sakuma James Peterson, Landscape Architects-Urban Planners, Founder & Prin. 1968-72; Private Practice, Designer.

JAMES, HENRY ■ AAR Trustee 1924-29 & 1944-48.

JAMESON, MICHAEL HAMILTON ■ FAAR Classics/Archaeology 59, RAAR Classics/Archaeology 89. b. Oct. 15, 1924, London, England. m. Virginia Broyles. c. Nicholas Andrew, Anthony David, John Timothy, David Richmond. BA 42, Univ. of Chicago; PhD 49, Univ. of Chicago. **Other Study:** ASCSA 1949-50; Inst. of Social Anthropology, Oxford Univ. 1953-54; archaeological surveys & excavations in Greece. **Research/Artistic Interests:** Greek history, epigraphy, religion. **Career & Employment:** Univ. of Missouri, Asst. Prof. 1950-53; Univ. of Pennsylvania, Asst. Prof. 1954-58, Assc. Prof. 1958-62, Prof. 1962-76, Univ. Museum, Research Assc. 1959-94, Graduate School Dean 1966-68; Stanford Univ., Prof. 1976-90, Prof. Emer. 1990-present; Visiting Positions: Bryn Mawr College 1957-58, Haverford College 1963, Florida State Univ. 1994. **Memberships & Offices:** APA, Pres. 1980-81; APS; AAAS, Fellow. **Fellowships, Honors & Awards:** Fulbright Fellowship 1949-50, 1958-59; Guggenheim Fellowship 1958-59; NEH Fellowship 1971-72, 1985-86; ACLS Grant 1977-78. **Publications:** "A Decree of Themistokles from Troizen," *Hesperia* 29 (1960): 198-223; "The Excavations of a Drowned Greek Temple," *Scientific American* 231.4 (Oct. 1974): 110-19; "Agriculture and Slavery in Classical Athens," *Classical Journal* 73 (1977-78): 122-45; "Sacrifice before Battle," in *Hoplites: The Classical Greek Battle Experience,* ed. Victor Hanson (London & New York: Routledge, 1992), 197-227; "Agricultural Labor in Ancient Greece," in *Agriculture in Ancient Greece: Proceedings of the Seventh International Symposium at the Swedish Institute at Athens, May 1990,* ed. B. Wells (Stockholm: Swedish Inst., 1992), 135-46; with David Jordan & Roy Kotansky, *A Lex Sacra from Selinous,* Greek, Roman & Byzantine Studies Monograph 11 (Durham, NC, 1994); with Tj. van Andel & C.N. Runnels, *A Greek Countryside: The South-*

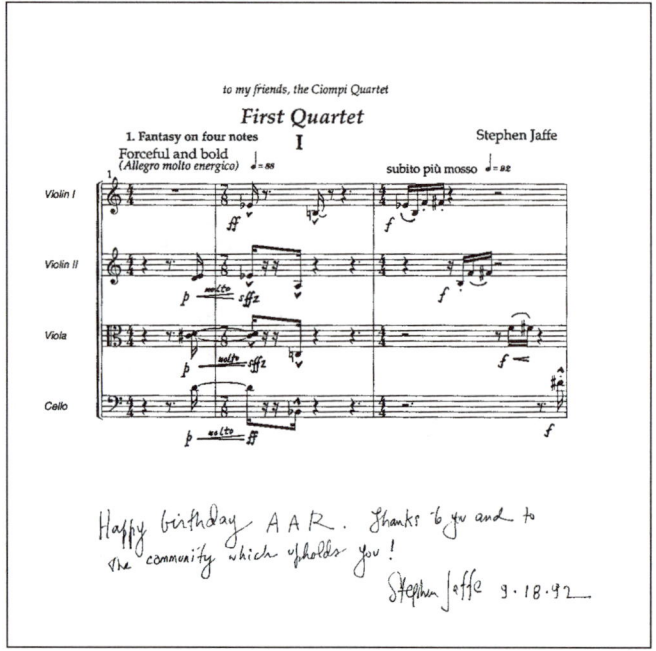

to my friends, the Ciompi Quartet

First Quartet

1. Fantasy on four notes   I   Stephen Jaffe
Forceful and bold
(Allegro molto energico)   ♩=88   subito più mosso ♩=92

Violin I

Violin II

Viola

Cello

Happy birthday A.A.R. Thanks to you and to the community which upholds you!
Stephen Jaffe 9·18·92

Stephen Jaffe

ern Argolid from Prehistory to the Present Day (Stanford: Stanford Univ. Press, 1994). **Bio-Bibliography:** *Directory of American Scholars.* **Home Address:** 647 Glenbrook Dr., Palo Alto, CA 94306.

JANEWAY, EDWARD G. ■ AAR Visitor 1959 — 1964, US Senator.

JANSON, HORST WOLDEMAR ■ RAAR History of Art 60. Oct. 4, 1913, St. Petersburg, Russia. d. Sept. 30, 1982. m. Dora Jane Heineberg. c. Anthony Frederick, Peter, Josephine, Charles. MA 38, Harvard Univ.; PhD 42, Harvard Univ. **Career & Employment:** Harvard Univ., Asst. Prof. 1936-37, Visiting Prof. 1967; Worcester Art Museum, Lect. 1936-38; State Univ. of Iowa, Instr. 1938-41; Washington Univ., St. Louis, Asst. Prof. & Curator 1941-48; NYU, Prof. 1949-79, Chair 1949-75; Prof. Emer. 1979-82; *Time-Life Library of Art*, Consulting Ed. **Memberships & Offices:** CAA, Ed.-in-Chief 1962-65, Pres. 1970-72; American Studies Assn. **Fellowships, Honors & Awards:** Guggenheim Fellow 1948-49, 1955-56. **Publications:** *Apes and Ape Lore in the Middle Ages and the Renaissance* (London: Warburg Inst., 1952); *The Story of Painting for Young People* (New York: Abrams, 1952); *The Sculpture of Donatello*, 2 vols. (Princeton: Princeton Univ. Press, 1957); with Dora Jane Janson, *The Picture History of Painting* (New York: Abrams, 1957); *History of Art* (New York: Abrams, 1962); *Form Follows Function – Or Does It?* (Maarssen, The Netherlands: G. Schwartz, 1982). **Bio-Bibliography:** "Bibliography," in *Art, The Ape of Nature: Studies in Honor of H.W. Janson*, ed. Mosche Barasch, et al. (New York: Abrams, 1981), 805-12; *NY Times,* Obit. (Oct. 3, 1982); *Burlington Magazine* 125 (1983): 226; *Contemporary Authors; Who Was Who in America; Who Was Who in American Art.*

JANSSEN, WERNER ■ FAAR Musical Composition 33. b. 1899. d. 1990. **Bio-Bibliography:** *NY Times,* Obit. (Sept. 21, 1990); *Baker's Biographical Dictionary of American Musicians; Contemporary American Composers.*

JAROS, SHEREE A. ■ FAAR Classics/Archaeology 90. b. Nov. 21, 1955, Detroit, MI. BA 79, Michigan State Univ.; MA 82, Univ. of Massachusetts. **Other Studies:** Columbia Univ. **Fellowships, Honors & Awards:** Columbia Univ., President's Fellowship 1984-85, Rudolf Wittkower Fellow 1988-89.

JARRARD, ALICE G. ■ FAAR History of Art 89. b. Jan 11, 1960, Lexington, VA. BA 82, Duke Univ. MA 85, Columbia Univ.; PhD 93, Columbia Univ. **Research/Artistic Interests:** Southern baroque art & architecture, focusing on ephemeral & theatrical works. **Career & Employment:** SITE Projects Research 1986-87; Columbia Univ., Preceptor 1986-87, 1989-90; Emory Univ., Instr. 1991-92; Univ. of Georgia, Asst. Prof. 1992-93; Smith College, Visiting Lect. 1994. **Memberships & Offices:** CAA 1989-present; SAH 1989-present. **Fellowships, Honors & Awards:** Columbia Univ., President's Fellow 1983-86, Milton Lewine Summer Travel Grant 1986, 1989; Kress Found. Fellow 1987-89; Whiting Found. Fellowship 1990-91. **Publications:** "Gordon Matta Clark and the Economy of Sight," in *Wealth of Nations,* exb. cat. (Warsaw: Center of Contemporary Art, 1993), 44-55. **Home Address:** 57 Huron Ave., No. 3, Cambridge, MA 02138.

JARRETT, JAMES R. ■ FAAR Architecture 59. b. Dec. 10, 1926, Springfield, IL. BA 50, Quincy College; BArch 55, Yale Univ. **Career & Employment:** John A. Benya, Architect, Draftsman-Designer 1948-54; Yale Univ., Design Critic 1955-; Paul

Schweikher, Architect 1956; Philip Johnson, Architect 1956; Univ. of Idaho, Prof.-Dept. Head 1967-. **Fellowships, Honors & Awards:** Yale Univ., William Wirt Winchester Fellowship 1955-56. **Important Works:** Park Avenue Synagogue, NYC.

JAVITCH, DANIEL ■ FAAR Post-Classical/Humanistic Studies 90. b. June 13, 1941, Cannes, France. BA 63, Princeton Univ.; BA 65, Pembroke College, Cambridge Univ.; MA 70, Pembroke College, Cambridge Univ.; PhD 71, Harvard Univ. **Research/Artistic Interests:** European Renaissance literature; history of literary theory to 1700; development of classical genres. **Career & Employment:** Harvard Univ., Tutor 1966-70; Columbia Univ., Asst. Prof. 1970-78; NYU, Assc. Prof. 1978-88, Prof. 1988-present. **Memberships & Offices:** New Directions Publishing, BoD 1972-present; RSA, Exec. Bd. 1992-present. **Fellowships, Honors & Awards:** Harvard Center for Renaissance Studies Fellowship, Villa I Tatti 1976-77; ACLS Research Fellowship 1977, 1990. **Publications:** *Poetry and Courtliness in Renaissance England* (Princeton: Princeton Univ. Press, 1978); *Proclaiming a Classic: The Canonization of Orlando Furioso* (Princeton: Princeton Univ. Press, 1991). **Bio-Bibliography:** *Directory of American Scholars; Who's Who in American Education.* **Business Address:** Dept. of Comparative Literature, NYU, 19 University Pl., 4th Floor, NYC 10003.

JAY, PIERRE ■ AAR Trustee 1938-44, Bank Exec.

JENNEWEIN, CARL PAUL ■ FAAR Sculpture 20. b. Dec. 2, 1890, Stuttgart, Germany. d. Feb. 26, 1978. m. Gina Pirra. c. Paolo Romano; Emilia Pirra van der Horst, Alexander Louis, James Joseph, Peter Gino. **Other Studies:** ASL. **Career & Employment:** American Red Cross, Italy, WWI; Independent Sculptor, NYC 1921-78. **Memberships & Offices:** NSS, Pres. 1960-63; ANS; AIA; NIAL; ALNY; Municipal Art Comm.; Fine Arts Comm.; Beaux Arts Inst.; Audubon Soc.. **Fellowships, Honors & Awards:** ALNY Prize 1912, Medal 1927; NAD, Saltus Medal for Merit 1942, Elizabeth Watrous Gold Medal 1960; PAFA, Gold Medal 1932; American Artists Professional League, Gold Medal 1968; NSS, 75th Annual Exb., Gold Medal 1968; NAD, Daniel Chester French Medal 1972. **Important Works:** Sculpture: Philadelphia Museum of Art; Washington Memorial, Valley Forge Tower; White House, Washington, DC; British Bldg., Rockefeller Center, NYC; New York World's Fair; MMA; Baltimore Museum of Art; Brooklyn Museum; Corcoran Gallery of Art, Washington, DC; Cincinnati Museum; Detroit Inst. of Art; Finance Bldg., Harrisburg, PA; Herron Art Inst.; US Dept. of Justice Bldg., Washington, DC; Museum of Fine Arts, Houston; Hartford Atheneum; Newark Museum; Pennsylvania Fine Arts Museum; Brookgreen Gardens, SC; Philadelphia Museum of Art; Eastman School of Music, Rochester. **Exhibitions/Performances:** Pearson Gallery of Sculpture; ALNY 1912, 1927; AIC 1921; Fairmont Park AA 1926; Concord AA, 1926; PAFA 1932; 1939; NAD 1942; Montclair Art Museum 1943; Tampa Museum 1980. **Bio-Bibliography:** *C. Paul Jennewein*, American Sculptors Series 11 (Athens, GA: Univ. of Georgia Press, 1950); *NY Times,* Obit. (Feb. 28, 1978); S.R. Howarth, *C. Paul Jennewein, Sculptor,* exb. cat. (Tampa, FL: Tampa Museum, 1980); *Who Was Who in America, Who Was Who in American Art.*

JENNY, C.O. ■ Cresson Fellow 1917, 1919-20.

JENSEN, BILL ■ RAAR Painting 89. b. Nov. 26, 1945, Turtle Lake, MN. m. Margrit Lewczuk. c. Russell. BFA 68, Univ. of Minnesota; MFA 70, Univ. of Minnesota. **Fellowships, Hon-**

ors & Awards: Creative Artists Public Service Program Grant 1979; NEA Fellowship 1985-86. **Exhibitions/Performances:** Solo: Fischbach Gallery, NYC 1973, 1975; Washburn Gallery, NYC 1980, 1981, 1982, 1984, 1986, 1987, 1988, 1989, 1991, 1992; MOMA 1986; Phillips Collection, Washington, DC 1987; Lannan Museum, Lake Worth, FL 1988; Margo Leavin Gallery, Los Angeles 1991; Grob Gallery, London 1991; Group: Davis-McClain Gallery, Houston 1988; Ledisflam Gallery, NYC 1990; John Berggruen Gallery, San Francisco 1991; André Emmerich Gallery, NYC 1991-92; Neilsen Galleries, Boston 1992; Pratt Manhattan Gallery, NYC 1992-93. **Bio-Bibliography:** Michael Brenson, "True Believers Who Keep the Flame of Painting," *NY Times* (June 7, 1987); Paul Richard, "Bill Jensen's Shadowy Meditations," *Washington Post* (Oct. 31, 1987); Jonathan Phillips, "Bill Jensen at Washburn," *Art World* (Apr.-May 1988); Stephen Westfall, "Into the Vortex," *Art in America* (Apr. 1988); John Yau, "Alone in a Pitiless Landscape," *Contemporanea* (June 1989); Roberta Smith, "Roughing it on 57th Street," *NY Times* (Mar. 17, 1991); Peter Schjeldahl, "Abstract Painting: The 90's," *Village Voice* (Jan. 13, 1992); Peter Plagens, "Last Minute Reprieve," *Newsweek* (Jan. 13, 1992); Holland Cotter, "Bill Jensen and Myron Stout," *NY Times* (May 1, 1992); Mary Sherman, "Exhibit Takes A Look at Landscape Art," *Boston Herald* (Aug. 19, 1992).

JENSEN, ROBERT EARL ■ FAAR Architecture 76. b. Nov. 24, 1938, Ravanna, NE. m. Kathleen Jensen. BArch 63, Univ. of Nebraska; MArch 69, Cornell Univ. **Career & Employment:** Sargent Webster Crenshaw & Folley, Architects 1964-66; NYSCA, Consultant 1967-68; J. Victor Bagnardi, Architect 1967-68; *Architectural Record*, Assc. Ed. 1968-73; Queens College, Adj. Inst. 1973; *Architecture PLUS*, Field Ed. 1974-75; NYIT, Adj. Inst. 1976-. **Fellowships, Honors & Awards:** NEA, Art Critics Fellowship 1976-77; Columbia School of Journalism Award. **Publications:** "Operation Breakthrough," *Architectural Record* (Apr. 1970); "Board and Batten Siding and the Ballroom Frame: Their Incompatibility in the 19th Century," *JSAH* 30 (1971): 40-50; "Urban Housing," *Architectural Record* (Apr. 1971); "Images for a New California City," *Architectural Record* (June 1971); "Shopping Malls in Suburbia," *Architectural Record* (Mar. 1972); "Italian Design Show at MOMA: A Post-Mortem," *Architectural Record* (Oct. 1972); "Mitchell/Giurgola Associates: Three Projects," *Architectural Record* (Oct. 1972); "Art Center as Artifact," *Architectural Forum* (Dec. 1973); "Buildings that Believe in Science," *Progressive Architecture* (Mar. 1974); with Patricia Conway, *Ornamentalism* (New York: Clarkson N. Potter Press, 1982). **Bio-Bibliography:** *American Architects Directory* (1970).

JERGENS, ROBERT J. ■ FAAR Painting 63. b. Mar. 18, 1938, Cleveland, OH. Dipl. 60, Cleveland Inst. of Art; BFA 61, Yale Univ.; MFA 64, Yale Univ. **Other Study:** Summers 1988-92, traveling & visiting artists in Japan. **Research/Artistic Interests:** Neon-sound. **Career & Employment:** Yale Univ., Asst. Prof. 1964-69; Univ. of Connecticut, Summers 1964, 1965; Cooper Union 1965-67; Yale Norfolk, Summers 1966-68; Cleveland Inst. of Art 1969-present, Summer Program 1969-present. **Fellowships, Honors & Awards:** Ranney Found. Grant 1970-72; Lilly Found. Grant for Computer Art 1989. **Important Works:** Cleveland Public Library, Main Branch mural; Jones, Day, Reavis, & Pougue, Main Lobby; National City Bank, OH; Cleveland Trust Bank, OH; Newman Religious Center, OH; Yale Univ.; B.P. America. **Exhibitions/Performances:** Solo: Butler Inst. of American Art, OH 1981, 1987; Rose Fried Gallery, NYC 1982, 1984, 1986; Walker Gallery, IL 1985; Akron Art Museum 1988; Wismer Gallery at Ursuline College, OH 1990; Group: Brook-

lyn Museum 1981; MOMA 1981; Contemporary Arts Center, OH 1984; Corcoran Gallery of Art, Washington, DC 1985; Great Northern Corporate Center, OH 1987; First Inst. of Art & Design, Hong Kong 1989. **Home Address:** 5356 Regency Dr., Parma, OH 44129-5961. **Business Address:** Cleveland Inst. of Art, 11141 East Blvd., Cleveland, OH 44106.

JIMENEZ, LUIS ALFONSO ■ AAR Visitor 80. b. July 30, 1940, El Paso, TX. m. Susan B. Jimenez. c. Eliza, Adam, Orion, Xochil. BS 85. **Other Study:** Asst. to Semore Lipton 1966. **Research/Artistic Interests:** Fiberglass public sculpture, drawings, prints, works on paper. The sculpture is visually accessible, using popular images; the material also comes from the popular culture. **Career & Employment:** Univ. of Arizona, Prof. 1985-present. **Home Address:** PO Box 7, Hondo, NM 88336.

JOHANNOWSKY, WERNER ■ Italian Fulbright Fellow 1956-57.

JOHANSEN, JOHN M. ■ RAAR Architecture 75. b. June 29, 1916, NYC. m. Beate Gropius. c. Christen, Deborah. BS 39, Harvard College; MArch 42, Harvard GSD. **Research/Artistic Interests:** Painting, printmaking, drawing, music & writing. **Career & Employment:** Marcel Breuer 1943; Skidmore Owings Merrill 1946-50; Own firm 1950-present; Harvard GSD, Visiting Critic 1953; Columbia Univ., Adj. Prof. 1962-64; Yale Univ., Adj. Prof. 1953-56; Pratt Inst., Adj. Prof. 1975-present. **Memberships & Offices:** AIA, Fellow; ALNY, Pres. 1968-70; NAD 1969; AAAL 1979. **Fellowships, Honors & Awards:** Hon. DFA: Maryland Inst. of Art 1965, Clark Univ. 1970; AAAL, Brunner Award 1968; AIA, Honor Award 1971; City of New York, Bard Award 1976; Graham Found. Grant 1990. **Publications:** "Avant Garde in Architecture Today," *Arts & Society* (1965); "Architecture for Electronic Age," *American Scholar* 35 (1966); "Johansen Declares Himself," *Architectural Forum* (1967); "Mummers Theater: A Fragment," *Architectural Forum* (1969): 69-72; "Architecture: Three Imperatives," *Architecture* (Mar. 1984): 156-57; "The New Modernity," *A + U Japan* (1989). **Important Works:** US Embassy, Dublin, Ireland 1963; Clownes Hall Opera House, Indianapolis 1964; Mechanic Theater, Baltimore 1967; Goddard Library, Clark Univ., Worcester, MA 1968; Oklahoma Theater Center, Oklahoma City 1970; Smith Elementary School, Columbus, IN 1970; New York State College, Old Westbury 1972; Roosevelt Island Neighborhood, NYC 1975; Quincey Office Bldg. 1986; 7 future-tech projects 1984, 1995. **Exhibitions/Performances:** MOMA 1952; "Transformations in Modern Architecture" MOMA 1979; Nat. Inst. of Architectural Education 1987. **Bio-Bibliography:** *Who's Who in America.* **Business Address:** 821 Broadway, NYC 10003.

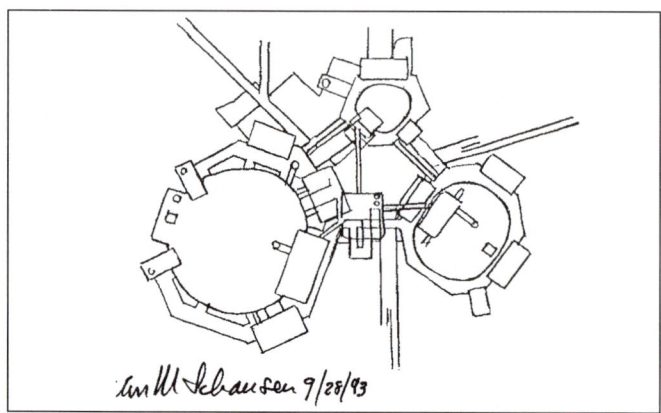

John M. Johansen

JOHNS, CHRISTOPHER M.S. ■ FAAR History of Art 84. b. Apr. 13, 1956, Portsmouth, VA. BA 77, Florida State Univ., Tallahassee; PhD 85, Univ. of Delaware. **Research/Artistic Interests:** Art history, architectural history & art theory in Italy, 1680-1870, with emphasis on Rome & the papacy. **Career & Employment:** Univ. of Virginia, Assc. Prof. 1985-present. **Memberships & Offices:** American Soc. for Eighteenth-Century Studies, Adv. Ed. for Art History 1990-93; CAA; SAH. **Fellowships, Honors & Awards:** Phi Beta Kappa; NGA, Chester Dale Fellowship 1983; Fulbright Fellowship 1984; ACLS Grant-in-Aid 1988; Univ. of Rome, "La Sapienza," Research Fellowship 1989; Univ. of Virginia, Teacher of the Year 1991. **Publications:** "Theater and Theory: Thomas Sully's 'George Frederick Cooke as Richard III,'" *Winterthur Portfolio* 18 (1983): 27-38; "Some Observations on Collaboration and Patronage in the Altieri Chapel: Bernini and Gaulli," *Storia dell'Arte* 50 (1984): 43-47; "Clement XI, Carlo Fontana and S. M. Maggiore in the Early Eighteenth Century," *JSAH* 45 (1986): 286-93; "Papal Patronage and Cultural Bureaucracy in Eighteenth-Century Rome," *Eighteenth-Century Studies* 22 (1988): 1-23; "Politics, Nationalism and Friendship in Van Dyck's 'Le Roi à la Ciasse,'" *Zeitschrift für Kunstgeschichte* 51 (1988): 243-61; "Antonio Canova's Drawings for 'Hercules and Lichas,'" *Master Drawings* 27 (1989): 358-67; "Illuminations of S. Maria Maggiore in the Early Settecento," *Burlington Magazine* 123 (1990): 528-34; "French Connections to Papal Art and Politics in the Rome of Clement XI, 1700-1721," *Storia dell'Arte* 67 (1990): 279-85; "Antonio Canova and Austrian Art Policy," in *Austria in the Age of the French Revolution*, ed. Kinley Brauer (Minneapolis: Univ. of Minnesota Press, 1990), 83-90; "Art and Science in Eighteenth-Century Bologna: Donato Creti's Astronomical Landscapes," *Zeitschrift für Kunstgeschichte* 56 (1992): 578-89; "Re-framing Art History: Text and Context," *Eighteenth-Century Studies* 25 (1992): 517-22; *Papal Art and Cultural Politics: Rome in the Age of Clement XI* (Cambridge & New York: Cambridge Univ. Press, 1993). **Business Address:** Dept. of Art, Univ. of Virginia, Charlottesville, VA 22903.

JOHNS, JASPER ■ AAR Trustee 1973-76, Trustee Emer.; Artist.

JOHNSEN, MILLICENT ■ AAR Trustee 1987-95; AAR Academy Award 1990. BA, Skidmore College. **Memberships & Offices:** Garden Club of America: Pres.; Medal Awards Com.; Long Range Planning on Flower Show & Judging Com., Chair; Bryant Park Flower Show Section, Chair; Autumn in the Atrium, NYC, Chair; Horticultural Soc. of New York, Dir.; World Wildlife Fund, Dir.; Passaic Collegiate School, BoT; Skidmore College, BoT; Riverview Hospital, Red Bank, NJ, Governor; Borough of Rumson Environmental Comm., Chair. **Fellowships, Honors & Awards:** Garden Club of America, Creative Leadership Award. **Important Works:** Twinlights of Highlands, NJ, rehabilitation and re-landscaping.

JOHNSON, ALLAN C. ■ AAR Trustee 1929-46, Classicist.

JOHNSON, DEAN A. ■ FAAR Landscape Architecture 66. b. May 29, 1937, South Bend, IN. c. Bryn, Kier, Todd, Teryn. BS 61, Michigan State Univ.; MLA 63, Univ. of Michigan. **Career & Employment:** Johnson, Johnson, & Roy, Inc. 1963-64; Peter Rolland Asscs. 1966-67; Currier, Andersen & Geda 1967-69; Johnson & Dee 1969-81; Johnson & Richter, Inc. 1981-92. **Memberships & Offices:** ASLA, Chap. Pres. 1981-83, Nat. VP 1986-88. **Fellowships, Honors & Awards:** ASLA, Design Award 1976, 1978, Fellow 1983; AIA Honor Award 1978, Connecticut Chap., Public Places Award 1979, 1981, 1989; Urban Land Inst.

Award for Excellence 1989. **Important Works:** Wolcott Park, West Hartford, CT 1976; New London Parade Area; New York Bar Center, Albany 1978; Barrier-Free Site Design Publication for HUD & ASLA 1978; Martin Luther King, Jr. Memorial & Center for Social Change, Atlanta 1978; Glastonbury Town Green, CT; Congress St. Historic Rehabilitation 1981; Wallingford Center Green, CT 1986; Windsor Train Station-Freight House Historic Rehabilitation 1989; Charleston Place, SC 1989; Hartford Insurance Parking Plaza 1990; Hockanum River 26 Mile Linear Park, Vernon, Manchester & East Hartford, CT 1994. **Home Address:** Avon Park North, No. 8, Avon, CT 06001. **Business Address:** Johnson & Richter, Inc., PO Box 567, Avon, CT 06001.

JOHNSON, DORA ■ FASCSR 1910-11; ASCSR Student 1909-10. b. Mar. 23, 1877. d. Mar. 23, 1912. AB 1899, Vanderbilt Univ.; MA 1900, Univ. of Chicago. **Career & Employment:** Girls' Latin School, Baltimore, Teacher 1901-6. **Fellowships, Honors & Awards:** Univ. of Chicago, Fellowship 1907-9. **Publications:** *The Expression of the Idea of Respect in Plautus and Terence* (Chicago: Univ. of Chicago Press, 1900).

JOHNSON, HAROLD F. ■ AAR Trustee 1952-63.

JOHNSON, HUNTER ■ FAAR Musical Composition 35. b. Apr. 14, 1906, Benson, NC. dec. BMus 29, Eastman School of Music. **Other Studies:** UNC 1924-26. **Career & Employment:** Univ. of Michigan, Faculty 1929-33; Univ. of Manitoba, Faculty 1944-47; Cornell Univ., Faculty 1948-53; Univ. of Illinois, Faculty 1959-65; Univ. of Texas, Faculty 1966-71. **Fellowships, Honors & Awards:** Guggenheim Fellowship 1941, 1945; NIAL Award; Fine Arts Award of North Carolina 1965. **Important Works:** *Symphony* 1931; *Piano Sonata* 1934; *Concerto for Piano & Chamber Orchestra* 1935; *Elegy*, for clarinet & strings 1937; *Violin Sonatina* 1937; *Music for Strings* 1939; *In Time of Armament*, a ballet 1939; *Letter to the World*, a ballet 1940; *Deaths and Entrances*, a ballet 1942; *Concerto for Orchestra* 1944; *Trio for Flute, Oboe & Piano* 1954; *North State*, for orchestra 1963; *Past the Evening Sun*, for orchestra 1964; *The Scarlet Letter*, a ballet 1975. **Bio-Bibliography:** *Baker's Biographical Dictionary of Musicians, New Grove Dictionary of American Music; Who's Who in America*.

JOHNSON, JERRY ■ Chicago Architectural Club, Burnham Prize 1989-90.

JOHNSON, PHILIP C. ■ AAR Trustee 1973-77, Trustee Emer.; Architect.

JOHNSON, RICHARD A. ■ FAAR Painting 68. b. Feb. 26, 1942, Minneapolis, MN. m. Donna Campbell Perret. c. Stephanie Johnson, Melanie Perret. BFA 65, Minneapolis College of Art & Design; MFA 67, Washington Univ., St. Louis. **Research/Artistic Interests:** Abstract painting, mixed media, acrylic. **Career & Employment:** East Texas Univ., Asst Prof. 1968-73; Indiana Univ., Bloomington, Asst. Prof. 1973-75; Univ. of New Orleans, Prof. 1978-present; Rockefeller Found., Southeastern Center for Contemporary Art, Artist-in-Residence 1980. **Important Works:** Public Commissions: *Stereoscope*, Texaco Bldg., New Orleans 1985; *Midnight Silhouette & Blue Ridge*, 99 High St., Keystone Center, Boston 1993; Public Collections: New Orleans Museum of Art; Longview Art Center, TX; Louisiana Art & Science Center, Baton Rouge; Louisiana State Arts Council, Baton Rouge; Birmingham Museum of Art, AL. **Exhibitions/Performances:** Solo: Galerie Simone Stern, New Orleans 1978, 1979, 1981 1982, 1984, 1986, 1988, 1991; Watson-DeNagy & Co.,

Houston 1981, 1983; Galerie Ninety-Nine, Bar Harbor Islands, FL 1983; Edith Baker Gallery, Dallas 1987; Galerie Joans Prats, NYC 1991; Maria-Villa-Chicago 1993; Alexandria Museum of Art, LA 1994. **Bio-Bibliography:** Henry Schwalb, "Trick & Treat," *Pittsburgher Magazine* 2.8 (Jan. 1979); John R. Clarke, "The Reality of Illusion: Eclipse or Realism?" *Arts Magazine* (Feb. 1981): 156-60; Towne Peabody, "Towards the Sanctuary," *New Orleans Art Review* (Mar.-Apr.-May 1984): 27; David Rive, "Richard Johnson's New Work," *New Orleans Art Review* (Feb. 1986): 14; Roger Green, "Johnson's New Works Need Savoring," *New Orleans Times-Picayune* (Jan. 17, 1986): 12; Terrington Calas, "On Abstraction," *New Orleans Art Review* (Feb.-Mar. 1987): 9-10; David Rosendorf, "Richard Johnson," *Atlanta Art Papers* 12.4 (July-Aug. 1988): 60; Edward Lucie-Smith, *Richard Johnson,* exb. cat. (New York: Galeria Prats, 1991); Terrington Calas, "Looking at Abstract Painting in a New Light," *Art, Times-Picayune* (Nov. 22, 1991); Terrington Calas, "Abstraction Redux," *New Orleans Art Review* 10.2 (Nov.-Dec. 1991); Roger Green, "Richard Johnson," *Art News* (Feb. 1992); Peter Frank, "Richard Johnson, Concrete Expressonist," in *Richard Johnson/ John Scott,* exb. cat. (Alexandria Museum of Art, 1993). **Home Address:** 518 Julia St., New Orleans, LA 70130.

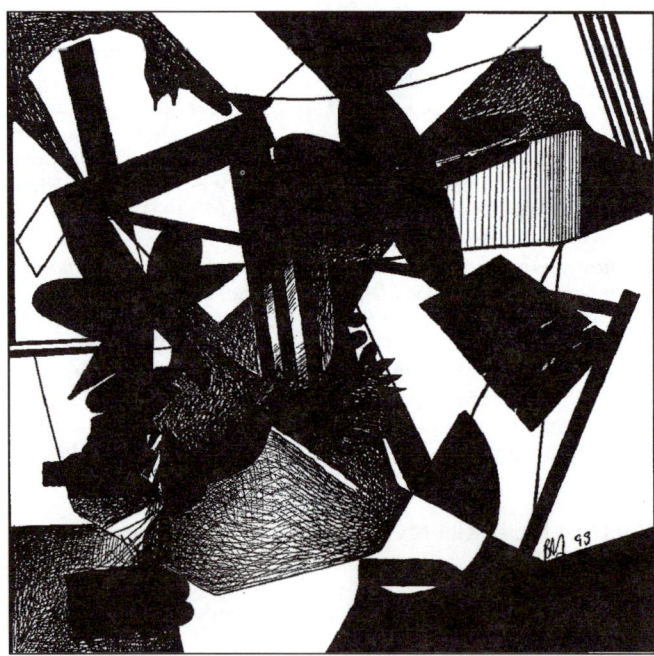

Richard A. Johnson

JOHNSON, T.L. ■ Winchester Fellow 1923-24.

JOHNSTONE, BURTON KENNETH ■ FAAR Architecture 32. b. Jan. 20, 1907, Chicago, IL. d. Jan 1, 1979. m. Helene Estelle Hetzel. c. Dorn Kenneth, Robert Philip. BS 28, Univ. of Illinois; BFA 29, Yale Univ. **Other Studies:** Lake Forest Found. for Architecture & Landscape Architecture 1928. **Research/ Artistic Interests:** Reconstruction of the Temple of Neptune and Hadrian's Villa; home planning for future home owners. **Career & Employment:** Granger & Bollenbacher, Draftsman 1924; Univ. of Illinois, TA 1928; Yale Univ., TA 1929; Penn. State College, Faculty 1933-45, Dept. Head 1938-45; Carnegie Inst. of Technology, College of Fine Arts, Dean 1945-52; Marlier, Wolf & Johnstone, Part. 1946-79. **Memberships & Offices:** Pennsylvania Soc. of Architects; Assn. of Collegiate Schools of Archi-

tecture, Pres.; Tau Beta Pi; Sigma Tau; Phi Eta Sigma; Pi Kappa Alpha; Scarab, Nat. Pres. **Fellowships, Honors & Awards:** Scarab Gold Medal 1941; AIA, Fellow. **Publications:** co-author, *Building or Buying a House, A Guide to Wise Investment* (New York: McGraw-Hill, 1945). **Bio-Bibliography:** *Who Was Who in America.*

JOHNSTONE, WILLIAM H. ■ AAR Trustee 1966-73, Lawyer.

JONES, CLIFFORD EDGAR ■ FAAR Painting 39. b. June 17, 1915, Greentown, IN. d. Mar. 30, 1975. m. Polly Soule. c. Laurinda J. Lee, Robert L. BFA 37, John Herron School of Art. **Other Studies:** D. Mattison, H. Mayer, John Herron, Univ. of Iowa, J. Charlot. **Career & Employment:** Instr.: Univ. of Iowa, John Herron Art School; Orchard School for Boys & Girls; United Aircraft Corp., Chance Vought Aircraft Division, WWII; Carnegie Inst. of Technology, Asst Prof. 1946-48; Univ. of Hartford, Instr.-Assc. Prof. 1948-75. **Memberships & Offices:** Artists Assn., Kokomo, IN. **Fellowships, Honors & Awards:** Beaux Arts 1st Medal for Mural Design; Connecticut Watercolor Soc. Prize; De Pauw Univ. Purchase Prize; Indianapolis News Watercolor Award; Hallmark Art Award. **Important Works:** Mural work, Hartford Electric Light Co., Middletown, CT; St. John's Church, Bridgeport CT. **Exhibitions/Performances:** Indiana State Fair 1936, 1940, 1941; All Iowa Exb. 1940; Indianapolis Art Museum 1941; Hoosier Salon 1941; New Haven PCC 1946. **Bio-Bibliography:** *Who Was Who in American Art.*

JONES, E. FAY ■ FAAR Architecture 81. b. Jan. 31, 1921, Pine Bluff, AR. m. Mary Elizabeth Knox. c. Janis Fay, Jean Cameron. BArch 50, Univ. of Arkansas, Fayetteville; MArch 51, Rice Univ. **Other Study:** Apprentice to Frank Lloyd Wright 1953, Mem. of Taliesin Fellowship. **Research/Artistic Interests:** Architecture. **Career & Employment:** Univ. of Oklahoma, Asst. Prof. 1951-53; Univ. of Arkanas 1953-88, Chair, Dept. of Architecture 1966-74, Dean, School of Architecture 1974-76; Univ. Prof. Emer. 1988-present. **Fellowships, Honors & Awards:** AIA Honor Award 1981, 1987, 1990; Gold Medal 1990; Tau Sigma Delta Gold Medal for Excellence in Design 1984; Assn. of Collegiate Schools of Achitecture, Distinguished Prof. 1985. **Important Works:** Don Edmondson House, Forrest City, AR 1980; Thorncrown Chapel, Eureka Springs, AR 1980; Roy Reed House, Hogeye, AR 1984; Pinecote Pavilion, Picayune, MS 1988; Cooper Memorial Chapel, Bella Vista, AR 1988; Worship Center, Eureka Springs, AR 1989. **Exhibitions/ Performances:** Iowa State Univ. 1967; Univ. of Oklahoma 1967; Auburn Univ. 1970; Hendrix College 1975; Univ. of Tennessee 1980; Notre Dame Univ. 1983; Kansas State Univ. 1984; Univ. of Arkansas 1984; Univ. of Michigan 1985; Florida A & M Univ. 1985; Univ. of Illinois 1988; Univ. of Utah 1989. **Bio-Bibliography:** William Marlin, "Truing Up," *Inland Architect* (Nov.-Dec. 1989): 27-39; Philip Langdon, "In the Wright Tradition," *The Atlantic* (Apr. 1989): 83-87; Andrea Oppenheimer Dean, "The Cathedral Builder Born 500 Years Too Late," *Smithsonian* (Aug. 1991): 102-11; Robert Ivy, Jr., "The Architecture of Fay Jones," *Architecture & Urbanism* (Feb. 1991): 57-120; Robert Ivy, Jr., *Fay Jones* (Washington, DC: AIA Press, 1992); *Who's Who in America.* **Home Address:** 1330 North Hillcrest, Fayetteville, AR 72703. **Business Address:** Fay Jones & Maurice Jennings, Architects, 619 W. Dickson, Fayetteville, AR 72701.

JONES, FRANCIS C. ■ AAR Trustee 1917-31.

JONES, FRANKLIN WEEKS ■ FAAR Classics/Archaeology 31. b. Sept. 25, 1905, Evanston, IL. d. May 31, 1991. m. Eve F. Caswell. BA 25, Harvard Univ.; MA 27, Harvard Univ.; MBA

34, Northwestern Univ.; PhD 42, Northwestern Univ. **Research/Artistic Interests:** Greek epic. **Career & Employment:** US Office of Strategic Services, Washington, DC 1942-45; US Army, Captain 1943-46; US State Dept., Research Analyst 1946-48; US Central Intelligence Agency, Intelligence Officer 1948-67. **Fellowships, Honors & Awards:** ASCSA, Charles Eliot Norton Fellowship 1925-26. **Publications:** "The Formation of the Revenge Motif in the *Odyssey*," *TAPA* 72 (1941): 195-202. **Bio-Bibliography:** Harvard Univ. Archives.

JONES, JEFFREY ■ FAAR Musical Composition 74. b. May 11, 1944, Santa Ana, CA. BMus 66, Immaculate Heart College; MFA 72, Brandeis Univ. **Other Studies:** Accademia di Santa Cecilia 1968-69. **Fellowships, Honors & Awards:** Fulbright Grant 1967-69; Accademia Chigiana, Scholarship 1968; Festival International du Son, 1st Grand Prize 1970; Marlboro Music Festival, Composer-in-Residence 1970; BMI Award 1970. **Important Works:** *Piece,* for 10 instruments 1966; *Trio,* for flute, clarinet, & bassoon 1966; *Expressions,* for guitar solo (Southern Music) 1967; *Trio,* for guitar, violin & viola 1968; *Variance,* for two violins, cello, harpsichord, piano & one or two percussionists (Editions Musicales Françaises) 1968-69; *Modi Movendi,* for 8 players 1970; *Tierces Mouvantes,* for piano solo 1971; *Rideau d'Amethystes,* for harp, cello & guitar 1971.

JONES, KRISTIN A. ■ FAAR Visual Arts 94. b. Aug. 1, 1956, Washington, DC. m. Andrew H. Ginzel, FAAR 94. BFA 79, RISD; MFA 83, Yale Univ. School of Art. **Other Study:** Travel has always been a major source of study & inspiration. A travel fellowship to India in 1990-91 allowed me to explore devotional architecture & performance. **Research/Artistic Interests:** I work in collaboration with Andrew Ginzel. Our work evolves from a fascination of dynamic opposites. We are concerned with the definition & interrelationships of polarities. We attempt to build seductive, contemplative work which challenges perception while endowed with a sense of reverence for the larger mysteries. Working with a range of evocative elements that propose concurrent realities, we attempt to present the drama & the extreme fragility of equilibrium. Both empirical & intuitive elements bring into question the tangibility of time. **Career & Employment:** Oxbow Summer School of Art, Saugatuck, MI 1976-82; Cooper Union, Lect. 1982-86; School of Visual Arts 1985-present; numerous visiting positions. **Fellowships, Honors & Awards:** Artists Grant, Artists Space, NYC 1985; NYSCA, Award 1986; NEA Fellowship 1986, Grant 1989, 1991, Scholarship 1994; The Bessie, New York Dance & Performance Award 1986; Yaddo, Fellowship 1987; NYFA, Fellowship 1987; Mass. Council on the Arts & Humanities, New Works Program Grant 1988; Art Comm. of the City of New York, Award for Excellenee in Design 1989; MacDowell Colony Fellowship 1989, 1991, 1993; Indo-American Fellowship, Council for Intl. Exchange of Scholars 1990; Louis Comfort Tiffany Found. Award 1991; American Center Paris, Cité Intl. des Arts, Residency 1993-94; Pollock-Krasner Found 1994. **Important Works:** *Moribus* (*Cruxis*), Museo d'Arte Contemporanea Permanent Collection Comm., Prato 1988; *Analemma,* Wadsworth Atheneum, Hartford, CT 1988; *Field and Figures,* for Merce Cunningham Dance Co., NYC 1989; *Mnemonics,* Battery Park City, NYC 1989-92; *Atol,* Univ. Art Museum, UC, Santa Barbara 1990; *Principia,* Oregon Convention Center, Portland 1990; *Diaxiom,* Commerce Sq. One, I.M. Pei & Partners, Philadelphia 1991; *Plethora,* 7th Triennale, India, USIS, New Dehli 1991; *Soundings,* Pennsylvania Convention Center, Philadelphia 1994; **Permanent Collections:** Brooklyn Museum; Centro per l'Arte Contemporanea Luigi Pecci, Prato, Italy; Kunsthalle Basel; Wadsworth Atheneum.

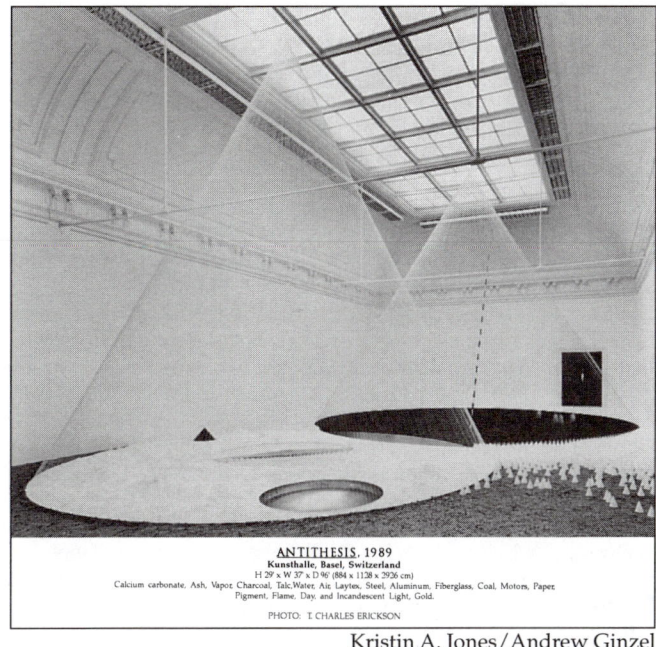

ANTITHESIS, 1989
Kunsthalle, Basel, Switzerland
H 29' x W 37' x D 96' (884 x 1128 x 2926 cm)
Calcium carbonate, Ash, Vapor, Charcoal, Talc, Water, Air, Laytex, Steel, Aluminum, Fiberglass, Coal, Motors, Paper, Pigment, Flame, Day, and Incandescent Light, Gold.
PHOTO: T. CHARLES ERICKSON

Kristin A. Jones / Andrew Ginzel

Bio-Bibliography: Douglas C. McGill, "Art People: Collaborators Depict Nature," *NY Times* (Nov. 21, 1986): C33; *Triptych* (New York: New Museum of Contemporary Art, 1987); Margot Crutchfield, *Installations,* exb. cat. (Richmond: Virginia Museum of Fine Arts, 1987); Andrea Miller-Keller, *Matrix 99,* exb. cat. (Hartford, CT: Wadsworth Atheneum 1988); Pam Lambert, "Art: The World According to Jones-Ginzel," *Wall Street Journal* (June 15, 1989): 11A; Dmitri L. Coromilas, "Kristin Jones + Andrew Ginzel: *Antithesis,*" *Tehni/Art* 1.1 (Nov. 28, 1989): 14-15, 38-39; Jim Jenkins & Dave Quick, *Motion-Motion Kinetic Art* (Salt Lake City: Gibbs Smith Publishers, 1989), 54-57; Thomas Kellein & Patricia C. Phillips, *Antithesis,* exb. cat. (Basel: Kunsthalle Basel, 1989); Thomas Kellein, "Jones + Ginzel: Künstler-paare," *Kunstforum International* (Mar.-Apr. 1990): 178-80; Phyllis I. Freeman, *New Art* (New York: Abrams, 1990), 97; "Plethora: A Project for Artforum," *Artforum* 29.9 (May 1991): 128; Andy Lansett, "Public Art," Nat. Public Radio, Weekend Edition (Sept. 1992). **Home Address:** 289 Bleecker St., NYC 10014.

JONES, THOMAS HUDSON ■ FAAR Sculpture 22. b. July 24, 1892, Buffalo, NY. d. Nov. 4, 1969. m. c. 2 daughters, 2 sons. **Other Studies:** Buffalo Art School; Albright Art School 10 years; MFA; Carnegie Technical School. **Career & Employment:** Columbia Univ., Instr. 1924-29. **Memberships & Offices:** NAD, Assc. Mem. 1932. **Fellowships, Honors & Awards:** Albright Scholarship Buffalo 1909-10; MFA School, Scholarship 1912. **Important Works:** Sculpture: Tomb of the Unknown Soldier, Arlington Nat. Cemetery; U.S. Grant Medal; War Memorial, Port Chester, NY; Doors, Brooklyn Public Library; NYU Hall of Fame; Memorial Reliefs, Holyoke, MA; St. Matthew's Church, Washington, DC; Mechanics Inst., NYC; Houston Texas Public Library; US Treasury Dept., Washington, DC; Park, Rochester, NY; Burmingham, AL; Trinity College, Hartford; Yellow Fever Medal, US Treasury; Memorial, Burlington, WI. **Bio-Bibliography:** *Who Was Who in America.*

JONES, WESLEY C. ■ FAAR Architecture 86. b. Jan. 27, 1958, Santa Monica, CA. m. Jean Young. BA 80, UC, Berkeley; MArch 83, Harvard GSD. **Other Study:** US Military Acad. 1978. **Career & Employment:** ELS Design Group 1980-85; Eisenman-

Robertson, Architects 1985-86; Holt & Hinshaw 1986-87; Holt Hinshaw Jones Architecture 1987-93; Jones Partners Architecture 1993-present; Visiting Prof.: Rice Univ. 1989, Harvard Univ. 1990, 1994, Columbia Univ. 1992. **Fellowships, Honors & Awards:** UC, Berkeley, Eisner, Bakewell Brown & Bakewell Weihle Prizes 1980, Phi Beta Kappa 1980; AIA, Certificate of Merit 1983; Graham Found. Scholarship 1983; NYFA, Architecture Fellowship 1987; *Progressive Architecture,* Citations 1988, 1990, 1991 (2), 1994, Award 1987, 1989; Astronauts Memorial Nat. Competition, Winner 1988; Columbus Convention Center Finalist 1989; US Pavillion, Expo 92, Finalist 1989; American Soc. of Architectural Perspectivists, Juror's Award 1989; Rene Debois Bioshelter Finalist 1991; Head Start Finalist 1994. **Important Works:** Altman & Manley Advertising, San Francisco, CA 1986; Tract House, Manhattan Beach, CA 1987; Bridgeway Science & Technology, Newark, CA 1987; Zaccho Dance Theater 1987; Alcatraz Island, San Francisco 1988; Astronauts Memorial, Kennedy Space Center, FL 1988; Right Away Redy Mix 1, Oakland, CA 1988; Lifeguard Station, Los Angeles 1988; Paramount Pictures Film & Tape Archives, Hollywood, CA 1989; Tarantino Residence, Los Angeles 1989; US Pavilion, Expo 92, Seville, Spain 1989; Columbus Convention Center 1989; House for a Corporate Family, Malibu, CA 1990; Lake Superior Aquarium, Duluth, MN 1991; Confluence Point Bridges & Ranger Station, San Jose, CA 1991; UCLA Chiller Plant-Facilities Complex 1991; San Jose Repertory Theater, San Jose, CA 1992; Oakville Ranch Winery, Napa, CA 1992; Univ. of Cinncinnati, Library Sq. Stair 1993, Edenscape Area Improvements 1993; Hesselink House 1994. **Exhibitions/ Performances:** ALNY 1985; Gallery 400, Univ. of Chicago 1985; AIA Conference on Homelessness, Washington, DC 1985; AIA Nat. Convention, San Francisco 1985; Storefront for Art & Architecture, NYC 1985, 1986, 1987; Inst. for Art & Urban Resources, PS 1, NYC 1986; Columbia Univ., Graduate School of Architecture 1987; Outdoor Chair Show, Sausalito, CA 1987; Kirsten Kiser Gallery, Los Angeles 1988; Harvard GSD 1989; Univ. of Virginia 1989; Steelcase Design Partnership 1990; Soc. for Arts & Crafts 1991; Leo Castelli-Gagosian Gallery, NYC 1992; San Francisco Museum of Modern Art 1993. **Bio-Bibliography:** "Storefront for Art and Architecture," *Architecture + Urbanism* (1986); "Building Machine," *Pamphlet Architecture* 12 (1987); "Hot Rods," *Progressive Architecture* (1988); "Mechanics," *Architectural Review* (1989); "Putting Names in the Sky," *Newsweek* (May 13, 1991); *Progressive Architecture* (July 1991); "Un Cielo de Cine," *A&V* (1991); "Architecture Mobili," *Casabella* (June 1992); "A Daring High-Tech Design," *San Jose Mercury News* (Feb. 14, 1993); "Notes Re:constitution," *Oz* 15 (1993); "Cool Chiller," *Architectural Record* (June 1994); "Boss Design: A Los Angeles Sketchbook," *NY Times* (June 12, 1994). **Home Address:** 461 2 St, No. 458, San Francisco, CA 94107.

JORDAN, JUNE M. ■ FAAR Design Arts 71. b. July 9, 1936, Harlem, NY. c. Christopher Meyer. **Study:** Barnard College 1953-55, 1956-57; Univ. of Chicago 1955-56. **Career & Employment:** *The Cool World,* Asst. to the Producer 1964; Mobilization for Youth, Research Assc., Writer 1965-66; Teachers & Writers Collaborative, Poet-in-Residence 1966-68; CCNY, Faculty 1967-70, 1972-75, 1977-78; Voice of the Children, Dir. 1967-70; Connecticut College, Faculty 1968; Sarah Lawrence College, Faculty 1971-75; Yale Univ., Faculty 1974-75; SUNY, Stony Brook, Assc. Prof. 1978-82, Prof. 1982-84; MacAlester College, Visiting Poet-in-Residence 1980; Loft Mentor Series, Minneapolis, Visiting Mentor Poet 1983; Poetry Center, Dir. 1986-89, Creative Writing Program, Dir. 1986; UC, Berkeley, Chancellor's Distinguished Lect. 1986, Prof. 1989-present; New Dramatist,

NYC Playwright-in-Residence 1987-88; Univ. of Wisconsin-Madison, Visiting Prof. 1988; Walt Whitman Birthplace, Huntington, NY, Poet-in-Residence 1988; *The Progressive,* Columnist 1989-present; *San Francisco Bay Guardian,* Contr. Ed. 1992-present. **Memberships & Offices:** Poets & Writers, Inc., BoD 1979-present; PEN American Center, Exec. Bd. 1980-84; American Writer's Congress, Exec. Bd. 1981-present; Acad. of American Poets, Judge, Lamont Prize 1981-83; Massachusetts Council on the Arts, Awards in Poetry, Judge 1984; Center for Constitutional Rights, BoD 1984-present; *American Heritage Dictionary of the English Language,* Usage Panel 1992; Scholastic Writing Awards, Judge 1992. **Fellowships, Honors & Awards:** Rockefeller Grant in Creative Writing 1969; Barnard College, Reid Lect. 1976; CAPS Grant in Poetry 1978; Yaddo Fellow 1979, 1980; NEA Fellowship 1982; NYFA Fellowship 1985; Massachusetts Council on the Arts Award in Contemporary Arts 1985; MacDowell Colony Fellow 1987; Nat. Assn. of Black Journalists Achievement Award; California Poets in the Schools 1990; Middle East-MERIP Award 1991; PEN Center USA West, Freedom to Write Award 1991; Arts Comm. of San Francisco, "Poem on a New Year's Eve" engraved on the sidewalk 1992; Middle East Children's Alliance Honor 1993; Northfield Mount Hermon School, Distinguished Service Award 1993; Nat. Black Women's Health Project, Founder's Award 1993. **Publications:** *Passion: New Poems 1977-1980* (Boston: Beacon Press, 1980); *Civil Wars: Selected Essays 1963-1980* (Boton: Beacon Press, 1981); *Things That I Do in the Dark: Selected Poems 1954-1977* (Boston: Beacon Press, 1981); *Kimako's Story* (Boston: Houghton Mifflin, 1981); *On Call: New Political Essays, 1981-85* (Boston: South End Press, 1985); *Living Room: New Poems 1980-1984* (Thunder's Mouth Press, 1985); *Naming Our Destiny: New and Selected Poems* (Thunder's Mouth Press, 1989); *Moving Towards Home: Selected Political Essays* (London: Virago Press, 1989); *Lyrical Campaigns: Selected Political Essays* (London: Virago Press, 1989); *Technical Difficulties: New Political Essays* (New York: Pantheon Press, 1992); *The Haruko: Love Poetry of June Jordan* (London: Virago Press, 1993); *A Place of Rage,* a film; *I Was Looking at the Ceiling and Then I Saw the Sky,* an opera 1995; Recordings: *Things That I Do in the Dark* (Spoken Arts, 1978); *For Somebody to Start Singing* (Watershed-Black Box, 1980). **Bio-Bibliography:** Peter Erickson, "June Jordan," in *Black Sister II: Essays on Black American Poets, 1746-1980,* ed. Earlene Stetson (Bloomington: Indiana Univ. Press, 1983); Peter Erickson, "The Love Poetry of June Jordan," *Callaloo* 9.1 (1986); "Women Talk," *Essence* (May 1990); Carla Freccero, "June Jordan," *African American Writers* (New York: Scribner's, 1991); Penelope Moffet, "Poetic Justice," *Los Angeles Times* (Jan. 21, 1993); *African-American Writers; Dictionary of Literary Biography; International Who's Who of American Women; Who's Who in America; Who's Who of Black Americans; Who's Who of Children's Book Authors; Who's Who of Women.* **Business Address:** Dept. of African American Studies, 3335 Dwinelle Hall, UC, Berkeley, CA 94720.

JORDY, WILLIAM HENRY ■ AAR Visitor 1951 — 1955, Art Historian. b. Aug. 31, 1917. **Career & Employment:** Brown Univ., Prof. 1960-, Chair 1963-66 & 1976-77. **Selected Publications:** *American Buildings and Their Architects,* 2 vols. (1972); as ed., *The Function of Ornament* (1986).

JORIO, STEFANIA ■ Italian Fulbright Fellow 1976-77.

JOSEPH, WENDY EVANS ■ FAAR Architecture 84; SOF, VP 1990-present. b. Nov. 23, 1955, NYC. m. Peter T. Joseph. c. Danielle, Nicholas. BA 77, Univ. of Pennsylvania; MArch 81, Harvard GSD. **Research/Artistic Interests:** Pencil drawings &

watercolors. **Career & Employment:** Pei Cobb Freed & Partners 1981-83, 1985-93; Wendy Evans Joseph, AIA, Private Practice 1994-present. **Memberships & Offices:** Univ. of Pennsylvania, School of Fine Arts, Bd. of Overseers 1992-present; Architects, Designers & Planners for Social Responsibility, New York Bd. 1991-present; AIA, Nat. Com. on Design, Steering Com. 1989-present; AIA, New York Chap., Exec. Bd. 1988-90; Harvard GSD, Alumni Council 1982-90, Sec. 1986-88, Pres. 1988-90; American Craft Museum, Nat. Adv. Com. 1991-present; NIAE, BoD, Sec. 1993-present; Second Stage Theater, NYC, BoD 1991-present; Salvadori Center on the Built Environment, VP 1993-present. **Fellowships, Honors & Awards:** Harvard Univ., AIA Henry Adams Medal 1981, John T. Kelley Prize 1981; Graham Found. Scholarship 1981. **Important Works:** Home for Contemporary Theatre & Arts, NYC 1986-91; American Business Center at Checkpoint Charlie, Competition Entry, Pei Cobb Freed & Partners, Project Architect 1992; US Holocaust Memorial Museum, Senior Assc. for Design. **Exhibitions/Performances:** Oberlin Bandstand Competition Exb. 1985; City Visions Competition Exb., Philadelphia 1986; American Soc. for Architectural Perspectivists 1987, 1988, 1992;

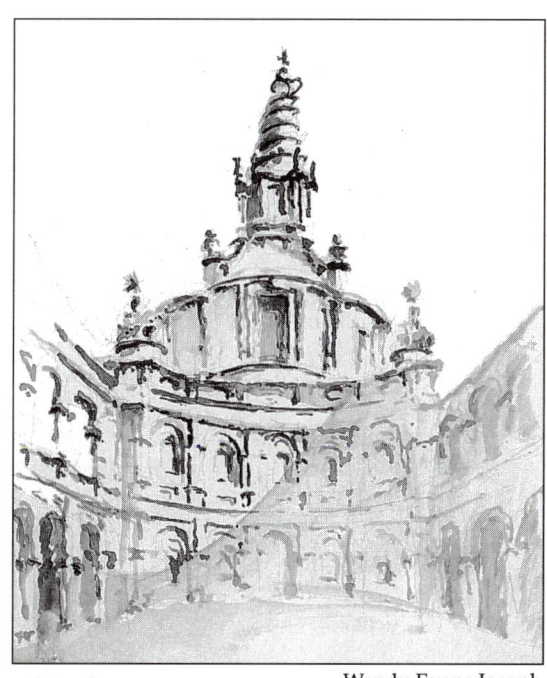

Wendy Evans Joseph

Bergdorf Goodman Architect's Windows, AIA Nat. Convention, NYC 1988; Columbia Univ., Avery Library Centennial Exb., NYC 1991; Kohn Pedersen Fox Gallery, NYC 1992; Checkpoint Charlie Competition Exb., Harvard Univ. 1993; African Burial Ground Competition 1994. **Bio-Bibliography:** *Glamour Magazine* (1988); *Self Magazine* (1989); *Contract Design Magazine* (1994). **Home Address:** 500 Park Ave., 40th Fl., NYC 10022.

JOSEPHSON, MATTHEW ■ RAAR Literature 60. Feb. 15, 1899, Brooklyn, NY. d. Mar. 13, 1978. m. Hannah Geffen. c. Eric, Carl. BA 20, Columbia Univ. **Career & Employment:** *Broom*, Ed. 1922-24; New York Stock Exchange, Acct. Rep 1924-26; *Transition*, American Ed. 1928-29; *New Republic*, Asst. Ed. 1931-32; Independent Writer 1932-68; UC, Irvine, Spec. Lect. 1968-69. **Memberships & Offices:** NIAL 1948. **Fellowships, Honors & Awards:** Soc. of American Historians, Francis Parkman Prize

1960; Van Wyck Brooks Prize 1969. **Publications:** *Zola and His Time* (London: Gollancz, 1929); *Portrait of the Artist as American* (New York: Harcourt, Brace, 1930); *Jean-Jacques Rousseau* (New York: Harcourt, Brace, 1931); *Nazi Culture* (New York: John Day, 1933); *The Robber Barons* (New York: Harcourt, Brace, 1934); *The Politicos 1865-1896* (New York: Harcourt, Brace, 1938); *The President Makers* (New York: Harcourt, Brace, 1940); *Victor Hugo* (New York: Doubleday, 1942); *Empire of the Air* (New York: Harcourt, Brace, 1944); *Stendhal: Or the Pursuit of Happiness* (New York: Doubleday, 1946); *Sidney Hillman: Statesman of American Labor* (Garden City, NY: Doubleday, 1952); *Union House, Union Bar: The History of the Hotel and Restaurant Employees and Bartenders International Union, AFL-CIO* (New York: Random House, 1956); *Edison: A Biography* (New York: McGraw-Hill, 1959); *Life among the Surrealists: A Memoir* (New York: Holt, Rinehart & Winston, 1962); *Infidel in the Temple: A Memoir of the 1930s* (New York: Knopf, 1967); *Al Smith: Hero of the Cities* (Boston: Houghton Mifflin, 1969); *The Money Lords: The Great Finance Capitalists 1925-1950* (New York: Weybright & Faley, 1972). **Bio-Bibliography:** *NY Times*, Obit. (Mar. 14, 1978); David E. Shi, *Matthew Josephson, Bourgeois Bohemian* (New Haven: Yale Univ. Press, 1981); *Oxford Companion to American Literature; Twentieth-Century Authors; Who's Who in the World; Who Was Who in America.*

JOVA, HENRI V. ■ FAAR Architecture 51. b. May 11, 1919, Newburgh, NY. BArch 49, Cornell Univ. **Research/Artistic Interests:** Architecture, interior design; acrylic painting. **Career & Employment:** Harrison & Abramowitz, Architects 1950-54; Abreu & Robeson, Chief of Design 1954-65; Jova-Daniels-Busby, Founding Part. & Chair 1966-present. **Memberships & Offices:** AIA; American Inst. of Interior Designers; Cornell Univ., College of Architecture, Bd. of Adv.; Century Club; Atlanta College of Art, Bd., Hon. Mem.; Atlanta Botanical Gardens, Bd., Life Mem. **Fellowships, Honors & Awards:** Fulbright Fellow 1951; AIA Fellow, Georgia Chap. Silver Medal 1985; Knight Corpus Christi de Toledo; American Soc. of Interior Designers, Georgia Chap., Design Archievement Award 1993. **Important Works:** Altanta Newspapers HQ Bldg. 1972; Colony Sq., Atlanta 1975; Monarch at Sea Pines 1985; Carter Presidential Center, Atlanta 1986; Day Butterfly Center, Callaway Gardens, Pine Mountain, GA 1988; Southern Progress Corp. HQ Bldg., Birmingham, AL 1989; First Presbyterian Church, Dalton, GA 1989; Atlanta City Hall Complex 1990; Home Mission Bd. of Southern Baptist Convention HQ, Alpharetta, GA 1995. **Bio-Bibliography:** *Who's Who in America.* **Home Address:** 861 Mentelle Dr. NE, Atlanta, GA 30308.

JUDSON, J. RICHARD ■ RAAR History of Art 82. b. July 5, 1925, Long Island, NY. m. Carolyn French. c. Pieter Moulton, Matthew Bowditch, Sarah Mercer, Nicolaas French. BA 48, Oberlin College; MA 53, IFA; PhD 56, Kunsthistorisch Instituut, Utrecht Univ. **Research/Artistic Interests:** *Rubens and the Passion of Christ* project. **Career & Employment:** US Naval Reserve, Midshipman 1943-44; Smith College, Prof. 1956-74; UNC, Wm. R. Kenan, Jr. Prof. 1974-93. **Fellowships, Honors & Awards:** Belgian-American Educational Found., C.R.B. Fellow 1953; Fulbright Fellow 1954-55, Prize Grant 1955-56; Guggenheim Fellow 1960-61; Univ. of Utrecht, Guest Prof. 1960-61; ACLS Grant-in-Aid 1974; Southeastern Inst. of Medieval & Renaissance Studies, Senior Fellow 1976; City of Antwerp Rubens Medal 1981-82; NGA Guest Curator 1983-86; Netherlands Inst. for Advanced Studies, Fellow 1986. **Publications:** *Gerrit van Honthorst: A Discussion of His Position in Dutch Art* (The Hague: Martinus Nijhoff, 1959); "Marine Symbols of Salvation in the Sixteenth Century," *Essays in Memory of Karl*

Lehmann, ed. Phyllis Williams Lehmann (Locust Valley, NY: J.J. Augustin, 1965), 136-52; *Rembrandt after Three Hundred Years: An Exhibition of Rembrandt and His Followers,* exb. cat. (Chicago, Minneapolis & Detroit: AIC, 1969); *Dirck Barendsz, 1534-1592* (Amsterdam: Van Gendt & Co., 1970); *The Drawings of Jacob de Gheyn* (Northampton, MA, Gehenna Press & New York:

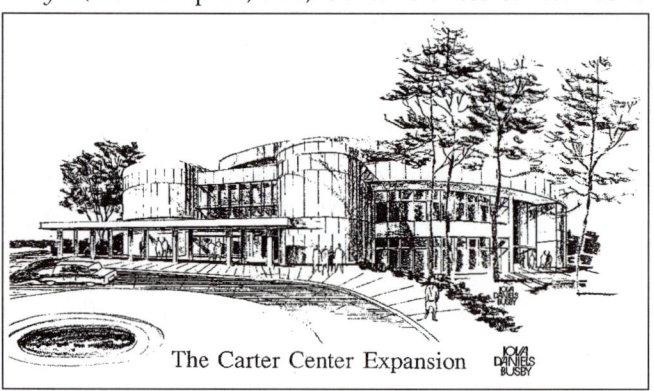

The Carter Center Expansion

Henri V. Jova

Grossman, 1973); "Rembrandt and Jacob de Gheyn II," *Album Amicorum J. G. van Gelder,* ed. J Bruyn, J A Emmens, F. de Jongh, D.P. Snoep (Utrecht: M. Nijhoff, 1973), 207-10; *P.P. Rubens als Boekillustrator* (Antwerp, Plantin-Moretus Museum, 1977); with C. Van de Velde, *Book Illustrations and Title Pages,* Part XXI, *Corpus Rubenianum Ludwig Burchard,* 2 vols. (London: Harvey Miller & Heyden Son, 1978); "Rubens & Moretus," *Medieval & Renaissance Studies* 7 (1979): 141-52; "Jan Gossaert, the Antique & the Origins of Mannerism in the Netherlands," in *Netherlandish Mannerism,* ed. Görel Cavalli-Björkman (Stockholm: Nat. Museum, 1985), 14-20; with J.O. Hand et al., *The Age of Bruegel: Netherlandish Drawings in the Sixteenth Century* (Washington, DC: NGA & Cambridge: Cambridge Univ. Press, 1986); "Utrecht, Rome, Leiden," *Nieuw Licht op de Gouden Eeuw,* exb. cat. (Utrecht-Braunschweig; Braunschweig, Limbach Druckerei & Verlagshaus, 1986-87); "Observations on the Use of the Antique in Sixteenth-Century Netherlandish Art," in *Rubens and His World: Bijdragen-Études-Studies-Beiträge Opgedragen ann Prof. Dr. Ir. R.-A. d'Hulst,* ed. Arnout Balis, Frans Baudoin, et al. (Antwerp: Het Gulden Cabinet, 1985), 49-59. **Home Address:** 4 Woods End Rd., Etna, NH 037450.

■ ■ ■

K

KACHADOORIAN, ZUBEL ■ FAAR Painting 59. b. Feb. 7, 1924, Detroit, MI. m. Deena Morguloff. c. Karina Kachadoorian, Nika Kachadoorian. **Other Study:** Meinzinger Art School, Detroit 1943-44; Apprenticeship with Francis De Erdely 1943-45; Ox Bow Summer School of Painting, Saugatuck, MI 1944-45; Skowhegan School of Painting & Sculpture 1946; Apprenticeship with Carlos Lopez 1946-50; Colorado Fine Arts Center, Colorado Springs 1947. **Career & Employment:** AIC, Artist-in-Residence 1960-61; Ox Bow Summer School of Painting, Faculty 1960-61, 1968-69; Norton Gallery School, West Palm Beach, FL, Artist-in-Residence 1961; Skowhegan School of Painting & Sculpture, Instr. 1964; Besser Museum School, Alpena, MI, Artist-in-Residence 1967; Wayne State Univ., Asst. Prof. 1967-73; Roeper City Country School for Gifted Children, Artist-in-Residence 1975-76; Camden-Frontier School, Artist-in-Residence 1979-84; Ferndale, MI, Public Schools, Artist-in-Residence; Private Studio classses, Detroit 1979-86. **Memberships & Offices:** Common Ground of the Arts, Visual Arts Adv. Panel 1965-66; Detroit Council of the Arts 1979-82; Detroit Rep-

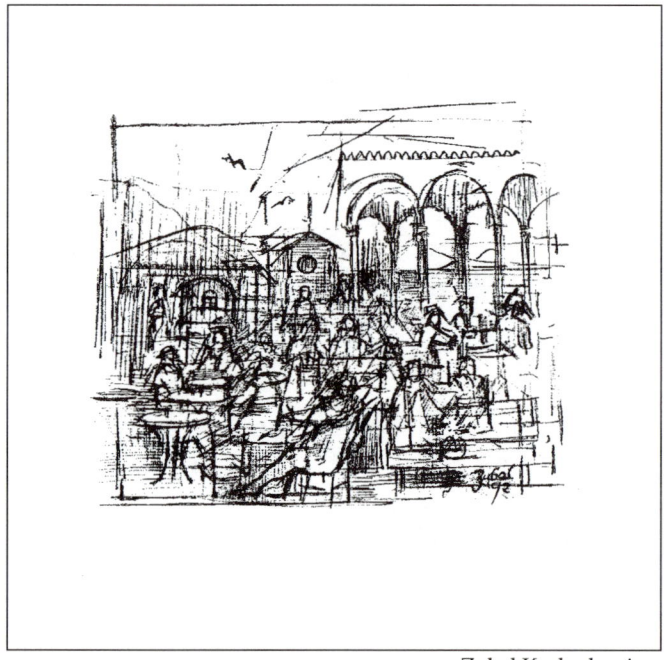

Zubel Kachadoorian

ertory Theatre, Art Dir. 1970-75. **Fellowships, Honors & Awards:** Pepsi-Cola Midwest Fellowship 1946-47; NIAL Richard & Linda Rosenthal Award 1961; Michigan Council for the Arts, Artist Apprenticeship Grant 1981, Creative Artists Grant 1983-84, 1990-91. **Important Works:** Michigan Physician Mutual, East Lansing; Detroit Inst. of Arts; AIC; Worcester Art Museum; Smithsonian Inst., Washington, DC; Tate Gallery, London; Norton Gallery of Art, West Palm Beach, FL; William Rockhill Nelson Gallery of Art, Kansas City, MO; Univ. of Michigan Art Museum; Muskegon Art Museum, MI; Wayne State Univ.; Henry Ford Community College, Dearborn, MI; Blue Cross-Blue Shield Bldg., Detroit; City Nat. Bank, Detroit; Kresge Intl. Center, Troy, MI; Michigan Bell, Detroit; Ball State Univ.; AAA Bldg., Dearborn, MI; Manufacturers Nat. Bank, Renaissance Center, Detroit; Arthur Andersen & Co., Renaissance Center, Detroit; Detroit Plaza, Renaissance Center; Portsmouth Community Arts Center, Portsmouth, VA; St. John's Armenian Church of Greater Detroit, Southfield, MI; Novi Hilton Hotel, Novi, MI; Oakland Univ., Rochester MI; Commissions: St. John's Armenian Church of Greater Detroit 1966-67; Michigan Bicentennial Fine Print Portfolio 1975; Detroit Repertory Theatre 1974-76; Henry Ford Community College, Dearborn, MI 1978. **Exhibitions/Performances:** Solo Museum: Kalamazoo Art Museum 1946; AIC 1961; Norton Gallery of Art, West Palm Beach, FL 1961; Besser Museum, Alpena, MI 1967; Battle Creek Art Center 1983; Solo Gallery: Civic Man's Center, Dearborn, MI 1943; Scarab Club, Detroit 1944, 1945; J.L. Hudson Gallery, Detroit 1945, 1946; Viviano Gallery, NYC 1946; Gallery Crueze, Paris 1952; Detroit Artist Market 1949, 1950, 1953, 1966, 1976; Delacorte Gallery, NYC 1956; Ann Werbe Gallery, Detroit 1958; Main Street Gallery, Chicago 1959, 1961; Nordness Gallery, NYC 1960, 1962, 1964; Forsythe Gallery, Ann Arbor 1953, 1957, 1961; 1965, 1969; Liggett School, Grosse Pointe, MI 1967; Westminster Church Gallery, Detroit 1969; Detroit Women's City Club, 1970; Henry Ford Community College, Dearborn MI 1971; Detroit Repertory Theatre Gallery 1972; Lockmoor Country Club Gallery, Grosse Pointe Woods, MI 1978; Univ. of Michigan, Dearborn 1986. **Bio-Bibliography:** *Contemporary Personalities, Detroit Artists Market, Dictionary of International Biography, International Directory of Arts, Oral History: Archives of American Art, Who's Who in America, Who's Who in American Art, Who's Who in Midwest Art, Who's Who in the World.* **Home Address:** 1214 Beaubien, Detroit, MI 48226.

KAHN, BEVERLY L. ■ FAAR Post-Classical/Humanistic Studies 85. b. June 24, 1947, Newton, MA. m. Robert M. Kahn. c. Adam, Crystal. BA 69, Dickinson College; MA 70, Columbia Univ.; PhD 76, Indiana Univ. **Research/Artistic Interests:** Italian political philosophy, Italian Marxism, contemporary Italian politics. **Career & Employment:** Indiana Univ., Assc. Instr. 1972-73; Univ. of South Carolina, Instr. 1973-76, Asst. Prof. 1976-77; Ohio State Univ., Mansfield, Asst. Prof. 1977-83, Assc. Prof. 1983-90; Fairfield Univ., Asst. Dean, College of Arts & Sciences & Assc. Prof. 1990-94, Assc. Dean 1994-present. **Memberships & Offices:** American Assn. for Higher Education; American Political Science Assn., Foundations of Political Theory Group; Midwest Political Science Assn.; Conference Group on Italian Politics & Soc.; Council for European Studies; Fulbright Alumni Assn.; Fulbright Assn., Connecticut Chap., BoD, Newsletter Ed. **Fellowships, Honors & Awards:** Pi Gamma Mu, Social Science Honorary 1969; Ford Found. Fellow 1970-71, 1971-72, Summer Grant 1972; Council for European Studies Grant 1972; Univ. of South Carolina, Amoco Distinguished Teaching Award, Semi-finalist 1974-75, Honors Program, Outstanding Teacher Award 1975-76, Research Grant 1976; NEH Summer Seminar 1980; Ohio State Univ., Research Grant 1980, Dean's Award for Special Services: Women's Week 1984, Faculty Professional Leave 1984-85, Distinguished Affirmative Action Award 1985; Fulbright Research Scholarship 1984-85; NAACP Mansfield Branch, Outstanding Service Award 1988; Phi Beta Delta, Honor Soc. for Intl. Scholars 1988; Fulbright Fellowship 1994. **Publications:** "Hegemony and Italian History: The Philosophy of Antonio Gramsci," *Italian Quarterly* 24.92 (Spring 1983): 75-93; "Antonio Gramsci on Reading Marx," *Quarterly Journal of Ideology* 7.1 (Spring 1983): 43-48; "Antonio Gramsci's Reformulation of Benedetto Croce's Speculative Idealism," *Idealistic Studies: An International Philosophical Journal* 15.1 (Jan. 1985): 18-40; "Le fondement ontologique et epistemologique du marxisme de Labriola," in *Labriola d'un siècle à l'autre*, ed. Georges Labica & Jacques Texier (Paris: Meridiens Klincksieck, 1988), 85-90; "Antonio Gramsci's Critique of Scientistic Marx-

ism," *Thought: Quarterly Review* 64.253 (June 1989): 158-75. **Home Address:** 369 Sigwin Dr., Fairfield, CT 06430. **Business Address:** College of Arts & Sciences, Fairfield Univ., Fairfield, CT 06430.

KAHN, LOUIS I. ■ RAAR Architecture 51. b. Feb. 20 1901, Island of Osel, Saarama, Estonia. d. Mar. 17, 1974. m. Esther Virginia Israeli. c. Sue Ann. BArch 24, Univ. of Pennsylvania. **Other Studies:** PAFA; Fleisher Memorial Art School; Public Industrial Art School, Philadelphia. **Career & Employment:** Hofman & Henan, Draftsman 1921; Hewitt & Ash Draftsman 1922; City Architects Dept., Philadelphia, Senior Draftsman 1924-27, Chief of Design for Sesqui-Centennial Exb. 1925-26; Paul Cret, Designer 1929-30; Borie & Medary, Designer 1930-32; Architectural Research Group, Organizer & Dir. 1932-33; WPA, City Planning Comm., Philadelphia, Housing Studies, Squad Head 1933-35; Alfred Kastner & Part., Asst. Prin. Architect 1935-37; Private Practice 1937-74; in assn. with George Howe 1941-42, Howe & Oscar Stonorov 1942-43, Stonorov 1943-48; Yale Univ., Prof. 1948-57; MIT, Albert Farwell Bemis Prof. 1956; Univ. of Pennsylvania, Prof. 1957-66, Paul Cret Prof. 1966-71, Prof. Emer. 1971-74. **Memberships & Offices:** Consulting Architect: Philadelphia Housing Authority 1937; US Housing Authority 1939; Philadelphia City Planning Comm. 1946-52, 1961-62; Philadelphia Redevelopment Authority 1951-54. **Fellowships, Honors & Awards:** AIA Fellow 1953; NIAL, Arnold Brunner Prize 1960; Graham Found. Fellowship 1961; Philadelphia Art Alliance Medal 1962; Franklin Inst., Frank P. Brown Medal 1964; NIAL 1964; Danish Architects Assn., Medal of Honor 1965; Philadelphia Sketch Club, Annual Award 1966; AAAS 1968; Univ. of Connecticut, Intl. Silver Medal 1969; AIA, Philadelphia Chap., Centennial Gold Medal 1969; AIA, New York Chap., Gold Medal of Honor; AIA Gold Medal 1971; Philadelphia Book Award 1971; Brandeis Univ., Creative Arts Medal 1972; Royal Inst. of British Architects, Royal Gold Medal 1972; AAAL 1973; NIAL Gold Medal 1973; plus numerous Hon. Degrees. **Publications:** with Oscar Stonorov, *Why City Planning is Your Responsibility* (New York, 1942); *The Travel Sketches of Louis I. Kahn: An Exhibition*, intro. by Vincent J. Scully (Philadelphia: PAFA, 1978); plus numerous articles. **Important Works:** with Paul Cret, Folger Library, Washington, DC 1929-32; with George Howe, Pine Ford Housing, Middletown PA 1941-42; with Howe & Oscar Stonorov, Carver Court Housing, Coatesville, PA 1941-43; with Howe & Stonorov, Pennypack Housing, Philadelphia 1942; with Howe & Stonorov, Lincoln Rd. Housing, Coatesville, PA 1943; with Howe & Stonorov, Lily Ponds Housing, Washington, DC 1943; Yale Univ. Art Gallery 1951-53; Salk Inst., Laboratory Buildings, La Jolla, CA 1959-65; with Preston M. Gerne & Asscs., Kimbell Art Museum 1966-72; Phillips Exeter Acad., Library & Dining Hall 1967-72; Family Planning Center, Katmandu, Nepal 1970-74; Yale Center for British Art & Studies 1969-74; Collections: Univ. of Pennsylvania, MOMA. **Exhibitions/Performances:** PAFA 1930, 1933, 1969; MOMA 1936, 1939, 1966, 1992; La Jolla Museum of Art 1965; Swiss Federal Inst. of Technology, Zurich 1969. **Bio-Bibliography:** Vincent J. Scully, *Louis I. Kahn* (New York: Braziller, 1962); Romaldo Giurgola & Jaimini Mehta, *Louis I. Kahn* (Boulder: Westview, 1975); August E. Komendant, *Eighteen Years with Architect Louis I. Kahn* (Englewood, NJ: Aloras, 1975); Ronnie Heinz, Sharad Jhaveri & Alessandro Vasella, *Louis I. Kahn: Complete Works 1935-74* (Boulder: Westview, 1977); Joan Lobell, *Between Silence and Light: Spirit in the Architecture of Louis I. Kahn* (Boulder: Shambala, 1979); Alexandra Tyng, *Beginnings: Louis I. Kahn's Philosophy of Architecture* (New York: John Wiley, 1984); A.

Latour, ed., *Louis I. Kahn, l'uomo, il maestro* (Rome: Kappa, 1986); P.C. Lord, *The Art Museums of Louis I. Kahn* (Durham, NC: Duke Univ. Press, 1989); "The Posthumous Adventures of Louis Kahn," *NY Times* (Feb. 25, 1990); "Wanted: A Little Less Respect," *NY Times* (June 23, 1991); "Louis Kahn," *Metropolis* (Dec. 1991); "Kahn-Temporary," *Travel & Leisure* (Sept. 1991); *The New Yorker* (July 27, 1992); "A Master of Masses, Last in a Long Line," *NY Times* (June 19, 1992); *Contemporary Architects; Who Was Who in America.*

KAHN, ROBERT ■ FAAR Architecture 82. BA 77, Washington Univ.; MArch 80, Yale Univ. **Career & Employment:** James Stirling, Michael Wilford & Asscs., London, Senior Designer 1982-84; Yale Univ., Graduate School of Architecture, Critic of Advanced Design Studio 1983, 1994, 1995; Columbia Univ., Graduate School of Architecture, Adj. Asst. Prof. 1985, 1986; Robert Kahn, Architects, NYC, Prin. 1986-present; Ohio State Univ., School of Architecture, Adj. Prof., Studio Critic 1986, 1988. **Fellowships, Honors & Awards:** Yale Univ., Glassman Prize for Design Excellence 1979, Alumni Award 1980; Council for the US & Italy, Young Leaders Conference, Milan, Participant 1980. **Important Works:** Cornell Univ., Performing Arts Center 1983; Nussbaum Residence, St. Louis 1987; Kahn Residence, St. Louis 1988; Stella Squash Ct., Amenia, NY 1989; Kline-Cates Residence, Cold Springs, NY 1989; Columbia Univ., John Jay & Carman Halls, Faculty Apartments 1989; De La Chaume Residence, NYC 1989; Lincoln Center, NYC, Office Renovation 1991, Vivian Beaumont Theater, Orchestra Pit 1992; Jacobs Residence, Apartment Renovation NYC 1992; with Frank Stella, Private Museum, The Negev, Israel 1993; Stella Residence, House Addition, Ipswich, MA 1993; Mamet Residence, Newtown, MA 1995. **Business Address:** Robert Kahn, Architects, 611 Broadway, Suite 201, NYC 10012.

KAISER, WALTER ■ AAR Visitor 1989-90; Villa I Tatti., Dir.

KAISH, LUISE ■ FAAR Sculpture 72; AAR Trustee 1973-80, Trustee Emer. b. Sept. 8, 1925, Atlanta, GA. m. Morton Kaish. c. Melissa. BFA 46, Syracuse Univ.; MFA 51, Syracuse Univ. **Other Study:** Escuela de Pintura y Escultura, Taller Grafico, Escuela de las Artes Libro, Mexico, painting with Jesus Guerrero Galvan & Alfedo Zalce & art history with Diego Rivera 1946-47; sculpture with Ivan Mestrovic, Syracuse 1951; bronze casting, Istituto Statale d'Arte 1951-52. **Research/Artistic Interests:** Brancacci Chapel, Florence; the interface of Masaccio's art with that of Brunelleschi & Donatello. **Career & Employment:** Dartmouth College, Artist-in-Residence 1974; Univ. of Washington, Seattle, Visiting Artist 1979; Columbia Univ., Prof. 1980-92, Prof. Emer 1993; Chair, Division of Painting & Sculpture 1980-86; Com. on Arts Properties 1982-88; Presidential Comm. on the Future of the University 1985-87; Univ. of Haifa, Artist-in-Residence 1985. **Memberships & Offices:** Carl Fischer Musical Instrument Co., BoD 1961-70; Sculptors Guild, VP, Chair of Membership Com., Exec. Bd. 1974-82; NYC Fine Arts Comm., Nominating Com. 1976-79; Augustus Saint-Gaudens Memorial, Nat. Park Service, BoT 1978-90, Fellowship Com., Chair 1980-90, Exec. Com. 1980-90; Syracuse Univ., College of Visual & Performing Arts, Bd. of Visitors 1980-84. **Fellowships, Honors & Awards:** Everson Museum, 1st Prize 1947; Rochester Memorial Art Gallery, Jurors Show Award 1951, H.H. Sullivan Award 1951; Louis Comfort Tiffany Grant 1951; NAWA, Bertha K. Barstow Award 1954; Emily Lowe Award 1957; Guggenheim Fellowship 1959; Church World Service, San Francisco, Nat. Exb. of Painting, Graphics & Sculpture, Award 1960; S. Shore Purchase & Louis Bergman

Awards; Soc. of Typographic Arts, Certificate of Excellence 1962; Audubon Artists, Gold Medal 1963; Augustus Saint-Gaudens Fellowship 1970; Westchester Fine Arts Council, Special Citation 1974; Honor Awards: GRA, AIA, Nat. Interfaith Conference on Religion & Architecture 1975; MacDowell Fellow 1975; Syracuse Univ., Arents Pioneer Medal 1989; Winsor & Newton Certificate of Achievement 1993. **Important Works:** Collections: Smithsonian Inst., Nat. Museum of American Art, Washington, DC; MMA; Whitney Museum, NYC; Jewish Museum, NYC; Minnesota Museum of Art, St Paul; Rochester Memorial Art Gallery; Export Khleb, Moscow; Container Corp. of America, Chicago; Continental Grain Co., NYC; General Mills Corp., Minneapolis; Lowe Museum, Coral Gables, FL; Syracuse Univ.; Central Synagogue, Milan; Vera & Albert A. List Collection, Hebrew Union College, Jerusalem; Atlantic Richfield, Los Angeles; Selected Commissions: Temple B'rith Kodesh, Rochester, NY 1961-64; AMOCO, NY; Temple Israel, Westport, CT 1965; Holy Trinity Mission Seminary, Silver Springs, MD 1965-66; Temple Beth Shalom, Wilmington, DE 1968; Beth-El Synagogue Center, New Rochelle, NY 1972-73; Temple B'nai Abraham, Essex County, NJ 1973; Jewish Museum, NYC 1974; Hebrew Union College, Jerusalem 1975; Continental Grain Co., NYC 1976. **Exhibitions/Performances:** Solo: Rochester Memorial Art Gallery 1954; Sculpture Center, NYC 1955, 1958; Staempfli Gallery, NYC 1968, 1981, 1984, 1988; Minnesota Museum of Art, St. Paul 1969; Jewish Museum, NYC 1973; Hopkins Center, Dartmouth College 1974; Univ. of Haifa, Israel 1985; Fine Arts Center, Fulbright College of Art, Univ. of Arkansas 1990. **Bio-Bibliography:** *Community Leaders; Noteworthy Americans: Bicentennial Memorial Edition; Who's Who in America; Who's Who in American Art; Who's Who in Education; Who's Who in International Art; Who's Who in the World; Who's Who of American Women; World's Who's Who of Women.* **Business Address:** 610 West End Ave., Apt. 9A, NYC 10024.

KALLMANN, GERHARD M. ■ RAAR Architecture 84. b. 1915, Berlin, Germany. Grad. 41, Architectural Assn., School of Architecture, London. **Career & Employment:** Inst. of Design, Illinois Inst. of Technology, Asst. Prof. 1948-51; Columbia Univ., Assc. Prof. 1958-62; MIT, Bemis Prof. 1963-64, 1981; Yale Univ., William Henry Bishop Visiting Prof. 1976, 1982; Harvard GSD, Prof. 1967-80, Prof. Emer. 1980-present; Kallmann McKinnell & Wood, Architects, Inc., Prin.; Visiting Critic & Lect.: Cornell Univ.; Washington Univ.; Univ. of Florida; Univ. of Tennessee; UNC; RISD; Univ. of Toronto; McGill Univ.; Dartmouth College; Architectural Assn., London; E.T.H., Zurich; Smithsonian Inst. **Memberships & Offices:** *Architectural Review*, London, Asst. Ed. & Contr.; AIA Honors & Awards Programs in Minnesota, Ohio & North Carolina, Chair; Boston Soc. of Architects, Harleston Parker Award Com.; Nat. Massey Price Jury, Ottawa, Canada; US Delegate, Ditchley Found. Conference on Artistic & Design Standards in Public Buildings, Oxford, England 1979; AAAL, Fellow 1986; AIA, Fellow; Royal Inst. of British Architects, Assc.; AAAS, Fellow. **Fellowships, Honors & Awards:** AIA Honor Awards 1969, 1981, 1990, 1993, 1994, Firm Award 1984; City of Boston, Harleston Parker Awards (5); Louis Sullivan Award 1987. **Publications:** Mr. Kallmann has published a number of theoretical articles in the national & international professional press & has lectured extensively in the US & abroad. **Important Works:** Boston Five Cents Bank 1967; Boston City Hall 1969; AAAS 1981; Becton Dickinson Corp. HQ 1986, Divisional HQ 1993; Asian Export Wing, Peabody Museum, Salem, MA 1988; US Embassy, Bangladesh 1988; Hynes Auditorium & Convention Center 1989; Harvard Univ., Shad Hall 1989, Holmes Field Bldg.

1994; Newton Free Library 1991; Yale Univ., Bass Center for Molecular Biophysics & Biochemistry 1993; US Chancery, Bangkok 1995. **Home Address:** 5 Concord Ave., Cambridge, MA 02138.

KAMMERER, HERBERT L. ■ FAAR Sculpture 51. b. July 11, 1915, NYC. d. May 9, 1985. m. Margaret. c. Mary Susan, Cornelia Ann, Seth Lewis. BFA 41, Yale Univ. School of the Fine Arts. **Other Studies:** NAD 1934-37; Apprentice Sculptor to Charles Keck & C.P. Jennewein 1933-37. **Career & Employment:** Paul Manship, Asst. 1945-48; Hackley School, Faculty; Westchester County Center, Faculty; Parsons School of Design, Faculty; SUNY, New Paltz, Prof. 1962-85. **Memberships & Offices:** Sculpture juries, including the Yonkers Art Assn. **Fellowships, Honors & Awards:** George D. Widener Memorial Medal; PAFA Annual 1948; Fulbright Fellowship.

KANT, LAURENCE H. ■ FAAR Classics/Archaeology 87. b. Jan. 15, 1956, Brookline, MA. m. Dianne M. Bazell. BA 78, Tufts Univ.; MTS 81, Harvard Divinity School; MA 83, Yale Univ.; PhD 93, Yale Univ. **Other Study:** ICCS 1977; Harvard Univ., Rabbinics 1983-84. **Research/Artistic Interests:** Religions of the Greco-Roman World: Christian, Jewish & pagan. **Career & Employment:** Cornell Univ., Lect. 1991-92, Asst. Prof. 1992-present. **Memberships & Offices:** American Acad. of Religion, AHA, APA, North American Patristic Soc., Soc. of Ancient Historians, Soc. of Biblical Literature. **Fellowships, Honors & Awards:** Pfeiffer Fellowship in Biblical Archaeology 1980; Yale Univ. Fellowship 1981-83, Leo & Elsa Guttman Links Fund 1983-85; Nat. Found. for Jewish Culture, Doctoral Dissertation Fellowship 1987-88; Fondazione Lemmermann, Borsa di studio 1987-88; Memorial Found. for Jewish Culture, Doctoral Scholarship 1987-89; Deutscher Akademischer Austauschdienst Fellowship 1988; Josephine de Karman Fellowship 1988-89; NEH Summer Stipend 1994. **Publications:** "Jewish Inscriptions in Greek and Latin," in *Aufstieg und Niedergang der römischen Welt II* 20.2 (1987): 671-713. **Home Address:** 900-20 Ivy Ridge Rd., Syracuse, NY 13210. **Business Address:** Dept. of Near Eastern Studies, 360 Rockefeller Hall, Cornell Univ., Ithaca, NY 14853.

KASS, SPENCE R. ■ FAAR Architecture 81. b. Dec. 20, 1955, Philadelphia, PA. m. Laura Martin. BA 77, RISD; BArch 78, RISD; MArch 85, Cornell Univ., Urban Design Program. **Other Study:** Pratt Inst., Brooklyn, Continuing Education Program-Alvar Aalto in Finland 1981. **Research/Artistic Interests:** Architecture, urban design, interior architecture-design. **Career & Employment:** Moore Grover Harper, Intern 1978-79; Cope Linder Asscs., Project Designer 1979-82; Kenneth Parker Asscs., Project Architect 1982-87; Cornell Univ., Asst. Lect. 1984, Studio Critic, Freshman Architecture Program 1983-84; Shapiro Petrauskas Gelber, Assc. 1987-89; Hillier Group, Project Architect 1989-90; Kass & Asscs., Prin. 1990-present; Spring Garden College, Philadelphia, Adj. Prof. 1990-92; Philadelphia College of Textile & Science, Asst. Prof. 1991-present; IEI Architects, Pres. 1994-present. **Memberships & Offices:** Philadelphia RISD Alumni Club 1986-present, VP 1989-90, Pres. 1992-present; AIA 1985-91, Philadelphia Chap., Urban Design Com. 1985-91; Pennsylvania Soc. of Architects 1985-91. **Fellowships, Honors & Awards:** NIAE, Lloyd Warren Fellowship 1980; 67th Paris Prize, 3d Prize, Arbeit Memorial Prize 1980; Washington Univ., Steedman Fellowship 1980; Cornell Univ., Sage Graduate Fellowship 1982-83, TA 1983-84, Sage Graduate Summer Fellowship 1984; Found. for Architecture, Philadelphia, City Visions Design Competition, Honorable Mention 1986. **Publications:** "Provident Mutual Returns to Center City," *Corporate*

Design & Realty (Jan. 1986); "The Voluminous Wall," *Cornell Journal of Architecture* 3 (Fall 1987): 44-55; "ARA Services Runs its Towers Like the Olympic Games," *Facilities Design & Management* (Sept. 1988): 32-39; "The Best New Restaurants of 1988," *Esquire* (Nov. 1988): 190-214. **Important Works:** with Kenneth Parker Asscs., Provident Mutual HQ, Philadelphia 1984; with Kenneth Parker Asscs., ARA Services HQ, Philadelphia 1986; with Kenneth Parker Asscs., ARCO Exec. Office Bldg., Newtown Square, PA 1988; with Shapiro Petrauskas Gelber, Meiji-En Japanese Restaurant, Philadelphia 1988; Buerger Residence, Wyndmoor, PA 1989; Dion Residence, Wynnewood, PA 1991; Ernst & Young, Philadelphia as Design Consultant for InterArch 1992; Dr. Shulman Office, Philadelphia 1992; Lewis-Semingson Residence, Philadelphia 1993; Weiss Residence, Merion, PA 1994; Burns Residence, Bryn Mawr, PA 1995; Sidewater Residence, Philadelphia 1995. **Exhibitions/Performances:** City Visions, Philadelphia 1986; Spring Garden College, Philadelphia 1990; Philadelphia College of Textile & Science, Faculty Show 1991. **Home Address:** 915 N. 20th St., Philadelphia, PA 19130. **Business Address:** Kass & Asscs., 915 N. 20th St., Philadelphia, PA 19130.

KATZ, ALEX ■ RAAR Painting 84. b. July 24, 1927, NYC. m. Ada Katz. c. Vincent. Cooper Union 1946-49; Skowhegan School for Painting & Sculpture 1949-50. **Career & Employment:** Brooklyn Museum, Art Instr. 1961-62; Yale Univ., Visiting Critic 1963-65; Pratt Inst. & School of Visual Arts, for brief appointments in the 1960s. **Fellowships, Honors & Awards:** New England Art Award 1971; Guggenheim Fellowship 1972; US-USSR Cultural Exchange Grant, US State Dept. 1972; Cooper Union Achievement Citation 1974, Alumni Award 1980, Augustus Saint-Gaudens Award 1980; Skowhegan School, Medal for Achievement in Painting 1980; Colby College, Hon. DFA 1984; Art in Public Places, Chicago Bar Assn. 1985; AAAL 1988. **Publications:** with John Ashbery, *Fragment* (Los Angeles: Black Sparrow, 1966); with Kenneth Koch, *Interlocking Lives* (New York: Kulchur Press, 1970); with Carter Ratcliff, *Give Me Tomorrow* (New York: Vehicle Editions, 1985). **Important Works:** In more than 65 public collections, including: MFA; AIC; Detroit Inst. of Art; Ft. Worth Art Museum; Los Angeles County Art Museum; MMA; MOMA; Whitney Museum, NYC; Philadelphia Museum of Art; Hirshhorn Museum, Washington, DC; Art Gallery of Ontario, Toronto; Staatliche Museen Preussichen Kulturbesitz Nationalgalerie, Berlin; Bayerische Stattsbibliothek, Munich; Tate Gallery, London; Hiroshima City Museum; Israel Museum, Jerusalem. **Exhibitions/Performances:** Selected Solo: Retrospective, Whitney Museum, NYC 1986; Marlborough Gallery, NYC 1986, 1988, 1991; Robert Miller Gallery, NYC 1987; Galerie Inge Baecker, Cologne 1987; Brooklyn Museum 1988; Galerie Daniel Templon, Paris 1988; Seibu Museum of Art, Tokyo 1988; Cleveland Museum of Art 1988; Galerie Bernd Klüser, Munich 1989; Galerie Emilo Mazzoli, Modena 1989; Fandon Galeria de Arte Moderno, Valencia, Spain 1990; Ascan Crone, Hamburg, Germany 1990; Orlando Museum of Art 1990; North Carolina Museum of Art, Raleigh 1990; Inst. of Contemporary Arts, London 1990; Marlborough Fine Art, Tokyo 1990; Museum of Art, Munson-Proctor Inst., Utica, NY 1991; Contemporary Museum of Honolulu 1991. **Bio-Bibliography:** Irving Sandler & William Berkson, eds., *Alex Katz* (New York: Praeger, 1971); Irving Sandler, *Alex Katz* (New York: Harry N. Abrams, 1979); Nicholas P. Maravell, *Alex Katz: The Complete Prints* (New York: Alpine Fine Arts, 1983); Richard Marshall, *Alex Katz* (New York: Whitney Museum & Rizzoli, 1986); Ann Beattie, *Alex Katz* (New York: Harry N. Abrams, 1987); Donald Kuspit, *Alex Katz* (New York: Harry N. Abrams, 1991). **Home Address:** 435 W. Broadway, NYC 10012.

KATZ, ROBERT ■ AAR Visitor 1965-66, Writer.

KAUFFMAN, MARY-BARBARA ■ AAR World War II Scholar 1943.

KAVELMAN, BUFF SUZANNE ■ AAR – New York, Dir. of Programs.

KAY, ULYSSES ■ FAAR Musical Composition 52. b. Jan. 7, 1917, Tucson, AZ. d. May 20, 1995. m. Barbara J. Kay. c. Virginia, Melinda, Hillary. BMus 38, Univ. of Arizona; MusM 40, Eastman School of Music. **Other Study:** Yale Univ. 1941-42, Tanglewood 1942, Columbia Univ. 1946-49. **Career & Employment:** US Navy, Musician 1942-46; Freelance Composer for film & TV 1948-64; BMI, Ed. Adv. 1953-68; Boston Univ., Visiting Prof. 1965; UCLA, Visiting Prof. 1966-67; Herbert H. Lehman College, CUNY, Prof. 1968-78, Distinguished Prof. 1972-95. **Memberships & Offices:** US Dept. of State, US Composers to USSR, Cultural Exchange Program 1958; Guest Conductor: Little Symphony, Tucson Symphony, Philadelphia Orchestra 1979; Corp of Yaddo; American Fed. of Musicians; League of Composers; NIAL; Phi Mu Alpha Sinfonia. **Fellowships, Honors & Awards:** Commendations from: Louisville Symphony Orchestra, Koussevitzky Music Found., DePaur Inf. Chorus, Quincy, IL Fine Arts Soc.; ABC Prize 1946; Alice M. Ditson Fellowship 1946; 3d Annual Gershwin Contest Award 1947; Julius Rosenwald Fellowship 1948; Fulbright Fellowship, Italy 1950-51; Guggenheim Fellowship 1964-65. **Important Works:** Operas: *The Boor* 1955; *The Juggler of Our Lady* 1956; *The Capitoline Venus* 1970; *Jubilee* 1974-76; *Frederick Douglass* 1980-85; *Danse Calinda,* a ballet; *Concerto for Orchestra; Three Pieces after Blake,* for soprano & orchestra; *Serenade for Orchestra; Triumvirate,* for male chorus; *Cantata; Song of Jeremiah; Inscriptions from Whitman.* **Bio-Bibliography:** *NY Times,* Obit. (May 24, 1995); *Who's Who in America.*

KAZIN, ALFRED ■ RAAR Literature 75. Critic, literary historian. **Publications:** "A Walker in the City-Again," *New York* (Jan. 19, 1987).

KEARNS, JERRY B. ■ FAAR Sculpture 70. b. Feb. 27, 1943, Petersburg, VA. BFA 66, UC, Santa Barbara; MFA 68, UC, Santa

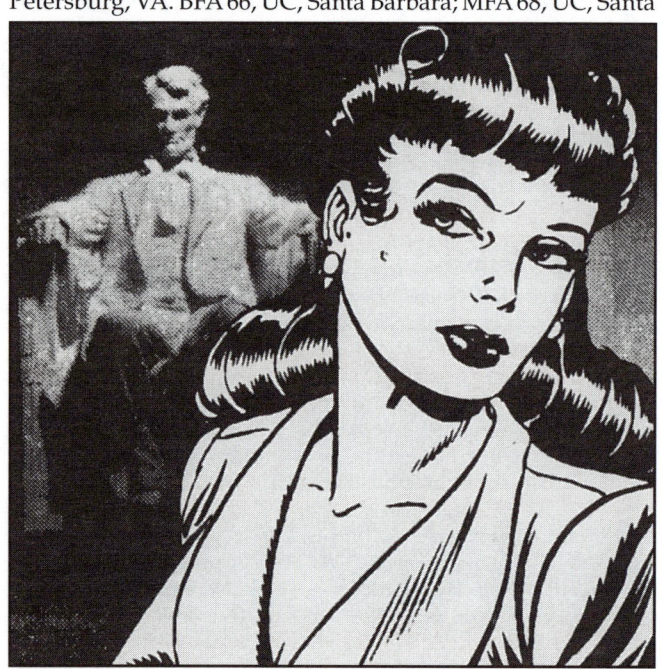

Jerry B. Kearns

Barbara. **Career & Employment:** UCLA, Lect. 1970-71; Univ. of Massachusetts, Amherst, Prof. 1971-present. **Memberships & Offices:** Exit Art, BoD 1987-present. **Fellowships, Honors & Awards:** NEA Grant 1974; NYSCA Grant 1987; Massachusetts Council for the Arts Comm. 1988, 1990; Public Art Fund Comm. 1988. **Exhibitions/Performances:** Selected Solo: Perimeter Gallery, Chicago 1986; Modernism Gallery, San Francisco 1986, 1994; Atrium Gallery, Univ. of Connecticut, Storrs 1987; Zone Art Gallery, Springfield, MA 1988; Meyers-Bloom Gallery, Los Angeles 1988, 1991; Kent Fine Art, NYC 1987, 1988, 1993; Galeria Temple, Valencia, Spain 1989; Galerie Fahnemann, Berlin 1991; Traveling Exb. 1991: Lehman College Art Gallery, NYC; Univ. Art Museum, UC, Santa Barbara; Univ. of Massachusetts, Amherst; City Gallery of Contemporary Art, Raleigh, NC; Tyler Galleries, Temple Univ., Philadelphia 1991; Benjamin Mangel Gallery, Philadelphia 1993; Jose Freire Fine Art, NYC 1993, 1994. **Home Address:** 183 E. Broadway, NYC 10002.

KECK, CHARLES ■ FAAR Sculpture 1904. b. Sept. 9, 1875, NYC. d. Apr. 23, 1951. m. J. Anne Collyer. c. James Collyer, John William, Charles Jr. **Other Studies:** NAD; ASL; with Augustus Saint-Gaudens. **Research/Artistic Interests:** Relief sculpture, medals. **Career & Employment:** Independent Sculptor 1905-50. **Memberships & Offices:** NAD 1928; ALNY 1929; NSA; American Federation of Arts; NSS, Pres. 1931-33; Nat. Arts Club. **Fellowships, Honors & Awards:** ALNY, Annual Gold Medal for Sculpture 1926. **Important Works:** Brookgreen Garden, SC; Hall of Fame NYU; Hall of Fame, Richmond, VA; Washington Mounument, Palermo Park, Buenos Aires 1913; Lewis & Clark Memorial, Charlottesville, VA 1921; Stonewall Jackson, Charlottesville, VA 1921; War Memorial, Brooklyn, NY 1922; War Memorial, Irvington, NJ 1922; Booker T. Washington, Tuskegee, AL 1922; Liberty Monument, Ticonderoga, NY 1925; Andrew Jackson, Kansas City, MO 1934; Francis D. Duffy, NYC 1937; St. Isaac Jogues, Lake George, NY 1937; Huey Long, Baton Rouge, LA 1940 & Washington, DC 1941; Harry S. Truman, US Senate 1947; Alfred E. Smith, NYC 1950; Triumph of Good Government, Bronx County Bldg., NYC. **Exhibitions/Performances:** NAD; Nat. Arts Comm.; ALNY; Century Association; State of New York 1940. **Bio-Bibliography:** *NY Times,* Obit. (Apr. 24, 1951); *National Cyclopedia of American Biography; Who Was Who in America; Who Was Who in American Art.*

KEECH, PAMELA ■ FAAR Sculpture 82; SOF, Council Mem. 1994-present, *Newsletter* Co-Ed. 1995-present. b. Sept. 21, 1947, Elyria, OH. BFA 78, Ohio State Univ.; MFA 80, Ohio State Univ. **Research/Artistic Interests:** Site-specific narrative installations with actual and/or fictional historic themes. **Career & Employment:** Univ. of Akron, Asst. Prof. 1989-90; Lower Eastside Tenement Museum, NYC, Artist-in-Residence 1993-present. **Memberships & Offices:** United Scenic Artists Local 829. **Fellowships, Honors & Awards:** NEA Fellowship 1982; Marie Walsh Sharpe Art Found., Space Program 1991. **Publications:** *Lust at Fox Gorge* (Columbus, OH: Cottier & Peirce, 1980); *The Conjuror and the Contortionist* (San Diego: Sushi, 1991). **Important Works:** *I Dreamed I Found Edmonia Lewis' Grave,* Installation, Spaces, Cleveland 1983; *Monstrance (Morning),* Installation, Ohio State Univ. Galleries, Newark, OH 1986; *Monstrance (Night),* Installation, C.A.G.E. (Cincinnati) 1986; *Trail of Lost Thoughts,* Installation, Art Museum of South Texas, Corpus Christi 1987; *The Conjuror and the Contortionist,* Installation, Sushi Visual Arts, San Diego 1991; *The Pursuance of Erotic Fate,* Installation, 1708 E. Main Gallery, Richmond, VA 1992; *Lust &*

Etiquette, Installation, Broadway Windows, NYC 1992; John Michael Kohler Art Center, Sheboygan, WI 1993; Lower Eastside Tenement Museum, NYC 1994; Antioch College, Yellow Springs, OH 1995. **Bio-Bibliography:** John R. Clarke, "Pamela Keech: Neglect, Infidelity and Poisoning," *Arts Magazine* (Oct. 1982): 76-77; Geraldine Wojno-Kiefer, "Pamela Keech," *New Age Examiner* (June 1983): 21; Leah Ollman, "Installation Conjures Up an Intrigue," *Los Angeles Times* (Dec. 4, 1991): F1, F4; "Powerful Secrets: An Interview with Pamela Keech," *Parabola* (Fall 1994): 34-42. **Home Address:** 35 W. 82 St., Apt. 9B, NYC 10024. **Business Address:** 451 Greenwich St., NYC. 10013

KEEFE, DANIEL T. ■ AAR – New York, Assc. Dir. of Development.

KEELEY, EDMUND L. ■ FAAR Literature 60; SOF, Exec. Com. 1973-75; Council Mem. 1984-87. b. Feb. 5, 1928, Damascus, Syria. m. Mary Stathatos-Kyris. BA 49, Princeton Univ.; DPhil. 52, Oxford Univ. **Research/Artistic Interests:** Creative writing in fiction & translation; historical writing (non-fiction). **Career & Employment:** American Farm School, Thessaloniki, Greece, Teacher 1949-50; Brown Univ., Instr. 1952-53; Univ. of Thessaloniki, Fulbright Lect. 1953-54, 1986; Princeton Univ.: Faculty 1954-present, Program in Comparative Literature, Co-Chair 1964-65; Creative Arts Program, Dir. 1965-71, McCarter Theatre Com. Chair 1969, Program in Creative Writing & Theater, Dir. 1971-74, Creative Writing Program, Dir. 1974-81, Charless Barnwell Straut Prof. of English 1992-94, Prof. Emer. 1994, Program in Hellenic Studies, Dir. 1985-94; Oxford Univ., Visiting Lect. 1960; Univ. of Iowa, Writers Workshop, Visiting Lect. 1962-63; Knox College, Writer-in-Residence 1963; New School for Social Research, Visiting Prof. 1980; Columbia Univ., School of the Arts, Visiting Prof. 1981; Univ. of Athens, Fulbright Lect. 1985; Univ. of the Aegean, Lect. 1988. **Memberships & Offices:** Modern Greek Studies Assn., Exec. Com., Chair 1968-69, Pres. 1970-73, 1980-82; *Byzantine & Modern Greek Studies,* Ed. Bd. 1974-82; Nat. Book Awards, Translation Jury 1976-77; Columbia Univ. Translation Center, BoD 1977-94; Poetry Soc.

> The best prose that I can offer as a tribute to the American Academy in Rome, in gratitude for what it gave me, is the first page of the novel I wrote while a Fellow in Writing during 1959-60. The novel was published as The Gold-Hatted Lover by Little, Brown in 1961.
>
> IT WAS A STRANGE SUMMER from the very start. In June it rained too much, as though it were March, so that the dirt roads in the north suddenly became impassable at the moment one wanted to move to the mountains for a weekend or head for a deserted beach on the far side of the peninsula. Early June was too hot, more like mid-August, so that any retreat proved vulnerable to the white sun and the maddening flies. And the air was always nervous, full of unexpected motion and the droning of restless cicadas. Then in the middle of the month there was a sudden spell of cool winds, cool enough to drive people inside at night and empty the open-air tavernas for a week. My Greek friends blamed the erratic weather on hydrogen bomb tests and secret experiments in the Antarctic, but I preferred to blame it on the gods. It looked to me as though they had chosen that particular summer to be capricious, to invert the normal order of things and then to withdraw from active engagement in human affairs so that they might see what would become of their mortal charges if chaos were permitted to rule for a time in place of the usual system — an experiment, ultimately, in arrogance. If this was so, I imagine even the gods were a bit disturbed (the ones who weren't simply amused) by the way a few of their mortal charges chose to behave under the circumstances.
>
> *Edmund Keeley*

Edmund L. Keeley

of America, VP 1977-79, 1981-83, Wesleyan Univ. Press Translation Award, Judge 1984; American Farm School, Thessaloniki, Greece, BoT 1978-present; *Translation Review,* Ed. Bd. 1978-present; PEN American Center, Exec. Bd. 1980-present; Intl. PEN Congress Delegate: Lugano 1987, Paris 1991, Vienna 1991, Barcelona 1992, Rio de Janeiro 1992, Santiago de Compostela 1993, VP 1989-91, Pres. 1991-93; *Journal of Modern Greek Studies,* Ed. Bd. 1983-91; American Literary Translators Assn., Exec. Council 1983-present; *Delos,* Adv. Ed. 1987-present; Aegean Univ. Intl. Program, BoD 1989-90; Acad. of American Poets, Landon Translation Award, Judge 1992. **Fellowships, Honors & Awards:** Oxford Univ., Woodrow Wilson Fellow 1950-51; Princeton Univ., Council of Humanities Fellow 1956-57, McCosh Faculty Fellow 1969-70; Guggenheim Fellow 1959-60, 1973; Columbia Univ. Translation Center-PEN Translation Award 1975; Ingram Merrill Found. Grant 1977-78; NEH Grant 1977-78, 1982; Acad. of American Poets, Harold Morton Landon Translation Award 1980; NEA Creative Writing Fellowship 1981-82, Arts Fellowship in Translation 1988; Rockefeller Found., Bellagio Residency 1982, 1989; Howard T. Behrman Award 1982; NEA-PEN Fiction Syndicate Award 1983; Pushcart Prize IX 1984-85; Fulbright Research Fellow, Athens 1987; Premier Prix Européen de Traduction de la Poésie 1987; AAAS, Fellow 1992-present. **Publications:** *The Libation* (New York: Scribner's, 1958); *The Gold-Hatted Lover* (Boston: Little, Brown, 1961); trans., with Philip Sherrard, *George Seferis: Collected Poems* (Princeton: Princeton Univ. Press, 1969); *The Impostor* (New York: Doubleday, 1970); *Voyage to a Dark Island* (Curtis Books, 1972); trans., with Philip Sherrard & George Savidis, *C.P. Cavafy: Collected Poems* (Princeton: Princeton Univ. Press, 1975); *Cavafy's Alexandria: Study of a Myth in Progress* (Cambridge, MA: Harvard Univ. Press, 1976); *Modern Greek Poetry: Voice and Myth* (Princeton: Princeton Univ. Press, 1983); *A Wilderness Called Peace* (New York: Simon & Schuster, 1985); *The Salonika Bay Murder: Cold War Politics and the Polk Affair* (Princeton: Princeton Univ. Press, 1989); trans., *Yannis Ritsos: Repetitions, Testimonies, Parentheses* (Princeton: Princeton Univ. Press, 1991); *School for Pagan Lovers* (New Brunswick, NJ: Rutgers Univ. Press, 1993). **Bio-Bibliography:** *Who's Who in America, Who's Who in the East.* **Home Address:** 140 Littlebrook Rd., Princeton, NJ 08540. **Business Address:** George Borchardt, 136 E. 57th St., NYC 10022.

KELLEHER, PATRICK JOSEPH ■ FAAR History of Art 49. b. July 26, 1917, Colorado Springs, CO. d. June 16, 1985. m. Marion Mackie. c. Maria. BA 39, Colorado College; MFA 42, Princeton Univ.; PhD 47, Princeton Univ. **Research/Artistic Interests:** Early Christian art, Ambrogio Lorenzetti, the Holy Crown of Hungary, museum curatorship. **Career & Employment:** US Army Office of Military Government for Germany, Greater Hesse Div., Monuments, Fine Arts & Archives, Head WWII; Los Angeles County Museum of Art, Chief Curator 1949; Univ. of Buffalo, Lect. 1950-51; Albright-Knox Art Gallery, Buffalo, Chief Curator 1950-54; Nelson-Atkins Museum of Art, Curator 1954-59; Princeton Univ., Prof. 1960-73, Dir. of Art Museum 1960-72. **Publications:** *The Holy Crown of Hungary,* AAR Papers & Monographs 13 (Rome: AAR, 1951); "Life and Death of Alexander Attributed to Carpaccio or His Immediate Circle," *Buffalo Gallery Notes* 16 (1952): 2-4, 7-10; "Gratiot Portraits by Thomas Sully," *Princeton Museum Record* 20 (1961): 49-56; *Living with Modern Sculpture: The John B. Putnam, Jr. Memorial Collection* (Princeton: Princeton Univ. Press, 1982). **Bio-Bibliography:** *Who Was Who in America.*

KELLER, DEANE ■ FAAR Painting 29. b. Dec. 14, 1901, New Haven, CT. d. Apr. 12, 1992. m. Katherine Parkhurst Hall. c.

Deane G., William B. BA 23, Yale Univ.; BFA 26, Yale School of Fine Arts. **Other Study:** Painting with Edwin C. Taylor, Eugene F. Savage & George Bridgman. **Research/Artistic Interests:** Portrait painting. **Career & Employment:** Yale Univ., School of Fine Arts 1930-70; US Fifth Army Fine Arts Officer, AMG 1943-46. **Memberships & Offices:** Connecticut Acad. of Fine Arts, Hon. Mem. 1972; Legion of Merit, Knight of the Order of the Crown, Italy; Mem. of the British Empire; Order of St. John Lateran. **Important Works:** Partial list of commissions: Two Murals, Shriver Hall, Johns Hopkins Univ.; *Dr. Harvey Cushing*, Salvador Hospital, Santiago, Chile; *Senator Robert A. Taft*, US Senate Reception Chamber, The Capitol, Washington, DC; *Postmaster General W. Marvin Watson*, US Post Office HQ, Washington, DC; *Chief Justice Raymond E. Baldwin*, Supreme Court Bldg., Hartford, CT; plus 78 paintings at Yale Univ. & 700 portrait commissions. **Bio-Bibliography:** *American Paintings at Yale University* (New Haven: Yale); Obituaries (Apr. 1992): *NYTimes, New Haven Register, Hartford Courant.*

KELLOGG, GEORGE DWIGHT ■ FASCSR 1900. b. June 28, 1873, St. Louis, MO. d. Sept. 19, 1955. m. Anna Mary Collins. c. Helen Stewart, George Dwight. BA 1895, Yale Univ.; PhD 1898, Yale Univ. **Other Studies:** In Germany 1899, 1913. **Career & Employment:** Yale Univ., Instr. 1896-99, Tutor 1900-1903; Williams College, Asst. Prof. 1903-5; Princeton Univ., Preceptor & Asst. Prof. 1905-11; Union College, Prof. 1911-43; Dept. Head 1923-26; Prof. Emer. 1943-55; Visiting Prof. & Lect.: Univ. of Chicago 1920; Syracuse Univ. 1926-28, 1930; Columbia Univ. 1931-32. **Memberships & Offices:** APA; Classical Assn. of Atlantic States, VP 1906-10, 1911-12; British Classical Assn.; Soc. for Promotion of Byzantine & Modern Greek Studies; AAUP; NY State Teachers' Assn., Classical Sect., Pres. 1917-19; Phi Beta Kappa, Alpha of New York, Pres. 1924-28; *Classical Weekly*, Assc. Ed. 1925-35. **Publications:** contr., *American Journal of Philology; Classical Weekly; TAPA.* **Bio-Bibliography:** *NY Times,* Obit. (Sept. 21, 1955); Briggs, 318-19; *Who Was Who in America.*

KELLUM, BARBARA ■ FAAR History of Art 80. b. Apr. 2, 1948, Los Angeles, CA. m. M. Hellman. BA 70, Univ. of Southern California; MA 74, Univ. of Southern California; MA 76, Univ. of Michigan; PhD 81, Harvard Univ. **Career & Employment:** Smith College, Assc. Prof. 1981-present. **Fellowships, Honors & Awards:** Univ. of Southern California, Phi Beta Kappa 1970, Phi Kappa Phi 1970; Kress-Harvard Fellowship 1978-1980; Smith College, Mellon Fellowship 1983, 1986, Junior Faculty Teaching Award 1988; NEH Grant 1986; CFCD Grant l991, 1992. **Publications:** "Infanticide in England in the Later Middle Ages," *History of Childhood Quarterly: The Journal of Psychohistory* 1 (1974): 367-88; "The Portrait Statue Program at the Forum of Augustus," in *On Judging the Merits of Augustus,* ed. E.A. Judge (Berkeley: Center for Hermeneutical Studies in Hellenistic & Modern Culture, 1984), 40-43; "Sculptural Programs and Propaganda in Augustan Rome: The Temple of Apollo on the Palatine," *Publications d'histoire de l'art et d'archéologie de l'Université de Louvain* 44 = *Archeologia Transatlantica* 5 (1985): 168-76; "The City Adorned: Programmatic Display at the *Aedes Concordiae Augustae,*" in *Between Republic and Empire: Interpretations of Augustus and His Principate,* ed. Kurt A. Raaflaub & Mark Toher (Berkeley: UC Press, 1990), 276-308; "What We See and What We Don't See: Narrative Structure and the Ara Pacis Augustae," *Art History* 17.1 (Mar. 1994): 26-45; "The Construction of Landscape in Augustan Rome: The Garden Room at the Villa *ad Gallinas,*" *Art Bulletin* 76.2 (June 1994): 211-24. **Business Address:** Dept. of Art, Smith College, Northampton, MA 01063.

KELLY, THOMAS FORREST ■ FAAR Post-Classical/Humanistic Studies 86. b. Apr. 20, 1943, Greensboro, NC. m. Peggy Badenhausen. c. Sarah Danforth French, Adam Christian French. BA 64, UNC; LRAM 66, Royal Acad. of Music; MA 71, Harvard Univ.; PhD 73, Harvard Univ. **Other Study:** Schola Cantorum, Paris, Diplôme de virtuosité, 1966; Institut Grégorien, Paris 1964-66. **Career & Employment:** St. Andrew's College, Instr. 1964; Smithsonian Inst., Div. of Musical Instruments, Research Asst. 1972; Wellesley College, Instr. 1972-73, Asst. Prof. 1973-79; Mt. Holyoke College, NEH Inst., Adj. Faculty 1981, 1983; Smith College, Asst. Prof. 1979-81, Assc. Prof. 1981-82; Amherst College, Assc. Prof. 1982-84; Five-College Early Music Program, Dir. 1979-84; Oberlin College Conservatory of Music, Prof. & Dana Faculty Fellow 1988-94, Acting Dean 1990-91; Harvard Univ., Prof. 1994-present. **Memberships & Offices:** Castle Hill Festival, Artistic Dir. 1973-83; *Journal of the Lute Society of America,* Ed. 1973; *Journal of the American Musical Instrument Society,* Ed.-in-Chief 1974-79; Cambridge Soc. for Early Music, Music Dir. 1977-78; Intl. Early Dance & Music Inst., Dir. 1982-84; Early Music America, BoD, Pres. 1988-94; American Musicological Soc., Council Mem. 1991-94, Oberlin Baroque Performance Inst., Artistic Adv. 1992-present; "Performance Today," Nat. Public Radio, Monthly Commentator; Cambridge Studies in Medieval & Renaissance Music, Ser. Ed.; Schirmer Books, Studies in Historical Performance Practice, Ser. Ed. **Fellowships, Honors & Awards:** Fulbright Grant 1964-66; Wellesley College Research Grant 1976-77; NEH Research Fellowship 1984-85, 1991-92; ACLS Grant 1987-88; H.H. Powers Fellowship 1989; American Musicological Soc., Otto Kinkeldey Award 1989; Oberlin College Research Grants 1991-92. **Publications:** "Montecassino and the Old-Beneventan Chant," *Early Music History* 5 (1985): 53-83; "Beneventan Fragments at Altamura," *Mediaeval Studies* 49 (1987): 465-79; "Beneventan and Milanese Chant," *Journal of the Royal Musical Association* 112 (1987): 173-95; "Orfeo da Camera," *Historical Performance* 1 (1987): 3-9; "The Beneventan Chant," *Studia Musicologica Academiae Scientiarum Hungaricae* 30 (1988): 393-97; "Early Music in Higher Education: A Major Challenge," *National Association of Schools of Music Proceedings* (1989): 124-29; "The EMA Survey of Early Music: A Preliminary Report," *Historical Performance* 2 (1989): 21-25; *The Benevantan Chant* (Cambrige: Cambridge Univ. Press, 1989); ed., *Plainsong in the Age of Polyphony* (Cambridge: Cambridge Univ. Press, 1992); *Les témoins manuscrits du chant bénéventain,* Paléographie musicale 21 (Solesmes: Abbaye St.-Pierre, 1992). **Home Address:** 31 Wendell St., Cambridge, MA 02138.

KELSEY, FRANCIS WILLEY ■ AAR Trustee 1911-19, Classicist.

KENDALL, WILLIAM MITCHELL ■ AAR Charter Mem., AAR Trustee 1911-41, elected Founder 1942.

KENFIELD, JOHN FAWCETT, III ■ FAAR Classics/Archaeology 77; School of Classical Studies, Adv. Council 1977-present. b. June 18, 1944, Evanston, IL. BA 66, Brown Univ.; MA 69, Princeton Univ.; PhD 72, Princeton Univ. **Other Study:** ASCSA 1965. **Career & Employment:** Excavations at Morgantina, Sicily, Professional Staff, 1969-present; Rutgers College, Asst. Prof. 1971-75, Assc. Prof. 1975-present; Indiana Univ., Excavations at Castle Copse, Assc. Dir. 1982-86. **Memberships & Offices:** ArIA, Princeton Soc., Pres. 1984-87; Roman Research Trust, Avebury, England, BoT 1987-present; *Lexicon Iconographicum Mythologiae Classicae,* Adv. Council 1982-present; NEH, Classical Art & Archaeology projects, Adv. 1979-present; *AJA,* Ed. Adv.; ArIA, Thompson Lecture Program Com. 1992-95;

Princeton Univ. Press, Ed. Adv. 1992-present. **Fellowships, Honors & Awards:** ASCSA, Fellow 1965-present; Ford Found. Travel Grants 1965, 1969; NDEA Fellowship at Princeton Univ. 1966-69; Princeton Univ. Graduate Fellowship 1970-71; Fulbright Fellowship 1970-71 (declined); ACLS 1979; Rutgers Univ., FASP Fellowship 1976-77, 1984-85, 1988, Summer Fellowship for Junior Faculty 1972, 1974, Research Council Summer Research Grants 1977-93, Rutgers College Parents Assn. Outstanding Teacher of the Year 1994; APS Grant 1980. **Publications:** "The Sculptural Significance of Early Greek Armor," *Opuscula Romana* 9 (1973): 149-56; "The Question of the Cleveland Kouros," *AJA* 78 (1974): 70-71; "An Alexandrian Samson: Observations on the New Catacomb on the Via Latina," *Rivista di Archeologia Cristiana* (1975): 179-92; "The Princeton Core," in *Echoes from Olympus*, ed. D.A. Amyx (Berkeley: UC Press, 1974), 77, no. 27, 83, fig. 27; "A Bronze Herakles in the Metropolitan Museum of Art: Drunkard or Wrestler?" *AJA* 80 (1976): 415-19; "Preliminary Report on Excavations of the Late Roman Villa at Castle Copse, Great Bedwyn, 1986," *Wiltshire Archaeological Magazine* 81 (1987): 52-56; with E.R. Hostetter & T.N. Howe, "An East Greek Master Coroplast at Late Archaic Morgantina," *Hesperia* 59 (1990): 265-74; "A Modelled Terracotta Frieze from Archaic Morgantina: Its East Greek and Central Italic Affinities," in *Deliciae Fictiles*, eds. C. Wikander & E. Rystedt (Stockholm, 1993), 21-28; "The Case for a Phokaian Presence at Morgantina as Evidenced by the Site's Archaic Architectural Terracottas," *Varia Anatolica* 3 (Paris 1993): 261-69; "High Classical and High Baroque in the Architectural Terracottas of Morgantina," *Hesperia*, supp. 27, ed. N.A. Winter (1994): 275-81. **Home Address:** 229 S. Harrison St., Princeton, NJ 08542.

KENNAN, KENT W. ■ FAAR Musical Composition 39. b. Apr. 18, 1913, Milwaukee, WI. BMus 34, Eastman School of Music, Univ. of Rochester; MMus 36, Eastman School of Music, Univ. of Rochester. **Other Study:** Univ. of Michigan 1930-32; Accademia di Santa Cecilia, Ildebrando Pizzetti, Rome 1938. **Research/Artistic Interests:** Composing & transcribing. Have made transcriptions for clarinet & piano of the following: Brahms, *Sonata* op. 100 for violin & piano, & Prokofieff, *Sonata* op. 94 for flute & piano or violin & piano. **Career & Employment:** Kent State Univ. 1939-40; Univ. of Texas, Austin 1940-46, 1949-83, Prof. Emer. 1983-present; US Military Service 1942-46; Ohio State Univ. 1947-49; Eastman School of Music, Univ. of Rochester 1954, 1956. **Memberships & Offices:** Soc. for Music Theory, Nat. Assn. of Composers, ASCAP, Pi Kappa Lambda, Phi Mu Alpha Sinfonia. **Fellowships, Honors & Awards:** Eastman School of Music, Univ. of Rochester, Alumni Achievement Award 1992. **Publications:** *The Technique of Orchestration* (Englewood Cliffs: Prentice-Hall, 1952, 4th ed., with Donald Grantham, 1990); *Counterpoint* (Englewood Cliffs:

Prentice-Hall, 1959, 3d ed. 1987). **Important Works:** *Night Soliloquy*, for flute with various possible accompaniments 1936; *Nocturne & Il Campo dei Fiori*, for orchestra, rev. as *From a Rome Diary: Notturno & Il Campo dei Fiori* 1988; *Dance Divertimento: Promenade, Air de Ballet, Jig*, for orchestra 1938, rev. 1988 with movements retitled *Grand March, Toe Dance, Jig*; *Andante*, for oboe & orchestra 1939, rev. 1988 as *Elegy*; *Three Preludes*, for piano 1939; *Scherzo, Aria and Fugato*, for oboe & piano 1942; *Concertino for Piano and Orchestra* 1947, rev. for piano & wind ensemble; *Two Preludes* for piano 1951; *Theme with Variations*, for organ 1952; *Sonata for Trumpet and Piano*, 1956; *A John Donne Prayer*, for chorus & piano 1982; *Retrospectives*, a set of 12 piano pieces 1939-60, rev. 1991; *Sail Forth*, for chorus & piano 1992; Publishers: Carl Fischer, G. Schirmer, T. Presser, & others; Recordings: Mercury, RCA Victor, Columbia, Summit Records, Helarc, Koch Intl., CRI & others. **Bio-Bibliography:** *Baker's Biographical Dictionary of Musicians; Grove's Dictionary of Music and Musicians; International Who's Who in Music; Who's Who in America*. **Home Address:** 1513 Westover Rd. Austin, TX 78703.

KENNEDY, CLARENCE ■ RAAR History of Art 61. b. Sept. 4, 1892, Philadelphia, PA. d. July 29, 1972. m. Ruth Wedgwood Doggett, RAAR 61. c. Melinda Norris, Robert Lawrence. BS 14, Univ. of Pennsylvania; MA 15, Univ. of Pennsylvania; PhD 24, Harvard Univ. **Other Studies:** ASCSA 1920-22. **Research/Artistic Interests:** Stereophotography and reproduction process for book illustration. **Career & Employment:** Smith College, Prof. 1930-60, Dir. of Graduate Study in Europe 1925-32; NYU, Visiting Prof. 1932; Toledo Museum of Art, Annual Prof. 1938-39; consultant to: Polaroid, Kodak, Meriden Gravure; Catina Press, Dir. **Fellowships, Honors & Awards:** Harvard Univ., Norton Fellow 1920-21; Guggenheim Fellow 1930; CAA, Research Fellow 1931-32. **Publications:** ed, *Studies in the History and Criticism of Sculpture*, 7 vols. (Northampton, MA: Smith College, 1927-33); "Documenti inediti su Desiderio da Settignano e la sua famiglia," *Rivista d'arte* 12 (1930): 243-96; "Selection of Copy for Illustrations," *Art Bulletin* 42 (1961): 57-61; with F. Hartt & G. Corti, *The Chapel of the Cardinal of Portugal* (Northampton, MA: Gehenna Press, 1962); with Ruth Kennedy, *Four Portrait Busts by Francesco Laurana, 1434-1459, at San Miniato in Florence* (Philadelphia: Univ. of Pennsylvania Press, 1964). **Bio-Bibliography:** *Clarence Kennedy: An Exhibition of his Photographs* (Northampton, MA: Smith College Museum of Art, 1967); "Obituary," *Art Journal* 32 (1973): 372; L. McGavin, *Clarence Kennedy: Scholar, Photographer*, exb. cat. (Williamstown, MA, 1980); *Who Was Who in America*.

KENNEDY, EUGENE FRANCIS, JR ■ Rotch Scholar 1924.

KENNEDY, GEORGE A. ■ AAR Trustee 1980, Trustee Emer., Classicist.

KENNEDY, RAYMOND MCCORMICK ■ FAAR Architecture 19. b. Apr. 12, 1891, New Brighton, PA. d. May 11, 1976. m. Myrtle Kennedy. c. Raymond M. Jr., Thomas A. BArch 15, Cornell Univ.; MArch 16, Cornell Univ. **Career & Employment:** York & Sawyer, Designer; Howard Greenley, Designer. **Memberships & Offices:** AIA, Pasadena, California Chap. **Fellowships, Honors & Awards:** AIA, School Medal for General Excellence 1915; John Plaut Fellowship. **Important Works:** Grauman's Chinese Theater, Hollywood.

KENNEDY, RUTH WEDGEWOOD ■ RAAR History of Art 61. b. 1896. d. 1968. **Bio-Bibliography:** Obit., *Art Journal* 29 (1969): 1001-10.

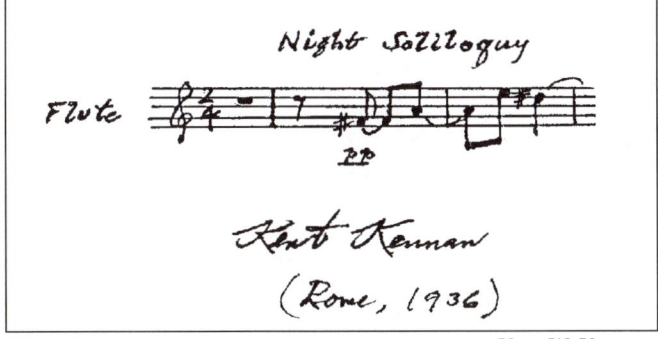

Kent W. Kennan

KENNEY, RICHARD L. ■ FAAR Literature 87. b. Aug. 10, 1948, Glens Falls, NY. m. Mary F. Hedberg. c. Hollis, Will. BA 70, Dartmouth College. **Research/Artistic Interests:** Poetry. **Career & Employment:** Univ. of Washington 1986-present. **Fellowships, Honors & Awards:** Yale Series of Younger Poets Prize, Yale Univ. Press 1983; Guggenheim Fellow 1984; MacArthur Fellow 1987-91; Lannan Literary Award 1994. **Publications:** *The Evolution of the Flightless Bird* (New Haven: Yale Univ. Press, 1984); *Orrery* (New York: Atheneum, 1985); *The Invention of the Zero* (New York: Knopf, 1993). **Bio-Bibliography:** *Who's Who in America.* **Home Address:** 1231 Jackson St., Port Townsend, WA 98368. **Business Address:** Dept. of English, Univ. of Washington, Seattle, WA 98195.

```
                        MYAMACADMY

    Here's Latin, inlaid:           E basta. Here's
                                    a burst memory: Amer-
    Ciao, bella! Lei— abrupt        ican Academy in Rome!— rhyme
    puff. A bus. Pellucid           that, amore: run
    diesel bloom upon               your finger round the heart's rim
    a peach.                        till it rings:
    A cappuccino. A cat. No
    pooch. No chains. No macadam:   And O, refills! Ciao, bella: label
    cobbles.                        all the hours, rung, umber
                                    days, those, and
    Opulence: lawns,                wine, and pollen lifting
    cyprus besoms sweeping          from the high umbrella pines, time
    pollen-yellow, lime-lip-lit skies.  passing, sifting through
    Christ's signs                  the thousand spilled belfry bells
    ubiquitous.                     of Rome—

    A Bic-                          Ring AMACADMY.
    scritch; cue-ball click. Clink  American Academy in Rome. No
    wine: I'm                       macadam, no, Ma'am,
    trying to write this poem for   cobbles. A cat. A dreamy cat
    the festschrift, ssshh.         in Rome. A merry cast: a demi-
                                    god or two, you,
    (Verse curdles across the cortile's  a cat, a poem, a damned
    cloistered unprintable post-    miracle! A room: a terracotta
    prandial amorous air-           room—
    hammers' merci-
    less converse.)                 Dimmer, now:
                                    a merry cast, a room, a poem,
    Verse: vespers. Vespasian. A    a rheumy memory:
    Vespa! Ciao, bella—
    puff—                           Me.
    a bus—                          In Rome.
```

Richard L. Kenney

KENWORTHY, RICHARD G. ■ FAAR Post-Classical/Humanistic Studies 70. b. June 21, 1943, Burlington, VT. BA 65, Univ. of Chicago; MA 68, UCLA; PhD 76, UCLA. **Career & Employment:** Troy State Univ., Asst. Prof. 1971-75, Assc. Prof. 1984-present; Auburn Univ., Instr. 1993-present. **Publications:** *The Italian Garden Transplanted,* exb. cat. (Troy, AL: Troy State Univ., 1988); *Writing on the Gardens of Italy* (Monticello: Vance Architectural Bibliographies, 1990); "Published Records of Italianate Gardens in America," *Journal of Garden History* 10 (1990): 10-70; "Bringing the World to Brookline: The Gardens of Larz and Isabel Anderson," *Journal of Garden History* 11 (1991): 224-41. **Business Address:** Dept. of Architecture, Auburn Univ., Auburn, AL 36849.

KEPES, GYORGY ■ RAAR Painting 75. b. Oct. 4, 1906, Sylep, Hungary. m. Juliet Appleby. c. Julie Stone, Imre Kepes. MA, Royal Acad. of Fine Arts, Budapest. **Career & Employment:** MIT, Prof. Emer.; Center for Advanced Visual Studies, Founding Dir. **Memberships & Offices:** AAAS, AAAL; NAD. **Fellowships, Honors & Awards:** Illinois Acad. of Fine Arts, IFA Award, Univ. of Washington, Walker Ames Prof.; Univ. of Hawaii, Visiting Artist; Univ. of Utah, Bicentennial Prof.; Rice Univ., Andrew Mellon Prof.; Hanover, NH, Artist-in-Residence; Washington Univ., St. Louis, Distinguised Visiting Prof.; Rochester Inst. of Technology, Kern Inst. Prof.; DFA: Art Inst., Bos-

ton; Illinois Acad. of Fine Arts; Lehigh Univ.; RISD. **Important Works:** Gyorgy Kepes Visual Center, Eger, Hungary; Collections: Addison Gallery of American Art; Albright-Knox Gallery; Brooklyn Museum; Museum of Art, Cleveland; Corcoran Gallery, Washington, DC; Museum of Fine Arts, Dallas; Houston Museum of Fine Arts; Phoenix Art Museum, etc. **Exhibitions/Performances:** Alpha Gallery, Boston 1994. **Home Address:** 90 Larchwood Dr., Cambridge, MA 92138.

KERNIS, AARON JAY ■ FAAR Musical Composition 85. b. Jan. 15, 1960, Philadelphia, PA. BMus 81, Manhattan School of Music. **Other Study:** San Francisco Conservatory 1977-78; Yale School of Music 1981-83. **Career & Employment:** Manhattan School of Music, Prof. 1992-present; Minnesota Public Radio, Minnesota Composers Forum, Composer-in-Residence 1993-94; St. Paul Chamber Orchestra, Composer-in-Residence 1993-96. **Fellowships, Honors & Awards:** BMI Student Composer Awards 1976, 1983, 1984; Guggenheim Fellowship 1984; NEA Fellowship 1984; Columbia Univ., Bearns Prize 1986; NYFA Grant 1987; ASCAP Composition Awards 1987; Chamber Music Soc. of Lincoln Center, Stoeger Chamber Music Prize 1993. **Important Works:** *Dream of the Morning Sky,* for soprano & orchestra 1983; *Love Scenes,* for soprano & cello 1987; *Invisible Mosaic III,* for orchestra 1988; *Symphony in Waves* 1989; *Songs of Innocents, Books I & II,* for high voice & piano 1989; *String Quartet – "musica celestis"* 1990; *Second Symphony* 1991; *Brilliant Sky, Infinite Sky,* for baritone, violin, percussion & piano 1991; *Still Movement with Hymn,* for piano, violin, viola, cello, American Public Radio Comm. 1993; *100 Greatest Dance Hits,* for guitar & string quartet, Music from Angel Fire Comm. 1993; *Colored Field,* for English horn & orchestra, San Francisco Symphony Comm. 1994; *Goblin Market,* for narrator & ensemble, Birmington Contemporary Music Group Comm. 1994. All published by Associated Music Publishers, Inc. **Home Address:** 116 Pinehurst Ave., Apt. D-25, NYC 10033. **Business Address:** G. Schirmer, 257 Park Ave. S., 20 Fl., NYC 10010.

KERR, WALTER ■ AAR Visitor 1959 — 1964, Critic.

KESSLER, HERBERT L. ■ FAAR History of Art 85. b. July 20, 1941, Chicago, IL. m. Johanna Zacharias. c. Morisa Kessler-Zacharias. BA 61, Univ. of Chicago; MFA 63, Princeton Univ.; PhD 65, Princeton Univ. **Research/Artistic Interests:** medieval art. **Career & Employment:** Univ. of Chicago, Asst. Prof.-Assc. Prof.-Prof. 1965-76; John Hopkins Univ., Charlotte Bloomberg Prof. 1976-present. **Memberships & Offices:** CAA 1965-present, Porter Prize Selection Com. 1974-77, Chair 1976-77, Program Dir. 1976, Annual Meeting Chair 1979, 1988, 1991; MAA 1968-present, Fellow 1991-present; Intl. Center for Medieval Art 1966-present, BoD 1974-77; Byzantine Studies Conference 1974-present, Organizing Com. 1975-78, Program Dir. 1976; Dumbarton Oaks Alumni Assn. 1976-present, VP 1977-79; Assn. Intl. des Études Byzantines, US Com. 1978-present; Dumbarton Oaks Center for Byzantine Studies, Adv. to the Byzantine Photograph Collection 1984-88; Mt. Holyoke College, Visiting Byzantinist 1985; Smithsonian Inst. & Biblioteca Apostolica Vaticana, Organizer of Symposium 1988; Società della storia di miniatura 1992-present. **Fellowships, Honors & Awards:** Dumbarton Oaks Center for Byzantine Studies, Junior Fellow 1965, Fellow 1979-80, Senior Fellow 1980-86; NEH Fellow 1967, Postdoctoral Fellow 1984-85; Univ. of Chicago, Quantrell Grant 1968; IAS, Herodotus Fellow 1969-70; Guggenheim Fellow 1972-73, 1984-85 (declined); ACLS Fellow 1979-80, 1988-89; APS Fellow 1980. **Publications:** *The Illustrated Bibles from Tours,* Studies in Manuscript Illumination 7

(Princeton: Princeton Univ. Press, 1977); "Christian Narrative Art" & 31 entries in *The Age of Spirituality: Late Antiquity and Early Christianity, Third to Seventh Century* (New York: MMA, 1979), 449-512 et passim; "Pictorial Narrative and Church Mission in Sixth-Century Gaul," *Studies in the History of Art* 16 (1985): 75-91; with Kurt Weitzmann, *The Cotton Genesis* (Princeton: Princeton Univ. Press, 1986); "On the State of Medieval Art History," *Art Bulletin* 70 (1988): 166-87; "*Caput et speculum omnium ecclesiarum:* Old St. Peter's and Church Decoration in Medieval Latium," in *Italian Church Decoration of the Middle Ages and Early Renaissance: Functions, Forms and Regional Traditions*, ed. W. Tronzo, Villa Spelman Colloquia 1 (Bologna: Nuova Alfa, 1989), 121-45; "An Apostle in Armor and the Mission of Carolingian Art," *Arte medievale*, ser. 2.4 (1989): 17-41; "L'antica basilica di San Pietro come fonte e ispirazione per la decorazione delle chiese medievali," in *Fragmenta picta: Affreschi e mosaici staccati nel medioevo romano*, exb. cat. (Rome: Argos, 1989), 45-64; with Kurt Weitzmann, *The Frescoes of the Dura Synagogue and Christian Art*, Dumbarton Oaks Studies 28 (Washington, DC: Dumbarton Oaks, 1990); "'Pictures Fertile with Truth' (How Christians Managed to Make Images of God without Violating the Second Commandment)," *Journal of the Walters Art Gallery* 49-50 (1991-92): 53-65; "A Lay Abbot as Patron: Count Vivian and the First Bible of Charles the Bald," in *Committenti e produzione artistico- letteraria nell'alto medioevo occidentale*, Settimane di studio del Centro italiano di studi sull'alto medioevo 39 (Spoleto: CISAM, 1992): 647-75; "Medieval Art as Argument," in *Iconography at the Crossroads*, ed. B. Cassidy (Princeton: Princeton Univ. Press, 1993), 59-70; *Studies in Pictorial Narrative* (London: Pindar Press, 1994); "'Facies bibliothecae revelata,' Carolingian Art as Spiritual Seeing," in *Testo e immagine nell'alto medioevo*, Settimane di studio del Centro italiano di studi sull'alto medioevo (Spoleto) 41 (CISAM, 1994), 533-84; "Gazing at the Future: the Parousia Miniature in the Vatican Cosmas," *Byzantine East, Latin West: Art Historical Studies in Honor of Kurt Weitzmann* (Princeton: Princeton Univ. Press, 1995), 365-71. **Bio-Bibliography:** *Who's Who in America*. **Home Address:** 211 Ridgewood Rd., Baltimore, MD 21210. **Business Address:** Johns Hopkins Univ., Baltimore, MD 21218.

KESSLER, MICHAEL C. ■ FAAR Painting 90. b. Oct. 23, 1954, Hanover, PA. m. Regina A. Merder. c. Celia. BFA 78, Kutztown Univ. **Other Study:** Whitney Museum, Independent Study Program 1977. **Research/Artistic Interests:** Painting: oil, watercolor, acrylic. **Fellowships, Honors & Awards:** Pennsylvania Council on the Arts Grant in Painting 1983; 5th Annual Awards in the Visual Arts 1985; Pollock-Krasner Found. Award 1992. **Important Works:** Selected Public Collections: Air Products & Chemicals, Allentown, PA; Albright-Knox Art Gallery, Buffalo; Allentown Art Museum; Bank of Boston; Broad Found., Los Angeles; Brooklyn Museum; Castellani Art Museum, Niagara Univ.; Chase Manhattan Bank, NYC, Columbus Museum of Art; Flint Inst. of Arts; Huntington Art Gallery, Austin, TX; Muhlenberg College, Allentown, PA; MFA; Newark Museum; New Museum of Contemporary Art, NYC; Pepsico, Purchase, NY; Philadelphia Museum of Art; Prudential Insurance, NYC; Rodale Press, Emmaus, PA; Santa Barbara Museum of Art; SOHIO, Cleveland; Sen. Specter's Office, US Senate Bldg., Washington, DC; Price-Waterhouse, Washington, DC; Vanderbilt Univ. **Exhibitions/Performances:** Solo: Castellani Art Gallery, Niagara Univ. 1983, 1992, 1994; Jack Tilton Gallery, NYC 1984, 1987, 1988, 1990; Art Now Gallery, Goteborg, Sweden 1986, 1989, 1991, 1993, 1995; Fabian Carlson Gallery, London 1986; Wolff Gallery, NYC 1986; Bar-

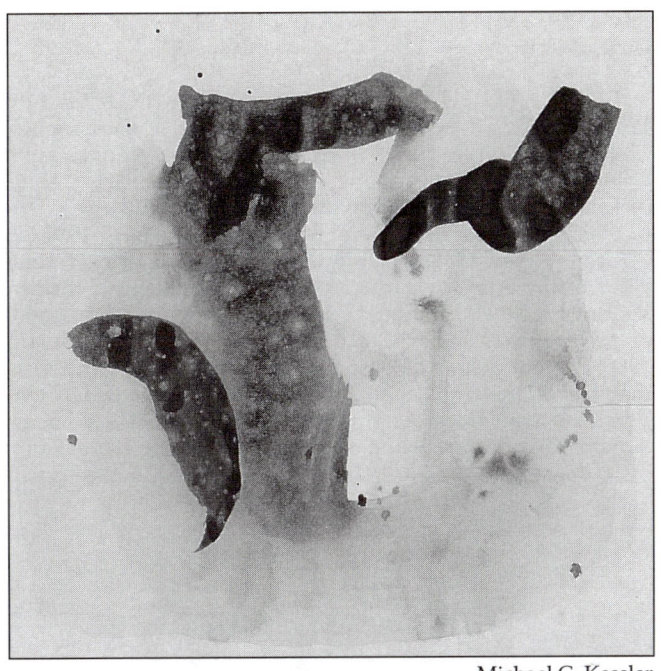

Michael C. Kessler

bara Krakow Gallery, Boston 1987; Virginia Miller Gallery, Coral Gables, FL 1988, 1994; Nina Freudheim Gallery, Buffalo 1990; Klein Artworks, Chicago 1990, 1994, 1995; Schmidt-Dean Gallery, Philadelphia 1990, 1992, 1993, 1994; Freyberger Gallery, Pennsylvania State Univ., Reading 1992; Mirmar Gallery, Sarasota, FL 1992. **Home Address:** Michael Kessler, Camino Ocate, Santa Fe, NM 87501.

KIANG, DAWSON ■ FAAR Classics/Archaeology 71. b. Mar. 10, 1933, Shanghai, China. BA 53, Harvard Univ.; PhD 68, Columbia Univ. **Other Study:** Cornell Univ., Cert. in Historic Preservation 1976. **Career & Employment:** Pennsylvania State Univ., Assc. Prof. 1964-82. **Fellowships, Honors & Awards:** FELS Found. Fellowship 1959; ANS Fellowship 1960; American Research Center in Egypt Fellowship 1962-63; NEH Fellowship 1971. **Publications:** "Bramante's Heraclitus and Democritus: the Frieze," *Zeitschrift für Kunstgeschichte* 51 (1988): 262-68; "Gasparo Visconti's Pasitea and the Sala delle Asse," *Achademia Leonardi Vinci, Journal of Leonardo Studies* 2 (1989): 101-9; "The 'Enigma of the Dice': A Bramante Sonnet Published by Lomazzo," *Achademia Leonardi Vinci, Journal of Leonardo Studies* 4 (1991): 196-99; "Josquin Desprez and a Possible Portrait of the Ottoman Prince Jem in Cappella Sistina Ms. 41," *Bibliothèque d'Humanisme et Renaissance* 54 (1992): 411-26; "The 'Mappamondo' in Bramante's Heraclitus and Democritus," *Achademia Leonardi Vinci, Journal of Leonardo Studies* 5 (1992): 128-35. **Home Address:** 465 S. New Hampshire Ave., Los Angeles, CA 90020.

KIBRE, ADELE JEANNE ■ FAAR Classics/Archaeology 32. b. Jan. 13, 1902, Philadelphia, PA. d. Mar. 24, 1976. BA 21, UC, Berkeley; MA 22, UC; PhD 30, Univ. of Chicago. **Research/Artistic Interests:** The library and scriptorium of Lorsch, the *Ars Grammatica* of Smaragdus, German. **Career & Employment:** UC, TA 1922-23, 1925-26; Univ. of Oregon, TA 1923-24; Independent Scholar, Rome 1933-38; Univ. of Chicago 1938-42; American Legation, Stockholm 1942-44; US Office of Strategic Services, Washington, DC, Field Representative 1944, Consular Officer, Spain 1949-52.

KIDDER-SMITH, G.E. ■ AAR Visitor 1943 — 1951; Brown Univ. Fellow.

KIERAN, STEPHEN J. ■ FAAR Architecture 81. b. Mar. 18, 1951, Englewood, NJ. m. Barbara De Grange. c. Christopher, Caitlin. BA 73, Yale Univ.; MArch 76, Univ. of Pennsylvania. **Other Study:** Urban planning, American, particularly perimeter cities. **Career & Employment:** Alan Greeenberg, Architect 1977-78; Venturi, Rauch & Scott Brown 1978-80, 1981-82; Princeton Univ. 1982-86; Univ. of Pennsylvania 1986-present; Kieran, Timberlake & Harris 1984-present; Yale Univ., Saarinen Visiting Prof. 1994; Visiting Lect.: Iowa State Univ. 1980; School of Architecture, Lisbon, Portugal 1982; Univ. of New Mexico 1986; Parsons School of Design 1992; Univ. of Karlsruhe, Germany 1992; Inst. for Urban Design, Philadelphia 1993. **Memberships & Offices:** AIA; Pennsylvania Soc. of Architects; American Collegiate Schools of Architecture; The Athenaeum;

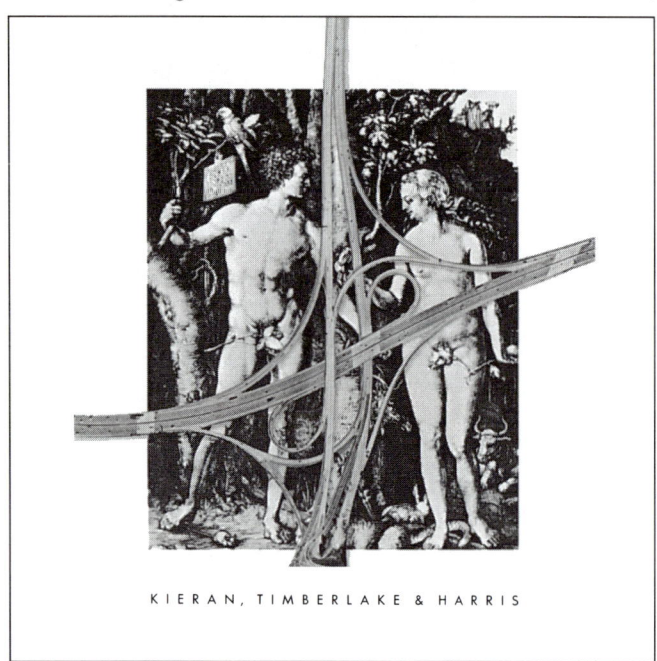

KIERAN, TIMBERLAKE & HARRIS

Stephen J. Kieran

Jury Critic: Drexel Univ. 1978-80; North Carolina State Univ. 1982; Columbia Univ. 1983; Univ. of Pennsylvania 1983-present; Univ. of Toronto 1984-85; Yale Univ. 1986-present; Temple Univ. 1987; New Jersey Inst. of Technology, Super Jury 1992. **Fellowships, Honors & Awards:** Yale Univ., Walter Louis Ehrich Prize 1973, H.E. Ellsworth Prize 1973; Univ. of Pennsylvania, Graduate School of Fine Arts Scholarship 1973-74, Arthur Spayd Brooke Bronze Medal 1976, Frank Miles Day Prize 1976, Alpha Rho Chi Medal; *Interiors Magazine*, Philadelphia Design Awards 1988; AIA, Philadelphia Chap. Merit Awards 1988, 1992, 1993, 1994, Gold Medal 1993; Graham Found. 1992; Pennsylvania Soc. of Architects, Merit Award 1993, Distinguished Bldg. Award 1994. **Publications:** ed., *Via III: Ornament* (Philadelphia: Journal of the Graduate School of Fine Arts, Univ. of Pennsylvania, 1977); "The Theory of Imitation," *Symposium Proceedings: American Collegiate Schools of Architecture* (Washington, DC: ACSA, 1979); "The United States Supreme Court Building, Washington, DC," *Antiques* (Oct. 1985): 760-69; "The Architecture of Plenty: Theory and Design in the Marketing Age," *Harvard Architecture Review: Patronage* (New York: Rizzoli, 1987), 102-13; "The Image in the Empty Frame: 'Wu

Hall and the Art of Representation,'" in *The Architecture of Robert Venturi*, ed. Christopher Mead (Univ. of New Mexico Press, 1989), 85-109; "Paradise Regained," *Architecture Magazine* (Dec. 1991): 48-51; "Die neue amerikanische Landschaft," *Arch +* (June, 1992): 30-35. **Important Works:** Chestnut Hill College Student Activity Center 1987; Shapiro Residence, Cherry Hill, NJ 1989; East Stroudsburg Univ., Old Dining Hall Renovation 1990, Univ. Center Addition & Renovation 1993; Scott Residence, Philadelphia 1991; Rider College, Lawrenceville, NJ, Admission & Financial Aid Center 1991, Science & Technology Center 1992, Olsen, Switlick & Hill Halls Renovations 1992-1994; Villanova Univ., Pedestrian Underpass 1993-94; Germantown Acad. Master Plan, Ft. Washington, PA 1993; Johnson Pavilion Laboratories, Univ. of Pennsylvania 1993; Tatnall Lower School Gymnasium 1995. **Exhibitions/Performances:** Graduate School of Fine Arts, Univ. of Pennsylvania 1982, 1994. **Bio-Bibliography:** "Columbus Parking Lot," *Landscape: The Princeton Journal* 2; "Chestnut Hill College, Student Activities Center," *Interiors Magazine* (1988); "From House to Campus," *Progressive Architecture* (Apr. 1990); "A City in Limbo," *Architectural Record* (Jan. 1993): 106-7; "University Center-East Strounsburg University," *Architectural Record* (Oct. 1993): 110-13; "AIA Medal Winners: Why They Think They Won," *Philadelphia Inquirer* (Oct. 17, 1993): L1, L6; "Serious about Systems," *Progressive Architecture* (Mar. 1994); "Tectonic Teaching," *Architecture* (July 1994): 68-73. **Home Address:** 402 Moylan Ave., Moylan, PA 19065. **Business Address:** Kieran, Timberlake & Harris, 20 N. 3d St., Philadelphia, PA 19106.

KILEY, DANIEL U. ■ RAAR Landscape Architecture 76. b. Sept. 2, 1912, Boston, MA. m. Anne L. Sturges. c. Kor, Kathleen, Christopher, Antonia, Timothy, Grace, Aaron, Caleb. Harvard GSD 1936-38. **Other Study:** Apprentice to Warren H. Manning 1932-38. **Career & Employment:** Concord, NH, City Planning Bd. 1938-40; Nat. Park Service, Architect 1938; US Housing Authority, L.A. Assc. Town Planning Architect 1940; Private Practice 1940-present. **Fellowships, Honors & Awards:** NAD, Academician 1968-present; US Army, Legion of Merit 1944; Jefferson Memorial, St. Louis, Competition Winner 1948; AIA Gold Medal Award 1966, Allied Professional Medal 1971, Collaborative Achievement Award 1972; Harvard GSD, Daniel Urban Kiley Lect. 1985; Thomas Jefferson Medal for World Architecture 1988; Nat. Landscape Award 1990; Brandeis Univ., Creative Arts Award 1990; Waterfront Center, Excellence of the Waterfront Award 1992; Green Mountain College, Hon. DHL. **Important Works:** Jefferson Memorial Arch, St. Louis, MO 1947; Irwin Miller Residence, Columbus, IN 1955; US Air Force Acad., Colorado Springs 1955; Dulles Intl. Airport, Chantilly, VA 1958; Independence Mall, Third Block, Philadelphia 1959; Lincoln Center, NYC 1960; Oakland Museum 1962; Ford Found. Bldg., NYC 1964; Halle Centrale, La Defense, Paris 1970; John F. Kennedy Library, Dorchester, MA 1978; Fountain Place, Dallas 1985; North Carolina Nat. Bank Plaza, Tampa, FL 1985; Nat. Sculpture Garden, NGA 1985-present; Henry Moore Sculpture Garden, Nelson-Atkins Museum, Kansas City, MO 1987-89. **Exhibitions/ Performances:** "Landscape Design: The Work of Dan Kiley," American Fed. of Arts Traveling Exb. 1959; Nat. Gallery of Design 1968; Harvard GSD 1980; "Built Landscapes: Gardens in the Northeast," Harvard Univ. Traveling Exb. 1984; ALNY 1987; Planning & Design Retrospective, Burlington, VT 1988; London Architectural Found Exb. 1994. **Bio-Bibliography:** "Landscape Design Works of Dan Kiley," *Process Architecture* 33; *Who's Who in America*. **Home Address:** PO Box 1812, East Farm, Charlotte, VT 05445. **Business Address:** Office of Dan Kiley, PO Box 1808, Charlotte, VT 05445.

KIMBALL, RICHARD ARTHUR ■ AAR, Dir. 1960-65, Architect.

KING, ANN RUTH ■ AAR World War II Scholar 1943.

KINNELL, GALWAY ■ RAAR Literature 87. **Fellowships, Honors & Awards:** MacDowell Colony Fellow. **Publications:** Poetry: *What a Kingdom It Was* (1960); *Flower Herding on Mount Monadnock* (1964); *Body Rags* (1968); *First Poems 1946-1954*; *The Book of Nightmares* (1971); *The Avenue Bearing the Initial of Christ into the New World: Poems 1946-1964* (1974); *Mortal Acts, Mortal Words* (1980); *Selected Poems* (1982); Prose: *Black Light* (1966); *Walking Down the Stairs: Selections from Interviews* (1978); Translations: Rene Hardy, *Bitter Victory* (1956); Yves Bonnefoy, *On the Motion and Immobility of Douve* (1968); Yvan Goll, *Lackawanna Elegy* (1970); *The Poems of François Villon* (1977). **Home Address:** RFD 1, Sheffield, VT 05866.

KINNEY, DALE ■ FAAR History of Art 72; NEH Summer Seminar Leader 1993; SOF Bd. 1979-86. b. May 10, 1944, NYC. m. Mark L. Darby. c. Aaron Kinney. BA 65, Syracuse Univ.; MA 67, IFA; PhD 75, IFA. **Career & Employment:** Bryn Mawr College, Lect. 1972-75, Asst. Prof. 1975-78, Assc. Prof. 1978-87, Prof. 1987-present; Univ. of Melbourne, Australia, Visiting Lect. 1986; Univ. of Delaware, Visiting Lect. 1988; George Washington Univ., Distinguished Visiting Prof. 1990. **Memberships & Offices:** *Marsyas: Studies in the History of Art*, Ed.-in-Chief 1967-68; *Byzantine Studies-Études Byzantines*, Book Review Ed. 1976-83; Byzantine Studies Conference 1979-83; AVISTA 1985-91; NEH, Museums Division, Juror 1986, Summer Seminar for College Teachers, Juror 1994; Intl. Center of Medieval Art, Domestic Adv. 1983-86, BoD 1987-96, Publications Com. Chair 1987-92, Program Com. Chair 1993-96; Delaware Valley Medieval Assn., Pres. 1987-88; Mellon Fellowships in the Humanities, Region II Selection Com. 1988-92; Byzantine Studies Conference, Program Com. Chair 1991; *Studies in Iconography*, Adv. Bd. 1992-present; SAH, Founder's Award Com. Chair 1994. **Fellowships, Honors & Awards:** Phi Beta Kappa 1964; Woodrow Wilson Fellowship 1965; Fulbright-Hays Grant 1969, 1977; NGA, Chester Dale Fellowship 1970; Bryn Mawr Grants 1976, 1980, 1982, 1984, 1985, 1989, Research Award 1977; NEH Summer Stipend 1979; APS Grant 1981; George A. & Eliza Gardner Howard Found. Fellowship 1982; IAS, Visiting Mem. 1982; Lindback Found. Award 1984; CASVA, Samuel H. Kress Senior Fellowship 1989. **Publications:** "'Capella Reginae': S. Aquilino in Milan," *Marsyas* 14 (1970-71): 13-35; "The Evidence for the Dating of S. Lorenzo in Milan," *JSAH* 31 (1972): 92-107; "Excavations in S. Maria in Trastevere, 1865-69: A Drawing by Vespignani," *Römische Quartalschrift* 70 (1975): 42-53; "Spolia from the Baths of Caracalla in S. Maria in Trastevere," *Art Bulletin* 68 (1986): 379-97; "Le chiese paleocristiane di Mediolanum," in *Milano, una capitale da Ambrogio ai Carolingi*, ed. C. Bertelli (Milan: Electa, 1987), 48-79; "Mirabilia urbis Romae," in *The Classics in the Middle Ages*, ed. A.S. Bernardo & S. Levin (Binghamton, NY: SUNY Press, 1990), 207-21; "The Apocalypse in Early Christian Monumental Decoration," in *The Apocalypse in the Middle Ages*, ed. R.K. Emmerson & B. McGinn (Ithaca & London: Cornell Univ. Press, 1992), 200-216; "The Iconography of the Ivory Diptych Nicomachorum-Symmachorum," *Jahrbuch für Antike und Christentum* 37 (1994): 64-96; "Ivory Diptychs," in *The Making of Art*, ed. M. Greenhalgh & A. Yarrington (in press); "A Late Antique Ivory Plaque and Modern Response," *AJA* 98 (1994): 457-72; "Rape or Restitution of the Past? Interpreting *Spolia*," in *The Art of Interpreting* (in press). **Home Address:** 757 Buck Lane, Haverford, PA 19041. **Busi-**

ness Address: Bryn Mawr College, 101 N. Merion Ave., Bryn Mawr, PA 19010.

KIRCHMER, PAUL JOSEPH ■ FAAR Sculpture 58. b. Apr. 17, 1921, Dayton, OH. d. after 1990. **Other Studies:** Dayton Art Inst. 1939-41; Cranbrook Acad. of Art 1946-48; Acad. of Fine Arts, Florence, Italy. **Career & Employment:** Independent Artist, Germantown, OH. **Fellowships, Honors & Awards:** Dayton Art Inst., Dayton Artists Annual, 1st Prize 1949. **Important Works:** MMA, Sculpture Collection 1951. **Exhibitions/Performances:** Intl. Exb. of Sacred Art, Vatican City 1950; Troy Community Park, Troy, OH 1962.

KIRCHNER, LEON ■ RAAR Musical Composition 74. b. Jan. 24, 1919, Brooklyn, NY. m. Gertrude Schoenberg. c. Paul, Lisa. BA 40, UC, Berkeley; MA 61, Harvard Univ. **Other Study:** with Bloch, Sessions, & Schoenberg. **Career & Employment:** UC, Berkeley, Lect. 1946-48; Univ. of Southern California, Los Angeles, Asst. Prof.-Prof. 1950-54; Mills College, Luther Brusie Marchant Prof. 1954-61; Harvard Univ., Prof. & Walter Bigelow Rosen Prof. 1961-89; Prof. Emer. 1989-present; Visiting Positions: SUNY, Buffalo, Slee Prof. 1959; Juilliard 1983; Yale Univ., Sanford Prof. 1984; Fellow or Performer & Conductor in Residence at: Marlboro; Blue Hill, ME; Tanglewood; Aspen; Aldeburgh, England; Music Today, Tokyo; Lincoln Center, NYC; Santa Fe; Stearns Inst., Ravinia; American Music Festival; Conductor & Pianist with: San Francisco Symphony; Boston Symphony; New York Philharmonic; St. Paul Chamber Symphony; Philadelphia Orchestra; Buffalo Symphony; Aldeburgh; Tanglewood; Tokyo Today; Ton Halle, Zurich; Baden Baden; Sudstfunk; Aspen. **Fellowships, Honors & Awards:** UC, Berkeley, Paris Prize 1942; Guggenheim Fellowship 1948, 1950; New York Critics Circle Award 1949-50, 1959-60; Naumburg Award 1952; AAAL 1962; Koussevitzky Award 1964; Pulitzer Prize 1967; Center for Advanced Study in the Behavioral Sciences, Fellow 1974-75; Music Industry, Nat. Music Award 1976; Brandeis Univ., Creative Arts Award Medal 1977; Kennedy Center, Friedheim Award 1994; & commissions from the New York Philharmonic, Boston Symphony, Phila-

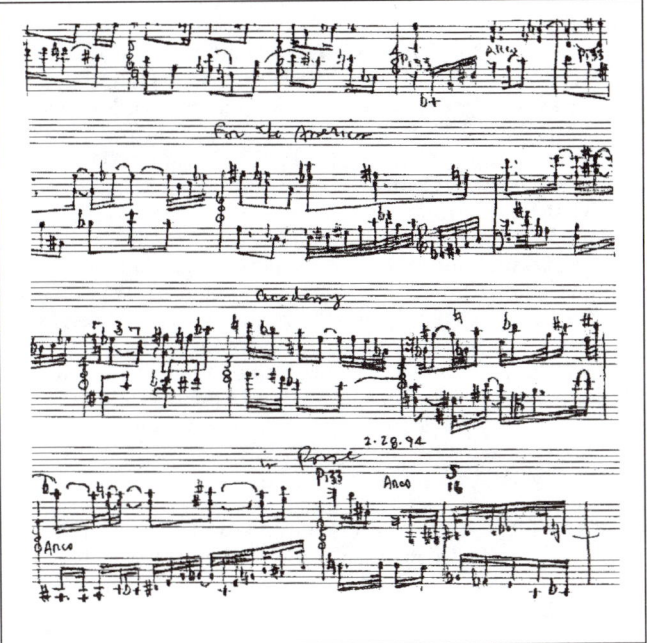

Leon Kirchner

delphia Orchestra, etc. Honorary Doctorates: Johns Hopkins-Peabody 1970; New England Conservatory. **Important Works:** *Duo for Violin & Piano* 1947; *Piano Sonata* (Bomart, Epic, Educo, CRI) 1948; *String Quartet No. 1* (CRI) 1949; *Trio*, for piano, violin & cello, Elizabeth Sprague Coolidge Comm. 1954; *Concerto for Violin, Piano & Percussion*, Baird Comm. 1960; *Toccata*, San Francisco Symphony Comm., Louisville Orchestra (First Edition Records) 1956; *Piano Concerto No. 1* 1953; *Piano Concerto No. 2* 1963; *Music for Orchestra No. 1*, New York Philharmonic Comm. 1969; *Music for Flute & Orchestra* 1978; *The Twilight Stood*, song cycle for piano & soprano, Kennedy Center- Lincoln Center-Santa Fe Festival Comm. 1982; *Triptych*, for violin & cello 1988; *Music for Orchestra No. 2*, NEC Comm. 1990; *Music for Cello & Orchestra*, Philadelphia Symphony Comm. 1992; *Trio No. 2*, for piano, violin & cello, Kennedy Center-YMMA-Purdue Univ. Comm. 1993. Publisher: Associated Music Publishers. Performances are numerous; & recording list is incomplete. **Bio-Bibliography:** *Current Biography; Musical Quarterly; Who's Who in America.* **Business Address:** Harvard Univ., Cambridge, MA 02138.

KIRKLAND, J. MICHAEL ■ FAAR Architecture 70. b. Mar. 31, 1943, Miami, FL. m. Ellis G. Kirkland. c. Lori Nicole, Gillian Crawford, Cleo. BArch 66, Univ. of Florida; MArch 68, Harvard GSD; M.Urban Design 71, Harvard GSD. **Career & Employment:** Columbia Univ., Asst. Prof. 1970-72; Urban Design Corp., NYC, Assc. Chief Arch. 1970-72, Dir. 1972-75; Harvard Univ., Visiting Prof. 1973, 1987; Univ. of Toronto, Prof. 1975-present; Univ. of Wisconsin, Distinguished Intl. Prof. 1988-89. **Memberships & Offices:** Canadian Prix de Rome Programme, Founder 1987. **Fellowships, Honors & Awards:** Fulbright Fellowship 1969; Harvard Univ., Sheldon Frederick Fellow 1969, Loeb Fellow 1973; *Progressive Architecture* Award 1975, Citation 1977, 1984; *Architectural Design* Award 1983, 1984; IAKS, Cologne, Silver Medal 1989; Governor General Award 1990; Ataratiri, Jean-Alaurent Grand Prix Award of Distinction 1991. **Publications:** *Mississauga City Hall* (New York: Rizzoli, 1984); "The Isms of Architecture," *C.C.H. Magazine* (Dec. 1991): 30-35; "Pain in the Belly of the Architect," *C.C.H. Magazine* (Mar. 1992): 12-15. **Important Works:** Low Rise High Density Housing Prototype, Brooklyn 1972-75; Ghent Sq. Houses, with Barton Myers, Norfolk, VA 1976-78; Fredericton Medical Centre, New Brunswick 1984-86; Mississauga City Hall, ONT, with Edward Jones 1982-87; North York Civic Pool, ONT 1983-87, Civic Sq. 1983-88; Nat. Film Bd. of Canada, Toronto 1989-92; Shanghai Culinary Centre, China 1992-95; Tianjin Teda Centre 1994-present; York Center 1994-present; North Markham 1995-present; Collections: Canadian Centre for Architecture, Montreal. **Exhibitions/Performances:** MOMA 1972; US Embassies, London, Moscow 1972; Sabel-Casteli Gallery, Toronto 1983; Harvard Univ. 1985; "Measure of Consensus, Canadian Architecture in Transition," Travelling to Vancouver, NYC, London, Paris, Rome, Tokyo 1986; "Le Nouveau Monde," Travelling to Paris, Toronto 1987; Triannale Milano 1988. **Bio-Bibliography:** *Who's Who in Canada.* **Home Address:** 225 Richmond St. N., Toronto, ONT M5V 1N2, Canada. **Business Address:** Kirkland Partnership Architects, 225 Richmond St. W., Toronto, ONT M5V 1W2, Canada.

KIRKPATRICK, JOHN F. ■ FAAR Landscape Architecture 39. b. Feb. 18, 1912, Cincinnati, OH. m. Harriet Ristvedt. c. Troy Hightower, Scott. BArch 34, Cornell Univ.; BL 37, Cornell Univ. **Career & Employment:** Clarence C. Combs, Landscape Architect 1939-40; US WPA 1940-41; Caribbean Architects-Engineers 1941-42; US Military Service, 603rd Combat Engineers

Battalion (Top Secret) 1942-45; Cincinnati Planning Comm. 1946; Office of Ladislaus Sego, Planner 1946-48; Skidmore, Owings & Merrill 1948-72; Nat. Capitol Development Comm., Canberra, Australia, Consultant 1957-72. **Memberships & Offices:** AILA. **Important Works:** Master Plan for Oak Ridge, TN; Master Plan for the US Air Force Acad., Colorado Springs; San Francisco Civic Center Master Plan; Stanford Area 6 Master Plan; San Francisco Depressed Embarcadero Freeway Study; San Francisco Area E Redevelopment Plan; Pennsylvania Ave., Washington, DC Development Plan; Alameda, CA, Tidelands Master Plan; Monterey Coast & Scenic Highway Master Plan; Univ. of Nevada, Reno Campus Master Plan; Univ. of Nevada, Las Vegas Campus Master Plan; Sacramento, West End Commercial Complex Redevelopment Plan; Washington, DC Mall Master Plan, Nat. Park Service; Black Hawk Ranch, Alameda County Master Plan; Carson City, Nevada, State Capitol Development Plan; Monterey Mall Development Projects; Work Ranch, Monterey Master Plan; Santa Fe to Taos Scenic Highway, NM; Redevelopment Plan for the Kern County Land Co., Bakersfield, CA; Subic Bay US Naval Base, Philippines; Master Plan for town & harbor facilities, French New Caledonia; Development Plans for Fowler McCormick Ranch, Scottsdale AZ; Development Design for 60,000-acre ranch, Maui, Hawaii; Washington, DC Mall Master Plan Update, US Capitol Reflecting Pool, Washington, DC; Boise, ID Central Business District Redevelopment; San Francisco Port Development for US Steel. **Home Address:** 2332 Washington St., San Francisco, CA 94115.

KIRKPATRICK, RALPH ■ AAR Visitor 1943 — 1951, Harpsichordist.

KIRSHNER, JULIUS ■ FAAR Post-Classical/Humanistic Studies 69. b. July 12, 1939, NYC. m. Judith Russi. c. Jessica, Alexander. BA 61, Pace College; PhD 70, Columbia Univ. **Other Study:** Vatican School for Diplomatics & Paleography 1967-69, Diploma. **Career & Employment:** Bard College, Asst. Prof. 1965-67, 1969-70; Univ. of Chicago, Prof. 1970-present. **Memberships & Offices:** *Journal of Modern History*, Ed. 1977-present. **Fellowships, Honors & Awards:** Soc. for Italian Historical Studies, Marraro Prize 1973; ACLS Grant 1975-76; AHA, Modern European History Section, Higby Prize 1978; NEH Fellow 1979-80, Research Grant 1979-81; Cambridge Univ., Clare Hall, Visiting Fellow 1983. **Publications:** *Pursuing Honor while Avoiding Sin: The* Monte delle doti *of Florence*, Quaderni di Studi Senesi 41 (Milan: QSS, 1978); gen. ed., with John Boyer, *University of Chicago Readings in Western Civilization*, 9 vols. (Chicago: Univ. of Chicago Press, 1986-87); ed. with Suzanne Wemple, *Women of the Medieval World: Essays in Honor of John H. Mundy* (Oxford: Basil Blackwell, 1985); "Wives' Claims against Insolvent Husbands in Late Medieval Italy," in *Women of the Medieval World: Essays in Honor of John H. Mundy* (Oxford: Basil Blackwell, 1985), 255-303; "Materials for a Gilded Cage: Non-dotal Assets in Florence (1300-1500)," in *The Family in Italy from Antiquity to the Present* (New Haven: Yale Univ. Press, 1991), 184-207; "*Maritus Lucretur Dotem Uxoris Sue Permortue* in Late Medieval Florence," *Zeitschrift der Savigny-Stiftung, Kanonistische Abteiling* 77 (1991): 111-55. **Home Address:** 5658 S. Blackstone Ave., Chicago, IL 60637. **Business Address:** Dept. of History, Univ. of Chicago, 1126 E. 59th St., Chicago, IL 60637.

KISELEWSKI, JOSEPH ■ FAAR Sculpture 29. b. Feb. 16, 1901, Browerville, MN. d. June 1986. **Other Studies:** Minneapolis School of Art; NAD; Beaux Arts Inst. of Design, NYC;

Julien Acad., Paris; with L. Lawrie, P. Landowski, & H. Bouchard. **Memberships & Offices:** NAD, Assc. 1936, Mem.; NSS; ALNY. **Fellowships, Honors & Awards:** Beaux Art Paris, Prize 1925-26; NAD, Gold Medal 1937. **Important Works:** Sculpture: John Peter Zenger, Public School 18, Bronx, NYC; General Accounting Bldg., Washington, DC; House Chamber, US Capitol Bldg., Washington, DC; Monument, Milwaukee; Bronx County Court House, NYC; Monument, Vincennes, IN; Monument, Fargo, ND; Monument, Tarrytown, NY; US War Dept., Washington, DC; Commerce Bldg., Washington, DC; Metropolitan Life Insurance Company, NYC; Rosary College, River Forest, IL; John Wesley Episcopal Church, Winston-Salem; Lyman Allyn Museum; Occidental College; Bryn Mawr College; New York World's Fair 1939. **Exhibitions/Performances:** James R. Marsh Galleries, Essex Fells, NJ; NAD 1937; Beaux Arts Inst. Paris 1925-26. **Bio-Bibliography:** *Who Was Who in American Art.*

KISSINGER, HENRY ■ AAR Visitor 1994, US Sec. of State.

KITAO, T. KAORI ■ AAR Visitor. b. Jan. 30, 1933, Tokyo, Japan. BA 58, UC, Berkeley; MA 61, UC Berkeley; PhD 66, Harvard Univ. **Research/Artistic Interests:** Bernini & baroque Rome, architectural theory, semiotics. **Career & Employment:** RISD, Asst. Prof. 1963-66; Swarthmore College, Asst. Prof. 1966-68, Assc. Prof. 1968-75, Chair 1975-81, Prof. 1975-present. **Home Address:** 540 Westminster Ave., Swarthmore, PA 19081. **Business Address:** Swarthmore College, 500 College Ave., Swarthmore, PA 19081.

KITCHEN, ROBERT SIEBER ■ FAAR Landscape Architecture 38. b. July 8, 1912, Dayton, OH. m. Priscilla Kitchen. BArch 35, Cornell Univ.; BLA, Cornell Univ. **Career & Employment:** Kitchen & Hunt, Architects, San Francisco 1950s. **Fellowships, Honors & Awards:** Baird Prize 1933; Knickerbacker Fellowship 1933-34, 1934-35; Charles Goodwin Sands Medal; Clifton Beckwith Brown Medal. **Bio-Bibliography:** *American Architects Directory.*

KITZINGER, ERNST ■ RAAR History of Art 89. b. Dec. 27, 1912, Munich, Germany. m. Margaret Susan Theobald. c. S. Anthony, M. Rachel, Adrian N. PhD 34, Univ. of Munich. **Other Study:** Univ. of Rome, La Sapienza 1931-32. **Research/Artistic Interests:** Late antique, Byzantine & early medieval art. **Career & Employment:** British Museum 1935-40; Dumbarton Oaks, Junior Fellow, Fellow, Asst. Prof., Assc. Prof., Prof. of Byzantine Art & Archaeology 1941-67, Dir. of Studies 1955-66; Harvard Univ., Kingsley Porter Univ. Prof. 1967-79. **Fellowships, Honors & Awards:** Guggenheim Fellowship 1953-54;

Swarthmore College, D.Litt. 1969; Warwick Univ., D.Litt. 1989; Univ. of Rome, La Sapienza, D.Litt. 1992. **Publications:** *Early Medieval Art in the British Museum* (London: British Museum, 1940); *The Mosaics of Monreale* (Palermo: Flaccovio, 1960); *The Art of Byzantium and the Medieval West* (Bloomington & London: Indiana Univ. Press, 1976); *Byzantine Art in the Making* (London: Faber & Faber, 1977); *The Mosaics of St. Mary's of the Admiral in Palermo* (Washington: Dumbarton Oaks, 1990); *I mosaici del periodo normanno in Sicilia* (Palermo: Accademia Nazionale di Scienze, Lettere e Arti, 1992-). **Bio-Bibliography:** W.E. Kleinbauer, "Foreword," in *The Art of Byzantium* (Bloomington & London: Indiana Univ. Press, 1976), vii ff.; H. Belting, "Laudatio," in *Studies in Honor of Ernst Kitzinger,* Dumbarton Oaks Papers 41, ed. William Tronzo & Irving Lavin (Washington, DC: Dumbarton Oaks, 1987), xii ff; *I mosaici del periodo normanno in Sicilia* (Palermo: Accademia Nazionale di Scienza, Lettere e Arte, 1992). **Home Address:** 14 Richmond Rd., Oxford, OX1 2JJ, England.

KLAIBER, SUSAN ELIZABETH ■ FAAR History of Art 90. b. Mar. 18, 1961, Little Rock, AR. BA 82, Kalamazoo College; MA 85, Columbia Univ.; MPhil 87, Columbia Univ. **Research/Artistic Interests:** History of baroque architecture. **Fellowships, Honors & Awards:** Univ. of Münster Exchange Fellowship 1982-83; Mellon Fellowship 1984-86; Columbia Univ. President's Fellowship 1986-87.

KLEPPER, DEEANA C. ■ FAAR Post-Classical/Humanistic Studies 90. b. Dec. 1, 1959, Chicago, IL. m. Jeffrey A. Klepper. c. Rachel, Liora. BA 83, Northland College; MA 88, Northwestern Univ.; PhD 95, Northwestern Univ. **Research/Artistic Interests:** Late medieval cultural & religious history. **Memberships & Offices:** AHA, MAA. **Fellowships, Honors & Awards:** Charlotte Newcombe Doctoral Dissertation Fellowship 1990-91; Northwestern Univ., Alumnae Assn. Dissertation Fellowship 1992-93. **Publications:** "The *Ingesso Ludovici Palatini Reni ad terram sanctam*: A Fifteenth-Century Response to Spiritual Crisis," *Fifteenth-Century Studies* 15 (1989): 209-31; "The Dating of Nicholas of Lyra's *Quaestio de Adventu Christi*," *Archivum Franciscum Historicum* 86 (1993): 297-312. **Home Address:** 1326 Washington St., Evanston, IL 60202.

KNAUER, GEORG N. ■ RAAR Classics/Archaeology 85; AAR Adv. Council 1978-88. b. Feb. 26, 1926, Hamburg, Germany. m. Elfriede R. Kezia, RAAR 94. c. Georg Lorenz. **Research/Artistic Interests:** Printed commentaries on Vergil in the 16th century & the Latin translations of Homer. **Career & Employment:** *Thesaurus Linguae Latinae,* Munich, Research Asst. 1952-54; Freie Universität, Berlin, Asst. Prof. 1954-61, Assc. Prof. 1964-66, Prof. 1966-74, 1985-88; Yale Univ., Visiting Prof. 1965; Oxford Univ., Nellie Wallace Lect. 1969; Univ. of Pennsylvania, Prof. 1975-88, Chair 1978-79, 1980-82, Prof. Emer. 1988; Columbia Univ., Visiting Prof. 1976. **Memberships & Offices:** Bund Freiheit der Wissenschaft, Bonn; APA; Berliner Wissenschaftliche Gesellschaft, Korrespondierendes Mitglied; RSA. **Fellowships, Honors & Awards:** British Council Scholarship 1957-58; IAS 1973-74; Guggenheim Fellowship 1978-79; NEH Fellowship 1984-85; Rockefeller Found., Bellagio Center, Resident 1989; Herzog August Bibliothek Wolfenbüttel, Fellow 1991. **Publications:** *Sarabara* (Dan. 3,94 [27] bei Aug., *mag.* 10.33.37), *Glotta* 33 (1954): 100-18; *Psalmenzitate in Augustins Konfessionen* (Göttingen: Vandenhoeck & Ruprecht, 1955); "Peregrinatio animae: Zur Frage der Einheit der augustinischen Konfessionen," *Hermes* 85 (1957): 216-48; *Die Aeneis und Homer: Studien zur poetischen Technik Vergils mit Listen der Homerzitate*

Cura hominum potuit tantam componere Romam
Quantam non potuit solvere cura deûm

Hildebert of Lavardin (A.D.1056-1134)

May the American Academy during the second century of its life continue to contribute to this cura as valiantly as it has done during the first.

Ernst Kitzinger

August 24, 1992

Ernst Kitzinger

in der Aeneis (Berlin: Habilitationsschrift 1961); "Vergil's *Aeneid* and Homer," *Greek, Roman and Byzantine Studies* 5 (1964): 61-84; "The *Georgics* and Homer (*Vergil and Homer II*)," in *Aufstieg und Niedergang der Römischen Welt*, ed. Hildegard Temporini & Wolfgang Haase, II.31.2 (Berlin-New York: Walter de Gruyter, 1981), 890-918; "Printed Commentaries on Vergil in the 16th Century," in *Catalogus Translationum et Commentariorum* (Washington, DC: Catholic Univ. Press, forthcoming); "The Latin Translations of Homer," in *Catalogus Translationum et Commentariorum* (Washington, DC: Catholic Univ. Press, forthcoming). **Bio-Bibliography:** *Wer ist Wer?*; *Who's Who in America*, **Home Address:** 3600 Conshohocken Ave., Apt. 1505, Philadelphia, PA 19131.

KNOOPS, JOHANNES MARINUS ■ NIAE, John Dinkeloo Traveling Fellow 1990-91.

KNOWLTON, P.C. ■ Appleton Fellow 1917, 1919-20.

KNOX, SEYMOUR ■ AAR Visitor 1959 — 1964; Knox-Albright Art Museum, Buffalo, NY, Founder.

KOBAYASHI, GRACE RICAKO ■ FAAR Architecture 90. b. Mar. 27, 1959, West Lafayette, IN. BArch 82, Cornell Univ.; MArch 86, Harvard GSD. **Career & Employment:** James Stirling-Michael Wilford & Asscs., Architects 1982-83; Fred Koetter & Asscs. 1984; Benjamin Thompson & Asscs. 1984; Freedenfeld & Asscs., Architects 1985; Archetype 1986; Richard Meier & Partners, Architects 1986-88. **Fellowships, Honors & Awards:** Student Agencies Design Competition, Ithaca, NY, 1st Prize Award 1980; Beinecke Memorial Scholarship 1981; Cornell Univ., Edwin A. Seipp Memorial Prize 1980, AIA-1st Certificate & Medal 1982, Clifton Beckwith Brown Memorial Medal 1982; Skidmore, Owings & Merrill Travelling Fellowship 1982; Harvard Univ., Letter of Commendation 1986. **Exhibitions/Performances:** Venice Biennale 1986.

KOCH, KENNETH ■ AAR Visitor 1977-78, Poet.

KOEPPEL, GERHARD M. ■ RAAR Classics/Archaeology 75; Classical Soc., Pres. 1991, Exec. Com. PhD 66, Univ. of Cologne. **Other Study:** Univ. of Tübingen 1959-62. **Career & Employment:** UNC, Asst. Prof. 1968-74, Assc. Prof. 1974-85, Prof. 1985-present; ICCS, Prof.-in-Charge & Dir. 1980-81, Prof.-in-Charge 1989-90. **Memberships & Offices:** ArIA; CAMWS; Deutscher Archäologenverband; Verein von Alterumsfreunden im Rheinlande; Deutches Archäologisches Institut, Corresponding Mem. **Publications:** "Die historischen Reliefs der römischen Kaiserzeit I: Stadtrömische Denkmäler unbekannter Bauzugehörigkeit aus augusteischer und julisch-claudischer Zeit," *Bonner Jahrbücher* 183 (1983): 61-144; "Two Reliefs from the Arch of Claudius in Rome," *Römische Mitteilungen* 90 (1983): 103-9; "Die historischen Reliefs der römischen Kaiserzeit II: Stadtrömische Denkmäler unbekannter Bauzugehörigkeit aus flavischer Zeit," *Bonner Jahrbücher* 184 (1984): 1-65; "Die historischen Reliefs der römischen Kaiserzeit III: Stadtrömische Denkmäler unbekannter Bauzugehörigkeit aus trajanischer Zeit," *Bonner Jahrbücher* 185 (1985): 143-213; "*Maximus Videtur Rex:* The Collegium Pontificum on the Ara Pacis Augustae," *Archaeological News* 14 (1985): 17-22; "The Role of Pictorial Models in the Creation of the Historical Relief during the Age of Augustus," in *The Age of Augustus: Brown University Conference 1982*, Publications d'histoire de l'art et d'archéologie de l'Université Catholique de Louvain 44 (Louvain: UCL, 1985), 89-106; "Die historischen Reliefs der römischen Kaiserzeit IV:

Stadtrömische Denkmäler unbekannter Bauzugehörigkeit aus hadrianischer bis konstantinischer Zeit," *Bonner Jahrbücher* 186 (1986): 1-90; "Die historischen Reliefs der römischen Kaiserzeit V: Ara Pacis Augustae, Teil 1 (Quellen, Beschreibung, Bibliographie)," *Bonner Jahrbücher* 187 (1987): 101-57; "Die historischen Reliefs der römischen Kaiserzeit V: Ara Pacis Augustae, Teil 2 (Quellen, Beschreibung, Bibliographie)," *Bonner Jahrbücher* 188 (1988): 97-106; "Die historischen Reliefs der römischen Kaiserzeit VI: Reliefs von behannten Bauten der augusteischen bis antoninischen Zeit," *Bonner Jahrbücher* 189 (1989): 17-71; "Die historischen Reliefs der römischen Kaiserzeit VII: Der bogen des Septimius Severus, Die Decennalienbasis und der Konstantinsbogen," *Bonner Jahrbücher* 190 (1990): 1-64; "Die historischen Reliefs der römischen Kaiserzeit VIII: Der Fries der Traianssäule, Teil 1: Der erste Dakische Krieg, Szenen I bis LXXVIII," *Bonner Jahrbücher* 191 (1991): 135-98; "Die historischen Reliefs der römischen Kaiserzeit VIII: Der Fries der Traianssäule, Teil 2: Der zweite Dakische Krieg, Szenen LXXIX bis CLV," *Bonner Jahrbücher* 192 (1992): 61-122. **Home Address:** 32 Clover Dr., Chapel Hill, NC 27514. **Business Address:** Classics Dept., CB 3145, 210 Murphey Hall, UNC, Chapel Hill, NC 27599.

KOHL, BENJAMIN GIBBS ■ FAAR Post-Classical/Humanistic Studies 71; AAR Jury for History of Art & Post-Classical/Humanistic Studies 1975-79; SOF Council 1984-87, VP 1987-89, Sec. 1989-91. b. Oct. 26, 1938, Middletown, DE. m. Judith A. Cleek. c. Benjamin G. Kohl, Jr.; Laura Kohl Ball. BA 60, Bowdoin College; MA 62, Univ. of Delaware; PhD 68, Johns Hopkins Univ. **Other Study:** Univ. of Padua for Latin palaeography 1964-65. **Research/ Artistic Interests:** Renaissance Italy, humanism. **Career & Employment:** Vassar College, Instr.-Assc. Prof. 1966-81; Prof. 1981-94; Andrew W. Mellon Prof. 1994-present; Chair 1979-82, 1988-89, 1993-present. **Memberships & Offices:** City of Poughkeepsie, Appointed Historian 1971-77; AAUP, Com. A, Academic Freedom & Tenure, NY Conference 1986-present, Chair, 1987-88; *Renaissance Studies*, Adv. Bd. 1990-present; MAA; RSA; American Friends of the Warburg Inst., Pres. 1994-present. **Fellowships, Honors & Awards:** Fulbright Fellowship 1964-65; Delmas Found. Fellow 1978; Columbia Univ. Renaissance Seminar, Assc. 1979-present; Folger Shakespeare Library Fellow 1980; Royal Historical Soc., Fellow 1980-present. **Publications:** "Government and Society in Renaissance Padua," *Journal of Medieval and Renaissance Studies* 2 (1972): 205-21; "The Works of Giovanni di Conversino da Ravenna," *Traditio* 31 (1975): 349-67; ed., with R.G. Witt, *The Earthly Republic: Italian Humanists on Government and Society* (Philadelphia: Univ. of Pennsylvania Press, 1978); ed. & trans., with H.L. Eaker, *Giovanni Conversini da Ravenna, Dragmalogia de eligibili vite genere* (Lewisburg, PA: Bucknell Univ. Press, 1980); with N.G. Siraisi, "The *De monarchia* Attributed to Apuleius," *Mediaevalia* 7 (1981): 1-39; *Renaissance Humanism 1300-1550: A Bibliography of Materials in English* (New York: Garland, 1985); ed. & trans., with J. Day, *Giovanni Conversini da Ravenna: Two Court Treatises* (Munich: Wilhelm Fink Verlag, 1987); ed. & trans., with H.L. Eaker, *Giovanni Conversini da Ravenna: Dialogue between Giovanni and a Letter* (Binghamton, NY: MRTS, 1989); "Fedeltà e tradimento dello stato carrarese," in *Istituzioni, società e potere nella Marca trevigiana e veronese*, ed. G. Ortalli & M. Knapton (Rome: Studi storici, 1988), 41-63; "Giusto de' Menabuoi e il mecenatismo artistico in Padova," in *Giusto de' Menatuoi e il Battistero di Padova*, ed. A.M. Spazzi (Trieste: Lint, 1990), 13-30; "The Changing Concept of the *Studia humanitatis* in the Early Renaissance," *Renaissance Studies* 6 (1992): 185-209; ed., with A.A. Smith, *Major Problems in the History of the Italian Renaissance* (Lexington, MA: D.C. Heath, 1995).

Bio-Bibliography: *Contemporary Authors, Dictionary of American Scholars; Who's Who in the East.* **Home Address:** 59 S. Grand Ave., Poughkeepsie, NY 12603.

KOKOSCHKA, OSCAR ■ AAR Visitor 1943 — 1951, Artist.

KOLB, BARBARA ANNE ■ FAAR Musical Composition 71, RAAR Musical Composition 76; AAR Trustee 1975-77, Trustee Emer. b. Feb. 10, 1939, Hartford, CT. BMus 61, Hartt College of Music, Univ. of Hartford; MMus 64, Hartt College of Music, Univ. of Hartford. **Other Studies:** Tanglewood 1960, 1964, 1968; Vienna Acad. of Music & Art 1966-67. **Career & Employment:** Marlboro Music Festival, Composer-in-Residence 1973; Brooklyn College, Asst. Prof. 1973-75; Temple Univ., Visiting Prof. 1978; Eastman School of Music, Visiting Prof. 1984-85. **Memberships & Offices:** "Music New to New York" Concert Series, Third Street Music School Settlement, NYC, Founder-Dir. 1979-82. **Fellowships, Honors & Awards:** Fulbright Scholarship 1966; MacDowell Colony Fellowship 1968, 1969, 1971, 1972, 1980, 1983, 1987-89; Koussevitzky Comm. 1971; Guggenheim Fellowship 1971, 1976-77; NIAL Award 1973; Hartt School of Music, Alumna of the Year 1978; NYFA Grant 1986; Kennedy Center Friedheim Award 1987; NEA Grant 1989. **Important Works:** *Trobar Claus*, Fromm Found. Comm. 1970; *Solitaire* 1971; *Soundings* 1972; *The Point That Divides the Wind* 1982; *Umbrian Colors* 1986; *Time...and Again* 1985; *Yet That Things Go Round*, Fromm Found. Comm. 1987; *Extremes*, for flute & piano 1989; *The Enchanted Loom* 1990; *Voyants* 1990. **Bio-Bibliography:** "Why Can't a Woman Compose Like a Man?," *NY Times* (June 17, 1973); Donal Henahan, "Rebel Who Found a Cause," *NY Times* (Nov. 17, 1976); Richard Dyer, "Composer Barbara Kolb Finds the Midas Touch," *Boston Globe* (Feb 18, 1978); Kenneth Fain, "Artists and Their Art," *Cultural Post* (May-June 1979).

KOLOSKI-OSTROW, ANN O. ■ AAR Visitor 1973-75. b. Oct. 13, 1949, Great Barrington, MA. m. Steven E. Ostrow, FAAR 75. c. Aaron, Benjamin. BA 71, Upsala College; MA 73, Univ. of Michigan; PhD 86; Univ. of Michigan. **Other Study:** Excavation experience: Herculaneum 1968; Heshbon, Jordan

> The Academy experience reminds me of the tapestry which the clever Penelope wove and dismantled and wove again while waiting for Odysseus. She was motivated by hope and acted with love in her heart. The intricate weave of scholars and artists -- together for a semester, for a year, or for two years -- is dismantled too, only to be reconstituted again and again with new life, new color, new strength. And just as it was for Penelope, the whole process is motivated by love and hope. I am so grateful to have been a part of it.

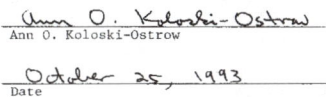
Ann O. Koloski-Ostrow

October 25, 1993
Date

Ann O. Koloski-Ostrow

1973; Carthage, Tunisia 1977, 1978. **Research/Artistic Interests:** Roman & Greek archaeology, Latin language & literature; Greek art & archaeology; Greek language & literature. **Career & Employment:** Colorado College, Lect. 1975; VSA, Assc. Dir. 1976, 1979, 1981; Dartmouth College, Lect. 1984; ICCS, Asst. Prof. 1989-90; Brandeis Univ., Visiting Lect. 1985-87, Lect. 1987-89, Asst. Prof. 1990-95. **Home Address:** 74 Angelica Dr., Framingham, MA 01701. **Business Address:** Dept. of Classical Studies, Rabb 140, PO Box 9110, Brandeis Univ., 415 S. St., Waltham, MA 02254.

KOMMERS, PETER ■ FAAR Architecture 76. b. Nov. 8, 1944, Billings, MT. m. Dianne M. Kommers. c. Faye, Warren. BArch 67, Montana State Univ.; MArch 72, Univ. of Oregon. **Research/Artistic Interests:** Intaglio printmaking, painting, drawing. **Career & Employment:** Kommers, McLaughlin & Leavengood, Architects 1972-82; Peter Kommers, Architect 1982-present; Montana State Univ., Prof. 1982-present. **Fellowships, Honors & Awards:** AIA, Montana Chap. Design Excellence Award 1981, 1986, 1993; State of Montana, Governor's Citation 1986; US Dept. of Energy, Design Excellence Award 1987; Graham Found. Grant 1989; NEA Design Arts Grant 1990; Montana State Univ., Creativity Grant 1994. **Important Works:** Kommers, McLaughlin & Leavengood, Architects Offices, Bozeman, MT 1972-82; Metcalf Bldg., Montana State Capitol Complex, Helena 1985; Kommers Residence, Bozeman, MT 1990; Lundberg Residence, W. Boulder Reserve, MT 1990; Copeland Residence, Bozeman, MT 1992; Northern Cheyenne Heritage Center Project, Lame Deer, MT 1992; Pryor Creek Painting Series 1994. **Bio-Bibliography:** L. Krantz, *A Survey of American Architects and Their Notable Works* (1990). **Home Address:** 54 Hitching Post Rd., Bozeman, MT 59715.

KOPFF, E. CHRISTIAN ■ FAAR Classics/Archaeology 79; AAR Publications, Asst. to the Dir. 1979. b. Nov. 22, 1946, Brooklyn, NY. m. Carmen Grace. c. Barrett Alexander, Theodore Frederick. BA 68, Haverford College; PhD 74, UNC, Chapel Hill. **Career & Employment:** ICCS, Asst. Prof. 1972-73; Univ. of Colorado, Boulder, Asst. Prof. 1973-77, Assc. Prof. 1977-present, Honors Program, Assc. Dir. 1990-present. **Memberships & Offices:** APA, Asst. to Sec. 1976-77; *Classical Journal*, Staff 1974-77, Book Review Ed. 1977-87; *Quaderni di Storia*, American ed. 1982-present; *Chronicles*, Contributing ed. 1985-present; *PEALS*, Ed. Bd. 1990-92. **Fellowships, Honors & Awards:** Univ. of Colorado, Faculty Fellowship 1978-79, 1986-87; Jacob van Eck Mentor 1981, 1984, 1994; Teacher Recognition Award 1983; Graduate School Com. on the Arts & Humanities, Faculty Essay Prize 1986; NEH Fellowship 1978-79, 1990-92. **Publications:** "Thomas Magister and the Text of Sophocles' *Antigone*," *TAPA* 106 (1976): 241-66; "Was Socrates Murdered? (Aristophanes, Nubes 1493 ff.)," *Greek, Roman and Byzantine Studies* 18 (1977): 113-22; ed., with J.H. D'Arms, *The Seaborne Trade of Ancient Rome: Studies in Archaeology and History*, Memoirs of the AAR 36 (Rome: AAR, 1980); "Virgil and the Cyclic Epics," *Aufstieg und Untergang der römischen Welt II* 31.2 (1981): 919-47; ed., Brooks Otis, *Cosmos and Tragedy* (Chapel Hill: UNC Press, 1981); ed., Euripides, *Bacchae* (Teubner: Leipzig, 1982); "Wilamowitz and Classical Philology in the United States," in *Wilamowitz nach 50 Jahren*, ed. W.M. Calder et al. (Darmstadt: Wissenschaftliche Buchgesellschaft, 1985), 558-80; "The Date of Aristophanes, Nubes II," *American Journal of Philology* 111 (1990): 318-29; "Troiano, ciclo," *Enciclopedia Virgiliana* 5 (Rome: Enciclopedia Italiana, 1990), 293-94; "Inventing Lost Worlds (on J.R.R. Tolkien)," *Chronicles of Culture* 9.4 (Apr. 1986): 6-8; "The Veterans of Future Wars," *Chronicles*

15.12 (Dec. 1991): 42-43; "Margaret Fuller in Rome," *Chronicles* 16.10 (Oct. 1992): 20-23. **Home Address:** 1331 Kennedy Ave., Boulder, CO 80027.

KOREN, GEORGE MATTHEW ■ FAAR Sculpture 41. b. Apr. 18, 1911. BA, Carnegie Inst. of Technology. **Other Studies:** Cranbrook Inst. **Fellowships, Honors & Awards:** Pittsburgh Associated Artists Sculpture Prize 1937; Russel Hewlitt Fellowship 1936-37. **Important Works:** Sculpture: *Three Rivers*; Johanna K. Woodwell Hailman Comm., Pittsburgh.

KOSTOF, SPIRO ■ AAR Visitor 1974-75, Scholar.

KOSUTH, JOSEPH ■ AAR Visitor 1990-91, Artist.

KOUNELLIS, JANNIS ■ AAR Visitor 1988-89, Artist.

KOUSSEVITZKY, SERGE ■ AAR Visitor 1943 — 1951, Conductor.

KOYL, GEORGE SIMPSON ■ FAAR Architecture 14; AAR Trustee 1934-51. b. Feb. 8, 1885, Evanston, WY. d. Mar. 14, 1975. m. Adelaide Wight. BArch 09, Univ. of Pennsylvania; MArch 11, Univ. of Pennsylvania. **Research/Artistic Interests:** Villa of Hadrian, Ortatorio of San Bernardino, Perugia. **Career & Employment:** Cass Gilbert 1915-17, 1918-19; US Army Air Corps, Lieut. 1917-18; McKim, Mead & White 1920-24; Columbia Univ., Critic in Design 1928; Princeton Univ., Critic in Design 1928-29; New York Univ., Instr.-Asst. Prof. 1928-32; Rich, Mathiesus & Koyl, Part. 1929-32; Univ. of Pennsylvania, School of Fine Arts, Dean 1932-50, Prof.-Prof. Emer. 1950-75. **Memberships & Offices:** AIA, Philadelphia Chap., VP; ArIA, Philadelphia Chap., Pres.; ALNY. **Fellowships, Honors & Awards:** Arthur Spayd Brooke Memorial Prize, Silver Medal, 1909; Univ. of Pennsylvania, Hon. DFA 44. **Publications:** ed., *American Architecture Directory* (1956 & 1962); ed., *American Architectural Drawings: Catalogue of Original and Measured Drawings of Buildings of the United States of America to December 31, 1917*, 5 vols. (Philadelphia: AIA, 1969). **Important Works:** County and City Bldg., Denver 1924-27; New Jersey Women's Club Bldg., Ridgewood 1928; Hospital, Littleton, NH 1930; James Cardinal Gibbons Memorial, Washington, DC 1930; AAR Bldg., Rome, revised scheme. **Bio-Bibliography:** *American Architects Directory; Who Was Who in America*; Obit., *ArIA Journal* 63 (1975): 62.

KRAMER, REUBEN R. ■ FAAR Sculpture 36. b. Oct. 9, 1909, Baltimore, MD. m. Perna Krick. Rinehart School, Baltimore 1927-34. **Other Study:** one year in London, six months in Paris. **Memberships & Offices:** Baltimore Art Center for Children, Founder & Dir. 1944-56. **Fellowships, Honors & Awards:** Maryland Inst. Scholarships 1931, 1933; Frederick Douglass Homes Competition 1st Prize 1940; Baltimore Museum of Art, All-Maryland Show: Wilson-Levering Medal 1940, 1st Sculpture Prize 1946, 1952, Grand Prize 1948, Anonymous Award 1949, Artists Prize 1951, Hutzler Award for Sculpture 1954; IBM Purchase Prize 1941; Sculptors Guild, 1st Prize 1947; Corcoran Gallery of Art, Purchase Prize 1952, Sculpture Prize 1958-60; Artists Prize, 1st Regional Artists Exb. 1953; Washington Sculptors Group, 4th Biennial of Contemporary Sculpture Exb., 1st Prize 1954; Peale Museum, Baltimore, Drawing Prize 1954; Baltimore City College Hall of Fame 1963; NIAL, Sculpture Award 1964; Maryland Inst. College of Art, Distinguished Alumni Award 1984. **Important Works:** Woodcarvings for US Post Office, St. Albans, WV 1940; Portrait of Pres. John F. Kennedy 1970; Portrait of Maryland Gov. & Baltimore Mayor

Theodore R. McKeldin 1972; H.L. Mencken; Thurgood Marshall, US Supreme Court Justice, Federal Courthouse, Baltimore 1977-80; "Standing Girl," Glen Rock School; drawings of many people in & around Baltimore. **Exhibitions/Performances:** Solo: Maryland Inst. College of Art, Baltimore 1937, 1985; Baltimore Museum of Art 1939, 1959, 1966; American Univ., Washington, DC 1953; Washington County Museum of Fine Arts, Maryland 1955; Corcoran Gallery of Art, Washington, DC 1959; Jewish Community Center, Baltimore 1974. **Bio-Bibliography:** *Who's Who in America, Who's Who in the World.* **Home Address:** 121 Mosher St., Baltimore, MD 21217.

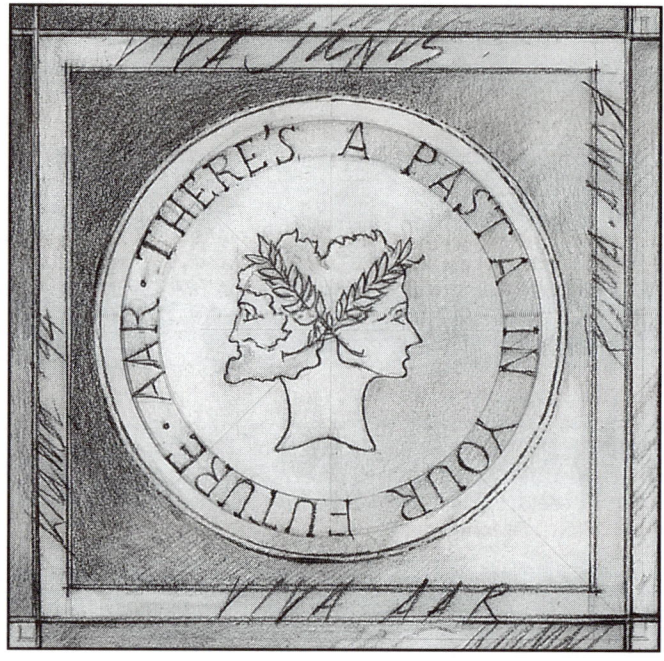

Robert E. Kramer

KRAMER, ROBERT E. ■ FAAR Design Arts 72. b. Mar. 8, 1940, Cleveland, OH. c. Aaron, Ann, Ami, Daniel, Jesse. MArch 74, MIT. **Other Study:** Apprenticeships with John Lautner 1958-59, 1963-65; Bruce Goff 1960-63. **Research/Artistic Interests:** Creating Places of Felicitous Meeting, i.e. piano-piano from the series Living Separately/Together....Two pianos (with keyboards lowered to receive residents) stand on a plateau above the sea.... A line of pure nickel, set into the floor of the passage between them, marks the exact midpoint of that corridor & is hidden from our approach by virtue of the double curving walls. The arrival of our dwellers (living separately together) at this line, marks a synchronistic moment of felicitous meeting. Should one of the two reach the line of nickel without the other appearing opposite at that exact instant, a maxim ruling conduct within Piano/Piano, requires that person to turn & walk back into their respective half of the double dwelling. **Career & Employment:** Private Practice, NYC 1973-80, Los Angeles 1980-present. **Home Address:** 476 36 St., Manhattan Beach, CA 90266.

KRAUSE, GEORGE ■ FAAR Painting 77; RAAR Design Arts 80. b. Jan. 24, 1937, Philadelphia, PA. c. George Jr., Kathryn Jane. Philadelphia College of Art 1954-57, 1959-60. **Career & Employment:** Brooklyn College, Instr. 1972-73; Bucks County Community College 1973-75; Univ. of Houston, Prof. 1975-present. **Memberships & Offices:** NEA Juror for Photography 1990. **Fellowships, Honors & Awards:** Fulbright-Hays Fellowship 1963; Guggenheim Fellowship 1967, 1976; NEA Fellowship 1977, 1979. **Publications:** with Rosellen Brown, *Qui Risposa* (Brown & Krause, 1987). **Important Works:** Public Collections: Addison Gallery of American Art, Andover, MA; Chrysler Museum, Norfolk, VA; Amon Carter Museum, Fort Worth; Center for Creative Photography, Univ. of Arizona, Tucson; AIC; Bibliotheque Nat., Paris; Carpenter Center for the Visual Arts, Harvard Univ.; George Eastman House, Rochester, NY; Gernsheim Collection, Univ. of Texas, Austin; Library of Congress, Washington, DC; Museo de Bellas Artes, Caracas; MFA; Museum of Fine Arts, Houston; Museum of Fine Arts, New Orleans; MOMA; Nat. Museum of American Art, Smithsonian Inst.; Philadelphia Museum of Art; Worcester Art Museum. **Exhibitions/Performances:** Witkin Gallery, NYC 1978; Focus Gallery, San Francisco 1981; PAFA 1982; Burton Gallery, Toronto 1982; Milwaukee Center for Photography 1982; Amarillo Art Museum 1982; Chrysler Museum, Norfolk, VA 1983; Film in the Cities, Minneapolis-St Paul 1987; Italian Festival of Photography, Turin 1987; Galeria Spectrum, Zaragoza, Spain 1990; Lichtbild Galerie, Worpswede, Germany 1991; Museum of Fine Arts, Houston 1992. **Bio-Bibliography:** Mark Power, *George Kraus 1* (Toll & Armstrong, 1972); Ann Krause, *George Krause: Universal Issues* (Houston: Rice Univ. Press, 1992); *Contemporary Photographers; Who's Who in America; Who's Who in the South and Southwest America.* **Home Address:** 420 E. 25th St., Houston, TX 77008. **Business Address:** Univ. of Houston, Houston, TX 77004.

KRAUTHEIMER, RICHARD ■ RAAR History of Art 56, 68. b. July 6, 1897, Fürth, Germany. d. Nov. 1, 1994. m. Trude Hess. PhD 23, Univ. of Halle-Wittenberg. **Other Studies:** Univ. of Munich 1919-20; Univ. of Berlin 1920-21. **Research/Artistic Interests:** Early Christian, Byzantine, Renaissance & baroque architecture & urbanism. **Career & Employment:** Univ. Marburg, Privatdozent 1928-33; Univ. of Louisville, Asst. Prof. 1935-37; Vassar College, Prof. 1937-52; IFA, Prof. 1952-72. **Memberships & Offices:** Deutsche Archäologisch Inst., Fellow; AAAS; MAA; Jewish Acad. of Arts & Science; APS; British Acad.; Max Planck Gesellschaft; American Research Inst., Turkey; Comité Intl. d'Histoire d'Art. **Fellowships, Honors & Awards:** Guggenheim Fellow 1950-51, 1963-64; CAA, Charles Rufus Morey Award 1956, ACLS Award 1961; SAH, Alice Davis Hitchcock Award 1965; Accademia Nazionale dei Lincei, Feltrinelli Prize 1975; NYU, Presidential Medal 1992; Citizen of Rome 1994; Hon. Doctorates: Univ. of Louisville 1959, Univ. of Frankfurt 1965; Pontifical Inst. of Christian Archaeology, Rome 1968. **Publications:** *Die Kirchen der Bettelorden in Deutschland* (Cologne: F.J. Marcan, 1925); *Mittelalterlichen Synagogen* (Berlin, 1927); *Corpus basilicarum christianarum,* 5 vols. (Vatican City: Pontificio Istituto di Archeologia cristiana, 1937-77); with Trude Krautheimer-Hess, *Lorenzo Ghiberti* (Princeton: Princeton Univ. Press, 1956; new ed., 2 vols, 1979); *Early Christian and Byzantine Architecture,* Pelican History of Art (Harmondsworth: Penguin, 1956; 4th ed., 1986); *Studies in Early Christian, Medieval and Renaissance Art: Collected Essays* (New York: NYU Press, 1969); *Ghiberti's Bronze Doors* (Princeton: Princeton Univ. Press, 1971) *Rome: Profile of a City, 312-1308* (Princeton: Princeton Univ. Press, 1980); *Three Christian Capitals: Topography and Politics* (Berkeley: UC Press, 1983); *The Rome of Alexander VII, 1655-1667* (Princeton: Princeton Univ. Press, 1985). **Bio-Bibliography:** R. Krautheimer, "And Gladly Did He Learn and Gladly Teach," in *Rome, Tradition, Innovation and Renewal* (Victoria, BC, 1991), 93-126; *NY Times,* Obit. (Nov. 3, 1994); *Feuilleton* 256 (3 Nov. 1994): 35; Nicholas Adams,

James Ackerman, Pamela Askew, Phyllis Lambert, John Coolidge, Craig Hugh Smyth, "In Memoriam: Richard Krautheimer (1897-1994)," *JSAH* 54 (1995): 4-7, 115-21; *Who's Who in America.*

KREIGER, ARTHUR V. ■ FAAR Musical Composition 80. b. May 8, 1945, New Haven, CT. BA 67, Univ. of Connecticut; MA 70, Univ. of Connecticut; DMA 77, Columbia Univ. **Other Study:** Composers Conference, Johnson, VT 1974; Berkshire Music Festival, Tanglewood 1975. **Research/Artistic Interests:** Music composition for all media. **Career & Employment:** Columbia Univ., Preceptor 1972-76; Columbia-Princeton Electronic Music Center, Technician 1976-78; Rutgers Univ., Adj. Instr. 1978; Columbia Univ., Lect. 1981-92; New York Univ., Instr. 1988; Baruch College, Adj. Asst. Prof. 1984-88, Substitute Asst. Prof. 1989, Adj. Assc. Prof. 1990-92. **Memberships & Offices:** American Composers Alliance, Bd. of Governors 1984-88; MacDowell Colony Fellows Com. 1989-92. **Fellowships, Honors & Awards:** Bourges, Intl. Electroacoustic Award 1977, 1978; Guggenheim Found. Fellowship 1981; Jerome Found. Fellowship 1981; ACA Recording Award 1982; NEA Fellowship 1982; New Calliope Singers-NYSCA Comm. 1983; NYFA Fellowship 1983, 1989; American Composers Orchestra Comm. 1987; CYGNUS Comm. 1991; Fromm Music Found. Comm. 1991; Brandeis Univ., Creative Arts Award 1993. **Important Works:** *Five Songs,* for soprano, flute, clarinet, violin 1974; *Short Piece: In Memory of My Father,* for electronic tape (Odyssey) 1974; *Dialogue for Steel Drums and Electronic Tape* 1974; *Dance for Sarah* 1976; *Theme and Variations* (CRI) 1977; *Fantasy for Piano and Electronic Tape* (Spectrum) 1979; *Passacaglia on Spring and All,* for chorus, electronic tape (Finnadar) 1981; *Remnants,* for symphony orchestra 1983; *Chamber Concerto for Piano and Twelve Instruments* 1986; *Riverside Variations,* for symphony orchestra 1989; *A Noiseless Patient Spider,* for children's chorus, electronic tape 1989; *Electronic Study: In Memoriam Ussachevsky,* for electronic tape 1990; *Uncommon Bonds,* for clarinet, electronic tape 1990; *Suitable Attachments,* for flute, clarinet, guitar, cello, electronic tape 1991. Publishers: American Composers Editions, Assn. for the Promotion of New Music. **Bio-Bibliography:** Morris Rosensweig, "Contemplated Balances: A Brief View of Arthur Kreiger and Peter Lieberson," *Contemporary Music Review,* "American Composers: The Emerging Generation" (Harwood Academic, 1994). **Home Address:** 173 Pond Hill Rd., Moosup, CT 06354. **Business Address:** Music Dept., 709 Dodge Hall, Columbia Univ., NYC 10027.

KREILICK, MARJORIE E. ■ FAAR Painting 63. b. Nov. 8, 1925, Oak Harbor, OH. m. Duncan Allen McNab. BA 46, Ohio State Univ.; MA 47, Ohio State Univ.; MFA 52, Cranbrook Acad. of Art. **Other Study:** Mosaic studio of Giulio Giovanetti, Rome, 1956-57; Corsi de cultura sull'Arte Ravennate e Bizantina, Univ. of Bologna 1970. **Research/Artistic Interests:** Optical mixing with iridescent paints & mosaics. **Career & Employment:** Toledo Museum of Art 1948-51; Univ. of Wisconsin, Prof. 1953-91. **Memberships & Offices:** Nat. Soc. of Mural Painters, Inter-Soc. Color Council, Intl. Assn. of Contemporary Mosaicists. **Fellowships, Honors & Awards:** Univ. of Wisconsin Research Grant 1961, 1965, 1968, 1970, 1976, 1979, 1980. **Important Works:** Architectural Comms.: Beth Aaron Synagogue, Detroit 1956; Wonderland Shopping Center, Livonia, MI 1959; Harlan Bldg, Birmingham, MI 1960; State Office Bldg, Milwaukee 1963; Science Bldg, Augustana Univ., Sioux Falls, SD 1967; Public Library, Mason City, IA 1968; Mayo Clinic, Rochester, MI 1969; St. Mary's Hospital, Wausau, WI 1969; Pritzker & Pritzker, First Nat. Bank Bldg, Chicago 1971; Telfair Acad. of Arts & Sciences,

Savannah 1973. **Exhibitions/Performances:** Solo: ALNY 1964; Minnesota Museum of Art, St. Paul 1973; Columbia Museum of Art, SC 1977; Theodore Lyman Wright Center, Beloit, WI 1980; Univ. of Illinois, Macomb 1980. **Bio-Bibliography:** Louis Redstone, *Art in Architecture* (New York: McGraw-Hill, 1968); *Mirror to Man: The Murals of the Mayo Clinic* (1976); *Art & Alchemy* (Wisconsin Alumni Research Found., 1980), 38-43; Brent Brolin, *Source Book of Architectural Ornament* (New York: Van Nostrand Reinhold, 1982); *Who's Who in American Art; Who's Who in the Midwest; Who's Who of Women.* **Home Address:** 2713 Chamberlain Ave., Madison, WI 53705. **Business Address:** Univ. of Wisconsin, 6241 Humanities Bldg., 445 N. Park St., Madison, WI 53706.

KRESSBACH, LISA ■ AAR – New York, Centennial Coordinator.

KREUTZ, ARTHUR RUDOLF ■ FAAR Musical Composition 42. b. July 25, 1906, La Crosse, WI. d. Mar. 11, 1991. m. Zoe Lund Schiller. BS 30, Univ. of Wisconsin; BMus 35, Univ. of Wisconsin; MEd 39, Columbia Univ.; Diploma 33, Royal Conservatory, Ghent, Belgium. **Career & Employment:** Central High & Vocational School, Madison, WI, Faculty 1936-38; Teachers College, Columbia Univ., Faculty 1938-40; Georgia State College, Milledgeville, Faculty 1940; Univ. of Texas, Austin, Faculty 1942-44; Univ. of Mississippi, Prof. 1952-64, Prof. Emer. 1972-91; Soloist: Ghent Symphony, Madison Civic Symphony, Milwaukee Symphony, Columbia Summer Symphony. **Fellowships, Honors & Awards:** Guggenheim Fellowship 1944-45. **Important Works:** *Winter of the Blue Snow* 1942; *Land Be Bright*, dance, Martha Graham Comm. 1942; Symphonies 1945, 1946; *New England Folksing*, for chorus & orchestra 1948; *Mosquito Serenade*, for orchestra 1948; *Acres of Sky*, a musical 1952; *The University Greys*, an opera 1954; *Dance Concerto* 1958; *Sourwood Mountain*, an opera 1959; *Violin Concerto* 1965; *Jazz Sonata*, for violin & piano (2). **Bio-Bibliography:** *Baker's Biographical Dictionary of Musicians; Contemporary American Composers.*

KRIER, LEON ■ RAAR Architecture 86. b. 1946, Luxembourg. **Other Studies:** Stuttgart Univ. **Career & Employment:** Architectural Assn., London, Faculty; Cornell Univ., Faculty; James Stirling, London 1968-70, 1973-74; Robert Krier, Stuttgart 1971; J.P. Kleihues, Berlin, Part. 1971-73; Princeton Univ., Faculty 1973-77. **Fellowships, Honors & Awards:** City of Jeddah, Gold Medal 1985; Jefferson Memorial Medal 1985. **Publications:** "Urban Transformations, 'The Blind Spot,'" *Architectural Digest* (Apr. 1978); "The Cities within a City II: Luxembourg, Capital of Europe," *Architectural Design* (1979); *Leon Krier: The Reconstruction of the European City* (Venice: Cluva Library, 1980). **Exhibitions/Performances:** Milan Triennale 1973; "Rational Architecture," (organizer), London, Barcelona, Vienna, Darmstadt, 1975; "Roma Interrota," Rome, NYC, Mexico City 1978; Galleria Jannone, Milan 1979; Max Protetch Gallery, NYC 1981. **Bio-Bibliography:** Ada Louise Huxtable, "Leon Krier's Call for a Return to Urban Classicism," *NY Tmes* (Feb. 1, 1981); Michael Sorkin, "A City Drawn and Quartered," *Village Voice* (Feb. 3, 1981); Wendy Steiner, "Calling for a Return to Sanity in Architecture," *NY Times* (May 19, 1991); Paul Goldberger, "Embracing Classicism in Different Ways," *NY Times.*

KRISTELLER, PAUL OSKAR ■ AAR Visitor 1981-82, Scholar.

KROB, R.M. ■ McKim Fellow 1926-27.

KROMER, GRETCHEN ■ FAAR Classics/Archaeology 73. b. June 11, 1946, Boston, MA. m. Paul W. Kuznets. BA 68,

Goucher College; PhD 73, Johns Hopkins Univ. **Other Study:** Indiana Univ., School of Education, Instructional Systems Technology. **Research/Artistic Interests:** Freelance design & photography; designing interative hypermedia products. **Career & Employment:** Mt. Holyoke College, Asst. Prof. 1973-77; Indiana Univ., Visiting Asst. Prof. 1977-79; Dunn Real Estate, Broker Assc. 1981-87; Remax Realtors, Broker 1987-89; Century 21 All Seasons Realtors, Broker 1989-present. **Publications:** "The Redoubtable PTYX," *Modern Language Notes* 86 (1971): 563-72; "The Value of Time in Pindar's Olympian 10," *Hermes* 110 (1976): 420-36; "The Didactic Tradition in Vergil's *Georgics*," in *Virgil's Ascraenan Song: Ramus Essays on the Georgics*, ed. A.J. Boyle (1980), 7-21. **Exhibitions/Performances:** "Other Worlds," photo exb., Uptown Café, Bloomington. **Home Address:** 708 Ballantine Rd., Bloomington, IN 47401.

KRUMHOLZ, NORMAN ■ FAAR Design Arts 87. b. June 17, 1927, Passaic, NJ. m. Virginia Martin. c. Daniel, Laura, Andrew. BA 52, Univ. of Missouri; MA 65, Cornell Univ. **Other Study:** Spent 25 years in city halls in Buffalo, Pittsburgh, & Cleveland learning urban politics & planning. **Research/Artistic Interests:** Issues of urban planning, housing, poverty, & race. **Career & Employment:** City of Ithaca, NY, Planning Comm., Asst. Dir. 1964-65; City of Pittsburgh, Planning Comm., Asst. Dir. 1965-69; City of Cleveland, Planning Comm., Dir. 1969-79; Cleveland Found., Program Officer 1980-81; Cleveland State Univ., Center for Neighborhood Development, Adj. Prof. & Dir. 1979-85; College of Urban Affairs, Prof. 1985-present. **Memberships & Offices:** Harvard Univ., Adv. Com. 1979-83; Cuyahoga Metropolitan Housing Authority, Vice Chair 1982-86; Cornell Univ., Adv. Com. 1985-90; MIT, Adv. Com. 1993-present; American Planning Assn., Pres. 1986-87, Bd. of Governors 1992-present. **Fellowships, Honors & Awards:** Nat. Comm. on Neighborhoods, Appointed 1979; American Planning Assn., Award for Distinguished Leadership 1990; Associated Collegiate Schools of Planning, Best Book of the Year Award 1991; Research supported by HUD, Ford Found., George Gund Found., Cleveland Found., & B.P. America 1979-present. **Publications:** "A Retrospective View of Equity Planning," *Journal of the American Planning Association* (Spring 1982): 163-74; "Twenty Years After Kerner: The Cleveland Case," *Journal of Urban Affairs* (Fall 1990): 285-97; with Dennis Keating & Keith Racey, "Community Development Corporations in the United States: Their Role in Housing and Urban Development," in *Governments and Housing: Developments in Developing Countries*, ed. Willem Van Vliet & Jan Van Weesep (Newbury Park, CA: Sage, 1990), 206-19; with John Forester, *Making Equity Planning Work: Leadership in the Public Sector* (Philadephia: Temple Univ. Press, 1990); with Dennis Keating & David Perry, "Cleveland's Muny Light: Public Power, Democratic Promise and Political Conflict," *Journal of Urban Affairs* (Winter 1991): 397-419; with Dennis Keating, "Downtown Plans of the 1980s: Lessons for the 1990s," *Journal of the American Planning Association* (Spring 1991): 172-93; with Dennis Keating & Phil Star, "Community-Based Housing Programs: Overview, Assessment and Agenda for the Future," *Journal of Planning Literature* 6.1 (Aug. 1991): 34-48; "Equity & Local Economic Development," *Economic Development Quarterly* (Nov. 1991): 291-300; "Roman Impressions: Contemporary City Planning in Rome," *Landscape & Urban Planning*, ed. B.V. Amsterdam (New York: Elsevier, 1992), 107-14; "The Kerner Commission: Twenty Years Later," in *The Metropolis in Black & White: Place, Power & Polarization*, ed. Edward W. Hill & George Galster (New Brunswick, NJ: Rutgers Univ. Press, 1993), 19-39; with Dennis Keating & David Perry, *Cleveland: A*

Metropolitan Reader (Kent, OH: Kent State Univ. Press, 1995); plus about 30 articles & chapters on urban planning & housing. **Bio-Bibliography:** Pierre Clavel, *Progressive Cities* (New Brunswick, NJ: Rutgers Univ. Press, 1988), chap. 4; Larry D. Terry, *The Administrator as Conservator: The Leadership of Public Bureaucracies* (Newbury Park, CA: Sage, forthcoming). **Business Address:** College of Urban Affairs, Cleveland State Univ., Cleveland, OH 44115.

KUBIC, PAUL A. ■ FAAR Sculpture 79. b. May 23, 1940, Lorain, OH. m. Erica J. Vegter. c. Saskia. BFA 66, Cleveland Art Inst.; MFA 68, Cranbrook Acad. of Art. **Other Study:** Cooper School of Art, Cleveland 1961; worked as assistant to Bill McVey, Cleveland; Julius Schmidt, MI; Peter Agostini, NC; Steven Antonakos, NC. **Research/Artistic Interests:** Primarily involved with the casting of bronze & painting. **Career & Employment:** UNC, Greensboro 1968-71; Penland School of Crafts, NC 1969-71; Humbolt State Univ. 1972-73; Maryland Inst. of Art, Baltimore 1973-74; San Jose State Univ. 1979-81, 1986-88; Mission College, Santa Clara, CA 1984-88; De Anza College, Cupertino, CA 1986. **Fellowships, Honors & Awards:** Cranbrook Acad., Student Sponsored Tuition Scholarship 1967, Carl Milles Tuition Scholarship 1968; Cleveland Museum of Art, Museum Purchase Prize 1968; UNC, Greensboro, Faculty Research Grant 1970; Maryland Council of the Arts Award 1976. **Important Works:** Cleveland Museum of Art; Atlantic Richfield Co.; Gordon Hanes, NYC; Karin Stephen; William Lacy, NYC; Dr. & Mrs. Robert Fenwick, Los Altos Hills, CA; Arnold Ashkenazy, Hermitage Hotels, Los Angeles. **Exhibitions/Performances:** Solo: Humbolt State Univ., Arcata, CA 1979; San Jose Museum of Art 1984; Metro Art Gallery, Foster City, CA 1989; NCRV Studios, Hilversum, Holland 1991; Galerie Wollebrandshof Culemborg 1993; Galerie Année, Haarlem 1994; Galerie de Brieder, Rotterdam 1995; Selected Group: Cleveland Museum of Art 1967, 1968; Weatherspoon Gallery, UNC 1969, 1970, 1971; Clemson Univ. 1970; Morris Mechanic Theatre, Baltimore 1978; Palo Alto Cultural Center 1980; Triton Museum of Art, Santa Clara, CA 1984; Joseph Chowning Gallery, San Francisco 1985; San Jose Inst. of Contemporary Art

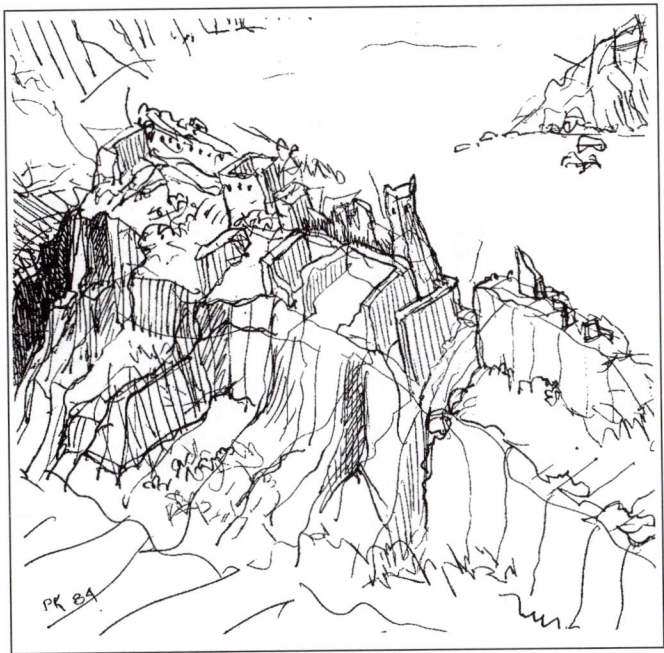

Paul A. Kubic

1985, 1987; First San Jose Biennial 1986; Monterey Peninsula Museum of Art 1987; Alonso-Sullivan Gallery, Seattle 1987; Sculpturepark Doorn 1990; Galerie Année, Haarlem 1993. **Bio-Bibliography:** Irene Chang, *San Jose Mercury News* (May 12, 1988); *San Mateo Times* (Mar. 15, 1989); Thea Figee, *Utrechts Nieuwsblad* (June 14, 1993); *De Gooi en Eembode* (Apr. 21, 1994); Bas Donher Van Meel, *Haarlems Dagblad* (Aug. 3, 1994). **Home Address:** Zuidereinde 78, 1243KJ 'S-Graveland, The Netherlands.

KUBIK, GAIL T. ■ FAAR Musical Composition 52. b. Sept. 5, 1914, South Coffeyville, OK. d. July 20, 1984. BMus 34, Eastman School of Music; MMus 36, American Conservatory of Music. **Other Studies:** Harvard Univ. with Walter Piston; with Nadia Boulanger in Paris. **Career & Employment:** Monmouth College, Faculty 1934; Dakota Wesleyan Univ., Faculty 1936-37; Teachers College, Columbia Univ. 1938-40; US Office of War Information, Motion Picture Bureau, Musical Dir. WW II; Scripps College, Composer-in-Residence 1970-80. **Fellowships, Honors & Awards:** Sinfonia Nat. Composition Award 1934; Chicago Symphony Award 1940; Jascha Heifetz Prize 1941; Soc. for the Publication of American Music Award 1943; Guggenheim Fellowship 1944, 1956; Acad. Award, Oscar 1951; Pulitzer Prize 1952; NY Film Critics' Award; Edinburgh Festival Award 1954; American Conservatory of Music, Hon. DFA 1983; MacDowell Colony Fellowship; ASCAP Award (3). **Important Works:** *A Mirror for the Sky*, a musical 1939; *Gerald McBoing Boing* 1950; film scores: *Memphis Belle* 1944, *Thunderbolt, Two Gals and a Guy* 1951, *Double for Della, C-Man* 1949, *Around the Atlantic, The Desperate Hours* 1955, *Transatlantic, The Miner's Daughter*; *Symphony Concertante*, for trumpet, viola, piano & orchestra 1952; *Music at Scripps* (Desto Records); *Five Theatrical Sketches, Divertimento No. 3* 1971; *Five Theatrical Sketches*, for piano, violin & cello 1973; *A Record of Our Time*. **Bio-Bibliography:** *Baker's Biographical Dictionary of Musicians, New Grove Dictionary of American Music*.

KUBY, ANDREW E., JR. ■ AAR World War II Prize 1942.

KUNTZ, MARGARET A. ■ FAAR History of Art 91. b. June 21, 1960, Greenwich, CT. **Home Address:** 226 Harrison Ave., Highland Park, NJ 08904.

KUPPER, EUGENE ■ FAAR Architecture 83. b. Apr. 2, 1939, Oakland, CA. m. Kathleen R. Kupper. c. Marc, Erik, Kirsten, Bryan, Selene. BArch 66, UC, Berkeley; MArch 67, Yale Univ. **Other Study:** Univ. of Illinois, Urbana, Center for Advanced Study 1968-69. **Career & Employment:** UCLA, Graduate School of Planning & Urban Architecture, Assc. Prof. 1969-present; Eugene Kupper, Architect, Prin. 1969-present; Frank O. Gehry & Asscs., Project Designer 1973-74. **Fellowships, Honors & Awards:** Fulbright Traveling Fellowship 1967 (declined); Univ. of Illinois, Urbana, Center for Advanced Study, Fellow 1967-69; *Progressive Architecture*, 1st Design Award 1972; AIA, Nat. Honor Award 1977; AIA Southern California Chap., Honor Award 1975, Citation Award 1977, Merit Award 1978; City of Los Angeles, Mayor's Commendation 1984; AIA Los Angeles Chap., Distinguished Achievement in Education Award 1989. **Publications:** "Nineteen Thoughts in the Model," in *Great Models* (North Carolina State Univ. Press, 1978); "Linee Occulte," in *Points of Reference* (Los Angeles, 1988). **Important Works:** California Inst. of Arts, Film & Drama School 1970; UCLA, Instruction & Conference Center Extension 1971; Mobil Theater Project 1971; Oberlin College, Multi-Arts Center 1972; Ferry Plaza Restaurant, San Francisco 1972; Handball Club,

Los Angeles 1972; South Shopping Center, Park Forest, IL 1973; Concord Pavilion, Concord, CA 1973; Westinghouse Office Bldg., El Monte, CA 1973; UCLA Extension Project 1975; Nilsson House, Los Angeles 1979; Wall House Project, Berkeley 1978; Starr House, Los Angeles 1979; Legal Offices, Santa Monica 1980-82; West Hollywood Civic Center 1987; Friant Ranch, Madera, CA 1988-89; Tennessee House, Los Angeles 1989. **Exhibitions/Performances:** San Francisco Museum of Art 1962; Oakland Art Museum Invitational 1963; Oakland Festival 1963; College of Environmental Design, UC, Berkeley 1965; Univ. of Illinois Center for Advanced Study 1969; Los Angeles Inst. of Contemporary Art 1978; AIA, California Council 1978; Architecture Gallery, Venice, CA 1979; Venice Biennale 1980; Festival d'Autumne, Paris 1981; Gallery, San Francisco 1982; Architectural Assn., London 1983; USC 1984; UCLA 1984, 1992; Los Angeles AIA, Museum of Science & Industry 1984; G.A. Gallery, Tokyo 1987. **Home Address:** 14925 Magnolia Blvd., No. 101, Sherman Oaks, CA 91403. **Business Address:** Graduate School of Planning & Urban Architecture, UCLA, 405 Hilgard Ave., Los Angeles, CA 90024.

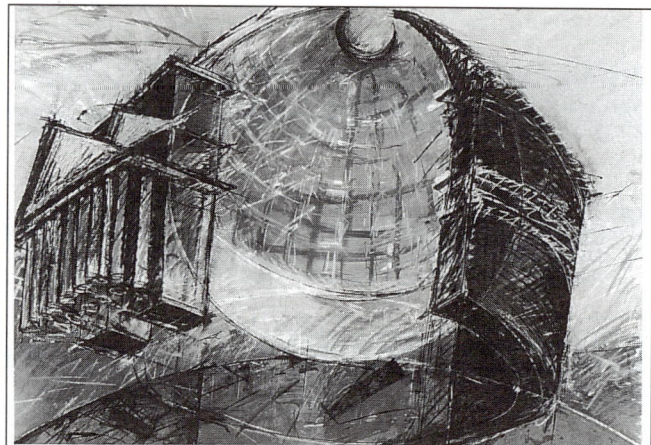

Pantheon III, Roma 1983   *E. Kupper FAAR '83*

THE PANTHEON MIRRORS A COSMOS. A CIRCULAR GRID MADE OF SQUARES IN PERSPECTIVE RECESSION SETS A CELESTIAL ARCHITECTURE IN MOTION. THE SEARCHLIGHT FINDS US BENEATH THE TANGENT PLANE OF THAT PLUMMETING SPHERE, THE SHARD OF ITS WEIGHTY SURROUND AND ITS OBLIGATORY PORTICO TORN AWAY FROM THAT GLOWING ORB. LEONARDO SECTIONED OUR SKULL THUS. OUR COSMIC MACHINERY HAS ESCAPED EARTH'S GRAVITY TO BEAM BACK A SPHERICAL RADIANCE, OUR MIRROR.

Eugene Kupper

■   ■   ■

L

LABALME, PATRICIA H. ■ AAR Trustee 1978-present. **Studies:** Bryn Mawr College, Harvard Univ. **Career & Employment:** Wellesley College, Faculty; Barnard College, Faculty; Hunter College of CUNY, Faculty; NYU, Lect.; IAS, Assc. Dir. 1982-, Corp. Sec., Asst. to Dir. **Memberships & Offices:** Lawrenceville School, BoT; Gladys Krieble Delmas Found., BoT; Brearley School, Hon. Trustee; RSA, Exec. Dir.; Phi Beta Kappa Asscs., Dir. **Publications:** *Bernardo Giustiniani: A Venetian of the Quattrocentro* (1969); ed. & contr., *Beyond Their Sex: Learned Women of the European Past* (1980); ed. & contr., *A Century Recalled: Essays in Honor of Bryn Mawr College* (1987).

LABATUT, JEAN ■ RAAR Architecture 53, 59, 65, 68. b. May 10, 1899, Martres-Tolosane, Haute-Garonne, France. d. Nov. 26, 1986. m. Mercedes Terradell. Dipl. 19, L'École des Beaux-Arts; Laureate, Inst. de France. **Career & Employment:** Private Practice 1924-26; Castillega de Gusman, Architect 1926-31; American Summer School of Fine Arts, Palais de Fountainbleau, France, Prof. 1927-38, Dir. 1945-48; Princeton Univ., Prof. 1928-67, Dir. of Graduate Studies, Bureau of Urban Research & Architectural Laboratory, Founder 1941; NY World's Fair, Design Consultant 1937-50. **Memberships & Offices:** American Society of Planning Officials; Academie d'Architecture; Ordre des Architectes; NAD; Acad. Languedoc. **Fellowships, Honors & Awards:** Thomas Jefferson Memorial Found., Medal 1973; Princeton Univ., LHD 75; AIA-Assn. Collegiate Schools of Architecture, Joint Award 1976; AIA, Fellow. **Publications:** *The Universities' Position with Regards to the Visual Arts* (Princeton, 1944); ed. with Wheaton J. Lane, *Highways in Our National Life: A Symposium* (Princeton: Princeton Univ. Press, 1950) **Important Works:** New York World's Fair 1937-50; designer, fountains for water, light and sound displays 1937-40; José Marti Monument, Plaza & Park, Havana, Cuba. **Bio-Bibliography:** *NY Times*, Obit. (Nov. 29, 1986), *Who Was Who in America*.

LACEY, JUANITA ELIZABETH ■ AAR World War II Scholar 1944.

LACY, BILL ■ AAR Pres. 1977-80, Architect; Cooper Union, Pres. 1980-; SUNY, Purchase, Pres. 1993-present.

LACY, INGRID ROWLAND ■ FAAR Post-Classical/Humanistic Studies 82. b. Aug. 19, 1953, Princeton, NJ. BA 74, Pomona College; MA 76, Bryn Mawr College; PhD 80, Bryn Mawr College. **Other Studies:** ASCSA 1976-77. **Fellowships, Honors & Awards:** ASCSA, James R. Wheeler Fellowship 1976-77; Mrs. Giles Whiting Found. Fellowship 1978-79.

LADERMAN, EZRA ■ FAAR Musical Composition 64, RAAR Musical Composition 83. b. June 29, 1924, NYC. m. Aimlee D. Laderman. BA, Brooklyn College; MA 52, Columbia Univ. **Career & Employment:** American Music Center, Pres. 1972-75; NEA, Dir. of Music Programs 1979-82; Nat. Music Council, Pres. 1983-87; American Composers Orchestra, BoD, Chair 1989-92; Yale School of Music, Dean 1989-present. **Fellowships, Honors & Awards:** Guggenheim Fellowship 1959, 1963, 1965. **Publications:** Fifty works published by Broudy, Oxford Univ. Press, & G. Schirmer. **Important Works:** 150 compositions; 20 recordings. **Bio-Bibliography:** *Grove Dictionary of Music*, etc. **Home Address:** 311 Greene St.,

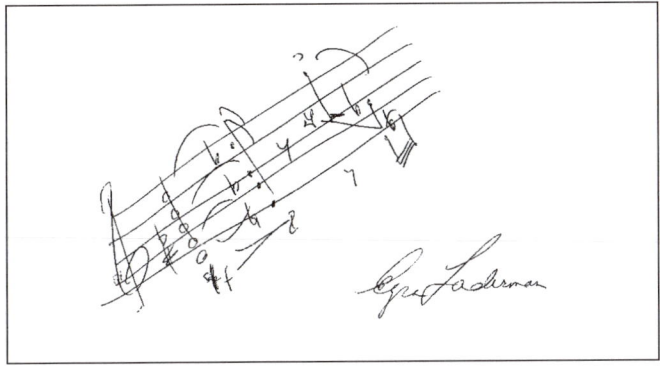

Ezra Laderman

New Haven, CT 06511. **Business Address:** School of Music, Yale Univ., New Haven, CT.

LAFARGE, C. GRANT ■ AAR Trustee 1909-38, Architect.

LAFARGE, JOHN ■ AAR Incorporator, Artist. b. March 31, 1835. d. 1910. Studied architectural decoration and then painting; turned focus to religious mural painting and became an innovator in glass staining. Instrumental in the creation of the original American School in Rome.

LA FOLLETTE, LAETITIA AMELIA ■ FAAR History of Art 84; AAR Summer School, Asst. Dir. 1984; SOF, Exec. Council, VP 1990-92; *Newsletter* Ed. 1986-91. b. Sept. 30, 1955, Lawrence, MA. m. George E. Ryan. c. Hannah Amelia La Follette Ryan, Sophia Alice La Follette Ryan. BA 77, Harvard-Radcliffe; MA 81, Princeton Univ.; PhD 86, Princeton Univ. **Other Study:** ASCSA 1977-78; Archaeological fieldwork: Halieis, Greece 1975; Tel Akko, Israel 1978, 1979; Athens, Agora 1981. **Research/ Artistic Interests:** Art, architecture & archaeology of the Greco-Roman world. **Career & Employment:** Princeton Univ., Lect. 1986-87; Univ. of Massachusetts, Amherst, Asst. Prof. 1987-93, Assc. Prof. 1994-present; Mt. Holyoke College, Visiting Asst. Prof. 1989, 1990. **Memberships & Offices:** ArIA, Western Massachusetts Soc., Exec. Council, VP 1991-93, Pres. 1994-present. **Fellowships, Honors & Awards:** Inst. of Intl. Education, ITT Fellowship 1977-78; Princeton Univ., Univ. Fellow 1978-82; NEH Summer Stipend 1988, Travel to Collections Grant 1991; Univ. of Massachusetts, Faculty Research Grant 1988-90, 1995-96, APS Grant 1991; ACLS Grant-in-Aid 1992; Graham Found. Grant 1992; Center for Teaching Lilly Fellowship 1994-95; Five Colleges, Inc.-Pew Charitable Trust Grant 1995. **Publications:** "Le terme Deciane sull'Aventino," *Archeologia Laziale* 7 (1985): 139-44; "The Chalkotheke on the Athenian Acropolis," *Hesperia* 55 (1986): 75-87; selected inscriptions in *Tituli 6, La collezione epigrafica dei musei capitolini: Inediti, revisioni, contributi al riordino,* ed. Silvio Panciera (Rome: Edizioni di Storia e Letteratura, 1987), 84-86, 329-30; with R. Wallace, "Latin *seni crines* and the Hair Style of Roman Brides," *Selecta Classica* 4 (1993): 43-48; "A Contribution of Andrea Palladio to the Study of Roman Thermae," *JSAH* 52 (1993): 189-98; "The Costume of the Roman Bride," in *The World of Roman Costume,* ed. L. Bonfante & J. Sebesta (Madison: Univ. of Wisconsin Press, 1994), 54-64; *The Baths of Trajan Decius on the Aventine,* Roman Papers I, *Journal of Roman Archaeology,* supp. ser. 11 (1994): 1-88. **Home Address:** 18 Dana St., Amherst, MA 01002. **Business Address:** Art History Program, Univ. of Massachusetts, Amherst, MA 01003.

LA GIOIA, ROBERTO ■ AAR – Rome, Bookkeeper.

LAIDLAW, ANNE ■ FAAR Classics/Archaeology 61, RAAR Classics/Archaeology 76; AAR Classical Summer School 1955; Cosa Excavations, Staff 1965-71; Council of Contributing Institutions, Exec. Com. 1970-73, Chair 1973, Hollins College Rep. 1963-present; Tatiana Warscher Award for Archaeological Research 1965; Classical Jury 1977-79; Classical Soc., Scholarship Com., Head 1988-90, 1992-present. b. Apr. 16, 1931, NYC. BA 52, Bryn Mawr College; MA 57, Yale Univ.; PhD 63, Yale Univ. **Other Study:** Excavation training: Cosa, Italy 1965; Corinth, Greece 1991. **Research/Artistic Interests:** Ancient painting, Pompeian studies. **Career & Employment:** Westtown School, Faculty 1952-53; George School, Faculty 1953-56; Hollins College, Instr. 1961-63; Asst. Prof. 1963-67; Assc. Prof. 1968-74; Prof. 1974-87; E. Marion Smith Prof. 1987-present; Chair 1961-67, 1971-72, 1974-75, 1979-81, 1982-83, 1984-87, 1988-93. **Memberships & Offices:** ArIA, Lynchburg Soc., Pres. 1967-68; Excavations in the House of Sallust in Pompeii, Dir. 1969-72; Joint organizer & instructor, Short Term in Rome 1969-73; Consultant for exb., "Pompeii A.D. 79," American Museum of Natural History 1978; German Archaeological Inst. in Rome, Mission in Carthage, Staff Mem. 1983, 1987-88, 1994; ASCSA, Senior Assc. Mem. 1983-84, 1990-91. **Fellowships, Honors & Awards:** Yale Univ., Kellogg-Univ. Fellowship 1957-58, Lewis-Farmington Fellowship 1958-59; Fulbright Fellowship 1959-60; Hollins College, Faculty Research Grant 1963, 1966, Ford Fund Grant 1970, 1971, Mellon Fund 1974-85; ACLS Grant-in-Aid 1967, 1971, 1974, 1983, Travel Grant 1973; NEH Younger Scholars Fellowship 1968-69; APS Grant 1969, 1971, 1974; NEH Research Grants 1970, 1972; Virginia Colleges, Mednick Memorial Fund Grant 1975. **Publications:** "The Tomb of Montefiore: A New Roman Tomb Painted in the Second Style," *Archaeology* (Spring 1964): 33-42; "Through Pompeii with Tape and Ladder," *Hollins College Bulletin* (Feb. 1967): 8-12; "A Reconstruction of the First-Style Decorations in the Alexander Exedra in the House of the Faun," in *Neue Forschungen in Pompeji,* ed. Bernard Andreae & Helmut Kyrieleis (Recklinghausen: Aurel Bongers, 1975), 39-46; "Reconstructions of the First-Style Decorations in the House of Sallust in Pompeii," in *In Memoriam Otto J. Brendel: Essays in Archaeology and the Humanities,* ed. Larissa Bonfante & Helga von Heintze (Mainz: Philipp von Zabern, 1976), 105-13; "When in Athens...," *Newsletter of ASCSA* (Fall 1984): 3; *The First Style in Pompeii: Painting and Architecture,* Archaeologica 57 (Rome: Giorgio Bretschneider, 1985); "Die erste Stil," in *Pompeianische Wandmalerei* I (Stuttgart: Belser Verlag, 1990), 205-12; "Pompei no Hekiga dai Ichi Yoshiki," in *Pompei no Hekigat* 1 (Tokyo: Iwanami Shoten, 1991), 211-18; "Le Ier style," in *La peínture de Pompei* (Paris: Éditions Hazan, 1993), 1:227-35; "Excavations in the Casa di Sallustio in Pompeii: A Preliminary Assessment," in Eius Virtutis Studiosi: *Classical and Post-Classical Studies in Memory of Frank Edward Brown,* ed. Russell Scott & Ann Scott, Studies in the History of Art 43 (Washington, DC: NGA, 1993), 216-33. **Bio-Bibliography:** *Directory of American Scholars; Directory of College & University Classicists in the United States & Canada* (*Classical World* 78.4 [1985]); *Who's Who in the South & Southwest.* **Business Address:** PO Box 9691, Hollins College, VA 24020.

LAING, GORDON JENNINGS ■ FASCSR 1897; ASCSR, Prof. 1911-12. b. Oct. 16, 1869, London, ONT. d. Sept. 1, 1945. m. Alice C. Judson. BA 1891, Univ. of Toronto; PhD 1896, Johns Hopkins Univ. **Career & Employment:** Bryn Mawr College, Lect. 1897-99; Univ. of Chicago, Instr. 1899-1902, Asst. Prof. 1902-7, Assc. Prof. 1907-13, Prof. 1913-21, Chair 1919-21; McGill

Univ., Prof.-Dept. Head-Dean 1921-23; Univ. of Chicago, Prof. 1923-35, Dean 1931-35, Alumni Dean 1940-43; Univ. of Chicago Press, General Ed. 1909-21, 1923-40. **Memberships & Offices:** *Classical Journal,* Managing Ed. 1905-8; *Classical Philology,* Assc. Ed. 1905-21, Ed. 1923-45; United Educators Inc., General Ed. 1944-45; ArIA, VP; APA, Pres; CAMWS, Pres. **Fellowships, Honors & Awards:** Univ. of Toronto, LittD 1923; Univ. of Western Ontario, LLD 1924; Univ. of Pittsburgh, LLD 1930; Johns Hopkins Univ, LLD 1938; Louisiana State Univ., LLD 1938. **Publications:** ed., *Masterpieces of Latin Literature* (New York: Houghton Mifflin, 1903); *Selections from Ovid* (New York: D. Appleton, 1905); *The Phormio of Terence* (Chicago: Scott Foresman, 1908); ed. with Paul Storey, *Horace: Odes and Epodes* (Boston: B.N. Sanborn, 1910); *The Genitive of Value in Latin and Other Constructions with Verbs of Rating* (Chicago: Univ. of Chicago Press, 1920); trans., A. Gentili, *De legationibus libri tres,* 2 vols. (New York: Oxford Univ. Press, 1924); trans., Cornelius van Bijnkershock, *De foro legatorum liber singularis* (Oxford: Oxford Univ. Press, 1946); *Survivals of Roman Religion* (New York: Longmans, Green, 1931). **Bio-Bibliography:** *NY Times,* Obit. (Sept. 3, 1945); Briggs, 335-36; *Who Was Who in America.*

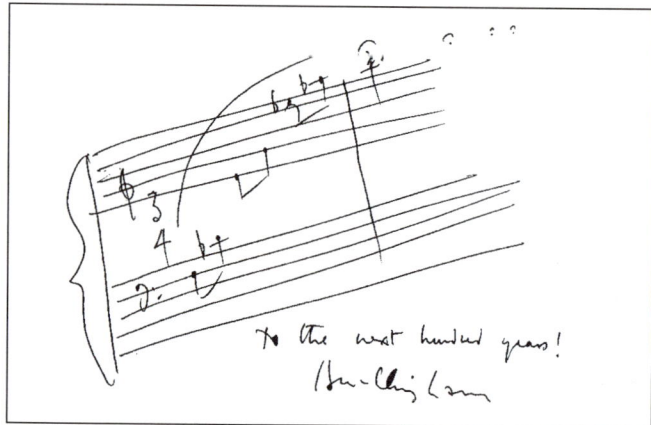

Bun-Ching Lam

LAM, BUN-CHING ■ FAAR Musical Composition 92. b. June 26, 1954, Macao. BA 76, Chinese Univ. of Hong Kong; MA 80, UC, San Diego; PhD 81, UC, San Diego. **Career & Employment:** Cornish College of the Arts, Seattle. **Memberships & Offices:** Washington Composers' Forum, VP 1985-86; Composers' Forum Inc., BoD 1992. **Fellowships, Honors & Awards:** Shanghai Intl. Competition, Highest Award 1987; Meet the Composer 1988, 1992; NEA Fellowship 1989; Bay Area Dance, Isadora Duncan Award 1990; NYFA Fellowship 1991-92. **Important Works:** *Wolken II,* for narrator, double choruses & chamber orchestra, King County Arts Comm. 1987; *Saudades de Macau,* for small orchestra, Macau Cultural Inst. Comm. 1987-89; *Another Spring,* for alto flute, cello & piano, Batschletes of Basel Comm. 1988; *Social Accidents,* for flute, bass clarinet, violin, accordion, piano & percussion, American Dance Festival Comm. 1988; *E.O. 9066,* for dance, Meet the Composer Comm. 1989; *Klang,* for solo percussion, Fritz Hauser Comm. 1990; *Similia/Dissimilia,* for trombone & electric violin,"Trombown" Comm. 1990; *Walking Walking Keep Walking,* for tenor & Chinese ensemble, Music from China Comm. 1991; *L'Air du Temps,* for string quartet 1991; *Circle,* for large orchestra 1992; *Last Spring,* for piano quintet, Composers' Forum Comm. for Ursula Oppens & the Arditti Quartet 1992; *The Child God,* a chamber opera, Bang on a Can Festival Comm. 1993; *Sudden Thunder,* for pipa & orchestra, American Composers Orches-

tra Comm. 1994. **Bio-Bibliography:** Barbara Miller, "Contemporary Chinese Composers" (PhD Diss., Univ. of Heidelberg, 1994); *New Grove Dictionary of Woman Composers.* **Home Address:** Spring Ave. Ext., Poestenkill, NY 12140.

LAMANTIA, JAMES R., JR ■ FAAR Architecture 49. b. Sept. 22, 1923, New Orleans, LA. BSArch 43, Tulane Univ.; MArch 47, Harvard GSD. **Career & Employment:** Wm. R. Burk & Asscs., Assc. 1951; Burk, Le Breton, Lamantia, Part. 1955-64; James Lamantia, Architect 1964-present; Tulane Univ., Prof. 1972-92, Richard Koch Prof. 1993-95, Prof. Emer. 1995; Univ. of Jordan, Amman, Fulbright Prof. 1949; Visiting Prof. & Critic: Harvard, Yale, Columbia, Notre Dame, etc. **Memberships & Offices:** Vieux Carré Comm. 1958-60. **Fellowships, Honors & Awards:** Fulbright Fellow 1940-51; AIA, NYC Chap. Environmental Award 1969; City Club of New York, Bard Award 1985; plus numerous honor awards from AIA & *Progressive Architecture.* **Important Works:** St. Catherine of Siena Church, New Orleans 1953-62; Presbytere Renovations & Reconstruction, Jackson Sq., New Orleans 1958-62; US Consulate Gen. Bldg., Madras, India 1960-64; Central Park Renovations: Tavern on the Green 1964, Dairy 1972-76, Belvedere 1972-77, Cop-Cot Pavilion 1972, Chess & Checkers House 1979; Prospect Park, Brooklyn Renovations: Tea House Pavilion 1980-87, Terrace Bridge 1985; Restaurants: Bethesda Fountain, Central Park, NYC 1968; Concourse Level, World Trade Center, NYC 1972; Outdoor Cafe, Lincoln Center, NYC 1984; Brasserie, NYC 1985; Kennedy Center Restaurant & Food Facilities, Washington, DC 1990. **Home Address:** 539 Bienville St., New Orleans, LA 70130. **Business Address:** James Lamantia, Architect, 539 Bienville St., New Orleans, LA 70130.

LAMB, ALBERT R., III ■ FAAR Landscape Architecture 70. b. Feb. 24, 1943, NYC. m. Nancy S. Lamb. BSLA 66, RISD; MLA 68, Univ. of Michigan. **Other Study:** Apprenticeship with Dimitri Hadzi 1993-present. **Research/Artistic Interests:** Urban spaces & culture, sculpture, drawing, gardening. **Career & Employment:** Clarke & Rapuano, Landscape Designer 1962-

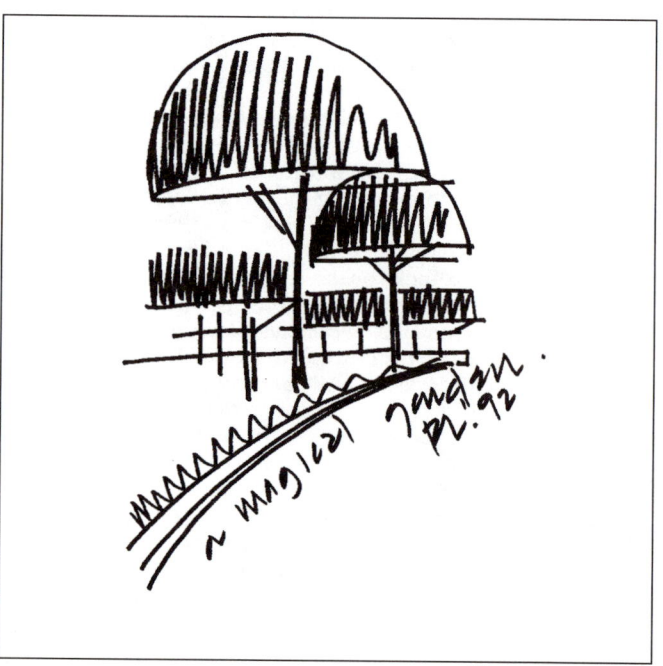

Albert R. Lamb, III

64; Architects Collaborative, Landscape Architect 1968-70; Dan Kiley & Part., Landscape Architect 1970-72; Benjamin Thompson & Asscs., Consulting Assc. 1974-79; Harvard GSD, Visiting Critic 1979-81, 1994; SWA Group, Design Prin. 1980-90; MIT, Center for Real Estate, Lect. 1982-present; Carr Lynch Hack & Sandell, Design Prin. 1990-present; Rick Lamb Asscs., Prin. 1990-present. **Memberships & Offices:** ASLA 1976-present; Urban Land Inst., Recreational Development Council 1986-91. **Fellowships, Honors & Awards:** ASLA, Merit & Honor Awards 1980-90. **Important Works:** La Defense, Central Mall, Paris 1970-72; New Seabury, MA, Resort Community 1972-present; Faneuil Hall Marketplace, Boston, Urbanscape 1975-77; Long Boat Key Master Plan & associated projects, Sarasota 1982-85; Santa Agueda Resort, Grand Canaria, Spain 1985-present; Cape Cod Acad., Osterville 1986; Trevor Zoo, Millbrook, NY 1989-present; Lincoln, NE, Revitalization 1989-90; Prudential Center Redevelopment, South Garden & Urbanscape, Boston 1990-present; Wilkens Residence, Oyster Harbors, MA 1991-92; Kasarjian Residence, Mahwaw, NJ 1992-present; McGraw Residence, Wiamo, MA 1993-present; Cavillon Historical Park, Dayton, OH 1994-present. **Home Address:** 21 Grant St., Cambridge, MA 02138.

LAMBERT, PHYLLIS ■ AAR Visitor 1986-87, Architect; Canadian Centre for Architecture, Montreal, Founder & Dir.

LAMBERTON, CLARK D. ■ FASCSR 08. b. June 18, 1881, Humboldt, ME. d. Apr. 24, 1965. BA 02, Dickinson College; MA 03, Princeton Univ.; PhD 08, Princeton Univ. **Other Study:** Berlin 1907. **Research:** Early Christian & medieval art. **Career & Employment:** Dickinson College Preparatory School, Carlisle, PA, Teacher 1902-3; Adelbert College, Western Reserve Univ., Instr. 1911-14, Asst Prof. 1914-24, Assc. Prof. 1924-28, Prof. 1928-52. **Memberships & Offices:** CAA, ArIA. **Fellowships, Honors & Awards:** Univ. of Pennsylvania, Harrison Fellow 1908-11. **Publications:** *Themes from St. John's Gospel in Early Roman Catacomb Painting* (Princeton: Princeton Univ. Press, 1905); "Development of Christian Symbolism as Illustrated in Roman Catacomb Painting," *AJA* 15 (1911): 507-17; *Art Estimate of Roman Catacomb Painting*, Western Reserve Univ. Bulletin, n.s. 33.16 (1930); abstract, *Art and Archaeology* 27 (1929): 91; "Accidental Factor in Constituting Isolation in Early Christian Art," *Art Bulletin* 32 (1950): 259-61. **Bio-Bibliography:** *Directory of American Scholars*, Princeton Univ. Archives.

LAMBETH, JAMES L. ■ FAAR Architecture 79. b. May 14, 1942, Kansas City, MO. m. Joyce T. Lambeth. c. Courtney. BS 64, Washington Univ.; BArch 66, Washington Univ.; MArch 67, Rice Univ. **Research/Artistic Interests:** Solar architecture & art. **Career & Employment:** Univ. of Arkansas, Prof. 1968-88. **Memberships & Offices:** AIA, Fellow 1976-present. **Publications:** *Solar Designing* (Pvt. Pub. 1976); *Solar 4* (Berlin: Amerika Haus, 1981); *Cuisine of the Creative* (San Francisco: Ten Speed Press, 1995). **Important Works:** Lambeth Residence, Fayetteville, AR 1969-92; Yocum Ski Lodge, Snowmass at Aspen, CO 1972; McKamey Residence, Fayetteville, AR 1973; Strawberry Fields Apts., Springfield, MO 1974; Delap Residence, Fayetteville, AR 1974; Benjamin Spock Residence, Beaver Lake, AR 1977; Ospedale dei Bambini, Civitavecchia, Italy 1980; Blevins HS, Blevins, AR 1982; Desert Compound, Amargosa Desert, NV 1983; Yaeger Residence, Estes Park, CO 1992; Inn at the Mill (Clarion Hotel), Johnson, AR 1995. **Exhibitions/Performances:** "Solar 4," Traveling Exb. 1981-86; Amerika Haus, Berlin, 1993. **Bio-Bibliography:** *Sundancing: The Art & Architecture of James Lambeth* (Miami: Miami Dog Press, 1993). **Home Address:** 1591

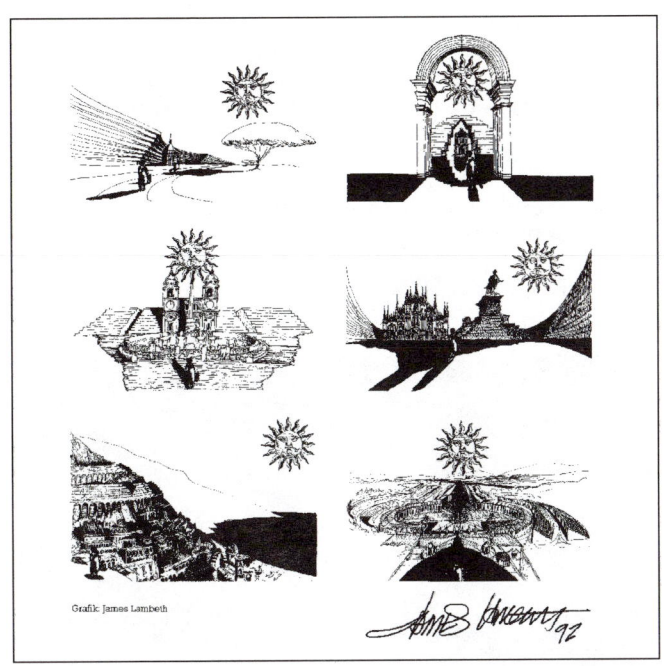

Grafik: James Lambeth

James L. Lambeth

Clark St., Fayetteville, AR 72701. **Business Address:** James Lambeth, Inc., PO Box 409, Johnson, AR 72741.

LAMBITTI, FABRIZIO ■ AAR – Rome, Housekeeping Staff.

LA MONTAINE, JOHN ■ RAAR Musical Composition 62. b. Mar. 17, 1920, Chicago, IL. BM 42, Eastman School of Music. **Fellowships, Honors & Awards:** Guggenheim Fellowships; Pulitzer Prize 1959; Koussevitzky Found. Comm.; William Inglis Morse Trust for Music Comm.; AAAL Grant; Eastman School Distinguished Alumni Award. **Important Works:** *Songs of the Rose of Sharon*, for soprano & orchestra 1956; *Piano Concertos I, II & IV* 1958, 1987 & 1989; *Fragments from the Song of Songs*, for soprano & orchestra 1959; *A Trilogy of Medieval Christmas Operas* 1961-69; *Birds of Paradise*, for piano & orchestra 1964; *Wonder Tidings*, for chorus, soloists & harp 1964; *Wilderness Journal*, for bass-baritone, organ & orchestra 1972; *The Nine Lessons of Christmas* 1975; *Be Glad Then America*, a Bicentennial opera 1976; *Symphonic Variations*, for piano & orchestra 1982; *The Lessons of Advent*, for chorus, harp, oboe, & guitar 1983; *The Solution to Elgar's Enigma*, for chorus & orchestra 1995. **Publisher:** Fredonia. **Bio-Bibliography:** *Baker's Dictionary of Music & Musicians.* **Home Address:** 3947 Fredonia Dr., Hollywood, CA 90068.

LANDON, ROBBINS ■ AAR Visitor 1970-71; Haydn Soc., Pres.

LANG, DAVID A. ■ FAAR Musical Composition 91. b. Jan. 8, 1957, Los Angeles, CA. BA 78, Stanford Univ.; MM 80, Univ. of Iowa; MMA 83, Yale School of Music; DMA 89, Yale School of Music. **Career & Employment:** Aspen Music Festival 1970s-81; Tanglewood 1983; New York Philharmonic, Revson Fellow, Asst. Composer-in-Residence 1985-86; Bang on a Can Festival, Co-Founder-Co-Artistic Dir. 1987-present. **Fellowships, Honors & Awards:** Guggenheim Fellowship 1986; NYFA Grant 1986; NEA Fellowship 1987; Kennedy Center, Friedheim Award 1989; BMW Music Theater Prize, Munich 1990. **Important Works:** *Illumination Rounds*, for violin & piano (CRI) 1982; *By Fire*, for choral group (CRI) 1984; *Eating Living Monkey*, for orchestra 1985; *Spud* (CRI) 1986; *Are You Experienced* (CRI) 1987-

88; *Orpheus Over & Under,* for 2 pianos (CRI) 1989; *International Business Machine,* for orchestra 1990; *Bonehead,* for orchestra 1990; *The Anvil Chorus,* for solo percussion 1991; *Judith & Holofernes,* a puppet opera. **Home Address:** 38 Barrow St., NYC 10014. **Business Address:** Novello & Co., c/o Bette Snapp, 1007 Glen Cove Ave., Glen Head, NY 11545.

LANGDON, TANNYS ■ Chicago Architectural Club, Burnham Prize 1984-85.

LANIER, CHARLES ■ AAR Charter Mem., Bank Exec.

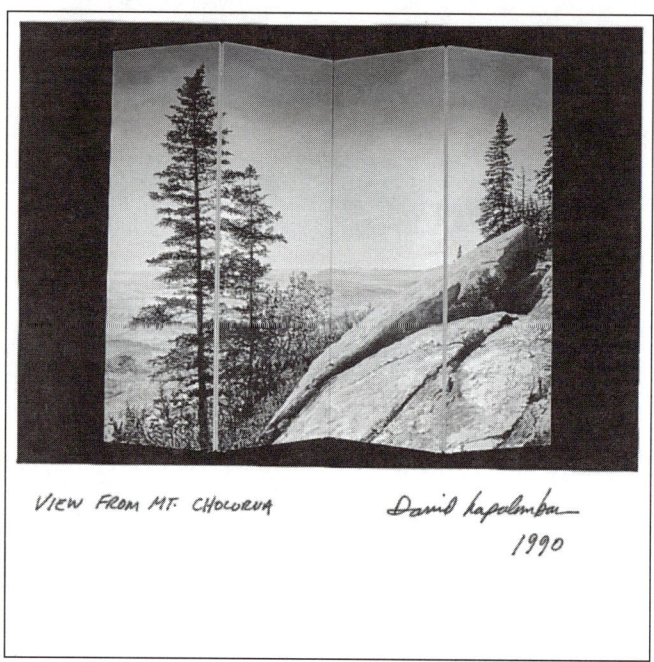

VIEW FROM MT. CHOCORUA

David Lapalombara
1990

David Lapalombara

LAPALOMBARA, DAVID ■ FAAR Sculpture 82. b. Apr. 28, 1957, Lansing, MI. m. Catherine Hinchey. c. Paia. BA 79, Oberlin College; MFA 81, Nova Scotia College of Art & Design. **Research/Artistic Interests:** Outdoor sculpture; the relationship of art & audience in selected plazas, parks, & churches in Rome; painted landscape screens. **Career & Employment:** Antioch College, Assc. Prof. 1986-present. **Fellowships, Honors & Awards:** Fulbright Fellowship 1982; Antioch College Faculty Fund 1987, 1989, 1990, 1993. **Important Works:** Allen Memorial Art Museum, Oberlin College; Graham Gund & Asscs.; Elizabeth B. Noyce; Douglas Dillon. **Exhibitions/Performances:** Allen Memorial Art Museum, Oberlin College 1979; Anna Leonowens Gallery, Nova Scotia College of Art & Design, Halifax 1981; American Studies Center, Naples, Italy 1982; Nat. Museum of Modern Art, Rome 1982; Richard Barreto Contemporary Art, Boston 1985; McKinley Park, Dayton 1987; Firelands Gallery, Oberlin 1991; Wingspread Gallery, Northeast Habor, ME 1991, 1992, 1994; Brendan Walker Gallery, Santa Monica 1992; Gallery 68, Belfast, ME 1992; ARA Gallery, Boston 1994. **Bio-Bibliography:** *Who's Who in American Education.* **Business Address:** Dept. of Art, Antioch College, Yellow Springs, OH 45387.

LAPALOMBARA, JOSEPH ■ AAR Trustee 1982-90, Trustee Emer.; Yale Univ., Prof.; Diplomat.

LAPATIN, KENNETH SHAPIRO ■ Broneer Fellow 1989-90.

LA REGINA, ADRIANO ■ AAR Visitor 1980-81, Superintendent for the Antiquities of Lazio.

LARICO, BENEDICT C. ■ FAAR Painting 85. b. Nov. 27, 1948, St. Louis, MO. BFA 72, Washington Univ.; MA 76, Bennington College. **Other Studies:** Whitney Independent Study Program 1973-74. **Career & Employment:** Bennington College, Instr. 1974-76; Bennington Summers, Program Coordinator 1976; Bryan Hunt, Casting Asst. 1978; DIA Art Found., Exhibition Asst. 1979-82. **Fellowships, Honors & Awards:** Helena Rubinstein Found. Award 1974.

LA ROCCA, EUGENIO ■ AAR Visitor, Archaeologist, Educator. **Career & Employment:** City of Rome, Superintendent for Monuments & Excavations; Univ. of Pisa, Prof. **Publications:** *Ara Pacis Augustae* (1983); *L'Auriga dell'Esquilino* (1987); *L'Esperimento della Perfezione: Arte e Società nell'Atene di Pericle* (1988).

LARSEN, NIELS HJALMAR ■ Rotch Scholar 1911.

LARSON, GARY H. ■ FAAR Architecture 83. Feb. 16, 1939, Amery, WI. c. Rachael. BArch 62, Washington State Univ. **Career & Employment:** Kallmann-McKinnell 1962-65; Walker-McGough 1965-68; Zimmer Gunsul Frasca 1968-77, Part. 1977-82; Parker-Larson, Part. 1984-90; Boucher Mouchka Larson, Part. 1990-present. **Important Works:** Kah-Nee-Ta Resort Hotel, Warm Springs, OR 1972; World Trade Center, Portland 1976; Veterans Administration Hospital, Portland 1981; Koin Tower, Portland 1981; Granpac Food Processing Plant, Portland 1992; Cooley Science Center, Oregon Graduate Inst., Portland 1992; Sony Disc Manufacturing Center, Springfield, OR 1994. **Business Address:** Boucher Mouchka Larson, 209 SW Oak, Suite 600, Portland, OR 97204.

LARSON, ROY FRANK ■ RAAR Architecture 62. b. Mar. 31, 1893, Minneapolis, MN. d. June 30, 1973. m. Olive Hathaway. c. Peter, David, John. BArch 23, Univ. of Pennsylvania. **Other Study:** Atelier Puckey, Chicago Architectural Club 1915-17. **Research/Artistic Interests:** Designs of educational & public buildings. **Career & Employment:** W. Carbys Zimmerman, Draftsman 1911-17; US Army 2nd Lieut.-1st Lieut. 1918-21; Paul Philippe Cret, Part. 1921-45; Habeson, Hough, Livingston & Larson, Part. 1945-70; Penn State Univ., Supervising Architect 1948-70; Rutgers Univ., Supervising Architect 1960-68. **Memberships & Offices:** Independence Hall Assn., Philadelphia, Co-Founder-VP 1942-73; Com. on Federal Public Works, Philadelphia Chap., Pres. 1938-40; Philadelphia Arts Comm., Pres. 1949-68; AIA; Royal Soc. of Arts, Great Britain; NAD. **Fellowships, Honors & Awards:** Chicago Architectural Club, Traveling Scholarship 1917; Univ. of Pennsylvania, Spayd Brooke Medal 1923, Faculty Medal 1923; Huckel Essay Prize; Art Alliance Medal for Distinguished Achievement 1955; Philadelphia Arts Festival Awards for Independence Hall 1962; Moore College of Art, Hon. DFA 1963. **Important Works:** Pennsylvania State Government Office Bldg., Philadelphia; Haverford College Library; Bethlehem Civic Center; Federal Reserve Office Bldg., Philadelphia; Malvern Senior HS, PA; US Military Acad., academic buildings, barracks & gymnasium; Boston Univ., residence hall; Pennsylvania State Univ., Van Pelt Library, Dietrich Graduate Library Center, Social Science Center, School of Medicine; Influential in planning in Philadelphia's historical area. **Bio-Bibliography:** *American Architects Directory; National Cyclopedia of American Biography; Who Was Who in America.*

LARSON, THOMAS NORMAN ■ FAAR Architecture 64. b. Aug. 7, 1935, St. Paul, MN. BArch 58, Univ. of Minnesota; MArch 62, Harvard Univ. **Career & Employment:** Ellerbe & Co., Designer 1956-59; Minoru Yamasaki, Sr. Designer 1959-60; Progressive Design Asscs., Part. 1960-61; Harvard GSD, Visiting Critic 1971-78; Architects Collaborative Inc., VP 1981-. **Fellowships, Honors & Awards:** Rotch Travelling Scholarship 1962; AIA Grant 1962. **Important Works:** Reid Residence, Lakeville, CT 1973, 1976; School of Law, Economics & Political Science, Tunis, Tunisia 1975; Grandberg Residence, Dover, MA 1976; Doyle Residence, Marblehead, MA 1978; Baghdad Sheraton Hotel, Iraq 1981.

LASCARI, SALVATORE ■ FAAR Painting 22. b. May 3, 1884, Sicily, Italy. d. Mar. 1967. m. Hilda Kristina Gustafson. **Study:** NAD. **Memberships & Offices:** Nat. Acad. of Fine Arts, Assc.; ALNY; NAD, Assc. **Fellowships, Honors & Awards:** NAD, Proctor Portrait Prize 1927. **Important Works:** Mosaics, St. Matthew's Cathedral, Washington, DC 1922; Dome, Welch Medical Library, Johns Hopkins Univ.; Mosaics, Currier Gallery of Art, Manchester, NH; Staircase Decoration, Washington Irving HS, NYC. **Exhibitions/Performances:** NAD. **Bio-Bibliography:** "Lascari, Well-Known Painter, Returns to Old Home in Lodi," *Passaic Herald News* (Apr. 1, 1941); *Who Was Who in America; Who Was Who in American Art.*

LASCH, PAT ■ FAAR Sculpture 83. b. Nov. 20, 1944, NYC. c. Melinda. BA 70, Queens College, CUNY; MFA 90, Georgia State Univ. **Research/Artistic Interests:** Mixed medium, most recently casting bronze; focus on context has been my relationship to death *(momento mori)*. **Career & Employment:** Parsons School of Design, Found. Faculty 1978-88; RISD, Asst. Prof. 1988-89; Univ. of Massachusetts, Assc. Prof., Dir. of Foundations 1991-present. **Fellowships, Honors & Awards:** Yaddo 1978, 1980, 1993; NYSCA, CAPS Grant 1980, Indiv. Project Grant 1985; NEA Grant 1980; Pollock Krasner Found. Grant 1987. **Important Works:** MMA; MOMA; Oberlin Museum, OH; Woman's Museum, Washington, DC; Rutgers Univ.; Queens College, CUNY; Prudential Insurance, NJ; Bouse Allen, NYC.

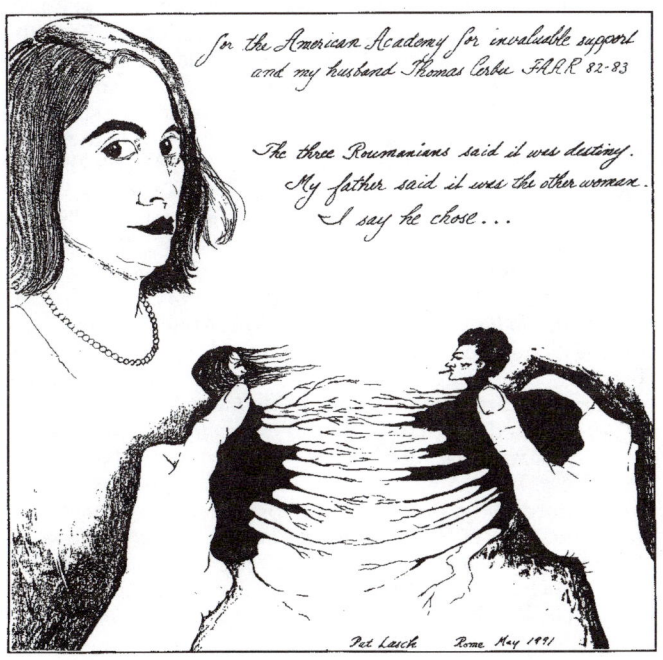

Pat Lasch

Exhibitions/Performances: Solo: AIR Gallery 1973, 1977, 1979, 1980; Zabriskie Gallery, NYC 1975; Galleruet, Lund, Sweden 1980; Galerie Ahlner, Stockholm, Sweden 1980; Kathryn Markel Gallery, NYC 1981, 1984, 1985; Lerner Heller Gallery, NYC 1981; Albright-Knox Gallery, Members' Gallery, Buffalo, NY 1984; McIntosh Drysdale Gallery, Washington, DC 1985; Marilyn Pearl Gallery 1988, 1990; Sculpture Center 1993; AIR 1994. **Bio-Bibliography:** *Who's Who in Art in America.* **Home Address:** 463 West St., Apt. 228G, NYC 10014.

LASH, STEPHEN S. ■ AAR Visitor 1990-91; Christie's, Senior VP.

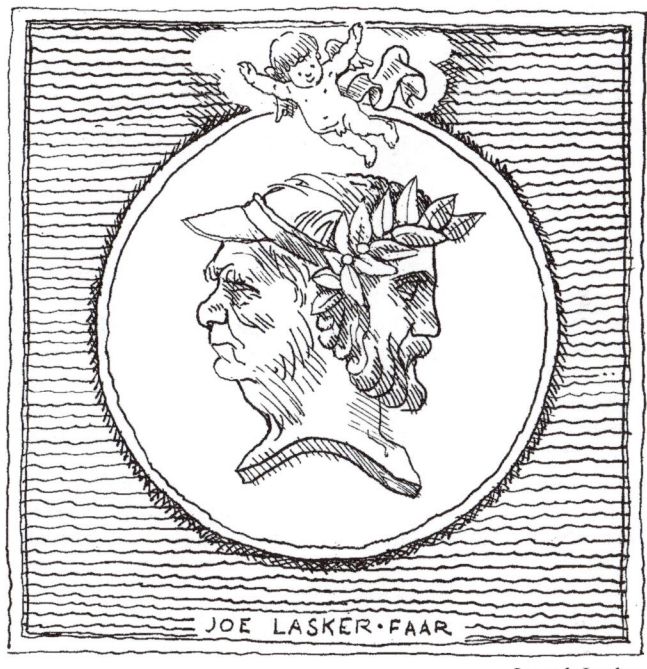

Joseph Lasker

LASKER, JOSEPH ■ FAAR Painting 51. b. June 26, 1919, NYC. m. Mildred Jaspen. c. David, Laura, Evan. Cert. 39, Cooper Union. **Research/Artistic Interests:** Book illustration. **Career & Employment:** Freelance painter & illustrator 1939-present; Univ. of Illinois, Visiting Assc. Prof. 1953-54. **Memberships & Offices:** NAD 1965-present, Council, Corresponding Sec. 1986-90, Mem. at Large 1992. **Fellowships, Honors & Awards:** NAD: Edwin Austin Abbey Memorial Scholarship 1947, 1948, 2d Altman Prize 1958, Clark Prize 1969, Isidore Gold Medal 1972, 1st Altman Prize 1980; Guggenheim Fellowship 1954; AAAL, Purchase Award 1965, 1968; NIAL Grant 1968; various awards for illustration & writing of children's books. **Important Works:** Whitney Museum, NYC; Hirshhorn Collection, Washington, DC; Philadelphia Museum; Baltimore Museum; Munson-Williams-Proctor Inst., Utica, NY; California Palace of the Legion of Honor, San Francisco; Springfield Museum, MA; Syracuse Univ., NY; Colgate Univ., Hamilton, NY; Univ. of Minnesota, Minneapolis; Notre Dame Univ.; Wichita Museum, KS; Mural Paintings: Calumet, MI Post Office; Millbury, MA Post Office; Henry St. Settlement Playhouse, NYC. **Exhibitions/Performances:** Solo: Kraushaar Galleries, NYC 1951-present; plus numerous annuals, biennials, theme shows. **Bio-Bibliography:** *Who's Who in America; Who's Who in Art.* **Home Address:** 20 Dock Rd., Norwalk, CT 06854.

LATTIMORE, RICHMOND ALEXANDER ■ FAAR Classics/Archaeology 35. b. May 6, 1906, Paotingfu, China. d. Feb. 26, 1984. m. Alice Bockstahler. c. Steven, Alexander. BA 26, Dartmouth College; MA 28, Univ. of Illinois; BA 32, Christ Church, Oxford Univ.; PhD 35, Univ. of Illinois. **Research/Artistic Interests:** Greek & Latin epitaphs, poetry, translations of Greek literature. **Career & Employment:** Wabash College, Asst. Prof. 1928-29; Bryn Mawr College, Prof. 1935-71; US Navy 1943-46. **Memberships & Offices:** AAAL, Literature Dept.; APS; NIAL; ArIA; AAAS; PEN. **Fellowships, Honors & Awards:** Oxford Univ., Rhodes Scholar 1929; Rockefeller Post-War Fellow 1946; Fulbright Fellowship 1951-52; NIAL Award 1954; Dartmouth Univ., LittD 1958; ACLS Award 1959; Oxford Univ., MA 1964; Acad. of American Poets, Annual Prize for Lifetime Poetic Achievement 1984; Bollingen Translation Prize; Phi Beta Kappa. **Publications:** *Themes in Greek & Latin Epitaphs* (Urbana: Illinois Univ. Press, 1942); trans., Pindar, *The Odes of Pindar* (Chicago: Univ. of Chicago Press, 1947); trans., *Greek Lyrics* (Chicago: Univ. of Chicago Press, 1955); trans., Homer, *The Iliad* (Chicago: Univ. of Chicago Press, 1951); ed. & trans. with David Grene, *The Complete Greek Tragedies,* 4 vols. (Chicago: Univ. of Chicago Press, 1953-56); *Poems* (Ann Arbor: Univ. of Michigan Press, 1957); *The Poetry of Three Decades* (Baltimore: Johns Hopkins Press, 1958); *The Poetry of Greek Tragedy* (Baltimore: Johns Hopkins Press, 1958); trans., Hesiod, *The Works & Days: Theogony* (Ann Arbor: Univ. of Michigan Press, 1959); *Sestina for a Far-Off Summer: Poems 1957-62* (Ann Arbor: Univ. of Michigan Press, 1962); trans., *The Frogs of Aristophanes* (Ann Arbor: Univ. of Michigan Press, 1962); *Story Patterns in Greek Tragedy* (London: Athlone Press, 1964); *The Stride of Time* (Ann Arbor: Univ. of Michigan Press, 1966); trans., Homer, *The Odyssey* (Chicago: Univ. of Chicago Press, 1967); *Poems from Three Decades* (New York: Scribner's, 1972); trans., Euripides, *Iphigeneia in Tauris* (New York: Oxford Univ. Press, 1973); trans., *The Four Gospels and the Revelation* (New York: Farrar, Straus & Giroux, 1979); *Continuing Conclusions: Poems* (Baton Rouge: Louisiana State Univ. Press, 1983); **Bio-Bibliography:** *NY Times,* Obit. (Feb. 28, 1984); Briggs, 344-46; *Who Was Who in America.*

LAURENT, ROBERT ■ RAAR Sculpture 55. b. June 29, 1890, Concarneau, France. d. Apr. 20, 1970. m. Marie Caraes. c. Jean Louis, Paul Robert. **Studies:** British Acad. of Fine Arts, Rome; with Hamilton Easter Field, Maurice Sterne. **Research/Artistic Interests:** Sculpture in wood & direct cutting in plaster, stone & marble. **Career & Employment:** US Naval Aviation Corps 1917-19; Ogunquit School of Painting & Sculpture, Dir.; Indiana Univ., Prof. **Memberships & Offices:** NIAL, American Soc. of Painters, Sculptors & Gravers; Modern Artists of America; Audubon Artists; Sculptors Guild; Salons of America, VP; Hamilton Easter Field Art Found., Pres. **Fellowships, Honors & Awards:** NSS, Fellow. **Important Works:** in large museums throughout US. **Exhibitions/Performances:** American Art Exb., Moscow 1959; Robert Laurent Memorial Exb., Durham, NH 1972-73. **Bio-Bibliography:** *Who Was Who in America.*

LAVIN, IRVING ■ RAAR History of Art 72, 79; AAR Jerome Lectures 1985-86. b. Dec. 14, 1927, St. Louis, MO. m. Marilyn Aronberg, RAAR. c. Amelia, Sylvia. BA 48, Washington Univ.; MA 52, IFA; MA 53, Harvard Univ.; PhD 55, Harvard Univ. **Other Study:** with Bertrand Russell, logic & history of philosophy, Cambridge Univ. 1948-49. **Career & Employment:** Vassar College 1959-61; NYU 1963-73; IAS 1973-present. Special Lectureships: Columbia Univ., Charles T. Mathews Lectures 1957; Pierpont Morgan Library, NYC, Franklin Jasper Walls Lectures 1975; Collège de France, "Bernini and the Unity

of the Visual Arts" 1984, 1990; Oxford Univ., Slade Lectures 1985; UC, Berkeley, Una's Lectures in the Humanities 1987. **Memberships & Offices:** Assn. Intl. pour l'étude des mosaïques antiques; SAH, BoD 1967-70, CAA Liaison Officer 1970-71, BoD 1976-80, Millard Meiss Publication Fund Com. 1976-83; RSA, Adv. Council Representative for the Visual Arts 1976-79; Verein zur Förderung des kunsthistorischen Instituts in Florenz; Columbia Univ., Seminar on the Renaissance; Washington Univ., Dept. of Art & Archaeology, Visiting Com. 1969-73; Corpus of the Ancient Mosaics of Tunisia, Steering Com. Sec. 1969-present; Dumbarton Oaks Research Library & Collections, Bd. of Scholars 1972-75; *Iconographical Lexicon of Classical Mythology,* Adv. Com. 1973-75; Princeton Univ., Dept. of Art & Archaeology, Adv. Council 1973-present; Com. on Renaissance Studies 1973-present; *Journal of Medieval and Renaissance Studies,* Adv. Bd. 1974-present; Nat. Com. for the History of Art 1975-present, Chair 1983-present; Comité intl. d'histoire de l'art 1975-present, VP 1982-86, Pres. 1986-89; Italian Emergency Relief Com., Friuli Arts & Monuments 1976-present; Harvard Univ., Dept. of Fine Arts, Visiting Com. 1977-88; CASVA, Adv. Bd. 1979-84; Seventeenth Century Soc., Adv. Com. 1980-present; Dante Soc. of America, Adv. Bd. 1980-present; *Quaderni d'italianistica,* Ed. Bd. 1980-present; *History of European Ideas,* Ed. Bd. 1981-present; J. Paul Getty Museum Trust, Com. of Adv. 1981-91; Intl. Research & Exchanges Bd., ACLS-Polish Acad. of Sciences Com. 1982-83; Canadian Centre for Architecture, Adv. Com. 1983-86, BoT 1986-present; *Art e Dossier,* Scientific Com. 1986-present; *Palladio, rivista di storia dell' architettura e restauro,* Ed. Bd. 1988-present. **Fellowships, Honors & Awards:** Belgian American Educational Found. Fellow 1949; Harvard Univ., Sheldon Traveling Fellowship 1953-54; Dumbarton Oaks, Senior Research Fellow 1957-59; Senior Fulbright Scholar 1961-63; ACLS, Senior Fellowship 1965-66; Guggenheim Fellow 1968-69; CAA, Arthur Kingsley Porter Prize 1959, 1962, 1968; AAAS, Fellow 1978; City of Rome, Medal of Honor, Tercentenary of Gianlorenzo Bernini 1980; City of Montevarchi, Tercentenary of Francesco Mochi, Medal of Honor 1981; Premio Daria Borghese, Rome 1981; Accademia Nazionale dei Lincei, Rome, Socio Straniero 1986; Accademia Clementina, Bologna, Accademico d'Onore 1986; City of Rome & Istituto di Studi Romani, Premio Cultori di Roma 1987. **Publications:** "The Sources of Donatello's Pulpits in San Lorenzo: Revival and Freedom of Choice in the Early Renaissance," *Art Bulletin* 41 (1959): 19-38; "The House of the Lord: Aspects of the Role of Palace Triclinia in the Architecture of Late Antiquity and the Early Middle Ages, "*Art Bulletin* 44 (1962): 1-27; "The Hunting Mosaics of Antioch and Their Sources: A Study of Compositional Principles in the Development of Early Mediaeval Style," *Dumbarton Oaks Papers* 17 (1963): 179-286; "Five Youthful Sculptures by Gianlorenzo Bernini and a Revised Chronology of His Early Works," *Art Bulletin* 50 (1968): 228-48; *Bernini and the Crossing in Saint Peter's,* Monographs on Archeology and the Fine Arts (New York: NYU Press, 1968); "Bernini's Death," *Art Bulletin* 54 (1972): 158-86; "Divine Inspiration in Caravaggio's Two *St. Matthews,*" *Art Bulletin* 56 (1974): 59-81; ed., with John Plummer, *Studies in Late Medieval and Renaissance Painting in Honor of Millard Meiss* (New York: NYU Press, 1977); *Bernini and the Unity of the Visual Arts* (Oxford: Oxford Univ. Press & New York: Pierpont Morgan Library, 1980); ed., et al., *Drawings by Gianlorenzo Bernini from the Museum der bildenden Kunste, Leipzig,* exb. cat. (Princeton: Princeton Univ. Press, 1981); ed., *Gianlorenzo Bernini: New Aspects of His Art and Thought. A Commemorative Volume* (State College, PA & London: Pennsylvania State Univ. Press, 1985); ed., with William Tronzo, *Studies on Art and Archeology in Honor* *of Ernst Kitzinger on his Seventy-Fifth Birthday*, Dumbarton Oaks Papers 41 (Washington, DC: Dumbarton Oaks, 1987); ed., *World Art: Themes of Unity in Diversity, Acts of the Twenty-Sixth International Congress of the History of Art*, 3 vols. (Univ. Park, PA & London: Pennsylvania State Univ. Press, 1989); *Past-Present: Essays on Historicism in Art from Donatello to Picasso* (Berkeley, 1993); ed., *Meaning in the Visual Arts: Views from the Outside. A Centennial Commemoration of Erwin Panofsky (1892-1968)* (Princeton, 1995); ed., *Erwin Panofsky: Three Essays on Style* (Cambridge, MA, 1995). **Bio-Bibliography:** *Directory of American Scholars; Who's Who in America; Who's Who in American Art.* **Home Address:** 56 Maxwell Ln., Princeton, NJ 08540. **Business Address:** IAS, Olden Ln., Princeton, NJ 08540.

LAVIN, MARILYN ARONBERG ■ RAAR History of Art 79. b. Oct. 27, 1925, St. Louis, MO. m. Irving Lavin, RAAR 72, 79. c. Amelia, Sylvia. BA 47, Washington Univ.; MA 49, Washington Univ.; Cert. 52, Univ. of Rome; PhD 73, IFA. **Other Study:** Univ. of Brussels 1949. **Research/Artistic Interests:** Italian Renaissance painting, computers & history of art (interactive electronic imaging, database construction). **Career & Employment:** Visiting Prof.: Yale Univ. 1978, Univ. of Maryland 1982-83; Princeton Univ., Visiting Lect.-Prof. 1976-present. **Memberships & Offices:** J. Paul Getty Trust, AHIP, Adv. Com. 1986-present; AITF-Getty (Computer Standards), Consultant 1989-present; CAA, Com. on Electronic Information, Chair 1991-present; Consortium of Art & Architectural Historians, Internet Listserver; IFA Alumni Assn., Treas. 1990-93. **Fellowships, Honors & Awards:** Fulbright-Hays Grant 1951-52; CAA, C.R. Morey Award 1977; NEH Grant 1985; Chicago Women in Publishing Award, 1st Place Winner 1991; US Dept. of Education, FIPSE Award 1992-94. **Publications:** "Giovannino Battista: A Study in Renaissance Religious Symbolism," *Art Bulletin* 37 (1955): 85-101; "Giovannino Battista: A Supplement," *Art Bulletin* 43 (1961): 319-35; "The Corpus Domini Altar of Urbino, Paolo Uccello, Joos van Ghent, Piero della Francesca," *Art Bulletin* 49 (1967): 1-24; "Piero della Francesca's 'Flagellation': The Triumph of Christian Glory," *Art Bulletin* 50 (1968): 321-42; "Piero della Francesca's Montefeltro Altarpiece: A Pledge of Fidelity," *Art Bulletin* 50 (1969): 367-71; "Piero della Francesca's Fresco of Sigismondo Pandolfo Malatesta before St. Sigismund," *Art Bulletin* 56 (1974): 345-74; *Ibid.,* 57 (1975): 307 & 607; *Seventeenth-Century Barberini Documents and Inventories of Art* (New York: NYU Press, 1975); "The Mystic Winepress in the Merode Altarpiece," *Studies in Late Medieval and Renaissance Painting in Honor of Millard Meiss*, ed. I. Lavin & J. Plummer (New York: NYU Press, 1977), 297-302; "The Joy of the Bridegroom's Friend: Smiling Faces in Fra Filippo, Raphael and Leonardo," *Art the Ape of Nature: Essays in Honor of H.W. Janson*, ed. M. Barasch, L.F. Sandler, & P. Egan, (New York: NYU Press, 1980), 193-210; *Piero della Francesca's "Baptism of Christ"* (New Haven: Yale Univ. Press, 1981); *The Place of Narrative: Mural Decoration in Italian Churches 431-1600 AD* (Chicago: Univ. of Chicago Press, 1990); ed., *IL 60: Essays Honoring Irving Lavin on his Sixtieth Birthday* (New York: Italica Press, 1990); *Piero della Francesca*, Masters of Art Series (New York: Harry N. Abrams, 1992); "Researching Visual Images with Computer Graphics," *Computers and the History of Art* 2 (1992): 1-5; "Piero's Meditation on the Nativity," *Monarca della Pittura: Piero and his Legacy*, Studies in the History of Art, ed. M.A. Lavin (Washington, DC: NGA), 127-42; "Iconographic Innovations at Arezzo," *Iconography at the Crossroads*, ed. Brendan Cassidy (Princeton: Princeton Univ. Press, 1993), 139-49; *Piero della Francesca: San Francesco, Arezzo* (New York: George Braziller, 1994). **Home Address:** 56 Maxwell Ln., Princeton, NJ 08540.

Business Address: Dept. of Art & Archaeology, Princeton Univ., Princeton, NJ 08544.

LAWLER, LILLIAN BEATRICE ■ FAAR Classics / Archaeology 26; AAR Classical Soc., VP 1941, 1943. b. June 30, 1898, Pittsburgh, PA. d. Dec. 13, 1990. BA 19, Univ. of Pittsburgh; MA 21, Univ. of Iowa; PhD 25, Univ. of Iowa. **Research/Artistic Interests:** Methods of the dance in Ancient Greece, remediability of English spelling with the study of Latin in secondary schools, art history. **Career & Employment:** Univ. of Iowa, Instr. 1923-25, 1961-67; Univ. of Kansas, Asst. Prof. 1926-29; Hunter College, Instr.-Prof. 1929-59, Prof. Emer. 1959. **Memberships & Offices:** *Classical Outlook*, Ed.-in-Chief 1936-57; APA; ArIA; Classical Assn. of the Atlantic States, Pres. 1947-49; American Classical League, Exec. Council, VP 1957-64; CAMWS; VSA. **Fellowships, Honors & Awards:** Phi Beta Kappa; Eta Sigma Phi, BoT 1949-55. **Publications:** "The Maenads: A Contribution to the Study of Dance in Ancient Greece," *Memoirs of the AAR* 6 (1927): 69-112; *Easy Latin Plays* (New York: AAR, 1929); *The Latin Club* (Nashville, 1929, 1957). *Adventures in Language* (Englewood Cliffs, NJ: Prentice-Hall, 1941); ed., *Studies in Honor of B.L. Ullman* (St. Louis: St. Louis Univ. Press, 1960); *The Dance of the Ancient Greek Theatre* (Iowa City: Univ. of Iowa Press, 1964); *The Dance in Ancient Greece* (London: A. & C. Black Co., 1965). **Bio-Bibliography:** Briggs, 246-48; *Contemporary Authors; Directory of American Scholars; Foremost Women in Communications; Who Was Who among North American Authors; Who's Who of American Woman.*

LAWSON, EDWARD GODFREY ■ FAAR Landscape Architecture 20. b. Oct. 29, 1884, Buffalo, NY. d. Jan. 4, 1968. BS, Cornell Univ.; MLA, Cornell Univ. **Research/Artistic Interests:** Garden details. **Career & Employment:** Cornell Univ., Prof.; American Red Cross, Italy, WWI; House of Herbs, Canaan, CT. **Important Works:** Fine Arts Comm., Washington, DC, Planner for American cemeteries in France, Belgium & England after WWI.

LAWSON, JOHN Q. ■ FAAR Architecture 81. b. Apr. 11, 1940, Tucumcari, NM. m. Lorna M. Katz. c. Bevan Eugene Lawson, Cary Augusta Lawson. BA 61, Rice Univ.; BSArch 62, Rice Univ.; MFAArch 64, Princeton Univ. **Other Study:** With O'Neil Ford, Preceptorship Program, Rice Univ. 1962; collaborated with artists on several projects: Richard Fleischner, sculptor 1983; Charles Fahlen, sculptor 1987-92; George Patton, landscape architect 1988; Audrey Flack, sculptor 1989; Stephen Berg, poet 1990; Warren Angle, artist 1992. **Career & Employment:** Frank Schlesinger Architect, Project Architect 1963-64; Kneedler, Mirick & Zantzinger Architects, Staff Architect 1964-65; Mitchell-Giurgola Architects 1965, Assc. 1971, Part. 1974-85; Univ. of Pennsylvania, Asst. Adj. Prof. 1972-87; Mitchell-Giurgola & Thorp Architects, Part. 1980-85; John Lawson Architects, Part. 1986-present. **Memberships & Offices:** Reynolds Aluminum Prize for Architecture Students, Juror 1982; AIA Design Awards Program, Washington Chap., Juror 1982, Chesapeake Bay Chap., Juror 1986; Nat. Council of Architectural Registration Exam, Grader 1985; *AS&U Magazine*, Architectural Portfolio Awards Program, Juror 1986; AIA Colorado Design Awards Jury, Chair 1990. **Fellowships, Honors & Awards:** Rice Univ., Tau Sigma Delta 1961, M. N. Davidson Award 1962; Princeton Univ., Lowell M. Palmer Fellowship 1962-64, Univ. Scholar 1963-64, Henry Adams Award 1964; AIA, Philadelphia Chap., Citation for Excellence 1971, Merit Award 1983, Silver Medal 1983, with Environmental Protection Agency, Citation 1978; Pennsylvania Soc. of Architects, Distinguished Building

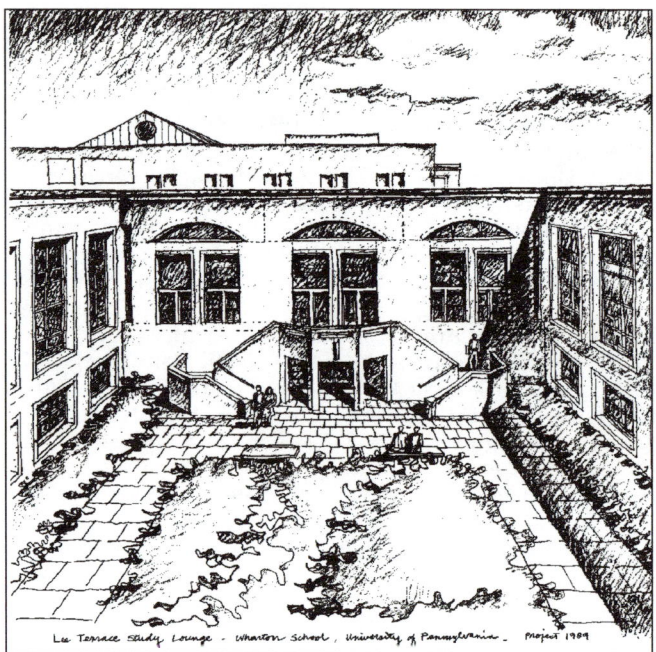

John Q. Lawson

Award 1971, 1975, Merit Award 1983; *American School & University Magazine*, Louis I. Kahn Citation 1985; Benjamin Franklin Bridge Lighting Com., 1st Runner-Up 1986; Redevelopment Authority of Philadelphia, Diamond Park Competition, 1st Prize 1987; Center City Residents' Assn., 1st Prize for Residential Renovation 1990. **Important Works:** with Mitchell-Giurgola Architects, United Way of Southeastern Pennsylvania, HQ Bldg., Philadelphia 1971; Swarthmore College, Lang Music Bldg. 1973, Tarble Pavilion, Physical Activities Bldg. 1978; Westinghouse Electric Corp., Central Services Bldg., Lester, PA 1974; US Interior Dept., Nat. Park Service, Independence Nat. Historical Park, Liberty Bell Pavilion, Philadelphia 1975, Maintenance Facility 1981; with Boney Architects, Walter Royal Davis Library, UNC, Chapel Hill 1984; in collaboration with Richard Fleischner, sculptor, Columbia Ave. Station Improvements-Columbia Plaza, Philadelphia 1985; with John Lawson, Evancich Residence, Additions & Renovations, Philadelphia 1988; Stepanian Residence, Additions & Renovations, Haddonfield, NJ 1990; Center for Animal Health & Productivity, School of Veterinary Medicine, Univ. of Pennsylvania, New Bolton Center, Kennett Sq. 1990; Wachs Residence, Loveladies, NJ 1991. **Exhibitions/Performances:** Rice Univ. 1962; Philadelphia College of Art 1976; Graduate School of Fine Arts, Univ. of Pennsylvania 1976-78; AIA Found., The Octagon, Washington, DC 1979; AIA Philadelphia Chap. 1985, 1991; Philadelphia Art Alliance 1985; NEXUS Gallery, Philadelphia 1987; Arthur Ross Architecture Gallery, Columbia Univ. 1990; Dyansen Gallery, NYC 1991. **Bio-Bibliography:** *Architectural Forum* (Jan. 1971); *L'Industria Italiana del Cemento* (Nov. 1971); *Progressive Architecture* (Apr. 1976); Aldredo De Vido, *Designing Your Client's House* (Whitney Library of Design, 1983); *Architectural Record* (July 1983); *Progressive Architecture* (Mar. 1985); *Architectural Record* (Aug. 1985); "She's Got What She Wanted," *Today Magazine, Philadelphia Inquirer* (July 12, 1989); "Into the Garden," *Qualified Remodeler* (Jan. 1992); *Who's Who in America; Who's Who in the East.* **Business Address:** John Lawson Architects, 812 Chestnut St., Philadelphia, PA 19107.

LAX, MICHAEL ■ FAAR Design Arts 78. b. Nov. 8, 1929, NYC. c. Jennifer, Rebecca. BFA 51, Alfred Univ. **Research/Artistic Interests:** Industrial design. **Career & Employment:** Independent Industrial Designer, NYC 1965-present; Lect.: Pratt Inst. 1970-71, RISD 1975-76. **Memberships & Offices:** Industrial Designers Soc. of America; American Inst. of Graphic Arts. **Fellowships, Honors & Awards:** Fulbright Fellowship 1953. **Important Works:** Major Clients: American Cyanamid, Copco, Champion Intl., Eastern Airlines, Formica, Kirk, Lightolier, Mikasa, & Salton, US; Christensell, Denmark; Coquet, France; Faveka, Netherlands; Amcor, Israel; Artemide, Italy; Takatsuki Diecasting, Japan; San Ignacio, Spain; Gullaskrufs Glasbruks, Sweden; Exb. Design: American Federation of Arts, Brooklyn Children's Museum, Ford Found., MMA, Nat. Aeronautics & Space Administration, Smithsonian Inst., US Commerce Dept., USIA. **Exhibitions/Performances:** MOMA 1952, 1968; Nat. Museum of Stockholm 1975; Stedelijk Museum, Amsterdam 1978; Musée des Arts Decoratifs, Paris 1980; Philadelphia Museum of Art 1983; Denver Museum of Art 1995. **Bio-Bibliography:** Jay Doblin, *One Hundred Great Product Designs* (New York, 1970); *Environment Design of the World* (Tokyo, 1971); E. Erikson, "Collaboration in Glass," *Craft Horizons* (Feb. 1971); *Design Review, Industrial Design Annual* (New York & London, 1978); ed. Kathryn B. Hiesinger & George Marcus, *Design Since 1945*, exb. cat. (Philadelphia, 1983). **Home Address:** 68 E. 91 St., NYC 10128.

LAYTON, BILLY JIM ■ FAAR Musical Composition 57; AAR Trustee 1969-78, Trustee Emer. b. Nov. 14, 1924, Corsicana, TX. m. Evro Zeniou. c. Alexis, Daphne. BMus 48, New England Conservatory of Music; MusM 50, Yale Univ.; MA 52, Harvard Univ.; PhD 60, Harvard Univ. **Career & Employment:** New England Conservatory of Music, Faculty 1959-60; Harvard Univ., Instr.-Asst. Prof. 1960-66; SUNY, Stony Brook, Prof. 1966-92, Chair 1966-72, 1982-85. **Memberships & Offices:** *Perspectives of New Music*, Ed. Bd. 1961-71; American Soc. of Univ. Composers, Founding Mem. 1965-84; Intl. Soc. for Contemporary Music, BoD USA Section 1968-70; College Music Soc., Council Mem. 1970-72; American Music Center, BoD 1972-74. **Fellow-**

My years at the Academy were the most important in my career, and certainly were the happiest in my life. How pleasant it is to remember all the wonderful friends I made then and the exciting events that we shared.

Thank you, Academy; thank you, for-sighted founders; thank all of you who have made the Academy what it has been and still is today!

Billy Jim Layton
F.A.A.R. 1957

September 1992

Billy Jim Layton

ships, Honors & Awards: NIAL Grant 1958; Brandeis Univ., Creative Arts Award 1961; Guggenheim Fellowship 1963-64; Thorne Music Fund Grant 1968-71. **Important Works:** *Five Studies for Violin & Piano* (CRI) 1952; *An American Portrait,* symphonic overture & orchestra 1953; *Three Dylan Thomas Poems,* for mixed chorus & brass sextet (G. Schirmer) 1954-56; *String Quartet in Two Movements* (CRI) 1956; *Three Studies for Piano* (G. Schirmer, CRI) 1957; *Divertimento,* for violin, clarinet, bassoon, violoncello, trombone, harpsichord & percussion (G. Schirmer) 1958-60; *Dance Fantasy,* for orchestra 1964. **Bio-Bibliography:** *Baker's Biographical Dictionary of Musicians, New Grove Dictionary of Music, Riemann Musik Lexikon; Who's Who in America.* **Home Address:** 1105 Mass Ave., No. 10A-B, Cambridge, MA 02138.

LAYTON, FREDERICK ■ AAR Charter Mem., Philanthropist, Art Collector.

LEACH, ELEANOR WINSOR ■ RAAR Classics/Archaeology 83; NEH Seminars, Dir. 1986, 1989; AAR Adv. Council 1978-present. b. Aug. 16, 1937, Providence, RI. c. Harriet Olney. BA 59, Bryn Mawr College; MA 60, Yale Univ.; PhD 63, Yale Univ. **Career & Employment:** Bryn Mawr College, Instr.-Asst. Prof. 1962-66; Villanova Univ., Asst. Prof.-Assc. Prof. 1966-71; Indiana Univ., Bloomington, Asst. Prof. 1977-80, Prof. 1980-present, Chair 1978-85; Visiting Prof.: Univ. of Texas, Austin 1972-74; Wesleyan Univ. 1974-76; Barnard College, Columbia Univ. 1981-82; Vassar College, Blegen 1987-88; Center for Renaissance & Baroque Studies, Univ. of Maryland, College Park 1990. **Memberships & Offices:** VSA, BoT 1978-83, 2d VP 1989; Indiana Classical Conference, 1st VP 1978-79, Pres. 1979-80; APA, BoD 1981-84, 1991-94, Program Com. 1981-84, Div. of Program, VP 1991-94, Ed. Bd. for Microforms 1984-87, Nominating Com. 1984-87, Chair 1987, Com. on the Classics in American Education 1987-89, Preservation Com. 1987-88, Publications Com. 1989-92; CAMWS, Exec. Com. 1984-88; ArIA, Central Indiana Soc., Pres. 1985-87; Ed. Bds.: *APA Monographs* 1989, *American Journal of Philology* 1989-present, *AJA* 1989-present. **Fellowships, Honors & Awards:** Bryn Mawr College, M. Carey Thomas Senior Essay Prize 1959; Woodrow Wilson Fellowship 1959-60; Yale Univ. Wilson Fellowships 1959-62; CUNY, Carnegie Teaching Internship 1961; Fulbright Award 1962 (declined); APS Grant-in-Aid 1971; ACLS Grant-in-Aid 1972, Fellowship 1992-93; Wesleyan Univ., Center for the Humanities Fellow 1974; Guggenheim Fellowship 1976-77; NEH Fellowship 1983-84; Nat. Humanities Center Fellowship 1992-93. **Publications:** "Georgic Imagery in the *Ars Amatoria,*" *TAPA* 95 (1964): 142-54; "*Ekphrasis* and the Theme of Artistic Failure in Ovid's *Metamorphoses,*" *Ramus* 3 (1974): 102-42; *Vergil's Eclogues: Landscapes of Experience* (Ithaca, NY: Cornell Univ. Press, 1974); "Neronian Pastoral and the World of Power," *Ramus* 4 (1975): 204-33; "Parthenian Caverns: Remapping of an Imaginative Topography," *Journal of the History of Ideas* 39 (1978): 539-60; "The Metamorphoses of the Myth of Acteon in Campanian Painting," *Mitteilungen des Deutschen Archaeologischen Instituts, Römische Abteilung* 88 (1981): 171-83; "The Anonymity of Romano-Campanian Painting and the Transition from the Second to the Third Style," in *Literary and Artistic Patronage in Augustan Rome,* ed. B. Gold (Austin: Univ. of Texas, 1982), 135-73; "The Punishment of Dirce: A Newly Discovered Continuous Narrative Painting in the Casa di Giulio Polibio and its Significance within the Visual Tradition," *Römische Mitteilungen* 93 (1986): 118-38; *The Rhetoric of Space: Literary and Artistic Representations of Landscape in Republican and Augustan Rome* (Princeton: Princeton Univ. Press, 1988); "The Politics of

Self-Presentation: Pliny's Letters and Roman Portrait Sculpture," *Classical Antiquity* 9 (1990): 19-39; "Polyphemus in a Landscape: Traditions of Pastoral Courtship," in *The Pastoral Landscape,* Studies in the History of Art 36, ed. John Dixon Hunt (Washington: NGA, 1992), 63-88; "Horace's Sabine Property in Lyric and Hexameter Verse," *American Journal of Philology* 114 (1993): 271-302. **Bio-Bibliography:** *Who's Who in the Midwest.* **Home Address:** 417 S. Henderson, Bloomington, IN 47401. **Business Address:** Dept. of Classical Studies, 547 Ballentine Hall, Indiana Univ., Bloomington, IN 47405.

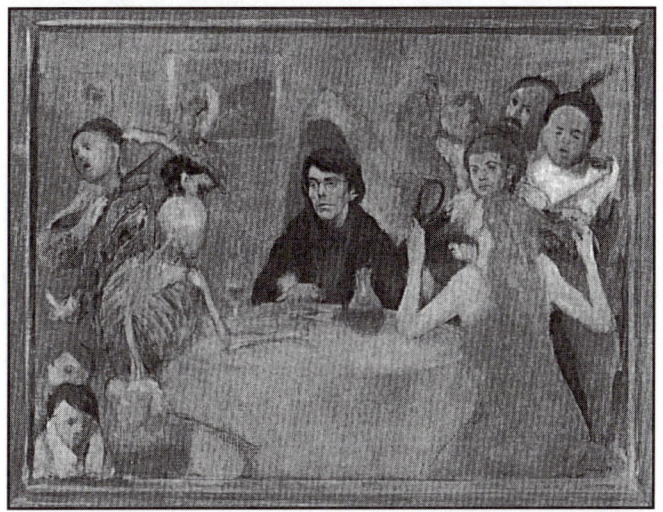

John C. Leavey

LEAVEY, JOHN C. ■ FAAR Painting 70. b. Mar. 21, 1937, Bronx, NY. m. Norma Leavey. **Study:** ASL, with George Grosz, Robert Beverly Hale & Edwin Dickinson 1955-61. **Research/Artistic Interests:** Figurative painting in oil. **Career & Employment:** United Scenic Artists Local 829, Scenic Painter 1979-present. **Fellowships, Honors & Awards:** ASL, Robert Ward Johnson Scholarship 1961; Louis Comfort Tiffany Grant 1965; Edwin Austin Abbey Fellowship 1969-71; NAD, Benjamin Altman Prize 1988. **Important Works:** Hirshhorn Collection, NGA, Washington, DC; Dickinson College, Carlisle PA; Museo della Città di Roma. **Exhibitions/Performances:** Solo: Columbia Univ., NYC 1965; Seamens Church Inst., NYC 1969; US Information Service, Rome 1973; St. Stephen's School, Rome 1974; Agostini Gallery, Rome 1974; Blue Mountain Gallery 1980, 1983, 1987-89; Group: NAD 1963, 1978, 1988-90; Gallery 88, Rome 1971-76; Forum Gallery, NYC 1973; Blue Mountain Gallery 1980-82, 1984-1986, 1988, 1990, 1991, 1992, 1993, 1994; Grand Central Gallery, NYC 1988, 1989; Atelier A/E, NYC 1994. **Bio-Bibliography:** *Americana* (USIS, Jan. 1975). **Home Address:** 30 Fifth Ave., NYC 10011.

LEAVITT, DAVID L. ■ FAAR Architecture 51. b. Aug. 26, 1918, Omaha, NE. BA 40, Univ. of Nebraska; BArch 40, Univ. of Nebraska; MArch 42, Princeton Univ. **Career & Employment:** Princeton Univ., Assc. Prof. 1940-41; Pratt Inst., Design Critic 1954-61; Antonin Raymond AIA, Chief Designer-Assc. Part. 1954-70; Hilton Intl. Co., Dir. of Architecture & Interiors 1970-78; MB Design Asscs., SA 1978-81; David T. Williams 1981-89; David L. Leavitt, Hotel Design Consultant 1989-present. **Memberships & Offices:** AIA, Emer.; AIA, New York State, Emer.; Nat. Council of Architecture Registration Bds.; Far East Assn. of Architects & Engineers. **Fellowships, Honors &**

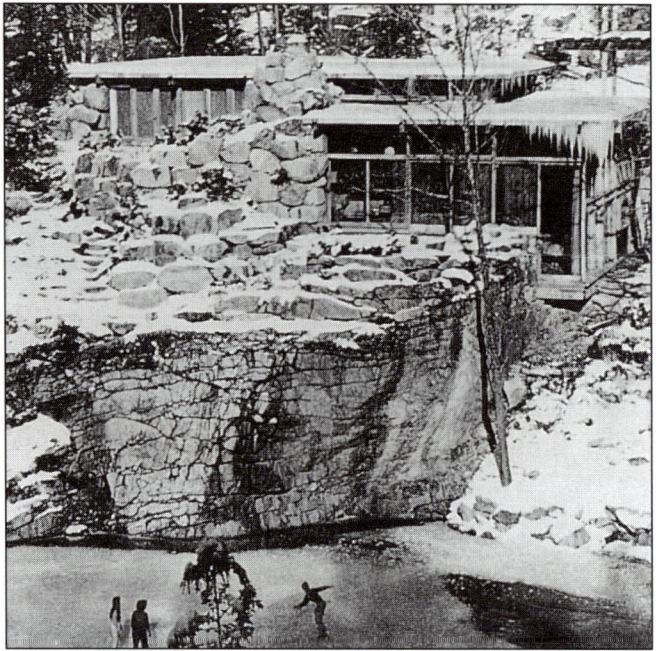

David L. Leavitt

Awards: Univ. of Nebraska Regents Scholarship 1936; Princeton Univ. Prize 1940. **Important Works:** Long Beach Shoreline Study, CA 1948; *Readers Digest* Bldg., Tokyo 1953; with Raymond & Rado, Yamaha Music Store, Ginza, Tokyo 1953; with Raymond & Rado, Russell Wright Residence, Garrison, NY 1962; with MB Design, Hilton Intl. Hotel, Strassburg, France 1970; with D.T. Williams, Drake Hotel, Chicago 1983; with S. Failla, Chicago Athletic Club 1988-91; with S. Failla, New York Athletic Club 1989; with D.T. Williams & G. Portero, Drake Hotel, NYC 1990; with S. Failla, Westchester County Country Club, NY 1992. **Address:** 118 W. 72 St., Apt. 903, NYC 10023.

LEBRUN, RICO ■ RAAR Painting 60. b. Dec. 10, 1900, Naples, Italy. d. May 10, 1964. m. Constance Johnson. c. David. **Study:** Acad. of Fine Arts, Naples 1919-21. **Career & Employment:** Italian Army 1917-18; ASL 1936-37; Chouinard Art Inst. 1938-39; Sophie Newcomb College, Faculty 1942-43; Colorado Springs Fine Arts Center 1945; Jepson Art Inst. 1947-50, Dir. 1951-52; Escuela de Bellas Artes, San Miguel de Allende, Mexico 1953; Yale Univ., Summer Art School 1956, Artist-in-Residence 1958-59; Santa Barbara Museum School 1962. **Memberships & Offices:** NIAL. **Fellowships, Honors & Awards:** NAD, Assc.; Guggenheim Fellow 1935-37, 1962-63; AIC, 1st Prize 1947; Los Angeles County Museum, 1st Prize 1948; Univ. of Illinois, Purchase Prize 1949; MMA, American Painting Today, 2d Prize 1950; AAAL, Award of Merit 1952; PAFA, Temple Gold Medal 1953, Walter Lippincott Prize 1962. **Publications:** *Drawings* (Berkeley: UC Press, 1961); *Illustrations from Dante's* Inferno, exb. cat. (Worcester, MA: Worcester Art Museum, 1962). **Important Works:** Comms.: Pomona College; Pennsylvania Station, NYC 1936-38; Collections: Phillips Acad., Andover; MFA; Colby College; de Young Museum; Denver Art Museum; Harvard Univ.; Univ. of Hawaii; Univ. of Illinois; Los Angeles County Museum of Art; MMA; MOMA; RISD; Pomona College; Santa Barbara Museum of Art; Syracuse Univ. **Exhibitions/Performances:** de Young Museum 1942; Santa Barbara Museum of Art 1942, 1947, 1951, 1956; Colorado Springs Museum of Fine Arts 1945; Philadelphia Art Alliance 1945, 1950; Jepson Art Inst. 1947, 1949; Los Angeles

County Museum of Art 1950, 1961, 1967; AIC 1955; Retrospective, Los Angeles County Museum of Art 1967. **Bio-Bibliography:** *NY Times,* Obit. (May 11, 1964); *Dictionary of Contemporary American Artists; Oxford Companion to Twentieth-Century Art; Who Was Who in America; Who's Who in American Art.*

LEDBETTER, CELIA MARGARET ■ FAAR Architecture 83. b. Nov. 22, 1955, Oklahoma City, OK. m. David Hamilton. c. Wesley Robert. BArch 78, Oklahoma State Univ.; MS 80, Georgia Inst. of Technology. **Career & Employment:** Diedrich Architects & Asscs., Apprentice Architect, 1980-.

LEDOUX, BARRY ■ FAAR Sculpture 87. b. Nov. 3, 1947, Mamou, LA. BA 68, Southwestern Louisiana State Univ. **Career & Employment:** School of Visual Arts, NYC, Faculty; Tyler School of Art, Faculty. **Fellowships, Honors & Awards:** Athena Corp. 1981; CAPS Grant 1983; NEA Grant 1984; NYFA Grant 1985; Guggenheim Fellowship 1992-93. **Exhibitions/Performances:** Solo: Clocktower, NYC 1981; Willard Gallery 1982; 2-person: Hayden Gallery, MIT 1983-84; Group: Henry Street Settlement, NYC 1980-84; PS 1, LIC, NY 1981; Indianapolis Museum of Art 1982; Milwaukee Art Museum 1982-83; John Berggruen Gallery, San Francisco 1983; Bette Stoler Gallery, NYC 1984-85; Willard Gallery, NYC 1985. **Bio-Bibliography:** Roberta Smith, "Spacewalk," *Village Voice* (June 10-16, 1981); John Perreault, "Good for the Figure," *Soho Weekly News* (Nov. 25, 1981); Cynthia Nadelman, "The New American Sculpture," *Art News* (Jan. 1984).

LEE, RENSSELAER WRIGHT ■ RAAR History of Art 55; AAR Trustee 1958-76, Pres. 1969-71. b. June 15, 1898, Philadelphia, PA. d. Dec. 4, 1984. m. Stella Garrett. c. Julia Rensselaer Lee; Mary Lee Muromcew; Rensselaer W. Lee, III. BA 20, Princeton Univ.; PhD 26, Princeton Univ. **Research/Artistic Interests:** Renaissance & baroque painting, art theory, English literature. **Career & Employment:** Princeton Univ., Instr. 1922-23, Visiting Prof. 1948, 1968-69, Chair 1955-64, Marquand Prof. 1961-66, Prof. Emer. 1966-84; Northwestern Univ., Assc. Prof.-Chair 1931-34, Prof. 1934-40, Harris Lect. 1966; Smith College, Prof. 1941-48; Columbia Univ., Prof. 1948-54; IFA, Prof. 1954-55. **Memberships & Offices:** *Art Bulletin,* Ed.-in-Chief 1942-44, Ed. Bd. 1945-70; CAA, Pres. 1944-46; Fogg Museum, Harvard Univ., Visiting Com. 1957-63; IAS 1939, 1942-44, 1946-47; MAA, Councilor 1961-64; RSA, Pres. 1977-78; Union Academique Intl., Pres. 1962-65; ACLS, BoT 1944-46. **Fellowships, Honors & Awards:** Carnegie Fellow 1927-29; ACLS Fellow 1929-30; Northwestern Univ., Hon. LHD 1971. **Publications:** "*Ut pictura poesis:* The Humanistic Theory of Painting," *Art Bulletin* 22 (1940): 197-269 (2d ed., New York: Norton, 1967); "Effect of War on Renaissance and Baroque Art in Italy," *Art Journal* 4 (1945): 81-91; "Vinloos Rinaldo and Armida in the Princeton Museum," *Princeton Museum Record* 19 (1961): 10-22; "Giambattista Tiepolo's Drawing of Rinaldo and Armida," *Smith College Museum Bulletin* 40 (1961): 10-22; *Names on Trees: Ariosto into Art* (Princeton: Princeton Univ. Press, 1977); "Ariosto's Roger and Angelica in Sixteenth-Century Art," *Essays in Late Medieval and Renaissance Painting in Honor of Millard Meiss,* ed. Irving Lavin & John Plummer (New York: NYU Press, 1977), 1:302-19; "Adventures of Angelica: Early Frescoes Illustrating *Orlando Furioso,*" *Art Bulletin* 59 (1977): 39-46. **Bio-Bibliography:** *NY Times,* Obit. (Dec. 7, 1984); *Contemporary Authors; Dictionary of American Scholars; International Who's Who; Who Was Who in America; Who's Who in the World.*

LEE, THOMAS OBOE ■ FAAR Musical Composition 87; SOF, Council Officer 1988-90. b. Sept. 5, 1945, Beijing, China. m. Kristin Beckwith. BA 72, Univ. of Pittsburgh; MusM 76, New

England Conservatory; PhD 81, Harvard Univ. **Other Study:** Tanglewood Fellowship 1976. **Career & Employment:** Swarthmore College, Asst. Prof. 1979-80; MIT, Lect. 1987-89; Duke Univ., Asst. Prof. 1989-90; Boston College, Assc. Prof. 1990-present. **Memberships & Offices:** BMI 1980-present; New England Conservatory, Alumni Assn., BoD 1987-90. **Fellowships, Honors & Awards:** Koussevitzky Tanglewood Composition Prize 1976; Massachusetts Artist Fellowship 1977, 1983; Guggenheim Fellowship 1983, 1986; NEA Fellowship 1983, 1987; AAAL, Charles Ives Fellowship 1985. **Important Works:** *Morango…Almost a Tango,* Kronos Quartet Comm. (Departed Feathers Music, Nonesuch, MCA) 1983; *Harp Concerto,* Pro-Arte Chamber Orchestra Comm. (Margun Music) 1985; *String Trio,* St. Paul Chamber Orchestra Comm. (Departed Feathers Music) 1985; *Marimolin* (Margun Music, GM) 1986; *Chôrinhos, Opus 38,* Pittsburgh New Music Ensemble Comm. (Departed Feathers Music) 1987; *Piano Quintet…Apple Strudel,* Apple Hill Chamber Players Comm. (Departed Feathers Music) 1988; *String Quartet in B-Flat,* Harvard Musical Assn. Comm. (Departed Feathers Music) 1990-91, rev. 1993; *I Never Saw Another Butterfly,* Amnesty Intl. Comm. (Departed Feathers Music) 1991; *That Mountain,* Thoreau Soc. Comm. (Departed Feathers Music) 1991-92; *Symphony No. 1…Fallen Angels,* Omaha Symphony Orchestra Comm. (Departed Feathers Music) 1992-93; *Piano Trio…Tangos,* Raphael Trio Comm. (Departed Feathers Music) 1994-95; *Eurydice…A Tone Poem for Cello & Orchestra,* Civic Symphony Orchestra of Boston Comm. (Departed Feathers Music) 1994-95. **Home Address:** 9 Remington St., Cambridge, MA 02138.

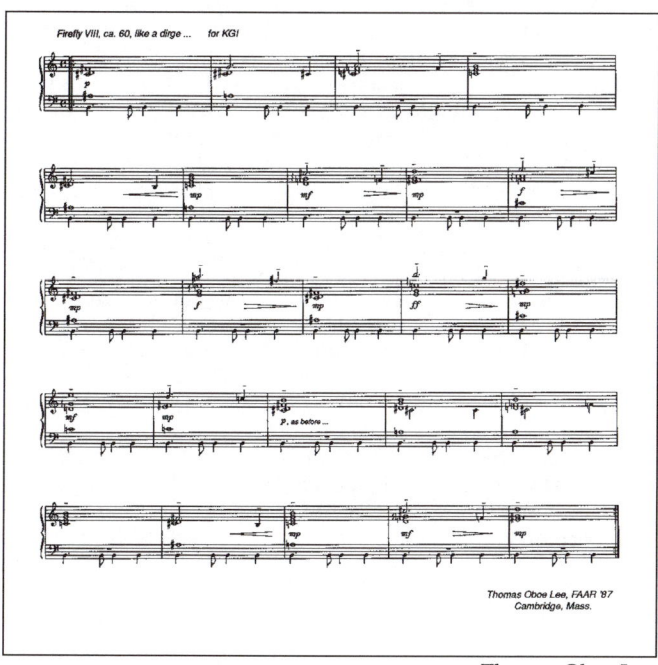

Thomas Oboe Lee

LEFTWICH, GREGORY VINCENT ■ FAAR Classics/Archaeology 91. b. May 28, 1951, Oklahoma. BA 73, NYU; MA 81, Princeton Univ.; PhD 87, Princeton Univ. **Other Studies:** ASCSA 1981-83. **Career & Employment:** Sarah Lawrence College, Faculty 1985-86; Vassar College, Visiting Instr. 1986; Boston Univ., Asst. Prof. 1987-. **Fellowships, Honors & Awards:** Fulbright Fellow 1981-83; Princeton Univ. Writing Fellow 1984-85.

LELLA, MARINA ■ AAR – Rome, Administrative Asst.

LENAGHAN, JOHN O. ■ FAAR Classics/Archaeology 59. b. Dec. 31, 1931, Clinton, IA. m. Lydia Lenaghan, FAAR 59. c. Patrick, Andrew, Julia, Matthew. BA; PhD 62, Princeton Univ. **Career & Employment:** Columbia Univ., 1959-61; Rutgers Univ., Asst. Prof.-Assc. Prof. 1961-present. **Home Address:** PO Box 2015, E. Millstone, NJ 08875.

LENAGHAN, LYDIA ■ FAAR Classics/Archaeology 59. b. Mar. 1, 1933, Emden, Germany. m. John O. Lenaghan, FAAR 59. c. Patrick, Andrew, Julia, Matthew. BA 54, Barnard College; MA 55, Bryn Mawr College; PhD 58, Bryn Mawr College. **Career & Employment:** Bryn Mawr College, Instr. 1959-62; Barnard College, Asst. Prof.-Prof. 1962-present. **Fellowships, Honors & Awards:** ANS, Fellow 1960; AAUW, Fellow 1969; APS, Summer Inst. 1975. **Home Address:** PO Box 2015, E. Millstone, NJ 08875.

LENNON, JOHN ANTHONY ■ FAAR Musical Composition 81. b. Jan. 14, 1950, Greensboro, NC. m. Camille Anne Goebel. BA 72, Univ. of San Francisco; MusM 75, Univ. of Michigan; AMusD 78, Univ. of Michigan. **Other Study:** Fellow at Tanglewood, Charles Ives Center, Composers Conference. **Research/Artistic Interests:** Music composition. **Career & Employment:** Emory Univ. 1994-present. **Fellowships, Honors & Awards:** Pi Kappa Lambda Honor Soc. 1975; AAAL, Charles Ives Prize 1977; Delius Festival Award 1979; Crofts Fellow in Composition, Tanglewood 1979; NEA Grant 1979, 1986; ACA Recording Award 1980; David Bates Award 1980; East & West Artists' Competition 1980; ACA, Elected Mem. 1980; Norlin Found. Fellow, MacDowell Colony 1980, 1984; BMI Grant 1980-1990; Knoxville Music Teachers' Assn., Composer of the Year 1981; Guggenheim Fellowship 1981-82; Meet-the-Composer Grants 1982-1987; Composers Conference Fellow 1983; Univ. of Tennessee, Faculty Development Grant 1983, Chancellor's Award 1988, Liberal Arts Creative Achievement Award 1991; Phi Beta Kappa 1985; Charles Ives Center for American Studies 1985, 1986; Harvard Univ., Fromm Found. Grant 1986; Deutscher Akademischer Austauschdienst (DAAD), Germany Residence 1986; Library of Congress, McKim Found. Grant 1986; Composers, Inc., 1st Place 1987; Spectri Sonori-Leoni Rothschild Award 1990; Composers Guild, 1st Place 1991; Phi Mu Alpha Sinfonia, Orpheus Medal 1991; Marian & Iwanna Kots Orchestral Competition 1992; Friedheim Award 1994. **Important Works:** *Symphonic Rhapsody,* concerto for alto saxophone & orchestra (C.F. Peters); *Metapictures,* for small orchestra (E.C. Schirmer); *Spectra,* for large orchestra (E.C. Schirmer); *Voices,* for string quartet (C.F. Peters, CRI); *Messiana,* for string quartet; *Death Angel,* for piano (Galaxy Music-Columbia Univ. Press, CRS, Composers Series-Capstone Records); *Another's Fandango,* for guitar (Mel Bay, Bridge Records); *Distances within Me,* for alto saxophone & orchestra (Woodwind Services, CRI); *Ghostfires,* for mezzo-soprano, harp, flute, guitar (ACA, Bridge Records); *Echolalia,* for flute (CRI); *Colors Where the Moon Never Could,* for soprano, violin, viola, cello, celesta, & percussion (ACA); *Far from These Things,* for chamber orchestra (E.C. Schirmer); *Ballade Belliss',* for violin & piano (CRI); *Suite of Fables,* for youth orchestra & narrator (E.C. Schirmer); *Seven Translations,* for soprano, piano, violin, & clarinet (E.C. Schirmer, CRI); *Zingari, Concerto for Guitar and Orchestra* (E.C. Schirmer, Bridge Records) 1993. **Bio-Bibliography:** *International Who's Who; Who's Who in America.* **Business Address:** Dept. of Music, Emory Univ., Atlanta, GA 30322.

LEON, ERNESTINE FRANKLIN ■ FAAR Classics/Archaeology 23; AAR Classical Soc., Pres. 1968. b. Aug. 10, 1895, NYC.

d. Jan. 9, 1968. m. Harry J. Leon, Sheldon Fellow 1919-20, 1921-22. c. Benjamin, Isabel Samfield, Judith Smith. BA 17, Hunter College, CUNY; MA 18, Columbia Univ. **Research/Artistic Interests:** Philology, archaeology. **Career & Employment:** HS Teacher 1917-21, 1923-24; Hunter College Summer Session 1919-21; Univ. of Texas 1925-50. **Memberships & Offices:** APA; CAMWS; Texas Classical Assn., VP 1963-64; Texas Fine Arts Assn.; League of Woman Voters; Nat. Council of Jewish Women. **Fellowships, Honors & Awards:** Drisler Fellow 1918-19; Phi Beta Kappa. **Publications:** "The *Imbecillitas* of the Emperor Claudius," *TAPA* 79 (1942): 79-86; "Cato's Cakes," *Classical Journal* 38 (1943): 213-21; "The *Instita* of The Roman Matron's Costume," *Classical Journal* 44 (1949): 278-81; "Scribonia and Her Daughters," *TAPA* 82 (1951): 168-75; "*Molochina* and a Fragment of Caecilius," *TAPA* 84 (1953): 176-80. **Bio-Bibliography:** *Who's Who of American Women*.

LEON, HARRY J. ■ Sheldon Fellow 1919-20, 1921-22; AAR Classical Soc., Pres. 1960.

LEONARDI, CLAUDIO ■ Italian Fulbright Fellow 1958-59.

LERDAHL, FRED ■ RAAR Musical Composition 87. b. Mar. 10, 1943, Madison, WI. m. Louise Litternick. c. Julia, Ruth, Sophia. BMus 65, Lawrence Univ.; MFA 67, Princeton Univ. **Career & Employment:** UC, Berkeley, Acting Asst. Prof. 1969-71; Harvard Univ., Asst. Prof. 1971-77, Assc. Prof. 1977-79; Univ. of Michigan, Assc. Prof. 1985-88, Prof. 1988-91; Chair 1988-90; Columbia Univ., Prof. 1991-present; Visiting Prof.: Yale Univ. 1981, Boston Univ. 1985. **Memberships & Offices:** Koussevitzky Music Found., BoD 1979-present, Comm. Com. 1985-present, VP 1985; *Contemporary Music Review*, US Ed. 1986-present; *Music Theory Spectrum*, Publications Com. 1989-91; Univ. of Michigan Inst. for the Humanities, Exec. Com. 1989-91; American Composers Orchestra, Adv. Bd. 1993-present. **Fellowships, Honors & Awards:** Marlboro Music Festival, Composer-in-Residence 1967-68; AAAL Composer Award 1971, 1988; Guggenheim Fellowship 1974-75; Naumburg Recording Award 1977; IRCAM, Resident Composer-Theorist 1981, 1984, 1991; Martha Baird Rockefeller Recording Award 1982; Wellesley Composers' Conference, Composer-in-Residence 1988; Michigan Council for the Arts, Creative Arts Award 1989; NEH Fellowship 1991; Center for Advanced Study in the Behavioral Sciences, Research Fellowship 1993. **Publications:** with Ray Jakendoff, *A Generative Theory of Tonal Music* (Cambridge: MIT Press, 1983); with Yves Potard, "La composition assistée par ordinateur," *IRCAM: Rapports de recherche* (1986); "Timbral Hierarchies," *Contemporary Music Review* 2.1 (1987); "Tonal Pitch Space," *Music Perception* 5.3 (1988): 315-50; "Cognitive Constraints on Compositional Systems," in *Generative Processes in Music*, ed. J. Sloboda (New York: Oxford Univ. Press, 1988); "Les relations chromatiques comme moyen d'extension d'une théorie générative de la musique tonale," *Analyse Musicale* 16 (1989): 54-60; "Atonal Prolongational Structure," *Contemporary Music Review* 3.2 (1989); "Whither Music Theory?" *Indiana Theory Review* 10 (1990); with John Halle, "Some Lines of Poetry Viewed as Music," in *Music, Language, Speech, and Brain*, Wenner-Gren Intl. Symposium Series, ed. J. Sundberg, L. Nord & R. Carlson (London: Macmillan, 1991); "Pitch-space Journeys in Two Chopin Preludes," in *Cognitive Bases of Musical Communication*, ed. M.R. Jones & S. Holleran (Washington, DC: American Psychological Assn., 1991); "Underlying Musical Schemata," in *Representing Musical Structure*, ed. I. Cross & P. Howell (New York: Academic, 1991); *Composition and Cognition* (New York: Oxford

Univ. Press). **Important Works:** *Chords,* for orchestra, Fromm Music Found. & Berkshire Music Center Comm. 1974-83; *Eros,* for mezzo-soprano & chamber ensemble, Koussevitzky Music Found. & Chamber Music Soc. of Lincoln Center Comm. (CRI) 1975; *Imitations,* for flute, viola, & harp, Orpheus Trio Comm. 1977, rev. 1992; *First String Quartet,* Juilliard Quartet & Joslyn Art Museum Comm. (CRI) 1978; *Second String Quartet,* Pro Arte Quartet & NEA Comm. (Laurel) 1980-82; *Waltzes,* for violin, viola, cello, & bass, Spoleto Festival USA Comm. (CRI) 1981; *Beyond the Realm of Bird,* for soprano & small orchestra, Univ. of Chicago Comm. 1981-84; *Fantasy Études,* for chamber ensemble, Musical Elements, Arch Ensemble, Contemporary Chamber Players, & Alea III, NEA Consortium Comm. (CRI) 1985; *Cross-Currents,* for orchestra 1987; *Waves,* for chamber orchestra, Orpheus, St. Paul & Los Angeles Chamber Orchestras, NEA Consortium Comm. (DGG) 1988; *Marches,* for chamber ensemble, Chamber Music Soc. of Lincoln Center Comm. 1992. Publisher: Boelke-Bomart. **Home Address:** 445 Riverside Dr., Apt. 21, NYC 10027.

LERNER, ROBERT E. ■ FAAR Post-Classical/Humanistic Studies 84. b. Feb. 2, 1940, NYC. m. Erdmut Lerner. c. Dietlind, Olivia. BA 60, Univ. of Chicago; MA 62, Princeton Univ.; PhD 64, Princeton Univ. **Other Study:** Westfälische Wilhelms-Universität, Münster 1962-63. **Research/Artistic Interests:** Medieval history: intellectual, cultural, religious history. **Career & Employment:** Western Reserve Univ., Asst. Prof. 1964-67; Northwestern Univ., Asst. Prof.-Prof. 1967-93, Peter B. Ritzma Prof. 1993-present. **Memberships & Offices:** MAA 1964-present, Fellow 1990-present; AHA 1964-present. **Fellowships, Honors & Awards:** Fulbright Senior Fellowship 1967-68; NEH Research Fellowship 1972-73; ACLS Fellowship 1979-80; Guggenheim Fellowship 1984-85; IAS, Fellow 1988-89; Rockefeller Found., Bellagio Study Grant 1989; Historisches Kolleg, Munich, Forschungspreis 1992. **Publications:** *The Age of Adversity: The Fourteenth Century* (Ithaca, NY: Cornell Univ. Press, 1968); *The Heresy of the Free Spirit in the Later Middle Ages* (Berkeley & Los Angeles: UC Press, 1972; 2d ed., Notre Dame Univ. Press, 1991); "A Collection of Sermons Given in Paris c. 1267, Including a New Text by Saint Bonaventura on the Life of Saint Francis," *Speculum* 49 (1974): 466-98; "Refreshment of the Saints: The Time after Antichrist as a Station for Earthly Progress in Medieval Thought," *Traditio* 32 (1976): 97-144; "The Black Death and Western European Eschatological Mentalities," *American Historical Review* 86 (1981): 533-52; *The Powers of Prophecy: The Cedar of Lebanon Vision from the Mongol Onslaught to the Dawn of the Enlightenment* (Berkeley & Los Angeles: UC Press, 1983); "A Case of Religious Counter-Culture: The German Waldensians," *The American Scholar* (Spring 1986):

> At the risk of sententiousness, I offer the following two quotations:
>
> Precipue in acquisitione litterarum humaniorum plerumque societas multorum sociorum prodest, quia interdum alter ignorat quod alius invenit.
> --Anon.
>
> Among the innumerable monuments of architecture constructed by the Romans. . . their greatness alone, or their beauty, might deserve our attention; but they are rendered more interesting by two important circumstances, which connect the agreeable history of the arts with the more useful history of human manners. Many of those works were erected at private expense, and almost all were intended for public benefit.
> --Edward Gibbon
>
> *Robert Lerner*
> *2 Sept. 1992*

Robert E. Lerner

234-47; "The Pope and the Doctor," *Yale Review* 78 (1988): 62-79; "Ernst Kantorowicz and Theodor E. Mommsen," in *An Interrupted Past: German-Speaking Refugee Historians in the United States,* ed. H. Lehmann & J. Sheehan (Washington, DC & Cambridge: Cambridge Univ. Press, 1991), 188-205; "Ecstatic Dissent," *Speculum* 67 (1992): 33-57; with Standish Meacham & E.M. Burns, *Western Civilizations,* 12th ed. (New York: W.W. Norton, 1993); "Himmelsvision oder Sinnendelerium? Franziskaner und Professoren als Traumdeuter im Paris des 13. Jahrhunderts," *Historische Zeitschrift* 259 (1994): 337-67. **Bio-Bibliography:** *Who's Who in America.* **Business Address:** Dept. of History, Northwestern Univ., 1881 Sheridan Rd., Evanston, IL 60208.

LESNICK, DANIEL R. ■ FAAR Post-Classical/Humanistic Studies 91. b. Jan. 17, 1946, Cleveland, OH. m. Linda J. Stone. c. Tommaso, Jane, Claire, Carey, Stacy. BA 71, Oberlin College; MA 73, Univ. of Rochester; PhD 76, Univ. of Rochester. **Research/Artistic Interests:** Crime & punishment in medieval Italy, preaching in medieval Italy. **Career & Employment:** Hiram College, Visiting Asst. Prof. 1977-79; Univ. of Alabama, Asst. Prof. 1980-87, Assc. Prof. 1987-present. **Memberships & Offices:** AHA 1973-present; Soc. for Italian Historical Studies 1984-present; RSA 1986-present. **Fellowships, Honors & Awards:** Fulbright-Hays Research Fellowship 1975, 1983; Villa I Tatti Research Fellowship 1976; NEH Fellowship 1979, 1988; APS Fellowship 1981. **Publications:** "Dominican Preaching and the Creation of Capitalist Ideology in Late-Medieval Florence," *Memorie Domenicane* ns 8-9 (1977-78): 199-247; "Religion and Social Transformation: Popular Preaching in Late-Medieval Florence," *Europa: A Journal of Interdisciplinary Studies* 3 (1979-80): 19-59; "How a Sermon Means: Preaching War in Late-Medieval Florence," *Allegorica* 6 (1982): 181-91; *Preaching in Medieval Florence: The Social World of Franciscan and Dominican Spirituality* (Athens: Univ. of Georgia Press, 1989); "Civic Preaching in the Early Renaissance," in *Christianity and the Renaissance,* ed. John Henderson & Timothy Verdon (Syracuse: Syracuse Univ. Press, 1990), 208-25; "Insults and Threats in Medieval Todi," *Journal of Medieval History* 17 (1991): 71-89. **Home Address:** 1516 Melrose Pl., Birmingham, AL 35209. **Business Address:** Dept. of History, Univ. of Alabama at Birmingham, Birmingham, AL 35294.

LEVAL, SUSANA TORRUELLA ■ AAR Trustee 1993-present. **Studies:** IFA. **Career & Employment:** MMA, Lect.; Museum of Contemporary Spanish Art, NYC, Chief Curator 1985-87; El Museo del Barrio, NYC, Exec. Dir. **Memberships & Offices:** MMA, BoT, Borough of Manhattan Trustee Representative.

LEVI, JULIAN EDWIN ■ RAAR Painting 68. b. June 20, 1900, NYC. d. Feb. 28, 1982. **Study:** PAFA with Henry Breckenridge, Arthur B. Carles, Jr. **Career & Employment:** ASL; New School of Social Research, Faculty 1945-66; PAFA, Faculty 1964-77. **Fellowships, Honors & Awards:** PAFA, Cresson Fellowship 1920, Fellowship 1954; AIC, M.V. Kohnstamm Prize 1942; Norman Wait Harris Medal 1943; Carnegie Hon. Mention 1945; NAD, Adolph & Clara Obrig Prize 1945; Univ. of Illinois 1948; NIAL Grant 1955, Fellow 1960. **Important Works:** Collections: Univ. of Arizona; Britannica; Albright Gallery, Buffalo; AIC; Cranbrook Inst.; Des Moines; Detroit Inst. of Art; Univ. of Georgia; Univ. of Illinois; MMA; MOMA; Michigan State Univ.; NAD; Univ. of Nebraska; Newark Museum; PAFA; Reed College; Santa Barbara Museum of Art; Scripps College; Springfield Museum of Fine Arts; Toledo Museum of Art; Whitney Museum, NYC. **Exhibitions/Performances:** Solo: Crillon Gal-

leries, Philadelphia 1933; Downtown Gallery, NYC 1940, 1942, 1945, 1950; Philadelphia Art Alliance 1953, 1963; Alan Gallery, NYC 1955; Lee Nordness Gallery, NYC 1961; Anna Werbe Gallery, Detroit 1961; Retrospective: Boston Univ., 1962; Rehn Galleries, NYC 1974. **Bio-Bibliography:** *NY Times,* Obit. (Mar. 2, 1982); *Contemporary Authors; Dictionary of Contemporary American Artists.*

LEVINE, DAVID A. ■ FAAR History of Art 78; SOF Council 1988-91. b. Dec. 2, 1951, NYC. m. Nicola Courtright, FAAR 83. c. Anna Tione, Luisa Cecilie. BA 73, Oberlin College; MFA 76, Princeton Univ.; PhD 84, Princeton Univ. **Career & Employment:** ICCS, Instr. 1978-79; Southern Connecticut State Univ., Asst. Prof. 1979-85, Assc. Prof. 1985-91, Prof. 1991-present, Art History Area Coordinator 1983-88, 1992-present; Brown Univ., Visiting Prof. 1992; Mt. Holyoke College, Visiting Prof. 1993. **Memberships & Offices:** CAA 1975-present; Connecticut Acad. of Arts & Sciences 1986-present; Yale Univ., Morse College, Assc. Fellow 1987-present; Art Center, Southern Connecticut State Univ., Adv. Bd. 1987-94. **Fellowships, Honors & Awards:** Mrs. Giles Whiting Found. Fellowship 1976-77; NGA, Chester Dale Fellowship 1977-78; Connecticut State Univ., Presidential Research Fellowship 1984-85, Research Grant 1985, 1987, 1988, 1989, 1990, 1992, 1994, Faculty Scholar Award 1992; Getty Fellowship 1985-86; IAS, Visitor 1985-86; Princeton Univ., Visiting Fellow 1985-86; NEH Travel to Collections Grant 1990. **Publications:** contr., *Dutch Drawings in American Collections,* exb. cat. (Washington, DC: NGA, 1977); with James H. Rubin, *Eighteenth-Century French Life-Drawings,* exb. cat. (Princeton: Princeton Univ. Press, 1977); "The Paradox of Rembrandt's 'Dr. Tulp'," *Art Bulletin* 68 (1986): 337-40; "Pieter van Laer's Artists' Tavern: An Ironic Commentary on Art," in *Holländische Genremalerei im 17. Jahrhundert: Symposium Berlin 1984,* ed. H. Bock & T.W. Gaehtgens (Berlin: Preussischer Kulturbesitz, 1987), 169-91; "The Roman Limekilns of the Bamboccianti," *Art Bulletin* 70 (1988): 569-89; "The Bentvueghels: 'Bande Académique,'" in *IL60: Essays Honoring Irving Lavin on his Sixtieth Birthday,* ed. Marilyn Lavin (New York: Italica Press, 1990), 207-25; with Ekkchard Mai et al., *I Bamboccianti: Niederländische Malerrebellen im Rom des Barock* (Milan: Electa, 1991). **Home Address:** 11 Blake Field, Amherst, MA 01002. **Business Address:** Art Dept., Southern Connecticut State Univ., 501 Crescent St., New Haven, CT 06515.

LEVINE, NEIL ■ AAR Visitor 1982-83, 1994, Architectural Historian.

LEVITAN, WILLIAM ■ FAAR Classics/Archaeology 88. b. Mar. 17, 1947, NYC. BA 70, Yale Univ.; PhD 83, Univ. of Texas. **Career & Employment:** Univ. of Southern California, Asst. Prof. 1982-85; Princeton Univ., Asst. Prof. 1985-93; Grand Valley State Univ., Prof. 1993-present.

LEVY, BROOKS EMMONS ■ FAAR Classics/Archaeology 56. b. Dec. 3, 1928, NYC. m. Kenneth Levy. BA 50, Radcliffe College; MA 52, Radcliffe Graduate School. **Career & Employment:** Brimmer & May School, Boston, Faculty 1954-55. **Fellowships, Honors & Awards:** Fulbright Fellowship 1952-53; Radcliffe Graduate School, Dana Scholarship 1950-52.

LEVY, EVONNE A. ■ FAAR History of Art 90. b. Nov. 12, 1961, NYC. BA 83, Brown Univ.; MA 84, Brown Univ.; MFA 87, Princeton Univ.; PhD 93, Princeton Univ. **Career & Employment:** Princeton Univ., Lect. 1992-93; UC, San Diego, Visiting Lect. 1994. **Fellowships, Honors & Awards:** Brown Univ.,

Graduate Tuition Fellowship 1983-84; Princeton Univ. Fellowship 1985-88, Italian Studies Com. Grant 1986, 1987, 1989, Whiting Fellowship 1990-91, Mellon Dissertation Fellowship 1991-92; Bibliotheca Hertziana, Kress Found. Fellowship 1988-90; Robert H. Lehman Fellowship 1988-90; Centro Internazionale di Studi sull'Architettura, 'Andrea Palladio,' Grant 1989; DAAD Fellowship 1993; MMA, Andrew Mellon Post-Doctoral Fellowship 1994-95; Woodrow Wilson Intl. Center Fellowship 1995. **Publications:** "Ideal and Reality of the Education of the Artist in the Sixteenth and Seventeenth Centuries," in *Children of Mercury: The Education of the Artist in the Sixteenth and Seventeenth Centuries*, exb. cat. (Providence: Bell Gallery, Brown Univ., 1984), 20-27; "Paolo De Matteis," and 5 entries in *A Taste for Angels: Neapolitan Painting in North America, 1650-1750*, exb. cat., ed. George Hersey & Judith Colton (New Haven: Yale Univ. Art Gallery, 1987), 215-28; "'A Noble Medley and Concert of Materials and Artifice': Jesuit Church Interiors in Rome, 1567-1700" and 25 entries in *Saint, Site, and Sacred Strategy: Ignatius, Rome, and Jesuit Urbanism*, exb. cat., ed. Thomas Lucas (Vatican City: Biblioteca Apostolica Vaticana, 1990), 46-61; "'Che Cos'è un (Architetto/)Autore?': Andrea Pozzo, la Cappella di Sant' Ignazio e il problema del disegnare in comitato," in *Atti del Convegno 'Andrea Pozzo e il suo tempo,' Trento, 1993* (Trento: QM Editore, 1995). **Home Address:** 35 Ellsworth Rd., Larchmont, NY 10538.

LEVY, MARVIN DAVID ■ FAAR Musical Composition 64. b. Aug. 2, 1932, Passaic, NJ. BA 54, NYU; MA 56, Columbia Univ. **Career & Employment:** American Opera Soc., Archivist 1952-58; Fort Lauderdale Opera Guild, Artistic Dir. 1990-; *Opera News*, Music Critic; *Musical America*, Music Critic; *American Record Guide*, Music Critic; *NY Herald-Tribune*, Music Critic. **Fellowships, Honors & Awards:** Guggenheim Fellowship 1960, 1964; Damrosch Grant 1961; Ford Found. Grant 1965; Scroll of the City of NY for Distinguished & Exceptional Service 1967; NEA Grants 1974, 1978. **Important Works:** *The Tower*, an opera 1956; *Sobota Komachi*, an opera 1957; *Escorial*, an opera 1958; *Mourning Becomes Elektra*, an opera, Ford Found. Comm. 1967; *Piano Concerto* 1970; *Trialogus*, for orchestra 1972; *Masada*, for voice, Nat. Symphony Comm. 1973; *Canto de los Maranos*, for orchestra 1977; *The Balcony*, an opera, rewritten as a musical, Metropolitan Opera Comm. 1981.

LEWINE, MILTON JOSEPH ■ FAAR History of Art 61, RAAR History of Art 73; SOF, Pres. 1973-75. b. Aug. 22, 1928, Atlantic City, NJ. d. July 30, 1979. m. Carol Filler. BA 52, Columbia Univ.; MA 55, Columbia Univ.; PhD 60, Columbia Univ. **Research/Artistic Interests:** Roman church architecture 1400-1800; mannerist & baroque art & architecture. **Career & Employment:** Columbia Univ., Lect. 1954-55, Instr.-Assc. Prof. 1955-69, Dir. of Graduate Studies 1969-72, Prof. 1969-79. **Fellowships, Honors & Awards:** ACLS Grant 1966; APS Grant 1966. **Memberships & Offices:** SAH, CAA. **Publications:** "Vignola's Church of Sant'Anna de' Palafrenieri in Rome," *Art Bulletin* 47 (1965): 199-229; ed. with others, *Essays in the History of Architecture Presented to Rudolf Wittkower* (London: Phaidon, 1967); *Masters of the Loaded Brushes: Oil Sketches from Rubens to Tiepolo* (pvt. printed, 1967); "Roman Architectural Practice during Michangelo's Maturity," in *Stil und Uberlieferung in der Kunst des Abendlandes* (Berlin: Gehr Mann, 1967); "Nanni, Vignola, e San Martino degli Svizzeri in Rome," *JSAH* 28 (1969): 27-40; "Vignola e Palladio: S. Andrea in Via Flaminia e la chiesa a Maser," *Bolletino del Centro Internazionale di Studi d'Architettura Andrea Palladio* 15 (1973): 121-29. **Bio-Bibliography:** "Obituary," *Burlington Magazine* 121 (1979): 728; *NY Times*, Obit. (Aug. 2, 1979); *Directory of American Scholars; Who's Who in American Art*.

LEWIS, DIANE HERMIONE ■ FAAR Architecture 77. b. June 16, 1951, NYC. BA 76, Cooper Union. **Other Study:** Apprenticeship at office of Richard Meier 1977-78; at office of I.M. Pei & Partners 1978-82. **Research/Artistic Interests:** The relationship of literature & architectural structure. **Career & Employment:** Univ. of Virgina, Asst. Prof. 1978; Yale Univ. School of Architecture, Visiting Prof. 1979-82, 1989, 1990; Cooper Union, Assc. Prof. 1982-present; Private Practice 1982-present; Harvard GSD, Visiting Prof. 1991-95; Architectural Assn., London, Resident Scholar 1995. **Fellowships, Honors & Awards:** Record Interior Award 1983; NYSCA Architecture Grant 1988-89; Graham Found. Fellowship 1991. **Publications:** "On Richard Meier," in *Richard Meier*, ed. V. Vaudou (Paris: Electa Moniteur, 1987); "Program the Literary Counterpart of the Architectural Work," *Journal of Architectural Education* 25 (Spring 1987); *The Education of an Architect*, 2 vols. (New York: Rizzoli 1988); "Introduction," in *Essays on The City: Notes from New York City, and Essay on the House*, ed. D. Lewis, J. Hejduk & K. Schapitch; "Kuriositatenkabinet," in *The Silent Baroque*, ed. Christian Leigh (New York: Rizzoli 1989); "The League for the Voice of the Critical Individual: A United Nations for Journalism Situated in Berlin," in *Denkmal oder Denkmodel: Galerie Aedes*, exb. cat. (Berlin: Feiress Galerie, 1988); "Young American Educators," *Arch Space Journal* (Korea); Aaron Betsky, *Violated Perfection*, (New York: Rizzoli, 1991); "Report from New York," *DQ* (Spring 1995); "Trip of Column through Wall," *New World Review* (Spring 1995). **Important Works:** Les Tuileries Restaurant, W. 59 St., NYC; Kent Gallery, E. 57 St., NYC 1984; Gauchos Basketball Found. Gym, South Bronx, NYC 1985; Painters Studio, 12 Harrison Street, NYC 1986; Private Library; 710 Broadway, NYC (project) 1986-87; Law Offices, 57C Lexington Avenue, NYC 1986-87; Honeymoon Miralda, Intl. Sculpture Installations 1987-88; Presentation Room; Condé Nast Publications, NYC (project) 1987-88; Factory Floor Domicile, 350 Manhattan Ave., NYC 1988-89; Washington Mews House Renovation, NYC 1988; Eccentric Motions Dance Co., Hydraulic Wall, Stage Set 1988; Century Paramount Hotel Renovation, NYC (project) 1988; Library Residence, 111 4th Ave., NYC 1988; Private Residence, Malibu, CA 1989; Bridge House, Astoria, OR 1989; Kunsthalle NY, Project 1991-93. **Exhibitions/Performances:** *Lezione in Inglese*, Stage Set for Fabio Mauri, Teatro di Roma 1977; Cooper Union 1980; Aedes Galerie, Berlin 1988; *Fuori le Mura*, Dance Performance Set, Pooh Kaye & the Eccentric Motions, La Mama, NYC & The Strand, Boston 1988-89; Knoll Intl., NYC 1989; Cooper-Hewitt Museum, NYC 1990. **Home Address:** 11 E. 10th St., NYC 10003. **Business Address:** Diane Lewis, Architect, 11 E. 10th St., NYC 10003.

LEWIS, DOUGLAS ■ FAAR History of Art 66. b. Apr. 30, 1938, Centreville, MS. BA (2) 59, 60, Yale Univ.; BA, MA 62, 66, Univ. of Cambridge; MA 63, Yale Univ.; PhD 67, Yale Univ. **Other Study:** German language, Columbia Univ. 1963 & Univ. of Vienna 1965. **Research/Artistic Interests:** Renaissance & baroque art & architecture, ancient architecture & sculpture, neo-classic & 19th-century art & architecture, American architecture, John James Audubon. **Career & Employment:** Bryn Mawr College, Asst. Prof. 1967-68; NGA, Curator 1968-present; UC, Berkeley, Visiting Lect. 1970, 1979; Johns Hopkins Univ., Adj. Prof. 1973-77; Georgetown Univ., Lect. 1980-93; Univ. of Maryland, Adj. Prof. 1988-present. **Memberships & Offices:** Centro Intl. di Studi di Architettura, Palladian Center, Adv. Council 1971-present; Mt. Holyoke College Art Museum, Art

Adv. Com., Subcom. Chair 1978-present; Smith College Art Museum, Visiting Com. 1979-present; US Postal Service, Citizens' Stamp Adv. Com., Vice-Chair 1979-present; Belgian-American Educational Found., American Fellowship Com. 1972-present; Bauman Family Found., Dir. 1989-94. **Fellowships, Honors & Awards:** Univ. of Cambridge, Clare College, Paul Mellon Fellow 1960-62, Hon. Scholar 1962; NGA, Chester Dale Fellow 1965-65, David E. Finley Fellow 1965-68; Smithsonian Inst., Copley Medal of Nat. Portrait Gallery 1981. **Publications:** *Late Baroque Churches of Venice* (New York & London: Garland, 1979); *The Drawings of Andrea Palladio* (Washington, DC: Intl. Exb. Found., 1981); with Manfred Leithe-Jasper, "Introduction," *Renaissance Master Bronzes* (London & Wshington, DC: Scala & S.I.T.E.S., 1986); with Pietro C. Marani, essays in *The Genius of the Sculptor in Michelangelo's Work,* exb. cat. (Montreal: Museum of Fine Arts, 1992); with Walter J. Boyne & David Finn, "Introduction," to *Art in Flight: The Sculptures of John Safer* (New York: Hudson Hills, 1992). **Bio-Bibliography:** *Who's Who in America; Who's Who in American Art.* **Business Address:** NGA, 4 St. at Constitution Ave. NW, Washington, DC 20565.

LEWIS, ELSIE ■ AAR World War II Scholar 1942.

LEWIS, ERNEST FARNUM ■ FAAR Architecture 11. b. July 13, 1883. dec. **Study:** Brown Univ., MIT.

LEWIS, NAPHTALI ■ FAAR Classics/Archaeology 36. b. Dec. 14, 1911, NYC. m. Helen L. Block. c. Judith L. Herman, John B. Lewis. BA 30, City College, CUNY; MA 32, Columbia Univ.; D.èsS. 34, Sorbonne, Univ. de Paris. **Research/Artistic Interests:** Social history of ancient Greece & Rome; Greek papyrology & epigraphy. **Career & Employment:** CUNY, Asst. Prof.-Distinguished Prof. 1947-76; Yale Univ., Visiting Prof., occasionally; NYU, Visiting Prof., occasionally. **Memberships & Offices:** APA 1938-present; Assn. Intl. de Papyrologues 1938-present, VP & Pres. 1965-83. **Fellowships, Honors & Awards:** American Field Service Fellow 1933. **Publications:** *L'Industrie du papyrus dans l'Egypte greco-romaine* (Paris: Rodstein, 1934); with Meyer Reinhold, *Roman Civilization,* 2 vols. (New York: Columbia Univ. Press, 1951, 3d ed. 1990); *Leitourgia Papyri* (Philadelphia: APS, 1963); *Greek Papyri in the Collection of New York University* (Leiden: E.J. Brill, 1967); *Greek Historical Documents: The 5th Century BC* (Toronto: Hakkert, 1971); *Papyrus in Classical Antiquity* (Oxford: Clarendon Press, 1974); *Greek Historical Documents: The Roman Principate* (Toronto: Hakkert, 1974); *The Compulsory Public Services of Roman Egypt* (Florence: Gonnelli, 1982); *Life in Egypt under Roman Rule* (Oxford: Clarendon. Press, 1983); *Greeks in Ptolemaic Egypt* (Oxford: Clarendon, 1986); *Papyrus in Classical Antiquity: A Supplement* (Brussels: Fondation Égyptologique Reine Élisabeth, 1989); *The Documents of the Bar Kokhba Period from the Cave of Letters: Greek Papyri* (Jerusalem: Israel Exploration Soc., 1989); plus some 150 articles & reviews in US & foreign journals. **Bio-Bibliography:** *Directory of American Scholars, Who's Who in America.* **Home Address:** RR 1, Box 291, Newport, NH 03773.

LEWIS, ROBERT HALL ■ RAAR Musical Composition 81. b. Apr. 22, 1926, Portland, OR. m. Barbara B. Lewis. c. Renata. BMus 49, Eastman School of Music, Univ. of Rochester; MusM 51, Eastman School of Music, Univ. of Rochester; Diploma 57, Vienna Acad. of Music; PhD 64, Eastman School of Music, Univ. of Rochester. **Other Study:** Paris Conservatory, conducting 1952-53; private study in composition with Nadia

Boulanger, Paris 1952-53, Hans Erich Apostel, Vienna 1955-57; Mozarteum, Salzburg, opera conducting 1956. **Research/Artistic Interests:** Have large body of music encompassing all media except opera. Thus, 4 symphonies, 4 string quartets, various concerti & diverse orchestra works. Chamber music ranging from duets to music for 12 players in diverse combinations. Solo works for piano, woodwind & brass instruments. Three works for chamber chorus. Some 80 compositions in toto. **Career & Employment:** Syracuse Univ., Instr. 1950-51, 1954; Oklahoma City Univ., Instr. 1951-52; Goucher College, Elizabeth Conolly Todd Distinguished Prof. 1957-present; Johns Hopkins Univ., Peabody Inst., Prof. 1964-66, 1972-present; Catholic Univ., Visiting Lect. 1967-68; Johns Hopkins Univ., Prof. 1969-80. **Memberships & Offices:** Chamber Music Soc. of Baltimore, Artistic Dir. 1964-1983, 1988-present; Baltimore Symphony Orchestra, Music Com. 1958-85, BoD 1968-83; American Soc. of Univ. Composers, Regional Chair 1971-73; American Music Center, BoD 1972-75; Ars Viva Concerts, Artistic Dir. 1981-present. **Fellowships, Honors & Awards:** Kosciuszko Found., Chopin Award 1951; Fulbright Scholarship 1955-57; Vienna Acad. of Music, Graduation Prize 1957; LADO Prize 1961; Guggenheim Fellowship 1966-67, 1980-81; ASCAP Awards 1969-95; Columbia Univ., Walter Hinrichsen Award 1972; Outstanding Educator of America 1974; AAAL Award 1976; NEA Grant 1976, 1986; Koussevitzky Music Found. Award 1977; Maryland State Artist Fellowship 1980, 1991; Rockefeller Found., Bellagio Study Center 1981; Baltimore City Arts Grant 1991. **Important Works:** *String Quartet No. 1* 1956; *Symphony No. 2* (Theodore Presser, CRI) 1971; *Concerto for Chamber Orchestra* (Theodore Presser, CRI) 1972; *Combinazioni II for Eight Percussionists and Piano* (Theodore Presser, Albany) 1974; *Duetto da Camera for Violin and Piano* (Theodore Presser, Albany) 1976; *Osservazioni II for Winds, Keyboard, Harp and Percussion* (Theodore Presser, CRI) 1978; *Combinazioni IV for Cello and Piano* (Theodore Presser, Albany) 1978; *Fantasiemusik II for Clarinet and Piano* (Theodore Presser, Albany) 1978; *Kantaten* (Theodore Presser, New World) 1980; *Symphony No. 3* 1981; *String Quartet No. 3* 1981; *Diptychon for Nine Players* 1984; *Archi for Piano Solo* (Theodore

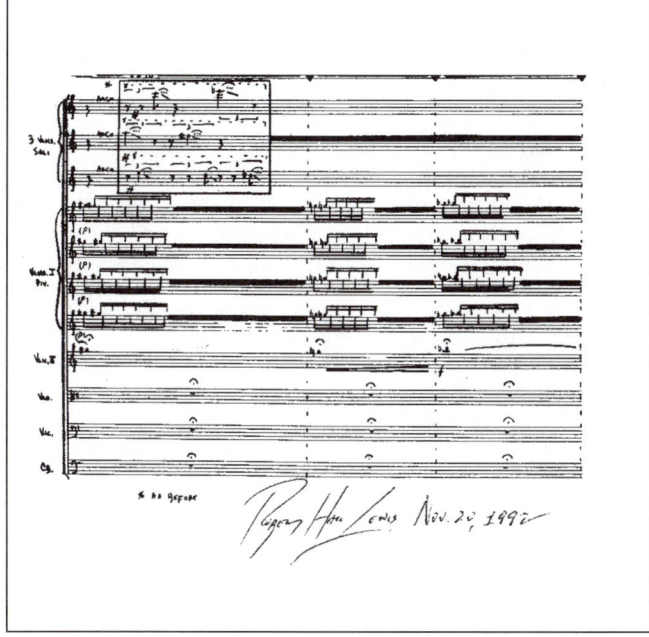

Robert Hall Lewis

Presser, New World) 1985; *Concerto for String Orchestra, Trumpets, Keyboard & Harp* (Theodore Presser, CRI) 1987; *Symphony No. 4* (Theodore Presser, New World) 1990; *Three Movements on Scenes of Hieronymous Bosch* (Theodore Presser) 1990; *Images & Dialogues for Orchestra* (Theodore Presser) 1992; *Nine Versions for Piano Trio* 1992; *String Quartet No. 4 "Seven Environments"* 1993; *Ottetto* 1994; *Soona for String Ensemble* 1995; *Ariosi for Orchestra* 1995. **Bio-Bibliography:** Luis Jorge Gonzalez, "Analytical Study of the Symphonies of R.H. Lewis" (D.M.A. Dissertation, Peabody Inst., 1977); Burchard Bulling, *Kurzgefasstes Tonkünstler-Lexikon* (Wilhelmshaven: Heinrichshofen Verlag, 1978); *ASCAP Biographical Dictionary; Contemporary American Composers; Index to Biographies of American Composers; International Who's Who in Music; New Grove Dictionary of American Music; Who's Who in American Music, Classical.* **Home Address:** 328 Broadmoor Rd., Baltimore, MD 21212. **Business Address:** Rosalie Calabrese Management, 700 Columbus Ave., NYC 10025.

LEWIS, ROY W. ■ FAAR Architecture 86. b. Jan. 16, 1954, Maracaibo, Venezuela. m. Marie Constance. c. Aaron. BA 76, Rice Univ.; BArch 80, Rice Univ.; PhD, Univ. of Pennsylvania. **Other Study:** Archaeological excavations in Latium. **Research/Artistic Interests:** The Augustan Pantheon as an institution & as a building. **Career & Employment:** Craig Morrison, AIA, Architects, Assc. 1988-90; Voith & Mactavish Architects, Project Architect 1990-91. **Fellowships, Honors & Awards:** *Progressive Architecture,* Design Award 1984; Washington Univ., Steedman Fellowship 1986; US Education Dept., Jacob Javits Fellowship 1992. **Important Works:** Gardosik Ranch House, Guadelupe Co., TX 1983-84; with Craig Morrison AIA, "Dolobran" Restoration 1989-90; with Voith & Mactavish, Thomas Great Hall Restoration, Bryn Mawr College 1990-92. **Home Address:** 244 Harrogate Rd., Wynnewood, PA 19096.

LEWITT, SOL ■ AAR Visitor 1985-86, Artist.

LICHT, GEORGE TIBBITS ■ FAAR Architecture 37. b. Sept. 20, 1907, Pelham, NY. m. Doris Ditmars Atkinson. BFA 32, Yale Univ. **Fellowships, Honors & Awards:** Beaux-Art Medals (8); Soc. of Illuminating Engineers Prize 1934; Fontainbleau Prize 1929.

LICHTENSTEIN, ROY F. ■ RAAR Painting 89; AAR Trustee 1989-95. b. Oct. 27, 1923, NYC. m. Dorothy Lichtenstein. c. David, Mitchell. BFA 46, Ohio State Univ.; MFA 49, Ohio State Univ. **Other Study:** ASL, with Reginald Marsh 1939. **Career & Employment:** SUNY, Oswego, Asst. Prof. 1957-60; Rutgers Univ., Douglas College, Asst. Prof. 1960-63. **Fellowships, Honors & Awards:** AAAS Fellow 1971; Skowhegan Medal for Painting 1977; California Inst. of the Arts, DFA 1977; AAAL 1979; Ohio State Univ., Hon. DFA 1988; Brandeis Univ., Creative Arts Award 1989; Amic de Barcelona 1993; Royal College of Art, London, Hon. DFA 1993. **Important Works:** Public Sculpture: Gilman Paper Co. Collection, St. Mary's, GA; Miami Beach Theater for the Performing Arts; Port Columbus, OH, Intl. Airport; Walker Art Center, Minneapolis; Steven Mazoh & Co., NYC; Caisse de Dépôts et Consignations, Paris; Barcelona, Spain; Tokyo, Japan; Public Murals: Worlds Fair, New York State Pavilion; Univ. of Dusseldorf, School of Medicine; Green St., NYC; Equitable Tower, NYC; Tel Aviv Museum, Israel; Creative Artists Agency, Beverly Hills, CA; Works in Public Collections: MOMA; Whitney Museum, NYC; Neue Galerie-Sammlung Ludwig, Aachen,

Germany; Stedelijk Museum, Amsterdam; Baltimore Museum of Art; Albright-Knox Art Gallery, Buffalo, NY; AIC; Wallraf-Richartz Museum, Cologne; Hessischen Landesmuseum, Darmstadt; Dayton Art Inst.; Denver Art Museum; Des Moines Art Center; Detroit Inst. of Arts; Kunstsammlung Nordhein-Westfälen, Dusseldorf; Univ. of Dusseldorf; Wadsworth Athenaeum, Hartford, CT; Louisiana Museum of Modern Art, Humlebaek, Denmark; William Rockhill Nelson Gallery of Art, Kansas City, KS; Mary Atkins Museum of Fine Arts, Kansas City, KS; Tate Gallery, London; Victoria & Albert Museum, London; Los Angeles County Museum of Art; Mittelrheinisches Landesmuseum, Mainz, Germany; Theatre of the Performing Arts, Miami. **Exhibitions/Performances:** Selected Solo: Leo Castelli Gallery, NYC 1962, 1963, 1964, 1967, 1971, 1973, 1974, 1975, 1977, 1981, 1983, 1984; Guggenheim Museum, NYC 1969, 1993; Centre Georges Pompidou, Paris 1975; MOMA 1987; Gagosian Gallery, NYC 1988; 65 Thompson St., NYC 1989; Mary Boone Gallery, NYC 1989; Galerie Beyeler, Basel 1991; Guild Hall Museum, East Hampton, NY 1992; Galerie Ulysses, Vienna 1992; Leo Castelli & 65 Thompson St., NYC 1992; FAE Musée d'Art Contemporain, Lausanne 1992. **Bio-Bibliography:** Alberto Boatto & Giordano Falzoni, eds., *Lichtenstein,* in *Fantazaria* 1.2 (July-Aug. 1966); Diane Waldman, *Roy Lichtenstein: Drawings and Prints* (New York & London: Chelsea House, 1969); Angel Crespo, *Roy Lichtenstein y el arte Pop* (Mayaguez: Univ. de Puerto Rico, 1970); John Coplands, ed., *Roy Lichtenstein* (New York & Washington, DC: Praeger, 1972); Diane Waldman, *Roy Lichtenstein* (New York: Harry N. Abrams, 1972); Lawrence Alloway, *Roy Lichtenstein* (New York: Abbeville, 1983); Bernice Rose, *The Drawings of Roy Lichtenstein* (New York: MOMA, 1987); Ernst A. Busche, *Roy Lichtenstein: Das Fruhwerk, 1942-1960* (Berlin: Gebr. Mann, 1988); *Roy Lichtenstein* (Tokyo: Kodansha, 1992); Diane Waldman, *Roy Lichtenstein* (New York: Rizzoli, 1993); Diane Waldman, *Roy Lichtenstein,* exb. cat. (New York: Guggenheim Museum, 1993); plus numerous reviews, articles, profiles. **Business Address:** c/o Cassandra Lozano, Fax: 212-727-3138.

LIEBMAN, THEODORE ■ FAAR Architecture 66. b. May 7, 1939, Newark, NJ. m. Nina Roskin. c. Sophia, Hanna, Tessa. BArch 62, Pratt Inst.; MArch 63, Harvard Univ. **Career & Employment:** Boston Redevelopment Authority, Project Design Officer 1963-64; Carlo Aymonino, Architect, Rome, Designer, 1964-65; David A. Crane, Architect, Philadelphia, Project Dir. 1966-69; New York State Urban Development Corp., NYC Chief of Architecture 1969-75; Harvard Inst. for Intl. Development, Teheran, Chief Urban Design Officer 1975-1977; HAUS Intl., NYC & Teheran, Pres. & Founding Prin. 1977-79; Liebman Melting Partnership, NYC, Part. & Founding Prin. 1979-present; ARCH (American Russian Consortium for Habitat) Development, LLC, Managing Dir.; Pratt Inst., Assc. Prof. 1983-86; UNC, Charlotte, Distinguished Visiting Prof. 1984-85; Studio Critic: Inst. for Architecture & Urban Studies 1975; Harvard Univ., Jerusalem Study 1981; Visiting Lect.: Baruch College, CUNY; Cornell Univ.; Columbia Univ.; Harvard Univ.; Univ. of Maryland; MIT; UNC, Charlotte; Pratt Inst.; Univ. of Pennsylvania; Rice Univ.; Architectural Assn., London; Univ. of Marseilles; Syracuse Univ.; Univ. of Colorado, Denver; Univ. of Miami. **Memberships & Offices:** Inst. for Urban Design, Bd. of Adv. 1970-present; *Progressive Architecture,* Adv. Panel 1972-75; AIA, New York Chap., Urban Planning Com. Chair 1981-83, Pres. 1983-84; Urban Land Inst. 1982-present, Intl. Council 1992-present; Brooklyn Heights Assn., NYC, Bd. of Governors, VP 1988-94, Pres. 1994-present. **Fellowships, Honors & Awards:** Harvard Univ., Wheelwright

Fellowship 1971; AIA, Fellow 1986, NYC Chap., Pioneer in Housing Award 1988; NYC Landmarks Conservancy Preservation Award 1990. **Important Works:** Grant St. Housing, Denver 1982; Crotona Terrace Housing, Bronx, NY 1994; Shorehaven Housing, Bronx NY 1987, 1995; Spring Creek Gardens Housing, Brooklyn, NY 1988; 55 White St., Tribeca, Cast Iron Restoration, NYC 1990; Ducat Place Office Bldg., Moscow, Russia 1993; 53 Leningradsky Prospect Office Bldg., Moscow, Russia 1994; PS 37 Elementary School, Bronx, NY 1994. **Exhibitions/Performances:** MOMA 1973; USIA, US Embassy, London 1973; Museum of Contemporary Art, Teheran 1978; Municipal Art Soc., NYC 1984; AIA, NYC Chap. 1989. **Bio-Bibliography:** *Who's Who in America*. **Home Address:** 105 Montague St., Brooklyn, NY 11201. **Business Address:** The Liebman Melting Partnership, 330 W. 42 St., NYC 10036.

LILLA, MARK ■ FAAR Post-Classical/Humanistic Studies 87. b. Sept. 17, 1956, Detroit, MI. m. Isabelle Frank, FAAR 87. BA 78, Univ. of Michigan; MPP 80, Harvard Univ., Kennedy School of Government; PhD 90, Harvard Univ. **Career & Employment:** NYU, Asst. Prof. 1990-present. **Memberships & Offices:** *The Public Interest*, Ed. 1980-87; *Partisan Review*, Contr. Ed. 1990-present; Princeton Univ. Press, "New French Thought" series, Gen. Ed. 1991-present; New York Inst. for the Humanities, Fellow 1992-present. **Fellowships, Honors & Awards:** Fulbright Fellow 1986; Woodrow Wilson Fellowship Found., Newcombe Fellow 1989-90; American Political Science Assn., Leo Strauss Award 1991; Alexander Van Humboldt Found. Fellow 1995-96. **Publications:** with Nathan Glazer, *The Public Face of Architecture: Civic Culture and Public Spaces* (New York: Free Press, 1987); *G.B. Vico: The Making of an Anti-Modern* (Cambridge: Harvard Univ. Press, 1993); ed., *New French Thought: Political Philosophy* (Princeton: Princeton Univ. Press, 1994). **Home Address:** 37 Washington Sq. W., NYC 10011. **Business Address:** Dept. of Politics, NYU, 715 Broadway, NYC 10003.

LINDROTH, SCOTT A. ■ FAAR Musical Composition 86. b. Jan. 16, 1958, Cincinnati, OH. BMus 80, Eastman School of

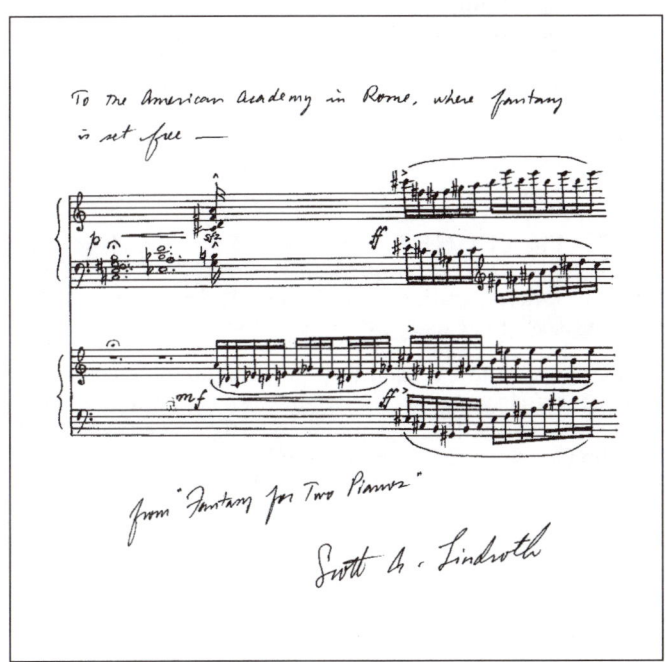

Scott A. Lindroth

Music; MusM 82, Yale School of Music; DMA 91, Yale School of Music. **Other Study:** Yale School of Music, Composers Seminar 1979. **Research/Artistic Interests:** I compose music for chamber ensembles, orchestra & electronic media; and I have been active as a pianist & conductor in my work. **Career & Employment:** Duke Univ., Asst. Prof. 1990-present. **Memberships & Offices:** ASCAP, Writer Mem. 1981-present. **Fellowships, Honors & Awards:** ISCM Nat. Composers Competition Winner 1983; NEA Fellowship 1984; New York Philharmonic-Revson Found. Fellowship 1984-85; NYFA Fellowship 1988; Koussevitzky Found. Comm. 1988; Guggenheim Fellowship 1988; Mellon Found. Fellowship 1991; Lila Wallace Found., *Readers' Digest* Consortium Comm. 1992; Duke Univ., Lilly Endowment Fellowship 1992. **Important Works:** *Chasing the Trane Out at Darmstadt*, for tenor sax & piano 1979-80; *A Fire's Bright Song*, for orchestra 1981, rev. 1987; *Pieces of Piano*, for solo piano 1982; *Relations to Rigor*, for six instruments & tape (CRI) 1986-87; *Stomp*, for ten instruments 1988; *Treatise on Tailors' Dummies*, Relâche-Pew Charitable Trust Comm. 1988-89; *In the Middle of the Road*, for alto, alto flute & piano, Sanae Nakayama Comm. 1989; *Duo for Violins*, Koussevitzky Found. Comm. 1990; *Light*, Corn Palace Festival Comm. 1991; *Fantasy for Two Pianos*, Double Edge Comm. 1992; *January Music*, for orchestra 1993; *Big Band*, for orchestra, Chicago Symphony Orchestra Comm. 1994. **Home Address:** 1412 Carroll St., Durham, NC 27707. **Business Address:** Music Dept., Duke Univ., Durham, NC 27708.

LINKER, WAYNE A. ■ AAR – New York, Exec. VP.

LINN, STEVEN ALLEN ■ FAAR Sculpture 76. b. May 3, 1943, Chicago, IL. c. Nadia. BS 65, Univ. of Illinois. **Career & Employment:** UC, Santa Cruz, Instr. 1971-74; Smith College, Instr. 1968-69. **Fellowships, Honors & Awards:** Univ. of Illinois, Design Fellowship 1964; Berkshire Museum, Priscilla S. Ward Sculpture Prize 1968; MacDowell Colony, Fellow 1980. **Exhibitions/Performances:** Berkshire Museum, Pittsfield, MA 1967, 1968; Ile-Ife Black Humanitarian Center, Philadelphia 1969; Eastern States Exb., Springfield, MA 1969; Contemporary Arts Found., Oklahoma City 1971; Louis K. Meisel Gallery, NYC 1974, 1976, 1979, 1981; Santa Barbara Museum 1974; Santa Cruz City Museum 1974; Whitney Museum, NYC 1979; Newport, RI Art Museum 1979.

LIPPMANN, WALTER ■ AAR Visitor 1959 — 1964, Journalist.

LIST, VERA ■ AAR Trustee 1977-79, Trustee Emer.; Art Patron.

LISTER, JAMES MACKENZIE ■ FAAR Landscape Architecture 37. b. Mar. 9, 1907, Cleveland, OH. d. Sept. 12, 1983. m. Barbara S. Lister. c. Michael, Geoffrey, Anthony, Margaret, Jane. BA 29, Harvard Univ.; BLA 33, Cornell Univ.; MLA 35, Cornell Univ. **Other Studies:** Williams College. **Research/Artistic Interests:** City planning, urban renewal. **Career & Employment:** City of Cleveland, Public Service 1938-79, Freeway Expeditor 1945-49, Planning Dir. 1949-79; Consultant, city planning 1979-83. **Fellowships, Honors & Awards:** Clifton Beckwith Brown Medal. **Bio-Bibliography:** "Planning Chief Paid to Dream," *Cleveland Plain Dealer* (June 5, 1953).

LITHGOW, KENNETH RICHARD ■ FAAR Painting 71. b. Mar. 18, 1941, Detroit, MI. d. Apr. 29, 1990. BFA 66, Wayne State Univ. **Other Studies:** ASL. **Research/Artistic Interests:** The theme of AIDS was predominant in most of his later work. **Fellowships, Honors & Awards:** MacDowell Colony, Resident; Wurlitzer Found. **Exhibitions/Performances:** Manchester Gallery, Taos 1968; Kendall Gallery, NYC 1988.

LIVESEY, ROBERT S. ■ FAAR Architecture 75. b. Jan. 25, 1947, Montclair, NJ. m. Diana M.J. Livesey. c. Jessica (Olin), Cecilia. BA 69, Princeton Univ.; MArch 72, Harvard GSD. **Career & Employment:** Collins Uhl Hoisington Anderson 1969-70; James Stirling & Part. 1975-76; I. M. Pei & Partners 1976-78; Yale Univ., Adj. Prof. 1976-83; Livesey-Rosenstein Asscs., Part. 1978-81; Stirling-Wilford Asscs. 1979-81; Univ. of Pennsylvania, Adj. Prof. 1979-80; CUH2A, Dir. of Architectural Design 1981-83; Ohio State Univ., Prof. 1983-present, Chair 1983-91; Robert Livesey, Architect 1983-present. **Fellowships, Honors & Awards:** Harvard Univ., Sheldon Traveling Fellowship 1972-73; *Progressive Architecture* Citation 1978; Yale Univ., Judith M. Capen Award 1980. **Important Works:** Turton Residence, Water Island, St. Thomas, VI 1991; Musi Residence, Boxley, OH 1991; Baroui Residence, Columbus, OH 1992; Bowman Residence, Blacklick, OH 1992; Harold Mettor Hall, Columbus State Community College 1993. **Home Address:** 9 Old Kings Hgwy., Weston, CT 06883. **Business Address:** Robert Livesey, Architect, 1049 City Park Ave., Columbus, OH 43206; Dept. of Architecture, Ohio State Univ., 190 W. 17 Ave., Columbus, OH 43210.

LIVINGSTON, PHILIP RUSH ■ FAAR Sculpture 81. b. Feb. 19, 1941, Chicago, IL. m. Lona Goodman Stein. c. Guy P., Hugh B. BA 64, Brown Univ.; MFA 65, Univ. of Wisconsin. **Career & Employment:** Univ. of Tennessee, Instr. 1965-66, Asst. Prof. 1966-72, Assc. Prof. 1972-78, Prof. 1978-. **Fellowships, Honors & Awards:** 15th Annual Ball State Small Sculpture & Drawing Show, Purchase Award 1969; Univ. of Tennessee, Faculty Research Grant 1973; Tennessee Arts Comm. Grant 1978; Ford Found. Purchase Award; *Minneapolis Star and Tribune* Award. **Exhibitions/Performances:** Solo: Adele Rosenberg Gallery, Chicago 1966; Univ. of Tennessee, Knoxville 1973; Zaks Gallery, Chicago 1989, 1992; 2-person: Ward-Nasse Gallery, NYC 1974; Rechenbach Gallery, Knoxville 1977; Group: NY World's Fair, American Express Pavilion, Young American Sculpture 1965; Southeastern Center for Contemporary Art 1975.

LOCKWOOD, DEAN PUTNAM ■ FASCSR 09; ASCSR, Prof.-in-Charge 1927-28. b. 1884. d. Feb. 7 1965. m. Esther G. Abercrombie. c. Robert. BA 03, Harvard Univ.; MA 04, Harvard Univ.; PhD 07, Harvard Univ. **Career & Employment:** Harvard Univ. Instr. 1909-10; Columbia Univ., Asst. Prof. 1911-15, Acting Librarian 1916-17; Haverford College, Prof. & Librarian 1918-49, Prof. Emer. 1949-65. **Memberships & Offices:** RSA, MAA. **Fellowships, Honors & Awards:** Phi Beta Kappa. **Publications:** "De Rinucio Aretino Graecarum litterarum interprete," *Harvard Studies in Classical Philology* 24 (1913): 51-110; "The Plot of the *Querolus* and the Folk-Tales of Disguised Treasure," *TAPA* 44 (1913): 215-32; "Two Thousand Years of Latin Translation from the Greek," *TAPA* 49 (1918): 115-29; *Survey of Classical Roman Literature* (New York: Prentice Hall, 1934); *Ugo Benzi, Medical Philosopher and Physician 1376-1439* (Chicago: Univ. of Chicago Press, 1951). **Bio-Bibliography:** *NY Times*, Obit. (Feb. 9, 1965); *Directory of American Scholars.*

LOCKWOOD, NORMAND ■ FAAR Musical Composition 32. b. Mar. 19, 1906, NYC. m. Dorothy Sanders. c. Deborah Riefstahl, Hedwig-Marie Small, Angeline-Rose Johnson. **Other Study:** Music instruction under father (Samuel Pierson Lockwood), mother (Angelina Smith), & uncle (Albert Lewis

Lockwood); student under Ottorino Respighi 1924-25; Nadia Boulanger 1925-28. **Career & Employment:** Prof.: Oberlin College; Columbia College, Columbia Univ.; Westminster Choir College; Union Theological Seminary, School of Sacred Music; Yale Univ.; Trinity Univ., San Antonio; Univ. of Oregon; Univ. of Hawaii; Univ. of Denver. **Memberships & Offices:** Phi Mu Alpha Sinfonia Fraternity, Hon. Mem.; ACA; Composers' Conferences, Middlebury-Bennington; Yaddo Music. **Fellowships, Honors & Awards:** Guggenheim Fellowship 1949-50, 1950-51; Soc. for the Publication of American Music Award; Swift Prize; G. Schirmer World's Fair Prize; Ernest Bloch Award; NIAL Award; AAAL, Marjorie Peabody Waite Award; Berea College, Hon. DMus; Univ. of Denver, Hon DHL. **Important Works:** *Trio*, for flute, harp & viola, Elizabeth Sprague Coolidge Comm.; *The Scarecrow*, an opera, Alice M. Ditson Fund Comm.; *Concerto for Organ & Brasses*, Oliver Daniel Comm. for CBS; *Second Concerto for Organ & Brasses*, Marilyn Mason Comm.; *Concerto for Organ & Chamber Orchestra*, Walter Blodgett Comm. for Cleveland Museum of Art; *Clarinet Quintet*, Walter Blodgett Comm. for Cleveland Museum of Art; *Concertina for Trumpet & Band*, Gerald Endsley Comm.; *Festive Service for the Organ*, American Guild of Organists Comm.; *Fantasy on Jesus My Joy*, for organ, Alexander Boggs Ryan Comm.; *Sonata for Two Pianos*, James Duncan Comm.; *Prelude to Western Star*, for voice & piano, Catheine Parker Comm.; *Donne's Last Sermon*, for chorus & organ, Gerald Lepinski Comm.; *Oratorio: Children of God*, Nat. Council of Churches & Berea College Comm; *Choreographic Cantata*, for choir, organ & percussion, Reuter Organ Co. & American Guild of Organists Comm.; *Mass for Children & Orchestra*, Duain Wolfe Comm. for Colorado Children's Chorale; *Thought of Him I Love*, for children & chamber orchestra, Duain Wolfe Comm. for Colorado Children's Chorale; *Symphony for Large Orchestra*, T. Gordon Parks Comm. for Arapaho Community Symphony; *Concerto for Oboe*, Richard Pointer Comm. for Orquesta Sinfonica Nacional Costa Rica; *Concerto for Two Harps*, Suzann & Deborah Davids Comm. for Orquesta Sinfonica Nacional Costa Rica; *Light Out of Darkness*, oratorio for chorus, bass solo, & orchestra, Buffalo Schola Cantorum Comm. **Bio-Bibliography:** Kay Norton, *Norman Lockwood: His Life & Music* (Metuchen, NJ: & London: Scarecrow); Bulletin of the ACA, Special Issue on Lockwood (New York: CRI, 1957); *Baker's Biographical Dictionary of American Musicians; Contemporary American Composers; New Grove Dictionary of American Music; Who's Who*; works archived at the Library of Music, Univ. of Colorado, Boulder. **Home Address:** PO Box 100053, Univ. Park Sta., Denver, CO 80250.

LOEFFLER, ELAINE PEMBROKE ■ FAAR Classics/Archaeology 53. b. June 30, 1928, Rochester, NY. BA 50, Smith College. **Other Studies:** IFA. **Career & Employment:** Mt. Holyoke College, Faculty; Brandeis Univ., Prof. (retired).

LOERKE, WILLIAM ■ Fulbright Resident Fellow 1952-53. b. Aug. 13, 1920, Toledo, OH. m. Helen L. Trautmann. c. Anna (Hurd), Timothy, Eric, Alison, Lisa, Ellen, Martha. BA 42, Oberlin College; MFA 48, Princeton Univ.; PhD 57, Princeton Univ. **Research/Artistic Interests:** Early Christian art, Roman architecture, theory of architecture. **Career & Employment:** Brown Univ., Instr.-Asst. Prof. 1949-59; Bryn Mawr College, Assc. Prof. 1959-64; Univ. of Pittsburgh, Prof. 1964-71, Chair 1964-68; Dumbarton Oaks, Prof. 1971-88, Center for Byzantine Studies, Dir. 1971-77; Visiting Prof.: Catholic Univ. of America 1978-88; Univ. of Maryland 1988-91. **Home Address:** 227 Gralan Rd., Catonsville, MD 21228-4835.

LONG, BERT L., JR ■ FAAR Painting 91. b. May 27, 1940, Houston, TX. m. Connie D. Kelly. c. Deborah D. Flowers, John A. Foster, Bertran L. Long III. UCLA, Teaching Credential for State of California. **Other Study:** Los Angeles Trade Technical Inst., Restaurant Management-Commercial Cooking 1962-72. **Research/Artistic Interests:** Art that reflects the impact of social issues upon society. **Career & Employment:** Hospitality Industry, Sous Chef-Exec. Chef. 1953-78: Houston Club; Ritz Carlton Hotel, Chicago; Las Vegas Hilton; Hyatt Regency Hotel, Houston; Hungry Tiger Restaurants, CA; Holiday Inns, Houston; *Houston Artscene,* Publisher 1979-88. **Memberships & Offices:** Chefs de Cuisine of America 1971-79; Artists in Action, Chair 1979-83; Houston Arts Alliance, Exec. Com.; Midtown Arts Center, Adv. Panel 1988; Cultural Arts Council, Houston, Visual Arts Panelist, Allocations Com. 1988; Texas Comm. on the Arts, Panelists 1990; Diverse Works, BoD 1989-91; Bemis Found., Intl. BoD 1992-present; Texas Fine Arts Assn., Intl. BoD 1992-present. **Fellowships, Honors & Awards:** Chefs de Cuisine Assn. of America, Gold Augie Award 1972; Texas Fine Arts Assn., La Gaguna Gloria Arts Museum, Citation Award 1977; Bayton, Texas Art League, 3d Place 1978; Cooperstown, NY Art Assn., Dorothy Oudin Mem. Prize 1978; E.O. Smith Jr. HS, Successful Alumnus 1985; Texas Senate Proclamation 1985; NEA Fellowship 1987; Bemis Found. Residency 1988; Art League of Houston, Texas Artist of the Year 1990; Phylis Wheatly HS, Successful Alumnus 1994; Texas House of Representatives, Outstanding Texan Award 1991; Inst. de Bachillerato, Dipl. 1994. **Important Works:** Contemporary Museum of Honolulu; Dallas Museum of Art; MMA; Bell Telephone, Houston; Museum of Fine Arts, Houston; Arkansas Art Center; Huntington Museum Gallery; Univ. of Texas, Austin; Fabric Workshop/Museum; Ayuntamiento de Berzocana, Caceres, Spain; Inst. de Bachillerato de Loerosan, Caceres, Spain; High Land Distributing, Houston. **Exhibitions/Performances:** Solo: Lawndale Annex, Univ. of Houston 1983; L.A. Louver Gallery, Venice 1987; Okane Gallery, Univ. of Houston 1987; Butler Gallery, Houston 1988; Art Museum of East Texas, Beaumont 1988; Dallas Museum of Art 1988; Barry Whistler Gallery, Dallas 1989; Allan Stone Gallery, NYC 1990; Lew Allen Gallery, Sante Fe 1991; Contemporary Arts Museum, Houston 1991-92; Lyons Matrix Gallery, Austin 1991; Fabric Workshop, Jive Plantation 1993; Two-Person: Butler Gallery, Houston, TX 1985; Group: Centro Washington Irving, US Embassy, Spain. **Bio-Bibliography:** *Showdown,* exb. cat. (New York: Alternative Museum, 1983); *Art: A Healing Force,* exb. cat. (Univ. of Houston, Lawndale Annex, 1983); *Fresh Paint* (Houston: Museum of Fine Arts, 1985); *Cinco Cinco,* exb. cat. (Paris: Gerard-Georges Lemaire, 1987); *Concentrations* (Dallas: Dallas Museum of Art, 1988); Lucy Lippard, *Mixed Blessings* (New York, 1990); *Mental Asylum* (Houston: Contemporary Museum, 1992); Susan Chadwick, "Artist Still Roaming," *Houston Post* (Jan. 25, 1992); *Texas Fine Arts Assn. News* (Feb.-Mar.-Apr. 1995). **Home Address:** PO Box 1254, Shepherd, TX 77371; c/o Pilar 10129, Berzocana Caceres, Spain.

LONG, HERBERT S. ■ FAAR Classics/Archaeology 41. b. Mar. 23, 1919, Dexter, NY. m. Charlotte D. Rider. c. Alison, George. BA 39, Hamilton College; MA 41, Princeton Univ.; PhD. 42, Princeton Univ. **Career & Employment:** Hamilton College, Instr. 1943-44, North Prof. 1952-68; Colgate Univ., Instr. 1944-46; Yale Univ., Asst. Prof. 1946-51; Case Western Reserve Univ., Prof. 1968-86, Chair 1983-86, Prof. Emer. 1986-present, Lect. 1986-present. **Memberships & Offices:** APA; Shaker Historial Soc., BoT 1969-71; Phi Beta Kappa. **Fellowships, Honors & Awards:** IAS 1951-52, 1965-66; ASCSA, Special Research Fellow 1958-59; APA, Award of Merit 1965; Hamilton College, LittD 1972. **Publications:** *Diogenes Laertius* (Oxford Classical Text, 1964). **Home Address:** 84 Kendal Dr., Oberlin, OH 44074.

LONG, JANET BLOW ■ FAAR Post-Classical/Humanistic Studies 81. b. Sept. 30, 1951, Fall River, MA. BA 72, Wheaton College; PhD 77, Duke Univ. **Career & Employment:** Catholic Univ. of America, Visiting Asst. Prof. 1977-78, 1979-80; Univ. of Iowa, Visiting Asst. Prof. 1978-79.

LONGOBARDI, INEZ ■ AAR Librarian 1961-75.

LORD, AUSTIN W. ■ AAR Charter Mem., American School of Architecture in Rome, Dir. 1894-96.

LORD, ISRAEL PIERRE ■ Rotch Scholar 1908.

LORD, LOUIS ■ AAR Classical Soc., Pres. 1945.

LORD, MILTON E. ■ RAAR Classics/Archaeology 72; AAR Librarian 1926-30; Librarian-in-Residence 1971-72, 1975-76. b. June 12, 1898. d. Feb. 12, 1985. m. Rosamond Lane. c. Peter, Joan, Mary, Anne, Sarah. BA 19, Harvard College. **Other Study:** Harvard Univ. 1921-24; École des Sciences Politiques, Paris 1925-26. **Career & Employment:** Harvard Union, Librarian 1919-23; Univ. of Iowa, Dir. of Libraries 1930-31; Boston Public Library, Dir. & Librarian 1932-65; Intl. Council of Monuments & Sites, Consultant 1969-78. **Memberships & Offices:** Council of Nat. Library Assn., Chair 1944-45; American Book Center for War-Devastated Libraries, Chair 1945-54; US Book, Simmons College, Chair 1957-65; US Com. for IOMOS 1970-78. **Fellowships, Honors & Awards:** Chevalier de la Légion d'Honneur; Royal Soc. of Arts, Benjamn Franklin Fellow; AAAS, Fellow.

LOSITO, MARIA ■ Italian Fulbright Fellow 1990-91.

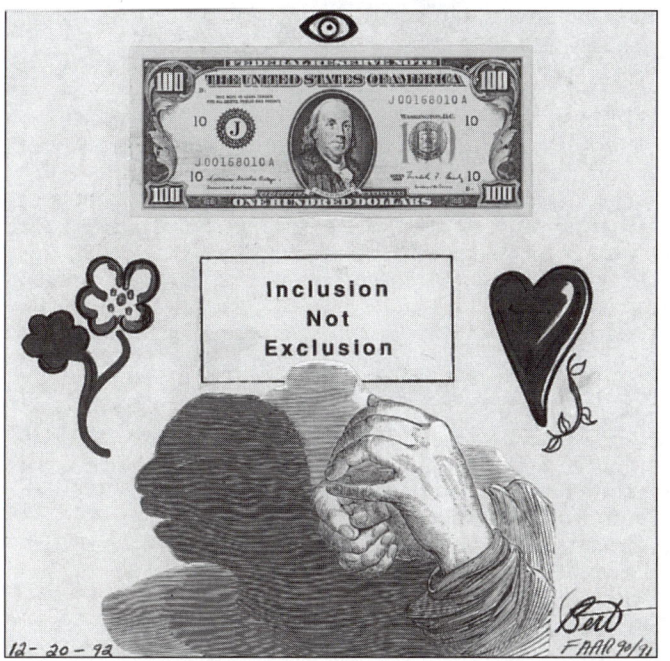

Bert L. Long, Jr.

LOWE, ELIAS AVERY ■ FASCSR 11. b. Oct. 15, 1879, Calvaria, Lithuania. d. Aug. 8, 1969. m. Helen Tracy Porter. c. Prudence Holcombe, Frances Beatrice, Patricia Tracy. BA 02, Cornell Univ; PhD 07, Univ. of Munich; MA 20, Oxford. **Other Studies:** City College of New York 1894-97; Univ. of Halle 1902-3. **Research/Artistic Interests:** Latin palaeography. **Career & Employment:** Carnegie Inst., Assc. 1911-13; Oxford Univ., Lect. 1913-27; Reader 1927-48; IAS, Prof. 1936-45; Library of Congress, Consultant. **Memberships & Offices:** Hispanic Soc. of America; Acad. of History of Madrid, Corresponding Mem.; Bayerische Akademie der Wissenschaften; Accademia dei Lincei, Rome; Inst. de France; Royal Irish Acad., Hon. Mem. **Fellowships, Honors & Awards:** Oxford Univ., Hon. DLitt 1936; UNC, Hon. LLD 46; Corpus Christi College, Honorary Fellow; MAA, Haskins Medal; Bibliographical Soc., London, Gold Medal Award 1959; MAA, Fellow; AAAS, Fellow; British Acad., Fellow; Phi Beta Kappa. **Publications:** *Die ältesten Kalendarien aus Monte Cassino* (Munich, 1908); *Studia palaeographica: A Contribution to the History of Early Latin Minuscule* (Munich, 1910); *The Beneventan Script* (Oxford: Clarendon Press, 1914; rev. ed., ed. Virginia Brown, Rome: Storia e Letteratura, 1980); *Codices lugdunenses antiquissimi* (Lyons, 1924); *Scriptura Beneventana*, 2 vols. (Oxford: Clarendon Press, 1929); *English Uncial* (Oxford: Clarendon Press, 1960); ed., *Codices Latini Antiquiores*, 12 vols. (Oxford: Clarendon Press, 1934-72); *Handwriting: Our Medieval Legacy* (Rome, 1969); *Palaeographical Papers, 1907-1965*, ed. L. Bieler, 2 vols. (Oxford: Clarendon Press, 1972). **Bio-Bibliography:** James J. John, "E.A. Lowe and *Codices Latini Antiquiores*," *ACLS Newsletter* 20.5 (Oct. 1969): 1-17; *Speculum* 45 (1970): 520-21; *Palaeographical Papers* 2:591-611; James J. John, "A Paleographer among Benedictines: A Tribute to E.A. Lowe," *American Benedictine Review* 21 (1970): 139-47; Bernhard Bischoff, "Elias Avery Lowe. 15.10.1879-8.8.1969," *Jahrbuch der Bayerischen Akademie der Wissenschaften* (1970): 1-4; Julian Brown, "E.A. Lowe and the *Codices Latini Antiquiores*," *Scrittura e Civiltà* 1 (1977): 177-97; Briggs, 276-78; *Who Was Who in America*.

LOWE, JEANNE R. ■ FAAR Literature 70. b. 1924. d. 1972. **Bio-Bibliography:** *NY Times*, Obit. (Apr. 29, 1972); *Contemporary Authors*.

LOWRIE, WALTER ■ FASCSR 1899-1900. b. April 26, 1868, Philadelphia, PA. d. Aug. 12, 1959. m. Barbara Armour. BA 1890, Princeton; MA 1893, Princeton Theological Seminary; DD 30, Princeton Univ. **Other Studies:** Univ. of Griefswald 1893-94; Univ. of Berlin 1894. **Research/Artistic Interests:** Church history, liturgy & architecture, translations of works of Søren Kierkegaard. **Career & Employment:** Protestant Episcopal Church, Deacon 1895, Priest 1897; Trinity Church, Southwark, Philadelphia, Rector 1903-4; Trinity Church, Newport 1905-7; St. Paul's American Church, Rome, Rector 1907-30. **Fellowships, Honors & Awards:** Trinity Cathedral, Trenton, Hon. Canon; Danish Order of Knights of Dannebrog 1948. **Publications:** *The Doctrine of St. John* (New York: Longmans, Green, 1899); *Monuments of the Early Church* (New York: Macmillan, 1901); *The Church and its Organization* (New York: Longmans, Green, 1904); *Abba, Father* (New York: Longmans, Green, 1908); *Problems of Church Unity* (New York: Longmans, Green, 1926); *Fifty Years of St. Paul's Church* (Rome, 1926); *The Birth of the Divine Child* (New York: Longmans, Green, 1926); *Jesus According to St. Mark* (New York: Longmans, Green, 1929); *Our Concern with Theology of Crisis* (Boston: Meader, 1937); *Kierkegaard* (New York: Oxford Univ. Press, 1937); *SS.*

Peter and Paul in Rome: An Archaeological Rhapsody (New York: Oxford Univ. Press, 1940); *A Short Life of Kierkegaard* (Princeton: Princeton Univ. Press, 1942); *The Short Story of Jesus* (New York: Scribners, 1943); *The Lord's Supper and the Liturgy* (New York: Longmans, Green, 1943); *Art in the Early Church* (New York: Pantheon, 1947); *Johann Georg Hamann: An Existentialist* (Princeton: Princeton Theological Seminary, 1950); *Enchanted Island* (New York: Philosophical Library, 1952); *Action in the Liturgy, Essential and Unessential* (New York: Philosophical Library, 1957); trans. 12 vols. from Kierkegaard's works published by Oxford Univ. Press and Princeton Univ. Press 1939-55. **Bio-Bibliography:** *NY Times*, Obit. (Aug. 14, 1959); *Newsweek* (Aug. 24, 1959); *Who Was Who in America*.

LUENING, OTTO ■ RAAR Musical Composition 58; AAR Trustee 1950-64; Trustee Emer. b. June 15, 1900, Milwaukee, WI. m. Ethel Codd, Catherine Brunson. **Study:** Royal Acad. of Music, Munich; Zurich Conservatory. **Career & Employment:** Tonhalle Orchestra, Zurich, flutist; Eastman School of Music 1925-28; WOR Conductor 1929-30; Univ. of Arizona, Asst. Prof. 1932-34; Bennington College, Music Dept. Head 1934-44; New York Philharmonic Symphony Chamber Orchestra, Assc. Cond. 1935-37; Barnard College, Joline Prof. 1944-64, Assc. Prof. 1944-64, Music Dept. Chair 1944-64; Columbia Univ., Brander Matthews Theatre, Music Dir. 1944-59, Prof. 1949-68, Prof. Emer. 1968, School of the Arts, Music Chair 1968-70; Columbia-Princeton Electronic Music Center, Co-Dir. 1959-80; Juilliard School 1971-73. **Memberships & Offices:** Opera in Our Language Found., Assc. Music Dir.; Vermont State Symphony, BoD, Soloist & Guest Cond.; ACA, Founding Mem. 1937; American Music Center, Co-Founder 1940, Chair 1940-60; Nat. Music Council, Charter Mem. 1940; Yaddo Music Com., late 30s & 40s; League of Composers, BoD 1943; UNESCO Music Adv. Com. 1953-61; Guggenheim Found., Educational Adv. Bd. 1964-69; *Making Your Own Music*, Silver-Burdett, Special Consultant 1963-65. **Fellowships, Honors & Awards:** Guggenheim Fellowship 1930-32; David Bispham Medal 1932; ACA, Laurel Leaf Award 1970; Brandeis Univ., Creative Arts Award 1981; Nat. Music Council, American Eagle Award 1985; BMI Distinguished Service Citation 1985; Soc. for Electro-Acoustic Music Citation 1990; Busoni Found. Award 1991; Hon. Degrees: Wesleyan Univ., MusD 1963; Univ. of Wisconsin, Parkside-Kenosha, Hon. Alumnus 1977; Univ. of Wisconsin, Madison, DFA 1977; Wisconsin Conservatory, MusD 1979; Columbia Univ., LittD 1981; Univ. of Wisconsin, Milwaukee, DFA 1984; Selected Commissions: Louisville Orchestra, Los Angeles Philharmonic, New York Philharmonic, American Mime Theatre. **Publications:** *The Odyssey of an American Composer* (New York: Charles Scribner's Sons, 1980). **Important Works:** *Sextet*, for mixed ensemble (Bardic Edition) 1918; *String Quartet No. 1* (Highgate Press) 1919-20; *Serenade for Three Horns & Strings*, Rochester Philharmonic Comm. (Highgate Press) 1927; *Preludes to a Hymn Tune by William Billings*, Yaddo Comm. (C.F. Peters) 1937; *Fantasy in Space*, for flute on tape recorder (Highgate Press, CRI, Folkways) 1952; *Low Speed*, for flute on tape recorder (Highgate Press, CRI) 1952; *Invention in Twelve Notes*, for flute on tape recorder (Highgate Press, CRI) 1952; with Vladimir Ussachevsky, *Rhapsodic Variations for Tape Recorder & Orchestra*, Louisville Orchestra Comm. (C.F. Peters, Louisville Orchestra First Edition Recordings) 1954; *Symphonic Fantasias 1-10*, for orchestra, Horace Mann School-Woodstock Chamber Orchestra Comms. (ACA, CRI) 1924-90; *No Jerusalem but This*, for chorus (C.F. Peters, CRI) 1982. **Bio-Bibliography:** Ralph Hartsock, *Otto Luening: A Bio-Bibliography*

(Westport, CT: Greenwood Press, 1991). **Home Address:** 460 Riverside Dr., NYC 10027. **Business Address:** BMI, 320 W. 57 St., NYC 10019.

LYNCH, KEVIN ■ AAR Visitor 1951 — 1955. City Planner. Educator. b. Jan. 7, 1918. d. April 24, 1984. **Career & Employment:** Frank Lloyd Wright, Apprentice 1937-39; MIT, Instr.-Prof. 1948-78; Carr Lynch Asscs., Part. 1977-84. **Honors & Awards:** American Inst. of Planners, 50th Anniversary Award 1967. **Selected Publications:** *What Time Is This Place* (1972); *A Theory of Good Form* (1981).

LYNDON, DONLYN ■ RAAR Architecture 78, 87. b. Jan. 7, 1936, Detroit, MI. m. Alice Wingwall. BA 57, Princeton Univ.; MFA 59, Princeton Univ. **Career & Employment:** Maynard Lyndon, Assc. 1960-62; UC, Berkeley, Asst. Prof. 1960-64, Prof. 1978-present; MLTW-Moore, Lyndon, Turnbull, Whitaker, Part. 1962-65; Univ. of Oregon, Assc. Prof. & Dept. Head 1964-67; MLTW-Lyndon, Prin. 1965-67; Moore, Lyndon, Turnbull, Part. 1967-71; MIT, Prof. 1967-77, Dept. Head 1967-75; Lyndon Asscs., Prin. 1971-78; Lyndon-Buchanan, Part. 1978-present; Visiting Prof.: Univ. College, London 1970; UC, Berkeley 1973; Univ. of Maryland 1975; Univ. of Texas, Austin 1982. **Memberships & Offices:** Intl. Laboratory of Architecture & Urban Design, BoD 1977-present; Sea Ranch, Design Com., Chair 1984-88; Kronos Performing Arts Assn., BoD 1987-present; Mayor's Inst. of City Design, Midwest, Minneapolis Resource Person 1989, Charlottesville Resource Person 1991, New Orleans Resource Person 1992, West, Berkeley Coordinator 1990-present; Gen. Services Administration, Nat. Acad. of Sciences Panel, Chair 1990; NEA Design Arts Policy Panel, Chair 1988-90; NEA State of the Arts, Review Panel 1988, 1991. **Fellowships, Honors & Awards:** Fulbright Scholar 1959-60; AIA Honor Award 1980 (2), 1983, 1991, Nat. Honor Award 1967, 1979, Fellow 1978, Award of Merit 1985, 25-Year Award 1991, CA Council, Excellence in Education Award 1991, CA Council, 25-Year Award 1992, Urban Design Award of Excellence 1992; Governors Design Award, CA 1967; *Progressive Architecture*, 1st Design Award 1970; Boston Soc. of Architects, Honor Award 1977; Graham Found. Study Grant 1978; Pacific Coast Builders, 1st Design Award 1983 (2); *Sunset Magazine*, Citation 1983; Inst. of Urban Design, Fellow 1992. **Publications:** with Charles W. Moore & Gerald Allen, *The Place of Houses* (New York: Holt, Rinehart & Winston, 1974); *The City Observed: Boston* (New York: Random House, 1982); ed., *Places* (Cambridge: MIT Press, 1982-89; Design History Found., 1989-present); "They're Putting the Arch Back in Architecture," *Boston Globe* (Aug. 28, 1988); "(Measure), Vary, Distinguish, Nurture, Inhabit, Be Festive," in *Yearbook 1989: The Contemporary Town* 1, ed. Connie Occhialini & Giancarlo De Carlo (Siena: Sagep Editrice, Intl. Laboratory of Architecture & Urban Design, 1989), 54-59; "Thoughts on Memorability," in *La Città Contemporanea*, ed. Connie Occhialini & Giancarlo De Carlo (Catania: Sagep Editrice, Intl. Laboratory of Architecture & Urban Design, 1989), 38-45; "Preface," to John Nolan & Duo Dickinson, *Common Walls-Private Homes* (New York: McGraw Hill, 1990); "About Being Somewhere," in *Yearbook 1992: Reading and Design of the Physical Environment*, ed. Connie Occhialini & Giancarlo De Carlo (Urbino: Quattro Venti, Intl. Laboratory of Architecture & Urban Design, 1992), 24-27; "Sea Ranch: Donlyn Lyndon's Assessment," *Progressive Architecture* (Feb. 1993): 94-95; "Distinction in Place," *Architecture* (May 1994): 105-6; with Charles W. Moore, *Chambers for a Memory Palace* (Cambridge: MIT Press, 1994). **Important Works:** Sea Ranch Condominiums, Sea Ranch, CA 1964-65; Brown Univ.,

Pembroke Dormitories 1968-75; Univ. Ave. Housing Cooperative, Berkeley 1979; Pasadena Civic Center Masterplan 1987-88; Miles Inc., Masterplan & Design Guidelines, Berkeley 1991; Miles Inc., Production Bldgs. 1991. **Bio-Bibliography:** Y. Futagawa, *Global Architecture, No. 3* (Tokyo: A.D.A. Edita, 1970); Y. Futagama, *MLTW; Houses by MLTW 1959-75* (Tokyo: A.D.A. Edita, 1975); S. Woodbridge, *Bay Area Houses* (New York: Oxford Univ. Press, 1976); R.A.M. Stern, "Architects of the New '40 under 40,'" *Architecture + Urbanism* 1 (1977): 113; "Pembroke Dormitories, Brown University," *Architecture + Urbanism* (Dec. 1978): 76-79; "MLTW/Lyndon Associates: Pembroke Dormitories," *Global Architecture Document*, Spec. Issue 1970-80 (Summer 1980): 180-81; *GA Houses* #7 (Spring 1981); Sally Woodbridge, "Two California Civic Centers," *Progressive Architecture* (Apr. 1993): 98-103. **Business Address:** Lyndon/Buchanan Asscs., 2604 Ninth St., Berkeley, CA 94710.

LYNES, RUSSELL, JR ■ AAR Trustee 1979-88, Ed., Author. b. Dec. 2, 1910. d. Sept. 15, 1991. **Career & Employment:** *Harper's Magazine*, Asst. Ed. 1944-47, Managing Ed. 1947-67, Contr. Ed. 1967-82. **Selected Publications:** *Highbrow, Lowbrow, Middlebrow* (1949); *The Tastemakers* (1954); *Confessions of a Dilettante* (1966); *Life in the Slow Lane* (1991).

■ ■ ■

M

MAAS, MICHAEL R. ■ FAAR Classics/Archaeology 81. b. Apr. 24, 1951, Wheeling, WV. BA 73, Cornell Univ.; MA 75, UC, Berkeley; PhD 82, UC, Berkeley. **Research/Artistic Interests:** Greek & Roman history, esp. late antiquity & early Byzantine history; Roman art & archaeology. **Career & Employment:** Dartmouth College, Visiting Asst. Prof. 1982-84; Rice Univ., Asst Prof. 1984-91, Assc. Prof. 1991-present; ICCS, Managing Com. 1990-95. **Memberships & Offices:** APA, AHA, Roman Soc., Soc. for the Promotion of Byzantine Studies. **Fellowships, Honors & Awards:** Dumbarton Oaks Center Fellow 1984-85; Fulbright Scholar 1988-89; Kings College, Univ. of London, Research Fellow 1988-89; Routledge Ancient History Prize 1990; Nat. Humanities Center Fellow 1992-93; ACLS Fellow 1992-93; Inst. for Advanced Studies, Hebrew Univ., Jerusalem, Fellow 1993. **Publications:** *John Lydus and the Roman Past: Antiquarianism and Politics in the Age of Justinian* (London, 1992). **Home Address:** 4037 Osby Dr., Houston, TX 77025. **Business Address:** Dept. of History, Rice Univ., Box 1892, Houston, TX 77251.

MACAULAY, LEO ■ AAR Visitor 1959 — 1964, Ambassador.

MACDONALD, WILLIAM L. ■ FAAR Classics/Archaeology 56; Juror 1986-87. b. July 12, 1921, Putnam, CT. c. Noel, Nicholas. BA 49, Harvard College; MA 53, Harvard Univ.; PhD 56, Harvard Univ. **Research/Artistic Interests:** The history of architecture with emphasis on classical architecture in its varied manifestations. **Career & Employment:** Boston Architectural Center, Lect. 1950-54; Wheaton College, Instr. 1953-54; Yale Univ., Instr.-Assc. Prof. 1956-65; Smith College, A.P. Brown Prof. 1965-80; Independent scholar & consultant 1980-present; Visiting Prof.: Harvard Univ.; MIT; UC, Berkeley; Emory Univ.; Univ. of Pennsylvania; Univ. of Maryland, Kea Distinguished Prof. 1973; Williams College, Clark Art Inst., C.J. Robinson Prof. 1981; George Mason Univ.; Georgetown Univ. **Memberships & Offices:** Byzantine Inst., Exec. Sec. 1950-54; SAH, Dir. 1965-68; J. Paul Getty Museum Com. 1990-present; CASVA, Bd. of Adv. 1992-93. **Fellowships, Honors & Awards:** Harvard Univ., Veterans Nat. Scholar 1948-50; Emerton, Shaw Fellow early 1950s; Yale Univ., Morse Fellow 1962-63; Dean Wm. Emerson Fund Award 1966-70; SAH, A.D. Hitchcock Prize 1987; MIT Dept. of Urban Studies, Kevin Lynch Award 1989; Getty Center for the Fine Arts and the Humanities, Getty Scholar 1985-86. **Publications:** *Early Christian and Byzantine Architecture* (New York: George Braziller, 1962); *The Architecture of the Roman Empire*, Vol. 1: *An Introductory Study* (New Haven: Yale Univ. Press, rev. ed 1986); *The Pantheon: Design, Meaning, and Progeny* (London: Penguin Books & Cambridge: Harvard Univ. Press, 1976); *Northampton Massachusetts Architecture and Buildings* (Northampton: City of Northhampton, 1976); assc. ed., *The Princeton Encyclopedia of Classical Sites* (Princeton: Princeton Univ. Press, 1976); *Piranesi's Carceri: Sources of Invention* (Northampton: Smith College, 1979); with B.M. Boyle, "The Small Baths at Hadrian's Villa," *JSAH* 39.1 (1980): 5-27; "Excavation, Restoration, and Italian Architecture of the 1930s," in *In Search of Modern Architecture: A Tribute to H.-R. Hitchcock*, ed. H. Searing (New York: Architectural History Found. & Cambridge, MA: MIT Press, 1982), 298-320; *The Architecture of the Roman Empire*, Vol. 2: *An Urban Appraisal* (New Haven: Yale Univ. Press 1986); "Hadrian's Circles," *CASVA Studies in the History of Art* 43 (Washington, DC: NGA, 1993); with John A. Pinto, *Hadrian's Villa and its Legacy* (New Haven: Yale Univ. Press, 1995). **Bio-**

Bibliography: *Who's Who in America, Who's Who in Art, Who's Who in the East.* **Home Address:** 3811 39th St. NW, Washington, DC 20016.

MACDOUGALL, ELISABETH BLAIR ■ AAR Visitor 1959 — 1964, Art-Architectural Historian. **Career & Employment:** Harvard Univ. Prof., Prof. Emer.; Dumbarton Oaks, Program of Studies in Landscape Architecture, Founder & Dir.

MACDOWELL, EDWARD A. ■ AAR Trustee 1905-6, Composer.

MACFADYEN, JOHN H. ■ FAAR Architecture 54. b. Mar. 5, 1923, Duluth, MN. m. Mary-Esther E. MacFadyen. c. John Tevere, William Loyall, Wile Sewall, Camilla Lewis. BA 45, Princeton Univ.; MFA 47, Princeton Univ. **Memberships & Offices:** NYSCA, Exec. Dir. 1961-64; American Council on the Arts, Pres. 1964-66. **Important Works:** Wolf Trap Family Park, Vienna, VA; Saratoga Performing Arts Center, Saratoga Springs, NY; Mann Music Center, Robin Hood Dell, Philadelphia; Snow King Inn, Jackson, WY. **Bio-Bibliography:** *Who's Who in America* **Home Address:** PO Box 246, Alna, ME 04535.

MACK SMITH, DENIS ■ AAR Visitor 1980-81, Historian.

MACKAY, CLARENCE H. ■ AAR Incorporator, Charter Mem., Trustee 1931-34, Industrialist.

MACKENDRICK, PAUL L. ■ RAAR Classics/Archaeology 58; AAR Trustee 1966-72, Trustee Emer.; Classical Soc., Pres. 1954; Summer School, Prof.-in-Charge 1956-59. b. Feb. 11, 1914, Taunton, MA. m. Dorothy G. Lau. c. Andrew, Sarah. BA 34, Harvard Univ.; MA 37, Harvard Univ.; PhD 38, Harvard Univ. **Other Study:** Balliol College, Oxford, Classical Honour Moderations 1934-36. **Research/Artistic Interests:** Archaeological research, Cosa. **Career & Employment:** Phillips Acad., Instr. 1938-41; Harvard Univ., Instr. 1946; Univ. of Wisconsin, Asst. Prof. 1946-48, Assc. Prof. 1948-52, Prof. 1952-58, Lily Ross Taylor Prof. 1958-84. **Memberships & Offices:** APA, Sec.-Treas. 1956-59; CAMWS, Pres. 1972. **Fellowships, Honors & Awards:** Fulbright Fellow 1950; Guggenheim Fellow 1957-58. **Publications:** with H.M. House, *Classics in Translation*, 2 vols. (Madison: Univ. of Wisconsin Press, 1952); *The Roman Mind at Work* (New York: Van Nostrand, 1958); *The Mute Stones Speak* (New York: St. Martin's, 1961, 1983); *The Greek Stones Speak* (New York: St. Martin's, 1962, 1981); *Athenian Aristocracy* (Cambridge: Harvard Univ. Press, 1966); *The Iberian Stones Speak* (New York: Funk & Wagnalls, 1969); *Roman France* (New York: St. Martin's, 1971); *Romans on the Rhine* (New York: Funk & Wagnalls, 1976); *The Dacian Stones Speak* (Chapel Hill: UNC Press, 1980); *The North African Stones Speak* (Chapel Hill: UNC Press, 1985); *Philosophical Books of Cicero* (London: Duckworth, 1989); *Cicero's Speeches: Context, Law, Rhetoric* (London: Duckworth, 1995). **Bio-Bibliography:** *Who's Who in America.* **Home Address:** 208 Bordner Dr., Madison, WI 53705.

MACLEISH, ARCHIBALD ■ RAAR Literature 57. b. May 7, 1892, Glencoe, IL. d. Apr. 20, 1982. m. Ada Hitchcock c. Kenneth, Brewster, Mary, William. BA 15, Yale Univ. **Career & Employment:** Librarian of Congress 1939-44; US Office of Facts & Figures, Dir. 1941-42; Cambridge Univ., Rede Lect. 1942; OWI, Asst. Dir. 1942-43; US Asst. Sec. of State 1944-45; Harvard Univ., Boylston Prof. 1949-62; Amherst College, Simpson Lect. 1963-67. **Fellowships, Honors & Awards:** Tufts College, Hon. MA

1955. **Publications:** *The Happy Marriage & Other Poems* (Boston: Houghton Mifflin, 1924); *The Pot of Earth* (Boston: Houghton Mifflin, 1925); *Nobodaddy, A Play* (Cambridge, MA: Dunster House, 1926); *Streets in the Moon, Poems* (1926); *The Hamlet of A. MacLeish* (Boston: Houghton Mifflin, 1928); *Einstein* (Paris: Black Son Press, 1929); *New Found Land, Fourteen Poems* (Boston: Houghton Mifflin, 1930); *Conquistador* (Boston: Houghton Mifflin, 1932); *Frescoes for Mr. Rockefeller's City* (New York: John Day Co., 1933); *Poems, 1924-1933* (Boston: Houghton Mifflin, 1933); *Union Pacific* (Boston: Houghton Mifflin, 1934); *Panic, A Play in Verse* (Boston: Houghton Mifflin, 1935); *The Fall of the City: A Verse Play for Radio* (New York: Farrar & Rinehart, 1937); *Air Raid: A Verse Play for Radio* (New York: Harcourt & Brace, 1938); *Land of the Free* (New York: Harcourt & Brace, 1938); *America Was Promises* (New York: Duell, Sloan & Pearce, 1939); *The Irresponsibles: A Declaration* (New York: Duell, Sloan & Pearce, 1940); *The American Cause* (New York: Duell, Sloan & Pearce, 1941); *A Time to Speak* (Boston: Houghton Mifflin, 1941); *A Time to Act* (Boston: Houghton Mifflin, 1942); *American Opinion & the War* (New York: Cambridge Univ. Press, 1942); *Act Five & Other Poems* (New York: Random House, 1948); *Freedom is the Right to Choose: An Inquiry into the Battle for America's Future* (Boston: Beacon Press, 1951); *Collected Poems, 1917-1952* (Boston: Houghton Mifflin, 1952); *J.B.: A Verse Play* (Boston: Houghton Mifflin, 1958); *Herakles: A Play in Verse* (Boston: Houghton Mifflin, 1967); *A Continuing Journey* (Boston: Houghton Mifflin, 1968); *The Human Season: Selected Poems 1926-72* (Boston: Houghton Mifflin, 1972); *New & Collected Poems, 1917-76* (Boston: Houghton Mifflin, 1976); *Archibald MacLeish: Reflections*, ed. B.A. Draheck & H.E. Ellis (Amherst: Univ. of Massachusetts Press, 1986). **Bio-Bibliography:** Edward J Mullaly, *Archibald Macleish: A Checklist* (Kent, OH: Kent State Univ. Press, 1973); Scott Donaldson & R.H. Winnick, *Archibald Macleish: An American Life* (Boston: Houghton Mifflin, 1992); *Who Was Who in America*.

MACMAHON, A. PHILIP ■ Sheldon Fellow 1915-16, 1916-17.

MACMONNIES, FREDERIC ■ AAR Charter Mem., Sculptor.

MACMULLEN, RAMSAY ■ RAAR History of Art. 80. b. 1928. **Research/Artistic Interests:** Late antiquity. **Career & Employment:** Yale Univ., Prof.

MACNEIL, ANNE ■ FAAR Post-Classical/Humanistic Studies 92. BA 81, Ithaca College; MS 85, Eastman School of Music; PhD 94, Univ. of Chicago. **Career & Employment:** Univ. of Chicago Press 1986-88; Univ. of Chicago 1987-91; Chicago State Univ. 1989-90; American Inst. of Indian Studies 1994-present. **Fellowships, Honors & Awards:** Univ. of Chicago, Century Scholarship 1985-88; American Musicological Soc., Midwest Chap. Hon. Mention 1987, Fellowship 1992-93; Special Music Fund Scholarship 1988-93; NEH Fellowship 1990, 1995; Gladys Krieble Delmas Fellowship 1992-93. **Publications:** "The Divine Madness of Isabella Andreini," *Journal of the Royal Music Association 120* (1995): forthcoming. **Home Addreess:** 5120 S. Hyde Park Blvd., Chicago, IL 60615.

MACNEIL, HERMON ATKINS ■ FAAR Sculpture 1899, AAR Trustee 1919-27. b. Feb. 27, 1866, Everett, MA. d. Oct. 2 1947. m. Carol Brooks, Cecelia W. Meunch. c. Claude Lash, Alden Brooks, Joie Katherine. **Other Studies:** Massachusetts State Normal Arts School 1886; with Chapu, Julien Acad., Paris; with Falguière, Beaux Arts Inst., Paris. **Career & Employment:** Cornell Univ., Instr. 1889; AIC, Instr. **Memberships & Offices:** NAD; NSS, Pres. 1910-12, 1922-24; American Federation of Arts; NIAL; ALNY; NY Municipal Arts Assn. **Fellowships, Honors & Awards:** Chicago Exposition, Designer's Medal 1893; Rinehart Fellowship 1896-1900; Paris Exposition, Silver Medal 1900; Buffalo Exposition, Gold Medal 1901; Charleston Exposition, Silver Medal 1902; Loiusana Purchase, Commerative Medal 1904; Panama Exposition, Gold Medal 1904; ALNY, Medal of Honor 1917; ANS, Saltus Medal 1923; Paris Salon, Bronze Medal 1933. **Important Works:** Main Cascade Fountain, Louisana Purchase Exposition; McKinley Memorial, Columbus; Soldiers & Sailors Monument, Albany, NY; Statue of George Washington, Washington Square Arch, NYC; US Supreme Court Bldg., Eastern Pediment, Washington, DC; Pony Express Statue, St. Joseph, MO; Ft. Sumter Memorial, Charleston, SC; *The Coming of the White Man*, Portland, OR; US Liberty 25-cent Coin 1916; *The Last Act of the Maqui Snake Dance*, Paris Exposition 1900; *Pioneer Woman; Primitive Chant; Lincoln the Lawyer; Out from Chaos Came the Dawn;* Collections: AIC; Peabody Inst., Baltimore; Cornell Univ.; MMA; Johns Hopkins Univ. **Exhibitions/Performances:** 1900 Intl. Universal Exposition, Paris; Pan American Exposition, Buffalo 1901. **Bio-Bibliography:** *National Cyclopedia of American Biography*.

MACSHANE, FRANK ■ RAAR Literature 82. b. Oct. 19, 1927, Pittsburgh, PA. BA 49, Harvard Univ.; MA 51, Yale Univ.; D.Phil. 55, Oxford Univ. **Career & Employment:** McGill Univ., Lect. 1955-57; Vassar College, Visiting Prof. 1958-59; UC, Berkeley, Asst. Prof. 1959-64; Williams College, Assc. Prof. 1964-67; Columbia Univ., School of the Arts, Writer, Prof. in the Writing Division, Translation Center, Dir. 1967-present, Dean 1972-73; Univ. of Rome, Visiting Prof. 1982. **Memberships & Offices:** Poets & Writers, Dir. 1970-80; PEN American Center; Nat. Book Critics' Circle; Center for Intl. Scholarly Exchange, Exec. Com. 1980-present; Authors Guild, Council Mem. 1982-present; Poets House, BoD 1987-92; Oxford & Cambridge Club, London; Century Assn., NYC. **Fellowships, Honors & Awards:** Fulbright Fellowship 1957, 1962, 1979; Guggenheim Fellow 1974; New York Humanities Inst., Fellow 1983-85; Cavaliere Ufficiale dell' Ordine al Merito della Repubblica Italiana 1987. **Publications:** *Many Golden Ages: Ruins, Temples and Monuments of the Orient* (Tokyo: Tuttle, 1962); ed., *Impressions of Latin America* (New York: Morrow, 1962); ed., *Critical Writings of Ford Madox Ford* (Univ. of Nebraska Press, 1964); ed., *The American in Europe* (New York: Dutton, 1965); *The Life and Work of Ford Madox Ford* (New York: Horizon Press & London: Routledge, 1965); ed., *Ford Madox Ford: The Critical Heritage* (London: Routledge, 1972); co-ed., *Borges on Writing* (New York: Dutton & London: Allen Lane, 1973); *The Life of Raymond Chandler* (New York: Dutton, 1976); ed., *The Notebooks of Raymond Chandler* (New York: Ecco & London: Weidenfeld, 1976); *The Life of John O'Hara* (New York: Dutton & London: Cape, 1981); ed., *Selected Letters of Raymond Chandler* (New York: Columbia Univ. Press, 1981); ed., *Collected Stories of John O'Hara* (New York: Random House, 1985); *Into Eternity: The Life of James Jones, American Writer* (Boston: Houghton Mifflin, 1985); plus numerous translations, introductions & contributions to books, as well as articles in periodicals. **Home Address:** 1326 Madison Ave., NYC 10128.

MAGOFFIN, RALPH VAN DEMAN ■ FASCSR 1907; AAR School of Classical Studies, Prof.-in-Charge 1920-21. b. Aug. 8, 1874, Rice County, KS. d. May 15, 1942. m. Lily Buckler, Kate H. Manning. c. Ralph. BA 02, Univ. of Michigan; PhD 08, Johns Hopkins Univ.; LLD 22, Washington College. **Other Studies:** Marburg, Berlin 1906-7. **Career & Employment:** Marietta College Acad., Teacher 1902-5; Johns Hopkins Univ., Instr.-Assc.

Prof. 1908-23; NYU, Prof.-Dept. Head 1923-39, Prof. Emer. 1939-42; US Military Service, Spanish-American War & WWI. **Memberships & Offices:** ArIA, Recorder 1914-21, Pres. 1921-31; AHA; APA; American Classical League, Pres. 1926-31, Hon. Pres. 1931-42; CAMWS; Classical Assn. of Atlantic States; Classical Club of NYC; Classical Assn. of Great Britain; Spanish American Veterans; American Legion; *AJA,* Ed. 1924-31; *Art and Archaeology,* Assc. Ed. 1914-25; Comitato Permanente per l'Etruria, Corresponding Mem. 1927-42; Intl. Mediterranean Research Assn. of Rome, Corresponding Mem., American Nat. Com., Pres. 1929-42; American Hellenic Com., Nat. Vice Chair 1930-42; Master Inst. of United Arts, Adv. **Fellowships, Honors & Awards:** Phi Beta Kappa; Omicron Delta Kappa; Commendatore della Corona d'Italia; Eta Sigma Phi; Pi Gamma Mu; Order of the Saviour, Greece, Knight. **Publications:** *A Study of the Topography and Municipal History of Praeneste* (Baltimore: Johns Hopkins Press, 1908); "Unpublished Inscriptions from Latium," *AJA* 14 (1910): 51-59; *The Quinquennales: A Historical Study* (Baltimore: Johns Hopkins Press, 1913); trans., H. Grotius, *The Freedom of the Seas* (1633) (New York: Oxford Univ. Press, 1916); co-author, *A Handbook of Economic Agencies of the War of 1917* (Washington, DC: Government Printing Office, 1919); with E.B. Garey, *American Guide Book to France and its Battlefields* (New York: Macmillan, 1920); ed., C.V. Bynkerrhock, *De dominio maris dissertatio* (New York: Oxford Univ. Press, 1923); trans., C.V. Bynkerrhock, *The Sovereignty of the Sea* (New York: Oxford Univ. Press, 1924); *The Roman Forum* (New York, 1928); with E.C. Davis, *Magic Spades: The Romance of Archaeology* (New York: Holt, 1929); *The Lure and Lore of Archaeology* (Baltimore: Williams & Wilkens, 1930); *Ancient and Medieval History* (New York: Silver, Burdett, 1939). **Bio-Bibliography:** *NY Times,* Obit. (May 17, 1942); *Who Was Who in America.*

MAGONIGLE, HAROLD VAN BUREN ■ Rotch Scholar 1894, Architect, b. Oct. 17, 1867. d. Aug. 29, 1935. **Career & Employment:** McKim, Mead & White 1888-94. One of the first men in residence at the Academy during its initial year of operation. **Important Works:** Kansas City War Memorial; Chicago War Memorial; Pan American Union Bldg., Washington, DC.

MAHONEY, JAMES OWEN ■ FAAR Painting 35; AAR Trustee 1951-54. b. Oct. 16, 1907, Dallas, TX. d. Oct. 19, 1987. BA 28, Southern Methodist Univ.; BFA 32, Yale Univ. **Research/ Artistic Interests:** Mural painting. **Career & Employment:** Cornell Univ., Prof. 1939-73, Chair 1963-68, Prof. Emer. 1973-87; US Army Air Corps, Capt. WWII. **Memberships & Offices:** Nat. Soc. of Mural Painters. **Important Works:** Murals: Texas Centennial Exb., Hall of State, Dallas 1936; NY World's Fair, Hall of Judiciary, Federal Bldg. & Communications Bldg. 1938; Adolphus Hotel, Dallas, Presidential Suite 1950; Johns Hopkins Univ., Shriver Hall 1957; All Saints Episcopal Church, Chevy Chase, MD 1958; Fairmont Hotel, Atlanta 1974; Acad. of Medicine, Atlanta 1983. **Exhibitions/Performances:** Grand Central Art Gallery 1935; ALNY 1936, 1938; PAFA 1942; Mace Gallery, Dallas 1946. **Bio-Bibliography:** "Tour of Home of Cornell Artist Mahoney Opens a Few Eyes," *Ithaca Journal* (June 27, 1988); *Who Was Who in America; Who Was Who in American Art.*

MALAMUD, MARTHA A. ■ FAAR Classics/Archaeology 88. b. May 20, 1957, Boston, MA. m. Donald T. McGuire. c. Frances. BA 78, Bryn Mawr College; MA 82, Cornell Univ.; PhD 85, Cornell Univ. **Research/Artistic Interests:** Late antique literature & Latin poetry. **Career & Employment:** Univ. of South-

ern California, Lect. 1984-85, Mellon Fellow 1985-86, Asst. Prof. 1986-91, Assc. Prof. 1991-present; SUNY, Buffalo, Assc. Prof. 1992-present. **Memberships & Offices:** *Arethusa,* Assc. Ed. 1993-present. **Fellowships, Honors & Awards:** Cornell Univ., A.D. White Univ. Fellowship 1979-82; Mellon Fellowship 1985-86; NEH Senior Fellowship 1988-89; Univ. of Southern California, Zumberge Research & Innovation Fund Fellowship 1992. **Publications:** with Patricia T. Johnson, "Ovid's *Musomachia,*" *Pacific Coast Philology* 23 (1988): 30-38; *A Poetics of Transformation: Prudentius and Classical Mythology* (Ithaca: Cornell Univ. Press, 1989); "Making a Virtue of Perversity: Prudentius and Classical Poetry," in *The Imperial Muse: Ramus Essays on Roman Literature of the Empire,* vol. 2, ed. A.J. Boyle (Victoria, 1989); with Donald T. McGuire, "Valerius Flaccus: Mythic Variant," in *Roman Epic: Critical Essays,* ed. A.J. Boyle (London & New York: Routledge, 1992); "Vandalizing Epic," *Ramus* (1993). **Home Address:** 308 Highland Ave., Buffalo, NY 14222. **Business Address:** Classics Dept., Clemens Hall, SUNY, Buffalo, NY 14260.

MALDARELLI, ORONZIO ■ AAR Trustee 1958-62.

MANCA DI MORES, GIUSEPPINA ■ Italian Fulbright Fellow 1984-85.

MANDELBAUM, ALLEN ■ AAR Visitor 1951-55, Scholar, Translator.

MANGRAVITE, PEPPINO ■ AAR Trustee 1947-49, Columbia Univ., Artist.

MANGURIAN, ROBERT EMERSON ■ FAAR Architecture 77. b. Apr. 15, 1941, Baltimore, MD. BArch 67, UC, Berkeley. **Career & Employment:** Conklin & Rossant, Architectural Designer-Planner 1967-68; Warner, Burns, Toan, Lunde, Architectural Designer-Planner 1968-69; Works, Prin. & Co-Founder 1969-76; City College, CUNY, Adj. Prof. 1969-76; UCLA, Visiting Lect. 1975. **Fellowships, Honors & Awards:** City Club of New York, Albert S. Bard Award 1970; *Progressive Architecture,* Citation 1972, Award 1976. **Important Works:** Reconstruction of Venzone, Italy, Plan Developer. **Exhibitions/Performances:** Group: NAD 1983. **Bio-Bibliography:** Paul Goldberger, "Rewarding What May Be, Rather Than What Is," *NY Times* (Feb. 2, 1986).

MANN, MORTON M. ■ Appleton Fellow 1913.

MANSHIP, PAUL HOWARD ■ FAAR Sculpture 12; AAR Trustee 1942-66. b. Dec. 25, 1886, St. Paul, MN. d. Jan. 31, 1966. m. Isabel McIlwain. c. John Paul, Pauline F.H. Natti, Elizabeth Solomon, Jane Murtha. **Other Studies:** St. Paul School of Fine Arts, MN; PAFA; ASL. **Research/Artistic Interests:** Bronze casting. **Career & Employment:** Studios of Solon Borglum & Isidore Konti, NYC. **Memberships & Offices:** AAAL, Pres. 1948-53; Smithsonian Inst., Fine Arts Com., Chair; NSS, Pres. 1939-42; NAD, Assc. Mem.; Argentine Acad. 1943; Century Club, Pres. 1950. **Fellowships, Honors & Awards:** NAD, Prizes 1913, 1917; PAFA, Widener Gold Medal 1914; ANS, Gold Medal 1924; Philadelphia Art Alliance, Gold Medal 1925; Sesqui-centennial Exposition, Philadelphia, Gold Medal 1926; Légion d'Honneur, Chevalier 1929; Paris Salon, Prize 1937; NSS, Prize 1943; NIAL, Gold Medal 1945; San Francisco Exposition, Gold Medal. **Publications:** "The History of Sculpture," and "Decorative Sculpture" in *Encyclopedia Britannica.* **Important Works:** Prometheus Fountain, Rockefeller Center, NYC 1934; Paul J. Rainey Memorial Gateway, Bronx Zoo, NYC 1934; *Armillary Sphere, Time* *and the Fates of Man, Day,* NY World's Fair 1939; William C. Osborn Memorial Playground Gateway, Central Park, NYC 1952; Seals, NY Coliseum, Columbus Circle 1956; Herbert Lehman Gateway, Children's Zoo, Central Park, NYC 1960; Fountain, Fairmont Park, Philadelphia; *The Four Elements,* former AT &T Co. Bldg., replica of 1914 panels. **Exhibitions/ Performances:** NAD 1913, 1917; PAFA 1914; Pan-Pacific Expo, San Francisco 1915; Peabody Gallery, Baltimore 1916; AIA 1921; ANS 1924; Philadelphia Art Alliance 1925; Carnegie Inst., Pittsburgh 1925; Numismatic Sesqui-centennial Exposition, Philadelphia 1926; Corcoran Gallery 1937; Paris Salon 1937; NSS 1943; AAAL 1945; MMA 1951; Chesterwood, Stockbridge, MA 1966; Arts & Science Center, St. Paul, MN 1967; Minnesota Museum of Art, St. Paul 1985; Tate Gallery, London; Retrospective: Smithsonian Inst. 1958. **Bio-Bibliography:** Edwin Murtha, *Paul Manship* (New York: Macmillan, 1957); Carol Hynning Smith, *The Drawings of Paul Manship* (St. Paul: Minnesota Museum of Art, 1987); Harry Rand, *Paul Manship* (Washington, DC: Nat. Museum of American Art, 1989); John Manship, *Paul Manship* (New York: Abbeville Press, 1989); Susan Rather, *Archaism, Modernism, and the Art of Paul Manship* (Austin: Univ. of Texas Press, 1993); *Encyclopedia of American Art; Who Was Who in America; Who Was Who in American Art.*

MANSO, LEO ■ RAAR Painting 80. b. Apr. 15, 1914, NYC. d. Feb. 5, 1993. m. Blanche Manso. c. Peter, Victor. **Other Studies:** NAD; New School for Social Research; MMA. **Career & Employment:** Cooper Union, Faculty 1947-; ASL, Faculty 1975-; Dartmouth Univ., Artist-in-Residence 1985. **Fellowships, Honors & Awards:** Audubon Artists, Emily Lowe Award 1951-52, 1955-56; Hudson River Museum, 1st Prize 1970; Guggenheim Fellowship 1981; AAAL Prize 1982-84; NAD 1985; Pollock-Krasner Found. Grant 1988. **Exhibitions/Performances:** Solo: Norlyst Gallery, NYC 1947; Babcock Gallery, NYC 1954, 1956; Philadelphia Art Alliance 1961, 1968; Rose Fried Gallery, NYC 1966, 1968, 1970; Frank Rehn Gallery, NYC 1974; Everson Museum, Syracuse 1976; Long Point Gallery, Provincetown 1977-92; Arras Gallery, NYC 1983; Provincetown Art Assn. & Museum 1987; Armstrong Gallery, NYC 1988; Alan Brown Gallery, Hartsdale, NY 1990; Stuart Levy Gallery, NY 1991; ASL 1992; Group: American Abstract Annual, NYC 1951, 1958, 1960; Hudson River Museum Annual, Yonkers, NY 1970; Alternative Museum, NYC 1980; AAAL 1981; Belltable Arts Center, Limerick, Ireland 1991.

MARANO, LIZBETH ■ FAAR Sculpture 86. b. Dec. 2, 1950, Newark, NJ. c. Francesca Bochner, Piera Bochner. BFA 72, Washington Univ. **Research/Artistic Interests:** Sculpture, drawing, photography. **Career & Employment:** MFA School 1982; Sarah Lawrence College 1982-83; Baruch College, CUNY 1983-84; Brandeis Univ. 1989-90; Cooper Union 1995. **Memberships & Offices:** Yaddo, Juror 1989. **Fellowships, Honors & Awards:** Change Inc. Grant 1975; NEA Grant 1978, 1985, 1988-89. **Publications:** "Robert Rauschenberg: Castelli & Sonnabend," *Art in America* (Jan. 1982): 182-83; "Anselm Kiefer: Culture as Hero," *Portfolio* (May-June 1983): 102-5; "Carol Brown: Witkin Gallery," *Art in America* (Sept. 1983): 170-71; *Two Presses-Two Processes: Parasol & Simca,* exb. cat. (Lewisburg, PA: Bucknell Univ., 1983); "Ruth Thorne-Thomsen: Marcuse Pfeiffer Gallery," *Art in America* (Apr. 1984): 188; "Anselm Kiefer," *Modern Arts Criticism,* vol. 1, ed. Joanne Prosynink (1991): 292-94. **Important Works:** Prints & drawings 1980-90 in: New York Public Library, MFA, Shearson-Lehman, Levi Strauss, IBM. **Exhibitions/Performances:** Daniel Weinberg Gallery, San Francisco 1982, Los

Angeles 1983, 1984; Baskerville & Watson Gallery, NYC 1984; Sculpture Center, NYC 1985; Artists Space, NYC 1985; Galleria Primo Piano, Rome 1986; Carnegie Mellon Univ. Art Gallery, Pittsburgh 1987; Laurie Rubin Galley, NYC 1987; Leubsdorf Art Gallery, Hunter College, NYC 1988; David Nolan Gallery, NYC 1988; MFA 1988; AAAL 1989; Molica GuidArte Gallery, NYC 1990, 1991; Galleria Molica, Rome 1992. **Bio-Bibliography:** Elizabeth Murray, "Personal Choices," *Bomb* (Jan. 1983); Ron Warren, "Brilliant Color," *Arts Magazine* (Apr. 1984); Douglas Dreishpoon, *Between Drawing and Sculpture,* exb. cat. (New York: Sculpture Center, 1986); "Opening the Circle: Lizbeth Marano," *891 International Arts Magazine* 1.3.7 (1986): 6-11; Susan Edwards, *A Debate on Abstraction, Systems and Abstraction,* exb. cat. (New York: Leubsdorf Art Gallery, Hunter College, 1988), 10, 12, 15; Gabriella Dalesio, "Lizbeth Marano 'Entropia'," *Segno* 111-112 (Feb.-Mar. 1992): 74-77; Paolo Balmas, *Lizbeth Marano: Entropia,* exb. cat. (Rome: Galleria Molica, 1992); *Roma in Mostra,* exb. cat. (Rome: Edizioni Carte Segrete, 1992): 178-79. **Home Address:** 108 Franklin St., NYC 10013.

MARCA-RELLI, CONRAD ■ RAAR Painting 76. b. June 5, 1913, Boston, MA. m. Anita Gibson. **Career & Employment:** Yale Univ., Prof. **Fellowships, Honors & Awards:** Guggenheim Award; AIC, 1st Prize 1954; Ford Found. Award 1970. **Exhibitions/Performances:** thirty solo; Whitney Museum, NYC, Retrospective 1967. **Bio-Bibliography:** M.A. Arnason, *Marca-Relli* (New York: Abrams, 1960); Daniel Miracle, *Marca-Relli* (New York: Rizzoli, 1976). **Home Address:** 132 Lionshead Dr. W., Wayne, NJ 07470. **Business Address:** Marisa del Re Gallery, 41 E. 57 St., NYC.

MARCEAU, HENRI GABRIEL ■ FAAR Architecture 25. b. June 21, 1895, Richmond, VA. d. Sept. 15, 1969. m. Rebecca Alvord. c. Elizabeth Bartlett. BArch 20, Columbia Univ. **Research/Artistic Interests:** Temple of Concord, Rome; Pozzi Chapel, Florence. **Career & Employment:** Univ. of Pennsylvania, Instr. 1926, Asst. Prof. 1927; John G. Johnson Collection, Curator 1927-29; Philadelphia Museum of Art, Curator 1929-33, Asst. Dir. 1933-45, Assc. Dir. 1945-55, Acting Dir. 1955-56, Dir. 1956-64. **Memberships & Offices:** Fairmount Park Art Assn., Sec. 1930, VP 1946; Philadelphia Art Alliance, Sec. 1932-33, VP 1933; Arts & Crafts Guild, Pres. 1937-39; Philadelpia Art Comm. 1940-69, VP 1945; Walters Art Gallery, Adv. Com. Chair 1946; Philadelphia Art Jury; APA; AIA, Hon. Mem.; Nat. Soc. of Art Directors; Assn. of Art Museum Directors; American Inst. of Designers, Hon. Mem. **Fellowships, Honors & Awards:** Order of the Belgian Crown, Chevalier 1940; French Order of Legion of Honor, Chevalier 1947; Intl. Inst. for Conservation of Museum Objects, Fellow. **Publications:** with Homer Rebert, "The Temple of Concord in the Roman Forum," *Memoirs of the AAR* 5 (1925): 53-78; *William Rush, the First American Sculptor* (Philadelphia: Pennsylvania Museum of Art, 1937). **Bio-Bibliography:** *NY Times,* Obit. (Sept. 16, 1969); *Current Biography Yearbook* (1970); *Who Was Who in America.*

MARINI, MARINO ■ AAR Visitor 1943 — 1951, Sculptor.

MARINO, LUCILLA ■ AAR Librarian 1977-92.

MARSH, DAVID R. ■ FAAR Post-Classical/Humanistic Studies 83. b. Sept. 25, 1950, Chicago, IL. m. Dorene A. O'Hara. c. Diana, Christina. BA 72, Yale Univ.; MA 73, Harvard Univ.; PhD 78, Harvard Univ. **Career & Employment:** Univ. of Michigan, Asst. Prof. 1978-84; Rutgers Univ., Asst. Prof. 1986-88, Assc.

Prof. 1988-present. **Memberships & Offices:** *Italian Quarterly,* Ed. Bd. 1988-present. **Fellowships, Honors & Awards:** Yale Univ., Nat. Scholarship & Nat. Merit Scholarship 1968-72, Phi Beta Kappa, Calhoun College Fellows' Cup 1972, Winthrop Prize 1972, Noyes-Cutter Prize 1972; Harvard Univ., Graduate Soc. Scholarship 1973, Bowdoin Graduate Prize 1974; Fulbright-Hays Grant 1976-77; Villa I Tatti Fellowship 1977-78; NEH Grant 1977-78; Univ. of Michigan, Matthews Underclass Teaching Award 1981, Rackham Faculty Grant & Fellowship 1982; Mellon Fellowship 1982-83; Newberry Library Fellowship 1984; NEH Postdoctoral Fellowship 1984-85; Rutgers Univ., Faculty Grant & Summer Fellowship 1987; APS Grant 1989. **Publications:** *The Quattrocento Dialogue: Classical Tradition and Humanist Innovation,* Harvard Studies in Comparative Literature 35 (Cambridge-London: Harvard Univ. Press, 1980); "Lorenzo Valla's Translation from Xenophon's *Cyropaedia,*" *Bibliothèque d'Humanisme et Renaissance* 46 (1984): 407-20; "Petrarch and Alberti," in *Renaissance Essays in Honor of Craig Hugh Smyth,* ed. Sergio Bertelli & Gloria Ramakus, 2 vols. (Florence: Giunti-Barbera, 1985), 1:363-75; "Struttura e retorica nel 'De vero bono' di Lorenzo Valla," in *Lorenzo Valla e l'Umanesimo italiano,* ed. Ottavio Besomi & Mariangela Regoliosi, Medioevo e Umanesimo 59 (Padua: Antenore, 1986), 311-26; *Leon Battista Alberti, Dinner Pieces: A Translation of the* Intercenales, Medieval and Renaissance Texts & Studies 45, RSA Renaissance Texts 9 (Binghamton, NY: SUNY Press, 1987); "Sannazaro's Elegy on the Ruins of Cumae," *Bibliothèque d'Humanisme et Renaissance* 50 (1988): 681-89; "Sparta and Quattrocento Humanism: Lilius Tifernas' Translation of Xenophon's Spartan Constitution," *Bibliothèque d'Humanisme et Renaissance* 53 (1991): 91-103; "Beyond the Pillars of Hercules: Voyage and Veracity in Exploration Narratives," *Annali d'Italianistica* 10 (1992): 134-49; "Ovid in Tuscany: Myth and Unity in Lorenzo's *Ambra,*" *Stanford Italian Studies* 11 (1992): 75-90; "Xenophon," in *Catalogus Translationum et Commentariorum: Mediaeval and Renaissance Latin Translations and Commentaries, Annotated Lists and Guides* 7, ed. Virginia Brown (Washington, DC: Catholic Univ. of America Press, 1992), 75-196; "Further Notes on Leon Battista Alberti's Dinner Pieces," *Allegorica* (1993): 23-37. **Home Address:** 11 Barrington Rd., Belle Mead, NJ 08502. **Business Address:** Italian Dept., Rutgers Univ., New Brunswick, NJ 08903.

MARTI, BERTHE M. ■ FAAR Classics/Archaeology 45; RAAR Classics/Archaeology 51. b. May 11, 1904. d. June 4, 1995. Bacc. 22, Gymnase Classique Cantonal, Lausanne; Lic. 25, Univ. of Lausanne; MA 26, Bryn Mawr College; PhD 33, Bryn Mawr College. **Other Study:** Univ. College, London 1924. **Research/Artistic Interests:** Literature of the Neronian age, history of the Latin epic, literature of the 12th century, history of medieval education. **Career & Employment:** Bryn Mawr College, Instr.-Asst. Prof.-Assc. Prof.-Prof. 1932-63; UNC, Chapel Hill, Prof. 1963-76; Southern Inst. of Medieval & Renaissance Studies, Seminar Dir. 1967. **Memberships & Offices:** *Mediaevalia et Humanistica,* Ed. Bd. 1970-80; *Catalogus Translationum et Commentariorum,* Ed. Bd. & Exec. Bd. 1960-95; APA, BoD 1959-62, Monograph Com. 1957-62, Rep. to *Thesaurus Linguae Latinae* 1962-67; UNC, Philological Club, Pres. 1973-74, School of Library Science, Adv. Bd. 1973-75. **Fellowships, Honors & Awards:** Bryn Mawr College, European Fellow 1925-26, 1928-29, Madge Miller Research Fund Grant 1952, 1961; Fulbright Grant 1946; Guggenheim Fellowship 1954-55; ACLS Grant 1957, Travel Grant 1974; APS, Primrose Research Fund Grants (3); MAA, Fellow 1977. **Publications:** "Place de l'Hercule sur l'Oeta dans le Corpus des Tragédies de Sénèque," *Revue des Études Latines* (1949): 188-210; "A Crux in Dante's

Inferno," *Speculum* 27 (1952): 67-70; "Seneca's *Apocolocyntosis* & Octavia," *American Journal of Philology* 73 (1952): 24-36; "Hugh Primas and Arnulf of Orleans," *Speculum* 30 (1955): 233-38; "Lucan's Invocation to Nero in the Light of the Medieval Commentaries," *Quadrivium* 1 (1956): 1-11; *Arnulfi Aurelianensis Glossulae super Lucanum,* Papers & Monographs of the AAR 18 (Rome: AAR, 1958); *The Spanish College at Bologna* (Philadelphia: Univ. of Pennsylvania Press, 1963); "Gomez versus the Spanish College at Bologna," in *Didascaliae: Studies in Honor of Anselm M. Albareda,* ed. S. Prete (New York: B.A. Rosenthal, 1963), 293-319; "Tragic History and Lucan's Pharsalia," *Classical and Renaissance Studies in Honor of Berthold Louis Ullman,* ed. C. Henderson (Rome: Storia e Letteratura, 1964), 165-204; "Cassius Scaeva and Lucan's Invention," in *The Classical Tradition: Literary and Historical Studies in Honor of Harry Caplan,* ed. L. Wallach (Ithaca: Cornell Univ. Press, 1966), 239-57; "The Founding of the Spanish College at Bologna," *Medieval and Renaissance Studies* (1967): 70-95; "Lucan's Narrative Techniques," *La Parola del Passato* 160 (1975): 74-90. **Bio-Bibliography:** *Directory of American Scholars; Who's Who of American Women.*

MARTIN, HAROLD C. ■ AAR Pres. 1974-77. b. Jan. 12, 1917, Raymond, PA. m. Elma H. Martin. c. Thomas, Joel, Ann, Rebecca. BA 37, Hartwick College; MA 42, Univ. of Michigan; PhD 54, Harvard Univ. **Career & Employment:** Adams HS, NY, Teacher 1937-39; Goshen HS, NY, Teacher & Asst. Prin. 1939-48; Harvard Univ., Gen. Ed. Dir., Lect. 1951-65; Union College & Univ., Pres. & Chancellor 1965-74; Trinity College, Hartford, Dana Prof. 1977-82. **Home Address:** 1317 Meadowlark Ln., Corrales, NM 87048.

MARTIN, JANET M. ■ FAAR Post-Classical/Humanistic Studies 72. b. Oct. 24, 1938, Bogalusa, LA. BA 61, Radcliffe College; MA 63, Univ. of Michigan; PhD 68, Harvard Univ. **Career & Employment:** Harvard Univ., Instr. 1968-69, Asst. Prof. 1969-72; Princeton Univ., Asst. Prof. 1973-76, Assc. Prof. 1976-present. **Memberships & Offices:** APA, Com. on the Status of Women & Minority Groups 1973-80, Founding Mem. Chair & author of annual reports 1978-80; Women's Classical Caucus, Steering Com. 1989-93, Co-chair 1992; Medieval Latin Studies Group 1982-present, Founding Mem., Chair 1990-93; MAA, Councillor 1980-83, Exec. Bd. 1982-83; *Toronto Medieval Latin Texts,* Ed. Bd. 1973-present. **Publications:** ed., with Giles Constable, *Peter the Venerable: Selected Letters,* Toronto Medieval Latin Texts 3 (Toronto: Pontifical Inst. of Mediaeval Studies, 1974); "John of Salisbury's Manuscripts of Frontinus and of Gellius," *Journal of the Warburg & Courtauld Institutes* 40 (1977): 1-26; "Uses of Tradition: Gellius, Petronius, and John of Salisbury," *Viator: Medieval and Renaissance Studies* 10 (1979): 57-76; with P.K. Marshall & Richard H. Rouse, "Clare College MS. 26 and the Circulation of Aulus Gellius 1-7 in Medieval England and France," *Mediaeval Studies* 42 (1980): 353-94; "Classicism and Style in Latin Literature," in *Renaissance and Renewal in the Twelfth Century,* ed. Robert L. Benson & Giles Constable, with Carol D. Lanham (Cambridge, MA: Harvard Univ. Press, 1982), 537-68; "John of Salisbury as Classical Scholar," in *The World of John of Salisbury,* Studies in Church History: Subsidia 3, ed. Michael Wilks (Oxford: Basil Blackwell & Ecclesiastical History Soc., 1984), 179-201; with Greta Mary Hair, "O Ecclesia: The Text and Music of Hildegard of Bingen's Sequence for St. Ursula," *Tjurunga: An Australasian Benedictine Review* 30 (1986): 3-62; "Cicero's Jokes at the Court of Henry II of England: Roman Humor and the Princely Ideal," *Modern Language Quarterly* 51 (1990): 144-66. **Business Address:** Dept. of Classics, 104 East Pyne, Princeton Univ., Princeton, NJ 08544.

MARTIN, ROGER B. ■ FAAR Landscape Architecture 64. b. Nov. 23, 1936, Virginia, MN. m. Janis A. Martin. c. Thomas E., Stephen B., Jonathan K. BS 58, Univ. of Minnesota; MLA 64, Harvard Univ. **Career & Employment:** UC, Berkeley, Asst. Prof. 1964-66; Univ. of Minnesota, Assc. Prof. 1966-72, Prof. 1972-present. **Memberships & Offices:** ASLA 1967-present, Nat. Pres. 1987. **Fellowships, Honors & Awards:** Sigma Lambda Alpha, Nat. Honorary Soc. 1978, Distinguished Educator Award 1990; MASLA, Merit Award 1978, 1980 (2), 1986 (2), 1989, Honor Award 1978, 1986, Public Service Award 1985, Landscape Architecture Awareness Award 1987, Lob Pine Award for Service to Landscape Architecture 1989; Minneapolis Com. on Urban Environment Award 1990; Univ. of Minnesota, College of Architecture & Landscape Architecture, Service to Profession Award 1990. **Publications:** "Goals for Education of Landscape Architects," *National Conference of Instructors in Landscape Architecture Proceedings* (1976); "Collaborative Practice," *Landscape Australia-Magazine* (Nov. 1980): 12-17; "Reflections on Australian Landscape," *Landscape Australia-Magazine* (Feb. 1981): 12-17; "Enhancing Creativity," Televised workshops (4) for classroom use, Minnesota Multimedia Center, 1984; "Enhancing Creativity in Landscape Architectural Education," *CELA Forum* (1985); with Jon Burley, "Home Owner Preference for Naturalistic Landscapes Tolerance of Wildlife," *Proceedings of the National Symposium on Urban Wildlife* (1986); "Metropolitan Park Systems," in *American Landscape Architecture: Designers and Places,* ed. William Tishler (Nat. Trust for Historical Preservation, 1989); *Writing as a Means to Design* (Minneapolis: Univ. of Minnesota, Center for Interdisciplinary Studies in Writing, 1990); *Writing in the Design Disciplines* (Minneapolis: Univ. of Minnesota, Center for Interdisciplinary Studies in Writing, 1992). **Important Works:** Shade Trees Exb., Univ. of Minnesota Arboretum, Chaska, MN 1988; Hennepin County Waste to Energy Plant, Minneapolis 1988; Community Center Site Development, Minnetonka, MN 1988; Reister Residence, Star Prairie, WI 1989; North Hennepin Community College Master Plan, Brooklyn Park, MN 1989; Downtown & River Front Study, River Falls, WI 1990; Main St. Urban Park Rehabilitation, Minneapolis 1990; Nicollet Island Circulation Master Plan, Minneapolis 1990; Federal Courts Plaza Context Master Plan Study, Minneapolis 1991; St. Anthony Falls Heritage Trail, Design Development, Minneapolis 1991; Longfellow Park Redevelopment, Minneapolis 1992; Nicollet Island Master Plan, Minneapolis 1993; Upper Iowa Univ. Sports Recreation Complex, Fayette 1993. **Bio-Bibliography:** *Who's Who in America.* **Home Address:** 2912 45th Ave. S., Minneapolis, MN 55406. **Business Address:** Dept. of Landscape Architecture, College of Architecture & Landscape Architecture, Univ. of Minnesota, 89 Church St., Minneapolis, MN 55455.

MARTIN, SUSAN D. ■ FAAR Classics/Archaeology 81; Classical Soc., Treas. 1994. b. Nov. 30, 1951, Oakland, CA. m. Paul E. Barrette. BA 73, UC, Berkeley; BA 76, UC, Berkeley; PhD 81, Univ. of Michigan. **Research/Artistic Interests:** Roman law, legal history. **Career & Employment:** Univ. of Tennessee, Asst. Prof. 1981-91, Assc. Prof. & Dept. Head 1991-present. **Fellowships, Honors & Awards:** Univ. of Michigan, Horace Rackham Graduate Fellowship 1979-80; Univ. of Tennessee Faculty Research Grant 1984; Harvard Law School, Liberal Arts Fellow 1988-89; NEH Summer Seminar 1991. **Publications:** *The Roman Jurists and the Organization of Construction in the Late Republic and Early Empire* (Brussels: Latomus, 1989); & other articles & reviews. **Business Address:** Dept. of Classics, Univ. of Tennessee, 710 McClung Twr., Knoxville, TN 37996.

MARTINELLI, EZIO ■ RAAR Sculpture 65, AAR Trustee. b. Nov. 27, 1912. d. 1981. **Career & Employment:** Sarah Lawrence College 1947-75; Parsons School of Design 1953-78. **Bio-Bibliography:** *Directory of Contemporary American Artists.*

MARTINŮ, BOHUSLAV (JAN) ■ RAAR Musical Composition 57. b. Dec. 8, 1890, Policka, Czechoslovakia. d. Aug. 28, 1959. m. Charlotta Quennehen. **Study:** Prague Conservatory 1906-9; with Suk; Prague Organ School 1909-10; with Albert Roussel, Paris 1923. **Career & Employment:** Czech Philharmonic, 1913-14, 1918-23; Princeton Univ., Visiting Prof. 1948-51. **Fellowships, Honors & Awards:** Elizabeth Sprague Coolidge Award 1932; New York Critics' Circle Award 1955. **Important Works:** *Preludium,* in the form of a scherzo, for orchestra 1930; *String Sextet* 1932; *Trio No. 2,* for violin, cello & piano 1934; *Comedy on the Bridge,* an opera 1935, rev. 1950; *Sinfonietta Giocosa,* for piano & chamber orchestra 1940-41; *Memorial to Lidice,* for orchestra 1943; *Toccata et Due Canzoni,* for small orchestra 1946; *Concerto da Camera,* String Quartet No. 7 1947; *Three Czech Dances,* for 2 pianos 1949; *Sinfonietta La Jolla,* for chamber orchestra & piano 1950; *Double Violin Concerto,* for orchestra 1950; *Fantaisies Symphoniques,* Symphony No. 6 1951-53; *What Men Live By,* an opera 1951-52; *Rhapsody Concerto,* for viola & orchestra 1952; *The Marriage,* an opera 1952; *Greek Passion,* an opera 1955-59. **Bio-Bibliography:** M. Safránek, *Bohuslav Martinů; His Life and Works* (London: A Wingate, 1962); H. Halbreich, *Bohuslav Martinů* (Zurich: Atlantis Verlag, 1968); Charlotta Martinů, *My Life with Bohuslav Martinů* (Prague: Orbis, 1971); Jiri Mihule, *Martinů* (Prague, 1972); Brian Large, *Martinů* (London: Duckworth, 1975); Guy Erismann, *Martinů: Un Musicien à l'eveil des sources* (Arles: Actes Sud, 1990); *Who Was Who in America.*

MARTIRANO, SALVATORE ■ FAAR Musical Composition 59. b. Jan. 12, 1927, Yonkers, NY. BMus 51, Oberlin Conservatory of Music; MMus 52, Eastman School of Music. **Fellowships, Honors & Awards:** Tanglewood, Crofts Award 1952, 1955, Sagalyn Prize. **Important Works:** *That Shakespearean Rag,* League of Composers-ISCM Comm. for Marion Bauer 1958; NEA-Koussevitzky Found., Library of Congress Comm. 1958; *Chansons Innocentes Ninna Nanna* 1958.

MARVIN, MIRANDA ■ AAR Classical Soc., Pres. 1977, 1978; NEH Summer Seminar Co.-Dir. 1994.

MARZOTTO, PAOLO ■ AAR Italian Com. 1994-present.

MASON, RICHARD ■ AAR Visitor 1992-93, Writer.

MASSEY, JOHN L. ■ FAAR Painting 61; RAAR Painting 79. b. Oct. 18, 1925, Pittsburgh, PA. Cert. 53, PAFA. **Other Study:** Carnegie Inst. of Technology, Barnes Found. **Research/Artistic Interests:** Painting, sculpture in various media. **Career & Employment:** PAFA 1963; RISD 1963-present, Honors Program in Rome, Dir.-Critic 1966-67, 1975-77. **Fellowships, Honors & Awards:** PAFA, Scheidt Fellowship 1952, Cresson Fellowship 1953, Special Prize Fellowship Exb. 1953; Museum of Art, Carnegie Inst., Purchase Award 1961; Associated Artists of Pittsburgh, Leisser Alumni Prize 1961; *Progressive Architecture* Magazine, Design Award 1965. **Important Works:** Collections: Museum of Art, Carnegie Inst., Pittsburgh; Philadelphia Museum of Art; Albright-Knox Gallery, Buffalo; Westmoreland, PA, County Museum of Art; FRIAM, Commune di Udine, Italy; Princeton Univ.; Colgate Univ.; MIT; Chase Manhattan Bank, NYC; Commissions & Corporations: Sage Mfg. Co., Providence; Hospital Trust Bank, Providence; Davol Corp., Providence; Quaker Fabric Corp., Fall River, MA; Nabisco Corp., NJ; Winsor Asscs., Providence; Colgate Hoyt Co., Milton, MA; Halpern Corp., NYC; First Nat. Bank, Boston; Shadyside Hospital, Pittsburgh; Jones & Laughlin Corp., Pittsburgh; Ford Motor Co., Dearborn; Colgate Univ. **Exhibitions/ Performances:** Woods-Gerry Gallery, Providence; Phillips Gallery, Philadelphia 1951; Pittsburgh Playhouse 1951; Philadelphia Art Alliance 1954; USIA Gallery, Naples 1960; Wesleyan Univ. 1968; Art Unlimited Gallery, Providence 1968; Westmoreland County Museum of Art, Greensburg, PA 1971; Colgate Univ. 1972; Newport Art Assn. 1974; Virginia Lynch Gallery, Tiverton, RI 1984; Lenore Gray Gallery, Providence 1986; Arts Center, Catanzaro, Italy 1988; Reynolds Gallery, Pittsburgh 1990; Museum of Art, RISD 1990, 1992, 1994. **Home Address:** 116 Chestnut St., Providence, RI 02903.

MASSON, GEORGINA ■ AAR Visitor 1977-78, Author. **Selected Publications:** *Italian Villas and Palaces* (1959); *Ancient Rome, From Romulus to Augustus* (1973); *The Companion Guide to Rome* (1983).

MASTERS, ELIZABETH ■ NIAE, John Dinkeloo Traveling Fellow 1981-82.

MATT, JOHN A. ■ FAAR Sculpture 72; AAR Sculpture Jury 1974. b. Jan. 2, 1935, Richmond, VA. m. Mary Billingsley. c. Andrew, Thomas. BFA 68, Yale Univ.; MFA 68, Yale Univ. **Other Study:** Ringling School of Art, Sarasota, FL 1955-57; PAFA 1957-59; Skowhegan School of Painting & Sculpture 1960-61. **Research/Artistic Interests:** Sculpture, fabrication of mixed mediums: metal, wood, glass, etc. **Career & Employment:** Chestnut Hill Creative Arts Center, Killingworth, CT, Instr. 1965-70; New Haven Creative Arts Workshop, Instr. 1969-70; Yale Univ., Instr. 1969-70; Trinity College, Hartford, Sculptor-in-Residence 1972-73; RISD, Instr. 1973-76; Univ. of Connecticut, Storrs, Instr. 1984. **Memberships & Offices:** Louis Comfort Tiffany Found., BoT 1976-83. **Fellowships, Honors & Awards:** Skowhegan School, Sculpture Prize 1960; Chaloner Prize Found. Award 1962-64; Louis Comfort Tiffany Found. Award 1965, 1973; San Francisco Civic Center Plaza, Intl. Competition, 3d Prize 1965; Blanche E. Coleman Award 1977. **Important Works:** Inst. for the Crippled & Disabled, NYC 1962; O. Henry Jr. HS, NYC 1965; Fairfield Univ. 1967; Evansville, IN, Day School 1969; John H. Doyle, NYC 1981; Howard Kaplan, Chester, CT 1982; Connecticut Percent for the Arts Competition, Bristol Technical School 1983-84; Andres & Mirja Kukk, Avon, CT 1994; D'Elia Asscs., NYC 1995. **Exhibitions/Performances:** Solo: Trinity College, Hartford 1972; Addison Gallery, Phillips Acad., Andover, MA 1976; Lamont Gallery, Phillips Acad., Exeter, NH 1977; Alexander F. Milliken Inc., NYC 1977, 1979; William W. Crapo Gallery, Swain School of Design, New Bedford, MA 1978; AAAL 1978-80; Showcase Gallery, Connecticut Commission for the Arts, Hartford 1984; Public Art Trust, Washington, DC 1986; Group: Wall Focus Gallery, Chester, CT 1986, 1991-95; 2-Person: Essex Art Gallery, Essex, CT 1994. **Home Address:** 80 W. Main St., Chester, CT 06412.

MATTESON, IRA ■ FAAR Sculpture 55. b. June 26, 1917, Hamden, CT. m. Helen D. Matteson. c. Abigail. **Study:** ASL with Mahonri Young & Arthur Lee 1937-42, with William Zorach & Arthur Lee 1946-53; NAD with John Flanagan 1946-47. **Research/Artistic Interests:** Clay, plaster, conté crayon, bronze, steel, wood, Japanese paper, frottage. **Career & Employment:** Florentine craftsman 1955-68; Kent State Univ. 1968-

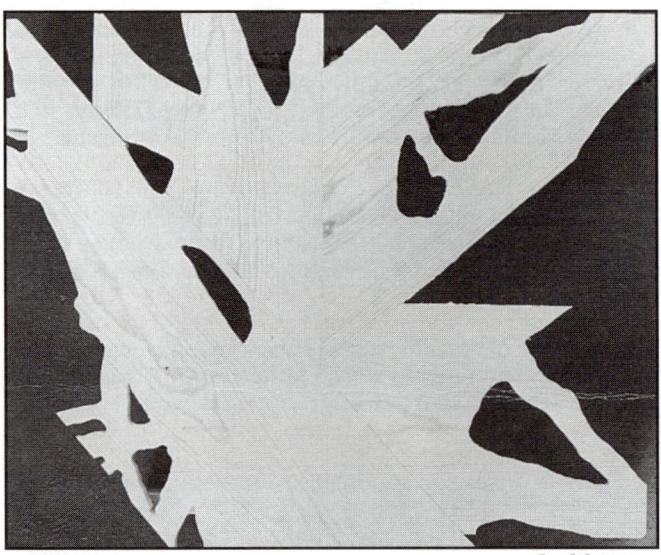

Ira Matteson

88, Emer. 1988-present. **Memberships & Offices:** Sculptors Guild 1966-70. **Fellowships, Honors & Awards:** Tiffany Found. Grant 1960, 1963; Ohio Arts Council Sculpture Grant 1978. **Important Works:** Walter P. Chrysler Museum, Norfolk, VA 1958; College of William & Mary 1958; Cleveland Museum of Art 1958; City of Akron, Akron Bar Assn. Comm. 1979; Case Western Reserve Univ., Campus Comm. 1981; Kent State Univ. 1988. **Home Address:** 621 S. DePeyster St., Kent, OH 44240.

MATTHEWS, EUGENE E. ■ FAAR Painting 60. b. Mar. 22, 1931, Davenport, IA. m. Wanda Miller. c. Anthony, Daniel. BFA 52, Univ. of Iowa; MFA 57, Univ. of Iowa. **Other Study:** Dradley Univ., Peoria, IL 1948-51. **Research/Artistic Interests:** Painting, acrylic & oil. **Career & Employment:** Univ. of Colorado, Asst. Prof. 1961-66, Assc. Prof. 1967-71, Prof. 1972-85, Visiting Artist Pgm. Dir. 1985-present. **Memberships & Offices:** Watercolor USA Honor Soc., Charter Mem. 1987-present. **Fellow-**

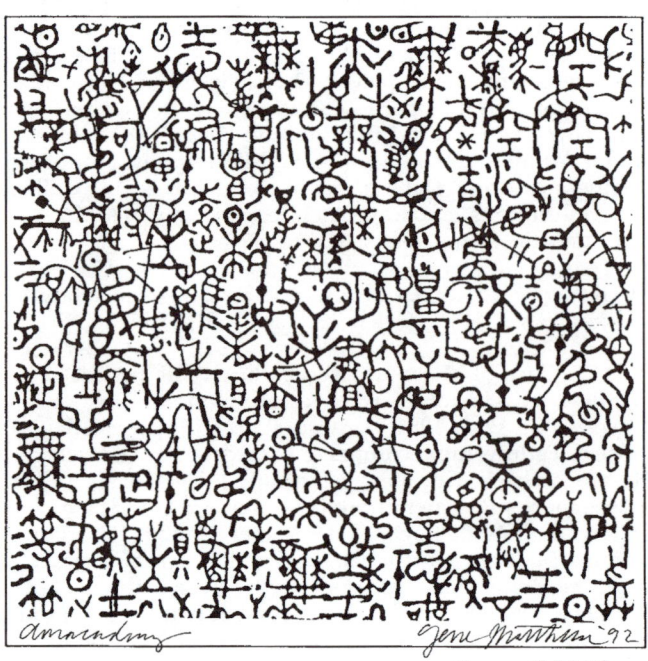

Eugene E. Matthews

ships, Honors & Awards: Univ. of Colorado, Faculty Fellowship 1966-67, Research Travel Grant 1989. Important Works: Poland Nat. Museum, Poznan; Nat. Collection of Fine Arts, Washington, DC; Denver Art Museum; Chrysler Art Museum, Youngstown, OH; Joslyn Art Museum, Omaha; Springfield Art Museum, MO; Fort Worth Nat. Bank; Sheldon Art Galleries, Univ. of Nebraska, Lincoln; Des Moines Art Center; Colorado Springs Fine Arts Center; Pepsi Cola Corp.; Lloyds of London. Exhibitions/ Performances: 1st Festival of Two Worlds, Spoleto 1958; Foreign Academies in Rome Joint Exb., Palazzo Nazionale di Esposizione 1959; Louvre, Paris 1960; Museum of Modern Art, Rijeka, Yugoslavia 1976; Intl. Drawing Biennale, Arts Council of Great Britain, Traveling Exb. 1977-79; Trade Mart Bldg. Galleries, New Orleans 1983; Taipei Fine Arts Museum, Taiwan 1985; São Paulo, Brazil 1987; Buda Castle Galleries, Budapest 1990; Kyoto Intl. Art Center 1992; Art in the Embassies Program 1967-92: Bogotá, Colombia; Amman, Jordan; Abidjan, Ivory Coast; Dacca, Bangladesh; Blantry, Malawi; Sophia, Bulgaria; Bangkok, Thailand; Katmandu, Nepal; Helsinki, Finland. Bio-Bibliography: *Dictionary of International Biography; Who's Who in America; Who's Who in American Art; Who's Who in the World.* Home Address: 3066 7 St., Boulder, CO 80304.

MATTISON, DONALD MAGNUS ■ FAAR Painting 31. b. Apr. 24, 1905, Beloit, WI. d. July 28, 1975. m. Catherine Lucille Morrison, Mary Gebhardt Wheeler. c. Georgia Coxe; Marianne Ullyott. BFA 28, Yale Univ. Research/Artistic Interests: Portraiture. Career & Employment: Columbia Univ., Instr. 1931-32; NY School of Design, Instr. 1931-32; NYU, Instr. 1931-33; John Herron School of Art, Dir. 1933-67, Dean 1967-75, Dean Emer. 1975. Memberships & Offices: Nat. Assn. of Schools of Design, Dir.; Midwest College Art Conference, Dir.; CAA; Mural Painters of America; North Carolina Professional Artists. Fellowships, Honors & Awards: Indianapolis Art Assn., Prize 1935, Directors Prize 1945; Holcomb Prize 1946; Delgado Museum, New Orleans, Nat. Exb., Annual Award. Important Works: Portraits: Thurgood Marshall, Sherman Minton, Paul McNutt, Harold W. Handley, Booth Tarkington; other works: Yale School of Fine Arts; Albert H. French Co., NYC; City Service Bldg., NYC; US Post Office, Tripton, Union City, IN. Exhibitions/Performances: Indianapolis Art Museum 1935; Hostess House, Marion, IN 1953. Bio-Bibliography: *Who Was Who in America; Who Was Who in American Art.*

MAULE, TALLIE BURTON ■ FAAR Architecture 52. b. July 7, 1917, Sand Springs, OK. BArch 40, Oklahoma A&M College; MFA 48, Princeton Univ. Career & Employment: Phillips Petro. Co., Architectural Draftsman 1939; Philip Wilber, Architect, Architectural Draftsman 1940-41; US Navy, Asst. Architect 1942-43; US Navy, General Line Officer 1943-46; George W. Edwards, Architect, Architectural Designer 1946-47; Skidmore, Owings & Merrill, Architectural Designer & Chief Designer 1947-. Fellowships, Honors & Awards: Alpha Rho Chi Architectural Award 1940; American Gas Assn. House Competition, Prize 1938; BAID Awards.

MAX, JERRY ■ AAR – New York, Board Liaison-Public Information Officer.

MAY, ARTHUR ■ FAAR Architecture 75. b. Mar. 4, 1940, NYC. m. Penny F. May. c. Elizabeth, Juliana. BArch 63, Rensselear Polytechnic Inst.; MArch 64, Univ. of Pennsylvania. Research/ Artistic Interests: Painting. Career & Employment: I.M. Pei & Partners, Designer 1964-69; Univ. of Kansas, Asst. Prof. 1970-71; John Carl Warnecke, VP 1973-76; Kohn Pedersen Fox 1977-

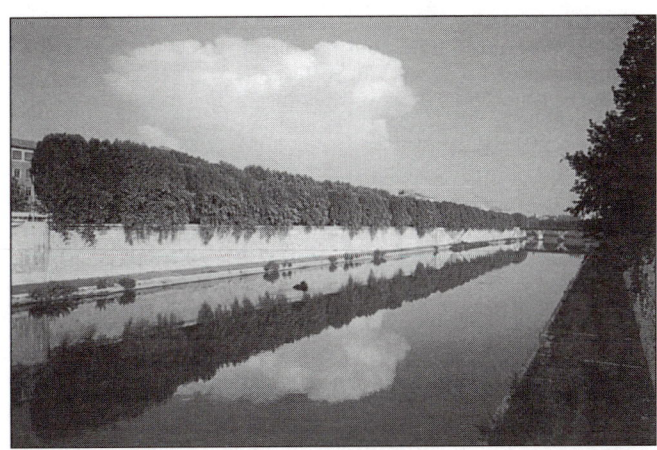

Arthur May

91; Rensselear Polytechnic Inst., Asst. Prof. 1990-91; May Whitelaw Pinska 1991-present. Memberships & Offices: AIA. Fellowships, Honors & Awards: Rensselear Polytechnic, Rickets Prize 1963; Univ. of Pennsylvania, Huckel Prize 1964; *Progressive Architecture* Design Award 1967; Arnold W. Brunner Memorial Prize 1985; AIA: Fellow, Architectural Merit Award, Silver Medal Design Award, Distinguished Design Award, Award for Design Excellence, Design Award of Merit. Important Works: Hercules Inc. HQ, Wilmington 1983; 1100 Ave. of the Americas Renovation, NYC 1983; Four Seasons, Logan Sq. Hotel & Office Tower, Philadelphia 1983; 188 E. 70th St., NYC 1986; ABC Phase II, NYC 1986; Hyatt Regency Hotel, Greenwich, CT 1986; Third Nat. Bank of Nashville 1986; 1000 Wilshire Blvd., Los Angeles 1987; AARP HQ, Washington, DC 1991; 8 Penn Center, Philadelphia 1991; Franklin Court, Washington, DC; New Federal Court House at Foley Sq., NYC 1995. Home Address: 1150 Park Ave., NYC 10128. Business Address: May Whitelaw Pinska, 22 W. 19th St., NYC 10011.

MAYERNIK, DAVID T. ■ FAAR Architecture 89. b. Apr. 8, 1960, Allentown, PA. m. Brette A. Jackson. BArch 83, Univ. of

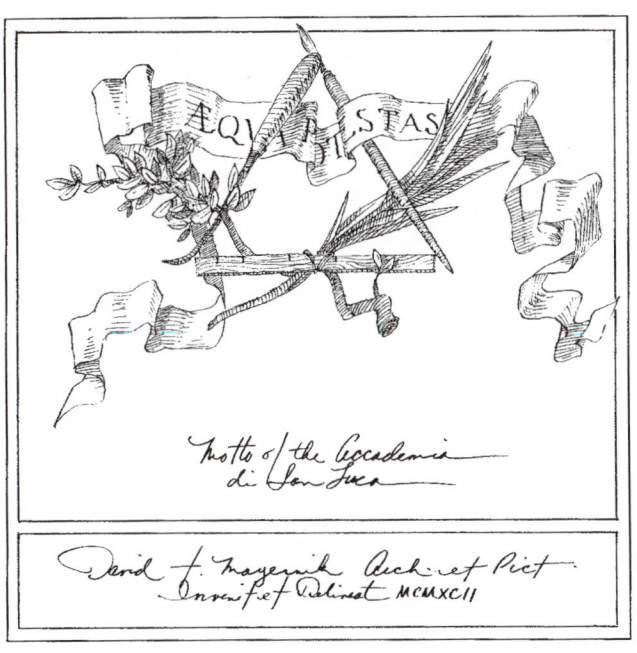

David T. Mayernik

Notre Dame. **Other Study:** Fresco technique with Leonetto Tintori, Prato 1989. **Research/Artistic Interests:** Artistic media: buon fresco, oil on canvas, watercolor wash (architectural), clay & wax models for sculptures in plaster, metals & wood; research: urban iconography & architecture as allegory. **Career & Employment:** Hammond Beeby & Babka 1984-85; John Blatteau Asscs. 1985-86; Private practice 1986-present. **Fellowships, Honors & Awards:** ASLA, Minnesota Chap. Design Award 1987; *Classical America*, Arthur Ross Award 1987; Graham Found., Fellowship 1988-89, 1992-93; Gabriel Prize 1993. **Publications:** "The City as Memory Theater and Architecture as Allegory," *Via* 12 (1995): 18-37. **Important Works:** with Thomas N. Rajkovich: Gardens & Pavilions Designs, Minnesota State Capitol Bldg.; Bridges & Railings, St. Paul. **Exhibitions/ Performances:** Stubbs Books & Prints, NYC 1990, 1991; New York School of Interior Design 1992, 1995; Chicago Cultural Center 1995. **Bio-Bibliography:** *Building Classical* (London: Academy Editions, 1993); *Composite Drawing* (New York: McGraw-Hill, 1995). **Business Address:** 25 Monroe Pl., No. 4A, Brooklyn, NY 11201.

MAZZOLANI, MATILDE ■ Italian Fulbright Fellow 1966-67.

MCBRIDE, RITA K. ■ FAAR Sculpture 92. b. Mar. 28, 1960, Des Moines, IA. BA 82, Bard College; MFA 87, California Inst. of the Arts. **Exhibitions/Performances:** Solo: Galeria Atlantica, Porto, Portugal 1989; Margo Leavin Gallery, Los Angeles 1990, 1992, 1995; Standard Graphik, Cologne 1990; Des Moines Art Center 1992; Michael Klein Gallery, NYC 1992, 1994; Studio Galleria, Budapest 1993; Ausstellungsburo Michael Schill, Stuttgart 1994; Selected Group: Artist Space, NYC 1991; Indianapolis Museum of Art 1991; New Langton Gallery, San Francisco 1992; Witte de With, Rotterdam 1994, 1995; Neuberger Museum, Purchase, NY 1995. **Bio-Bibliography:** Juliao Sarmento, *Rita McBride*, exb. cat. (Porto, Portugal: Galeria Atlantica, 1989); Antonio Cerveria Pinto, "Paisagens Urbanas," *O Independente* (Jan. 5, 1990); Amelia Jones, "Rita McBride," *Artscribe* (Mar.-Apr. 1991); Eleanor Heartney, *Rita McBride*, exb. cat. (Des Moines: Des Moines Art Center, 1992); Eliot Nusbaum, "Parts Exhibition a Playful Contradiction," *Des Moines Sunday Register* (July 26, 1992): 7F; Connie Butler, "Rita McBride," *Art and Text* (Jan. 1993); Terry Myers, "Rita McBride," *Tema Celeste* (Winter 1993); Diana Kingsley, "Rita McBride," *Art Today* (Budapest, Sept. 1993); Ingrid Schaffner, "Rita McBride," *Art Forum* (Jan. 1995); Faye Hirsch, "Rita McBride," *Art in America* (Feb. 1995); William Zimmer, "Neuberger's Anniversary Exhibit," *NY Times Sunday* (Feb. 5, 1995); Jody Zellen, "A Stroll through Santa Monica," *Art Press* (Paris, Apr. 1995); *Who's Who in American Art*. **Home Address:** 9 W. 64 St., Apt. 2B, NYC 10023.

MCCALL, DEBRA A. ■ FAAR Design Arts 89. b. Nov. 1, 1950, Butler, PA. c. Adrian. BA 72, Jackson College, Tufts Univ.; MA 76, NYU. **Other Study:** Laban movement analysis, Laban Inst. NYC; ballet with Maggie Black, Zena Rommet, Finis Jhung, Tokunaga; modern dance with Martha Graham & company members, José Limón, Hanya Holm-Nikolais-Lewis, Merce Cunningham, Viola Farber; improvisation & composition with Steve Paxton, Kei Tekei, Anna Halprin. **Research/ Artistic Interests:** Dance as related to the visual arts & architecture, dance ethnology. **Career & Employment:** NYU, Adj. Prof. 1976-83; Laban Inst. of Movement Studies, Faculty 1979-82, 1990-93; Pratt Inst., Asst. Prof. 1979-87; Adelphi Univ., Visiting Prof. 1982-86; Choreographic Research, Dir. 1982-93; Art Italiana, Coordinator for Dance-Movement 1984-93. **Fellow-

ships, Honors & Awards:** New England Film Festival, 1st Prize 1972; NEA Fellowships 1981, 1984, 1985; NEH Grant 1983; NYSCA Grant 1984. **Publications:** "Reconstructing Oskar Schlemmer's Bauhaus Dances: A Personal Narrative," in *Oskar Schlemmer,* ed. Arnold L. Lehman & Brenda Richardson, exb. cat. (Baltimore: Baltimore Museum of Art, 1986), 149-59; *Oskar Schlemmer's Bauhaus Dances of the 1920s: A Reconstruction,* a film (1986); "Dance and the Bauhaus," in *International Encyclopedia of Dance,* ed. Selma Jeanne Cohen (New York: Charles Scribner's Sons, forthcoming); "A Choreography of Soul," *ADTA Journal* (forthcoming). **Important Works:** Choreography: *Shadows*, film by Martin Beck 1972; *Les Troyennes*, film sequence for Boston Opera production 1972; *Harbor Roll, Warehouse Walk & Common Ground*, site specific performance pieces, Boston 1972; *Summer Blues*, Boston City Dance Theater 1973; *Geometricité*, Choreographers' Lab Workshop 1978; *Oskar Schlemmer's Bauhaus Dances of the 1920s: A Reconstruction*, Goethe House, Choreographic Research & The Kitchen 1982, 1984, 16mm film 1986; *Classical Rap*, Independent Choreographers 1983; *Cairo*, Teatro Viola, Rome 1988; *Iseum*, Choreographic Research, Mediterranean Nights 1992. **Exhibitions/Performances:** The Kitchen NYC 1982; Cornell Univ. 1983; Guggenheim Museum, NYC 1984; Traveling exb.: Meervart Theater, Amsterdam 1984; Schounburg, Rotterdam 1984; Toneelschur, Haarlem 1984; HOT, The Hague 1984; Stadsschouwburg, Utrecht, Groningen, Tilburg, Eindhoven 1984; 1st Intl. Biennale de la Danse, Theatre Celestin, Lyon 1984; Alabama Halle, Munich 1984; Walker Center for the Arts, Minneapolis-St. Paul 1984; Williams College 1985; Baltimore Museum of Art 1986; Gusman Cultural Center, Miami 1986; IBM Gallery of Science & Art, NYC 1986; AIC & Columbia Univ. Dance Center 1986; Goethe House, NYC 1987; Laforet Museum, Tokyo, 1987; The Bauhaus, Dessau, Germany 1995. **Bio-Bibliography:** Anna Kiselgoff, "They Created Dance Works at the Bauhaus, Too," *NY Times* (Oct. 31, 1982); Anna Kiselgoff, "The Year's Best: 1982 in Review," *NY Times* (Dec. 26, 1982); Elizabeth Schwartz, "Reconstruction des Danses du Bauhaus," *Pour La Danse* (Jan. 1983); Donald Kuspit, "Oskar Schlemmer's Bauhaus Dances," *Artforum* (Feb. 1983); Craig Bromberg, "Bauhaus Dances," *Art in America* (Feb. 1983); David Vaughan, "Reviews," *Dancemagazine* (Apr. 1984); D.S. Moynihan with Leigh George Odom, "Oskar Schlemmer's Bauhaus Dances: Debra McCall's Reconstructions," *Drama Review* 28.3 (Fall 1984); Rob Baker, "Artists Design for the Theater," *Theater Crafts* (Apr. 1984); Celia Ipiotis, "Voice of Dance," *Eye on Dance* (162); Doris Albrecht, "Wenn ein Wohnzimmer zur Buhne wird," *Ambiente* (July 1984); Mindy Aloff, "Dance," *Nation* (Mar. 17, 1984). **Home Address:** 103 Reade St., NYC 10013.

MCCANN, ANNA MARGUERITE ■ FAAR Classics/Archaeology 66; Classical Soc., Pres. 1975-76; SOF, BoD 1979-81; Roman Port Excavations, Cosa, Dir. 1965-87. b. May 11, 1933, NYC. m. Robert D. Taggart. BA 54, Wellesley College; MA 57, IFA; PhD 65, Indiana Univ. **Other Study:** ASCSA 1954-55; Archaeological field work: Kenchreai, Greece; Cosa, Rome, Taranto, Populonia & Pyrgi, Italy; Bodrum, Turkey. **Research/ Artistic Interests:** Greek & Roman art & archaeology, underwater archaeology, exploration of ancient harbors, deep-sea archaeology & robotic technology, Roman sculpture. **Career & Employment:** Swarthmore College, Instr. 1957-59; Barnard College, Instr. 1959-61; Tuscan Port Survey, Dir. 1965-74; Univ. of Missouri, Asst. Prof. 1966-71; NYU, Adj. Prof. 1983-86; Jason Project, Woods Hole Oceanographic Inst. 1989-present; Visiting positions: UC, Berkeley 1971-74; Trinity College, Hartford 1989; Univ. of Washington, Seattle 1992; Williams College 1994. **Memberships & Offices:** ArIA, BoT 1977-86, 1989-

present, Co-Chair, Archives Com. 1991-present; Nat. Com. for Underwater Archaeology, Founder & Chair 1985-88, Nominating Com. 1977, 1983, 1986, 1991, Com. for Development 1980-present; Com. for Archaeological Outreach 1982-present, New York Chap., BoD & VP 1976-84; *Archaeology* Magazine, Ed. Bd. 1983-89; Shelburne Museum, BoT 1987-present, Educational Task Force Com., Chair 1989-91; Wellesley College, Com. for Friends of Art 1976-92; Marine Technology & Historic Shipwrecks Com., WHOI & NOAA 1990-present. **Fellowships, Honors & Awards:** Fulbright Scholarship 1954-55; Univ. of Missouri Grant 1968, 1969, 1970; ACLS Grant 1969, 1973; NEH Grant 1971, 1972, 1973, 1974-76, 1981-82; American Assn. for the Advancement of Science Award 1989; Woods Hole Oceanographic Inst. Research Grant 1989-90; Computer World-Smithsonian Award 1989, 1990; ArIA, Norton Lect. 1994-95. **Publications:** *The Portraits of Septimius Severus (A.D. 193-211)*, Memoirs of the AAR 30 (1968); "A Re-Dating of the Reliefs from the Palazzo della Cancelleria," *Mitteilungen des Deutschen archaeologischen Instituts, Römische Abteilung* 79 (1971): 249-76; with John Oleson, "Underwater Excavations at the Etruscan Ports of Populonia & Pyrgi," *Journal of Field Archaeology* 1 (1974): 398-402; "Aerial Views for Probes under the Sea," in *The Etruscans*, ed. D.J. Hamblin (New York: Time-Life, 1975), 147-53; "Underwater Excavations at the Etruscan Port of Populonia," *Journal of Field Archaeology* 4 (1977): 275-96; *Roman Sarcophagi in the Metropolitan Museum of Art* (New York: MMA, 1978); "Beyond the Classical in Third-Century Portraiture," *Aufsteig und Niedergang der römischen Welt* 12.2 (1981): 623-45; with I.E.M. Edlund & C.R. Sherman, "Gisela Maria Augusta Richter (1882-1972): Scholar of Classical Art & Museum Archaeologist," in *Women as Interpreters of the Visual Arts, 1820-1979*, ed. C.R. Sherman (Westport, CT: Greenwood, 1981), 275-300; "The Portus Cosanus: A Center of Trade in the Late Republic," *Rei Cretariae Romanae Fautorum Acta* 25-26 (1987): 21-70; with J. Bourgeois, E.K. Gazda, J.P. Oleson & E.L. Will, *The Roman Port and Fishery of Cosa: A Center of Ancient Trade* (Princeton: Princeton Univ. Press, 1987); "The Roman Port of Cosa," *Scientific American* 256.3 (Mar. 1988): 102-9; "Diving into Our Past," World Ocean Floors Atlantic Ocean, *National Geographic* (Jan. 1990); with R.D. Ballard & R. Archbold, *The Lost Wreck of the ISIS* (Toronto: Scholastic-Madison Press, 1990); with J. Freed, *Deep Water Archaeology: A Late Roman Ship from Carthage and an Ancient Trade Route near Skerki Bank off Northwest Sicily*, Journal of Roman Archaeology, supp. ser. 13 (1994); "ROV's for Archaeology," *Intervention/ROV '91* (Marine Technology Soc., 1991) :13; "Underwater Archaeology," in *An Encyclopedia of the History of Classical Archaeology*, ed. N. de Grummond (Westport, CT: Greenwood Press, 1995). **Home Address:** 200 E. 66 St., NYC 10021.

MCCARTHY, MARY ■ RAAR Literature 79. b. June 21, 1912, Seattle, WA. d. Oct. 25, 1989. m. Harold Johnsrud, Edmund Wilson, Bowden Broadwater, James West. c. Reuel Wilson. BA 33, Vassar College. **Research/Artistic Interests:** Woman of letters, social & cultural criticism. **Career & Employment:** *Partisan Review*, Ed. 1937-38; Drama Critic 1937-62; Reviewer: *The Nation, The New Republic* 1937-48; Bard College, Instr. 1945-46; Sarah Lawrence College, Instr. 1948. **Memberships & Offices:** NIAL, Phi Beta Kappa. **Fellowships, Honors & Awards:** Horizon Prize 1949; Guggenheim Fellow 1949-50, 1959-60; NIAL Grant 1957; Hon. D. Letters: Univ. of Hull 1974, Bard College 1976, Univ. of Aberdeen 1979; Hon. D. Literature: Bowdoin College 1981, Univ. of Maine 1982; Edward MacDowell Medal 1984; Harold K. Guinzburg Found., Nat. Medal for Literature 1987. **Publications:** *The Company She Keeps* (New York: Simon

& Schuster, 1942); *The Oasis* (New York: Random House, 1949); *Cast a Cold Eye* (New York: Harcourt, Brace & World, 1952); *The Groves of Academe* (New York: Harcourt, Brace & World, 1952); *A Charmed Life* (New York: Harcourt, Brace & World, 1955); *Sights & Spectacles, 1937-1956* (New York: Farrar, Straus, 1956); *Memories of a Catholic Girlhood* (New York: Harcourt, Brace & World, 1957); *The Stones of Florence* (New York: Harcourt, Brace & World, 1959); *Venice Observed* (London: Heineman, 1961); *On The Contrary: Articles of Belief 1946-61* (New York: Farrar, Straus, 1961); *Mary McCarthy's Theatre Chronicles, 1937-1962* (New York: Harcourt, Brace & World, 1963); *The Group* (New York: Harcourt, Brace & World, 1963); *The Humanist in the Bathtub* (New York: Signet, 1964); *Vietnam* (New York: Harcourt, Brace & World, 1967); *Hanoi* (New York: Harcourt, Brace & World, 1968); *Birds of America* (New York: Harcourt, Brace, Jovanovich 1971); *Cannibals and Missionaries* (New York: Harcourt, Brace, Jovanovich 1979); *Occasional Papers* (San Diego: Harcourt, Brace, Jovanovich 1985); *How I Grew* (San Diego: Harcourt, Brace, Jovanovich 1987); *Intellectual Memoirs* (New York: Harcourt, Brace, Jovanovich 1992). **Bio-Bibliography:** Willene Schaefer Hardy, *Mary McCarthy* (New York: Ungar, 1981); Carol W. Gelderman, *Mary McCarthy: A Life* (New York: St. Martin's Press, 1988); Joy Bennett, *Mary McCarthy: An Annotated Bibliography* (New York: Garland, 1992); Carol Brightman, *Writing Dangerously: Mary McCarthy and Her World* (New York: C. Potter, 1992); *Contemporary Authors*.

MCCARTNEY, EUGENE STOCK ■ FAAR Classics/Archaeology 16. b. March 1, 1883, Wilmington, DE. d. Jan. 8, 1959. BA 06, Univ. of Pennsylvania; PhD 11, Univ. of Pennsylvania. **Research/Artistic Interests:** Roman military organization, warfare in antiquity, folklore. **Career & Employment:** Univ. of Pennsylvania, Instr. 1906-14; Univ. of Texas, Instr. 1916-19; Northwestern Univ., Instr. 1920-22; Univ. of Michigan Press, Ed. 1922-53; Papers of the Michigan Acad. of Science, Arts & Letters, Ed. 1923-50. **Memberships & Offices:** Michigan Acad. of Science, Arts & Letters, Pres. 1931. **Fellowships, Honors & Awards:** Univ. of Pennsylvania, Harrison Fellowship 1909. **Publications:** *Figurative Uses of Animal Names in Latin and Their Application to Military Devices* (Lancaster, PA: New Era Printing, 1912); "The Genius of Rome's Military Equipment," *Classical Weekly* 6 (1912-13): 74-79; "The Military Indebtedness of Early Rome to Etruria," *Memoirs of the AAR* 1 (1918): 121-68; *Warfare by Land and Sea*, Our Debt to Greece and Rome 23 (Boston: Marshall Jones, 1923); "Greek and Rome Lore of Animal-Nursed Infants," *Papers of the Michigan Academy of Science, Arts and Letters* 4 (1924): 15-42; "Longevity and Rejuvenation in Greek and Roman Folklore," *Papers of the Michigan Academy of Science, Arts and Letters* 5 (1925): 37-72; ed., *Studies in Shakespeare, Milton and Donne* (Ann Arbor: Univ. of Michigan Press, 1925); "Folklore Heirlooms," *Papers of the Michigan Academy of Science, Arts and Letters* 16 (1932): 105-210; *Recurrent Maladies in Scholarly Writing* (Ann Arbor: Univ. of Michigan Press, 1953). **Bio-Bibliography:** Briggs, 380-81.

MCCLELLAN, GEORGE B. ■ AAR Charter Mem., AAR Trustee 1911-40.

MCCLOSKEY, ROBERT ■ FAAR Painting 49. b. Sept. 15, 1914, Hamilton, OH. **Study:** In the studios of Francis Bradford, FAAR, & Jerry Farnsworth. **Bio-Bibliography:** *Who's Who in America*. **Home Address:** PO Box 57, Little Deer Isle, ME 04650.

MCCLOY, JOHN J. ■ AAR Visitor 1959 — 1964, US High Comm., Germany; Harvard Univ., Pres.

MCCORMACK, ELIZABETH ■ AAR Trustee 1990-present. **Studies:** Manhattanville College, Purchase; Fordham Univ. **Career & Employment:** Manhattanville College, Purchase, Pres.; Rockefeller Family & Asscs.; Rockefeller Family Philanthropic Office; Rockefeller Brothers Fund; John D. & Catherine T. MacArthur Found., Chair. **Memberships & Offices:** United HealthCare Corp., Dir; Memorial Sloan-Kettering Cancer Center, Manager; Alliance Capital, BoD; Asian Cultural Council, BoT; Hamilton College, BoT. **Fellowships, Honors & Awards:** Hon. Degrees: CUNY, Brandeis Univ., Princeton Univ., Marlboro College, American Univ. of Paris.

MCCOY, ANN ■ FAAR Painting 90. b. July 8, 1946, Boulder, CO. m. Dominique Nahas. BFA 69, Univ. of Colorado; MA 72, UCLA. **Career & Employment:** School of Visual Arts, Faculty 1977-; Barnard College, Faculty 1980-; Columbia Univ., Faculty 1985-. **Fellowships, Honors & Awards:** Los Angeles County Museum of Art, Contemporary Art Council New Talent Award 1972; AIC, 71st American Exb., Norman Wait Harris Award 1974; AAUW 1976; Berliner Kunstlerprogramm, DAAD 1977; NEA 1978, 1989; AVA (Awards in the Visual Arts) 1989. **Publications:** "Alice Baber: Light as Subject," *Art International* 24.1-2 (Sept.-Oct. 1980); "Maura Sheehan's Urban Artifacts," *Arts* (Nov. 1985). **Exhibitions/Performances:** Solo: Margo Leavin Gallery, Los Angeles 1976; Portland Center for Visual Arts, OR 1979; Brooke Alexander, Inc., NYC 1979, 1981, 1985; MMA, Mezzanine Gallery 1982; Galerie Kornfeld, Bern 1983; Ruth Bachofner Gallery, Los Angeles 1984; Eugene Binder Gallery, Dallas 1986; ACA Contemporary, NYC 1988; Arnold Herstand & Co., NYC 1990. Group: San Francisco Museum of Modern Art 1986; Sherry French Gallery, NYC 1988; Santa Barbara Museum of Art 1988. **Bio-Bibliography:** Melinda Terbell, "The Strangeness of Reality," *ArtNews* (Nov. 1973); "Deep Sea Diver: Ann McCoy," *Bulletin of the Analytic Psychology Club of NY* (Mar. 1980); Helen Harrison, "Large-Scale Montages that Reflect the World of Dreams," *NY Times* (Jan. 2, 1983); Mark Schipper, "Ann McCoy," *Art Scene* (Los Angeles, Dec. 1984); Peter Selz, "Alternative Aesthetics: Quests for the Spiritual Quintessence," *Arts* (Oct. 1987); Cordelia Oliver, "Classicism in Rags," *The Guardian* (Jan. 1988); John Russell Taylor, "Art Which Feeds on Itself," *The Arts* (Scotland, 1988).

MCCRACKEN, GEORGE ENGLERT ■ FAAR Classics/Archaeology 31. b. Feb. 6, 1904, Dunmore, PA. dec. BA 26, Princeton Univ.; MA 28, Lafayette College. **Career & Employment:** Drake Univ., Faculty; Otterbein College, Faculty. **Bio-Bibliography:** *Contemporary Authors*; *Directory of American Scholars*.

MCCRINDLE, JOSEPH F. ■ AAR Trustee 1980-94, Trustee Emer.; Art Collector.

MCDONALD, JOHN J., JR ■ FAAR Architecture 83. b. Mar. 20, 1956, Highland Park, MI. m. Debi Lacey McDonald. BArch 80, Cornell Univ.; MArch 88, Harvard GSD. **Career & Employment:** Skidmore, Owings & Merrill 1980-82; WZMH Group 1983-86; Hisaka & Asscs. 1988-92; Clark, Bonins, & Asscs. 1992; Cannon 1994-present. **Memberships & Offices:** Boston Soc. of Architects 1986-present; AIA 1986-present. **Fellowships, Honors & Awards:** with Debi Lacey McDonald & Jeffrey Clark, Northeastern Univ., Urban Design Charrette 1992; Boston Soc. of Architects Award 1992; AIA, Washington, DC Chap. Award 1992. **Important Works:** with Skidmore, Owings & Merrill: Royal Dutch Shell HQ, The Hague 1980-81; San Francisco Federal Savings & Loan, Banking Hall & Office Bldg. 1981-82; with WZMH Group: Dallas Design District Master Plan & Renova-

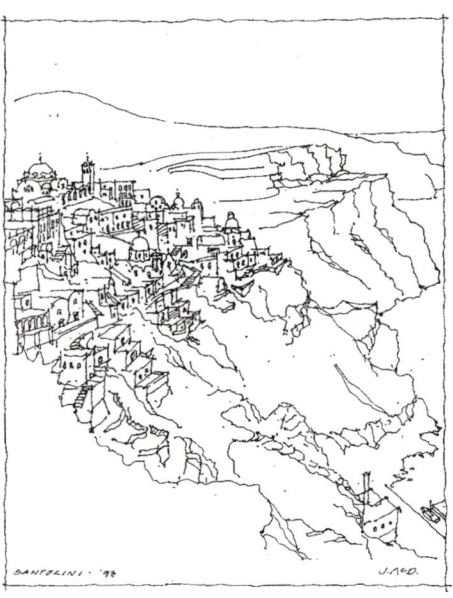

John J. McDonald, Jr.

tion 1985-86; with Cannon: Children's Medical Center, Tel Aviv 1987; with Hisaka & Asscs.: 1150 18th St., Washington, DC 1988-91; Old Orchard Golf Club Clubhouse, Ibaraki, Japan 1988-91; Loeb Library Renovation, Harvard GSD 1991-92. **Exhibitions/Performances:** Cornell Univ. 1980; Harvard GSD 1986; Northeastern Univ., Urban Design Charrette 1992; Boston Soc. of Architects 1992. **Home Address:** 1640A Massachusetts Ave., Cambridge, MA 02138. **Business Address:** Cannon, 148 State St., Boston, MA 02109.

MCDONNELL, JOE H. ■ McKim Fellow 1918-19.

MCGINN, THOMAS A.J. ■ FAAR Classics/Archaeology 85; Summer School, Asst. Dir. 1986. b. Nov. 11, 1956, Staten Island, NY. m. Eileen A. Nee. c. Thomas A. BA 78, Harvard College; MA 80, Cambridge Univ.; PhD 86, Univ. of Michigan. **Research/Artistic Interests:** Roman law & social history. **Career & Employment:** RISD, Instr. 1985; Vanderbilt Univ., Asst. Prof. 1986-93, Assc. Prof. 1994-present; ICCS, Mellon Prof.-in-Charge 1996-97. **Memberships & Offices:** APA, Com. of Placement 1986-87; ICCS, Managing Com. 1991-95; NEH, Summer Seminars Evaluation Panel, Division of Research Programs, Reviewer. **Fellowships, Honors & Awards:** Harvard Univ., Woodbury Scholarship 1975-76, Clark Prize 1978, Landon Scholarship 1978; Cambridge Univ., Koumoulides Prize 1979; Michigan Univ., Rackham Fellowship 1980-81, 1983-84; Fulbright Fellowship 1984-85; NEH Summer Fellowship 1987, 1989, 1991; Vanderbilt Univ., Research Council Award 1988, 1989-90, 1993; Kenan Venture Fund Com. Award 1993. **Publications:** co-ed. & contr., "*Puteolana Analecta:* Seven Inscriptions in the Kelsey Museum," *Puteoli* 9-10 (1985-86): 41-78; "The Taxation of Roman Prostitutes," *Helios* 16 (1989): 79-110; "*Ne Serva Prostituatur:* Restrictive Covenants in the Sale of Slaves," *Zeitschrift der Savigny-Stiftung für Rechtsgeschichte* 107 (1990): 315-53; "Concubinage & the *Lex Iulia* on Adultery," *TAPA* 121 (1991): 335-74; "The *SC* from Larinum & the Repression of Adultery at Rome," *Zeitschrift für Papyrologie & Epigraphik* 93 (1992): 273-95; "Prostitution," in *Encyclopedia of Social History*, ed. P.N. Stearns (New York & London: Garland, 1994), 588-91; *Prostitution and Roman Society* (Ann Arbor: Univ. of Michigan

Press, forthcoming); *Prostitution and the Law: The Formation of Social Policy in Ancient Rome* (New York: Oxford Univ. Press, forthcoming). **Home Address:** 1212 Bedfordshire Ct., Nashville, TN 37221.

MCGINNESS, FREDERICK J. ■ FAAR Post-Classical/ Humanistic Studies 78. b. Sept. 10, 1944, Cleveland, OH. m. Carole E. Straw. BA 66, Univ. of Detroit; MA 76, UC, Berkeley; PhD 82, UC, Berkeley. **Other Study:** Loyola Univ., Cert. in Philosophy 1966-68; Hochschule Sankt Georgen, Frankfurt-am-Main, Baccalaurate in Theology 1970-73; Universidad de Comillas, Madrid, theological studies 1973-74. **Career & Employment:** Univ. of Detroit HS, Teacher 1968-70; Graduate Theological Union, Berkeley, Adj. Prof. 1977; Mt. Holyoke College, Lect. 1981-82, Visiting Asst. Prof. 1985; Smith College, Asst. Prof. 1982-85, Visiting Lect. 1988, Complex Organizations Pgm., Dir. & Lect. 1985-present; Univ. of Massachusetts, Amherst, Visiting Asst. Prof. 1992. **Memberships & Offices:** Academia Latinitati Fovendae, AHA, Catholic Historical Assn., Intl. Medieval Sermons Studies Soc., Intl. Soc. for the History of Rhetoric, RSA, Sixteenth-Century Historical Studies, Soc. for Italian Historical Studies. **Publications:** "Preaching Ideals and Practice in Counter-Reformation Rome, *Sixteenth Century Journal* 11 (1980): 109-27; "The Rhetoric of Praise and the New Rome of the Counter Reformation," in *Rome: The City and the Myth*, ed. Paul A. Ramsey (Binghamton: SUNY, 1982), 355-70; "Roma Sancta and the Saint: Eucharist, Chastity, and the Logic of Catholic Reform," *Historical Reflections-Réflexions historiques* 15.1 (1988): 99-116; "Renaissance in Europe," "Reformation and Counter-Reformation," "The Age of Discovery: 1450-1700," "Europe: 1648-1789," in *History of the World*, gen. ed. John Whitney Hall, ed. John Grayson Kirk (New York: Gallery Books, 1988), 2:6-67; "The Counter Reformation in Italy," in *Reformation Europe: A Guide to Research II*, ed. William S. Maltby (Saint Louis: Center for Reformation Research, 1991), 307-39; *Right Thinking: Sacred Oratory and the Culture of Counter-Reformation Rome* (Princeton: Princeton Univ. Press, 1995); ed., Erasmus, *Exomologesis sive modus confitendi*, and *Ecclesiastes sive de ratione concionandi*, in the Collected Works of Erasmus 67-68 (Toronto, Buffalo, London: Univ. of Toronto Press, forthcoming); "Gregory Martin," in *The Oxford Encyclopedia of the Reformation* (New York: Oxford Univ. Press, forthcoming). **Home Address:** 29 Silver St., S. Hadley, MA 01075-1615. **Business Address:** Complex Organizations Program, Mt. Holyoke College, S. Hadley, MA 01075.

MCGINNISS, JOSEPH ■ Rotch Scholar 1910.

MCGOODWIN, ROBERT R. ■ Cresson Fellow 1913.

MCGREGOR, JAMES H.S. ■ FAAR Post-Classical/ Humanistic Studies 82. b. Oct. 1, 1946, Frostburg, MD. m. Sarah Spence, FAAR 82. c. Raphael, Edward. BA 68, Princeton Univ.; PhD 75, Princeton Univ. **Career & Employment:** Onondaga Community College, Lect. 1973-75; Syracuse Univ., Instr. 1977-79; Colgate Univ., Visiting Asst. Prof. 1979-80; Univ. of Georgia, Asst. Prof. 1981-87, Assc. Prof. 1988-present; UC, Berkeley, Visiting Asst. Prof. 1984-85. **Memberships & Offices:** American Assn. for Italian Studies; American Assn. of Teachers of Italian; American Boccaccio Assn.; Associazione Intl. per gli Studi di Lingua e Letteratura Italiana; MLA; Southeastern Renaissance Soc. **Fellowships, Honors & Awards:** NDEA Fellowship 1969-72; Princeton Univ. Fellowship 1976; Southeastern Inst. of Medieval & Renaissance Studies, Fellow 1976; Univ. of Georgia, Sarah Moss Traveling Fellowship 1981, Research Found.

Grant 1989, 1992. **Publications:** "The Iconography of Chaucer in Hoccleve's *De Regimine Principium* and in the Troilus Frontispiece," *Chaucer Review* 11 (1978): 338-50; "Ovid at School," *Classical Folia* 32 (1978): 29-52; "Tragedy in Buchanan's *Jephthes*," *Humanistica Lovaniensia* 31 (1982): 120-40; "The Theater of Theseus: Form and Function of an Ancient Monument in Boccaccio's *Teseida*," *Modern Language Notes* 99 (1984): 1-42; "Boccaccio's Knowledge of Lactantius Placidus and his Glosses to *Teseida*," *Studi sul Boccaccio* 14 (1983-84): 302-9; "The Medieval Art of Imitation and Chaucer's *Legenda Tesbe*," *Medievalia* 9 (1986 for 1983): 181-202; "Troilus' Hymn to Venus in Boccaccio's *Filostrato*," *Romance Philology* 41 (1987): 48-57; "Is Beatrice Boccaccio's Most Successful Fiction?" *Texas Studies in Language and Literature* 32 (1990): 137-51; *The Shades of Aeneas: The Imitation of Vergil and the History of Paganism in Boccaccio's* Filostrato, Filocolo *and* Teseida (Athens & London: Univ. of Georgia Press, 1991); *The Image of Antiquity in Boccaccio's* Filostrato, Filocolo *and* Teseida (New York & Bern: Peter Lang, 1991); ed., Luigi Guicciardini, *The Sack of Rome* (New York: Italica Press, 1993). **Bio-Bibliography:** *Contemporary Authors; Who's Who in the South & Southeast; Who's Who in the World*. **Home Address:** 778 Hill St., Athens, GA 30606. **Business Address:** Dept. of Comparative Literature, Univ. of Georgia, Athens, GA 30602.

MCGREW, C.B. ■ Plym Fellow 1921-22, 1922-23.

MCILHENNY, HENRY P. ■ RAAR History of Art 47, 48. b. Oct. 7, 1910, Philadelphia, PA. d. May 11, 1986. BA 33, Harvard Univ. **Career & Employment:** Philadelphia Museum of Art, Decorative Arts, Curator 1935-64, BoT 1964-76, VP 1968-76, Chair BoD 1976-85; USNR, Officer 1942-46. **Memberships & Offices:** Philadelphia Orchestra Assn., BoD 1940-82; Philadelphia Soc. Preservation Landmarks, Dir.; American Italy Soc. of Philadelphia, Dir.; Smithsonian Art Comm. 1957-77. **Bio-Bibliography:** *NY Times*, Obit. (May 13, 1986); *French Masterpieces of the Nineteenth Century from the Henry P. McIlhenny Collection* (Allentown, PA: The Museum, 1977); Jo Durden-Smith & Diane de Simone, "Meet the Marvelous Mr. McIlhenny," *Connoisseur* 214 (Aug. 1984): 84-90; *Who's Who in America*.

MCKIBBEN, WILLIAM T. ■ FAAR Classics/Archaeology 51; Classical Soc., Pres. 1959. b. Sept. 30, 1916, Seattle, WA. m. Elizabeth P. McKibben. c. Andrew. BA 37, Stanford Univ.; MA 38, Stanford Univ.; PhD 42, Univ. of Chicago. **Career & Employment:** Univ. of Utah, Asst. Prof. 1946-49; Grinnell College, Assc. Prof. 1952-58, Prof. 1958-82, Prof. Emer. 1982-present. **Memberships & Offices:** Classical League; CAMWS 1952-present; APA 1952-present; ArIA, c.1953-c.1982; Iowa Foreign Language Assn., Pres. 1995. **Fellowships, Honors & Awards:** Phi Beta Kappa, Stanford Univ. 1936; Univ. of Chicago, Classical Fellow 1938-41. **Home Address:** 916 7th Ave., Grinnell, IA 50112.

MCKIM, CHARLES FOLLEN ■ AAR Founder, Pres. 1894-1909, Architect. b. Aug. 24, 1847. d. 1909. In 1894, established the American School of Architecture in Rome, predecessor of the Academy, & continued to lead the institution's development until his death. **Career & Employment:** McKim, Mead & White, Founding Part. 1879-1909. **Important Works:** Pennsylvania Station, NYC 1909; White House Restoration (various rooms), Washington, DC 1900-1902; Boston Public Library; many buildings at Columbia Univ. & Amherst College.

MCKINNELL, NOEL MICHAEL ■ RAAR Architecture 89. b. Dec. 25, 1935, Salford, England. BA 58, Univ. of Manchester;

MA 60, Columbia Univ. **Career & Employment:** Kallmann McKinnell & Wood Architects, Inc., Founding Part. 1962-present; Harvard GSD, Asst Prof. 1963-66, Assc. Prof. 1966-71, Prof. 1971-83, Nelson Robinson Jr. Prof. 1983-88. **Memberships & Offices:** Presidential Comm. on Education in the Visual Arts 1964; Boston Soc. of Architects, Honors & Awards Com., Chair 1975, Design Commissioner 1977; AIA, Fellow, Honors & Awards Program, Chair 1986; AAAS, Fellow. **Fellowships, Honors & Awards:** Columbia Univ., William Hale Kendall Fellowship 1960; NIAL, Arnold W. Brunner Prize 1969; Harvard GSD, Hon. MA 1978. **Important Works:** Boston City Hall 1967; Phillips Exeter Acad. Athletic Facility, Exeter, NH 1970; Boston Five Cents Savings Bank 1972; AAAS, HQ, Cambridge, MA 1982; Washington Univ., Olin School of Business, St. Louis 1986; Becton Dickinson & Co., Corp. HQ, Franklin Lakes, NJ 1986, Divisional HQ & Laboratories, Franklin Lakes, NJ 1992; Back Bay Station, Boston 1987; Hynes Convention Center, Boston 1989; Peabody Museum, Asian Export Art Wing, Salem, MA 1988; Newton, MA, Free Library 1991; Arrow Intl. Corp. HQ, Reading, PA 1992. **Exhibitions/ Performances:** Harvard Univ. 1988, 1989, 1994; Yale Univ. 1993; Princeton Univ. 1994; Alfred Univ. 1995. **Bio-Bibliography:** Alex Krieger, *The Architecture of Kallmann McKinnell & Wood,* exb. cat. (Cambridge: Harvard GSD, 1988); *Who's Who in America.* **Home Address:** 939 Boylston St., Boston, MA 01225. **Business Address:** Kallmann McKinnell & Wood Architects, Inc., 939 Boylston St., Boston, MA 02115.

MCKNIGHT, ROBERT J. ■ FAAR Sculpture 35. b. Feb. 26, 1905, Bayside, NY. dec. m. Patricia McKnight. BFA, Yale Univ., College of Art; PhD 27, Yale Univ. **Career & Employment:** Memphis Acad. of Art., Dir. 1936-42; Brooks Memorial Art Gallery, Dir. 1964-71. **Fellowships, Honors & Awards:** Lake Forest Found. Scholarship. **Exhibitions/Performances:** Millesgarden, Stockholm 1986.

MCLANATHAN, RICHARD B.K. ■ FAAR History of Art 49. b. Mar. 12, 1916, Methuen, MA. m. Jane Fuller. BA 38, Harvard Univ.; PhD 51, Harvard Univ. **Research/Artistic Interests:** Medieval, Renaissance, & American arts. **Career & Employment:** Allen-Stevenson School, Instr. 1938-43; MFA, Asst. Curator 1946-54, Museum Sec. 1949-56, Curator 1954-57; Munson-Williams Proctor Inst., Utica, NY, Museum of Art, Dir. 1957-61; American Assn. of Museums, Washington, DC, Dir. 1976-78. **Memberships & Offices:** Boston Arts Festival, BoT Exec. Com. 1954-59; Albany Inst. of History & Art, Bd. of Adv. 1958-70; USIA, American Nat. Art Exb., Moscow, Curator 1959; Boys Club of Boston, Bd. of Adv. 1959-61; Boys Club of Utica, BoT 1959-61; Corcoran Biennial Jury 1960; NYSCA, Initial Mem. 1960-64; US State Dept., American Specialist, W. Germany, Poland, Denmark 1959, Jugoslavia 1961; Brandywine River Museum, BoT 1970-75; US Nat. Com. for UNESCO 1976-79; Maine Maritime Museum, BoT 1984-88. **Fellowships, Honors & Awards:** Harvard Univ., Soc. of Fellows; USIA, Distinguished Service Award 1959; MMA, Rockefeller Senior Fellow 1975-76. **Publications:** *Images of the Universe: Leonardo da Vinci, The Artist as Scientist* (New York: Doubleday, 1966); *The Pageant of Medieval Art* (New York: Westminster, 1966); *The American Tradition in the Arts* (New York: Harcourt, Brace, 1968; college text ed., 1970); *Guide to Civilisation: The Kenneth Clark Films on the Cultural Life of Western Man* (Washington: NGA & New York: Time-Life, 1970); *Art in America: A Brief History* (New York: Harcourt, Brace & London: Thames & Hudson, 1973); *The Art of Margaret Stix* (New York: Abrams, 1977); *The National Gallery of Art, East Building: A Profile* (Washington, DC: NGA, 1978); *World Art in American Museums: A Personal Guide* (New York:

Doubleday, 1983); *Gilbert Stuart* (New York: Harry N. Abrams & Washington, DC: Smithsonian Inst., 1986); *Leonardo da Vinci: First Impressions* (New York: Harry N. Abrams, 1990); *Michelangelo: First Impressions* (New York: Harry N. Abrams, 1993); *Ruben's First Impressions* (New York: Harry N. Abrams, 1995). **Bio-Bibliography:** *Who's Who in America, Who's Who in the Arts, Who's Who in the East, Who's Who in the World.* **Home Address:** The Stone School House, Phippsburg, ME 04562.

MCMANAMON, JOHN M., SJ ■ FAAR Post-Classical/Humanistic Studies 83. b. May 20, 1951, Cleveland, OH. BA 73, Univ. of Detroit; MA 75, Univ. of Detroit; PhD 84, UNC, Chapel Hill. **Other Study:** Theology at Pontifical Gregorian Univ., Rome 1977-80. **Research/Artistic Interests:** Italian humanism, Renaissance history. **Career & Employment:** St. Ignatius HS, Instr. 1975-77; Loyola Univ., Asst. Prof. 1984-90, Assc. Prof. 1990-present. **Memberships & Offices:** RSA, Council for History of Classical Scholarship 1991-93; American Catholic Historical Assn., Marraro Prize Com. 1990-92. **Fellowships, Honors & Awards:** UNC, Pogue Fellowship 1980-82; NEH Fellowship 1986, Summer Stipend 1988; Loyola Univ., Research Leaves 1986, 1989, 1992; Gladys Krieble Delmas Found. Research Fellowship 1989. **Publications:** "The Ideal Renaissance Pope: Funeral Oratory from the Papal Court," *Archivum Historiae Pontificiae* 14 (1976): 9-70; "Renaissance Preaching: Theory and Practice. A Holy Thursday Sermon of Aurelio Brandolini," *Viator* 10 (1979): 355-73; "Innovation in Early Humanist Rhetoric: The Oratory of Pier Paolo Vergerio (the Elder)," *Rinascimento* ns 22 (1982): 3-32; "Pier Paolo Vergerio the Elder and the Beginnings of the Humanist Cult of Jerome," *Catholic Historical Review* 71 (1985): 353-71; *Funeral Oratory and the Cultural Ideals of Italian Humanism* (Chapel Hill & London: UNC Press, 1989); "Continuity and Change in the Ideals of Humanism: The Evidence from Florentine Funeral Oratory," in *Life and Death in Fifteenth-Century Florence,* ed. Marcel Tetel, Ronald G. Witt & Rona Goffen (Durham, NC: Duke Univ. Press, 1989), 68-87; "Marketing a Medici Regime: The Funeral Oration of Marcello Virgilio Adriani for Giuliano de' Medici (1516)," *Renaissance Quarterly* 44 (1991): 1-41. **Business Address:** History Dept., Loyola Univ., Chicago, IL 60626.

MCMILLAN, WILLIAM C. ■ AAR Charter Mem.

MCMILLEN, LOUIS A. ■ RAAR Architecture 69. b. Oct. 24, 1916, St. Louis, MO. m. Persis W. McMillen. c. Leander, Louis, Michael. BFA 40, Yale Univ.; MArch 47, Harvard GSD. **Career & Employment:** The Architects Collaborative, Founding Part., Prin. Dir., Pres. 1946-80; also TAC Intl., Vaduz, Liechtenstein, Pres. **Fellowships, Honors & Awards:** AIA, Fellow. **Important Works:** Partial list of projects with TAC: Various private houses; USAF, Airbase planning: SAC, ADC, ARDC; West Point Military Acad., Master Plan Update; Schools: Concord; Chelmsford; Attleboro; Univ. of Baghdad, Iraq; Univ. of Mosul, Iraq; King Feisal Univ., Saudi Arabia; Military towns (3), Saudi Arabia; Raytheon Housing, Jeddeh, Saudi Arabia; School of Government Administration, Riyadh, Saudi Arabia; Cultural Center, Abu Dhabi, UAE; Commercial areas (3), Kuwait; Kuwait Fund for Arab Economic Development, HQ; Kuwait Found. for Advancement of Science, HQ; Emiri Diwan Preliminary Design, Kuwait; Al Ghanim House, Kuwait. **Bio-Bibliography:** *Who's Who in America.* **Home Address:** PO Box 490, 80R Eastern Ave., Essex, MA 01929.

MCMINN, WILLIAM GENE ■ FAAR Architecture 81. b. Aug. 17, 1931, Abilene, TX. m. Joan Gentry. c. Kevin, Tracy. BA

52, Rice Univ.; BArch 53, Rice Univ.; MArch 54, Univ. of Texas. **Other Study:** Architectural studio with Harwell, Hamilton, Harris. **Career & Employment:** Clemson Univ., Asst. Prof. 1959-63; Auburn Univ., Asst. to Dean 1963-65, Dept. Head & Prof. 1965-68; Six Asscs. Inc., Dir. of Design 1968-71; Louisiana State Univ., Head & Prof. 1971-74; Mississippi State Univ., Founding Dean & Prof. 1974-84; Cornell Univ., Dean & Prof. 1984-present. **Memberships & Offices:** Assn. of Collegiate Schools of Architecture, Dir. 1976-79; Nat. Architectural Accrediting Bd., Pres. 1983; Adv. Council, Schools of Architecture, Rice Univ., Univ. of Miami, Carnegie Mellon Univ., Univ. of Petroleum & Minerals, Dhahran, Saudi Arabia. **Fellowships, Honors & Awards:** AIA, Fellow; Tau Sigma Delta, Distinguished Architectural Alumni Award 1990; Assn. of Collegiate Schools of Architecture, Distinguished Prof. Award 1990-91. **Publications:** "A New School for the Middle East," *University of Jordan* (1979); "Architectural Education: NAAB Sets New Accrediting Rules for the Schools," *Architectural Record* (Mar. 1984); "The Architects Handbook of Professional Practice," *AIA Education and Licensing Handbook* (Washington, DC: AIA, 1988). **Important Works:** Chemical & Life Science, Research Triangle, NC; Duke Univ. Divinity School; Enka Office Bldg., Asheville, NC. **Home Address:** 1351 Slaterville Rd., Ithaca, NY 14850. **Business Address:** Cornell Univ., Ithaca, NY 14853.

MCNALL, CAMERON C. ■ FAAR Architecture 92. b. Mar. 19, 1956, Coronado, CA. m. Margaret B. Reeve. c. Reeve. BA 78, UCLA; MArch 85, Harvard GSD. **Research/Artistic Interests:** Architecture, site-specific public art, installations, films & teaching about light. **Career & Employment:** Texas A&M, Visiting Critic 1988; Harvard GSD, Visiting Critic 1989; UCLA, Lect. 1991-present; Self-employed, 1990-present. **Fellowships, Honors & Awards:** PS 1 Studio Artists Fellowship 1987; ALNY, Young Architect Award 1988; NEA Sculpture Fellowship 1988; NYFA, Architecture Fellowship 1989; Saint-Gaudens Sculpture Fellowship 1990; AIA, Brunner Grant 1993, 1994. **Exhibitions/Performances:** Harvard GSD 1986, 1989; Art on the Beach, Long Island City, NY 1987; PS 1, Long Island City, NY 1988; ALNY 1988; 2AES Gallery, San Francisco 1989; Design Center, San Francisco 1991; Parsons School of Design, NYC 1991; Intl. Design Festival, Osaka, Japan 1991; Saint-Gaudens Nat. Site, Cornish, NH 1991; Artpark, Lewiston, NY 1991. **Home Address:** 12034 Navy St., Los Angeles, CA 90066.

MCPHEE, SARAH C. ■ FAAR History of Art 92. b. June 3, 1960, NYC. m. Alexander Stille. BA 82, Harvard Univ.; MA 88, Columbia Univ.; MPhil 89, Columbia Univ. **Career & Employment:** MMA, Editor-Writer 1984-86; Freelance Writer-Editor 1985-90. **Fellowships, Honors & Awards:** Harvard Univ., James Bowdoin Writing Prize 1982; Mellon Found. Fellowship 1986-88, 1988, 1992-93, Grant 1986; Columbia Univ., Presidents Fellow 1988-89; Kress Fellowship (declined) 1990; Fulbright-Hays Fellowship (declined) 1990; MMA, Jane & Morgan Whitney Fellowship 1993-94, Chester Dale Fellowship 1994-95. **Publications:** "Starting from Scratch," *ArtNews* (Nov. 1985); "One Man's Museum," *ArtNews* (Apr. 1986); "Life into Art," *ArtNews* (May 1986); "A New Sketch-Book by Filippo Juvarra," *Burlington Magazine* (May 1993): 346-50; "Filippo Juvarra: A New Sketch-Book from the Roman Years," *Studi Piemontesi* (Nov. 1993): 377-83; *Filippo Juvarra: Drawings from the Roman Period 1704-1714*, Part II, ed. Henry A. Millon (forthcoming). **Home Address:** 915 W. End Ave., Apt. 7C, NYC 10025.

MCTIGHE, SHEILA ■ FAAR History of Art 90. b. Oct. 24, 1955, Bethesda, MD. m. Frederick M. Biggs. c. Lily. BA 78,

Georgetown Univ.; MA 82, Yale Univ.; PhD 87, Yale Univ. **Career & Employment:** Yale Univ., Lect. 1986; Cornell Univ., Asst. Prof. 1986-90; Barnard College, Columbia Univ., Asst. Prof. 1990-present. **Memberships & Offices:** CAA; RSA; Assn. of Art Historians, UK. **Fellowships, Honors & Awards:** Yale Univ., Council of West European Studies Graduate Fellowship 1980-82, Grant 1982, John Roberts Memorial Fellowship 1982-83; Fulbright-Hays Grant (declined) 1983-84; Art Dealers Assn. of America, Doctoral Fellowship 1983-85; Cornell Univ. Research Grant 1987; Mellon Grant 1987; Getty Found. Fellowship 1989 (declined), 1993-94. **Publications:** essay on Nicholas Poussin's landscapes, in *Claude to Corot: The Development of Landscape Painting in France*, ed. A. Wintermute, exb. cat. (New York: Colnaghi Gallery, 1990), 50-56; "Nicolas Poussin's Storm Landscapes and Seventeenth-Century Libertinage," *Word & Image* 5 (1989): 333-61; "Perfect Deformity, Ideal Beauty, and the *Imaginaire* of Work: The Reception of Annibale Carracci's *Arti di Bologna* in 1646," *Oxford Art Journal* 16 (1993): 75-91; *The Late Allegories of Nicolas Poussin* (Cambridge Univ. Press, forthcoming). **Home Address:** 241 Central Park W., Apt. 13A, NYC 10024. **Business Address:** Dept. of Art History, Barnard College, NYC 10027.

MEAD, WILLIAM RUTHERFORD ■ AAR Charter Mem., Trustee 1905-28, Pres. 1910-28, Architect. b. Aug. 20, 1846. d. June 20, 1928. **Career & Employment:** McKim, Mead & White, Part. 1879-1928. **Honors & Awards:** NIAL, Gold Medal. **Important Works:** Boston Public Library; many buildings for Columbia Univ.; Pennsylvania Station, Tiffany Building, Bellevue Hospital, all NYC.

MEADER, CLARENCE LINTON ■ FAAR Classics / Archaeology 98. b. Aug. 12, 1868, Battle Creek, MI. d. June 1, 1967. m. Virginia D. Farmer, Xenia Ethel Burt. BA 1891, Univ. of Michigan; PhD 02, Univ. of Michigan. **Other Studies:** ASCSA 1892-93, Univ. of Bonn 1893, Univ. of Munich 1898-99. **Career & Employment:** Univ. of Michigan, Instr.-Prof. 1893-1938, Prof. Emer. 1938-67. **Memberships & Offices:** APA; MLA; American Dialect Soc.; Linguistic Soc. of America; Univ. of Michigan Research Club; Technocracy Inc.; Delta Upsilon. **Fellowships, Honors & Awards:** Univ. of Michigan, Elisha Jones Classical Fellow 1891-93; Univ. of Munich, Fellow 1898-99. **Publications:** *The Latin Pronouns is, hic, iste, ipse: A Semiological Study* (New York: Macmillan, 1901); ed., *Latin Philology*, Univ. of Michigan Studies, Humanistic Series, vol. 3 (New York: Macmillan, 1910); "The Development of Copulative Verbs in the Indo-European Languages," *TAPA* 43 (1912): 173-200; trans. with F.N. Scott, *Plays by Leonid Andreyev* (New York: Scribners, 1915); with Walter B. Pillsbury, *The Psychology of Language* (New York: Appleton, 1929). **Bio-Bibliography:** Briggs, 402; *Who Was Who in America*.

MEEKS, EVERETT V. ■ AAR Trustee 1928-49, Architect.

MEIER, RICHARD ■ RAAR Architecture 73. b. Oct. 12, 1934, Newark, NJ. c. Joseph, Ana. BArch 57, Cornell Univ. **Career & Employment:** Davis, Brody, Wisniewski, NYC 1959; Skidmore, Owings, Merrill, NYC 1960; Marcel Breuer, NYC 1961-63; Richard Meier & Partners 1963-present. **Memberships & Offices:** Architects Inst. for Architecture & Urban Studies, BoT 1972-84; AIA, Fellow 1976-present; ALNY, Dir. 1982-present; AAAL 1983-present; Intl. Competition for La Defense, Paris, Juror 1983; Intl. Competition, Convention Hall, Nara, Japan, Juror 1992; Spreebogen, Berlin, Intl. Competition, Juror 1993. **Fellowships, Honors & Awards:** AAAL, Arnold Brunner Prize 1972;

AIA, Nat. Honor Awards (11) 1968-92, New York Chap., Medal of Honor 1980, Chap. Awards (30) 1965-94; Pritzker Architecture Prize 1984; Royal Inst. of British Architects, Royal Gold Medal 1988, Hon. Fellow 1988-present; Guild Hall, Lifetime Achievement Award 1991; French Republic, Order of Arts & Letters, Commander 1992; Royal Inst. of Scottish Architects, Hon. Fellow 1994-present. **Important Works:** Smith House, Darien, CT 1965-67; Bronx Developmental Center 1970-77; Douglas House, Harbor Springs, MI 1971-76; Atheneum, New Harmony, IN 1975-79; Hartford Seminary 1978-81; Museum for Decorative Arts, Frankfurt 1979-85; High Museum of Art, Atlanta 1980-83; Des Moines Art Center 1982-85; Getty Center, Los Angeles 1985-97; City Hall & Central Library, The Hague 1986-95; Museum of Contemporary Art, Barcelona 1987-95; Canal+ Television HQ, Paris 1988-92. **Exhibitions/Performances:** "40 Under 40," American Federation of Arts, NYC 1966; XV Triennale de Milano 1973; MOMA 1975; "Five Architects," Cooper Union, NYC & traveling to Geneva, Paris, Brussels, Helsinki 1976; Leo Castelli Gallery, NYC 1977, 1994; Gallery of Contemporary Art, New Harmony, IN 1979; Whitney Museum, NYC 1982; Des Moines Art Center 1984; Colby College, ME 1984; Knoll Intl., Tokyo 1988; October Gallery, London 1990; Palazzo Reale, Naples 1991; Palazzo delle Esposizioni, Rome 1993. **Bio-Bibliography:** Kenneth Frampton & Colin Rowe, *Five Architects: Eisenman, Graves, Gwathmey, Hedjuk, Meier* (New York: Wittenborn, 1972); Kenneth Frampton & Colin Rowe, *Richard Meier, Architect: Buildings and Projects 1966-1976* (New York: Oxford Univ. Press, 1976); Joseph Rykwert & John Kejduk, eds., *Richard Meier* (New York: Rizzoli, 1984); Valerie Vaudou, ed., *Richard Meier* (Paris: Electa Moniteur, 1986); Werner Blaser, *Richard Meier: Building for Art* (Basel: Birkhäuser, 1990); Lois E. Nesbitt, *Richard Meier: Collages* (New York: St. Martin's, 1990); *Richard Meier* (London: Academy Editions, 1990); Ferruccio Izzo & Alessandro Gubitosi, *Richard Meier Architetture-Projects 1986-1990* (Florence: Centro Di, 1991); Kenneth Frampton, Joseph Rykwert & Frank Stella, *Richard Meier Architect 2* (New York: Rizzoli, 1991); Gloria Gerace, ed., *The Getty Center Design Process* (Los Angeles: J. Paul Getty Trust, 1991); *Richard Meier/Frank Stella: Arte e Architettura* (Milan: Electa, 1993); Lois E. Nesbitt, *Richard Meier, Sculpture* (New York: Rizzoli, 1994); *Contemporary Architects; Current Biography; Encyclopedia of Architecture; Encyclopaedia Universalis; Who's Who in America; Who's Who in American Art; Who's Who in World Jewry.* **Business Address:** Richard Meier & Partners, 475 10th Ave., NYC 10018.

MELCHERT, JAMES F. ■ AAR Dir. 1984-88. b. Dec. 2, 1930, New Bremen, OH. m. Mary Ann Hostetler. c. Christopher, David, Renee Thorpe. BA 52, Princeton Univ.; MFA 57, Univ. of Chicago; MA 61, UC, Berkeley. **Career & Employment:** San Francisco Art Inst., Ceramics Dept., Head 1961-65; UC, Berkeley, Prof. 1965-92; NEA, Visual Arts Program, Dir. 1977-81. **Home Address:** 6077 Ocean View Dr., Oakland, CA 94618.

MELLON, EDWARD P. ■ AAR Trustee 1917-23, Architect.

MELLON, PAUL ■ AAR Visitor 1959 — 1964, Philanthropist.

MELTING, R. ALAN ■ FAAR Design Arts 70. b. June 2, 1940, Breckenridge, MN. m. Elizabeth G. Miller. c. Sarah, Benjamin, Andrew, Kate. BA 62, Univ. of Minnesota; BArch 64, Univ. of Minnesota; MCP 69, MIT. **Career & Employment:** Detroit City Planning Comm., Urban Design, Head 1965-72; Arrowstreet, Project Architect 1972-73; New York State Urban Development Corp., Assc. Architect 1973-75; Gruzen & Partners, Project Ar-

chitect 1975-78; Haus Intl., Assc. for Planning 1978-79; The Liebman Melting Partnership, Part. 1979-present; Pratt Inst., Adj. Asst Prof. 1983-86; Columbia Univ., Adj. Asst. Prof. 1985-86. **Memberships & Offices:** American Planning Assn. 1981-present; American Inst. of Certified Planners 1981-present; AIA 1983-present; Irwin Sweeney Miller Found., Dir. 1983-present. **Fellowships, Honors & Awards:** AIA Student Medal 1964, Citation for Excellence 1965; US Dept. of Housing & Urban Development, Urban Design Award 1971; *Progressive Architecture* Design Award 1971; NEA Architecture-Environmental Arts Grant 1972-73; Harvard GSD, Loeb Fellow 1977-78; New York Landmarks Conservancy, Lucy G. Moses Preservation Award 1990; AIA, Fellow 1995. **Important Works:** Streets for People, Washington, DC 1973; Southtown Master Plan, Roosevelt Island, NYC 1975; Reza Pahlavi New Community, Shah Reza, Iran 1978; Housing Development Strategies, Denver 1980; Grant St. Housing, Denver 1983; Shorehaven, Bronx, NYC 1988; Spring Creek Gardens, Brooklyn, NYC 1989; Sawyer's Walk, Miami 1990; Arverne New Community, Far Rockaway, Queens, NYC 1992; Ducat Pl., Moscow, Russia 1993, 1995; PS 37, Bronx, NYC 1995. **Business Address:** The Liebman Melting Partnership, 330 W. 42 St., NYC 10036.

MENDELL, CLARENCE WHITTLESLEY ■ RAAR Classics/Archaeology 50; Annual Prof. 1933; AAR Trustee 1928-53. b. June 3, 1883, Norwood, MA. d. Dec. 14, 1976. m. Katharine DeFord Webb, Elizabeth B. Lawrence. BA 04, Yale Univ.; MA 05, Yale Univ.; PhD 10, Yale Univ. **Career & Employment:** Yale Univ., Instr. 1907-11, Asst. Prof. 1911-19, Dunham Prof. 1919-47, Sterling Prof. 1947-53; Yale College, Bd. of Athletic Control, Chair 1919-25, Dean 1926-37; Branford College, Master 1932-43; US Military Intelligence, Paris 1918-19; US Navy Reserve, Lieut. Commander 1942-44, Commander 1944. **Memberships & Offices:** APA; Classical Assn. of Great Britain; Salisbury School, BoT, Chair; Beta Theta Pi. **Fellowships, Honors & Awards:** Legion of Merit 1945; Phi Beta Kappa. **Publications:** *Sentence Connection in Tacitus* (New Haven: Yale Univ. Press, 1911); *Latin Sentence Connection* (New Haven: Yale Univ. Press, 1917); trans., Aeschylus, *Prometheus* (New Haven: Yale Univ. Press, 1926); ed., *Livy, XXX-XXXIII* (New York: Century, 1928); *Jeanne d'Arc at Rouen* (New Haven, 1931); *Our Seneca* (New Haven: Yale Univ. Press, 1941); *Tacitus: The Man and His Work* (New Haven: Yale Univ. Press, 1960); *Latin Poetry, The New Poets and the Augustans* (New Haven: Yale Univ. Press, 1965); *Latin Poetry, The Age of Rhetoric and Satire* (New Haven: Yale Univ. Press, 1967); *Latin Poetry Before and After* (Hamden, CT: Archon Books, 1970). **Bio-Bibliography:** *Yale Classical Studies* 23 (1973): vii-ix; Briggs, 403-4; *Who Was Who in America.*

MENDIETA, ANA MARIA ■ FAAR Sculpture 84. b. Nov. 18, 1948, Havana, Cuba. d. Sept. 8, 1985. m. Carl Andre. BA 69, Univ. of Iowa; MA 72, Univ. of Iowa; MFA 73, Univ. of Iowa. **Career & Employment:** SUNY, Old Westbury, Instr. 1979-80; AIC, Visiting Artist 1980. **Fellowships, Honors & Awards:** Creative Artists Public Service Grant 1978; Guggenheim Fellowship 1980; NEA Grant 1982. **Exhibitions/Performances:** Solo: Iowa Memorial Union, Univ. of Iowa 1971; 112 Greene Street, NYC 1976; A.I.R. Gallery, NYC 1979, 1981; Museo de Arte Contemporanea, São Paulo, Brazil 1980; Yvonne Seguy Gallery, NYC 1982; Lowe Art Museum, Univ. of Miami, Coral Gables, FL 1982; Museo Nacional de Bellas Artes, Havana 1983; Primo Piano, Rome 1984; Gallery AAM, Rome 1985; New Museum of Contemporary Art, NYC 1987-88; Los Angeles Contemporary Exhibitions 1988; Terne Gallery, NYC 1988;

Carlo Lamagna Gallery, NYC 1989; Aspen Art Museum 1990; Pat Hearn Gallery, NYC 1990; Galerie Lelong, NYC 1991; Group: Inst. of Contemporary Art, Philadelphia 1991; Inst. of Contemporary Art, Boston 1991; Cleveland Center for Contemporary Art 1992. **Bio-Bibliography:** Janet Heit, "Ana Mendieta," *Arts* (Jan. 1980); Judith Wilson, "Ana Mendieta Plants Her Garden," *Village Voice* (Aug. 13-19, 1980); John Perreault, "Manifesto Destiny," *Soho News* (Jan. 19, 1982).

MENOTTI, GIAN CARLO ■ AAR Visitor 1943 — 1951, 1994; AAR *Academy Award* in The Year of Music 1991; Composer. b. July 7, 1911. **Career & Employment:** Festival of Two Worlds, Spoleto, Italy, Founder 1958; Spoleto Festival USA, Composer-Artistic Dir. 1988-. **Honors & Awards:** Guggenheim Fellowship 1946, 1947; Pulitzer Prize for Music 1950, 1955; Drama Critics' Circle Award 1955; Musical America, Musician of the Year 1991. **Important Works:** *The Medium* 1945; *Amahl and the Night Visitors* 1951; *The Saint of Bleeker Street* 1954.

MENUHIN, YEHUDI ■ AAR Visitor 1943 — 1951, Violinist. b. Apr. 22, 1916. **Career & Employment:** Bath Festival, England, Dir. 1958-68; debut as conductor of symphony orchestra in America with American Symph. Orch., Carnegie Hall 1966. **Honors & Awards:** Mendelssohn Prize 1986; Glenn Gould Found., Glenn Gould Prize 1990; Wolf Prize in Arts 1991; 10 Grammy Awards.

MERITT, LUCY SHOE ■ FAAR Classics/Archaeology 37, 50; Classical Soc., Treas. 1942-46, VP 1951, Pres. 1952. b. Aug. 7, 1906, Camden, NJ. m. Benjamin Dean Meritt. BA 27, Bryn Mawr College; MA 28, Bryn Mawr College; PhD 35, Bryn Mawr College. **Other Study:** ASCSA, Fellow 1929-32, Research Mem. 1932-34, 1950, 1961, 1969-70. **Research/ Artistic Interests:** Classical archaeology: Greek, Etruscan, & Roman architecture, specifically profiles of mouldings. **Career & Employment:** Mt. Holyoke College, Asst. Prof. 1937-41, Assc. Prof. 1941-50, Counsellor-Chief Counsellor of Students 1943-48; Washington Univ., Visiting Prof. 1958, 1960; Princeton Univ., Visiting Lect. 1959; Univ. of Texas, Austin, Prof. 1973-74, 1975-76, 1990, Visiting Scholar 1973-present. **Memberships & Offices:** IAS 1948-49, 1950-73; ASCSA, Managing Com. 1937-present, Alumni Assc., Sec. 1940-75, Exec. Com. 1948-52, Publications Ed. 1950-72; Intl. Assn. of Classical Archaeology, USA Correspondent 1952-72; ArIA, Recorder 1960-68, 1971, Acting Gen. Sec. 1967; Princeton Soc., Sec. 1953-56, Pres. 1963-67; Austin Soc., VP 1976-78; German Archaeological Inst., Corresponding Mem. **Fellowships, Honors & Awards:** APS Grant 1961; Brown Univ., Hon. LHD 1974; ArIA, Gold Medal 1976; AAUW, Austin Branch, Outstanding Woman of Texas in Humanities 1980; Hamilton College, Hon. LHD 1994. **Publications:** *Profiles of Greek Mouldings* (Cambridge: ASCSA, 1936); "Architectural Mouldings of Doura-Europos," *Berytus* 9 (1948): 1-40; "Greek Mouldings of Kos & Rhodes," *Hesperia* 19 (1950): 338-69; *Profiles of Western Greek Mouldings*, AAR Papers & Monographs 14 (Rome: AAR, 1952); "The Roman Ionic Base in Corinth," in *Essays in Memory of Karl Lehmann*, Marsyas, suppl. 1 (1964): 300-303; *Etruscan & Republican Roman Mouldings*, Memoirs of the AAR 28 (Rome: AAR, 1965); "The Geographical Distribution of Greek and Roman Ionic Bases," *Hesperia* 38 (1969): 186-204; "Architectural Mouldings from Murlo," *Studi Etruschi* 38 (1970): 13-25; "Some Ionic Architectural Fragments from the Athenian Agora," *Hesperia*, suppl. 20 (1982): 82-92; *History of the American School of Classical Studies at Athens 1939-80* (Princeton: ASCSA, 1984); "The Athenian Ionic Capital," in *Eius Virtutis Studiosi: Studies in Memory of Frank Edward Brown*, ed. Russell Scott & Ann Scott,

Studies in the History of Art 43 (Washington: NGA, 1992), 315-25. **Bio-Bibliography:** *Archaeology* 30 (1977): 74-75; *AJA* 71 (1977): 238; *Dictionary of International Biography; Directory of American Scholars; Personalities of the South; Who's Who in America; Who's Who of American Women; Who's Who in the South & Southeast; Who's Who in the World; World Who's Who of Women*. **Home Address:** 712 W. 16 St., Austin, TX 78701.

MERRILL, JOHN O. ■ AAR Visitor 1951 — 1955, Architect.

MERTZ, STUART M. ■ FAAR Landscape Architecture 40; AAR Centennial Medal 1994. b. Dec. 4, 1915, Wayne, PA. m. Constance Buck, Theodora Lucks. c. Stuart Jr., Maurice. BS 37, Pennsylvania State Univ.; BLA 38, Cornell Univ. **Other Study:** Washington Univ., St. Louis, German Language; Meramec Community College, St. Louis, French & Spanish languages. **Research/Artistic Interests:** Pencil sketching. **Career & Employment:** John Noyes 1940; Harland Bartholomew & Asscs., Chief Designer 1941-49; Stuart M. Mertz & Asscs. 1949-83; Austin Tao & Asscs., Sen. Assc. 1984-94. **Memberships & Offices:** ASLA 1947-present, Missouri Valley Chap., Sec.-Treas. 1954-60, St. Louis Chap., Pres. 1960-63, Fellow 1961-present, Nat. Sec.-Treas. 1963-67, Nat. 2d VP 1967-69, Found. Bd. 1965-69, 1971-75, Sec.-Treas. 1967-69, Council of Fellows, Chair 1977-79; Cornell Club of St. Louis, Pres. 1955-56; People's Art Center Assc. Bd. 1959-63, Pres. 1960-62; Spirit of St. Louis Fund Bd. 1960-62; Missouri Assn. of Landscape Architects 1961-present, Pres. 1966-86; Univ. of Missouri, School of Forestry, Fisheries & Wildlife, Adv. Council 1974-83. **Publications:** "Pencil Sketches," *Pencil Points* 18 (1937): 123; "Bal Harbour, Florida, Plans for the Development of a Winter Community," *Landscape Architecture* 38 (1948): 61-67; "Office and Warehouse Buildings in St. Louis," *Landscape Architecture* 42 (1952): 126-27; "Unit Pieces: St. Louis's Schools and Semi-Public Building Grounds," *Landscape Architecture* 44 (1954): 147-50; "Appreciation of the IFLA Exhibit at Zurich," *Landscape Architecture* 47 (1957): 326-27; "Big Debate over Schools Neglects Important Site," *Landscape Architecture* 48 (1958): 226-27; "Residential Designs, Step-by-Step," *Landscape Architecture* 53 (1962): 38-41; "The 64th Annual Meeting: American Society of Landscape Architects, Pittsburgh, PA," *Landscape Architecture* 54 (1963): 62-68. **Important Works:** Bellerive Country Club, St. Louis Co., MO 1959-61; Missouri Baptist Hospital, Town & Country, MO 1961-70; Parkway S. Senior HS, St. Louis Co., MO; St. Andrews Golf Club, St. Charles, MO 1964-65; Greensfelder Memorial County Park, St. Louis Co., MO 1965; Sioux Passage County Park, St. Louis Co., MO 1966-68; Parkway W. Senior HS, St. Louis Co., MO 1967-69; Florissant Valley Community College, Florissant, MO 1968-78; Meramec Community College, Kirkwood, MO 1968-70; R.S. Barnwell Memorial Art & Garden Center, Shreveport, LA 1969-71; St. Joseph Hospital, Kirkwood, MO 1970-75; St. Luke's West Hospital, Chesterfield, MO 1970-80. **Bio-Bibliography:** *Who's Who in America*. **Home Address:** 9009 Sedgwick Pl. Dr., St. Louis, MO 63124. **Business Address:** Austin Tao & Asscs., 1709 Washington, 8 Fl., St. Louis, MO 63103.

MESSER, WILLIAM STUART ■ FAAR Classics/Archaeology 22. b. Aug. 19, 1882, Washington, DC. d. Dec. 21 1960. m. Winifred Irish, Edna E. Wilson. BA 05, Columbia Univ.; MA 09, Columbia Univ.; PhD 17, Columbia Univ. **Research/Artistic Interests:** History & literature, Greek & Roman tragedy. **Career & Employment:** Barnard College, Dept. Head 1905-9; Columbia Univ., Instr. 1911-19; Dartmouth College, Asst. Prof. 1919-23, Prof. 1923-38, Daniel Webster Prof. 1938-51, Dept.

Chair 1926-30, 1937-41, 1947-51; Whitney Found., Whitney College, Visiting Prof. 1953. **Memberships & Offices:** APA; American Classical League; NECA; AAUP. **Fellowships, Honors & Awards:** Phi Beta Kappa; Columbia Univ., Gottsberger Fellow 1910-11; Order of Redeemer, Greece, Decorated Officer; Univ. of Padua, Hon. PhD 1922; Dartmouth College, Hon. MA 1923. **Publications:** "Ad Cic. *Tusc. Disp.* III.19,45," *Mnemosyne* ns 45 (1917): 78-92; *Dream in Homer and Greek Tragedy* (New York: Columbia Univ. Press, 1918); "A Mutiny in the Roman Army: The Republic," *Classical Philology* 15 (1920): 158-75; "The Roman World of Caesar, Cicero and Vergil," *Classical Journal* 19 (1923-24): 356-68; "The New Rome and Archaeology," *Classical Journal* 22 (1926-27): 177-88; "Classical Art from Ancient Shipwrecks," *Art and Archaeology* 23 (1927): 147-59; "Martial IX,15," *Classical Journal* 36 (1940-41): 226-29. **Bio-Bibliography:** *NY Times,* Obit. (Dec. 23, 1960); Briggs, 409-10; *Who Was Who in America.*

MEWSHAW, MICHAEL ■ AAR Visitor 1975-76, Writer.

MEYER, ALVIN ■ Cresson Fellow 1920-21, 1921-22; FAAR Sculpture 26. b. Dec. 31, 1892, Bartlett, IL. d. May 9, 1976. m. Edith Meyer. **Study:** Maryland Inst. of Art & Design; PAFA. **Career & Employment:** WWII, Douglas Aircraft; Saugatuck Summer School, Teacher 1935. **Fellowships, Honors & Awards:** PAFA, Cresson Travelling Scholarship; Rinehart Scholarship. **Important Works:** Peabody Inst.; Maryland Inst.; Chicago Daily News; Chicago Board of Trade; Ohio State Office Bldg., Columbus; Archives Bldg., Springfield IL; Natural History Bldg., Urbana IL. **Bio-Bibliography:** *Who Was Who in American Art.*

MEYER, MELISSA ■ FAAR Painting 81. b. May 4, 1947, NYC. BS 68, NYU; MA 75, NYU. **Career & Employment:** MMA, Education Dept. 1978-79, Young People's Programs 1981-84; Parsons School of Design, NYC 1982-91; Columbia Univ. 1989; RISD 1992, 1994; Vermont Studio Center 1992, 1994; School of Visual Arts, NYC 1993-present; Visiting Artist at: Franconia College 1978; Converse College 1982; Bennington College 1982, 1985; AIC 1985; Univ. of Iowa 1985; Syracuse Univ. 1985, 1986; Provincetown Art Museum 1985, 1986; Univ. of Buffalo 1986; Middlebury College 1986; Fort Hays State Univ., KS 1986; Dartmouth College 1995. **Fellowships, Honors & Awards:** Provincetown Workshop, with Leo Manso & Victor Candell 1972, 1973, 1974; Yaddo 1974, 1975, 1979, 1982, 1983, 1994; Palisades Interstate Project-America the Beautiful Fund 1978; Edward F. Albee Found. Grant 1979, 1980; CAPS Grant 1981-82; NEA Grant 1983-84, 1993; NYFA 1992. **Important Works:** MOMA; MMA; Guggenheim Museum, NYC; Brooklyn Museum; Jewish Museum; Aldrich Museum of Contemporary Art, Ridgefield, CT; Arkansas Art Center, Little Rock; Rose Art Museum, Waltham, MA; Arthur Andersen & Co., Chicago; Best Products, Richmond, VA; Chemical Bank, NYC; Citibank, NYC; Connecticut Bank & Trust Co., Stamford; County Federal Savings, Westport, CT; Estée Lauder, NYC; Fidelity Management, Boston; Robert Half Co., Buffalo; Hallmark Cards, Kansas City, MO; IBM, Stamford, CT; Johnson & Johnson, New Brunswick, NJ; Progressive Corp., Pepper Pike, OH; Mobil Oil, NYC & Richmond, VA; Needham, Harper Worldwide, NYC; Nichols, Carter, Seary, & Grant, Atlanta; Paine Webber, NYC; Proskauer, Rose, Goetz, & Mendelsohn, NYC; Prudential Life Insurance, Newark, NJ; Reich & Tang, NYC; Shearson Lehman Hutton, NYC; Sonesta Intl., Boston; Yaddo; Zale Corp., Dallas. **Exhibitions/Performances:** Solo: Cornell Club, NYC 1976; Frank Marino Gallery, New York 1979; Milliken Gallery, Converse College 1982; Maples Gallery, Fairleigh Dickinson Univ. 1982;

Douglas College, New Brunswick 1983; Exit Art, NYC 1984; Janet Steinberg Gallery, San Francisco 1985; R.C. Erpf Gallery, NYC 1986, 1987; Leslie Cecil Gallery, NYC 1987; J.J.L. Becker-East End Gallery, Provincetown 1987, 1988; Moss-Thorns Gallery, Fort Hays State Univ. 1988; Holly Solomon Gallery, NYC 1988, 1993; Ellen Miller Fine Art, Boston 1991; Montgomery Glasoe Fine Arts, Minneapolis 1993; Galerie Renée Ziegler, Zurich 1993; Miller-Block Gallery, Boston 1994. **Bio-Bibliography:** Judy K. Collischan Van Wagner, *Lines of Vision: Drawings by Contemporary Women* (New York: Hudson Hills Press), 99. **Home Address:** 186 Franklin St., NYC 10013. **Business Address:** Holly Solomon Gallery, 172 Mercer St., NYC 10012.

MEZZATESTA, MICHAEL P. ■ FAAR History of Art 79. b. June 9, 1948, NYC. m. Nancy L. Kitterman. c. Philip, Alexander, Marya. BA 70, Columbia College; MA 74, NYU; PhD 80, NYU. **Research/Artistic Interests:** Renaissance & baroque art, 20th-century art. **Career & Employment:** Kimbell Art Museum, Curator 1980-86; Duke Univ. Museum of Art, Dir. 1987-present. **Fellowships, Honors & Awards:** Ford Found. Fellow 1974-77; American Council on Germany, John J. McCloy Fellow 1982; IAS, Visitor 1986. **Publications:** ed., *The Art of Gianlorenzo Bernini: Selected Sculpture,* exb. cat. (Fort Worth: Kimbell Art Museum, 1982); "Marcus Aurelius, Fray Antonio de Guevara and the Ideal of the Perfect Prince in the Sixteenth Century," *Art Bulletin* 66.4 (1984): 620-33; ed., *Henri Matisse: Sculptor-Painter,* exb. cat. (Fort Worth: Kimbell Art Museum, 1984); "The Facade of Leone Leoni's House in Milan, the Casa degli Omenoni: The Artist and the Public," *JSAH* 44.3 (1985): 233-49; "Giambologna's Altar of Liberty in Lucca: Civic Patriotism and the Counter-Reformation," *Antologia di Belle Arti,* ns 23-24 (1985); ed., *Kimbell Art Museum: In Pursuit of Quality* (Ft. Worth: Kimbell Art Museum, 1987); ed., *On the Edge: The Sculpture of Leonid Lerman,* exb. cat. (Durham, NC & London: Duke Univ. Museum of Art, Duke Univ. Press, 1988); "Foreword," to *The Art Museums of Louis I. Kahn,* exb. cat. (Durham, NC & London, Duke Univ. Press & Duke Univ. Museum of Art, 1989), viii-x; "The King, the Poet, and the Nation: A French 16th-Century Relief and the Pléiade," in *IL60: Essays in Honor of Irving Lavin on His 60th Birthday,* ed. Marilyn A. Lavin (New York: Italica Press, 1990), 227-52; "Foreword," to *Lines of Light and Shadow: The Drawings of Federico Garcia Lorca,* exb. cat. (Durham, NC & London: Duke Univ. Museum of Art, Duke Univ. Press & Madrid: Taba Press, 1991), 7; "Foreword," to *Jackson Pollock: "Psychoanalytic" Drawings,* exb. cat. (Durham, NC & London: Duke Univ. Museum of Art & Duke Univ. Press, 1992), vii-viii; "Foreword," to *Painting the Maya Universe, The Royal Ceramic Tradition,* exb. cat. (Durham, NC & London: Duke Univ. Museum of Art & Duke Univ. Press, 1994), ix-x; "Gianlorenzo Bernini," in *The Dictionary of Art.* **Home Address:** 118 Porter Pl., Chapel Hill, NC 27514. **Business Address:** Duke Univ. Museum of Art, 6845 College Station, Durham, NC 27705.

MICHELS, AGNES KIRSOPP LAKE ■ FAAR Classics/Archaeology 33; AAR Adv. Council, Chair. b. July 31, 1909, Leiden, Netherlands. d. Nov. 1993. m. Walter Christian Michels. c. Leslyn (Mrs. C. Howard Goodrich). BA 30, Bryn Mawr College; MA 31, Bryn Mawr College; PhD 34, Bryn Mawr College. **Career & Employment:** Bryn Mawr College, Instr. 1934-38, Asst. Prof. 1938-46, Assc. Prof. 1946-55, Prof. 1955-70, Mellon Found. Prof. 1970-75; Oberlin College, Martin Lect. 1969. **Memberships & Offices:** APA, 2d VP 1970; AHA; ArIA; Soc. for the Promotion Roman Studies; Intl. Archaeological Assn. **Fellowships, Honors & Awards:** Ford Faculty Fellow 1953-54; Guggenheim Fellow 1960-61; APA, Goodwin Merit Award

1970. **Publications:** "Campana Supellen, the Pottery Deposit at Minturnae," *Bollettino dell'Associazione internazionale Studi Mediterranei* 5 (1934-35); "Origin of the Roman House," *AJA* 41(1937): co-ed., *Quantulacumque: Studies Presented to Kirsopp Lake* (London: Christopher, 1937); 598-601; "Note on the Pediment of the Tuscan Temple," *AJA* 45 (1941): 71-72; *The Calendar of the Roman Republic* (Princeton: Princeton Univ. Press, 1967). **Bio-Bibliography:** Russell T. Scott, "Nan Michels," *Bryn Mawr Classical Review* (Dec. 1993); *Directory of American Scholars; Who's Who in America; Who's Who of American Women.*

MICHENER, CHARLES ■ AAR Visitor 1987-88, Writer.

MICHENER, DIANA ■ AAR Visitor 1987-88, Photographer.

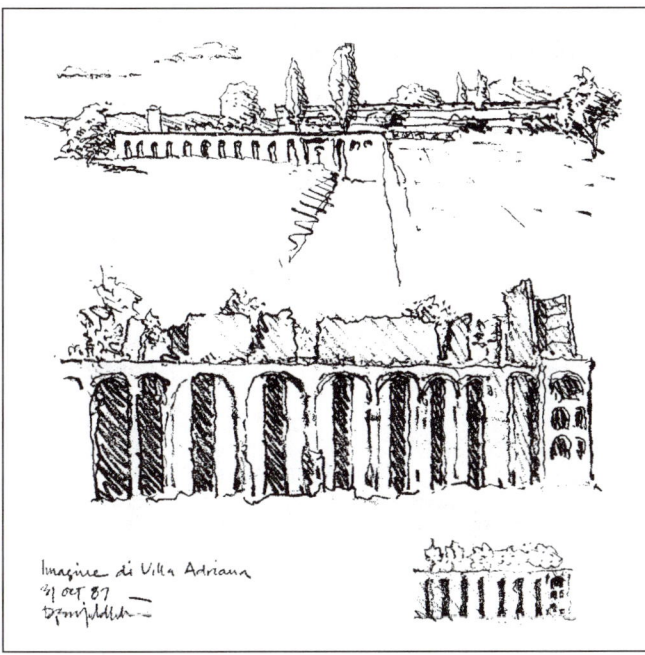

imagine di Villa Adriana
21 ocT 87
B?nvldllh—

D.B. Middleton

MIDDLETON, D.B. ■ FAAR Architecture 82. b. May 26, 1956, Cambridge, MA. m. Martha Hart Eddy. BArch 78, Cornell Univ.; MArch 81, Cornell Univ. **Career & Employment:** Polshek & Partners, Architects, Assc. Part. 1984-present; Syracuse Univ., Florence Pre-Architecture Pgm., Dir. 1982-83; Visiting Critic: Harvard Univ. 1985-86, Univ. of Virginia 1990, Yale Univ. 1991; Univ. of Toronto, Asst. Prof. 1987; California College of Arts & Crafts, Adj. Prof. 1994-present. **Memberships & Offices:** AIA; ALNY; NIAE; *Cornell Journal of Architecture*, Guest Ed. 1983; Nat. Council of Architectural Registration Bds. **Fellowships, Honors & Awards:** New York Soc. of Architects, Del Gaudio Memorial Award 1979. **Publications:** "The Combining of the Modern City and the Traditional City," *Lotus International* 27 (1980): 47; with J.K. Smith, "Baltimore: Strategy for Urban Design," *Design Quarterly* 113-14 (1980): 34-35; with G. Berti, W. Hunziker & J. Tice, "Tre propositi dal Lungotevere di Roma," in *La Rinascita della Città* (Bologna: Centro di Architettura, 1984). **Important Works:** As Design Assc. for Polshek & Partners: Santa Barbara County Bowl; Santa Fe Opera Theater; Akron Convention Center; Nat. Inventors' Hall of Fame, Phase I; Center for Wine, Food & Arts, Napa, CA; Han Jung Industrial Data & Information Center, Seoul, Korea. **Exhibitions/Performances:** Centro di Architettura, Bologna 1984. **Business Address:** Polshek & Partners, Architects, 250 Sutter St., Suite 600, San Francisco, CA 94108.

MILES, MARGARET M. ■ FAAR Classics/Archaeology 88. b. Sept. 16, 1952, Detroit, MI. BA 73, Univ. of Michigan; MA 76, Princeton Univ.; PhD 80, Princeton Univ. **Other Study:** Goethe Inst., Radolfgill 1975; ASCSA 1976-79, 1980-82. **Research/Artistic Interests:** Greek & Roman archaeology & architecture, western Greek architecture & religion. **Career & Employment:** UC, Berkeley, Visiting Asst. Prof. 1982-87; ICCS, Visiting Asst. Prof. 1988-90; Smith College, Visiting Asst. Prof. 1991-92; UC, Irvine, Asst. Prof. 1992-94, Assc. Prof. 1994-present. **Memberships & Offices:** ArIA; CAA; APA; ASCSA, Alumni Assn., Pres. 1995-97. **Fellowships, Honors & Awards:** ASCSA, White Fellow 1976-77; AAUW 1979-80; APS, Penrose Travel Grant 1983; ACLS, Grant-in-Aid 1985; IAS, Mellon Fellow 1990-91. **Publications:** "A Reconstruction of the Temple of Nemesis at Rhamnous," *Hesperia* 58 (1989): 131-249; *The Athenian Agora: The City Eleusinion* (Princeton: ASCSA, forthcoming). **Home Address:** 77 Whitman Ct., Irvine, CA 92715-4065. **Business Address:** Dept. of Art History, School of Humanities, UC, Irvine, CA 92717.

MILLER, J. IRWIN ■ AAR Trustee 1982-84, Corp. Exec.

MILLER, MARGARET KOONS ■ FAAR History of Art 51. b. Aug. 23, 1917, Seoul, Korea. d. Feb. 13, 1994. m. William B. Miller, FAAR 51. c. Charlotte D., Katherine B. BA 38, Wooster College. **Other Study:** Oberlin College 1939-40. **Career & Employment:** Columbia Univ., Resident Scholar 1941-43, Univ. Fellow 1947-50; Rhode Island State College, Instr. 1940s; Smith College, Instr. 1950-51; Colby College, Instr. 1956-60, Asst. Prof. 1960-94. **Fellowships, Honors & Awards:** Carnegie Fellowship 1940.

MILLER, WILLIAM BLACKALL ■ FAAR History of Art 51. b. May 7, 1916, Cambridge, MA. m. Margaret Koons Miller, FAAR 51. c. Charlotte D., Katherine B. BA 39, Harvard Univ.; MA 48, Columbia Univ.; PhD 62, Columbia Univ. **Research/Artistic Interests:** Palaeography-calligraphy: workshops with several British & American master scribes; the Franciscan legend in 13th-century Italian art. **Career & Employment:** RISD, Instr. 1946-51; Amherst College, Instr. 1952-56; Colby College, Prof. 1956-82. **Memberships & Offices:** CAA; Maine League of Historical Societies & Museums, Pres.; Maine Citizens for Historic Preservation, VP, Adv. Trustee; Calligraphers of Maine,

LA BELLEZZA *risulterà dalla bella forma e dalla corrispondenza del tutto alle parti, delle parte fra loro, e di quelle al tutto: conciosiache gli edificii habbiamo da parere uno intiero, e ben finito corpo: nel quale l'un membro all'altro convenga, e tutte le membra siano necessarie à quello, che si vuol fare.*

Andrea Palladio
I quattro libri dell'architettura, I, i.
1570

William Blackall Miller

Pres., BoD. **Publications:** contr., *Maine Forms of American Architecture*, ed. D. Thompson (Camden, ME: Down East, 1976); plus numerous museum catalogs & book reviews. **Exhibitions/ Performances:** Colby College Library 1989. **Home Address:** 3 Mt. Merici Ave., Waterville, ME 04901.

MILLET, FRANCIS DAVIS ■ AAR Charter Mem., Trustee 1905-12, Exec Sec. & Chief Administrator 1911-12; Journalist, Artist. b. Nov. 3, 1846. d. April 15, 1912. **Career & Employment:** *New York Herald, London Times* and *London Daily News.*

MILLON, HENRY A. ■ FAAR History of Art 60, RAAR History of Art 66; AAR Dir. 1974-77; AAR Trustee 1977-present, Vice-Chair 1982-present. b. Feb. 22, 1927, Altoona, PA. m. Judith Rice. c. Henri, Hadrian, Phoebe, Aaron. BA 47, Tulane Univ.; BS 49, Tulane Univ.; BArch 53, Tulane Univ.; MA 54, Harvard Univ.; MArch, 55, Harvard Univ.; PhD 64, Harvard Univ. **Other Study:** Belgian-American Educational Found. Seminar 1956. **Research/Artistic Interests:** History & architecture & art. **Career & Employment:** Boston Architectural Center, Lect. 1954, Design Instr. 1956-57; MIT, Instr. 1955-57, Asst. Prof. 1960-1964, Assc. Prof. 1964-1970, Prof. 1970-1980, Visiting Prof. 1981-present; Harvard Univ., Teaching Fellow 1956-57; Univ. Extension Courses, Boston, Lect. 1960-62, 1964-65; Brown Univ., Visiting Lect. 1961; *Boston Globe*, Architecture Feature Writer 1962-63; Pennsylvania State Univ., Visiting Prof. 1965; NGA, CASVA, Dean 1979-present. **Memberships & Offices:** SAH, BoD 1963-66, VP 1966-67, Pres. 1968-69; Boston Landmarks Comm. 1969-73, Vice-Chair 1971-73; Intl. Union of Academies of Archaeology, History & History of Art in Rome, Pres. 1974; AAAS 1975-present; Società Subalpina di Storia Patria, Turin, Foreign Corresponding Mem. 1975-present; Accademia delle Scienze, Turin, Foreign Mem. 1978-present; IAS 1978; *Macmillan Encyclopedia of Architects*, Ed. Bd. 1978-82; US Nat. Com. for the History of Art 1980-present; Intl. Com. for the History of Art, Alternate 1981-85, Delegate 1985-present; Dumbarton Oaks, Program in History of Landscape Architecture, Senior Fellows Com., Chair. 1983-89; Architectural Drawings Adv. Group, Convener 1983-present; Council on American Overseas Research Centers, Vice Chair. 1984-91; Getty Art History Information Program, Adv. Com. 1986-91; Architectural History Found., Ed. Bd. 1986-present; Nat. Bldg. Museum, BoT 1988-94; APS 1989-present. **Fellowships, Honors & Awards:** Frick Symposium Lect. 1956; Belgian-American Educational Found. 1956; Fulbright Fellow 1957-58; Oberlin College, Baldwin Seminar 1963; with J.J. Schiffer & I. Galantay, Boston Architectural Center Design Competition, 1st Hon. Men. 1964; ACLS Fellowship 1966, 1973; NEH Research Grant 1972, Summer Stipend Award 1978. **Publications:** "The Architectural Theory of Francesco di Giorgio," *Art Bulletin* 40 (1958): 257-61; "L'Altare maggiore della Chiesa di San Filippo Neri a Torino," *Bollettino della Società Piemontese di Archaeologia e Belle Arte* 14-15 (1960-61): 83-91; *Baroque and Rococo Architecture* (New York: Braziller, 1961); *Key Monuments of the History of Architecture* (New York: Abrams, Prentice Hall, 1964); "The Role of History of Architecture in Fascist Italy," *JSAH* 24 (1965): 53-59; "Michelangelo Garove and the Chapel of the Beato Amedeo of Savoy in the Cathedral of Vercelli," in *Essays in the History of Architecture Presented to Rudolf Wittkower*, ed. Howard Hibbard (London: Phaidon, 1967), 2:134-42; with Craig Hugh Smyth, "Michelangelo and St. Peter's I: Notes on a Plan of the Attic as Originally Built on the South Hemicycle," *Burlington Magazine* 111 (1969): 484-500; "La geometria nel linguagio architettonico di Guarino Guarini," in *Guarino Guarini e l'internazionalità del barocco*, vol. 2, ed. V. Viale (Turin: Accademia delle Scienze, 1970), 35-60;

"Rudolf Wittkower, Architectural Principles in the Age of Humanism: Its Influence on the Development and Interpretation of Modern Architecture," *JSAH* 31 (1972): 83-91; with Craig Hugh Smyth, "A Design by Michelangelo for a City Gate: Further Notes on the Lille Sketch," *Burlington Magazine* 117 (1975): 162-66; with Craig Hugh Smyth, "Michelangelo and St. Peter's II: Observations on the Interior of the Apses, a Model for the Apse Vault and Related Drawings," *Römisches Jahrbuch für Kunstgeschichte* 16 (1976): 137-206; "Vasi – Piranesi – Juvarra," in *Piranese et les Français*, ed. Georges Brunel (Rome: Edizioni dell'Elefante, 1978), 345-62; "Some New Towns in Italy in the 1930s," in *Art and Architecture in the Service of Politics*, ed. L. Nochlin & H. Millon (Cambridge, MA: MIT Press, 1978), 326-41; "A Note on Michelangelo's Facade for a Palace for Julius III in Rome: New Documents for the Model," *Burlington Magazine* 121 (1979): 770-74; "Guarino Guarini," "Filippo Juvarra," "Bernardo Vittone" & 37 other architects in *Macmillan Encyclopedia of Architects* (New York: Macmillan, 1982); *Filippo Juvarra: Drawings from the Roman Period 1704-1714* (Rome: Edizioni dell'Elefante, 1984); with Craig Hugh Smyth, *Michelangelo Architect* (Milan: Olivetti, 1988); with Craig Hugh Smyth, "Pirro Ligorio, Michelangelo, and St. Peter's," in *Pirro Ligorio Artist and Antiquarian*, ed. Robert W. Gaston (Milan: Silvana Editoriale, 1988), 216-86; "Filippo Juvarra, New Drawings," in *An Architectural Progress in the Renaissance and Baroque*, ed. H. Millon & G.S. Munshower (University Park: Pennsylvania State Univ., Dept. of Art History, 1992), 2:566-610; ed., with Vittorio Lampugnani, *The Renaissance from Brunelleschi to Michelangelo* (Milan: Bompiani, 1994). **Bio-Bibliography:** *Who's Who in America.* **Business Address:** CASVA, NGA, Washington, DC 20565.

MINNICH, NELSON H. ■ FAAR Post-Classical/Humanistic Studies 80. b. Jan. 15, 1942, Cincinnati, OH. BA 65, Boston College; MA 69, Boston College; STB 70, Gregorian Univ., Rome; PhD 77, Harvard Univ. **Career & Employment:** Loyola Acad., Wilmette, IL, Instr. 1966-68; Harvard Univ., TF & TA 1972-73, 1974-77; Catholic Univ., Asst. Prof. 1977-83, Assc. Prof. 1983-93, Prof. 1993-present, Acting Chair 1978, 1985, Chair 1979,

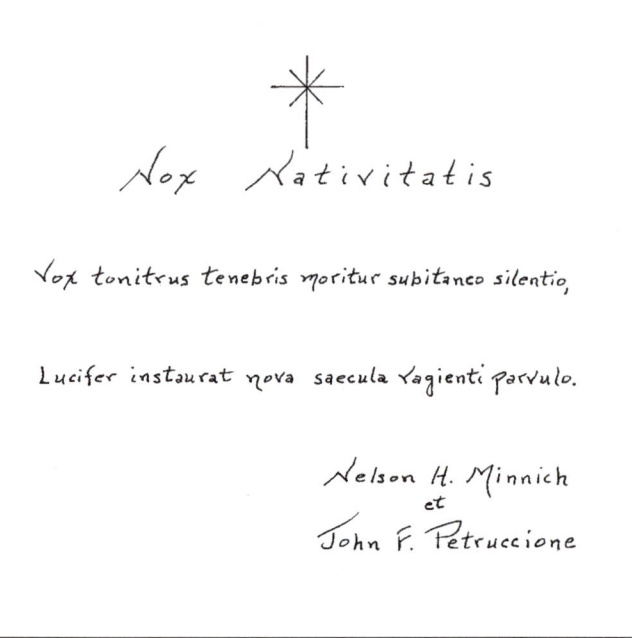

Nelson H. Minnich

1987-89. **Memberships & Offices:** *Catholic Historical Review,* Assc. Ed. 1977-90, Adv. Ed. 1991-present; *Melville Studies in Church History,* Ed. 1988-present. **Fellowships, Honors & Awards:** Found. for Reformation Research, Junior Fellow 1971; Harvard Univ. Scholarship 1971-73, 1974-76, Emerton Fellowship 1972-73, Traveling Fellowship 1973-74; Sixteenth-Century Studies Conference, Carl Meyer Prize 1977; NEH, Summer Stipend 1978, Translation Grant 1986; Villa I Tatti, Fellowship 1979; ACLS, Research Fellowship 1979-80, Travel Grant 1986, Research Fellowship 1990; Richard Krautheimer Scholarship, Research Grant 1980; APS, Research Grant 1984; Catholic Univ., Faculty Research Grant 1990, 1993, 1994. **Publications:** with William W. Meissner, M.D. "The Character of Erasmus," *American Historical Review* 83 (1978): 598-624, 84 (1979): 907-909; "The Healing of the Pisan Schism (1511-13)," *Annuarium Historiae Conciliorum* 16 (1984): 59-192; ed., with Robert B. Eno, S.S., & Robert Trisco, *Studies in Catholic History in Honor of John Tracy Ellis* (Wilmington, DE: Michael Glazier, 1985); "The Autobiography of Antonio degli Agli (ca. 1400-77), Humanist and Prelate," *Renaissance Studies in Honor of Craig Hugh Smyth,* ed. Andrew Morrogh et al., 2 vols., Villa I Tatti: Harvard University Center for Italian Renaissance Studies 7 (Florence: Giunti Barbera, 1985), 1:177-91; "Erasmus and the Fifth Lateran Council (1512-17)," in *Erasmus of Rotterdam, The Man and the Scholar: Proceedings of the Symposium Held at the Erasmus University, Rotterdam, 9-11 November 1986,* ed. Jan Sperna Weiland & Willem Th.H. Frijhoff (Leiden: E.J. Brill, 1988), 46-60; "On the Origins of Eck's 'Enchiridion,'" in *Johannes Eck (1486-1543) im Streit der Jahrhunderte: Internationales Symposium der Gesellschaft zur Herausgabe des Corpus Catholicorum aus Anlass des 500. Geburtstages des Johannes Eck vom 13. bis 16. November 1986 in Ingolstadt und Eichstätt,* ed. Erwin Iserloh, Reformationsgeschichtliche Studien und Texte 127 (Münster: Aschendorff, 1988), 37-73; "The Proposals for an Episcopal College at Lateran V," in *Ecclesia Militans: Studien zur Konzilien und Reformationsgeschichte. Remigius Bäumer zum 70. Geburtstag gewidmet,* ed. Walter Brandmüller, Herbert Immenkötter & Erwin Iserloh, 2 vols. (Paderborn: Ferdinand Schöningh, 1988), 1:213-32; "Alexios Celadenus: A Disciple of Bessarion in Renaissance Italy," *Culture, Society and Religion in Early Modern Europe: Essays by the Students and Colleagues of William J. Bouwsma,* ed. Ellery Schalk, Historical Reflections 15 (1988): 47-64; "The Debate Between Desiderius Erasmus of Rotterdam and Alberto Pio of Carpi on the Use of Sacred Images," *Annuarium Historiae Conciliorum* 20 (1988): 379-413; "Prophecy and the Fifth Lateran Council (1512-17)," in *Prophetic Rome in the High Renaissance Period,* ed. Marjorie E. Reeves, Oxford-Warburg Studies (Oxford: Clarendon Press, 1992), 63-87; *The Fifth Lateran Council (1512-17): Studies on Its Membership, Diplomacy, and Proposals for Reform* (Aldershot, England: Variorum, 1993); *The Catholic Reformation: Council, Churchmen, and Controversies* (Aldershot, England: Variorum, 1993). **Bio-Bibliography:** *Directory of American Scholars; Who's Who in the East.* **Home Address:** 5713 37th Ave., Hyattsville, MD 20782.

MINOTT, CHARLES I. ■ FAAR History of Art 64; AAR Juror 1972. b. June 16, 1932, Melrose, PA. c. Alexander, Nicolas. BFA 54, Massachusetts College of Art; MA 59, UNC, Chapel Hill; MFA 60, Princeton Univ.; PhD 67, Princeton Univ. **Research/Artistic Interests:** Medieval & northern Renaissance art history. **Career & Employment:** Univ. of Pittsburgh, Instr. 1964-66; Univ. of Pennsylvania, Asst.-Assc.-Prof. 1966-present. **Memberships & Offices:** CAA; Intl. Center for Medieval Art; IAS, Assn. of Members. **Fellowships, Honors & Awards:** CAA, Arthur Kingsley Porter Prize 1969; IAS 1972-73. **Publications:**

Martin Schöngauer (New York: Collectors Editions, 1971); *Albrecht Durer: The Early Graphic Work,* exb. cat. (Princeton: Museum of Art, 1971); *History of Art* (New York: Harper Collins, 1992). **Home Address:** 708 S. Mildred St., Philadelphia, PA 19147. **Business Address:** Dept. of History of Art, Univ. of Pennsylvania, 3440 Market St., No. 560, Philadelphia, PA 19104.

MIRICK, HENRY D. ■ FAAR Architecture 33. b. Aug. 6, 1905, Washington, DC. m. Marion Winsor. c. Marion, Dustin, Heath, Richard. BA 27, Princeton Univ.; BArch 30, Univ. of Pennsylvania; MArch 31, Univ. of Pennsylvania. **Other Study:** Harry Sternfeld 1931-33. **Career & Employment:** Self-employed 1933-35; Kneedler, Mirick & Zantzinger 1935-42; US Army 1942-45; Mirick Pearson, Batcheler 1945-present. **Memberships & Offices:** AIA, Philadelphia Chap., Pres. 1970. **Fellowships, Honors & Awards:** AIA, Fellow 1971; various awards for completed architectural projects. **Publications:** "Large Bath," in *Hadrian's Villa,* Memoirs of the AAR (1932). **Important Works:** Penwalt Tower, Philadelphia; Nat. Bd. of Medical Examiners, Philadelphia; Friends Select School, Philadelphia; Shipley School & Episcopal Acad., Suburban Philadelphia; Dunwoody, Cathedral Village, Medford Leas Retirement Communities; Humming Bird House, African Plains, Philadelphia Zoo; Bryn Mawr, Jefferson Methodist, Univ. of Pennsylvania Hospitals; St. Christopher's Church, Gladwyn, PA; Church of the Redeemer, Bryn Mawr, PA; Home & Museum for Dr. Albert Barnes, Art Collector. **Exhibitions/Performances:** AIA, Philadelphia Chap. 1987. **Bio-Bibliography:** *Who's Who in America.* **Home Address:** 101 Cherry Ln., Box 671, Ardmore, PA 19003. **Business Address:** Mirick Pearson Batcheler, Philadelphia, PA 19003.

MIRRA, TINA ■ AAR – Rome, Library Asst.

MISS, MARY M. ■ RAAR Architecture 89; AAR Trustee 1989-present. b. May 27, 1944, NYC. m. George Peck. BA 66, UC, Santa Barbara; MFA 68, Maryland Art Inst. **Career & Employment:** Yale Univ., Davenport Visiting Prof 1991; School of Visual Arts, NYC; Cooper Union; Sarah Lawrence College; Hunter College, CUNY; Pratt Inst.; Univ. of Rhode Island, Visiting Lect. **Fellowships, Honors & Awards:** NYSCA, CAPS Grant 1973, 1976; Mott Community College, Flint, MI, Project Grant 1974; NEA 1974, 1975, 1984; Brandeis Univ., Creative Arts Award 1982; Guggenheim Fellowship 1986; AIA, Medal of Honor 1990; with Studio Works, *Progressive Architecture,* Urban Design Award 1992; NYC Parks Council, Philip N. Winslow Landscape Design Award 1992. **Publications:** *On a Redefinition of Public Sculpture,* Perspecta 21 (1984). **Important Works:** 13th Winter Olympics, Veiled Landscape, Lake Placid, NY 1979; Hills & Dales Park, Staged Gates, Dayton, OH 1979; Fogg Museum, Harvard Univ., Mirror Way 1980; Governor's State Univ., Field Rotation, Park Forest South, IL 1980-81; Laumeier Sculpture Park, Pool Complex, Orchard Valley, St. Louis, MO 1982-85; Inst. of Contemporary Art, Study for a Courtyard, London 1983; with Stanton Eckstut & Susan Child, Battery Park City Waterfront Park, NYC 1983-88; Univ. Hospital, Reflecting Pools, Walkways & Pergola, Seattle 1986-90; Architectural Assn., Pavilion-Locator, London 1987; with Michael Kelly, Hayden Sq., Tempe, AZ 1987; with Adele Santos, Albright College, Art Center Grounds & Central Court, Reading, PA 1987-91; with Billie Tsien & Tod Williams, Three-Sided Telephone Booth, American Crafts Museum, NYC 1988. **Exhibitions/Performances:** 55 Mercer Gallery, NYC 1971, 1972; Salvatore Ala Gallery, Milan 1975; Rosa Esman Gallery, NYC 1975; MOMA 1976; Max Protetch Gallery, NYC 1980; Arts Roslyn, NY 1980; Brown Univ. & Univ. of Rhode Island,

Kingston 1981; Laumeier Sculpture Park, St. Louis, MO 1982; Inst. of Contemporary Art, London 1983; Protetch-McNeil Gallery, NYC 1984; Danforth Museum of Art, Framingham, MA 1986; Architectural Assn., London 1987; Harvard GSD 1990, 1991. **Bio-Bibliography:** Lucy Lippard, "In and Out of the Public Domain," *Studio International* 193.986 (Mar.-Apr. 1977): 85-89; Ronald J. Onorato, *Mary Miss: Perimeters/Pavilions/Decoys*, exb. cat. (Roslyn, NY: Nassau County Museum, 1979); Rosalind E. Krauss, "Sculpture in the Expanded Field," *October* 8 (Spring 1979); Phyllis Tuchman, *Mary Miss: Interior Works 1966-1980* (Kingston, RI: Bell Gallery, Univ. of Rhode Island, 1981); Kate Linker, *Mary Miss*, exb. cat. (London: Inst. of Contemporary Art, 1983); Joseph Giovaninni, *Mary Miss: Projects 1966-1987* (London: Architectural Assn., 1987); Hugh M. Davies & Ronald J. Onorato, *"Sitings,"* exb. cat. (La Jolla, CA: Museum of Contemporary Art, 1986); Roberta Smith, *On Site 3: St. Louis Sculptures*, exb. cat. (St. Louis, MO: First Street Forum, 1986); Alvin Boyarsky, *Mary Miss: Projects 1966-1987*, exb. cat. (London: Architectural Assn., 1983). **Home Address:** PO Box 304, NYC 10013.

MITCHELL, CHARLES ■ RAAR History of Art 66. b. Jan. 25, 1912, Ealing, London, England. m. Prudence Yalden Thomson, Jean Flower. c. Simon Edward, John Burnett. BA 34, St. Johns College; B.Litt. 39, St. Johns College; MA 43, St. Johns College. **Career & Employment:** Warburg Inst., Univ. of London, Lect. 1945-60; Bowdoin College, Visiting Prof. 1956-57, 1980-82; Bryn Mawr College, Visiting Prof. 1959-60, Prof. 1960-80, Andrew Mellon Prof. 1975-80, Prof. Emer. 1980-present; Smith College, Visiting Prof. 1975; Williams College, Visiting Prof. 1982; NGA, Kress Prof. 1984-85. **Fellowships, Honors & Awards:** Royal Historical Soc., Fellow; ACLS Fellow 1964-65; Guggenheim Fellow 1970-71; Bowdoin College, Hon. Degree 1970; Lindback Found. Award 1974. **Publications:** *Seaman's Portrait* (London: Collins, 1939); *A Book of Ships* (Harmondsworth: Penguin, 1940); *Hogarth's Peregrination* (Oxford: Clarendon, 1952); *A Fifteenth-Century Italian Plutarch* (London: Faber & Faber, New York: Yoseloff, 1961); *Felice Feliciano Antiquarius* (London: British Acad., 1962); with Erna Mandowsky, *Pirro Ligorio's Roman Antiquities* (London: Warburg Inst., 1963); with E.W. Bodner, *Cyriacus of Ancona's Journeys in the Propontis and the Northern Aegean 1444-1445* (Philadelphia: APS, 1976); and numerous articles. **Home Address:** 21 Cowley Rd., Littlemore, Oxford OX4 4LE, England.

MITCHELL, S. WEIR ■ AAR Charter Mem.

MITTELSTADT, ROBERT J. ■ FAAR Architecture 64. b. Aug. 16, 1935, Racine, WI. c. Paul, Sarah. BA 59, Univ. of Minnesota, Minneapolis; MArch 64, Yale Univ. **Career & Employment:** Harry Weese & Asscs., Designer 1960; Eero Saarinen & Asscs., Drafter 1960-62; Paul M. Rudolph, Architect, Drafter 1962-64; Robert Mittelstadt, Architect, Owner 1966-pressent; UC, Berkeley, Lect. 1968-79; Stanford Univ. Architecture Pgm., Assc. Prof. & Dir. 1973-77; California Polytechnic Univ., Prof. & Chair 1977-79; Hellmuth Obata & Kassabaum, Senior VP, Design Dir. 1980-81; Catholic Univ., Lect. 1982-83; Gensler & Asscs., Designer 1983-84; Okamoto Murata Mittelstadt, Part. 1985-90. **Fellowships, Honors & Awards:** Fulbright Fellow 1964. **Publications:** "Homage to the Mall," *Archetype* (Summer 1980): 7-8; "Casa Mittelstadt," *Arquitectura* (Jan. 1980): 43. **Important Works:** Freemont Civic Center, CA 1969; Cantor Rodin Sculpture Garden, Stanford Univ. 1985; Hawthorne Plaza Office Tower, San Francisco 1988; Weersing Residence, Pescadero,

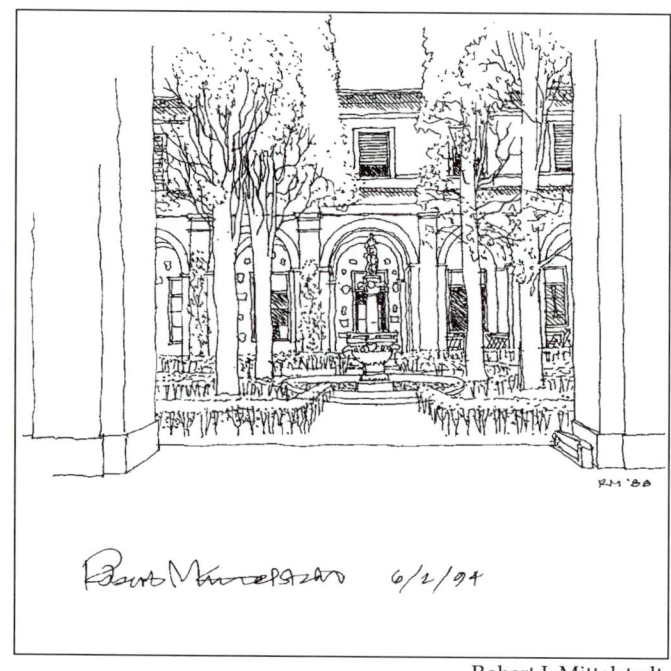

Robert J. Mittelstadt

CA 1995. **Exhibitions/Performances:** San Francisco Museum of Art; San Jose Museum of Art; ALNY 1966. **Bio-Bibliography:** *Architecture + Urbanism* (Jan. 1977); *Public Landscape* (New York: McGraw-Hill, 1978); *Global Architecture* 11. **Business Address:** 725 Filbert St., San Francisco, CA 94133.

MOBBERLEY, JAMES C. ■ FAAR Musical Composition 90. b. June 10, 1954, Des Moines, IA. m. Laura S. Moore. c. Lucas, Jacob. BA 78, UNC, Chapel Hill; MM 80, UNC, Chapel Hill; DMA 82, Cleveland Inst. of Music. **Career & Employment:** Cleveland Inst. of Music 1980-82; Webster Univ., Visiting Asst. Prof. 1982-83; Univ. of Missouri, Kansas City, Asst. Prof. 1983-88, Assc. Prof. 1988-91, Prof. 1992-present, Music Production & Computer Technology Center, Dir. 1988-present; Kansas City Symphony, Composer-in-Residence 1991-present. **Memberships & Offices:** ASCAP; College Music Soc.; Music Teachers Nat. Assn.; Soc. of Composers; Soc. for Electro-Acoustic Music in the US; American Music Center; Composers Forum; Missouri Music Teachers Assn. **Fellowships, Honors & Awards:** Mid-America State Universities Assn., Honor Lect. 1987-88; Missouri Music Teachers Assn., Composer of the Year 1987; Music Teachers Nat. Assn., Distinguished Composer of the Year 1988; ASCAP Award 1988-89, 1990-91, 1991-92, 1992-93; UKC Trustees Faculty Research Award 1991; Lee Ettelson Composer's Award 1991; Guggenheim Fellowship 1992; Barlow Endowment Comm. 1992-93; NEA Composers Fellowship 1993-94, Meet-the-Composer Residency 1994-97. **Publications:** with Earl Henry, *Musicianship* (New York: Prentice-Hall, 1986). **Important Works:** *A Plurality of One*, for clarinet & electronic tape (MMB Music) 1982; *Going with the Fire*, for flute & electronic tape, Mary Posses Comm. (EDIPAN) 1985; *#2146 in a Series*, dance & electronic tape, Susan Warden Dancers Comm. (Cautious Music) 1986; *Beams!*, for trombone & electronic tape (Modern Editions) 1986; *Caution to the Winds*, for piano & electronic tape (EDIPAN) 1987; *Critical Mass*, for organ & electronic tape, Cleveland Museum of Art Comm. (Cautious Music) 1989; *Soggiorno*, for violin & electronic tape, St. Louis Symphony Orchestra Comm. (EDIPAN) 1989; *Spontaneous Combustion*, for saxophone & tape, Timothy Timmons Comm. (Cautious Music) 1991; *Toccatas & Interludes,* for chamber ensemble, SUNY, Stony Brook Comm. (Cautious Music) 1991; *Déjà Voyages,* for orchestra, Kansas City Symphony Comm. 1992; *Concerto for Piano and Orchestra,* Guggenheim & Barlow Comm. 1994; *TNT (Turetzky 'N' Tape),* for contrabass & electronic tape, NEA & Guggenheim Comm. 1994. **Home Address:** 3715 Harrison, Kansas City, MO 64109.

MOE, HENRY ALLEN ■ AAR Trustee 1942-75; Guggenheim Found., Lawyer; Found. Pres.

MOEVS, MARIA TERESA MARABINI ■ FAAR Classics/ Archaeology 64; Fulbright Fellow to Academy 1951-52; AAR, Italian Fulbright Awards, Selection Com. 1964. b. Jan. 31, 1926, Rome, Italy. m. Robert Moevs, FAAR 55. c. Marina, Christian. Dipl. 43, Liceo Classico; Laurea 47, Univ. of Bologna; PhD 51, Univ. of Rome. **Other Study:** Italian Archaeological School, Athens 1950-51; Archaeological excavations: Phaistos, Crete 1950, Cosa 1952. **Career & Employment:** Liceo Classico, Rome, Teacher 1947-52; Inspector of Antiquities, Ministry of Education, Italy, Syracuse & Padua 1952-53; Central Restoration Inst., Rome, Inspector 1953-55; Harvard Univ., Instr. 1956-57; Douglass College, Instr. 1965-68, Asst. Prof. 1968-72, Assc. Prof. 1972-77, Prof. 1977-81; Rutgers Univ., Prof. 1981-91. **Memberships & Offices:** ArIA; Rei Cretariae Romanae Fautores; Mary Bunting Inst., Soc. of Fellows; IAS, Assn. of Members; Fulbright Grants, National Screening Com. 1978-79, 1982-83; ArIA, Princeton Soc., Pres. 1986-89. **Fellowships, Honors & Awards:** Italian Archaeological School, Rome, Italian Government Fellowship 1947-50; Italian Archaeological School, Athens, Fellow 1950-51; Italian Foreign Ministry Research Scholarship 1952; APS Grant 1961, 1979; Radcliffe Inst., Assc. Scholar 1962-64; Univ. of Bologna, Carduccci Prize 1967; Rutgers Univ., Research Council Grant 1967, 1971, 1984; Goffredo Bellonci Special Prize for Literary Criticism 1977; IAS 1977-78; NEH Grant 1986-87. **Publications:** *Fra Marmo Pario e Archeologia: L'Antichità nella vita e nell'opera di Giosuè Carducci* (Bologna: Cappelli, 1971); *The Roman Thin-Walled Pottery from Cosa (1948-1954),* Memoirs of the AAR 32 (Rome: AAR, 1973); *Gabriele D'Annunzio e le estetiche della fine del secolo* (L'Aquila: Japadre, 1976); "The Italo-Megarian Ware from Cosa," *Memoirs of the AAR* 34 (1980): 157-228; "Aco in Northern Etruria," *Memoirs of the AAR* 34 (1980): 231-80; "Le Muse di Ambracia," *Bollettino d'Arte* 12 (1981): 1-59; "Gabriele D'Annunzio e L'Arte Classica," in *D'Annunzio, la Musica e le Arti Figurative,* Quaderni del Vittoriale 6 (1982): 151-70; Il Kalathos Alessandrino di Bologna," *Bollettino d'Arte* 22 (1983): 1-42; "Gabriele D'Annunzio fra Winckelmann e Schliemann," in *D'Annunzio e la Cultura Germanica* (Pescara: Centro Nazionale di Studi Dannunziani, 1984), 63-74; "Penteterìs e le Tre Horai nella Pompa di Tolomeo Filadelfo," *Bollettino d'Arte* 42 (1987): 1-36; "D'Annunzio e Schopenhauer," in *D'Annunzio a Yale,* Quaderni Dannunziani 3-4 (1988): 263-82; "Ephemeral Alexandria: The Pagentry of the Ptolemaic Court and Its Documentation," in Eius Virtutis Studiosi, *Classical and Postclassical Studies in Memory of Frank Edward Brown,* ed. R.T. Scott & Ann Scott (Washington, DC: NGA, 1993): 123-47; "Strategos and Savior: A Portrait of Ptolemy I in Baltimore," *Bollettino d'Arte* 77 (1993): 1-28. **Home Address:** 1640 River Rd., Blackwell's Mills, Belle Mead, NJ 08502.

MOEVS, ROBERT W. ■ FAAR Musical Composition 55, RAAR Musical Composition 61; AAR Composition Jury 1956, 1962. b. Dec. 2, 1920, La Crosse, WI. m. Maria T. Marabini, FAAR 64. c. Marina, Christian. BA 42, Harvard College; MA 52, Harvard Univ. **Other Study:** with Walter Piston, Harvard 1938-42, Écoles

d'Art, Fontainebleau 1946; Nadia Boulanger, Paris 1946-51; Conservatoire National de Musique, Paris 1947-51. **Career & Employment:** US Air Force, Pilot 1942-47; Harvard Univ., Instr. 1955-57, Asst. Prof. 1957-63, Dir. of Undergraduate Studies in Music 1958-60, Curator of Ancient Instruments Collection; Rutgers Univ., Assc. Prof. 1964-67, Prof. 1968-75, Workshop Dir. of Contemporary Chamber Ensemble 1966-68, Chair of Music, New Brunswick 1974-80, Prof. II 1975-90, Prof. Emer. 1991-present. **Memberships & Offices:** Concours Intl. de Composition, Prince Ranier III de Monaco, Pre-Jury & Jury Mem. 1961; ISCM, Exec. Com. American Section 1967-70; American Soc. of Univ. Composers, Founding Mem.; ASCAP; AMC; New Jersey Guild of Composers. **Fellowships, Honors & Awards:** AAAS Award 1956; Guggenheim Fellowship 1963-64; ASCAP Award 1967 & successive years; Stockhausen Intl. Prize in Composition, Italy 1978. **Publications:** "Some Observations on Instruction in Music Theory," *College Music Symposium* 6 (1966): 69-71; "Music and Liturgy," *Liturgical Arts* 38.1 (1969): 4-9; "Intervallic Procedures in Debussy," *Perspectives of New Music* 8.1 (1969): 82-101; "Mannerism and Stylistic Consistency in Stravinsky," *Perspectives of New Music* 9.2 (1971): 92-103; with Ellen Rosand, "Nadia Boulanger," *Nineteenth Century Music* 3.3 (Mar. 1980): 276-78; "Music and the Liturgy," *CCICA Annual* (Notre Dame, IN: CCICA, 1983), 39-40. **Important Works:** *Fourteen Variations for Orchestra,* Koussevitzky Found. Comm. 1952; *Three Symphonic Pieces,* Cleveland Orchestra Comm. 1955; *Attis,* for chorus, percussion & orchestra, Boston Symphony Orchestra Comm. 1958; *Attis, Part II,* 1963; *Et Occidentem Illustra,* for chorus & orchestra, Rutgers Univ. Comm. for Boston Symphony Orchestra 1964; *Main-Travelled Roads, Symphonic Piece No. 4,* Wisconsin American Revolution Bicentennial Comm. 1973; *The Aulos Player,* for soprano solo, 2 choruses & 2 organs Trinity Church, NYC Comm. 1975; *Ludi Praeteriti: Games of the Past,* for 2 pianos, Middelsex County (NJ) Cultural & Heritage Comm. 1976; *Una Collana Musicale,* for piano (CRI) 1977; *Prometheus: Music for Small Orchestra,* Harvard Univ. Bach Soc. Orchestra Comm. 1980; *Trio for Violin, Cello and Piano,* Naumburg Found. Comm. 1980; *Three Pieces for Violin and Piano,* Auriol-Fauchet Duo Comm. 1982; *String Quartet No. 2,*

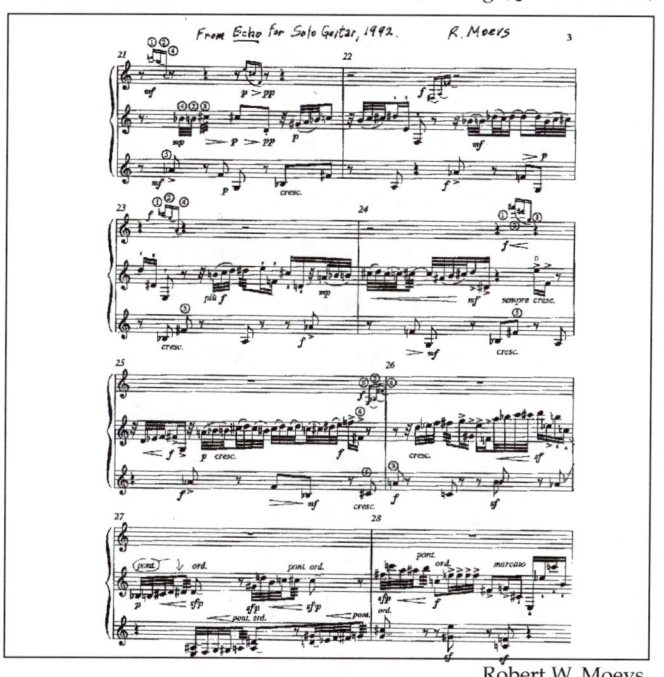

Robert W. Moevs

SUNY, Stony Brook Comm. 1989; *Musica da Camera III: Daphne,* Bennington, VT, Composers Forum Comm. 1992; *Conun.drum,* for 5 percussion players, NJ Percussion Ensemble Comm. 1993. **Bio-Bibliography:** N. Slonimsky, *Music Since 1900* (1971); James Boros, "The Systematic Chromaticism of Robert Moevs," *Perspectives of New Music* 28.1 (1990): 294-323, 324-35; H. Pollack, *Harvard Composers: Walter Piston and His Students* (Metuchen, NJ, 1992), 323-32; *Baker's Dictionary; Dictionary of American Composers; Dictionary of Contemporary Music; Dictionary of International Biography; Harvard Concise Dictionary of Music; New Grove's Dictionary of Music; Who's Who in America; Who's Who in American Music; Who's Who in Entertainment.* **Home Address:** 1640 River Rd., Blackwell's Mills, Belle Mead, NJ 08502.

MOHOLY-NAGY, SIBYL ■ AAR Visitor 1959 — 1964.

MOIR, ALFRED ■ RAAR History of Art 70, 80; AAR Adv. Council 1983-88. b. Apr. 14, 1924, Minneapolis, MN. BA 48, Harvard Univ.; MA 49, Harvard Univ.; PhD 53, Harvard Univ. **Other Study:** Univ. of Rome 1950-51. **Research/Artistic Interests:** Baroque art, particularly drawing & painting; Caravaggio & his followers, Anthony Van Dyck, Old Master drawings. **Career & Employment:** Newcomb College, Tulane Univ., Instr. 1952-54, Asst. Prof. 1954-58, Assc. Prof. 1958-62; UC, Santa Barbara, Prof. 1962-91, Prof. Emer. 1991-present, Chair 1963-69, Education Abroad Program in Italy, Dir. 1978-80, Art Museum, Adj. Curator 1987-93. **Memberships & Offices:** Delgado Museum, New Orleans, Acquisitions Consultant 1953-59; Art Assn. of New Orleans, BoD 1957-62; Harvard Club of Louisiana, VP & Pres. 1957-62; Friends of Louisiana State Museum, VP 1960-62; Art Affiliates, Santa Barbara, BoD 1963-71; NEH Consultant 1971-78; Southern California Art Historians, Pres. 1960s; Blake School, Outstandng Alumnus Award 1993. **Fellowships, Honors & Awards:** Fulbright Fellowship 1950-51; Harvard Univ., Edward R. Bacon Fellowship 1950-52; Tulane Univ., Hon. Alumnus 1962. **Publications:** *The Italian Followers of Caravaggio* (Cambridge, MA: Harvard Univ. Press, 1967); *Drawings by Seventeenth-Century Masters from the Collection of Janos Scholz* (Santa Barbara: UC Art Galleries, 1974); *European Drawings in the Santa Barbara Museum of Art* (Seattle: Univ. of Washington Press, 1976); *Caravaggio and His Copyists,* CAA Monograph (New York: NYU Press, 1976); *Regional Styles of Drawing in Italy* (Santa Barbara: UC Museum, 1977); *Caravaggio,* Library of Great Painters Series (New York: Abrams, 1982); *Old Master Drawings from the Feitelson Collection* (Santa Barbara: UC Museum, 1983); *Old Master Drawings from the Collection of John & Alice Steiner* (Santa Barbara: Santa Barbara Museum of Art, 1986); *Van Dyck's Antwerp* (Antwerp: Stedlijke Museum, 1991); *Anthony Van Dyck* (New York: Abrams, 1994). **Bio-Bibliography:** *Who's Who in America, Who's Who in American Art.* **Home Address:** 51 Seaview Dr., Santa Barbara, CA 93108.

MONDALE, JOAN ADAMS ■ AAR Visitor 1977-78, Wife of US Vice President.

MONFASANI, JOHN ■ FAAR Post-Classical/Humanistic Studies 71. b. July 5, 1943, NYC. m. Adrianne J. Fazio. c. Alex, Cristina, Mark. BA 65, Fordham Univ.; MA 66, Columbia Univ.; PhD 73, Columbia Univ. **Other Study:** Scuola Vaticana di Paleografia e Diplomatica 1971. **Career & Employment:** Rutgers Univ., Lect. 1968-69; SUNY, Albany, Lect. 1971-73, Asst. Prof. 1973-80, Assc. Prof. 1980-87, Prof. 1987-present. **Memberships & Offices:** RSA, Exec. Dir. 1995-present; American Reformation Soc.; Intl. Soc. for the History of Rhetoric; MAA; Soc. for the History of Medieval & Renaissance Philosophy; AHA.

Fellowships, Honors & Awards: Woodrow Wilson Found. Fellowship 1969-70 (declined); Fulbright Fellowship 1969-70; SUNY, Research Found. Fellowship 1973, Travel Grant 1975, 1987, 1988, 1991; Villa I Tatti Fellow 1973-74, 1982-83; NEH Junior Fellowship 1976, Travel Grant 1991, Senior Fellowship 1993; ACLS Fellowship 1977; MAA, John Nicholas Brown Prize 1980; Guggenheim Fellow 1980-81; SUNY, Albany, Excellence in Research Award 1982; Leopold Schepp Found. Fellow 1982-83; APS Travel Grant 1987; IAS, Fellow 1987-88; RSA, William Nelson Prize 1988; Venetian Acad. of Science "Ateneo Veneto," Fellow 1992. **Publications:** *George of Trebizond: A Biography and a Study of His Rhetoric and Logic,* Columbia Studies in the Classical Tradition 1 (Leiden: E.J. Brill, 1976); *Collectanea Trapezuntiana: Texts, Documents, and Bibliographies of George of Trebizond,* Medieval & Renaissance Texts & Studies 25; RSA, Renaissance Texts Series 8 (Binghamton, NY: SUNY Press, 1984); ed., with J. Hankins & F. Purnell, Jr., *Supplementum Festivum: Studies in Honor of Paul Oskar Kristeller,* Medieval & Renaissance Texts & Studies 49 (Binghamton, NY: SUNY Press, 1987); ed., with Ronald G. Musto, *Renaissance Society and Culture: Essays in Honor of Eugene F. Rice. Jr.* (New York: Italica Press, 1991); "Hermes Trismegistus, Rome, and the Myth of Europa: An Unknown Text of Giles of Viterbo," *Viator* 22 (1991): 311-42; "A Theologian at the Roman Curia in the Mid-Quattrocento: A Bio-bibliographical Study of Niccolò Palmieri, O.S.A.," *Analecta Augustiniana* 54 (1991): 321-81, 55 (1992): 5-98; *Fernando of Cordova: A Biographical and Intellectual Profile,* Transactions of the APS 82.6 (Philadelphia: APS, 1992); *Language and Learning in Renaissance Italy: Selected Essays* (Adershot, Hampshire: Variorum, 1994); "The Averroism of John Argyropoulos and His *Quaestio utrum intellectus humanus sit perpetuus,*" *I Tatti Studies: Essays in the Renaissance* 5 (1993): 157-208; "Aristotelians, Platonists, and the Missing Ockhamists: Philosophical Liberty in Pre-Reformation Italy," *Renaissance Quarterly* 46 (1993): 247-76; "L'insegnamento di Teodoro Gaza a Ferrara," in *Alla corte degli Estensi: Filosofia, arte e cultura a Ferrara nei secoli XV e XVI. Atti del convegno internazionale di studi, Ferrara, 5-7 marzo 1992,* ed. Marco Bertozzi (Ferrara: Università degli Studi, 1994): 5-17; *Byzantine Scholars in Renaissance Italy: Cardinal Bessarion and Other Emigrés: Selected Essays* (Aldershot, Hampshire: Variorum, 1995). **Business Address:** Dept. of History, SUNY, Albany, NY 12222.

MONGAN, AGNES ■ RAAR History of Art 50, 51. b. 1905, Somerville, MA. BA 27, Bryn Mawr College; MA 29, Smith College; LHD 41, Smith College; LittD 54, Wheaton College. **Other Study:** Fogg Museum 1928-29; Univ. of Massachusetts, LHD 1970. **Career & Employment:** Fogg Art Museum, Research Asst 1929-37, Keeper of Drawings 1937-47, Curator of Drawings 1947-75, Asst. Dir. 1951-64, Assc. Dir. 1964-68, Acting Dir. 1968-69, Dir. 1969-71, Consultant 1972-present; Harvard Univ., Martin A. Ryerson Lect. 1960-75; Timken Art Gallery, San Diego, Visiting Dir. 1971-72; Northwestern Univ., Kreeger-Wolf Distinguished Visiting Prof. 1976; Univ. of Louisville, Bingham Visiting Prof. 1976; Univ. of Texas, Austin, Waggoner Visiting Prof. 1977, Visiting Prof. 1981; NGA, Samuel H. Kress Prof.-in-Residence 1977-78; UC, Santa Barbara, Visiting Prof. 1979; Metropolitan Museum and Art Centers, Coral Gables, FL, Visiting Dir. 1980. **Fellowships, Honors & Awards:** Inst. of Intl. Education Grant 1935; Palms d'Academie, Paris 1949; Oberlin College, Baldwin Seminar Lecture Series 1966; Mt. Holyoke College, Amy Sackler Memorial Lectureship 1966-67; Hon. DFA: LaSalle College 1973, Colby College 1973, Univ. of Notre Dame 1980, Boston College 1985; Cavaliere Ufficiale, Italy 1971; St. Botolph Club Award 1977; Julius Stratton Award 1978;

Harvard Univ., Signet Soc. Medal 1986, 350th Anniversary Medal 1986; Vatican, Benemerenti Medal 1987; Women's Caucus for the Arts 1987. **Publications:** with Paul J. Sachs, *Drawings in the Fogg Museum of Art*, 2 vols. (Cambridge, MA: Harvard Univ. Press, 1940); *Ingres: Twenty-four Drawings* (New York: Pantheon, 1947); ed., *One Hundred Master Drawings* (Cambridge, MA: Harvard Univ. Press, 1949); *French Drawings from the Thirteenth Century to 1919*, Great Drawings of All Times, ed. Ira Moskowitz, vol. 3 (New York: Shorewood, 1962); "On Silverpoint Drawings and the Subject of Left-Handedness," in *Drawings Defined* (New York: Abaris, 1987); "A Brief History of Italian Drawings at Harvard," in *The Famous Italian Drawings at the Fogg Art Museum in Cambridge* (Milan: Riunione Adriatica di Sicurtà, 1988); "Recollections of French Drawings from Clouet to Matisse," *Master Drawings* 28.3 (1990); plus numerous journal articles. **Home Address:** c/o Harvard Univ. Art Museums, 32 Quincy St., Cambridge, MA 02138.

MONTANA SICARI, MARA FRANCESCA ■ Italian Fulbright Fellow 1960-61.

MOORE, ANNA M. ■ FAAR Classics/Archaeology 90; AAR Classical Soc. b. May 7, 1949, Shreveport, LA. m. Jack P. Janetatos. c. Lydia. Schoeck. BA 82, George Washington Univ.; MA 86, Princeton Univ. **Other Study:** ASCSA 1984. **Career & Employment:** FBI, Sec. 1968-72; ITT-Electrophysics Lab, Sec. 1972-73; Baker & McKenzie, Legal Sec. 1973-82; Smithsonian Inst., Research Asst. 1990-92; *Archeomaterials*, Staff Ed. 1992-93; George Washington Univ., Lect. 1993-95. **Memberships & Offices:** ArlA. **Fellowships, Honors & Awards:** Ione May Spears Travel Grant 1987; Stanley J. Seeger Found. Fellowship 1984, 1986; Robert Simpson Fund, Fellowship 1985. **Home Address:** 206 Wolfe St., Alexandria, VA 22314.

MOORE, CHARLES ■ AAR Charter Mem., Trustee 1905; Bank Exec.

MOORE, CHARLES W. ■ RAAR Architecture 75, 81. b. Oct. 31, 1925, Benton Harbor, MI. d. Dec. 16, 1993. BArch 47, Univ. of Michigan; MFA 56, Princeton Univ.; PhD 57, Princeton Univ. **Career & Employment:** Mario Corbett, Clark & Beuttler, Joseph Allen Stein, Draftsman 1947-49; Univ. of Utah, Salt Lake City, Asst. Prof. 1950-52; US Army Corps of Engineers, Lieut. 1952-54; Princeton Univ., Asst. Prof. 1957-59; Clark & Beuttler, Assc. 1959-62; UC, Berkeley, Assc. Prof. 1959-65, Chair 1962-65; Moore Lyndon Turnbull Whitaker, Part. 1962-65; MLTW-Moore Turnbull, Part. 1965-69; Yale Univ., Prof. 1965-75, Chair 1965-69, Dean 1969-71; Charles W. Moore Asscs., Prin. 1970-75; Urban Innovations Group 1974-present; Moore Grover Harper, Part. 1975-85; UCLA, Prof. 1975-85, Program Head 1978-82; Centerbrook Architects 1975-present; Moore Ruble Yudell, Part. 1976-present; Harvard GSD, Visiting Prof. 1982; Univ. of Texas, Austin, O'Neil Ford Centennial Chair in Architecture 1984-present; Charles W. Moore, Architect, Prin. 1985-1990; Moore-Andersson Architects, Part. 1991-present. **Fellowships, Honors & Awards:** *Architectural Record*, Award of Excellence 1962, 1969, House of the Year 1982; *Progressive Architecture*, Citation 1962, 1966, 1970, 1977, 1st Honor Award 1970; AIA-*Sunset* Award 1962, Special Award 1963-64, Award of Merit 1967, 1968, Gold Medal 1991; NEA Grant 1976; Guggenheim Fellowship 1976; AIA, Honor Award 1987, 1988, California Council, Honor Award 1988, Firm of the Year Award 1992; AIA-Assn. of Collegiate Schools of Architecture, Topaz Medallion 1989, Los Angeles Chap. Honor Award 1990, Austin Chap., Citation of Honor 1990, 1992, 25 Year Award 1991,

AIA-American Library Assn., Library Buildings Award 1991; Cornell College, Hon. DFA 1989; AIA, American Wood Council Honor Award 1991; Univ. of Michigan, Hon. Doctor of Architecture 1992. **Publications:** with Nicholas Pyle, *The Yale Mathematics Building Competition* (New Haven, Yale University Press, 1974); with G. Allen & D. Lyndon, *The Place of Houses* (New York: Holt, Rinehart, Winston, 1974); with G. Allen, *Dimensions: Space, Shape and Scale in Architecture* (New York: Architectural Record Books, 1976); with K.C. Bloomer, *Body, Memory and Architecture* (New Haven, 1977); with P. Becker & K. Smith, *Home Sweet Home: American Domestic Vernacular Architecture* (New York, 1983); with P. Becker, R. Campbell, *Los Angeles, The City Observed* (New York: Random House, 1984); with S. Woodbridge, *The Cabin the Temple the Trailer* (1985); with W.J. Mitchell & W. Turnbull, *The Poetics of Gardens* (Cambridge, MA: MIT Press, 1988); *Beauty and the Beast* (New York, Rizzoli, 1991); with Jane Lidz, *Water and Architecture* (New York: Harry N. Abrams, 1994); with Donlyn Lyndon, *Chambers for a Memory Palace* (Cambridge, MA: MIT Press, 1994). **Important Works:** Jobson Cabin, Palo Colorado Canyon, CA 1961; Orinda House, Orinda, CA 1962; Sea Ranch Condominium, Sea Ranch, CA 1965; Santa Barbara Faculty Club, Santa Barbara, CA 1968; Kresge College, Santa Cruz, CA 1974; Tegal Harbor Housing, Berlin 1981; St. Matthew's Church, Pacific Palisades, CA 1983; Hood Museum, Dartmouth, MA 1985; Beverly Hills Civic Center. **Bio-Bibliography:** Eugene Johnson, ed., *Charles W. Moore, Architect* (New York: Rizzoli, 1987); James Steele, ed., *Moore Ruble Yudell* (London: Academy Editions, 1993); Michael Crosbie, ed., *Centerbrook* (Washington, DC: AIA Press, 1993); Kevin Keim, ed., *Charles W. Moore: A Life in Architecture* (Boston: Bullfinch Press, forthcoming).

MOORE, DEREK A.R. ■ FAAR History of Art 84. b. Nov. 7, 1956, Denver, CO. m. Charlotte F. Nichols, FAAR 83. c. Olivia Isabella. BA 78, Amherst College; MA 80, IFA; PhD 88, IFA; MArch 88, Columbia Univ. **Other Study:** Univ. degli Studi-Smith College, Florence 1976-77; Summer Latin Inst. 1979; Centro Intl. di Studi di Architettura Andrea Palladio, Vicenza 1983; Accademia Nazionale dei Lincei, Rome 1982. **Research/ Artistic Interests:** Italian art & architectrual history. **Career & Employment:** I.M. Pei & Partners 1988-90; William Nicholas Bodouva & Asscs. 1992-present; Columbia Univ., Adj. Asst. Prof. 1989-present. **Memberships & Offices:** SAH; CAA. **Fellowships, Honors & Awards:** Amherst College, Anna Baker Heap Prize, John Woodruff Fellowship 1978; Accademia Nazionale dei Lincei, Wolfgang Lotz Memorial Found. 1982; IFA, Lehman Fellow 1980-82, 1984-85, Post-Graduate Fellow 1991. **Publications:** "Sanmicheli's Tornacoro in Verona Cathedral: A New Drawing and Problems of Interpretation," *JSAH* 44 (1985): 221-32; "Carlo Borromeo, Milan, and the Sacri Monti," *Zodiac* 9 (1993): 12-51; "Notes on the Use of *Spolia* in Roman Architecture from Bramante to Bernini" (forthcoming). **Bio-Bibliography:** *Outstanding Young Men of America, 1990*. **Home Address:** 45 Woodland Ave., Summit, NJ 07901.

MOORE, DOUGLAS STUART ■ RAAR Musical Composition 47; AAR Trustee 1945-67. b. Aug. 10, 1893, Cutchogue, NY. d. July 25, 1969. m. Emily Bailey. c. Mary, Sarah. BA 15, Yale Univ.; BMus 17, Yale Univ. **Other Studies:** Schola Cantorum with Vincent d'Indy & Nadia Boulanger, Paris 1921; Cleveland Inst. of Music with Ernest Bloch 1924. **Career & Employment:** Cleveland Museum of Art, Music Dir. 1921; Columbia Univ., Assc. 1926, Asst. Prof. 1927, Assc. Prof. 1928, Prof. & Chair 1940; MacDowell Prof. 1943-62, Prof. Emer. 1962-69. **Memberships & Offices:** Yale Alumni Council 1947; AAAL, Pres. 1951-62;

ASCAP; NIAL, Pres. 1941-53. **Fellowships, Honors & Awards:** Pulitzer Traveling Scholarship 1925; Guggenheim Fellow 1934; Hon. DMus: Cincinnati Conservatory of Music 1946, Univ. of Rochester 1947, Yale Univ. 1955; Pulitzer Prize 1951; New York Critics' Circle Award 1958; Huntington Hartford Found. Award 1960; Columbia Univ., Hon. LHD 1963. **Publications:** *Listening to Music* (New York: Norton, 1932); *From Madrigal to Modern Music* (New York: Norton, 1942). **Important Works:** 11 operas; 3 film scores; 9 orchestral works; *Greek Games,* a ballet 1930; *The Devil and Daniel Webster,* music for Stephen Vincent Benet's opera 1939; *Wind Quintet* 1942-rev. 1948; *Giants in the Earth,* an opera 1950; *Cotillion,* suite for strings 1952; *The Ballad of Baby Doe,* an opera 1956; *Gallantry: A Soap Opera* 1957; *The Wings of the Dove,* an opera 1961; *Carry Nation,* an opera 1966. **Bio-Bibliography:** Jack Beeson, "In Memoriam Douglas Moore," *Perspectives of New Music* (1969); H. Gleason & W. Becker, "Douglas Moore," *Twentieth-Century Composers* (Bloomington: Indiana Univ. Press, 1981); *Baker's Biographical Dictionary of Musicians; New Grove Dictionary of American Music; Who Was Who in America.*

MOORE, EDWARD C., JR ■ AAR Trustee 1923-31.

MOORE, HENRY ■ AAR Visitor 1951 — 1955, Artist.

MOORE, JOHN E. ■ FAAR History of Art 85. b. May 1, 1958, Brooklyn, NY. BA 80, Cornell Univ.; MA 82, Harvard Univ.; PhD 92, Harvard Univ. **Career & Employment:** Smith College, Instr. 1989-92, Asst. Prof. 1993-present. **Memberships & Offices:** CAA, SAH. **Fellowships, Honors & Awards:** Cornell Univ., Frances Sampson Prize 1980; DAAD Fellowship 1981; Harvard Univ., Certificate of Distinction in Teaching 1984; Fondazione Lemmerman, Borsa di Studio 1986-87; NEH Summer Grant 1990, 1994; Getty Center Grant 1995. **Publications:** "Prints, Salami and Cheese: Savoring the Roman Festival of the Chinea," *Art Bulletin* (forthcoming). **Business Address:** Dept. of Art, Smith College, Northampton, MA 01063.

MORAVEC, PAUL ■ FAAR Musical Composition 85. b. Nov. 2, 1957, Buffalo, NY. m. Wendy Lamb. BA 80, Harvard Univ.; MA 82, Columbia Univ.; DMA 87, Columbia Univ. **Research/Artistic Interests:** Composition in orchestral, chamber, music theater, film, electro-acoustic media. **Career & Employment:** Tobeason-Moravec Music, VP 1986-89; Darmouth College, Assc. Prof. 1987-present. **Fellowships, Honors & Awards:** Bearnes Prize 1983; AAAL, Ives Fellowship 1986, Lieberson Fellowship 1991; Rockefeller Found. Fellowship 1993; NEA Composers Fellowship 1994; Camargo Found. Fellowship 1994. **Important Works:** *Music Remembers,* for piano (CRI) 1985; *The Open Secret,* for violin, cello & piano (CRI) 1985); *The Kingdom Within,* for flute, clarinet, violin, cello & piano (CRI) 1987; *Devices and Desires,* for synthesizer (Centaur) 1989; *Spiritdance,* for orchestra (Vienna Modern Masters) 1989; *Ancient Lights,* for orchestra 1990; *Circular Dreams,* for clarinet, violin, cello & piano, Chamber Music America Comm. (CRI) 1991; *Sempre Diritto! (Straight Ahead!),* for chamber orchestra 1991; *Third String Quartet, "Claritas"* 1992; *Sonata for Violin and Piano,* Philadelphia Network for New Music Comm. (BMG/RCA Classics) 1992; *Northern Lights Electric,* for flute, clarinet, piano & string quintet, NH State Council on the Arts Comm. 1993; *Lyric Concerto for Violin and Orchestra* 1994; *Aubade,* for string orchestra. **Business Address:** Music Dept., Dartmouth College, Hanover, NH 03755.

MORAVIA, ALBERTO ■ AAR Visitor 1977-78, Writer.

MORELAND, FLOYD LEONARD ■ FAAR Classics/Archaeology 69. b. Oct. 18, 1942, Passaic, NJ. BA 64, Middlebury College; PhD 71, UC, Berkeley. **Other Studies:** ICCCS 1966-67. **Career & Employment:** Reed College, Asst. Prof.; Brooklyn College & CUNY Graduate Center, Prof., Latin-Greek Inst., Dir. **Memberships & Offices:** Classical Assn. of the Atlantic States, Exec. Bd.; APA. **Fellowships, Honors & Awards:** APA Award 1979; Stanford Univ., ICCCS Fellowship; UC, Berkeley, Woodrow Wilson Fellowship 1964-65. **Publications:** with R.M. Fleischer, *Latin: An Intensive Course* (Berkeley: UC Press, 1977).

MORETTI, MARINA ■ Italian Fulbright Fellow 1980-81.

MOREY, CHARLES RUFUS ■ FASCSR 03; AAR Prof.-in-Charge 1925-26; Acting Dir. 1945-47. b. Nov. 20, 1877, Hastings, MI. d. Aug. 28, 1955. m. Sara Tupper. c. Jonathan. BA 1899, Univ. of Michigan; MA 1900, Univ. of Michigan. **Research/Artistic Interests:** Index of Christian art, early Christian & medieval art. **Career & Employment:** Princeton Univ., Instr. 1905-7, Preceptor 1906-15, Asst. Prof. 1915-18, Prof. 1918-38, Marquand Prof. 1938-45, Chair 1925-45; US Embassy, Rome, Cultural Attaché 1945-52. **Memberships & Offices:** CAA; Pontifical Acad. of Archaeology; ArIA; Virtuosi del Pantheon, Pres.; Intl. Union of Archaeological & Historical Insts. **Fellowships, Honors & Awards:** APS, Fellow; MAA; Pierpont Morgan Library, Fellow; AAAS, Fellow; Accademia dei Lincei, Corresponding Fellow; Hon. Degrees: Oberlin College, LHD 1932; Univ. of Michigan, LittD 1938; Univ. of Chicago LHD 1941; NYU, DFA 1942; Yale Univ., LittD 1951; Princeton Univ., LittD 1954; Dante Alighieri Soc., Silver Medal; Order of the Crown of Belgium, Chevalier; Silver Cross of the Vatican; Stella d'Oro of Italy, Ordre de Merite Syrien, 1st Class. **Publications:** *Early Christian Art in the Freer Collection* (New York: Macmillan, 1914); *The Sarcophagus of Claudia Antonia Sabina and the Asiatic Sarcophagi, Sardis,* Publications of the American Society for the Excavation of Sardis 5 (Princeton: Princeton Univ. Press, 1924); *The Miniatures of the Manuscripts of Terence,* 2 vols. (Princeton, Princeton Univ. Press, 1930-31); *Christian Art* (New York: Longmans, 1935); ed., *Catalogo del Museo Sacro della Biblioteca Apostolica Vaticana* (Vatican City: Bibl. Apostolica Vaticana, 1936); *The Mosaics of Antioch* (New York: Longmans, 1938); "The Byzantine Renaissance," *Speculum* 14 (1939): 139-59; *Early Christian Art* (1941.; 2d ed., Princeton: Princeton Univ. Press, 1953); *Medieval Art,* 2 vols. (New York: Norton, 1942). **Bio-Bibliography:** *NY Times,* Obit. (Aug. 30, 1955); *Art Bulletin* 37 (1955): iii-vi; *AJA* 60 (1956): 63-64; *College Art Journal* 15 (1956): 139-43; *Speculum* 32 (1957): 645-46; *Directory of American Scholars; Who Was Who in America.*

MORGAN, EDWIN D. ■ AAR Charter Mem.

MORGAN, JOHN PIERPONT ■ AAR Founder, Trustee 1905-13; Financier. b. Apr. 17, 1837. d. Mar. 31, 1913. **Career & Employment:** Drexel, Morgan & Co. 1871. Financier in reorganizations of railways. Collector and philanthropist, he made repeated large donations to the Academy & was instrumental in assembling the present site of the AAR.

MORIARTY, STACY T. ■ FAAR Landscape Architecture 84. b. Mar. 3, 1956, Amarillo, TX. m. Patrick M. Condon. c. Kathleen Condon-Moriarty. BS 78, Univ. of Massachusetts; MLA 82, Univ. of Massachusetts. **Career & Employment:** Johnson & Ruchter, Landscape Architect 1982-83; Univ. of Minnesota, Asst. Prof. 1985-91; Moriarty-Condon Landscape Architects, Pres. 1985-present; Univ. of British Columbia, Adj. Prof. 1992-present.

Memberships & Offices: *Inform, Journal of Design Arts,* Ed. Bd. 1989-91. **Fellowships, Honors & Awards:** ASLA Merit Award 1982. **Important Works:** Private Residences, Minnesota 1985-92; Basilica of St. Mary, Minneapolis, Master Plan 1988; Minnesota Landscape Arboretum, Sensory & Horticultural Therapy Garden 1988; Church of St. Stephen, Columbianum Garden, Edna, MN 1989; Warroad Public Library, MN 1990; Upper Iowa Univ., Fayette Campus Masterplan 1991, Campus Renovation 1992-95. **Exhibitions/Performances:** Harvard GSD 1982; Univ. of Massachusetts 1984; Memphis Botanical Garden 1992.

MORRIS, MARY ■ FAAR Literature 80. b. May 14, 1947, Chicago, IL. m. Larry O'Connor. c. Kate. BA 69, Tufts College; MA 74, Columbia Univ.; MPhil 77, Columbia Univ. **Research/Artistic Interests:** Fiction, travel literature. **Career & Employment:** Princeton Univ. 1980-87, 1991-93. **Memberships & Offices:** American PEN, Exec. Bd; Freedom-to-Write. **Fellowships, Honors & Awards:** Columbia Univ., President's Fellowship 1977-78; NEA Fellowship 1978; Creative Artists Public Service Award 1980; Guggenheim Fellowship 1981; Princeton Univ., Council of the Humanities, George W. Perkins Fellowship 1982; American Council for the Arts, 1st Prize 1983; NYFA Prize 1985; Friends of American Writers, Distinguished Award 1986. **Publications:** *Vanishing Animals and Other Stories* (Boston: David Godine, 1979); *Crossroads* (Boston: Houghton Mifflin, 1983); *The Bus of Dreams* (Boston: Houghton Mifflin, 1985); *Nothing to Declare: Memoirs of a Woman Travelling Alone* (Boston: Houghton Mifflin, 1988); *The Waiting Room* (New York: Doubleday, 1989); *Wall to Wall: From Beijing to Berlin by Rail* (New York: Doubleday, 1992); *Maiden Voyage: The Journeys of Women* (New York: Vintage, 1993); *A Mother's Love* (New York: Doubleday, 1993). **Bio-Bibliography:** Ihab Hassan, *Selves at Risk* (Madison, WI: Univ. of Wisconsin Press, 1990); *Contemporary Authors; International Authors and Writers Who's Who; World Authors.* **Business Address:** Amanda Urban, ICM, 40 W. 57 St., NYC 10019.

Before she left, my mother used to practice her leaving on me. She'd say, "Come on. Let's go for a ride." "What about Sam?" I'd ask, for I always wanted my sister, Samantha, along. But Sam was not yet five, and my mother would drop her off at Dottie's trailer before heading with me into the desert. We'd get into the car and my mother would drive. She'd put the radio on High Desert Rock, roll down the windows, and sing all the way. I'd rest my head back, a girl of no more than seven, felling the wind through my own dense red curls, wishing that I had my mother's thick, black hair.

After a while I'd just sit beside her in the passenger seat and stare at the desert, across the expanse of dust and sand. It was as if we were living on the edge of the moon and not the state of Nevada. The light moved across the contours of the arid, red land and its beauty was otherworldly. At times it was a soft pink like a baby's flesh. At other times it appeared as if the world were on fire.

My mother would drive until she found a scenic place where she wanted to stop. She'd peer into the bottom of canyons and toss pebbles down the dark crevasses, counting the seconds until we heard the plop as it hit. Or she'd stand at the rim of the meteorite crater and gaze across its cavernous hole. *Mary Morris, Sept. 15, 1992*

Mary Morris

MORRIS, PAULINE M. ■ AAR World War II Scholar 1945.

MOSCA, ANNAPAOLA ■ Italian Fulbright Fellow 1991-92.

MOSES, ROBERT ■ AAR Visitor 1959 — 1964, Urban Planner, State & Municipal Officer.

MOSMAN, WARREN TOWLE ■ FAAR Sculpture 34. b. July 18, 1908. d. June 21, 1968. m. Luree Griffin Cory. BFA, Yale Univ. **Other Study:** NSS. **Career & Employment:** Minneapolis School of Art 1935-42; US Navy, Lieut., WWII; Independent Artist, IN 1950-68. **Exhibitions/Performances:** Minneapolis Inst. of Art; NY World's Fair 1939. **Bio-Bibliography:** *Who Was Who in American Art.*

MOSS, CHRISTOPHER FREDERICK ■ FAAR Classics/Archaeology 80.

MOST, GLENN W. ■ FAAR Classics/Archaeology 83. b. June 12, 1952, Miami, FL. m. Angela Citernesi. c. Corinna, Miranda. BA 72, Harvard College; PhD 80, Yale Univ.; D.Phil. 80, Univ. of Tübingen. **Other Study:** Corpus Christi College, Oxford 1972-73; Univ. of Tübingen 1976-78. **Career & Employment:** Yale Univ., Visiting Lect. 1978; Univ. of Heidelberg 1979-80, Prof. 1991-present; Princeton Univ., Asst. Prof. 1980-86; Univ. of Michigan, Visiting Assc. Prof. 1986-87, Visiting Prof. 1993; Univ. of Innsbruck 1987-91. **Memberships & Offices:** Ed. Bd.: *Philosophia naturalis* 1989-present, *Arion* 1990-present, *Phoenix* 1991-present, *Internationale Zeitschrift für Philosophie* 1992-present, md. *Materiali e discussioni per l'analisi dei testi classici* 1992-present. **Fellowships, Honors & Awards:** Harvard Univ., Detur Prize & J.O. Sargent Prize 1970, Knox Fellowship 1972-73; Yale Univ. Fellowship 1973-74, Samuel Botwinik Fellowship 1974-75; Danforth Found., Kent Fellowship 1975-76; Deutscher Akademischer Austauschdienst 1976-78; Andrew W. Mellon Fellowship 1982-83; Wissenschaltliches Mitglied, Wissenschaftskolleg zu Berlin 1988-89; Univ. of Michigan, Inst. for Humanities, Visiting Fellow 1993; Deutsche Forschungsgemeinschaft, Leibniz Preis 1994-99. **Publications:** ed., with W.W. Stowe, *The Poetics of Murder* (New York: Harcourt, Brace, Jovanovich, 1983); "The Hippocratic Smile: John le Carré and the Traditions of the Detective Novel," in *The Poetics of Murder,* (New York: Harcourt, Brace, Jovanovich, 1983), 341-65; *The Measures of Praise: Structure and Function in Pindar's Second Pythian and Seventh Nemean Odes,* Hypomnemata 83 (1985); with A.T. Grafton & J.E.G. Zetzel, *F.A. Wolf: Prolegomena to Homer* (Princeton: Princeton Univ. Press, 1985); "Alcman's 'Cosmogonic' Fragment (Fr. 5, Page 81 Calame)," *Classical Quarterly* 37 (1987): 1-19; "Cornutus and Stoic *Allegoresis*: A Preliminary Report," *Aufstieg und Niedergang der römischen Welt* 2.36.3 (1989): 2014-65; "The Stranger's Stratagem: Self-Disclosure and Self-Sufficiency in Greek Culture," *Journal of Hellenic Studies* 109 (1989): 114-33; "Zur Archäologie der Archaik," *Antike und Abendland* 35 (1989): 1-23; "Canon Fathers: Literacy, Morality, Power," *Arion* n.s. 31 (1990): 35-60; "Daphnis in Grasmere: Wordsworth's Romantic Pastoral," in *Cabinet of the Muses: Essays on Classical and Comparative Literature in Honor of Thomas G. Rosenmeyer,* ed. M. Griffith & D.J. Mastronarde (Atlanta: Univ. of Georgia Press, 1990), 361-85; "Ansichten über einer Hund: Zu einigen Strukturen der Homerrezeption zwischen Antike und Neuzeit," *Antike & Abendland* 37 (1991): 144-68; ed., with A. Laks, Théophraste, *Métaphysique* (Paris: Belles Lettres, 1993); "The Language of Poetry," *New Literary History* 24 (1993): 545-62. **Home Address:** Unterer Fauler Pelz 2, Heidelberg D-69117, Germany. **Business Address:** Universität Heidelberg, Heidelberg, Germany.

MOTHERWELL, ROBERT ■ AAR Trustee 1980, Artist.

MOTL, MARK ■ NIAE, John Dinkeloo Traveling Fellow 1986-87.

MOUCHLY-WEISS, HARRIET ■ AAR Trustee 1982-84, Trustee Emer.; Exec, Pub. Rel.

MOUTON, GROVER E., III ■ FAAR Architecture 73. b. 1946, Lafayette, LA. m. Bitsie Werlein. BArch 71, Tulane Univ. School of Architecture; MArch 74, Harvard GSD. **Other Study:** Skowhegan School of Painting & Sculpture 1970; Architectural Assn., London 1971; MIT, Center for Advanced Visual Studies 1977. **Career & Employment:** Urban Designer 1980-91; Tulane School of Architecture, Visiting Assc. Prof. 1985-91; Urban Design Studio & Charrette, New Orleans, Visiting Prof. 1985-91; Independent Artist, Architectural Drawing 1985-91; Pascagoula Public Library Public Art Program, Project Dir. 1985-86; Mayor's Inst. on City Design, South, Exec. Dir. 1989-92. **Fellowships, Honors & Awards:** Architectural Assn., London, Research Fellowship Award 1970-71; William Rutherford Mead Fellowship 1971-73; MIT, Center for Advanced Visual Studies, Fellow 1975-77; NEA Individual Fellowship Award 1979; New Orleans Museum of Arts, Sculpture Competition, 1st Prize 1979; New Orleans, Urban Design Grant Award 1985-91; NEA, Mayor's Inst. on City Design 1989-91. **Important Works:** Aquarium of the Americas Riverfront Park, New Orleans 1987-91; Sculpture Garden, Duncan Plaza Public Open Space, New Orleans 1985-86; New Orleans City Park Arboretum Design Competition 1985-86; Phoenix Arts Comm. Master Plan 1987-88; Kenner, LA, Civic Center & Lakefront Park 1988-89; Birmingham Urban Design Charrette 1989; Newcomb-Tulane Univ., Arts Center, Master Plan 1989; New Orleans Union Passenger Terminal, Urban Design Master Plan 1989-91; Birmingham Civil Rights District 1989-91; Monroe, LA, Downtown Master Plan 1989-91. **Exhibitions/Performances:** Hirshhorn Museum & Sculpture Garden, Smithsonian Inst., Washington, DC 1981; Sarah Campbell Blaffer Gallery, Univ. of Houston 1981; Blum Helman Gallery, NYC 1982; Gallery of Milano, Milan 1982; Drawing Center 1982; Contemporary Arts Center, New Orleans 1985; Southeast Center for Contemporary Arts, Winston-Salem, NC 1985; Louisiana World Exposition 1985; Fendrich Gallery, Washington, DC 1985, 1988; Simone Stern Gallery, New Orleans 1986; Morgan Gallery, Boston 1988; Malborough Gallery, NYC 1988, 1990; Art Museum at Florida Intl. Univ. 1989; University of New Orleans 1989; Alexandria Art Museum, LA 1990. **Address:** Tulane Univ. School of Architecture, 6823 St. Charles Ave., New Orleans, LA 70118; Arthur Q. Davis, Architects, 335 Julia St., New Orleans, LA 70130.

MOWBRAY, H. SIDDONS ■ AAR Charter Mem., Trustee 1911-21; American School of Architecture in Rome, Dir. 1903-6; Artist.

MOYNIHAN, DANIEL P. ■ AAR Visitor 1964-65, Scholar, US Senator.

MOYNIHAN, ROBERT ■ FAAR Post-Classical/Humanistic Studies 86. b. Nov. 12, 1953, Meriden, CT. m. Priscilla Hart. BA 77, Harvard Univ.; MA, Yale Univ.; MPhil, Yale Univ. **Career & Employment:** *Manchester CT Journal Inquirer*, News Reporter 1977-80. **Fellowships, Honors & Awards:** Associated Press, 1st Prize 1978; Charlotte E. Newcombe Fellowship 1983-84.

MUEHLEMANN, JAMES R. ■ FAAR Painting 82; SOF, Treas. 1983-89. b. Nov. 1, 1944, St. Louis, MO. m. Kathy Muehlemann, FAAR 88. BFA 71, Univ. of Illinois; MFA 73, Syracuse Univ.

Career & Employment: Randolph-Macon Women's College, Adj. Prof. **Memberships & Offices:** Creative Arts Project Series, New York State 1979. **Fellowships, Honors & Awards:** Adolph & Ethel Gottlieb Found. 1995. **Exhibitions/Performances:** Solo: Paul Cava Gallery, Philadelphia 1986, 1990; Althea Viafora Gallery, NYC 1986; Penine Hart Gallery 1994; Group: Max Hutchinson Gallery, NYC 1983; Huhlenberg & Lafayette, Easton, PA 1984; Kent Gallery, Kent, CT 1985; Condeco-Lawler, NYC 1985; CDS Gallery, NYC 1986, 1989. **Bio-Bibliography:** *Art in America, Arts Journal, ArtNews, Arts Magazine, Flash Art, New Art Examiner, NY Times, Philadelphia Inquirer.* **Home Address:** 6 Quinlan St., Lynchburg, VA 24503.

MUEHLEMANN, KATHY ■ FAAR Painting 88; SOF, VP 1991-present. b. Feb. 9, 1950, Austin, TX. m. James R. Muehlemann, FAAR 82. BFA 79, SUNY, Empire State College. **Research/Artistic Interests:** Oil painting, watercolor, printmaking, drawing. **Career & Employment:** Randolph Macon Women's College, Asst Prof. **Fellowships, Honors & Awards:** NEA Fellowship 1988; Guggenheim Fellowship 1994. **Important Works:** Ackland Art Museum, UNC, Chapel Hill; Cleveland Museum of Art; Contemporary Museum, Honolulu; Lannan Found., Los Angeles; Nelson-Atkins Museum of Art, Kansas City, MO; Grey Art Gallery, NYU; Santa Barbara City College, CA; Milwaukee Art Museum. **Exhibitions/Performances:** Solo: Oscarsson Hood Gallery, NYC 1984; Oscarsson Siegeltuch Gallery, NYC 1986; Lannan Museum, Lake Worth, FL 1988; Pamela Auchincloss Gallery, NYC 1989, 1991, 1993; Virginia Zabriskie Gallery, NYC 1989; Museum of Contemporary Art, Honolulu 1991; Nelson-Atkins Museum of Art, Kansas City, MO 1991; Cedar Rapids Museum of Art, IA 1994; Maier Museum of Art, Lynchburg, VA 1995. **Bio-Bibliography:** Nelson Atkins Museum of Art, exb. cat.; Lannan Museum, exb. cat.; *Art Forum; Art in America; ArtNews; Arts Magazine; Who's Who in American Art; Who's Who in the East.* **Home Address:** 6 Quinlan St., Lynchburg, VA 24503. **Business Address:** Pamela Auchincloss Gallery, 558 Broadway, NYC 10012.

MUELLER, JEANETTE RUTH ■ AAR World War II Scholar 1943.

MUELLER, MICHAEL JOSEPH ■ FAAR Painting 28. b. Dec. 3, 1893, Durand, WI. d. July 6, 1931. BFA 25, Yale Univ. **Study:** ASL; Minneapolis School of Fine Arts; S. Kendall, Ezra Winter & Savage, E.C. Taylor, Rittonberg, Bridgman, Dubois. **Research/Artistic Interests:** Northwest landscapes. **Career & Employment:** Univ. of Oregon, Dept. Head. **Fellowships, Honors & Awards:** Beaux Arts Inst., Competition Medal; Northwest Annual Prize 1930. **Exhibitions/Performances:** Northwest Annual, Seattle 1930. **Bio-Bibliography:** "Humble Beginning Does Not Stifle Ambitions of Honor Art Student at Yale," *New Haven Times-Leader* (Dec. 15, 1922); *Artists of the American West; Who Was Who in American Art.*

MULCAHY, VINCENT JOSEPH ■ FAAR Architecture 77. b. Apr. 4, 1949, Ithaca, NY. m. Cynthia Livermore. BA 71, Cornell Univ.; MArch 75, Harvard Univ. **Career & Employment:** Cornell Univ., Asst. Prof.; Professional Practice, Ithaca, NY. **Fellowships, Honors & Awards:** Harvard Univ., Special Commendation 1975.

MULLER, JEFFREY M. ■ FAAR History of Art 79. b. Dec. 19, 1948, NYC. m. Deborah Del Gais. c. Celia. BA 69, Queens College, CUNY; MA 72, Yale Univ.; PhD 77, Yale Univ. **Career & Employment:** Yale Univ., Instr. 1974-75; Bowdoin College, Instr.

1975-77, Asst. Prof. 1977-80; Brown Univ., Asst. Prof. 1980-86, Assc. Prof. 1986-present. **Fellowships, Honors & Awards:** Phi Beta Kappa 1969; Yale Univ., NDEA Title IV Fellowship 1969-72; Samuel H. Kress Found., Fellowship 1971, Traveling Fellowship 1972-73; Deutscher Akademischer Austauschdienst Stipendium 1972-73; Paul Mellon Centre for Studies in British Art Research Grant 1976; Bowdoin College, Humanities Fund Grant 1978-79; IAS 1980-81; *Art Bulletin*, Arthur Kingsley Porter Prize 1982; ACLS, Grant-in-Aid 1986; Fulbright Senior Research Fellowship 1989-90; NGA, Senior Fellowship 1989-90 (declined); NEH, Fellowship for Univ. Teachers 1992-93. **Publications:** "Oil Sketches in the Rubens Collection," *Burlington Magazine* 117 (1975): 371-77; "Rubens's Museum of Antique Sculpture: An Introduction," *Art Bulletin* 59 (1977): 571-82; "An Introduction to Rubens's Museum of Antique Sculpture," *Gentse Bijdragen tot de Kunstgeschiedenis* 24 (1976-78): 169-70; "Rubens's Emblem of the Art of Painting," *Journal of the Warburg & Courtauld Institutes* 44 (1981): 221-22; "The Perseus and Andromeda on Rubens's House," *Simiolus* 12 (1982): 131-46; "Rubens's Theory and Practice of the Imitation of Art," *Art Bulletin* 64 (1982): 229-46; "The Phaedran Charioteer in Two Early Paintings by Rubens," *Essays in Northern European Art Presented to Egbert Haverkamp-Begemann* (Doornspijk, 1983), 220-25; "'Con diligenza, Con studio* and *Con Amore':* Terms of Quality in the Seventeenth Century," in *Rubens and His World* (Antwerp, 1985), 273-78; "Rubens's Cupids and Andrians: The First Documents and What They Tell Us," in *Bachanals by Titian and Rubens* (Stockholm, 1987), 75-80; *Rubens: The Artist as Collector* (Princeton: Princeton Univ. Press, 1989); "Measures of Authenticity: the Detection of Copies in the Early Literature on Connoisseurship," *Studies in the History of Art* 20 (1989): 141-50; "The Quality of Grace in the Art of Anthony van Dyck," in *Anthony Van Dyck* (Washington, DC: NGA, 1990), 27-38; "Rubens, Italy and England: The Testimony of Edward Norgate," in *Rubens dall'Italia all'Europa* (Vicenza, 1992), 113-20. **Home Address:** 33 Everett Ave., Providence, RI 02906. **Business Address:** Brown Univ., Box 1855, Providence, RI 02912.

MUMFORD, LEWIS ■ AAR Visitor 1964 — 1968. Author, Urbanist. b. Oct. 19, 1895. d. Jan. 26, 1990. **Honors & Awards:** National Book Award 1961; Presidential Medal of Freedom 1964; NIAL, Gold Medal, Belles Lettres 1970; Nat. Medal for Literature 1972; Nat. Medal of Arts 1986. **Selected Publications:** *The Culture of Cities* (1938); *The Condition of Man* (1944); *From the Ground Up* (1956); *The City in History* (1961).

MURDOCK, RICHARD COOLIDGE ■ FAAR Landscape Architecture 33. b. Feb. 8, 1905, Malden, MA. dec. m. Marion Waterworth. BA 29, Cornell Univ. **Career & Employment:** Clarke & Rapuano. **Memberships & Offices:** ASLA. **Bio-Bibliography:** *Who's Who in the East.*

MURPHY, CHARLES THEOPHILUS ■ FAAR Classics/Archaeology 54. b. June 14, 1909, Philadelphia, PA. d. July 25, 1985. m. Fannie Bixler, Elizabeth Parkhurst. c. Charles Thorton, Arthur Bixler. BA 31, Harvard Univ.; PhD 35, Harvard Univ. **Other Studies:** ASCSA 1931-32. **Research/Artistic Interests:** Greek comedy, especially Aristophanes, comedy as a social phenomenon, Commedia dell'Arte. **Career & Employment:** Harvard Univ., Instr. 1935-40; Princeton Univ., Instr.-Asst. Prof. 1940-47; Oberlin College, Assc. Prof.-Prof.-Dept. Chair 1947-75; Univ. of Texas, Visiting Prof. 1957; VSA, Summer School, Dir. 1958, 1960, 1962, 1966, 1970, 1971, 1974, 1975; ICCS, Prof.-in-Charge 1968-69. **Memberships & Offices:** VSA, Sec.-Tres.

1954-60, Pres. 1970-; APA; ArIA; CAMWS; AAUP. **Fellowships, Honors & Awards:** ASCSA, Norton Fellowship 1931-32; Fulbright Fellowship 1953-54; Ford Found. Fellowship 1953. **Publications:** with W.J. Oates, *Greek Literature in Translation* (New York: Longmans, Green, & Co., 1944); with Kevin Guinagh & W.J. Oates, *Greek and Roman Classics in Translation* (New York: Longmans, Green, & Co., 1947); "Aristophanes and the Art of Rhetoric," *Harvard Studies in Classical Philology* 49 (1938): 69-113; "The Political Tendency of Aristophanes' *Knights,*" *TAPA* 69 (1938); "The Job of Classical Education in the Colleges," *Classical World* 39 (1945); "The Use of Speeches in Caesar's Gallic Wars," *Classical Journal* 45 (1949): 120-27; "A Survey of Recent Work on Aristophanes and Old Comedy (1957-1967)," *Classical World* 65 (1971-72): 261-73. **Bio-Bibliography:** Briggs, 432-33; *Dictionary of American Scholars; Who's Who in America; Who Was Who in America.*

MURPHY, FRANKLIN ■ AAR Visitor 1977-78; Kress Found., Chair.

MURRAY, ELIZABETH ■ RAAR Painting 91. m. Bob Holman. c. Dakota, Sophie, Daisy. **Exhibitions/Performances:** ArtistSpace, NYC 1992; Paula Cooper Gallery, NYC 1992; Group: Daniel Weinberg Gallery, NYC 1991; Anne Plumb Gallery, NYC 1991. **Bio-Bibliography:** Deborah Solomon, "Elizabeth Murray: Celebrating Paint," *NY Times Magazine* (Mar. 31, 1991); Corinne Robins, "Elizabeth Murray: Deconstructing Our Interiors," *Art Journal* (Spring 1991).

MURRILL, GWYNN ■ FAAR Sculpture 80. b. June 15, 1942, Ann Arbor, MI. m. David Faron. BA 67, UCLA; MA 70, UCLA; MFA 72, UCLA. **Fellowships, Honors & Awards:** Los Angeles County Art Museum, New Talent Purchase Award 1978; NEA Grant 1984-85; Guggenheim Fellowship 1986. **Important Works:** Los Angeles County Art Museum; Plaza Park Towers, Sacramento, CA; Ronald Reagan Bldg., Los Angeles; Grand Hope Park, Los Angeles; Home Savings Bank, San Francisco; TransAmerica Corp., San Francisco; City of Santa Monica; Culver City, CA; Trammell Crow Corp., Minneapolis; Hyatt Regency Hotels, Tampa, FL; United Bank of Denver; Hugo Neuhaus Memorial Park, Houston; Palos Verde Peninsula Library, CA. **Exhibitions/Performances:** Solo: Asher Faure Gallery, Los Angeles 1981, 1983, 1985, 1987, 1990, 1991; Municipal Art Gallery, Los Angeles 1982; John Berggruen Gallery, San Francisco 1987; Gail Severn Gallery, Ketchum, ID 1988, 1992; Rutgers Barclay Gallery, Santa Fe 1990; Group: Long Beach Museum of Art, CA 1987; Gallery at the Plaza, Los Angeles 1989; Sezon Museum of Art, Tokyo 1991; Leigh Yawley Woodson Art Museum, Wausau, WI. **Bio-Bibliography:** William Wilson, "Everything is New Again," *Los Angeles Times* (Oct. 27, 1987): 1; "Los Angeles' Astonishing Art Everywhere Scene," *Sunset Magazine* (Nov. 1988): 89-97; Peter Clothier, "Gwynn Murrill, Animal Magnetism," *Angeles* (Aug. 1989): 89-99; Suvan Geer, Review, *Los Angeles Times* (Jan. 13, 1990). **Home Address:** 29012 Crest, Agoura, CA 91301.

MURROW, EDWARD R. ■ AAR Visitor 1959 — 1964, Journalist.

MUSA, TOMASSO ■ AAR – Rome, Grounds Staff.

MUSCA, GIOSUE ■ Italian Fulbright Fellow 1966-67.

MUSHO, THEODORE J. ■ FAAR Architecture 61. b. Aug. 22, 1932, Peckville, PA. m. Sara R. Loos. c. Theodore, Paul, Suzanne, Sarah. BSArch 58, Univ. of Cincinnati; MArch 59, MIT.

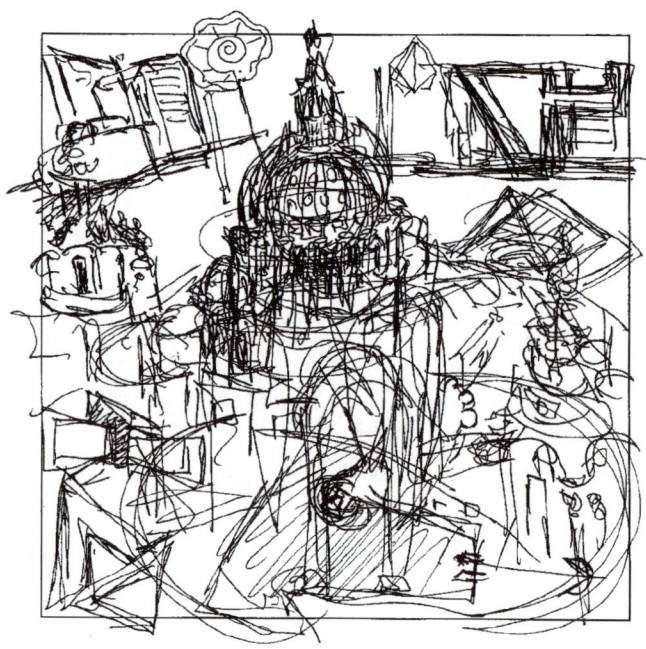

Theodore J. Musho

Career & Employment: I.M. Pei & Asscs., I.M. Pei & Partners, Pei Cobb Freed & Partners 1961-present, Assc. Part. 1980-present. **Important Works:** with H.N. Cobb, Pei & Partners, Fredonia College, SUNY; with Mr. Pei, Pei & Partners, Dallas City Hall; with Mr. Pei, Pei & Partners, John F. Kennedy Library, Boston; with Mr. Pei, Pei & Partners, Univ. of Indiana Art Museum, Bloomington; with H.N. Cobb, Pei & Partners, Mobil Research Laboratory, TX; with H.N. Cobb, Pei & Partners, Pitney Bowes World HQ, Stamford, CT; with H.N. Cobb, Pei & Partners, IBM Office Bldg., Somers, NY; with I.M. Pei, Pei Cobb Freed & Partners, Friedrichstadt Passagen, Quartier 206, Berlin; with H.N. Cobb, Pei & Partners, CSFB Office, Canary Wharf, London; with H.N. Cobb, Pei & Partners, Tan Shui Apt., Taipei, Taiwan. **Home Address:** 300 E. 33 St., Apt. 4J, NYC 10016. **Business Address:** Pei Cobb Freed & Partners, 600 Madison Ave., NYC 10022.

MUSKAT, DOROTHY B. ■ AAR World War II Scholar 1942.

MUSTO, RONALD G. ■ FAAR Post-Classical/Humanistic Studies 79. b. May 24, 1948, NYC. m. Eileen Gardiner. BA 69, Fordham College; MA 70, Columbia Univ.; PhD 77, Columbia Univ. **Other Study:** Manuscript research & paleography with Gino Corti, Florence 1974. **Research/Artistic Interests:** Medieval & Renaissance reform movements, history of Naples, history of peacemaking, book arts. **Career & Employment:** NYU, Visiting Asst. Prof. 1976; Columbia Univ., Graduate Faculties, Visiting Asst. Prof. 1980; Duke Univ., Asst. Prof. 1980-81; Freelance Ed., Humanities Reference, NYC 1981-85; Knowledge Industry Publications, *Overseas Assignment Directory,* Ed. 1983-86; Italica Press, Inc., NYC, Co-Publisher 1985-present. **Memberships & Offices:** Fellowship of Reconciliation 1972-present; Brooklyn Heights SANE 1973-78, *Newsletter,* Co-ed. 1977-78; Pax Christi, USA 1978-94, Book Award Com. 1989-94; AHA 1980-present; American Catholic Historical Assn. 1980-present; MAA 1980-present; RSA 1980-present, *Renaissance News & Notes,* Ed. 1988; Roosevelt Island Community Library, NYC, BoD 1987-90, Pres. 1989-90; Ciné Soleil Productions, NYC, Consultant, film project on religious roots of Haitian revolution 1989-93; Garland Publishing, Series Ed., "A Documentary History of Peace" 1992-present. **Fellowships, Honors & Awards:** New York State Teaching Fellowship 1969-74; RSA, Fellowship in Manuscript Research 1974; Columbia Univ. Dissertation Distinction 1977; NEH Fellowship 1978-79; Andrew W. Mellon Found. Fellowship 1980-81; US Catholic Press Assn., Best Book Award, for *The Catholic Peace Tradition* 1987. **Publications:** "Angelo Clareno's *Preparantia Christi Iesu habitationem,*" *Archivum Franciscanum Historicum* 73 (1980): 69-89; "Angelo Clareno, O.F.M.: Fourteenth-Century Translator of the Greek Fathers. An Introduction and a Checklist of Manuscripts and Printings of his *Scala paradisi,*" *Archivum Franciscanum Historicum* 76 (1983): 215-38, 589-645; "Queen Sancia of Naples (1286-1345) and the Spiritual Franciscans," in *Women of the Medieval World: Essays in Honor of John H. Mundy,* ed. Julius Kirshner & Suzanne Wemple (Oxford: Basil Blackwell, 1985), 179-214; ed., Petrarch, *The Revolution of Cola di Rienzo,* 2d ed. (New York: Italica Press, 1986); *The Catholic Peace Tradition* (Maryknoll, NY: Orbis Books, 1986); "Daniel Papebroch, S.J. and the Letters of Angelo Clareno, O.F.M.," *Archivum Franciscanum Historicum* 79 (1986): 392-410; *The Peace Tradition in the Catholic Church: An Annotated Bibliography* (New York: Garland Publishing, 1987); *Liberation Theologies: A Research Guide* (New York: Garland Publishing, 1991); "Just Wars and Evil Empires: Erasmus and the Turks," in *Renaissance Society and Culture: Essays in Honor of Eugene F. Rice, Jr.,* ed. John Monfasani & Ronald G. Musto (New York: Italica Press, 1991), 197-216; "Historical Introduction," in Enrico Bacco, *Naples: An Early Guide,* ed. & trans. Eileen Gardiner (New York: Italica Press, 1991), xix-lxii; *Catholic Peacemakers: A Documentary History,* Vol. 1: *From the Bible to the Crusades* (New York: Garland Publishing, 1993); Vol. 2: *From the Renaissance to the Twentieth Century* (New York: Garland Publishing, 1995); "Naples: Art Life and Organization Before 1455," & "Naples: Art Life and Organization 1455-c.1600," *The Dictionary of Art;* plus several dozen other introductions, occasional pieces & articles on contemporary politics & religion. **Bio-Bibliography:** Olga Rothschild, "Italica Press Celebrates Its Tenth," *Small Press Center News* (Spring 1995): 2-5, 7; *Contemporary Authors; Dictionary of International Biography; International Authors and Writers Who's Who; Who's Who in the East; Who's Who in the World.* **Business Address:** Italica Press, Inc., 595 Main St., 605, NYC 10044.

MUZZI, FRANCO ■ AAR Visitor 1980-81; RAI, Music Dir.

MYERS, ROBERT L. ■ FAAR Architecture 54. b. May 29, 1926, Macon, GA. BArch 50, Cornell Univ., College of Architecture, Art & Planning; MArch 51, Harvard GSD. **Career & Employment:** UNC, Chapel Hill 1942-44; Architects Collaborative, Designer 1951-53; Cornell Univ., Instr. 1955-56; Lashmit James Brown & Pollack, Designer 1957-58; Robert Myers, AIA, Architect 1959-60; Philip Johnson Asscs., Architects Designer 1960; Russell Gibson Von Dohlen, Architectural Designer 1977-88. **Memberships & Offices:** Nat. Council of Architectural Registration Bds.; Ackland Art Museum, UNC, Chapel Hill, Visiting Com. **Fellowships, Honors & Awards:** Cornell Univ., College of Architecture, Eidlitz Travel Fellowship 1950. **Important Works:** Stanley Works World Corp. HQ, New Britain, CT 1987; Hartford Group of ITT Expansion, Hartford, CT 1988; *Hartford Courant* Expansion, Hartford CT. **Home Address:** 144 Curtiss Rd., New Preston, CT 06777.

MYHERS, JOHN ■ GI Resident 1945-47, Singer.

■   ■   ■

N

NABOKOV, NICOLA (NIKOLAI) ■ RAAR Musical Composition 54, 68. b. Apr. 17, 1903, Lubcha, Novogrudok, Russia. d. Apr. 6, 1978. m. Dominique Cibiel. c. Ivan, Peter, Alexander. BA 26, Sorbonne, Paris. **Other Study:** With Rebikov in St. Petersburg & Yalta 1913-20; Stuttgart Conservatory 1920-22; Berlin Hochschule für Musik 1922-23 with Paul Juon & Ferruccio Busoni. **Career & Employment:** Wells College, Prof. 1936-41; St. John's College, Annapolis, Prof. 1941-44; Peabody Conservatory, Prof. 1943-45, 1947-52; Congress for Cultural Freedom, Sec. Gen. 1951-63; Berlin Music Festival, Art. Dir. 1963-68; SUNY, Buffalo, Lect. 1970-71; Aspen Inst. for Humanistic Studies 1970-73; NYU, Lect. 1972-73. **Fellowships, Honors & Awards:** NIAL 1970. **Publications:** *Old Friends & New Music* (Boston: Little Brown, 1951); *Igor Stravinsky* (Berlin, 1964); *Bagazh: Memoirs of a Russian Cosmopolitan* (London: Secker & Warburg, 1975). **Important Works:** *Ode: Méditation sur la majesté de Dieu,* a ballet-oratorio 1927; *Symphonie Lyrique,* No. 1, 1930; *La vie de Polichinelle,* a ballet 1934; *Union Pacific,* a ballet 1934; Symphonies 1930, 1941; *The Last Flower,* a ballet 1941; *The Holy Devil,* an opera 1958; *The Wanderer,* a ballet 1966; *Don Quixote,* a ballet 1966; *A Prayer,* Symphony No. 3, 1968; *Love's Labours Lost,* an opera 1973. **Bio-Bibliography:** *Baker's Biographical Dictionary of Musicians, New Grove Dictionary of American Music, Who Was Who in America.*

NAGINSKI, CHARLES ■ FAAR Musical Composition 40. b. May 29, 1909, Cairo, Egypt. d. Aug. 4, 1940. **Study:** Juilliard Graduate School with Rubin Goldmark 1928-33. **Important Works:** *Sinfonietta; The Minotaur,* a ballet for orchestra 1938; *Divertimento for Wind Instruments; Nocturne and Pantomime* 1938; *Five Pieces from a Children's Suite* 1940; *Three Poems by Walt Whitman; Concerto for Harpsichord; To Martha Graham,* for solo piano; *Conte Amusant,* for solo piano; *Gavotte,* for solo piano; Songs: *Reuben Bright; Sorrow; The Centaurs; The Pasture; The Woman with a Mirror; Mother and Babe; Under the Harvest Moon; Trickle Drops; Night Song at Amalfi.* **Bio-Bibliography:** *Contemporary American Composers.*

NAGY, HELEN ■ FAAR Classics/Archaeology 86. b. May 17, 1945, Igrici, Hungary. m. Eric W. Lindgren. c. Judith, Éva. BA 69, UCLA; MA 73, UCLA; PhD 78, UCLA. **Other Study:** Bryn Mawr College 1964-66. **Research/Artistic Interests:** Etruscan votive art, Greek Archaic sculpture. **Career & Employment:** Western Illinois Univ., Asst. Prof. 1977-79; Linfield College, Assc. Prof. 1979-87; Univ. of Puget Sound, Prof. 1987-present. **Memberships & Offices:** Classical Assn. of the Pacific Northwest, Ed. 1988-94; ArIA, Seattle Chap., Pres. 1992-94; Phi Beta Kappa, Delta Chap., Puget Sound, Pres. 1992-94. **Fellowships, Honors & Awards:** NEH, Summer Seminar in Rome 1979, Travel to Collections Grant 1983. **Publications:** *Votive Terracottas from the Vignaccia in the Lowie Museum* (Rome: Bretschneider, 1988); "Typological and Iconographic Analysis of the Vignaccia Deposit of Cerveteri," *Scienze dell' Antichità* 3-4 (1989-90): 729-39; "Divinities in the Context of Sacrifice and Cult on Caeretan Votive Terracottas," in *Murlo and the Etruscans,* ed. R.D. de Puma & J.P. Small (Madison, WI, 1994): 211-23. **Home Address:** 7720 Goodman Dr. NW, Gig Harbor, WA 98332. **Business Address:** Univ. of Puget Sound, Tacoma, WA 98416.

NATUNEWICZ, CHESTER F. ■ FAAR Classics/Archaeology 59. b. Mar. 13, 1932, Bristol, CT. m. Mary Ann Tustin. c. Ann, Cecily. BA 53, Yale Univ.; MA 54, Yale Univ.; PhD 57, Yale

My two years (1957-1959) at the American Academy in Rome were certainly among the happiest years of my life. I shall always be grateful for the opportunity of meeting and working with such distinguished scholars as Herbert Bloch, Lily Ross Taylor, George Duckworth, Paul MacKendrick, Axel Boethius, and Ferdinando Castagnoli, to name just a few. I remember with deep gratitude the kindness and generosity of so many people closely tied to the Academy, from our Director Lawrence Roberts and Mrs. Roberts, our New York Secretary Mary Williams, our Rome administrator Margherita Rospigliosi, our dear librarian Mrs. Longobardi to even the many loyal workers and servants at the Academy (our chef Signor Gentile, our driver Signor Nicola, our concierge Signor Giuseppe, and our factotum Signor D'Ettore). I treasure the fact that through the Academy I got to know better or meet for the first time people who already then were or since then have become scholars with distinguished reputations (Frank Brown, Eric Sjöqvist, Michael Jameson, Silvio Panciera and his lovely wife Mara, Giancarlo Susini, Giovanni Scichillone, Paolo Siniscalco, among others). Because of my association with the Academy I came in touch with many scholars from all over the world by being a translator and interpreter at the International Congress of Classical Archaeology. During that assignment I had the privilege of meeting with Amedeo Maiuri, Massimo Palottino, Giuseppe Lugli, Pietro Romanelli, Nevio DeGrassi, Fernanda Bertocchi, and especially East European colleagues from Poland, the Soviet Union, Bulgaria, Romania, Yugoslavia, Czechoslovakia, and East Germany, with whom I have had ties for over 34 years. It was a great experience for me to get to know so many American Fellows in various humanistic fields, to have Rome, as it were, in the "palm of my hand" for two full years, to get to know the Catholic Church better through frequent Vatican visits, and, one of the very best things of all, to meet at the American Academy the young lady, Mary Ann Tustin, who would later become my wife and to whom I have now been married for over twenty-six years. Much more could be said about how much I owe the Academy, but I'm running out of space.

Chester F. Natunewicz

Univ. **Research/Artistic Interests:** Foreign languages & literatures: Latin, ancient Greek, Italian, Polish, Russian & several others. **Career & Employment:** As teacher and/or administrator: Yale Univ. 1959-66, Wells College 1966-67, Dartmouth College 1967-68, Trinity College 1968, Goucher College 1968-76, Johns Hopkins Univ. 1976, Community College of Baltimore 1976, Univ. of Wisconsin Center, Manitowoc County 1976-84, Bellaire (TX) Senior HS 1985-present. **Memberships & Offices:** APA, American Classical League, Texas Classical Assn., Texas Foreign Language Assn. **Fellowships, Honors & Awards:** Phi Beta Kappa; Fulbright Fellow in Italy 1957-58. **Publications:** Over 75 articles & reviews in professional journals relating to the Greek & Latin classics; over 700 programs or interviews relating to the Greek and Latin over various radio & television stations. **Home Address:** 2107 Teague Rd., Houston, TX 77080. **Business Address:** Bellaire Senior HS, 5100 Maple St., Bellaire, TX 77401.

NAUGHTON, JOHN R. ■ FAAR Architecture 85. b. Oct. 25, 1946, Chicago, IL. m. Carol M. Naughton. BArch 70, Univ. of Illinois; MArch 83, Univ. of Illinois. **Career & Employment:** Chicago Associates, Planners and Architects, Prin. Designer 1972-80; A. Epstein & Sons, Senior Designer 1981-82; Yale Univ., Visiting Prof. 1983; Inst. for Architecture & Urban Studies, Teaching Fellow 1983. **Fellowships, Honors & Awards:** AIA, Univ. of Illinois, Chicago, School Medal 1983.

NAUMAN, BRUCE ■ RAAR Painting 87. b. Fort Wayne, IN. m. Susan Rothenberg. BA 64, Univ. of Wisconsin; MFA 66, UC, Irvine. **Fellowships, Honors & Awards:** Ohio State Univ., Wexner Center for the Arts Prize 1994. **Exhibitions/Performances:** Retrospectives: Los Angeles County Museum of Art & Whitney Museum, NYC 1972; Walker Art Center 1994, traveled to Los Angeles, Washington, DC, & MOMA; Leo Castelli Gallery, NYC 1994; First solo : Leo Castelli Gallery, NYC 1968.

NEBEL, BERTHOLD ■ FAAR Sculpture 17. b. Apr. 19, 1889, Basel, Switzerland. d. Apr. 4, 1964. m Marie Lucontoni. c. Emile, Lucia White. **Study:** ASL; Student Mechanics Inst.; NAD. **Ca-**

reer & Employment: Carnegie Inst. School of Sculpture, Head 1920-23. **Memberships & Offices:** NAD; NSS. **Fellowships, Honors & Awards:** Virginia War Memorial Competition Prize 1926. **Important Works:** Doors, Hispanic Museum, NYC; Doors, Museum of American Indian, NYC; Doors, Geographical Soc. of America, NYC; Connecticut State Capitol; US Capitol; Brown Bros. Bank, NYC; *Gen. Joseph Wheeler*, Hall of Fame, Washington, DC; *Alexander Brown*, Wall & Nassau Sts., NYC. **Bio-Bibliography:** *Who Was Who in America, Who Was Who in American Art*.

NEFF, AMY L. ■ FAAR History of Art 76. b. Dec. 17, 1947, Philadelphia, PA. m. Brian F. Griffin. c. Ezra, Miriam. BA 69, Barnard College; MA 71, Univ. of Pennsylvania; PhD 77, Univ. of Pennsylvania. **Research/Artistic Interests:** Medieval art, especially 13th-century Italian. **Career & Employment:** Univ. of Tennessee, Asst. Prof. 1978-86, Assc. Prof. 1986-present; Univ. of Virginia, Visiting Prof. 1989. **Memberships & Offices:** Phi Beta Kappa, CAA, Intl. Center for Medieval Art, MAA. **Fellowships, Honors & Awards:** Gladys Krieble Delmas Found. Fellowship 1978, 1988; ACLS Travel Grant 1979; Lilly Found., Post-Doctoral Teaching Award 1979-80; CASVA, Senior Fellowship 1982-83; Villa I Tatti, Senior Fellowship 1983-84; NEH Fellowship 1990, Mentor, Younger Scholars Award 1994. **Publications:** "A New Interpretation of the *Supplicationes Variae* Miniatures," in *Il Medio Oriente e l'Occidente nell' arte del xiii secolo*, ed. H. Belting (Bologna: C.L.U.E.B., 1982), 173-79; "The *Dialogus Beatae Mariae et Anselmi de Passione Domini*: Toward an Attribution," *Miscellanea Francescana* 86 (1986): 105-8; "Wicked Children on Calvary and the Baldness of St. Francis," *Mitteilungen des Kunsthistorischen Institut in Florenz* 34 (1990): 215-44; "Miniatori e 'arte dei cristallari' a Venezia nella seconda metà del Duecento," *Arte Veneta* 45 (1993): 6-19. **Home Address:** 2003 Island Home Blvd., Knoxville, TN 37920. **Business Address:** Art Dept., Univ. of Tennessee, Knoxville, TN 37996.

NEIL, WILLIAM ■ FAAR Musical Composition 83. b. Jan. 12, 1954. m. Linda Lupsor. c. Christopher, Sean. BA 77, Cleveland Inst. of Music; MA 79, Cleveland Inst. of Music; DMA 86, Univ.

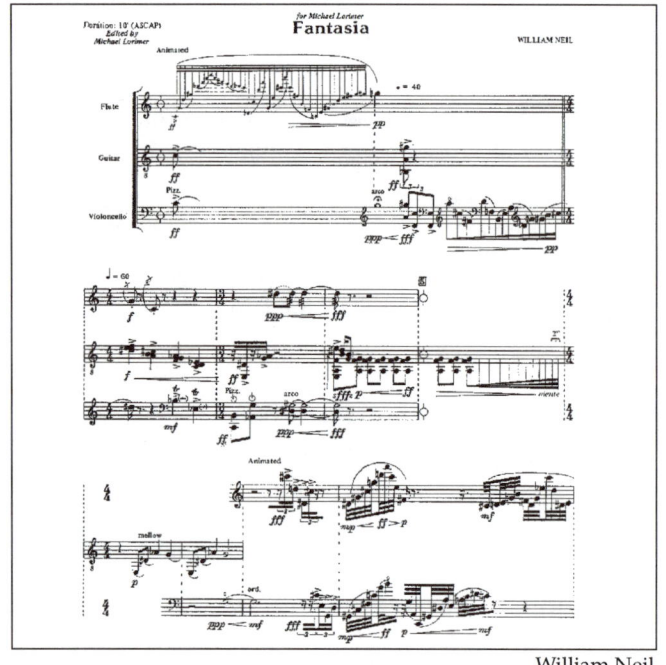

William Neil

of Michigan. **Other Study:** Hochschule für Musik, Cologne 1978-79. **Career & Employment:** De Pauw Univ., Instr. 1981-82; Socrates Bilingual School, Rome, Instr. 1982-83; Ambrit School, Rome, Dir. of Music 1983-84; Lyric Opera of Chicago, Composer-in-Residence 1984-86; New Music Chicago Fetival, Artistic Dir. 1987-88; Guest Conductor: Pontino Festival, Latina 1983. **Memberships & Offices:** Fellow: American Symphony Orchestra League, Chicago; Indianapolis Symphony; Grand Rapids Symphony 1989-present; Valentino Intl. Competition, Juror 1983; Experimental Sound Studio, Founding Mem. **Fellowships, Honors & Awards:** Fulbright Scholar 1978-79; BMI, Composition Award 1980; ASCAP Award 1980; AAAL, Charles Ives Scholarship Award 1981. **Important Works:** *Limites*, for orchestra 1977; *Oboe Concerto in One Movement*, for orchestra 1977; *Fantasia*, for flute, guitar & cello 1979; *Routine*, for clarinet & tape 1980; *Sumi II*, for piano & winds 1981; *Harlem Dances*, for guitar 1983; *Deserted Places* 1984; *A Play of Poems*, for soprano, baritone & orchestra 1984; *The Guilt of Lillian Sloan*, opera 1986; *Concerto for Piccolo Clarinet* 1987; *Guitar Concerto*, for orchestra 1987; *Dragon-töter*, for orchestra 1988. **Home Address:** 5455 N. Sheridan Rd., Chicago, IL 60640.

NELSON, GEORGE HAROLD ■ FAAR Architecture 34. b. May 29, 1908, Hartford, CT. d. Mar. 1986. m. Jacqueline Nelson. c. Mico. BA 28, Yale Univ.; BFA 31, Yale Univ. **Other Study:** Catholic Univ. of America. **Research/Artistic Interests:** Temple of Apollo, Corinth; house design. **Career & Employment:** Yale Univ., Instr. 1931-32; *Architectural Forum*, Assc. Ed. 1935-43, Co-Managing Ed. 1943-44, Consultant 1944-49; William Hamby, Part. 1936-41; Columbia Univ., Faculty 1942-45; Herman Miller Furniture Co., Design Dir. 1946; George Nelson & Co., Prin. 1947-53; *Interiors*, Ed. 1948-75; Nelson & Chadwick, Part. 1953-86; Harvard GSD, Visiting Critic 1972-73. **Memberships & Offices:** MOMA, Architecture Com.; US Housing Authority, Architectural Advising Com.; NY State Council on Architecture 1968-75; Intl. Design Conference, Program Chair 1965, BoD 1965; Industrial Designers Soc. of America, BoD 1967-69, 1972-86; Massachusetts College of Art, Visual Technology Center, Adv. 1982-86. **Fellowships, Honors & Awards:** Scarab Gold Medal 1941; Benjamin Franklin Fellow 1960; AIA, Fellow 1963; Industrial Arts Medal 1964; Industrial Designers Soc. of America, Fellow 1968, Distinguished Contribution Award 1974, Personal Recognition Award 1981; Royal Soc. of Arts, London, Hon. Royal Designer for Industry 1973; American Soc. of Interior Designers, Elsie Wolfe Award 1975; AIA, NY Chap., Medal of Honor 1979; Parsons School of Design, DFA 1979; Minneapolis College of Art & Design, DFA 1980. **Publications:** *Industrial Architecture of Albert Kahn Inc.* (New York: Architectural Book Publishing Co., 1939); with Henry Wright, *Tomorrow's House* (New York: Simon & Schuster, 1945); ed., *Living Spaces* (New York: Whitney Publications, 1952); ed., *Storage* (New York: Whitney Publications, 1954); *Problems of Design* (New York: Whitney Publications, 1957); *How to See: Visual Adventures in a World God Never Made* (Boston: Little, Brown, 1977); *George Nelson on Design* (New York: Whitney Publications, 1979). **Important Works:** Information Center, Colonial Williamsburg 1956; NYU Loeb Student Center Interiors 1959; NY Worlds Fair 1964: Chrysler Exb., Irish Pavilion, & US Dept. of State Hall of Presidents; USIA Industrial Design USA Exb. 1967; Rosenthal Studio, NYC 1968; US Treasury Exb. 1970; USIA Research & Development in the US Exb. 1970-72; Children's Place, West Hartford, CT, & Echelon & Willowbrook, NJ 1972; American Revolution Bicentennial Administration USA '76: The First Two Hundred Years Exb. 1974-76; Inter-American Cultural & Trade Center Latin American Exb. 1976;

Philadelphia Museum of Art, Design Since 1945 Exb. 1983. **Exhibitions/Performances:** Walker Art Center 1975-76. **Bio-Bibliography:** *Contemporary Architects.*

NELSON, PAUL ■ FAAR Musical Composition 60. b. 1929, Phoenix, AZ. m. Else Maria Wohlmuth. BS 54, Teachers College, Columbia Univ.; MA 57, Harvard Univ. **Other Study:** Arizona State Univ., Tempe 1947-50; Univ. of Vienna 1958-60; composition with Paul Creston 1948, Paul Hindemith 1949, Lukas Foss 1952, Walter Piston & Randall Thompson 1954-55, 1956-57. **Career & Employment:** Phoenix Symphony, Prin. Trumpet 1949-50; Monterey County Symphony, Prin. Trumpet 1950-51; US Army Band Training Unit., Instr. 1950-51; US Military Acad. Band, Staff Arranger-Composer 1951-53, Post Chapel Choir Cond. 1952-53; Univ. of Louisville, Instr. 1955-56; Bass Chorister: Church of the Advent, Boston 1956-57; American Church Choir, Paris 1959-60; Choeur Philharmonique, Paris 1959-60; Brown Univ., Asst. Prof. 1964-66, Assc. Prof. 1967-83. **Fellowships, Honors & Awards:** Arizona Soc. of Composers Award 1950; Friends of Harvey Gaul Competition, 1st Prize 1952; Louisville Orchestra Student Award 1953; Harvard Univ., Francis Boott Prize 1957; John Knowles Paine Traveling Fellowship 1957-58; Arizona Anniversary Music Project Award 1962; Inter-American Music Award 1965; NEA Composers Grant 1977; ASCAP, Rudolf Nissim Award 1987; Rhode Island State Council on the Arts Fellowship 1990-91. **Important Works:** *Variations on a Western Folksong,* Phoenix Symphony Comm. 1949; *Erzählung für Orchester* (Edition Modern, Munich) 1956; *Songs of Life,* for mixed chorus & strings (Carl Fischer) 1957, rev. 1992; *Horn Sonata,* Christopher Leuba Comm. (Horn Realm) 1958; *Divertimento for Clarinet,* Contemporary Music Soc. of Houston Comm. 1960; *Sinfonietta* (Galaxy Music) 1960; *Cantata da Camera,* for soprano, baritone & chamber ensemble 1962; *Thy Will Be Done,* for men's chorus, brass & percussion, Brown Univ. Glee Club Comm. (Boosey & Hawkes) 1964; *A 'Quad'libet on traditional Songs for Brown University,* for mixed chorus, baritone & orchestra, Brown Univ. Comm. 1970; *Aria & Scherzo,* for string quartet, Intl. String Quartet Comm. 1982; *Vox Aeterna Amoris,* for mezzo-soprano & orchestra 1987; *Cantata Psalmorum,* for mixed chorus, soprano & orchestra, Rhode Island Civic Chorale & Orchestra Comm. 1990. **Home Address:** 247 Williams St., Providence, RI 02906.

NEUERBURG, NORMAN ■ FAAR Classics/Archaeology 57. b. Feb. 3, 1926, Los Angeles, CA. BA 53, UCLA; MA 55, IFA; PhD 60, IFA. **Career & Employment:** UC, Berkeley, Lect. 1958; UC, Riverside, Instr. 1960-61; UC, Santa Barbara, Asst. Prof. 1964-65; UCLA, Lect. 1967-69; California Inst. of the Arts, Lect. 1965-66; California State College, Assc. Prof. 1966-70; California State Univ., Prof. 1971-82, Prof. Emer. 1982-present; Southwest Museum, Curator of Spanish Colonial Art 1982-83; Fototeca d'Archeologia e Topografia dell'Italia Antica, Rome, Dir. 1961-64; Mission San Fernando Restoration 1941-44, 1950-60, 1983-84, 1987-89. **Memberships & Offices:** Historical Consultant: J. Paul Getty Museum, Malibu 1970-74; Mission San Juan Capistrano 1978-present; Mission San José 1981; Santa Barbara Presidio 1982-present; Mission San Juan Bautista 1983-84; Santa Cruz State Historic Park 1985; El Pueblo de Los Angeles 1986-88; BoD: Santa Barbara Mission Archive-Library; Friends of the Archival Center, Archdiocese of Los Angeles; Citizens Adv. Bd. of Mission La Purissima State Historical Park; California Historical Soc. 1988-93; Serra Bicentennial Comm. 1983-84; Santa Cruz Island Found. **Publications:** "Some Considerations on the Architecture of the Imperial Villa at Piazza Armerina," *Marsyas* 8 (1959): 22-29; *L'Architettura delle fontane*

e dei ninfei nell'Italia Antica, Memorie dell'Accademia di archeologia e belle arti di Napoli 5 (1965); "Building the J. Paul Getty Museum," *Classical America* 4 (1977): 54-74; "The Angel on the Cloud, or 'Anglo-American Myopia' Revisited: A Discussion of the Writings of James L. Nolan," *Southern California Quarterly* (1980): 1-48; "The Function of Prints in the California Missions," *Southern California Quarterly* (1985): 263-80; "The Changing Face of Mission San Diego," *Journal of San Diego History* 32.1 (1986): 1-26; *The Decoration of the California Missions* (Santa Barbara: Bellerophon, 1987); *Agustín V. Zamorano Architect* (Santa Barbara: Bellerophon, 1988); *The Saints of the California Missions* (Santa Barbara: Bellerophon, 1989); "Saint Bonaventure, Seraphic Doctor," *Ventura County Historical Society Quarterly* 37.1 (1991): 1-28; "Indians as Artists in California Before and After Contact," *Congrés Internacional d'Estudios Històricos les Illes Balears i Amèrica* (Palma: Institut d'estudis Baleárics, 1992), 2:41-60; with Bartolomé Font Obrador, *Fr. Junipero Serra: Mallorca-México-Sierra Gorda-Californias* (Mallorca: Comissió de Cultura, Consell Insular de Mallorca, 1992). **Home Address:** 4153 Tracy St., Los Angeles, CA 90027.

NEWHOUSE, VICTORIA ■ AAR Trustee 1986-present. **Study:** Bryn Mawr College, Columbia Univ. **Memberships & Offices:** MOMA, Com. on Architecture & Design; Jewish Heritage Council Com., World Monuments Fund; Samuel H. Kress Found., BoT. **Publications:** *Wallace K. Harrison, Architect* (1989).

NEWMAN, LAURA M. ■ FAAR Painting 80. b. July 16, 1956, Cleveland, OH. m. Charles M. Hagen. c. Anna Adele Hagen. BFA 78, Cooper Union School of Art. **Other Study:** Nova Scotia College of Art & Design, Halifax 1981. **Research/Artistic Interests:** Painting, oil & watercolor. **Career & Employment:** Cooper Union School of Art, Adj. Instr. 1978-92; Nova Scotia College of Art, Instr. 1988-92; NYU, Adj. Instr. 1992; Yale Univ., Asst. Prof. 1994-present. **Fellowships, Honors & Awards:** Guggenheim Fellowship 1981-82; New Jersey State Council on the Arts Fellowship 1984-85; AAAL, Rosenthal Award 1992. **Exhibitions/Performances:** Solo: Victoria Munroe Gallery 1987, 1989; Group: New Museum, NYC 1985; Anne Plumb Gallery, NYC 1986; Rutgers Univ. 1988; Anna Leonowens Gallery, Halifax 1990, 1992; Victoria Munroe Gallery, Metrotech Center, Brooklyn 1990, 1991, 1993, 1994; Cooper Union 1992; Tribeca 148, NYC 1992; AAAL 1992; David Beitzel Gallery, NYC 1992, 1993. **Business Address:** 705 Driggs Ave., Brooklyn, NY 11211.

NEWTON, CARLTON ■ FAAR Sculpture 81. b. May 6, 1946, Boston, MA. m. Elizabeth King. BFA 72, San Francisco Art Inst.; MFA 78, San Francisco Art Inst. **Other Study:** Art History, UC, Berkeley 1974. **Career & Employment:** San Francisco Art Inst., Sculpture Dept., Technical Supervisor 1979-80; College of William & Mary, Asst. Prof. 1982-86; Princeton Univ., Lect. 1983; Univ. of Richmond, Visiting Asst. Prof. 1986-87; Virginia Commonwealth Univ., Faculty 1987-94, Asst. Prof. 1994-present. **Fellowships, Honors & Awards:** NEA Fellowship 1980. **Exhibitions/Performances:** Solo: Seigfred Gallery, Ohio Univ., Athens 1984; 1708 East Main, Richmond, VA 1986; Peninsula Fine Arts Center, Newport News, VA 1989; 1708 Gallery, Richmond, VA 1994; Group: New Museum, NYC 1979; Tyler Art School, Philadelphia 1982; Art Museum, Princeton Univ. 1985; Contemporary Arts Center, New Orleans 1988; City Gallery of Contemporary Art, Raleigh, NC 1987; Virginia Museum of Fine Arts, Richmond 1990; OAS Museum, Washington, DC 1994; Bennington College 1995. **Home Address:** PO Box 8062, Richmond, VA 23223. **Business Address:** Sculpture Dept., Virginia Commonwealth Univ., 1001 W. Broad St., Richmond, VA 23284.

NEWTON, NORMAN T. ■ FAAR Landscape Architecture 26, RAAR Landscape Architecture 67. b. Apr. 21, 1898, Corry, PA. d. Sept. 12, 1992. m. Lyyli E.E. Lamsa. BS 19, Cornell Univ.; MLD 20, Cornell Univ. **Research/Artistic Interests:** Reconstruction of Monte Cassino Abbey. **Career & Employment:** Bryant Flemming, Landscape Architect 1920-23; Ferruccio Vitale, Landscape Architect 1926-31, Assc. 1930-31; Private Practice, NYC 1931-42; US Nat. Park Service, Assc. Landscape Architect 1933-39; US AAF 1942-46; Harvard GSD, Asst. Prof.-Prof. 1939-66, Charles Eliot Prof. 1963-66, Charles Eliot Prof. Emer. 1966-92; Harvard College, Dept. of Architectural Science, Chair 1949-64. **Memberships & Offices:** AAUP; New England Historic Genealogical Soc.; Gamma Delta Psi; Theta Delta Chi; Century Assn. 1937; ASLA, Nat. Pres. 1957-61. **Fellowships, Honors & Awards:** Boy Scouts of America, Nat. Gold Medal 1914; US Air Force Service Medal; Commander, Sts. Maurice and Lazarus, Grand Officer, Crown of Italy 1946; Order, Star of Solidarity, Italy 1950; Harvard Univ., Hon. MA 1957; ASLA, Bradford Williams Medal 1975, ASLA Medal 1979, Fellow; Sigma Lambda Alpha Distinguished Mem. Award 1984; Hubbard Educational Trust, Distinguished Educator Award 1991; Accademia delle Arti del Disegno, Florence 1979; Harvard GSD, Lifetime Teaching Award (Posthumous) 1992. **Publications:** ed., *State Park Master Planning Manual* (1937); *War Damage to Monuments and Fine Arts of Italy* (1946); *Structure of Design, Preliminary Notes* (1949); *An Approach to Design* (Cambridge, MA: Addison-Wesley, 1951); *Design on the Land: The Development of Landscape Architecture* (Cambridge, MA: Harvard Univ. Press, 1971). **Important Works:** Liberty Island Master Plan 1937; Salem Maritime Nat. Historic Site; Saratoga Battlefield Historic Site. **Exhibitions/Performances:** ASLA 1926; ALNY 1932; Gund Gallery, Harvard GSD 1988. **Bio-Bibliography:** *Landscape Architecture* (Mar.-Apr. 1989); *Who's Who in America, Who Was Who in America;* Video Biography, Hubbard Educational Trust.

NICASSIO, SUSAN V. ■ FAAR Post-Classical/Humanistic Studies 94. b. March 25, 1941, Muscogee, OK. m. Anthony R. Nicassio. c. Alexander Raymond. BA 83, Louisiana State Univ.; MA 85, Louisiana State Univ.; PhD 89, Louisiana State Univ. **Research/Artistic Interests:** 18th-century social & cultural history, specifically popular theater & social cohesion in papal Rome. Also, 18th- & 19th-century musical theater. **Career & Employment:** Elon College, Asst. Prof. 1989-91; Univ. of Alabama, Asst. Prof. 1991-present. **Memberships & Offices:** AHA 1988-present; Soc. for Italian Studies 1989-present; American Soc. for 18th-Century Studies 1988-present; S.E. American Soc. for 18th-Century Studies, Planning Com. 1989-present; New England Historical Assn. 1991-present. **Fellowships, Honors & Awards:** Fulbright Fellowship 1986-87; Louisiana State Univ., T. Harry Williams Fellow 1987-88, Distinguished Dissertation Award 1989; Newberry Library, American Soc. for 18th-Century Studies Fellow 1990; NEH Faculty Grant 1991; Univ. of Alabama Graduate Research Grant 1991, 1992. **Publications:** "The Pain Doesn't Matter: Tosca and the Law," *Opera Quarterly* 7.4 (Winter 1990): 39-43; "A Tale of Three Cities: Perceptions of Eighteenth-Century Modena," *Journal of Interdisciplinary History* 21.3 (Winter 1991): 415-45; "'For the Benefit of My Soul...': Mass Obligations in an Eighteenth-Century Italian City," *Catholic Historical Review* 77.2 (Apr. 1992): 175-96; "Lodovico Antonio Muratori," in *The Directory of Medieval Scholars*, ed. Helen Damico & Joseph B. Zavadil (New York: Garland Publishers, 1993); *The Italian Bach* (Stony Brook, NY: Bach Aria Group, SUNY, 1994); "The Lively Steeets: Art, Status and Social Control in the Streets of Eighteenth-Century Modena,"

in *Absolutism and Urban Space in Early Modern Italy,* ed. R. Burr Litchfield & Geoffrey Symcox (Princeton: Princeton University Press); "Giacomo Puccini," in *Research Guide to Europe Biography* (Beacham); "A Model for Enlightened Absolutism: The Long-Distance Restructuring of Modena," *Proceedings of the Consortium on Revolutionary Europe,* pp. 320-27. **Home Address:** 2117 Grayson Valley Dr., Birmingham, AL 35235. **Business Address:** Univ. of Alabama, 1212 Univ. Blvd., Birmingham, AL 3529.

NICHOLS, CHARLOTTE F. ■ FAAR History of Art 83; SOF, Council 1992-present. b. June 15, 1954, Springfield, MA. m. Derek A.R. Moore, FAAR 84. c. Olivia. BA 76, Smith College; MA 80, IFA, PhD 88, IFA. **Other Study:** Univ. of Florence 1974-75. **Research/Artistic Interests:** History & art of the Italian Renaissance, especially of Naples. **Career & Employment:** RISD, Rome, Lect. 1984; Syracuse Univ., Florence, Adj. Lect. 1984; Frick Collection, Lect. & Curatorial Asst. 1985-88; Mt. Holyoke College, Asst. Prof. 1988-89; Seton Hall Univ., Asst. Prof. 1990-present. **Memberships & Offices:** CAA, SAH, RSA. **Fellowships, Honors & Awards:** IFA, Grants 1976-80, Bernard Berenson Fellowship 1980-81, Florence Waterbury Fellowship 1983-84; ACLS Grant-in-Aid 1989; NEH Summer Seminar 1990. **Publications:** *The Caracciolo di Vico Chapel in Naples and Early Cinquecento Architecture* (Ann Arbor: University Microfilms, 1988). **Home Address:** 45 Woodland Ave., Summit, NJ 07901.

NITZE, SUSAN ■ AAR Trustee 1987-present. BA Wellesley College. **Memberships & Offices:** Groton School, BoT; New York Philharmonic Volunteer Council, Chair 1985-; Girl Scouts Council of Greater New York, BoT; MMA, HS Program, Course Chair.

NIVOLA, CONSTANTINO ■ RAAR Sculpture 72, 77. b. July 5, 1911, Orani, Sardinia. d. May 5, 1988. MA 36, Istituto Superiore d'Arte. **Career & Employment:** Olivetti Co., Art Dir. 1936-39; *Interiors Magazine,* Art Dir. 1941-45; Harvard GSD, Faculty 1953-57; Columbia Univ., Faculty 1961-63; Harvard Univ. 1970-73; Intl. Univ. of Art, Florence 1971; Dartmouth College 1978; UC, Berkeley 1978-79. **Memberships & Offices:** Artists' Equity; ALNY; NIAL; Vietnam Veterans Memorial, Washington, DC, Juror 1982. **Fellowships, Honors & Awards:** Philadelphia Decorators Club Award 1959; Carborundum Major Abrasive Marketing Award 1962; Municipal Arts Soc. of NY, Certificate of Merit 1962; Cagliari Regional Exb., Gold Medal; Federation of Graphic Arts, Diploma; Park Assn. of NY, Certificate of Commendation 1965; AIA, Fine Arts Medal 1968. **Important Works:** Milan Triennial 1933; Paris World's Fair, Italian Pavillion 1937; Olivetti Showroom 1953-54; Four Chaplains Memorial Fountain, Falls Church, VA 1955; 1025 Fifth Ave. 1955, William E. Grady Vocational HS, Brooklyn 1957; Mutual Insurance Co., Hartford, Facade 1957; PS 46 Brooklyn 1959; McComick Place Exposition Hall, Chicago 1960; Motorola Bldg., Chicago 1960; Yale Univ., Saarinen Dorms 1962; Memorial Plaza, Nuoro, Italy 1966; PS 320, Brooklyn 1967; Sculpture, Mexico City-Nacional Olympiad 19th 1968; 15 sculptures, Government Bldg, Cagliari, Italy 1986-87. **Exhibitions/Performances:** Solo: Sassary Gallery, Sardinia 1927; Betty Parsons Gallery 1940; Tibor de Nagy Gallery 1950; Peridot Gallery 1954, 1957; Harvard Univ. 1956; Bertha Schaefer Gallery 1958; ALNY 1958; Galleria Il Milione, Milan 1959; Arts Club of Chicago 1959; American Federation of Arts 1960; Galleria dell'Ariete 1962; Byron Gallery 1964-67; Andrew-Morris Gallery, NYC; Marlborough Galleria d'Arte, Rome 1973; Willard Gallery 1973; Cagliari Univ. 1973; ICA, Boston 1974; Gallery Paule Anglim, San Francisco 1978; Duchamp Gallery, Cagliari, Italy 1982;

Washburn Gallery Inc. 1984, 1987. **Bio-Bibliography:** *Who Was Who in America, Dictionary of Contemporary American Artists;* Fred Licht, *Nivola, Scultóre* (Milan: Jaca, 1991).

NOGUCHI, ISAMU ■ AAR Visitor 1943 — 1951, Artist. b. Nov. 17, 1904. dec. **Honors & Awards:** President's Medal 1985. **Exhibitions/Performances:** Solo Shows: MOMA; Whitney Museum, NYC; André Emmerich Gallery, NYC. **Important Work:** MMA; MOMA; San Francisco Museum of Modern Art; Isamu Noguchi Garden Museum, Long Island City, NY.

```
Ille terrarum mihi praeter omnis angulus ridet (That corner
of the world has a smile for me beyond all others) says
Horace with his customary felicity. He is speaking of
Tarentum, but his words often come to mind when I think
of the American Academy in Rome. That corner of the
Janiculum has been for me a place of learning, a center
from which to explore Rome, the rest of Italy, and many
other parts of the ancient Mediterranean world, and since
my first visit, in the vintage year of 1953-54, it has
introduced me to an unforgettable throng-Fellows, visiting
scholars and artists, birds of passage of variegated
plumage- who have defined for me the meaning of amicitia.

                         Helen F. North

                    Helen F. North
                    January 6, 1993
```

Helen F. North

NORTH, HELEN F. ■ RAAR Classics/Archaeology 80; World War II Fellow 1942; AAR Trustee 1977-94; Trustee Emer.; AAR Adv. Council Trustee 1972-75; Com. on the Classical School, Chair 1982-94; Classical Soc., Pres. 1961. b. Jan. 31, 1921, Utica, NY. BA 42, Cornell Univ.; MA 43, Cornell Univ.; PhD 45, Cornell Univ. **Research/Artistic Interests:** Classical philology, especially Greek & Roman ethical philosophy, ancient rhetoric & literary criticism. **Career & Employment:** Rosary College, Instr. 1946-48; Swarthmore College, Asst. Prof.-Prof. 1948-91, Prof. Emer. 1991; Visiting Positions: Barnard College 1954-55, La Salle College 1965, ASCSA 1975, 1987, Vassar College 1979. **Memberships & Offices:** APA, BoD 1972-77, 1992-95, Pres. 1976, Series of College Texts, ed. 1969-77, Nominating Com., Chair 1979, 1980, BoD 1972-77, 1992, Research Div., VP 1992, Com. on Publications 1990-93, Delegate to ACLS 1991-95; Phi Beta Kappa, Bd. of Visiting Scholars 1975-76, Senate 1991-97; ACLS, BoD 1977-84, Search Committee for Pres., Chair 1985-86, Nominating Com., Chair 1979, 1983, 1985, Exec. Com., Bd. of Delegates 1992-95; La Salle Univ., BoT 1973-present, Chair 1991-92. **Fellowships, Honors & Awards:** Mary Isabel Sibley Fellowship 1945-46; Fulbright Fellowship 1953-54; Ford Found. Fellowship 1953-54; Guggenheim Fellowship 1958-59, 1975-76; NEH Fellowship 1967-68, 1983-84; APA, Charles J. Goodwin Award 1969; ACLS Fellowship 1971-72, 1987-88; Martin Classical Lectures 1972; AAAS 1975; Distinguished Daughter of Pennsylvania 1989; APS 1991; Hon. degrees: Rosary College, Trinity College (Dublin), La Salle Univ., Yale Univ. **Publications:** "A Period of Opposition to *Sophrosyne* in Greek Thought," *TAPA* 78 (1947): 1-17; "The Concept of *Sophrosyne* in Greek Literary Criticism," *Classical Philology* 43 (1948): 1-17; "The Use of Poetry in the Training of the Ancient Orator," *Traditio* 8 (1952): 1-33; Sophrosyne: *Self-Knowledge and Self-Restraint in Greek Literature* (Ithaca, NY: Cornell Univ. Press, 1966); trans., John Milton, *Defensio Secunda pro Populo Anglicano,* Complete Prose Works of John Milton, vol. 4 (New Haven: Yale Univ. Press, 1966); ed., with Anne King, Harry Caplan, *Of Eloquence: Studies in Ancient and Mediaeval Rhetoric* (Ithaca, NY: Cornell Univ. Press, 1969); "Swimming Upside Down in the Wrong Direction: Plato's Criticism of Sophistic Rhetoric on Technical & Stylistic Grounds," *Traditio* 32 (1976): 11-29; ed., *Interpretations of Plato* (Leiden: Brill, 1977); *From Myth to Icon: Reflections of Greek Ethical Doctrine in Literature and Art* (Ithaca, NY: Cornell Univ. Press, 1979); "Combing and Curling: *Orator Summus Plato,*" *Illinois Classical Studies* 16 (1991): 201-19; "Emblems of Eloquence," *Proceedings of the American Philosophical Society* 137 (1993): 406-30; "The Acropolis of the Soul," *Nomodeiktes: Greek Studies in Honor of Martin Ostwald* (Ann Arbor; Univ. of Michigan Press, 1993): 423-33; "Opening Socrates: The *Eikon* of Alcibiades," *Illinois Classical Studies* 19 (1994): 89-98. **Bio-Bibliography:** *Directory of American Scholars, Who's Who in America.* **Home Address:** 604 Ogden Ave., Swarthmore, PA 19081.

NORTON, CHARLES D. ■ AAR Trustee 1913-21, Bank Exec.

NORTON, RICHARD ■ ASCSR, Dir. 1899-1907, Archaeologist.

NUSSDORFER, LAURIE ■ FAAR Post-Classical/Humanistic Studies 81; AAR SOF Council 1990-92, VP 1992-96, *Newsletter,* Ed. 1990-94. b. Feb. 1, 1950, Oak Park, IL. m. Fred Travisano, FAAR 82. BA 72, Yale Univ.; MSc 74, London School of Economics; PhD 85, Princeton Univ. **Other Study:** Vassar College. **Research/Artistic Interests:** Social history of early modern Rome (16th-18th centuries). **Career & Employment:** NYU, Visiting Asst. Prof. 1985-86; Wesleyan Univ., Assc. Prof. 1986-present. **Memberships & Offices:** Soc. for Italian Historical Studies, Award & Citation Com. 1990-91, Exec. Council 1994-present; New England Historical Assn., Book Award Com. 1992. **Fellowships, Honors & Awards:** Mellon Post-Doctoral Fellowship 1985; ACLS Research Fellowship 1987, Grant-in-Aid 1991; NEH Grant for College Teachers 1991, Summer Inst., Newberry Library 1993. **Publications:** *Civic Politics in the Rome of Urban VIII* (Princeton: Princeton Univ. Press, 1992); "Writing and the Power of Speech: Notaries and Artisans in Baroque Rome," in *Culture and Identity in Early Modern Europe 1500-1800,* ed. Barbara Diefendorf & Carla Hesse (Ann Arbor: Univ. of Michigan Press, 1993), 103-18; with Nicholas Adams, "The Italian City, 1400-1600," in *The Renaissance from Brunelleschi to Michelangelo: The Representation of Architecture,* ed. Henry A. Millon & Vittorio Magnago Lampugnani (Milan: Bompiani, 1994), 205-31. **Business Address:** History Dept., Wesleyan Univ., Middletown, CT 06459.

■ ■ ■

O

OBERLIN, RUSSELL ■ AAR Visitor 1987-88, Musicologist, Counter-tenor.

O'BOYLE, NANCY M. ■ AAR Trustee 1984-present. BA, Smith College. **Memberships & Offices:** Modern Art Museum, Ft. Worth, Adv. Trustee; Whitney Museum, NYC, Drawing Com.; Smith College Museum, Visiting Com.; American Federation of the Arts, BoT.

O'BRIEN, EUGENE J. ■ FAAR Musical Composition 73. b. Apr. 24, 1945, Paterson, NJ. BM 67, Univ. of Nebraska; MM 69, Univ. of Nebraska; DMA 83, Case Western Reserve Univ., Cleveland Inst. of Music. **Other Study:** Staatliche Hochschule für Musik, Cologne 1969-70. **Career & Employment:** Cleveland Inst. of Music, Teacher 1973-81, Composer-in-Residence 1981-85; Catholic Univ. of America, Assc. Prof. 1985-87; Indiana Univ., Prof. 1987-present. **Memberships & Offices:** Juror: Cuyahoga Co. Cultural Council 1981-84; Ohio Arts Council 1983-85; Michigan Council for the Arts 1984; Minnesota Composers Forum 1984; Adv.: Bascom Little Fund 1977-85, Cleveland Arts Prize 1980-85, Contemporary Music Forum 1985-87. **Fellowships, Honors & Awards:** Fulbright Fellowship 1969-70; NEA Fellowship 1977, 1979; NIAL, Music Award 1980; Ohio Arts Council Fellowship 1980; Guggenheim Fellowship 1984-85; Rockefeller Found., Bellagio Fellowship 1984. **Important Works:** *Ambages* (G. Schirmer, Golden Crest) 1975; *Dédales,* for soprano & orchestra, Koussevitzky Found. Comm. (MMB Music) 1973; *Lingual* (Crystal Records) 1977; *Embarking for Cythera,* chamber ensemble (Boosey & Hawkes, CRI) 1978; *Allures,* for percussion trio (CRI) 1979; *Dreams & Secrets of Origin,* for soprano & orchestra 1983; *Taking Measures,* chamber ensemble, Cleveland Modern Dance Assn. Comm. (MMB Music, Capstone) 1985; *Mysteries of the Horizon,* for chamber orchestra, Fromm Found. Comm. (MMB Music) 1987; *Tristan's Lament* (MMB Music) 1991; *Black Fugatos* (MMB Music) 1991; *Concerto for Alto Saxophone & Orchestra,* John Sampen Comm. (MMB Music) 1992. **Bio-Bibliography:** *Baker's Biographical Dictionary of Musicians; New Grove Dictionary of American Music.* **Business Address:** School of Music, Indiana Univ., Bloomington, IN 47405.

O'BRYAN, MARK J. ■ NIAE, John Dinkeloo Traveling Fellow 1984-85. b. Mar. 20, 1958, Louisville, KY. m. Mary Lee O'Bryan. c. Charles Xavier, Abigail Lee. BArch 82, Univ. of Kentucky; MArch 87, Cornell Univ. **Career & Employment:** Ohio State Univ., Adj. Asst. Prof. 1987-present; Univ. of Kentucky, Assc. Prof. 1989-present. **Home Address:** 1103 Old Cannons Ln., Louisville, KY 40207.

OBUCK, JOHN F. ■ FAAR Painting 89. b. Aug. 20, 1946, Detroit, MI. BFA 68, Wayne State Univ.; MFA 72, AIC. **Research/Artistic Interests:** Painting, printmaking. **Career & Employment:** Univ. of Texas, Austin, Lect. 1988, 1990-91; Princeton Univ., Lect. 1989; RISD, Visiting Artist 1990; Tyler School of Art, Visiting Artist 1992; Princeton Univ., Lect. 1992-95. **Memberships & Offices:** American Abstract Artists 1991-present. **Fellowships, Honors & Awards:** Art Matters Inc. 1986; Louis Comfort Tiffany Grant 1987; NEA Grant 1979, 1980, 1987; NYFA Grant 1988; Pollock-Krasner Found. Grant 1992. **Important Works:** Museum of Contemporary Art, Chicago; Cincinnati Museum of Art; Chase Manhattan Bank, NYC; General Electric Corp., NYC; John Hilberry & Asscs., Detroit. **Exhibitions/**

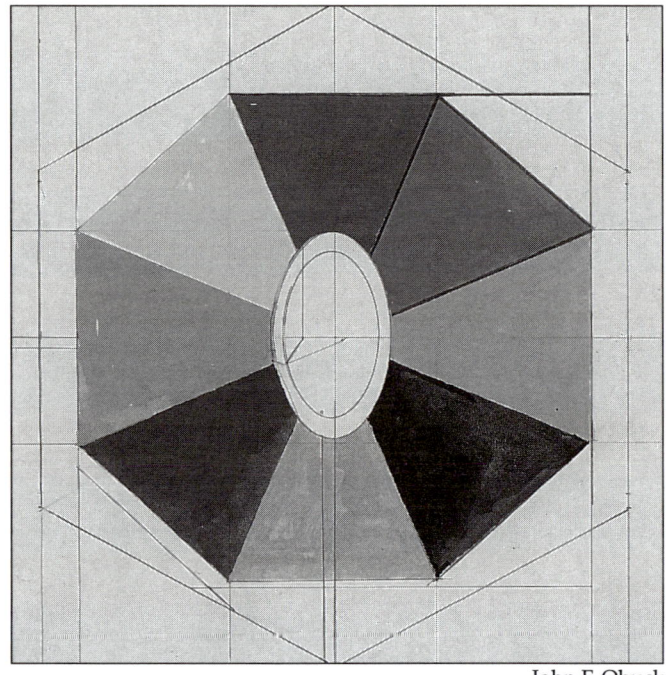

John F. Obuck

Performances: Solo: N.A.M.E. Gallery, Chicago 1979; Young-Hoffman Gallery, Chicago 1980, 1981, 1983; Barbara Gladstone Gallery, NYC 1980, 1982; Delahunty Gallery, Dallas 1981; Hanes Artcenter, UNC, Chapel Hill 1987; Feigenson-Preston Gallery, Birmingham, MI 1990, 1992; Jack Hanley Gallery, San Francisco 1991. **Home Address:** PO Box 1148, Church St. Sta., NYC 10008.

OENSLAGER, DONALD MITCHELL ■ RAAR Design Arts 54. b. Mar. 7, 1902, Harrisburg, PA. d. June 21, 1975. m. Mary Osborne Polak. BA 23, Harvard Univ. **Career & Employment:** Provincetown Playhouse & Greenwich Village Theatre 1924-25; Yale Univ., Instr. 1925-71, Prof.-Prof. Emer. 1971-75. **Memberships & Offices:** Master Drawing Assn., Dir., VP; Neighborhood Playhouse School of Theater, Pres., BoD 1928-63; Municipal Art Soc., Dir. 1954-68; Parsons School of Design, BoD 1958-70; MacDowell Assn., BoD 1962-67; US State Dept., Adv. Comm. on the Arts, Drama Panel Cultural Presentations Program 1963-66; ANTA, BoD 1964-68, VP 1962-69; American Acad. of Dramatic Arts, BoD 1964-75; Museum of City of New York, BoD 1964-75; Art Comm. of the City of New York 1965-75, Pres. 1969-75; UNESCO, US Nat. Comm. 1966-69; American Federation of Arts, BoD 1966-75. **Fellowships, Honors & Awards:** Sachs Traveling Fellowship 1923-24; US State Dept., Lecture Grant, South America 1950, Yugoslavia 1953, Ireland-Iceland-Finland 1955; Colorado College, Hon. AFD 1953; Ford Found. Grant 1960; Antoinette Perry Award 1963-68; Royal Soc. of Arts, London, Benjamin Franklin Fellow. **Publications:** ed., *Notes on Scene Painting; The Theatre of Donald Oenslager* (Middletown, CT: Wesleyan Univ. Press, 1978); *Stage Design: Four Centuries of Scenic Invention* (New York: Viking, 1975). **Important Works:** Set Designs for: *Good News, Brand, Overture, The Winter's Tale, The Emperor Jones, Uncle Tom's Cabin, The Lady from the Sea, The Farmer Takes a Wife, First Lady, Stage Door, Johnny Johnson, You Can't Take It with You, A Doll's House, I'd Rather Be Right, Of Mice & Men, The Circle, The American Way, Candida, The Man Who Came to Dinner, Claudia, The Doctor's Dilemma, L'Histoire du Soldat* (for League of Composers), *Three To Make Ready, Pygmalion, Born Yesterday,* etc.; Designed fountains &

lighting for NY World's Fair 1964-65; Consultant in theater architecture for: American Pavilion Theater, Brussels World Fair 1958; Montreal Cultural Center 1961; Philharmonic Hall, Lincoln Center, NYC 1962; New York State Theater, Lincoln Center, NYC 1964; John F. Kennedy Center for the Performing Arts, Washington, DC 1968. **Bio-Bibliography:** Frederick Tollini, "Donald Oenslager, Stage Designer and Teacher," (Diss., Yale Univ., 1972); *Donald Oenslager, with a Catalogue from His Collections* (Austin, TX: College of Fine Arts, Univ. of Texas, 1977); *Contemporary Authors; National Cyclopedia of American Biography; Oxford Companion to American Theatre; Who Was Who in America.*

OFFNER, RICHARD ■ FASCSR 13. b. June 30. 1889, Vienna Austria. d. Aug. 25, 1965. m. Phillippa Gerry Whiting. c. Antonia, Paul Phillip Nathaniel. BA 12, Harvard Univ.; PhD 14, Univ. of Vienna. **Career & Employment:** US Army, 2d Lieut., WWI; NYU, Prof. 1923-60, Prof. Emer. 1960-65. **Fellowships, Honors & Awards:** Harvard Univ., Sachs Fellow 1920-22. **Publications:** *Italian Primitives at Yale University* (New Haven: Yale Univ. Press, 1927); *Studies in Florentine Painting* (New York: F.F. Sherman, 1927); *A Critical and Historical Corpus of Florentine Painting,* 7 vols. (New York: NYU Press, 1930-58); "The Barberini Panels and their Painter," in *Medieval Studies in Memory of A. Kingsley Porter,* ed. W.R.W. Koehler (Cambridge, MA: Harvard Univ. Press, 1939), 1:205-53; "Giotto, non-Giotto," *Burlington Magazine* 74 (1939): 259-68, 75 (1939): 96-113; *A Critical and Historical Corpus of Florentine Painting: A Legacy of Attributions* (New York: IFA, 1981). **Bio-Bibliography:** "Bibliography of Richard Offner," in *An Exhibition of Italian Panels and Manuscripts from the Thirteenth and Fourteenth Centuries in Honor of Richard Offner* (Hartford: Wadsworth Atheneum, 1965), 59-60; *National Cyclopedia of American Biography; Who's Who among English and European Authors; Who Was Who in Literature; Who Was Who in America.*

OGLE, MARBURY BLADEN ■ School of Classical Studies, Prof.-in-Charge 1931-34.

OHL, RAYMOND THEODORE ■ FAAR Classics/Archaeology 30. b. Nov. 11, 1899, Philadelphia, PA. d. Mar. 5, 1983. BA 21, Haverford College; MA 22, Haverford College; PhD 28, Univ. of Pennsylvania. **Research/Artistic Interests:** Latin epigraphy, ancient literature. **Career & Employment:** Haverford College, Instr. 1921-28, 1943-44; Lebanon Valley College, Dept. Head 1930-32; Newberry College, Prof. 1934-36; Michigan State College, Asst. Prof. 1936-42; William Penn Charter School, Master 1944-46; Temple Univ., Prof. 1946-70. **Fellowships, Honors & Awards:** Univ. of Pennsylvania, Harrison Fellow 1925-26. **Publications:** "A Litterateur in the Age of the Antonines," *Classical World* 20 (1927): 99-105; ed. & trans., *The Enigmas of Symphosius* (Philadelphia, 1928); "The Inscriptions at the American Academy in Rome," *Memoirs of the AAR* 9 (1931): 89-134; "Classical Archaeology, 1941," *Classical World* 35 (1941-42): 135-36; "Some Remarks on the Latin Anthology," *Classical World* 42 (1948-49): 146-53; "Ironic Reserve in Horace," *Classical World* 43 (1949-50): 35-40. **Bio-Bibliography:** *Directory of American Scholars.*

OLCOTT, GEORGE N. ■ FASCSR 1899; Carnegie Inst. Research Fellow, ASCSR 1911-13. b. Sept. 19, 1869, Brooklyn, NY. m. Zita Ledderucci. d. Mar. 2, 1913. BA 1893, Columbia Univ.; PhD 1899, Columbia Univ. **Research/Artistic Interests:** Latin epigraphy, Etruscan vases. **Career & Employment:** Columbia Univ., Lect. 1898-1904, Asst. Prof. 1901-4, Prof. 1905-13. **Fel-**

lowships, Honors & Awards: Columbia Univ., Fellow 1894-96, Drisler Travelling Fellow 1896-97. **Publications:** *Studies in the Word-Formation of the Latin Inscriptions: Substantives and Adjectives with Special Reference to the Latin Sermo Vulgaris* (Rome, 1898); "Some Unpublished Inscriptions from Rome," *AJA* 3 (1899): 229-39; *Thesaurus Linguae Latinae Epigraphicae: A Dictionary of Latin Inscriptions,* 22 fasc. (1904-12); "Latin Inscriptions: Inedited or Corrected," *AJA* 10 (1906): 154-58; "Unpublished Latin Inscriptions," *AJA* 12 (1908): 39-46. **Bio-Bibliography:** Ingrid E.M. Edlund, "The Iron Age and Etruscan Vases in the Olcott Collection at Columbia University," *Transactions of the APS* 70.1 (1981): 6-8; *Who Was Who in America.*

OLDENBURG, CLAES ■ AAR Trustee 1972-75, Trustee Emer.; Artist.

OLDHAM, ELLEN MCQUILKIN ■ AAR World War II Scholar 1943.

OLDS, IRVING S. ■ AAR Trustee 1962-65; Lawyer; US Steel Corp. BoD, Chair.

OLIN, LAURIE D. ■ FAAR Landscape Architecture 74; AAR Trustee 1982-present. b. Oct. 12, 1938, Marshfield, WI. m. Victoria M. Steiger. c. Jessica, Nathaniel. BArch 61, Univ. of Wisconsin. **Other Study:** Civil Engineering, Univ. of Alaska 1956-57; Univ. of Washington with Theodore Roethke 1962-63; **Research/Artistic Interests:** Landscape & architectural history & theory; drawing & painting, writing on history, theory of landscape architecture & architectural design. **Career & Employment:** Bureau of Public Roads & Alaska State Highway Dept., Anchorage, Engineer 1956-60; Richard Haag Asscs., Asst. Landscape Architect 1957-61; Port Authority of Seattle, Planner-Designer 1962; Edward Larrabee Barnes, Architects, Architect, Project Designer 1964-70; George Bartholick, Architects & Planners, Project Architect & Prin. Designer 1969-72; Univ. of Washington, Seattle, Lect. 1970-72; Derek Lovejoy & Partners, Croydon, England, Landscape Architect 1973-74; Joseph Passonneau & Partners, Part. 1974-76; Univ. of Penn-

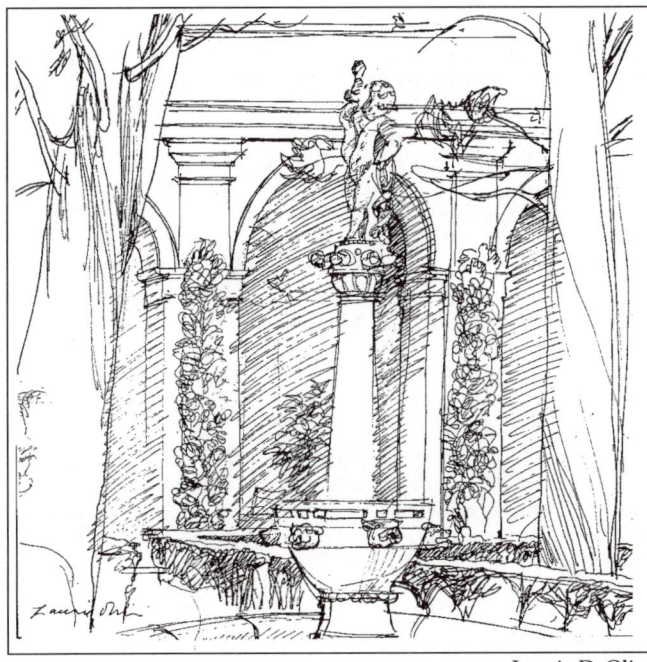

Laurie D. Olin

sylvania, Lect. 1974-76, Center for Environmental Design, Graduate School of Fine Arts, Deputy Dir. 1976-77, Adj. Assc. Prof.-Asst. Prof. 1980-82; Hanna-Olin, Ltd., Prin. 1976-present; Harvard GSD, Chair. & Adj. Prof. 1982-87. **Memberships & Offices:** ASLA 1982-present; NEA, Design Arts Adv. Council 1979-83; Harvard GSD, Visiting Com. 1988-94; Gateway Nat. Park, San Francisco, Adv. Council 1991-94. **Fellowships, Honors & Awards:** Univ. of Alaska, College, Sears Roebuck Scholarship 1956-57; Fulbright-Hays Fellowship 1972-73 (declined); Guggenheim Fellowship 1972-73; Intl. Design Conference, Aspen, Eliot Noyes Fellow 1978; Dumbarton Oaks, Senior Fellow 1982-89; AIA, Hon. Mem. 1989; Bradford Williams Medal 1991; NAD 1994. **Publications:** *Breath on the Mirror, Seattle's Skid Road Community* (Seattle, WA: L. Olin, 1972); "Reflections on Domitian's Palace," *Modulus* 4 (1982): 18-25; "Place: Memory, Poetry, Drawing," *Places* 2.3 (1985): 33-49; "Singing the Praise of Canary Wharf," *Landscape Design* 163 (Oct. 1986): 69-73; "Form, Meaning, and Expression in Landscape Architecture," *Landscape Journal* 7.2 (Fall 1987): 149-68; "Landscape Design in Cities," *Places* 4 (1988): 91-94; "Wide Spaces and Widening Chaos," *Landscape Architecture* 80.10 (Oct. 1990): 76-83; "Landscape Design as a Catalyst for Development," *Landscape Institute Conference, Durham 1990* (London: ILA, 1991), 26-35; "Open Space and the Public Life," *Design & Values*, Conference Proceedings, CELA 4 (Washington, DC: Landscape Architectural Found., 1992), 16-24; "Landscaftsgestaltung am Rebstock Park," *Frankfurt: Rebstock Park, Folding in Time* (Munich: Volker Fischer, 1992), 25-25; Frederick Steiner & Todd Johnson, "Perfecting the Ordinary," *Landscape Architecture* (Mar. 1992): 68-77; "Regionalism in American Landscape Architecture and the Work of Hanna-Olin, Ltd.," *Regional Garden Design in the United States* (Washington, DC: Dumbarton Oaks, 1992). **Important Works:** 16th St. Transitway-Pedestrian Mall, Denver 1979; Battery Park City, NYC, Masterplan, South Park Esplanades 1979-83; Playa Vista Master Plan, Los Angeles 1985-present; Ohio State Univ., Wexner Center for the Arts 1987; Abigail House, New Albany, OH 1987-94; Exchange Sq., London 1987; Univ. of Washington, Allen Library, Quad & Greig Garden, Seattle 1989; AAR, Campus Restoration 1990-present; Villa Olympia, Barcelona 1990-92; Bryant Park, NYC 1992; Pershing Sq., Los Angeles 1994; Hermann Park Restoration, Houston 1994. **Exhibitions/Performances:** MOMA 1966; Henry Gallery, Univ. of Washington, Seattle 1968; Richard White Gallery, Seattle 1969; Western Washington State College, Bellingham 1969; Washington State Museum, Olympia 1970; ACT Theater, Seattle 1971; Polly Friedlander Gallery, Seattle 1972; Nat. Visitor Center, Washington, DC 1977-1978; Whitney Museum, NYC 1980; 9H Gallery, London 1987; Univ. of Virginia 1988; Univ. of Pennsylvania 1988, 1990; Harvard GSD 1992, 1993; Roger Williams College 1994. **Business Address:** Hanna/Olin Ltd., 421 Chestnut St., Philadelphia, PA 19106.

OLIVER, JAMES HENRY ■ FAAR Classics/Archaeology 30. b. Apr. 26, 1905, Brooklyn, NY. d. Apr. 3, 1981. m. Janet Carnochen. BA 26, Yale Univ.; PhD 31, Yale Univ. **Other Study:** Univ. of Bonn, Germany 1928. **Research/Artistic Interests:** Roman government in the provinces, Greek historical texts & epigraphy, Athens in antiquity. **Career & Employment:** Yale Univ., Instr. 1930-32; Agora Excavations, Athens, Excavator-Epigraphist 1932-36; Barnard College, Asst. Prof. 1936-42; US Army, Major 1943-1945; Johns Hopkins Univ., Prof. 1946-70, Francis White Prof. 1957-70. **Memberships & Offices:** APA, Dir. 1965-70, VP 1972-74, Pres. 1974-75; *Ameri-*

can Journal of Philology, Hon. Ed.; *Greek, Roman and Byzantine Studies,* Adv. 1958-81; ArIA; American Soc. of Papyrologists; Soc. for the Promotion of Roman Studies; Austrian Archaeology Inst. **Fellowships, Honors & Awards:** Guggenheim Fellow 1946, 1955; Fulbright Fellow 1963-64; NEH Senior Fellow. **Publications:** "The Augustan Pomerium," *Memoirs of the AAR* 16 (1932): 45-182; *The Sacred Gerusia* (Baltimore: ASCSA, 1941); *The Athenian Expounders of the Sacred and Ancestral Law* (Baltimore: Johns Hopkins Press, 1950); *The Ruling Power* (Philadelphia: APS, 1953); *Demokratia: The Gods of the Free World* (Baltimore: Johns Hopkins Press, 1960); *The Civilizing Power* (Philadelphia: APS, 1968); *Marcus Aurelius: Aspects of Civil and Cultural Policy in the East* (Princeton: ASCSA, 1970); *The Civil Tradition and Roman Athens* (Baltimore: Johns Hopkins Univ. Press, 1983); *Greek Constitutions of Early Roman Emperors from Inscriptions and Papyri,* APS Memoirs 179 (Philadelphia: APS, 1989). **Bio-Bibliography:** Briggs, 461-63; *Who Was Who in America.*

OLIVER, REVILO P. ■ AAR Classical Soc., Pres. 1956.

OLIVETTI, ROBERTO ■ AAR Visitor 1982-83; Olivetti Found., Pres.

OLMSTED, FREDERICK LAW ■ AAR Charter Mem.; Landscape Architect. b. 1822. d. 1903. **Important Works:** Central Park, NYC; Prospect Park, Brooklyn, NY; South Park, Chicago; The Fenway, Boston.

OLMSTED, FREDERICK LAW, JR ■ AAR Adv. Council; Landscape Architect. b. 1870. d. 1957. **Career & Employment:** Harvard Univ., Prof. of Landscape Architecture. Helped create Landscape Architecture as an AAR discipline.

OLSEN, ERLING C. ■ FAAR Classics/Archaeology 39. b. August 8, 1913, Chicago, IL. d. July 28, 1944. BA 35, Harvard Univ.; MA 37, Princeton Univ. **Other Studies:** Institut d'Art et d'Archéologie, Université de Paris. **Research/Artistic Interests:** Archaeology, Arch of Septimus Severus, portraiture, late antique art. **Career & Employment:** US Nat. Guard 1939; US Infantry Intelligence Service 1942-44. **Fellowships, Honors & Awards:** Carnegie Fellowship 1936. **Publications:** "An Interpretation of the Hephaisteion Reliefs," *AJA* 42 (1938): 276-87; "Two Roman Portrait Heads in the Museum of the American Academy in Rome," *Memoirs of the AAR* 15 (1938): 82-86; with Karl Lehmann, *Dionysiac Sarcophagi in Baltimore* (New York: IFA, NYU, 1942). **Bio-Bibliography:** *College Art Journal* 4 (1945): 107.

OLSEN, O.M. ■ Stewardson Memorial Fellow 1923-24.

OLSON, DON H. ■ FAAR Landscape Architecture 62. b. Oct. 11, 1932, Chicago, IL. m. Jacqueline M. Olson. BS 55, Iowa State Univ; MLA 56, Harvard Univ. **Career & Employment:** Philadelphia City Planning Comm. 1956-57; US Army 1957-59; Rogers Toliafero & Lamb, Architects 1959-60; Harvard GSD, Assc. Prof. 1962-69; Sasaki Asscs., Prin. 1962-present. **Memberships & Offices:** ASLA; Boston Soc. of Landscape Architects. **Fellowships, Honors & Awards:** Tau Sigma Delta 1955; Gamma Sigma Delta 1955; ASLA, Student Award 1955, Fellow 1991; Iowa State Univ., Honor Award 1955, Christian Peterson Design Award 1989. **Important Works:** Pennsylvania Ave., Washington, DC; Nationwide Plaza, Columbus; Baltimore Museum of Art Sculpture Garden; Ismaili Center Roof Garden, London; Excelsior Hotel Courtyard Garden, Venice; Harbortown at Sea Pines Plantation, Hilton Head Island, SC;

Landings at Skidaway Island, Savannah, GA; Zanzibar Tourism Improvements, Tanzania; Kingsmill at the James Community, Williamsburg, VA; Pocantico Hills Estate, Tarrytown, NY; Aiglemont Estate, Gouvieux, France; Costa Smeralda, Sardinia. **Home Address:** 30 Forest St., Lexington, MA 02173. **Business Address:** Sasaki Asscs. Inc., 64 Pleasant St., Watertown, MA 02172.

O'MALLEY, JOHN W. ■ FAAR Post-Classical/Humanistic Studies 65; RAAR Post-Classical/Humanistic Studies 83; *Memoirs of the AAR,* Consulting Ed. b. June 11, 1927, Wheeling, WV. BA 51, Loyola Univ.; MA 57, Loyola Univ.; STL 60, Loyola Univ.; PhD 66, Harvard Univ. **Research/Artistic Interests:** The religious culture of the Italian Renaissance, history of rhetoric & preaching, Erasmus, the early Jesuits. **Career & Employment:** Univ. of Detroit, Asst. Prof.-Prof. 1965-79; Univ. of Michigan, Visiting Prof. 1972-73; Weston School of Theology, Prof. 1979-present; Boston College, Visiting Prof. 1992-93. **Memberships & Offices:** Catholic Historical Assn., Pres. 1991; RSA, Council Mem. 1976-82, 1984-88; Villa I Tatti, *Renaissance Studies,* Consulting Ed. 1988-present. **Fellowships, Honors & Awards:** Villa I Tatti, Research Fellow 1966-68; Guggenheim Fellowship 1975-76; AHA, Best Book 1979; Loyola Univ., Hon. Doctorate 1982; NEH Research Fellow 1983; ACLS Research Fellow 1988-89; APS, Best Book 1993. **Publications:** *Giles of Viterbo on Church and Reform: A Study in Renaissance Thought* (Leiden: Brill, 1968); *Praise and Blame in Renaissance Rome: Rhetoric, Doctrine, and Reform in the Sacred Orators of the Papal Court, ca. 1450-1520* (Durham, NC: Duke Univ. Press, 1979); *Rome and the Renaissance: Studies in Culture and Religion* (London: Variorum, 1981); *Tradition and Transition: Historical Perspectives on Vatican II* (Wilmington, DE: Glazier, 1989); ed., *Catholicism in Early Modern History: A Guide to Research* (St. Louis: Center for Reformation Research, 1989); *Spiritualia,* Collected Works of Erasmus 66 (Toronto: Univ. of Toronto Press, 1988); *The First Jesuits, 1540-1565* (Cambridge, MA: Harvard Univ. Press, 1993); *Religious Culture in the Sixteenth Century: Preaching, Rhetoric and Reform* (London: Variorum, 1993); co-ed., *Images of Humanity and Divinity: Pursuing the Holy in the Age of Renaissance and Reform: Essays in Honor of Charles Trinkaus* (Leiden: Brill, 1993). **Business Address:** Weston School of Theology, 3 Phillips Pl., Cambridge, MA 02138.

ORIGO, BENEDETTA ■ AAR Italian Com. 1994-present.

ORLANDO, RUGGERO ■ AAR Visitor 1980-81, Radio Commentator.

ORR, D.W. ■ Winchester Fellow 1919-20.

ORR, DAVID GERLAD ■ FAAR Classics/Archaeology 73. b. Sept. 8, 1942, Warren, OH. m. Linda Orr. BA 64, Ohio State Univ.; MA 69, Univ. of Maryland.

ORTONA, EGIDIO ■ AAR Visitor 1977-78, Italian Ambassador to US.

OSHEIM, DUANE J. ■ FAAR Post-Classical/Humanistic Studies 76. b. May 28, 1942, Story City, IA. m. Yvonne Nelson. c. Erik, Christina. BA 64, Luther College; MA 67, Univ. of Nebraska; PhD 73, UC, Davis. **Research/Artistic Interests:** Medieval & Renaissance Italian history; social & institutional history. **Career & Employment:** Univ. of Virginia, Prof. 1976-present. **Memberships & Offices:** MAA 1976-present; AHA 1976-present; RSA 1985-present; Soc. for Italian Historical Stud-

ies 1976-present. **Fellowships, Honors & Awards:** Istituto Storico Lucchese; Soc. for Italian Historical Studies, Dissertation Prize 1974; ACLS Research Fellowship 1980-81; Fulbright Fellowship 1985-86; NEH Summer Fellowship 1987. **Publications:** "The Episcopal Archive of Lucca in the Middle Ages," *Manuscripta* 17 (1973): 131-46; "Rural Population and the Tuscan Economy in the Late Middle Ages," *Viator* 7 (1976): 329-46; *An Italian Lordship: the Bishopric of Lucca in the Late Middle Ages* (Berkeley: UC Press, 1977); with Thomas W. Blomquist, "The First Consuls at Lucca: 10 July 1119," *Actum Luce* 7 (1978): 31-40; "Conversion, *Conversi,* and the Christian Life in Late-Medieval Tuscany," *Speculum* 56 (1983): 368-93; "Sentimenti religiosi dei Lucchesi al tempo di Castruccio," *Atti del Convegno Internazionale su Castruccio Castracane e il suo tempo* (Lucca: Istituto Storico Lucchese, 1987), 99-111; "Countrymen and the Law in Late Medieval Tuscany," *Speculum* 64 (1989): 317-37; *A Tuscan Monastery and its Social World: San Michele of Guario (1156-1348)* (Rome: Herder, 1989); "The Place of Women in the Late Medieval Church," in *That Gentle Strength,* ed. Lynda L. Coor et al. (Charlottesville, VA: Univ. of Virginia Press, 1990), 79-96; "Benedictines and the Laity in Thirteenth-Century Italy," in *Proceedings of the Sewanee Mediaeval Colloquium* 4 (Sewanee, TN: Press of the Univ. of the South, 1990), 93-103; "Sutri, Synod of," and "Matilda of Tuscany," in *The Dictionary of the Middle Ages,* ed. Joseph R. Strayer (New York: Scribner's, 1982-88). **Business Address:** Univ. of Virginia, Charlottesville, VA 22903.

OSLUND, THOMAS R. ■ FAAR Landscape Architecture 92. b. Aug. 21, 1956, Stanton, VA. m. Nancy E. Oslund. c. Ingrid. BLA 80, Univ. of Minnesota; MLA 86, Harvard GSD. **Career & Employment:** Hammel Green & Abrahamson, Dir. of Landscape Architecture 1986-present; Michael Van Valkenburgh Asscs., Design Prin. 1989; Harvard GSD, Visiting Prof. 1989-91; Univ. of Minnesota, Visiting Prof. 1993-present. **Fellowships, Honors & Awards:** ASLA, Minnesota Chap., Honor Award 1987, 1989, 1992, 1993, Merit Award 1988, 1993, Design Merit Award 1993; *International Design* Magazine Annual, Hon. Men. 1993. **Important Works:** Weesner Family Amphitheater, Birds of Prey, Minnesota Zoological Gardens, Apple Valley; IBM Facility, Rochester, MN; Garden of Time, Shakopee Women's Correctional Facility; Courtyard Colonial Church of Edina, MN; Rooftop Garden, St. Therese Residence, MN. **Exhibitions/Performances:** Harvard GSD 1986; Walker Art Center, Minneapolis 1991; Temple Univ. Gallery, Rome 1992; Tho-

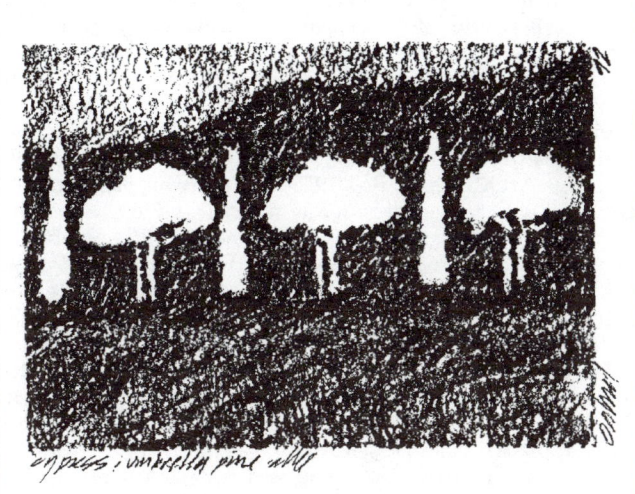

Thomas R Oslund

mas Barry Fine Art, Minneapolis 1993. **Bio-Bibliography:** "Conceiving a Courtyard," *Places* 6.3 (1990); *Contemporary Landscapes of the World* (Tokyo: Pricess Architecture, 1990), 120-21; "A Winter Garden in Minneapolis," *Brooklyn Botanic Garden Record* 47.4 (1991): 70-73; Amphitheater Takes Wing," *Architectural Record* 180.6 (1992); "A Wing and a Prey(er)," *Inland Architect* 36.2 (1992); *Landscape Architecture* (Apr. 1993); *International Design* (July-Aug. 1993). **Home Address:** 4808 Garfield Ave. S., Minneapolis, MN 55419. **Business Address:** HGA Inc., 1201 Harmon Pl., Minneapolis, MN 55403.

OSTROW, STEVEN E. ■ FAAR Classics/Archaeology 75. b. Mar. 14, 1946, Worcester, MA. m. Ann O. Koloski-Ostrow. c. Aaron, Benjamin. BA 68, Brown Univ.; MA 69, Univ. of Michigan; PhD 77, Univ. of Michigan. **Other Study:** ICCS 1966-67; archaeological field work: Satrianum, Graviscae, Italy; Cyrene, Libya; El-Djem, Carthage, Tunisia; Kourion, Cyprus. **Career & Employment:** Woodmere Acad., Teacher 1969-70; ICCS, TA 1970-71, Asst. Prof. 1989-90; VSA, Dir. of Summer School 1979, 1981, 1995; Univ. of Colorado, Asst. Prof. 1975-77; Dartmouth College, Asst. Prof. 1977-84; College of Holy Cross, Visiting Lect. 1986, 1991, Asst. Prof. 1987-89; Tufts Univ., Visiting Asst. Prof. 1987; Wayland HS, Teacher 1990-91; Univ. of Massachusetts, Boston, Lect. 1991, 1994; MIT, Instr. 1991, Visiting Lect.-Asst. Prof. 1992-94, Lect. 1995. **Memberships & Offices:** ArlA 1967-present, Ann Arbor Soc., Sec. 1972-73, Boulder Soc., VP 1976-77; APA 1973-present; VSA 1974-present; Amici di Pompei 1975-present; CANE 1978-present; Soc. for Roman Studies 1982-present. **Fellowships, Honors & Awards:** Brown Univ., Wayland Prize 1965; Univ. of Michigan, Fellowships 1968-69, 1971-72, 1972-73; NEH Summer Stipend 1980, Fellowship 1985. **Publications:** "The Topography of Puteoli and Baiae," *Puteoli* 3 (1979): 77-140; "Augustales along the Bay of Naples: A Case for Their Early Growth," *Historia* 34 (1985): 64-101; "The Augustales in the Augustan Scheme," in *Between Republic and Empire: Interpretations of Augustus and His Principate*, ed. K. Raaflaub & M. Toher (Berkeley : UC Press, 1990), 364-79. **Home Address:** 74 Angelica Dr., Framingham, MA 01701. **Business Address:** History Faculty, MIT, E51-210, Cambridge, MA 02139.

OSTWALD, MARTIN ■ AAR Visitor 1955 — 1959, Scholar.

OSVER, ARTHUR ■ FAAR Painting 54, RAAR Painting 58; AAR Trustee 1961-73, Trustee Emer. b. July 26, 1912, Chicago, IL. m. Ernestine B. Betsberg. **Other Study:** Northwestern Univ.; AIC under Boris Anisfeld. **Career & Employment:** Brooklyn Museum Art School 1947; Columbia Univ. 1950-1951; Univ. of Florida, Artist-in-Residence 1954; Cooper Union 1955, 1958; Washington Univ., St. Louis 1960, Prof. Emer. 1981. **Memberships & Offices:** Intl. Fulbright Comm. 1956; Yale Univ., Visiting Critic 1956-57; Guggenheim Adv. Bd. 1959-70; St. Louis Art Museum, BoT 1975-78. **Fellowships, Honors & Awards:** AIC, James Nelson Raymond Traveling Fellowship 1936-38; Guggenheim Fellowships 1948-49; NEA Sabbatical Leave Grant 1967-68; AAAL Award 1991. **Important Works:** MMA; MOMA; Whitney Museum, NYC; PAFA; Philadelphia Museum; Walker Art Center; Toledo Museum of Art; New Orleans Museum of Modern Art; Colorado Springs Fine Arts Center; Museum of Modern Art, Rio de Janeiro; Houston Museum of Fine Arts; Peabody Museum; Montclair Art Museum, NJ; Duncan Phillips Collection; St. Louis Art Museum; Davenport Art Gallery; AIC; Smithsonian Inst.; Univ. of Illinois; Univ. of Michigan; Univ. of Minnesota; Univ. of Nebraska; Southern Illinois Univ., Carbondale; Syracuse Univ.; Rochester Memorial Art Gallery; Des Moines Art Center;

Washington Univ.; Univ. of Georgia; Univ. of Cincinnati; Wilmington Art Museum, DE; Mulvane Art Center, Topeka; St. Petersburg Museum of Fine Arts, FL; John Burroughs School; Ringling Art Museum, Sarasota; St. Louis Univ.; Laura Mussert Gallery, Muscatine, IA; Albrecht Art Gallery, St. Joseph, MO; Hunter College, NYC. **Exhibitions/Performances:** Group: AAAL; John Herron Art Inst.; MMA; AIC; MOMA; Brooklyn Museum; Museum of Modern Art, Rio de Janeiro; Carnegie Inst.; PAFA; Corcoran Gallery; Philadelphia Museum; Des Moines Art Center; Toledo Art Museum; Detroit Inst.; Venice Biennale; Duncan Phillips Gallery; Virginia Museum; Galleria Nazionale, Rome; Walker Art Center; Gallery of Modern Art, Tokyo; Whitney Museum, NYC. **Bio-Bibliography:** *Who's Who in America*. **Home Address:** 465 Foote Ave., St. Louis, MO 63119.

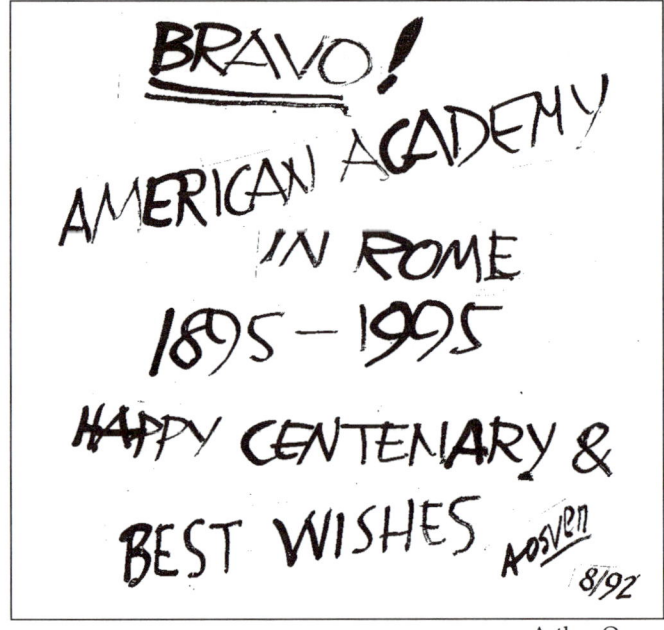

Arthur Osver

O'TOOLE, W.G. ■ Appleton Fellow 1920-21, 1921-22.

OTTONE, PIERO ■ AAR Italian Com. 1994-present.

OUELLETTE, WILLIAM ■ FAAR Painting 65. b. Sept. 16, 1938, Springfield, MA. BFA 60, RISD; MFA 62, Cranbrook Acad. of Art. **Other Study:** London School of Film Technique 1965-66; Karolyi Found., Vence, France, painting 1967; Hagen-Berghof Studio, NYC, theater 1971-73. **Research/Artistic Interests:** Informal study of Japanese art, gardens & architecture during four trips to Japan 1983-86; current projects: a book on unusual aspects of Japanese aesthetics, & adapting Japanese design concepts to Western gardens. **Fellowships, Honors & Awards:** Louis Comfort Tiffany Found. Grant 1962. **Publications:** *Fantasy Postcards* (New York: Doubleday, 1975; London: London Editions, 1975); *Cartes Fantasques* (Paris: Henri Veyrier, 1975); *Erotic Postcards* (London: London Editions, 1977, New York: Excalibur Books, 1977; Australia: Cassell, 1977). **Important Works:** Painting in private collections in the US, England, France & Japan. **Home Address:** Rensselaerville, NY 12147.

OWENS, CHARLES A. ■ FAAR Painting 48. b. June 21, 1917, Shepherdstown, WV. dec. **Study:** ASL. **Fellowships, Honors & Awards:** Cumberland Valley Artists, 1st Prize 1942, 1944,

1947. **Exhibitions/Performances:** Group Show, Betty Parsons Gallery, NYC 1947.

OWINGS, NATHANIEL ALEXANDER ■ RAAR Architecture 59; AAR Trustee 1961-72. b. Feb. 5, 1903, Indianapolis, IN. d. June 13, 1984. m. Emily Otis, Margret Wentworth. c. Emily, Natalie, Jennifer, Nathaniel Jr. BS 27, Cornell Univ. **Other Study:** Univ. of Illinois 1921-22. **Career & Employment:** Skidmore & Owings, Founding Part. 1936-39; Skidmore, Owings & Merrill, Part. 1939-84. **Memberships & Offices:** Chicago Planning Comm., Chair 1948-51; California Highway & Scenic Roads Comm. Vice-Chair 1964-67; Comm. on the Design of Pennslyvania Ave., Washington, DC 1964-82; US Sec. of the Interior, Adv. Bd. on Nat. Parks, Historic Sites, Bldgs. & Monuments, Washington, DC 1966-70, Chair 1970-72. **Fellowships, Honors & Awards:** US Interior Dept., Conservation Service Award 1968; Ball State Univ., LLD 1970; Indiana Univ., LHD 1973; AIA Fellow, Gold Medal 1983; Butler Univ. LHD 1976; Sierra Club, Hon. Life Mem. **Publications:** "New Materials and Building Methods for the Chicago Exposition," *Architectural Record* (Apr. 1932); "Economics of Department Store Planning," *Architectural Record* (Feb. 1947); "What's New in Planning an Office Building" *Building* (Dec. 1947); "Do We or Do We not Orient the Bedroom?" *Royal Arch. Inst. of Canada Journal* (Sept. 1948); "Two Looks at Preservation," *AIA Journal* (Feb. 1962); *The American Aesthetic* (New York: Harper & Row, 1969); *The Spaces in Between: An Architect's Journey* (Boston: Houghton-Mifflin, 1973). **Important Works:** Reflecting Basin, US Capitol Bldg.; Lever House, NYC; Chase Manhattan Bank, NYC; Crown Zellerbach Office Bldg.; Alcoa Bldg.; Hartford Insurance Bldg., San Francisco; Equitable Life Bldg., Chicago; Oakland Coliseum, CA; Mauna Kea Hotal, HI. **Exhibitions/Performances:** MOMA 1950. **Bio-Bibliography:** E. Danz, *Architecture of Skidmore, Owings and Merrill, 1950-62* (London: Architectural Press, 1963); E. Danz, *Architecture of Skidmore, Owings and Merrill, 1963-73* (London: Architectural Book Co., 1974); Albert Bush-Brown, *Skidmore, Owings and Merrill, Architecture and Urbanism, 1973-83* (New York: Van Nostrand Reinhold, 1984); *Contemporary Architects; Who Was Who in America.*

OXHANDLER, S. ■ McKim Fellow 1920-21, 1921-22.

■   ■   ■

P

PACKER, JAMES E. ■ FAAR Classics/Archaeology 63; AAR Adv. Council 1964. b. Dec. 25, 1937, Los Angeles, CA. BA 59, UC, Berkeley; MA 60, UC, Berkeley; PhD 64, UC, Berkeley. **Other Study:** Model-making with Caviliere Pietro di Carlo, Rome 1972. **Research/Artistic Interests:** Roman imperial architecture, city planning, archaeology; Greek & Roman history. **Career & Employment:** UC, Berkeley, TA 1960-62; California State Univ., Northridge, Asst. Prof. 1964-66; Northwestern Univ., Asst. Prof. 1966-71, Assc. Prof. 1971-90, Prof. 1990-present. **Memberships & Offices:** ArIA 1966-present; Soc. of Ancient Historians 1980-present; AAUP 1964-present; Soc. for Classical America 1964-present. **Fellowships, Honors & Awards:** APS, Grant-in-Aid 1965, 1969, 1982, 1983; Northwestern Univ., Faculty Research Grant 1966, 1968-70, 1973, 1975-76, 1978, 1981-83, 1989, President's Fund 1988-89; ACLS Grant-in-Aid 1965, 1973, 1975; NEH Research Grant 1970, 1972; Graham Found., Research Grant 1988-89, Publication Grant 1990; Samuel H. Kress Found., Research Grant 1989-90; Getty Grant Program, Publication Grant 1990. **Publications:** *The Insulae of Imperial Ostia,* Memoirs of the AAR 31 (New York & Rome: AAR, 1971); "La Casa di Via Giulio Romano," *Bullettino della Commissione Archeologica Comunale di Roma* 81 (1968-69): 127-48; "Middle and Lower Class Housing in Pompeii and Herculaneum: A Preliminary Survey," in *Neue Forschungen in Pompeji,* ed. B. Andreae & H. Kyrieleis (Recklinghausen, 1975), 133-42; "Review Essay: Ancient Cities," *Maryland Historian* 6.2 (1975): 117-23; "Inns at Pompeii: A Short Survey," *Cronache Pompeiane* 4 (1978): 5-51; "Lively Last Days and Nights [of Pompeii]," *Natural History* 88.4 (Apr. 1979): 72-77; "Pierino di Carlo, Master Model-Builder: The Man and His Craft," *Curator* 22.3 (Sept. 1979): 185-98; "Some Numismatic Evidence for the Southeast (Forum) Facade of the Basilica Ulpia," in *Coins, Culture and History in the Ancient World: Numismatic and Other Studies in Honor of Bluma Trell,* ed. L. Casson & M. Price (Detroit: Wayne State Univ. Press, 1981), 57-68; with K.L. Sarring & R. Sheldon, "A New Excavation in Trajan's Forum," *AJA* 87 (1983): 165-72; "Imperial Construction: Rome and Central Italy," in *Civilization of the Ancient Mediterranean* I, ed. M. Grant (New York: Scribner's, 1988), 299-321; "Politics, Urbanism and Archaeology in 'Roma capitale,' a Troubled Past and a Controversial Future," *AJA* 93.1 (1989): 137-41; *The Forum of Trajan: A Study of the Monuments* (Berkeley: UC Press, forthcoming); "FORVM TRAIANI," in *Lexicon Urbis Romae* (Rome: Quasar, forthcoming). **Business Address:** Dept. of Classics, Northwestern Univ., 1859 Sheridan Rd., Evanston, IL 60208.

PADOVANO, ANTHONY J. ■ FAAR Sculpture 62. b. July 19, 1933, Brooklyn, NY. m. Gerarda S. Padovano. c. Robert, Lea, Nicole, Francesca, Gina. BFA 57, Columbia Univ.; MA 80, Hunter College. **Other Study:** Worked as an assistant to Theodore Roszack & Oronzio Maldarelli. **Career & Employment:** Univ. of Connecticut, Instr. 1962-64; Columbia Univ., Asst. Prof. 1965-71; Queens College 1971-73; Sarah Lawrence College, Asst. Prof. 1974-80; Kingsborough Community College, Assc. Prof. 1980-92; ASL 1983-91. **Memberships & Offices:** Sculptor's Guild 1975-92, Selection Com. 1978; Audubon Artists 1985-92; Millay Colony, Juror 1985-92. **Fellowships, Honors & Awards:** Guggenheim Fellow 1964; NIAL 1980; NAD, Gold Medal 1980; NSS, Fellow 1994. **Publications:** *The Process of Sculpture* (New York: Doubleday, 1981). **Important Works:** Whitney Museum, NYC; Nat. Collection of Fine Art, Smithsonian Inst.; Port Authority of New York & New Jer-

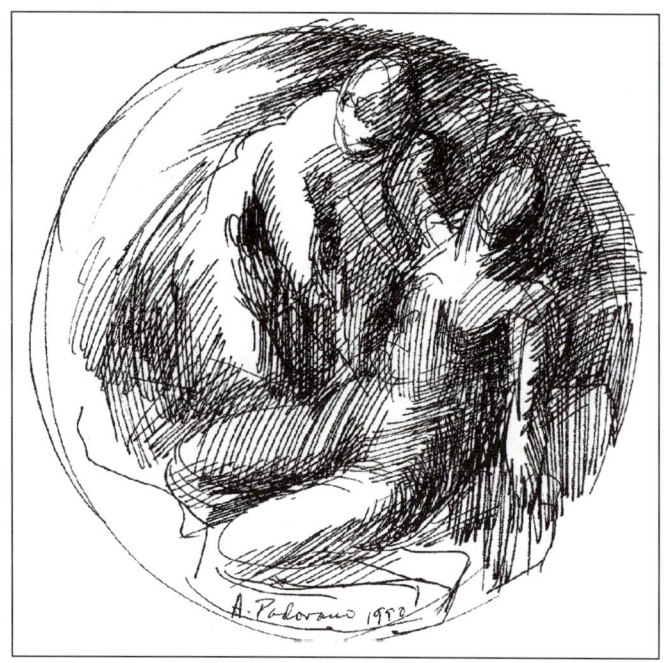

Anthony J. Padovano

sey; Storm King Art Center, NY; Larry Aldrich Museum, Ridgefield, CT; Wichita Art Museum; Cornell Univ. Hospital, NYC; First Nat. City Bank, Chicago; Herron Museum of Art, IN; Newark Museum of Art; Kingsborough Community College, Brooklyn; Sheldon Gallery, Univ. of Nebraska. **Exhibitions/Performances:** Solo: Lincoln Memorial Gallery 1954; Columbia Univ. 1957, 1965; Sculptor's Studio, Washington, DC 1958; George Lester Gallery, Rome 1962; Ruth White Gallery, NYC 1962; Richard Feigen Gallery, NYC 1962; Univ. of Connecticut 1964; Bertha Schaefer Gallery, NYC 1968; Galerie Simons Stern, New Orleans 1968; Graham Gallery, NYC 1972, 1975, 1979, 1981-82; IFA Gallery, Washington, DC 1976; Alwin Gallery, NYC 1986, 1988, 1990; Vorpal Gallery, NYC 1986, 1988, 1990; & numerous group exhibitions. **Bio-Bibliography:** James Mellow, "For Public Spaces," *NY Times* (1970); Judy Valente, "A Work of Art," *Newark Star Register* (1975); J. Taylor Basker, "The Silent Language of Sculpture," *Artspeak* (1986); Kathy Grantham, "Anthony Padovano," *Gannett Suburban News* (1991); Dennis Wepman, "The Heroic Women of Anthony Padovano," *Artspeak* (1988); *Who's Who in America*. **Home Address:** 34 Lover's Lane, Putnam Valley, NY 10579.

PAGE, GEORGE BISPHAM ■ Univ. of Pennsylvania Travelling Fellowship to the American School of Architecture in Rome 1894; one of the first men in residence at the Academy during its initial year of operation. **Career & Employment:** Page & Stewardson, Philadelphia.

PAIST, PHINEAS ■ Cresson Fellow 1911-12, 1913.

PALAIA, FRANC D. ■ FAAR Painting 86. b. Sept. 18, 1949, New Rochelle, NY. m. Eve D'Ambra, FAAR 86. BA 71, Newark State College; MFA 73, Univ. of Cincinnati. **Career & Employment:** Newark State College, Adj. Instr. 1975-76, 1979-82; Essex County College, Adj. Instr. 1976-77; Upsala College, Adj. Instr. 1976-77. **Fellowships, Honors & Awards:** Univ. of Cincinnati Scholarship 1973; NJ State Council on the Arts Grant 1982, 1992; Louis Comfort Tiffany Found. Grant 1984; Polaroid Photography Sponsorship 1985-89; Ludwig

Vogelstein Found. Grant 1988; Rutgers Univ. Grant 1988; Painted Bridge Grant 1992. **Publications:** *Nightlife: Photographs of Wall Paintings by Richard Hambleton* (Elizabeth, NJ: Handmade Books, 1982); *Great Walls of China* (Westfield, NJ: Eastview Editions, 1984); *Italian Series* (Rome: Carta Segrete, 1986); *Berlin Wall Coloring Book* (Jersey City, NJ: Handmade Books, 1991). **Important Works:** Polaroid Corp., Boston; Newark Museum; Port Authority of New York & New Jersey; New Jersey State Museum, Trenton; Prudential Insurance Co., Nat. HQ, Newark; Stedelijk Museum, Amsterdam; New Museum, NYC; McDonald's Corp., Chicago; Coopers & Lybrand, Newark; Brooklyn Museum; Smithsonian Inst., Washington, DC; Univ. of Cincinnati. **Exhibitions/Performances:** Solo: OK Harris Gallery, NYC 1978; Helander Gallery, Palm Beach 1984; Gabrielle Bryers Gallery, NYC 1987; Rutgers Univ., Newark 1988; Galerie D'Eendt, Amsterdam 1989; New Jersey State Museum, Trenton 1993; Broadway Windows, NYC 1993; Selected Group Shows: Newark Museum 1991; Artists' Space, NYC 1990; Alternative Museum, NYC 1990; Clocktower, NYC 1990; Studio Museum of Harlem, NYC 1990. **Bio-Bibliography:** *Who's Who in American Art*; *Who's Who in the Northeast*. **Home Address:** 371 4th St., Jersey City, NJ 07302.

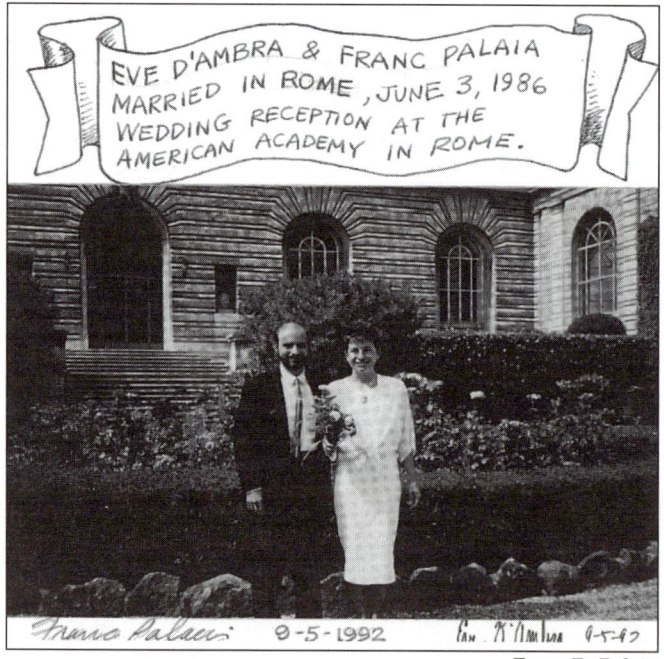

Franc D. Palaia

PALANGE PORTEN, FRANCESCA PAOLA ■ Italian Fulbright Fellow 1961-62.

PALLADINO, ANTONIO ■ AAR – Rome, Library Asst.

PALLAVICINI, ELVINA ■ AAR Visitor 1981-82.

PALMER, HAZEL ■ AAR World War II Scholar 1943.

PALMER, ROBERT E.A. ■ RAAR Classics/Archaeology 79. b. Aug. 15, 1932, Boise, ID. BA 53, Johns Hopkins Univ.; MA 54, Johns Hopkins Univ.; PhD 56, Johns Hopkins Univ. **Career & Employment:** Univ. of Illinois, Instr. 1958-59, Asst. Prof. 1959-61; Univ. of Pennsylvania, Asst. Prof.-Prof. 1959-present, Chair 1973-78, Acting Chair 1979-80; Princeton Univ., Visiting Prof.

1975-76. **Fellowships, Honors & Awards:** NEH Research Fellow 1978-79. **Publications:** *The King and the Comitium,* Historia Einzelschrift 11 (Weisbaden: Steiner, 1969); *The Archaic Community of the Romans* (Cambridge: Cambridge Univ. Press, 1970); *Roman Religion and Roman Empire* (Philadelphia: Univ. of Pennsylvania Press, 1974); "Silvanus, Sylvester and the Chair of St. Peter," *APS Proceedings* 122 (1978): 222-47; "Octavian's First Attempt to Restore the Constitution (36 B.C.)," *Athenaeum* 55 (1978): 315-28; "C. Verres' Legacy of Charm and Love to the City of Rome," *Pontificia Accademia Romana di Archeologia. Rendiconti* 51-52 (1978-79, 1979-80): 111-36; "Customs on the Market Goods Imported into the City of Rome," *Memoirs of the AAR* (1980): 217-33; "The Topography and Social History of Rome's Trastevere (Southern Sector)," *APS Proceedings* 125 (1981): 368-97; "Martial," in *Ancient Writers: Greece and Rome,* ed. T.J. Luce (New York: Scribner's, 1982), 887-915; "On the Track of the Ignoble," *Athenaeum* 61 (1983): 343-61; "A New Fragment of Livy Throws Light on the Roman Postumii and the Latin Gabii," *Athenaeum* 78 (1990): 5-18; *Studies in the Northern Campus Martius in Ancient Rome,* APS Transactions 80.2 (1990). **Home Address:** 1045 Montgomery Ave., Narberth, PA 19072. **Business Address:** 720 Williams Hall, Univ. of Pennsylvania, Philadelphia, PA 19104.

PANCIERA, SILVIO ■ Italian Fulbright Fellow 1958-59; Univ. of Rome, La Sapienza, Prof. of Epigraphy & Roman Antiquity.

PANDIRI, THALIA ALEXANDRA ■ FAAR Classics/Archaeology 67. b. Mar. 12, 1943, NYC. BA 64, City College of CUNY. **Other Studies:** Free Univ. of Berlin 1962-63.

PANICELLI, IDA ■ AAR Visitor 1984-85; Galleria Nazionale d'Arte, Rome, Dir.

PANSKY, STANLEY H. ■ FAAR Architecture 53. b. Dec. 29, 1923, NYC. m. Hazel May Borne, Iris A. Barron. c. Thomas, Jane. BEng. 44, NYU; MArch 50, Harvard GSD. **Other Study:** Private study of historic pressures for city formation & the necessary physical parameters of cities & social needs of city dwellers & how to restore cities to modern life. **Career & Employment:** Skidmore, Owings & Merrill, Assc. 1950-75; Daniel Mann Johnson & Mendenhall, Manager 1975-80; Battelle Northwest Laboratory, Senior Research Architect 1982-86. **Memberships & Offices:** Portland Civic Theater, BoD, Chair late 60s & early 70s. **Fellowships, Honors & Awards:** *Progressive Architecture* Award 1985. **Publications:** Miscellaneous articles in technical & trade periodicals all on the subject of energy conservation in building design & operation (1980-86). **Bio-Bibliography:** *Who's Who in the West.* **Home Address:** 2647 S.W. Vista Ave., Portland, OR 97201.

PAPPAS, JOHN NICK ■ FAAR Sculpture 67. m. Mary Irene Borns. c. Anna, Nick, Andy, Cathy. BFA 58, Wayne State Univ.; MA 59, Wayne State Univ. **Career & Employment:** Eastern Michigan State Univ., Prof. 1960-present. **Fellowships, Honors & Awards:** Phi Kappa Phi; Michigan State Comm. for Art in Public Places. **Important Works:** Univ. of Michigan Medical Center, Ann Arbor; McAuley Cancer Care Center, Ann Arbor; Chelsea Harbour, London; Catherine McAuley Health Center, Ann Arbor; Perry Child Development Center, Ypsilanti; "Maryanne Gray," Lighthouse Point, FL; St. Nicholas Greek Orthodox Church, Troy, MI; Beth Israel Congregation, Ann Arbor; William Weatherford, Bloomfield Hills, MI; "Donald Petersen," Chair, Ford Motor Co., World HQ, Dearborn, MI; Kresge Eye Center, Ann Arbor; Planned Parenthood of Mid-

Michigan, Ann Arbor; Detroit Osteopathic Hospital; Miller Gallery, Cincinnati; "Ralph Fletcher," West Palm Beach; Wayne State Univ.; City of Hillsdale, MI; Beyer Memorial Hospital, Ypsilanti, MI; Wayne State Univ.; Blue Cross & Blue Shield of Michigan, Detroit; Collections: Detroit Inst. of Arts; Kresge Art Center, Michigan State Univ., Lansing; Bendix Corp., Detroit; Michigan Bell Telephone Co., Detroit; Ex-Cello Corp., Troy. **Exhibitions/Performances:** Chelsea Harbour Intl. Sculpture Exb., London; Baystreet Gallery, Northport, MI; Wayne State Univ. Alumni Exb., Detroit; Freeman Gallery, Lansing; Phoenix Gallery, Ann Arbor; "Mainstreams USA 69," Marietta, OH; Nat. Religious Art Show, Cranbrook Acad.; US State Dept., Worldwide Traveling Exb.; PAFA; Ball State Annual, Muncie, IN; Michigan Artists Annual, Detroit Inst. of Art; Michiana, South Bend, IN; Forme Humaine, Paris; Forsythe Gallery, Ann Arbor; Hanamura Gallery, Detroit; Temple Israel Show, Detroit; Wayne State Centennial Exb., Detroit; Sill Gallery, Eastern Michigan Univ., Ypsilanti; Drawings USA, Minneapolis; Solo: Arwin Gallery, Detroit (7); Preston Burke Galleries, Farmington Hills, MI; Welna Gallery, Chicago. **Business Address:** 6 W. Cross, Ypsilanti, MI 48197.

PARK, NEIL HAMILL ■ FAAR Landscape Architecture 33. b. May 12, 1904, Lansing, MI. d. Feb. 4, 1986. m. Lois Eva Linebarier. BA 24, Little Rock College; BLA 28, Cornell Univ. **Career & Employment:** Highberger & Park, Landscape Architects, Memphis, TN.

PARSLOW, CHRISTOPHER C. ■ FAAR Classics/Archaeology 88; AAR Summer Session, Asst. Dir. 1987. b. Sept. 1, 1958, Chicago, IL. BA 80, Grinnell College; MA 83, Univ. of Iowa; PhD 89, Duke Univ. **Other Study:** ASCSA, Summer School 1982; ICCS 1979. **Research/Artistic Interests:** Roman art & archaeology, archaeology of Pompeii & Herculaneum. **Career & Employment:** Univ. of Iowa, Instr. 1982-83; Duke Univ., Instr. 1985-86; Rice Univ., Asst. Prof. 1989-90; Univ. of Toronto, Asst. Prof. 1990-91; Wesleyan Univ., Asst. Prof. 1991-present. **Memberships & Offices:** ArIA. **Fellowships, Honors & Awards:** ArIA, Olivia James Traveling Fellowship 1986-87; Duke Univ., Mellon Fellow 1988-89; NEH Summer Stipend 1990. **Publications:** "Documents Illustrating the Excavations of the Praedia of Julia Felix," *Rivista di Studi Pompeiani* 2 (1989): 37-48; "Herculaneum: A New Bibliography and Recent Work," *Journal of Roman Archaeology* 3 (1990): 248-52; "Karl Weber and Pompeian Archaeology," in *Ercolano 1738-1988: 250 Anni di Ricerca Archeologica,* (Rome: Bretschneider, 1993), 51-56; "The Forum Frieze in Pompeii in its Archaeological Context," in *The Shapes of City Life in Rome and Pompeii,* ed. Harry Evans & Mary T. Boatwright (New Rochelle, NY: Caratzas, 1995); *Rediscovering Antiquity: Karl Weber and the Excavation of Herculaneum, Pompeii, and Stabiae* (New York: Cambridge Univ. Press, 1995). **Home Address:** 101 High St., Middletown, CT 06457. **Business Address:** Wesleyan Univ., Middletown, CT 06459.

PARTRIDGE, LOREN W. ■ FAAR History of Art 68, RAAR History of Art 85. b. Apr. 11, 1936, Raton, NM. m. Rosemary Partridge. c. Wendy, Amy. BA 58, Yale Univ.; MA 65, Harvard Univ.; PhD 69, Harvard Univ. **Other Study:** Univ. of Buenos Aires 1958-59, Cert. in Latin American Literature; Army Language School, Monterey, CA 1960-61, Dipl. in Russian. **Research/Artistic Interests:** Italian Renaissance art. **Career & Employment:** Harvard Univ., TF 1964-66; UC, Berkeley, Lect. 1968, Acting Asst. Prof. 1969-70, Asst. Prof. 1970-76, Assc. Prof. 1976-80, Prof. 1980-present, Chair 1978-87, 1990-93. **Fellowships, Honors & Awards:** Fulbright Fellowship 1958-59; Kress

Found. Grant 1968-69, 1971-72; IAS, Kress Fellow 1974-75; Fulbright Research Fellowship 1975; Guggenheim Fellowship 1981-82; Getty Senior Research Grant 1988-89. **Publications:** *John Galen Howard and the Berkeley Campus: Beaux-Arts Architecture in the "Athens of the West"* (Berkeley: BAHA, 1978; rpt. 1988); with Randolph Starn, *A Renaissance Likeness: Art and Culture in Raphael's "Julius II"* (Berkeley: UC Press, 1980); *Caprarola, Palazzo Farnese*, Grand Tour Series (Milan: Franco Maria Ricci Editore, 1988); with Randolph Starn, *Arts of Power: Three Halls of State in Italy 1300-1600* (Berkeley: UC Press, 1992); "Vignola and the Villa Farnese at Caprarola, Part I," *Art Bulletin* 52 (1970): 81-87; "The Sala d'Ercole in the Villa Farnese at Caprarola, Part I and Part II," *Art Bulletin* 53 (1971): 467-486, and 54 (1972): 50-62; "Divinity and Dynasty at Caprarola: Perfect History in the Room of Farnese Deeds," *Art Bulletin* 60 (1978): 494-530; with Randolph Starn, "Representing War in the Renaissance: The Shield of Paolo Uccello," *Representations* 5 (1984): 33-65; with Randolph Starn, "Triumphalism and the Sala Regia in the Vatican," *Papers in Art History from the Pennsylvania State University* 6 (1990): 22-81; "The Room of Maps at Caprarola, 1573-75," *Art Bulletin* (1995); "Discourse of Asceticism in Bertoja's Room of Penitence in the Villa Farnese at Caprarola," *Memoirs of the AAR* (forthcoming). **Home Address:** 1012 The Alameda, Berkeley, CA 94707. **Business Address:** Dept. of History of Art, UC, Berkeley, CA 94720.

PASCAL, PAUL ■ FAAR Classics/Archaeology 52. b. Mar. 26, 1925, NYC. m. Naomi Brenner. c. David, Janet. BA 48, Univ. of Vermont; PhD 53, UNC. **Research/Artistic Interests:** Latin language & literature, Roman art, medieval Latin. **Career & Employment:** Univ. of Washington, Asst. Prof.-Prof. 1953-91, Prof. Emer. 1991-present. **Fellowships, Honors & Awards:** Univ. of Washington, Distinguished Teaching Award 1987. **Publications:** "The *Institutionum Disciplinae* of Isidore of Seville," *Traditio* 13 (1958): 425-31; "The Conclusion of the *Pervigilium Veneris*," *Neophilologus* 43 (1959): 142-47; ed. & trans., *The Julius Exclusus of Erasmus* (Bloomington: Univ. of Indiana Press, 1968); "The Ancient Romans and Ourselves," *Social Education* 43 (1979): 529-31; *Hrotsvitha: Dulcitius and Paphnutius* (Bryn Mawr: Bryn Mawr Commentaries, 1985); "Dialogus Bilinguium ac Trilinguium," *The Correspondence of Erasmus* 7 (1987): 334-47; *The Poem of Letaldus: A New Edition* (Ann Arbor: Univ. of Michigan Press, 1987). **Home Address:** 10702 Robinhood Dr., Edmonds, WA 98020.

PASQUANTONIO, PINA ■ AAR – Rome, Asst. Dir. for Operations.

PATTERSON, WILLIAM J. ■ FAAR Painting 67. b. Mar. 16, 1941, Albany, NY. m. Linda B. Patterson. c. Catherine, Jeremiah, Aaron, Sarah. BFA 65, Hartford Art School; MFA 69, Syracuse Univ. **Other Study:** Yale-Norfolk Summer Scholarship Program 1964. **Research/Artistic Interests:** Painting, printmaking; I am a "contemporary realist." **Career & Employment:** Hartford Art School 1969-71; Univ. of Massachusetts 1971-83, Prof. 1983-present. **Memberships & Offices:** Soc. of American Graphic Artists; Connecticut Acad. of Fine Arts. **Fellowships, Honors & Awards:** Massachusetts Council on the Arts, Creative Artists Fellowship 1975; Univ. of Massachusetts, Faculty Research Grant 1974, 1980, 1983, 1984, 1990, 1992, Humanities & Fine Arts College Outstanding Teacher Award 1992-93; plus numerous awards for prints & paintings. **Important Works:** Public Collections: Library of Congress, New Britain Museum, New Jersey State Museum, De Cordova Museum, Honolulu Acad. of Art, Springfield Museum, Holyoke Museum, New York

William J. Patterson

Public Library, Univ. of New Hampshire, Arizona State Univ., Northern Illinois Univ., Mt. Holyoke College Museum. **Exhibitions/Performances:** Solo: NAD 1968; Masruden Gallery, Boston 1977; Swain School of Art, New Bedford, MA 1979; New Britain Museum of Art 1981; Marietta College 1989; Group: Assn. of American Artists Gallery, NYC 1970; Connecticut Acad. 1972; Brooklyn Museum 1974-75; NAD 1978; Contemporary American Graphics Traveling Exb. 1984, 1985, 1986, 1987, 1988, 1989; Hart Gallery, Northampton, MA 1992, 1994; Univ. of New Hampshire 1992; Univ. of Massachusetts 1994. **Bio-Bibliography:** *American Artist* (Oct. 1989): 44-49, 93-96; *Who's Who in American Art*. **Home Address:** 24 Applewood Ln., Amherst, MA 01002. **Business Address:** Art Dept, Univ. of Massachusetts, Amherst, MA 01033.

PATTON, FRANCIS L. ■ AAR Charter Mem.

PATTON, GEORGE ERWIN ■ FAAR Landscape Architecture 51. b. Mar. 18, 1920, Franklin, NC. d. Mar. 6, 1991. m. Sidney Ott Belleville. BS 48, North Carolina State College. **Career & Employment:** US Marine Corps, WWII 1943-46; George E. Patton & Asscs. 1954-91; Univ. of Pennsylvania, Faculty 1955-65; Simonds & Simonds, Pittsburgh; MGM Studios, Scenic Artist. **Memberships & Offices:** Philadelphia Art Comm. 1960-68; *Landscape Architecture*, Publication Bd. 1975-81; ASLA, Nat. Design Awards, Juror 1982; ASLA, VP-Chair 1967-69. **Fellowships, Honors & Awards:** Fulbright Scholarship; Garden Club of America Fellowship 1949-50; plus numerous ASLA & AIA Awards. **Publications:** contributed to *Landscape Architecture, Architectural Record, & Garden Design*. **Important Works:** Locust Walk, Univ. of Pennylvania; Independence & Rittenhouse Squares Restorations, Philadelphia, Kimbell Art Museum, Ft. Worth. **Bio-Bibliography:** *Who's Who in America; Who Was Who in America*.

PAUL, CAROLE ■ FAAR Classics/Archaeology 86. b. Dec. 4, 1956, Philadelphia, PA. m. Robert J. Williams, FAAR 91. c. Julia Helen Williams. BA 78, Barnard College; MA 82, Univ. of Pennsylvania; PhD 89, Univ. of Pennsylvania. **Research/Artistic Interests: History of 17th- & 18th-century Italian art. Career & Employment: Philadelphia Museum of Art, Print Dept., Asst. 1987; Rosenbach Museum, Research Asst. 1987-88; UC, Santa Barbara, Asst. Research Art Historian 1990, Lect. 1992, 1995. Fellowships, Honors & Awards: Guggenheim Museum, Intern Fellowship 1978; Univ. of Pennsylvania, Teaching Fellowship 1980-83, Kress Fellowship 1983-84; Penn-L'Aquila Italian Studies Center Fellowship 1984-85. Publications: "Mariano Rossi's Camillus Fresco in the Borghese Gallery," *Art Bulletin* 75 (1992): 297-326. Home Address: 206 Ravenscroft Dr., Santa Barbara, CA 93117.

PAWLOWSKI, PAUL R.V. ■ FAAR Landscape Architecture 69; SOF, Adv. Council, VP 1978, 1989. b. Aug. 31, 1942, NYC. m. Ingrid Anderson. c. Allegra S., Tess W. BArch 65, Univ. of Virginia; MLArch 67, Univ. of Michigan. Career & Employment: Sasaki Asscs., Sen. Assc. & Projects Dir., Middle East 1969-79; Dedham, MA, Zoning Bd. of Appeals 1978-84; Pawlowski Asscs., Pres. & Founder 1979-present; RISD, Asst. Prof. 1982-89, Dept. Head 1983-86; Kuwaiti Engineers Office, Dir. of Design & Planning 1989-90. Memberships & Offices: AIA, Interiors Comm. 1986-present; Little Compton, RI, Conservation Comm. 1992-present.; ASLA, RI Chap., Pres. 1995. Fellowships, Honors & Awards: ASLA, RI Chap., Merit Award 1989; AIA, RI Chap., Merit Award 1989; *Interiors,* Honor Award 1991. Publications: ed., Piero Santogo, *Prolegomena to the Higher Educational Environment* (Rome: pvt. ptg. 1963). Important Works: El Kantaoui Resort, Sousse, Tunisia 1970-72; State Park at Rockwood Hall, Tarrytown & Mt. Pleasant, NY 1972-74; Costa Sur Resort, La Romana, Dominican Republic 1975; Costa Smeralda Resort, Sardinia 1969-76; Kuwait Waterfront Competition, Master Plan, Final Design, with Frank James 1975-79; Bush Apt., NYC 1982; Peat Marwick Main Providence Office 1987-88; Cookson America Corp. HQ, Providence 1988-89; Gulf Investment Corp. HQ Tower Competition, Kuwait 1990; Abdulla al Ahmed St., Kuwait, Competition, with Frank James 1990; Hasbro Industries, Renovations & Landscape Improvements 1991-94; Narragansett Indian Casino 1992-present. Business Address: Pawlowski Asscs. Inc., 1 Allens Ave., Providence, RI 02903.

PAYSON, MRS. CHARLES S. ■ AAR Visitor 1959 — 1964, Philanthropist.

PEABODY, ROBERT SWAIN ■ AAR Charter Mem., Architect.

PEACOCK, CLIFFTON S. ■ FAAR Painting 95. b. Oct. 21, 1953, Chicago, IL. BFA 75, Boston Univ.; MFA 77, Boston Univ. Career & Employment: College of Charleston, Asst. Prof. 1991-present. Fellowships, Honors & Awards: Massachusetts Artist Fellowship 1980, 1986, 1989; NEA Grant 1981, 1983, 1987; Engelhard Found. Fellowship 1986; Award in the Visual Arts VII 1988; Louis Comfort Tiffany Grant 1989. Important Works: MFA; MIT; Rose Art Museum, Waltham, MA; Hood Art Museum, Dartmouth College; Carnegie-Mellon Univ. Art Gallery. Exhibitions/Performances: Thomas Segal, Boston 1986, 1988, 1990; Inst. of Centemporary Art, Boston 1986; Germans Van Eck, NYC 1988, 1990, 1993; Greenville County Museum of Art, SC 1991, 1993; Jan Baum Gallery, Los Angeles 1991; William Halsey Gallery, College of Charleston 1991; Southeastern Center for Contemporary Art, Winston-Salem 1992. Business Address: Studio Art, College of Charleston, Charleston, SC 29424.

PEARLSTEIN, PHILIP ■ RAAR Painting 82. b. 1924, Pittsburgh, PA. m. Dorothy Cantor. c. William, Julia, Ellen. BFA 49,

Carnegie Inst. of Technology; MA 55, IFU. Career & Employment: Pratt Inst., Instr. 1959-63; Yale Univ., Visiting Critic 1962-63; Brooklyn College, Prof. 1963-88, Dist. Prof. Emer. 1988. Fellowships, Honors & Awards: Fulbright Hays Fellow 1956-59; NEA Fellowship 1968; Guggenheim Fellowship 1969. Important Works: Selected AIC; MFA; Brooklyn Museum; Carnegie Inst., Pittsburgh; Cleveland Museum of Art; Corcoran Gallery, Washington, DC; Hirshhorn Museum & Sculpture Garden, Washington, DC; Kansas City Art Inst; MMA; Milwaukee Art Inst; MOMA; Nat. Gallery, Berlin; Philadelphia Museum of Art; San Antonio Museum of Art; Toledo Museum of Art; Whitney Museum, NYC. Exhibitions/Performances: Recent Solo: Weatherspoon Art Gallery, UNC 1981; Retrospective 1983: Milwaukee Art Museum, Brooklyn Museum, PAFA, Toledo Museum of Art, Carnegie Inst. Museum of Art; Univ. of Northern Iowa, Cedar Falls 1983; Il Ponte Galleria, Rome 1983; Fay Gold Gallery, Atlanta 1984; Hirschl & Adler Modern, NYC 1985, 1988, 1993; Art Gallery, Northern Illinois Univ. 1987; Galerie Rudolf Zwirner, Cologne 1989; Brooklyn Museum 1989; Printworks Gallery, Chicago 1990; Butler Inst. of American Art., Youngstown 1992; Donald Morris Gallery, Birmingham, MI 1994; Robert Miller Gallery, NYC 1995. Bio-Bibliography: Russell Bowman, *Philip Pearlstein: The Complete Paintings* (New York: Alpine Fine Arts Collection, 1983); John Perreault, *Philip Pearlstein: Drawings & Watercolors* (New York: Harry N. Abrams, 1988); *International Who's Who; Who's Who.* Home Address: 361 W. 36 St., 6th Fl., NYC 10012.

PECK, JOHN F. ■ FAAR Literature 79. b. Jan. 13, 1941, Pittsburgh, PA. c. Ingrid. BA 62, Allegheny College; PhD 73, Stanford Univ. Other Study: C.G. Jung Inst., Kusnacht, Switzerland, Dipl. Analytical Psychology 1992. Research/Artistic Interests: Poetry, critical essays, exploratory essays. Career & Employment: Princeton Univ., Instr. 1968-71, Lect. 1972-75; Mt. Holyoke College, Asst Prof. 1977-80, Assc. Prof. 1980-82; Univ. of Zurich, Lect.-Prof. 1985-92; Private Practice 1993-present. Fellowships, Honors & Awards: AAAL Award 1975; Guggenheim Fellowship 1981; NYU, Delmore Schwartz Award 1995; Ingram Merrill Award 1995. Publications: *Shagbark* (New York

```
To the Gods the Shades: diis manibus ◆ Johannes Felbermeyer

        MUUUscia! A greybeard
    at garden's end with leavings
        for the stiff-tailed queens--

        had danced for the Kaiser,
    photographed Marcus' column
        from mounting sandbags,

        graphed visions behind
    those Etruscan bronze pre-dawn
        Giacomettis,

        guaged the suns rising
    from the south portal, Shiva's,
        of the gods' ocean:

        these do not sum up
    love in the eyes of one man--
        when did it start there?--

        whom the iron Lupa
    suckled without poisoning,
        Rome, mam, dug, slut, witch.

        Thus called time's father
    in morning's origin, thus
        were the mists nourished,

        thus the animals
    pricked their ears in attunement
        as the chanter passed.
```

John F. Peck

& Indianapolis: Bobbs-Merrill, 1972); *The Broken Blockhouse Wall* (Boston: Godine, 1977 & Manchester: Carcanet, 1979); *Poems and Translations of Hi-Lo* (Manchester: Carcanet, 1991 & New York: Sheep Meadow, 1993); *ARGVRA* (Manchester: Carcanet, 1993 & New York: Sheep Meadow, 1995); *Selva Morale* (Manchester: Carcanet: 1995); trans., with Frank Nisetich, Euripides, *Orestes* (New York: Oxford Univ. Press, 1995). **Bio-Bibliography:** Donald Davie, "John Peck's Shagbark," in *Trying to Explain* (Ann Arbor: Univ. of Michigan & Manchester: Carcanet, 1979); James Powell, "The Rope of Twined Lifetimes: The Poetry of John Peck," *Occident* (Spring 1980): 26-31; Joan Landis, "Shipwreck, Autochthony and Nostos: The Poetry of John Peck," *Salmagundi* 47-48 (Winter-Spring 1980): 159-200; Clive Wilmer, in *Oxford Companion to Twentieth-Century Poetry in English* (New York & Oxford: Oxford Univ. Press, 1991); Clive Wilmer, "In a Chinese Mirror," *Times Literary Supplement* (Aug. 8, 1991); Patrick McGuinness, "Trajectories," *PN Review* 94.20.2 (Nov.-Dec. 1993): 53-54; interview with Clive Wilmer, *PN Review* 98.20.6 (July-Aug. 1994): 56-59 & *Poets Talking* (Manchester: Carcanet, 1994): 136-45; *Contemporary Poets; International Who's Who in Poetry; Who's Who in America.* **Home Address:** 4 Bullock St., Brattleboro, VT 05301.

PECK, TRACY ■ ASCSR, Dir. 1898-99.

PEDERSEN, WILLIAM ■ FAAR Architecture 67. b. 1938, St. Paul, MN. m. Elizabeth Essex. c. Kia Pederson, Lea Pedersen. BArch 61, Univ. of Minnesota; MArch 63, MIT. **Career & Employment:** I.M. Pei & Partners 1967-71; John Carl Warnecke, VP 1971-76; Kohn Pedersen Fox, Founder & Prin. 1976-present. Visiting Appointments: RISD, Columbia Univ., Harvard Univ. **Memberships & Offices:** ALNY, NY State Assn. of Architects, SAH. **Fellowships, Honors & Awards:** Univ. of Minnesota, Gargoyle Club Prize 1961; MIT, Whitney Fellow 1963; AIA, Nat. Honor Award 1984, 1987 1995, NY Chap. Gold Medal 1989, Nat. Architectural Firm of the Year Award 1990; AAAL, Arnold W. Brunner Memorial Prize 1985; Yale Univ., Eero Saarinen Prof. 1986; *Progressive Architecture* Award 1987, 1988, 1989, 1991; Univ. of Illinois, Chicago, Herbert Greenward Dist. Prof. 1989; Univ. of Minnesota, Alumni Achievement Award 1990. **Important Works:** with I.M. Pei, NGA 1970; with John Carl Warnecke, Aid Assn. for Lutherans HQ, Appleton, WI 1976; 333 Wacker Dr., Chicago 1983; Procter & Gamble Gen. Office Complex, Cincinnati 1986; Rockefeller Plaza West, NYC 1991; IBM HQ, Montreal 1992; Mainzer Landstrasse 58, Frankfurt 1993; Federal Reserve Bank, Dallas 1993; Carwill House, Stratton Mountain, VT 1993; World Bank, Washington, DC 1994; US Federal Court, Portland, OR 1995; Greater Buffalo Intl. Airport 1995. **Bio-Bibliography:** *Kohn Pederson Fox: Buildings & Projects 1976-1986* (New York: Rizzoli, 1987); "Kohn Pederson Fox Associates," *Process Architecture* (Nov. 15, 1989); "Methods and Intentions 1976-1989," *Process Architecture* (Nov. 15, 1989); *Kohn Pederson Fox: Architecture and Urbanism 1986-1992* (New York: Rizzoli, 1993). **Home Address:** 7 W. 81 St., NYC 10024.

PEDLEY, JOHN GRIFFITHS ■ RAAR Classics/Archaeology 90; Classical Studies Jury 1990-92. b. July 19, 1931, Burnley, England. m. Mary G. Sponberg. BA 53, Cambridge Univ.; MA 59, Cambridge Univ.; PhD 65, Harvard Univ. **Other Study:** ASCSA 1963-64. **Research/Artistic Interests:** Greek sculpture; art & archaeology of Asia Minor; art & archaeology of South Italy & Sicily. **Career & Employment:** Univ. of Michigan, Asst. Prof. 1965-68, Assc. Prof. 1968-74, Prof. 1974-present, Graduate Program in Classical Art & Archaeology, Chair 1971-82; Kelsey Museum of Archaeology, Dir. 1973-86. **Memberships**

& Offices: ArIA, Exec. Com. 1972-75, Nominating Com. 1979-80, 1986-87, Fellowship Com. 1981-84; Monographs Com. 1992-present, Program Com. 1994-present; ICCS, Managing Com. 1985-90; ASCSA, Council Mem. 1975-present. **Fellowships, Honors & Awards:** American Research Inst., Turkey, Fellow 1967; ACLS Fellow 1972; NEA Grant 1974, 1975, 1977, 1979; NEH Grants 1967, 1975, 1977, 1983, 1984; Univ. of Michigan, Senior Faculty Distinguished Achievement Award 1978; APS Grant 1979; NEH Fellow 1986-87. **Publications:** with G.M.A. Hanfmann, "The Statue of Meleager," *Antike Plastik* 3 (1964): 61-66; "The Archaic Favissa at Cyrene," *AJA* 75 (1971): 39-47; *Ancient Literary Sources on Sardis* (Cambridge: Harvard Univ. Press, 1972); *Greek Sculpture of the Archaic Period: The Island Workshops* (Mainz: Philip von Zabern, 1976); "Cycladic Influences in the Sixth-Century Sculpture of Attica," in *Athens Comes of Age* (Princeton: Princeton Univ. Press, 1978), 53-72; ed., *New Light on Ancient Carthage* (Ann Arbor: Univ. of Michigan Press, 1980); "A Group of Early Sixth-Century Korai and the Workshop on Chios," *AJA* 86 (1982): 183-91; "Excavations at Paestum 1984," *AJA* 89 (1985): 53-60; "Reflections of Architecture in Sixth-Century Attic Vase-Painting," in *J. Paul Getty Museum Papers on the Amasis Painter and His World* (Malibu: J. Paul Getty Museum, 1987), 63-81; *Paestum: Greeks and Romans in Southern Italy* (London: Thames & Hudson, 1990); *Greek Art and Archaeology* (New York: Harry N. Abrams & London: Cassell, 1992): "Field Archaeology and Professional Training: Excavation and the University," *Eutopia* 1 (1992): 89-97; with M. Torelli et al., *The Sanctuary of Santa Venera at Paestum* I (Rome: Bretschneider, 1993). **Bio-Bibliography:** *Who's Who in America.* **Home Address:** 1233 Baldwin, Ann Arbor, MI 48104. **Business Address:** Dept. of Classical Studies, Univ. of Michigan, Ann Arbor, MI 48109.

PEEBLES, BERNARD MANN ■ FAAR Classics/Archaeology 34. b. Jan. 1, 1906, Norfolk, VA. d. Nov. 22, 1976. m. Cary Christian Taliaferro. c. Elizabeth Mann Brownstein, Lucien Taliaferro. BA 26, Univ. of Virginia; MA 28, Harvard Univ.; PhD 40, Harvard Univ. **Research/Artistic Interests:** Latin paleography, Church Fathers, writings of Sulpicius Severus. **Career & Employment:** Univ. of Virginia, Faculty 1928-29; Fordham Univ., Faculty 1934-35, 1939-41; Harvard Univ., Faculty 1937-39; St. John's College, Annapolis, Faculty 1941-48; US Army 1943-45; Catholic Univ., Assc. Prof.-Prof.-Dept. Chair 1948-70. **Memberships & Offices:** APA; MAA; ArIA; RSA; Assn. Internationale d'Études Patristiques; Catholic Comm. on Intellectual & Cultural Affairs; Washington Classical Soc., Pres; *The Fathers of the Church: a New Translation*, Ed. Dir. 1946-68; *Traditio*, Ed. 1952-73; Mediaeval & Renaissance Latin Translations & Commentaries, Exec. Com. 1961-76. **Fellowships, Honors & Awards:** Harvard Univ., William Watson Goodwin Fellowship 1928-32. **Publications:** "Girolamo da Prato and His Manuscripts of Sulpicius Severus," *Memoirs of the AAR* 13 (1936): 8-65; *The Poet Prudentius* (New York: Macmillen, 1951). **Bio-Bibliography:** Briggs, 489-90; *Directory of American Scholars; Who Was Who in America.*

PEI, TING ■ AAR Visitor 1990-91, Architect.

PELL, F. LIVINGSTON ■ McKim Scholar 1911-12, 1913.

PELLECCHIA, LINDA A. ■ FAAR History of Art 92. b. Oct. 20, 1946, Leominster, MA. BA 68, Smith College; MA 73, Harvard Univ.; PhD 83, Harvard Univ. **Other Study:** Boston Univ. 1964-66. **Research/Artistic Interests:** Renaissance architectural history, Giuliano da Sangallo, Renaissance & antiquity, Vitruvius & the Renaissance, palaces & villas. **Career &**

Employment: Davidson College, Asst. Prof. 1983-85; Univ. of Delaware, Visiting Asst. Prof. 1985-87, Asst. Prof. 1987-present; NGA, Found. for Documents of Architecture, Architectural Historian 1988-89. **Career & Employment:** NEH, Reviewer-Juror 1988, 1989, 1991; US Congress, Office of Technology Assessment, Consultant 1991. **Fellowships, Honors & Awards:** Davidson College, Mellon Found. Award 1984, Grant 1985; NEH Summer Stipend 1986; Univ. of Delaware, Research Grant 1986, 1990. **Publications:** "The First Observant Church of San Salvatore al Monte in Florence," *Mitteilungen des Kunsthistorischen Institutes in Florenz* 23 (1979): 273-96; "The Patron's Role in the Production of Architecture: Bartolomeo Scala and the Scala Palace," *Renaissance Quarterly* 42 (1989): 258-91; "Architects Read Vitruvius," *JSAH* (forthcoming). **Home Address:** 141 W. Main St., Newark, DE 19711.

PELS, MARSHA S. ■ FAAR Sculpture 85. b. Dec. 24, 1950, Brooklyn, NY. BFA 72, RISD; MFA 74, Syracuse Univ. **Other Study:** Apprenticed in founderies in Italy & NYC. **Career & Employment:** Bennington College, Visiting Prof. 1987-88; Tyler School of Art, Asst. Prof. 1988-90; RISD, Adj. Prof. 1990-91; Queens College, Adj. Prof. 1990-91; Sarah Lawrence College, Guest Appt. 1992-93; Univ. of Iowa, Iowa City, Visiting Prof., Chair. & Dir. of Graduate Studies 1993-94. **Important Works:** "Of the Cities," from the Crucifixion Series 1985, United Jewish Appeal, Corporate HQ, NYC 1985; "Acheron," Grounds for Sculpture, Hamilton, NJ 1985-93. **Exhibitions/Performances:** Oscarsson-Siegeltuch, NYC 1986; Beaver College, Glenside, PA 1986; Aldrich Museum of Contemporary Art, Ridgefield, CT 1986; Suzanne Usdan Gallery, Bennington College 1987; Univ. Museum, S.I.U., Carbondale, IL 1988; Proctor Art Center, Bard College 1988; Sally Hawkins Gallery, NYC 1989; Burlington County College Sculpture Garden, Pemberton, NJ 1990; Brooklyn Waterfront Museum 1990; Ashawagh Hall, East Hampton 1990; Rockland Center for the Arts, Nyack, NY 1990; Kouros Gallery, NYC 1992; Socrates Sculpture Park, NYC 1993; La Fonda del Sol Visual Arts Center, Washington, DC 1994. **Home Address:** 99 Commercial St., Brooklyn, NY 11222.

PEÑA, J. THEODORE ■ FAAR Classics/Archaeology 85; AAR Summer School, Asst. Dir. 1985. BA 78, Wesleyan Univ.; MA 81, Univ. of Michigan; PhD 87, Univ. of Michigan. **Other Study:** Istituto di Archeologia, Università degli Studi, Perugia 1980-81; Archaeological field work: Capalbiaccio, Albegna Valley, Fregellae, Morgantina, Cetamura del Chianti, Roman Palatine, & Turano Valley, Italy; Carthage, Tunisia; Tel Amafa, Israel. **Research/Artistic Interests:** Art & archaeology of Roman & pre-Roman Italy; ancient city of Rome; ancient economy, settlement archaeology, archaeological ceramics, ceramic technology. **Career & Employment:** ICCS, Visiting Lect. 1981-82, Visiting Asst. Prof. 1992-93; SUNY, Albany, Lect. 1985-87, Asst. Prof. 1987-94; SUNY, Buffalo, Asst. Prof. 1994-present. **Fellowships, Honors & Awards:** Danforth Fellowship 1978-83; SUNY, Albany, Faculty Merit Award 1987-88, 1989-90, Faculty Grant 1990-91; NEH Travel Grant 1990; USIA, Exchange Grant 1991; Smithsonian Inst. Fellowship 1991. **Publications:** *Latin Inscriptions in the Kelsey Museum*, ed. M. Torelli & M. Baldwin (1979), 83-94; "The Generation & Interpretation of the Archaeological Record of the Seri," *Michigan Discussions in Anthropology* 5.1-2 (1980): 100-16; "P. Giss. 69: Evidence for Supplying of Stone Transport Operations in Roman Egypt and the Production of Fifty-foot Monolithic Column Shafts," *Journal of Roman Archaeology* 2 (1980): 126-32; "Internal Red-slip Cookware (Pompeian Red Ware) from Centamura, Italy: Mineralogical Composition

and Provenience," *AJA* 94 (1990): 647-61; "The Reconstruction of Ancient Ceramic Technology through the Comparative Analysis of Ancient and Contemporary Potters' Materials: A Case Study from the Central Tiber Valley of Italy," *Proceedings of the Materials Research Society* 184 (1991): 511-21; "Neutron Activation Analysis of Materials from the Vasanello Ceramic Production Workshop," in *La civiltà dei Falisci: Atti del XV Convegno di Studi Etruschi ed Italici* (1991), 272-74; "Raw Material Use among Nucleated Industry Potters: The Case of Vasarello, Italy," *Archeomaterials* 6.2 (1992): 93-122; "Two Studies of the Provenience of Roman Pottery through Neutron Activitation Analysis," in *The Inscribed Economy: Production and Distribution in the Roman Empire in Light of* instrumentum domesticum, ed. W.V. Harris, *Journal of Roman Archaeology*, supp. ser. 6 (1993): 107-20; with E. Hostetter et al., "A Late Roman Domus with Apsidial Hall on the NE Slope of the Palatine: 1989-91 Seasons," *Journal of Roman Archaeology*, supp. ser. 11 (1994): 135-85. **Business Address:** Dept. of Classics, 712 Clemens Hall, SUNY, Buffalo, NY 14260.

PENNELL, HENRY B. ■ Rotch Scholar 1897.

PEPPER, BEVERLY ■ RAAR Sculpture 86. b. Dec. 20, 1924, Brooklyn, NY. m. Curtis B. Pepper. c. Jorie Graham, John Pepper. **Study:** Industrial Design at Pratt Inst. 1940s; sculpture & painting, ASL with Fernand Léger & Andre L'hote; Grand Chaumière, Paris 1940s. **Research/Artistic Interests:** Site-specific earth works, public sculpture, cast iron, cast bronze, stainless steel, painting, etching. **Fellowships, Honors & Awards:** Mostra Internazionale, Gold Medal & Sculpture Purchase Award 1966; Jacksonville Art Museum, 1st Prize & Purchase Award 1970; Iron & Steel Industry, New York, Best Art in Steel Award 1970; Reynolds Metal Company, R.S. Reynolds Memorial Award 1974; GSA Grant, Washington, DC 1975, 1993; NEA Award 1975, 1979; Hon. Degrees: DFA, Pratt Inst. 1982 & Maryland Inst. 1983; Prof. Emer., Univ. of Perugia 1987. **Important Works:** San Diego Federal Bldg. 1975; North Park, Dallas 1971; AT&T Long Lines Bldg., Bedminster, NJ 1974-76; Dartmouth College 1975-77; Four-Leaf Towers, Houston 1982; Laumeier Intl. Sculpture Park, St. Louis 1983-85; Sol i Ombra Park, Barcelona 1986-91; Ville Celle, Pistoia 1989-91; Detroit Inst. of Arts 1991; Nat. Arboretum, Washington, DC 1992; Gotanno Community Park, Adachi-ku, Tokyo 1992; "Palingenesis," Zurich 1992-94; Garden at 26 Federal Plaza, General Services Administration, NYC 1993-95; Jerusalem Found 1994. **Exhibitions/Performances:** Albright-Knox Art Gallery 1968; San Francisco Museum of Modern Art 1976; Seattle Museum of Contemporary Arts 1977; Princeton Art Museum 1978; Seattle Museum of Art 1979; Intl. Sculpture Conference, Washington, DC 1980; Nat. Collection of Fine Arts, Smithsonian Inst. 1980; Laumeier Intl. Sculpture Park, St. Louis 1982; traveling exb. Albright-Knox Art Gallery 1986-87; Contemporary Sculpture Center, Tokyo 1991; Mezzanine Gallery, MMA 1991; Narni alla Rocca, Narni, Italy 1991. **Bio-Bibliography:** Robert Hughes, *Time* (June 16, 1975): 28; Phyllis Tuchman, *Bennington Review* 14 (1982): 41-43; Kenneth Baker, *Art in America* (Apr. 1984): 176-79; Kay Larson, *New York Magazine* (June 8, 1987): 46-58; Deborah Solomon, *ArtNews* (Dec. 1987): 112-17; Barbara Rose, *The Journal of Art* (Nov. 1989): 3; Michael Brenson, *NY Times* (Sept. 21, 1990): C24; Robert Hobbs, *Sculpture* (Nov.-Dec. 1994): 20-25; Barbara Rose, *Amphisculpture* (film) 1977; Vittorio Armentano, *Beverly Pepper Making Sculpture* (film) 1970; *Contemporary Artists; Who's Who in America; Who's Who in American Art.* **Home Address:** Torre Gentile di Todi, PG 06059, Italy; 84 Thomas St., NYC 10013. **Business Address:** André Emmerich Gallery, 41 E. 57 St., NYC 10022.

PEPPER, CURTIS BILL ■ AAR Visitor 86. b. Aug. 20, 1920, Huntington, WV. m. Beverly Pepper, RAAR 86. c. Jorie Graham, John Pepper. **Study:** Univ. of Florence, Univ. of Illinois. **Career & Employment:** US Military, MIS-X, WW II; United Press; CBS; *Newsweek,* Rome Bureau Chief 1956-67. **Home Address:** Torre Gentile di Todi, PG 06059, Italy. **Business Address:** IMG-Julian Bach Literary Agency, 22 E. 71 St., NYC 10021.

PEREIRA, WILLIAM LEONARD ■ RAAR Architecture 71. b. Apr. 25, 1909, Chicago, IL. d. Nov. 13, 1985. m. Margret McConnell, Bronya Kester. c. William L., Monica I. BArch 31, Univ. of Illinois, School of Architecture. **Other Studies:** Otis Art Inst. 1964; Art Center, College of Design 1971. **Career & Employment:** Holabird & Root, Assc. 1930-32; Private Practice, Chicago & Los Angeles; Univ. of Southern California, Prof. 1949-57; William L. Pereira & Asscs. 1958-85. **Memberships & Offices:** California Governor's Task Force on Transportation, Chair 1967-68; Nat. Council of the Arts 1967-68; California Governor's Comm. on Ocean Resources 1967; Aeronautics & Space Engineering Bd., Nat. Acad. of Engineering, Adv. 1969-70; Science & Technology Council of the California Assembly 1970; Crocker Nat. Bank, Adv. Com. 1965-85; Urban America Inc., Dir. 1965-85; American Film Inst., Washington, DC, Dir. 1965-85. **Fellowships, Honors & Awards:** AIA, Fellow 1958, Southern California Chap., Honor Award 1963 (2); American Library Assn., Merit Award 1963; Otis Art Inst., Hon. PhD 1964; Art Center College of Design, DFA 1971; Univ. of Illinois, Alumni Achievement Award 1973; Pepperdine Univ., DL 1974; Acad. of Motion Picture Arts & Sciences, Fellow; Order of the Ivory Coast, Commander. **Publications:** "The Architect and the Entrepreneur," *AIA Journal* (July 1962); "Campus Planning, Univ. of Cailfornia," *Architectural Record* (Nov. 1964). **Important Works:** CBS Television City, Los Angeles 1952; UC, Santa Barbara 1953-58; Los Angeles Intl. Airport 1959-62; Los Angeles County Museum of Art 1964; UC, Irvine, Library, Halls & Humanities-Social Science Bldg. 1965, Fine Arts Library 1970; Dickenson Art Center, UCLA 1965; Booth Memorial Hall, Univ. of Southern California 1965; Central Library, UC, San Diego 1970; Transamerican Bldg., San Francisco 1972; Sheraton Hotel & Conference Center, Doha, Qatar 1981; Tom Bradley Intl. Airport Terminal, Los Angeles 1984. **Bio-Bibliography:** *Contemporary Architects; Current Biography Yearbook: Who Was Who in America.*

PERLIN, BERNARD ■ FAAR Painting 51. b. Nov. 21, 1918, Richmond, VA. **Study:** New York School of Design 1936; New York Acad. of Design Art School 1936; ASL 1937-38, 1939-40. **Career & Employment:** US War Information Office, Graphics Div. 1942-43; *Life,* War Correspondent 1943-44; *Fortune Magazine* 1945; Brooklyn Museum Art School, Instr. 1946-48. **Fellowships, Honors & Awards:** Kosciuszko Found. Scholarship 1938; Chaloner Found. Award 1948, 1949; Fulbright Fellow 1950; Guggenheim Fellow 1954-55, 1959; NIAL Award 1964. **Exhibitions/Performances:** Knoedler Galleries, NYC 1948; Solo: Catherine Viviano Gallery, NYC 1955, 1958, 1963, 1966; Group: Inst. of Contemporary Arts, London 1950; Palazzo Venezia, Rome 1950; MMA 1950; Museum of Art, Springfield, MA 1950; Corcoran Gallery of Art, Washington, DC 1953, 1959; Whitney Museum, NYC 1951, 1955, 1956; Cincinnati Art Museum 1958; Detroit Inst. of Arts 1960; PAFA 1960, 1966; New York World's Fair 1964-65; Arkansas Art Center, Little Rock 1970.

PERLONGO, DANIEL J. ■ FAAR Musical Composition 72. b. Sept. 23, 1942, Gaastra, MI. BMus 64, Univ. of Michigan; MusM 66, Univ. of Michigan; Dipl. 68, Accademia di Santa Cecilia, Rome. **Career & Employment:** Indiana Univ. of Pennsylvania, Assc. Prof. 1968-92. **Memberships & Offices:** American Music Center; ACA; BMI; Fulbright Comm., Nat. Screening Com. for Composition, Juror 1985-87. **Fellowships, Honors & Awards:** Bearns Prize 1966; Fulbright Grant 1966-68; AAAL 1975; NEA Grant 1981, 1995; Guggenheim Fellow 1982. **Important Works:** *Concertino,* for chamber orchestra 1980; *Concerto,* for piano & orchestra 1992; *Ricercar,* for wind trio (CRI) 1981; *Fragments,* for flute & cello (CRI) 1981; *Tapestry,* for organ 1981; *String Quartet II* (ISCM) 1983; *Montalvo Overture,* for wind ensemble 1984; *A Day at Xochimilco,* for woodwind quintet & piano 1987; *Novella,* for trombone & organ 1988; *Suite,* for piano 1988; *By Verse Distills,* for mezzosoprano, clarinet, violin, & piano 1989; *First Set,* for piano 1990; *Lake Breezes,* for chamber orchestra 1990; *Preludes and Variations,* for wind ensemble 1991; *Arcadian Suite,* for horn & harp 1993; *Shortcut from Bratislava,"* for piano & orchestra 1994; *Antique Seranade,* for orchestra 1994. **Bio-Bibliography:** *Baker's Biographical Dictionary of American Musicians; Who's Who in America.* **Home Address:** 18 N. Third St., Indiana, PA 15701.

PERRIELLO-SHARON, LAURIE ■ NIAE, John Dinkeloo Traveling Fellow 1990-91.

PERRONE, CARLO ■ AAR Italian Com. 1994-present.

PERRY, CHARLES O. ■ FAAR Architecture 66, RAAR Sculpture 71. b. Oct. 18, 1929, Helena, MO. m. Sheila A. Henry. c. Paul, Carlo, Daniela, Patrick, Marco. MArch 58, Yale Univ. **Other Study:** Columbia Univ. 1953; UC, Berkeley 1953. **Career & Employment:** Skidmore, Owings & Merrill, Architect 1958-63; Self-Employed, Sculptor & Designer 1964-present. **Memberships & Offices:** Century Assn. 1974; Yale Univ., Architectural Juror 1981, 1986; NAD; Katonah Museum of Art; Sculptors' Guild; Silvermine Guild Center for the Arts. **Publications:** "On the Edge of Science," *Leonardo* 25 (1992). **Important Works:** Collections: MOMA; AIC; Art Museum at Dartmouth College; Univ. of Michigan; Phillips Acad., Andover, MA; San Francisco Museum of Modern Art; De Young Museum, San Francisco; Smithsonian Inst., Washington, DC; Contemporary Arts Soc., London; Oakland Museum; Cummer Gallery of Art, Jacksonville, FL; Commissions: Masco Corp., Taylor, MI; Shell Oil Co., Melbourne, Australia; Barnett Plaza, Tampa, FL; Lincoln Center, Dallas; IBM Univ. Research Park, Charlotte, NC; Saudi Arabian Airlines, Jeddah; Nat. Air & Space Museum, Washington, DC; Harvard Business School, Boston; Dartmouth College; General Electric HQ, Fairfield, CT; Hyatt Regency Hotel, San Francisco; Federal Reserve Bank, Minneapolis; Peachtree Center, Atlanta. **Exhibitions/Performances:** Numerous Solo; Group Shows: Whitney Museum Annual 1964, 1966; "Festival of the Two Worlds, Spoleto 1968; Venice Art Biennale 1970; Quadriennale d'Arte di Roma 1977; Sculptors' Guild, Lever House, NYC 1984; Katonah Gallery, NY 1986, 1989; Sculpture as Public Art, ISC, Washington, DC 1987; NAD 1988; Dartmouth College 1988. **Bio-Bibliography:** *Who's Who in America; Who's Who in American Art.* **Home Address:** 20 Shoreham Rd., Norwalk, CT 06855.

PERRY, ELLEN ■ Broneer Fellow 1993-94.

PERRY, MARILYN ■ AAR Visitor 1981-82; Samuel H. Kress Found., Pres.

PERUSINO, FRANCA ■ Italian Fulbright Fellow 1961-62.

PETERDI, GABOR ■ FAAR Painting 77. b. Sept. 17, 1915, Pestjuhely, Hungary. m. Joan Peterdi. **Study:** Acad. of Fine Arts, Budapest 1929; Acad. of Fine Arts, Rome 1930; Acad. Julien, Paris 1931; Acad. Scandinave, Paris 1932; Atelier 17, Paris 1933-39, NYC 1947. **Research/Artistic Interests:** Painting, printmaking, writing. **Career & Employment:** Brooklyn Museum Art School 1948-52; Hunter College, Assc. Prof. 1952-60; Yale Univ., Visiting Prof. 1954-60, Prof. 1960-87. **Memberships & Offices:** Accademia Fiorentina delle Arti del Disegno 1963; NAD 1979. **Fellowships, Honors & Awards:** Prix de Rome, Hungary 1929; Yale Univ., MA Honoris Causae 1965; Paris World's Fair, Gold Medal 1937; Sesnan Gold Medal for Oils 1958; Ford Found. Fellowship 1960; Pennel Medal 1961; Guggenheim Fellowship 1964-65; AAAL, Louise Nevelson Award 1991. **Publications:** *Printmaking: Methods Old and New* (New York: Macmillan, 1959-80); "A Biography of My Landscape," *Art in America* 51.3 (June 1963): 38-43; *Great Prints of the World* (New York: Macmillan, 1969); "Printmaking," *Encyclopedia Britannica* (1974). **Important Works:** Collections: MMA; MOMA; AIC; NGA; Whitney Museum, NYC; Galleria degli Uffizi, Florence; Brooklyn Museum; Cleveland Art Museum; Corcoran Gallery of Art, Washington, DC; High Museum of Art, Atlanta; Library of Congress, Washington, DC; Yale Univ. Art Gallery. **Exhibitions/Performances:** Over 200 solo exhibitions in the U.S. & abroad, including 20 retrospectives. **Bio-Bibliography:** Stanley W. Hayter, *About Prints* (London: Oxford Univ. Press, 1962); Ralph E. Shikes, *The Indignant Eye* (Boston: Beason Press, 1969); Una E. Johnson, *Gabor Peterdi: Graphics 1934-69* (New York: Touchstone, 1970); *Viewpoints* (Washington, DC: Library of Congress, 1975); Fritz Eichenberg, *The Art of the Print* (New York: Abrams, 1976); Paul Cummings, *A Dictionary of Contemporary American Artists* (New York: St. Martin's, 1977); Una E. Johnson, *American Prints and Printmakers* (New York: Doubleday, 1980); Burt Chernow, *Gabor Peterdi: Paintings* (New York: Taplinger, 1982); Claude Marks, *World Artists 1950-1980* (New York: H.W. Wilson, 1984); Riva Castleman, *Prints Since Pollack* (New York: Knopf, 1985); *The Landscape in Twentieth-Century American Art* (New York: Rizzoli, 1991); *Who's Who in American Art.* **Home Address:** 108 Highland Ave., Rowayton, CT 06853. **Business Address:** Grace Borgenicht Gallery, 724 5th Ave., NYC 10019.

PETERSON, WARREN A. ■ FAAR Architecture 55. b. June 3, 1928, Jamestown, NY. BArch 52, Yale Univ.; MArch 53, Yale Univ. **Research/Artistic Interests:** Architecture, architectural history, architectural restoration, painting, music, drama, history & literature. **Career & Employment:** Cull, Robinson & Green 1955-57; Pietro Belluschi 1958-60; Meyer & Ayers 1961-63; Warren A. Peterson, Prin. 1963-65; Peterson & Brickbauer, Prin. 1963-94; Warren Alfred Peterson, Architect 1995-present. **Fellowships, Honors & Awards:** Yale Univ., Magnus T. Hopper Fellowship 1953. **Important Works:** RISD Quadrangle 1965; Sullivan-Dorr House Restoration, Providence 1966; Sun Life Insurance, Baltimore 1966; Mercantile Safe Deposit & Trust, Baltimore 1970; Blue Cross & Blue Shield of Maryland, Towson 1976; Bankers Trust Plaza, NYC 1978; Baltimore-Washington Intl. Airport Terminal 1980; Devon Hill Apartments & Condominiums, Baltimore 1985; Washington College, Casey Academic Center, Chestertown, MD 1990; Baltimore City Life Museums 1990; F&G Life Insurance HQ, Baltimore 1990. **Exhibitions/Performances:** US State Dept. Traveling Exb. 1973; MOMA 1979; Maryland Historical Soc. 1992. **Bio-Bibliography:** Lieberman, *Award Winning Architecture* (1973); Kidder-Smith, *Architecture in America* (1978); Drexler, *Transformations in Modern Architecture* (1979); Kidder-Smith, *The Architecture of the United States* (1979). **Home Address:** 361 Homeland Southway, Baltimore, MD 21212.

PETING, DONALD LEE ■ FAAR Design Arts 78. b. Dec. 18, 1939, Chicago, IL. m. Betty Peting. c. Mark, Linda. BArch 62, Univ. of Illinois, MArch 63, UC, Berkeley. **Career & Employment:** Univ. of Oregon, Faculty 1963-1974, Assc. Prof.-Asst. Dept. Head 1974-; Daniel Herbert, Architect 1964; Wilmsen, Endicott & Unthank 1966; Paul Thiry, Architect 1966-67; Skilling, Helle, Christiansen & Robertson 1967; Private Practice 1968-. **Memberships & Offices:** AIA, SW Oregon Chap.; AAUP; Soc. for Industrial Archaeology. **Fellowships, Honors & Awards:** Gargoyle Architectural Hon. 1961; Univ. of Oregon Graduate School Research Award 1965, 1970.

PETRASSI, GOFFREDO ■ RAAR Musical Composition 56. b. July 16, 1904, Zagarolo, Italy. **Other Studies:** Piano with Bastini; harmony with Donato 1925; Conservatorio di Santa Cecilia: composition with Bustini, Dipl. 1932; organ with Germani, Dipl. 1933; with Molinari. **Career & Employment:** Accademia di Santa Cecilia 1934-36, 1959-74; Teatro La Fenice, Gen. Dir. 1937-40; Conservatorio di Santa Cecilia 1939-59; Accademia Chigiana 1966-67. **Important Works:** *Concertos* 1934, 1951, 1953, 1955, 1956, 1957, 1964, 1972; *Magnificat,* for soprano, chorus & orchestra 1940; *La follia di Orlando,* a ballet 1942-43; *Il Cordonavo,* an opera 1944-48; *Il ritratto di Don Chisciotte,* a ballet 1945; *La Morte dell'Aria,* an opera 1949-50; *String Trio* 1959; *Mottetti per la Passione,* for chorus 1966; *Four Odi,* for string quartet 1975. **Bio-Bibliography:** J. Weissman, *Goffredo Petrassi* (Milan, 1957; English ed. 1980); C. Annibaldi, *Goffredo Petrassi: Catalogo delle opere e bibliografia* (Milan, 1971); G. Zosi, *Ricerca e sintesi nell'opera di Goffredo Petrassi* (Rome, 1978); E. Restagno, ed., *Petrassi* (Turin, 1986); *Baker's Biographical Dictionary of Musicians; International Who's Who; New Grove Dictionary of Music & Musicians; Who's Who in the World.*

PETRUCCIONE, JOHN FRANCIS ■ FAAR Post-Classical/Humanistic Studies 91. b. Feb. 13, 1950, Westfield, NJ. BA 72, Dartmouth College; MA 79, Oxford Univ.; PhD 85, Univ. of Michigan. **Career & Employment:** Seton Hall Prep School, S. Orange, NJ, Faculty 1975-77; Priory School, St. Louis, MO, Faculty 1977-80; Catholic Univ., Asst. Prof. 1985-. **Fellowships, Honors & Awards:** H.H. Rackham Fellowship 1980-81, 1984-85; A.W. Mellon Fellowship 1983-84. **Publications:** "The Text of Sophocles' Ajax in the Codex Ienensis (Bos. Q.7)," *Zeitscrhift für Papyrologie und Epigraphik* 53 (1983): 37-52; "The Role of the Poet and His Song in Nemean 1," *American Journal of Philology* 107 (1986): 34-45.

PFAFF, JUDY ■ RAAR Sculpture, 88. b. Sept. 19, 1946, London, England. BFA 71, Washington Univ.; MFA 73, Yale Univ. **Other Study:** Wayne State Univ. 1965; Southern Illinois Univ. 1968; Norfolk Summer School of Music & Art 1970. **Career & Employment:** School of Visual Arts 1986-91; Columbia Univ., Prof. 1992-94; Skowhegan School of Painting & Sculpture 1994; Bard College, Prof. & Co-Chair 1995-present. **Fellowships, Honors & Awards:** Creative Artist Public Service 1976; NEA Fellowship 1979, 1986; Guggenheim Fellowship 1983. **Important Works:** Selected Public Collections: Albright-Knox Gallery, Buffalo; Brooklyn Museum; Detroit Art Inst.; High Museum of Art, Atlanta; MOMA; Sammlung Ludwig, Aachen; Whitney Museum, NYC. **Exhibitions/Performances:** Selected Solo: Whitney Museum, NYC 1981, 1987; Venice Biennale 1982; Univ. Art Gallery, Univ. of Massachusetts, Amherst 1982; Weinberg Gallery, Los Angeles 1984; Spokane City Hall 1984; Wacoal Art Center Spiral, Tokyo 1985; Nat. Museum of Women in the Arts, Washington, DC 1989; St. Louis Art Museum 1989; Thomas Solomon's Garage, Los Angeles 1990; Max Protetch

Gallery, NYC 1990; Cleveland Center for Contemporary Art 1990; Morris Gallery, PAFA 1991; Susanne Hilberry Gallery, Birmingham, MI 1991; Usdan Gallery, Bennington College 1992; Rotunda Gallery, Brooklyn 1993; Nancy Drysdale Gallery, Washington, DC 1993; Exit Art, NYC 1994; Denver Art Museum 1994; Columbus Museum of Art 1994; Rose Art Museum, Waltham, MA 1995; Williamson Gallery, Pasadena 1995. **Home Address:** 319 Greenwich St., 5F, NYC 10013.

PFEIFFER, HOMER FAY ■ FAAR Architecture 30. b. Aug. 6, 1898, Diamond Springs, KS. d. Mar. 30, 1981. c. George, Dorrit Castle, Beth McNay. BArch 25, Univ. of Illinois; BFA 26, Yale Univ. **Research/Artistic Interests:** Restoration, Roman library & theater, painting. **Career & Employment:** US Navy Dept., District Public Works Officer 1942-45; US Navy, Lieut. Commander 1945. **Memberships & Offices:** ArIA. **Fellowships, Honors & Awards:** Société des Architectes, Diplomes Medal 1926-27. **Exhibitions/Performances:** Community Art Center Gallery, Greenville, NC 1944; Laurel Gallery, NYC 1947; Catherine Hood Gallery, Guilford, CT 1970.

PHILLIPS, KYLE M., JR ■ RAAR Classics/Archaeology 77. b. May 20, 1934, Cabot, VT. d. Aug. 7, 1988. BA 56, Bowdoin College; MA 59, Princeton Univ.; PhD 62, Princeton Univ. **Research/Artistic Interests:** Sicilian & Etruscan archaeology, Hellenistic & Roman mosaics; Greek vase painting; Roman wall painting. **Career & Employment:** Univ. of Michigan, Instr. 1960-62; Bryn Mawr College, Asst. Prof. 1962-67, Assc. Prof. 1967-73, Prof. 1973-82; UCLA, Visiting Prof. 1986; Tuscany Excavations 1961, 1964, 1966-88. **Memberships & Offices:** ArIA; Istituto Studi Etruschi, Corresponding Mem.; University Museum, Univ. of Pennsylvania, Research Assc. **Fellowships, Honors & Awards:** Samuel R. Fels Fellowship 1959-60; Univ. of Michigan, Rackham Research Grant 1960; APS, Summer Research Grant 1961; ACLS Grant 1969; NEH Fellow 1976-77; Cavaliere dell'Ordine della Stella della Solidarietà Italiana 1976; Dignitario dell'Ordine dei Dignitari dell'Ombra della Sera, Volterra 1979; German Archaeological Inst., Berlin, Visiting Scholar 1985. **Publications:** "Subject and Technique in Hellenistic-Roman Mosaics: A Ganymede Mosaic from Sicily," *Art Bulletin* 42 (1960): 243-62; "Bryn Mawr College Excavations in Tuscany," *AJA* 71 (1967): 133-39, 72 (1968): 121-23, 73 (1969): 333-39, 74 (1970): 241-44, 75 (1971): 257-61, 76 (1972): 249-44, 77 (1973): 319-26, with E.O. Nielsen 78 (1974): 265-78, with E.O. Nielsen 79 (1975): 357-66, with E.O. Nielsen 81 (1977): 85-101; "Perseus and Andromeda," *AJA* 72 (1968): 1-23; ed., *Poggio Civitate (Murlo, Siena), il santuario arcaico*, exb. cat. (Florence: Olschki, 1970); with A.H. Ashment, *Corpus Vasorum Antiquorum, the United States*, Bryn Mawr College, fasc. 1 (Princeton: Princeton Univ. Press, 1971); co-author, *Classical Vases* (Providence, RI: RISD Museum of Art, 1976); *In the Hills of Tuscany: Recent Excavations at the Etruscan Site of Poggio Civitate (Murlo, Siena)*, exb. cat. (Philadelphia: Univ. of Pennsylvania Museum, 1993). **Bio-Bibliography:** "Memoir," *AJA* 93 (1989): 239-40; *Murlo and the Etruscans*, ed. R.D. De Puma & J.P. Small (Madison: Univ. of Wisconsin Press, 1994): xxvi-xxxi; *Directory of American Scholars*.

PHILLIPS, MARIA A. ■ FAAR History of Art 83. b. Rome, Italy. m. Robert Max Klang. c. Jennifer Phillips, Susan Phillips. BA 74, California State Univ.; MA 77, UCLA; PhD 93, UCLA. **Career & Employment:** Univ. of Wyoming, Visiting Lect. 1981; California State Univ., Dominguez Hills, Lect. 1987; Foothill-DeAnza Community College, Instr. 1988-89; California State Univ., Chico, Lect. 1990-93; Georgia State Univ., Asst. Prof. 1993-

present. **Memberships & Offices:** CAA, SAH. **Fellowships, Honors & Awards:** Dickson Travel Grant 1979, 1980, Support Fellowship 1979-82; UC Travel Grant 1980; Kress Found. Research Travel Stipend 1981; Getty Center Dissertation Fellowship 1985-86. **Publications:** "Nuove richerche sul codice ambrosiano sulle rovine di Roma," *Arte Lombarda* n.s. 65 (1983): 5-14; "The Ambrosiana's Sketchbook on the Ruins of Rome: Its Function and Meaning," in *Les Traités d'Architecture*, ed. J. Guillaume (Paris: Picard, 1988), 151-67; *Text, Image, and Art as "primum mobile,"* exb. cat. (Santa Monica: Getty Center, 1990); "Antonio Labacco," in *The Dictionary of Art*. **Home Address:** 13 Lakeshore Dr., Avondale Estates, GA 30002.

PIANO, RENZO ■ AAR Italian Com. 1994-present, Architect.

PILLSBURY, EDMUND P. ■ AAR Trustee 1992-present. BA Yale Univ.; PhD, Courtauld Inst., Univ. of London. **Career & Employment:** Yale Univ. Art Gallery, Staff 1972-; Yale Univ., Lect.1972-; Yale Center for British Art, Dir.; Paul Mellon Centre for Studies in British Art, CEO; Kimbell Art Museum, Ft. Worth, Dir. 1980-. **Memberships & Offices:** Villa I Tatti Council, Founding Chair; *Burlington Magazine* Found., BoT; Yale Univ. Art Gallery, Bd. of Governors; Assn. de Soutien et de Diffusion d'Art, Paris, Minda de Gunzburg Prize, Juror; State Hermitage Museum, St. Petersburg, UNESCO Consultant. **Publications:** *The Graphic Art of Federico Barocci: Selected Drawings and Prints; Sixteenth-Century Italian Drawings: Form and Function; Florence and the Arts: Five Centuries of Patronage, a Critical Catalogue of Florentine Arts in Cleveland Collections.*

PINE, JOHN B. ■ AAR Trustee 1910-23, Lawyer.

PINNEY, GLORIA FERRARI ■ Italian Fulbright Fellow 1965-66.

PINTO, JOHN A. ■ FAAR History of Art 75; NEH Summer Seminar Leader 1992. b. Feb. 28, 1948, Cincinnati, OH. m. Margaret Hopkin. c. Nicholas, James. BA 70, Harvard Univ.; PhD 76, Harvard Univ. **Other Study:** Art & architectural history of

I greatly value the time I've spent at the American Academy, the friends I've made there, and the shared experiences of Rome. By bringing artists and scholars together, by providing them with a stimulating setting for exchange, and by encouraging them to reflect on the cultural tradition embodied by Rome, the Academy is unique among American institutions. But beyond its larger purpose, the Academy enriches lives -- has certainly enriched my life -- through countless personal associations and memories: there I encounter the benign ghosts of Frank Brown and Johannes Felbermeyer, Tony Clark and Babs Johnson, Ben Brower and Meryl Mathis. I relive my older son's discovery of aqueducts and my younger son's first steps in the Chiaraviglio garden; my mind's eye retains the picture of an Easter game of croquet by the Casa Rustica. And especially I think of the Library, which for over twenty-five years has nourished my fascination with Rome. There is a timeless quality to the sunlight slanting through the windows of the Reading Room on a summer's afternoon. In no other setting do I feel so intensely the links binding the past to the present.

John Pinto

9.III.93

John A. Pinto

Italy 1400-1750, especially Rome. **Career & Employment:** Smith College, Asst. Prof., Prof., Chair 1976-88; Princeton Univ., Prof. 1988-present. **Memberships & Offices:** SAH 1976-present; CAA 1980-present; Dumbarton Oaks, Senior Fellows Com. 1988-91. **Fellowships, Honors & Awards:** ACLS 1981; CASVA Senior Fellow 1984, 1991; Dumbarton Oaks Fellow 1987; Program for Art on Film 1987. **Publications:** "Origins and Development of the Ichnographic City Plan," *JSAH* 25 (1976): 34-50; "Filippo Juvarra's Drawings Depicting the Capitoline Hill," *Art Bulletin* 71 (1980): 598-616; *The Trevi Fountain* (New Haven & London: Yale Univ. Press, 1986); *Hadrian's Villa and Its Legacy* (New Haven & London: Yale Univ. Press, 1995). **Home Address:** 6 Greenhouse Dr., Princeton, NJ 08540.

PIPPENGER, ROBERT ■ FAAR Sculpture 42. b. May 26, 1912, Nappanee, IN. m. Mary Pippenger. BFA 38, John Herron Art School. **Fellowships, Honors & Awards:** Mary Milliken Award 1938; Indiana State Fair 1st & 2d Prizes.

PIRIE, ROBERT S ■ AAR Trustee 1993-present. **Studies:** Harvard College, Harvard Law School. **Career & Employment:** Skadden, Arps, Slate, Meagher & Flom, Part.; Rothschild North America, Inc., Co-Chair & CEO; Rothschild Inc., Chair & CEO; Rothschild Canada Inc., Vice Chair; Bear, Stearns & Co., Inc., Managing Dir. **Memberships & Offices:** AAAS, Fellow; American Antiquarian Soc., Fellow; Asian Cultural Council, BoT; Asia Soc., BoT; Rosenbach Museum, BoT; MFA, Bd. of Overseers; New York Public Library, Com. of the Research Libraries; Howard Florey Biomedical Found., BoT, Pres.

PISTOLETTO, MICHELANGELO ■ AAR Visitor 1992-93, Artist.

PLAIN, GERALD H. ■ FAAR Musical Composition 76. b. Nov. 30, 1940, Sacramento, KY. m. Marilyn V. Plain. BME 63, Murray State Univ.; MM 66, Butler Univ. **Other Study:** Univ. of Michigan 1966-70; Woodworking at School of American Craftsman, Rochester Inst. of Technology. **Career & Employment:** Texas Tech. Univ., Visiting Asst. Prof. 1971-72; Roosevelt Univ., Instr. 1973-74; De Paul Univ., Instr. 1973-74; Univ. of Wisconsin, Stevens Point, Instr. 1977-78; Eastman School of Music, Asst. Prof 1978-81. **Memberships & Offices:** American Music Center. **Fellowships, Honors & Awards:** NEA Fellowship Grant 1977; Prince Pierre of Monaco Musical Composition Prize 1980; Millay Colony for the Arts, Resident 1987; AAAL, Charles Ives Fellowship 1988; NYFA Fellowship 1990-91. **Important Works:** *3 Sec,* for piano 1965; *Arrows,* for orchestra 1968; *Golden Wedding,* for mangetic tape 1969; *Showers of Blessings,* for clarinet & tape 1972; *Raccoon Song,* for cello 1973; *and left ol' joe a bone, AMAZING!,* for orchestra 1975; *Violin Concerto,* for violin & orchestra 1979; *Portrait I: Sally Goodin,* for flute, violin, cello & harp 1986; *Portrait II: Pretty Polly,* for orchestra 1987; *Portrait I: Sally Goodin,* for orchestra 1989; *Clawhammer,* for chamber orchestra 1992; *Fireworks,* for orchestra 1993. Publisher: Oxford Univ. Press. **Bio-Bibliography:** *Contemporary American Composers; International Who's Who in Music and Musicians' Directory.* **Home Address:** 30 Doncaster Rd., Rochester, NY 14623.

PLATER-ZYBERK, ELIZABETH M. ■ RAAR Architecture 88. b. Dec. 20, 1950, Bryn Mawr, PA. m. Andres M. Duany. BA 72, Princeton Univ.; MArch 74, Yale Univ. **Career & Employment:** Arquitectonica, Founder & Part. 1976-80; Univ. of Maryland, Visiting Prof. 1978; Univ. of Miami, Prof. 1979-present, MArch Program, Dir. 1988-90; Harvard GSD, Visiting Prof.

1984, 1990; Yale Univ. School of Architecture, Bishop Chair 1987; Prince of Wales's Summer School, Visiting Faculty 1990; MIT, Visiting Com. 1990-94. **Memberships & Offices:** Architectural Club of Miami, Founder & Pres. 1977-86; *Journal of Architectural Education,* Ed. Bd. 1982-84; Princeton Univ. School of Architecture, Adv. Council 1982-present; Miami Beach Design Preservation League, BoD 1986-present; Princeton Univ., BoT 1987-91; numerous juries including: NEA 1984, *Progressive Architecture* Annual Awards 1984, Louis Sullivan Award for Architecture 1985, AIA Awards 1991. **Fellowships, Honors & Awards:** American Library Addition, Berlin, Purchase Award 1989; FACE Award 1990; *Metropolitan Home* Design 100, Editorial Award 1990; Governor's Urban Design Award, FL 1990; AIA, Miami Chap. Award 1990; *Time,* Best of the Decade 1991; *Time,* Best of 1991, 1992; Chapel Hill, NC, "Key to the City" 1991; AIA, Inst. Honors for Urban Design 1991; AIA Survey, "Ten Best Works of American Architecture since 1980," 1991; Manhattanville College, Castle Award 1991; Maryland State Planning Comm., Award for Excellence 1992; *Builder's Magazine,* Builder's Choice Merit Award for Excellence in Design 1992; *Progressive Architecture,* Urban Design Citation 1992; Seaside Prize 1993. **Important Works:** Regional Plans: North Area Urban Expansion Study, Sacramento, CA 1991; Marion County, FL 1991; Southport, CA 1991; Markham Center, ONT 1992; New S. Dade, FL 1992; New Towns: Seaside, FL 1979-82; Tanin, AL 1986; Friday Mountain, TX 1987; Bedford Three Corners, NH 1987; Disney Prototypical Town, FL 1987-88; Blount Springs, AL 1988; Crab Creek, MD 1988; Deerfield, IN 1988; Sturbridge, NY 1988; St. Lucie W., FL 1988; Kentlands, MS 1988; Belmont, VA 1988; Marineland, FL 1988; Sandy Spring, MD 1989; South Hill, NY 1989; Windsor, FL 1989; Ingraham Corner, ME 1989; Nicholson Quarter, VA 1989; Poundbury, Dorset, England 1989; Riverlands, NH 1989; Wellington, FL 1989; Avalon Park, FL 1989; Haymount, VA 1989; Rancho del Sol, FL 1990; Nassau Forest, FL 1990; Nance Canyon, CA 1990; McKenzie Town, ALB 1990; Southlake, FL 1990; Rosa Vista, AZ 1991; Fort Erie, Canada 1991; Balmoral, FL 1991, Overoaks, FL 1991; Kemer Country, Turkey 1991-92; Bamberton, BC 1992; Oyster Bay, Jamaica 1992; Ninth Line Area Study, ONT 1992; Egmont-Amelia Park, FL 1992, Highland Park, MI 1992; Daniel Island, SC 1992; New Atlantis, Dominican Republic 1992; plus urban redevelopment & neighborhood plans. **Exhibitions/ Performances:** Victoria & Albert Museum 1989; Amerika-Gedenkbibliothel Competition, Berlin 1989; Univ. of Miami School of Architecture 1989; Miami Dade County College 1990; *Metropolitan Home* Exb., NYC 1990; Harvard GSD 1990; N. Miami Center of Contemporary Art 1991; Syracuse Univ. School of Architecture 1991; Found. pour l'Architecture, Brussels 1991; Parrish Art Museum, Southampton, NY 1991; Bologna 1992; Center for the Fine Arts, Miami 1992; Nat. Archives, Washington, DC 1993. **Bio-Bibliography:** David Mohney & Keller Easterling, *Seaside: Making a Town in America* (New York: Princeton Architectural Press); plus numerous magazine & newspaper articles. **Home Address:** 1023 SW 25 Ave., Miami, FL 33135. **Business Address:** Andres Duany & Elizabeth Plater-Zyberk, Architects, 1023 SW 25 Ave., Miami, FL 33135.

PLATNER, WARREN ■ FAAR Architecture 55. b. June 18, 1919, Baltimore, MD. BArch 41, Cornell Univ. **Fellowships, Honors & Awards:** Advanced Research Fulbright 1955; Graham Found. Award 1962; 1st NY Designers Lighting Forum Award 1975; AIA Fellow 1975; RISD President's Fellow 1980; *Interior Design* Hall of Fame 1985. **Publications:** *Ten by Warren Platner* (New York: McGraw-Hill, 1975); *Creating an Interior* (Englewood Cliffs, NJ: Prentice-Hall, 1980); *The Office Book*

(New York: Facts on File, 1982); *Dining by Design: More Places for People* (New York: McGraw-Hill, 1983). **Important Works:** Sea Containers, HQ, London; MGIC, Milwaukee; Porter, Wright, Morris & Arthur, Columbus; Teknor-Apex, Pawtucket; Met Life Bldg. Additions, NYC; *Providence Journal,* RI; Shopping Centers: Water Tower Place, Chicago; Heart of Atlanta; Restaurants: Windows on the World, NYC; American Restaurant, Kansas City, MO; Wildflower Restaurant, Vail, CO; Apex Center, Providence; Compass Rose, Singapore; Ground Floor, NYC; Hotels: Lodge at Vail, CO; Carlyle, NYC; Showrooms: Steelcase, Chicago; Georg Jensen Design Center, NYC; Libraries: Kent Memorial Library, Suffield, CT; Providence Athenaeum, RI; Schools: Princeton Prospect Center, NJ; Wesleyan Athletic Center, Middletown, CT; Ships: "Fantasia," "Fiesta," "European Waters"; Research: Standard Brands Research Center, Wilton, CT. **Bio-Bibliography:** *Who's Who in America.* **Business Address:** 18 Mitchell Dr., New Haven, CT 06511.

PLATT, CHARLES ADAMS ■ AAR Trustee 1920-33, AAR Pres. 1928-33, Architect, Art Patron.

PLATT, WILLIAM ■ AAR Trustee 1942-74, Architect.

PLIMPTON, FRANCIS T.P. ■ AAR Visitor 1959 — 1964; Lawyer, Ambassador.

PLUMB, WILLIAM LANSING ■ FAAR Design Arts 86. b. July 13, 1932, Malone, NY. m. Catherine Plumb. c. Abigail, Christian. BFA 54, Cornell Univ. **Other Studies:** Politecnico di Milano, Italy 1958-59. **Career & Employment:** Studio Gio Ponti, Milan, Apprentice Designer 1957-58; La Rinascente, Milan, Designer 1958-59; Eliot Noyes & Asscs., Designer 1959-63; Plumb Design Group, Inc., Pres. 1963-; Philadelphia College of Art, Faculty; RISD, Faculty. **Memberships & Offices:** Inst. for Ecological Studies, Co-Founder; Industrial Designers Soc. of America 1964-, Chair; NY Bronze Apple Award, Dir.-at-Large 1983, 1984; *ID,* Ed. Bd. **Fellowships, Honors & Awards:** IBM Fellow, Intl. Design Conference, Aspen 1966; Industrial Designers Soc. of America, Fellow 1983; Hannover Fair, "Gute Form" Design Awards (2). **Important Works:** Collections: MOMA. **Exhibitions/Performances:** Brooklyn Museum; Philadelphia Museum of Art; Jewish Museum, NYC; Smithsonian Inst., Washington, DC. **Bio-Bibliography:** *ID, Contract, Interiors, Fortune, Domus.*

PODDIGHE, ELISABETTA ■ Italian Fulbright Fellow 1990-91, Oscar Broneer Fellowship 1991-92.

POLAK, EMIL J. ■ FAAR Post-Classical/Humanistic Studies 63; School of Classical Studies, Adv. Com. 1960. b. Aug. 16, 1936, Bayshore, NY. m. Patricia F. Leuzzi. BA 57, SUNY, Albany; MA 58, Columbia Univ.; PhD 70, Columbia Univ. **Research/Artistic Interests:** Ancient, medieval & Renaissance history; classical tradition, medieval & Renaissance rhetoric & epistolography, *Ars dictaminis, Ars epistolandi,* Latin palaeography. **Career & Employment:** Brooklyn College, CUNY Lect. 1961-62, 1963-65; St. John's Univ., Instr. 1965-66; Staten Island Community College, CUNY, Instr. 1966-67; City College of New York, CUNY, Lect. 1967-70; Queensborough Community College, CUNY, Instr.-Prof. 1970-present. **Memberships & Offices:** APA 1959-present; AHA 1960-present; MAA 1971-present; Intl. Soc. for the History of Rhetoric 1978-present; Intl. Assn. for Neo-Latin Studies 1979-present; RSA 1980-present; Soc. for Textual Scholarship 1982-present; CUNY Acad. for the Humanities & Sciences, BoD 1988-89; Intl. Soc. for the Classical

Emil J. Polak

Tradition 1990-present. **Fellowships, Honors & Awards:** PSC-CUNY Research Awards 1977-93; Intl. Research & Exchanges Bd. Fellowships 1978-79, 1981; ACLS-USSR Acad. of Sciences Exchange Grant 1981. **Publications:** *A Textual Study of Jacques de Dinant's* Summa dictaminis, Études de philologie et d'histoire 28 (Geneva: Librairie Droz, 1975); "Medieval and Renaissance Epistolography in Poland: the Manuscript Evidence," *Eos* 73 (1985): 349-62; *Medieval and Renaissance Letter Treatises and Form Letters: A Census of Manuscripts Found in Eastern Europe and the Former U.S.S.R.,* Davis Medieval Texts & Studies 8 (Leiden: Brill, 1993); *Medieval and Renaissance Letter Treatises and Form Letters: A Census of Manuscripts Found in Part of Western Europe, Japan, and the United States of America,* Davis Medieval Texts and Studies 9 (Leiden: Brill, 1994). **Bio-Bibliography:** *Dictionary of American Scholars; Répertoire International des Médiévistes; Who's Who in the East.* **Business Address:** Dept. of History, Queensborough Community College, CUNY, Bayside, NY 11364.

POLASEK, ALBIN ■ FAAR Sculpture 13. b. Feb. 14, 1879, Frenstat, Moravia, Czechoslovakia. d. May 19, 1965. m. Emily Muska Kuhat. **Other Studies:** PAFA. **Research/Artistic Interests:** Bronze sculpture. **Career & Employment:** AIC, Sculpture Dept., Head 1916-43. **Memberships & Offices:** NSS; ALNY; Assn. of Chicago Painters & Sculptors; State of Illinois, Bd. of Art Adv. **Fellowships, Honors & Awards:** Paris Salon, Hon. Mention 1913; PAFA, Widener Gold Medal 1914; San Francisco Expo, Silver Medal 1915; AIC, Logan Medal 1917, 1922, 1925; Chicago Soc. of Artists, Silver Medal 1922; NAD 1933; Order of White Lion, Czechoslovakia 1938; Nat. Inst. of Immigrant Welfare Award 1939; Assn. of Chicago Painters & Sculptors, Gold Medal. **Important Works:** *Woodrow Wilson,* Vrychlicky Park, Prague; *J.G. Batterson,* Hartford, CT; *Governor Yates Memorial,* Springfield, IL; *Theodore Thomas Memorial*; Bohemian Nat. Cemetery; *Father Pierre Gibault,* Vincennes, IN; Collections: PAFA; MMA; AIC; Vanderpoel Museum; Detroit Museum. **Exhibitions/Performances:** Paris Salon 1913; PAFA 1914, 1925; Panama-Pacific Exposition, San Francisco 1915; AIC 1917, 1922; Milwaukee Art Inst. 1917; Chicago Soc. of Artists 1922; Assn.

of Chicago Painters & Sculptors 1933; Chicago Gallery Assn. 1937. **Bio-Bibliography:** Ruth Sherwood, *Carving His Own Destiny: The Story of Albin Polasek* (Chicago: Ralph Fletcher Seymour, 1954); Emily M.K. Polasek, *Albin Polasek: Man Carving His Own Destiny* (Winter Park, FL, 1970); *Who Was Who in America; Who Was Who in American Art.*

POLLACK, PETER M. ■ FAAR Landscape Architecture 71. b. Dec. 3, 1939, Philadelphia, PA. m. Eleanor Whitney. c. David, Michael, Johonna. BSLA 63, Pennsylvania State Univ.; MLA 65, Harvard GSD. **Career & Employment:** Sasaki, Dawson, DeMay Asscs., Staff 1963-65, Senior Staff 1965-67, Assc. 1967-73; Univ. of Michigan, Asst. Prof. 1973-76, Assc. Prof. 1976-87, Visiting Lect. 1987-present; Adj. Prof. 1992-present; Walker Williams Partnership, Prin. 1974-77; Pollack Design Asscs., Dir. of Design 1976-present. **Memberships & Offices:** Council of Educators in Landscape Architecture, *The Newsletter*, Ed. & Designer 1974-77, Exec. Com. 1975-77; Citizens Assn. for Area Planning, Ann Arbor, BoD 1978-81; ASLA Roster of Visiting Evaluators, Accreditation Bd., MI Chap., Pres. 1989, BoT 1991-present, Legislative Fly-In 1993; Annadear Area Chamber of Commerce, BoT 1989-92; State of Michigan, Dept. of Natural Resources, State Parks & Citizen Adv. Com. 1992-present; Nat. Trust for Historic Preservation; Historic Soc. of Michigan; Washtenaw County Historic Soc.; Michigan Soc. of Planning Officials; Michigan Recreation & Parks Assn. **Fellowships, Honors & Awards:** Copley Sq. Competition, 1st Prize, 1966; AAN, Landscape Award 1968, 1974; *Progressive Architecture*, Citation-Urban Design 1970; AIA, Merit Award 1975; Michigan Honor Award 1983; Michigan Merit Award 1984, 1988; ASLA, Merit Award 1985, 1986, 1987, Fellow 1993; Michigan Soc. of Planning Officials, Honor Award 1994. **Important Works:** College Park, Indianapolis 1966-70; Christian Science Church Center, Boston 1966-73; Baxter Laboratories Corp. HQ, Deerfield, IL 1971-73; Gandy Dancer Restaurant, Ann Arbor 1974-75; Independence Lake Park, Washtenaw County, MI 1978-88; Haithco Recreation Area, Saginaw, MI 1988-present; Heritage Park & Civic Center Complex, Canton Township, MI 1990-92; Powder Coat Technology-Herman Miller, Spring Lake, MI 1991-92; Phoenix Designs-Herman Miller 1993-present. **Home Address:** 515 Detroit St., Ann Arbor, MI 48104. **Business Address:** Pollack Design Asscs., 220 S. Main St., Ann Arbor, MI 48104.

POLSKY, CYNTHIA HAZEN ■ AAR Trustee 1992-present. BA, Marymount College; MBA, Fordham Univ. **Memberships & Offices:** MMA, BoT; Asia Soc., President's Circle, Chair; Asia Soc., Gallery Adv. Bd.; Storm King Art Center, VP; The McKim Soc., Chair, Pierpont Morgan Library. **Important Works:** Paintings in Public Collections: Corcoran Museum, Washington, DC; Fogg Museum, Cambridge, MA; Johnson Museum, Cornell Univ.; AAAS; Rockefeller Univ.

POLVERINI, LEANDRO ■ Italian Fulbright Fellow 1962-63.

POOR, HENRY VARNUM, III ■ RAAR Painting 50, 51. b. Sept. 30, 1888, Chapman, KS. d. Dec. 8, 1970. m. Elizabeth Breuer. c. Josephine Lydia, Anne, Peter. BA 10, Stanford Univ. **Other Studies:** Slade School, London, with Walter Sickert 1910; Académie Julian, Paris 1911 with Jean Paul Laurens. **Research/Artistic Interests:** Pottery, painting, tile decoration. **Career & Employment:** Stanford Univ.; Mark Hopkins Art School 1917; Colorado Springs Fine Arts Center 1937; Skowhegan School; Columbia Univ., Prof. 1952. **Memberships & Offices:** Skowhegan School of Painting & Sculpture, Pres.; San Francisco Intl. Exposition, Awards Jury 1939; Comm. of Fine Arts,

Washington, DC 1944-45; US State Dept., Unit of Artists, Art Adv. Comm., Alaska Theater of War; NIAL; Artists Equity Assn., 1st VP 1953. **Fellowships, Honors & Awards:** AIC Landscape Prize; Norman Wait Harris Silver Medal 1932; Carnegie Inst., 3d Prize 1933; Syracuse-Everson, 1st Prize 1937; ALNY, Gold Medal of Honor 1938. **Publications:** *An Artist Sees Alaska* (New York: Viking, 1945); *A Book of Pottery, from Mud to Immortality* (Englewood Cliffs, NJ: Prentice-Hall, 1958). **Important Works:** Tile Ceiling, Union Dime Savings Bank, NYC; Murals, US Dept. of Justice Bldg., Washington, DC; *Conservation of American Wildlife Mural*, US Interior Dept. Bldg., Washington, DC; *Land Grant Mural*, Pennsylvania State College 1941; Fresco, *New Courier-Journal* Bldg., Louisville. **Important Works:** Collections: Rehn Gallery, NYC; MMA; Whitney Museum, NYC; AIC; Newark Museum; San Francisco Museum; Cleveland Museum; Addison Memorial Museum, Andover; Brooklyn Museum; Wichita Art Museum; Univ. of Kansas; Univ. of Nebraska. **Bio-Bibliography:** N.E. Dickson, *Henry Varnum Poor, 1888-1970: A Retrospective Exhibition* (University Park: Pennsylvania State Univ. Museum, 1983); Richard Porter, "Henry Varnum Poor, 1887-1970: A Biography and Study of His Paintings" (Diss., Pennsylvania State Univ., 1983); *Dictionary of Contemporary American Artists, Who Was Who in America.*

POPE, JOHN RUSSELL ■ FAAR Architecture 1897; AAR Trustee 1926-37; AAR Pres. 1934-37. b. Apr. 24, 1874, NYC. d. Aug. 19, 1937. m. Sadie Jones. c. Jane London. 1892, College of the City of New York; 1894, Columbia Univ. **Other Studies:** École des Beaux Arts, Paris 1900. **Career & Employment:** Bruce Price, Architect 1900-1903; Private Practice 1903-37. **Memberships & Offices:** AIA; Beaux Arts Inst. of Design; ALNY; AAAL; NIAL; Intl. Congress of Architects; US Comm. of Fine Arts 1917-22. **Fellowships, Honors & Awards:** Schermerhorn Travelling Fellow 1898-1900; Jean Leclaire Inst. of France, Medal 1900; ALNY, Medal of Honor 1916; AIA, New York Chap., Gold Medal 1918; French Legion of Honor, Chevalier 1922. **Important Works:** Scottish Rite Temple, Washington, DC 1910; Lincoln Memorial, Hodgenville, KY 1925; Baltimore Museum of Art 1927-29, 1937; Constitution Hall, Daughters of the American Revolution, Washington, DC 1929; Payne Whitney Gymnasium, Yale Univ. 1932; Nat. Archives Bldg., Washington, DC 1933-35; Tate Gallery, Sculpture Wing 1937; War Memorial, Montfaucon, France 1937; British Museum, Sculpture Gallery 1937; Jefferson Memorial 1937; NGA 1937. **Exhibitions/Performances:** NGA 1991. **Bio-Bibliography:** Herbert Croly, "Recent Works of John Russell Pope," *Architectural Record* 29 (1911): 441-511; J.R. Pope, *The Architecture of John Russell Pope*, 3 vols. (New York: W. Helburn, 1924-30); Joseph Hudnut, "The Last of the Romans: Comment on the Building of the National Gallery of Art," *Magazine of Art* 34 (1941): 169-73; *Dictionary of American Biography; Encyclopedia of Amercian Architects; Macmillian Encyclopedia of Architects; Who Was Who in America.*

PORTER, HENRY KIRKE ■ AAR Charter Mem., Industrialist.

PORTNOFF, COLLICE HENRY ■ FAAR Classics/Archaeology 30. b. Dec. 9, 1899, San Luis Obispo, CA. dec. m. George E. Portnoff. c. Lisa Crehan. BA 21, UC, Berkeley; MA 22, UC, Berkeley; PhD 27, Stanford Univ. **Research/Artistic Interests:** Works of Maria Martinez Sierra, philology, poetry, Latin, English, Spanish literature. **Career & Employment:** Belmont Military Acad., Instr. 1922-23; Stanford Univ., Instr. 1923-27; Arizona State College, Flagstaff, Instr. 1930-41; US Signal Corps., Washington DC, Cryptanalyst 1942; Allied Military Government, Washington DC, Trans. 1942-43; Arizona State Univ.,

Tempe, Prof. 1945-69, Prof. Emer. after 1969, Dept. Chair 1957-58. **Memberships & Offices:** AAUP; Nat. Soc. of Arts & Letters; Nat. Council of Teachers of English; Rocky Mountain Modern Language Assn., Pres. 1964; Nat. Council of Teachers of English; Phoenix Chamber Music Soc., BoD; Centro Studi e Scambi Internazionali; American Trans. Assn.; *Arizona Republic,* Contr. Ed. **Fellowships, Honors & Awards:** Arizona State Univ., Alumni Assn., Distinguished Teacher Award; Carter Memorial Fellowship 1927-28; Phi Beta Kappa; Sigma Delta Pi; Alpha Lambda Delta; Gamma Phi Beta. **Publications:** with Samuel R. Golding, *Naked Came I: A Play* (1957). **Bio-Bibliography:** *Directory of American Scholars, Who's Who in America; Who's Who in the World; Who's Who of American Women.*

PORTOGHESI, PAOLO ■ AAR Visitor 1977-78, Architect.

POSNER, DONALD ■ FAAR History of Art 61, RAAR History of Art 69. b. Aug. 30, 1931, NYC. c. Anne Posner. BA 56, Queens College, CUNY; MA 57, Harvard Univ., PhD 62, NYU. **Research/Artistic Interests:** Art history, 17th & 18th centuries, Italian & French art. **Career & Employment:** Columbia Univ., Asst. Prof. 1961-62; IFA, Ailsa Mellon Bruce Prof. 1962-present; Williams College, Robert Sterling Clark Prof. 1973; Univ. of Virginia, Wm. R. Kenan Jr. Prof. 1976-77; Univ. of Washington, Seattle, Visiting Prof. 1991. **Memberships & Offices:** CAA 1957-present, Dir. 1970-74, *Art Bulletin,* Ed.-in-Chief 1968-71; American Soc. for 18th-Century Studies. **Fellowships, Honors & Awards:** CAA, Charles Rufus Morey Prize 1972; IAS 1976; NEH Fellowship 1983. **Publications:** *Annibale Carracci. A Study in the Reform of Italian Painting around 1590* (London: Phaidon, 1971); with J. Held, *Seventeenth and Eighteenth-Century Art* (New York: Harry N. Abrams & Prentice Hall, 1972); *Watteau: A Lady at Her Toilet* (London & New York: Penguin, 1973); *Antoine Watteau* (London, Ithaca, Berlin: Weidenfeld & Nicolson, Cornell Univ. Press, Frölich u. Kaufmann, 1984). **Bio-Bibliography:** *Directory of American Scholars; Who's Who in America; Who's Who in American Art.* **Business Address:** IFA, 1 E. 78 St., NYC 10021.

POST, CHANDLER R. ■ AAR Trustee 1930, Educator, Prof. of Greek.

POST, GEORGE B. ■ AAR Charter Mem., Architect.

POTOFF, REEVA B. ■ FAAR Sculpture 81. b. Oct. 12, 1941, Waterbury, CT. BFA 63, Pratt Inst.; MFA 65, Yale Univ. **Career & Employment:** Fieldston School 1971; St. Ann's School 1972-78; Bennington College 1977; Parsons School of Design 1979; Princeton Univ., Visiting Artist 1980-86; Vermont Studio School 1985; Columbia Univ. 1981-present. **Fellowships, Honors & Awards:** Skowhegan School of Art Scholarship 1961; Provincetown School of Art Scholarship 1962; Yale Univ. Scholarship 1964-65, Griggs Prize 1965; CAPS Grant 1975, 1980; NEA Fellowship 1977, 1980; Yaddo Fellowship 1985, 1987, 1991; MacDowell Fellowship 1986, 1987; Djerassi Found. Fellowship 1989; Ludwig Vogelstein Found. Grant 1991. **Exhibitions/Performances:** Solo: Louis Meisel Gallery, NYC 1976-80; Forefront Gallery, Indianapolis Museum of Art 1992; Group: Aldrich Museum, Ridgefield, CT 1971; Inst. of Contemporary Art, Philadelphia 1972; MOMA 1978; Albright-Knox Gallery, Buffalo 1980; Princeton Museum 1985; Newhouse Center for Contemporary Art, Staten Island, NY 1989; Artpark, Lewiston, NY 1990-91; Brooklyn Museum 1991; Wallach Gallery, NYC 1992; Evanston Art Center 1993. **Home Address:** 101 Prince St., NYC 10012.

POUND, EZRA ■ AAR Visitor 1939-40, Poet.

POWELL, GORDON ■ FAAR Sculpture 88. b. May 4, 1947, Decatur, IL. m. Linda Crabtree. BFA 75, AIC School; MFA 80, Univ. of Illinois. **Fellowships, Honors & Awards:** ArtPark, Lewiston, NY, Artist-in-Residence 1985; Illinois Arts Council Fellowship 1985; NEA Grant 1986. **Exhibitions/Performances:** Solo: Illinois Arts Council 1977; A. Montgomery Ward Gallery, Univ. of Illinois, Chicago 1980; Roy Boyd Gallery, Chicago 1982, 1983, 1985, 1986; Kirkland Gallery, Millikin Univ., Decatur, IL 1984; Susan Cummins Gallery, Mill Valley, CA 1991; Group: Northeastern Univ., Boston 1984; AIC 1985; Cultural Center, Chicago, 1986; Mulvane Art Museum, Topeka, KS 1992.

POWELL, PADGETT ■ FAAR Literature 88. b. Apr. 25, 1952, Gainesville, FL. BA 75, College of Charleston; MA 82, Univ. of Houston. **Career & Employment:** Univ. of Tennessee 1975; Univ. of Houston, Faculty 1980, 1983-84; Univ. of Florida, Asst. Prof. 1984-88; Assc. Prof. 1988-92, Prof. 1992-present; Istanbul Univ., Senior Fulbright Lect. 1989-90. **Memberships & Offices:** PEN; Authors Guild; Screenwriters Guild of America, East. **Fellowships, Honors & Awards:** Henfield Found. *Transatlantic Review* Award 1981; *Time Magazine,* Best-of-Year Fiction 1984; American Book Award Nominee 1984; Whiting Found. Writers' Award 1986; Pushcart Prize 1990; *Paris Review,* John Train Humor Prize 1991. **Publications:** *Edisto* (New York: Farrar, Straus, Giroux, 1984); *A Woman Named Drown* (New York: Farrar, Straus, Giroux, 1987); *Typical* (New York: Farrar, Straus, Giroux, 1991); "Hitting Back," in *A World Unsuspected: Portraits of Southern Childhood,* ed. Alex Harris (Chapel Hill: UNC Press, 1987), 14-35; "Voice from the Grave," *Esquire* (Jan. 1987): 100-103; "Flood," *Grand Street* (Winter 1988): 29-31; "Typical," *Grand Street* (Spring 1989): 7-17; "Dr. Ordinary," *Harper's* (Oct. 1989): 42; "The Modern Italian," *The Gettysburg Review* (Autumn 1989): 612-29; "Texas/Kansas," *Grand Street* (Spring 1990): 7-10; "Mr. Irony" and "Mr. Irony Renounces Irony," *Paris Review* (Summer 1990): 162-93; "Our South in Words and Pictures," *Southern Living* (Jan. 1990): 92-93; "Grinace," *Harper's* (Feb. 1990): 47-48; "The Allure of Southern Women," *Gentlemen's Quarterly* (Mar. 1990): 296-99; "The Winnowing of Mrs. Schuping," *The New Yorker* (Jan. 7, 1991): 26-31; "No Place Like Home: Two American Palaces," *NY Times Magazine, Sophisticated Traveler* (Oct. 20, 1991): 25, 52-55. **Bio-Bibliography:** "Powell, Padgett," *Contemporary Literary Criticism* 34 (1984): 97-101; Helen Dundar, "Portrait of the Novelist as Lucky Stiff," *Wall Street Journal* (Nov. 26, 1986): 19; *Contemporary Authors.* **Business Address:** English Dept., Univ. of Florida, Gainesville, FL 32611.

POWERS, PAMELA "PIKE" ■ FAAR Sculpture 88. b. Mar. 26, 1956, Providence, RI. BFA 81, RISD; MFA 87, Yale Univ. **Other Study:** Glass-working artist at Pilchuck Glass School & J. & L. Lobmeyer (Austria) 1976-80; Architectural drafting 1989. **Research/Artistic Interests:** Contemporary sculpture & critique, contemporary glass art, circus history. **Career & Employment:** Parsons School of Design, Instr. 1988-present; Pilchuck Glass School, Artistic Pgm. Dir. 1993-present. **Fellowships, Honors & Awards:** NYFA Fellowship 1991. **Publications:** *Contemporary Glass* (Corning, NY, 1989). **Important Works:** Collections: Corning Museum Collection. **Exhibitions/Performances:** Solo: Woods-Gerry Gallery, Providence 1981; Moore College of Art, Philadelphia 1985; Smith-Goodrich Gallery, Providence 1985; Yale Art & Architecture Gallery, New Haven 1987; East-West Center, Honolulu 1990; Old Chatham

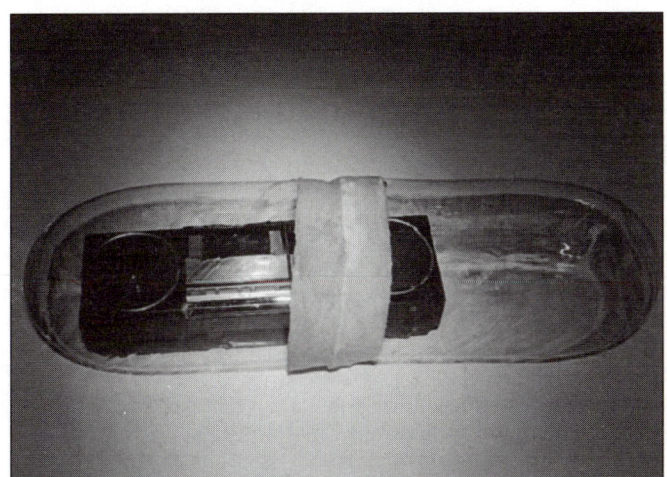

Pamela "Pike" Powers

Gallery, Chatham, NY 1992; plus numerous group exhibitions. **Business Address:** Pilchuck Glass School, 1201 316 St., NW, Stanwood, WA 98292.

PRADELLA, MASSIMO ■ AAR Visitor 1977-78, Conductor.

PRATT, FREDERIC B. ■ AAR Trustee 1932-45, Industrialist.

PRATT, KENNETH JAMES ■ FAAR Post-Classical/Humanistic Studies 63. b. May 17, 1924, Salt Lake City, UT. BA 47, UCLA; MA 49, UCLA; PhD 54, UCLA. **Career & Employment:** Immaculate Heart College, Los Angeles, Prof. 1952-59; UCLA, Visiting Prof. 1954-55, 1963; California State Univ., Los Angeles, Prof. 1959-. **Memberships & Offices:** MAA; Dante Alighieri Soc. of America. **Fellowships, Honors & Awards:** Soc. for Italian Historical Studies Prize 1964. **Publications:** "Roman Anti-Militarism," *Classical Journal* 51 (1955): 21-25; "Motivation and Learning in Medieval Writings," *The American Psychologist* 18 (1962): 496-500; "Rome As Eternal," *Journal of the History of Ideas* 26 (1965): 25-44; "The Dialect of Rome," *Italica* 43 (1966): 167-79; "Plutarch as Psychologist," in *Panhellenica: Historical and Historiographical Essays in Honor of T.S. Brown* (Lawrence, KS, 1979), 143-62.

PRATT, RICHARDSON ■ AAR Trustee 1940-59; Corp. Exec, Financier.

PRAY, JAMES STURGIS ■ AAR Trustee 1915-19.

PREDOCK, ANTOINE ■ FAAR Architecture 85; Juror 1987. b. June 24, 1936, Lebanon, MO. c. Hadrian, Jason. BArch 62, Columbia Univ. **Other Study:** Univ. of New Mexico 1957-61. **Career & Employment:** Antoine Predock Architect, Prin. 1967-present. **Memberships & Offices:** NIAE Paris Prize; *Architectural Design* Competition, Author & Juror 1987; AIA Awards Jury, Honor Awards Juror 1982, California Chap. 1984, Dallas Chap. 1984; Minnesota Soc. of Architects, Honor Awards Juror 1983. **Fellowships, Honors & Awards:** Columbia Univ., William Kinne Fellows Memorial Traveling Fellowship 1962-63; AIA Fellow 1981; Nissan Intl. Fellow, Aspen Design Conference 1991. **Publications:** *Italian Sketchbook* (1985); with David St. John, *Terraces of Rain: An Italian Sketchbook* (Santa Fe: Recursos Press, 1991); *Antoine Predock, Architect* (New York: Rizzoli, 1994). **Important Works:** Rio Grande Nature Center, Master Plan & Visitor Center, Albuquerque 1982; Nelson Fine Arts Center, Arizona State Univ., Tempe 1986; American Heritage Center & Art Museum, Univ. of Wyoming, Laramie 1987;

Las Vegas Central Library & Children's Discovery Museum 1987; Classroom-Laboratory-Administration Bldg., California Polytechnic Univ., Pomona 1987; Mandell Weiss Forum, UC, San Diego 1987; Hotel Santa Fe, Euro Disney, Paris 1988; Turtle Creek House, Dallas 1988; Thousand Oaks Government Center & Civic Auditorium, CA 1989; Social Sciences & Humanities Bldg., UC, Davis 1990; Music Facility, UC, Santa Cruz 1990; Museum of Science & Industry, Tampa 1991. **Exhibitions/Performances:** Solo: John Nichols Gallery, NYC 1988; Univ. of Wyoming Art Museum, Laramie 1993-94; Group: Centre Georges Pompidou, Paris 1981; Urban Center, NYC 1987; Architects-Designers-Planners for Social Responsibility: Max Protetch Gallery, NYC 1988; Bienal '89 Arquitectura, Buenos Aires; Cooper-Hewitt Museum, NYC 1988; Des Moines Art Center 1989; Nelson Fine Arts Center Project in NYC & Moscow 1990; "St. John the Divine South Transept," Urban Center, NYC 1991; Contemporary Architectural Drawing, GA Gallery, Tokyo 1992; Centre Canadien d'Architecture, Montreal 1992. **Bio-Bibliography:** *GA Document* 24 (Aug. 1989): 6-19; *GA Houses* 30 (Dec. 1990): 118-21; Jory Johnson & Felice Frankel, *Modern Landscape Architecture: Redefining the Garden* (New York: Abbeville Press, 1991), 131-41; Charles Jencks, *The Language of Post-Modern Architecture: The Sixth Edition* (New York: Rizzoli, 1991), 192-95; Bill Lacy, *100 Contemporary Architects* (New York: Harry Abrams, 1991): 186-87; Miriam Horn, "The Rise of the Desert Rat," *Vanity Fair* (Mar. 1992): 112-22; Kurt Gustmann, "Antoine Predock," *Hauser* (Apr. 1992): 59-70; Philip Jodidio, *Contemporary American Architects* (Benedikt Taschen, 1993): 141-51; Michael Webb, "Mandell Weiss Forum," *A+U* (Jan. 1993): 30-45; Joseph Giovannini, "Western Frontiers: Myth and Spirit," *Architecture* (Dec. 1993): 47-61; Kurt Anderson, "Architecture: Antoine Predock, Serious Modernism in Dallas," *Architectural Digest* (Mar. 1994): 104-11. **Home Address:** 300 12 St. NW, Albuquerque, NM 87102. **Business Address:** Antoine Predock Architect, 300 12 St. NW, Albuquerque, NM 87102.

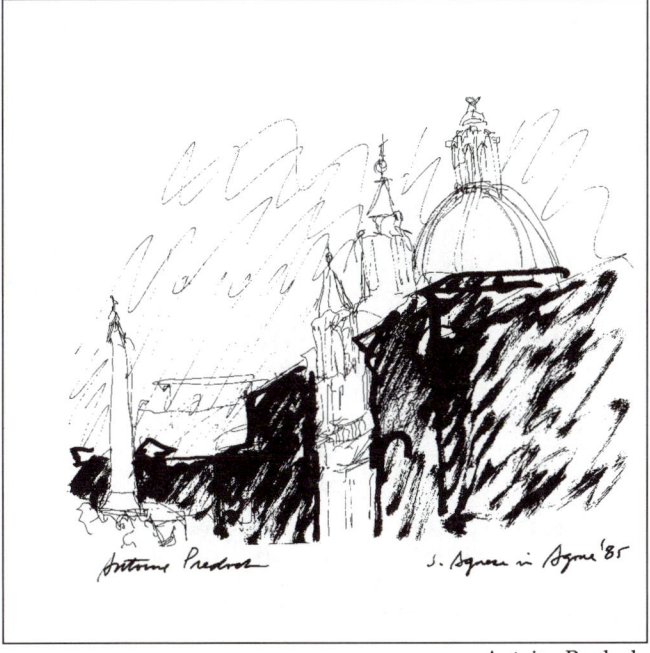

Antoine Predock

PRESTANDREA, DANIELA ■ AAR – Rome, Sec.

PRESTON, THOMAS JEX, JR ■ FASCSR 09. b. Oct. 26, 1862, Hasting-on-Hudson, NY. d. Dec. 23, 1955. m. Frances Folsom Cleveland. BA 1880, Poly. Inst. of Brooklyn; LittB 06, Princeton Univ.; MA 07, Princeton Univ.; PhD 10, Princeton Univ. **Other Studies:** Columbia Univ., The Sorbonne & Univ. of Rome. **Career & Employment:** T.J. Preston & Co. Linseed Oil, Newark, NJ 1885-1902; Princeton Univ., Prof. 1911-12; Wells College, Pres. Pro Tem. 1912; Independent Scholar 1912-55. **Memberships & Offices:** ArIA, Life Mem. **Publications:** *The Bronze Doors of the Abbey of Monte Cassino and of St. Paul's, Rome* (Princeton: Princeton Univ. Press, 1915). **Bio-Bibliography:** *Who Was Who in America; NY Times*, Obit. (Dec. 26, 1955).

PRESTOPINO, GREGORIO ■ RAAR Painting 72. b. June 21, 1907, Brooklyn, NY. d. Dec. 16, 1984. m. Elizabeth Dauber. c. Gregory, Paul. **Other Studies:** NAD. **Career & Employment:** School for Artists Studies, NYC, Faculty; Veterans Art Center, MOMA, Faculty 1946-48; Brooklyn Museum School, Faculty 1946-59; New School for Social Research, Faculty 1949-56, 1957, 1965; Federal A.P. **Memberships & Offices:** MacDowell Colony, BoD 1972-80. **Fellowships, Honors & Awards:** PAFA, Temple Gold Medal; Youngstown-Butler 1st Prize 1958; Cannes Film Festival, 1st Prize 1958; NIAL Grant 1961; NAD, Benjamin Altman Prize 1972, 1984, Emily Goldsmith Award 1977. **Important Works:** Collections: Whitney Museum, NYC; MOMA; Walker Art Center; Univ. of Rochester; Univ. of Nebraska; Univ. of Texas; Trenton State Museum; Currier Art Inst.; Albright-Knox Art Gallery; AIC; Univ. of Alabama; Phillips Acad., Andover; Brandeis Univ.; Univ. of Hawaii; IBM; Univ. of Illinois; Martha Washington Univ.; Mary Washington College. **Exhibitions/Performances:** Corcoran Gallery of Art 1937; Worcester Museum of Art 1938; NY World's Fair 1939; MOMA 1940, 1941, 1943-46; AIC 1941, 1943; St. Louis Art Museum 1945; Walker Art Gallery; Pepsi-Cola 1946; Whitney Museum, NYC. **Bio-Bibliography:** *Dictionary of Contemporary Artists, Who Was Who in American Art.*

PRICE, JESSIE H. ■ AAR Trustee 1993-present. BA, Newcomb College, Tulane Univ.; Univ. of Colorado Law School. **Memberships & Offices:** Texas Bar Assn.; Oklahoma Bar Assn.; Dallas Museum of Art, BoT, Sec., Exec. Com.; Whitney Museum, NYC, Nat. Com., Drawing Com.; Texas Nature Conservancy, Adv. Bd.; Modern Art Museum, Ft. Worth, Adv. Bd.

PRICE, THOMAS DREES ■ FAAR Landscape Architecture 32. b. May 18, 1901, Porto Alegre, Brazil. d. Mar. 29, 1989. BS 24, Ohio State Univ.; MLA 26, Harvard Univ. **Other Studies:** Copley Soc., Boston 1928-29. **Career & Employment:** Olmsted Brothers, Landscape Architects 1930-39. **Fellowships, Honors & Awards:** Charles Eliot Travelling Fellowship 1927; Brewster Fellowship of Landscape Architecture.

PRICE, VINCENT ■ AAR Visitor 1959 — 1964, Actor.

PRIMOSCH, JAMES ■ Philadelphia Regional Visiting Artist 1994.

PRINCE, DIANA ■ AAR Trustee 1986-present. **Study:** Vassar College. **Memberships & Offices:** Lyric Opera of Chicago, BoT; AIC, BoT; Rehabilitation Inst. of Chicago, BoT; Washington Opera, BoT; NGA Trustees Council; *Poetry Magazine*, BoT.

PRINDLE, LESTER MARSH ■ Sheldon Fellow 1918-19.

PRITCHETT, HENRY S. ■ AAR Charter Mem., Astronomer, Educator.

PROCTOR, GIFFORD MACGREGOR ■ FAAR Sculpture 35. b. Feb. 9, 1912, NYC. m. Ann Proctor. BFA, Yale Univ. **Fellowships, Honors & Awards:** Yale Univ., Fanny Pardee Prize. **Important Works:** George Washington, Valley Forge, PA. **Bio-Bibliography:** Albert Stern, "Washington in the Wind," *Americana* (Aug. 1986); Laurie A. O'Neill, "Sculptor Achieves a 50-Year Dream," *NY Times* (Feb. 16, 1986).

PROWN, JULES D. ■ AAR Visitor 1992-93, Art Historian.

PUGLISI, CATHERINE R. ■ FAAR History of Art 80. b. Apr. 8, 1953, NYC. m. William L. Barcham. c. Raphael, Arianna. BA 75, Radcliffe College; MA 76, Univ. of London; PhD 83, IFA. **Research/Artistic Interests:** Italian baroque painting. **Career & Employment:** Univ. of Pittsburgh, Asst. Prof. 1982-84; Rutgers Univ., Asst. Prof. 1984-90, Assc. Prof. 1990-present. **Fellowships, Honors & Awards:** Delmas Found. Research Fellowship 1984, 1990; ACLS Grant 1986; NEH Travel Grant 1988; APS Research Grant 1989. **Publications:** "Early Works by Francesco Albani," *Paragone* 381 (1981): 26-47; "Two Newly Identified Drawings by Annibale Carracci," *Master Drawings* 20 (1984): 310-15; "The Cappella di San Domenico in SS. Giovanni e Paolo, Venice," *Arte Veneta* 40 (1986): 230-38; "Piazzetta's 'Glory of St. Dominic,'" *Arte Veneta* 41 (1987): 210-17; *Francesco Albani* (forthcoming); *Caravaggio* (London: Phaidon, forthcoming). **Home Address:** 218 Harrison Ave., Highland Park, NJ 08904. **Business Address:** Art History Dept., Voorhees Hall, Rutgers Univ., New Brunswick, NJ 08903.

PUGLISI, CRISTINA ■ AAR – Rome, Asst. Dir. for Properties.

PULSIFER, HARRY ■ Rotch Scholar 1899.

PURYEAR, MARTIN ■ AAR Trustee 1995-present. b. May 23, 1941. BA, Catholic Univ. of America; MFA, Yale Univ. **Other Studies:** Catholic Univ.; Swedish Royal Acad., Stockholm. **Honors & Awards:** Louis Comfort Tiffany Grant 1981; Guggenheim Fellowship 1982; São Paulo Bienal Grand Prize 1989; MacArthur Fellowship 1989; Calder Atelier, Residence, Saché, France. **Important Works:** ArtPark Comm., Lewiston, NY 1977; Battery Park City Authority Comm.; New School for Social Research Comm. **Exhibitions/Performances:** Solo: Corcoran Gallery of Art 1977; Univ. Gallery, Amherst 1984; Brooklyn Museum 1988; Museum of Contemporary Art, Chicago; Univ. Art Museum, Matrix program, Berkeley; AIC Traveling Retrospective 1991-92 to Hirshhorn Museum, Los Angeles Museum of Contemporary Art, Philadelphia Museum of Art; Group: Whitney Museum, NYC 1979, 1981, 1989; Guggenheim Museum 1978, 1985, 1987; MOMA 1984; St. Louis Art Museum 1988; Palais du Luxembourg, Paris 1993; Museum for African Art, NYC 1994.

PUTNAM, MICHAEL C.J. ■ FAAR Classics/Archaeology 64, RAAR Classics/Archaeology 70; AAR Trustee 1991-present; School of Classical Studies, Andrew W. Mellon Prof.-in-Charge 1989-91. b. Sept. 20, 1933, Springfield, MA. BA 54, Harvard Univ.; MA 56, Harvard Univ.; PhD 59, Harvard Univ. **Research/Artistic Interests:** The literature of Greece & Rome with the poetry of the Republican & Augustan period as a particular specialty, along with the relationship of Latin literature to the Western humanistic tradition. **Career & Employment:** Smith College, Instr. 1959-60; Brown Univ., Instr. 1960-61, Asst. Prof. 1961-64, Assc. Prof. 1964-67, Prof. 1967-present, Macmillan Prof. 1985-present, Chair 1970-72 & 1977-78; Cornell Univ., Townsend Prof. 1985. **Memberships & Offices:** Center for

Hellenic Studies, Acting Dir. 1961, Senior Fellow 1971-86; Acad. of Literary Studies 1986-present; Accademia Nazionale Virgiliana 1983-present; APA, Dir. 1972-75, Com. on the Award of Merit 1975-78, Pres. 1982, Delegate to ACLS 1984-87; Keats-Shelley Memorial Assn., Honorary Sec., Rome Com. 1989-91; Lowell Observatory, Sole Trustee 1967-87, Bd. of Adv. 1988-present; VSA, BoT 1969-73, VP 1974-76. **Fellowships, Honors & Awards:** Guggenheim Fellowship 1966-67; APA, Goodwin Award of Merit 1971; NEH, Senior Fellowship 1973-74; ACLS Fellowship 1983-84; IAS 1987-88; Lawrence Univ., LLD Hon. 1985. **Publications:** *The Poetry of the Aeneid* (Cambridge MA: Harvard Univ. Press, 1965); *Virgil's Pastoral Art: Studies in the Eclogues* (Princeton: Princeton Univ. Press, 1970); *Tibullus: A Commentary* (Norman: Univ. of Oklahoma Press for APA, 1973); *Virgil's Poem of the Earth* (Princeton: Princeton Univ. Press, 1979); ed. with G. Bowersock & W. Burkert, *Arktouros: Hellenic Studies Presented to Bernard M.W. Knox* (Berlin: De Gruyter, 1979); ed., *Fifteen Odes of Horace,* trans. Cedric Whitman (Cambridge: Pvt. Printed, 1980); ed., *Virgil: 2000 Years,* Arethusa 14 (1981); *Essays on Latin Lyric, Elegy, and Epic* (Princeton: Princeton Univ. Press, 1982); *Artifices of Eternity: Horace's Fourth Book of Odes* (Ithaca: Cornell Univ. Press, 1986); *Virgil's Aeneid: Interpretation and Influences* (Chapel Hill: UNC Press, 1995); plus 50 articles & 70 reviews. **Bio-Bibliography:** *Who's Who in America.* **Business Address:** Dept. of Classics, Brown Univ., Providence, RI 02912.

The American Academy in Rome claims a special place in the hearts and minds of those who have been touched by her magic. In my experience the Academy comes the closest possible to exemplifying in real life the happy, verdant landscape that, for Virgil, defined the Elysian Fields. The intellectual freedom, the chance for artists and scholars to exchange ideas and friendship, the library as beautiful as it is rich, the glorious setting -- all this and much more contributes to making the Academy unique. May the second century be as fruitful and flourishing as the first!

Michael Putnam
Michael C. J. Putnam
November 29, 1994

Michael C.J. Putnam

PYLE, CYNTHIA M. ■ FAAR Post-Classical/Humanistic Studies 78. b. Dec. 30, 1940, NYC. m. Richard S. Kayne. BS 62, Jackson College, Tufts Univ.; MA 67, Middlebury College; PhD 76, Columbia Univ. **Research/Artistic Interests:** Renaissance studies (15th & 16th centuries): history of Italian culture, history of theater, history of science (esp. zoological natural history & illustration). **Career & Employment:** Harvard School of Public Health, Research Asst. 1965-66; MIT, Research Asst. 1962-64, 1967; Columbia Univ. & Barnard College, Graduate Asst. 1970-71; Vassar College, Visiting Asst. Prof. 1978-79; Centre National de la Recherche Scientifique, Paris, Researcher 1979-81; Univ. of Texas, Austin, Visiting Scholar 1982, Visiting Asst. Prof. 1983, Visiting Assc. Prof. 1984; Università di Parma, Prof. 1984; Harvard Univ., Assc. 1986-88; Graduate School & Univ. Center of CUNY, Renaissance Forum Dir. 1989-93, Renaissance Studies Concentration & Coordinator 1988-91, Renaissance Studies Certificate Program 1991-93, Assc. Prof. 1988-93, Research Assc. 1993-present. **Memberships & Offices:** Società Storica Lombarda; Columbia Univ. Seminar in the Renaissance, RSA. **Fellowships, Honors & Awards:** Columbia Univ., President's Fellowship 1969-70; New York State Regents Fellowship 1970-71; Austin Oldrini Travelling Fellowship 1971-

72; National Science Found., Individual Research Grant 1987-89; PSC-CUNY Research Award l991-92, 1992-94. **Publications:** with T.J. Hall, "Binaural Interaction in Single Units of the Accessory Superior Olivary Nucleus in Cat," *Quarterly Progress Report, Research Laboratory of Electronics, MIT* 68 (Jan. 15, 1963): 207-18; "Le thème d'Orphée dans les oeuvres latines d'Ange Politien," *Bulletin de l'Association Guillaume Budé* 39 (1980): 408-19; "Towards Vernacular Comedy: Gaspare Visconti's *Pasithea,*" *Il teatro Italiano del Rinascimento,* Acts of the Congress, Renaissance Theater in Northern Italy: The Court and the City 1400-1600, New York, Nov. 1978 (Milan: Edizioni di Comunità, 1980), 349-60; "Il tema di Orfeo, la musica e le favole mitologiche del tardo Quattrocento," *Ecumenismo della cultura,* II. Atti del XIII Convegno Internazionale di Studi Umanistici, Montepulciano, 1976, ed. G. Tarugi (Florence: Olschki, 1981), 121-39; *Das Tierbuch des Petrus Candidus: Codex Urbinas Latinus 276. Eine Einführung* (Zurich: Belser Verlag, 1984); "Pier Candido Decembrio and Rome," *Umanesimo a Roma nel Quattrocento,* Acts of the Congress, New York, Dec. 1981 (Rome, Istituto di Studi Romani, 1984), 295-307; "Neoplatonic Currents and Gaspare Visconti's *Fragmentum* (MS Triv. 1093)," *Supplementum Festivum: Studies in Honor of Paul Oskar Kristeller,* ed. J. Monfasani, J. Hankins & F. Purnell (Binghamton: MRTS, 1987), 457-67; "Harvard MS Richardson 23: A 'Pendant' to Vatican MS Urb. Lat. 276 and a Significant Exemplar for P.C. Decembrio's *Opuscula Historica,*" *Scriptorium* 42.2 (1988): 191-98; "Teodoro Ghisi," "Paul Oskar Kristeller," "Gaspare Visconti," in *The Dictionary of Art*; "Renaissance Humanism and Science," *Studi umanistici Piceni* 11 (1991): 197-202; "Per la biografia di Baldassare Taccone: Con un appendice di documenti nuovi," *Archivio storico lombardo* 117 (1991): 391-413; "L'entrée de Charles VIII dans Paris (1484) racontée par Baccio Ugolini a Lorenzo di Pierfrancesco de' Medici," *Bibliothèque d'Humanisme et Renaissance* 53 (1991): 727-34; "Per un'iconologia dello spettacolo: Dalle nozze sforzesche del 1489 alle favole mitologiche," *Metodologia della Ricerca: Orientamenti attuali. Congresso Internazionale in onore di Eugenio Battisti,* Milan, May 1991, *Arte lombarda* 105-7 (1993): 84-87; "A New Sixteenth-Century Depiction of the Aurochs (Bos primigenius+1627): Evidence from Vatican MS Urb. Lat. 276," *Archives of Natural History* 21 (1994): 275-88; *Milan and Lombardy in the Renaissance: Essays in Cultural History* (Rome, 1995); "Una relazione sconosciuta delle nozze di Isabella d'Aragona con Giangaleazzo Sforza nel febbraio 1489: Giovanni II Tolentino a Baldassare Taccone," *Libri e documenti* (Milan: Biblioteca Trivulziana, forthcoming); "Towards the Biography of Gaspar Ambrogio Visconti," *Bibliothèque d'Humanisme et Renaissance* (forthcoming). **Home Address:** 470 West End Ave., NYC 10024. **Business Address:** Graduate Center, CUNY, 33 West 42 St., NYC 10036.

■   ■   ■

Q

QUAYLE, DOROTHY V. ■ Oberlin Fellow 1928-29.

QUAYTMAN, REBECCA ■ FAAR Visual Arts 92. b. May 30, 1961, Boston, MA. BA 83, Bard College. **Other Study:** Skowhegan School of Painting & Sculpture 1982; Nat. College of Art & Design, Dublin 1984; Inst. Hautes Études en Arts Plastiques, Paris 1989. **Research/Artistic Interests:** Painting. **Career & Employment:** Inst. for Contemporary Art-PS 1 Museum & Clocktower Gallery 1987-91. **Fellowships, Honors & Awards:** John Bard Scholar 1983. **Exhibitions/Performances:** Grapevine Gallery, Dublin 1984; Drawing Center, NYC 1984; Soho Center for Visual Arts, NYC 1988; RealArt, Inc., NYC 1989; White Columns, NYC 1989, 1991; Russian Museum, St. Petersburg 1990; Julian Pretto Gallery, NYC 1990 (solo), 1992; Galleria d'Arte Moderna, Spoleto 1992. **Bio-Bibliography:** Meaning (1989, 1994); Peggy Cyphers, *Arts Magazine* (Sept. 1990); Jon Etra, *ArtNews* (May 1991); Kathleen Fraser, *Black Bread* 2 (1993); Ausilia Binda, *Artedomani 1992, Punti di Vista Cat.* (1993). **Home Address:** 231 Bowery, NYC 10002.

QUERAL, GEORGE L. ■ FAAR Architecture 88. b. Jan. 16, 1953, Havana, Cuba. BArch 83, Boston Architectural Center. **Other Study:** Paris 1985-86. **Research/Artistic Interests:** Exploration of the architecture of the city & its influence on it through an analysis of particular monuments & urban spaces. Theoretical work in architecture & urban design with particular attention to the creation of neighborhoods & housing. Drawing & painting as it relates to my architectural studies, seen as a reflection of personal expression. Film, art director to film shot in Paris. Music, punk band in Rome, "Superfetazione," with Corey Brennan, FAAR 88. **Career & Employment:** James Stewart Polshek & Partners 1983-85; Skidmore, Owings & Merrill 1985-87, 1988-90; David Smotrich & Partners 1990-present; City College of CUNY, Adj. Prof. 1991-present. **Memberships & Offices:** Municipal Art Soc., Fellow; NIAE. **Fellowships, Honors & Awards:** NIAE, William Van Alen, 3d Prize 1982; Paris Prize 1985-86; Steedman Fellowship 1987-88. **Important Works:** with Skidmore, Owings & Merrill, Islamic Cultural Center, NYC; Chase Manhattan Bank, Operational Bldg., Metrotech, Brooklyn; with David Smotrich & Partners, PS 153, NYC; with David Smotrich & Partners, Oneida Indian Nat. Commercial Complex. **Exhibitions/Performances:** Soc. of the Four Arts Annual, Palm Beach, FL 1974, 1976; Helen Shlien Gallery, Boston 1982 (2); Gallery 8, Miami 1982; Miami Dade Gallery, Miami 1984; New World Library Gallery, Miami 1984; Artmart Gallery, NYC 1984, 1985; Inter/Prise Gallery, Salerno, Italy 1988; FIT Gallery, NYC 1988; Inter American Art Gallery, Miami 1989; Urban Center, NYC 1990. **Home Address:** PO Box 1987, NYC 10009. **Business Address:** David Smotrich & Partners, 227 E. 45 St., NYC 10017.

QUILICI, LORENZO ■ Italian Fulbright Fellow 1965-66.

QUINN, PATRICK J. ■ FAAR Architecture 80. b. Jan. 15, 1931, Dublin, Ireland. m. Máirín P. Kennedy. c. Ciarán, Paul, Diarmuid, Aidan, Aoife, Siobhán. BArch 54, Univ. College, Dublin; MArch 59, Univ. of Pennsylvania. **Other Study:** Inst. of Advanced Architectural Studies, York, England 1964; Mount Athos 1981, 1983. **Research/Artistic Interests:** Church architecture, Irish architecture, urban design, residential design, museum design. **Career & Employment:** Pvt. Practice, San Francisco 1959-71, Troy, NY 1971-present; UC, Berkeley, Asst. Prof. 1962-67, Assc. Prof. 1967-71; Rensselaer Polytechnic Inst., Dean of Architecture 1971-79, Inst. Prof. 1982-present. **Memberships & Offices:** Assn. of Collegiate Schools of Architecture, BoT 1984-86, 1990-93, Pres. 1991-92; AIA, Eastern NY Chap., Pres. 1975-

Patrick J. Quinn

76, Honor Awards, Juror 1973, New England Awards, Juror 1974, Reynolds Award, Juror 1976, Topaz Medallion, Juror 1992. **Fellowships, Honors & Awards:** New Cathedral, Liverpool, Intl. Competition, Hon. Mention 1960; York Univ., Hon. Fellowship 1964; Graham Found. Fellowship 1968; AIA, Nat. Design Honor Award 1971; Bartlett Award 1971, Fellowship 1981; Royal Soc. for Arts Fellowship 1981; Notre Dame de la Source, Compiègne-Sud, France, Competition Finalist 1991. **Publications:** ed., "The Spirit of Home," *Association of Collegiate Schools of Architecture Annual Meeting Proceedings* (Washington, DC: ACSA, 1986); "Sixties to Eighties: Environmental Attitudes," *Association of Collegiate Schools of Architecture Annual Meeting Proceedings,* ed. Paul Heyer & Stephen Grabon (Washington, DC: ACSA, 1984); "Future of Church Architecture," *APS Yearbook* (Philadelphia: APS, 1965); "Future of American Church Architecture," *Looking to the Future*, ed. J.G. Davies (Birmingham: Univ. of Birmingham Press, 1977); "Design as Inquiry," *ACSA Annual Meeting Proceedings,* ed. with Thomas Regan (Washington, DC: ACSA, 1985); "Some Notes on the Church & Academy of St. Jude, Boca Raton," *Interfairth Forum on Religion, Art and Architecture Journal* 22 (1988): 20-28; "La Monumentalité Intérieur," *Actes des Rencontres Internationale d'Evry, 1989* (Paris: ABCD, 1990); "Drawing on Mount Athos: The 1000-Year Lesson," *Places* (Spring 1985): 32-47. **Important Works:** Church of St. Jude, Marina, CA 1966; Eden House, Sky Ranch, Philo, CA 1967; Elmhurst Methodist Church, Oakland, CA 1969; Rice House, Tiburon, CA 1969; St. Michael's Church, Boulder Creek, CA 1969; Church of Our Divine Saviour, Chico, CA 1970; Master Plan, Graduate Theological Union, Berkeley 1971; St. Jude Church & School, Boca Raton, FL 1987; Furlong House Addition, Sand Lake, NY 1989. **Exhibitions/Performances:** Univ. of Pennsylvania 1960; Liverpool Cathedral Competition Exb., Liverpool & London 1960; An Comhairle Ealaoin, Dublin 1962; All-University Arts Festival, Berkeley 1963; Crocker Art Museum, Sacramento, CA 1966; AIA Convention, Detroit 1971; Vietnam Veterans Memorial Competition Exb. 1981; Rensselaer Polytechnic Gallery, Troy, NY 1985; Astronauts Memorial Competition Exb., Cape Canaveral, FL 1988; Ulugh Beg Memorial Competition Exb., Samarkand, Uzbekistan 1992. **Bio-Bibliography:** *Who's Who in America; Who's Who in the World.* **Home Address:** 12 Whitman Ct., Troy, NY 12180. **Business Address:** School of Architecture, Rensselaer Polytechnic Inst., Troy, NY 12180.

R

RABB, MAXWELL ■ AAR Visitor 1981-82, US Ambassador to Italy.

RADDING, CHARLES M. ■ FAAR Post-Classical/Humanistic Studies 86. b. Aug. 2, 1946, Springfield, MA. m. Maureen A. Flanagan. c. Sarah, Jonah. BA 67, Univ. of Chicago; PhD 73, Princeton Univ. **Research/Artistic Interests:** Intellectual & cultural history, especially of the Middle Ages. **Career & Employment:** Lewis & Clark College, Asst. Prof. 1971-73; Loyola Univ. Asst. Prof.-Assc. Prof. 1976-88; Michigan State Univ, Prof. 1988-present. **Fellowships, Honors & Awards:** NEH Fellowship 1979-80, 1991-92; APS Grant 1984; American Catholic Historical Assn., Howard R. Marraro Prize 1988. **Publications:** *A World Made by Men: Cognition and Society 400-1200* (Chapel Hill: UNC Press, 1985); *The Origins of Medieval Jurisprudence: Pavia and Bologna, 850-1150* (New Haven: Yale Univ. Press, 1988); with William W. Clark, *Medieval Architecture, Medieval Learning: Builders and Masters in the Age of Romanesque and Gothic* (New Haven: Yale Univ. Press); plus articles in *American Historical Review, Annales: E.S.C., Speculum, Quaderni Storici* & other journals. **Home Address:** 1014 Huntington, E. Lansing, MI 48823.

RADKE, GARY M. ■ FAAR History of Art 84. b. Mar. 10, 1951, Buffalo, NY. m. Nancy R. Radke. c. Lydia E. BA 73, Syracuse Univ.; MA 75, Michigan State Univ.; PhD 80, IFA. **Research/Artistic Interests:** Italian medieval & Renaissance art; 13th-century papal architecture, late 15th-century Florentine sculpture. **Career & Employment:** Syracuse Univ., Asst. Prof. 1980-86, Assc. Prof. & Chair 1986-89, Honors Program Dir. 1989-present. **Memberships & Offices:** Italian Art Soc., VP 1991-93, Pres. 1993-95; CAA; SAH. **Fellowships, Honors & Awards:** Syracuse Univ., Phi Beta Kappa 1973, Faculty Research Fellowship 1981, 1985; Michigan State Univ. Scholarship 1974; MMA, Cloisters Fellow 1976; IFA Fellowship 1976-77; NYU Scholarship 1976-77; NGA, David E. Finley Fellowship 1977-80; Fulbright-Hays Fellowship 1977-78; Andrew W. Mellon Fellowship 1983-84; Kress Found. Travel Grant 1990; ACLS Travel Grant 1990. **Publications:** "An Early Byzantine Head in the MSU Collection," *Kresge Art Center Bulletin* 8.4 (Jan. 1975); "A Note on the Iconographical Significance of St. John the Baptist in the Ghent Altarpiece," *Marsyas* 18 (1975-76): 5-11; biographies of 10 Italian architects, *Macmillan Encyclopedia of Architects* (New York: Macmillan, 1982); "The Plan of St. Gall and Medieval Ecclesiastical Palaces," *Cuyahoga Review* 1 (1983): 23-33; "Medieval Frescoes in the Papal Palaces of Viterbo and Orvieto," *Gesta* 23 (1984): 27-38; "The Plan of St. Gall: A Blueprint to the Middle Ages," *The Plan of St. Gall: A Context for Understanding*, exb. cat., 15-18; "The Sources and Composition of Benedetto da Maiano's San Savino Monument in Faenza," *Studies in the History of Art* 12 (1985): 7-27; catalogue entries, *Renaissance Sculpture in the Time of Donatello*, exb. cat. (Detroit: Detroit Inst. of Art, 1985); catalogue entries, *Donatello e i suoi, Scultura fiorentina del primo rinascimento*, exb. cat. (Florence, 1986), 234-35, 244-46; "The Impact of Seeing" & "The Liberation of the Humanities" in *Contesting the Boundaries of Liberal and Professional Education: The Syracuse Experiment* (Syracuse, 1988), 99-107, 192-99; "Benedetto da Maiano, the S. Croce Pulpit," *International Dictionary of Art and Artists* (London, 1990); "Benedetto da Maiano and the Use of Full-Scale Preparatory Models in the Quattrocento," in *Verrocchio and Late Quattrocento Italian Sculpture*, ed. Steven Bule (Florence, 1992), 217-24. **Home Address:** 233 DeWitt St., Syracuse, NY 13203. **Business Address:** Honors Program, Syracuse Univ., 306 Bowne Hall, Syracuse, NY 13244.

RAFFO, STEVE ■ FAAR Painting 55. b. Aug. 21, 1912, Hoboken, NJ. **Other Studies:** Cooper Union School of Art 1930-38. **Career & Employment:** Cooper Union, Instr. 1939-43, 1947-50; US Army 1943-46; Parsons School of Design, Instr. 1956-63. **Fellowships, Honors & Awards:** Guggenheim Fellowship 1950, 1951; PAFA Annual, Scheidt Memorial Prize 1948. **Exhibitions/Performances:** Solo: Rehn Gallery, NYC 1949, 1951, 1952, 1958, 1966; Art Alliance, Phialdelphia 1951; Group: Corcoran Gallery Biennial, Washington, DC 1947-51; Whitney Museum, NYC Annual Exhibits 1947, 1948, 1949, 1951; Carnegie Inst., Pittsburgh 1949; Ohio Museum, Toledo 1950, 1952; AAAL 1951, 1958, 1960; AIC Annual Exb. 1952-1961; Butler Art Inst., Youngstown, OH 1954, 1956; Rhode Island Museum of Art, Providence 1955; Museum, Ogunquit, ME 1962.

RAGGIO, OLGA ■ RAAR History of Art 84. b. Feb. 5, 1926, Rome, Italy. BA 44, Liceo E.Q. Visconti, Rome; BA 45, Lycée Chateaubriand, Rome; PhD 49, Univ. of Rome. **Career & Employment:** IFA, Adj. Prof. 1965-present; MMA, Dept. of European Sculpture & Decorative Arts, Chair 1971-present. **Fellowships, Honors & Awards:** Columbia Univ., Fulbright Fellowship 1950; Seminar on the Renaissance, Assc. 1959-present; Belgian-American Found. Fellow 1952; ACLS Fellow 1962, Grant 1976-77; MMA Trustee Fellowship 1969; Mellon Found. Grant 1990-1994. **Publications:** *El Patio de Velez Bianco: Un monumento Senero del Renacimiento* (Murcia: Publicaciones de la Universidad de Murcia, 1968); co-ed. & contr., *The Vatican Collections: Papacy and Art* (New York: MMA, 1982), 40-46, 49, 80-91, 110-15; with J. Draper & J. Hecht, *Die Bronzen der Furstlichen Sammlungen Liechtenstein* (Frankfurt: Liebieghaus, 1986); "Alessandro Algardi e gli stucchi de Villa Pamphili," *Paragone* 251 (1971): 3-38; "Vignola, Fra Damiano et Gerolamo Siciolante à la Chapelle de le Batie d'Urfe," *La Revue de l'Art* 15 (1972): 29-52; "A New Bacchic Group by Bernini," *Apollo* 108 (Dec. 1978): 406-17; "Bernini and the Collection of Cardinal Flavio Chigi," *Apollo* 117 (May 1983): 368-79; "New Galleries for French and Italian Sculptures at the MMA," *Gazette des Beaux-Arts* 118 (Dec. 1991): 231-52; "Rethinking the Collections," *Apollo* 139 (Jan. 1994): 3-19. **Bio-Bibliography:** *Who's Who in American Art.* **Home Address:** 64 E. 94 St., NYC 10128. **Business Address:** MMA, 1000 5th Ave. NYC 10028.

RAJKOVICH, THOMAS NORMAN ■ Burnham-Chicago Architectural Club Prize 1985-86. b. Oct. 8, 1960, Hammond, IN. m. Susan Barbara Spear. c. Thoman Norman Rajkovich the

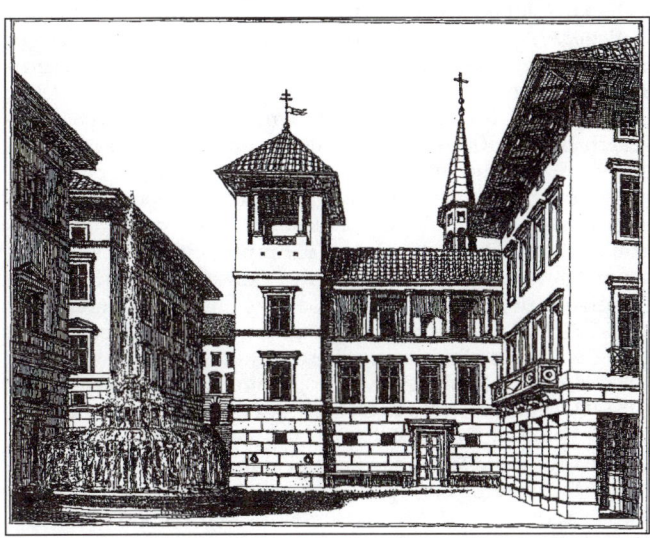

Thomas Norman Rajkovich

Younger. BArch 83, Univ. of Notre Dame. **Career & Employment:** Christopher H. Rudolph, AIA, Architect, Apprentice 1983-84; Hammond Beeby & Babka, Inc., Apprentice 1984-86; Univ. of Illinois at Chicago Circle, Adj. Asst. Prof. 1987-89; Univ. of Notre Dame, Visiting Asst. Prof. 1989-90, 1991-92; Thomas Norman Rajkovich, Architect, Prin. 1986-present. **Business Address:** Thomas Norman Rajkovich, Architect, 817 Judson Ave., 1-W, Evanston, IL 60202.

RAKOSKY, LEWIS E. ■ FAAR Sculpture 79. b. Jan 11, 1947, New London, CT. d. Sept. 15, 1991. BA 69, Antioch College; MFA 72, Indiana Univ. **Career & Employment:** Antioch College, Faculty 1969-70; Indiana Univ., Assc. Instr. 1971-72; Reed College, Visiting Asst. Prof. 1972-73, Asst. Prof. 1973-75; Humboldt State Univ., Visiting Lect. 1977-78. **Fellowships, Honors & Awards:** Indiana Univ., Gradute Research Grant 1971, 1972. **Exhibitions/Performances:** Solo: Evergreen State College, Olympia, WA 1973; Wentz Gallery, Museum Art School, Portland Art Museum, OR 1975; And/Or, Seattle 1976; California Gallery, San Francisco 1976; Northwest Artists Workshop, Portland, OR 1976; UC, Davis 1978; Group: Oten Gallery, Yellow Springs, OH 1970; Annual Mid-States Art Exb., Evansville, IN 1971.

RAMOS, JASON H. ■ FAAR Architecture 91. b. Oct. 11, 1964, Manila, Philippines. BArch 88, Cornell Univ. **Career & Employment:** Hillier Group Architecture Firm, Project Designer 1988-. **Fellowships, Honors & Awards:** Cornell Univ., Bronze Medal Award 1988; Ithaca Bridge Competition, 1st Place 1988.

RANALLI, GEORGE ■ AAR Visitor 1990-91, Architect.

RAND, CALVIN G. ■ AAR Pres. 1980-84. b. May 15, 1929, Buffalo, NY. m. Patricia Andrew Rand. BA 51, Princeton Univ.; MA 53, Columbia Univ. **Career & Employment:** Riverdale Country School, History Dept. Head 1955-60; SUNY, Buffalo, Lect. 1961-68, Cultural Affairs Dir. 1968-71, Adj. Prof. 1988-present; Niagara Inst., Pres. 1971-80; Consultant in Arts Education 1985-present. **Bio-Bibliography:** *Who's Who in America*. **Home Address:** 16 St. Andrews Walk, Buffalo, NY 14222.

RAND, EDWARD K. ■ AAR Trustee 1911-29, Classicist.

RAPHAEL, BETTINA A. ■ FAAR Conservation and Historic Preservation 94. b. May 15, 1946, Los Angeles, CA. c. Lilliana. AA 66, American College in Paris; BA 69, Barnard College; MA 73, SUNY, Oneonta. **Other Study:** Università per Stranieri, Perugia 1968; Walters Gallery, conservation internship 1972; Smithsonian Inst., conservation internship 1973; Univ. of British Columbia 1985; Univ. of London 1986. **Research/Artistic Interests:** Preventive conservation & its applications & teaching in Latin America; technology & preservation of pueblo Indian pottery in the American Southwest; ethnography & archaeological collections, their care, conservation & ethical concerns. **Career & Employment:** College Museum, Hampton Inst., Ethnographic Conservator 1973-75; Birmingham City Museum & Art Gallery, England, Conservator 1975-77; Rocky Mountain Regional Conservation Center, Dir. 1977-79; School of American Research, Resident Conservator 1982-94; Museum of New Mexico, Senior Artifact Conservator 1984-93. **Memberships & Offices:** American Inst. for Conservation, Fellow 1972-94; Nat. Inst. for Conservation, Study Com. on Ethnographic & Archaeological Conservation, Chair 1982-84; ICOM Working Group of Ethnographic Conservation 1985-94; Western Assn. of Art Conservators 1992-94. **Fellowships,**

Honors & Awards: Rockefeller Found. Fellowship 1970-73; Smithsonian Inst. Fellowship 1971. **Publications:** "The Edwards Papers," in *The Camelot Years* (Cooperstown, NY: Cooperstown Graduate Program, 1981), 75-83; with K. Laitner & M. Surovik-Bohnert, "Field Conservation Manual," *Archaeological Resources in Southwestern Colorado* 13 (1982): 210-34; ed., *Ethnographic and Archaeological Conservation in the United States* (Washington, DC: Nat. Inst. for Conservation, 1984); *Manual de Instrucción para la Conservación de las colecciones de Artesiania y Arte Popular* (Mexico City: Museo Nacional de Artes & Industrias Populares, 1987); *Preservation Conditions in Museums in Argentina: Ethnographic and Archaeological Collections* (Buenos Aires: O.A.S. & Nat. Directorate of Argentinian Museums, 1992). **Home Address:** 611 Cortez St., Sante Fe, NM 87501. **Business Address:** School of American Research, 660 Garcia St., Santa Fe, NM 87501.

RAPP, CHARLES A. ■ FAAR Landscape Architecture 72. b. Oct. 22, 1941, Evanston, IL. m. Eleanor M. Rapp. c. Jennifer, Alisa. BLA 63, Syracuse Univ. & State of New York College of Forestry; MLA 67, UC, Berkeley. **Other Study:** oil painting with Frank Reilly, ASL, Woodstock, NY. **Research/Artistic Interests:** Water-color painting. **Career & Employment:** Royston-Hanamoto, Project Mgr. 1967-69; Univ. of Oregon, Asst. Prof. 1969-70; Edaw, Inc., VP 1972-81; Rapp & French, Pres. 1981-86; Rapp & Asscs., Pres, 1986-present. **Fellowships, Honors & Awards:** AIA, Rocky Mountain Chap., Merit Award 1984; NEA, Chandler, AZ Civic Plazas Design Competition, 1st Place 1985; ASLA, Nat. Merit Award 1988; US Army Chief of Engineers, Honor Award 1991. **Home Address:** 24682 Aquilla Dr., Dana Point, CA 92629.

RAPUANO, MICHAEL ■ FAAR Landscape Architecture 30; AAR Trustee 1947-74; AAR Pres. 1958-69. b. Mar. 16, 1904, Warner, NY. d. Sept. 13, 1975. m. Catherine Reid Peck. c. Marge Reid, Michael Reid. BLA 27, Cornell Univ. **Research/Artistic Interests:** Home gardens. **Career & Employment:** Vitale & Geiffert; Gilmore D. Clarke; Clarke & Rapuano, Landscape Architects 1939-75. **Memberships & Offices:** New York Municipal Art Comm., Sec. 1939-47; ASLA, NY Chap., Pres.; NIAL, Com. on Fine Arts. **Fellowships, Honors & Awards:** ASLA, Fellow; NAD. **Publications:** "These Gardens and Homes Were Developed Together," *American Home* (Mar. 1947). **Bio-Bibliography:** *NY Times*, Obit. (Sept. 15, 1975); *Memorial Exhibition: Thomas Hart Benton, George L.K. Morris, Michael Rapuano*, exb. cat. (New York: AAAL, 1976); *Who Was Who in America*.

RATHBONE, PERRY ■ AAR Visitor 1951 — 1955; MFA, Dir.

RAUSCHENBERG, ROBERT ■ AAR Trustee 1980, Trustee Emer.; Artist.

RAYMO, ROBERT R. ■ AAR World War II Scholar 1945.

RAYMOND, W.O. ■ McKim Fellow 1911-12, 1913.

READ, HERBERT ■ AAR Visitor 1951 — 1955, Art Critic.

REARDON, JOHN T. ■ FAAR Classics/Archaeology 17. b. 1890, Dorchester, MA. d. Dec. 14, 1969. m. Louise Brower. BA 12, Dartmouth Univ. **Other Studies:** Yale Univ., History. **Career & Employment:** Taft School, CT, Faculty 1917-54, Dept. Head 1928-54; Crosby HS, CT, Faculty 1954. **Memberships & Offices:** Chamber of Commerce Economic Discussion Group, Discussion Leader; Connecticut Historical Assn., Founder 1956;

Watertown Found. Scholarship Com., Chair; Secondary School Soc. for Intl. Cooperation, Founder. **Fellowships, Honors & Awards:** Dartmouth Univ., Tuck Fellowship.

REBERT, HOMER FRANKLIN ■ FAAR Classics/Archaeology 24. b. Feb. 8, 1891, Littlestown, PA. d. Aug. 26, 1961. BA 12, Franklin & Marshall College; MA, Cornell Univ.; PhD 23, Cornell Univ. **Research/Artistic Interests:** Epigraphy, Latin literature, history, Greek vases. **Career & Employment:** Franklin & Marshall College, Instr. 1912-18, 1919-20; Western Reserve Univ., Prof. 1923-27; Amherst College, Prof. 1927-45. **Publications:** with H. Marceau, "The Temple of Concord in the Roman Forum," *Memoirs of the AAR* 5 (1925): 53-77; "The Velia: A Study in Historical Topography," *TAPA* 56 (1925): 54-69; "The Literary Influence of Cicero on Juvenal," *TAPA* 57 (1926): 181-94; "The Felicity of *Infelix* in Virgil's *Aeneid*," *TAPA* 59 (1928): 57-71; *Virgil and Those Others* (Amherst, MA, 1930).

REED, JOSEPH VERNER ■ AAR Visitor 1959 — 1964, Philanthropist.

REED, WILLIAM ■ FAAR Design Arts 67, FAAR Architecture 68. **Other Study:** School of Design, Chicago; Harvard Univ.; Yale Univ.; Univ. of Minnesota. **Research/Artistic Interests:** Community redevelopment, rehabilitation & restoration, industrially-oriented approaches to single- and multiple-family housing & commercial construction. **Career & Employment:** Univ. of Chicago & Inst. of Design of Illinois Inst. of Technology; Private Practice 1953-present. **Memberships & Offices:** Com. of Five; Lincoln Park Conservation Assn., Found. & Dir.; Planning Com., Chair; AIA, Chicago Chap.-Chicago Assn. of Commerce & Industry, Annual Honor Awards Jury; AIA. **Exhibitions/Performances:** MOMA; AIC; Inst. of Design of Illinois Inst. of Technology; Exb. Momentum, Chicago; Bordelon Gallery, Chicago; Colorado Springs Fine Arts Center. **Home Address:** 630 W. Surf St., Chicago, IL 60657.

REICHART, WALTER LOUIS ■ FAAR Architecture 33. b. June 4, 1908, Los Angeles, CA. m. Isabel Virginia McLain. c. Louis French, Thomas Clark. BArch 30, Univ. of Pennsylvania. **Other Study:** UCLA 1933; California Inst. of Technology 1934. **Career & Employment:** Eugene Weston, Jr., Reginald D. Johnson, Claude Beelran, Gordon B. Kaufmann, Ralph Fleweling, Samuel F. Lunden 1934-39; Paul R. Hunter, Part. 1939-41; US War Dept. 1941-43; California Inst. of Technology 1942-44; Private Practice 1943-present. **Memberships & Offices:** AIA 1934-present; Town Hall of Los Angeles 1934-present. **Fellowships, Honors & Awards:** Univ. of Pennsylvania, Arthur Spayd Brooke Medal 1930; AIA Medal 1930, Faculty Medal 1930. **Publications:** ed., with Paul R. Hunter, *Residential Architecture in Southern California* (AIA, Southern California Chap., 1939). **Important Works:** John Tracy Clinic, Los Angeles; Residences and schools in southern California; Military housing in San Diego, San Pedro, & Camp Pendleton. **Exhibitions/Performances:** Various exhibitions with AIA. **Home Address:** 4210 Oakwood Ave., La Canada, CA 91011.

REICHEK, JESSE ■ RAAR Painting 72. b. Aug. 16, 1916, NYC. m. Laure Reichek. c. Jonathan, Joshua. **Career & Employment:** Univ. of Michigan, Instr. 1946-47; Illinois Inst. of Design 1951-53; UC, Berkeley 1953-87. **Home Address:** 5925 Red Hill Rd., Petaluma, CA 94952.

REID, MABEL DOUGLAS ■ FASCSR 01. b. c.1876. d. after 1960. m. George L. Nussey. BA 1900, Cornell Univ. **Career &**

Employment: Independent Scholar, England 1930s-60s. **Bio-Bibliography:** Cornell Univ. Archives.

REINHOLD, MEYER ■ FAAR Classics/Archaeology 35. b. Sept. 1, 1909, NYC. m. Diane Roth. c. Robert, Helen Barrett. BA 29, CUNY; MA 30, Columbia Univ.; PhD 33, Columbia Univ. **Career & Employment:** Brooklyn College, Asst. Prof. 1938-45, Assc. Prof. 1945-55; Southern Illinois Univ., Prof. 1965-67; Univ. of Missouri-Columbia, Prof. 1967-80; Boston Univ., Univ. Prof. 1980-present. **Memberships & Offices:** APA, Chair, Com. on the Classical Tradition in N. America 1984-89; Inst. for the Classical Tradition, Dir. 1983-present; Intl. Soc. for the Classical Tradition, Co-Pres. 1991-present; VSA; CAMWS; CANE; American Assn. of Ancient Historians. **Fellowships, Honors & Awards:** Phi Beta Kappa, Alpha, New York 1929; Columbia Univ., Drisler Fellow 1931, Univ. Fellow 1932; Univ. of Missouri-Columbia, Byler Distinguished Prof. 1978; CAMWS, Award of Merit 1987. **Publications:** *Marcus Agrippa: A Biography* (Geneva, New York: Humphrey, 1933); ed., with N. Lewis, *Roman Civilization*, 2 vols. (New York: Columbia Univ. Press, 1951-55, 3d ed. 1990); "Historian of the Classic World: A Critique of Rostovtzeff," *Science and Society* 10 (1946): 361-91; *History of Purple as a Status Symbol in Antiquity* (Brussels: Latomus, 1970); *Past and Present: The Continuity of Classical Myths* (Toronto: Samuel/Stevens, 1972); *The Classic Pages: Classical Reading of Eighteenth-Century Americans* (Chico, CA: APA, 1975); *The Golden Age of Augustus* (Toronto: Samuel/Stevens, 1978); "Usurpation of Status and Status Symbols in the Roman Empire," *Historia, Zeitschrift für Alte Geschichte* 20 (1981): 275-302; *Diaspora: The Jews among the Greeks and Romans* (Toronto: Samuel/Stevens, 1983); *Classica Americana: The Greek and Roman Heritage in the United States* 10 (Detroit: Wayne State Univ. Press, 1984); "Thomas Jefferson and the Classical World," in *Thomas Jefferson: A Reference Biography*, ed. Merrill D. Peterson (New York: Scribner's, 1986), 135-56; *From Republic to Principate: A Historical Commentary on Cassius Dio's Roman History Books 49-52*, APA Monograph 34, Intl. Cassius Dio Project 6 (Atlanta: APA, 1988); ed., Annual Bibliographies of Publications on the Classical Tradition published 1988-present in *Classical and Modern Literature* (Spring). **Bio-Bibliography:** William M. Calder III, *Preface to Classica Americana* (1984); *Biographical Directory of American Scholars; Directory of International Biography; Outstanding Educators of America; Who's Who in America; Who's Who in the Midwest.* **Home Address:** 63 Sparks St., Cambridge, MA 02138.

REISER, JESSE ■ FAAR Architecture 85. b. Apr. 12, 1958, NYC. m. Nanako Umemoto. c. Zeke. BArch 81, Cooper Union; MArch 84, Cranbrook Acad. **Other Study:** worked for John Hejduk, Aldo Rossi. **Career & Employment:** Reiser-Umemoto, Prin. 1986-present; Yale Univ., Critic 1990-93; Columbia Univ., Adj. Asst. Prof 1992-present; Guest Instr.: Tulane Univ., Illinois Inst. of Technology 1991. **Fellowships, Honors & Awards:** Nat. Scholastic Art Awards, Gold Medal 1976; New York State Student Awards Gold Medal 1976; I.A.U.S. Columbus Circle Competition, 2d Prize 1981; NYFA, Gregory Millard Fellowship 1988; NEA Grant 1990; NYSCA, Project Grant 1992; with N. Umemoto, Graham Found. Grant 1993. **Important Works:** Wooden Tower, Yeshiva Univ. Museum, NYC 1985; Mr. & Mrs. Milton Brechner, Garden Bronzes, Sands Point, NY 1986-87; Globe Theater Project 1986-88; Dan Brechner Co., Courtyard 1987; Shadow Theater, Globe Theater Project, NYC 1988; Drummers Collective, Space & Video Offices, NYC 1989; Schwartz Residence & Studio, Taos, NM 1989; Icarus Project, Marui Co. Ltd., Kyoto 1989; Aktion Poliphile, House Competition,

Wiesbaden 1990; Venice Gateway Competition 1990; J. Jadow Residence, Landscape Design 1991; H. Jadow Pavilion, Bridge, Pool, Pergola 1992; Boros Residence Enclosure 1992; Leonard Brechner, apartment & furniture, NYC 1993; Cardiff Bay Opera House Competition 1994. **Exhibitions/Performances:** Terminal New York 1983; Venice Biennale 1985; Yeshiva Univ. Museum, NYC 1985; John Nichols Gallery, NYC 1987; London Project, Artist Space, NYC 1988; Griffin McGear Gallery, NYC 1989; Galerie ZB, Frankfurt 1990; Royal Inst. of British Architects, London 1990; NIAE 1991; Yale Univ. 1991; Princeton Univ. 1991; Ohio Univ., Miami 1991; Cartier Found., Paris 1992; Architectural Assn., London 1994; World Architecture Triennale, Nara, Japan 1995. **Bio-Bibliography:** "Last x-ray Picture of Architecture," *New Observations* (July 1987); "Harbingers of Change," *Metropolis Magazine* (Nov. 1987); *The London Project* (New York: Princeton Architectural Press, 1989), chap. 2; "Reiser & Umemoto," *Architectural Review* (Feb. 1989): 59-61; "Reiser & Umemoto," *Architecture +Urbanism* (Nov. 1990): 38-61; "Hypnerotomachia Ero/Machia, Hypnia, House" *Assemblage* 13 (1991) 88-105; *Machines d'Architecture* (Found. Cartier, 1992); "A Plurality of Worlds," *AA Files* 24 (1993); "The Folded, Pliable and Supple in Architecture," *AD*, Special issue (Feb. 1993); *Semiotexte Architecture-Facade Writing* (May 1993); "The New East Coast Movement," *Space Design* (Aug. 1994); "Cardiff Bay Opera House: Some Notes on Geodetics," *Assemblage* 26 (1995). **Home Address:** 200 W. 92nd St., Apt. 4B, NYC 10025.

RENIER, JOSEPH EMILE ■ FAAR Sculpture 20. b. Aug. 11, 1887, Union City, NJ. d. Oct. 8, 1966. m. Margaret Carey. c. Margaret Josephine Donner. **Other Studies:** ASL; in Paris; with M. Victor Rousseau in Brussels. **Career & Employment:** American Red Cross, 1st Lieut. WWI; Private Practice, NYC 1928-66. **Memberships & Offices:** NAD, Assc. Mem. 1937; NSS; Garden Club of America. **Fellowships, Honors & Awards:** Garden Club of America, 2 prizes; American Artists Professional League, NY State Chap., Gold Medal for Sculpture 1959; Nat. Arts Club, Bronze Medal 1960; NAD, Samuel F.B. Morse Medal 1962, Elizabeth N. Watrous Gold Medal 1965; NYU Hall of Fame, Mark Hopkins Medal 1964; Daniel Chester French Medal 1966. **Important Works:** *Speed*, Court of Communication, NY World's Fair 1939; Domestic Relations Court, Brooklyn; Civil War Commemorative Medallion 1961; Metopes, Postal Administration Bldg, Washington, DC; Relief, State of Texas Bldg., Dallas; *Pomona & Boy with Snails*, Brookgreen Gardens, SC. **Bio-Bibliography:** *NY Times*, Obit. (Oct. 9, 1966); *Who Was Who in America*, *Who Was Who in American Art*.

RESTON, JAMES ■ AAR Visitor 1992-93, Writer.

RHINELANDER, FREDERICK W. ■ AAR Charter Mem.

RHINELANDER, PHILIP HAMILTON ■ RAAR Classics/ Archaeology 64. b. Jan. 1, 1908, Cambridge, MA. d. Mar. 20, 1987. m. Virginia Roberts. c. Helen, K. Virginia, K. Philip, M. Elizabeth. BA 29, Harvard Univ.; LLB 32, Harvard Univ.; PhD 49, Harvard Univ. **Research/Artistic Interests:** Philosophy, humanities. **Career & Employment:** Choate Hall & Stewart, Legal Assc. 1932-40; US Naval Reserve, Lt. Commander 1941-45; Harvard Univ., Instr. 1949-51, Dir. of General Education, Lect. 1952-55; Stanford Univ., School of Humanities & Sciences, Prof. & Dean 1956-61, Olive Plame Prof. 1961-73, Prof. Emer. 1973-87. **Memberships & Offices:** APA; MAA; Tavern Club, Boston, Pres. 1952-56; Century Assn., NY; Bohemian Club, San Francisco. **Fellowships, Honors & Awards:** Phi Beta Kappa; Stanford Univ., Dinkelspiel Award 1963; Church Divinity

School of the Pacific, Hon. DD 1977. **Publications:** *Is Man Incomprehensible to Man?* (San Francisco: W.H. Freeman, 1973). **Bio-Bibliography:** J.B. Stockdale, "The World of Epictetus," *Atlantic Monthly* (Apr. 1978); *NY Times*, Obit. (Mar. 25, 1987); *Directory of American Scholars, Who's Who in America, Who Was Who in America*.

RHODEN, JOHN WALTER ■ FAAR Sculpture 54. b. Mar. 3, 1916, Birmingham, AL. m. Richanda Phillips. **Other Study:** Talledega College, AL; Columbia Univ. **Research/Artistic Interests:** Research with jewel glass & welding techniques, casting & varous techniques with sculpture. **Career & Employment:** NYC Bd. of Education. **Memberships & Offices:** Muncipal Art Soc., Life Mem.; American Soc. of Contemporary Artists; Archives of American Art; Hays-Fulbright Comm. for Selection of Grants; NY Arts Comm. **Fellowships, Honors & Awards:** Rosenwald Fellow; Columbia Univ., 1st in Sculpture; Atlanta Univ., Tiffany Award in Sculpture; Skowhegan School Student Scholarship; Painters & Sculptors of New Jersey Prize; Fulbright Fellowship; Howard Univ., Rockefeller Grant; Guggenheim Fellowship; Harlem School of Arts, Humanitarian Award. **Important Works:** *Rev. Frederick Shuttleworth*, Freedom Park, Birmingham, AL; *Frederick Douglass*, Lincoln Univ., PA; *The Family*, Harlem Hospital, NYC; *Mitochrondria*, Bellevue Hospital, NYC; Metropolitan Hospital, NYC; *Clifton Senior HS*, Baltimore; Afro-American Museum, Philadelphia; *Wall of Universal Symbols*, Sheraton Hotel, Philadelphia. **Exhibitions/Performances:** MMA; Audubon Annuals; PAFA; American Acad. of Arts; British-American Gallery; AIC; Univ. of Illinois Annual; Howard Univ. Museum; Exb. of Foreign Academies in Rome; Camino Gallery; Schneider Galleria, Rome; Fairweather-Hardin Gallery, Chicago; Saidenberg Gallery, NYC; Fisk Univ; Frick Museum, Pittsburgh; MFA; Brooklyn College; Whitney Museum, NYC; Afro-American Historical & Cultural Museum, Philadelphia; Nat. Urban League, Gallery 62; Birmingham Museum of Art, AL; Kenkeleba Gallery, NYC; Montclair State College, NJ. **Bio-Bibliography:** *Who's Who in the East*. **Home Address:** 23 Cranberry St., Brooklyn, NY 11201. **Business Address:** Rhoden Studios, 23 Cranberry St., Brooklyn, NY 11201.

RICCO, ROGER R. ■ FAAR Painting 65. b. Feb. 11, 1940, Milwaukee, WI. m. Cia L. Ricco. BFA 63, Univ. of Wisconsin. **Career & Employment:** Ricco/Maresca Gallery, Part. **Publications:** with Frank Maresca, *American Primitive: Discoveries in Folk Sculpture* (New York: Knopf, 1988); with Frank Maresca, *Bill Traylor: His Art, His Life* (New York: Knopf, 1991); with Frank Maresca, *American Self-Taught: Paintings by Outsider Artists* (New York: Knopf, 1993). **Home Address:** 92 B Wittenberg Rd., Woodstock, NY. **Business Address:** Ricco/Maresca Gallery, 152 Wooster St., NYC 10012.

RICE, EUGENE F., JR ■ RAAR History of Art 75. b. Aug. 20, 1924, Lexington, KY. m. Charlotte Bloch. c. Eugene, John, Louise. BA 47, Harvard Univ.; MA 48, Harvard Univ.; PhD 53, Harvard Univ. **Other Study:** École Normale Supérieure, Paris 1951-53. **Career & Employment:** Harvard Univ.; Cornell Univ., Prof. 1955-63; Columbia Univ., Prof. 1963-present, Chair 1970-73. **Memberships & Offices:** RSA, Exec. Dir. 1966-82, 1985-87, *Renaissance Quarterly*, Ed. Bd.; ACLS, BoD; AHA, VP for Research; *Journal of the History of Ideas*, Ed. Bd. **Fellowships, Honors & Awards:** AAAL, Fellow; ACLS Grant; Fulbright Found. Grant; Guggenheim Found. Fellowship; IAS; NEH Fellowship. **Publications:** "The Patrons of French Humanism, 1490-1520," in *Renaissance Studies in Honor of Hans Baron*, eds. A. Molho &

J. Tedeschi (Florence: G.C. Sansoni, 1971), 687-702; *The Prefatory Epistles of Jacques Lefevre d'Etaples and Related Texts* (New York & London: Columbia Univ. Press, 1972); contr., *Columbia History of the World*, eds. J. Garraty & P. Gay (New York: Harper & Row, 1972), chap. 39-43; *The Renaissance Idea of Wisdom* (orig. ed. 1958; new ed. Westport CT: Greenwood Press, 1973); adv. ed., *The Western Experience*, by M. Chambers, R. Grew, D. Herlihy, T. Rabb, & I. Woloch, 2 vols. (New York: Alfred A. Knopf, 1974); "The Idea of the Evangelical," in *The Pursuit of Holiness in Late Medieval and Renaissance Religion*, ed. C. Trinkaus & H. Oberman (Leiden: Brill, 1974), 472-76; "The 'De magia naturali' of Jacques Lefevre d'Etaples," in *Philosophy and Humanism: Renaissance Essays in Honor of Paul Oskar Kristeller*, ed. E. Mahoney (New York: Columbia Univ. Press, 1976), 19-29; "The Humanist Idea of Christian Antiquity and the Impact of Greek Patristic Work on Sixteenth-Century Thought," in *Classical Influences on European Culture, A.D. 1500-1700*, ed. R.R. Bolgar (Cambridge: Cambridge Univ. Press, 1976), 199-203; "The Social World of Jean Grolier," *Gazette of the Grolier Club*, n.s. 30-31 (1979): 51-66; "Paulus Aegineta," in *Catalogus Translationum et Commentariorum* 4, ed. P.O. Kristeller & F.E. Cranz (Washington, DC: Catholic Univ. of America Press, 1980), 145-91; "St. Jerome's 'Vision of the Trinity': An Iconographical Note," *Burlington Magazine* 66 (1983): 151-55; *Saint Jerome in the Renaissance* (Baltimore & London: Johns Hopkins Univ. Press, 1985); "Philosophy," in *A Critical Bibliography of French Literature: The Sixteenth Century*, ed. R. La Charité (Syracuse, NY: Syracuse Univ. Press, 1985), 93-107; "The Renaissance Idea of Christian Antiquity: Humanist Patristic Scholarship," and "Humanism in France," in *Renaissance Humanism: Foundations, Forms, and Legacy*, ed. A. Rabil, 3 vols. (Philadelphia: Univ. of Pennsylvania Press, 1988), 1:17-28, 2:109-22. **Bio-Bibliography:** John Hine Mundy, "Eugene F. Rice, Jr.: An Appreciation," in *Renaissance Society and Culture*, ed. John Monfasani & Ronald G. Musto (New York: Italica Press, 1991), xvii-xx.

RICE, LOUISE ■ FAAR History of Art 86. b. Apr. 29, 1958, Ithaca, NY. BA 80, Harvard Univ.; MA 82, Columbia Univ.; PhD 92, Columbia Univ. **Research/Artistic Interests:** Italian baroque art. **Career & Employment:** Univ. of Illinois, Champaign-Urbana, Visiting Lect. 1988-91; Duke Univ., Asst. Prof. 1992-present. **Publications:** "A Newly Discovered Landscape by Pietro da Cortona," *Burlington Magazine* 129 (1987): 73-77; ed., with Joseph Connors, *Specchio di Roma barocca: Una guida inedita del XVII secolo* (Rome: Edizioni dell'Elefante, 1990); with Ruth Eisenberg, "Angelica Kauffmann's Uffizi Self-Portrait," *Gazette des Beaux-Arts* 117 (1991): 123-26; "Urban VIII, the Archangel Michael, and a Forgotten Project for the Apse Altar of St. Peter's," *Burlington Magazine* 134 (1992): 428-34. **Home Address:** 209 Watts St., Apt. 3, Durham, NC 27701. **Business Address:** Dept. of Art & Art History, Duke Univ., E. Duke Bldg., Durham, NC 27708.

RICH, DANIEL CATTON ■ AAR Trustee 1959-63, Museum Dir.

RICHARDSON, EMELINE H. ■ FAAR Classics/Archaeology 52, RAAR Classics/Archaeology 79; NEH Summer Seminar Leader 1979. b. June 6, 1910, Buffalo, NY. m. Lawrence Richardson, jr, FAAR 50. BA 32, Radcliffe College; MA 35, Radcliffe College; PhD 39, Radcliffe College. **Career & Employment:** Wheaton College, Instr.-Assc. Prof. 1941-49; Visiting Lect.-Prof.: Yale Univ. 1955-65, Stanford Univ. 1962, IFA 1969, UNC, Chapel Hill 1968-79. **Memberships & Offices:** ArIA, BoD 1965-67; German Archaeological Inst., Corresponding Mem; AAAS, Fellow; Istituto di Studi Etruschi ed Italici, Rome,

Membro Straniero. **Fellowships, Honors & Awards:** Phi Beta Kappa 1930; APS Grant 1958; Radcliffe Graduate Soc. Medal for Distinguished Achievement 1969; UNC Grant 1975; ArIA, Norton Lect. 1976-77; Dignitario della Società dell'Ombra della Sera, Volterra, Italy 1980. **Publications:** *The Etruscan Origins of Early Roman Sculpture*, Memoirs of the AAR 21 (Rome & New York: AAR, 1953); *Cosa II: The Temples of the Arx, Part 3, Terracotta Sculpture*, Memoirs of the AAR 26 (Rome & New York: AAR, 1960); *The Recurrent Geometric in the Sculptures of Central Italy*, Memoirs of the AAR 27 (Rome & New York: AAR, 1962); *The Etruscans: Their Art and Civilization* (Chicago: Univ. of Chicago Press, 1964); Prepared O.J. Brendel., *Etruscan Art*, Pelican History of Art Series (New York: Penguin, 1978); *Etruscan Votive Bronzes: Geometric, Orientalizing, Archaic* (Mainz: Philipp von Zabern, 1983); articles on Blera, Centum cellae (Città Vecchia), Clusium (Chiusi), Falerii Novi (Santa Maria di Falleri), Falerii Veteres (Civita Castellana), Fanum Fortunae (Fano), Narce, Norchia, Picentia (Pontecagnano), Pisaurum (Pesaro), Punicum (Santa Marinella), Sala Consilina, Tarquinii (Tarquinia), in the *Princeton Encyclopedia of Classical Sites* (Princeton: Princeton Univ. Press, 1976). **Bio-Bibliography:** *Directory of American Scholars*. **Home Address:** 1103 N. Gregson St., Durham, NC 27701.

RICHARDSON, JAMES D. ■ AAR Charter Mem.

RICHARDSON, LAWRENCE, JR ■ FAAR Classics/Archaeology 50, RAAR Classics/Archaeology 79; AAR Trustee 1969-92, Trustee Emer.; Field Archaeologist 1952-55; Com. of Classical School, Chair 1972-81; Library Com., Chair 1981-present; Exec. Com.; Com. on Plant & Planning; Com. on Publications; Summer Seminar 1978; Andrew W. Mellon Prof.-in-Charge 1980-81; Jury on Classics Fellowships 1972-80, 1990; Jury on Mellon Fellowships 1981-1984. b. Dec. 2, 1920, Altoona, PA. m. Emeline Hill, FAAR 52. BA 42, Yale Univ.; PhD 52, Yale Univ. **Career & Employment:** Yale Univ., Instr. 1946-47, Instr.-Assc. Prof. 1955-66; Duke Univ., Prof. 1966-78, James B. Duke Prof. of Latin 1978-91. **Memberships & Offices:** NEH Jury on Fellowships in Archaeology 1982, 1988; *AJA*, Adv. Bd. 1986-present; Associazione Internazionale "Amici di Pompei," Ed. Bd. 1982-present; Deutsches Archaeologisches Inst., Corresponding Mem. 1964-present. **Fellowships, Honors & Awards:** Fulbright Fellow 1949-50; Guggenheim Fellow 1958-59; IAS 1967; ACLS Fellow 1967, 1972-73; NEH Fellow 1979-80. **Publications:** *Pompeii: The Casa dei Dioscuri and Its Painters*, Memoirs of the AAR 23 (Rome & New York: AAR, 1955); with F.E. Brown & E.H. Richardson, *Cosa II: The Temples of the Arx*, Memoirs of the AAR 26 (Rome & New York: AAR, 1960); ed., *Propertius: Elegies I-IV* (Norman: Univ. of Oklahoma Press, 1977); *Poetical Theory in Republican Rome* (New Haven: Yale Univ. Press, 1944; rpt. ed. New York: Garland, 1978); *Pompeii: An Ar-*

chitectural History (Baltimore: Johns Hopkins Univ. Press, 1988); *A New Topographical Dictionary of Ancient Rome* (Baltimore: Johns Hopkins Univ. Press, 1992); with F.E. Brown & E.H. Richardson, *Cosa III: The Buildings of the Forum*, Memoirs of the AAR 37 (University Park: Pennsylvania State Univ. Press, 1993). **Bio-Bibliography:** *Directory of American Scholars, Who's Who in America.* **Business Address:** Dept. of Classical Studies, 229B Allen Bldg., Duke Univ., Durham, NC 27708.

RICHMOND, ISIDOR ■ Rotch Scholar 1923.

RICHTER, GISELA MARIE AUGUSTA ■ AAR Jerome Lecturer 1952-53; Medal for Outstanding Service to Academy 1964; Archaeologist. b. Aug. 15, 1882. d. Dec. 24, 1972. **Career & Employment:** MMA, Curator, Dept. of Greek & Roman Art 1925-48. **Honors & Awards:** ArIA, Gold Medal 1968. **Publications:** Author of many books on classical art & archaeology. Bequeathed her apartment in Rome to the Academy.

RIEFLER, JULIE M. ■ FAAR Design Arts 87. b. May 19, 1955, Dallas, TX. m. James F. Cali. BFA 76, Texas Tech Univ. **Career & Employment:** Eisenberg & Pannell, Designer 1977; Bright & Asscs., Design Dir. 1977-82; Art Center College of Design, Pasadena, Instr. 1981-82; Donovan & Green, Asscs. 1982-. **Exhibitions/Performances:** *Graphis Magazine* Show; *Communication Arts Magazine* Shows; Art Directors Club of New York Shows; Art Directors Club of California Shows; *Art Direction Magazine*; AIGA Graphic Design USA Show & Annuals 1980-83. **Bio-Bibliography:** *Regional Design Annual* (1983); *Print Magazine* (1985).

RIFKIND, CAROLE ■ AAR Visitor 1990-91, ALNY.

ROBATHAN, DOROTHY M. ■ FAAR Classics/Archaeology 49; AAR Classical Jury 1959-60. b. May 11, 1898, Scranton, PA, d. Dec. 29, 1991. BA 19, Wellesley College; MA 21, Columbia Univ.; PhD 29, Univ. of Chicago. **Research/Artistic Interests:** Palaeography, history of classical texts, topography & archaeology of Rome, Renaissance humanism. **Career & Employment:** Walnut Hill School, Natick, MA, Teacher 1921-25; Northampton, MA, School, Latin Dept. Head 1926-27; Wells College, Instr. 1930-31; Wellesley College, Instr.-Prof. 1931-63, Dept. Chair 1939-48. **Memberships & Offices:** APA, Pres. 1964-65. **Publications:** "Two Unreported Persius Manuscripts," *Classical Philology* 26 (1931): 284-301; "A Fifteenth-Century History of Latin Literature," *Speculum* 7 (1932): 239-48; "The Catalogues of the Princely and Papal Libraries of the Italian Renaissance," *TAPA* 68 (1937): 138-49; "A Reconsideration of the Roman Topography in the *Historia Augusta,*" *TAPA* 70 (1939): 515-34; "Libraries of the Italian Renaissance," in *The Medieval Library*, ed. James W. Thompson (Chicago: Univ. of Chicago Press, 1939), 130-44; *The Monuments of Ancient Rome* (Rome: Bretschneider, 1950); "Another Fifteenth-Century Manuscript of the *Germania,*" *American Journal of Philology* 71 (1950): 225-38; "Introduction to the Pseudo-Ovidian *De Vetula,*" *TAPA* 88 (1957): 197-207; *The Pseudo-Ovidian* De Vetula (Amsterdam: 1968). **Bio-Bibliography:** Briggs, 525-26; *Contemporary Authors; Directory of American Scholars; Who's Who of American Women.*

ROBERSON, NORMAN ■ AAR – Rome, Gate Reception.

ROBERTS, EILEEN L. ■ FAAR History of Art 81. b. Oct. 27, 1945, Cleveland, OH. BA 71, Ohio State Univ.; MA 76, Ohio State Univ.; PhD 84, SUNY, Binghamton. **Career & Employment:** Northern Michigan Univ., Assc. Prof. 1986-present. **Fel-**

lowships, Honors & Awards: Samuel H. Kress Found., Dissertation Research Grant 1981-82, 1982-83. **Publications:** "The Exultet Hymn in Twelfth-Century Sicily as an Indicator of Manuscript Provenance," *Ecclesia Orans* 5.2 (1988): 157-64; "Replicas of Italian Medieval Sculpture at Cranbrook," *Source: Notes in the History of Art* 9.4 (1990): 23-29; "Ionic Order Restored: The Greek Theatre at Cranbrook," *Inland Architect* 35.4 (1991): 21-22, 25. **Home Address:** PO Box 485, Marquette, MI 49855. **Business Address:** Dept. of Art & Design, Northern Michigan Univ., Marquette, MI 49855.

ROBERTS, LAURENCE P. ■ AAR Dir. 1946-60; AAR Trustee 1973-76, Trustee Emer. b. Oct. 1, 1907, Bala-Cynwyd, PA. m. Isabel Roberts. BA 29, Princeton Univ. **Career & Employment:** Philadelphia Museum of Art, Asst. Curator 1930-32; Brooklyn Museum, Curator 1934-38, Dir. 1938-42. **Home Address:** 1310 Bolton St., Baltimore, MD 21217.

ROBIN, DIANA ■ FAAR Post-Classical/Humanistic Studies 88. b. Sept. 12, 1935, Passaic, NJ. c. Robin Benning, Anne Benning. BA 57, Sweet Briar College; MA 69, Columbia Univ., Teachers College; PhD 79, Univ. of Iowa. **Career & Employment:** Univ. of New Mexico, Asst. Prof. 1979-85, Assc. Prof. 1985-92, Prof. 1992-present, Chair 1992-present, Comparative Literature & Cultural Studies, Dir. 1992-present. **Memberships & Offices:** CAMWS, State VP 1984-present; RSA, Discipline Councilor, 1989-present; APA, Women's Classical Causus, Co-Chair 1993; *Frontiers: A Journal of Women's Studies*, Ed. 1993-present. **Fellowships, Honors & Awards:** Univ. of New Mexico Research & Allocations Com., Faculty Research Grants 1980, 1981, 1982, 1983, 1984; Mellon Post-Doctoral Fellowship 1984; Exxon Education Found. Fellowship, Newberry Library 1985; Gladys Krieble Delmas Found. Research Fellowship 1987-88 (declined), 1991; Newberry Library Fellowship 1991; NEH Fellowship 1993-95. **Publications:** "The Manuscript Tradition of Oppian's *Halientica,*" *Bollettino dei Classici dell'Accademia Nazionale dei Lincei*, ser. 3, 2 (1981): 28-94; "Alcaeus, Frag. 113 and Euripides, I.T. 1138-51," *Classical Outlook* 60 (Oct.-Nov. 1982): 15; "A Reassessment of the Character of Francesco Filelfo (1398-1481)," *Renaissance Quarterly* 36 (Summer 1983): 202-24; "Unknown Greek Poems of Francesco Filelfo," *Renaissance Quarterly* 37 (Summer 1984): 173-206; "Humanist Politics or Vergilian Poetics?" *Rinascimento* 25 (1985): 101-25; *Filelfo in Milan: Writings, 1451-1477* (Princeton: Princeton Univ. Press, 1991); "Film Theory and the Gendered Voice in Seneca," in *Feminist Theory and Classics*, ed. A. Richlin & N. Rabinowitz (London & New York: Routledge, 1993), 102-21; "Cassandra Fedele," in *Italian Women Writers: A Biographical Sourcebook*, ed. R. Russell (Westport, CT: Greenwood Press, 1993), 119-27; "Sexual Harassment in the Classics Workplace: Evaluating the Testimony," *Women's Classical Newsletter* 20 (Spring 1993): 28-41; ed. with Ira Jaffe, *Women Filmmakers and the Politics of Gender in Third Cinema*, Frontiers 15.1 (1994); "Cassandra Fedele's *Epistolae* (1488-1521): Biography as Ef-facement," in *Rhetorics of Life: Writing in Early Modern Europe*, ed. T. Mayer & D.R. Woolf (Ann Arbor: Univ. of Michigan Press, 1995), 187-203; "Culture, Imperialism, and Humanist Criticism in the Italian City-States," in *Cambridge History of Literary Criticism*, Vol. 3: *The Renaissance, c. 1500-1700*, ed. Glyn P. Norton (Cambridge: Cambridge Univ. Press, forthcoming); "Space, Woman and Renaissance Discourse," in *Sex and Gender in Medieval and Renaissance Texts: The Latin Tradition*, ed. Barbard K. Gold, Paul Allen Miller & Charles Platter (Albany: SUNY Press, forthcoming). **Home Address:** 1331 Park Ave. SW, No. 1205, Albuquerque, NM 87102. **Business Address:** Dept. of Foreign Languages & Literatures, Univ. of New Mexico, Albuquerque, NM 87131.

ROBIN, E.J. ■ Columbia Scholar 1915.

ROBINSON, CHARLES ALEXANDER, JR ■ FAAR Classics/Archaeology 26. b. Mar. 30, 1900, Princeton, NJ. d. Feb. 23, 1965. m. Celia Sachs. c. Charles Alexander III, Samuel Sachs, Franklin Westcott. BA 22, Princeton Univ.; MA 23, Princeton Univ. **Other Studies:** ASCSA 1923-25. **Research/Artistic Interests:** Greek inscriptions, archaeology, Pericles' Athens, scenery in the plays of Sophocles, Alexander the Great; archaeological field work: ASCSA at Corinth, Nemea, Philius, Prosymma. **Career & Employment:** Brown Univ., Instr. 1928-29, Asst. Prof 1929-35, Assc. Prof 1935-45, Prof. 1945-59, David Benedict Prof. 1959-65; ASCSA, Annual Prof. 1934-35, 1948, 1962. **Memberships & Offices:** Shakespeare & Review Clubs of Providence; Amateurs of Ancient Greece, Founder; Comm. for Excavation of the Athenian Agora; Com. on Agora Museum; Providence Athenaeum, Dir. 1936-40; Intl. Inst. of Arts & Letters; ANS, Fellow. **Fellowships, Honors & Awards:** Princeton Univ., John Harding Page Fellow 1926. **Publications:** *Alexander the Great* (New York: Dutton, 1947); ed., *An Anthology of Greek Drama* (New York: Rinehart, 1949); *Ancient History* (New York: Macmillan, 1951); ed., *The Portable Gibbon* (New York: Viking, 1952); *History of Alexander the Great*, 2 vols. (Providence: Brown Univ. Press, 1953, 1963); *Spring of Civilization: Periclean Athens* (New York: Dutton, 1954); with G.W. Botsford, *Hellenic History*, 4th ed. (New York: Macmillan, 1956); *Athens in the Age of Pericles* (Norman: Univ. of Oklahoma Press, 1959); ed., *Selections from Greek and Roman Historians* (New York: Rinehart, 1957); *Plutarch* (New York: Rinehart, 1960). **Bio-Bibliography:** Briggs, 527-28; *Who Was Who in America.*

ROBINSON, EDWARD ■ AAR Charter Mem., AAR Trustee 1906-31, Art Historian.

ROBINSON, JETHRO ■ AAR World War II Fellow 1943.

ROBINSON, RODNEY POTTER ■ AAR School of Classical Studies, Prof.-in-Charge 1935-37.

ROCHBERG, GEORGE ■ FAAR Musical Composition 51. b. July 5, 1918, Paterson, NJ. m. Gene Rosenfeld. c. Paul (dec.), Francesca. **Study:** Mannes School of Music; Curtis Inst. of Music 1948-54. **Career & Employment:** Univ. of Pennsylvania 1960-83, Chair, Dept. of Music to 1968; Annenberg Prof. Emer. **Fellowships, Honors & Awards:** Brandeis Creative Arts Award, Gold Medal in Music 1985; AAAL 1985; Univ. of Pennsylvania, Hon. DMus 1985; AAAS 1986; Lancaster Symphony Composers Award 1986; Alfred I. du Pont Award 1987; Andre & Clara Mertens Contemporary Composer Award 1987; Curtis Inst. of Music, Hon. DMA 1988. **Important Works:** *String Quintet,* for double cello, Concord String Quartet Comm. 1982; *The Confidence Man,* an opera, Santa Fe Opera Comm. 1982; *Quartet,* for piano, violin, viola, & cello, Frank Taplin Comm. 1983; *Concerto for Oboe and Orchestra,* New York Philharmonic Orchestra Comm. 1983; *Symphony No. 5,* City of Chicago Sesquicentennial Comm. 1984; *Four Short Sonatas,* for piano, USIA Comm. 1984; *Trio,* for piano, violin, & cello, Elizabeth Sprague Coolidge Found. in the Library of Congress Comm. 1985; *To the Dark Wood,* for wind quintet, Earle Page College Found., Univ. of New England, Armidale, Australia Comm. 1985; *Symphony No. 6,* Pittsburgh Symphony Soc. Comm. 1986; *Sonata for Violin and Piano,* McKim Fund in the Music Division of the Library of Congress & Concert Artists Guild Comm. 1988; *Summer 1990, Trio No. 3,* for violin, cello & piano, Philadelphia Chamber Music Soc. Comm. 1989; *Muse of Fire,* for flute & guitar,

Carnegie Hall Comm. 1990; *Concerto for Clarinet and Orchestra,* Philadelphia Orchestra Comm. 1994. **Bio-Bibliography:** *George Rochberg: A Bio-Bibliography to His Works* (Pendragon); *Baker's Biographical Dictionary of Musicians; Grove's Dictionary; Who's Who.* **Home Address:** 285 Aronimink Dr., Newtown Sq., PA 19073.

ROCHE, KEVIN ■ AAR Trustee 1968-71, Trustee Emer.; Architect.

ROCKBURNE, DOROTHEA ■ RAAR Painting 91. b. Oct. 18, 1934, Montreal, Canada. c. Christine Williams. **Study:** Black Mountain College 1951-56. **Research/Artistic Interests:** Painting: oil, watercolor, photography, fresco; work on paper. **Career & Employment:** Skowhegan School of Painting & Art, Visiting Artist 1984; Bard College, Distinguished Prof. 1986. **Fellowships, Honors & Awards:** Guggenheim Fellowship 1972; AIC, Painting Award 1972; NEA Fellowship 1974. **Important Works:** Highhold Intl., South Africa; Art Gallery of Ontario, Toronto; MOMA; Whitney Museum, NYC; Guggenheim Museum, NYC; Brooklyn Museum; MMA; Philadelphia Museum of Art; Albright-Knox Art Gallery, Buffalo, NY; Houston Museum of Fine Arts; Ludwig Museum, Aachen; Aldrich Museum, Ridgefield, CT; High Museum of Art, Atlanta; Auckland City Art Museum; Corcoran Gallery, Washington, DC. **Exhibitions/Performances:** Bykert Gallery, NYC 1970, 1973; Sonnabend Gallery, Paris 1971; Art Club of Chicago 1973; Galleria Schema, Florence 1973, 1975, 1992; Galleria Toselli, Milan 1974; John Weber Gallery, NYC 1976, 1978; Texas Gallery, Houston 1979, 1981; MOMA 1981; Xavier Fourcade, NYC 1981, 1982, 1985, 1986; Margo Leavin Gallery, Los Angeles 1982; André Emmerich Gallery, NYC 1988, 1991, 1992, 1994, 1995; Rose Art Museum, Brandeis Univ. 1989; d. P. Fong & Spratt Galleries, San Jose 1991. **Bio-Bibliography:** *Who's Who in America; Who's Who in American Art; Who's Who in the East; Who's Who of American Women.* **Home Address:** 140 Grand St., 2F, NYC 10013.

ROCKEFELLER, JOHN DAVISON, JR ■ AAR Charter Mem.; Philanthropist, Financier. b. Jan. 29, 1874. d. May 11, 1960. Active philanthropist who demonstrated generous support of the Academy with a donation of $200,000 in 1922; the Academy was also supported by his foundations.

RODGERS, RICHARD ■ AAR Visitor 1959 — 1964, Composer.

RODRIGUEZ, MARINA ■ AAR – New York, Program Assc.

ROETHKE, THEODORE ■ AAR Visitor 1951 — 1955, Poet.

ROGERS, M.R. ■ Sheldon Fellow 1919-20.

ROGERS, ROBERT SAMUEL ■ FAAR Classics/Archaeology 24. b. Dec. 5, 1900, Madison, NJ. d. Jan. 2, 1968. m. Dorothy Elizabeth Taylor. c. Robert, David. BA 20, Univ. of Pennsylvania; MA 21, Princeton Univ.; MA 22, Columbia Univ.; PhD 23, Princeton Univ. **Research/Artistic Interests:** Ancient history, philology. **Career & Employment:** Princeton Univ., Instr. 1924-28; Columbia Univ., Faculty 1926-27; Western Reserve Univ., Asst. Prof. 1928-37; Duke Univ., Prof. 1937-62, Dept. Chair 1940-62, Classical Studies, Chair 1962-66. **Memberships & Offices:** APA, Dir. 1953-58, VP 1958-60, Pres. 1961; ANS; CAMWS; consulting ed., *The Corpus of Roman Law.* **Fellowships, Honors & Awards:** Princeton Univ., Page Fellowship 1921-22, Procter Fellowship 1922-23; Phi Beta Kappa. **Publications:**

Criminal Trials and Criminal Legislation under Tiberius (Middleton, CT: APA, 1935); *Studies in the Reign of Tiberius* (Baltimore: Johns Hopkins Press, 1943); "The Roman Emperors as Heirs and Legatees," *TAPA* 78 (1947): 140-58; "A Tacitean Pattern in Narrating Treason-Trials," *TAPA* 83 (1952): 279-311; "The Neronian Comets," *TAPA* 84 (1955): 190-212; "The Deaths of Julia and Gracchus, A.D. 14," *TAPA* 98 (1967): 283-90; ed. with Kenneth Scott & Margret M. Ward, *Caesaris Augusti Res Gestae et Fragmenta*, 2d ed. (Detroit, Wayne State Univ. Press, 1990). **Bio-Bibliography:** *TAPA* 99 (1968) xx-xxii; Briggs, 534-35; *Who Was Who in America.*

ROLFE, JOHN C. ■ AAR Trustee 1918-40, Prof. of Latin.

ROLLAND, PETER G. ■ FAAR Landscape Architecture 78; SOF, Pres. 1992-present; Trustee Ex-officio 1991-95. b. July 2, 1930, Frankfurt A/M, Germany. m. Wendy Altschul. c. David, Seth, Janna. BS 52, Delaware Valley College; MLA 55, Harvard GSD. **Career & Employment:** Perkins & Will Architects 1955, 1958-60; US Army 1956-58; Lawrence Halprin & Asscs. 1960-63; Peter G. Rolland & Asscs. 1963-87; Yale Univ., Faculty 1973-93; Rolland/Towers 1987-present; Visiting Faculty: Harvard Univ., Cornell Univ., Univ. of Virginia, Univ. of Utah. **Memberships & Offices:** NY State Bd. of Landscape Architects Chair 1972-82; NYSCA 1979-82; Delaware Valley College, BoT 1991-present. **Fellowships, Honors & Awards:** ASLA Awards for Design 1966-93; AIA, Awards for Design 1970-94; Museum & Park, Frankfurt, Germany, 1st Prize 1979; New Parliament House, Australia, 1st Prize 1980; Yale Univ., Mellon Visiting Prof. 1980; ASLA Fellow 1982; Building Stone Inst., "Tucker Award" 1982, 1990; Yale Univ., Pierson College Fellow 1982-93; Australian Inst. of Landscape Architects, Honor Landmark Award 1988; Royal Australian Inst. of Architects, Award for Design 1989; AIA, Inst. Honor Award 1990; NAD 1991. **Important Works:** SUNY, Purchase 1972; Crown Center Redevelopment, Kansas City, MO 1972; A.I.U. HQ, Tokyo, Japan 1975; IBM AF/E HQ, Tarrytown, NY 1975; Corning Glass Works, Master Plan & R&D Facility, Corning, NY 1982; Volvo HQ & Manufacturing Facilities, Gothenburg, Sweden 1988; New Par-

Peter G. Rolland

liament House, Canberra, Australia 1989; IBM Conference Center, Palisades, NY 1991; Conway Farms Development, Lake Forest, IL 1991; Suffolk County Courthouse Complex, Islip, NY 1992; Dartmouth Hitchcock Medical Center, Hanover, NH 1992; US Embassy, Caracas, Venezuela 1994. **Exhibitions/Performances:** ASLA Traveling Exb. 1970, 1971, 1973, 1977, 1985, 1992; MOMA 1971; Whitney Museum, NYC 1972; Intl. Exb. of Landscape Architecture, Amsterdam, Holland 1972; AIA Annual Exb. 1972, 1976, 1986, 1989, 1990, 1994; ASLA, NY Chap. 1977, 1978, 1979, 1985, 1989; Urban Center, NYC 1980; New Parliament House, Canberra, Australia, Permanent-Traveling Exb. 1981-present. **Bio-Bibliography:** *Who's Who in America.* **Home Address:** 731 Milton Rd., Rye, NY 10580.

ROLLINS, HENRY CLIFFORD ■ FAAR Sculpture 66. b. June 8, 1937, Kansas City, KS. BA 62, Univ. of Washington; MFA 64, RISD. **Fellowships, Honors & Awards:** Puget Sound Group of Northwest Painters Award 1962; RISD Fellowship 1962-63; Chester Dale Fellowship 1964. **Important Works:** *The Sum* 1968; *Blue Totem* 1970. **Exhibitions/Performances:** Paul Art Center, Univ. of New Hampshire 1965; Whitney Museum, NYC 1968, 1971; Oakland Museum 1970. **Bio-Bibliography:** *Afro-American Artitsts*; J. Tarshis, "San Francisco," *Artforum* 9 (Oct. 1970): 81.

ROMANO, SERGIO ■ AAR Italian Com. 1994-present.

ROMUALDI, ANTONELLA ■ Italian Fulbright Fellow 1974-75.

RONQUIST, EYVIND C. ■ FAAR Post-Classical/Humanistic Studies 70. b. Nov. 13, 1939, NYC. BA 61, St. John's College, Annapolis; MA 64, Univ. of Chicago; PhD 75, Univ. of Chicago. **Research/Artistic Interests:** Medieval studies. **Career & Employment:** Univ. of Chicago, Lect. 1965-68; Concordia Univ., Assc. Prof. 1972-present. **Fellowships, Honors & Awards:** Fulbright Fellowship 1968-69; Research Council of Canada, Social Science & Humanities Fellowship 1978-79. **Publications:** "Friendship in Laurence of Durham," *Classica et Mediaevalia* 35 (1984): 191-213; "The Powers of Poetry in Sir Orfeo," *Philological Quarterly* 64 (1985): 99-117; "The Early-Thirteenth-Century Monastic Encyclopedia in Verse of Gregorius de Monte Sacro," *Studi Medievali* ser. 3, 29.2 (1988): 841-71; "Learning and Teaching in Twelfth-Century Dialogues," *Res Publica Litterarum* 13 (1990): 239-56. **Business Address:** Dept. of English, Concordia Univ., 1455 Boul. de Maisonneuve Ouest, Montreal, QUE H3G 1M8, Canada.

ROOT, ELIHU ■ AAR Charter Mem.; US State Dept., Sec.

RORIMER, ANNE ■ AAR Trustee 1973-76, Trustee Emer.

ROSBOROUGH, RUSKIN R. ■ FAAR Classics/Archaeology 24. b. Feb. 12, 1893, Columbus, MS. d. Oct. 18, 1980. BA 15, John B. Stetson Univ.; MA 16, Univ. of Pennsylvania; PhD 20, Univ. of Pennsylvania. **Other Studies:** Univ. of Toulouse; Univ. of Brussels & Louvain 1921-22. **Research/Artistic Interests:** Latin & Roman studies, epigraphy, archaeology. **Career & Employment:** Spartanburg HS, SC, Faculty 1916-17; US Expeditionary Forces, France 1918-19; Univ. of Pennsylvania, Instr. 1920-21; Duke Univ., Prof. 1925-42; Cornell Univ., Visiting Prof. 1927-30. **Fellowships, Honors & Awards:** Univ. of Pennsylvania, Harrison Fellow 1917-18, 1919-20; C.R.B. Fellowship, Belgium 1921. **Publications:** *An Epigraphic Commentary on Suetonius's Life of Gaius Caligula* (Philadelphia: Univ. of Pennsylvania Press, 1920). **Bio-Bibliography:** *Dictionary of American Scholars.*

ROSE, C. BRIAN ■ FAAR Classics/Archaeology 92; AAR Adv. Council, Sec.-Treas. 1992-present; Classical Soc., *Newsletter*, Ed. 1994. b. Aug. 8, 1956, Marietta, OH. BA 78, Haverford College; MA 80, Columbia Univ.; PhD 87, Columbia Univ. **Other Study:** ICCS 1977. **Research/Artistic Interests:** Roman art & archaeology, numismatics, Anatolian archaeology. **Career & Employment:** Univ. of Cincinnati, Asst. Prof. 1987-94, Assc. Prof. 1994-present; Troy, Post-Bronze Excavations, Head 1990-present. **Fellowships, Honors & Awards:** Samuel H. Kress Found. Fellowship 1984-86; American Research Inst. in Turkey, Fellow 1985; ArIA., Helen Woodruff Fellowship 1991-92; NEH 1993-96; Max Planck Research Prize 1994. **Publications:** "Princes & Barbarians on the Ara Pacis," *AJA* 94 (1990): 453-67; "The Arch at Pavia & the Einsiedeln Manuscript," *Journal of Archaeology* 3 (1990): 163-68; "The Theater at Ilion," *Studia Troica* 1 (1991): 69-77; "Greek & Roman Excavations at Troy, 1991," *Studia Troica* 2 (1992): 43-60: *Dynastic Art & Ideology in the Julio-Claudian Period* (Cambridge: Cambridge Univ. Press, 1995). **Business Address:** Dept. of Classics, Univ. of Cincinnati, Cincinnati, OH 45221.

ROSENZWEIG, IRENE ■ FAAR Classics/Archaeology 30. b. July 26, 1903, Pine Bluff, AR. dec. BA 24, Washington Univ.; MA 26, Bryn Mawr College; PhD 33, Bryn Mawr College.

ROSS, ARTHUR ■ AAR Trustee 1982-93. **Studies:** Univ. of Pennsylvania, Columbia Univ. **Career & Employment:** Central Nat.-Gottesman, Inc., Vice Chair; Cenro Corp., Pres. **Memberships & Offices:** UN Assn. of USA, Vice Chair; Council on Foreign Relations; Foreign Policy Assn., Dir. & Governor; Center for Strategic Intl. Studies, Washington, DC; Intl. Inst. for Strategic Studies, London; New York Landmarks Conservancy, BoT; Spanish Inst., Dir. & VP; Barnard College, BoT; American Museum of Natural History, BoT; Central Park Conservancy, BoT; Mt. Sinai Medical Center, Hon. Life Trustee; Asia Soc., Hon. Life Trustee; Riverdale Country School, Hon. Life Trustee; New York Botanical Garden, BoD; Cooper-Hewitt Museum, BoD; Bryant Park Restoration Corp., BoD; Parks Council, BoD. **Fellowships, Honors & Awards:** Appeal of Conscience Annual Award 1987; Central Park Conservancy, Frederick Law Olmsted Award 1987; Nat. Inst. of Social Sciences, Gold Medal Award 1982; City of New York, Mayor's Award of Honor for Arts & Culture 1983; Parks Council Award 1984; Spanish Government, *Orden de Isabel la Catolica* 1986; Republic of Italy, Order of Merit, Commendatore 1992.

ROSS, DAVID O. ■ FAAR Classics/Archaeology 66. b. June 25, 1936, NYC. c. Ian, Eric, Peter. BA 58, Yale Univ.; PhD 66, Harvard Univ. **Career & Employment:** Yale Univ., Asst. Prof.-Assc. Prof. 1966-74; Univ. of Michigan, Assc. Prof.-Prof. 1974-present. **Publications:** *Style and Tradition in Catullus* (Cambridge, MA: Harvard Univ. Press, 1969); *Backgrounds to Augustan Poetry: Gallus, Elegy and Rome* (New York: Cambridge Univ. Press, 1975); *Virgil's Elements: Physics and Poetry in the Georgics* (Princeton: Princeton Univ. Press, 1987). **Address:** Dept. of Classical Studies, Univ. of Michigan, Ann Arbor, MI 48109.

ROSZAK, THEODORE J. ■ AAR Trustee 1969-72, Artist.

ROTHKO, MARK ■ AAR Visitor 1943 — 1951, Artist. b. Sept. 25, 1903. d. Feb. 25, 1970. **Honors & Awards:** Brandeis Univ., Creative Arts Award 1964, 1965. **Important Works:** MOMA; Whitney Museum, NYC; Tate Gallery, London; Centre Georges Pompidou, Paris.

ROUSE, STEVE ■ FAAR Musical Composition 88. b. July 9, 1953, Moss Point, MS. BMus 76, Univ. of Southern Mississippi; MMus 82, Univ. of Michigan; DMA 87, Univ. of Michigan. **Career & Employment:** Eastern Michigan Univ., Music Dir., Dance 1979-82; Univ. of Michigan, Teaching Fellow 1982-85; Univ. of Utah, Asst. Prof. 1985-86; Univ. of Louisville, Assc. Prof. & New Music Ser. Dir. 1988-present. **Memberships & Offices:** League-ISCM, Nat. Adv. Bd. 1990-present; Soc. of Composers; CMS 1985-present. **Fellowships, Honors & Awards:** Univ. of Michigan, Halick Award 1980; AAAL, Ives Composition Fellowship 1985, Hinrichsen Award 1995; Dartmouth Univ., New Choral Music, 1st Prize 1986; Kentucky Arts Council, Al Smith Artist's Fellowship 1990; NEA Composition Fellowship 1990. **Publications:** "Hexachords and Their Trichordal Generators: An Introduction," *In Theory Only* 8.8 (Dec. 85): 19-43. **Important Works:** *Freedom's Ring*, for orchestra (PPP) 1979; *Dense Pack*, for chorus (PPP) 1983; *Crosswinds*, for organ & 12 players (PPP) 1984; *Symphony: Light Descending*, for orchestra (PPP) 1987; *Diamonds*, for violin solo (PPP) 1989; *Short Stories*, for orchestra (PPP) 1990; *The Avatar*, for trumpet & piano (MMB) 1990; *Ribbons*, for string orchestra (PPP) 1988-91; *Into the Light*, for orchestra (MMB) 1991; *Violin Sonata*, for violin & piano (PPP) 1992; *Bone to Be Wild*, for trombone & piano (PPP) 1993; *Light Fantastic*, for orchestra (PPP) 1994. **Bio-Bibliography:** Glenn Watkins, *Soundings: Music in the Twentieth Century* (New York: Schirmer), 499, 664. **Business Address:** School of Music, Univ. of Louisville, Louisville, KY 40292.

ROWE, COLIN ■ RAAR Architecture 70.

ROWELL, HENRY THOMPSON ■ RAAR Classics/Archaeology 67; AAR Trustee 1946-74; AAR School of Classical Studies, Prof.-in-Charge 1961-63; Classical Soc., Pres. 1949; AAR Pres. 1971-74. b. Mar. 12, 1904, Stamford, CT. d. Feb. 4, 1974. m. Tanja Ramm. c. Louisa, Margit-Ruth. BA 26, Yale Univ.; PhD 33, Yale Univ. **Research/Artistic Interests:** Dura-Europos, Roman army & history, Augustan Rome. **Career & Employment:** Dura-Europos Excavations, Asst. 1929-31; Yale Univ., Instr. 1931-35, Asst. Prof. 1935-40; US Army, Major-Lieut. Colonel 1942-45; Johns Hopkins Univ., Prof. 1940-71, Dept. Chair 1946-71; Asst. excavations: Harvard Univ., Visiting Prof. 1965. **Memberships & Offices:** *American Journal of Philology*, Ed. 1940-46, Ed.-in-Chief 1946-71; ACLS, Delegate 1953-55; ArIA, Pres. 1953-56; German Archaeology Inst.; Assn. Intl. d'Archéologie Classique; APA; Soc. for the Promotion of Roman Studies; Classical Assn. of Atlantic States. **Fellowships, Honors & Awards:** Philippine Liberation Medal; 5 Battle Stars; Cavaliere Ufficiale della Corona d'Italia; Univ. of South, Hon. LittD 1958. **Publications:** "The *Honesta Missio* from the *Numeri* of the Roman Imperial Army," *Yale Classical Studies* 6 (1939): 71-108; "The Forum and Funeral *Imagines* of Augustus," *Memoirs of the AAR* 17 (1940): 131-43; ed. & revisor, Jerome Carcopino, *Daily Life in Ancient Rome* (New Haven: Yale Univ. Press, 1940); "Vergil and the Forum of Augustus," *American Journal of Philology* 63 (1941): 261-76; "The 'Campanian' Origin of Cn. Naevius and Its Literary Attestation," *Memoirs of the AAR* 19 (1949): 15-34; "The Gladiator Petraites and the Date of the *Satyricon*," *TAPA* 89 (1958): 14-24; *Rome in the Augustan Age* (Norman: Univ. of Oklahoma Press, 1962); "Ammianus Marcellinus: Soldier-Historian of the Late Roman Empire," in *Semple Lectures, First Series* (Cincinnati, 1964), 261-313; ed. with D.C. Allen, *The Poetic Tradition* (Baltimore: Johns Hopkins Press, 1968). **Bio-Bibliography:** *American Journal of Philology* 94 (1973): 229-30; Herbert W. Benario, *Classical Outlook* 69.2

(Winter 1991-92): 61; Briggs, 547-48; *Contemporary Authors; Who Was Who in America.*

RUBIN, H.L. ■ Stewardson Memorial Fellow 1919-20.

RUBINGTON, NORMAN JOSEPH ■ FAAR Painting 53. b. June 20, 1921, New Haven, CT. d. Jan. 1, 1991. **Study:** Yale School of Fine Arts 1939-43; Academie de la Grande Chaumière 1948; École des Beaux Arts, Paris 1949-50. **Fellowships, Honors & Awards:** Tiffany Fellowship 1954-55; Guggenheim Fellowship 1958. **Publications:** *Fuzz against Junk* (Paris: Olympia Press, 1959); *The Hero Maker* (Paris: Olympia Press, 1961); *The Boiler-Maker* (Paris: Olympia Press, 1961); illus., *Olympia Reader* (Paris: Olympia Press, 1965). **Important Works:** Hirshhorn Gallery, Washington, DC; San Francisco Museum of Art; Mary Washington College; Grace Cathedral, San Francisco; Syracuse Univ. **Exhibitions/Performances:** Galerie aux Impressions d'Art, Paris 1948; Galerie '8', Paris 1950; Galerie Schneider, Rome 1951-53; Galerie Craven, Paris 1953; Galerie Il Camino, Rome 1953; City Center, NYC 1954-55; Corcoran Biennial, Washington, DC 1955; Museum of Fine Arts, San Francisco 1955; Univ. of Illinois Biennial 1955, 1957, 1959; Carl Siembab Gallery, Boston 1957; Washington Irving Gallery, NYC 1958; AIC 1961; Salon des Réalités Nouvelles, Paris 1963. **Bio-Bibliography:** *Sept Americains de Paris,* exb. cat. (Paris, 1962); *Who's Who in American Art.*

RUBINS, DAVID KRESZ ■ FAAR Sculpture 31. b. Sept. 5, 1902, Minneapolis, MN. d. 1985. **Study:** Minneapolis School of Art; Beaux Arts Inst. of Design, NYC; École des Beaux Arts, Paris; Academie Julien, Paris. **Career & Employment:** Herron School of Art, Prof.-Chair-Prof. Emer. 1935-85. **Fellowships, Honors & Awards:** Beaux Arts Inst. of Design, Paris Prize 1921; ALNY Prize 1932. **Publications:** *The Human Figure: An Anatomy for Artists* (New York: Viking, 1953). **Important Works:** *Gov. Henry Schhricker,* Indiana State House; *Abraham Lincoln as a Youth,* Indiana State House Plaza; *Caroline Marmon Fesler,* Indianapolis Museum of Art. **Exhibitions/Performances:** MMA, NAD, ALNY, Minneapolis Inst. of Art, Indianapolis Museum of Art. **Bio-Bibliography:** *Dictionary of American Painters, Sculptors and Engravers.*

RUBINSTEIN, ALICE L. ■ FAAR Post-Classical/Humanistic Studies 78. b. Dec. 15, 1951, Cleveland, OH. m. Robert Rubinstein. c. Joseph R., Max R. BA 73, Swarthmore College; PhD 79, Princeton Univ. **Publications:** "The Notes to Poliziano's *Iliad,*" *Italia Medioevale e Umanistica* 25 (1982); "Imitation and Style in Angelo Poliziano's *Iliad* Translation," *Renaissance Quarterly* 36 (1983). **Home Address:** 300 Lincoln Blvd., Cleveland Hgts., OH 44118.

RUDELL, JEFFERY ■ AAR – New York, Asst. to the Pres.

RUDENSTINE, ANGELICA ■ AAR Trustee 1979-91, Trustee Emer.; Art Historian.

RUDOLPH, PAUL ■ AAR Visitor 1943 — 1951 on Wheelright Traveling Fellowship in Architecture; Architect. b. Oct. 23, 1918. **Career & Employment:** Paul Rudolph Architect, Prin. 1952-; Yale Univ., Dept. of Architecture, Chair 1958-65.

RUSCHE, CAROL A. ■ FAAR History of Art 94. b. May 23, 1957, St. Louis, MO. m. Paul L. Bentel. c. Lukas, Michela, Nikolas. BA 79, Washington Univ.; MArch 81, N. Carolina State Univ., Raleigh. **Other Study:** Università di Venezia, Istituto

d'Architetura 1985; MIT 1986-present. **Research/Artistic Interests:** Italian architecture 1920s, 1930s. **Career & Employment:** Architects Collaborative 1981-83; Don Hisaka & Asscs., Architect 1983-84; Georgia Inst. of Technology, Asst. Prof. 1984-85; Bentel & Bentel Architects, Prin. 1985-present; Visiting Lect.: Architectural Assn., London 1988-89; Harvard Univ. 1990-91. **Memberships & Offices:** AIA 1985-present, Nat. Com. on Design 1990-present; SAH; AHA; Long Island Traditions, BoD 1991-present. **Fellowships, Honors & Awards:** N. Carolina State Univ., Graduate Student Teaching Award 1981; AIA School Medal 1981; with Paul Bentel, Municipal Arts Soc., Times Sq. Competition, 1st Place 1985; Fulbright Hays Grant 1985-86; with Paul Bentel, AIA, Long Island Chap., Archi Award 1990, 1991. **Publications:** "The Palazzo del Littorio Competition," *Architecture Today* 3 (1989); "Der Wettbewerb für den Palazzo Littorio im Jahre 1934: Projekt A und Projekt B," in *Giuseppe Terragni 1904-1943,* ed. Stefan Germer (Munich, 1991). **Important Works:** with Bentel & Bentel Architects: Suffolk County Court House Competition, Finalist 1985; Simpson Residence, Long Island, NY 1989; Bressler Residence Renovation, NYC 1989-90; Lynbrook Public Library, NY 1990; Meilman Residence Renovation, NYC 1994; Public School 150 Addition, Queens, NYC 1994-95. **Exhibitions/Performances:** North Carolina State Univ., Raleigh 1983; Atlanta Arts Alliance 1984; NESA & D Gallery, Boston 1984; NYIT 1991. **Bio-Bibliography:** "Times Square Competition," *Urban Design International* 5.2 (Winter 1985); Michael Crosbie, "Sacred Traditions," *Architecture* (June 1992): 66-69; "Walk to Work," *Interior Design* (June 1992): 164-67; Paolo Righetti, "In a Forest of Steel Columns," *L'Arca* 70 (April 1993): 12-17. **Home Address:** 22 Buckram Rd., Locust Valley, NY 11560. **Business Address:** Bentel & Bentel, 22 Buckram Rd., Locust Valley, NY 11560.

RUSH, LOREN ■ FAAR Musical Composition 71. b. Aug. 23, 1945, Fullerton, CA. BA 57, San Francisco State Univ.; MA 60, UC, Berkeley; DMA 69, Stanford Univ. **Other Study:** with Robert Erickson 1954-60, Dwight Peltzer 1960s. **Career & Employment:** Stanford Univ. Center for Computer Research in Music & Acoustics, Founding Dir. 1974-86. **Fellowships, Honors & Awards:** Concours de Composition Musicale de Royaumont, Highest Award 1965; Guggenheim Fellowship 1971; Prince Pierre of Monaco Musical Composition Award 1971; several NEA Composer's Fellowships. **Important Works:** *String Quartet in C# Minor* (CRI) 1961; *Nexus 16,* for 16 instruments, Fromm Music Found. & Berkshire Music Center Comm. (Wergo) 1964; *Dans le Sable,* for soprano, speaker, 4 altos & chamber orchestra 1968, orchestral version 1970; *The Cloud Messenger,* for orchestra 1970; *I'll See You in My Dreams,* for amplified orchestra & stereo audio tape, Nildaus Wyss & San Francisco Symphony Comm. 1973; *Song and Dance,* for amplified orchestra with computer-generated quadraphonic audio tape, Seiji Ozawa & San Francisco Symphony Comm. 1975; *Vita d'un Uomo,* for soprano, baritone, pianist, trombonist, narrator & orchestra 1982; *The Digital Domain,* for digitally recorded & synthesized stereo tape (Electra) 1983; *A Little Traveling Music,* a new version for piano in just intonation with digital audio disk playback (Wergo) 1988; *Dreaming Susanna,* for orchestra 1990; *Slow Blues in Five-Limit Tuning and Slow Blues in Seven-Limit Tuning,* for enhanced pianos, enhanced bass, enhanced sitar, drums 1992; *soft music HARD MUSIC '92* 1992; *Della Vita d'un Uomo,* for baritone & enhanced piano in just intonation, Thomas Buckner Comm. 1993. Recordings on Wergo, Electra, & CRI. Publishers: Editions Jobert & others. **Home Address:** 2995 Woodside Rd., No. 400, Woodside, CA 94062.

RUSSI, ANGELO BARTOLO ■ Italian Fulbright Fellow 1973-74.

RUTELLI, FRANCESCO ■ AAR Visitor 1994, Mayor of Rome.

RUTLAND GILLISON, LINDA W. ■ FAAR Classics/Archaeology 81. b. Jan. 26, 1948, Versailles, KY. m. James H. Gillison, III. c. Aulica Rutland, Robert Gillison, James H. Gillison, IV. BA 68, Univ. of Louisville; MA 71, Univ. of Minnesota; PhD 75, Univ. of Minnesota. **Other Study:** Ruprecht Karl Univ., Heidelberg 1971-73. **Research/Artistic Interests:** The urban parks (*horti*) of ancient Rome, their survival in the cityscape tradition, their appearance in & influence on Rome in the Renaissance. **Career & Employment:** Univ. of Washington, Asst. Prof. 1976-83; Northwestern Univ., Lect. 1990-91, Visiting Asst. Prof. 1991-92; Univ. of Montana, Missoula, Visiting Asst. Prof. 1992-present. **Memberships & Offices:** APA; CAMWS 1990-present; Classical Assn. of the Pacific Northwest 1976-83, 1992-present. **Fellowships, Honors & Awards:** Northwestern Univ., Faculty Honor Roll 1990-91. **Publications:** "Women as Makers of Kings in Tacitus' *Annals*," *Classical World* 72.1 (1978): 15-29; "*Fortuna sola invocatur*: Pliny's Statement," *Classical Bulletin* 56.2 (Dec. 1979): 28-31; "Irrationality in the Early Republic: Livy Editorializes," *Classical World* 72.2 (1979): 416-17; "*In hortum aedium, esbas de es arouran*: Consultation Scenes in Livy and Herodotus," *Eranos* 82 (1984): 199-203; "Hope Springs Eternal: Disaster in Thucydides," *Echos du Monde Classique/Classical Views* n.s. 3.1 (1984): 15-22; "*Institutio oratoria* 10.3.25: A Suggestion," *Rheinisches Museum für Philologie* n.f. 128.2 (1985): 191-94; "The Tacitean Germanicus: Suggestions for a Re-evaluation," *Rheinisches Museum für Philologie* n.f. 130.2 (1987): 153-64. **Business Address:** Dept. of Foreign Languages, Univ. of Montana, Missoula, MT 59812.

RUTLEDGE, HARRY ■ AAR Classical Soc., Pres. 1995.

RYBERG, INEZ GERTRUDE SCOTT ■ FAAR Classics/Archaeology 26; AAR Classical Society, Sec. b. Nov. 2, 1901, Grimes, IA. d. Sept. 15, 1980. m. Milton E. Ryberg. BA 21, Univ. of Minnesota; MA 21, Univ. of Minnesota; PhD 24, Univ. of Wisconsin. **Research/Artistic Interests:** Roman archaeology, art, & religion. **Career & Employment:** Wilson College, Instr. 1922-23; Smith College, Instr. 1926-27; Vassar College, Asst. Prof. 1927-37, Assc. Prof. 1937-42, Prof. 1942-65, Dept. Chair 1942-49, 1952-65. **Memberships & Offices:** APA, Pres. 1962; ArIA, Exec. Commissioner 1950-56; APS; VSA, BoT 1957-62, VP 1964. **Fellowships, Honors & Awards:** Guggenheim Fellowship 1960-61; Phi Beta Kappa. **Publications:** *The Grand Style in the Satires of Juvenal*, Smith College Classical Studies 8 (1927); "Early Roman Traditions in the Light of Archaeology," *Memoirs of the AAR* 7 (1929): 77-118; *An Archaeological Record of Rome, from the Seventh to the Second Centuries B.C.* (Philadelphia: Univ. of Pennsylvania Press, 1940); *Rites of the State Religion in Roman Art*, Memoirs of the AAR 22 (1955); "Vergil's Golden Age," *TAPA* 89 (1958): 112-31; *Panel Reliefs of Marcus Aurelius* (New York: ArIA, 1966). **Bio-Bibliography:** "Biographical Memoir," *APS Yearbook* (1983); Briggs, 550-51; *Who's Who of American Women*.

RYLAND, ROBERT KNIGHT ■ FAAR Painting 06. b. Feb. 10, 1873, Grenada, MS. d. Nov. 9, 1951. BA 1892, Bethel College. **Other Studies:** NAD & ASL 1894-1900. **Research/Artistic Interests:** Mural painting. **Career & Employment:** *Syracuse Herald*, Staff Artist 1898-1900; Tiffany Studios, Designer c.1906-7; Cooper Union, Instr. 1908-19; New York Evening School of Industrial Art, Instr. 1923-36. **Memberships & Offices:** NAD, Assc.; American Soc. of Mural Painters; Sigma Alpha Epsilon Club, Salmagundi Club. **Fellowships, Honors & Awards:** NAD, Altman Prize 1924; AIC, Hon. Mention 1926. **Important Works:** Murals: US Capitol Bldg; Municipal Bldg., NYC; *School Yard at 8:30*, Museum of Fine Arts, Syracuse; Washington Irving HS, NYC; State Supreme Court, NYC; Newark Museum. **Exhibitions/Performances:** NAD 1924; AIC 1926; Fifteen Gallery, NYC c.1948; Corcoran Gallery of Art; St. Louis Art Museum; Brooklyn Museum; Brooklyn Soc. of Artists; Salmagundi Club. **Bio-Bibliography:** *National Cyclopedia of American Biography*; *Who Was Who in America*.

■   ■   ■

S

SAARINEN, EERO ■ AAR Visitor 1951 — 1955, Architect.

SACCHETTI, GIULIO & GIOVANNA ■ AAR Italian Com. 1994-present.

SACKS, GLEN ■ FAAR Visual Arts 91. BFA 76, Philadelphia College of Art; MFA 90, Bard College. **Career & Employment:** Mt. Sinai Hospital, NYC, Art Program 1992-present; Visiting Artist: Pennsylvania State Univ. 1990, Temple Univ. in Rome 1992, Middlebury College 1993. **Fellowships, Honors & Awards:** Organization of Independent Artists Grant 1990; Artists Space Project Grant 1991; NEA-Arts Intl. Travel Grant 1993. **Exhibitions/Performances:** Kennedy Airport, NYC 1990; Blum Gallery, Annendale-on-Hudson, NYC 1990; Ex-Convent of San Domenico, Spoleto 1991; Fonti di Clitunno, Campello, Italy 1991; BACA Downtown, NYC (solo) 1991; Framart Studio Galleries, Milan 1992; Lehman College Art Gallery, NYC 1992; Four Walls, NYC 1992; Artists Space, NYC 1992, 1994; Jersey City Museum 1993. **Home Address:** 112 Franklin St., NYC 10013.

SADEK, GEORGE ■ AAR Visitor late 1970s and 1980s, Designer, Educator. b. Oct. 12, 1928. **Career & Employment:** Cooper Union, Prof.-Dean of the School of Art 1966-81; Center for Design & Typography, Dir. 1981-92; Lubalin Study Center, Dir. 1983-92. **Memberships & Offices:** CAA, Pres. 1976-78. **Important Works:** MMA; Library of Congress, Washington, DC; MOMA.

SAINT-GAUDENS, AUGUSTUS ■ AAR Charter Mem., Sculptor. b. Mar. 1, 1849, Dublin, Ireland. d. 1907. **Study:** École des Beaux Arts, Paris, 1867-70. **Career & Employment:** Studio: NYC 1873-85; Cornish, NH 1885-1907. **Selected Works:** *Adoration of the Cross*, St. Thomas Church, NYC; *Diana*, Madison Square Garden, NYC; *The Puritan; General Sherman; Amor Caritas*, Paris.

SALER, KAREN ■ FAAR Painting 68. b. Oct. 16, 1942, Philadelphia, PA. BFA 64, Philadelphia College of Art; MFA 66, Maryland Inst. College of Art. **Other Study:** Johns Hopkins Univ., Temple Univ. **Career & Employment:** Univ. of the Arts, Assc. Prof. **Fellowships, Honors & Awards:** Venture Fund Grant; American Scholars in Israel Grant. **Exhibitions/Performances:** Philadelphia Art Alliance; Gianetta Gallery; Woodmere Gallery; Univ. of the Arts. **Home Address:** 418 S. 26 St., Philadelphia, PA 19146. **Business Address:** Univ. of the Arts, Broad & Pine Sts., Philadelphia, PA 19102.

SALERNO, LUIGI ■ Italian Fulbright Fellow 1967-68.

SALISBURY, HARRISON ■ AAR Visitor 1988-89, Writer.

SALLER, RICHARD ■ NEH Summer Seminar Dir. 1991, Classicist.

SALZER, DONNA MARIE ■ FAAR History of Art 88. b. Feb. 13, 1951, Charlotte, NC. d. Oct. 31, 1992. BS 74, Univ. of Virginia School of Architecture; MA 85, Harvard Univ. **Other Studies:** Mary Washington College 1969-71; Cornell Univ., College of Architecture 1980-82. **Career & Employment:** Architects' Collaborative, Landscape Architect; Carol R. Johnson & Asscs., Landscape Architect; Halvorson Co., Landscape Ar-

chitect; Brown & Rowe, Landscape Architect; Boston Architectural Center, Instr. 1980; Herbert H. Johnson Museum, Asst. 1981-82; Univ. of Michigan, Asst. Prof. **Fellowships, Honors & Awards:** Alpha Phi Sigma Nat. Honorary Scholastic Fraternity 1972; Dumbarton Oaks Fellowship in Washington.

SALZMAN, MICHELE RENEE ■ FAAR Classics/Archaeology 87; Boston Univ. Representative to Adv. Council. b. Aug. 2, 1952, Brooklyn, NY. m. Steven G. Brint. c. Juliana Brint, Benjamin Brint. BA 73, Brooklyn College; MA 75, Bryn Mawr College; PhD 81, Bryn Mawr College. **Career & Employment:** Swarthmore College, Lect. 1980; Columbia Univ., Asst. Prof. 1980-82; Boston Univ., Asst. Prof. 1982-90, Assc. Prof. 1990-present. **Memberships & Offices:** Referee: *AJA, Classical Antiquity, Helios, Journal of Ancient History, TAPA*; Columbia Univ., NEH Summer Seminar, Consultant 1981; APA, Nat. Com. on Job Placement 1982-84; CANE, Com. for Publications 1986; APA; Assn. for Ancient Historians; Byzantine Studies Conference; New York Classical Club. **Fellowships, Honors & Awards:** Columbia Univ. Research Grant 1981, 1982; Boston Univ., Research Grant 1983, Humanities Found. Junior Fellow 1988-89; ACLS Research Fellowship 1983, Travel Grant 1990; APS Research Grant 1983; Richard Krautheimer Fellowship 1987; Yale Univ., Visiting Fellow 1990-91; UCLA, Visiting Scholar 1993. **Publications:** "New Evidence for the Dating of the Calendar at Santa Maria Maggiore in Rome," *TAPA* 111 (1981): 215-27; "Cicero, the Megalenses, and the Defense of Caelius," *American Journal of Philology* 103 (1983): 299-304; "Magna Mater: Great Mother of the Roman Empire," in *The Book of the Goddess: Past and Present*, ed. C. Olson (New York, 1983), 60-68; "The Representation of April and the Calendar of 354," *AJA* 88 (1984): 43-50; "*Superstitio* in the Codex Theodosianus and the Persecution of Pagans," *Vigiliae Christianae* 41 (1987): 172-88; with Steven Brint, "Reflections on Political Space: The Roman Forum and Capitol Hill, Washington D.C.," *Places* (Mar. 1988): 1-15; "Reflections on Symmachus' Idea of Tradition," *Historia* 38.3 (1989): 348-64; "Aristocratic Women: Conductors of Christianity in the Fourth Century?," *Helios* 16.2 (1989): 207-20; *On Roman Time: The Codex-Calendar of 354 and the Rhythms of Urban Life in Late Antiquity* (Berkeley: UC Press, 1990); "How the West Was Won: The Christianization of the Roman Aristocracy in the West in the Years after Constantine," *Studies in Latin Literature and Roman History* 6, ed. Carl Deroux, *Latomus* 217 (1992): 451-79; "The Evidence for Conversion in Book 16 of the Theodosian Code," *Historia* 42.3 (1993): 362-78; "The Calendar of 354," "The Vatican Vergil," in *Historical Dictionary of Classical Archaeology* (Westport, CT: Greenwood Press, forthcoming). **Home Address:** 76 Parkman St., Apt. 1, Brookline, MA 02146. **Business Address:** Dept. of Classical Studies, Boston Univ., 745 Commonwealth Ave., Boston, MA 02215.

SAMUELS, DANNY M. ■ FAAR Architecture 86. b. Jan. 19, 1947, Memphis, TN. BA 69, Rice Univ.; BArch 71, Rice Univ. **Career & Employment:** Taft Architects, Part. 1972-present; Rice Univ., School of Architecture, Prof. 1973-present, Dir. 1993-present; Yale Univ., Davenport Chair Prof. 1984. **Fellowships, Honors & Awards:** with partners, AIA Honor Awards 1981, 1982, 1983, local & state chapters over 50 honor awards since 1975, Fellow 1991; Venice Biennale 1980; Graham Found. Fellowship 1985-86. **Important Works:** Hendley Bldg., Galveston 1977-79; Municipal Control Bldg., Quail Valley 1978-79; YWCA Masterson Branch & Office Bldg., Houston 1979-81; Talbot House, Nevis 1980-81; River Crest Country Club, Fort Worth 1981-84; Water Resources Bldg., The Woodlands 1982-85; Corpus Christi City Hall 1984-88; Hope Elementary School, TX 1986-88; Olson House, Nevis 1987-88; Rothwell House, Houston 1988-93; Lycée Technique Bernard Palissy, Saintes, France 1990-94; Penn-Plax Assembly Plant, Saintes, France 1991; Rice School, Houston 1991-94; Tribune & Educational Bldg., Sogndal, Norway 1992-94. **Bio-Bibliography:** ed., Charles Jencks, *Post Modern Classicism* (London: Academy Editions, 1980); Venice Biennale, *Architecture 1980: The Presence of the Past* (New York: Rizzoli, 1980); Charles Jencks, *Architecture Today* (New York: Abrams, 1982); E. McCoy & B. Goldstein, *Guide to US Architecture: 1940-1980* (Santa Monica: A + A Press, 1982); Paolo Portoghesi, *After Modern Architecture* (New York: Rizzoli, 1982); ed., Charles Jencks, *Abstract Representation* (London: Academy Editions, 1983); Robert Jensen & Patricia Conway, *Ornamentalism* (New York: Potter, 1983); *101 Contemporary Architects in the World* (Tokyo: Kajima Publishers, 1985); Architectural League, *Emerging Voices: A New Generation of Architects in America* (New York: Princeton Architectural Press, 1986); Charles Jencks, *Post-Modernism* (New York: Rizzoli, 1987); ed., Stanley Tigerman, *The Chicago Tapes* (New York: Rizzoli, 1987); Robert A.M. Stern, *Post-Modern Classicism* (New York: Rizzoli, 1988); Sylvia Hart Wright, *Sourcebook of Contemporary North American Architecture* (New York: Van Nostrand, 1989); Roberto Masiero, *Neoclassico* (Venice: Marsilio Editori, 1990); ed., Stephen Fox, *Houston Architectural Guide* (Houston: Houston AIA-Herring Press, 1990); *Architecture Address Book* (New York: Rizzoli, 1992); Sydney LeBlanc, *20th Century American Architecture* (New York: Whitney Library of Design, 1993); Ben E. Graves, *School Ways* (New York: McGraw Hill, 1993). **Home Address:** 361A Montrose Blvd., No. 1105, Houston, TX 77006. **Business Address:** Taft Architects, 807 Peden, Houston, TX 77006.

SANDERS, HENRY ARTHUR ■ AAR School of Classical Studies, Prof.-in-Charge 1915-16, 1928-31.

SANDERS, ROBERT LEVINE ■ FAAR Musical Composition 29. b. July 2, 1906, Chicago, IL. d. Dec. 26, 1974. m. Marie Hiebl. c. Timothy Bosworth, Barrett. BMus 24, Bush Conservatory; MusM 25, Bush Conservatory; MusD 39, Chicago Conservatory. **Other Studies:** Accademia Conservatorio Santa Cecilia, Rome. **Career & Employment:** North Shore Univ., Organist & Choir Dir.; Chicago Conservatory, Faculty 1929-38; Meadville Theological School, Instr. 1930-38; First Unitarian Church, Organist & Musical Dir. 1930-38; Chicago Civic Orchestra, Asst. Conductor 1933-36; Univ. of Chicago, Instr. 1937-38; School of Music at Indiana Univ., Dean 1938-47; Brooklyn College, Prof. 1947-72, Chair 1947-54; Port Singers, Port Washington, NY, Conductor 1952-54. **Fellowships, Honors & Awards:** New York Philharmonic Symphony Soc. Prize; Guggenheim Fellow 1954-55. **Publications:** co-ed., *Hymns of the Spirit*; contr., *Hymns for the Celebration of Life* (1964). **Important Works:** *Piano Trio* 1926; *Saturday Night* 1933; *Scenes of Poverty and Toil*, for orchestra 1934-35; *Violin Concerto* 1936; *Little Symphonies* 1936-37, 1953, 1963; *The Mystic Trumpeter*, for narrator, baritone, chorus & orchestra 1939-41; *Brass Quintet* 1942; *Symphony for Concert Band* 1942-43; *L'Ag'ya*, a ballet 1943; *Brass Quartet* 1949; *Brass Trio* 1958; *Song of Myself*, for reciter, soprano, chorus, brass & percussion 1966-70. **Bio-Bibliography:** *Baker's Biographical Dictionary of American Musicians, New Grove Dictionary of American Music, Who Was Who in America*.

SANFELICE DI MONTEFORTE, MARCHESE & MARCHESA ■ AAR Visitors 1990-91, Owners, Cosa.

SANFORD, EVA M. ■ Whitney Fellow 1923-24.

SANTANGELO, MARIA ■ Italian Fulbright Fellow 1951-52.

SANTEE, FREDERICK LAMOTTE ■ FAAR Classics/Archaeology 27. b. Sept. 17, 1906, Wapwallopen, PA. BA 24, Harvard Univ. **Other Studies:** Wadham College, Oxford Univ. **Career & Employment:** Vanderbilt Univ., Faculty; Kenyon College, Assc. Prof. **Fellowships, Honors & Awards:** Harvard Univ., Sheldon Traveling Fellowship.

SARGENT, JOHN T. ■ AAR Trustee 1980-present, Treas. 1987, Sec. 1995-present; AAR Pres. 1988. **Studies:** Harvard Univ. **Career & Employment:** Air Transport Command, WW II; Doubleday & Co., Copywriter – Chair. **Memberships & Offices:** Amer. Assn. of Publishers, Officer; Intl. Publishers Assn., VP; US Information Agency, Private Sector Book & Library Com., Chair; Atlantic Mutual Insurance Co., Dir.; River Bank of America, Dir.; Alger Fund, Dir.; New York Public Library, BoT; American Acad. of Poets, BoT; Freedom Inst., BoT; New York Zoological Assn., Adv.

SARTOGO, PIERO ■ AAR Visitor 1977-78, Architect.

SAUNDERS, RAYMOND ■ FAAR Painting 66. b. Oct. 28, 1934, Pittsburgh, PA. BFA 60, Carnegie Inst. of Technology; MFA 61, California College of Arts & Crafts. **Other Studies:** PAFA 1953-57. **Fellowships, Honors & Awards:** PAFA, Awards-1st Prizes 1953-57, Catherine Grant Memorial Prize, Thomas Eakins Prize, Thouron Oil Painting Prize, Cresson European Travel Scholarship 1956; 80th San Francisco Art Annual, Schwabacher-Frey Award 1961. **Exhibitions/Performances:** Pittsburgh Playhouse Invitational 1961; PAFA 1962, 1963; School for Social Research, NYC 1963; Terry Dintenfass Gallery, NYC 1964, 1962, 1969; Stephen Wirtz Gallery, San Francisco 1983, 1988.

SAVAGE, EUGENE FRANCIS ■ FAAR Painting 15; AAR Trustee 1928-47. b. Mar. 29, 1883, Covington, IN. d. Oct. 19, 1978. m. Matilda M. Freitag. c. Dorothy Ann Crawford. BFA 24, Yale Univ.; MA 27, Yale Univ.; DFA 63, Univ. of Hartford. **Other Studies:** AIC; Chicago Acad. of Fine Arts; Corcoran Art Gallery; Reynolds & Henderson. **Research/Artistic Interests:** Figure, portrait, mural & landscape painter. **Career & Employment:** Yale Univ., William Leffingwell Prof. 1923-58. **Memberships & Offices:** US Commissioner of Fine Arts, 1933-41; NAD, BoT; Nat. Soc. of Mural Painters. **Fellowships, Honors & Awards:** ALNY Medal of Honor 1921; AIC, W.M.R. French Memorial Gold Medal 1921; Norman Waite Harris Silver Medal & Prize 1922; NAD, Saltus Medal of Merit & T.B. Clark Prize 1923; 2d Altman Prize 1924; All-American Biannual, Chicago, Frank G. Logan 1st Prize & Medal 1924; John C. Shaffer Prize 1925; Centennial Medal Artists Fellowship 1968; American Sculpture Soc., Diamond Jubilee Medal 1969. **Publications:** "On Art Education," *American Magazine of Art* (Sept. 1929). **Important Works:** Bailey Memorial Fountain, Grand Army Plaza, Brooklyn; collections: Elks Nat. Memorial HQ, Chicago; First Nat. City Bank, NYC; Los Angeles Museum of Art; State Museum of Nebraska; Herron Art Inst.; Oshkosh Fine Arts Museum, WI; Sterling Library, Yale Univ.; South Hall, Columbia Univ.; Centennial Hall of Texas, Dallas; USPO Bldg., Washington, DC; Communications Bldg. & US Government Bldg, NY Worlds Fair; Pennsylvania Treasury, Harrisburg; Courthouse, Covington, IN; Home State Tabernacle, Honolulu; NY State Court of Appeals, Albany;

Foyer Memorial Center, Purdue Univ.; US Memorial, Epinal, France. **Exhibitions/Performances:** ALNY 1921; AIC 1922, 1924; NAD 1922, 1924; Grand Central Gallery 1929; Ferargil Gallery, NYC 1945; Mattatuck Museum, Waterbury, CT 1966. **Bio-Bibliography:** "Our Famous Neighbors," *New Rochelle Standard* (May 20, 1931); *Encyclopedia of American Artists; Who Was Who in America; Who Was Who in American Art.*

SAVAGE, SUSAN MAY ■ FAAR Classics/Archaeology 38. b. Nov. 11, 1911, Mt. Holly, NJ. dec. BA 33, Bryn Mawr College; MA 34, Bryn Mawr College; PhD 40, Bryn Mawr College. **Other Studies:** Univ. of Pennsylvania 1935-36. **Research/Artistic Interests:** Topography, numismatics, history of Janiculum. **Career & Employment:** Rockford College, Prof. 1943-46; Univ. of Pennsylvania Press, Ed., after 1946. **Fellowships, Honors & Awards:** Univ. of Pennsylvania, Bennett Fellow 1935-36. **Publications:** "The Cults of Ancient Trastevere," *Memoirs of the AAR* 17 (1940): 26-56; *"Remotum a Notitia Vulgari,"* TAPA 76 (1945): 157-65.

SAWARD, SUSAN VIRGINIA ■ FAAR History of Art 71. b. Oct. 27, 1942, Boston, MA. m. Ronald Filson. c. Timothy, Lily. BA 64, Sarah Lawrence College; MA 68, Bryn Mawr College; PhD 73, Bryn Mawr College. **Career & Employment:** Newcomb College, Tulane Univ., Faculty. **Fellowships, Honors & Awards:** Bryn Mawr College, Samuel H. Kress Fellowship 1968-69. **Publications:** *The Golden Age of Marie De' Medici* (Ann Arbor: Univ. of Michigan Press).

SAWYER, JOHN ■ AAR Visitor 1982-83; Mellon Found., Pres.

SAWYER, MARGO L. ■ FAAR Sculpture 87. b. May 6, 1958, Washington, DC. BA 80, Chelsea School of Art; MFA 82, Yale Univ. **Other Studies:** Skowhegan School of Painting & Sculpture 1980. **Career & Employment:** Chelsea School of Art, London, Visiting Artist 1982; Sir J.J. School of Art, Bombay, India, Visiting Artist 1982-83; Baroda School of Art, Gujarat, India, Visiting Artist 1983; West Surrey College of Art & Design, England, Visiting Artist 1983; School of Visual Arts, Visiting Artist 1983; Yale Univ., Visiting Artist 1985. **Fellowships, Honors & Awards:** Ford Found. Travel Grant 1981; Fulbright Fellowship 1982-83. **Exhibitions/Performances:** Solo: British Council, Bombay, India 1983; Group: Hyde Park, London 1978; Whitechapel Gallery, London 1979; I.C.A. London 1979, 1980; Courtyard, Hong Ning Apartments, NYC 1986. **Bio-Bibliography:** Mick Brown, "Dead Trees Become Something to Enjoy," *London Sunday Times* (May 28, 1978); Peter Rippon, "On Making It; CAA & ICA," *Artscribe* 17 (1979); Stuart Morgan, "New Contemporaries," *Artscribe* (1980); Lakshmi Lal, "Beginning and End," *Sunday Times of India* (Apr. 1983).

SCALFERO, LUIGI ■ AAR Visitor 1994, President of Italy.

SCARAVAGLIONE, CONCETTA MARIA ■ FAAR Sculpture 50. b. July 9, 1900, NYC. d. Sept. 6, 1975. **Study:** NAD; ASL 1952-67. **Career & Employment:** Sarah Lawrence College 1925-47; Vassar College, Prof. 1952-67; Masters Inst., NYC; Black Mountain College. **Memberships & Offices:** Nat. Assn. of Women Painters & Sculptors; Salons of America; NSS; AAAL. **Fellowships, Honors & Awards:** PAFA, Widener Gold Medal; NAD, Bronze Medal & Silver Medal. **Important Works:** MOMA; Whitney Museum, NYC; PAFA. **Exhibitions/Performances:** MOMA; AIC; Fairmont Park, Philadelphia; NY World's Fair 1939; Virginia Museum of Fine Arts 1941; NY World's Fair 1964; Vassar College; Dartmouth College; Univ.

of Colorado. **Bio-Bibliography:** *The Sculpture of Concetta Scaravaglione,* exb. cat. (Richmond, VA: Virginia Museum of Fine Arts, 1941); Ralph M. Pearson, *The Modern Renaissance in American Art* (New York: Harper & Brothers, 1954); *Seven American Women: The Depression Decade,* exb. cat. (Poughkeepsie, NY: Vassar College Art Gallery, 1976); *Dictionary of Painters, Sculptors and Engravers; National Cyclopedia of American Biography; Who's Who in American Art.*

SCARPITTA, SALVATORE ■ GI Resident 1945-47, Painter.

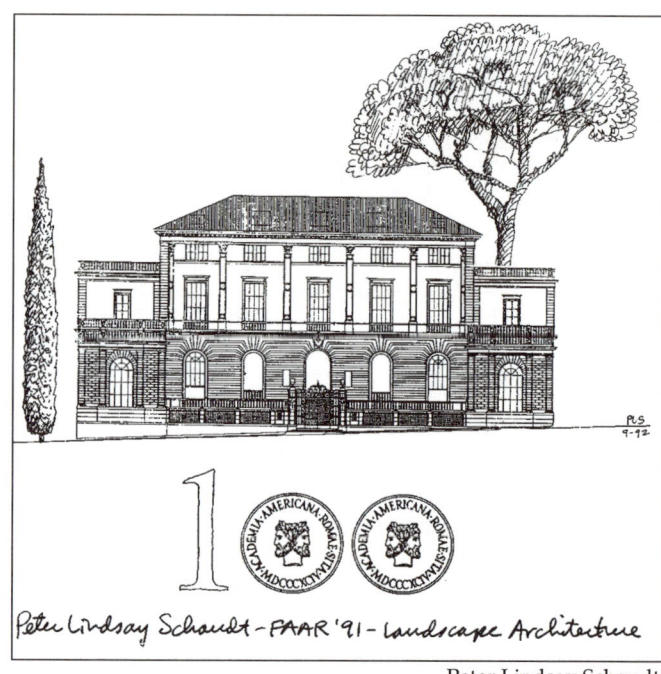

Peter Lindsay Schaudt - FAAR '91 - Landscape Architecture

Peter Lindsay Schaudt

SCHAUDT, PETER LINDSAY ■ FAAR Landscape Architecture 91. b. May 10, 1959, LaGrange, IL. m. Janet L. Bratschun. c. Elaine Schaudt, Elliot Schaudt. BArch 82, Univ. of Illinois at Chicago; MLA 84, Harvard GSD. **Career & Employment:** Office of Dan Kiley, Assc. Landscape Architect 1984-87; Clark Tribble Harris & Li Architects, Dir. of Landscape Architecture 1987-90; Peter Lindsay Schaudt Landscape Architecture, Prin.-Owner 1991-present. **Memberships & Offices:** ASLA 1988-present; Morton Arboretum 1991-present; Chicago Architectural Club, BoT 1994-present. **Fellowships, Honors & Awards:** Vietnam Veterans Memorial Nat. Design Competition, Meritorious Design Award 1981; Copley Sq. Nat. Design Competition, 2d Place Award 1984; Kent State May 4 Memorial Nat. Design Competition, 3d Place Award 1986; Innovations in Housing Nat. Design Competition, Citation of Merit Award 1986; Graham Found. Grant 1991. **Important Works:** with Office of Dan Kiley, NCNB Plaza Florida HQ, Tampa 1986; with Clark Tribble Harris & Li Architects, "Tapis Vert" Gateway Center, Charlotte, NC 1989; Spartan Food Systems Corp. HQ Plaza, Spartanburg, SC 1990; Carolinas NFL Stadium, Charlotte, NC 1991; St. Meinrad Monastery Master Plan, St. Meinrad, IN 1992; Chicago Historic Blvds. Master Plan 1992; Manilow Residence, Chicago 1992; Belmont Univ. Master Plan, Nashville 1994; Prairie Crossing, Grayslake, IL 1994. **Exhibitions/Performances:** Vietnam Veterans Memorial Nat. Design Exb., Washington, DC 1981; Kent State May 4 Memorial Design Exb. 1986. **Bio-Bibliography:** Heidi

Landecker, "Rome Prize Winner," *Landscape Architecture* (July 1990): 18. **Business Address:** Peter Lindsay Schaudt Landscape Architecture, 410 S. Michigan Ave., Suite 612, Chicago, IL 60605.

SCHERMERHORN, F. AUGUSTUS ■ AAR Charter Mem.

SCHIFF, JEFFREY A. ■ FAAR Sculpture 77. b. Aug. 23, 1952, Rolla, ND. m. Blair J. Tate. c. Walker Schiff, Clayton Schiff. BA 74, Brown Univ.; MFA 76, Univ. of Massachusetts, Amherst. **Career & Employment:** Wesleyan Univ., Assc. Prof. 1987-present. **Fellowships, Honors & Awards:** Massachusetts Artist Found. Fellowship 1975, 1980, 1985; NEA Fellowship 1976, 1979, 1984; Boston-Kyoto Sister City Traveling Grant 1984. **Important Works:** Commissions: Inst. of Contemporary Art, Boston 1983; Liberty Sq., Market Center Intersection, Baltimore 1985-present; Thomson Sq., Charleston, MA 1986-95; South Station Railroad Terminal, Boston 1990-95; Public Collections: Williams College Museum of Art; San Diego Museum of Contemporary Art; Rose Art Museum, Brandeis Univ. **Exhibitions/Performances:** Solo: Stux Gallery, NYC 1986; San Diego Museum of Contemporary Art 1987; Williams College Museum of Art, Williamstown, MA 1988; Wesleyan Univ., Zilkha Gallery, Middletown, CT 1989; Sculpture Center, NYC 1992; Selected Group: Inst. of Contemporary Art, Boston 1979; Washington Project for the Arts, DC 1980; Hayden Gallery, MIT 1983; Rose Art Museum, Brandeis Univ. 1986; Atlanta Arts Festival 1986; Snug Harbor Sculpture Festival, NYC 1991. **Home Address:** 209 Clinton St., Apt. 2R, Brooklyn, NY 11201.

SCHLITT, MELINDA WILCOX ■ FAAR History of Art 86. b. 1959, Norfolk, VA. BA 81, SUNY, Purchase; Dipl. 82, Greek & Latin Inst., Brooklyn College; MA 83, Johns Hopkins Univ.; PhD 91, Johns Hopkins Univ. **Career & Employment:** Loyola Univ., Rome, Instr. 1985; Bates College, Instr. 1987-89; Bates College Museum of Art, Acting Dir. 1989-90; Dickinson College, Asst. Prof. 1990-present. **Fellowships, Honors & Awards:** Johns Hopkins Graduate Fellowships 1982, 1983, 1984; Fulbright Fellowship 1984; Getty Fellowship 1986-87; Dickinson College Grants 1991, 1993. **Publications:** "The Patronage of Style: Francesco Salvati's Frescos of 'Camillus' and Cosimo I de' Medici," in *The Search for a Patron in the Middle Ages and Renaissance*, ed. David Wilkins (1995): 159-79. **Business Address:** Dept. of Fine Arts, Dickinson College, Carlisle, PA 17013.

SCHMELING, GARETH L. ■ FAAR Classics/Archaeology 78; AAR Trustee 1984-87, Trustee Emer.; Juror 1981; SOF, VP 1980-83. b. May 28, 1940, Algoma, WI. m. Karen Weiss. BA 63, Northwestern College; MA 64, Univ. of Wisconsin; PhD 68, Univ. of Wisconsin. **Research/Artistic Interests:** Ancient novel, literary criticism, textual criticism. **Career & Employment:** Univ. of Virginia, Asst. Prof. 1968-70; Univ. of Florida, Assc. Prof. 1970-75, Prof. 1975-present; Univ. of Colorado, Visiting Prof. 1992. **Memberships & Offices:** CAMWS, Sec.-Treas. 1975-81, Pres. 1985-86; Petronian Soc. Newsletter, Ed. 1970-present. **Fellowships, Honors & Awards:** APS Grant 1970, 1971, 1972, 1977, 1978, 1984, 1985; NEH Fellowship 1973-74; ACLS Fellowship 1974; CAMWS Ovatio 1981. **Publications:** "Pythagorean Element of the Subterranean Basilica at the Porta Maggiore," *Latomus* 28 (1969): 1071-73; "Trimalchio's Menu & Wine List," *Classical Philology* 65 (1970): 248-51; *Cornelius Nepos: Lives of Famous Men* (Lawrence: Coronado, 1971); "The *Exclusus Amator* Motif in Petronius," in *Fons Perennius* (Torino: Baccola & Gili, 1971), 333-57; *Chariton* (New York: Twayne, 1974); "T.S. Eliot & Petronius," *Comparative*

Literature Studies 12 (1975): 393-410; *A Bibliography of Petronius* (Leiden: Brill, 1977); *Xenophon of Ephesus* (Boston: Twayne, 1980); *Historia Apollonii Regis Tyri* (Leipzig: Teubner, 1989); "Manners and Morality in the *Historia Apollonii*," in *Piccolo mondo antico*, ed. A. Scarcella (Perugia: Università di Perugia, 1989), 197-215; "The *Satyricon*: The Sense of an Ending," *Rheinisches Museum* 134 (1991): 352-77; "Apollonius of Tyre: The Last of the Troublesome Latin Novels," *Aufstieg & Niedergang der Römischen Welt* II 34.4 (Berlin: Walter de Gruyter, 1995), 864-90. **Bio-Bibliography:** *Contemporary Authors; Directory of American Scholars; Who's Who in America.* **Business Address:** Dept. of Classics, Univ. of Florida, Gainesville, FL 32611.

SCHMIDT, BENNO, JR ■ AAR Visitor 1992-93; Yale Univ., Pres.

SCHMIDT, EDWARD W. ■ FAAR Painting 83. b. Apr. 14, 1946, Ann Arbor, MI. m. Cheryl Ginenthal. BFA 71, Pratt Inst.; MFA 74, Brooklyn College. **Other Study:** ASL, with Robert Beverly Hale 1966-71; Skowhegan School of Painting 1967; École des Beaux Arts, Paris 1967-68; printmaking with S.W. Hayter, Atelier 17, Paris 1978. **Career & Employment:** Suffolk County Community College, Instr. 1973-79; Catholic Univ., Instr. 1979-80; New York Acad. of Art, Assc. Prof. 1982-present; Queens College, Instr. 1982; ASL, Instr. 1984. **Fellowships, Honors & Awards:** Greenshields Found. Grant 1972; Ingram Merrill Found. Grant 1984; NEA Grant 1985; San Francisco Museum of Modern Art, Clos Pegase Competition Winner 1985; Gottlieb Found. Grant 1994. **Important Works:** Bayley Museum of Art, Univ. of Virginia, Charlottesville; NAD; Elizabeth Greenshields Memorial Found., Montreal; Crown American Corp., Johnstown, PA. **Exhibitions/Performances:** Solo: Salve Regina Gallery, Catholic Univ. 1980; Bayley Museum, Univ. of Virginia 1980; Robert Schoelkopf Gallery, NYC 1982; Brooklyn College of Art 1988; Suffolk Community College, Brentwood, NY 1990; Stiebel Modern, NYC 1992; Contemporary Realist Gallery, San Francisco 1993, 1995; Group: Le Salon Nat. des Beaux Arts, Paris 1968; Robert

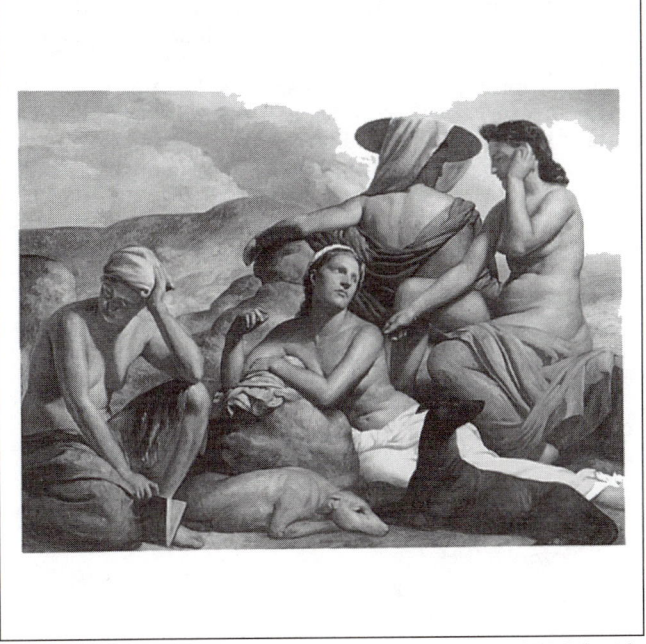

Edward W. Schmidt

Schoelkopf Gallery, NYC 1982, 1987; Museum of Modern Art, San Francisco 1985; Carl Solway Gallery, Cincinnati 1986; Centre Georges Pompidou, Paris 1988. **Bio-Bibliography:** George M. Tapley, Jr., "The Arcadian Ethos in Contemporary Painting," *Arts Magazine* (Feb. 1983); Martin Filler, *Art & Architecture & Landscape*, exb. cat. (San Francisco: San Francisco Museum of Modern Art, 1985); Edward Lucie-Smith, *American Art Now* (New York: William Morrow, 1985); Patricia Phillips, "Figure in Architecture: Michael Graves, Edward Schmidt," *Artforum* (Mar. 1986); Charles Jencks, *Post-Modernism* (London: Academy Editions, 1987); Caroline Cass, *Grand Illusions: Contemporary Interior Murals* (London: Phaidon, 1989); Thomas Wolfe, "The New Radicals in the Fine Arts," *American Arts Quarterly* (Fall 1990); John Hollander, *The Italian Tradition in Contemporary Landscape Painting 1960-1990*, exb. cat. (Charleston, SC: Gibbs Museum, 1990); Thomas Bolt, *New American Figure Painting*, exb. cat. (San Francisco: Contemporary Realist Gallery, 1992); Karen Stanger, "Edward Schmidt: Images of Arcadia," *American Artist* (Dec. 1993); Mark Helprin, "In Appreciation of Edward Schmidt," *The Classicist* (1994); *Who's Who in American Art.* **Home Address:** 79 Circuit Rd., Tuxedo Park, NY 10987. **Business Address:** New York Acad. of Arts, 111 Franklin St., NYC 10013.

SCHMIT, MARIAN A. ■ AAR Classical Soc., Pres. 1967.

SCHMITT, PETER MILLER ■ FAAR Architecture 72. b. Apr. 19, 1942, Washington, DC. m. Lydia R. Hancock. c. Emily Schmitt, Samuel Schmitt, Patrick Schmitt, John Schmitt. BA 64, Georgetown Univ.; MArch 70, Yale Univ. **Research/Artistic Interests:** Research into law & order for the Lord Chancellor's Dept. (UK Judiciary) including critical appraisal of Design Guides & Standards for Crown & County Courts (criminal & civil courts) & for Magistrate Courts, & produced the design & specification for an idealized County Court bldg. with Probation Service. **Career & Employment:** Howell Killick Partridge & Amis, Chartered Architects 1972-92; Marlborough College 1988-93; Univ. of Brighton 1993-present; Univ. of London 1993-94; Royal Acad. of Arts, Surveyor 1994-present. **Memberships & Offices:** Royal Inst. of British Architects 1979-present. **Fellowships, Honors & Awards:** Government of Trinidad & Tobago, Hall of Justice Competition Winner 1978; Civic Trust Commendation 1981; Royal Fine Art Comm. Approval, for Courthouse 1985. **Publications:** "The Lost Staircase," *Royal Academy Magazine* (Autumn 1994). **Important Works:** Middlesex Polytechnic Faculty of Art & Design, Enfield 1972-79; Medway Magistrates' Court, Chatham, Kent 1975-80; Hall of Justice, Trinidad 1978-85; Finsbury Leisure Center Squash Courts, Islington 1983-87; Warrington Crown & County Courthouse, Cheshire 1985-92; Japanese

Peter Miller Schmitt

Univ. College, Univ. of Kent, Canterbury 1989-92. **Exhibitions/Performances:** Heinz Gallery, London 1982. **Home Address:** 12 Lydon Rd., Clapham Old Town, London, SW4 0HW England.

SCHNACKE, MAHLON K. ■ AAR Librarian 1933-38.

SCHNACKENBERG, GJERTRUD C. ■ FAAR Literature 84. b. Aug. 27, 1953, Tacoma, WA. m. Robert Nozick. BA 75, Mt. Holyoke College. **Fellowships, Honors & Awards:** Radcliffe College, Bunting Fellowship 1979; Mt. Holyoke, Hon. LLD 1985; NEA Fellowship 1986; Guggenheim Found. Fellowship 1987; Brandeis Univ., Creative Arts Awards Citation 1989; Literary Lion, New York Public Library 1993. **Publications:** *Portraits and Elegies* (Boston: Godine, 1982); *The Lamplit Answer* (New York: Farrar, Straus, Giroux, 1985); *A Gilded Lapse of Time* (New York: Farrar, Straus, Giroux, 1992). **Bio-Bibliography:** Glyn Maxwell, *Contemporary Poets; Dictionary of Literary Biography; Who's Who in America; World Authors, 1985-90.*

SCHNADELBACH, R. TERRY ■ FAAR Landscape Architecture 66. b. Jan. 29, 1939, New Orleans, LA. m. Maxine B. Lepp. c. Erin Schnadelbach, John Lepp, Pier Schnadelbach. BArch 62, Louisiana State Univ.; MLA 64, Harvard GSD. **Career & Employment:** Philadelphia City Planning Comm., Planning Trainee 1961; Boston Redevelopment Authority, Architect & Urban Designer 1962-64; Schnadelbach & Asscs., Landscape Architects, Part. 1963-65; NASA, Marshall Space Flight Center, Urban Designer 1964; Alexander E. Rattray, Landscape Architect, Project Dir. 1966-68; David A. Crane, Architect, Landscape Architect 1967-69; Schnadelbach Asscs., Founder & Prin. 1968-present. **Memberships & Offices:** AIA, Assc. Mem.; Nat. Assn. for Olmsted Parks; ASLA 1971-present; Niagara Falls Civic Center, NY Juror 1972; AIA RUDAT, Macon, GA, CBD Renewal, Panelist 1973; Harvard GSD, Alumni Council, Treas. 1976, Mem. 1992; AIA RUDAT, Birmingham, AL, Five Inner-City Neighborhoods, Panelist 1978; AIA RUDAT, Healdsburg, CA, wine country tourist center development, Chair 1981; Carscape Competition, Columbus, IN, Juror 1985; Buffalo Bayou Competition, Houston, Chair 1987; Prix de Paris, NIAE, Juror 1988; Urban Land Inst., Ft. Wayne, IN, Panelist 1990; Inst. de Management Hotelier Intl., Cergy-Pontoise, Val d'Oise, France, Panelist 1990; Urban Land Inst. 1990-present; Real Estate Bd. of NYC, Landscape Design Com. 1991; Urban Land Inst., Los Angeles, Panelist 1992; *Garden Design Magazine*, Juror 1993; Urban Land Inst., Krakow, Poland, Panelist; Republic of Slovenia, Design of Nations Highways, Panelist. **Fellowships, Honors & Awards:** City Club of NY, Bard Award 1971; NY State Architects Assn., Award of Merit 1974; HUD Urban Design Award 1976; *Urban Design Magazine* Award 1978; American Steel Inst. Award 1983; Nat. Assn. of Home Builders, Inst. of Residential Marketing Award 1989; Parks Council, NYC, Philip N. Winslow Landscape Design Award 1991. **Publications:** "Fairmont Park: Philadelphia's Largest Asset," *The Green Scene* (Nov. 1973); with Kathleen Kelly, *Landscaping the Saudi Arabian Desert* (Philadelphia: Delancey Press, 1975); with Kathleen Kelly, "Dry Prospects in Saudi Arabia: Desert Ecology," *Landscape Architecture* (Oct. 1975); "Parks that Pay for Themselves," *Urban Land* (July 1991): 21-24; "Washington, Pennsylvania Avenue: Grand-Rue à l'Americaine," *Urbanismes & Architecture* 252 (Nov. 1991): 82-83. **Important Works:** USTA Nat. Tennis Center, Flushing Meadows Park, Queens, NYC 1976; Bausch & Lomb HQ, Rochester, NY 1992; Quai de Saone Waterfront Park, Lyons, France 1992; A8 Bis Autoroute Environmental &

Landscape Study Section Siagne-Var 1992; A1 & A25 Autoroute Connections to Centre Ville, Lille, France 1992; Antiker Archaeology Park, Cambodia 1994; Place Charles Hornu, Villeurbourg, France 1993; Brooklyn Bridge Park, Brooklyn, NYC 1994. Competitions: Copley Sq., Boston 1984; Nelson-Atkins Museum, Henry Moore Collection, Kansas City, MO 1985; Centre Thomson, Gennevilliers, France 1986; Auto Route de Soleil, Lyons, France 1989; ZAC Industrielle, St. Denis, Paris 1989; Plaine de l'Est Regional Plan, Lyons, France 1990; "La Nautile" Oceanographic Museum, Calais, France 1990. **Exhibitions/Performances:** ASLA Centennial Nat. Traveling Exb. 1964; MFA 1967; MOMA 1973; Whitney Museum, NYC 1973; Nelson-Atkins Museum, Kansas City, MO 1986; Urban Center, NYC 1990. **Bio-Bibliography:** J. Ritchie Smith, Jr., "Ain't That Beautiful," *Landscape Architecture* (May 1983): 50; "Tony Garnier Nous Viola!," *Le Progres Daily* (Dec. 21, 1988): 1, 5; "L'Invention d'un Site," *Techniques et Architecture* (Jan. 1989): 128-37; "Contemporary French Architecture: Big Projects in Paris," *Space Design* (Aug. 1989): 54-55; "La Nobile Arte del Riusso," *Spazio & Società* (Sept. 1990): 47-49; Philip Langdon, "In Pursuit of Affordability," *Landscape Architecture* (Apr. 1991): 42-47; Karen Tetlow, "En France," *Landscape Architecture* (Aug. 1991): 22, 47-51; Eve Kahn, "Riverscape Reshaped," *Garden Design* (July-Aug. 1992); Bert McClure, "Concours Interne," *Urbanisme & Architecture* (Aug. 1992); Eve Kahn, "Global Landscape: Sunday in the Corporate Park," *Landscape Architecture* (Aug. 1993): 33; Pierre Clement, "La Voirie Support de Projet Du Batia la a Ville," *Reflexions et Enjeux* (May 1993): 102-7. **Home Address:** 139 W. 19 St., NYC 10011. **Business Address:** The Schnadelbach Partnership, 5 W. 19 St., NYC 10011.

SCHREIBER, EARL GEORGE ■ FAAR Post-Classical/ Humanistic Studies 77; SOF, Bd. 1980-82. b. May 20, 1944, San Francisco. d. May 12, 1993. CA. BA 65, SUNY, Albany; MA 66, Johns Hopkins Univ.; PhD 69, Univ. of Illinois. **Career & Employment:** Summer Arts Festival, Roxbury, NY, Prod. Dir. 1964-65; The Depot, Inc., Urbana, IL, Man. Dir. 1966-69; SUNY, Stony Brook, Asst. Prof. of English 1969-76, Adj. Asst. Prof. 1973-76; Univ. of Illinois, Instr. 1966-67, Visiting Asst. Prof. 1970; Everyman Street Theatre Company of NYC at SUNY, Stony Brook, Presenter-Producer 1972; Port Jefferson (NY) Summer Playhouse, Man. Dir. 1972-76; New School for Social Research, Asst. to the Dean 1977-78; Arts Council of Tampa, Exec. Dir. 1978-84; Univ. of South Florida, Tampa, Theatre Dept., Lect. 1979; ArtsReports, WUSF-FM, NPR, Tampa, Producer-Writer-On-Air Talent 1979-84; *Mixed Media*, WEDU-TV, PBS, Tampa, Assc. Producer & Host 1981-83; Arts & Entertainment Reporter-Critic, WTVT-TV, CBS, Tampa 1982-85; Consultant in marketing, strategic & long-range planning & management 1984-89; Durham (NC) Arts Council, Inc., Exec. Dir. 1989-92; Duke Univ., Visiting Instr. Spring 1992. **Memberships & Offices:** Assn. of College., Univ., & Community Arts Administrators, BoD 1980-83, Exec. Com. 1980-81; Florida Assembly of Community Arts Agencies, BoD & VP 1980-82; Florida Cultural Action Alliance, BoD 1982-84, VP 1982-83; Triangle Arts Planning Consortium, BoD 1989-92; North Carolina Assn. of Arts Councils, BoD 1990-92. **Fellowships, Honors & Awards:** NY State Regents College Teaching Fellowship 1965-69; Woodrow Wilson Dissertation Fellowship 1968-69. **Publications:** with Diane Darrow & Thomas E. Maresca, *Three Plays for Readers Theatre* (produced at SUNY, Stony Brook, 1971); "Everyman in America," *Comparative Drama* 9 (1975): 99-115; "Venus in the Medieval Mythographic Tradition," *Journal of English and Germanic Phi-*

lology 74 (1975): 519-35; with Virginia L. Bush, *Lira-Wise Guide to the American Academy in Rome* (Rome: AAR, 1977 & 1978); trans., with Thomas E. Maresca, *Bernardus Silvestris, Commentary on Six Books of the* Aeneid (Lincoln: Univ. of Nebraska Press, 1979); "What the Arts Really Need," *Tampa Bay Magazine* (Oct. 1981): 100; "A Primer for Advocacy" and "An Advocacy Case Study," in *Advocates for the Arts: A Citizen Action Manual* (New York: American Council for the Arts, 1980); "A Reader's Guide to Better Graphics," *American Arts* (Jan. 1982): 26-27; *Promoting Your Product* (Madison: ACUCAA, 1983 & 1985); "Marketing," in *Contact! A Guide to Presenting the Performing Arts in California* (California Arts Council, 1984); "Six Myths about the Arts," *American Arts* (May 1984): 14-15; "To Market, To Market," *American Arts* (July 1984): 10-11; "Getting Your Way with the Media," *ACUCAA Bulletin Supplement* 104 (Mar. 1985); "New Approaches to Consumer Behavior and Their Implications for Communications," *Journal of Arts Management and Law* 15 (1985): 40-48; "You Should Plan on It," *ACUCAA Bulletin Book Supplement* (Nov.-Dec. 1988): 1, 8; "Arts in a Sunshine State: The Extraordinary Growth of Performing Arts Centers in Florida," *International Arts Manager* (Mar.-Apr. 1989); "Mismatched Expectations: Boards, Managers and Artists," in *Work Papers* (New York: FEDAPT, 1991); "Arts Are Basic to a Thriving City," *Durham Herald Sun* (Feb. 23, 1992). **Important Works:** Producer-Writer-Ed., *How Long Does It Take You To Write A Play?* 1987.

SCHULLIAN, DOROTHY MAY ■ FAAR Classics/Archaeology 34. b. May 19, 1906, Lakewood, OH. d. Apr. 1, 1989. m. Howard B. Adelmann. BA 27, Western Reserve Univ.; PhD 31, Univ. of Chicago. **Research/Artistic Interests:** Edition of Rodulfus Tortarius, Valerius Maximus, history of medicine. **Career & Employment:** Albion College, Instr. 1939-44; Nat. Library of Medicine, Cleveland, History of Medicine Division, Asst. to Chief Curator 1944-61; Cornell Univ. Library, Curator of History of Science 1961-72. **Memberships & Offices:** American Assn. of History of Medicine; History of Science Soc.; Medical Library Assn.; Intl. Acad. of the History of Medicine; MAA; RSA; APA; ArIA; American Classical League. **Fellowships, Honors & Awards:** Univ. of Chicago, Ryerson Fellowship in Archaeology 1931-32; Phi Beta Kappa; American Assn. of the History of Medicine, Garrison Lect. 1953; Fulbright Fellow 1953-54. **Publications:** *External Stimuli to Literary Production in Rome 90 B.C.-27 B.C.* (Chicago, 1932); ed. with Marbury B. Ogle, *Rodulfi Tortarii Carmina*, AAR Papers & Monographs 8 (1933); "The Excerpts of Hieric 'Ex Libris Valeris Maximi Memorabilium Dictorum vel Factorum,'" *Memoirs of the AAR* 12 (1935): 155-84; with Max Schoen, *Music and Medicine* (New York: H. Schuman, 1948); ed. with Francis E. Sommer, *Catalogue of Incunabula and Manuscripts in the Army Medical Library* (New York, 1950); ed. with Luigi Belloni, *Carlo Francesco Cogrossi: New Theory of the Contagious Disease among Oxen* (Milan: IGIS, 1953); ed. with Luigi Belloni, *Tortellii de Medicina et Medicis, Iacopi Batholoti de Antiquitate Medicinae* (Milan: IGIS, 1954); ed. & trans., Alessandro Benedetti, *Diaria de Bello Carolino* (New York: Ungar, 1967); ed., *The Baglivi Correspondence from the Library of Sir William Osler* (Ithaca: Cornell Univ. Press, 1974); " A Revised List of the Manuscripts of Valerius Maximus," *Miscellanea Augusto Campana* (Padua: Editrice Antenore, 1981), 695-728; "Valerius Maximus," in *Catalogus Translationum et Commentariorum* 4, ed. F. Edward Cranz (Washington, DC; Catholic Univ. Press, 1984), 287-403. **Bio-Bibliography:** *NY Times*, Obit. (Apr. 6, 1989); *Directory of American Scholars; Who Was Who in America; Who's Who of American Women*.

SCHUMACHER, THOMAS L. ■ FAAR Architecture 69, RAAR Architecture 92. b. Nov. 7, 1941, Bronx, NY. m. Patricia E. Sachs. BArch 63, Cornell Univ.; MArch 66, Cornell Univ. **Research/Artistic Interests:** Architectural theory, history, methodology, Renaissance to present; emphasis on 20th century. **Career & Employment:** I.M. Pei & Partners, Architects 1969-71; Inst. for Architectural & Urban Studies 1971-72; Princeton Univ., Asst. Prof. 1972-78; Univ. of Virginia, Assc. Prof. 1978-84; Univ. of Maryland, Prof. 1984-present. **Fellowships, Honors & Awards:** NEA, Individual Grant 1984, 1987; Graham Found., Individual Grant 1988; Assn. of Collegiate Schools of Architecture, Distinguished Prof. Award 1993. **Publications:** *Il Danteum di Terragni* (Rome: Officina Edizioni, 1980); *The Danteum* (Princeton: Princeton Architectural Press, 1985); *Surface & Symbol: Giuseppe Terragni and the Architecture of Italian Rationalism* (New York: Princeton Architectural Press, 1991). **Business Address:** School of Architecture, Univ. of Maryland, College Park, MD 20742.

SCHURMAN, J.G. ■ AAR Charter Mem.; Cornell Univ., Pres.

SCHURZ, CARL ■ AAR Charter Mem., Publisher, Diplomat.

SCHWAB, HARVEY ■ Stewardson Memorial Scholar 1913.

SCHWARTING, JON MICHAEL ■ FAAR Architecture 70; AAR Trustee 1988-92, Trustee Emer.; SOF, Sec.-Treas 1984-88, Pres. 1988-92. b. Apr. 17, 1943, Columbus, OH. m. Beyhan Karahan. c. Jessica, Sinan. BArch 66, Cornell Univ.; MArch-UD 68, Cornell Univ., Inst. of Architecture & Urban Studies. **Career & Employment:** Richard Meier & Asscs. Architects, Assc. 1970-73; Cooper Union, Adj. Assc. Prof. 1972-84; Columbia Univ., Assc. Prof. 1974-83; Design Colaborative Architects, Part. 1978-83; Karahan-Schwarting Architecture Co., Part. 1983-present; Univ. of Pennsylvania, Adj. Assc. Prof. 1984-86; Inst. for Architecture & Urban Studies, Dir. of Education 1985-86; Yale Univ., Visiting Lect. 1986-87; NYIT, Assc. Prof. & Chair. 1987-present. **Memberships & Offices:** ALNY, Exec. Com. 1974-78, 1980-84; NIAE, BoT 1991-present. **Fellowships, Honors & Awards:** Cornell Univ., Charles Goodwin Sands Memorial Award 1966; NEA Grant 1975, 1987; Graham Found. Grant 1984; NYSCA Grant 1986, 1988, 1989, 1995. **Publications:** "The Olivetti Prototype," *Domus* 3 (1974); "Reconstruction of a Postulation," *Progressive Architecture* 5 (1974); "The Lesson of Rome," *Harvard Review* 2 (1981); "Battery City Park Will Rise," *Progressive Architecture* 2 (1984); "In Reference to Habermas," in *Architecture Criticism and Ideology* (Princeton: Princeton Architectural Press, 1985); "Postscript," in *Architecture Re-production* (Princeton: Princeton Architectural Press, 1988); "'Morality and Reality': In Search for a Better Argument," *Via* 10 (1990); "Ulterior Motives: The Possibility of a Second Agenda in Architecture," *Modulus* 21 (1991). **Important Works:** 473 Broome St. Loft, NYC 1974; Fire Station, Naticoke, PA 1975; Bulgari Apartment, NYC 1977; Les Halles Competition 1980; FIT Campus Plan 1981; Italian Trade Center, NYC 1981; Kallista Showroom, NYC 1984; Kohler Showroom, NYC 1986; Todos Santos Plaza Competition 1987; Affordable Housing Competition, Greenwich, CT 1988; Tribeca Open Space Study, NYC 1989; Franklin St. Subway Renovation & Canopy 1990; Stuyvesant Cove Park Master Plan 1994; Roosevelt Island Tram Station 1995. **Exhibitions/Performances:** Inst. for Architecture & Urban Study, NYC 1975; Univ. of Virginia 1979; NAD & Syracuse Univ. 1980; "Urban Design for Les Halles," Traveling Exb. 1980; Cooper Union 1982; Municipal Arts Soc., NYC 1983, 1991; Harvard Univ. 1985; Storefront for Art & Architecture 1986; ALNY 1987; Columbia Univ. 1990; Bronx Museum of Art 1990; Clock Tower, NYC 1991. **Home Address:** 55 Greene St., NYC 10013. **Business Address:** Karahan-Schwarting Architecture Co., 55 Greene St., NYC 10013.

SCHWARTZ, ANDREW THOMAS ■ FAAR Painting 02. b. Jan. 1867, Louisville, KY. d. Sept. 16, 1942. **Study:** Cincinnati Art Acad., with Frank Duveneek; ASL with H. Siddons Mowbray. **Memberships & Offices:** ALNY; American Watercolor Soc.; Allied Artists of America; Nat. Soc. of Mural Painters; Circolo Artistico di Roma; Union Intl. des Beaux Artes et Lettres, Paris. **Fellowships, Honors & Awards:** Lazarus Scholarship 1899. **Career & Employment:** H. Siddons Mowbray, Asst. for Univ. Club & J.P. Morgan's private library. **Important Works:** Baptist Church, S. Londonderry, VT; Kansas City Life Insurance Co. Bldg., MO; Atkins Memorial Museum, Kansas City; West Side YMCA, NYC. **Exhibitions/Performances:** New York, Chicago, Philadelphia, Pittsburgh, Cincinnati, Boston. **Bio-Bibliography:** *National Cyclopedia of American Biography.*

SCHWARTZ, FREDERIC D. ■ FAAR Architecture 86. b. Apr. 1, 1951, NYC. BArch 73, UC, Berkeley; MArch 78, Harvard GSD. **Career & Employment:** Skidmore, Owings & Merrill 1976-78; Venturi, Rauch & Scott Brown, Assc. 1978-80, Dir. 1980-84; Columbia Univ., Adj. Asst. Prof. 1982-84; Anderson/Schwartz Architects, Part. 1984-present; Visiting Prof.: Univ. of Miami 1982; Yale Univ. 1987; Harvard Univ. 1989; Princeton Univ., Lect. 1992. **Memberships & Offices:** *Harvard Architecture Review,* Assc. Ed. 1980; ALNY, BoD 1990; Ruby Shang Dance Co., BoD 1990. **Fellowships, Honors & Awards:** Phi Beta Kappa, UC Berkeley 1972; Harvard GSD, Graham Found. Scholar 1976-78; *Progressive Architecture* Award, at VSBA 1980, 1982, 1983; Columbus Circle Competition, Prize Winner 1981; NEA Design Fellowship 1983; Harvard Gate Competition, Prize Winner 1983; 40 Under 40, *Interiors Magazine* 1986; NYC Arts Comm. Award of Honor 1988; *ID Magazine,* Annual Design Review Awards 1988; ALNY, Emerging Voices in Architecture 1990; *AD 100: "Architectural Digest World Top 100 Architects"* 1991; Intl. Competition for the Regional Capitol of Southwest France, Winner 1992; Intl. Competition for the Staten Island Ferry Terminal, NYC, Winner 1992; NYC/AIA Award 1994. **Publications:** *Mother's House: The Evolution of Vanna Venturi's House in Chestnut Hill* (New York: Rizzoli, 1992); *Venturi, Scott Brown Associati* (Milan: Zanichelli, 1992). **Important Works:** Block Island Houses, RI 1980; with Venturi, Scott Brown & Asscs., Westway, NYC 1980-85; *The Big Apple,* Times Sq., NYC 1985; with ASA, Finlandia Vodka Offices, NYC 1987; Cogan Apt., NYC 1988; Lake Sebago House, ME 1988; Parkside Restaurant, Atlanta 1989; Roses, Vines, & Lily Plates for Swid Powell, NYC 1989-92; Goldman House, East Hampton, NY 1990; Rolling Stone Offices, NYC 1990; Chelsea Pictures, NYC 1991; Baltimore Orioles Spring Training Camp, Naples, FL 1992; Greenberg House, Bronx, NYC 1994; Lightstone House, Southampton, NY 1995. **Exhibitions/Performances:** Paris Biennale 1982; Venice Biennale 1985; "New York Architecture 1970-90," Deutsches Architektur Museum, Germany 1989-90; Cooper-Hewitt Museum, NYC 1990; De Quito BiennaleVII, Ecuador 1990; Taipei Fine Arts Museum, Japan 1991; Wallach Art Gallery, Columbia Univ. 1991; 1st Parrish Art Museum Design Biennale, Southampton, NY 1991; Home Rooms Installation, Arts Center, Univ. of Massachusettes 1991; Sci Arc, Los Angeles 1993; AIA Convention, Chicago 1993. **Home Address:** 12 Greene St., NYC 10013.

SCHWARTZ, MARTHA ■ RAAR Landscape Architecture 92. BFA 73, Univ. of Michigan; MLA 77, Univ. of Michigan. **Other Study:** Harvard GSD 1976-77. **Career & Employment:** SWA Group East, Boston 1976-78; SWA Group, Boston 1978-80; Martha Schwartz Inc., Boston 1980-82; Office of Peter Walker-Martha Schwartz, Landscape Architects, NYC & San Francisco 1982-90; Martha Schwartz-Ken Smith-David Meyer, Inc., San Francisco 1990-92; Martha Schwartz, Inc., Cambridge, MA, San Francisco 1992-present; Harvard GSD, Adj. Prof. 1992-present; Visiting Critic: Harvard GSD; RISD; UC, Berkeley. **Memberships & Offices:** Villa Romana, Florence, Visiting Artist in Residence 1983; Radcliffe College, Artist in Residence 1987. **Fellowships, Honors & Awards:** Urban Design Award, Atlanta, GA 1987; ASLA Design Award 1989, Merit Award 1989, Honor Award 1991 (2); Urban Design Inst., Fellow 1990. **Important Works:** Ahmanson Theater, Los Angeles; Baltimore Inner Harbor; Chelsea District Courthouse, Chelsea, MA; Delano Hotel, Miami Beach; Intl. Jazz Hall of Fame-Parade Park Master Plan, Kansas City, MO; Jacob Javits Federal Bldg., East Plaza, 26 Federal Plaza, NYC; World Trade Center Plaza, NYC; HUD Plaza, Washington, DC; Lincoln Rd. Mall, Miami Beach; Minneapolis Federal Courthouse. **Exhibitions/Performances:** Hayden Gallery, MIT 1983; Chicago Inst. of Contemporary Art 1983; New Gallery of Contemporary Art, Cleveland 1984; Main Art Gallery, California State Univ., Fullerton 1986; Urban Design Center, NYC 1986; Harvard GSD 1986; Topher-Delaney, Sausalito, CA 1987; Inst. of Business Design 1987; Vanguard Gallery, Philadelphia 1987; Olympia & York, NYC 1988; Henry Art Gallery, Univ. of Washington 1991; Max Protetch Gallery, NYC 1991. **Home Address:** 167 Pemberton St., Cambridge, MA 02140. **Business Address:** Martha Schwartz, Inc., 167 Pemberton St., Cambridge, MA 02140.

SCHWARTZMAN, MADELINE K. ■ NIAE, John Dinkeloo Traveling Fellow 1987-88. b. Jan. 29, 1962, NYC. BA 83, Barnard College; MArch 86, Yale Univ. **Research/Artistic Interests:** Film & architecture, sculpture, drawing, architecture. **Career & Employment:** Yale Univ., Instr. 1989; Columbia Univ., Adj. Asst. Prof. 1989-95; Parsons School of Design, Adj. Asst. Prof. 1991-95. **Home Address:** 248 Third Ave., No. 4, NYC, 10010. **Business Address:** Ascending Pictures, 248 Third Ave., No. 4, NYC 10010.

SCHWARTZMAN, PAUL D. ■ FAAR Design Arts 77. b. May 31, 1950, NYC. BA 72, Univ. of Pennsylvania; MAH 74, Univ. of Buffalo. **Other Study:** Harvard Univ. 1974; UCLA 1974 & 1977. **Career & Employment:** Intl. Creative Management, Senior VP 1979-90; Independent literary agent. **Publications:** "Fellini," *NY Times Sunday Magazine* (Feb. 1977); "Bertolucci," *Film Comment* (May 1979). **Home Address:** 940 Centinela Ave., Santa Monica, CA 90403.

SCHWARZ, FRANK HENRY ■ FAAR Painting 24. b. June 21, 1894, NYC. d. Sept. 5, 1951. **Study:** Chicago Acad. of Fine Arts; AIC. **Career & Employment:** Columbia Univ., Faculty 1928-31. **Memberships & Offices:** ALNY; Nat. Arts Club. **Fellowships, Honors & Awards:** Tiffany Found. Fellowship 1921; Guggenheim Fellow 1926-27; Salmagundi Club, Isidor Prize.

SCHWARZENBERG, LUDMILA ■ AAR – New York, Dir. of Development.

SCHWERIN, RONALD J. ■ FAAR Painting 64. b. Oct. 28, 1940, Pittsburgh, PA. m. Guna Petersons. c. Carla, Peter. BFA

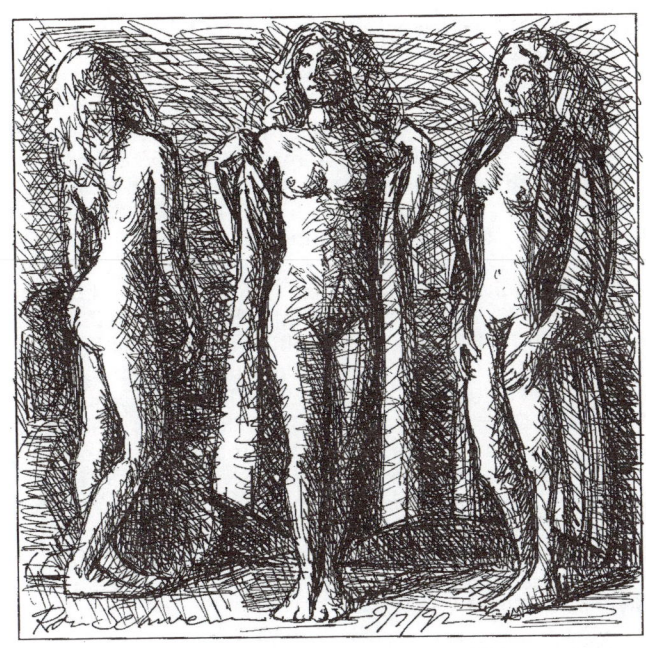

Ronald J. Schwerin

62, Pratt Inst. **Career & Employment:** NYIT, Instr. 1965-68; Pratt Inst., Instr. 1966-67; Univ. of Rhode Island, Instr. 1967; Mike Cuesta Photography Studio 1968-70; Ron Schwerin, Inc., Photography 1970-89. **Exhibitions/Performances:** Univ. of Rhode Island 1967; Ellis Gallery, NYC 1981; OK Harris Invitational, NYC 1991; Alan Stone Gallery Invitational 1991; Sherry French Gallery, Boca Raton, FL 1993; Zenith Gallery, Washington, DC 1993, 1994; Heckscher Museum, Huntington, NY 1994; Bruce L. Lewin Gallery, NYC 1995. **Bio-Bibliography:** Anna C. Noll, *American Arts Quarterly* (Summer-Fall 1994). **Home Address:** 70 Hollywood Pl., Huntington, NY 11743. **Business Address:** 889 Broadway, NYC 10003.

SCICHILONE, GIOVANNI ■ Italian Fulbright Fellow 1958-59.

SCORSESE, MARTIN ■ AAR Visitor 1974-75, Film Dir.

SCOTT, ANN R. ■ FAAR Classics / Archaeology 67. b. Apr. 20, 1938, NYC. m. Russell T. Scott, FAAR 66. c. Charles. BA 60, Radcliffe College; MA 70, Harvard Univ.; PhD 93, Bryn Mawr College. **Research/Artistic Interests:** Latin & Greek literature, archaeology, transmission of classical texts in Italy; Latin paleography, codicology & papal diplomatics. **Career & Employment:** ICCS, Instr. 1988, 1992; Univ. of Delaware, Instr. 1989-present. **Fellowships, Honors & Awards:** Anne Radcliffe Scholar 1956-57; Fulbright Fellow 1965-66; AAUW Grant 1970. **Publications:** with L. Richardson, jr & R.T. Scott, *Cosa III: The Buildings of the Forum*, Memoirs of the AAR (University Park: Penn State Press, 1994); ed. with R.T. Scott, Eius Virtutis Studiosi: *Classical and Post-Classical Studies in Memory of Frank Edward Brown* (Washington, DC: NGA, 1993). **Home Address:** 907 New Gulph Rd., Bryn Mawr, PA 19010.

SCOTT, JOHN BELDON ■ FAAR History of Art 81. b. Aug. 3, 1946, Scottsburg, IN. m. Katherine H. Tachau. BA 68, Indiana Univ.; MA 75, Rutgers Univ.; PhD 82, Rutgers Univ. **Research/Artistic Interests:** Renaissance & baroque art & architecture in Italy. **Career & Employment:** Univ. of Pennsylvania, Lect. 1981-82; Univ. of Iowa, Asst. Prof.-Assc. Prof. 1982-

present. **Memberships & Offices:** CAA, RSA, SAH, Sixteenth-Century Studies Conference, AHA, Midwest Art History Soc., Italian Art Soc. **Fellowships, Honors & Awards:** Gladys Krieble Delmas Found. Grant 1979, 1986; ACLS Research Fellow 1984; Andrew W. Mellon Fellow 1984-85; APS Research Grant 1984, 1989; NEH Travel Grant 1986; IAS, Visiting Mem. 1991-92. **Publications:** "The Catafalques of Philip II in Saragosa," *Studies in Iconography* 5 (1979): 107-34; "S. Ivo alla Sapienza and Borromini's Symbolic Language," *JSAH* 41 (1982): 294-317; "Urban VIII, Bernini, and the Countess Matilda," in *L'âge d'or du Mécénant (1598-1661)* (Paris: Éditions du CNRS, 1985), 119-27; "The Counter-Reformation Program of Borromini's Biblioteca Vallicelliana," *Storia dell'Arte* 47 (1985): 295-304; "The Meaning of Perseus and Andromeda in the Farnese Gallery and on the Rubens House," *Journal of the Warburg & Courtauld Institutes* 51 (1988): 25-60; "Pietro da Cortona's Payments for the Barberini Salone," *Burlington Magazine* 131 (1989): 416-18; *Images of Nepotism: The Painted Ceilings of Palazzo Barberini* (Princeton: Princeton Univ. Press, 1991); "The Art of the Painter's Scaffold, Pietro da Cortona in the Barberini Salone," *Burlington Magazine* 135 (1993): 327-37. **Business Address:** School of Art & Art History, Univ. of Iowa, Iowa City, IA 52242.

SCOTT, RUSSELL T. ■ FAAR Classics/Archaeology 66, RAAR Classics/Archaeology 79; School of Classical Studies, Andrew W. Mellon Prof.-in-Charge 1984-88; AAR School of Classical Studies, Summer-Session Dir. 1974-76; Cosa Publications, Ed. 1984-present. b. Dec. 9, 1938, Lewiston, ID. m. Ann R. Scott, FAAR 67. c. Charles. BA 60, Stanford Univ.; MA 62, Yale Univ.; PhD 64, Yale Univ. **Research/Artistic Interests:** Roman archaeology & history of the republican & imperial periods with special reference to Italy & the western provinces. **Career & Employment:** Bryn Mawr, Asst. Prof. 1966-72, Assc. Prof. 1972-78, Prof. 1978-present, Chair 1976-82. **Memberships & Offices:** ArIA, Lect. 1969-70, 1973-74, 1988-89; Fasti Archaeologici, Correspondent 1972-present; AIAC Rep. 1983-present; Nat. Geographic Soc., Consultant 1982; *CP* Referee; *AJA* Referee, Adv. Com., Adv. Ed. 1982-85; NEH Referee; American Comm. for Cultural Exchange with Italy 1984-88; Villa Massenzia, Bryn Mawr College, Rome, Dir. 1982-84; ICCS, Andrew W. Mellon Prof. 1991-92. **Fellowships, Honors & Awards:** Yale Univ., Sterling Fellowship 1963-64; Fulbright Fellowship 1964-65; APS, Summer Research Grants 1968, 1972, 1977; ACLS, Summer Research Grants 1968, 1969, Fellowship 1972; Bryn Mawr College, Summer Research Grants 1969, 1972; NEH Senior Research Fellowship 1990. **Publications:** *Religion and Philosophy in the Histories of Tacitus,* AAR Papers & Monographs 22 (1968); with L.R. Taylor, "Seating Space in the Roman Senate and the *Senatores Pedarii*," *TAPA* 100 (1969): 529-82; "Providentia Aug.," *Historia* 23 (1982): 436-59; "The Text of Tacitus Ann. 14.60-61 and Octavia," *Classical Journal* 79 (1983): 39-43; "The Decorations in Terracotta from the Temples at Cosa," *La coroplastica templare etrusca fra il iv e il ii secolo a.c. Atti del XVI convegno de studi etruschi ed italici, Orbetello 1988*; "Excavations in the Roman Forum: The *Area Sacra* of Vesta," *AJA* 94 (1990): 304-12; "A New Corpus of Gladiatorial Inscriptions in the West," *Journal of Roman Archaeology* 3 (1990): 310ff; "Cosa," *Enciclopedia Italiana*, 315-17; "A New Fragment of Serpent Ware from Cosa," *Journal of Glass Studies* 34 (1992) 58-180; with V.J. Bruno, *Cosa IV: Houses,* Memoirs of the AAR 38 (University Park: Penn State Univ. Press, 1993); "Lavori e ricerche nell'area sacra di Vesta 1990-91," *Archeologia laziale XI, QuadAEI* 21 (1993): 11-17; ed., *Cosa III: The Buildings of the Forum* (University Park: Penn State

Univ. Press, 1994); "Excavations in the *Area Sacra* of Vesta 1988-89," in Eius Virtutis Studiosi: *Studies in Memory of Frank Edward Brown,* ed. with Ann R. Scott (Washington, DC: NGA, 1993); "Atrium Vestae," *Lexicon Topographicum Urbis Romae* I, A-C (Rome: Edizioni Quasar, 1993). **Home Address:** 907 New Gulph Rd., Bryn Mawr, PA 19010. **Business Address:** Dept. of Latin, Bryn Mawr College, Bryn Mawr, PA 19010.

SCUDDER, ROGERS V. ■ AAR Librarian 1976-83. b. Nov. 16, 1912, St. Louis, MO. BA 34, Harvard Univ.; MA 58, Univ. of Wisconsin. **Other Study:** Oxford Univ., Dipl. in Classical Archaeology. **Career & Employment:** Brooks School, Faculty 1936-66; Groton School, Faculty 1968-94. **Business Address:** Groton School, PO Box 991, Groton, MA 01450.

SCULLY, DANIEL V. ■ FAAR Architecture 70. b. Oct. 24, 1943, New Haven, CT. m. Carol J. Scully. c. Michael. BArch 70, Yale Univ.; MArch 70, Yale Univ. **Other Study:** Union College, Schenectady 1963-66; Louis I. Kahn, Architect, 4 summer interships. **Career & Employment:** Main Street Development Corp., Pre-fab Housing Designer 1972-73; Total Environmental Action. Inc., BoD & VP for Design 1974-81; Equinox, Architect & Founding Prin. 1981-83; Daniel V. Scully Architect 1983-present. **Memberships & Offices:** Augustus Saint-Gaudens Nat. Historic Site, BoT; Museum of Transportation, Boston, Incorporator, Exb. Design Com.; PLAN NH, BoD; Soc. for Commercial Archaeology, Founder 1977, Pres. 1991; Dublin Historical Soc., Bldg. Com. 1988; Nat. Register Review Com. 1989; Town of Harrisville, NH, Selectman 1978-81, 1981-84, Planning Bd. 1980-84, Historic District Comm. 1980-84, Fire Station Bldg. Com., Chair 1981-84. **Fellowships, Honors & Awards:** *Progressive Architecture* Annual Design Awards, Citation 1972; *Architecture & Urbanism* Magazine "40 Under 40" (1977); HUD Cycle 3 Solar Demonstration Design Awards (2) 1978; Intl. Solar Energy Assn., Best Built Institutional Commercial Design Award 1980; American Soc. of Engineers, New England Chap., Excellence Award 1987; Bush-Gate Design Competition, Hon. Mention 1989; Gateway Gas Design Competition, Hon. Mention 1990; Soc. for Commercial Archeology, Pres. Award for Initiative 1990; American Wood Council, Design Honor Award 1991; Detroit Auto Show Design Seminar, Luncheon Speaker 1994; "Electric Vehicle and the American Community" Competition, Small Community Award & Special Logo Award 1st Place. **Publications:** "Animus," *Journal of Architectural Education* 29.1; *The Fuel Savers: A Kit of Solar Ideas for Existing Homes; Solar Energy Home Design in Four Climates.* **Important Works:** NERWI Bldg., Southern Maine Vocational Training Inst. 1980; Good Shepherd Lutheran Church, Peterborough, NH 1991; Savidge Library Access Walk, MacDowell Colony, Peterborough, NH 1989 (Nat. Registry); College of the Atlantic, Kaelber Hall, Bar Harbor, ME 1986; Munsonville School, Nelson, NH; Flat Rock Brook Nature Center, NJ 1980; Music & Arts Center Renovation, Dwight Englewood School, Englewood, NJ; Peter Pap Oriental Rugs, Dublin, NH; Barker Residence, Renovation, Dublin, NH; Moran Residence, Harvard, NH; J.A. Wright Silver Polish Co., Renovations 1994; Wollaeger Residence, Stoddard, NH 1995. **Exhibitions/Performances:** Exeter Acad. 1978; "New Americans," Traveling Exb. in Italy 1979; "Emerging Architectural Ideas" 1983; Washington Art Assn. 1985; Univ. of New Hampshire 1991. **Bio-Bibliography:** "Steamboat Ashore," *Solar Age Magazine* (Mar. 1981): 42-45; Robert Storr, "Fast & Slow," *Art Press* 151: 30-35; "Works of Dan Scully," *Automobile Magazine* (Jan. 1992): 114-19; *Autoweek Magazine* (Jan. 11, 1994): 27. **Business Address:** Daniel V. Scully, Architect, 44 Main St., Peterborough, NH 03458.

SCULLY, VINCENT ■ AAR Visitor 1951 — 1955; AAR *Academy Award* in The Year of Architecture 1994. **Career & Employment:** Yale Univ., Sterling Prof. Emer.; Univ. of Miami, Distinguished Visiting Prof. **Selected Publications:** *Architecture: The Natural and the Manmade; The Earth, The Temple, and the Gods: Greek Sacred Architecture; The Shingle Style: Architectural Theory and Design from Richardson to the Origins of Wright.*

SEABLOM, SETH H. ■ FAAR Landscape Architecture 68. b. Nov. 10, 1937, Seattle, WA. m. Victoria M. Battaglia. c. Angela Kristine. BArch 61, Univ. of Washington, Seattle; MArch 63, Univ. of Pennsylvania; MCP 63, Univ. of Pennsylvania. **Other Study:** Royal Danish Acad., Town Planning Dept. **Career & Employment:** NBBJ 1973-80; Callison Partnership 1980-82; TRA 1982-85; 2s2m 1984-87; Seth Seablom Architects 1986-present. **Fellowships, Honors & Awards:** Tau Sigma Delta 1960; AIA Student Medal Award 1961; Fulbright-Danish Royal Acad. 1963-64. **Publications:** *Bonytt* (1967); with Erik Huttberg, "A House is a House...." *Ark* (1968); *Casabella* (1968); "Education is a Personal Endeavor," *Arkitekten* (1969); "Kobenhavn," G.E.C. *Gads Forlag* (1969), 297-99; "The Development of a Socio-Critical Institution: The University of Trondheim," *Arkitekten* 23 (1970): 609-27; with Victoria Seablom, "Klassisk Akademisk Modell-eller et Universitet integrert in bysamfinnit?," *Nye Bonytt* (1971); with Mark Ashley, "Five New Architectural Offices," *Arcade* (1984); "Plan og Frihed," *Danish Town Planning* 33 (1985): 22-25; "Tag over Hovedet," *Arkitektens Forlag*, 200-2. **Important Works:** 3rd Ave. South Transit Station, Seattle; Washington State Convention & Trade Center, Seattle; Orthopedic Physicians, Inc. P.S. Offices, Nordstrom Tower, Seattle; Valley Internal Medical Offices, Renton, WA; 2d Ave. Bank of Puget Sound Remodeling, Seattle; Mercer Island Civic Center, WA; Baltimore Convention Center; West Amager Project, Copenhagen; Angel Kingdom, Ueno, Japan; Paul Henningsen Housing Competition, Copenhagen; Tivoli Office Complex, Copenhagen. **Exhibitions/Performances:** Exb. of Northwest Illustrator 1992. **Bio-Bibliography:** *Who's Who in the West.* **Home Address:** 2106 2 Ave. N., Seattle, WA 98109.

SECCHIA, PETER F. ■ AAR Visitor 1990-91, US Ambassador to Italy.

SEGAL, CHARLES P. ■ FAAR Classics/Archaeology 63, RAAR Classics/Archaeology 86. b. Mar. 19, 1936, Boston, MA. m. Nancy A. Jones. c. Joshua, Thaddeus, Cora. BA 57, Harvard College; PhD 61, Harvard Univ. **Other Study:** ASCSA 1957-58. **Research/Artistic Interests:** Greek & Roman literature, comparative literature. **Career & Employment:** Harvard Univ., TF & Tutor 1959-61, Instr. 1963-64; Univ. of Pennsylvania, Asst.-Assc. Prof. 1964-67; Brown Univ., Assc. Prof.-Prof. 1968-78, Prof. of Classics & Comparative Literature 1978-80, Chair 1978-81, David Benedict Prof. 1980-86; Princeton Univ., Prof. 1987-90; Harvard Univ., Prof. 1990-present; Visiting Appointments: ICCS, Visiting Prof. 1970-71, Prof.-in-Charge 1971-72; Brandeis Univ., Visiting Prof. 1974; École des Hautes Études, Directeur d' Études Associés 1975-76; Univ. of Melbourne, Australia, Fulbright Exchange Prof. 1978; Columbia Univ., Visiting Prof. 1979; École Normale Supérieure, Paris, Visiting Prof. 1982. **Memberships & Offices:** Società Italiana per lo Studio dell'Antichità Classica, Corresponding Mem. 1981-present; APA, Pres. 1993. **Fellowships, Honors & Awards:** Harvard Univ., Bowdoin Prize (4) 1955-57, 1960, Richardson Prize in Greek and Latin 1957; ASCSA Fulbright Fellowship 1957-58; Center for Hellenic Studies, Washington, DC, Junior Fellow 1967-68, Senior Fellow 1987-92; Martin

Classical Lecturership 1974; ACLS Fellowship 1974-75; NEH Summer Stipend for Research 1977; ACLS-IREX Travel Grant, 1st USA-USSR Conference on Semiotics, Moscow, USSR 1980; Guggenheim Fellowship 1981-82; NEH Fellowship 1985-86; IAS, Visiting Scholar 1985; Center for Advanced Study in the Behavioral Sciences, Stanford, CA, Fellow 1989-90; AAAS, Fellow 1992; Nat. Humanities Center, Fellow 1993-94. **Publications:** *Landscape in Ovid's* Metamorphoses: *A Study in the Transformation of a Literary Symbol*, Hermes Einzelschriften 23 (Wiesbaden: Franz Steiner Verlag, 1969); *The Theme of the Mutilation of the Corpse in the* Iliad, Mnemosyne, supp. 17 (Leiden: Brill, 1971); *Tragedy and Civilization: An Interpretation of Sophocles*, Martin Classical Lectures 26 (Cambridge, MA: Harvard Univ. Press, 1981); *Poetry and Myth in Ancient Pastoral: Essays on Theocritus and Virgil* (Princeton: Princeton Univ. Press, 1981); ed., Cedric H. Whitman, *The Heroic Paradox: Essays on Homer, Sophocles and Aristophanes* (Ithaca: Cornell Univ. Press, 1982); *Dionysiac Poetics and Euripides'* Bacchae (Princeton: Princeton Univ. Press, 1982); *Pindar's Mythmaking: The Fourth Pythian Ode* (Princeton: Princeton Univ. Press, 1986); *Language and Desire in Seneca's* Phaedra (Princeton: Princeton Univ. Press, 1986); *Interpreting Greek Tragedy: Myth, Poetry, Text* (Ithaca: Cornell Univ. Press, 1986); ed., G.B. Conte, *A Rhetoric of Imitation: Literary Memory in Virgil and Other Latin Poets* (Ithaca: Cornell Univ. Press, 1986); *La musique du Sphinx: Poesie et structure dans la tragedie grecque*, trans. C. Malamoud & M.-P. Gruenais (Paris: Éditions de la découverte, 1987); ed., Alison Goddard Elliott, *Roads to Paradise: Reading the Lives of the Early Saints* (Hanover, NH: Univ. Press of New England & Brown Univ. Press, 1987); *Orpheus: The Myth of the Poet* (Baltimore: Johns Hopkins Univ. Press, 1989); *Lucretius on Death and Anxiety: Poetry and Philosophy in* De Rerum Natura (Princeton: Princeton Univ. Press, 1990); *Ovidio e la poesia del mito: Saggi sulle "Metamorfosi"* (Venice: Marsilio, 1991); *Sophocles'* Oedipus Tyrannus: *Tragic Heroism and the Limits of Knowledge*, Twayne Masterworks Series (New York: Macmillan, 1993); *Euripides and the Poetics of Sorrow: Art, Gender, and Commemoration in Alcestis; Hippolytus, and Hecuba* (Durham, NC: Duke Univ. Press, 1993); plus, approximately 250 essays in

As the years pass, I look back on my two-year fellowship at the Academy as one of the most enriching and valuable experiences of my life. The time to read, study, write in the unique atmosphere of the Academy, both lively and peaceful, has loomed larger and larger in its importance for my work and growth as a scholar and a person. The daily associations with so many creative scholars and artists are a remarkable stimulus and provide a perspective on one's own work that can be found nowhere else. For a classicist to live and work in Rome, with its extraordinary artistic riches and cultural continuities, is the greatest of joys, and to have that experience in one's formative years is a great good fortune. Although life in Rome becomes more and more difficult and demanding, the Academy provides a haven and a center where what this great city offers can be appreciated and drawn upon for our own struggles toward creative and useful lives in the ever more turbulent and less certain modern world. It is very important that the Academy survive as the superb, unique institution that it is; and all who have been touched by it should make some effort to assure that survival, however modest the support is.

Charles P. Segal

books & journals. **Bio-Bibliography:** *Who's Who in America.* **Business Address:** Dept. of Classics, Boylston Hall 319, Harvard Univ., Cambridge, MA 02138.

SEGAL, GEORGE ■ AAR Trustee 1984, Trustee Emer.; Sculptor.

SEGENNI, SIMONETTA ■ Italian Fulbright Fellow 1981-82.

SELIGMANN, WERNER ■ FAAR Architecture 81. b. Mar. 3, 1930, Osnabrück, Germany. m. Jean L. Liberman-Seligmann. c. Raphael John, Sabina Charlotte. BArch 55, Cornell Univ. **Other Study:** with Friedrich Wilhelm Kraemer, Technische Hochschule Braunschweig 1958-59. **Research/Artistic Interests:** History of modern architecture, especially housing. **Career & Employment:** Univ. of Texas, Austin, Instr. 1956-58; E.T.H. Zurich, Asst. 1959-61, Visiting Prof. 1990-93; Cornell Univ., Asst. Prof.-Prof. 1961-74; Harvard Univ., Prof. 1974-76; Syracuse Univ., Dean & Prof. 1976-90; Harvard GSD, Eliot Noyes Visiting Prof. 1986; Yale Univ., William Bishop Visiting Prof. 1988; E.T.H. Zurich, Prof. 1990-93; Univ. of Virginia, Thomas Jefferson Prof. **Publications:** *Schirn am Ruomerberg,* exb. cat. (Frankfurt, 1986); *The Poetics of Counterpoint: Works of Mario Campi* (New York: Rizzoli, 1987); "Le Corbusier as Engineer," *Architectural Record* (Oct. 1987); "The Evolution of the Prairie House: A Primer in Architectural Principles," in *Frank Lloyd Wright* (New York: Princeton Architectural Press, 1989); "The Texas Years and the Beginning at the E.T.H., 1956-61," *Architecture Lehren* (Zurich: G.T.A. 1989). **Important Works:** Willard Administration Bldg., Willard, NY 1971; Elm Street Housing, Ithaca, NY 1973; Olean Central Fire Station, NY 1980; Center Ithaca, NY 1982. **Exhibitions/Performances:** Prinz Albrecht Site Design Competition, Martin Gropius Bldg., Berlin 1984; Inst. Français d'Architecture, Paris 1985; Harvard GSD 1986; Columbia Univ. 1986; XVII Triennale di Milano 1987. **Bio-Bibliography:** *Contemporary Architects; Who's Who in America.* **Home Address:** 11 Homer Ave., Cortland, NY 13045.

SELZ, PETER H. ■ RAAR History of Art 72. b. Mar. 27, 1919, Munich, Germany. m. Carole Marks. c. Tanya Nicole, Gabrielle. MA 49, Univ. of Chicago; PhD 54, Univ. of Chicago. **Other Study:** Columbia Univ. 1937-38; Univ. of Paris 1949-50. **Career & Employment:** Inst. of Design, Chicago 1949; Pomona College, Chair 1955-58; MOMA, Chief Curator, Painting & Sculpture Exbs. 1958-65; UC, Berkeley, Univ. Art Museum, Dir. 1965-73, Prof. 1965-89; Hebrew Univ., Jerusalem, Visiting Prof. 1976; Peoples Republic of China, Visiting Lect. 1986; CUNY, Grad. Center 1987. **Memberships & Offices:** CAA 1948-present, Dir. 1959-64, 1966-71; Intl. Assn. of Art Critics 1960-present; American Assn. of Art Museum Directors 1965-73; *Art in America,* Ed. Bd. 1966-present; *Archives of American Art,* Adv. Com. 1979-present; American Crafts Council, BoT 1983-89. **Fellowships, Honors & Awards:** Fulbright Grant 1949-50; NY Public Library, Medal for American Scholars 1961; Federal Republic of Germany, Order of Merit, 1st Class 1963; California College of Arts & Crafts, Hon. DFA 1967; NEH, Senior Fellowship 1972-73; Bauhaus Archiv & DAAD, Research Grant 1976; Rockefeller Found., Bellagio Study Center, Resident 1994. **Publications:** *German Expressionist Painting* (Berkeley & Los Angeles: UC Press, 1957); *New Images of Man* (New York: MOMA, 1959); *Art Nouveau: Art and Design at the Turn of the Century,* exb. cat. (New York: MOMA, 1960); *Mark Rothko,* exb. cat. (New York: MOMA, 1961); *The Work of Jean Dubuffet,* exb. cat. (New York: MOMA, 1962); *Emil Nolde,* exb. cat. (New York: MOMA, 1963); *Max*

Beckmann, exb. cat. (New York: MOMA, 1964); *Ferdinand Hodler* (Berkeley: University Art Museum & New York: Guggenheim Museum, 1972); *Sam Francis* (New York: Harry N. Abrams, 1975); *Art in Our Times: A Visual History 1890-1980* (New York: Harry N. Abrams, 1981); *Art in a Turbulent Era* (Ann Arbor, UMI Press, 1985); *Chillida* (New York: Harry N. Abrams, 1986); *Max Beckmann: The Self Portraits* (New York: Rizzoli, 1992). **Bio-Bibliography:** *Contemporary Authors; Directory of American Scholars; International Authors and Writers Blue Book; Who's Who in America; Who's Who in American Art; Who's Who in the West; Who's Who in the World; The Writers Directory.* **Home Address:** 861 Regal Rd., Berkeley, CA 94708. **Business Address:** Dept. of Art History, UC, Berkeley, CA 94720.

SEMPLE, WILLIAM T. ■ AAR Trustee 1933-46.

SENNETT, RICHARD ■ AAR Visitor 1992-93, Art Historian.

SEREBRIER, JOSE ■ AAR Visitor 1989-90, Composer.

SESSIONS, ROGER ■ FAAR Musical Composition 31. b. Dec. 28, 1896, Brooklyn, NY. d. Mar. 16, 1985. m. Elizabeth Franck. c. John Porter, Elizabeth Pease. BA 15, Harvard Univ.; BMus 17, Yale Univ. **Other Studies:** with Ernest Bloch. **Career & Employment:** Smith College 1917-21; Cleveland Inst. of Music, Dept. Head 1921-25; Boston Conservatory 1933-35; New Jersey College for Women 1935-37; Princeton Univ. 1935-44, Conant Prof. 1953-66; UC, Berkeley 1944-53, Bloch Prof. 1966-67; Columbia-Princeton Electronic Music Center, Co-Dir. 1959; Juilliard School 1965-83; Harvard Univ., Norton Prof. 1968-69. **Memberships & Offices:** Berkeley Fellows, Charter Mem. 1968; AAAS; Intl. Soc. of Contemporary Music, Hon. Mem., Co-Chair US Section; AAAL; League of Composers; BMI; NIAL. **Fellowships, Honors & Awards:** Guggenheim Fellow 1926, 1927; Carnegie Found. Grant 1931; Pulitzer Award Com., Special Citation 1974, Pulitzer Prize 1982; Brandeis Univ., Creative Arts Award 1958; Wesleyan Univ., Hon. MusD 1958; Akademie der Künste, Berlin 1960; NIAL, Gold Medal 1961; Harvard Univ., Hon. MusD 1964; Academia Nacional de Bellas Artes, Argentina 1965. **Publications:** *The Musical Experience of Composer, Performer, Listener* (Princeton; Princeton Univ. Press, 1950); *Harmonic Practice* (New York: Harcourt, Brace, 1951); *Questions about Music* (Cambridge, MA: Harvard Univ. Press, 1970); ed., E. Cone, *Roger Sessions on Music: Collected Essays* (Princeton: Princeton Univ. Press, 1979). **Important Works:** *Symphonies* 1927, 1946, 1957, 1958, 1964, 1966, 1967, 1968, 1978; *Montezuma,* an opera 1941-1963; *The Trial of Lucullus,* an opera 1947; *Divertimento,* for orchestra 1959-60; *Psalm 140,* for soprano & orchestra 1963; "When Lilacs Last in the Dooryard Bloom'd," cantata for soloists, chorus & orchestra 1964-70; *Piano Sonata No. 3* 1965; *Six Pieces for Violoncello Solo* 1966; *Rhapsody,* for orchestra 1970; *Double Concerto for Violin, Violoncello & Orchestra* 1970-71; *Concertino for Chamber Orchestra* 1972; *Three Choruses on Biblical Texts,* for chorus & orchestra 1972; *Five Pieces for Piano* 1974; *Concerto for Orchestra* 1979-81. **Bio-Bibliography:** Andrea Olmstead, *Roger Sessions and His Music* (Ann Arbor: UMI Research, 1985); A. Olmstead, *Conversations with Roger Sessions* (Boston: Northeastern Univ. Press, 1987); *New Grove Twentieth-Century American Masters* (New York: Norton, 1987); A. Olmstead, *The Correspondence of Roger Sessions* (Boston: Northeastern Univ. Press, 1992); *Baker's Biographical Dictionary of American Musicians, Who Was Who in America.*

SETTIS, SALVATORE ■ Italian Fulbright Fellow 1967-68.

SHACOCHIS, ROBERT G. ■ FAAR Literature 90. b. Sept. 9, 1951, West Pittston, PA. m. Barbara Petersen. BA 73, Univ. of Missouri; MA 79, Univ. of Missouri; MFA 82, Univ. of Iowa. **Career & Employment:** Peace Corps, Agricultural Journalist 1975-76; *Palm Beach Evening Times,* Reporter 1980; Univ. of Missouri, Visiting Lect. 1984-85; Univ. of Iowa, Visiting Lect. 1985-86. **Memberships & Offices:** Poets and Writers. **Fellowships, Honors & Awards:** *Playboy* Award 1982; NEA Literary Fellowship 1982; Iowa Writers Workshop, James Michener Award 1983; Bread Loaf Writers Conference, Scholarship & Fellowship 1983, 1985; Pushcart Press, Pushcart Prize 1985; Assn. of American Publishers, American Book Award 1985; Best Stories from the South, Award 1986. **Publications:** *Easy in the Islands* (New York: Crown, 1985); *The Next New World* (New York: Crown, 1989); "Soup Therapy," *Gentlemen's Quarterly* (Mar. 1990); *Swimming in the Volcano* (New York: Crown).

SHAILOR, BARBARA A. ■ AAR Visitor 1973-74. b. Jan. 27, 1948, New Haven, CT. m. Harry W. Blair II. BA 69, Wilson College; MA 71, Univ. of Cincinnati; PhD 75, Univ. of Cincinnati. **Career & Employment:** Bucknell Univ., Asst. Prof. 1975-82, Assc. Prof. 1982-88, Prof. 1988-present, Assc. Dean, College of Arts & Sciences 1986-88, Assc. Provost 1988-89, Affirmative Action Officer & Special Asst. to the Pres. 1990-91, VP for Student Services l99l-present. **Home Address:** RD 6, Box 278B, Lewisburg, PA 17837. **Business Address:** Bucknell Univ., 209 Marts Hall, Lewisburg, PA 17837.

SHAPERO, HAROLD S. ■ AAR World War II Prize 1941; RAAR Musical Composition 71. b. Apr. 19, 1920, Lynn, MA. m. Esther B. Geller. c. Hannah. BA 41, Harvard Univ. **Other Study:** Berkshire Music Center, Musical Composition with Paul Hindemith 1940-41; Longy School, Cambridge, MA; Musical Composition with Nadia Boulanger 1942-43. **Career & Employment:** Brandeis Univ., Prof., Dir. of Electronic Studio 1951-88. **Fellowships, Honors & Awards:** Harvard Univ., Paine Fellowship 1942-43; Columbia Univ., Bearns Prize 1946; Gershwin Prize 1946; Guggenheim Fellowship 1947, 1948; Fulbright Fellowship, Junior 1949-50, Senior 1962-63. **Home Address:** 9 Russell Circle, Natick, MA 01760.

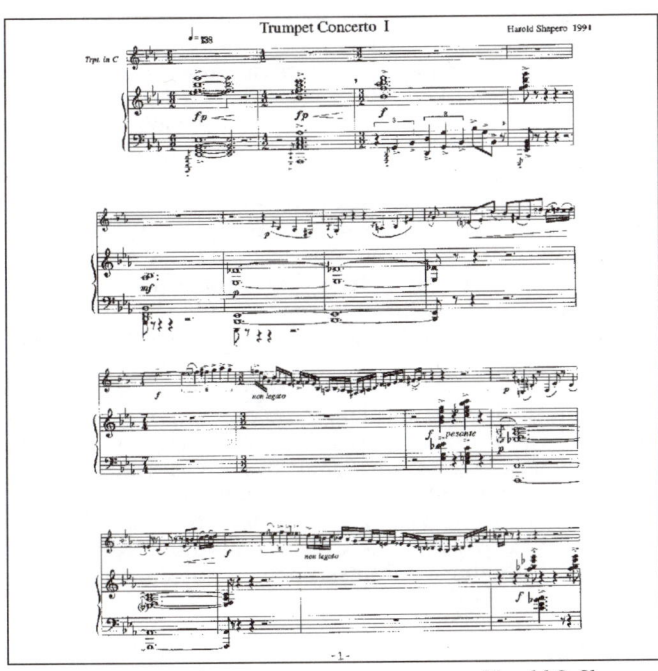

Harold S. Shapero

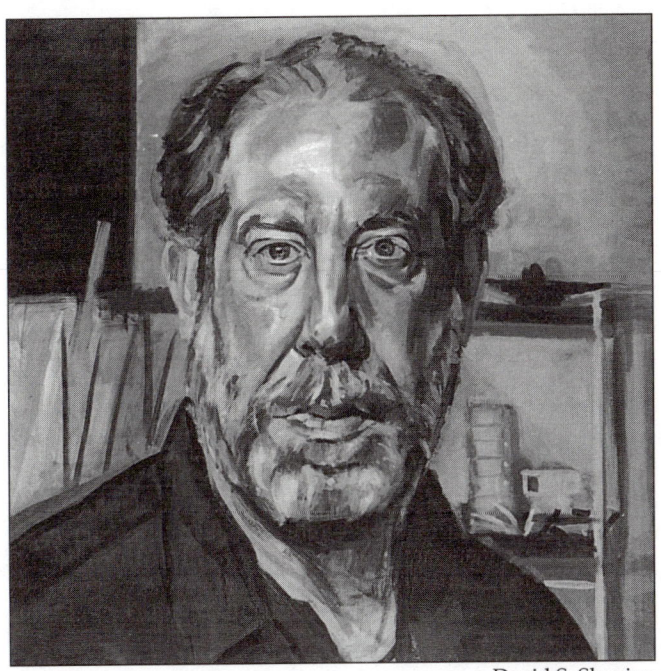

David S. Shapiro

SHAPIRO, DAVID S. ■ FAAR Painting 73. b. Mar. 3, 1943, Cambridge, MA. **Study:** Vesper George School of Art, Boston 1961-64; MFA School 1964-65; Maryland Inst. of Art, Baltimore 1967-68; New York Studio School 1968-71. **Career & Employment:** SUNY, Binghamton, Assc. Prof. 1973-present. **Fellowships, Honors & Awards:** MFA School, Scholarship 1964-65; New York Studio School, Scholarship 1968-71; SUNY Research Grant 1975. **Exhibitions/Performances:** Solo: Forum Gallery, St. Mary's Creative Arts Forum, Lexington Park, MD 1978; Lycoming College Art Gallery, Williamsport, PA 1980; City Hall Gallery, Metropolitan Art Project, Binghamton, NY 1983; Jewish Community Center, Binghamton, NY 1990; Group: Studio Gallcry, SUNY, Binghamton 1986; "Artists of the Southern Tier," Norwich, NY 1990; Pyramid Gallery, NYC 1990; Helio Gallery, NYC 1991; New York Studio School Gallery 1992; Univ. Art Museum, SUNY, Binghamton 1992. **Home Address:** RD 1, Box 115E, Friendsville, PA 18818. **Business Address:** SUNY, Binghamton, NY 13901.

SHAPIRO, ELLEN R. ■ FAAR History of Art 78. b. July 20, 1951, Boston, MA. m. Roberto Pietroforte. c. Alexander. BA 73, Brandeis Univ.; MA 76, Yale Univ.; PhD 85, Yale Univ. **Career & Employment:** Northeastern Univ., Lect. 1981-85; RISD, Lect. 1984; Boston College, Lect. 1984-85; Connecticut College, Asst. Prof. 1985-91; *Assemblage,* Assc. Ed. 1985-87; Massachusetts College of Art, Assc. Prof. 1992-present. **Memberships & Offices:** AHA, CAA, Fulbright Alumni Assn., SAH. **Fellowships, Honors & Awards:** Kress Found. Fellowship 1975; Council on Western European Studies Research Fellowship 1976; Fulbright-Hays Scholar 1977-78; NEH Travel Fellowship 1990; Graham Found. Grant 1992. **Publications:** "Architecture I; Architecture II; The Foreigners–Il Gruppo Sette," *Oppositions* 6 (Fall 1976): 85-102; "Architecture III: Unpreparedness–Incomprehension–Prejudices: Architecture IV: A New Archaic Era," *Oppositions* 12 (Spring 1978): 88-105; "The Emergence of Italian Rationalism," *Architectural Design* 51 (1981): 5-9; "Cesare Bazzani," "Luigi Broggi," "Mario Chiattone," "Gustavo Giovannoni," "Ernesto Bruno La

Padula," "Giovanni Battista Meduna," "Ludovico Quaroni," "Giuseppe Samona," in *Macmillan Encyclopedia of Architects* (New York: Free Press, 1982); **"Ernesto Basile," "Gruppo Sette," "Gio Ponti,"** & "Giuseppe Sommaruga," in *International Dictionary of Architects and Architecture* (Detroit & London: St. James Press, 1993); "Ogetti e Terragni," in *Giuseppe Terragni,* ed. Giorgio Ciucci (Milan: Electa, 1995). **Business Address:** Massachusetts College of Art, 621 Huntington Ave., Boston, MA 02115.

SHAPIRO, H. ALAN ■ RAAR Classics/Archaeology 79, 87, 92. b. Aug. 3, 1949, NYC. BA 71, Swarthmore College; MA 72, UC, Berkeley; PhD 77, Princeton Univ. **Research/Artistic Interests:** Greek art & archaeology. **Career & Employment:** Columbia Univ., Asst. Prof. 1977-78; Tulane Univ., Asst. Prof. 1978-81; Stevens Inst. of Technology, Assc. Prof. 1981-92; Univ. of Canterbury, Prof. 1994-present. **Fellowships, Honors & Awards:** Guggenheim Fellow 1992-93. **Publications:** *Art and Cult under the Tyrants in Athens* (Mainz: Verlag Philipp von Zabern, 1989); *Personifications in Greek Art* (Kilchberg-Zurich: Akanthus Verlag, 1993); *Myth into Art: Poet and Painter in Classical Greece* (London: Routledge, 1994). **Business Address:** Dept. of Classics, Univ. of Canterbury, Christchurch, New Zealand.

SHAPIRO, JOEL ■ AAR Visitor 1984-85, Artist.

SHAPLEY, JOHN ■ FAAR Classics/Archaeology 13. b. Aug. 7, 1890, Jasper County, MO. d. Sept. 8, 1978. BA 12, Univ. of Missouri; MA 13, Princeton Univ.; PhD 14, Univ. of Vienna. **Career & Employment:** Brown Univ., Asst. Prof. 1919-24; NYU, Asst. Prof. 1925-29; Univ. of Chicago, Prof. 1929-39; Catholic Univ. of America, Prof. 1952-60; Univ. of Baghdad, Prof. 1960-63; Howard Univ., Prof. 1963-70; George Washington Univ., Prof. 1972-74. **Memberships & Offices:** CAA, Founder & Treas. 1918; *Art Bulletin,* Founding Ed., Ed. 1921-39; *Survey of Persian Art,* Ed. Bd. 1933. **Fellowships, Honors & Awards:** Carnegie Corp. Medal; Shah of Iran, Decoration 1960. **Publications:** trans., W. Worringer, *Form Problems of the Gothic Art* (New York: Stechert, 1918); " A Note in Purgatorio X, 55-63," *Art Bulletin* 4 (1921): 19-26; "Another Sidamara Sarcophagus," *Art Bulletin* 5 (1922): 61-75; "A Lost Cartoon for Leonardo's Madonna with St. Anne," *Art Bulletin* 7 (1925): 96-102; "English Manuscripts at the British Museum," *Parnassus* 3 (Feb. 1931): 18-23; "More Masters at the Fair," *Parnassus* 12 (May 1940): 6-11; co-author, *Comparisons in Art* (New York: Praeger, 1957). **Bio-Bibliography:** *Washington Post,* Obit. (Sept. 13, 1978); *Contemporary Authors; Who Was Who in America; Who's Who in American Art.*

SHARP, CURT ■ AAR – New York, Dir. of Finance & Administration.

SHARPLEY, W.W. ■ Stewardson Memorial Scholar 1911-12, 1913.

SHAW, STUART MACLAREN ■ FAAR Architecture 28. b. Apr. 3, 1899, Emerson, IA. d. Feb. 11, 1985. BA 21, Simpson College; BArch 25, Columbia Univ. **Research/Artistic Interests:** Market of Sertiu, Timgad, excavation & reconstruction of the Arsinoen, Samothrace. **Career & Employment:** MMA, Staff Architect-Instr.-Senior Lect. 1924-39; NYU Expedition to Samothrace, Staff Architect 1939-59; US War Dept., Research Analyst, WWII. **Memberships & Offices:** ArIA, ASCSA. **Fellowships, Honors & Awards:** AIA Medal 1925; Simpson College, Hon. DFA 1962; Perkins-Boring Traveling Fellowship. **Publications:** contr., *Samothrace,* ed. Karl Lehmann & Phyllis W. Lehmann, 4 vols. (Princeton: Bollingen Series & New York:

Pantheon Books, 1959). **Important Works:** Designer, Museum & Hotel, Samothrace.

SHAW, WILL V. ■ FAAR Design Arts 68. b. Apr. 12, 1924, Los Angeles, CA. m. Mary M. Shaw. BA 50, UC, Berkeley. **Career & Employment:** Private practice 1968-present; Visiting Lect. UC, Santa Cruz; School of Architecture & Environmental Design, California Polytechnic State Univ., St. Luis Obispo. **Memberships & Offices:** AIA, Monterey Bay Chap., Pres. & Co-Founder; AIA College of Fellows 1984; Big Sur Found., Pres.; California 7th Agricultural District, Pres; Monterey History & Art Assn., Pres; Design Adv. Com. for Monterey County, Chair; Found. for Environemntal Design, Exec. Dir; Monterey Peninsula Museum of Art, BoD; Monterey Bay Aquarium, BoD. **Fellowships, Honors & Awards:** AIA California Council Honor Award, Monterey Bay Chap. Honor Award, Monterey Bay Chap. Award of Merit, Nat. 1st Honor Award; AIA & *Sunset Magazine,* Western Home Award Citation; American Soc. of Interior Design Award; General Electric Edison Award; *Progressive Architecture,* Urban Design Award; City of Monterey, Certificate of Appreciation; State of California, Certificate of Excellence; Governor's Design Award. **Important Works:** 11 Pelicano Masterplan, Algrave, Portugal; Alvarado St. Semi-Mall, Monterey, CA; Buddhist Temple, Seaside, CA; California Market, Carmel Highlands; Carmel Valley Ranch, CA; Casa de la Torre, Monterey, CA; Cascade Ranch, San Mateo County, CA; Church of the Good Shepard, Richmond, CA; Community Church of Monterey, CA; Control Tower, Monterey Peninsula Airport, CA; Cooper-Molera Adobe, Monterey, CA; Custom House Plaza Urban Design Plan, Monterey, CA; Del Monte Center, Monterey, CA; Del Monte Forest, Monterey County, CA; Enterprise Cannery Bldg., Monterey, CA; Estrada Medical Center, Monterey, CA; First Presbyterian Church, Hollister, CA; Garland Park Visitor Center, Carmel Valley, CA; Golf Instruction Facility, Monterey County, CA; Grass Valley Group, Nevada City, CA; High Meadow Terrace, Monterey County, CA; Highlands Inn, Carmel Highlands, CA; Huckleberry Ridge, Monterey, CA; Lobos Lodge, Carmel, CA; Mary L. Johnson Music Center, Santa Catalina School, Monterey, CA; Merrit House Offices, Monterey, CA; Monterey Bay Inn, Monterey, CA; Mountain Valley, Fukushima Prefecture, Japan; Naval Postgraduate School Exchange Bldg., Monterey, CA; Northern California Savings & Loan, Carmel, CA; Ohmurawan Golf Clubhouse, Nagasaki, Japan; Old Capitol Site, Monterey, CA; Pacific 1001 Professional Bldg., Monterey, CA; Pacific Edge, Carmel Highlands, CA; Pacific Medical Center, Monterey, CA; Pebble Beach Co. Lot Program, Monterey County, CA; Pebble Beach Equestrian Center Study & Equestrian Trails, CA; Polytechnic State Univ., San Luis Obispo, CA; Pueblo Uno Masterplan, San Jose, CA; Quitos Addition, Salinas, CA; Salinas Center Urban Mall, CA; San Francisco Zoo, Koala Habitat; School of Architecture & Environmental Design, CA; Shell Gas Station, Carmel, CA; Sherwood Gardens Shopping Center, Salinas, CA; Spanish Bay Masterplan, Pebble Beach, CA; Spyglass Woods, Pebble Beach, CA; St. John's Episcopal Church, Monterey, CA; Forest Club, Pebble Beach, CA; Toro Environmental Science Center, Monterey County, CA; Vista Lobos Apts., Carmel, CA; Whispering Pines Professional Bldg., Monterey, CA; White House Creek Campground, San Mateo County, CA. **Business Address:** Shaw Architecture Planning, Inc., 225 Cannery Row, Monterey, CA 93940.

SHEARER, ALLEN R. ■ FAAR Musical Composition 80. b. Oct. 5, 1943, Seattle, WA. m. Barbara Strunk. BA 65, UC, Berkeley; Dipl. 68, Akademie Mozarteum; MA 70, UC, Berkeley; PhD 73, UC, Berkeley. **Other Study:** with Max Deutsch, Paris 1974. **Career & Employment:** UC, Berkeley, Lect. 1968-present; San Francisco State Univ., Lect. 1972, 1973, 1983; Univ. of British Columbia, Asst. Prof. 1974-76; Hayward State Univ., Lect. 1988-91. Composers Inc., Artistic Dir. 1987-present. **Memberships & Offices:** Nat. Assn. of Teachers of Singing; California Music Teachers Assn. **Fellowships, Honors & Awards:** UC, Alfred Hertz Scholarship 1966; NIAL, Charles Ives Scholarship 1974; NEA Grant 1978, 1994; MacDowell Colony Resident 1987, 1989, 1990, 1993. **Important Works:** *Fantasy for Cello & Piano,* (Fallen Leaf Press) 1974; *Five Poems of Wallace Stevens,* for baritone & piano, (Fallen Leaf Press, CRS) 1980; *Nude Descending a Staircase,* for male sextet (Chanticleer Records) 1980; *Fantasy for Piano & Orchestra* 1981; *Beauty is a Shell from the Sea,* for chamber chorus, Perfect Fifth Comm. (Fallen Leaf Press) 1983; *Mushrooms* and *The Illusion of Eternity,* Chanticleer Comm. (Chanticleer Records) 1985; *Ages of Day,* for mixed chorus, NEA Consortium Comm. (Chanticleer Records) 1987; *Fantasy for Piano & Chamber Ensemble,* Earplay Comm. 1986; *We Three,* for flute, cello & piano, Meet the Composer Comm. 1989; *King Midas* 1990; *Travel Notes,* for trumpet, percussion & double bass 1993. **Bio-Bibliography:** *International Who's Who in Music.* **Home Address:** 6440 Regent St., Oakland, CA 94618.

SHEERIN, DANIEL JOSEPH ■ FAAR Post-Classical/Humanistic Studies 80. b. Dec. 26, 1943, St. Louis, MO. BA 65, St. Louis Univ.; PhD 69, UNC. **Other Studies:** Cardinal Glennon College 1961-62. **Career & Employment:** Univ. of Delaware, Asst. Prof. 1969-70; Catholic Univ. of America, Asst. Prof. 1970-74, Sec. of the Faculty 1973-74; UNC, Chapel Hill, Asst. Prof. 1974-76, Assc. Prof. 1976-, Assc. Dean of Graduate School 1976-79. **Fellowships, Honors & Awards:** NDEA Fellowship 1966-69; MAA Fellowship 1971. **Publications:** "John Leland and Mildred of Winchester," *Manuscripta* 21 (1977): 172-80; "Turpilius and St. Jerome in Anglo-Saxon England," *Classical World* 70 (1976): 183-85; "Gervase of Chichester and Thomas Becket," *Mediaeval Studies* 38 (1976): 468-82.

SHEETS, GEORGE A. ■ FAAR Classics/Archaeology 85. b. 1947, Buenos Aires, Argentina. m. Janet Dornberger. c. Benjamin Sheets, Penelope Sheets. BA 70, UNC, Chapel Hill; PhD 74, Duke Univ.; JD 90, William Mitchell College of Law, St. Paul, MN. **Other Study:** ICCS 1968. **Career & Employment:** Portsmouth Abbey School, RI, Instr. 1970-71; Univ. of Texas, Visiting Asst. Prof. 1974-75; Southwest Educational Development Laboratory, Austin, Research Assc. & Technical Writer 1975-76; Univ. of Minnesota, Asst. Prof. 1977-82, Assc. Prof. 1982-present. **Fellowships, Honors & Awards:** Bryn Mawr College, Andrew Mellon Fellow 1976-77. **Publications:** "Palatalization in Greek," *Indogermanische Forschungen* 80 (1975): 118-68; "The Dialectological Implications of Secondary Mid-Vowels in Greek, *American Journal of Philology* 100 (1979): 559-67; *A Grammatical Commentary to Book I of the Histories of Herodotus* (Bryn Mawr: Bryn Mawr College, 1981); "The Dialect Gloss, Hellenistic Poetics, and Livius Andronicus," *American Journal of Philology* 102 (1981): 58-78; "Ennius Lyricus," *Illinois Classical Studies* 8.1 (1983): 22-33; "Plautus and Early Roman Tragedy," *Illinois Classical Studies* 8.2 (1983): 195-209; "Conceptualizing International Law in Thucydides," *American Journal of Philology* 115 (1994): 51-73; *Carmina Catulli Selecta: A HyperBook* (New Haven: Yale Univ. Press, in preparation). **Home Address:** 6 S. Deep Lake, N. Oaks, MN 55217. **Business Address:** Dept. of Classical & Near Eastern Studies, Univ. of Minnesota, 330 Folwell Hall, Minneapolis, MN 55455.

SHELDON, ROSE MARY ■ FAAR Classics/Archaeology 81. b. Oct. 22, 1948, Newark, NJ. m. Jeffrey L. Aubert. BA 69, Trenton State College; MA 76, Hunter College; PhD 87, Univ. of Michigan. **Research/Artistic Interests:** Ancient & modern intelligence studies. **Career & Employment:** Adj.: Georgetown Univ. 1984-88, 1990; Defense Intelligence College 1986-89; American Univ. 1987-90; Montana State Univ., Asst. Prof. 1990-91; Norwich Univ., Asst. Prof. 1991-93; Virginia Military Inst., Asst. Prof. 1993-present. **Memberships & Offices:** *International Journal of Intelligence and Counterintelligence,* Ed. Bd. 1988-present; Assn. of Former Intelligence Officers, Life Mem.; AHA; Assn. of Ancient Historians; VSA; Classical Assn. of Virginia; Nat. Military Intelligence Assn.; Soc. for the Promotion of Roman Studies; Soc. for the Promotion of Hellenic Studies. **Fellowships, Honors & Awards:** NJ State Scholarship 1965-69; Trenton State College, Travel Fellowship 1968; Univ. of Michigan, A.E.R. Boak Fellowship 1976-77; AAUW, Dissertation Grant 1980-81; Nat. Intelligence Book Award 1988; Trenton State College, Alumna of the Year Award 1989. **Publications:** "The Polygraph, Adultery and the Romans or Fluttering in Antiquity," *Foreign Intelligence Literary Scene* 5.2 (1986): 2; "Hannibal's Spies," *Espionage* 2.3 (1986): 149-52; "Tinker, Tailor, Caesar, Spy: Intelligence in Ancient Rome," *American Intelligence Journal* (June 1986): 3-5; "The Ill-fated Trojan Spy," *Studies in Intelligence* 31.1 (1987): 35-39; "Hannibal's Spies," *International Journal of Intelligence and Counterintelligence* 1.3 (1987): 53-70; "A Quirk of Fate," *Intelligence Quarterly* 3.4 (1988): 6; "Spying in Mesopotamia: The World's Oldest Classified Documents," *Studies in Intelligence* 33.1 (1989): 7-12; "L'Occhio di Roma," *Storia e Dossier* (Jan. 1989): 46-49; "Spies & Mailmen & the Royal Road to Persia," *American Intelligence Journal* (1992-93): 37-40; "The Spartacus Rebellion: A Roman Intelligence Failure?," *International Journal of Intelligence and Counterintelligence* 6.1 (1993): 69-84; "Taking on Goliath: Low-Intensity Conflict in the Great Jewish War," *Small Wars & Insurgencies* 5.1 (1994); "Go Spy the Land," *Journal of Military History* (1994): 139-40; "Toga and Dagger: Espionage in Ancient Rome," *Military History Quarterly.* **Bio-Bibliography:** *Who's Who of American Women.* **Home Address:** 1990 Rt. 6, Box 98, Lexington, VA 24450. **Business Address:** Virginia Military Inst., Lexington, VA 22450.

SHEN, LILY ■ AAR – New York, Development Asst.

SHEPARDSON, WHITNEY H. ■ AAR Trustee 1946-66. b. Oct. 30, 1890, Worcester, MA. d. May 29, 1966. m. Eleanor MacPherson Cargin. c. J.W. Shepardson. BA 10, Colgate Univ.; BA 13, Oxford; LLB 17, Harvard Univ. **Career & Employment:** St. Mark's School, Southborough, MA, Instr. 1913-14; US Shipping Bd., Attorney 1917; US Army Air Corp Comm., 2d Lieut. 1918; American Comm. to Negotiate Peace, Asst. to Colonel House, Paris 1919; League of Nations Secretariat, London 1919; P.N. Gray & Co. 1920-23; Intl. Education Bd. 1923-27; Gen. Education Bd. 1925-27, Dir. 1927; Bates Intl. Bag Co., Pres. 1928-30; Intl. Rys. Central America, VP 1931-42; US Embassy, London, Special Asst. to Ambassador 1942, OSS & SSU, Washington, DC, Secret Intelligence Branch, Chief 1943-46; Carnegie Corp., British Dominions & Colonies Fund, Dir. 1946-53; Free Europe Com., Pres. 1953-56. **Memberships & Offices:** Phi Beta Kappa 1910-66, Treas., United Societies 1934-37; Council on Foreign Relations, Dir. 1921-66, Treas. 1933-42; Athenaeum, London; Century Assn., NY, 1st VP 1951-53; Metropolitan, Washington, DC. **Fellowships, Honors & Awards:** Rhodes Scholar, NY 1910; Oxon, 1st Class, Gladstone Memorial Prize 1913; US Medal for Merit, Légion d'Honneur; Croix de Guerre avec Palme, France; Order of Orange Nassau, Netherlands 1947.

Publications: *The United States in World Affairs,* Annual 1934-40; *The Interests of the United States as a World Power* (1942); plus contributions to periodicals, including *Foreign Affairs* & *The Round Table.*

SHEPLEY, HENRY R. ■ AAR Trustee 1939-62, Architect.

SHERMAN, C.L. ■ Sheldon Fellow 1919.

SHERMAN, STUART ■ FAAR Visual Arts 92. b. Nov. 9, 1945, Providence, RI. **Fellowships, Honors & Awards:** *Village Voice* Obie 1978; DAAD Grant, Berlin 1986; MacDowell Residency 1989; Asian Cultural Council Fellowship 1988; Guggenheim Fellowship 1991; NYSCA Grants, NEA Grants, Art Matters Grants, & NYFA Grants. **Publications:** "Imperfect Notes for a Perfect Manifesto, and Oedipus," *Drama Review* 27.4 (1983): 77-83; *One-Acts and Two Trilogies,* VRI Theater Library: Series 1: *Contemporary Scripts* 10 (1987). **Important Works:** *The Tenth Spectacle; The Eleventh Spectacle; The Twelfth Spectacle; The Thirteenth Spectacle; Silent Film Series; Hamlet; Classical Trilogy; Chekhov.* **Home Address:** 166 W. 22 St., NYC 10011.

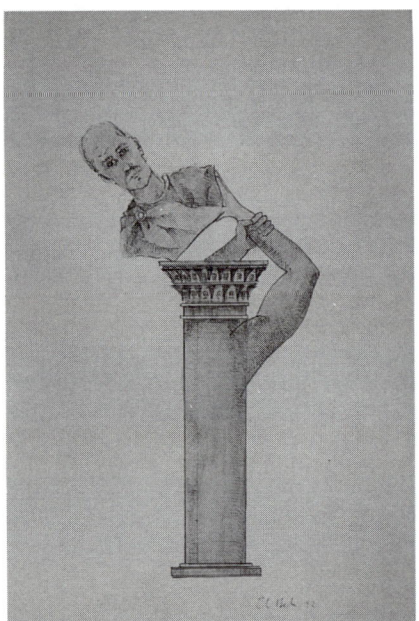

Idea: Stuart Sherman. Drawing: Eli Balser

SHERROD, PHILIP L. ■ FAAR Painting 86. b. Oct. 12, 1935, Pauls Valley, OK. m. Helena Alicia Decastro. c. Sandro Arentino Mateos Sherrod. BS 57, Oklahoma State Univ.; BA 59, Oklahoma State Univ. **Other Study:** ASL. **Research/Artistic Interests:** Street painter, street poet. **Career & Employment:** Brentano's Book Store 1960-72; Morristown Art Assn., Prof. 1973-74; NJ Center for Visual Arts, Prof. 1977-present; ASL, Prof. 1984-present. **Memberships & Offices:** NAD; Professional Street Painters, Founder 1977-present; Acad. of American Poets, Assc. Mem. **Fellowships, Honors & Awards:** Oklahoma State Univ., 1st Award 1959; ASL, Federation of Arts & Letters Scholarship 1963; AAAL, Childe Hassam Purchase Award 1967, 1969, 1974; Creative Artists Public Service Award 1980; Accademia Italia delle Arti e del Lavoro, Fellow-Gold-Medal 1980; Adolph & Esther Gottlieb Found. Grant 1981, 1988; NEA Grant 1982; Pollock-Krasner Found. Grant 1989. **Publications:** *30 Mentaltalia, Poems and Paintings* (Spring-

```
well..

      he's art's up
      onetwothree spins..
      thendownagain-

      without a grin
      to the tidewater.

   wasn't right?
                    oil-oozing-
                    from Newarkbed-rock

                    -bluedblack to bluer?
                    his leathermind..tethe-(red!)

      but fluttered-
      flew-the-coup!?
                    headon..'n hit!!
                    pinheaded- & redeyed-
      the Erie
            L A C K A W A N N A..
              from..Hoboken..
                            and fell-
                            likea-
                                 (paper-
                                     cutout!!)
```

Philip L. Sherrod

field, NJ: Merging Media, 1980); *Black Truck* (New York: Mirronic Publishers, 1981); *Mr Wigley Cums* (New York: Mirronic Publishers, 1983); *(69) /mages be/ow the Belt* (Springfield, NJ: Carrousel Publications, 1984); *Sex(/)Con!* (Springfield, NJ: Carrousel Publications, 1985). **Important Works:** American Broadcasting Corp. (ABC); Paramount Pictures Productions; Newcombe College Museum, Tulane Univ.; Everhart Museum, Scranton, PA; Almsford House, Fine Arts Center, Anderson, IN; Rose Art Museum, Brandeis Univ.; Hirshhorn Museum, Washington, DC; Worcester Fine Arts, MA; Phillips Exeter Acad., NH; Museum of the City of New York; Newark Museum, NJ; Museum of Fine Arts, Springfield, MA. **Exhibitions/Performances:** Solo: Selected Artists Gallery, NYC 1968; Sonraed Galleries, NYC 1971; Joan Michelman Home, Long Island, NY 1971; Artemis East Gallery, NYC 1972; Pace Univ., NYC 1972; Allan Stone Gallery, NYC 1973, 1976, 1983; Gallery 100, Princeton, NJ 1975; Cone Gallery, NYC 1976; Susan Montezinos Gallery, Philadelphia 1984; Herbert Johnson Museum, Cornell Univ. 1985. **Bio-Bibliography:** *American Artists of Renown; Dictionary of International Biography; International Who's Who of Intellectuals; Men of Achievement; Noteworthy Americans; Personalities of America; Who's Who in America; Who's Who in the East.* **Home Address:** 41 W. 24 St., 4 Fl., NYC 10010. **Business Address:** Allan Stone Gallery, NYC.

SHESTAK, ALAN ■ AAR Visitor 1984-85; Yale Art Gallery, Dir.

SHICOFF, ROCHELLE M. ■ FAAR Painting 81. b. Feb. 5, 1943, Brooklyn, NY. BA 65, Brooklyn College, CUNY; MA 70, Hunter College, CUNY. **Career & Employment:** Springfield Technical Community College, MA, Instr. 1975-77; Walter Vincent Smith Art Museum, Springfield, MA, Instr. 1977-78; Mt. Holyoke College, Instr. 1979; Univ. of Massachusetts, Instr. 1977-80; Museum of Fine Arts, Springfield, MA, Consultant 1978-80; Summer Arts Inst., Murals Instr., Brooklyn, NY 1984, 1985, Bronx, NY 1988, 1989; Parsons School of Design, Instr. 1984-85; Children's Museum of Manhattan, NYC, Public Programs Coordinator 1989-90; Washington Irving HS, NYC, Murals Instr. 1991-92, 1993; Hostos Community College, CUNY 1992-95; Hunter College, CUNY, Instr. 1993-95; Lehman College, CUNY, Instr. 1993-95. **Memberships & Offices:** Hestig Art Collective, MA 1979-80; Playzone Inc., MA & NYC; Playspaces, Consultant 1985-present; Artmakers Inc., NYC 1991-present. **Fellowships, Honors & Awards:** Found. for the Humanities & Public Policy, Mural Project Grant 1979;

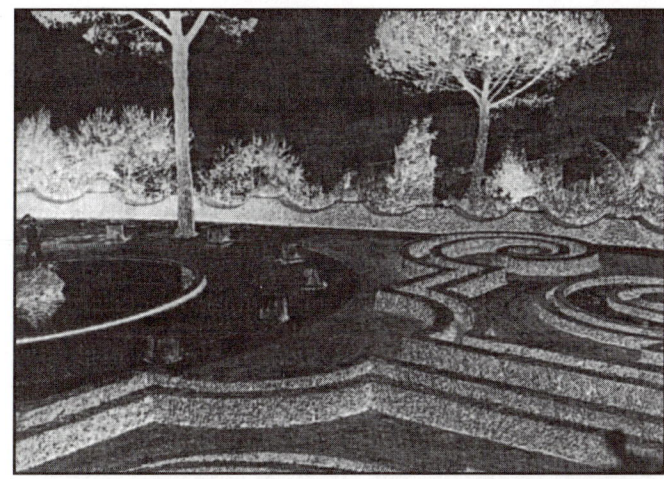

Rochelle M. Shicoff

Astraea Found. Mural, NYC 1979; Massachusetts Council for the Arts 1980; Artists Found., Boston 1981; Dominican College Fellowship, San Rafael, CA 1982; Artists Space Grant 1987, 1988, 1991; UNC, Visiting Artist 1988; John A. Spooner Award 1988; NYFA 1993; Lower East Side Print Shop, Special Editions Program, NYC 1989; Art in Action Grant, Mural 1993; Loomis Chaffee School, Windsor, CT, Visiting Artist 1993. **Important Works:** Head Start Graphics Pgm., Turners Falls, MA 1977; Westfield Area Mental Health & Retardation Center, Agawam, MA, Mural 1978; New England Telephone Co. Mural, Northampton, MA 1978-80; Bellevue Hospital Center Collection, NYC 1986; West Bronx Youth Center Mural 1991, 1992; Auburn Homeless Shelter Mural , Brooklyn, NY 1992; Women: Uniting Against Violence Murals 1993; United Community Centers Mural, Brooklyn, NY 1993-95. **Exhibitions/ Performances:** Solo: Image Gallery, Stockbridge, MA 1980, 1991; Springfield Museum of Fine Arts, MA 1980; Dominican College, San Rafael, CA 1982; A.I.R. Gallery, NYC 1986; BACA Downtown, Brooklyn, NY 1987; Hanes Art Center, Chapel Hill, NC 1988; Canal Gallery, Holyoke, MA 1991; SITES for Students 1993-95; Ladies' Center Mural, Pensacola, FL 1994; plus numerous group shows. **Home Address:** 410 3rd St., Brooklyn, NY 11215.

SHIELDS, DONALD CARL ■ FAAR Painting 80. b. Oct. 3, 1948, Albuquerque, NM. m. Michele Rowe. BFA 73, Washington Univ.; MFA 77, Southern Methodist Univ. **Research/ Artistic Interests:** Computer animation. **Career & Employment:** Industrial Transit Service, Truck Driver 1974-75; Richland College, Instr. 1977; Midwestern Truck Lines, Truck Driver 1977-78; Austin Products, Truck Driver 1978; Univ. of Michigan, Visiting Instr. 1984. **Fellowships, Honors & Awards:** NEA Grant; Guggenheim Fellowship 1980; MacDowell Colony Fellow. **Exhibitions/Performances:** Solo: Haber Theodore Gallery, NYC 1984; Nawara Gallery, Walled Lake, MI 1987. **Bio-Bibliography:** "Painter Drawn to Computer Animation," *Dallas Morning News* (Apr. 14, 1991).

SHIFFLET, JOEL A. ■ NIAE, John Dinkeloo Traveling Fellow 1993-94.

SHIRER, WILLIAM ■ AAR Visitor 1959 — 1964, Writer.

SHOEMAKER, INNIS HOWE ■ FAAR History of Art 73. b. Feb. 7, 1942, Reading, PA. BA 64, Vassar College; MA 68, Columbia Univ.; PhD 75, Columbia Univ. **Research/Artistic Interests:** Prints & drawings, primarily Italian Renaissance & contemporary. **Career & Employment:** Vassar College, Curator of the Art Gallery 1966-68, 1973-76; UNC, Chapel Hill, Adj. Asst. Prof. 1977-83, Adj. Prof. 1983-86; Ackland Art Museum, Asst. Dir. 1977-83, Dir. 1983-86; Philadelphia Museum of Art, Senior Curator of Prints, Drawings & Photographs 1986-present. **Memberships & Offices:** Assn. of Art Museum Directors 1983-86; Print Council of America, BoT 1984-present, BoD 1986-89; Conservation Center, Philadelphia, BoD 1987-present. **Publications:** "Drawings after the Antique by Filippino Lippi," *Master Drawings* 16 (1978): 35-43; *Drawings about Drawing Today* (Chapel Hill, NC: Ackland Museum, 1978); with Elizabeth Broun, *The Engravings of Marcantonio Raimondi* (Lawrence, KS: Univ. of Kansas Press, 1981); with Theodore Reff, *Paul Cézanne: Two Sketchbooks* (Philadelphia: Philadelphia Museum of Art, 1989); "Some Observations on the Development of Filippino Lippi's Figure Drawings," in *Florentine Drawings at the Time of Lorenzo the Magnificent* (Bologna: Nuova Alfa Editoriale, 1994), 255-64. **Bio-Bibliography:** *Who's Who in America*; *Who's Who in American Art*. **Business Address:** Philadelphia Museum of Art, Box 7646, Philadelphia, PA 19101.

SHOWERMAN, GRANT ■ FASCSR 1900; AAR Prof. 1922-23; AAR Summer School, Dir. 1923-32. b. Jan. 9, 1870, Brookfield, WI. d. Nov. 13, 1935. m. Zilpha Marie Vernon. c. Anita May, John Parker. BA 1896, Univ. of Wisconsin; MA 1897, Univ. of Wisconsin; PhD 1900, Univ. of Wisconsin. **Career & Employment:** Univ. of Wisconsin, Prof. 1900-35. **Fellowships, Honors & Awards:** Phi Beta Kappa; ArIA, Fellow 1898-1900; Univ. of Padua, Hon. PhD 1922. Ufficiale Cavaliere della Corona d'Italia. **Publications:** "The Great Mother of the Gods," *Bulletin of the University of Wisconsin, Philology and Literature Series* 1 (1901): 221-333; *With the Professor* (New York: Holt, 1910); trans., Ovid, *Heroides and Amores* (Cambridge, MA: Loeb Classical Library, 1914); *The Indian Stream Republic and Luther Parker* (Concord: New Hampshire Historical Soc., 1915); *A Country Chronicle* (New York: Century, 1916); *A Country Child* (New York: Century, 1917); *Horace and His Influence* (Boston: Marshall Jones, 1922); *Eternal Rome* (New Haven: Yale Univ. Press, 1924); *Century Readings in Ancient Classical Literature* (New York: Century, 1925); *Rome and the Romans* (New York: Macmillan, 1931); *Moments and Men of Ancient Rome* (New York: Appleton-Century, 1935). **Bio-Bibliography:** Briggs, 586-88; *National Cyclopedia of American Biography*; *Who Was Who in America*.

SHUTZE, PHILIP TRAMMELL ■ FAAR Architecture 20. b. Aug. 18, 1890, Columbus, GA. d. Oct. 17, 1982. BArch 12, Georgia Inst. of Technology; BArch 13, Columbia Univ. **Research/Artistic Interests:** Classical architecture, restoration of Hadrian's Villa. **Career & Employment:** Hentz, Reid & Adler, Designer 1920; Hentz, Adler & Shutze, Part. 1926; Hentz, Adler & Shutze, Prin. Architect 1927-35; Shutze & Armistead, Architects, Prin. Architect 1935-50. **Fellowships, Honors & Awards:** AIA Fellow 1950; AIA, Georgia Assn., Bronze Medal 1974. **Important Works:** Memorial Gate, Rich Bldg., Emory Univ.; Calhoun-Thornwell House, The Pink Palace 1919-22; Swan House, Atlanta Historical Soc. 1926-28; English-Chambers House 1929; Raymond Demere House, Savannah c.1930; Temple of the Hebrew Benevolent Congregation 1931-32; Whitehead Memorial Annex, Univ. Hospital, Emory Univ. 1940; Acad. of Medicine, Fulton County Medical Soc. 1940; Julian Hightower Residence, Thomaston, GA 1947-48; Charles

Daniel House, Greenville, SC 1954. **Exhibitions/Performances:** Low Memorial Library, Columbia Univ. 1979. **Bio-Bibliography:** "The Classic Lines of Philip Shutze," *Atlanta Constitution* (Mar. 12, 1979); *NY Times*, Obit. (Oct. 19, 1982); "Ball Theme Honors Swan House Architect," *Vinings Neighbor* (Marietta, GA, June 15, 1988); *Who Was Who in America.*

SIEFERT, GEORGE JOSEPH, JR ■ FAAR Classics/Archaeology 36. b. Aug. 25, 1910, Philadelphia, PA. d. Oct. 13, 1984. m. Mary W. Siefert. BA 30, Univ. of Pennsylvania; MA 32, Univ. of Pennsylvania. **Research/Artistic Interests:** Cults of greater Latium, Varro's *De vita populi Romani.* **Career & Employment:** Catholic Univ., Prof. 1936-42; US Army 1942-45. **Fellowships, Honors & Awards:** Univ. of Pennsylvania, Harrison Fellowship 1931-33; Italian Government, Gold Medal in Latin 1933. **Publications:** *Meter and Case in the Latin Elegias Pentameter,* Language Dissertations 49 (Baltimore: Linguistic Soc. of America, 1952).

SILK, EDMUND TAITE ■ FAAR Classics/Archaeology 31, RAAR Classics/Archaeology 56; AAR Classical Soc., Pres. 1958. b. Aug. 16, 1901, West Haven, CT. d. Apr. 12, 1981. m. Eleanor Smith. c. Edmund O.T., John K. BA 24, Yale Univ.; MA 27, Yale Univ.; PhD 31, Yale Univ. **Research/Artistic Interests:** Latin literature, Boethius, English literature, Horace & Augustan literature. **Career & Employment:** Yale Univ., Instr. 1927-33, Asst. Prof. 1933-40, Assc. Prof. 1940-48, Prof. & Dunham Prof. 1949-70; Yale Univ. Library, Curator, Classical & Medieval Manuscripts 1944-59. **Memberships & Offices:** APA; MAA; CANE. **Fellowships, Honors & Awards:** Guggenheim Fellowship; Yale Univ., John Addison Porter Fellowship 1925-26, Larned-Bidwell Fellowship 1924-25. **Publications:** *Saeculi Noni Auctoris in Boetii consolationem philosophiae commentarius,* AAR Papers & Monographs 9 (Rome: AAR, 1935); "Boethius' *Consolatio Philosophiae* as a Sequel to Augustine's Dialogues and Soliloquia," *Harvard Theological Review* 32 (1939): 19-39; "Notes on Cicero and the Odes of Horace," *Yale Classical Studies* 13 (1952): 145-58; "A Fresh Approach to Horace, II, 20," *American Journal of Philology* 77 (1956): 255-63; "Pseudo-Johannes Scottus, Adalbard of Utrecht and the Early Commentaries on Boethius," *Mediaeval and Renaissance Studies* 3 (1954): 1-40; "Bacchus and the Horation *Recusatio,*" *Yale Classical Studies* 21 (1969): 195-212; "Towards a Fresh Interpretation of Horace, Carm. III, 1," *Yale Classical Studies* 23 (1972): 131-45. **Bio-Bibliography:** "Ancient Languages Refuse to Die but Play Major Role in 1954, Says Yale Professor," *New Haven Register* (Nov. 21, 1954); Briggs, 589-90; *Directory of American Scholars; Who's Who in America.*

SILK, GERALD D. ■ FAAR Post-Classical/Humanistic Studies 82. b. Dec. 29, 1947, Fall River, MA. m. Marguerite H. O'Brien. c. Caitlin. BA 70, Brandeis Univ.; PhD 76, Univ. of Virginia. **Research/Artistic Interests:** Modern art, Italian Futurism. **Career & Employment:** Columbia Univ., Lect. 1975-76, Asst. Prof. 1976-83; Univ. of Pensylvania, Asst. Prof. 1983-87; Temple Univ., Tyler School, Assc. Prof. 1988-present. **Memberships & Offices:** *Arts Magazine,* Assc. Ed. 1983-88; *Art Journal,* Ed. Bd. 1990-present; Craft & Folk Art Museum, Los Angeles; Center for Advanced Study in Art & Culture, Nat. Adv. Bd. 1990-present; Getty Art History Information Program, Consultant 1988-present. **Fellowships, Honors & Awards:** Univ. of Virginia, Fellowship 1970-74; Nat. Museum of American Art, Smithsonian, Fellowship 1974-75; CAA Grant 1983; Univ. of Pennsylvania Fellowship 1984; CASVA, Ailsa Mellon Bruce Fellow 1987-88; Temple Univ. Grant 1990, 1995; Tyler

School of Art, Mellon Award 1991; NEH Stipend 1991. **Publications:** "Ed Kienholz's Back Seat Dodge '38," *Arts Magazine* 52 (Jan. 1978): 112-18; "Fu Balla e Balla Futurista," *Art Journal* 41 (1981): 328-36; *Museums Discovered: The Wordsworth Atheneum* (New York: Penshurst-Shorewood Fine Art Books, 1982); *Automobile & Culture* (New York & Los Angeles: Harry N. Abrams & Museum of Contemporary Art, 1984); *Investigations/Robert Colescott: The Artist & His Model* (Philadelphia: Inst. of Contemporary Art, Univ. of Pennsylvania, 1984); "The Integration of Music, Art, and Theater in Italian Futurist Performance," in *XXVth Internationaler Kongress für Kunstgeschichte: Kunst, Musik, Schaispiel* 2 (Vienna, 1985): 115-20; "Flight; Futurism; Aeropittura," in *Futurism Aeropittura* (Rome: Stilgraf, 1989), n.p.; "Futurism and the Automobile," in *Twentieth-Century Art Theory: Urbanism, Politics, and Mass Culture,* ed. Richard Hertz & Norman M. Klein (Englewood Cliffs, NJ: Prentice Hall, 1990), 28-42; "F3: The Synergy of Futurism, Fascism & Flight," in *World War II: A Fifty Year Perspective on 1939,* ed. Robert W. Hoeffner (Loudonville, NY: Siena College Press, 1992); "Away from a Theory of Public Art," in *art-public,* ed. Valentine Anker & Claude Ritschard (Geneva: Acts of the Intl. Assn. of Art Critics, 1992), 169-80; guest ed., "Uneasy Pieces: Controversial Works in the History of Art, 1830-50," *Art Journal* 51.1 (1992); *The Elegant Auto: Design & Fashion in the 1930s* (Portland, ME: Portland Museum of Art, 1992). **Bio-Bibliography:** *National Faculty Directory.* **Home Address:** 3718 Hamilton St., Philadelphia, PA 19104. **Business Address:** Tyler School of Art, Temple Univ., Philadelphia, PA 19027.

SILVA, THOMAS P. ■ FAAR Architecture 89. b. Dec. 17, 1965, Sacramento, CA. m. Ina Nouel. BArch 84, Cooper Union. **Career & Employment:** Office of the State Architect, Sacramento, Drafter 1977-78; Nubar Corp., Senior Designer & Project Manager 1978-80; Tecon Pacific, Detailer 1980-81; Wank Adams Slavin Asscs., in assn. with James Stirling, Michael Wilford & Asscs., Project Architect 1981-85; Eisenman Architects, Project Architect 1985-86; Richard Meier & Partners, Project Designer 1987-88; Vicente Wolf Asscs., Project Manager 1990-92; Polshek & Partners, Project Architect 1995-

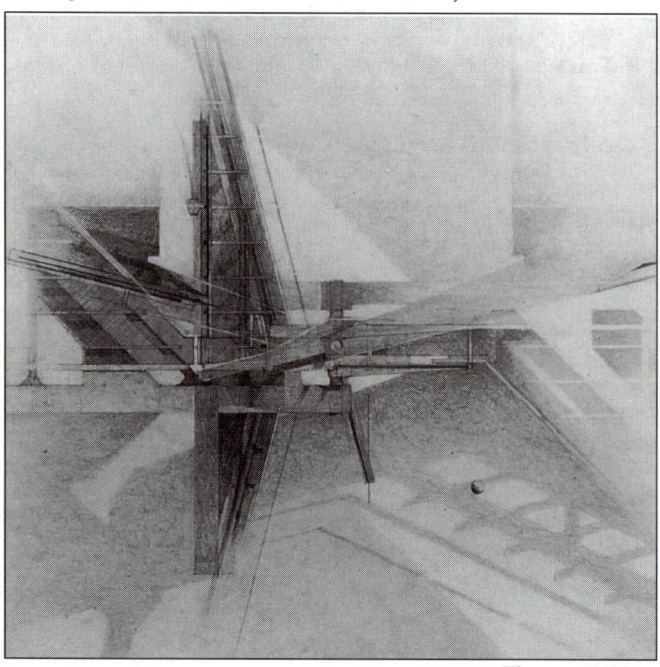

Thomas P. Silva

present. **Fellowships, Honors & Awards:** AIA, New York Chap., Elanor Allwork Scholarship 1984, 1985, 1986; AIA Nat. Found. Scholarship 1985; NY Soc. of Architects, Mathew del Gaudio Award for Excellence 1987; AIA Henry Adams Certificate of Merit 1987; Graham Found. Grant 1989. **Exhibitions/Performances:** Rotterdam Nat. Museum of Architecture 1985; Houghton Gallery, NYC 1987; Clocktower Gallery, NYC 1989; Museum of Modern Art, San Francisco 1990. **Home Address:** 41 Sutter St., Suite 1274, San Francisco, CA 94108. **Business Address:** Polshek & Partners Architects, 250 Sutter St., Suite 600, San Francisco, CA 94108.

SILVER, JUDY ■ FAAR Painting 78. b. Nov. 30, 1950, NYC. BFA 72, Philadelphia College of Art; MFA 74, Maryland Inst. College of Art. **Career & Employment:** Maryland Inst. College of Art 1972-74; Northern Virginia Community College 1974-75; Community College of Baltimore 1976; Canberra School of Art 1981-85; ABC, Canberra (2CN), Art Critic 1984-85; Australia Council 1986-87; City Art Inst., Sydney 1987; Charles Stuart Univ., Wagga Wagga, NSW 1989; 2SER, Sydney, Co-Producer, Presenter 1991-present. **Fellowships, Honors & Awards:** Links Soc. of New York, Fine Arts Award 1967; Fairfax County Council of the Arts, VA Grand Prize, Maryland Inst. College of Art, Hoffberger Scholarship 1974; Jabberwock Paper Mill, TAS, School of Art, Guest Artist 1982; *Canberra Times*, Nat. Art Award 1985; NY Intl. Radio Competition, Finalist 1994. **Important Works:** Resort Hotel Macquarie, "Parrots" Restaurant, Sydney 1988; Art Bank; Resort Hotel Macquarie; Hyatt Hotel, Melbourne; New Parliament House, Canberra; Queen Victoria Museum & Art Gallery, Launceston, TAS; Burnie Art Gallery, Burnie, TAS; Ararat Gallery, Ararat, VIC; European-American Bank, NYC; Gold Coast City Art Collection; Amalgamated Bank, NYC; Rutgers Univ.; Northern Virginia Community College; US Embassy in Tunisia. **Exhibitions/Performances:** *Side Show*, weekly arts program, Radio 2SER FM, Sydney 1990-93; "All Night Long," radio documentary, Australia 1993; "The Tarot Reader" & "The Third Runway," Two Interactive-Sound Installation works for the Newtown Festival 1993; "Angels in Australia," Sound piece for radio 1994; Solo: Walker Street Gallery, NYC 1975; Gallery 641, Washington DC, 1976; Gallery A, Sydney 1981; Gallery Huntly, ACT 1981; Christine Abrahams Gallery, Melbourne 1983; Council Gallery & Gallery Huntly, ACT 1984; Rex Irwin Art Dealer, Sydney 1984, 1987, 1989; "Wedding Blues," Sound Installation, Newtown Festival 1994; "Chimera," Radio Documentary, 2SER Nat. Broadcast 1995. **Home Address:** 47 Baltic St., Newtown, NSW 2042 Australia.

SILVER, SHEILA J. ■ FAAR Musical Composition 79; SOF Bd. 1994-97. b. Oct. 3, 1946, Seattle, WA. m. John Isaac Feldman. BA 68, UC, Berkeley; MFA 74, Brandeis Univ.; PhD 76, Brandeis Univ. **Other Study:** Hochschule für Musik, Stuttgart. **Career & Employment:** Brandeis Univ., Lect. 1976-77; Phillips Exeter Acad., Instr. 1976-77; SUNY, Stony Brook Assc. Prof. 1979-present. **Memberships & Offices:** American Music Center, BoD 1993-96; New York Women Composers. **Fellowships, Honors & Awards:** Intl. Soc. for Contemporary Music, Winner 1981, 1983; AAAL Composers Award 1986. **Important Works:** *Galixidi*, for chamber orchestra, Seattle Philharmonic Orchestra Comm. 1976; *Chariessa*, for soprano & piano, Radcliffe Inst. Comm. 1978, for soprano & orchestra, RAI Orchestra of Rome Comm. 1980; *Dynamis*, for French horn 1978; *Canto*, for baritone & chamber ensemble, Fromm Found. Comm. (Mode Records) 1979; *Fantasy Quasi Theme and Variation*, for piano 1980; *Theme and Variation for Bowed Vibraphone*

(Studio 4 Productions) 1980; *Ek Ong Kar*, for chorus 1981; *The Thief of Love*, an opera 1986; *Dance Converging*, for chamber ensemble, Speculum Musicae Comm. (CRI) 1987; *Song of Sarah*, for string orchestra 1987; *G Whiz*, for 2 violins & marimba (Studio 4 Productions) 1988; *Sonata for Cello and Piano* (CRI) 1988; *Dance of Wild Angels*, for chamber orchestra, Los Angeles Philharmonic New Music Group Comm. 1990; *Six Préludes pour Piano*, Heckscher Museum Comm. (CRI) 1990; *Bless the Lord, Oh My Soul*, for choirs & piano, Gregg Smith Singers Comm. (Gregg Smith Singers) 1990; *Three Preludes for Orchestra*, American Composers Orchestra Comm. 1992; *To the Spirit Unconquered*, Chamber Music America Comm. (CRI) 1992; *Harp Quintet*, NEA Comm. 1995. Publisher: MMB Music Publishers. **Bio-Bibliography:** *International Who's Who; International Who's Who of Women; Who's Who in America; Who's Who of American Women*. **Home Address:** 68-37 Dartmouth St., Forest Hills, NY 11375.

SILVETTI, JORGE ■ FAAR Architecture 86. b. Jan. 5, 1942, Buenos Aires, Argentina. Dipl. Arch. 66, Universidad de Buenos Aires; MArch 69, UC, Berkeley. **Other Study:** Conservatorio de Musica de Buenos Aires, music & performance (piano) 1948-59. **Career & Employment:** UC, Berkeley, Lect. 1969-73; Carnegie-Mellon Univ., Asst. Prof. 1973-75; Machado & Silvetti, Asscs., Founding Part. 1975-present; Harvard Univ., Asst. Prof. 1975-78, Assc. Prof. 1978-83, Prof. 1983-90, Nelson Robinson Jr. Prof. 1990-present, GSD Architecture Dept. Chair 1995. **Fellowships, Honors & Awards:** *Progressive Architecture*, Citations 1976, 1978, 1993, Awards 1985, 1st Awards 1980, 1985, 1991, Research Award 1991; Intl. Competition for Renovation of La Villete, Paris, 2d Prize 1976; DOM-Sicherheits-Techik Corp. HQ, Cologne, Intl. Competition, Hon. Mention 1980; Piazza Dante Intl. Competition, 1st Award 1990; Boston Soc. of Architects, Award for Excellence 1990, Citation for Excellence 1990; AAAL, 1st Award in Architecture 1991; Quinta Mostra Internazionale di Architettura, Venice, Citation 1991; AIA, New England Regional Council, Awards for Excellence 1992 (3), Nat. Assn. Honor Award 1993. **Publications:** "The Beauty of Shadows," *Oppositions* 9 (1977); "On Realism in Architecture," *Harvard Architecture Review* 1 (1980); "Perspektive und der neidische Blick auf die Renaissance," *Daidalos: Berlin Architectural Journal* 11 (1984): 10-21; "Four Public Squares in the City of Leonforte, Sicily," *Assemblage* 1 (1986): 54-71; "Contemporary Tendences of U.S.A. Architecture," *Metamorfosi* 6-7 (1987): 4-10; "Aires de la Pampa: An Introduction to the Work of Amancio Williams," in *Amancio Williams*, ed. Jorge Silvetti (New York: Rizzoli, 1987), 4-10; "The Work of Campi-Pessina," in *Mario Campi — Franco Pessina, Architects* (New York: Rizzoli, 1987), 4-9; ed., *The Architecture and Urban Environments of Sicily* (Cambridge: Harvard GSD, 1989); "Special Feature: Works of Machado and Silvetti," *Architecture + Urbanism* (1990): 65-138; with Rodolfo Machado, "War Memorial, Parking Structure, Commercial Residential Building and Piazza Dante," *Composicion Arquitectonica* 7 (1990): 61-108; "Discussion," in *Thinking the Present: Recent American Architecture*, ed. K. Michael Hays & Carol Burns (New York: Princeton Architectural Press, 1990), 123-34; ed., *Interactive Realms, The Bridge of San Francesco and the Palazzo Sant'Elia*, vol. 2 (Cambridge, MA: Harvard GSD, 1992). **Important Works:** Municipal Cemetery, Polizzi-Generosa, Italy 1987; Palermo Exb. Hall, Italy 1988; Parking Structure, Princeton Univ. Campus 1988; Donald Brecher Residence, Boston 1989; Piazza Dante, Genoa 1989; Piazzale Roma, Venice 1990; Nordbahnhofgelande Master Plan, Vienna 1991; Seaside Mix-Use Bldg. 1990; Cranbrook Educational Community, Entrance Gate Competition, Bloomfield Hills, MI 1991; Feldberg Residence, Concord, MA 1992; South Park, Battery Park City, NYC 1992; Princeton Univ. Master Plan 1993; Getty Villa, Malibu, CA 1994. **Exhibitions/Performances:** Leo Castelli Gallery, NYC 1983; Corcoran Gallery, Los Angeles 1984; Sala de Exposiciones de Ministerio de Obras Publicas, Madrid 1984; Martin-Gropius Bau, Berlin 1984; Biennale di Venezia 1985; XVII Triennale di Milano 1987; Harvard GSD 1989; Palazzo Comunale, Trieste 1990; Center de Arte y Communcacion, Buenos Aires 1990; AAAL 1991; Fondation pour l'Architeture, Brussels 1991; ALNY 1991; "Banffire": A Public Place, Banff (Alberta, Canada) 1992; Stadt Raum-Remise, Vienna 1992. **Bio-Bibliography:** Peter G. Rowe, *Rodolfo Machado and Jorge Silvetti: Buildings for Cities* (New York: Rizzoli, 1989); K. Michael Hays, *Unprecedented Realism: The Works of Machado and Silvetti* (New York: Princeton Architectural Press, 1994). **Business Address:** Machado & Silvetti, 560 Harrison Ave., Boston, MA 02118.

SIMON, JANET LYNN ■ NIAE, John Dinkeloo Traveling Fellow 1991-92.

SIMON, SIDNEY ■ RAAR Sculpture 70. b. May 21, 1917, Pittsburgh, PA. m. Renee Adriance. c. Mark, Teru, Rachel, Nora, Juno, Nicholas, Tony. BFA 40, Pennsylvania Acad. of Art, Univ. of Pennsylvania. **Other Study:** Carnegie Inst. of Technology, Pittsburgh 1933-36; Barnes Found. 1937-39; Asst. to George Harding, mural painter 1938-40; Grand Chaumière, Paris 1949. **Research/Artistic Interests:** Mural & sculpture for public places. **Career & Employment:** Skowhegan School of Painting & Sculpture, Co-Founder 1945-59, Acad. Dir. 1981-83; Cooper Union, Instr. 1946-48; Brooklyn Museum Art School, Instr. 1950-52, 1954-56; New School for Social Research, Instr. 1964-76; Sarah Lawrence College 1971-72; ASL, Instr. 1973-present; Visiting Artist: Univ. of Pennsylvania, Columbia Univ. **Memberships & Offices:** Sculpture Guild, BoD; Artists Equity Assn., Founder, Mem. 1946-present; Skowhegan School of Painting & Sculpture, Governor 1964-present; Castle Hill Center for the Arts, BoD 1968-present;

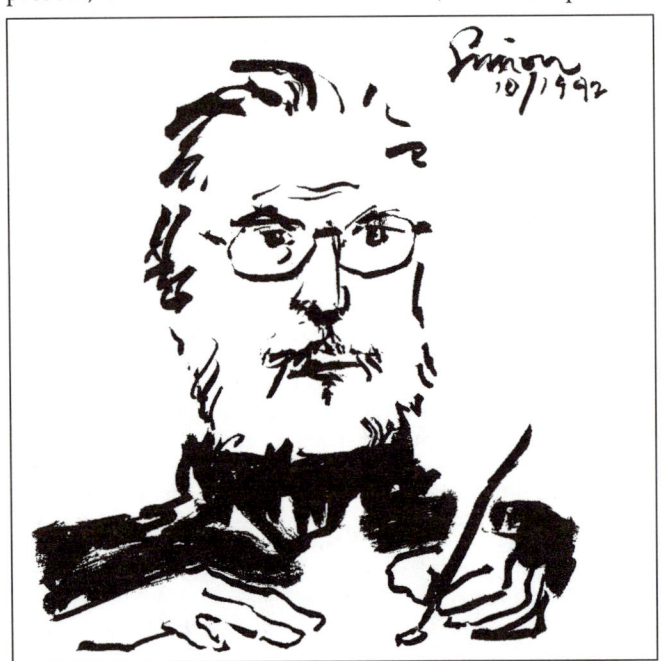

Sidney Simon

City of New York Art Comm. 1974-79; NAD, Council Mem. 1986-present; NSS, Fellow 1988-present. **Fellowships, Honors & Awards:** PAFA, Cresson Travel Fellowship 1940; NAD, Edwin Austin Abbey Award 1940, Gold Medal 1981, Maynard Award 1987; AAAL Grant 1976; NSS, Wexler Award 1989. **Important Works:** Paintings & Drawings from World War II included in US Defense Dept. Historical Collection & Australian War Memorial, Canberra; Four Seasons Fountain, World Wide Plaza, NYC; Graham Bldg. Fountain, City Hall Plaza, Philadelphia; West Point Jewish Chapel, West Point, NY; Hakone Open Air Museum; Loma-Nettleton Bldg., Dallas; 747 Third Ave., NYC; St. Luke's, NYC; Prospect Park, Brooklyn; Downstate Medical Center, Brooklyn; Our Lady of the Angels; Walt Whitman HS, Yonkers, NY; Temple Beth Abraham, Tarrytown, NY; Solon Meeting House, Maine. **Exhibitions/Performances:** Exhibiting in solo & group shows since 1938 at MOMA; MMA; NAD; Nat. Arts Club; PAFA; Corcoran Gallery, Washington, DC; Retrospective, Princeton Art Museum 1995; plus museums in Australia, & galleries in NYC, Paris, Rome & elsewhere. **Bio-Bibliography:** *Who's Who in America; Who's Who in Art.* **Home Address:** 95 Bedford St., NYC 10014.

SIMONDS, CHARLES F. ■ RAAR Sculpture 86. b. Nov. 14, 1945, NYC. BA 67, UC, Berkeley; MFA 69, Douglas College, Rutgers Univ. **Research/Artistic Interests:** clay sculpture. **Publications:** with Lucy Lippard, "Microcosm to Macrocosm/Fantasy World to Real World," *Artforum* (1974); *Three Peoples,* exb. cat. (Samanedizione, 1975, Chicago: Museum of Contemporary Art, 1982); with Daniel Abadie, *Art/Cahier 2,* SMI (1975); with Herbert Molderings, *Charles Simonds: Schwebende Stadte und andere Architekturen/Floating Cities and Other Architectures,* exb. cat. (Munster: Westfalischer Kunstverein, 1978); with Annelie Pohlen, "Interview mit Charles Simonds," *Heute Kunst/Flash Art* (1979). **Important Works:** Denver Museum of Art; Allen Memorial Art Museum, Oberlin College; Art Gallery of South Australia, Adelaide; Georges Pompidou Centre, Paris; Israel Museum, Jerusalem; Kunsthaus, Zurich; Museum of Contemporary Art, Chicago; Wallraf-Richartz Museum, Museum Ludwig, Cologne; MOMA; Storm King Art Center, NY; Walker Art Center, Minneapolis; Whitney Museum, NYC; Des Moines Art Center; Guggenheim Museum, NYC. **Exhibitions/Performances:** Solo: Centre National d'Art Contemporain, Paris 1975-76; MOMA 1976; Albright-Knox Art Gallery, Buffalo 1977; Westfalischer Kunstverein, Munster 1978; Bonner Kunstverein, Bonn 1978; Wallraf-Richartz Museum 1979; Museum Ludwig, Cologne 1979; Nationalgalerie, Berlin 1979; Museum of Contemporary Art, Chicago 1981-83; Los Angeles County Museum of Art 1981-83; Fort Worth Art Museum 1981-83; Contemporary Art Museum, Houston 1981-83; Phoenix Museum of Art 1981-83; Brooks Memorial Art Gallery, Memphis 1981-83; Guggenheim Museum, NYC 1981-83; Leo Castelli Gallery, NYC 1984, 1989; Galerie Maeght Lelong, Paris 1986; Architekturmuseum, Basel 1987; Corcoran Gallery of Art, Washington, DC 1988; Retrospective, Fondació "La Caixa," Spain & Galerie Nat. du Jeu de Paume, Paris 1994-95; and numerous group exhibitions. **Bio-Bibliography:** *Who's Who in America; Who's Who in American Art; Who's Who in the East.* **Home Address:** 26 E. 22 St., NYC 10010.

SIMONS, LANGDON S., JR ■ AAR Trustee 1972.

SIMPSON, LOUIS M. ■ FAAR Literature 58. b. Mar. 27, 1923, Jamaica, West Indies. m. Miriam Butensky. c. Matthew,

Anne, Anthony. BS 48, Columbia Univ.; MA 50, Columbia Univ.; PhD 59, Columbia Univ. **Career & Employment:** Bobbs-Merrill Publishing Company, Assc. Ed. 1950-55; Columbia Univ., Instr. 1953-59; New School for Social Research, Instr. 1955-59; UC, Berkeley, Prof. 1959-67; SUNY, Stony Brook, Prof. 1967-92, Distinguished Prof. 1992-present. **Memberships & Offices:** Pulitzer Prize for Poetry, Chair several times; Nat. Book Award for Poetry, Jury Chair 1993; Poets' Prize, Pres. 1988-93. **Fellowships, Honors & Awards:** *Hudson Review* Fellowship 1957; Columbia Univ., Distinguished Alumnus Award 1960; Guggenheim Fellowship 1962, 1970; Pulitzer Prize 1964; Columbia Univ., Medal for Excellence 1965; Eastern Michigan Univ., Hon. DHL 1977; Phi Beta Kappa, Hon. Mem. 1980; Inst. of Jamaica, Centenary Medal 1980; Jewish Book Council Award 1981; Rockefeller Found., Bellagio, Italy, Residency 1982; Elmer Holmes Bobst Award 1987; Hampden-Sydney College, Hon. DL 1990. **Publications:** *Good News of Death and Other Poems,* in *Poets of Today II* (New York: Scribner's, 1955); *Riverside Drive* (New York: Atheneum, 1962); *At the End of the Open Road* (Middletown, CT: Wesleyan Univ. Press, 1963); *Adventures of the Letter I* (New York: Harper & Row, 1971); *North of Jamaica* (New York: Harper & Row, 1972); *Three on the Tower: The Lives and Works of Ezra Pound, T.S. Eliot and William Carlos Williams* (New York: William Morrow, 1975); *Searching for the Ox* (New York: William Morrow, 1976); *Caviare at the Funeral* (New York: Franklin Watts, 1980); *The Best Hour of the Night* (New York: Ticknor & Fields, 1983); *Collected Poems* (New York: Paragon House, 1988); *Selected Prose* (New York: Paragon House, 1989); *Ships Going into the Blue* (Ann Arbor: Univ. of Michigan Press, 1994); *The King My Father's Wreck* (Brownsville, OR: Story Line Press, 1995); **Bio-Bibliography:** Ronald Moran, *Louis Simpson* (New York: Twayne, 1972); William H. Roberson, *Louis Simpson: A Reference Guide* (Boston: G.K. Hall, 1980); Peter Stitt, *The World's Hieroglyphic Beauty: Five American Poets* (Athens, GA: Univ. of Georgia Press, 1985); Hank Lazer, ed., *On Louis Simpson: Depths Beyond Happiness* (Ann Arbor: Univ. of Michigan Press, 1988); *Contemporary Authors; Current Biography; Dictionary of Literary Biography; Who's Who in America.* **Home Address:** 186 Old Field Rd., Setauket, NY 11733.

Since that time, with many visits to Italy, my idea of the Italians has changed. What I took to be frivolity I now see as a wish to offset poverty, illness, and old age. Not to mention volcanic eruptions, and the wars that sweep across the land, leaving ruins. In the face of these things, the young promenade with their arms around each other, and an old man and woman go by on a two-seater bicycle, pedaling with dignity.

The women who tend my mother's sickbed, Miriam says, are angels. Their patience is incredible; they go about their tasks with affection for the sufferer. Perhaps they really are angels: there couldn't be much difference between Grazia, Vincenza, Alessandra, Angela and the beings we see depicted in paintings who inhabit a higher sphere of existence. Perhaps there is no difference at all, and a Fra Angelico, a Giotto, are saying, "Look at the faces around you."

And the land is so beautiful! At the moment I'm sitting with Miriam on the back porch. On the porch itself there are flower pots with red roses, flowers the color of fuschia, whose name we don't know, and geraniums. Cherries are hanging a few feet away--the porch is level with the boughs. There is also a tree laden with apricots. In the garden below, white, rose-colored, blue, and lavender hydrangeas . . .

The King My Father's Wreck
Louis Simpson 9/25/93

Louis Simpson

SIMPSON, R.S. ■ Stewardson Memorial Scholar 1920-21, 1921-22.

SIMPSON, SHELLEY A. ■ FAAR Painting 88. b. Feb. 9, 1954, La Chapel, France. m. Graham B. Campbell. c. Robin. BFA 77, Univ. of Texas, Austin; MFA 79, Yale Univ. **Research/Artistic Interests:** Oil painting, drawing. **Fellowships, Honors & Awards:** Univ. of Texas, Ford Found. Grant 1975-77; Yale Univ. 1978, 1979; Skowhegan School of Painting & Sculpture 1976; Alice Kimball English Traveling Fellowship 1979; Fine Arts Work Center Fellowship 1979; Hudson D. Walker Annual Fellowship 1980; Louis Comfort Tiffany Found. Grant 1986. **Important Works:** Samual P. Horn Museum of Art, Univ. of Florida. **Exhibitions/Performances:** Solo: Hudson D. Walker Gallery, Provincetown, MA 1980, 1981; Group: Long Point Gallery, Provincetown, MA 1980; 14 Sculpture Gallery, NYC 1980; Annex Gallery, Provincetown, MA 1985; Leo Castelli Gallery, NYC 1986; 80 Washington Sq. E. Gallery, NYC 1987; Univ. Gallery, Ohio State Univ., Columbus 1988; Samuel P. Horn Museum of Art, Gainesville 1991-92; Montserrat Gallery, NYC 1992. **Bio-Bibliography:** *Who's Who among Rising Young Americans; World's Who's Who of Women.* **Home Address:** 270 Water St., Apt. 2, NYC 10038.

SIMPSON, WILLIAM MARKS, JR ■ FAAR Sculpture 33. b. Aug. 24, 1903, Norfolk, VA. d. Oct. 1958. BA 24, Virginia Military Inst. **Other Studies:** Rinehart School of Sculpture; Maryland Inst. of Fine Arts. **Career & Employment:** Rinehart School of Sculpture, Dir.; Virginia Military Inst., Faculty. **Memberships & Offices:** Norfolk Soc. of Artists. **Fellowships, Honors & Awards:** Sloane Prize 1920, 1921, 1923, 1924; Norfolk Soc. of Artists, Ferguson Prize 1923. **Important Works:** US Army HQ, Honolulu; Horace Commemorative Medal, Horace Bimillennium 1935-36; Patrick Henry Bust, Patrick Henry School, Norfolk, VA. **Bio-Bibliography:** *Dictionary of Painters, Sculptors & Engravers.*

SINISCALCO, PAOLO ■ Italian Fulbright Fellow 1957-58.

SINNIGEN, WILLIAM G. ■ FAAR Classics/Archaeology 54. b. Sept. 12, 1928, Paterson, NJ. BA 49, Univ. of Michigan; MA 50, Univ. of Michigan; PhD 54, Univ. of Michigan. **Research/Artistic Interests:** Roman & Byzantine history. **Career & Employment:** UC, Berkeley, Asst. Prof. 1956-62; Hunter College, CUNY, Assc. Prof. 1962-65, Prof. 1965-91, Chair 1971-75. **Memberships & Offices:** AHA, APA, ArIA. **Fellowships, Honors & Awards:** ACLS Fellowship 1959-60. **Publications:** *Officium of the Urban Prefecture* (Rome: AAR, 1957); with A.E.R. Boak, *A History of Rome to AD 565,* 6th ed. (New York: Macmillan, 1977); with C.A. Robinson, Jr., *Ancient History,* 3d ed. (New York: Macmillan, 1981). **Home Address:** PO Box 126, Westminster, VT 05158.

SIPORIN, MITCHELL ■ FAAR Painting 50, RAAR Painting 67. b. May 5, 1910, NYC. d. June 11, 1976. m. Miriam Tane. c. Judith, Rachel. **Other Studies:** AIC; studied with Todros Geller. **Career & Employment:** Brandeis Univ., Prof. 1951-76; Boston Museum School 1949; Columbia Univ. 1951. **Memberships & Offices:** Brandeis Univ. Awards Comm.; WPA; American Artists Congress; United American Artists; New England Contemporary Artists, Exec. Bd. **Fellowships, Honors & Awards:** AIC, Bertha Aberle Florsheim Prize 1942, Logan Prize & Gold Medal 1947; Guggenheim Fellowships 1946-47; PAFA, Pennell Memorial Medal 1946; Hallmark Intl. Competition, 2d Prize 1949; Boston Arts Festival, 2d Prize 1954, 3d Prize

1955; AAAL 1955; Youngstown Butler, 1st Prize 1961. **Important Works:** Bloom Township HS, Chicago; Lane Technical HS, Chicago; US Post Office, Decatur, IL; US Post Office, St. Louis, MO; Berlin Chapel, Brandeis Univ.; Collections: MMA; Smith College Museum; Univ. of Iowa; Newark Museum; Phillips Acad., Andover; Univ. of Arizona; Auburn Univ.; Brandeis Univ.; Britannica; AIC; Cranbrook Acad.; Univ. of Georgia; MOMA; NY Public Library; Whitney Museum, NYC; Allan Gallery. **Exhibitions/Performances:** Solo: Downtown Gallery 1940, 1942, 1946, 1947, 1957; Springfield (MA) Museum of Fine Arts; AIC 1947; Philadelphia Art Alliance 1949; Jewish Community Center, Cleveland 1953; Boris Mirski Gallery 1952; Nordness Gallery, NYC 1960; Retrospective: Rose Museum, Brandeis Univ. 1976; Babcock Galleries, NYC 1990. **Bio-Bibliography:** *Mitchell Siporin: A Retrospective,* exb. cat. (Waltham, MA, 1976); *Mitchell Siporin: The Early Years, 1930-1950,* exb. cat. (New York: Babcock Galleries, 1990); *Dictionary of Contemporary Artists, Who Was Who in American Art.*

SISTO CANALI, CARLA ■ Italian Fulbright Fellow 1964-65.

SITTON, JOHN MELZA ■ FAAR Painting 32. b. Jan. 9, 1906, Forsyth, GA. d. Apr. 29, 1993. m. Selma Koller. c. Carol Ann Kehm. BFA 29, Yale Univ. **Other Studies:** ASL; NAD; studied with I. Olinsky & E. Savage. **Research/Artistic Interests:** Mural painting, engraver, designer, etcher. **Career & Employment:** NYU, Faculty 1932; Columbia Univ., Instr. 1934-37; Finch Junior College, Dept. Head 1934-38; NY School of Applied Design for Women, Critic 1938-41; Cornell Univ., Asst. Prof. 1941-44. **Memberships & Offices:** Allied Artists of America; Nat. Soc. of Mural Painters; Municipal Art Soc., NY; Boca Raton Museum of Art, BoD; *Bendix Radio Engineer Magazine,* Art Ed.; Grand Central Art Gallery. **Fellowships, Honors & Awards:** NAD, Suydam Art Medal; High Museum Medal 1946; Florida Tri-Co Awards, Watercolor Prize 1978. **Publications:** *Radio Sketchbook of Personal Aviation for Bendix Radio;* "Painting of My Silk Decorations," *Art Instruction Magazine* (1938). **Important Works:** NY World's Fair 1939; Federal Reserve Bank, Atlanta 1941; Yale Univ. Art Gallery; Addison Gallery of American Art; Phillips Acad., Andover; Mint Art Museum; IBM College; US Post Office, Clifton, NJ; Elks War Memorial, Chicago; Nat. Archives Bldg., Washington, DC. **Exhibitions/Performances:** NAD 1932; Whitney Museum, NYC 1937; Grand Central Art Galleries 1942, 1945; Pepsi-Cola 1943; Southern States Art League 1943-46; Allied Artists of America 1944; Audubon Soc. 1945; Deerfield Beach Public Library 1970; Baltimore Museum of Art; Mint Art Museum, Charlotte, NC; High Art Museum, Atlanta; Lighthouse Gallery, Tequesta, FL 1971; Parker Playhouse, Ft. Lauderdale 1976. **Bio-Bibliography:** "Railroad Radio Employs New Advertising Medium," *Bendix Beam* (Nov. 1945); *Who Was Who in American Art.*

SJÖQVIST, ERIK ■ RAAR Classics/Archaeology 63; Jerome Lect. 67. b. July 15, 1903, Ronneby, Sweden. d. July 16, 1975. m. Gurli Wallbom. BA 23, Uppsala Univ.; MA 23, Uppsala Univ.; PhD 40, Uppsala Univ. **Research/Artistic Interests:** Greek sculpture; Roman topography; archaeological field work: Swedish expedition to Greece 1926; Swedish Cyprus Expedition, Field Dir. 1927-31; Princeton excavations at Morgantina, Co-Dir. 1955-68. **Career & Employment:** Royal Library, Stockhom 1933-39; Univ. of Stockholm, Assc. Prof. 1940-50; Swedish Inst. of Classical Studies in Rome, Dir. 1940-48; Private Secretary to H.R.H. The Crown Prince of Sweden 1949-50, then to H.M. the King of Sweden 1950-51; Keeper of

King's Book Collection 1951; Princeton Univ., Visiting Prof. 1948-49, Prof. 1951-71. **Memberships & Offices:** Intl. Assn. of Classical Archaeology at Rome; Accademia dei Lincei. **Fellowships, Honors & Awards:** North Star, Sweden, Commander; Crown of Italy, Commander; Order of the British Empire; Swedish Archaeology Soc., Fellow. **Publications:** "Some Cypriot Iron Age Tombs," *Corolla Archaeologica principi hereditario Regni Sueciae Gustavo Adolpho dedicata,* Skrifter Utgivna av Svenska Institutet i Rom 2 (1932): 189-207; *The Swedish Cyprus Expedition,* vol. 1-2 (Stockholm, 1934-35); *Problems of the Late Cypriote Bronze Age* (Stockholm, 1940); *Studi archeologici e topografici intorno alla Piazza del Collegio romano* (Lund: C.W.K. Gleerup, 1946); *Rom, en vandring genom seklerna,* 3d ed. (Stockholm: Norstedt, 1949); *Sicily and the Greeks* (Ann Arbor: Univ. of Michigan Press, 1973); Semple Lectures and articles on Lysippus; articles on Roman monuments & topography; articles & field reports on excavations at Morgantina. **Bio-Bibliography:** Bibliography, *Opuscula Romana* 9 (1973): 217-20; *NY Times,* Obit. (July 19, 1975); *Opuscula Romana* 18 (1990): 222-35; *Directory of American Scholars; Who Was Who in America.*

SKY, ALISON ■ FAAR Design Arts 78. b. Aug. 1, 1946, NYC. BA 67, Adelphi Univ. **Other Study:** ASL with Jose de Creeft & John Hovannes 1967-69; Columbia Univ. with Anatole Broyard; sculpture with Peter Lipman-Wulf 1964-67. **Career & Employment:** SITE/Sculpture in the Environment, Co-Founder, VP, Sec. 1969-91; SITE Projects, Co-Founder, Prin. 1970-91. **Fellowships, Honors & Awards:** *Interiors,* Best Showroom Design 1983, 1985; NEA Fellowship 1984, 1990; Pollock-Krasner Found. Sculpture Fellowship 1991; Winning Design Competition Entries: Highway 86 1985; Ansel Adams Museum 1985; Pershing Sq. 1986; Fulbright Indo-American Fellowship 1992. **Publications:** *Sky Book* (Profile Press, 1972); *Unbuilt America, ONSITE 7* (New York: McGraw-Hill, 1976); *ONSITE,* Series 1-7 (New York: SITE, 1971-76). **Important Works:** "AIR," Smithsonian Inst. 1972; "CATERPILLAR," Smithsonian Inst. 1972; "York Rest Stop," Comm.-Concept for Interstate 80, Nebraska 1974; "Highrise of Homes," Concept

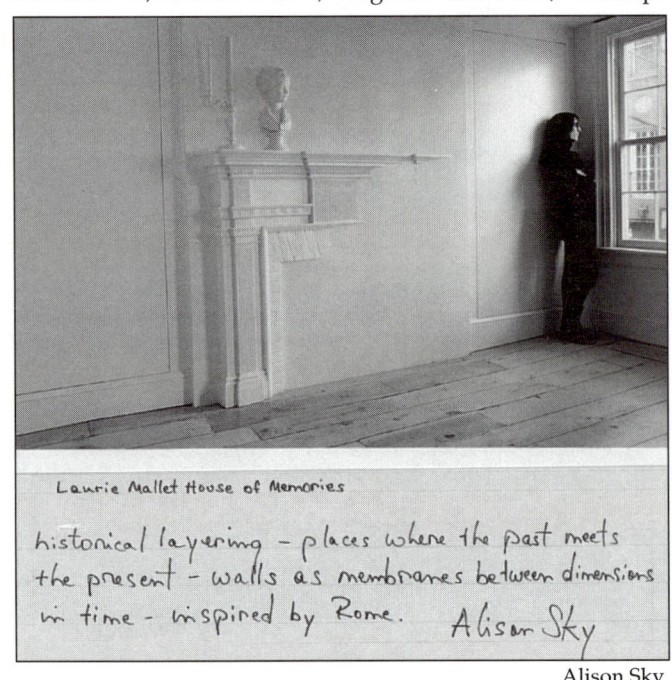

Laurie Mallet House of Memories

historical layering - places where the past meets the present - walls as membranes between dimensions in time - inspired by Rome. Alison Sky

Alison Sky

1981; Williwear Showrooms & Offices, Shops, NYC & London 1982-89; Best Products Showrooms, Richmond, Houston, Sacramento, Towson, Miami, Milwaukee 1979-84; SITE Studio, Gallery & Offices, NYC 1984; "Highway 86," EXPO 86, Vancouver 1985; "Laurie Mallet House of Memories," NYC 1986; "Pershing Square," Los Angeles 1986; Swatch Shop, Nantucket, NYC, Zurich 1988-90; "1989: The Year of Democracy," New York Public Library 1990. **Exhibitions/Performances:** Venice Biennale 1975; Pompidou Centre, Paris 1975; MOMA 1979; Ronald Feldman Fine Arts, NYC 1980, 1983; Virginia Museum of Fine Arts, Richmond 1980; Victoria & Albert Museum, Boiler House Projects, London 1984; Nat. Museum of Modern Art, Tokyo & Kyoto 1985-86; Whitney Museum, NYC 1985-86. **Studio Address:** 60 Greene St., NYC 10012.

SMETHURST, MAE J. ■ b. May 28, 1935, Hancock, MI. m. Richard J. Smethurst. BA 57, Dickinson College; MA 61, Univ. of Michigan; PhD 68, Univ. of Michigan. **Other Study:** Tutorial study of medieval *noh* texts in Japan. **Research/Artistic Interests:** Comparative theatre: ancient Greek & medieval Japanese. **Career & Employment:** Univ. of Pittsburgh, Instr. 1967-68, Asst. Prof. 1968-74, Assc. Prof. 1974-88, Prof. 1988-present, Chair 1988-94, Joint Prof. in East Asian Languages & Literatures 1992-present. **Business Address:** 1518 CL, Dept. of Classics, Univ. of Pittsburgh, Pittsburgh, PA 15260.

SMIT, LEO ■ RAAR Musical Composition 73. b. Jan. 21, 1921, Philadelphia, PA. **Study:** With Kolman Smit, Dmitri Kabalevsky at Moscow Conservatory, Isabella Vangerova & Nicolas Nabokov. **Career & Employment:** SUNY, Buffalo, Prof. Emer. **Fellowships, Honors & Awards:** Guggenheim Fellowship 1950; Fulbright Fellowship 1950; New York Critics' Circle Award 1958. **Important Works:** *Virginia Sampler*, Ballet Russe de Monte Carlo Comm. 1947; *Symphony No. 1 in E Flat*, Koussevitzky Found. Comm. 1955; *Copernicus – Narrative and Credo*, Nat. Acad. of Sciences Comm. 1973; *The Ecstatic Pilgrimage*, 80 songs for voice & piano 1989-92; *The Last Hour*; *Alone*, for female violinist-reciter 1988-90. **Exhibitions/Performances:** Solo pianist, Aaron Copland, *The Young Pioneers* (Sony). **Bio-Bibliography:** *Dictionary of American Composers*. **Home Address:** 39 Dorchester Rd., Buffalo, NY 14222.

SMITH, CLEMENT LAWRENCE ■ ASCSR, Dir. 1897-98, Educator.

SMITH, J. KELLUM, JR ■ AAR Trustee 1964-94; Trustee Emer. **Career & Employment:** John Simon Guggenheim Memorial Fund, Asst. Sec. 1960-62; Rockefeller Found., Sec. 1964-74; Andrew W. Mellon Found., VP & Sec. 1974-90, Senior Fellow 1990-present. **Memberships & Offices:** NSS, BoT; Nat. Inst. for Architectural Education, BoT; St. Bernard's School, BoT; Found. for Child Development, BoT; Brearley School, Pres., BoT; Century Assn.

SMITH, JAMES KELLUM ■ FAAR Architecture 23; AAR Trustee 1933-61; AAR Pres. 1938-58; AAR Hon. Pres. 1958-61. b. Oct. 3, 1893, Towanda, PA. d. Feb 18, 1961. m. Elizabeth Dexter. c. James Kellum, Jr.; Anne Dexter. BA 15, Amherst College; BArch 19, Univ. of Pennsylvania; MS Arch 20. **Research/Artistic Interests:** Restoration, collegiate architecture, Roman marble. **Career & Employment:** McKim, Mead & White 1924-29, Part. 1929-61; US Army Air Corps, 2d Lieut., WWI, Joint Intelligence Com., Lt. Col., WWII 1942-46. **Memberships & Offices:** Pratt Inst., BoT 1946-61; NIAL 1947; NAD. **Fellowships, Honors & Awards:** Phi Beta Kappa; John

Stewardson Memorial Fellowship 1919; Amherst College, Eminent Service Medal 1935, Hon. DHL 1946; Bowdoin College, Hon DHL 1951; AIA, Fellow. **Publications:** "A Restoration of the Temple of Zeus at Olympia," *Memoirs of AAR* 4 (1924): 153-68. **Important Works:** Amherst College: Alumni Gymnasium 1935, Kirby Theater 1937, Mead Art Bldg. 1948, Edward W. Chapin Hall 1957, Alumni House 1954, & 11 others; bldgs. at colleges, including: Bowdoin College, Middlebury College, Wesleyan Univ., Univ. of Pennsylvania, Univ. of Connecticut, Univ. of Vermont, Aldelphi Univ., Union College, Northwestern Univ., Johns Hopkins Univ., Colgate Univ.; US Military Cemetery, Florence; US Army Infantry School, Ft. Benning, GA; Commercial Nat. Bank Bldg., Shreveport, LA; Museum of History & Technology, Smithsonian Inst., Washington, DC; American Univ., Beirut, Lebanon; Architect to: Bethlehem Steel Co, 1st Nat. Bank of NY. **Bio-Bibliography:** *NY Times*, Obit. (Feb. 19, 1961); *National Cyclopedia of American Biography; Who Was Who in America.*

SMITH, LUCIAN ■ McKim Fellow 1911-12, 1913.

SMITH, PETER F. ■ FAAR Architecture 69. b. July 4, 1944, Bronx, NY. BArch 67, Pratt Inst. **Other Study:** Pratt Inst., 18th-century American architecture & urban design 1985; New York Botanical Soc., soil science 1992, botany & plant propagation 1993. **Career & Employment:** Edward Larrabee Barnes, Project Designer 1969-73; Peter Smith, Architecture 1973-present; NYIT, Adj. Asst. Prof. 1975-77. **Memberships & Offices:** Garrison Art Center, BoT 1975-80, Treas. 1978; Westchester Regional Theater, BoT 1977-82; Andrew Jackson Downing Memorial Park, Planning Com., BoT 1987-present, Treas. 1992, VP 1993; Steering Com. for Restorations, Chair 1990-present; City of Newburgh, Historic Survey Project, Liason 1993. **Fellowships, Honors & Awards:** Graham Found. Research Grant 1975. **Home Address:** 225 Montgomery St., Newburgh, NY 12550. **Business Address:** Peter Smith, Architecture Carriage House, 221 Montgomery St., Newburgh, NY 12550.

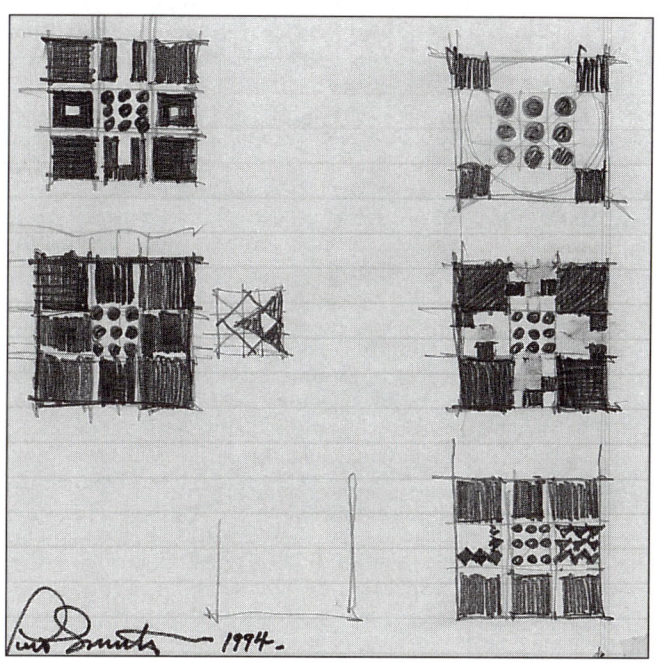

Peter F. Smith

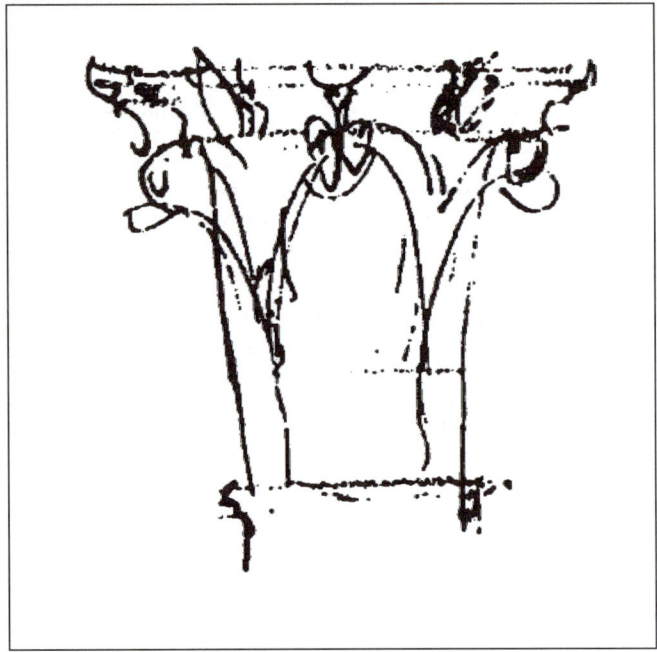

Thomas Gordon Smith

SMITH, THOMAS GORDON ■ FAAR Architecture 80. b. Apr. 23, 1948, Oakland, CA. m. Marika Wilson. c. Alan, Stuart, Demetra, Andrew, Philip, Duncan. BA 70, UC, Berkeley; MArch 75, UC, Berkeley. **Other Study:** American College in Paris 1966-67; California State Univ., Hayward 1967-68. **Research/Artistic Interests:** Theory & application of Vitruvian principles & forms of architecture as practiced in antiquity, the Renaissance, today; Grecian architecture & furniture of the 1820-50 period in the USA & Britain. **Career & Employment:** Thomas Gordon Smith Architect 1980-present; Univ. of Illinois, Chicago, Assc. Prof. 1986-89; Univ. of Notre Dame, Prof. & Chair 1989-present. **Memberships & Offices:** SAH; San Francisco Architectural Club, Pres; AIA. **Fellowships, Honors & Awards:** Graham Found. Grant 1984, 1987; APS Grant 1987; I.A. O'Shaughnessy Found. Grant 1988, 1989, 1991. **Publications:** *Classical Architecture: Rule and Invention* (Layton, VT: Gibbs M. Smith, Inc., 1988); *Two Pattern Books of American Architecture by Aster Benjamin* (New York: Da Capo, 1994); *The Modern Style of Cabinet Work Exemplified by Thomas King* (New York: Dover, 1995); *John Hall and the Grecian Domestic Environment* (New York: Acanthus, 1995). **Important Works:** Richmond Hill House, Richmond, CA 1981-83; Altarpiece-Frame for El Greco's *Assumption of the Virgin*, AIC 1988-89; Vitruvian House, South Bend, IN 1989-91; James & Demetra Wilson Residence, Livermore, CA 1990-93; Thomas & Theresa Kulb Residence, Bloomington, IL 1991-94; Univ. of Notre Dame, School of Architecture Renovation & Addition 1992-96. **Exhibitions/Performances:** Santa Barbara Museum of Art 1977; Cooper-Hewitt Museum, NYC 1978, 1979; AIC 1980; Venice Biennale, Venice 1980, San Francisco 1982; Smith College Museum of Art 1982; La Jolla Museum of Art 1982; Deutsches Architekturmuseum, Frankfurt 1984; IBM Gallery, NYC 1987; Avery Centennial, Buell Center, Columbia Univ. 1990, 1991. **Home Address:** 1903 Dorwood Dr., South Bend, IN 46617. **Business Address:** School of Architecture, Univ. of Notre Dame, Notre Dame, IN 46556.

SMITH, WILLIAM LEO ■ Rotch Scholar 1913.

SMITH, WILLIAM O. ■ FAAR Musical Composition 58, RAAR Musical Composition 80. b. Sept. 22, 1926, Sacramento, CA. m. Virginia Paquette. c. Mark, Greg, Matthew, Rebecca. BS 51, UC, Berkeley; MA 53, UC, Berkeley. **Other Study:** Juilliard School 1945-46; Mills College, Oakland, CA 1946-47; Paris Conservatory 1951-52. **Career & Employment:** UC, Berkeley, Instr. 1953-54; San Francisco Conservatory, Instr. 1954-55; Univ. of Southern California, Asst. Prof. 1955-60; Univ. of Washington, Prof., Prof. Emer. 1966-92. **Fellowships, Honors & Awards:** Prix de Paris 1951-53; Guggenheim Fellowship 1960-61, 1961-62; AAAL 1972; NEA Award 1975; Jazz Pioneer Award 1985; Jazz All-Stars Award 1990; Seattle Artists Award 1991. **Important Works:** *String Quartet* 1952; *Concerto for Jazz Soloist and Orchestra* (MJQ Music) 1962; *Variants for Clarinet Alone* (Universal Editions) 1963; *Interplay*, for jazz combo & orchestra 1964; *Chronos*, for string quartet 1975; *Elegia*, for clarinet & strings 1976; *Fragments*, for double clarinet (Edi-Pan) 1977; *Eternal Truths*, for woodwind quartet 1979; *Twelve*, for clarinet & string quartet 1983; *Pente*, for clarinet & string quartet 1983; *Trio*, for clarinet, violin & piano 1984; *Music for Five Players* (Ravenna Editions) 1987. Discography: Contemporary Composers Series; CRI; Crystal; Mark Records; New World Records; Orion Master; Edi-Pan; Advance Recordings. Publisher: Universal Editions, MJ Music, Shal-U-Mo, Ravenna Editions, Edi-Pan. **Bio-Bibliography:** *Baker's Biographical Dictionary; Introduction to Contemporary Music; New Grove Dictionary of American Music; New Grove Dictionary of Music & Musicians; New Grove Dictionary of Music; Who's Who in American Music.* **Home Address:** 5607 16 NE, Seattle, WA 98105.

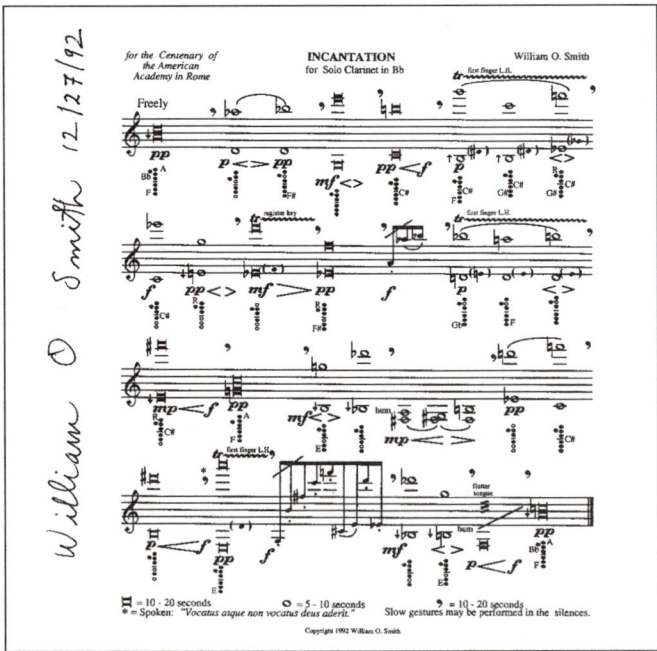

William O. Smith

SMITH-MILLER, HENRY ■ AAR Visitor 1967-68, Architect.

SMYLY, SUSAN V. ■ FAAR Sculpture 67. b. Oct. 16, 1940, Detroit, MI. m. Thomas A. Bullard. BFA 63, Memphis Acad. of Art; MFA 65, Cranbrook Acad. of Art. **Research/Artistic Interests:** As a sculptor I maneuver form through distortion & exaggeration with intent to create pieces with comic, ironic or tragic implications. The images have evolved from oozing

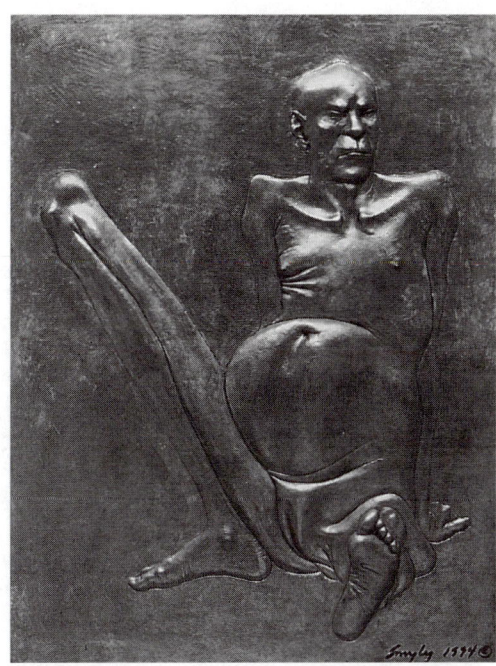

Susan V. Smyly

& opulent flesh of full bodied women into delicately balanced startlingly posed androgynous skeletal forms. **Career & Employment:** Self-employed, co founder of I.S. Intl., Inc. a corporation created to develop & market visual art educational curriculum & products; 25+ years of uninterrupted teaching appointments within noteworthy college & university systems. Assignments ranged from elementray drawing instruction to graduate studies in figurative sculpture. **Fellowships, Honors & Awards:** Fulbright Fellowship 1966; AAAL Award 1977. **Important Works:** Hirshhorn Museum & Sculpture Garden, Washington, DC; Prospect Park, Brooklyn, NYC; Steuben Glass; Garden Sculpture, Memphis, TN; Patents: design & utility patents for a portable drawing bench for home & institutional environments. **Exhibitions/Performances:** Early in 1980s I made a conscious decision to hold my work back from public display. My beliefs guided me to continue working in my studio while dedicating all non-studio time to the creation of educational programs. Awareness & appreciation of complex, figurative form has been overlooked too long in our educational system. My body of work consists of over 100 pieces of sculpture. Arrangements are in process for casting in bronze, exhibiting & marketing by 2005. **Home Address:** 165 William St., NYC 10038.

SMYTH, CRAIG HUGH ■ RAAR History of Art 59. b. July 28, 1915, NYC. m. Barbara Linforth. c. Alexandra, Edward Linforth. BA 38, Princeton Univ.; MFA 41, Princeton Univ.; PhD 56, Princeton Univ. **Research/Artistic Interests:** History of Italian Renaissance art & architecture of the 15th & 16th centuries. **Career & Employment:** NGA, Research Asst. 1941-42; US Naval Reserve, Ensign–Lieut. 1942-46; Central Art Collecting Point, Munich, Officer-in-Charge 1945; Frick Collection, Lect. 1946-50; IFA, Asst. Prof.-Prof 1950-73, Acting Dir. & Dir. 1951-73; Harvard Univ., Prof. 1973-85, Prof. Emer. 1985; Harvard Univ., Center for Italian Renaissance Studies, Villa I Tatti, Dir. 1973-85. **Memberships & Offices:** CAA, BoD 1953-57, Sec. 1956; Harvard Univ., Dept. of Fine Arts, Visiting Com. 1953-57; US Nat. Com. for the History of Art 1955-85; Princeton Univ., Dept. of Art & Archaeology, Visiting Com.

1956-73, 1985-89; Comité Intl. d'Histoire de l'Art, Alternate Mem. 1970-83, Mem. 1983-85; IFA, BoT 1973-present; Com. on Educational & Cultural Exchange between Italy & USA 1979-83; APS 1979-present; Organizing Com., 400th Anniversary of Uffizi Gallery, Invited Mem., Keynote Speaker 1981; J. Paul Getty Center for the History of Art & the Humanities, Adv. Com., Consultative Chair 1982-present, Architect Selection Com. 1983-84; *Burlington Magazine,* BoT 1987-present. **Fellowships, Honors & Awards:** Phi Beta Kappa 1937; Chevalier, Legion of Honor, France 1946; US Army Commendation Medal 1946; Senior Fulbright Fellowship 1949-50; MMA, Hon. Trustee 1968-present; Harvard Univ., Hon. MA 1975; AAAS, Fellow 1979-present; Accademia Fiorentina delle Arti del Disegno, Assc. Academician 1980-present; NGA, Samuel Kress Prof. 1987-88; Harvard Univ., I Tatti Mongan Prize 1992. **Publications:** "The Earliest Works of Bronzino," *Art Bulletin* 21 (1949): 184-211; *Mannerism and Maniera* (Locust Valley, NY: J.J. Augustin, 1963; rev. ed. Vienna: Irsa, 1992); with H.A. Millon, "Michelangelo and St. Peter's, I: Notes on a Plan of the Attic as Originally Built on the South Hemicycle," *Burlington Magazine* 111 (1969): 484-501; *Bronzino as Draughtsman* (Locust Valley, NY: J.J. Augustin, 1971); with H.A. Millon, "Michelangelo and St. Peter's: Observations on the Interior of the Apse, a Model of the Apse Vault and Related Drawings," *Römisches Jahrbuch für Kunstgeschichte* 15 (1976): 137-206; with H.A. Millon, "A Design by Michelangelo for a City Gate," *Burlington Magazine* 117: 162-66; "Venice and the Emergence of the High Renaissance in Florence: Observations and Questions," in *Florence and Venice, Comparisons and Relations,* ed. S. Bertelli, N. Rubinstein, C.H. Smyth, 2 vols. (Florence: La Nuova Italia Editrice, 1979), 2:209-49; "Gli Uffizi e i problemi dei grandi musei," *Gli Uffizi: Quattro secoli di una galleria, Atti del Convegno Internazionale di Studi,* ed. P. Barocchi & G. Ragioneri (Florence: Olschki, 1983), 2:545-56; "Osservazioni intorno a 'Il Carteggio di Michelangelo,'" *Rinascimento,* ser. 2, 25 (1985): 3-17; with H.A. Millon, "The Drum and Dome of St. Peter's," in H.A. Millon & C.H. Smyth, *Michelangelo Architect, the Facade of San Lorenzo and the Drum and Dome of St. Peter's,* exb. cat. (Milan: Olivetti, 1988), 92-187; *Repatriation of Art from the Central Collecting Point in Munich after World War II, Background and Beginnings* (Maarsen-The Hague: Gary Schwartz, SDU Publishers, 1988); with H.A. Millon, "Pirro Ligorio, Michelangelo and St. Peter's," in *Pirro Ligorio, Artist and Antiquarian,* ed. G. Gaston (Milan: Silvana Editoriale, 1988); "Charles Rufus Morey (1877-1955): Roma, archeologia

The privilege of working at the American Academy in Rome and absorbing its traditions, the amount one can accomplish there (not least in its library), the scholars, artists and architects encountered there who became friends, even close colleagues, have made the Academy for me a most special place. I like to think that our son has perhaps been the Academy's youngest fellow· eleven years old when we lived as a family in the mezzanine apartment for a semester, he learned in the Academy that artists are people, saw them at work, became imbued with Rome and its monuments (even while riding the bus to school)—in short, took in impressions important later when without hesitation he chose sculpture as a career.

Craig Hugh Smyth

September 1992

Craig Hugh Smyth

e storia dell'arte," in *Roma centro ideale della cultura dell' antico nei secoli xv e xvi: Da Martino V al Sacco di Roma 1417-1527*, ed. S. Danesi Squarzina (Milan: Electa, 1989); "The Princeton Department in the Time of Morey," "The Department of Fine Arts for Graduate Students at New York University," & "Concerning Charles Rufus Morey," in *The Early Years of Art History in the United States*, ed. C.H. Smyth & P.M. Lukehart (Princeton: Princeton Univ. Press, 1993). **Bio-Bibliography:** Rensselaer W. Lee. "Introduction," in *Renaissance Studies in Honor of Craig Hugh Smyth*, ed. A. Morrogh, F. Superbi Gioffredi, P. Marselli, E. Borsook, 2 vols. (Florence: Giunta Barbèra, 1985), 1:xiii-xvi; *International Who's Who; Who's Who in America; Who's Who in the World*. **Home Address:** PO Box 39, Cresskill, NJ 07626.

SMYTHE, RICHARD HAVILAND ■ FAAR Architecture 13. b. June 8, 1889, Brooklyn, NY. d. Aug. 25, 1965. BA, Columbia Univ. **Research/Artistic Interests:** Historic restoration, Roman Forum. **Career & Employment:** US Army, Lieut. WWI; Private Practice, NYC 1940-65. **Memberships & Offices:** ALNY. **Important Works:** Restoration: Village of Stony Brook, NY 1940, including Suffolk Museum, carriage house, municipal structures, restaurants & stores; Caroline Episcopal Church, Stony Brook; Thom McAn Shoe Store Chain, Storefront Design 1922. **Bio-Bibliography:** "Catalogs May Peddle Homes of the Future," *NY World-Telegram & Sun* (Aug. 31, 1955); *NY Times*, Obit. (Aug. 26, 1965).

SMYTH-PINNEY, JULIA MORGAN ■ NIAE, John Dinkeloo Traveling Fellow 1979. b. Apr. 30, 1951, Iowa City, IA. m. Paul Pinney. c. David. BFA 73, Cornell Univ.; BArch 76, Cornell Univ.; MArch 79, Harvard Univ. **Research/Artistic Interests:** Italian Renaissance & baroque architecture, modern architecture, architectural drawings. **Career & Employment:** Edward Bing & Asscs., Intern Architect 1976-77; Perry, Dean, Rogers, Intern Architect 1977-79; WZMH-Habib, Architect 1980-81; Univ. of Kentucky, Asst. Prof. 1981-87, Assc. Prof. 1987-present. **Home Address:** 472 W. 3 St., Lexington, KY 40508. **Business Address:** College of Architecture, Univ. of Kentucky, Pence Hall, Lexington, KY 40506.

SNOWDEN, GEORGE HOLBURN ■ FAAR Sculpture 30. b. Dec. 17, 1902, Yonkers, NY. d. Dec. 15, 1990. m. Louise Weider. c. George Holburn, Jr.; Mary Louise. BFA 26, Yale Univ. **Career & Employment:** Yale School of Fine Arts, Faculty 1930s; Private Practice, New York & Los Angeles. **Memberships & Offices:** NAD, Assc. 1937, Mem. 1941; NSS; ALNY. **Fellowships, Honors & Awards:** Pardee Prize 1923, 1925; Otis Elevator Prize; New Haven Paint & Clay Prize 1926; Beaux Arts Inst. of Design Prize 1926, 1935; Yale Univ., A.K. English Fellowship. **Important Works:** NY World's Fair 1939; Saratoga Springs, NY; Armonk, NY; Yale Memorial; Pershing Hall, Paris; *Clarence Ransom Edward Memorial*, State Capitol, Hartford; St. Theresa Church, Alhambra, CA; St. Francis Church, Catalina, CA; Nat. Shrine of Immaculate Conception, St. Francis Church, NYC. **Exhibitions/Performances:** New Haven Paint & Clay Club 1926; Beaux Arts Inst. of Design 1926, 1935; NY World's Fair 1939. **Bio-Bibliography:** *Who's Who in America; Who Was Who in American Art*.

SNYDER, DAN ■ FAAR Sculpture 75. b. July 23, 1948, Philadelphia, PA. m. Linda Maxwell Snyder. c. Zuzu, Sandy. BFA 70, Pennsylvania State Univ.; MFA 72, UC, Davis. **Other Study:** In 1973 I made visits to the Lascaux Cave in France & the rock engravings at Val Camonica, Italy, among other sites.

I presented collections & interpretations of my findings in Rome & San Francisco; 19th-century sculpture; prehistoric & ancient ceramic sculpture; fountains. **Career & Employment:** Pennsylvania State Univ., Instr. 1975-76; UC, Santa Cruz, Instr. 1987-90; San Francisco State Univ., Instr. 1991-92. **Fellowships, Honors & Awards:** NEA Special Projects Grant 1973. **Important Works:** San Francisco Intl. Airport, Gensler & Asscs; TRW HQ, Cleveland; Coca Cola Corp. HQ, Visitor's Center, Atlanta; Stanley Elementary School, Tacoma, WA; Bateman-Eichler Corp., San Francisco; Spectrum Foods-Prego Restaurant, San Diego; Oliver Carr Co., Ballston VA; Hyatt Hotels Corp., Scottsdale, AZ; Oakland Museum; Lannan Found., Palm Beach & Los Angeles; E.B. Crocker Museum, Sacramento. **Exhibitions/Performances:** Wenger Gallery, La Jolla 1973, 1981; Allrich Gallery, San Francisco 1977, 1981, 1982, 1985, 1990, 1991; Monterey Peninsula Museum of Art 1983, 1992. **Home Address:** 1449 66 St., Berkeley, CA 94702. **Business Address:** Allrich Gallery, 251 Post St., San Francisco, CA 94108.

SNYDER, WALTER FIFIELD ■ FAAR Classics/Archaeology 38. b. Apr. 9, 1912, Northfield, NJ. d. Feb. 9, 1993. m. Ruth Jespersen. BA 32, Swarthmore College; PhD 36, Yale Univ. **Research/Artistic Interests:** Greek & Roman history, exact chronology in period of the Roman Empire; public anniversaries in the Roman Empire. **Career & Employment:** Hunter College, CUNY, Instr. 1940-41; Univ. of Richmond, Assc. Prof. 1941-43, 1946-67; USNR 1943-46; Clarion State College, Prof. 1967-78, Prof. Emer. 1978-93. **Memberships & Offices:** APA; ArIA; AHA; American Soc. of Papyrologists; ANS. **Publications:** "Quinto Nundinas Pompeis," *Journal of Roman Studies* 26 (1936): 12-18; "Hemerai Sebastai," *Aegyptus* 18 (1938): 197-237; "Note on the Irregular Evidence upon the Date of the Beginning of the Year of Tribunician Power during the Reigns of Septimius Severus and Caracalla," *Memoirs of the AAR* 15 (1938): 62-69; "On Chronology in the Imperial Books of Cassius Dio's Roman History," *Klio* 7 (1940): 39-56; "Public Anniversaries in the Roman Empire," *Yale Classical Studies* 7 (1940): 223-317; "When Was the Alexandrian Calendar Established?" *American Journal of Philology* 64 (1943): 385-98; co-ed, *Current Issues in New Testament Interpretation: Essays in Honor of O.A. Piper* (New York: Harper, 1962); "Progress Report on the Hemerai Sebastai," *Aegyptus* 44 (1964): 145-69. **Bio-Bibliography:** *St. Petersburg Times*, Obit. (Feb. 21, 1993); *APA Newsletter* 16.3 (June 1993): 10-11; *Directory of American Scholars*.

SOKOLOWSKI, THOMAS ■ AAR Visitor 1976-77; Grey Art Gallery & Study Center, NYU, Dir.

SOLLBERGER, HARVEY D. ■ RAAR Musical Composition 89. b. May 11, 1938, Cedar Rapids, IA. c. Margot F. Harrison, Eva Sollberger. BA 60, Univ. of Iowa; MA 64, Columbia Univ. **Research/Artistic Interests:** Composition, conducting, instrumental performance: flute. **Career & Employment:** Columbia Univ., Adj. Prof. 1965-83; Manhattan School of Music, Contemporary Ensemble, Dir. 1972-83; Indiana Univ., Prof. 1983-92; UC, San Diego, Prof. 1992-present; Visiting Prof.: SUNY, Stony Brook 1978; Temple Univ. 1979; SUNY, Purchase 1979; Philadelphia College of the Performing Arts 1980-82; City College, CUNY 1982; Amherst College, Valentine Visiting Prof. 1992. **Memberships & Offices:** ACA, Ed. Bd. 1965-68, Bd. of Governors 1966-68, Finance Com. 1971-72, Admissions Com. 1971-72, 2d VP 1971-73; American Soc. of Univ. Composers, Treas. 1967-68, Exec. Com. Pres. & Chair 1968-69; CRI, BoD & 1st VP 1971-73; Martha Baird Rockefeller Fund for Music, Composition & Performance Panels 1977-

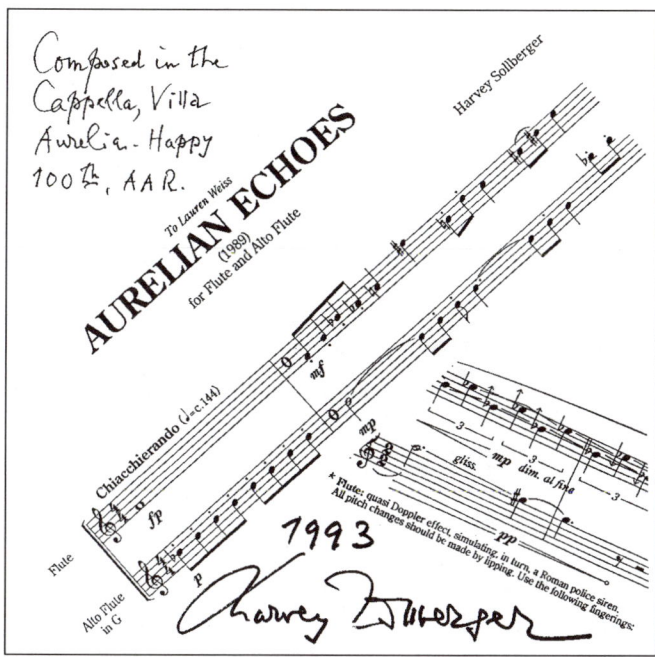

Harvey D. Sollberger

82; Pulitzer Prize Jury 1989, 1992; Fromm Music Found., Comm., Adv. Council 1990-present, Jury 1992, BoD 1994-99; NEA Adv. Panel 1991; League of Composers-Intl. Soc. for Contemporary Music, Adv. Bd. 1991; Judge: Nat. Flute Assn. 1983, BMI Awards 1988. **Fellowships, Honors & Awards:** Joseph Bearns Prize 1963; AAAL 1965; Koussevitzky Comm. 1966; Guggenheim Fellowship 1969, 1973; ACA Recording Award 1976; Fromm Music Found. Grant 1981; NEA Comm. 1989; Musica Sacra Contemporanea Comm. 1990; Amherst College Comm. 1991. **Important Works:** *Chamber Variations,* for 12 players, Fromm Found. Comm. (ACA, CRI) 1964; *Riding the Wind I,* for flute solo & 4 instruments, Walter W. Naumburg Found. & NYSCA Comm. (ACA, Neuma) 1974; *Hara,* for solo alto flute (C.F. Peters) 1978; *Angel & Stone,* for flute & piano (C.F. Peters, CRI) 1981; *Life Study,* for mezzo-soprano, flute & harp (ACA) 1982; *Double Triptych,* for flute & percussion (C.F. Peters, CRI) 1984; *Three or Four Things I Know about the Oboe,* chamber concerto for oboe & 13 instruments, NEA Comm. 1986; *Persian Golf,* for string orchestra (ACA) 1987; *Quodlibetudes,* for solo flute (McGinnis & Marx) 1988; *Trio (...from Winter's Frozen Stillness),* for violin, cello, piano (ACA) 1990; *Passages,* for soloists, chorus, & orchestra (Rugginenti-Milan) 1990; *The Advancing Moment,* for flute, clarinet, violin, cello, piano & percussion 1993; *In Terra Aliena,* for 5 soloists & orchestra, Assn. Romana di Musica Sacra e Religiosa Comm. 1995. **Bio-Bibliography:** *Baker's Biographical Dictionary of Musicians; Dictionary of Contemporary Music; Grove Dictionary of Music; New Grove Dictionary of American Music; Who's Who.* **Home Address:** 1543 Law St., San Diego, CA 92109. **Business Address:** Dept. of Music, UC San Diego, 9500 Gilman Dr., La Jolla, CA 92093.

SOLLMANN, MARY A. ■ AAR Visiting Student 1932 — 1934, Classicist. d. 1984. Bequeathed a gift to the Academy in support of the Academy's Classical Summer School.

SOLODOW, JOSEPH B. ■ FAAR Classics/Archaeology 81. b. Nov. 13, 1946, Brooklyn, NY. m. Graziella Patrucco. BA 67, Columbia Univ.; MA 69, Harvard Univ.; PhD 71, Harvard

Univ. **Research/Artistic Interests:** Latin literature & philology, Greek literature, historiography, Romance philology, comparative literature. **Career & Employment:** Columbia Univ., Asst. Prof. 1971-77; Bard College, Assc. Prof. 1977-83; Yale Univ., Visiting Research Scholar 1985-87; UC, Berkeley, Assc. Prof. 1988-89; Stanford Univ., Assc. Prof. 1989; UCLA, Assc. Prof. 1989-90; SUNY, Buffalo, Visiting Assc. Prof. 1990-92; S. Connecticut State Univ., Assc. Prof. 1992-present. **Publications:** *"Poeta Impotens*: the Last Three Eclogues," *Latomus* 36 (1977): 757-71; "Ovid's *Ars Amatoria*: The Lover as Cultural Ideal," *Wiener Studien* 90, n.f. 11 (1977): 106-27; "Cato, *Orationes,* Frag. 75," *American Journal of Philology* 98 (1977): 359-61; "A Note on Castiglione," *Notes and Queries* 222, n.s. 24 (1977): 492-93; *The Latin Particle* Quidem, American Classical Studies 4 (Boulder: APA, 1978); "Livy and the Story of Horatius, 1.24-26," *TAPA* 109 (1979): 251-68; "RAVCAE, TVA CVRA, PALVMBES: Study of a Poetic Word Order," *Harvard Studies in Classical Philology* 90 (1986): 129-53; "On Catullus 95," *Classical Philology* 82 (1987): 141-45; *The World of Ovid's* Metamorphoses (Chapel Hill: UNC Press, 1988); "Forms of Literary Criticism in Catullus: Polymetric vs. Epigram," *Classical Philology* 84 (1989): 312-19; "Persistence of Virgilian Memories," *Liverpool Classical Monthly* 4.8 (1989): 119-21; trans., Gian Biagio Conte, *Latin Literature: A History* (Baltimore: Johns Hopkins Univ. Press, 1994). **Home Address:** 127 W. Rock Ave., New Haven, CT 06515.

SOLOMON, BARBARA STAUFFACHER ■ FAAR Architecture 83. b. San Francisco, CA. c. Nellie King Solomon, Chloe Stauffacher. BA 78, UC, Berkeley; MArch 81, UC Berkeley. **Other Study:** Graphics at Kunstgewerteschule, Basel; painting at San Francisco Art Inst. **Career & Employment:** San Francisco Art Inst., Instr. 1961-62; UC, Berkeley, Lect. 1966-69, 1989; Yale Univ., Visiting Instr. 1968; Harvard GSD, Visiting Instr. 1986; ILAUD Architectural Program, Siena, Italy, Visiting Instr. 1989; Rice Univ., Visiting Instr. 1990. **Fellowships, Honors & Awards:** AIA, various awards 1966-70; State of California, Governor's Design Award 1966; Industrial Arts Medal 1970; Commonwealth Club of San Francisco, Silver

Barbara Stauffacher Solomon

Medal for "Green Architecture" 1989; ASLA Honor Award 1989; NEA Distinguished Design Fellow 1990. **Publications:** "Green Architecture," *Design Quarterly* 120 (1982); "2 Fields + 3 Houses = A Landscape," in *Transforming the America Garden*, ed. Michael Van Valkenburgh (Cambridge, MA: Harvard GSD, 1986); *Green Architecture and the Agrarian Garden* (New York: Rizzoli, 1988); *Good Mourning California* (New York: Rizzoli, 1992); "My Private Eden," *Eden Magazine*. **Important Works:** Supergraphics 1966-70; Sea Ranch, CA 1966; *Scanlon's Magazine*, Art Dir. 1971; landscape design for Taller de Arquitectura-Ricardo Bofill, El Jardin del Turia, Valencia, Spain 1982; landscape design for San Francisco Intl. Airport, Central Terminal, Arthur Gensler, Architect 1983; with Williams, Roberts & Todd, Guadalupe Corridor Project, San Jose 1984; with Ricardo Bofill & Daniel Solomon, Clos Pegase Winery for San Francisco Museum of Modern Art 1985; with Lars Lerup & Vito Acconci, ARTS PARK/LA, Natural History Museum 1988; with Michael Van Valkenburgh, "The Sculpture Garden" at Dayton-Hudson, Minneapolis 1988; with Daniel Solomon, Lee's Orchard, CA 1988; with Michael Van Valkenburgh, Edward L. Barnes, Architect, Regis Garden, Cowles Conservatory, Walker Art Center 1988; Visionary San Francisco Installation, San Francisco Museum of Modern Art 1990; with Vito Acconci & Stanley Saitowitz, public art, Embarcadero Promenade, San Francisco 1991; with Pascal Cribier & Louis Benech, Jardin des Tuileries, Paris 1991. **Exhibitions/Performances:** Solo: ALNY 1968; Green Architecture at AIA, San Francisco, RISD; Univ. Gallery, Amherst; Octagon, Washington, DC 1982-84; Walker Art Center, Minneapolis 1982; Philippe Bonnafont Gallery, San Francisco 1984; Urban League, NYC 1984; Gallerie Jamileh Weber, Zurich 1985; Max Protetch Gallery, NYC 1988; Spazio Piu Gallery, Vicenza 1989; Antonio Jannone Gallery, Milan 1989; Group: Whitney Museum, NYC 1974, 1985; Biennale de Venezia 1985; Walker Art Center 1989-90; San Francisco Museum of Modern Art 1990. **Bio-Bibliography:** C. Ray Smith, "Golden Gate Grids," *Supermannerism* (1977). **Home Address:** 30 Bellair Pl., San Francisco, CA 94133.

SONTAG, SUSAN ■ AAR Visitor 1981-82, Writer.

SOVERN, MICHAEL I. ■ AAR Trustee 1993-present, Bd. Chair 1994-present. **Studies:** Columbia College, Columbia Law School. **Career & Employment:** Columbia Univ., Law School Dean, Univ. Provost, Chancellor Kent Prof., Pres. 1980-93, Pres. Emer. **Memberships & Offices:** AAAS; Japan Soc., Chair; Asian Cultural Council, BoT; AT&T, BoD; Chemical Bank, BoD; Warner-Lambert Co., BoD; Shubert Found., BoT; Shubert Organization, BoT; State-City Comm. on Integrity in Government, Chair; New York City Charter Revision Comm., Chair. **Publications:** books & articles on labor relations, employment discrimination, conflict resolution. **Exhibitions/Performances:** Public Television, *Leading Questions*, host.

SOWERBY, LEO ■ FAAR Musical Composition 24; AAR Trustee 1938-49. b. May 1, 1895, Grand Rapids, MI. d. July 7, 1968. MusM 18, American Conservatory in Chicago. **Career & Employment:** American Conservatory of Music, Faculty 1925-62; US Army, Bandmaster WWII; College of Church Musicians, Washington, DC, Founder 1962, Dir. 1962-68; St. James Episcopal Cathedral, Chicago, Organist. **Memberships & Offices:** NIAL 1935; ASCAP; Cosmos Club. **Fellowships, Honors & Awards:** Soc. for the Publication of American Music, Annual Publication Award 1921, 1927, 1931, 1943; Univ. of Rochester, Hon. MusD 1934; Pulitzer Prize 1946; Royal

School of Church Music, London, Fellow 1963. **Publications:** *Ideals of Church Music* (1956). **Important Works:** *Violin Concerto* 1913; *Sonata*, for organ 1914-17; *Serenade*, for string quartet 1916; *Comes Autumn Time*, overture 1917; *From the Northland*, for orchestra 1924; *Florida Suite*, for piano 1929; *Prairie*, a symphonic poem 1929; *Symphony in G*, for organ solo 1930; *Concerto in C*, for organ & orchestra 1938; *The Canticle of the Sun*, for chorus & orchestra 1944; *Symphony No. 4* 1949; *Christ Reborn*, cantata for chorus & organ 1950; *Church Sonata*, for organ 1956; *Ark of the Covenant*, cantata for chorus & organ 1959; *Triptych of Diversions*, for organ, 2 violins, double bass, oboe & percussion 1962; *Solomon's Garden*, cantata for tenor, chorus & orchestra 1964; *La Corona*, for chorus & orchestra 1967; *Dialog*, for organ & piano 1967. **Bio-Bibliography:** *Leo Sowerby: A Short Biography and a Complete List of His Compositions* (Chicago, 1979); *Baker's Biographical Dictionary of American Musicians; New Grove Dictionary of American Music; Who Was Who in America.*

SPAETH, BARBETTE ■ Broneer Fellow 1990-91.

SPAFFORD, MICHAEL C. ■ FAAR Painting 69. b. Nov. 6, 1935, Palm Springs, CA. m. Elizabeth A. Sandvig. c. Michael Andrew Spafford. BA 59, Pomona College; MA 60, Harvard Univ. **Research/Artistic Interests:** Painting using oil & mixed media, also woodcuts. **Career & Employment:** Univ. of Washington, Prof. 1963-present. **Fellowships, Honors & Awards:** Louis Comfort Tiffany Found. Grant 1965-66; AAAL Award 1983. **Important Works:** Bellevue Art Museum, Bellevue, WA; Cheney Cowles Memorial Museum, Spokane, WA; Microsoft Corp., Redmond, WA; King County Arts Comm., Seattle; Seattle Art Museum; Swedish Hospital, Seattle; Univ. of Washington, Seattle; Washington State Collection, Olympia; Museum of Art, Washington State Univ., Pullman; House of Representatives Chamber, Olympia, WA; Kingdome, Seattle; Seattle Opera House. **Exhibitions/Performances:** Selected Solo: Mexican-North American Cultural Inst., Galerias Norte y Sur, Mexico City 1962; Francine Seders Gallery, Seattle 1967, 1969, 1972, 1976, 1977, 1980, 1983, 1986, 1991, 1993; Tacoma Art Museum 1966, 1975; Utah Museum of Fine Arts, Salt Lake City 1975; Vollum College Center Gallery, Reed College, Portland,

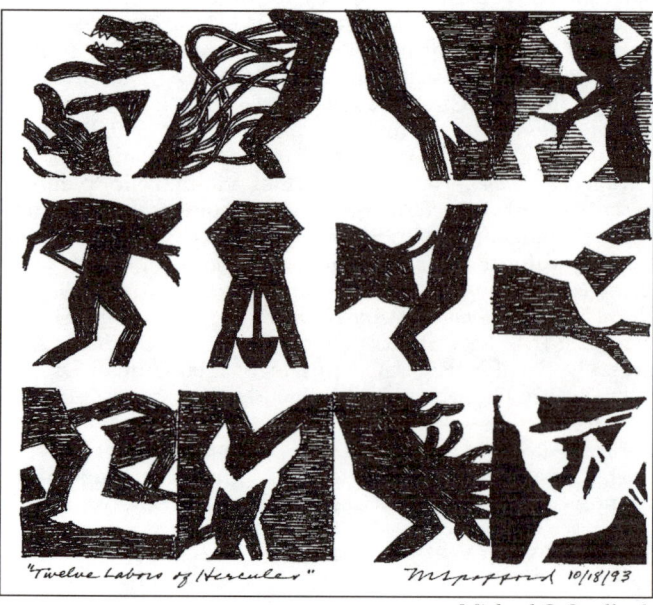

"Twelve Labors of Hercules"   MSpafford 10/18/93

Michael C. Spafford

OR 1984; Seattle Art Museum 1986; Whatcom Museum & Western Washington Univ. Art Gallery, Bellingham 1987; Bellevue Art Museum, WA 1991; Sheehan Gallery, Whitman College, Walla Walla, WA 1992. **Bio-Bibliography:** *Who's Who in America; Who's Who in American Art; Who's Who in the West.* **Home Address:** 2418 E. Interlaken Blvd., Seattle, WA 98112. **Business Address:** Francine Seders Gallery, 6701 Greenwood Ave., Seattle, WA 98103.

SPALDING, WALTER P. ■ AAR Trustee 1925.

SPANN, PHILIP O. ■ FAAR Classics/Archaeology 78. b. Aug. 13, 1941, Iowa City, IA. m. Jeanne Spann. c. Jessica. BA 65, Northwestern Univ.; MA 73, Univ. of Texas, Austin; PhD 76, Univ. of Texas, Austin. **Other Study:** Archaeological Field Work: Peñaflor, Sevilla; Garabato, Córdoba. **Career & Employment:** Univ. of Florida, Gainesville, Visiting Asst. Prof. 1978-81, Visiting Lect. 1985-91; Univ. of Arkansas, Fayetteville, Asst. Prof. 1981-85; Aegean Inst., Galatas, Visiting Prof. 1989; Univ. of Utah, Assc. Prof. 1991-present. **Fellowships, Honors & Awards:** NEH Fellowship 1980; Fulbright Fellowship 1981-82, 1992; Univ. of Florida, Teacher of the Year 1989-90, Outstanding Achievement & Performance Award 1989-90; Univ. of Utah Research Grant 1992. **Publications:** "Sallust, Plutarch and the Isles of the Blest," *Terrae Incognitae* 9 (1977): 75-80; "M. Perperna and Pompey's Spanish Expedition," *Hispania Antiqua* 7 (1977): 45-60; "Lacobriga Expugned: Of Renaissance Forgeries and the Sertorian War," *TAPA* 3 (1981): 229-35; "Saguntim vs. Segontia: A Note on the Topography of the Sertorian War," *Historia* 33.1 (1984): 116; "Sertorius in Drama: Or Shakespeare Manqué," *University of Florida Comparative Drama Papers* 6 (1985): 187-98; "C. Cotta & the 'Unspeakable' L. (?) Fufifius: A Note on Sulla's *Res Publica Restituta*," *Classical Journal* 82.4 (1987): 306-9; *Quintus Sertorius and the Legacy of Sulla* (Fayetteville: Univ. of Arkansas Press, 1987); "Ad Aras en El Garabato (Córdoba)?," *Revista de Arqueología* (Madrid) 108 (1990): 34-47; 4 articles on Roman Spain in *Dictionary of the History of Classical Archaeology*, ed. Nancy T. de Grummond (Westport, CT: Greenwood Press, 1995); "Informe sobre de la Prospección Arqueológica en El Garabato (Córdoba), Julio 1992," *Anuario Arqueológico de la Consejería de Cultura de la Junta de Andalucía* (forthcoming). **Home Address:** 1125 E 300 S, Salt Lake City, UT 84102. **Business Address:** Dept. of Languages & Literature, Univ. of Utah, Salt Lake City, UT 84112.

SPEAR, RICHARD E. ■ RAAR History of Art 88; AAR History of Art Jury 1984; NEH Summer Seminar 1994. b. Feb. 3, 1940, Michigan City, IN. m. Athena Tacha. BA 61, Univ. of Chicago; MFA 63, Princeton Univ.; PhD 65, Princeton Univ. **Research/Artistic Interests:** 17th-century Italian painting. **Career & Employment:** Oberlin College, Instr.-Assc. Prof. 1964-75, Allen Memorial Art Museum, Dir. 1972-83, Prof. 1975-83; Mildred C. Jay Prof. 1983-present, Acting Chair 1984-85, 1989-90; George Washington Univ., Distinguished Visiting Prof. 1983-84. **Memberships & Offices:** Intermuseum Conservation Assn., BoT 1972-83, Pres. 1975-77; Assn. of Art Museum Directors 1973-81; Ohio Arts Council, Visual Arts Adv. Bd.; American Civil Liberties Union, Regional Exec. Bd.; CAA, Session Chair 1977, 1984; Nominating Com. 1983; *Art Bulletin*, Ed.-in-Chief 1985-88, Chair, Ed. Bd. 1989-92; J. Paul Getty Postdoctoral Fellowships, Review Panel 1985; *The Dictionary of Art*, Field Adv. **Fellowships, Honors & Awards:** Princeton Univ., McCann, Wilson, & A.M. Friend Fellow 1961-64; Fulbright-Hays Research Scholarship 1966-67; NEH Grant 1968, Fellow 1980-81, Summer Seminar 1994; ACLS-NEH

Travel Grant 1969; ACLS Fellow 1971-72, Travel Grant 1979; Premio Daria Borghese 1972; Oberlin College, Research Status Grant 1977-78; Ossabaw Found. Project, Ossabaw Island, GA, Fellow 1980; CASVA, Ailsa Mellon Bruce Senior Fellow 1983-84; Djerassi Found. Fellow 1985; Guggenheim Found. Fellow 1987-88; Nat. Humanities Center, Fellow 1992-93. **Publications:** "The 'Raising of Lazarus': Caravaggio and the Sixteenth-Century Tradition," *Gazette des Beaux-Arts* 65 (1965): 65-70; "The Literary Source of Poussin's 'Realm of Flora,'" *Burlington Magazine* 107 (1965): 563-69; "Baciccio's Pendant Paintings of 'Venus and Adonis,'" *Allen Memorial Art Museum Bulletin* 23 (1966): 98-112; "Some Domenichino Cartoons," *Master Drawings* 5 (1967): 144-58; "The Cappella della Strada Cupa: A Forgotten Domenichino Chapel," *Burlington Magazine* 111 (1969): 12-23; *Caravaggio and His Followers* (Cleveland: Cleveland Museum of Art, 1971; rev. ed., New York: Harper & Row, 1975); *Renaissance and Baroque Paintings from the Sciarra and Fiano Collections* (Univ. Park, PA, & Rome: Ugo Bozzi, 1972); "Johann Liss Reconsidered," *Art Bulletin* 58 (1976): 582-93; "A Forgotten Landscape Painter: Giovanni Battista Viola," *Burlington Magazine* 122 (1980): 298-315; *Domenichino*, 2 vols. (New Haven & London: Yale Univ. Press, 1982); "Art History and the 'Blockbuster' Exhibition," *Art Bulletin* 68 (1986): 358-59; "Discussion: 'On Art History and the "Blockbuster" Exhibition,'" *Art Bulletin* 69 (1987): 297-98; "Leonardo, Raphael, and Caravaggio," in *Light on the Eternal City*, Papers in Art History from the Pennsylvania State Univ. 2, ed. H. Hager & S. Munshower (1987): 59-90; "Domenichino Addenda," *Burlington Magazine* 131 (1989): 5-16; "Re-viewing the 'Divine Guido,'" *Burlington Magazine* 131 (1989): 367-72; "Reni contre Dominiquin dans la litterature d'art française du XVIIe siècle," in *Rencontres de l'École du Louvre. Seicento: La peinture italienne du XVIIe siècle et la France* (Paris, 1990), 190-98; "La Necessità of Guido Reni," in *Il luogo ed il ruolo della città di Bologna tra Europa continentale e mediterranea*, Atti del Colloquio C.I.H.A. 1990 (Bologna 1992), 313-40; "Guercino's 'Prix-fixe': Observations on Studio Practices and Art Maketing in Emilia," *Burlington Magazine* 136 (1994): 592-602. **Bio-Bibliography:** *Who's Who in America.* **Home Address:** 291 Forest St., Oberlin, OH 44074. **Business Address:** Oberlin College, Oberlin, OH 44074.

SPEICHER, EUGENE ■ AAR Trustee 1955-58, Artist.

SPENCE, SARAH ■ FAAR Post-Classical/Humanistic Studies 82. b. Aug. 14, 1954, NYC. m. James H. Mc Gregor, FAAR 82. c. Edward. BA 76, Brown Univ.; MA 77, Columbia Univ.; PhD 81, Columbia Univ. **Research/Artistic Interests:** Classical tradition, especially in the Middle Ages; Vergil. **Career & Employment:** California State Univ., Long Beach, Asst. Prof. 1982-87; Univ. of Georgia, Asst. Prof. 1987-89, Assc. Prof. 1989-present. **Memberships & Offices:** *Tenso: Bulletin of the Société Guilhem IX*, Managing Ed. 1989-present. **Fellowships, Honors & Awards:** Whiting Fellow 1979-80; Harvard Univ., Mellon Faculty Fellow 1984-85; Bunting Inst. Fellow 1992-93; Rockefeller Found., Bellagio Research Center 1993. **Publications:** *The Chansons of Charles d'Orléans* (New York: Garland, 1986); *Rhetorics of Reason and Desire: Vergil, Augustine and the Troubadours* (Ithaca: Cornell Univ. Press, 1988). **Business Address:** Univ. of Georgia, Park Hall, Athens, GA 30602.

SPENDER, STEPHEN ■ AAR Visitor 1943 — 1951, Poet.

SPEYER, JAMES ■ AAR Charter Mem., Bank Exec.

SPOERL, C.G. ■ Stewardson Memorial Scholar 1911-12, 1913.

SPOFFORD, EDWARD WASHBURN ■ FAAR Classics/
Archaeology 64. b. Apr. 12, 1931, Lee, MA. BA 54, Amherst
College; MA 58, Cornell Univ. **Other Studies:** Harvard Univ.
1960-62. **Career & Employment:** Smith College, Faculty 1957-
60. **Fellowships, Honors & Awards:** Amherst College, James
I. Merrill Fellowship 1954-55.

SPRINGER, CAROLYN E. ■ FAAR Post-Classical/Human-
istic Studies 84; SOF Council, Regional Rep. 1988-present. b.
Oct. 2, 1952, Pullman, WA. BA 74, Wesleyan Univ.; MA 77,
Yale Univ.; PhD 81, Yale Univ. **Career & Employment:** Rutgers
Univ., Asst. Prof. 1981-85; Stanford Univ., Asst. Prof. 1985-88,
Assc. Prof. 1988-present; Wesleyan Univ., Visiting Assc. Prof.
1990. **Memberships & Offices:** *Stanford Italian Review,* Ed. Bd.
1985-present; Fulbright Comm., Juror 1985-present; MLA,
Delegate Assembly 1990-92; *Stanford Literature Review,* Ed. Bd.
1991-present. **Fellowships, Honors & Awards:** Fulbright-
Hays Grant 1975-76; Stanford Univ., Andrew H. Mellon Fel-
lowship 1984-85; Ford Found. Grant 1989; Harvard Univ., Villa
I Tatti Fellowship 1989-90. **Publications:** "Verso un'
iconografia 'democratica' del Risorgimento: romanzo e pittura
in Beatrice Cenci," *Versus: Quaderni di studi semiotici* 19-20
(1978); "Far from the Madding Crowd: Wordsworth and the
News of Robespierre's Death," *Wordsworth Circle* 12.4 (1981);
"Vico and Foscolo," *NEMLA Italian Studies* 6 (1982); "Rome
Souterraine: The Classical Landscape in the Risorgimento
from Didier to Garibaldi," *Stanford Italian Review* 3.2 (1983);
"Archaeology in Belli's Roman Sonnets," *Gradiva: International
Journal of Literature* 3.2-3 (1984-85); "Textual Geography: The
Role of the Reader in *Invisible Cities*," *Modern Language Studies* 15.4 (1985); *The Marble Wilderness: Ruins and Representation
in Italian Romanticism, 1775-1850* (Cambridge: Cambridge
Univ. Press, 1987); "Petrarch and Leopardi: The Two Canzoni
all'Italia," *Canadian Journal of Italian Studies* 10.34 (1987); ed.
with Pietro Frassica & Giovanni Pacchiano, *Immagini del
novecento italiano* (New York: Macmillan, 1987); "Fellini's Aesthetics of Fragmentation: Images of Rome in *La dolce vita*,"
Canadian Journal of Italian Studies 11 (1988); ed., *History and
Memory in European Romanticism,* Stanford Literature Review
6.1 (1989); "History, Fantasy and Fraud: The Status of Historical Representation in Sciascia's *Il Consiglio d'Egitto*," *Italica*
66.2 (1989). **Business Address:** Dept. of French & Italian,
Stanford Univ., Stanford, CA 94206.

SPURZA, JOANNE MARIE ■ FAAR Classics/Archaeol-
ogy 88. b. Feb. 19, 1956, Gloversville, NY. BA 79, Bryn Mawr
College; MA 82, Bryn Mawr College; MA 84, Princeton Univ.
Other Studies: ICCS 1978. **Fellowships, Honors & Awards:**
Princeton Univ., Stanley Seeger Travel Grant 1983, Albert C.
Hencken Travelling Fellowship 1986, Graduate Fellowship
1986-87.

ST. FLORIAN, FRIEDRICH ■ FAAR Architecture 85. b.
Dec. 21, 1932, Graz, Austria. m. Livia Campanella. c. Alisia,
Ilaria. Dipl. Ing. 58, Technische Universitaet, Graz; MArch 62,
Columbia Univ. **Career & Employment:** Columbia Univ.,
Instr. 1962-63; RISD 1963-present, Prof. 1980-present, Dean
of Architecture 1977-88, Acting VP for Academic Affairs 1981-
84; St. Florian Asscs., Architects, Prin. 1978-present; Visiting
Appointments: MIT; Architectural Assn., London; Univ. of
Utah; Univ. of Texas, Austin; McGill Univ. **Memberships &
Offices:** Juror: Intl. Design Competition "Trigon," Graz 1969;
Art Council, City of Cambridge, MA 1978; Panelist: MIT 1972,
1974; Soc. for Art, Religion & Culture, NYC 1972; Museum of
Science & Industry, Chicago 1972; Museum of Science, Bos-

ton 1973; Carpenter Center for Visual & Environmental Stud-
ies, Harvard Univ. 1973; Univ. of Texas, Austin 1975; Optical
Soc. of America, Boston 1975; Art Net, London. 1976; Univ. of
Utah, Salt Lake City 1978; Organizer: RISD Intl. Symposia
1976, 1977, 1978; Miami University, Coral Gables, School of
Architecture, Visiting Com. 1982-86. **Fellowships, Honors &
Awards:** with R. Abraham, Ex Equo, Intl. Architectural Competition for Cultural Center, Leopoldville, 2d Prize 1959;
Fulbright Fellowship 1961-62; MIT, Center for Advanced Visual Studies Fellow 1970-76; with R. Abraham, Intl. Architec-
tural Design Competition, Pompidou Centre, Paris, 2d Prize
1972; *Progressive Architecture,* Excellence in Design Award
1981. **Publications:** "Frederick Kiesler, Architekt der
Unendlichkeit," *Bau* 1/2 (1966); "On My Imaginary Architec-
ture," *Leonardo* (Paris) 11 (1978). **Important Works:** with R.
Abraham, Dapra House, Salzburg 1959-61; with R. Abraham,
Pless House, Vienna 1960-62; with R. Abraham & J. Thornley,
for the Pompidou Centre, Paris, Competition 1972; Edwards
Residence, Providence, RI 1982; Villa Shein, Seekonk, MA
1982; Villa Morgenthau, North Kingstown, RI 1987; Studio
Residence Congdon-Lichtman, Rehoboth, MA 1988; Studio
Residence Burgess, Hull, MA 1989; Studio Residence St.
Florian, Providence, RI 1989; Providence River Market, RI
1991; MOMA; MIT; Museum of Art, RISD. **Exhibitions/Per-
formances:** Galerie St. Stephan, Vienna 1966; Nat. Inst. of Ar-
chitects, Rome 1967; 4th Triennale di Milano 1968; Moderna
Museet, Stockholm 1969; Hayden Gallery, MIT 1970, 1973; Bell
Memorial Art Gallery, Brown Univ. 1972; Inst. of Contemporary Art, London 1973; Museum of Art, Univ. of Texas, Austin 1975; Memorial Gallery, Graduate School of Architecture,
Univ. of Utah, Salt Lake City 1975; MOMA 1975; Inst. of Contemporary Art, Boston 1975; Drawing Center, NYC 1979; Walker
Art Center, Minneapolis 1980. **Bio-Bibliography:** *L'Architettura
Sperimentale,* exb. cat. (Rome: Istituto Nazionale di Architettura,
1967); *Friedrich St. Florian, Imaginary Architecture,* exb. cat. (Stock-
holm: Moderna Museet, 1969); Gyorgy Kepes, *Friedrich St. Florian,
Projects,* exb. cat. (Cambridge, MA: MIT, Com. on the Visual Arts,
1973); Peter Cook, *Friedrich St. Florian, Projects 1961-76,* exb. cat.
(Austin: Art Museum, Univ. of Texas, 1976); *Who's Who in America.*
Home Address: 137 Univ. Ave., Providence, RI 02906. **Business
Address:** Dept. of Architecture, RISD, Providence, RI 02903.

ST. JOHN, DAVID ■ FAAR Literature 85. b. July 24, 1949,
Fresno, CA. m. Molly Bendall. c. Vivienne. BA 72, California
State Univ.; MFA 74, Univ. of Iowa, Writers' Workshop. **Re-
search/Artistic Interests:** 20th-century world poetry, contemporary American poetry. **Career & Employment:** Oberlin College, Asst. Prof. 1975-77; Johns Hopkins Univ., Asst. Prof. 1977-
81, Assc. Prof. 1981-87; Univ. of Southern California, Prof.
1987-present. **Memberships & Offices:** *Field,* Assc. Ed. 1975-
77; *Seneca Review,* Assc. Ed. 1977-81; Wesleyan Univ. Press,
Poetry Consultant 1982-90; *Poet & Critic,* Contr. Ed. 1981-89;
Antioch Review, Poetry Ed. 1981-present. **Fellowships, Honors & Awards:** *The Nation-Discovery,* Contest Winnner 1975;
Great Lakes College Assn., New Writers Award 1976; NEA
Fellowship 1976, 1984, 1993; Guggenheim Fellowship 1977-
78; San Francisco Found., James D. Phelan Prize 1980; Mary-
land Arts Council Fellowship 1980; Ingram Merrill Found.
Grant 1984; Nat. Book Award, Poetry Nomination 1994. **Pub-
lications:** *Hush* (Boston: Houghton Mifflin, 1976); *The Shore*
(Boston: Houghton Mifflin, 1980); *No Heaven* (Boston:
Houghton Mifflin, 1985); *Terraces of Rain: An Italian Sketch-
book,* illus. Antoine Predock, FAAR (Santa Fe: Recursos Books,
Santa Fe Literary Arts Center, 1991); *Study for the World's Body:
New and Selected Poems* (Harper Collins, 1994). **Bio-Bibliog-**

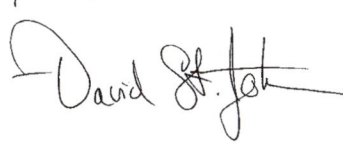

SHADOW

I am the shadow you once blessed

Though I was told later you meant only
To bless a small monkey carved of ebony
On the leg of a particular chair

Didn't you notice.
That when you fell to your knees I too
Fell & kissed this scarlet earth

Blackened by the lyre of your wings

David St. John

David St. John

raphy: Ian Hamilton, *Oxford Companion to Twentieth-Century Poetry* (1994). **Home Address:** 440 Rialto Ave., Venice, CA 90291. **Business Address:** English Dept., Univ. of Southern California, Los Angeles, CA 90089.

STAHR, FREDERICK CHARLES ■ FAAR Painting 15. b. June 9, 1878, NYC. d. Mar. 9, 1946. **Study:** NAD; Columbia Univ.; Royal Acad. of Bavaria, Germany; Lazarus School 1911-14. **Research/Artistic Interests:** Murals. **Memberships & Offices:** NAD; ALNY; Nat. Soc. of Mural Painters. **Important Works:** Moravian Church, New Dorp, Staten Island 1944. **Bio-Bibliography:** *Who Was Who in American Art.*

STALEY, EARL V. ■ FAAR Painting 82. b. 1938, Oak Park, IL. m. Suzanne Crowley. BFA 60, Illinois Wesleyan Univ.; MFA 63, Univ. of Arkansas. **Career & Employment:** Washington Univ., Asst. Prof. 1963-66; Rice Univ. 1966-69; Univ. of St. Thomas, Assc. Prof. 1969-81; Univ. of Texas, San Antonio, Visiting Artist 1990; Louisiana State Univ., Visiting Artist 1991; Tom Ball College, Art Instr. 1992-present. **Fellowships, Honors & Awards:** NEA Fellowship 1975, 1978, 1985; City of Houston, Mayor's Award 1985. **Important Works:** Chase Manhattan Bank, NYC; Chemical Bank, NYC; Dallas Museum of Fine Arts; First Nat. Bank of Chicago; Frito Lay, Dallas; Home Savings of America, Los Angeles; Museum of Fine Arts, Houston; New Museum of Contemporary Art, NYC; Paine Webber, NYC; Philip Morris, NYC; Prudential Insurance Co., Newark; El Paso Museum, TX. **Exhibitions/Performances:** Solo: Illinois Wesleyan Univ., Bloomington 1960, 1963; Rice Univ., Houston 1967; Meredith Long & Co., Houston 1970; Texas Gallery, Houston 1974, 1975, 1977, 1978; Sarah Campbell Blaffer Gallery, Univ. of Houston 1974; Contemporary Arts Museum, Houston 1980, 1983; Phyllis Kind Gallery, NYC 1981, 1983; Watson-de Nagy & Co., Houston 1980 (2), 1982, 1983, 1985; Sewall Art Gallery, Rice Univ. 1982; New Museum of Contemporary Art, NYC 1983; Texas Gallery, Houston 1987; La Jolla Museum of Modern Art, CA 1988; Moody Gallery, Houston 1990, 1991; & numerous group shows. **Bio-Bibliography:** *Comtemporary Art in Texas; Earl Staley: 1973-1983,* exb. cat.;

50 Texas Artists. **Home Address:** PO Box 1288, Houston, TX 77251. **Business Address:** Moody Gallery, Houston, TX.

STALEY, GREGORY A. ■ FAAR Classics/Archaeology 84. b. Aug. 12, 1948, Hagerstown, MD. m. Mary Ann Staley. c. Mark. BA 70, Dickinson College; MA 73, Princeton Univ.; PhD 75, Princeton Univ. **Career & Employment:** Dickinson College, Instr. 1974-75, Asst. Prof. 1978-79; Fordham Univ., Asst. Prof. 1975-76; Univ. of Alberta, Lect. 1976-78; Univ. of Maryland, Asst. Prof. 1979-85, Assc. Prof. 1985-present; Research Center for Arts & Humanities, Acting Deputy Dir. 1988-90. **Memberships & Offices:** American Classical League; *Classical Outlook,* Assc. Ed.; APA; Classical Assn. of the Atlantic States; VSA; Washington Classical Soc., Treas., Pres. **Fellowships, Honors & Awards:** Dickinson College, Phi Beta Kappa, Omicron Delta Kappa, Filler Prize, Rusler Prize, Junior & Senior Sophister 1968-70; Princeton Univ., NDEA-Proctor Fellowship 1971, 1973; Fulbright Fellowship 1977; NEH Grant 1980-83, 1989-91; Maryland Com. for the Humanities Citation 1982. **Publications:** "Latin Days Show Maryland's Commitment," *Prospects* (Fall 1980): 1-2; "Seneca's Thyestes: 'Quantum Mali Habeat Ira,'" *Grazer Beiträge* 10 (1981): 233-46; "*Speculum Iratis*: Philosophy and Rhetoric in Senecan Tragedy," *University of Florida Comparative Drama Conference Papers* 2 (1982): 93-105; "What Happened to Latin? Do Bother to Ask," *Association of Departments of Foreign Languages Bulletin* 14.4 (Sept. 1982): 20-22; "'But Ancient Violence Longs to Breed': Robinson Jeffers' 'The Bloody Sire' and Aeschylus' *Oresteia,*" *Classical and Modern Literature* 3.4 (Summer 1983): 193-99; Speculum Romanum: *A Collection of Latin Mini-Lessons on Roman Culture* (Oxford, OH: American Classical League, 1984); "The Literary Ancestry of Sophocles' 'Ode to Man,'" *Classical World* 78.6 (1985): 561-70; *Language 30: Latin Phrase Dictionary and Study Guide* (Washington, DC: Educational Services Corp., 1986); "The Univ. of Maryland *Speculum Romanum* Project," in *The Teaching of Latin in American Schools: A Profession in Crisis,* ed. Richard A. La Fleur (Decatur, GA: Scholars Press, 1987), 93-98; "Beyond Basic Mythology: The Complex Oedipus," in *Teaching Classical Mythology,* ed. Joseph F. O'Connor & Robert J. Rowland, Jr., APA Education Papers 5 (1987), 54-68; "Aeneas' First Act 1.180-4," *Classical World* 84.1 (1990): 25-38. **Home Address:** 10153 Rope Maker Dr., Ellicott City, MD 21042. **Business Address:** Dept. of Classics, 2407 Marie Mount Hall, Univ. of Maryland, College Park, MD 20742.

STANTON, MICHAEL ■ Steedman Fellow 1990.

STAPLEFORD, RICHARD W. ■ FAAR History of Art 67. b. Jan. 4, 1939, Woodbury, NJ. m. Judith Herron. c. Alessandra, Julian. BA 61, Duke Univ.; MA 63, IFA; PhD 74, IFA. **Research/Artistic Interests:** History of architecture, esp. medieval, Italian Renaissance & American; art history, esp. early medieval, Italian Renaissance & baroque; archaeology. **Career & Employment:** Hunter College, Asst. Prof.-Prof. 1967-present. **Publications:** with John Potter, "Velázquez' *Las Hiluderas,*" *Artibus et Historiae* 8 (1987): 159-81; "Botticelli's Portrait of a Young Man Holding a Trecento Medallion," *Burlington Magazine* 129 (1987): 428-36; *Temples of Illusion: The Atmospheric Theaters of John Eberson,* exb. cat. (New York: Leubsdorf Art Gallery, Hunter College, 1988); *The Age of Lorenzo de' Medici: Patronage and the Arts in Renaissance Florence* (Washington, DC: NGA, 1992). **Home Address:** 160 E. 84th St., NYC 10028.

STARBUCK, GEORGE E. ■ FAAR Literature 63. b. June 15, 1931, Columbus, OH. **Career & Employment:** Boston

Univ., Faculty; SUNY Buffalo, Librarian- Lect. **Fellowships, Honors & Awards:** *Nation* Poetry Prize, Lenore Marshall 1982. **Publications:** *Bone Thoughts* (New Haven: Yale Univ. Press, 1960). **Bio-Bibliography:** Ernest Herbert, "Words That Taste Just Right," *Boston Globe Magazine* (Apr. 24, 1983).

STARR, CHESTER G. ■ FAAR Classics/Archaeology 40. b. Oct. 5, 1914, Centralia, MO. BA 34, Univ. of Missouri; MA 35, Univ. of Missouri; PhD 38, Cornell Univ. **Research/Artistic Interests:** Ancient history. **Career & Employment:** Univ. of Illinois 1940-70; Univ. of Michigan 1970-85. **Memberships & Offices:** AHA, Chair of Com. on Ancient History. **Fellowships, Honors & Awards:** Guggenheim Fellowship 1950, 1958-59; Univ. of Washington, Walker Ames Lect. 1979; LLD: Univ. of Missouri 1981, Univ. of Illinois 1984, St. Michael's College 1992; AHA, Distinguished Scholar, Distinguished Teacher 1991. **Publications:** *The Roman Imperial Navy, 30 B.C.-A.D. 324* (Ithaca: Cornell Univ. Press, 1941); *The Emergence of Rome as Ruler of the Western World* (Ithaca: Cornell Univ. Press, 1950); *Civilization and the Caesars, The Intellectual Revolution in the Roman Empire* (Ithaca: Cornell Univ. Press, 1954); co-author, *A History of the World,* 2 vols. (Chicago: Rand McNally, 1960); *The Origins of Greek Civilization, 1100-650 B.C.* (New York: Alfred A. Knopf, 1961); *A History of the Ancient World* (New York: Oxford Univ. Press, 1965); *Rise and Fall of the Ancient World* (Chicago: Rand McNally, 1965); *The Awakening of the Greek Historical Spirit* (New York: Alfred A. Knopf, 1968); *Athenian Coinage, 480-449 B.C.* (Oxford: Clarendon Press, 1970); *The Ancient Greeks* (New York: Oxford Univ. Press, 1971); *The Ancient Romans* (New York: Oxford Univ. Press, 1971); *Early Man: Prehistory and the Civilizations of the Ancient Near East* (New York: Oxford Univ. Press, 1973); *Political Intelligence in Classical Greece,* Mnemosyne, supp. 31 (Leiden, 1974). **Bio-Bibliography:** *Storia del Mondo Antico* (Rome: Editori Riunite, 1977); *Craft of the Ancient Historian* (Lanham, MD: Univ. Press, 1985); *Who's Who in America.* **Home Address:** Ann Arbor, MI 48109.

STARR, LILLIAN ■ FAAR Classics/Archaeology 27. b. Sept. 1, 1900, Taunton, MA. d. Mar. 27, 1958. BA 24, Wellesley College; MA 26, Bryn Mawr College. **Other Study:** Bryn Mawr 1927-29. **Research/Artistic Interests:** Roman cut-stone construction. **Career & Employment:** Brown Univ., Graduate Asst. 1924-25; Elmira College, Instr. 1929-31; Independent Scholar after 1931. **Fellowships, Honors & Awards:** Wellesley College, Goldmark Fellowship. **Bio-Bibliography:** Bryn Mawr College Archives; Wellesley College Archives.

STARR, PAMELA F. ■ FAAR Post-Classical/Humanistic Studies 84. b. NYC. BA, Harpur College; MLS, Columbia Univ.; PhD 87, Yale Univ. **Other Study:** Private instruction: voice, viola da gamba. **Research/Artistic Interests:** Renaissance music, Classical period music, esp. Mozart. **Career & Employment:** Oberlin College, Visiting Instr. 1986; Univ. of Nebraska, Asst. Prof. 1987-93, Assc. Prof. 1993-present. **Memberships & Offices:** American Musicological Soc. Com., Program Chair 1980-present; College Music Soc. 1987-present. **Fellowships, Honors & Awards:** Fulbright Fellowship (declined) 1983-84; AAUW Fellowship 1984-85; NEH Fellowship 1988; Maude Hammond Fling Fellowship 1989; ACLS Grant 1989; APS Grant 1993. **Publications:** "The Ferrara Connection: A Case Study of Musical Recruitment in the Renaissance," *Studi musicali* 18 (1989): 3-17; "Rome as the Centre of the Universe: Papal Grace & Music Patronage," *Early Music History* 11 (1992): 223-62; "The Other Side of the Looking-Glass: Using the Vatican Archives in the Study of Music in

the Low Countries," in *Musicology and Archival Research,* ed. Barbara Haggh (Archiev-en-Bibliothekwesen in Belgie, 1994); "Towards the Cappella Sistina: A Profile of the Papal Chapel under Four Popes, 1447-71," in *Studien zur Geschichte der Päpstlichen Kapelle. Tagingsbericht Heidelberg,* ed. Bernhard Janz (Vatican City); "Strange Obituaries: The Historical Uses of the *Per Obitum* Supplication," in *Proceedings of the Library of Congress Conference, Music, Musicians, and Musical Culture in Renaissance Rome,* ed. Richard Sheer (Oxford: Oxford Univ. Press); "Storia della Cappella Pontificia, dal Concilio di Costanza al Pontificato di Giulio II: Palestrina," Fondazione Palestrina (forthcoming). **Business Address:** Univ. of Nebraska, 120 Westbrook, Lincoln, NE 68588.

STEEGMULLER, FRANCIS ■ AAR Visitor 1981-82, Writer, Translator.

STEGNER, WALLACE E. ■ RAAR Literature 60. b. Feb. 18, 1909, Lake Mills, IA. d. Apr. 13, 1993. m. Mary Page. c. Stuart Page Stegner. BA 30, Univ. of Utah; MA 32, Univ. of Iowa; PhD 35, Univ. of Iowa. **Career & Employment:** Augustana College, Rock Island, IL, Faculty 1934; Univ. of Utah, Faculty 1934-37; Univ. of Wisconsin, Faculty 1937-39; Harvard Univ., Faculty 1939-45; Stanford Univ., Jackson E. Reynolds Prof. 1945-71, Stanford Creative Writing Program, Dir. 1946-71. **Memberships & Offices:** AAAS; AAAL; Soc. of American Historians; Antiquarian Soc. **Fellowships, Honors & Awards:** Little-Brown Novelette Prize 1937; Houghton Mifflin Life-in-America Award 1945; O. Henry Memorial Short Story Awards, 1st Prize 1950; Rockefeller Found. Fellowship 1950; Guggenheim Fellowship 1950-51, 1959; NEA Senior Fellowship 1950, 1990; Wenner-Gren Found. Fellowship 1954; Commonwealth Club of California, Gold Medal 1967, 1976; US State Dept. Lecture Tour 1969; Pulitzer Prize 1972; Nat. Book Award 1977; *Los Angeles Times,* Robert Kirsch Prize 1980; PEN West Lifetime Achievement Award 1989; California Arts Council, Governor's Award for the Arts 1991; Hon. PhD: Univ. of California; Utah State Univ.; Univ. of Saskatchewan; Santa Clara Univ.; Montana State Univ.; Univ. of Wisconsin. **Publications:** *Remembering Laughter* (1937); *The Potter's House* (1938); *On a Darkling Plain* (1939); *Fire and Ice* (1941); *The Big Rock Candy Mountain* (1943); *One Nation* (1945); *Second Growth* (1947); *The Women on the Wall* (1950); *The City of the Living* (1956); *A Shooting Star* (1961); *Wolf Willow* (1962); *The Gathering of Zion* (1964); *All the Little Live Things* (1967); *The Sound of Mountain Water* (1969); *The Preacher and the Slave,* reissued as *Joe Hill* (1969); *Angle of Repose* (1971); *The Spectator Bird* (1976); *Recapitulation* (1979); *American Places* (1981); *One Way to Spell Man* (1982); *Crossing to Safety* (1987); *The American West as Living Space* (1987); *Collected Stories* (1990); *Where the Bluebird Sings to the Lemonade Springs* (1992).

STEIGER, RAND P. ■ FAAR Musical Composition 86. b. June 18, 1957, NYC. m. D. Vibeke Sorensen. BMus 80, Manhattan School of Music; MFA 82, California Inst. of the Arts. **Other Study:** IRCAM Stage 1982, computer music. **Career & Employment:** California Inst. of the Arts 1982-87; UC, San Diego, Assc. Prof. & Chair 1987-present. **Memberships & Offices:** California EAR Unit, Co-founder. **Fellowships, Honors & Awards:** NEA Composers Fellowship; Los Angeles Philharmonic Composer Fellow, Meet the Composer. **Important Works:** *Dialogues II,* for solo marimba & orchestra 1979-80; *Mirrors,* for piano 1981; *Quintessence,* for 12 cl., percussion, piano, el.pno.,vc 1981; *In Nested Symmetry,* for 2 flutes, 2 cl., 2 trp., 2 percussion, 2 piano, 2 violin., 2 vc., bs., electronics 1982; *Kennedy Sketches,* for marimba-vibraphone 1982; *Currents Ca-*

price, for electronics 1982; *Dialogues III,* for piano, percussion, electronics, 1983; *Hexadecathlon,* for solo horn, flute, cl., 2 percussion, piano, vln., vc, John Cerminaro Comm. 1984; *Fanfare erafnaF,* for double chamber orchestra, Los Angeles Philharmonic Comm. 1985; *ReSonata,* for cello & piano, Music Teachers Nat. Assn. Comm. 1985; *Tributaries,* for chamber orchestra, St. Paul Chamber Orchestra Comm. 1986; *Double Concerto* for solo piano & percussion with double chamber orchestra, Pasadena Chamber Orchestra Comm. 1987; *Tributaries for Nancarrow,* for computer controlled pianos 1987; *Druckman Tributary,* for fl, ob, cl, hrn, trb, perc, pno, harp, vln, vla,vc, Musical Elements Comm. 1988; *Thirteen Loops,* for solo flute, bass cl., perc., vln., vc, Fromm Found. Comm. 1988; *Trio in Memoriam,* for piano, percussion, & violacello, Mass. Arts Council Comm. for the Aequalis Ensemble 1989; *NLoops,* synthesized score for video installation by Vibeke Sorensen 1989; *Z Loops,* for clarinet, piano, 2 percussion, Jerome Found. Comm. for Zeitgeist 1989; *Woven Serenade,* for clarinet & string quartet, Los Angeles Chamber Orchestra Comm. 1991; *Nested Études,* for solo piano, Alan Feinberg Comm. 1992; *The Burgess Shale,* for large orchestra, Los Angeles Philharmonic Comm. 1993; *Resonant Vertices,* for solo perc., solo clarinet, fl., vln., vc, New York New Music Ensemble Comm. Recordings: CRI, New Albion Records, New World Records, Inc., Crystal Records. **Home Address:** 2322D La Costa Ave., Carlsbad, CA 92009. **Business Address:** Dept. of Music, 0326, UC, San Diego, La Jolla, CA 92093.

STEINBERG, ARTHUR RICHARD ■ FAAR Classics/ Archaeology 64. b. Mar. 23, 1937, Zurich, Switzerland. m. Frederica Steinberg. BA 58, Harvard Univ. **Other Studies:** ASCSA 1958-59; Univ. of Pennsylvania c.1961. **Career & Employment:** Haverford College, Teacher 1960-61; MIT, Prof. 1964-. **Fellowships, Honors & Awards:** Harvard Univ., Corey Traveling Fellow 1958-59; Univ. of Pennsylvania, Harrison Fellow 1959-60, 1960-61.

STEINBERG, BERNARD NORMAN ■ FAAR Architecture 63. b. Dec. 16, 1932, Toledo, OH. BArch 55, Cornell Univ.; MArch 56, UC. **Career & Employment:** US Army 1956-58; Sherwood, Mills, & Smith, Architects 1959-60; Norval C. White, Architect 1960. **Fellowships, Honors & Awards:** L'Ogive Prize 1954.

STEINBERG, LEO ■ RAAR History of Art 76. b. July 9, 1920, Moscow, Russia. Dipl. 40, Slade School; BS 54, NYU; PhD 60, IFA. **Career & Employment:** Parsons School of Design, Instr. 1949-60; Hunter College, CUNY, Assc. Prof.-Prof. 1961-75; Univ. of Pennsylvania, Univ. Prof. 1975-91, Univ. Prof. Emer. 1975-present. **Memberships & Offices:** CAA, BoD 1968-72. **Fellowships, Honors & Awards:** CAA, Frank Jewett Mather Award 1956, 1984; AAAS, Fellow 1978; Univ. College, London, Fellow 1979; AAAL, Literature Award 1983; MacArthur Found. Fellowship 1986; Hon. Doctorates: Philadelphia College of Art 1981, Parsons School of Design-The New School 1986, Massachusetts College of Art 1987, Bowdoin College 1995. **Publications:** *Other Criteria: Confrontations with Twentieth-Century Art* (New York: Oxford Univ. Press, 1972); "Leonardo's *Last Supper*," *Art Quarterly* 36 (1973): 297-410; "Michelangelo's *Last Judgment* as Merciful Heresy," *Art in America* 63 (Nov.-Dec. 1975): 49-63; *Michelangelo's Last Paintings* (New York: Oxford Univ. Press, London: Phaidon, 1975); *Borromini's San Carlo alle Quattro Fontane: A Study in Multiple Form and Architectural Symbolism* (New York: Garland, 1977); "Resisting Cézanne: Picasso's Three Women of 1908," *Art in*

America 66 (Nov.-Dec. 1978): 114-33; "A Corner of the Last Judgment," *Daedalus* 109 (Spring 1980): 207-73; "The Line of Fate in Michelangelo's Painting," *Critical Inquiry* 6 (Spring 1980): 411-54; *The Sexuality of Christ in Renaissance Art and in Modern Oblivion* (New York: Pantheon, 1983); "The Philosophical Brothel: Picasso's *Demoiselles d'Avignon*," *October* no. 44 (1988): 7-74; "Michelangelo's Florentine *Pietà*: The Missing Leg Twenty Years After," *Art Bulletin* 71 (Sept. 1989): 480-505; "Who's Who in Michelangelo's *Creation of Adam*," *Art Bulletin* 74 (Dec. 1992): 552-66; "All About Eve," *Art Bulletin* 75 (June 1993): 340-44. **Bio-Bibliography:** *Who's Who; Who's Who in American Art.* **Home Address:** 165 W. 66 St., 17A, NYC 10023.

STEINBERG, PAUL L. ■ FAAR Design Arts 82. b. Nov. 24, 1946, NYC. BFA 67, Pratt Inst.; Dipl. A.D. 71, Central School of Art & Design, London. **Research/Artistic Interests:** Set & costume design; primarily opera. **Career & Employment:** Parsons School of Design, Instr. 1973-81, 1988-91; NYU, Tisch School of the Arts, Instr. 1992-present; Nat. Theatre School of France, Strasbourg, Master Classes 1994. **Fellowships, Honors & Awards:** Arts Council of Great Britain Award 1971-72. **Important Works:** Set & Costume Design: *Flying Dutchman,* Dallas Civic Opera 1978; *I Capuletti ed i Montecchi,* Washington Opera 1979; *Count Ory,* NYC Opera 1979; *Ariadne auf Naxos,* Long Beach Opera 1987; *The Seven Deadly Sins,* London Sinfonietta 1988; *Dr. Miracle, Djameleh, & Don Procopio,* Opera Comique, Paris 1990; *Don Giovanni,* Seattle Opera 1991; *The Sailor Who Fell from Grace with the Sea,* San Francisco Opera 1991; *The Beggar's Opera,* Santa Fe Opera 1992; *I Vespri Siciliani,* San Francisco Opera 1993; *Turandot,* Welsh Nat. Opera 1994; Set Design: *The Duchess of Malfi,* Wolf Trap Festival Premiere 1978; *The Visit,* Goodman Theatre 1991; *Mozart-Da Ponte Cycle,* Chicago Symphony Orchestra 1992; *Tania,* American Music Theatre Festival Premiere 1992; *Cavelleria Rusticana & I Pagliacci,* New Israeli Opera 1992; *Lohengrin, Domengo,* Grand Théâtre de Généve 1994; *The Demon,* Wexford Festival 1994; *Madam Butterfly,* Antwerp 1994; *Harvey Milk,* Houston Grand Opera & New York City Opera 1995; *Otello,* Cologne Opera 1996. **Home Address:** 63 Perry St., Apt. 24, NYC 10014.

STEINER, GEORGE ■ AAR Visitor 1989-90, Writer.

STEINERT, ALEXANDER LANG ■ FAAR Musical Composition 30. b. Sept. 21, 1900, Boston, MA. d. July 7, 1982. BA 22, Harvard Univ. **Other Studies:** with Loeffler in Boston, with Koechlin and d'Indy in Paris; Conservatoire Nat., Paris, 2 years. **Career & Employment:** Russian Opera Co., NYC, Conductor 1934-35; US Army Air Forces, Motion Picture Unit, Music Head 1942. **Memberships & Offices:** ASCAP. **Important Works:** *Nuit méridionale,* for orchestra 1926; *Leggenda Sinfonica,* for orchestra 1930; *Concerto Sinfonico,* for piano & orchestra 1935; *Rhapsody,* for clarinet & orchestra (G. Schirmer) 1945; *The Nightingale and the Rose,* for speaker & orchestra 1950; plus various scores for motion pictures, radio programs, & television shows. **Bio-Bibliography:** *Baker's Biographical Dictionary of American Musicians.*

STELLA, FRANK ■ RAAR Painting 83; AAR Trustee 1987-89, Trustee Emer. b. May 12, 1936, Malden, MA. m. Harriet McGurk. **Study:** Princeton Univ. 1954-58. **Career & Employment:** Dartmouth College, Artist-in-Residence 1963; Brandeis Univ., Visiting Artist 1969; Harvard Univ., Charles Eliot Norton Prof. 1983-84. **Fellowships, Honors & Awards:** Andover-Phillips Acad., Claude M. Fuess Award, Distinguished Service Award 1979; Bezalel Acad., Jerusalem, Hon.

Fellowship 1981; Skowhegan Medal for Painting 1981; NYC Mayor's Award of Honor for Arts & Culture 1982; Harvard Univ., Charles Eliot Norton Prof. 1983-84; Princeton Univ., Hon. DFA 1984; Council for the United States & Italy, Bd.; NYU Soc. of Fellows, Resident Fellow; Dartmouth College, Hon. Degree 1985; PAFA, Award of American Art 1985. **Publications:** "An Artist Writes to Correct and Explain," *New York Herald Tribune* (Dec. 22, 1959), sec. 4, p. 7; appendix, in Robert Rosenblum, *Frank Stella* (New York: Penguin Books, 1971); "On Caravaggio," *New York Times Magazine* (Feb. 3, 1985): 38-39, 56-57, 59, 60-71; *Working Space*, Charles Eliot Norton Lectures 1983-84 (Cambridge, MA & London: Harvard Univ. Press, 1986). **Important Works:** Addison Gallery of American Art, Phillips Acad.; Albright-Knox Art Gallery, Buffalo, NY; AIC; Baltimore Museum; Rose Art Museum, Brandeis Univ.; Brooklyn Museum; List Art Center, Brown Univ.; Cleveland Art Museum; Contemporary Art Museum, Houston; Corcoran Gallery of Art, Washington, DC; Dallas Museum of Fine Art; Denver Museum of Art; Des Moines Art Center; Detroit Inst. of Arts; Fogg Art Museum, Cambridge, MA; Fort Worth Art Center; Guggenheim Museum, NYC; High Museum, Atlanta; Hirshhorn Museum & Sculpture Garden, Washington, DC; Indiana Univ. Art Museum, Bloomington; Jacksonville Art Museum, FL; Kitakyushu Municipal Museum, Japan; Kunstmuseum, Basel; Los Angeles County Art Museum; Luisiana Museum, Humlebaek, Denmark; MMA; Milwaukee Art Center; Minneapolis Inst. of Arts; Museum Boymans-von Beuningen, Rotterdam; Museum of Contemporary Art, Los Angeles; Moderna Museet, Stockholm; Nagoaka Museum of Art, Japan; Nat. Collection of Fine Art, Smithsonian Inst., Washington, DC; NGA; Nelson-Atkins Museum of Art, Kansas City, MO; Newport Harbor Museum, CA; Mary & Leigh Block Gallery, Northwestern Univ.; Philadelphia Museum; Phillips Collection, Washington, DC; Pompidou Centre, Paris; One Seaport Plaza, NYC; Portland Center of Visual Arts, OR; Princeton Univ. Art Museum; San Francisco Museum; Seibu Art Museum, Tokyo; Stedelijk Museum, Amsterdam; Tate Gallery, London; Toledo Museum of Art; Univ. of Michigan Art Museum, East Lansing; Vancouver Art Museum; Wadsworth Atheneum, Hartford, CT; Wallraf-Richartz Museum, Cologne; Whitney Museum, NYC. **Exhibitions/Performances:** Selected Solo: Pasadena Art Museum 1966; Washington Gallery of Modern Art 1968; Rose Art Museum, Brandeis Univ. 1969, 1979; MOMA 1970, 1979; Phillips Collection, Washington, DC 1973; Portland Center for the Visual Arts 1974; Kunsthalle Basel 1976; Baltimore Museum of Art 1976; Kunsthalle Bielefeld, Germany 1977; Museum of Modern Art, Oxford, England 1977; Fort Worth Museum 1978; Kunstmuseum Basel 1980; Addison Gallery of American Art, Phillips Acad. 1982; Kitakushu Municipal Museum of Art, Japan 1982; Museum of Modern Art, San Francisco 1983; Jewish Museum, NYC 1983; Fogg Art Museum, Harvard Univ. 1983; Albright-Knox Gallery, Buffalo 1983; ICA Gallery, Inst. of Contemporary Arts, The Mall, London 1985. **Bio-Bibliography:** William S. Rubin, *Frank Stella* (New York: MOMA, 1970); Robert Rosenblum, *Frank Stella*, Penguin New Art 1 (Baltimore-Harmondsworth, England: Penguin Books, 1971); Brenda Richardson, *Frank Stella: The Black Paintings* (Baltimore: Baltimore Museum of Art, 1976); *Frank Stella: Werke 1958-76* (Bielefeld: Richard Kaselowsky Haus Kunsthalle der Stadt Bielefeld, 1977); Philip Leider, *Stella Since 1970* (Fort Worth: Fort Worth Art Museum, 1978); *Frank Stella: Recent Works* (Nagoya, Japan: Galerie Valeur, 1980); Christian Geelhaar, *Frank Stella: Working Drawings Zeichnugun 1956-70* (Basel: Kunstmuseum, 1980); *Frank Stella: Working Drawings 1956-82 from the Artist Collection* (Kitakyushu:

Municipal Museum of Art, 1982); Richard Axsom, *The Prints of Frank Stella: A Catalogue Raisonné* (New York: Hudson Hills Press, Ann Arbor: Univ. of Michigan, 1983); *Frank Stella: Illustrations after El Lissitzky's Had Gadya 1982-84* (London: Waddington Graphics, 1985); Lawrence Rubin, *Frank Stella: Paintings 1958 to 1965: A Catalogue Raisonné* (New York: Stewart, Tabori & Chang, Publishers, 1986). **Business Address:** M. Knoedler & Co., 19 E. 70 St., NYC 10021.

STERNFELD, HARRY ■ NIAE, John Dinkeloo Traveling Fellow 1916, 1919-20.

STERNFELD, JOEL ■ FAAR Visual Arts 91. b. June 30, 1944, NYC. BA 65, Dartmouth College. **Career & Employment:** Stockton State College 1971-84; Yale Univ. 1984-85; Sarah Lawrence College 1985-present. **Fellowships, Honors & Awards:** Guggenheim Fellowship 1978, 1982; NEA Fellowship 1980; Higaskikawa, Japan, Festival of Photography, Grand Prize 1985; Dartmouth College Artist-in-Residence 1987-88; Lyndhurst Prize 1994-96. **Publications:** *American Prospects; Campagna Romana: The Countryside of Ancient Rome.* **Important Works:** MOMA; Museum of Modern Art, San Francisco; Houston Museum of Modern Art; Seattle Art Museum; Dallas Art Museum; High Museum of Art, Atlanta; Hallmark Collections, Kansas City, MO; AIC; Fotomuseum, Winterthur, Switzerland. **Exhibitions/Performances:** Solo: PAFA 1976; Daniel Wolf, NYC 1981, 1984; Friends of Photography, Carmel, CA 1984; Visual Studies Workshop 1984; Higaskikawa Intl. Festival, Japan 1985; Dartmouth College 1985; Museum of Fine Arts, Houston; Detroit Inst. of Art; Baltimore Museum of Art; Museum of Contemporary Art, La Jolla, CA; Nat. Gallery of Canada, Ottawa; Pace-Macgill Gallery, NYC 1989, 1991, 1994; AIC 1992; MFA 1992. **Home Address:** 70A Greenwich Ave., NYC 10011. **Business Address:** Pace-Macgill Gallery, 32 E. 57 St., NYC 10022.

STEVENS, GORHAM PHILLIPS ■ AAR Dir. 1912-13, 1917-32, Acting Dir. occasionally 1913-17. **Career & Employment:** McKim, Mead & White. **Fellowships, Honors & Awards:** ASCSA, Fellow 1903-5.

STEVENS, LAWRENCE TENNEY ■ FAAR Sculpture 25. b. July 16, 1896, Brighton, MA. d. Dec. 18, 1972. m. Bea Stevens. c. Marc Stevens, Sara Stevens, Sylvia Stevens, Chad Stevens. **Study:** MFA School; with Charles Grafly & Bela Pratt. **Career & Employment:** Philbrook Art Center, Tulsa Faculty. **Memberships & Offices:** NSS; Soc. of Medalists; ALNY. **Important Works:** Congregational Church, Brighton, MA; Fairmont Park, Philadelphia; St. Matthew's Church, Bedford, NY; Brook Green Gardens, SC; Univ. of Pennsylvania; Brooklyn Museum; Will Rogers Memorial, Clarence, OK; Texas Centennial; Colgate Univ.; Roscoe Turner Airport, Minneapolis; Music Hall, Rockefeller Center, NYC; Collections: Palm Springs Ramon Rd. Branch, Palm Springs, CA; Valley Nat. Bank of Arizona; NSS; ALNY. **Exhibitions/Performances:** PAFA 1929; Grand Central Art Galleries, NYC 1929; MFA; Philbrook Art Center; NAD. **Bio-Bibliography:** *Dictionary of Painters, Sculptors & Engravers, Who's Who in American Art.*

STEVENSON, ADLAI E. ■ AAR Visitor 1959 — 1964; Statesman, Ambassador.

STEWART, DAN ROBERT ■ FAAR Architecture 57. b. Jan. 8, 1926, Detroit, MI. dec. m. Donna Stewart. Cert. in Arch. 49, Cooper Union; BArch 52, Univ. of Cincinnati; MArch 55, MIT.

Research/Artistic Interests: Architect & painter. **Career & Employment:** Raymond & Rado 1953-54; Caudill, Rowlett, Scott, Assc. Part. 1961-69; Mayer, Ayres Saint Stewart Inc., Baltimore after 1969. **Memberships & Offices:** AIA, Baltimore Chap. 1966. **Bio-Bibliography:** *American Architects Directory (1970).*

STICKROTH, HARRY I. ■ FAAR Painting 17. b. 1890. d. Oct. 1922. **Other Studies:** Lazarus School for Mural Painting 1914-17. **Research/Artistic Interests:** Mural Decoration. **Career & Employment:** AIC, Faculty. **Important Works:** with B. Faulkner, Cunard Bldg., NYC. **Bio-Bibliography:** *National Cyclopedia of American Biography; Who Was Who in American Art.*

STIFTER, CHARLES THOMAS ■ FAAR Architecture 63. b. Aug. 29, 1935, Detroit, MI. BArch 59, Illinois Inst. of Technology; MArch 60, MIT. **Other Studies:** Univ. of Chicago 1951-54. **Career & Employment:** Skidmore, Owings, & Merrill 1956-59; Eero Saarinen & Asscs., 1960-; Washington Univ., Faculty 1964-. **Fellowships, Honors & Awards:** MIT, Emerson Grant 1959, Rotch Prize 1960.

STILLMAN, JAMES ■ AAR Charter Mem., Bank Exec.

STIRLING, CLAIRE ■ AAR Visitor 1981-82, Art Critic.

STIRLING, JAMES FRAZER ■ RAAR Architecture 83. b. Apr. 22, 1926, Glasgow, Scotland. d. June 25, 1992. m. Mary Shand. c. Benjamin, Kate, Sophie. Dipl. Arch. 50, Liverpool Univ. **Other Studies:** School of Town Planning & Regional Research, London 1950-52. **Career & Employment:** Lyons, Israel & Ellis 1953-56; Architectural Assn., London, Visiting Instr. 1955; Private Practice, with James Gowan 1956-63; Regent St. Polytech., Visiting Instr. 1956-57; Cambridge Univ. School of Architecture, Visiting Instr. 1958; Private Practice, London 1964-1970; Michael Wilford, James Stirling & Part. 1971-92; Royal Inst. of British Architects, Visiting Instr. 1965; Yale Univ., Visiting Davenport Prof. 1967. **Memberships & Offices:** Assn. of the Royal Inst. of British Architects 1950. **Fellowships, Honors & Awards:** Akademie der Künste, Berlin, Hon. Mem. 1969; NIAL, Brunner Award 1976; AIA, Hon. Fellow 1976; Alvar Aalto Medal, Finland 1978; Royal College of Art, London Hon. DFA 1979; Royal Soc. of Arts, London, Fellow 1979; Accademia delle Arti, Florence, Hon. Mem. 1979; Accademia Nazionale di San Luca, Rome, Hon. Mem. 1979; Royal Inst. of British Architects, Gold Medal 1980; Pritzker Architecture Prize 1981; Bund Deutscher Architekten, Germany, Hon. Mem. 1983. **Publications:** with Robert Maxwell, *James Stirling* (New York: Thames & Hudson, 1983); *James Stirling and Michael Wilford* (New York: St. Martin's Press, 1993). **Important Works:** Engineering Bldg., Leicester Univ. 1959-63; History Faculty Bldg., Cambridge, England 1964-67; Olivetti Training School, Haslemere, England 1969; Southgate Housing Project 1972-77; Museum of Science & Technology, Teheran 1977; Dresdner Bank, Marburg, Germany 1977; Neue Staatsgalerie, Stuttgart 1977-84; Fogg Museum, New Building, Cambridge, MA 1979-84; Tate Gallery Extension, London 1980-85; Designed bldgs. for Rome, Berlin, Stuttgart, Tokyo, as well as for Harvard Univ., Rice Univ., Cornell Univ. and UC, Irvine. **Exhibitions/Performances:** MOMA 1969; Heinz Gallery, Royal Inst. of British Architects, London 1974; Biennale, Venice 1976; Leo Castelli Gallery, NYC 1977; Walker Art Center, Minneapolis 1977; *Roma Interotta* 1978; Dortmund Univ., Germany 1979; Manhattan Townhouses, NY 1980; Three German Projects, Royal Inst. of British Architects, London 1980; Inst. of Contemporary Arts, London 1983; Fogg Museum, Cam-

bridge, MA 1989. **Bio-Bibliography:** *James Stirling: Buildings and Projects 1950-74* (New York: Oxford Univ. Press, 1975); *James Stirling: Buildings and Projects 1950-1980,* ed. Peter Arnell & Ted Bickford (New York: Rizzoli, 1984); Paul Goldberger, "James Stirling Made an Art Form of Bold Gestures," *NY Times* (July 19, 1992); *Who Was Who in America.*

STOKES, ANSON PHELPS, JR ■ AAR Trustee 1911-19, Philanthropist.

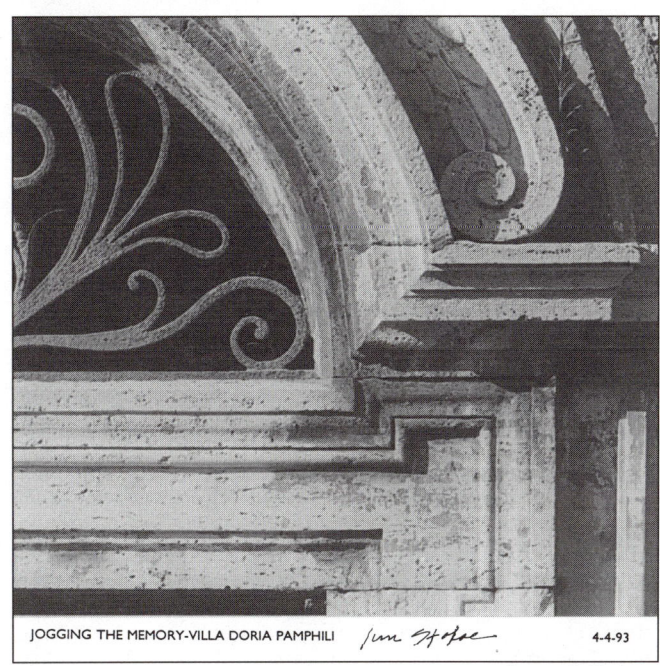

JOGGING THE MEMORY-VILLA DORIA PAMPHILI

James S. Stokoe

STOKOE, JAMES S. ■ FAAR Architecture 79. b. Apr. 24, 1951, Auburn, NY. m. Caroline S. Lee. c. Nathaniel, Madeline. BA 73, Washington Univ.; MArch 76, Washington Univ. **Career & Employment:** Charles W. Moore Asscs., Centerbrook, Designer 1973-74; Richard Claybour & Asscs., Project Architect 1977-78; Pearce Corp., Design Architect 1978; Hartman-Cox Architects, Project Architect 1979-84; Stokoe-Callison Architects, Pres. 1984-present. **Memberships & Offices:** AIA 1978-present. **Fellowships, Honors & Awards:** Washington Univ., Widmann Prize 1973; Found. for Architecture, Philadelphia, Hon. Men. 1986; AIA, Washington Chap. Award of Excellence 1990. **Publications:** "Caryatides and Atlantes Rediscovered," *International Architect* 2.1 (1979): 9; *Decorative and Ornamental Brickwork* (New York: Dover, 1982); "Fictional History in Rome," *Architecture* 73.11 (Nov. 1984): 76-79. **Important Works:** Mount Vernon Inn Retail Space, VA 1989; Lowell School Remodeling, Washington, DC 1989; Smithsonian Nat. Museum of American Art Bookstore, Washington, DC 1991; John F. Kennedy Center for Performing Arts Retail Shops, Washington, DC 1992; American Film Inst. Lobby Renovation 1992; Smithsonian Nat. Museum of Natural History, Museum Store, Washington, DC 1993; Valentine Riverside Museum Lobby Renovation & Museum Store, Richmond, VA 1994. **Exhibitions/Performances:** Decorative Brickwork, Glen-Gery Corp. 1987. **Home Address:** 3519 Cummings Ln., Chevy Chase, MD 20815.

STOLLER, EZRA ■ AAR Visitor 1991-92, Photographer.

STONE, EDWARD DURELL ■ RAAR Architecture 60. b. Mar. 1902, Fayetteville, AR. d. Aug. 6, 1978. m. Orlean Vandiver, Maria Torchio, Violet Campbell Maffat. c. Edward Jr., Robert, Benjamin, Maria, Fiona. **Study:** Univ. of Arkansas 1920-23; Harvard Univ. 1925-26; MIT 1925-26. **Career & Employment:** Rockefeller Center, NYC, with consortium of architects 1929-35; Edward Durell Stone & Asscs., Pres. 1935-78; NYU, Instr. 1935-40; Yale Univ., Assc. Prof. 1946-52; Princeton Univ., Visiting Critic 1953; Univ. of Arkansas, Visiting Critic 1955, 1957-59. **Memberships & Offices:** American Federation of the Arts, BoT; American Nat. Theater & Acad., BoD; Whitney Museum, NYC, BoD; NAD; NIAL. **Fellowships, Honors & Awards:** ALNY Medal 1937, 1950, 1953; Pittsburgh Glass Competition, Grand Prize 1938; *House & Garden,* 1st Prize 1939; Univ. of Arkansas, Hon. DFA 1951; AIA, Gold Medal 1955, Honor Award 1958, 1967; Colby College, Hon. DFA 1959; AAAS, Fellow 1960; Royal Soc. of Arts, London, Fellow 1960; Otis Art Inst., Hon. MFA 1961; Hamilton College, Hon. DFA 1962; Copper & Brass Reserve Assn., Architectural Achievement Award 1963; Univ. of South Carolina, Hon. LHD 1964; Metropolitan Washington Bd. of Trade, Architectural Excellence Award 1965; Inst. of North American Studies, Barcelona, John F. Kennedy Award 1966; *Business Magazine,* Building Award 1966; ASLA, 1st Prize 1973. **Publications:** *The Evolution of an Architect* (New York: Horizon Press, 1962); "Kitchens: Efficency is not Enough," *Architectural Record* (May 1962); *Recent and Future Architecture* (New York: Horizon Press, 1967). **Important Works:** Mandel House, Mt. Kisco, NY 1933; 4 Buckingham St., Cambridge, MA 1937; Goodyear House, Old Westbury, Long Island 1939; with Philip Goodwin, MOMA 1939; El Panama Hotel, Panama City 1946; American Federation of the Arts Bldg. Conversion, NYC 1959; SUNY, Albany 1963; Nat. Geographic Soc., Washington, DC 1964; Bush Memorial Stadium, St. Louis 1966; with Emerby Roth & Sons, General Motors Bldg., NYC 1968; John F. Kennedy Center for the Performing Arts, Washington, DC 1971; PepsiCo World HQ, Purchase, NY 1973; Standard Oil Bldg. & Plaza, with Perkins & Will, Chicago 1974. **Bio-Bibliography:** *Contemporary Architects, Who Was Who in America.*

STONE, GILBERT LEONARD ■ FAAR Painting 67. b. Sept. 9, 1940, Brooklyn, NY. d. Jan. 16, 1984. m. Carol Stone. **Study:** Parsons School of Design 1958-60, 1961-62. **Career & Employment:** School of Visual Arts, Faculty 1958. **Fellowships, Honors & Awards:** *Sports Illustrated* Comm.; 3 AIGA Awards; 3 Gold Medals; Soc. of Illustrators Awards of Excellence (2). **Important Works:** featured in: *McCalls, Graphis, Redbook, The London Times;* Collections: Brooklyn Museum, Smithsonian Inst., Joseph Hirshhorn Collection, Time Corp.

STONE, MICHELLE ■ FAAR Design Arts 78. b. Jan. 28, 1949, New Britain, CT. m. Yoshifumi Fujii. BA 69, NYU. **Career & Employment:** SITE (Sculpture in the Environment) 1970-present. **Fellowships, Honors & Awards:** Art Director's Club, Book Design 1977. **Publications:** *On Energy* (New York: Scribner's, 1974); *Unbuilt America* (New York: McGraw Hill, 1976); *De-Architetturizzazione: Progetti e Teorie 1969-78* (Bari: Dedalo Libri, 1978); *Architecture As Art* (London: Academy Editions, 1980); *SITE* (Tokyo: A + U, 1986); *SITE* (New York: Rizzoli, 1989). **Important Works:** Indeterminate Facade, Best Products Co., Houston 1974; Ghost Parking Lot, Nat. Shopping Centers, Hamden, CT 1977; WilliWear Women's Showroom, WilliWear, Ltd., NYC 1982; McDonald's Restaurant, McDonald's Corp., Chicago 1984; Museum of the Borough of Brooklyn 1985; Mallet Residence, NYC 1985; Highway 86,

Expo 86 Assn., Vancouver, Canada 1986; Swatch Retail Store, Swatch Watch U.S.A., NYC 1987; Four Continents Bridge, Country Communications, Hiroshima 1989; Saudi Arabian Pavilion, Kingdom of Saudi Arabia, Seville, Spain 1992; Avenue V, Expo 92 Assn., Seville, Spain 1992; Ross's Landing Park & Plaza, River City Co., Chattanooga, TN 1992. **Exhibitions/Performances:** Whitney Museum Biennial, NYC 1974; Centre Pompidou, Paris 1975; Venice Biennale 1975; MOMA 1975; Virginia Museum of Fine Arts, Richmond 1980; Los Angeles Inst. of Contemporary Art 1980; Whitney Museum, NYC 1981; Chrysler Museum, Norfolk, VA 1984; Victoria & Albert Museum, London 1984; Architectural Assn., London 1985; Treinnale di Milano 1986; Documenta 8, Kassel, Germany 1987. **Home Address:** 356 W. 23 St., NYC 10011.

STONE, SYLVIA ■ RAAR Sculpture 81. b. 1928. **Bio-Bibliography:** *Dictionary of Contemporary American Artists; Who's Who in American Art.*

STONEHILL, JOHN T. ■ FAAR Architecture 60. b. Aug. 1, 1933, NYC. m. Judith Stonehill. c. Alexandra, David S. BA 55, Dartmouth College; MArch 59, Yale Univ., School of Architecture. **Career & Employment:** Paul Rudolph, Architect, Draftsman 1960-61; Associated Architects & Engineers, Chief Designer 1961-63; Katz, Waisman, Weber, Strauss & Blumenkranz, Architects, Chief Designer 1963-64; Lundquist & Stonehill, Architects, Part. 1964-85; Stonehill & Taylor Architects, Part. 1985-present. **Memberships & Offices:** NIAE, BoT 1964-94, Chair, Vice-Chair. **Important Works:** Bellevue Hospital Parking Garage, Chief Designer, NYC 1963; Bellevue Hospital, Chief Designer, NYC 1964; WorldWide Motors Distribution HQ, Chief Designer, Orangeburg, NY 1965; NYC Parks Dept., Combined Recreation Center & Amphitheater, NYC 1965; Hoffman LaRoche, HQ, Nutley, NJ 1966; Hoffman LaRoche, Distribution Center, Bellevidere, NJ 1966; FDC Narcotic Rehabilitation Center, Fishkill, NY 1967; CUNY, Kingsborough Community College Arts & Science Center, NY 1970; NYC Bd. of Education IS 383, Brooklyn, NY 1971; FDC Glen Oaks School for the Severely & Profoundly Retarded, Queens, NY 1971; Sotheby's Auction House Facility, NYC 1980; NYC Bd. of Education IS 75, Staten Island, NYC 1981; Bard College Stone Row Dormitory Alterations, Annendale-on-Hudson, NY 1983; Residences: Mr. & Mrs. Richard Rodgers, Fairfield, CT 1965; Mr. & Mrs. Robert Nagler, Quogue, NY 1969; Mr. & Mrs. Ame Vennema, NY 1975; Mr. & Mrs. Ame Vennema, Houston, TX 1980; Mrs. Barbara Pintauro, Sag Harbor, NY 1985; Mr. & Mrs. Lionel Pincus, NY 1985; Mr. & Mrs. Donald Blinken, NYC 1989; Mr. & Mrs. Benjamin Sher, Franklin Lakes, NJ 1990. **Home Address:** 131 Charles St., NYC 10014. **Business Address:** Stonehill & Taylor, 270 Lafayette St., NYC 10012.

STORY, WALDO ■ AAR Charter Mem., Artist.

STOTT, DEBORAH ■ FAAR History of Art 81. b. June 11, 1942, Minneapolis, MN. BA 64, Wellesley College; MA 66, Columbia Univ.; PhD 75, Columbia Univ. **Research/Artistic Interests:** Italian Renaissance art, especially sculpture; history of women artists, especially Renaissance & baroque; history of imagery of women. **Career & Employment:** Wheaton College, Instr. 1970-75; ICCS, Asst. Prof. 1975-76; Univ. of Texas, Dallas, Assc. Prof. 1976-present, Assc. Dean for Undergratuate Studies 1993-present. **Memberships & Offices:** Dallas Museum of Art, Educational Planning Com. 1981-82. **Fellowships, Honors & Awards:** ACLS Grant-in-Aid 1980; Delmas Found. Grant 1980, 1982; Bunting Fellowship 1982-83. **Publications:** *Jacques Lipchitz and Cubism* (New York: Garland, 1978); "Fatte à

Sembianza di pittura: Jacopo Sanzovino's Bronze Reliefs in San Marco," *Art Bulletin* 64 (1982): 370-88. **Home Address:** 711 Gaylewood, Richardson, TX 75080. **Business Address:** Univ. of Texas at Dallas, Box 830688, Richardson, TX 75083.

The following translation of Leopardi was done while I was at the American Academy in the fall of 1983.

Mark Strand.

FEAR OF THE NIGHT

Alcetus: I'm telling you, Melissus,
            Looking at the moon just now
            Reminds me of a dream I had last night.
            I stood at the window, looking at the sky,
            And suddenly the moon began to fall.
            I came straight at me, getting nearer
            And nearer until it crashed
            Like a bowl beside the house.
            Then it burst into flame, then fizzled
            Like a hot coal dropped in water.
            It turned black, and the grass was singed.
            And that was the way the moon went out.
            But there was more to it than that.
            When I looked up, I saw an opening in the dark.
            It was the hole from which the moon
            Had rolled down out of the sky.
            I'm telling you, Melissus,
            I was scared and still am.

Melissus: And why shouldn't you be?
            After all, the moon could fall at any time.

Alcetus: That's right, look at the stars,
            They fall all summer long.

Melissus: But there are lots of stars,
            And if a few of them fall, so what?
            There are thousands left.
            But there is only one moon in the sky
            And no one has seen it fall but in dreams.

Mark Strand

STRAND, MARK ■ RAAR Literature 83. b. Apr. 11, 1934, Summerside, PEI, Canada. m. Julia Garretson. c. Jessica, Tom. BA 57, Antioch College; BFA 59, Yale Univ.; MA 62, Univ. of Iowa. **Career & Employment:** Univ. of Utah, Distinguished Prof. 1981-present. **Memberships & Offices:** Fulbright Fellowship 1960-61; Ingram Merrill Fellowship 1966; NEA Fellowship 1967-68, 1977-78, 1986-87; Rockefeller Fellowship 1968-69; Guggenheim Fellowship 1974-75; Edgar Allen Poe Prize 1974; AAAL Award 1975; Acad. of American Poets, Fellowship 1979; AAAL 1981-present; MacArthur Fellowship 1987-92; US Poet Laureate 1990-91; Utah Governors Award in the Arts 1992; Bobbit Prize 1992; Bollingen Prize 1993. **Publications:** *Reasons for Moving* (New York: Atheneum, 1968); *Darker* (New York: Atheneum, 1970); *The Owl's Insomnia* (New York: Atheneum, 1973); *The Story of Our Lives* (New York: Atheneum, 1973); *The Late Hour* (New York: Atheneum, 1978); *Selected Poems* (New York: Atheneum, 1980; rpt., New York: Knopf, 1990); *The Art of the Real* (New York: Clarkson Potter, 1985); *Mr. and Mrs. Baby* (New York: Knopf, 1985); *Traveling in the Family* (New York: Random House, 1986); *William Bailey* (New York: Abrams, 1987); *The Continuous Life* (New York: Knopf, 1990); *Dark Harbor* (New York: Knopf, 1993); *Hopper* (Ecco, 1994). **Bio-Bibliography:** David Kirby, *Mark Strand and the Poet's Place in Contemporary Culture* (Columbia: Univ. of Missouri Press, 1990); and many articles. **Business Address:** c/o Henry Ford, Alfred Knopf Publishers, Inc., 201 E. 50 St., NYC 10022.

STREET, (CURRY) TISON ■ FAAR Musical Composition 74. b. May 20, 1943, Cambridge, MA. BA 65, Harvard Univ.; MA 72, Harvard Univ. **Career & Employment:** UC, Berkeley, Lect. 1971-72; Freelance Violinist, Boston 1972-73, 1974-80; Harvard Univ., Music Comp., Instr. 1973-74, Praeceptor in Chamber Music 1976-77, Assc. Prof. c. 1980. **Fellowships, Honors & Awards:** Harvard Univ. Soc. of Fellows; Naumburg

Recording Award; Brandeis Award; Fromm Comm.; Koussevitzky Comm.; NIAL Award 1973. **Important Works:** *String Quartet* (G. Schirmer) 1972; *Three Sacred Anthems* (G. Schirmer); *Variations for Flute Guitar & Cello* (G. Schirmer); *Adagio for Oboe & Strings* (Associated Music).

STRIKER, CECIL L. ■ RAAR History of Art 71. b. July 15, 1932, Cincinnati, OH. m. Ute Stephan. BA 56, Oberlin College; MA 60, IFA; PhD 68, IFA. **Career & Employment:** Vassar College, Asst. Prof. 1962-68; Univ. of Pennsylvania, Assc. Prof. 1968-78, Prof. 1978-present. **Home Address:** 2046 Waverly St., Philadelphia, PA 19146. **Business Address:** Dept. of History of Art, Univ. of Pennsylvania, 3405 Woodland Walk, Philadelphia, PA 19104.

STRINI, ROBERT LOUIS ■ FAAR Sculpture 72. b. Mar. 22, 1942, Hayward, CA. BA 67, San Jose State College; MA 68, San Jose State College; MFA 70, UC, Berkeley. **Career & Employment:** UC, Berkeley, Instr.; San Jose State College 1968, 1969, 1970, 1971. **Memberships & Offices:** San Francisco Potters Assn. **Fellowships, Honors & Awards:** San Francisco Potters Asscs., Dr. Elizabeth Moses Memorial Award 1966, 1968; Annual College of San Mateo Ceramics Show Awards 1967 (3); Los Gatos Summer Arts Festival Award 1967. **Exhibitions/Performances:** Oakland Museum of Art 1970; Museum of Contemporary Crafts, NYC 1970; San Francisco Potters Asscs. Show, De Young Museum, San Francisco 1966, 1968.

STRUNK, OLIVER ■ AAR Visitor 1943 — 1951. Educator, Musicologist. b. Mar. 22, 1901. d. Feb. 24, 1980. **Career & Employment:** Princeton Univ., Faculty 1937-66. **Honors & Awards:** ACLS Award for Distinguished Scholarship in the Humanities 1961. Donated his private library of c. 950 volumes to the Academy in 1974. **Publications:** *Source Readings in Music History* (1950).

STRZELEC, PATRICK ■ FAAR Sculpture 89. b. Mar. 17, 1956, Chicago, IL. m. Amy L. Strzelec. c. Samuel, Lucas. BFA 79, Southern Illinois Univ.; MFA 87, Rutgers Univ. **Career & Employment:** School of Visual Arts 1991-present. **Fellow-**

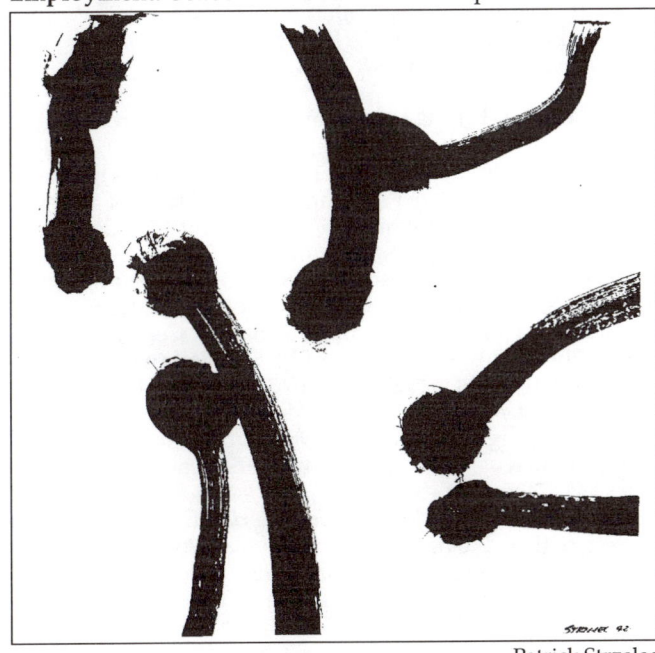

Patrick Strzelec

ships, Honors & Awards: New Jersey State Council on the Arts Fellowship 1985, 1989; NEA Grant 1988; Guggenheim Fellowship 1990-91. **Important Works:** Rutgers Univ.; Toledo Museum; Aldrich Museum, Ridgefield, CT; Newark Museum; Trenton Museum; US Holocaust Museum, Washington, DC. **Exhibitions/Performances:** Munson Williams Proctor Museum, Utica, NY 1985; Susanne Hillberry Gallery, Birmingham, MI 1986; Perkins Art Center, Moorestown, NJ 1986; Birmingham Museum, AL 1988; Princeton Gallery of Fine Art, NJ 1988; Zimmerli Museum, New Brunswick, NJ 1989; Morris Museum, Morristown, NJ 1989; Noyes Museum, Oceanville, NJ 1990; Barbara Toll Fine Arts, NYC 1990, 1991, 1992; Lawrence Olivier Gallery, Philadelphia 1991; James Michener Art Museum, Doylestown, PA 1991; Strauss Collection, Franklin Marshall, PA 1992. **Home Address:** 3698 Aquetong Rd., Carversville, PA 18913.

STUBBS, JOHN H. ■ AAR Visitor 1976-77; World Monuments Fund., Program Dir.

STUBBS, JOSEPHINE R. ■ AAR Trustee 1978-84, Trustee Emer.; Art Patron.

STUCCHI, SANDRO ■ Italian Fulbright Fellow 1961-62.

STYRON, WILLIAM C. ■ FAAR Literature 53. b. June 11, 1925, Newport News, VA. m. Rose Burgunder. c. Tommy, Alexandra, Susanna, Polly. AS 47, Duke Univ. **Career & Employment:** US Marine Corps, 1st Lieut. WWII. **Research/Artistic Interests:** NIAL; Signet Soc. of Harvard. **Fellowships, Honors & Awards:** Pulitzer Prize 1968; AAAL, Howells Medal 1970; Nat. Book Critics' Circle Award, Nominee 1980; American Book Award 1980. **Publications:** *Lie Down in Darkness* (Bobbs-Merrill, 1951); *The Long March* (New York: Vintage Press, 1957); *Set This House on Fire* (New York: Random House, 1960); *The Confessions of Nat Turner* (New York: Random House, 1967); *In the Clap Shack* (New York: Random House, 1973); *Sophie's Choice* (New York: Random House, 1979); ed., *Paris Review's Best Short Stories*. **Bio-Bibliography:** Miriam Schlicht, "Styron Wins Pulitzer Award," *New Milford Times* (May 9, 1968); Richard Robbins, "Pulitzer Prize Winner Shaped by a Uniontown He Barely Knew," *Greensburg Sunday Tribune Review* (June 19, 1994).

SULLIVAN, CHIP ■ FAAR Landscape Architecture 85. BA 74, Univ. of Florida, Gainesville; MA 77, Univ. of Florida, Gainesville. **Other Study:** ASL 1982. **Career & Employment:** Richard Tarbox Land Planning 1972-74; Univ. of Florida, Gainesville, Div. of Planning & Analysis 1973-76, Center for Wetlands 1977; Sasaki Asscs., Landscape Architect & Planner 1977-86; UC, Berkeley, Assc. Prof. 1987-present; Visiting Critic: UC, Davis; SUNY, Buffalo; California College of Arts & Crafts; Toronto Univ.; Radcliffe College; Palladian Center, Vicenza, Italy; Florida Intl. Univ; Univ. of Miami. **Fellowships, Honors & Awards:** ASLA Nat. Student Merit Award 1974, Florida Chap., Merit Award 1979, Nat. Merit Award 1986; Univ. of Florida, Distinguished Alumni 1984. **Publications:** "The Garden of Linnaeus," *Oblong* 3; "Garden Energies: Classic Gardens Take New Shapes," *Landscape Architecture Magazine* (Mar. 1979); "Balcony Gardens," *South Florida Home and Garden Magazine* (Fall 1984); "Sketchbook of Garden Design," *Environmental Design Center Magazine* (Fall 1984); "The Garden of the Rose: A Celestial Garden," *Places* 3.3 (1986); "The Garden of the Rose: A Celestial Garden," *Transforming the American Garden; 12 New Landscape Designs* (Cambridge, MA: Harvard

GSD, 1986); *The Historical Garden as a Passive Architectural Element* (Miami: Miami-Dade Community College, 1986); *New Forms of the Garden to Heat and Cool Your Home* (Miami: Miami-Dade Community College, 1986); "Garden as Reliquary," *Conference Proceedings, Meaning of the Garden, University of California at Davis, 1987*; "The Historical Garden as a Passive Solar Device," *Conference Proceedings, National Passive Solar Conference, 1989*; "The Garden as an Art Form," in *The Avant Garde and the Landscape; Can They Be Reconciled?*, ed. Patrick Condon & Lance Neckar (Landworks Press, 1990); "Garden as Reliquary," *Meanings of Garden,* ed. Mark Francis & Randy Hestor (Cambridge, MA: MIT Press, 1990); "California Garden Series," *Landscape Architecture Magazine* (Dec. 1990); "Landscape as Tattoo," Abstract, *CELA Proceedings* 1991; *Double Imperative Landscapes,* with text by Stephen Rodefer (Berkeley, CA: Poltroon Press, 1992). **Exhibitions/Performances:** Harvard GSD 1986; Hodgell-Gillman Gallery, Tampa 1987; Barbara Gillman Gallery, Miami 1987; Architecture Gallery, College of Environmental Design, UC, Berkeley 1988, 1992; Site 375, San Francisco 1989; Gallery 181, College of Design, Iowa State Univ. 1990; with Frances Butler, Capp Street Project, San Francisco 1990; Rmoc HQ, Ontario Assn. of Landscape Architects 1991; School of Architecture, McGill Univ., Montreal 1991; Gallery of Architecture & Landscape Architecture, Univ. of Toronto 1991; Architecture Hall, Univ. of Washington 1991; Grinnell Community Art Gallery, IA 1992; LaVerne Krause Gallery, Univ. of Oregon, Eugene 1992; BC Soc. of Landscape Architects & Univ. of British Columbia Landscape Architecture Program 1992; Tenth Floor Gallery, Univ. of Calgary 1992. **Home Address:** 1234 Stannage Ave., Berkeley, CA 94706. **Business Address:** Dept. of Landscape Architecture, College of Environmental Design, 202 Wurster Hall, UC, Berkeley, CA 94720.

SULLIVAN, JOHN B. ■ FAAR Landscape Architecture 83. b. Apr. 12, 1952, Berea, OH. m. Susan G. McWilliams. c. Margaret A. Sullivan. BFA 75, Ohio State Univ.; MLA 80, Univ. of Virginia. **Research/Artistic Interests:** Urban development, historic landscapes, city gardens (public & private), the architecture of the street. **Career & Employment:** SWA Group, Boston 1984-88; Jack Sullivan, ASLA 1988-90; Radcliffe Seminars, Cambridge 1988-91; RISD 1989-91; Wallace, Floyd Architects, Boston 1990-91; California Polytechnic State Univ. 1991-94: Univ. of Maryland 1994-present. **Fellowships, Honors & Awards:** ASLA, Honor Award 1985; James V. Crockett Award 1990. **Important Works:** with Oldham & Seltz, Curtis Center Fountain Court, Philadelphia 1985; with Robert A.M. Stern, Gustav Stickley-Craftsman Farms Residences, Parsippany, NJ 1986; with Robert A.M. Stern, Shops at Primrose Brook, Bernardsville, NJ 1987; with Hugh Newell Jacobsen, Waterwood Estate, Pvt. Residence, Vermilion, OH 1988; with SWA Group, Convention Center Plaza, Indianapolis 1988; with Anthony Belluschi, Galleria at Erieview, Cleveland 1989; Central Artery-Tunnel Project, Boston Master Plan at Downtown Waterfront 1991; William G. Dana Historic Adobe & Ranch, Master Plan, Nipomo, CA 1992-93. **Exhibitions/Performances:** New England Spring Flower Show, Roof Garden Exb. 1990; Memphis Botanical Garden Drawing Exb. 1992. **Home Address:** 215 Hodges Ln., Takoma Pk., MD 20912. **Business Address:** Landscape Architecture Program, Univ. of Maryland, College Park, MD 20742.

SUSINI, GIANCARLO ■ Italian Fulbright Fellow 1954-55.

SUSSMAN, WENDY ■ FAAR Painting 87. b. June 3, 1949, NYC. m. Juan Rodriguez. c. Gabriel Rodriguez. BA 77, Empire State College; MFA 79, Brooklyn College. **Other Studies:** New York Studio School 1974. **Career & Employment:** Staten Island College, Slide Librarian 1982-83; NYU, Guest Lect. 1983. **Important Works:** Cover Photograph, Artist Choice Museum Magazine 1982. **Exhibitions/Performances:** Bowery Gallery Annual, NYC 1979-1985; Sherry French Gallery 1982; Loch Haven Art Center, Orlando, FL 1982; New York Studio School 1984.

SUTTMAN, PAUL ■ FAAR Sculpture 68. b. July 16, 1933, Enid, OK. d. Apr. 21, 1993. m. Virginia L. Bush, FAAR 77. c. Mark Berlin, Jeffrey Berlin. BFA 56, Univ. of New Mexico; MFA 58, Cranbrook Acad. **Other Study:** with Giacomo Manzù; Kokoschka School of Vision, Salzburg. **Research/Artistic Interests:** Sculpture in bronze, marble, & other materials. **Career & Employment:** Univ. of Michigan, Instr. & Museum of Art, Asst. Dir. 1958-60, Asst. Prof. 1961-62; Dartmouth College, Artist-in-Residence 1973; State Inst. of Art, Istanbul, Ankara & Izmir, Turkey, Guest Lect. 1973; Univ. of New Mexico, Visiting Assc. Prof. 1975-79; Texas A&M Univ., Artist-in-Residence & Assc. Prof. 1980-82; Columbia Univ., Adj. Assc. Prof. 1983-85. **Fellowships, Honors & Awards:** General Motors-Fisher Body Scholarship 1948-51; Cranbrook Acad., West Scholarship 1957; Rackham Found. Grant for European Study 1959; Kokoschka School of Vision, Salzburg, 1st Prize 1960; Fulbright Fellowship 1963; Univ. of Michigan 150th Anniversary Award 1966; Ingram Merrill Found. Grant 1972; NSS, Fellow 1991. **Important Works:** Hirshhorn Museum & Sculpture Garden, Washington, DC; Fine Arts Gallery of San Diego; Museum of Art, Univ. of Michigan; Museum of Art, Princeton Univ.; Museum of Art, Dartmouth College; John Herron Art Inst., Indianapolis; Museum of Art, McComb College, Detroit; Layton School of Art, Milwaukee; Roswell Museum of Art, NM; Inst. of Fine Arts, Kalamazoo; Westland Center, Detroit; Martha Cook Garden, Univ. of Michigan; Fine Arts Collection, Texas A&M Univ.; Museum of Art, Univ. of Houston; Arizona State Univ., Tempe; Albuquerque Museum, NM; L.B. Johnson Library & Museum, Austin, TX; Montclair Museum, NJ; Middlebury College Gal-

lery, VT; Mt. Holyoke College Museum. **Exhibitions/Performances:** Solo: Donald Morris Gallery, Detroit 1959, 1962, 1965, 1967, 1969; Museum of Art, Univ. of Michigan 1962; Roswell Museum of Art, NM 1962; Terry Dintenfass Gallery, NYC 1962, 1964, 1965, 1967, 1969, 1971, 1973; Felix Landau Gallery, Los Angeles 1970; Robinson Gallery, Houston 1971, 1973, 1982; Galleria Nuovo Carpine, Rome 1972; McNamara O'Connor Museum, Victoria, TX 1972; Museum of Art, Dartmouth College 1973; Jodi Scully Gallery, Los Angeles 1974, 1977; Museum of Art, Redlands College, CA 1975; City of Los Angeles Municipal Gallery 1977; Adam Mekler Gallery, Los Angeles 1979; Marilyn Butler Gallery, Scottsdale, AZ 1980; Fine Arts Gallery, Texas A&M Univ. 1981; Paris-NYC-Kent Gallery, Kent, CT 1989, 1993, 1994; Franz Bader Gallery, Washington, DC 1990, 1994; Philippe Staib Gallery, NYC 1991. **Bio-Bibliography:** "The Bronze Man," Nat. Educational TV Film 1960; *Archives of American Art; Who's Who in American Art; Who's Who in International Art.*

SUTTON, CHARLES REUEL ■ FAAR Landscape Architecture 32. b. Mar. 8, 1900, Ottawa, IL. d. Sept. 13, 1963. m. Theodora Stone. c. Charles R. Jr., Jonathan. BS 21, Univ. of Illinois; BLA 26, Univ. of Illinois. **Career & Employment:** Ferruccio Vitale, Landscape Architect 1926-29; Ohio State Univ., Asst. Prof. 1932-37, Assc. Prof. 1937-51, Prof. 1951-63; Private Practice, Columbus, OH & Old Saybrook, CT 1932-63. **Memberships & Offices:** Roadside Council; Highway Research Board; Columbus Gallery of Fine Arts, Bd. of Managers; American Soc. of Planning Officials; American Planning & Civic Assn. Research Bd.; Alpha Rho Chi; Tau Sigma Delta. **Fellowships, Honors & Awards:** ASLA, Fellow. **Bio-Bibliography:** *Who Was Who in America.*

SVENSON, ERIK ALBIN ■ FAAR Landscape Architecture 58. b. Apr. 2, 1933, Mount Vernon, NY. BArch 56, Cornell Univ. **Career & Employment:** Sven A. Svenson & Son, Design Part. 1948-56; MIT, Faculty 1965-. **Fellowships, Honors & Awards:** Skidmore, Owings & Merrill Scholarship 1955-56.

SWEENEY, JAMES JOHNSON ■ AAR Trustee 1962-77; MMA, Dir.

SWERDLOW, NOEL M. ■ RAAR History of Art 90. b. Sept. 12, 1941, Los Angeles, CA. m. Nada Deretak. c. Dorian. BA 64, UCLA; MA 67, Yale Univ.; PhD 68, Yale Univ. **Research/Artistic Interests:** History of exact science, antiquity through the 17th century. **Career & Employment:** Univ. of Chicago, Asst. Prof. 1968-74, Assc. Prof. 1974-82, Prof. 1982-present. **Memberships & Offices:** APS 1988-present; Acad. Intl. d'Histoire des Sciences 1990-present. **Fellowships, Honors & Awards:** Pfizer Prize, History of Science Soc. 1985; MacArthur Fellow 1988. **Publications:** "The Derivation and First Draft of Copernicus's Planetary Theory; A Translation of the *Commenariolus* with Commentary," *APS Proceedings* 117 (1973): 423-512; with O. Neugebauer, *Mathematical Astronomy in Copernicus's De Revolutionibus*, 2 vols. (New York: Springer-Verlag, 1984); with A.T. Grafton, "Calendar Dates and Ominous Days in Ancient Historiography," *Journal of the Warburg & Courtauld Institutes* 51 (1988): 14-42; "Shadow Measurement: the *Sciametria* from Kepler's *Hipparchus*: A Translation with Commentary," in *The Investigation of Difficult Things*, ed. P.M. Harmon & A.E. Shapiro (New York: Cambridge Univ. Press, 1992), 19-70; "Science and Humanism in the Renaissance: Regiomontanus on the Dignity and Utility of the Mathematical Sciences," in *World Chances: Thomas Kuhn*

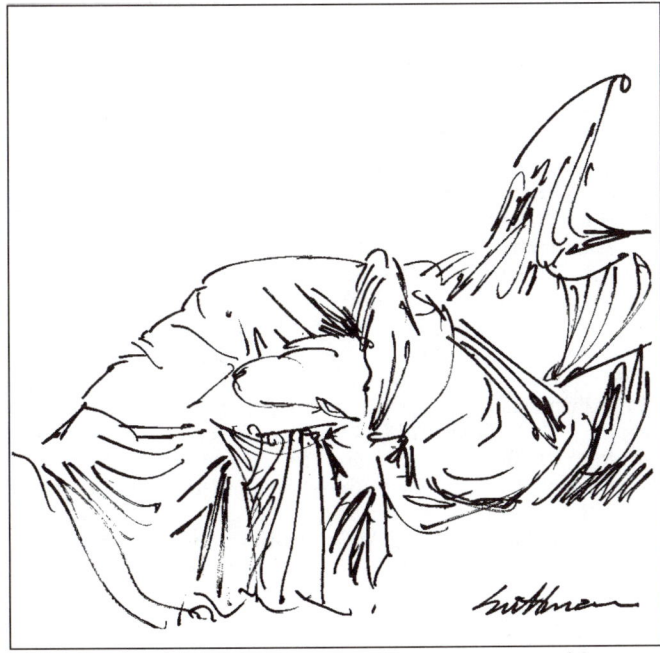

Paul Suttman

and the Nature of Science, ed. P. Horwich (Cambridge, MA: MIT Press, 1993), 131-68. **Business Address:** Univ. of Chicago, 5640 S. Ellis Ave., Chicago, IL 60637.

SZWEYKOWSKI, ZYGMUNT M. ■ Mellon East-Central European Visiting Scholar 1994.

SZYMANSKI, CAROL ■ FAAR Sculpture 89. b. 1955, Charlotte, NC. BA 77, UNC, Chapel Hill; MFA 82, San Francisco Art Inst. **Other Study:** Whitney Museum Independent Study Studio Pgm. 1982-83. **Fellowships, Honors & Awards:** NYSCA Grant 1984; NEA Fellowship 1988. **Publications:** "Forum: On Art, Motherhood, and Apple Pie," *Meaning* (Nov. 1992). **Exhibitions/Performances:** Otis Art Inst. Gallery, Los Angeles 1983; Emanuel Walter Gallery, San Francisco Art Inst. 1983; Inst. of Contemporary Art, Boston 1987; Loughelton Gallery, NYC 1987, 1989; Pence Gallery, Los Angeles 1988; Amy Lipton Gallery, NYC 1991, 1993; Sue Spaid Fine Art, Los Angeles 1993; Elga Wimmer Gallery, NYC 1995. Performances: *Untitled Performance,* by Dewey Redman, Pat Hearn Gallery, NYC 1991; *Antiphony,* Thread Waxing Space, NYC 1991; *Untitled Performance,* by Leo Smith, East Hampton, NY 1992; *Untitled Performance,* by Monique Buzarte, Brooklyn, NY 1992; *Tongue Tied,* Drawing Center, NYC 1993; *The King of Thule,* by Ben Neill, Thread Waxing Space, NYC 1993. **Bio Bibliography:** Michael Anderson, "Carol Szymanski at Pence," *LA Weekly* (Apr. 1-7, 1989); Peggy Cyphers, "New York in Review," *Arts* (Dec. 1989); David Carrier, "Carol Szymanski," *Tema Celeste* (Feb.-Mar. 1992); Brooks Adams, "Carol Szymanski at Amy Lipton Gallery," *Art in America* (Mar. 1992); Alain Kirili, "Who is Afraid of Abstract Modeling," *Tema Celeste* (Autumn 1992); Robert C. Morgan, *After the Deluge: Essays on Art in the Nineties* (New York: Red Bass Press, 1993). **Home Address:** 284 Prospect Pk. W., Brooklyn, NY 11215.

■ ■ ■

T

TAFURI, MANFREDO ■ AAR Visitor 1989-90; Univ. of Venice, Architecture Faculty.

TALBERT, RICHARD J.A. ■ RAAR Classics/Archaeology 91. b. Apr. 26, 1947, Purley, Surrey, England. BA 68, Cambridge Univ.; MA, PhD 72, Cambridge Univ. **Career & Employment:** Queen's Univ., Belfast, Lect. 1970-85; McMaster Univ., Prof. & Chair 1985-88; UNC, Chapel Hill, Distinguished Prof. 1988-present. **Fellowships, Honors & Awards:** APA, Goodwin Award of Merit 1987; Univ. of Alabama, Eminent Scholar in the Humanities 1993. **Publications:** *The Senate of Imperial Rome* (Princeton: Princeton Univ. Press, 1984); *Atlas of the Greek & Roman World* (Princeton: Princeton Univ. Press, forthcoming). **Business Address:** Dept. of History, UNC, Chapel Hill, NC 27599.

TALBOT, WILLIAM ■ AAR World War II Prize 1941.

TALESE, GAY ■ AAR Visitor 1981-82, Writer.

TALMA, LOUISE J. ■ AAR Visitor 1959 — 1964, Composer.

TANNER, WARREN SAUL ■ FAAR Painting 83. b. Sept. 24, 1942, Brooklyn, NY. d. Mar. 1, 1985. m. Renée Meyer. c. Sharon. BFA 64, Hunter College, CUNY; MA 70, Hunter College, CUNY. **Research/Artistic Interests:** Futurism, Cubism. **Career & Employment:** NYC Bd. of Education, Teacher 1969-74; NYIT, Instr. 1975; Baruch College, CUNY, Instr. 1975; Organization of Independent Artists, Founder 1976, Dir. 1976-82. **Fellowships, Honors & Awards:** *Soho Weekly News,* Most Challenging Art Concept Award 1978. **Exhibitions/Performances:** *Arte Fiere,* Bologna 1978; Dyansen Gallery, NYC 1981; Soho Center for Visual Arts, NYC 1981; Mokichi Okada Assn. Gallery, NYC 1982; Aldrich Museum, Ridgefield, CT 1982; Just Above Mid-Town Gallery. **Bio-Bibliography:** *NY Times,* Obit. (Mar. 16, 1985); *Who's Who in American Art.*

TATE, ALLEN J. ■ RAAR Literature 54. b. Nov. 19, 1899, Clark County, KY. d. Feb. 9, 1979. m. Caroline Gordon, Isabella Gardner, Helen Heinz. c. Nancy, John, Benjamin. BA 22, Vanderbilt Univ. **Career & Employment:** Southwestern Univ., Lect. 1934-36; UNC, Woman's College, Prof. 1938-39; Princeton Univ., Resident Fellow in Writing 1939-42; Library of Congress, Poetry Chair 1943-44; NYU, Lect. 1947-51. **Memberships & Offices:** AAAL; NIAL, Pres. 1968-69; AAAS; Soc. of American Historians; Southern Historical Assn.; Phi Beta Kappa. **Fellowships, Honors & Awards:** Guggenheim Fellow 1928-30; Midland Author's Prize, Chicago 1933; Bollingen Prize in Poetry 1956; Brandeis Univ., Medal for Poetry 1961; American Acad. of Poets Award 1963; Oscar Williams Award 1976; Ingram Merrill Award 1976; Nat. Medal for Literature 1976. **Publications:** *My Pope and Other Poems* (New York: Minton, 1928); *Stonewall Jackson, The Good Soldier* (New York: Minton, 1928); *Jefferson Davis: His Rise and Fall* (New York: Minton, 1929); *Three Poems* (New York: Minton, 1930); *Poems 1928-31* (New York: Scribner's, 1932); *Reactionary Essays on Poetry and Ideas* (New York: Scribner's, 1936); *Selected Poems* (New York: Scribner's, 1936); *The Fathers* (New York: Putnam, 1938); *Reasoning in Madness: Critical Essays* (New York: Putnam, 1941); *A Winter Sea* (New York: Cunnington, 1944); *On the Limits of Poetry* (New York: Swallow Press, 1948); *The Hovering Fly* (New York: Cunnington, 1949); *The Forlorn De-*

mon (Chicago: Regnery, 1953); *The Man of Letters in the Modern World* (Cleveland: Meridian, 1955); *Collected Essays* (Denver: Swallow Press, 1960); *Essays of Four Decades* (Denver: Swallow Press, 1969); *The Swimmers & Other Selected Poems* (New York: Oxford Univ. Press, 1970); *Memoirs & Opinions* (Chicago: Swallow Press, 1975); *The Fathers and Other Fiction* (Baton Rouge: Louisiana State Univ. Press, 1977); *Collected Poems, 1919-1976* (New York: Farrar, Straus, Giroux, 1977). **Bio-Bibliography:** Ferman Bishop, *Allen Tate* (Boston: Twayne, 1967); Robert S. Dupress, *Allen Tate and the Augustan Imagination* (Baton Rouge: Louisiana State Univ. Press, 1983); Walter Sullivan, *Allen Tate: A Recollection* (Baton Rouge: Louisiana State Univ. Press, 1988); *Contemporary Authors; Who Was Who in America.*

TAYLOR, DEEMS ■ AAR Trustee 1930-45; Composer, Music Critic.

TAYLOR, FRANCIS HENRY ■ AAR Trustee 1941-51, 1954-57; Art Historian, Museum Dir.

TAYLOR, GILBERT HAWTHORNE ■ FAAR Classics/Archaeology 20. b. July 11, 1883, Hardinsburg, KY. d. Oct. 1960. BA 09, DePauw Univ.; PhD 14, Univ. of Michigan. **Career & Employment:** Southwestern College, KS, Prof. 1923-27; Westminster College, PA, Prof. 1927-45.

TAYLOR, H.A.C. ■ AAR Charter Mem.

TAYLOR, LILY ROSS ■ FAAR Classics/Archaeology 18; AAR School of Classical Studies, Acting Prof.-in-Charge 1934-35, Prof.-in-Charge 1952-55. b. Aug. 12, 1886, Auburn, AL. d. Nov. 18, 1969. BA 06, Univ. of Wisconsin; PhD 12, Bryn Mawr College. **Research/Artistic Interests:** Religious & political history of republican Rome. **Career & Employment:** Vassar College, Instr.-Prof. 1912-27; American Red Cross, Italy & Balkans 1918-19; Bryn Mawr College, Prof. 1927-52, Prof. Emer. 1952-69, Dean of Graduate School 1942-52; UC, Sather Prof. 1947; US Office of Strategic Services, Social Science Analyst 1943-44; Phi Beta Kappa, Visiting Lect. 1956-57; Harvard Univ., Visiting Prof. 1959; Univ. of Wisconsin, Visiting Prof. 1962-63. **Memberships & Offices:** APA, Pres. 1942; IAS 1959; ArIA; ANS. **Fellowships, Honors & Awards:** AAAS, Fellow; APS, Fellow; Soc. for the Promotion of Roman Studies, Hon. Mem.; British Acad., Corresponding Fellow; Pontificia Accademia Romana di Archeologia, Fellow; Guggenheim Fellow 1952, 1958; AAUW, Award of Merit 1952; APA, Award of Merit 1962; "Cultore di Roma," Gold Medal 1962; LittD: Wilson College 1944, Mills College 1947, Univ. of Wisconsin 1950, Columbia Univ. 1954; Smith College 1961. **Publications:** *The Cults of Ostia* (Bryn Mawr: Bryn Mawr College, 1912); *Local Cults in Etruria*, AAR Papers & Monographs 2 (Rome, 1923); *The Divinity of the Roman Emperor* (Middletown, CT: APA, 1931); *Party Politics in the Age of Caesar* (Berkeley: UC Press, 1949); *The Voting Districts of the Roman Republic*, AAR Papers & Monographs 20 (Rome, 1960); *Assemblies from the Hannibalic War to the Dictatorship of Caesar* (Ann Arbor: Univ. of Michigan Press, 1966); plus 70 articles & 60 reviews. **Bio-Bibliography:** *NY Times*, Obit. (Nov. 27, 1969); T.R.S. Broughton, "Lily Ross Taylor," *APS Yearbook* (1971), 172-79; A.K. Michels, "Taylor, Lily Ross," in *Notable American Women: The Modern Period*, ed. B. Sicherman & C.H. Green (Cambridge, MA: Harvard Univ. Press, 1980), 677-78; A.K. Michels, "Lily Ross Taylor," *Classical Outlook* (Winter 1990-91): 52-53; Briggs, 636-38; *Who Was Who in America; Who's Who of American Women.*

TAYLOR, MYRON C. ■ AAR Trustee 1930-53; Corp. Exec, Diplomat.

TAYLOR, RENWICK ■ Pulitzer Fellow 1925-26.

TAYLOR, WAYNE ■ FAAR Architecture 62. b. Aug. 30, 1931, Maple, NC. m. Mary Lilla Hawkins. c. Anna Maria Taylor, Lilla Maria Taylor, Wayne Taylor Jr., Walter Hawkins Taylor. BArch 58, North Carolina State College, School of Design. **Other Study:** Extensive study & practice in structures, geometry, color & light, creative building & art history. These topics are especially pertinent to my interests & have reinforced the content of my teaching. I have engaged in funded & non-funded research in lightweight, thin concrete structures. I have painted since the 1950s & continue to do so today, & from time to time make sculpture. **Career & Employment:** US Coast Guard 1951-54; North Carolina State College, Instr. 1958-59, Asst. Prof. 1962-66; Univ. of Puerto Rico, Assc. Prof. 1966-68; North Carolina State Univ., Asst. Prof. 1968-76, Assc. Prof. 1976-82, Prof. 1982-present. **Important Works:** Public Collections: North Carolina Museum of Art, Raleigh; North Carolina State Univ., Raleigh; Wachovia Bank & Trust, Winston-Salem; Texas-Gulf, Raleigh; Southern Life Insurance Co., Greensboro; GE Microelectronics, Research Triangle Park, NC; College of the Albemarle, Elizabeth City, NC; North Carolina Microelectronics Center, Research Triangle Park. **Exhibitions/Performances:** Exhibitions of painting and graphic work in the Eastern US 1953-60; Solo shows, exhibitions & publications of paintings, sculpture & graphic works in North Carolina, Virginia, Washington, Massachusetts, Georgia, Florida, NYC, Rome, Spain, Puerto Rico & California 1962-present. **Home Address:** 215 Hillcrest Rd., Raleigh, NC 27605.

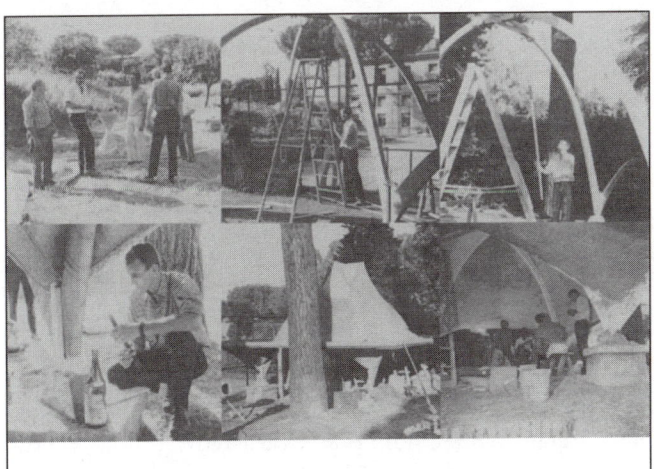

Thanks to all who made my two years at the American Academy so worthwhile. Rome, 1962. Wayne Taylor 1992

Wayne Taylor

TAZZI, PIER LUIGI ■ AAR Visitor 1992-93, Designer.

TEEGEN, O.J. ■ Appleton Fellow 1925-26, Architect.

TELLEEN, MELANY ■ Chicago Architectural Club, Burnham Prize 1990-91.

TEMPLE, SETH JUSTIN ■ McKim Fellow 1911-12, 1913.

TEPASKE-KING, SUSAN L. ■ FAAR Classics/Archaeology 92. b. July 16, 1955, Flint, MI. m. William E. TePaske-King. BA 77, Stanford Univ. **Other Study:** Stanford in Italy 1975-76; Univ. of Michigan 1985-94. **Research/Artistic Interests:** Art history of classical Greece & Rome, ancient Near East influence in Mediterranean. **Publications:** "A Lekythos by the Bowdoin Painter," *Bulletin of the Museums of Art & Archaeology, University of Michigan* 9 (1989-91): 30-47. **Home Address:** 1311 Marlborough Dr., Ann Arbor, MI 48104. **Business Address:** Student Academic Affairs, LS & A, 1213 Angell Hall, Univ. of Michigan, Ann Arbor, MI 48109.

THEK, PAUL ■ AAR Visitor 1967-68, Artist.

THIRY, PAUL ■ RAAR Architecture 69. b. 1904. **Bio-Bibliography:** *American Architects Directory; Contemporary Architecture; Who's Who in America; Who's Who in American Art.*

THOMPSON, CLARA LOUISE ■ FASCSR 09. b. Sept. 28, 1884, Lehigh, OK. d. July 28, 1963. BA 05, Univ. of Pennsylvania; MA 07, Univ. of Pennsylvania; PhD 11 Univ. of Pennsylvania; Dipl. 22, Centro di Estudios Historicos, Madrid. **Career:** Mary Inst., MO, Faculty 1909-10; Belmont College 1911-13; Rockford College, Prof. 1914-19; Shorter College, Rome, GA, Prof. 1919-53, Prof. Emer. 1953-63. **Memberships & Offices:** MLA, South; CAMWS; Georgia Classical Assn., Pres. 1939. **Publications:** Taedium vitae *in Roman Sepulchral Inscriptions* (Saint Louis: New Era Printing, 1911); ed., Seneca, *Octavia* (Boston, Stratford Co., 1921). **Bio-Bibliography:** *Directory of American Scholars; Shorter College Archives.*

THOMPSON, MILO H. ■ FAAR Architecture 65. BA 57, Univ. of Minnesota; BArch 62, Univ. of Minnesota; MArch 63, Harvard GSD. **Career & Employment:** Thorshov & Cerny, Minneapolis, Design Draftsman; Cerny Asscs. Inc., Designer; Carl Koch, Boston, Designer; Brown, Dallas Asscs., Rome, Designer; Cerny Asscs., Inc., Minneapolis, VP & Chief Designer; Frederick Bentz-Milo Thompson-Robert Rietow, Inc., Prin.; Univ. of Minnesota, School of Architecture & Landscape Architecture, Prof. **Memberships & Offices:** AIA; Minnesota Soc. of Architects Honor Awards Com., Publications Com., BoD; Regional Urban Design Assistance Teams: McMinnville, OR; New Rochelle, NY; Healdsburg, CA; Minnesota Architects Forum, Founding Mem.; Minnesota Urban Design Forum, Founding Mem.; Community Design Center of Minnesota, Founding Mem.; Walker Art Center; Minneapolis Inst. of Arts. **Fellowships, Honors & Awards:** AIA, Fellow; Ellerbe Prize in Architecture; Structural Clay Products Prize; Univ. of Minnesota, Gargoyle Prize in Architecture 1962; AIA Medal; Graham Found. Scholar; Harvard Univ Scholarship. **Important Works:** Blue Cross & Univac Office Bldgs., Eagan; Radisson South Hotel, Bloomington; Church of the Holy Name, Minneapolis; Prince of Peace Lutheran Church, Burnsville; St. Olaf Catholic Church Chapel, Minneapolis; Wooddale Church, Eden Prairie; Greenway Gables Townhouses, Minneapolis; Summit Bluff Townhouses, St. Paul; Elliot Park Community Bldg., Minneapolis; Hyland Park Community Bldg., West Bloomington; Jamestown College Library, ND; Univ. of Minnesota, St. Paul Campus Library; Plymouth Library, MN; Library for the Blind & the Physically Handicapped, Faribault, MN; Winona State Univ. Library; 1221 Nicollet Office Bldg., Minneapolis; Regency Center Conference Center, Hotel & Office Bldg., Green Bay, WI; Embassy Suites Hotels in Lowertown, St. Paul & Minneapolis; Restoration Projects: Minneapolis City Hall-Courthouse; Basilica of St. Mary, Minneapolis; Temple Israel, Minneapolis; Lake Harriet Band Shell & Refectory, Minneapolis; Campus Center, Univ. of Minnesota, Duluth; Metropolitan State Univ., St. Paul; City Hall, Rochester; Urban Design Studies for McMinnville, OR; New Rochelle, NY; Healdsburg, CA; Lowertown, St. Paul; Burlington Northern, Minneapolis Riverfront. **Home Address:** 510 Groveland, Minneapolis, MN 55403. **Business Address:** Frederick Bentz-Milo Thompson-Robert Reitow, Inc., 2600 Foshay Tower, Minneapolis, MN 55402.

THOMPSON, RANDALL ■ FAAR Musical Composition 25, RAAR Musical Composition 52, AAR Trustee 1954-69. b. Apr. 21, 1899, NYC. d. July 9, 1984. m. Margret Quail Whitney. c. Varney, Edward Samuel Whitney, Rosemary, Randall Jr. BA 20, Harvard Univ.; MA 22, Harvard Univ.; MusD 33, Univ. of Rochester. **Other Studies:** with Ernest Bloch, NYC 1920-21. **Career & Employment:** Wellesley College, Asst. Prof., Organist, Choir Dir. 1927-29, Lect. 1936-37; Harvard Univ., Lect. 1929, Prof. 1948-65, Walter Bigelow Prof. Emer.; Assn. of American Colleges, College Music Study, Dir. 1932-35; UC, Berkeley, Prof.-Chorus Dir. 1937-39; Curtis Inst. of Music, Dir. 1939-41; Univ. of Virginia, Dept. Head 1941-46; Princeton Univ., Prof. 1945-48; Dept. Chair 1952-57. **Memberships & Offices:** NIAL; AAAS; ASCAP; Century Club; Intl. Soc. for Contemporary Music, US Section, Dir. 1934-35; League of Composers, Exec. Bd. 1939-41, Dir. 1945-48. **Fellowships, Honors & Awards:** Guggenheim Fellowship 1929, 1930; Elizabeth Sprague Coolidge Award 1941; Republic of Italy, Cavaliere Ufficiale al Merito; Ditson Award 1944; Yale School of Music, Sanford Medal; Univ. of Pennsylvania, Hon. MusD 1969; New England Conservatory, Hon. MusD 1975. **Publications:** *College Music* (New York: Macmillan, 1935). **Important Works:** *Pierrot and Cothurnus,* for orchestra 1922; *The Piper at the Gates of Dawn,* symphonic prelude 1924; *Five Odes of Horace* 1924; *Jazz Poem,* for piano & orchestra 1928; Symphonies 1929, 1931, 1949; *Americana,* for 4 voices & piano or orchestra 1932; *The Peaceable Kingdom,* for chorus a cappella 1936; *Alleluia,* for chorus 1940; String quartets 1941, 1967; *Solomon and Balkis,* an opera 1942; *Jabberwocky,* a ballet 1951; *The Battle of Dunster Street,* for stage 1953; *A Trip to Nahant,* for orchestra 1954; *The Nativity According to St. Luke,* an opera 1961; *The Passion According to St. Luke,* an oratorio 1965; *The Place of the Blest,* a cantata 1969; *A Concord Cantata,* for 4 voices & orchestra 1975. **Bio-Bibliography:** H. Gleason & W. Becker, "Randall Thompson," *Twentieth-Century American Composers* (Bloomington: Indiana Univ. Press, 1981); Carolino Cepin Benser, *Randall Thompson: A Bio-Bibliography* (Westport, CT: Greenwood Press, 1991); *Baker's Biographical Dictionary of Musicians; New Grove Dictionary of American Music; Who Was Who in America.*

THOMSON, VIRGIL ■ AAR Visitor 1951 — 1955, Composer.

THON, WILLIAM E. ■ FAAR Painting 48, RAAR Painting 56, 65; AAR Trustee 1968-70. b. Aug. 8, 1906, NYC. m. Helen W. Thon. **Fellowships, Honors & Awards:** NAD, Academician 1968; AAAL 1967; American Watercolor Soc.; Audubon Artists; State of Maine Award Citation; Bates College, AFD 1957. **Important Works:** Farnsworth Museum, Rockland, ME; California Palace of the Legion of Honor; Michener Found.; Honolulu Acad. of Fine Arts; Univ. of Michigan Museum; PAFA; MMA; Brooklyn Museum; Whitney Museum, NYC; Wilmington Soc. of Fine Arts; High Museum, Atlanta; Portland Museum of Art, ME; City Art Museum of St. Louis; Morse

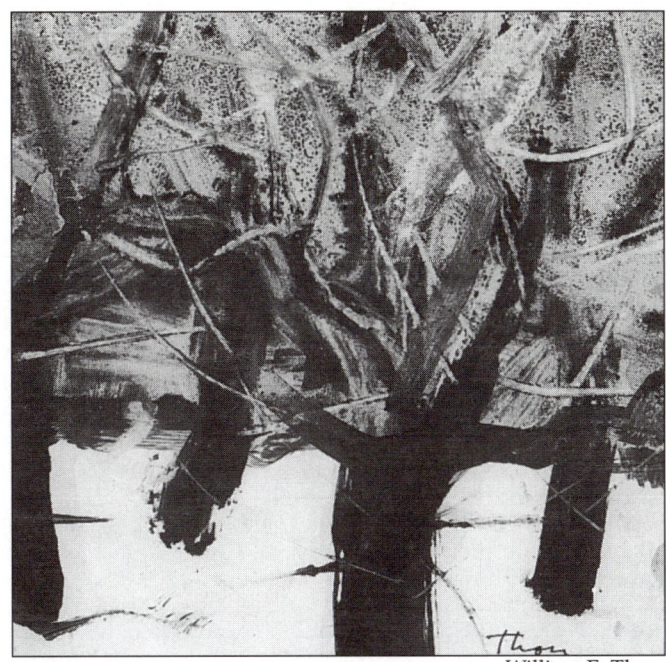

William E. Thon

Gallery, Rollins College, Winter Park, FL; Bates College; Univ. Club, NYC; Butler Inst., Youngstown, OH; Sara Roby Found., Smithsonian Found., Washington, DC; Rochester Memorial Art Gallery; Fleet Bank, Portland, ME; Irving Trust Co., NYC; Fuji Bank, Tokyo; NASA Collection, Eyewitness to Space, Smithsonian Inst., Washington, DC. **Exhibitions/ Performances:** Numerous, including NYC exhibitions every 2 to 3 years since 1944. **Bio-Bibliography:** *Who's Who in America*; *Who's Who in American Art*. **Home Address:** PO Box 22, Port Clyde, ME 04855.

THORBECK, DUANE ■ FAAR Architecture 64. b. Oct. 31, 1935, Bagley, MN. m. Sharon A. Mueffelman. c. Chad

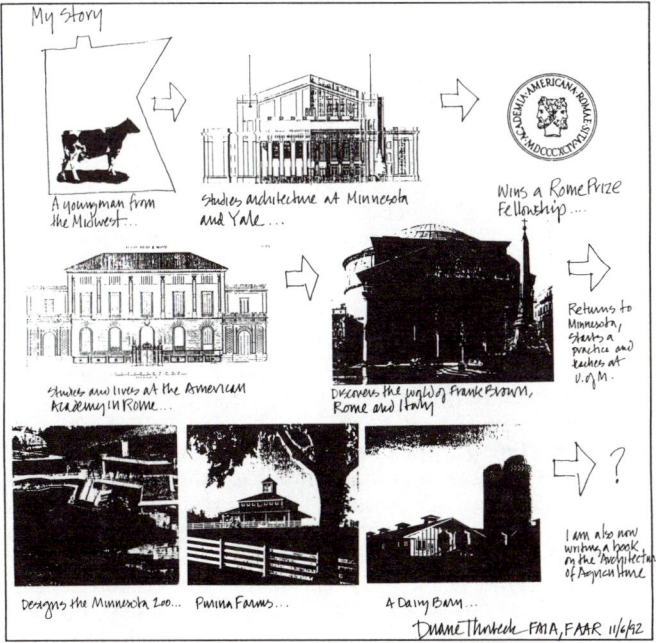

Duane Thorbeck

Abraham, Amy Abraham, Alexandra Stefanska-Thorbeck. BArch 60, Univ. of Minnesota; MArch 61, Yale Univ. **Career & Employment:** Univ. of Minnesota, Adj. Prof. 1965-present; Thorbeck Architects Ltd. 1969-present. **Memberships & Offices:** AIA 1965-present. **Fellowships, Honors & Awards:** AIA Fellow 1985; Graham Found. Grant 1990; plus numerous architectural design awards. **Publications:** *The Architecture of Agriculture* (in progress); plus articles in architectural magazines in US & abroad. **Important Works:** Housing System for HUD; National effort to develop industrialized housing 1970; Minnesota Zoological Garden, Apple Valley 1973-79; St. Cloud Public Library, MN 1978; Purina Farms for Ralston Purina Co., St. Louis 1985; Amphitheater for Northstar Financial Corp., Minneapolis 1986; Minnetonka Police Station & City Hall Remodeling, MN 1987; Master Plan, Minneapolis College of Art & Design 1989; Agricultural Industry & Research Facility, Pennsylvania State Univ., State College 1990; Sons of Norway Intl., Minneapolis 1992; Agricultural Operations Management Center, Univ. of Minnesota, Crookston 1993; Intl. Wolf Center, Ely, MN 1993. **Exhibitions/ Performances:** Architecture USA, Traveling Exb. by US Information Center 1970; Purina Farms, Carlton College 1987; various design award programs. **Business Address:** Thorbeck Architects, 1409 Willow St., Minneapolis, MN 55403.

THORNE, JOAN ■ FAAR Painting 87. b. Aug. 3, 1943, Brooklyn, NY. BS, NYU; MA, Hunter College. **Fellowships, Honors & Awards:** Aldrich Found., Artist of the Year 1972; Rhode Island State Council on the Arts Grant 1974, 1976; NYSCA Grant 1975, 1979; NEA Fellowship 1979, 1983; Pollock-Krasner Found. Grant 1986, 1972; Yaddo Residency 1974, 1976, 1979, 1991; Edward Albee Found. Residency 1977, 1978; Edna St. Vincent Millay Colony Residency 1977; MacDowell Colony 1981. **Important Works:** Albright-Knox Art Gallery, Buffalo; Aldrich Museum of Contemporary Art, Ridgefield, CT; Brooklyn Museum; Dallas Museum of Art; Krannert Museum, Univ. of Illinois, Champaign; Museum of Fine Arts, Houston; Portland Museum, ME; Smorgon Family Collection of Contemporary Art, Melbourne, Australia. **Exhibitions/ Performances:** Solo: Corcoran Gallery of Art, Washington, DC 1973; Fischbach Gallery, NYC 1974; Alfred Univ., Alfred, NY 1975; Galerie Veith Turske, Cologne Art Fair, Germany 1977; Clocktower, Inst. for Art & Urban Resources, NYC 1979; Willard Gallery, NYC 1980, 1982; Dart Gallery, Chicago 1980, 1983; Nina Freudenheim Gallery, Buffalo, NY 1982; Gloria Luria Gallery, Bay Harbor Island, FL 1983; Lincoln Center Gallery, NYC 1983; Graham Modern 1985, 1988, 1990; Ruth Bachofner Gallery, Los Angeles 1986, Santa Monica 1989; William Halsey Gallery, Simon Center for the Arts, College of Charleston, SC 1986. **Bio-Bibliography:** Ronny H. Cohen, "Drawing Now in N.Y.C.: The Pictorial Image of the 1980s," *Drawing Magazine* (1986); Nancy Smith, "Thorne Exhibition Assaults the Senses," *Charleston (SC) News and Courier* (Apr. 27, 1986); Leonore Malon, "Joan Thorne," *ArtNews* (Oct. 1988): 184; Orville O. Clarke, "Joan Thorne," *ArtScene* (May 1989); Ann Dumas, "Joan Thorne," *Arts Magazine* (Jan. 1991); Patricia Arache, "Los Artistas Residentes," *El Siglo* (Santa Domingo, Dominican Republic, Aug. 21, 1993). **Home Address:** 169 Mercer St., NYC 10012.

THORNE, LANDON K., JR ■ AAR Trustee 1967-79; Banker; *Rome Daily American*, Publisher.

THORNE, NICHOLAS C.K. ■ FAAR Musical Composition 82. b. Nov. 7, 1953, Copenhagen, Denmark. m. Elizabeth

Thorne. BMus 76, Berklee College of Music; MMus 79, New England Conservatory. **Career & Employment:** Norwich Univ.-Vermont College, Instr. 1976; Vermont Conservatory, Montpelier Instr. 1978-; Johnson State College, Instr. 1980-; Univ. of Michigan, Visiting Prof. 1989; Yale School of Music, Visiting Prof. 1990. **Fellowships, Honors & Awards:** Vermont Council on the Arts Grant 1979; Tanglewood Koussevitzky Composition Prize 1979, Tanglewood Fellowship 1979, 1980; Univ. of Michigan, Michigan Soc. of Fellows, Prof.-Postdoctoral Scholar 1985; Philadelphia Orchestra Comm. 1987. **Important Works:** *Aria Improvisations*, op. 5 1978; *From the Dying Earth*; *Night Elegy*, op. 8 1979; *Three Tales for Eleven Players*, op. 11 1980; *Eight Paintings*, op. 13 1980; *Four Fall Etchings*, op. 15 1980; *Trombone Concerto*, David Taylor Comm. 1986; *Quartet*, for clarinet, piano, violin & violincello, NEA Consortium Comm. 1986.

THOW, JOHN H. ■ FAAR Musical Composition 78. b. Oct. 6, 1949, Los Angeles, CA. m. Margaret W. Thow. c. Diana, Caroline. BMus 71, Univ. of Southern California; MA 73, Harvard Univ.; Dipl. 74, Accademia Musicale Chigiana, Siena; PhD 77, Harvard Univ. **Other Study:** Burnett Atkinson, flute 1961-67; Adolph Weiss, harmony, counterpoint & composition 1963-67; Luciano Berio 1973-74; Luigi Dallapiccola 1973-74. **Research/Artistic Interests:** Music composition, history & theory of 20th-century music. **Career & Employment:** Boston Univ., Asst. Prof. 1978-80; UC, Berkeley, Asst. Prof. 1981-86, Assc. Prof. 1986-90, Prof. 1990-present. **Fellowships, Honors & Awards:** Fulbright-Hays Fellowship 1973-74; Yaddo Fellowship 1976, 1980; Young Musicians Found. Award 1976; Harvard Univ., John Knowles Paine Fellowship 1977; Meet the Composers Grants 1980, 1982, 1986, 1987, 1992; Dorland Mountain Colony Fellowship 1981; UC Regents Fellowship 1983; AAAL, Goddard Lieberson Fellowship 1994; Guggenheim Fellowship 1986, 1987; Djerassi Found. Fellowship 1986, 1987; NEA Grant 1991; AAAL Award 1994. **Important Works:** *Divergences*, for flute, clarinet, viola & cello (Pembroke Music Editions) 1974; *Siempre*, for soprano & orchestra 1978; *Phoenix Music*, for solo flute, 9 strings, piano & percussion, Alea

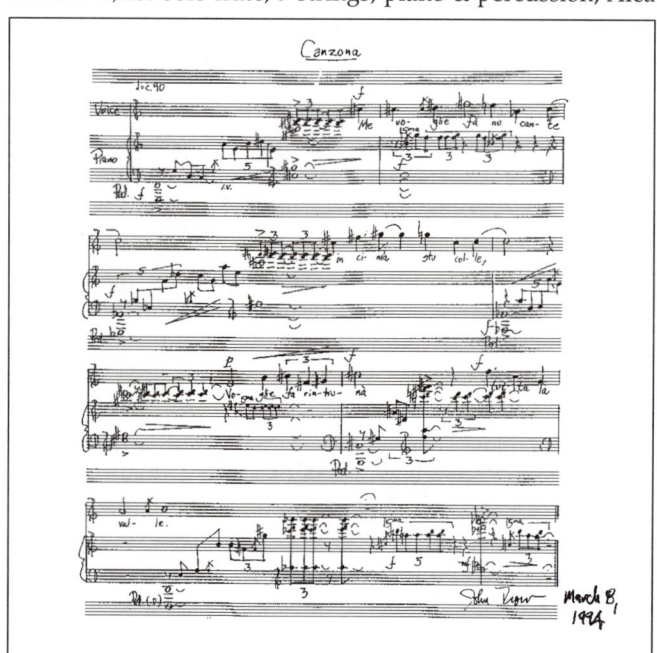

John H. Thow

III Comm. 1981; *All Hallows*, for flute, clarinet, violin, viola, cello, piano & percussion, Boston Musica Viva Comm. (Pembroke Music Editions, Neuma) 1982; *Live Oak*, for 10 players, Musical Elements Comm. 1983; *Resonance*, for orchestra 1986; *Three Elements for Two Pianos*, Alea III Comm. 1986; *Madrone*, for 14 players, (Pembroke Music Editions) 1987; *Into the Twilight*, 3 movements for orchestra, San Francisco Symphony Comm. 1988; *Concerto for Trombone & Orchestra*, 1990-93; *A Water Cycle*, for baritone & chamber ensemble 1991; *Songs for the Earth*, for mezzo-soprano & 6 instruments (Music & Arts) 1994. **Bio-Bibliography:** *Who's Who in America; Who's Who in the West.* **Home Address:** 1045 Ordway St., Albany, CA 94706. **Business Address:** Dept. of Music, UC, Berkeley, CA 94720.

THRASHER, HARRY D. ■ FAAR Sculpture 14. b. 1883. d. 1918. **Bio-Bibliography:** *Who Was Who in American Art.*

TIGERMAN, STANLEY ■ RAAR Architecture 80; AAR Midwest Asscs., Co-Founder. b. Sept. 20, 1930, Chicago, IL. m. Margaret I. McCurry. c. Judson, Tracy. BArch 60, Yale Univ.; MArch 61, Yale Univ. **Other Study:** MIT 1948-49; Inst. of Design, Chicago 1949-50. **Career & Employment:** S.O.M. 1957-59; Paul Rudolph 1959-61; Harry Weese 1961-62; Private Practice 1962-present; Univ. of Illinois, Chicago School of Architecture 1965-71, 1980-93, Dir. 1985-93; Yale School of Architecture, Davenport Prof. 1979-80, 1992-93, Bishop Prof. 1984-85; Harvard GSD, Visiting Prof. 1982-83, Davenport Prof. 1992-93; Archblocks, Co-Found. 1994-present. **Memberships & Offices:** 1962-94: over 625 lectures, juries, interviews, symposia; Yale School of Architecture, Adv. Com. 1975-80; AIC, Adv. Com. 1980-95; SAH, BoD 1984-87. **Fellowships, Honors & Awards:** AIA, Nat. Awards 1982, 1984, 1987 1991 (2), 1992, 1994, Chicago Chap. Design Awards (44) 1970-94, Distinguished Service Award 1983, Illinois Chap. Design Awards (3) 1976; HUD Low-Cost Housing Awards 1970, 1974; *Progressive Architecture*, Design Awards 1980 (2), 1988; *Architectural Record*, Record Houses Awards (6) 1980-90; various design awards (30) 1971-94; Masonry Inst., Masonry Awards 1982-91; Yale Univ. Arts Award 1985; Merchandise Mart, Dean of Architecture Award 1989; *Interior Design Magazine* Hall of Fame 1990; Domino's Gold 30 Award 1991; Illinois Acad. of Fine Arts 1992. **Publications:** *Chicago Tribune Tower Competition & Late Entries* (New York: Rizzoli, 1980); "Modernism & The Canonical Chicago Architecture Condition," in *Beyond the Modern Movement*, Harvard Architecture Review 1 (1980): 170-79; with Dorothy Metzer Habel & Ross Miller, *Versus: An American Architect's Alternatives* (New York: Rizzoli, 1982); *The Postwar American Dream* (Chicago: AIC, 1985); "Mies van der Rohe and His Disciples, or the American Architecture Text and Its Reading," in *Mies Reconsidered, His Career, Legacy, and Disciples*, ed. John Zukowsky (Chicago, 1986); *Chicago Tapes* (New York: Rizzoli, 1987); *The Architecture of Exile* (New York: Rizzoli, 1988); with Margaret McCurry, & Tracy Tigerman, *Dorothy in Dreamland* (New York: Rizzoli, 1991). **Important Works:** Woodlawn Garden Apartments, Chicago 1963-69; Polytechnic Institutes (5) for the People's Republic of Bangladesh 1966-75; St. Benedict's Abbey Church, Benet Lake, WI 1969-73; Illinois Regional Library for the Blind & Physically Handicapped, Chicago 1975-78; Anti-Cruelty Soc., Chicago 1977-78; "Chicago Architecture 1872-1922" Installation Design, AIC 1985-88; Camp Hoover for Differently Abled Boy Scouts, Yorkville, IL 1985-92; Commonwealth Edison Substation, Chicago 1986-89; Exb. Installation, Gulbenkian Found., Lisbon 1987-89; Momochi Housing Project, Fukuoka City, Kihshu, Japan 1988-89; Chicago Bar Assn. 1989-90; Power-

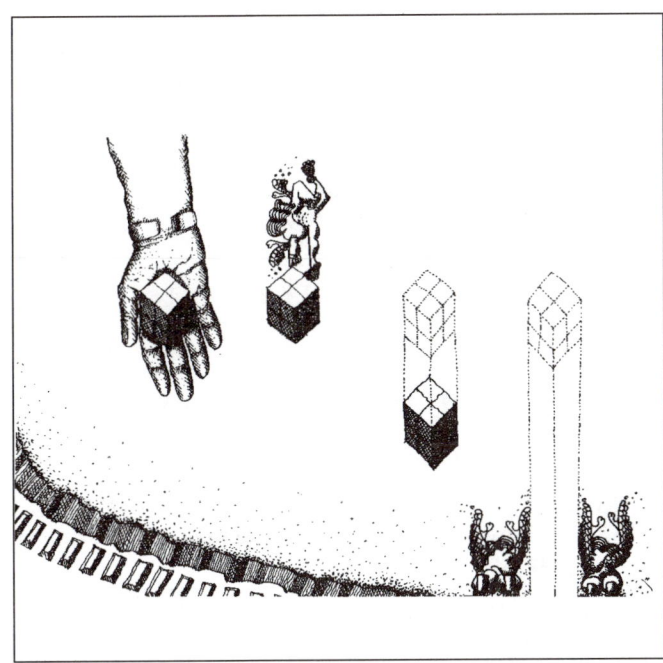

Stanley Tigerman

house Energy Education Center (Museum), Zion, IL 1987-92; Permanent Collections: AIC; MCA; MOMA; Deutsches Architektur Museum, Frankfurt. **Exhibitions/ Performances:** Exhibited 258 times in museums & galleries including: São Paulo, Brazil 1976; Harvard Univ. 1976; Venice Biennale 1976, 1980; Drawing Center, NYC 1977; Otis Art Inst., Los Angeles 1977; PS 1, NYC 1978; Teheran Museum of Contemporary Art, Iran 1978; MOMA 1979 (2); Collegio de Arquitectura, Bilbao, Vitoria & San Sebastian, Spain 1980; Museum of Finnish Architecture, Helsinki 1980; Castelvecchio, Verona 1981; Corcoran Gallery of Art, Washington, DC 1982; Deutsches Architektur Museum, Frankfurt 1984, 1988; Victoria & Albert Museum, London 1984; Renwick Gallery, Washington, DC 1985; Museum of Science & Industry, Chicago 1985; Cooper-Hewitt Museum, NYC 1987; MCA 1988; Gulbenkian Found., Lisbon 1989. **Bio-Bibliography:** *Stanley Tigerman, Buildings and Projects 1966-89,* ed. Sarah Moreman Underhill (New York: Rizzoli, 1989); *Who's Who in America; Who's Who in American Art; Who's Who in Interiors.* **Business Address:** 444 N. Wells, Chicago, IL 60610.

TIMBERLAKE, JAMES HARRISON ■ FAAR Architecture 83. b. Oct. 24, 1952, Findlay, OH. BES 74, Univ. of Detroit; MArch 77, Univ. of Pennsylvania. **Research/Artistic Interests:** Perimeter-center research in Houston-Uptown, Galleria; Philadelphia-King of Prussia; Washington, DC-Tyson's Corner, VA; Los Angeles-Irvine, CA; Atlanta-Perimeter Center, GA, in collaboration with Stephen Kieran, ongoing, since Fall 1987; drawing & restoration, relationship between drawing & design, subject of AAR research ongoing since 1980. **Career & Employment:** Univ. of Pennsylvania, TA 1975-77, Jury Critic 1977-present, *Design Week* Critic 1983, Studio Critic 1979, 1992, Studio Critic & Seminar Instr. 1989-91; Louis Sauer Asscs. 1976-77; Venturi, Rauch & Scott Brown 1977-1984, Assc. 1983-84; Drexel Univ., Jury Critic 1978-88; UNC, Charlotte, Studio Critic 1981; Kieran, Timberlake & Harris, Part. 1984-present; Univ. of Texas, Austin, Visiting Studio Critic 1984; Pennsylvania State Univ., Visiting Studio Critic 1985; Princeton Univ., Studio Critic 1986-88; Yale Univ., Eero Saarinen Prof. 1994.

Memberships & Offices: Classical America Soc. 1978-86; Soc. for Commercial Archeology 1979-present; AIA, Philadelphia Chap., BoD 1986-89; John Stewardson Memorial Competition Com., Sec. 1986-93; Business Volunteers for the Arts, Philadelphia 1987-present; Artspace Collaborative, Philadelphia 1990-present; Athenaeum, Philadelphia 1991-present. **Fellowships, Honors & Awards:** Cope Memorial Competition, 1st Prize 1975; John Stewardson Competition, 1st Prize 1976; Univ. of Pennsylvania, E. Lewis Dales Travelling Fellowship 1976, Paul Phillipe Cret Design & Thesis Prize 1976, 1977; *Interiors Magazine,* Philadelphia Design Awards 1988; AIA, Philadelphia Chap., Merit Award 1988, 1992, 1993, 1994; Graham Found. Grant 1992; Pennsylvania Soc. of Architects Award 1993. **Publications:** "Learning from Architectural Drawings," *Dichotomy* (1984); Photographs of Aldo Rossi Cemetery, *Architecture Magazine* (Sept. 1984); "The Value of Architecture and Campus Image to Collegiate Marketing Strategies," *SCUP Journal* (1985); "Personal Choices, Juried Selection of Contemporary Philadelphia Architectural Drawings," PAFA 1986; with Stephen Kieran, "Columbus Parking Lot," *Landscape* 2 (1986); with Stephen Kieran, "Paradise Regained," *Architecture Magazine* (Dec. 1991); with Stephen Kieran, "Die neue amerikanische Landschaft," *ARCH* + (June 1992); with Stephen Kieran, "The Form and Fabric of the Emerging Regional City, Perimeter Center-Atlanta," *Site/Sight* (Oct. 1992); "Tale of Two Cities: Atlanta/Perimeter Center Georgia," *The Periphery, AD* (Apr. 1994). **Important Works:** Architectural Comms.: Agricultural Museum, State of New Jersey, New Brunswick, Exb. Design 1988; Allingham Residence, Chestertown, MD 1989; Tully Residence, Centerville, DE 1989; Woodberry Forest School, VA, Master Plan 1990; Greenberg Residence, Wrightstown Twp., Bucks County, PA 1991; Kegler Residence, Philadelphia 1992; Shipley School, Bryn Mawr, PA, Master Plan, Additions & Renovations, Middle School 1993; West Chester Univ., PA, Sykes Union Bldg. 1994; Temple Univ., Philadelphia, Feasibility Study 1995. **Exhibitions/Performances:** AIA, Philadelphia Chap. Design Exbs. 1988-present; PAFA 1986; "The Suburbs," PBS segment produced by WHYY, Philadelphia 1992; Forum, Royal Acad. of Arts,

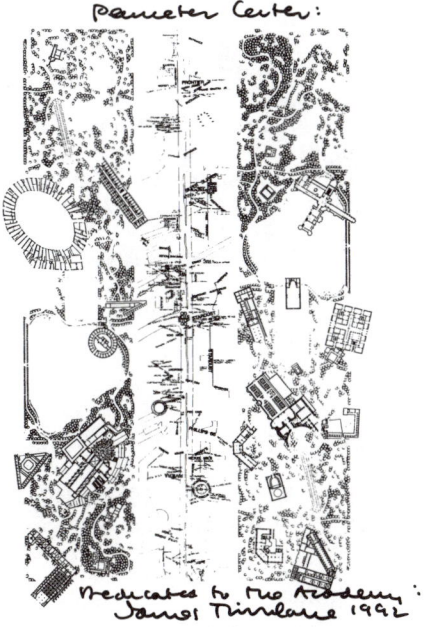

James Harrison Timberlake

London 1994. **Home Address:** 210 Locust Walk, 31C, Philadelphia, PA 19106. **Business Address:** Kieran, Timberlake & Harris, Daniel Bldg., 5th Fl., 20 N. Third St., Philadelphia, PA 19106.

TIMME, ROBERT H. ■ FAAR Architecture 86. b. Jan. 18, 1945, Houston, TX. m. Candace Timme. c. Elizabeth. BA 69, Rice Univ.; BArch 71, Rice Univ.; MArch 78, Rice Univ. **Career & Employment:** Taft Architects, Part. 1972-present; Univ. of Houston, College of Architecture, Prof. 1972-present, Dean 1992-present. **Fellowships, Honors & Awards:** with partners, AIA Honor Awards 1981, 1982, 1983, local & state chapters over 50 honor awards since 1975, Fellow 1991; Venice Biennale 1980; Yale Univ., Davenport Chair Prof. 1984; Graham Found. Fellowship 1985-86. **Important Works:** Hendley Bldg., Galveston 1977-79; Municipal Control Bldg., Quail Valley 1978-79; YWCA Masterson Branch & Office Bldg., Houston 1979-81; Talbot House, Nevis 1980-81; River Crest Country Club, Fort Worth 1981-84; Water Resources Bldg., The Woodlands 1982-85; Corpus Christi City Hall 1984-88; Hope Elementary School, TX 1986-88; Olson House, Nevis 1987-88; Rothwell House, Houston 1988-93; Lycée Technique Bernard Palissy, Saintes, France 1990-94; Penn-Plax Assembly Plant, Saintes, France 1991; Rice School, Houston 1991-94; Tribune & Educational Bldg., Sogndal, Norway 1992-94. **Bio-Bibliography:** Charles Jencks, ed., *Post Modern Classicism* (London: Academy Editions, 1980); Venice Biennale, *Architecture 1980: The Presence of the Past* (New York: Rizzoli, 1980); Charles Jencks, *Architecture Today* (New York: Abrams, 1982); E. McCoy & B. Goldstein, *Guide to US Architecture: 1940-1980* (Santa Monica: A + A Press, 1982); Paolo Portoghesi, *After Modern Architecture* (New York: Rizzoli, 1982); ed., Charles Jencks, *Abstract Representation* (London: Academy Editions, 1983); Robert Jensen & Patricia Conway, *Ornamentalism* (New York: Potter, 1983); *101 Contemporary Architects in the World* (Tokyo: Kajima Publishers, 1985); Architectural League, *Emerging Voices: A New Generation of Architects in America* (New York: Princeton Architectural Press, 1986); Charles Jencks, *Post Modernism* (New York: Rizzoli, 1987); ed., Stanley Tigerman, *The Chicago Tapes* (New York: Rizzoli, 1987); Robert A.M. Stern, *Post-Modern Classicism* (New York: Rizzoli, 1988); Sylvia Hart Wright, *Sourcebook of Contemporary North American Architecture* (New York: Van Nostrand, 1989); Roberto Masiero, *Neoclassico* (Venice: Marsilio Editori, 1990); ed., Stephen Fox, *Houston Architectural Guide* (Houston: Houston AIA-Herring Press, 1990); *Architecture Address Book* (New York: Rizzoli, 1992); Sydney LeBlanc, *20th Century American Architecture* (New York: Whitney Library of Design, 1993); Ben E. Graves, *School Ways* (New York: McGraw Hill, 1993). **Home Address:** 2617 Talbot, Houston, TX 77005. **Business Address:** Taft Architects, 807 Peden St., Houston, TX 77006.

TIRELLI, MARCO ■ AAR Visitor 1989-90, Artist.

TOLLEFSON, E.A. ■ Winchester Fellow 1924-25.

TOMASI, GIOACCHINO LANZA ■ AAR Visitor 1984-85; La Scala Opera House, Dir.

TONETTI, CLAUDIA ■ AAR – Rome, Housekeeping Staff.

TONGUE, WILLIAM RICHARD ■ FAAR Classics/Archaeology 38, RAAR Classics/Archaeology 48. b. Jan. 1, 1911, Haverstraw, NY. d. Nov. 28, 1977. BA 33, Univ. of Pennsylvania; MA 34, Duke Univ.; PhD 36, Univ. of Pennsylvania. **Other Studies:** Yale Univ., Visiting Research Fellow 1939-40. **Career & Employment:** Univ. of Missouri, Instr. 1936-37; Allegheny College, Instr. 1937-41, Asst. Prof. 1941-44; St.

Bonaventure Univ., Dir. of Classics Summer Session 1941-47; College of the Holy Cross, Asst. Prof. 1944-48; Univ. of Oklahoma, Assc. Prof. 1948-53, Prof. 1953-60, Dept. Chair 1952-56; Catholic Univ., Prof. 1960-75. **Memberships & Offices:** APA; American Classics League; Classical Assn. of Atlantic States; ArIA. **Fellowships, Honors & Awards:** Univ. of Pennslyvania, Harrison Scholar 1934-1936. **Publications:** contr., *New Catholic Encyclopedia* (1967). **Bio-Bibliography:** *Directory of American Scholars; Who's Who in Amercia*.

TONNER, GORDON DAWLEY ■ FAAR Post-Classical/Humanistic Studies 74. b. Feb. 22, 1945, Oberlin, OH. BA, MA 68, Oberlin College. **Other Studies:** Univ. of Michigan.

TOR, MICHAEL ■ GI Resident 1945-47, Singer.

TORRE, L. AZEO ■ FAAR Landscape Architecture 76. b. Mar. 30, 1948, New Orleans, LA. m. Regina Torre. c. Azeo, Marco. BLA 71, Louisiana State Univ. **Other Study:** Harvard GSD 1977. Line drawing & architectural rendering, furniture design, scupture, music (keyboard composition & performance). **Career & Employment:** Louisiana State Univ., Asst. Prof. 1973-74, Assc. Prof. 1980; Charles Caplinger Planners, Inc.-Perez Architects 1976-77; Tulane Univ., Visiting Prof. 1976, 1979; MLTA-EDAW, Prin. 1978; L. Azeo Torre, Ltd., Prin. 1979; Cashio, Cochran, Torre Design Consortium, Prin. 1980-present; Graphics & Design Consultant to: Ambrosette e Metz, Rome 1976; Agenzia de Publicità, Promos, Rome 1976; Design Consultant to: New Orleans City Planning Comm. 1971-73; Cashio, Cochran, Inc. 1972-73; New Orleans Planning Comm. on Urban Affairs 1972-73; Charles Caplinger & Asscs., New Orleans 1972-74; Louisiana Bicentennial Comm., Ft. Bute Memorial Park, Baton Rouge 1973; Costa Smeralda Developments, Sardinia 1974-75; Dick Bell Asscs., Landscape Architect 1975. **Memberships & Offices:** ASLA; ASLA Louisiana Chap., Pres. 1984-85; American Assn. of Zoological Parks & Aquariums; AIA; Intl. Soc. of Interior Designers; American Assn. of Museums; American Planning Assn.; Assn. of Zoological Horticulture; Louisiana Assn. of Architects; New Orleans Musicians Alumni; US Yacht Racing Union. **Fellowships, Honors & Awards:** ASLA, Honor Award 1982, Merit Award 1983, 1987, Merit Award of Excellence 1985; ASLA, Louisiana Chap., Honor Award 1984 (3), 1989, 1991, Merit Award 1989, 1990; US Transportation Dept., Biennial Award for Excellence 1984; American Assn. of Nurserymen, Nat. Landscape Award 1984, Nat. Special Judges Landscape Award 1984; Copley Square, Boston, Nat. Design Competition, Merit Award 1984; US Housing & Urban Devlopment Dept., Certificate of Nat. Recognition 1984; American Assn. of Zoological Parks & Aquariums, Exb. of the Year Award 1985; Hillsborough County, FL, Outstanding Contribution Award 1988; ASLA, Tennessee Chap., Honor Award 1989, 1991; ASLA, Florida Chap., Honorable Mention 1989, Merit Award 1989, Honor Award of Excellence 1989; AIA, New Orleans Chap., Peoples Choice Award 1989; Waterfront Center, Honor Award 1989, 1990; ASLA Fellow 1992. **Publications:** *Site Perspective* (New York: Van Nostrand, Reinhold, 1987); *Water Front Development* (New York: Van Nostrand, Reinhold, 1988); *The Business of Recreation* (New York: Van Nostrand, Reinhold, forthcoming). **Important Works:** Lower Algiers New Town, New Orleans; CBD Study, Planning, New Orleans, City Planning Comm.; with Cashio, Cochran, French Market Complex, New Orleans; Scotlandville By-Pass Study, New Orleans; St. Tammany Open Space & Recreation Interim Sketch Plan, New Orleans; New Milneburg Park, New Orleans City Planning

Comm; Brechtel Park, Design & Master Plan, New Orleans; Exchange Alley, Interim Design & Graphics, New Orleans; Visual Environmental Design Study, Prototype Urban Design Solutions, New Orleans; UNC, Plaza Design; Costa Smeralda, Sardinia, Design & Planning; Porto Cervo Park; Widen Canal St. Sidewalks, Preliminary Designs, New Orleans; Ochsner Hospital, Fountain & Plaza Design, Jefferson, LA; Wimbledon Playground, New Orleans; Laurence Sq. for Park & Parkway Comm., New Orleans; with Folse-HDR Architects, Saudi Arabian Prisons & Communities; Bayou Segnette State Park & Marina, Jefferson Parish, LA; with Curtis & Davis-DMJM, EXPO 1981, Los Angeles; with Curtis & Davis-DMJM, Louisiana World Exposition 1984, Festival Park, Preliminary Master Plan; St. Charles St. Transit Mall, New Orleans; Information Transferal System, Downtown Development District, New Orleans; Audubon Park & Zoological Garden, New Orleans; Lowry Park Zoo, Master Plan & Exb. Design, Tampa; Louisiana Nature Center, Master Plan & Site Improvements, New Orleans; Shreveport Zoo, Master Plan, Shreveport, LA; Memphis Zoo & Aquarium, Master Plan & Exb. Design; Pascagoula Waterfront Master Plan & Sand Beach Study, State of Mississippi Gulf Coast; Biloxi Waterfront Master Plan, MS; Southbank Riverwalk, Master Plan & Design, Jacksonville, FL; Missoula Waterfront Master Plan, MN; New Orleans Aquarium & Riverfront Park, Preliminary Master Plan, Park Design & Production; Fort Worth Zoo, Master Plan & Exb. Design; Woodland Park Zoo, Asian Tropical Forest Exb., Seattle; Sacramento Zoo, Rare Feline Exb.; El Paso Zoo, Master Plan & Exb. Design; Brookside Park & Comprehensive Plan, Master Plan & Site Improvements, Maitland, FL; Louisiana Purchase Gardens & Zoo, Master Plan, Monroe, LA; Chehaw Wild Animal Park, Master Plan & Exb. Design, Albany, GA; Louisiana State Univ., Hilltop Arboretum, Master Plan, Baton Rouge; Busch Gardens, Exb. Design, Tampa; Langford Park, Master Plan, Orlando, FL; Warner Park Zoo, Master Plan, Chattanooga, TN; Louisville, KY Zoo, Master Plan; Birmingham, AL Zoo, Master Plan; Jackson, MS Zoo, Master Plan & Exb. Design; Washington Park Zoo, Master Plan & Exb., Portland, OR; Cameron Park Zoo, Master Plan, Exb. & Facility Design, Waco, TX; Bayshore Blvd. Waterfront Plan, Master Plan & Construction, Tampa; Adventure Island, Water Park Master Plan, Busch Gardens, Tampa; New Orleans Intl. Airport, Master Plan; Bourbon Steet Revitalized Plan, Vieux Carré Comm., New Orleans; General DeGaulle Corridor, New Orleans; Jefferson Parish, LA Recreation Master Plan; Williams Blvd. Urban Corridor Master Plan, Kenner, LA; US Fish & Wildlife Dept., Bayou Sauvage Wildlife Refuge. **Exhibitions/Performances:** ASLA Convention, FL 1974; Annual Exb. of Yachts, Genoa 1976; Intl. Boat Show, Hamburg, Germany 1976; Louisiana State Univ. 1986. **Home Address:** 18 Swallow St., New Orleans, LA 70124. **Business Address:** Cashio-Cochran-Torre, Design Consortium Ltd., 5005 Magazine St., New Orleans, LA 70115.

TOVISH, HAROLD ■ RAAR Sculpture 66. b. 1921, NYC. m. Marianna Packard. c. Margo Mack, Aaron Tovish, Nina Tovish. **Study:** WPA Art Program, NYC 1936-40; Columbia Univ. 1940-43; Ossip Zadkine School of Sculpture, Paris 1949-50; Académie de la Grande Chaumière, Paris 1950-51; Stanley Hayter, Atelier 17, Paris 1951. **Career & Employment:** Alfred Univ., New York State College of Ceramics, Asst. Prof. 1947-49; Univ. of Minnesota, Asst. Prof. 1951-54; School of MFA, Instr. 1957-65; Skowhegan School of Painting & Sculpture, Instr. 1957, 1958, 1971; MIT, Center for Advanced Visual Studies, Research Fellow 1967-68; Univ. of Hawaii, Visiting Prof.

1969-1970; Boston Univ., Prof. 1971-84, Prof. Emer. 1984-present. **Fellowships, Honors & Awards:** Village Art Center, Hon. Men. 1946; Walker Art Center, Purchase Prize 1951; Minneapolis Art Inst., 1st Prize 1952, 1954; Portland Soc. of Art, Hon. Men. 1957; Boston Arts Festival, 1st Prize 1957, 1959; Boston Arts Festival, 1st Prize 1958; Inst. of Contemporary Art, Boston Selection 1958, Margaret Brown Award 1959; AAAL Grant 1960, 1971; Boston Arts Festival, 2d Prize 1964; Guggenheim Fellowship 1967. **Publications:** "Introduction," in *Sculpture of Germaine Richier*, exb. cat. (Boston: Boston Univ. School of Fine & Applied Art, 1959); "Sculpture: The Sober Art," *Atlantic Monthly* 208.3 (Sept. 1961); "Introduction," in *Contemporary European Sculpture*, exb. cat. (Boston: Boston Univ. Art Gallery, School for the Arts, 1975). **Important Works:** Public Collections: Addison Gallery of American Art, Phillips Acad., Andover; Guggenheim Museum, NYC; Hirshhorn Museum & Sculpture Garden, Smithsonian Inst., Washington, DC; Hunter Museum of Art, Chattanooga, TN; Minneapolis Inst. of Arts; MFA; MOMA; NAD; Nat. Museum of American Art, Smithsonian Inst., Washington, DC; Philadelphia Museum of Art; Univ. Art Museum, Univ. of Minnesota, Minneapolis; Virlane Found.; Walker Art Center, Minneapolis; Whitney Museum, NYC; Worcester Art Museum. **Exhibitions/Performances:** Solo: Walker Art Center, Minneapolis 1953; Swetzoff Gallery, Boston 1957, 1960, 1965; Fairweather Hardin Gallery, Chicago 1960; Terry Dintenfass Gallery, NYC 1965, 1972, 1974, 1980, 1985; Retrospective: Addison Gallery of American Art, Phillips Acad., Andover 1965, 1988; Retrospective: Watson Gallery, Wheaton College, Norton, MA 1966; Guggenheim Museum, NYC 1968; Alpha Gallery, Boston 1972, 1986; Honolulu Acad. of Arts 1979; Wiggin Gallery, Boston Public Library 1982. **Bio-Bibliography:** *Who's Who*. **Home Address:** 380 Marlborough St., Boston, MA 02115.

TRAHMAN, CARL R. ■ FAAR Classics/Archaeology 42; AAR Adv. Council, Sec. & Chair. b. Mar. 10, 1917, Irvington, NJ. BA 38, Union College; PhD 42, Univ. of Cincinnati. **Career & Employment:** Yale Univ., Asst Prof. 1946-48; Univ. of Cincinnati, Asst. Prof.-John M. Burnam Prof. 1948-82. **Fellowships, Honors & Awards:** Union College, Phi Beta Kappa 1938; Univ. of Cincinnati, Graduate Fellowships 1938-42. **Bio-Bibliography:** *Classical Texts and Their Traditions: Studies in Honor of C.R. Trahman*, ed. David F. Bright & Edwin S. Ramage (Chico, CA: Scholars Press, 1984); *Who's Who in America*. **Home Address:** 36 Williamson Ave., Bloomfield, NJ 07003.

TRAINA, GIUSTO ■ Italian Fulbright Fellow 1983-84. b. Sept. 19, 1959, Palermo, Italy. m. Antonietta Zucconi. c. Giacomo. Laurea 81, Univ. degli Studi, Pisa; PhD 87, Univ. de Paris; Dottorato 91, Univ. of Pisa, Pavia, Perugia. **Career & Employment:** Storia Geofisica Ambiente, Bologna 1983-93; Univ. of Perugia, Researcher 1993-present. **Home Address:** Via Costantino Beltrami, 10a, Rome 00154, Italy. **Business Address:** Univ. of Perugia, Facoltà di Magistero, Piazza Giuseppe Ermini Perugia, Italy 06123.

TRAUTMANN, JOHN P. ■ NIAE/Dinkeloo Fellow 1985-86. b. Aug. 13, 1961, Los Angeles, CA. BArch 84, California Polytechnic State Univ., San Luis Obispo; MArch 88, Harvard Univ. **Career & Employment:** Elias Torres & José António Martínez Lapeña, Architect 1986; Hodgetts & Fung, Project Architect 1988-90; Parsons Overseas Co., Sen. Architect 1990-94; Private Practice 1994-present. **Home Address:** 580 Agate St., Laguna Beach, CA 92651. **Business Address:** John Trautman, Architect, 1433 Yale St., Santa Monica, CA 90404.

TRAVISANO, FRED ■ FAAR Architecture 82; SOF Council 1994-95. b. Sept. 9, 1940, Newark, NJ. d. Mar. 30, 1995. m. Laurie Nussdorfer, FAAR 81. c. Simone Travisano, Mikel Travisano. BArch 67, Cooper Union. **Career & Employment:** Skidmore, Owings & Merrill 1967-70; John Hedjuk Architect 1970-71; Trenton, NJ, Dir. of Development 1971-78; Clarke & Travisano Architects 1978-81; Fred Travisano Architect 1981-85; Michael Mostoller-Fred Travisano Architects 1985-95. **Memberships & Offices:** AIA Central New Jersey, Pres. 1992-93. **Fellowships, Honors & Awards:** US Housing & Urban Development Dept., Urban Design Concept Honor Award 1976; *Progressive Architecture* Award 1978; Monroeville Civic Center, PA, 1st Prize 1982; AIA, NYC, Project Honor Award 1985; Excellence in Downtown Development 1990; NJ Soc. of Architects, Excellence in Architecture 1991. **Important Works:** Cube House Project, Cooper Union 1967; Mill Hill Historic Park, Trenton, NJ l976; Cooper Field Bathhouse, Trenton, NJ 1977; Monroeville Civic Center, PA 1982; Cityside Housing, Trenton, NJ 1990; Amandla Crossing, Edison, NJ 1991; 179-183 Nassau St., Princeton, NJ 1993; Riese Saint Gerard Senior Citizen Housing, Paterson, NJ 1993; Mario Gonzalez Child Care Facility, New Brunswick, NJ 1994; Escher St. Residential Hotel, Trenton, NJ 1995; Community Center, Princeton Community Village, NJ 1995; West Dr. Houses, Princeton Housing Authority, NJ 1995. **Exhibitions/Performances:** MOMA 1971; Deutsches Architekturmuseum, Frankfurt-am-Main 1989; Taipei Fine Arts Museum 1990-91.

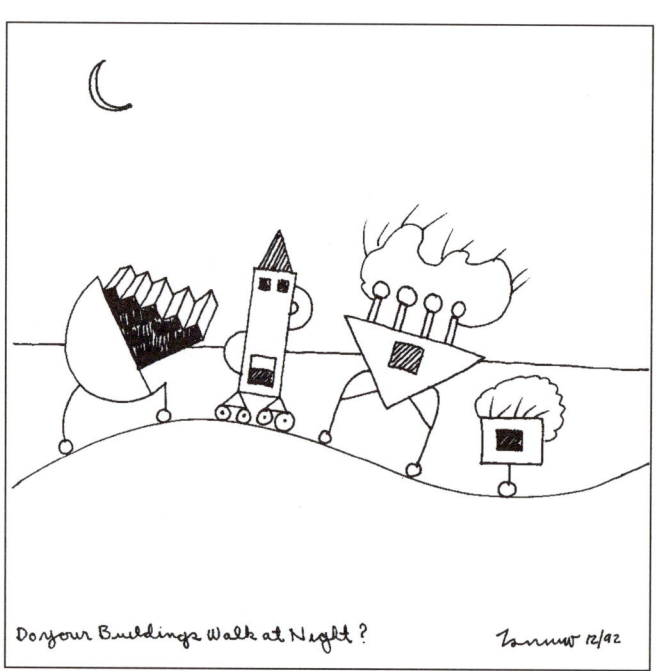

Do your Buildings Walk at Night?   Travino 12/92

Fred Travisano

TREIB, MARC ■ FAAR Landscape Architecture 85. b. Sept. 1, 1943, NYC. m. Dorothee Imbert. BArch 66, Univ. of Florida; MArch 68, UC, Berkeley; MA 69, UC, Berkeley. **Other Study:** Finland 1966-67. **Research/Artistic Interests:** Design: graphic, landscape architecture; history: graphic design, landscape, architecture; geographic research areas: Scandinavia, Japan, US. **Career & Employment:** UC, Berkeley, Asst-Assc. Prof. 1968-81, Prof. 1981-present. **Memberships & Offices:** SAH 1971-present. **Fellowships, Honors & Awards:** Fulbright Fellowship 1966-67, 1982, 1993; UC, Berkeley, Distinguished Teach-

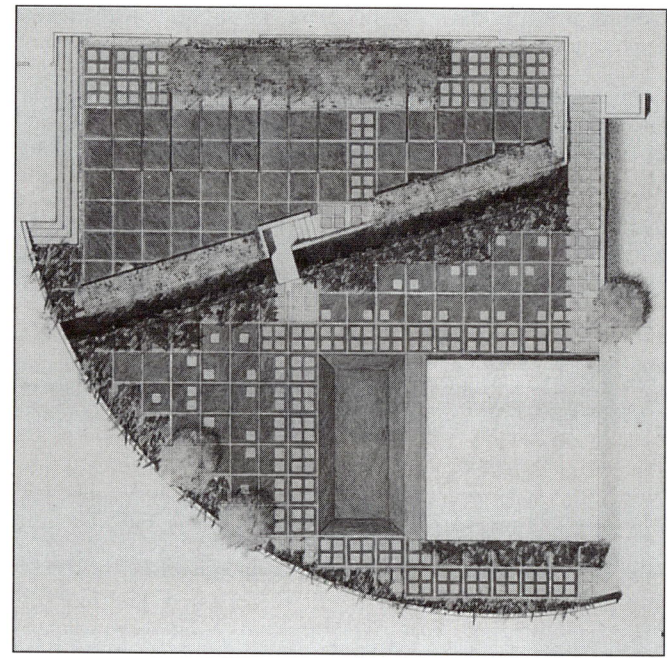

Marc Treib

ing Award 1987; Guggenheim Fellowship 1993-94. **Publications:** with Ron Herman, *A Guide to the Gardens of Kyoto* (Tokyo: Shufunotomo, 1980); "Mapping Experience," *Design Quarterly* 115 (1983); "The Dichotomies of Dwelling: Edo-Tokyo," in *Tokyo: Form and Spirit*, ed. Mildred Friedman (Minneapolis: Walker Art Center & New York: Abrams, 1988); *Sanctuaries of Spanish New Mexico* (Berkeley: UC Press, 1993); *Modern Landscape Architecture: A Critical Review* (Cambridge: MIT Press, 1993); ed., with Theres O'Malley, *The Regional Garden* (Washington: Dumbarton Oaks, 1995); ed., *An Everyday Modernism: The Houses of William Wurster* (San Francisco: San Francisco Museum of Modern Art, 1995). **Important Works:** Sculpture: Relay, Baltimore Subway System 1984; Various Lights, with Frances Butler & Peter Reiquam, Univ. Hospital, Univ. of Washington, Seattle 1989. **Business Address:** Dept. of Architecture, 232 Wuster Hall, UC, Berkeley, CA 94720.

TRINKAUS, CHARLES ■ RAAR Post-Classical/Humanistic Studies 77. b. Oct. 25, 1911, Brooklyn, NY. m. Pauline Moffitt Watts. BA 33, Wesleyan Univ.; PhD 40, Columbia Univ. **Research/Artistic Interests:** Renaissance intellectual history. **Career & Employment:** Sarah Lawrence College 1936-70; Univ. of Michigan, Prof. 1970-82; Visiting Prof.: Long Island Univ., NYU, UCLA. **Memberships & Offices:** Columbia Univ., Seminar on the Renaissance, Life Assc. 1945-present; RSA 1955-present, Pres. 1973-76; MAA; American Soc. for Reformation Research; AHA. **Fellowships, Honors & Awards:** Wesleyan Univ., Citation for Distinction in Scholarship & Teaching 1965; ACLS Fellow 1965-66; NEH, Senior Fellow 1972-73; Guggenheim Fellowship 1976-77; AAAS, Fellow 1976-present; Univ. of Michigan, Distinguished Faculty Achievement Award 1980. **Publications:** *Adversity's Noblemen: The Humanists on Happiness* (New York: Columbia Univ. Press, 1940); "The Problem of Free Will in the Renaissance and the Reformation," *Journal of the History of Ideas* 10 (1949): 51-62; "A Humanist's Image of Humanism: The Inaugural Orations of Bartolommeo della Fonte," *Studies in the Renaissance* 7 (1960): 90-147; "Humanism" and "Humanism and Renaisance Art," *Encyclopedia of World Art* (New York: McGraw-Hill, 1959-

87), 7:702-21, 721-34; *In Our Image and Likeness: Humanity and Divinity in Italian Humanist Thought*, 2 vols. (London: Constable, & Chicago: Univ. of Chicago Press, 1970); "The Renaissance Idea of the Dignity of Man," *Dictionary of the History of Ideas* (New York: Scribner's, 1973-74), 4:136-47; ed., with Heiko A. Oberman, *The Pursuit of Holiness in Late Medieval and Renaissance Religion: Papers from the University of Michigan Conference* (Leiden: Brill, 1974); "The Religious Thought of the Italian Humanists and the Reformers: Anticipation or Autonomy," in *Pursuit of Holiness* (Leiden: Brill, 1974), 339-66; *The Poet as Philosopher: Petrarch and the Formation of Renaissance Consciousness* (New Haven: Yale Univ. Press, 1979); *The Scope of Renaissance Humanism* (Ann Arbor: Univ. of Michigan Press, 1983); "Marsilio Ficino and the Ideal of Human Autonomy," in *Marsilio Ficino e il ritorno di Plaone: Studi e documenti*, ed. Gian Carlo Garfagnini, 2 vols. (Florence: Olschki, 1986), 1:197-201; "Coluccio Salutati's Critique of Astrology in the Context of His Natural Philosophy," *Speculum* 64 (1989): 46-68; "Humanistic Dissidence: Florence versus Milan, or Poggio versus Valla," in *Florence and Milan, Comparisons and Relations*, ed. Craig Hugh Smyth & Gian Carlo Garfagnini, 2 vols. (Florence: La Nuova Italia, 1989), 1:17-44; "Lorenzo Valla's Anti-Aristotelian Natural Philosophy," *I Tatti Studies* 5 (1993); 279-325. **Bio-Bibliography:** Festschrift: *Humanity and Divinity in Renaissance and Reformation*, ed. John O'Malley et al. (Leiden: Brill, 1993); *Who's Who in America.* **Home Address:** 59 Langdon Terrace, Bronxville, NY 10708.

TRONZO, WILLIAM ■ FAAR History of Art 79. b. Mar. 6, 1951, Detroit, MI. m. Gail Feigenbaum, FAAR 80. c. Phoebe. BA 73, Haverford College; MA 74, Harvard Univ.; PhD 82, Harvard Univ. **Career & Employment:** Dumbarton Oaks Center for Byzantine Studies, Research Assc. 1982-84; American Univ., Asst. Prof. 1982-84; Johns Hopkins Univ., Asst. Prof. 1984-86, Assc. Prof. 1986-90; Bibliotheca Hertziana, Prof. 1990-91; Duke Univ., Visiting Assc. Prof. 1992-present. **Fellowships, Honors & Awards:** Harvard Univ., Fellowship 1973-75, 1975-76; Dumbarton Oaks Center for Byzantine Studies, Robert Woods Bliss Fellowship 1975-76; Univ. of Pennsylvania, Lilly-Pennsylvania Program Fellowship 1981-82; NEH Summer Stipend 1988; ACLS Grant-in-Aid 1988-89, 1991-92; IAS 1990-91; CASVA, Samuel H. Kress Senior Fellowship 1991-92. **Publications:** "Moral Hieroglyphs: Chess and Dice at San Savino in Piacenza," *Gesta* 16.2 (1977): 15-26; "The Hildesheim Doors: An Iconographic Source and Its Implications," *Zeitschrift für Kunstgeschichte* 46 (1983): 357-66; "The Prestige of St. Peters: Observations on the Function of Monumental Narrative Cycles in Italy," *Studies in the History of Art of the National Gallery of Art* 16 (1985): 93-112; "Two Icons of St. Peter (Dumbarton Oaks & British Museum): Conclusions and Questions for Further Research," exb. guide (Washington, DC: Dumbarton Oaks, 1986); *The Via Latina Catacomb: Imitation and Discontinuity in Fourth-Century Roman Painting*, CAA Monographs 38 (University Park, PA & London: Penn State Univ. Press, 1986); ed. with Irving Lavin, *Studies on Art and Archaeology Presented to Ernst Kitzinger*, Dumbarton Oaks Papers 41 (Washington, DC: Dumbarton Oaks, 1987); "Setting and Structure in Two Roman Wall Decorations of the Early Middle Ages," *Dumbarton Oaks Papers* 41 (1987): 477-92; "Between Icon and Monumental Decoration of a Church: Notes on Duccio's Maestà and the Definition of the Altarpiece," *Icon* (1988): 36-47; ed., *Italian Church Decoration of the Middle Ages and Early Renaissance: Functions, Forms and Regional Traditions*, Villa Spelman Colloquia 1 (Bologna: Nuova Alfa, 1989); "Apse Decoration, the Liturgy and the Perception of Art in Medieval Rome: S. Maria in Trastevere and S.

Maria Maggiore," in *Italian Church Decoration of the Middle Ages and Early Renaissance: Functions, Forms and Regional Traditions*, Villa Spelman Colloquia 1 (Bologna: Nuova Alfa, 1989), 167-93; "The Medieval Object-Enigma, and the Problem of the Cappella Palatina in Palermo," *Word and Image* 9 (1993): 197-228; ed., *Intellectual Life at the Court of Frederick II, Hohenstaufen*, Studies in the History of Art of the National Gallery of Art 44 (Washington, DC: NGA, 1994). **Home Address:** 332 Suffolk Rd., Baltimore, MD 21218.

TROTTER, MORRIS EARLY ■ FAAR Landscape Architecture 35. b. July 11, 1906, Charlotte, NC. d. Jan. 4, 1982. BLA 32, Cornell Univ.; MLA 33, Cornell Univ. **Career & Employment:** Landscape Architect, Planning Consultant, Washington, DC 1950s.

TROWBRIDGE, SAMUEL BRECK PARKMAN ■ AAR Charter Mem., AAR Trustee 1906-24, Architect.

TRYON, ALBERT R. ■ AAR World War II Prize 1941.

TRYTHALL, RICHARD A. ■ FAAR Musical Composition 67, RAAR Musical Composition 70; AAR Music Liaison 1974-present. b. July 25, 1939, Knoxville, TN. BMus 61, Univ. of Tennessee; MFA 63, Princeton Univ. **Other Study:** Hochschule für Musik, Berlin 1963-64; studies with Boris Blacher & Josef Rufer 1964-69; Ferienkurse für Neue Musik, Darmstadt; studies with Pierre Boulez, Karlheinz Stockhausen, Bruno Maderna, Maurizio Kagel, Gyorgy Ligeti & others. **Research/ Artistic Interests:** Composition for orchestra, chamber ensembles, piano & tape. **Career & Employment:** St. Stephen's School, Arts Dept., Chair 1966-present; SUNY, Buffalo, Creative Assc. 1972-73; UC, Davis, Faculty 1976. **Memberships & Offices:** ASCAP 1969-present; Phi Beta Kappa 1981-present; Società Italiana di Autori ed Editori 1984-present. **Fellowships, Honors & Awards:** Fulbright-Hays Fellowship Grant 1963-64; Guggenheim Fellowship 1967-68; Ferienkursen für Neue Musik, Darmstadt, Kranichsteiner Musikpreis, Piano 1969; Naumburg Found. Recording Award 1973. **Important Works:** *Penelope's Monologue*, concert aria for soprano & orchestra 1966; *Costruzione per Orchestra* 1967; *Continuums*, for orchestra, Fromm Music Found.-Tanglewood Festival Comm. 1968; *Coincidences*, for piano (Suvini Zerboni Ed., Milan) 1970; *Verse*, for slides, film & tape 1972; *Omaggio a Jerry Lee Lewis*, for stereo tape 1975; *Variations on a Theme by Franz Josef Haydn*, for woodwind quintet & tape, Dorian Woodwind Quintet Comm. 1976; *Bolero*, for 4 percussion (Hartelu Publishers) 1979; *Recital*, 12 works for piano 1981; *Ballad*, for piano & orchestra 1982; World's Fair "Festival of Entertainment" (Knoxville, TN) Comm. 1982; *Arabesque 2*, for piano 1983; *Parts Unknown*, for piano 1991. **Bio-Bibliography:** *American Keyboard Artists; ASCAP Composers; Dictionary of American Composers; World Who's Who of Musicians.* **Home Address:** Via Quattro Novembre 96, 00187 Rome, Italy.

TUCKER, RICHARD ■ AAR Visitor 1969-70, Opera Singer.

TUNNARD, CHRISTOPHER ■ AAR Visitor 1959 — 1964, City Planner.

TURNBULL, WILLIAM, JR ■ FAAR Architecture 80. b. Apr. 1, 1935, NYC. m. Mary E. Griffin. c. Ramsay, Connor, William, Andrew. BA 56, Princeton Univ.; MFA 59, Princeton Univ. **Other Study:** École des Beaux Arts de Fontainebleau 1956; Enology Extension Program UC, Davis. **Research/Artistic Interests:** Viticulture & enology. **Career & Employment:** Skidmore, Owings & Merrill, San Francisco 1960-63; Moore

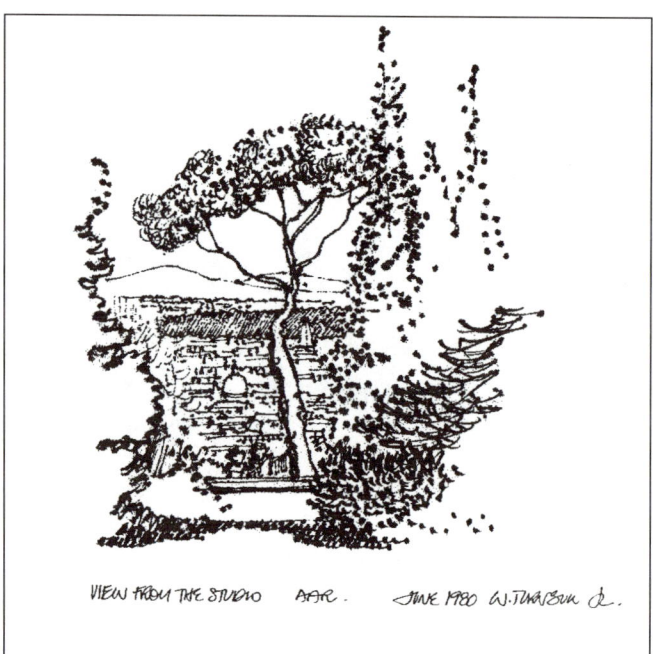

VIEW FROM THE STUDIO AFAR.   JUNE 1980 W.TURNBULL Jr.

William Turnbull, Jr.

Lyndon Turnbull Whitaker, Founding Part. 1962-65; Pres. Kennedy's Adv. Council, Design Group for Pennsylvania Ave., Washington, DC 1963; MLTW-Moore Turnbull, Part. 1965-69; UC, Berkeley, Lect. 1965-69, 1978-81; Univ. of Oregon 1967, 1968; William Turnbull Asscs., Dir. 1970-present; MIT 1976; Yale Univ., Visiting Critic 1977, Mobil Prof. 1982, Bishop Prof. 1986. **Memberships & Offices:** Citizen's Technical Adv. Com. to the California Legislative Joint Com. on Open Space Lands 1968-71; MIT, Council on the Arts 1976-80; City of Sausalito, CA, Design Review Bd. 1976-78; World Savings & Loan, Design Consultant 1976-present; Formica Corp., Design Adv. Bd., Founding Mem. 1977-84; AIA, Com. on Design 1980-85; Public Sculpture Public Places, Dir. 1981-84; AIA, Northern California Chap., Dir. 1982-83; *Architecture California*, Ed. Bd. 1987-92; UC, San Diego, Design Review Bd. 1988-93; NAD 1993-present; US State Dept., Foreign Bldg. Office, Design Adv. Bd. 1992-present. **Fellowships, Honors & Awards:** State of California, Governor's Award for Planned Communities 1966; AIA, Nat. Honor Award 1967, 1968, 1973, 1990, 1991; AIA, Bay Region Award of Merit 1967 1978, Honor Award 1978, Centennial Design Award 1982 (2); AIA, California Council, Community Design Award 1970, Honor Award 1982 (3), Firm of the Year 1986; Honor Award 1988, 1989, 1993, Merit Award 1989, 1993, Maybeck Award 1993; AIA, East Bay Award of Honor 1983, 1987 (2); AIA, San Francisco, Honor Award 1988, 1991; AIA, Redwood Empire Honor Award 1988, Merit Award 1994 (2), AIA-American Library Assn., Award of Merit 1978; *Progressive Architecture* Design Awards, Citation 1965, 1966, 1970, 1981, Honor Award 1974; *Architectural Record*, House of the Year 1972, 1973, 1983; San Francisco Art Comm., Award of Honor 1982; American Wood Council, Design Award 1984, Honor Award 1985, 1988, 1989, 1992, 1993 (2), 1994, Merit Award 1991. **Important Works:** Lovejoy Fountain, Portland OR 1964; Sea Ranch Condominium I, Sea Ranch, CA 1965; Sea Ranch Swim & Tennis Club, Sea Ranch, CA 1966; Kresge College, UC, Santa Cruz 1973; Zimmermann Residence, VA 1975; Biloxi Library, MS 1977; American Club, Hong Kong 1987; Johnson Turnbull Winery, Oakville, CA 1987; Foothill Student Housing, UC, Berkeley 1991; High Ridge Ranch,

Sonoma, CA 1991; Mountain View City Hall & Community Theater, CA 1991; St. Andrew Church, Sonoma, CA 1992. **Exhibitions/ Performances:** ALNY 1966; Oakland Museum, CA 1972; Triton Museum of Art 1976; Louisiana Museum, Denmark 1977; San Francisco Museum of Modern Art 1977; New York Inst. for Architecture & Urban Studies 1977; 1st Belgrade Triennial of World Architecture 1985; Color & Architecture 1986; Museum Boymans-Van Beuningen, Rotterdam 1986; "The Experimental Tradition, 25 Years of American Architectural Competitions" 1988; Chateau Bordeaux Exb., Pompidou Centre, Paris 1988; College of Environmental Design, UC, Berkeley 1991; William Turnbull, Jr.: A Regional Perspective, Contemporary Arts Center, Cincinnati 1992. **Bio-Bibliography:** James Shay, *New Architecture San Francisco* (1989); *William Turnbull, Jr.: A Regional Perspective*, exb. cat. (Cincinnati: Contemporary Arts Center, 1992); *Who's Who in America*. **Business Address:** William Turnbull Asscs., Pier 1 1/2, San Francisco, CA 94111.

TURNER, JAMES R. ■ FAAR Landscape Architecture 76. b. Feb. 27, 1942, Osyka, MS. m. Meriget Winans. BSLA 68, Louisiana State Univ.; MLA 70, Univ. of Michigan. **Research/ Artistic Interests:** Watercolor, native plant movement, Xeriscape, environmentally-sensitive living. **Career & Employment:** Reynolds Smith & Hills, Proj. Mgr. 1970-72, VP of Design 1990-present; Louisiana State Univ., Assc. Prof. 1972-82; Myrick, Newman Dahlberg, EDAW, others, consultant 1979-83; Richardson Verdoorn, VP 1983-87; James Turner Consulting Service, Prin. 1987-90. **Memberships & Offices:** Phi Kappa Phi 1968; ASLA, Florida Chap., Sec. 1971-72; Sigma Lamda Alpha, Founder 1974; ASLA 1978-present; Landscape Architecture Registration Bd., Louisiana, Chair 1972-74; Austin Lyric Opera, Founding BoD 1986-91; American Soc. of Architectural Perspectivists 1986-present. **Fellowships, Honors & Awards:** Fulbright Lectureship 1980; Nat. Prairie Assn., 1st Place Award 1986; New Orleans Arboretum, 1st Place Intl. Competition 1986; American Soc. of Architectural Perspectivists, Honor Award 1987; ASLA, Honor Award 1992. **Publications:** *Drawing with Confidence: A Manual for Architects, Landscape*

My studio at the Academy, the colors, the textures, the vistas, the powerful symmetry, come to me in memory as clearly as if I were there still. And in disheartening times, when caught up in the chaos of living, I find that that memory stays me, gives me direction and purpose, lets me remember who and what I have become, and be glad. What a grand thing to be part of a circle of artists and friends who have in common the nurturing guidance and encouragement of the Academy.

Because it has helped us to find our way in this world, my wife, Meriget Winans Turner, and I will leave our worldly goods to the Academy so that it may continue to enrich the lives of those who follow.

Narrativa degna di tal compenso è impensabile

James R. Turner
FAAR, 1975

James R. Turner

Architects, and Artists (New York: Van Nostrand Reinhold, 1984); *Identification, Selection and Use of Southern Plants for Landscape Design* (Claritors, 1987); as illustrator, *Earthscape: A Physical Geography*, by William M. Marsh (New York: John Wiley, 1987); *Hill Country Almanac: A Guide to Environmentally Sensitive Living* (Barton Creek, 1991). **Important Works:** Inverness Master Plan, Birmingham, AL 1970; Palm Coast Master Plan, Flagler County, FL 1971; Plaquemine Locks State Commemorative Area, Design & Historical Restoration, LA 1979; Univ. of Jordan, Master Plan 1980-81; Louisiana World Exposition Design Team 1982-84; San Jacinto Center & Four Seasons Hotel, Austin, TX 1983-85; Republic Sq. Park Master Plan, Austin 1984-86; Johnson Settlers Cabin, Historic Restoration, Bee Cave, TX 1985-86; Shield Ranch Master Plan, Bee Cave, TX 1987-89; Newfield House Garden (Xeriscape), Austin 1984-90; Leroy Melcher Jr. Plaza & Memorial Fountain, M.D. Anderson Cancer Center, Univ. of Texas, Houston 1988-89; with Penelope Hobhouse, Robinson House & Garden Historic Restoration, & New Garden, Austin 1990-92; with Penelope Hobhouse, Bass Residence, Ft. Worth 1991-92; Treaty Oak at Jessie Ball duPont Park, Jacksonville, FL 1991-95. **Exhibitions/Performances:** Solo: Hattiesburg, MS 1972; Union Gallery, Louisiana State Univ. 1976; Campus Gallery, Univ. of Texas, Arlington 1982; Group Shows: American Soc. of Architectural Perspectivists, Dallas 1987; Earth Summit Exb., Rio de Janiero, Brazil 1992. **Home Address:** 9209 Augusta Ct., Jacksonville, FL 32256.

TURPIN, WILLIAM N. ■ FAAR Classics/Archaeology 90. MA 75, Univ. of St. Andrews; MA 76, Univ. of Toronto; PhD 82, Cambridge Univ. **Other Study:** Vassar College 1971-73. **Career & Employment:** Madeira School for Girls 1981-82; Swarthmore College, Asst. Prof. 1982-89, Assc. Prof. 1989-present. **Fellowships, Honors & Awards:** Bedford College, London, Research Studentship 1979-80; Dumbarton Oaks, Jr. Fellowship 1980-81, Fellowship 1993-94; NEH Fellowship 1985-86. **Publications:** "*Apokrimata Decreta*, and the Roman Legal Procedure," *BASP* 18 (1981): 145-60; "The Law Codes and Late Roman Law," *RIDA3* 32 (1985): 339-53; "Death by Water: Horace, *Odes* 1.28," *Arethusa* 19 (1986) 79-86; "The Purpose of Law Codes in the Roman Empire," *ZRG* 104 (1987): 620-30; "*Adnotatio* and Imperial Rescript in Roman Legal Procedure," *RIDA3* 35 (1988); "Imperial Subscriptions and the Administration of Justice," *JRS* 81 (1991): 101-18. **Home Address:** 404 Elm Ave., Swarthmore, PA 19081. **Business Address:** Swarthmore College, Swarthmore, PA 19081.

TUTTLE, DAN ■ FAAR Landscape Architecture 88. b. Oct. 16, 1953, El Paso, TX. BFA 84, RISD; BLA 85, RISD. **Other Study:** Apprentice-Journeyman Saddler: Norton Holster & Saddle Co. Hamilton, MA & Grand Junction, CO 1973-78. **Career & Employment:** SWA Group, Designer 1985-87, Prin. 1989-present; Carr, Lynch, Hack & Sandell, Designer 1988-89; California College of Arts & Crafts, Adj. Prof. 1990-present. **Important Works:** La Città d'Este, Venice Biennale 1985; Playa Vista Master Plan, Los Angeles 1986; Huntington Memorial Hospital, Master Plan & Design, Pasadena 1986; Proposal for Piazza Venezia & il Vittoriano, Rome 1987; Marin City Master Plan & Design, Marin County, CA 1988-94; Pers-Stein Garden, Oakland, CA 1992; Kadivar House, Palo Alto 1992; Copas-Holland House, Oakland, CA 1993; Barclay Simpson Sculpture Studio, C.C.A.C., Oakland, CA 1993; Becker House, Oakland, CA 1993; Bischoff House, Oakland, CA 1993; Silicon Graphics, Shoreline Entry Site, Mountain View, CA 1994; Silicon Graphics, Farmer's Field Site, Mountain View, CA

1995. **Bio-Bibliography:** *Catalogue of the Venice Biennale of Architecture* (1985); "The SWA Group," *Process Architecture* (1989). **Home Address:** 31 Natick St., San Francisco, CA 94131.

TUTTLE, J.D. ■ Plym Fellow 1924-25, 1925-26.

TWOMBLY, CY ■ AAR Visitor 1980-81, Artist.

TWORKOV, JACK ■ RAAR Painting 73; AAR Trustee 1973-76. b. Aug. 15, 1900, Biala, Poland. d. Sept. 4, 1982. m. Helen, Hermine. **Study:** Columbia Univ. 1920-23; NAD 1923-25 with Ivan Olinsky, C.W. Hawthorne; with Ross Moffett 1924-25; ASL 1925-26 with Guy Pene Du Bois, Boardman Robinson. **Career & Employment:** Fieldston School, NYC 1931; WPA 1935-41; American Univ. 1948-51; Black Mountain College, Summer 1952; Univ. of Indiana, Summers 1954-55; Univ. of Mississippi 1954; Pratt Inst. 1955-58; Yale Univ., Visiting Artist 1962, Dept. Chair 1963-69, William Leffingwell Prof. Emer.; Cooper Union 1970-71; Dartmouth College 1973; Columbia Univ. 1973; Royal College of Art, London 1974. **Memberships & Offices:** Century Assn.; AAAL. **Fellowships, Honors & Awards:** Corcoran Gallery, Gold Medal-William L. Clark Prize 1963; Guggenheim Fellowship 1970; Maryland Inst. of Art, Hon. DFA 1971; Columbia Univ., Hon. LHD 72; Skowhegan School, Painting Award 1973; RISD, Hon. DFA 1979. **Important Works:** Marine Hospital, Carville, IA; Collections: AAAL; Allentown Art Museum; Amerada-Hess Corp, NYC; American Univ.; Brooklyn Museum; Albright, Baltimore; Albright, Buffalo; UC, Santa Barbara; Cleveland Museum of Art; Dartmouth College; Denison Univ.; Detroit Inst. of Art; Storm King Art Center; Chase Manhattan Bank, NYC; MOMA; MMA; NGA; RISD; Whitney Museum, NYC; Walker Art Center; Yale Univ. **Exhibitions/Performances:** Selected Solo: UC, Santa Barbara 1977; Baum-Silverman Gallery, Los Angeles 1979; RISD 1980; Middlebury College 1981; AAAL 1983; Provincetown Art Assn. 1983; Nancy Hoffman Gallery, NYC 1983; Adams Middleton Gallery, Houston 1985; PAFA 1986-87; Retrospective: Whitney Museum, NYC 1964; Retrospectives: Third Eye Center, Glasgow 1979; PAFA 1987; André Emmerich Gallery, NYC 1991. **Bio-Bibliography:** Edward Bryant, *Jack Tworkov*, exb. cat. (New York: Whitney Museum of Art, 1964); Andrew Forge, *Jack Tworkov: Fifteen Years of Painting*, exb. cat. (New York: Solomon R. Guggenheim Found., 1982); Richard Armstrong, *Jack Tworkov: Paintings, 1928-82*, exb. cat. (Philadelphia: PAFA, 1987); *Jack Tworkov: Paintings from 1930 to 1981*, exb. cat. (New York: André Emmerich Gallery, 1991; *Dictionary of Contemporary Artists*; *Who Was Who in America*; *Who Was Who in American Art*.

■ ■ ■

U

UCKMAR, VICTOR ■ AAR Italian Com. 1994-present.

UGGERI, GIOVANNI ■ Italian Fulbright Fellow 1965-66.

UHLFELDER, MYRA L. ■ FAAR Classics/Archaeology 50. b. Sept. 16, 1923, Cincinnati, OH. BA 45, Univ. of Cincinnati; MA 46, Univ. of Cincinnati. **Other Studies:** Bryn Mawr College. **Career & Employment:** Univ. of Iowa, Faculty; Sweet Briar College, Faculty. **Fellowships, Honors & Awards:** Univ. of Cincinnati, Taft Teaching Scholarship 1946-47; Bryn Mawr College, Fellowship 1947-48.

ULLMAN, B.L. ■ AAR Classical Soc., Pres. 1940.

ULRICH, ROGER B. ■ FAAR Classics/Archaeology 82. b. Mar. 2, 1955, Norwalk, CT. m. Imogen A. Mason. c. Emily Ulrich, Thea Ulrich. BA 77, Dartmouth College; MA 79, Yale Univ.; PhD 84, Yale Univ. **Other Study:** Archaeological field work: Aghios Stephanos, Laconia; Forum of Caesar, Rome; Via Gabina, Rome; Gigthis & Sbeitla, Tunisia. **Career & Employment:** Rice University, Asst. Prof. 1984-89; Dartmouth College, Asst. Prof. 1989-present. **Memberships & Offices:** ArIA, Houston Chap., Pres. 1988-89; CANE. **Fellowships, Honors & Awards:** Yale University Research Fellowships 1979-81; Fulbright-Hays Scholar 1981-82; M. Aylwin Cotton Found. Fellowship 1986-87; NEH Summer Seminar 1987, Individual Grant 1988-89. **Publications:** "The Rostrum and the Fountain of the Temple of Venus Genetrix in the Forum of Caesar," *AJA* 90 (1986): 190; "The Appiades Fountain in the Forum of Caesar in Rome," *Römische Mitteilungen* 96 (1986): 309-23; "Imperial Oratory and the Roman Templum-Rostratum," *AJA* 91 (1987): 283-84; "The Many Faces of Venus Genetrix, *AJA* 94 (1990): 312; "Julius Caesar and the Creation of the Forum Iulium," *AJA* 97 (1993): 49-80; *The Roman Orator and the Sacred Stage* (Brussels: Latomus, 1994); "Archaeological Reference Texts and the Information Age," *AJA* 99 (1995): 147-50. **Home Address:** PO Box 639, Wilder, VT 05088. **Business Address:** Dept. of Classics, 311 Reed Hall, Dartmouth College, Hanover, NH 03755.

V

VACCARO, MARY ■ FAAR History of Art 92. b. Nov. 12, 1964, Brooklyn, NY. BA 86, Williams College; MA 88, Columbia Univ.; PhD 94, Columbia Univ. **Other Study:** Italian Renaissance art. **Career & Employment:** Piero Corsini Art Gallery, Intern 1986-90; Columbia Univ., Preceptor 1989-90; Univ. of Texas, Arlington, 1994-present. **Fellowships, Honors & Awards:** Cornell Univ, Telluride Assn. 1981; Williams College, Tyng Fellow 1982-86; Columbia Univ. Fellowship 1986-90, President's Fellow 1992-93; Fulbright Fellow 1990-91; MMA, Whitney Fellow 1993-94. **Publications:** "Documents for Parmigianino's 'Vision of St. Jerome,'" *Burlington Magazine* 125 (1993): 22-27. **Business Address:** Art Dept., Univ. of Texas, Box 19089, Arlington, TX 76019.

VALENTINE, ALAN & LUCIA ■ AAR Visitors 1959 — 1964. Authors of *The American Academy in Rome 1894-1969* (Univ. of Virginia).

VALENTINO, PAUL ■ GI Resident 1945-47, Painter.

VALERIO, WILLIAM R. ■ FAAR History of Art 91. BA 85, Williams College; MA 87, Univ. of Pennsylvania; PhD 94, Yale Univ. **Other Study:** Syracuse Univ., Florence Program 1983-84. **Fellowships, Honors & Awards:** Yale Univ. Fellowship 1987-1988, 1989-90; Paul C. Ginigliat Fellowship 1988-1989; Josef Albers Grant, Travel Award 1989; Fondazione Roberto Longhi, Florence, Borsa di Studio 1991-92; Mellon Found. Grant 1992-93. **Publications:** "The Futurist State of Mind," *Art in America* 76.12 (Dec. 1988): 126-31; *Umberto Boccioni: The Graphic Works*, exb. cat. (New Haven: Yale Univ. Art Gallery, 1988); "The Villino Bellacci in Rome," *Architectural Digest* (Jan. 1993); "Primal Scene in Italian Futurism," in *Sexuality in the Painting and Theory of the Avant-Garde, Around 1910*, ed. S. Deicher (Limborg: Rijksuniversiteit Press, 1993). **Home Address:** 112 Franklin St., NYC 10013.

VALLAURI GALLUPPI, GIOVANNA ■ Italian Fulbright Fellow 1959-60.

VAN BUREN, ALBERT WILLIAM ■ FASCSR 1906; ASCSR, Librarian 1908-13; Lect. 1908-11; AAR Librarian 1913-26; Assc. Prof. of Archaeology 1911-23; Prof. 1923-46; Ed.-in-Chief, Curator of AAR Museum 1926-1946; Juridicial Custodian of Library, WWII; AAR Gold Medal 1962. b. Feb. 17, 1878, Milford, CT. d. Feb. 4, 1968. m. Elizabeth Douglas. BA 1900, Yale Univ.; PhD 15, Yale Univ. **Career & Employment:** Yale Univ., Instr. 1906-8. **Fellowships, Honors & Awards:** Royal Numismatic Soc., London, Fellow; Soc. for the Promotion of Hellenic Studies; German Archaeological Inst.; Pontificia Accademia Romana di Archeologia; Virtuosi del Pantheon, Hon. Mem.; Keats-Shelley Memorial Com., Rome. **Publications:** "Inscription of the Charioteer Menander," *AJA* 11 (1907): 179-81; *The Palimpsest of Cicero's* De Republica, Supplementary Papers of the ASCSR 2 (New York, 1908); "Inscriptions from Rome," *AJA* 16 (1912): 97; "The Geography of Ancient Italy," *Classical Journal* 8 (1912-13): 286-92, 327-40; "The Ara Pacis Augustae," *Journal of Roman Studies* 3 (1913): 134-41; "Studies in the Archaeology of the Forum at Pompei," *Memoirs of the AAR* 2 (1918): 67-76; "Further Studies in Pompeian Archaeology," *Memoirs of the AAR* 5 (1925): 103-13; "Epigraphical Salvage from Pompeii," *American Journal of Philology* 47 (1926): 177-79; Annual "News Items from Rome," *AJA* 30-46 (1926-42); compiler with Sir James George Frazer, *Graecia Antiqua, Maps and Plans to Illustrate Pausanias's Description of Greece* (London: Macmillan, 1930); "Antiquities of the Janiculum," *Memoirs of the AAR* 11 (1933): 69-79; *Ancient Rome as Revealed by Recent Discoveries* (London: L. Dickson, 1936); "Pinocothecae, with Special Reference to Pompeii," *Memoirs of AAR* 15 (1938): 70-81; *A Companion to the Study of Pompeii and Herculaneum* (Rome: AAR, 1938); "Laurentinum Plinii Minoris (Ep. II, 17)," *Rendiconti della Pontificia Accademia Romana di Archeologia* 20 (1944): 166-192; Annual "News from Italy," *AJA* 52-56 (1948-52); *A Bibliographical Guide to Latium and Southern Etruria*, 5th ed. (Rome: AAR, 1953); Annual "News Letter from Rome," *AJA* 57-70 (1953-70); "Alcune osservazioni riguardanti materiale pompeiano," *Rendiconti della Pontificia Accademia Romana di Archeologia* 28 (1956): 31-43. **Bio-Bibliography:** Frank E. Brown, "Albert William Van Buren," *Rendiconti della Pontificia Accademia Romana di Archeologia* 42 (1969-70): 31-36; *Who Was Who in America*.

VAN DEMAN, ESTHER BOISE ■ FASCSR 1909. b. Oct. 1, 1862, S. Salem, OH. d. May 3, 1937. BA 1891, Univ. of Michigan; MA 1892, Univ. of Michigan; PhD 1898, Univ. of Chicago. **Other Study:** ASCSR 1901-3. **Career & Employment:** Wellesley College, Instr. 1893-95; Bryn Mawr School, Baltimore, Teacher 1895-96; Mt. Holyoke College, Assc. Prof. 1898-1901; Goucher College, Assc. Prof. 1903-6; Carnegie Inst., Washington, DC, Assc. 1910-25; Univ. of Michigan, Carnegie Research Prof. 1925-30. **Fellowships, Honors & Awards:** Bryn Mawr College, Fellow 1892-93; Univ. of Chicago, Fellow 1896-98; Carnegie Fellow 1906-10; ArIA, Charles Eliot Norton Lect. 1926; Univ. of Michigan., Hon. LLD 1936. **Publications:** "The Value of the Vestal Statues as Originals," *AJA* 12 (1908): 324-42; Notes on a Few Vestal Inscriptions," *American Journal of Philology* 39 (1908): 171-78; *The Atrium Vestae* (Washington, DC: Carnegie Inst., 1909); "The So-Called Flavian Rostra," *AJA* 13 (1909): 170-86; "Methods of Determining the Date of Roman Concrete Monuments," *AJA* 16 (1912): 230-51, 387-427; "The Porticus of Gaius et Lucius," *AJA* 27 (1913): 14-28; "The Sullan Forum," *Journal of Roman Studies* 12 (1922): 383-424; "The Neronian Sacra Via," *AJA* 27 (1923): 383-424; "The House of Caligula," *AJA* 38 (1924): 368-98; "The Sacra Via di Nero," *Memoirs of the AAR* 5 (1925): 115-26; *The Building of the Roman Aqueducts* (Washington, DC: Carnegie Inst., 1934). **Bio-Bibliography:** Marion E. Blake, "Esther Van Deman," *Dictionary of American Biography* 22 (1958): 676-77; Lucy Shoe Meritt, "Van Deman, Esther Boise," *Notable American Women* 3 (1971): 507-8; Karin Einaudi, "Esther Boise Van Deman: Una archeologa americana," in *L'Archeologia in Roma: Capitale tra Sterro e Scavo* (Venice, 1983), 41-47; Karin Einaudi, "E. Van Deman and the Roman Forum," *Places* 3 (1988): 62-70; Karin Einaudi & Katherine A. Geffcken, *Esther B. Van Deman: Images from the Archive of an American Archaeologist in Italy at the Turn of the Century,* exb. cat. (Rome: AAR, 1991); Karen Einaudi, "E. Van Deman, collaboratione e corrispondenza con Thomas Ashby," *Atti del Convegno "Il Trionfo dell'Acqua"* (Rome, 1992), 21-34; *Who Was Who in America.*

VAN EYCK, ALDO ■ RAAR Architecture 66. b. 1918. **Bio-Bibliography:** *Contemporary Architects; Macmillan Encyclopedia of Architects; Who's Who in America.*

VAN HOESEN, HENRY BARTLETT ■ FASCSR 1908. b. Dec. 25, 1885, Truxton, NY. d. Jan. 6 1965. m. Ruth Sarah Hutchinson. c. Alice Lura, Martha Corrin, Drusilla Ruth. BA 05, Hobart College; MA 06, Princeton Univ.; PhD 12, Princeton Univ. **Other Studies:** Univ. of Munich 1908-9. **Career & Employment:** Princeton Univ., Instr. 1909-11, Rare Books Curator 1915-16, Asst. Librarian 1916-29; Western Reserve Univ., Instr. 1912-15; Brown Univ., Assc. Librarian 1929-30, Librarian 1930-49, John Hay Prof. 1930-49; Univ. of Chicago, Graduate Library, Instr. 1929-31. **Memberships & Offices:** Princeton Public Library, BoT 1920-28; American Library Assn.; APA; ArIA; MAA; Bibliographical Soc. of America, Sec. 1933-40; American Library Inst., Pres. 1934-36; Abraham Lincoln Assn.; Rhode Island Historical Soc.; Rhode Island Library Assn. **Fellowships, Honors & Awards:** Hobart College, Hon. LittD 1934; Phi Beta Kappa; Phi Phi Delta. **Publications:** *Roman Cursive Writing* (Princeton: Princeton Univ. Press, 1915); *Bibliography, Practical, Enumerative and Historical* (New York: Scribner's, 1928); ed., *Selective Cataloguing* (New York: H.W. Wilson, 1928); with A.C. Johnson, *Papyri in the Princeton University Collections* (Providence, 1931); *Brown University Library 1765-82* (Providence, 1939); with Otto Neugebauer, *Greek Horoscopes,* APS Memoirs 48 (Philadelphia: APS, 1959). **Bio-Bibliography:** *Who's Who in Library Services,* 3d ed. (New York: Grolier Soc, 1955); *NY Times,* Obit. (Jan. 7, 1965); *Dictionary of*

American Library Biography, ed. B.S. Wynar (Littleton, CO: Libraries Unlimited, 1978); *Who Was Who in America.*

VAN SICKLE, JOHN B. ■ AAR Classical Soc., Pres. 1981, 1982. b. Sept. 30, 1936, Freeport, IL. m. Gail Levin. BA 58, Harvard College; MA 59, Univ. of Illinois; PhD 66, Harvard Univ. **Career & Employment:** Brooklyn College, CUNY, Assc. Prof. 1976-78, Prof. 1979-present. **Home Address:** 85 Woodbine Dr., E. Hampton, NY 11937. **Business Address:** Dept. of Classics, Brooklyn College, Brooklyn, NY 11210.

EVER SINCE 1958
Some American Academy Vignettes

Steele Commager bemused over burnt toast at breakfast around the long tables set up in the courtyard.

Niccola (the old driver) telling me that the Fiat 600 I had bought from Charles Segal was *una macchina sfruttata.*

Michael Putnam arriving like Castor and Pollux rolled into one, insisting that I move from *fuori Piazza del Popolo* and get to know the *Campo de'Fiori* and environs.

Frank Brown at Cosa making my students from the Intercollegiate Center see and feel how the Roman surveyors had taken sightings out to landmarks on the horizons and how the colonists had marched up, each with his bit of turf from home to cast into the founding pit on the new site.

Larry Richardson, for another group of *Centro* students, populating an *atrium* in Pompeii with the throng of clients arriving early to greet their patron, reading the austere stones back and up into their original social frame.

Henry Rowell, his last spring in Rome, generous with praise after a shop talk that suggested a new way of linking Virgil and Theocritus; or again, over cocktails in high ceilinged rooms, quoting with gusto famous lines from Virgil's *Georgics.*

Spring lawns dense with little white flowers. Purple branches in the early sunlight out the kitchen window and the curve of Castel Sant'Angelo down beyond. Suddenly crisp air and fresh snow, visible as it always used to be up behind Tivoli on the hills.

J. Van Sickle 30/09/93

John B. Van Sickle

VAN VALKENBURGH, MICHAEL R. ■ FAAR Landscape Architecture 88. b. Sept. 5, 1951. m. Carol Doyle. c. Sibyl Alexander. BS 73, Cornell Univ.; MLArch 77, Univ. of Illinois. **Career & Employment:** Moriece & Gary, Inc. 1973-75; Univ. of Illinois, Urbana-Champaign, Instr. 1975-77; Carol R. Johnson & Asscs., Inc. 1977-79; RISD, Visiting Critic 1978-79; Carr, Lynch Asscs., Inc., Consulting Assc. 1979-84; Radcliffe Seminars in Landscape Architecture, Instr. 1979-83; Michael Van Valkenburgh, Landscape Architect 1979-; Harvard GSD, Asst. Prof. 1982-85, Assc. Prof. 1985-1991, Chair 1991-. **Memberships & Offices:** ASLA; Council of Educators of Landscape Architects. **Fellowships, Honors & Awards:** Dumbarton Oaks Summer Garden Fellowship 1973; Environmental Design Research Assn. Conference, 1st Award 1978; ASLA Design Merit Award 1983, 1985, Design Communication Award 1986; Graham Found. Award 1984, 1985; NEA Fellowship 1985, Design Exploration Grant 1986. **Publications:** "Garden Spot for Half a House," *Landscape Architecture* (Mar. 1981); "Notating Nature's Process," *Landscape Architecture* (Jan. 1983); "Planting Design," *Garden Design Book,* ed. Norman Johnson (New York: Simon & Schuster, 1984); with Douglas Lake, Susan Frey, et al., *Garden Design* (New York: Simon & Schuster, 1985); "Two Views of Landscape Design: A.E. Bye and Dan Kiley," *Orion Quarterly* (Spring 1985). **Bio-Bibliography:** Jory Johnson, "P/A Profile Michael Van Valkenburgh," *Progressive Architecture* (July 1989); Paula Deitz, "Landscapes that Recall Simplicity," *NY Times.*

VANDERBILT, WILLIAM KISSAM ■ AAR Founder; Capitalist. b. Dec. 12, 1849. d. July 22, 1920. **Career & Employment:** Dir. of many railroads, including the New York Central Rail Road. **Memberships & Offices:** Metropolitan Opera Co., Dir. Generous supporter of the Academy.

VARNEY, RALPH W. ■ Appleton Fellow 1911-12, 1913.

VASALY, ANN C. ■ FAAR Classics/Archaeology 83. b. Mar. 14, 1949, Minneapolis, MN. m. Richard A. Young. BA 72, Univ. of Minnesota; MA 75, Univ. of Minnesota; PhD 83, Indiana Univ. **Research/Artistic Interests:** Latin literature, Roman topography, ancient rhetoric, Cicero. **Career & Employment:** Boston Univ., Asst. Prof. 1983-present. **Fellowships, Honors & Awards:** Fulbright Grant 1982-83; Alexander von Humboldt Fellowship 1988; Boston Univ., Research Grant 1984, Humanities Found. Junior Fellow 1986-87. **Publications:** "Transforming the Visible," *Res* 16 (1983): 65-71; "The Masks of Rhetoric: Cicero's *Pro Roscio Amerino*," *Rhetorica* 3 (1985): 1-20; "Personality and Power: Livy's Depiction of the Appii Claudii in the First Pentad," *TAPA* 117 (1987): 203-26; "*Ars Dispositionis*: Cicero's Second Speech Against Rullus," *Hermes* 116 (1988): 409-27; *Representations: Images of the World of Ciceronian Oratory* (Berkeley: UC Press, 1993). **Home Address:** 117 Beach St., Quincy, MA 02170. **Business Address:** Classics Dept., Boston Univ., 745 Commonwealth Ave., Boston, MA 02215.

VAUGHN, JOHN WILLIAM ■ FAAR Classics/Archaeology 74. b. Jan. 11, 1947, Hackensack, NJ. d. Nov. 28, 1989. c. John, Corinna. BA 69, St. Peter's College; PhD 73, Johns Hopkins Univ. **Research/Artistic Interests:** The language of Theocritus, Greek dialects, Greek philology. **Career & Employment:** Johns Hopkins Univ., Teaching Asst. 1970-72; Ohio State Univ., Prof. c.1974. **Fellowships, Honors & Awards:** Johns Hopkins Univ., Woodrow Wilson Fellowship 1972-73. **Publications:** *The Megara (Moschus IV)* (Bern: P. Haupt, 1976).

VAUGHN, W.S. ■ Appleton Fellow 1923-24, 1924-25.

VECCHI, GIUSEPPE ■ Italian Fulbright Fellow 1954-55.

VELLECO, JAMES A. ■ FAAR Design Arts 77. b. June 26, 1944, RI. m. Linda Velleco. c. Anthony. BArch 67, Univ. of Notre Dame. **Other Studies:** Fontainebleau School of Fine Arts 1966. **Career & Employment:** Detroit Planning Comm., Design Staff 1967-69; Stull Asscs., Assc. 1969-; Grazado-Velleco Architects, Part. 1974-; Harvard GSD, Guest Critic 1975. **Fellowships, Honors & Awards:** Portland Inst., Traveling Scholar 1966; *Progressive Architecture* Design Award 1971; AIA, New England Chap. Award of Merit 1972, Housing Design Award 1973; Boston Soc. of Architects, Annual Design Award 1975.

VENTSCH, LESLIE ■ Chicago Architectural Club, Burnham Prize 1986-87.

VENTURI, ROBERT ■ FAAR Architecture 56, RAAR Architecture 66; AAR Trustee 1969-76, Trustee Emer. b. June 25, 1925, Philadelphia, PA. m. Denise Scott Brown. c. James. BA 47, Princeton Univ.; MFA 50, Princeton Univ. **Career & Employment:** Oskar Stonorov, Designer 1950-51; Eero Saarinen & Asscs., Designer 1951-53; Louis I. Kahn, Designer 1957; Univ. of Pennsylvania, Instr.-Assc. Prof. 1957-65; Venturi, Cope & Lippincott, Prin. 1958-61; Venturi & Short, Prin. 1961-64; Venturi & Rauch, Prin. 1964-80; UCLA, School of Architecture & Urban Planning, Panel of Visitors 1966-67; Yale Univ., Char-

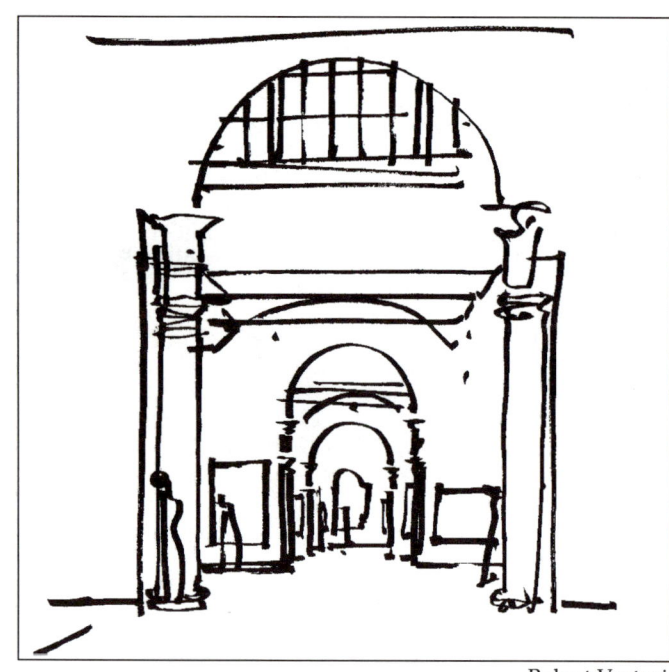
Robert Venturi

lotte Shepherd Davenport Prof. 1966-70, Eero Saarinen Visiting Prof. 1986-87; Rice Univ., Visiting Critic 1969; Princeton Univ., Bd. of Adv. 1977-81; Venturi, Rauch & Scott Brown, Prin. 1980-89; Harvard GSD, Walter Gropius Lect. 1982; Venturi, Scott Brown & Asscs., Prin. 1989-present. **Memberships & Offices:** Old Philadelphia Development Corp., BoT 1983-85; Nat. Bldg. Museum, Washington, DC, BoT 1983-87; Sir John Soane's Museum Found., Adv. BoD 1994. **Fellowships, Honors & Awards:** AIA, Fellow; Accademia Nazionale di San Luca, Fellow; Royal Incorporation of Architects in Scotland, Hon. Fellow; AAAS, Fellow; AAAL; US State Dept. Grant 1965; Arnold W. Brunner Memorial Prize 1973; Oberlin College, Hon. DFA 1977; Yale Univ., Hon. DFA 1979; Univ. of Pennsylvania, Hon. DFA 1980; Univ. of Virginia, Thomas Jefferson Memorial Found. Medal 1983; Princeton Univ., Hon. DFA 1983, James Madison Medal 1985; Republic of Italy, Commendatore of the Order of Merit 1986; ALNY, President's Medal 1986; UNC, Chapel Hill, LittD 1989; Hyatt Found., Pritzker Architecture Prize 1991; Architectural Assn., London, Reyner Banham Award 1991; Nat. Medal of Arts, US Presidential Award 1992; Bard College, Hon. Doctor of Arts 1993; Royal Soc. for the Encouragement of Arts, Manufactures & Commerce, Benjamin Franklin Medal 1993; Univ. of Roma, "La Sapienza," Laurae honoris causa in Architettura 1994; Royal Inst. of British Architects, Hon. Fellow. **Publications:** *Complexity and Contradiction in Architecture* (New York: MOMA, 1966); *Learning from Las Vegas,* with Denise Scott Brown & Steven Izenour (Cambridge, MA: MIT Press, 1972); "The Annual RIBA Discourse, July 1981," *Transactions* 1 (May 1982): 47-56; "Diversity, Relevance and Representation in Historicism, or *Plus ça Change*," *Architectural Record* (June 1982): 114-19; with Denise Scott Brown, *A View from the Campidoglio: Selected Essays, 1953-1984* (New York: Harper & Row, 1984); "From Invention to Convention in Architecture," *Royal Society of Arts Journal* (Jan. 1988); "Architecture as Elemental Shelter, the City as Valid Decon," *New Museums, Architectural Design Profile* 94 (London: Academy Group Ltd., 1991); numerous articles in periodicals. **Important Works:** Vanna Venturi House, Philadelphia 1961; Guild House, Philadelphia 1961;

Fire Station No. 4, Columbus, IN 1966; Allen Memorial Art Museum, Addition & Renovation, Oberlin, OH 1973; Furniture, Knoll Intl., NYC 1979; Princeton Univ., Gordon Wu Hall 1980; Seattle Art Museum 1984; with Payette Asscs., Univ. of Pennsylvania, Clinical Research Bldg. 1985; with Payette Asscs., UCLA, Gordon & Virginia MacDonald Medical Research Laboratories 1986; Princeton Univ., Fisher-Bendheim Halls 1986; Nat. Gallery, Sainsbury Wing, London 1986; Harvard Univ., Memorial Hall 1992; Regional Government Bldg., Toulouse, France 1992; Kirifuri Resort Facilities, Nikko, Japan 1992. **Exhibitions/Performances:** ALNY 1965, 1991; Whitney Museum, NYC 1971; "Roma Interotta," Incontri Internazionali d'Arte, Rome 1977-78; Kunstgewerkemuseum, Zurich & traveling 1979-81; Max Protetch Gallery, NYC 1982; Triennale di Milano, Italy 1985; Design Center, Stuttgart 1985; Pennsylvania Governor's Residence, Harrisburg 1987; Galleria di Architettura, Venice 1988; Knoll Showroom, Tokyo 1991; Nat. Museum of Modern Art, Kyoto, Japan 1991; Hokkoku Shimbun Art Forum, Kanazawa, Japan 1991; Museum of Contemporary Art, Sapporo, Japan 1991. **Bio-Bibliography:** Stanislaus Van Moos, *Venturi, Rauch & Scott Brown: Buildings and Project* (New York: Rizzoli, 1987); ed., Christopher Mead, *The Architecture of Robert Venturi* (Albuquerque: Univ. of New Mexico Press, 1989); Kenjiro Takagaki, Akira Sawamura & Nakihiro Maruyama, *Architecture and Decorative Arts: Two Naifs in Japan* (Tokyo: Kajima Inst. Publishing Co., 1991); Carolina Vaccaro & Frederic Schwartz, *Venturi, Scott Brown e Associati* (Bologna: Zanichelli Editore, 1991); Amadeo Belluzzi, *Venturi, Scott Brown e Associati* (Bari: Editori Laterza, 1992); Frederic Schwartz, *Mother's House: The Evolution of Vanna Venturi's House in Chestnut Hill* (New York: Rizzoli Intl., 1992); *Contemporary Architects; International Who's Who; Who's Who; Who's Who in America.* **Business Address:** Venturi, Scott Brown & Asscs., Inc., 4236 Main St., Philadelphia, PA 19127.

VERGASON, E. MICHAEL ■ FAAR Landscape Architecture 80; Jury Chair 1990. b. June 1, 1950, Richmond, VA. m. Sandi A. Chesrown. BSArch 72, Univ. of Virginia; MLArch 77, Univ. of Virginia. **Research/Artistic Interests:** Drawing,

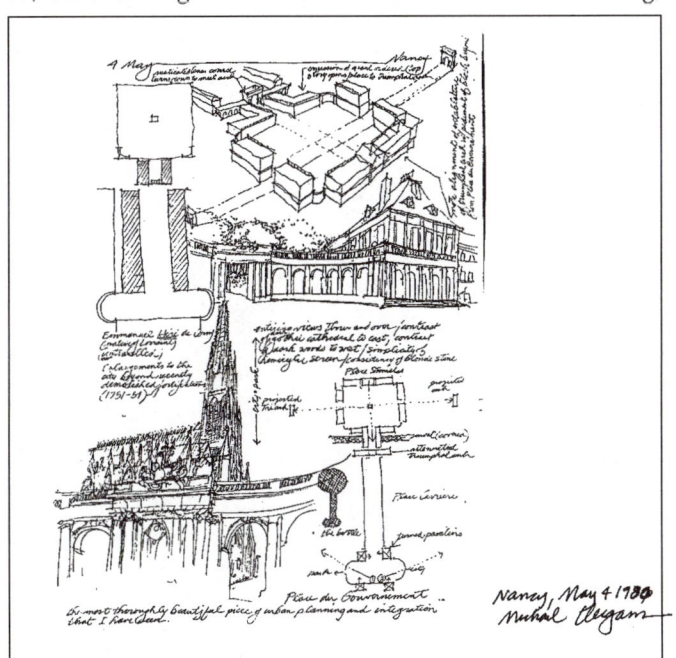

E. Michael Vergason

watercolor. **Memberships & Offices:** Dumbarton Oaks, Roundtable Lect. 1992; *LA Magazine*, Residential Design Awards Juror 1993. **Career & Employment:** Carol R. Johnson, & Asscs., Landscape Architect 1978-79; EDAW, Inc., Landscape Architects & Planners, Prin. 1980-87; Michael Vergason Landscape Architects, Prin. 1987-present. **Fellowships, Honors & Awards:** Vietnam Veterans Memorial, 3rd Place. **Important Works:** American Assn. for the Advancement of Science, Washington, DC; NIH Master Plan, Bethesda, MD; Huntsville Golf Course Club House, Huntsville, PA; Columbus School of Law, Catholic Univ., Washington, DC; Ft. Worth Childrens Medical Center; Ericsson Center, Ericsson Management Inc. & Gerald Hines Interests, Dallas; Intl. Trade Center, Barcelona, Spain; Master Plan for Kourion & Kouklia Archaeological Sites, Nicosia, Cyprus; St. Mary's College Master Plan, St. Mary's College, MD; IBM Rockspring, Bethesda, MD; George Washington Univ., Amenities Master Plan, Hospital; Virginia Polytechnic Inst., South Campus Master Plan, Blacksburg, VA. **Exhibitions/Performances:** PADC, Catholic Univ., Franklin Sq., & Fendrick Gallery, Washington, DC; Phillipe Bonaronte Gallery, San Francisco; Arlington Arts Center, Arlington, VA; George Mason Univ.; Harvard Univ. **Home Address:** 4517 16 St., N. Arlington, VA 22207. **Business Address:** Michael Vergason Landscape Architecture, 4517 16 St., N. Arlington, VA 22207.

VIDAL, GORE ■ AAR Visitor 1977-78, 1994, Writer. b. Oct. 3, 1925. **Honors & Awards:** Nat. Book Critics' Circle Award 1982. **Publications:** *Burr* (1973); *Lincoln* (1984); *Empire* (1987).

VINCIGUERRA, ALESSANDRA ■ AAR – Rome, Superintendent of Grounds.

VINYARD, WILLIAM K. ■ FAAR Architecture 90. b. May 6, 1961, Portland, OR. BS 84, Portland State Univ.; MArch 88, Yale Univ. **Other Study:** Univ. of Oregon, Eugene, Music Performance 1978-81; Univ. of Virginia 1984. **Career & Employment:** Allan Greenberg, Architect, Designer 1983-84; Cesar Pelli & Asscs., Architects, Designer 1984-89; Univ. of Texas, Austin, Asst. Prof. 1990-93; William K. Vinyard, Architect, Prin. 1990-present; Kohn Pederson Fox Asscs., Senior Designer 1993-present. **Home Address:** 81 Irving Pl., Apt. 9F, NYC 10003.

VITALE, FERRUCCIO ■ AAR Trustee 1920-33, Landscape Architect.

VITI, PAOLO ■ AAR Italian Com. 1994-present.

VITOLS, AUSTRIS J. ■ FAAR Architecture 65. b. July 12, 1940, Valmiera, Latvia. m. Gundega A. Vitols. c. Mara, Andris. BArch 63, Univ. of Minnesota; MArch 65, MIT. **Career & Employment:** Leonard Parker, Architect 1962-64; Belluschi-Catalano, Architects 1964-65; Brown-Daltas Architects 1966-68; Eduardo Catalano, Architect 1968-71; Frank L. Hope & Asscs. 1971-86; Austris Vitols 1986-present. **Memberships & Offices:** AIA 1971-present; Boston Architectural Center, Juror 1970; UC, Berkeley, Visiting Critic & Lect. 1975. **Fellowships, Honors & Awards:** Univ. of Minnestoa, Intl. Milling Co. Scholarship 1959, Minnegasco Prize 1962, Knudson Realty Co. Prize 1962, Chemstrand Corp. Prize 1962, Best Thesis 1963, Ellerbe Co. Prize 1963; MIT, Best Thesis 1965, Whitney Fellowship 1965; *Progressive Architecture* Design Award 1971; City of Palo Alto Design Award 1974; GSA Design Award 1975, 1978; AIA, ACA Design Award 1975, 1982, 1986, San Diego

Chap. Award 1976, San Francisco Chap. Design Citation 1977, San Luis Obispo Chap. Award 1983; Precast Concrete Inst. Award 1978; Rancho Mirage Civic Center, 5 Finalist Award 1990; Mobile County, City Government Center, AL, Hon. Mention 1991. **Important Works:** Alice Tully Hall, Juilliard School, Lincoln Center, NYC; Jewish Community Center, St. Paul, MN; Lytton Gardens, Palo Alto; Pleasanton Federal Correctional Facility, CA; Federal Office Bldg, Santa Rosa, CA; San Luis Obispo County Government Center, CA; Mobile County, City Government Center Competition, AL; Rancho Mirage Civic Center Competition. **Bio-Bibliography:** *Who's Who in California; Who's Who in the West.* **Home Address:** 367 Carrera Dr., Mill Valley, CA 94941. **Business Address:** Austris Vitols, FAAR, 367 Carrera Dr., Mill Valley, CA 94941.

VOELKEL, LAURA B. ■ AAR World War II Scholar 1942, 1943.

VON BLANCKENHAGEN, PETER ■ AAR Trustee 1984, Art Historian.

VREELAND, FREDERICK ■ AAR Visitor 1981-82, Political Affairs Officer.

VREELAND, THOMAS R. ■ RAAR Architecture 74. b. Jan. 1, 1925, Albany, NY. m. Nancy S. Vreeland. c. Daisy V. Zickerick, Phoebe A. Vreeland. BA 50, Yale Univ.; MArch 54, Yale School of Architecture. **Other Study:** École des Beaux Arts, Paris 1949-50; Sorbonne, Univ. of Paris 1949-50; Univ. of Rome 1952-53. **Career & Employment:** Univ. of Pennsylvania, Asst. Prof. 1955-65; Univ. of New Mexico, Chair 1965-68; UCLA, Architecture & Urban Design Program Head 1968-72, Prof. 1972-present. **Fellowships, Honors & Awards:** AIA, Philadelphia Chap., Honor Award 1963, Los Angeles Chap., Design Award 1980, Fellow 1981, Teaching Award 1988. **Important Works:** Rittenhouse Swim Club, Philadelphia 1961; Univ. of Pennsylvania, Therapeutic Research Laboratory 1963; City Center Urban Renewal, Camden, NJ 1965; Cooper's Point-Pyne Point Redevelopment, Camden, NJ 1965; Sierra del Sol Condominium, Taos Ski Valley, NM 1968; First Island Shopping Center, Hallandale, FL 1973; Marion Pike Studio, Los Angeles 1973; World Savings & Loan Branch Office, Santa Ana 1979; World Savings & Loan Branch Office, Cerritos 1980; Home Savings Bank of America Tower, Los Angeles 1989; California Inst. of Technology, Beckman Inst. 1990; Whittier College Performing Arts Center, Ruth Shannon Theater 1991; UCLA, Science & Technology Building 1993; Zonnick Residence, Los Angeles 1993. **Home Address:** 2179 Century Woods Way, Los Angeles, CA 90067. **Business Address:** A.C. Martin & Asscs., 811 W. 11 St., Los Angeles, CA 90017.

■   ■   ■

W

WADDY, PATRICIA A. ■ FAAR History of Art 70. b. July 29, 1941, Cannelton, IN. BA 63, Rice Univ.; MA 65, Tulane Univ.; PhD 73, IFA. **Research/Artistic Interests:** 17th-century Italian architecture. **Career & Employment:** Carnegie-Mellon Univ., Visiting Lect. 1970-71, Asst. Prof. 1971-77; Cornell Univ., Visiting Lect. 1977, Visiting Assc. Prof. 1981; Syracuse Univ., Assc. Prof. 1977-91, Prof. 1991-present. **Memberships & Offices:** *JSAH*, Foreign Book Review Ed. 1985-88, Assc. Ed. 1989-90, Ed. 1990-93; SAH, 2d VP 1993-94, 1st VP 1994-96; CAA; RSA. **Fellowships, Honors & Awards:** Fulbright-Hays Grant 1968-69; Samuel H. Kress Found. Grant 1971; NYU Founders' Day Award 1973; SAH Founders' Award 1976, Alice Davis Hitchcock Book Award 1992; NEH Summer Stipend 1977, 1994; ACLS Fellowship 1978; Syracuse Univ. Grant 1980; Nat. Humanities Center Fellowship 1984-85; CASVA, Samuel H. Kress Senior Fellow 1994-95. **Publications:** "Brunelleschi's Design for S. Maria degli Angeli in Florence," *Marsyas* 14 (1971): 36-45; "Michelangelo Buonarroti the Younger, Sprezzatura, and Palazzo Barberini," *Architectura* 5 (1975): 101-22; "The Design and Designers of Palazzo Barberini," *JSAH* 35 (1976): 151-85; "Luigi Arrigucci" and "Giovanni Battista Soria," *Macmillan Encyclopedia of Architects* (New York: Free Press & London: Collier Macmillan, 1982); "Francesco Borromini, *Opus architectonicum...,*" in *Architectural Theory and Practice from Alberti to Ledoux,* ed. Dora Wiebenson (Architectura Publications, 1982), III-D-6; "Taddeo Barberini as a Patron of Architecture," in *L'Age d'or du Mécenat (1598-1661),* Colloque Intl. CNRS (Mar. 1983) (Paris: CNRS, 1985), 191-99; *Seventeenth-Century Roman Palaces: Use and the Art of the Plan* (New York: Architectural History Found., 1990); "Maderno and Borromini: Plan and Section," in *An Architectural Progress in the Renaissance and Baroque: Sojourns in and out of Italy: Festschrift in Honor of Hellmut Hager,* ed. Henry A. Millon & Susan Scott Munshower (University Park, PA: Pennsylvania State Univ. Press, 1992), 194-223; "The Roman *appartamento nobile* by 1600," in *Architecture et vie sociale: L'Organisation intérieure des grandes demeures à la fin du moyen âge et à la Renaissance,* (De architectura), Actes du Colloque, Centre d'Études Superieures de la Renaissance, Tours, June 6-9, 1988 (Paris: Picard, 1994), 155-66; "Luigi Arrigucci," "Giovanni Battista Soria," "Carlo Maderno," "Michelangelo Buonarroti the Younger," and "Palazzo Barberini," in *The Dictionary of Art.* **Home Address:** 342 Fellows Ave., Syracuse, NY 13210. **Business Address:** Syracuse Univ., Syracuse, NY 13244-1250.

WAGENER, ANTHONY PELZER ■ FASCSR 11. b. May 27, 1887, Charleston, SC. d. Jan. 31, 1972. m. Frances Rebecca Keister. c. Anthony Pelzer, Frances Keister. BA 1906, College of Charleston; PhD 10, Johns Hopkins Univ. **Career & Employment:** Williams College, Instr. 1912-13; College of Charleston, Acting Prof. 1913-14; Roanoke College, Prof. 1914-19, 1919-26; US Infantry Reserve, 2d Lieut. 1918, Capt. 1930-40; West Virginia Univ., Prof. 1926-29; College of William & Mary, Prof.-Dept. Head 1929-58, Chancellor Prof. 1955-58. **Memberships & Offices:** APA; ArlA; Comm. on Present Status of Classical Education, Chair 1935-45; CAMWS, Pres. 1948-49; Scabbard & Blade; American Legion, 3d Dist. Dept. of Virginia, Commander. **Fellowships, Honors & Awards:** Austin College, John Hay Whitney Found. Scholar 1958-59; Phi Beta Kappa; Pi Kappa Phi, Nat. Pres.; Eta Sigma Phi; Omicron Delta Kappa. **Publications:** *Popular Associations of Right and Left in Roman Literature* (Baltimore: J.H. Furst, 1912); "Stylistic Qualities of the Apostrophe to Nature as a Dramatic Device," *TAPA* 62 (1931): 78-100; with Thornton Jenkins, *Latin and the Romans*, 2 vols. (Boston: Ginn, 1941-42); *Learning through Latin* (Boston: Ginn, 1944); ed., *Course of Study in Latin for High Schools of Virginia* (Richmond, 1945). **Bio-Bibliography:** Briggs, 669-70; *Who Was Who in America*.

WAITES, MARGARET C. ■ FASCSR 13. b. Dec. 5, 1883. d. Mar. 15, 1923. BA 05, Radcliffe College; MA 06, Radcliffe College; PhD 12, Radcliffe College. **Research/Artistic Interests:** Etruscan & Greek archaeology & mythology. **Career & Employment:** Rockford College, Classical Dept., Head 1910-14; Mt. Holyoke College, Assc. Prof. 1916-24. **Publications:** "Some Features of Allegorical Debate in Greek Literature," *Harvard Studies in Classical Philology* 23 (1912): 1-46; "The Meaning of the Dokana," *AJA* 23 (1919): 1-18; "Nature of the Lares and their Representation in Roman Art," *AJA* 24 (1920): 241-61; "Deities of the Sacred Axe," *AJA* 27 (1923): 25-56. **Bio-Bibliography:** Radcliffe College Archives.

WALKER, JOHN, III ■ AAR, School of Fine Arts, Prof.-in-Charge 1935-39; AAR Trustee 1940-74, Trustee Emer.; AAR Centennial Medal; NGA, Dir.; Art Historian.

WALKER, PETER ■ RAAR Landscape Architecture 92. b. 1933, Berkeley, CA. BS 55, UC, Berkeley; MLArch 57, Harvard Univ. **Other Study:** Univ. of Illinois 1956. **Career & Employment:** Peter Walker & Partners, Landscape Architecture; The SWA Group; Sasaki, Walker, Asscs., Inc.; Harvard GSD., Adj. Prof. 1981-, Chair 1978-81. **Memberships & Offices:** *Landscape Architecture*, Ed. Bd. 1988-. **Fellowships, Honors & Awards:** AIA, Inst. Honor 1992, Award; ASLA, Fellow, Award; Urban Land Inst., Research Fellow; Federal Housing Authority Award; American Inst. of Planners Award; ALNY Award; San Francisco Gold Balloon Award; NEA Award; Harvard Univ., Weidenmen Prize 1957. **Publications:** articles in: *Landscape Architecture, Architectural Record, Process: Architecture, Japan, Avant Garde, Progressive Architecture, SD Magazine, Japan, Sculpture, Quaderns, Architectural Review, England, architektur + wohner, Modern Gardens, Museum of Modern Art, Architectural Forum*. **Exhibitions/Performances:** California State Univ., Fullerton 1986; Harold Reed Gallery, NYC; Harvard Univ. 1989-; Jernigan Wicker Gallery; Hemicycle-Corcoran Gallery of Art; Centre Georges Pompidou, Paris.

WALKER, RALPH E. ■ AAR Visitor 1943 — 1951, Architect.

WALKER, RALPH THOMAS ■ Rotch Scholar 1916.

WALLACE, REX E. ■ FAAR Classics/Archaeology 85; Broneer Fellow 1984-85. b. Sept. 13, 1952, Wilmington, NC. BS 74, Univ. of Nebraska; MA 76, Univ. of Nebraska; MA 81, Ohio State Univ.; PhD 84, Ohio State Univ. **Career & Employment:** Univ. of Massachusetts, Asst. Prof. 1985-91, Assc. Prof. 1992-present. **Publications:** "A Note on the Development of *e and *ei in Anatolian," *Zeitschrift für vergleichende Sprachforschung* 96 (1983): 50-55; "The Development of *e in Palaic," *Die Sprache* 30 (1983): 153-63; "An Illusory Substratum Influence in Pamphylian," *Glotta* 61 (1983): 5-12; with Brian Joseph, "Latin Morphology: Another Look," *Linguistic Inquiry* 15 (1984): 319-28; "The Deletion of s in Plautus," *American Journal of Philology* 105 (1984): 213-25; "Volscian *sepu*/Oscan *sipus*," *Indogermanische Forschungen* 90 (1985): 123-28; "The Etymology of Umbrian and Paelignian *bio*," *Classical Philology* 80 (1986): 337-40; with Brian Joseph, "Latin *sum*, Oscan *sum, sim, esum*," *American Journal of*

Philology 108 (1987) 675-93; "Dialectal Latin *fundatid, parentatid, proiecitad*," *Glotta* 66 (1988): 211-20; "The Origins and the Development of the Latin Alphabet," in *The Origins of Writing*, ed. W. Senner (Lincoln: Univ. of Nebraska Press, 1989): 121-35; "The Etruscan *Gentilicia kurtinas* and *kuritianas*," *Beiträge zur Namenforschung* 25 (1990): 145-48; with Brian Joseph, "Is Faliscan a Local Latin Patois?" *Diachronica* 8 (1991): 159-86. **Home Address:** 87 Logtown Rd., Amherst, MA 01003. **Business Address:** Dept of Classics, Univ. of Massachusetts, 520 Herter Hall, Amherst, MA 01003.

WALSH, JOSEPH J. ■ FAAR Classics/Archaeology 86. b. Aug. 20, 1953, Rockville Centre, NY. BA 75, Fairfield Univ.; MA 78, SUNY, Buffalo. **Other Studies:** Univ. of Texas, Austin; Univ. of Augsburg, Germany 1981-83. **Research/Artistic Interests:** Greek and Roman history; Roman archaeology. **Fellowships, Honors & Awards:** Univ. of Texas, William Battle Fellowship 1981, Fellowship 1984-85; Fulbright Fellowship (declined) 1981-82; Deutscher Akademischer Austauschdienst Stipendium 1981-83; Oscar Broneer Fellowship 1986-87.

WALSH, THOMAS JOHN ■ FAAR Sculpture 74. b. July 10, 1937, Chicago, IL. m. Linda Wynne Walsh. c. Michael. MFA 62, Univ. of Michigan. **Career & Employment:** Murray State Univ., Asst. Prof. 1962-67; Southern Illinois Univ., Prof. 1967-92; Humboldt State Univ., Artist-in-Residence 1977-78. **Fellowships, Honors & Awards:** Tiffany Found. Grant 1971; Illinois Arts Council Project Completion Grant 1976; Kresge Challenge Grant 1979; NEA Project Grant 1980; Residencies: Handhollow Found. 1981; Virginia Center for the Creative Arts 1981; Caldwell Resident in the Arts, Indiana Univ. 1982; Ragdale Found. 1982, 1983, 1985, 1987; Millay Colony; Kohler Arts-Industry Program 1988. **Important Works:** Kalamazoo Art Center; *Louisville Courier-Journal*, KY; Mint Museum, Charlotte, NC; Speed Museum, Louisville, KY; Berea College; Murray State Univ., KY; St. Paul Art Center, MN; Mer Museum, Tyler, TX; Pembroke State Univ., NC; Lafayette Art Center, LA; Univ. of Evansville, IN; Del Mar College, Corpus Christi, TX; Montana State Univ.; Southern Illinois Univ.; Illinois State Museum, Springfield; Ball State Univ.; Chattanooga Univ., TN. **Exhibitions/Performances:** Recent Solo Shows: Berea College 1980; Bethany College, Lindsborg, KS 1981; Emporia State Univ., Emporia, KS 1981; Sangamon State Univ., Springfield, IL 1983; Mitchell Museum, Mount Vernon, IL 1985; Anden Gallery, St. Louis, MO 1985; Anderson College, Anderson, IN 1985; Governor's State Univ., Park Forest, IL 1985; Contemporary Art Workshop, Chicago 1986; Arc Gallery, Chicago 1987; Toledo Museum School of Art 1987; Triton Museum of Art, Santa Clara 1988; Millikin Univ. 1988; Fairweather Hardin Gallery, Chicago 1989; Southern Illinois Univ. 1989; Univ. of Richmond 1989; Webster Univ., St. Louis, MO 1990. **Home Address:** 96 Caretaker Rd., Makanda, IL 62958.

WALTERS, HENRY ■ AAR Founder, Trustee 1905-30; Financier, Art Patron. b. Sept. 26, 1848. d. Nov. 30, 1931. First major donor to the Academy. **Career & Employment:** Dir. of Railroads. **Memberships & Offices:** MMA, Trustee; New York Public Library, Trustee.

WALTON, CRAIG H. ■ FAAR Architecture 82. b. Aug. 31, 1950, Lancaster, PA. m. Virginia H. Walton. c. Drew, Julia. BArch 73, Univ. of Virginia; MCPUD 79, Harvard Univ. **Home Address:** 1043 Wheatland Ave., Lancaster, PA 17603. **Business Address:** RLPS Architects, 1910 Harrington Dr., Lancaster, PA 197601.

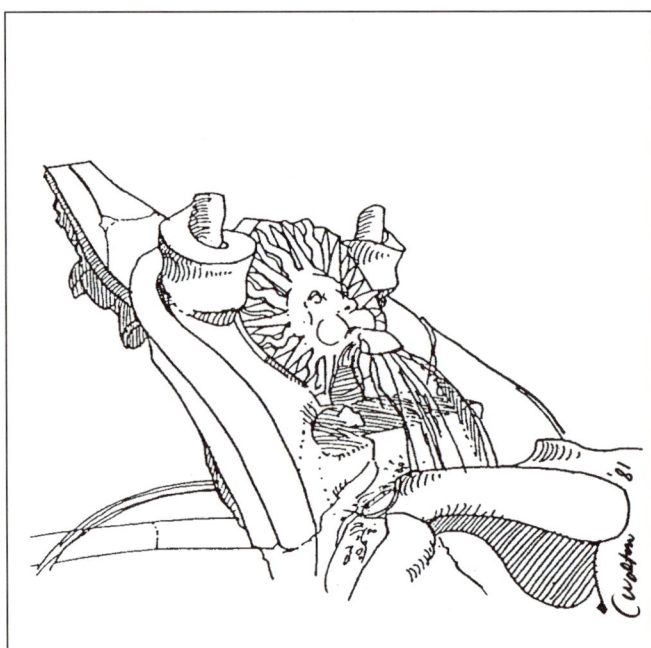

Craig H. Walton

WALTON, FRANCIS REDDING ■ FAAR Classics / Archaeology 37. b. Nov. 8, 1910, Philadelphia, PA. d. Oct. 11, 1989. m. Mary Sabin Walton. c. Sarah Jane Clark, David Ford Walton. BA 32, Haverford College; MA 33, Harvard Univ.; PhD 38, Harvard Univ. **Research/Artistic Interests:** Ancient art, ancient cults & religions. **Career & Employment:** Haverford College, Instr. 1938-40; Williams College, Instr. 1940-42, Asst. Prof. 1946-47; Univ. of Minnesota, Faculty 1947-48; Univ. of Chicago, Prof. 1948-52; Florida State Univ., Tallahassee, Prof. 1952-61; Cornell Univ., Visiting Prof. 1960-61; ASCSA, Gennadius Library, Librarian-Dir. 1961-76. **Memberships & Offices:** APA, Ed. 1952-58; ArIA. **Fellowships, Honors & Awards:** Fulbright Research Fellow 1956-57; Assn. Intl. de Bibliophilie, Hon. Mem. 1977; Order of the Phoenix, Greece, Commander 1977. **Publications:** ed. & trans., *Diodorus of Sicily, Books XXI-XL* (Cambridge, MA: Loeb Classical Library, 1957); co-ed., *Catalogue of the Gennadius Library* (1968); contr., *Oxford Classical Dictionary, Encylopedia Britannica*; "Incunabula in the Gennadius Library," *Mediaevalia et Humanistia* 2 (1971): 1-20; contr., *The Greek Book, 1476-1825* (Athens, 1979); *The Gennadius Library: A Survey of the Collections* (Athens: ASCSA, 1981). **Bio-Bibliography:** Brenda Marder, "Francis Walton at the Gennadeion," *The Athenian* (Oct. 1979): 24-27; *Francis R. Walton: A Memorial Evening, March 29, 1990* (Athens: ASCSA, 1991); *Directory of American Scholars;* Haverford College Archives.

WALTON, JAMES M. ■ AAR Trustee 1977-79, Trustee Emer.; Banker.

WARD, J.Q.A. ■ AAR Charter Mem., Sculptor.

WARNER, GEOFFREY CAMPBELL ■ NIAE, John Dinkeloo Traveling Fellow 1989-90.

WARREN, H. LANGFORD ■ AAR Trustee 1911-17.

WARREN, HARRY EDWARD ■ FAAR Architecture 09; Appleton Fellow 1911-12, 1913. b. Mar. 20, 1882, Rochester, NH. d. June 7, 1973. BArch 04, Harvard Univ.; MArch 05, Harvard

Univ. **Research/Artistic Interests:** Restoration, measurement of drawings. **Exhibitions/Performances:** Bronxville Women's Club 1970.

WARREN, MINTON ■ ASCSR, Dir. 1896-98; Educator.

WARREN, ROBERT PENN ■ RAAR Literature 57. b. Apr. 24, 1905, Guthrie, KY. d. Sept. 15, 1989. m. Emma Brescia, Eleanor Clark. c. Rosanna Phelps Scully, Gabriel Penn. BA 25, Vanderbuilt Univ.; MA 27, UC, Berkeley; BLitt 30, Oxford Univ. **Other Studies:** Yale Univ. 1927-28. **Career & Employment:** Southwestern College, Asst. Prof. 1930-31; Vanderbilt Univ., Asst. Prof. 1931-34; Louisiana State Univ., Asst.-Assc. Prof. 1934-42; Univ. of Minnesota, Prof. 1942-50; Yale Univ., Prof. 1950-73, Prof. Emer. 1973-89. **Memberships & Offices:** *The Southern Review,* Co-Founder & Co-Ed. 1935-42; *Kenyon Review,* Adv. Ed. 1938-61. **Fellowships, Honors & Awards:** Rhodes Scholar 1928-30; *Poetry Magazine,* Levinson Prize 1936, Union League Civic & Arts Found. Prize 1953; Guggenheim Fellowship 1939-40, 1947-48; Shelly Memorial Prize 1942; Pulitzer Prize 1947, 1958, 1979; Southern Prize 1947; Sidney Hillman Award 1957; Edna St. Vincent Millay Memorial Award 1958; Nat. Book Award 1958; Bollingen Prize for Poetry 1970; Nat. Medal for Literature 1970; Copernicus Award 1976; MacArthur Found. Award 1980, AAAL, Gold Medal for Poetry 1985; Poet Laureate 1986-87; Nat. Medal of Arts 1987. **Publications:** with Cleanth Brooks, *Understanding Poetry* (New York: Holt 1938); *Night Rider* (New York: Houghton, 1939); *Eleven Poems on the Same Theme* (New York: New Directions, 1942); with Cleanth Brooks, *Understanding Fiction* (New York: Appleton-Century-Crofts, 1943); *Heaven's Gates* (New York: Harcourt, 1943); *Selected Poems 1923-1943* (New York: Harcourt, 1944); *All the King's Men* (New York: Harcourt, 1946); *World Enough and Time* (New York: Random House, 1950); *Brother to Dragons* (New York: Random House, 1953); *Band of Angels* (New York: Random House, 1955); *Segregation: The Inner Conflict in the South* (New York: Random House, 1956); *Promises: Poems 1954-56* (New York: Random House, 1957); *Selected Essays* (New York: Random House, 1958); *The Cave* (New York: Random House, 1959); *You, Emperors and Others: Poems, 1957-1960* (New York: Random House, 1960); *Wilderness: A Tale of the Civil War* (New York: Random House, 1961); *Flood: A Romance of Our Time* (New York: Random House, 1964); *Who Speaks for the Negroes* (New York: Random House, 1965); *Incarnations: Poems 1966-68* (New York: Random House, 1968); *Audubon: A Vision* (New York: Random House, 1969); *Meet Me in the Green Glen* (New York: Random House, 1971); *Or Else-Poems: Poems 1968-74* (New York: Random House, 1974); *A Place to Come To* (New York: Random House, 1977); *Now and Then: Poems 1976-78* (New York: Random House, 1978); *New and Selected Poems (1923-1985)* (New York: Random House, 1985). **Bio-Bibliography:** Barnett Guttenberg, *Web of Being: The Novels of Robert Penn Warren* (Nashville: Vanderbilt Univ. Press, 1975); Neil Nakadate, *Robert Penn Warren: A Reference Guide* (Boston: G. K. Hall, 1977); James H. Justus, *The Achievement of Robert Penn Warren* (Baton Rouge: Louisiana State Univ. Press, 1981); *NY Times,* Obit. (Sept. 16, 1989); Randolph Runyan, *The Taciturn Text: The Fiction of Robert Penn Warren* (Columbus: Ohio State Univ. Press, 1990); William Bedford Clark, *The American Visions of Robert Penn Warren* (Lexington: Univ. of Kentucky Press, 1991); *Contemporary Authors; Contemporary Literary Criticism; Current Biography; Dictionary of Literary Biography.*

WARREN, S.D. ■ AAR Charter Mem.

WASSON, R. GORDON ■ AAR Trustee 1956-63, Banker.

WATKINS, FRANKLIN C. ■ AAR Trustee 1954-58, Artist.

WATTS, PAULINE M. ■ FAAR Post-Classical/Humanistic Studies 77. b. Dec. 8, 1948, San Francisco, CA. m. Charles Trinkaus. BA 70, Sarah Lawrence College; PhD 76, Univ. of Michigan. **Other Study:** Religious & intellectual history of ancient, late medieval, early modern Mediterranean cultures; evangelization of 16th-century Mexico. **Career & Employment:** Pomona College, Visiting Asst. Prof. 1984-85; Sarah Lawrence College, Prof. 1985-present. **Fellowships, Honors & Awards:** Harvard Univ., Villa I Tatti Fellow 1981-82; John Carter Brown Library, NEH Research Fellow 1987; ACLS Fellow 1988. **Publications:** *Nicolaus Cusanus: A Fifteenth-Century Vision of Man* (Leiden: Brill, 1982); "Prophecy & Discovery: On the Spiritual Origins of Christopher Columbus's 'Enterprise of the Indies,'" *American Historical Review* (1985): 79-102; *The Game of Spheres: A Translation of Nicolaus Cusanus: De Ludo Globi* (New York: Abaris, 1986); "Dionysius the Areopagite and Three Renaissance Platonists: Cusanus, Ficino, and Pico on Mond and Cosmos," in *Supplementum Festivum: Studies in Honor of Paul Oskar Kristeller*, ed. John Monfasani, J. Hankins, & F. Purnell (Binghamton, NY: SUNY Binghamton Press, 1987), 279-98; ed. with Silvio Bedini et al., *The Christopher Columbus Encyclopedia*, 2 vols. (New York: Simon & Schuster, 1991); "Talking to Spiritual Others: Ramon Lull, Nicholas of Cusa, Diego Valadés," in *Nicholas of Cusa in Search of God and Wisdom*, ed G. Christianson & T.M. Izbicki (Leiden: Brill, 1991), 203-18; "Hieroglyphs of Conversion: Alien Discourses in Diego Valadés's *Rhetorica Christiana*," *Memorie Domenicane* n.s. 22 (1991): 405-33; "The New World and the End of the World: Evangelizing Sixteenth-Century Mexico," in *Imagining the New World: Columbian Iconography*, ed., Gianni Eugenio Viola & Franca Rovigotti (New York & Rome, 1991-92), 28-39. **Business Address:** History Dept., Sarah Lawrence College, Bronxville, NY 10708.

WATTS, WINTTER ■ FAAR Musical Composition 25. b. Mar. 14, 1884, Cincinnati, OH. d. Nov. 1, 1962. Cert. 14, Inst. of Musical Art. **Other Study:** with Percy Goetschius. **Fellowships, Honors & Awards:** Loeb Prize 1919; Pulitzer Traveling Award 1923. **Important Works:** *Pied Piper*, an opera; music to *Alice in Wonderland; Bridal Overture* 1916; *Etchings*, suite 1921; *Young Blood*, symphonic poem 1923; *Vignettes of Italy*, song cycle; *Wings of Night; Like Music on the Water*, song cycle. **Bio-Bibliography:** W.T. Upton, *Art-Song in America* (New York, 1930); *NY Times*, Obit. (Nov. 2, 1962); *Baker's Biographical Directory of Musicians; Contemporary American Composers; New Grove Dictionary of American Music*.

WAUGH, SIDNEY BIEHLER ■ FAAR Sculpture 32; AAR Trustee 1953-63. b. Jan. 17, 1904, Amherst, MA. d. June 30, 1963. m. Elizabeth Pettigrew Lake. **Other Studies:** MIT; Massachusetts State College; Amherst College; École des Beaux Arts, with Henri Bouchard, Paris 1925-28. **Career & Employment:** Steuben Glass, Chief Assc. Designer; US Army Air Forces, Capt. WWII; Rinehart School of Sculpture, Teacher & Dir.; WPA Artist. **Memberships & Offices:** NIAL 1941; NAD, 1st VP; NSS, Pres.-Council Mem.; ANS, Fellow; American Geographic Soc.; NYC Art Comm.; Parsons School of Design, BoT; Municipal Art Soc.; Shakespeare Assn. of America; Kappa Sigma. **Fellowships, Honors & Awards:** US Bronze Star; US Silver Star; French Croix de Guerre (2); Cavaliere Ufficiale della Corona d'Italia; Paris Salon, Bronze Medal 1928, Silver Medal 1929; Amherst College, Hon. MA 1939; Univ. of Massachusetts, Hon. AFD 1950; Saltus Medal; Herbert Adams Memorial Medal. **Publications:** *The Art of Glass Making* (New York: Dodd, Mead, 1938); *The*

Making of Fine Glass (New York: Dodd, Mead, 1947). **Important Works:** Collections: MMA; AIC; Cleveland Museum of Fine Art; Toledo Museum, John Herron Inst., Indianapolis; Johns Hopkins Univ.; Victoria & Albert Museum, London; US Nat. Archives Bldg, Washington, DC; USPO Bldg. Pediment Group, Washington, DC; Federal Reserve Bd. Bldg., Washington, DC; District Court of Appeals Bldg., Washington, DC; Mellon Memorial Fountain, Washington, DC; Mead Art Bldg., Amherst College; Bethlehem Steel Co.; Bank of Manhattan; Lamar Monument, Richmond, TX; Buhl Planetarium, Pittsburgh; Pulaski Monument, Philadelphia; Federal Trade Comm. Bldg., Washington, DC; US Justice Dept. Bldg., Washington, DC; Smith College; Corning Bldg., NYC. **Bio-Bibliography:** Sidney Waugh, *Sidney Waugh* (New York: Norton, 1948); *NY Times*, Obit. (July 1, 1963); *Dictionary of American Biography; National Cyclopedia of American Biography; Who Was Who in America; Who Was Who in American Art*.

WEAVER, WILLIAM ■ AAR Visitor 1985-86, Translator, Writer.

WEBB, EDWARD ■ Chicago Architectural Club, Burnham Prize 1991-92.

WEBEL, RICHARD K. ■ FAAR Landscape Architecture 29, RAAR Landscape Architecture 63. b. July 5, 1900, Germany. m. Pauline D. Webel. c. Richard C. BS 23, Harvard Univ.; MA 26, Harvard Univ. **Career & Employment:** Harvard Univ., Asst. Prof. 1930-39; Innocenti & Webel, private practice 1931-present. **Memberships & Offices:** ASLA, Fellow 1954, New York Chap., Pres. 1954; NAD; Fine Arts Comm.; ALNY; General Services Administration, Public Adv. Panel. **Fellowships, Honors & Awards:** Sheldon Fellow 1926-27; Garden Club, Oakleigh Thorne Medal 1970; Nat. American Assn. of Nurserymen Award 1981; Hon. Doctorates: Wofford College 1979; Furman Univ. 1983. **Important Works:** Redesign of Washington Mall & Lincoln Memorial Areas, Washington, DC. **Bio-Bibliography:** *Who's Who in America*. **Home Address:** 1089 Cedar Swamp Rd., Glen Head, NY 11545. **Business Address:** Innocenti & Webel, 85 Forest Ave., Box 506, Locust Valley, NY 11560.

WEED, WILLIAM ■ AAR Trustee 1983-92, Trustee Emer.; Corp. Exec.

WEESE, HARRY M. ■ RAAR Architecture 73; AAR Architecture Com. Juror 1966. b. June 30, 1915, Evanston, IL. m. Kate Baldwin Weese. c. Shirley, Marcia, Kate. BArch 38, MIT. **Other Study:** Yale Univ. 1936-37; Cranbrook Acad. of Art 1938-39; MIT, Bemis Housing Found. Research Asst. 1939-40. **Research/Artistic Interests:** Method of constructing modular buildings (U.S. patent); modular building construction system using segmented column assembly (U.S. patent); interstitial space frame system (US patent); hinged slab system of building (U.S., U.K., & Italy patents); airport passenger loading & unloading machine (U.S. patent). **Career & Employment:** Skidmore, Owings & Merrill, Designer 1939-40, 1946-47; Private Practice with Benjamin Baldwin 1941; USNR (Ret.) Engineering Officer, Lt.(E) 1941-46; Harry Weese & Asscs., Chair 1947-92; *Inland Architect Magazine*, Publisher 1977-91. **Memberships & Offices:** Metropolitan Housing & Planning Council, Chicago, Bd. of Governors 1964-present; Open Lands Project, Chicago, Bd. of Governors 1964-present; Pres. Johnson's Citizens' Adv. Com. on Recreation & Natural Beauty 1966-69; Pres. Nixon's Citizens' Adv. Com. on Environmental Quality 1969-71; AIA Capitol Adv. Com. 1972, Task Force on Rebuilding the City 1973, Delegation-Study Mission to Peoples' Republic of China, Chair 1974; Nat. Council of the Arts 1974-80; American Revolution Bicentennial Comm., Creative & Visual Arts Adv. Panel 1972-76; US State Dept., Foreign Bldgs. Program 1973; NEA Task Force on Federal Architecture 1973; AIA, Chicago Chap., Pres. 1975; Chicago, Mayor's Architectural Adv. Com., Co-Chair 1979-83, Mayor's Task Force on Navy Pier 1985; Architect of the Capitol, Adv. 1980; Nat. Council of the Arts, Design Arts Com. 1982-present; San Jose Redevelopment Agency, Urban Design Review Bd. 1984-90; Nat. Assn. of Housing & Redevelopment Officials, Adv. Bd. 1985-90. **Fellowships, Honors & Awards:** Cranbrook Acad., Fellowship 1938-39; AIA, Fellow 1961; NAD, Assc. 1968, Academician 1975; American Soc. of Interior Designers, Illinois Chap., Total Design Award 1975; Tau Sigma Delta, Gold Medal 1977; Chicago Press Club, Chicagoan of the Year 1978; AIA Firm of the Year Award 1978, Chicago Chap., Distinguished Service Award 1981; Union of Architects, Bulgaria, Diplome de Lauret, Biennale Mondale de l'Architecture 1983; *Architectural Record* Magazine & Illinois Council, AIA, Chicago Architecture Award 1987; Landmarks Preservation Council of Illinois, Distinguished Illinois Preservationist Award 1991; Hon. Doctorates: Northwestern Univ. 1979; Catholic Univ. 1980; Columbia College 1980; DePauw Univ. 1980. **Important Works:** US Embassy, Accra, Ghana 1958; First Baptist Church, Columbus IN 1965; Washington Metropolitan Area Transit System, Washington, DC, VA, MD 1965-present; Adler-Sullivan Auditorium Theatre Restoration, Chicago 1967; *Time & Life* Bldg., Chicago 1970; Univ. of Wisconsin, South Lower Campus Project, Madison 1970; Milwaukee Center for the Performing Arts 1970-present; Crown Center Hotel, Kansas City, MO 1973; US Courthouse Annex, Federal Correctional Center, Chicago 1975; Stanford Univ., Terman Engineering Center 1977; Miami Dade County Transit System 1982; 200 S. Wacker Dr. Office Bldg., Chicago 1982; Union Underwear Co., Corp. HQ, Bowling Green, KY 1982; US Embassy Staff Housing, Tokyo 1984; Chinatown, Master Plan & Architectural Design, Chicago 1985. **Exhibitions/Performances:** Galerie Daniel Gervis, Paris 1983; Belgrade Triennial of World Architecture 1985, 1988, 1991; Museum of Science & Industry, Chicago 1986; ALNY-NAD, NYC 1988, traveling through 1991; Gulbenkian Found., Lisbon 1989; Columbia Univ. 1991; Tavern Club, Chicago 1992; Chicago Architecture Found. 1993; AIC 1993. **Bio-Bibliography:** "Harry Weese: Humanism and Tradition," *Process Architecture* 11 (1979); Betty Blum, "An Oral History by Harry Weese," Taped 1987-88-89 (Chicago: AIC, American Archives of Art, 1982); Kitty Baldwin Weese, *Harry Weese Houses* (Chicago: Chicago Review Press, 1987); *Crazy Critters to Color: Drawings by Harry Weese from A to Z* (1989); Balthazar Korab, "Columbus, Indiana" in *Weese in Columbus* (Documan Press, 1989), 82-89; Bill Lacy, *100 Contemporary Architects and Their Drawings* (1991); *International Who's Who*; *Who's Who in America*; *Who's Who in the Midwest*. **Business Address:** Harry Weese Asscs., 10 W. Hubbard St., Chicago, IL 60610.

WEI, WESLEY ■ Philadelphia Regional Visiting Artist 1994.

WEIL, MARK S. ■ RAAR History of Art 85. b. May 26, 1939 St. Louis, MO. m. Phoebe D. Weil. c. Daniel D., Alexander P. BA 61, Washington Univ.; MA 64, Columbia Univ.; PhD 68, Columbia Univ. **Career & Employment:** Colgate Univ. 1957-59; Washington Univ., Asst. Prof. 1968-74, Assc. Prof. 1974-85, Prof. 1985-present, Chair 1982-88. **Memberships & Offices:** CAA; SAH; Midwest Art History Soc., Acting Sec.-Treas. 1979-80; St. Louis Art Museum, BoT 1981-84. **Fellowships, Honors & Awards:** NEH Junior Humanist Fellowship 1972-73. **Publications:** *The History and Decoration of the Ponte S. Angelo* (University Park: Pennsylvania State Univ. Press, 1974); "Salvator Rosa's St. John the Baptist Preaching in the Wilderness," *Museum Monographs* 3 (St. Louis: St. Louis Art Museum, 1974), 57-70; "The Pamphili Chapel in Sant'Agostino," *Römisches Jahrbuch für Kunstgeschichte* 15 (1974): 183-98; with Rudolph Primesberger, "The Devotion of the Forty Hours and Roman Baroque Illusions," *Journal of the Warburg & Courtauld Institutes* 37 (1974): 218-48; "The Serra Sculpture: How Public is a Public Monument?" *St. Louis Literary Supplement* 1.5 (1977): 6-8; *Baroque Theatre and Stage Design*, exb. cat. (St. Louis: Washington Univ. Gallery of Art, 1983); "Un fauno molestato da cupidi: forma e significato," in *Gian Lorenzo Bernini e le arti visive* (Rome, 1987), 73-84; with Margaretta Darnall, "Il Sacro Bosco di Bomarzo: A Literary and Antiquarian Interpretation," *Journal of Garden History* 4 (1984): 1-94; "A Bronzetto of Scipione Borghese by Bernini," *Source: Notes in the History of Art* 8-9 (1989): 34-39; with Roger Ward, *Master Drawings from the Nelson-Atkins Museum of Art*, exb. cat. (St. Louis: Washington Univ. Gallery of Art, 1989); "The Relationship of the Cornaro Chapel to Mystery Plays and Italian Court Theatre," *Art and Pageantry in the Renaissance and Baroque*, Papers in Art History from Pennsylvania State Univ. 6 (University Park: Pennsylvania State Univ., 1990), 458-86; "Love, Monsters, Movement and Machines: The Marvelous in Theaters, Festivals and Gardens," in *The Age of the Marvelous* (Hanover, NH: Hood Museum of Art, Dartmouth College, 1991), 159-78. **Home Address:** 7 Univ. Ln., St. Louis, MO 63105.

WEIN, ALBERT W. ■ FAAR Sculpture 49. b. July 27, 1915, NYC. d. Mar. 30, 1991. Dipl., Beaux Arts Inst. of Design, NYC. **Other Studies:** Maryland Inst., Baltimore; NAD; Grand Central Inst., NYC. **Career & Employment:** Univ. of Wyoming, Visiting Prof. 1965-67, NAD, Faculty 1977-78; Pace Univ. Adj. Prof. 1979. **Fellowships, Honors & Awards:** NSS, Fellow; Huntington Hartford Found., Fellow; Intl. Inst. of Arts & Letters, Fellow; Metropolitan Life Insurance Competition, 2d Hon. Mention 1938; Chaloner Found. Scholarship, 2d Hon. Mention 1940; US War Dept. Competition, Hon. Mention 1941; Mrs. Louis Bennet Prize 1942; Avery Prize 1944; Lindsey Morris Prize 1946; NAD Artist Fund Prize 1976, 1980, Certificate of Merit 1978, 1983, Gold for Sculpture 1979, Agopoff Award 1986, Gold Medal 1986; NSS, John Cavanaugh Memorial Prize 1988, Herbert Adams Memorial Medal 1989; Tiffany Found. Grant; Rockefeller Grant for Bellagio Center. **Important Works:** Vatican Museum Numismatic Collection; Jewish Museum, NYC; Brookgreen Gardens, SC; Palm Springs Desert Museum, CA; Post Office, Frankfort, NY; Gramercy Park Memorial Chapel, NYC; Natural Habitats Design, Bronx Zoo, NYC; NYU Hall of Fame; Hillside Memorial Park, Los Angeles 1960-68; St. Michael's Episcopal Church, Anaheim 1967; The Gardens, Palm Beach; Univ. of Wyoming Physical Science Center 1968; UN, 25th Anniversary Medal 1970; Libby Dam Treaty Tower, MT 1975; Libby Dam Dedication Medal 1975; Korean & Vietnam War Memorial, NYC; NY Athletic Club, NYC 1985. **Exhibitions/Performances:** Palma Gallery, Rome; Salon d'Automne, Paris; Whitney Museum, NYC 1950; Argent Galleries 1951; MMA 1951; San Francisco Museum of Art 1957; Jewish Museum, NYC 1958; Heritage Gallery 1969; Palm Springs Desert Museum 1969; Grand Central Art Galleries 1983; ALNY; NAD; Palace of Legion of Honor, San Francisco. **Bio-Bibliography:** Janice Lovoos, "The Art of Albert Wein," *American Artist* (Jan. 1963); *Albert Wein: Classic Modern Sculpture*, exb. cat. (Boston: Childs Gallery, 1990); *Who's Who in American Art*.

WEINBERG, ELBERT ■ FAAR Sculpture 53. b. May 27, 1928, Hartford, CT. d. Dec. 27, 1991. c. Julia Weinberg. BFA 51, RISD; MFA 55, Yale Univ. **Other Studies:** Hartford Art School with Henry Kreis 1946-48. **Career & Employment:** Cooper Union, Instr. 1956-59; Dartmouth Univ., Visiting Prof. 1969; Boston Univ., Visiting Prof. 1969-71, 1980-91. **Fellowships, Honors & Awards:** Tate Gallery, Political Prisoner Competition, Hon. Mention 1953; *Progressive Architecture* Award 1954; Guggenheim Fellowship 1959; Yale Univ., Silver Medal for Achievement in the Arts 1959; AAAL Sculpture Award 1968; Soc. of Medallists Award 1971. **Important Works:** Holocaust Memorial, W. Hartford, CT; Holocaust Memorial, Wilmington, DE; School of Law, Boston Univ.; Brandeis Univ.; Colgate Univ.; Federal Reserve Bank, Atlanta; Jewish Museum, NYC; Portman San Francisco Hotel; Collections: MOMA; Jewish Museum, NYC; Whitney Museum, NYC; MFA; Brooklyn Museum; RISD Museum; Addison Gallery, Phillips Acad., Andover; Wadsworth Athenaeum, Hartford, CT. **Exhibitions/Performances:** Solo: Providence Art Club 1951, 1954; Borgenicht Gallery, NYC 1957-66, 1969, 1970, 1975, 1982, 1986; Alpha Gallery, Boston 1966, 1969, 1971; Dartmouth College 1969; Menges Museum, Berkeley 1974; Schenectady Museum, NY 1977; Retrospective: Boston Univ. Art Gallery 1991. **Bio-Bibliography:** Kim Sichel, *Elbert Weinberg, 1928-1991*, exb. cat. (Boston: Boston Univ. Art Gallery 1991); *Contemporary American Artists*.

WEINBERG, HENRY ■ FAAR Musical Composition 70. b. June 7, 1931, Philadelphia, PA. BFA 52, Univ. of Pennsylvania; MFA 61, Princeton Univ.; PhD 66, Princeton Univ. **Other Studies:** Cherubini Conservatory 1961-62. **Career & Employment:** Queens College, CUNY, Faculty; Marlboro Music Festival, Residence 1968. **Fellowships, Honors & Awards:** Princeton Univ., R.D. Welch Fellowship 1960-61; Italian Government-Fulbright Travel Grant 1961; Berkshire Music Center-Fromm Found. Comm. 1966; ASCAP Award 1966, 1967; Walter Naumburg Award for Chamber Music 1967; Brandeis Univ., Creative Arts Award 1969. **Important Works:** *Vox in Rama*, for mixed chorus a capella (Presser Co.) 1956; *Five Haiku*, for voice & 5 instruments (MCA Music) 1958; *Movement for String Quartet* (Apogee Press) 1959; *Song Cycle*, for voice & piano (MCA Music) 1960; *String Quartet No. 2* (MCA Music) 1960-64; *Cantus Commemorabilis I*, for chamber orchestra (MCA Music) 1966.

WEINGARDEN, LOUIS SMITH ■ FAAR Musical Composition 70. b. July 23, 1943, Detroit, MI. d. June 8, 1989. BMus 71, Juilliard School of Music. **Other Studies:** Columbia Univ. 1961-63; Jewish Theological Seminary with Miriam Gideon 1961-63. **Career & Employment:** Architectural Firm, Part. 1972-89. **Fellowships, Honors & Awards:** NEA Grant 1968; Charles Ives Award; NIAL; Elizabeth Sprague Coolidge Award. **Important Works:** *Evening Liturgy of Consolation*; *Violin Sonata* 1959; *The Sorrows of David* 1967; *Fantasy and Funeral Music*, for 2 pianos & percussion 1967; *Ghirlande*, for soprano & orchestra 1975; *Four Pieces for Piano Trio* 1975; *Piano Concerto* 1975; *Things Heard and Seen in Summer*, piano trio; *Cello Sonata*; *Suite for Violin*; *Vox clamens in deserto*, for organ & brass; *The Sorrows of David*, cantata with soli & orchestra; *Three Short Sacred Songs*, for women's voices a cappella. **Bio-Bibliography:** *Contemporary American Composers*.

WEINSTEIN, RICHARD ■ AAR Visitor 1991-92; UCLA, Graduate School of Architecture & Urban Planning, Dean.

WEIS, HARRIETT ANNE ■ FAAR Classics/Archaeology 80. b. Oct. 16, 1947, Moberly, MO. BA 68, Univ. of Missouri; MA 71, Univ. of Missouri; PhD 76, Bryn Mawr College. **Other Study:** ASCSA 1970; VSA Program on Coinage 1974. **Research/Artistic Interests:** Roman Republican art & archaeology, esp. sculpture & architecture. **Career & Employment:** Univ. of Pittsburgh 1976-present. **Memberships & Offices:** ArIA; CAA; VSA; Asmosia. **Publications:** *The Hanging Marsyas Statue: Roman Innovations in a Hellenistic Sculptural Tradition* (Rome: Bretschneider, 1992). **Business Address:** 104 Frick Fine Arts Bldg., Univ. of Pittsburgh, Pittsburgh, PA 15260.

WEISGALL, HUGO DAVID ■ RAAR Musical Composition 67. b. Oct. 13, 1912, Ivancice (Eibenschütz), Czechoslovakia. m. Nahalie Shulman. c. Jonathan M. Weisgall, Deborah Weisgall-Wilder. Dipl. (2) 38, 39, Curtis Inst.; PhD 40, Johns Hopkins Univ. **Other Study:** Peabody Conservatory 1927-32; with Roger Sessions 1932-41. **Research/Artistic Interests:** Operas & large-scale song cycles. **Career & Employment:** US Military Service 1941-47; Military Attaché, London 1945-46; Cultural Attache, Prague 1946-47; Chamber Soc. of Baltimore, Founder & Conductor 1948-present; Johns Hopkins Univ. 1951-57; Cantors Inst. of Jewish Theological Seminary, Chair 1952-present; Hilltop Opera Co., Founder & Conductor 1952-present; Juilliard School 1957-70; Queens College, CUNY, Prof. 1961-79, Dist. Prof. 1979. **Memberships & Offices:** American Music Center, Pres. 1963-73; AAAL 1993, Pres. 1990-93. **Fellowships, Honors & Awards:** Guggenheim Fellowship (3); NIAL 1975; AAAL, Gold Medal 1993. **Important Works:** *Overture in F* 1942-43; *Soldier Songs*, for baritone & orchestra 1944-46; *Outposts*, a ballet 1947; *The Tenor*, an opera 1948-50; *The Stronger*, an opera 1952; *Six Characters in Search of an Author*, an opera, Ditson Fund Comm. 1953-56; *Purgatory*, an opera 1958; *Athaliah*, an opera, Thomas Scherman & Little Orchestra Comm. 1960-63; *The Golden Peacock*, a song cycle 1960, rev. 1976; *Nine Rivers from Jordan*, an opera 1964-68; *Fancies & Inventions*, song cycle 1970; *Translations*, a song cycle, Shirley Verrett Comm. 1971-72; *End of Summer*, a song cycle 1973-74; *Jennie, or the Hundred Nights*, an opera, Juilliard School-NEA Comm. 1975-76; *The Gardens of Adonis*, an opera 1959, rev. 1977-81; *Esther*, an opera, New York City Opera Comm. 1993. Principal Publisher: Presser. **Bio-Bibliography:** *New Grove Dictionary of American Music*. **Home Address:** 81 Maple Dr., Great Neck, NY 11021.

WEISMAN, FREDERICK R. ■ AAR Visitor 1992-93, Art Collector.

WEISSMAN, GEORGE ■ AAR Trustee 1982-90, Trustee Emer.; Corp. Exec.

WELCH, KATHERINE E. ■ FAAR Classics/Archaeology 94; AAR, Summer School, Asst. Dir. 1993. b. Oct. 4, 1961, New Haven, CT. BA 84, Cornell Univ.; MA 88, IFA; PhD 94, IFA. **Other Study:** ICCS 1981; archaeological experience: Alambra 1982, San Giovanni di Ruoti 1983, Sardis 1984-87, Samothrace 1988-89, Aphrodisias 1991-present. **Research/Artistic Interests:** Roman art & archaeology, Greek art & archaeology, Roman social history. **Career & Employment:** Stevens Inst. of Technology, Adj. Prof. 1989-90; Harvard Univ., Asst. Prof. 1994-present. **Fellowships, Honors & Awards:** IFA, Shelby White & Leon Levy Fellowship 1988, Charles & Rosanna Batchellor Fellowship 1987-91; ASCSA, Oscar Broneer Fellowship 1992-93; ArIA, Kenan T. Erim Award 1993; American Research Inst. in Turkey, Fellow 1995. **Publications:** "Roman Amphitheatres Revived," *Journal of Roman Archaeology* 4 (1991): 271-82; "The Roman Arena in Late Republican Italy: A New Interpretation," *Journal of Roman Archaeology* 7 (1994): 59-80. **Business Address:** Harvard Univ., Dept. of Fine Arts, Cambridge, MA 02138.

WELLS, CHARLES ARTHUR, JR ■ FAAR Sculpture 66. b. Dec. 24, 1935, NYC. BA 59, Amherst College. **Other Studies:** Apprentice to Leonard Baskin 1961-64. **Fellowships, Honors & Awards:** NAD, Gold Medal 1987; NIAL Grant; John Taylor Arms Award. **Exhibitions/Performances:** Forum Gallery, NYC 1989; Solo: Hinckley & Brohel 1964; Far Gallery, NYC 1967, 1969; Forum Gallery, NYC 1988.

WENGER, JOHN H. ■ FAAR Painting 72. b. June 4, 1940, Salem, OR. c. Tuscany. BA 68, Univ. of Colorado; MFA 74, Univ. of Arizona. **Other Study:** with Philip Guston, Jack Tourkof, James Davis, plus many others; AIC, Univ. of Oregon, Eugene Wagner College of New York in Austria. **Research/Artistic Interests:** Figurative oil painting, political, ecological, social themes; also research into emerging chaos theory as related to non-mechanistic cultures & creativity. **Career & Employment:** Univ. of New Mexico, Lect. 1974-75, Asst. Prof. 1975-84, Assc. Prof. 1984-present. **Fellowships, Honors & Awards:** Univ. of New Mexico Grant 1983, Presidential Lectureship Award 1988. **Important Works:** Public Collections: Tucson Art Museum; Phoenix Art Museum; Museum of New Mexico, Santa Fe; Univ. Art Museum, Univ. of New Mexico, Albuquerque; Albuquerque Museum; Atlantic Richfield Co., Dallas; Amoco Production Co., Houston; Susman Godfrey McGowan, Houston; Republic Bank, Houston; Henderson-Massengill, Houston. **Exhibitions/ Performances:** Solo Shows: Harr Studio, Chicago 1966; URBA Studio, Chicago 1967; Sheffield Studio, Chicago 1968; Foothill's Art Center, Golden, CO 1969; Gallery 1309, Boulder 1969; Art Museum, Univ. of Colorado, Boulder 1970; Univ. of Arizona, Tucson 1973; Art Museum, Univ. of Montana, Missoula 1974; Harlan Gallery, Tucson 1976; L.A. Number One, Los Angeles Museum of Science & Industry 1976; Ten Take Ten, Colorado Springs Fine Arts Center 1977; Hill's Gallery, Santa Fe 1979; Yares Gallery, Scottsdale, AZ 1981; Davis-McClain Gallery, Houston 1983, 1985; Univ. Art Museum, Albuquerque 1986; Joseph Gross Gallery, Univ. of Arizona, Tucson 1986; Cafe Gallery, Albuquerque 1992. **Home Address:** SR 1092, Sandia Park, NM 87047.

WEPPNER, ROBERT A., JR ■ FAAR Architecture 36. b. Nov. 2, 1906, Cleveland, OH. d. Dec. 19, 1994. m. Dorothy. c. Christina, Robert, III. BArch 29, Catholic Univ. **Other Study:** Notre Dame Univ.

WERLICK, STEPHEN G. ■ FAAR Sculpture 64. b. June 29, 1932, Bronx, NY. m. Dorte Christjansen. c. Eve Valentina Lunt. BFA 56, Cooper Union; MFA 60, Tulane Univ., Newcomb Art School. **Other Study:** Skowhegan School of Painting & Sculpture 1953; studio asst. to Milton Hebald 1952-53; sculpture & bronze casting with Heinrich Kirchner, Akademie der Bildenden Künste, Munich 1956-57. **Research/Artistic Interests:** All areas of the visual arts: special emphasis & expertise in figurative sculpture, lost wax bronze casting & wood carving & fabrication. **Career & Employment:** UC, Santa Barbara, Asst. Prof. 1960-61; California State Univ., Long Beach, Prof. 1964-present. **Fellowships, Honors & Awards:** Fulbright Fellowship 1956. **Important Works:** 1972 Munich Olympic Games Comm.; Fort Lauderdale Sports Hall of Fame Museum; Memorial Relief Sculpture Comm., Reverend Nitsiotis, St. Catherine's Greek Orthodox Church, Redondo Beach, CA 1978; Edward A. Filene Memorial Portrait Sculpture, California Credit Union League Comm., Pomona, CA 1981; *The Holocaust,* Temple Judea Comm., Laguna Hills CA 1982; St Josephs Cathedral Comm., Los Angeles 1988; Loyola Marymount Univ. Comm., Los Angeles 1992. **Exhibitions/Performances:** Solo:

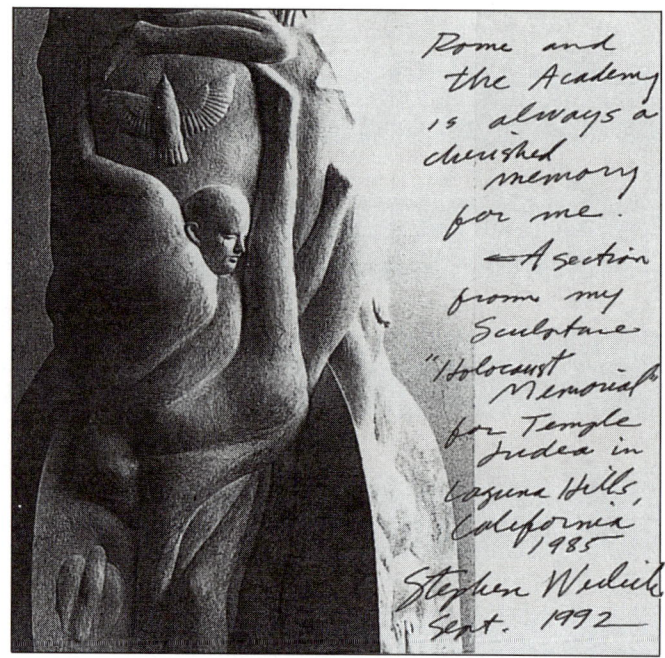

Stephen G. Werlick

Rex Evans Gallery, Los Angeles 1967; Retrospective, Golden West College, Huntington Beach, CA 1980. **Home Address:** 4450 E. 4th St., Long Beach, CA 90814. **Studio Address:** 2501 E. 10 St., Long Beach, CA 90804.

WESCOAT, BONNA D. ■ FAAR History of Art 92. b. May 1, 1954, Westfield, NJ. m. F. Bailey Green. c. Hugh Henry W. Green, Abigail Bailey W. Green. BA 76, Smith College; MA 77, Univ. of London, Inst. of Archaeology; MPhil 79, Oxford Univ.; PhD 83, Oxford Univ. **Research/Artistic Interests:** Greek architecture & urban planning, Greek iconography, history of architecture in general. **Career & Employment:** Kenyon College, Visiting Instr. 1980-82; Emory Univ., Asst. Prof. 1982-89, Assc. Prof. 1989-present. **Fellowships, Honors & Awards:** Marshall Scholarship 1976-79; Getty Fellowship 1986-87. **Publications:** *Poets and Heros: Scenes from the Trojan War* (Atlanta: Emory Univ. Museum, 1986); "Designing the Temple of Athena at Assos: Some Evidence from the Capitals," *AJA* 91 (1987): 553-68; *Syracuse, the Fairest Greek City* (Rome: de Luca, 1989); "Wining and Dining on the Temple of Athena at Assos," *Papers in the History of Art 9*, ed. S. Munshower (University Park, PA: Penn State Univ. Press, forthcoming); *The Temple of Athena at Assos* (Oxford: Oxford Univ. Press, forthcoming). **Home Address:** 32 Kingston Rd., Kensington, CA 94707. **Business Address:** Art History Dept., Emory Univ., Atlanta, GA 30322.

WEST, ANDREW F. ■ AAR Trustee 1911-27, Classicist.

WEST, REBECCA J. ■ FAAR Post-Classical/Humanistic Studies 79. b. Dec. 14, 1946, Butler, PA. BA 68, Univ. of Pittsburgh; PhD 74, Yale Univ. **Research/Artistic Interests:** 20th-century Italian literature, Italian women writers, film, Dante, literary theory. **Career & Employment:** Univ. of Chicago, Asst. Prof. 1974-81, Assc. Prof. 1981-89, Prof. 1989-present, Chair 1987-94. **Memberships & Offices:** Ed. Bd.: *Italica, Annali d'Italianistica, World Literature Today, Forum Italicum*; MLA; Midwest Modern Language Assn.; American Assn. of Italian Studies; American Assn. of Teachers of Italian; Dante Soc.; Associazione Internazionale di Studi Italiani. **Fellowships,**

Honors & Awards: MLA, Howard Marraro Prize 1982; Guggenheim Fellowship 1985-86; Univ. of Chicago, Burlington Northern Faculty Achievement Award 1992. **Publications:** "Montale's *Forse*: The Poetics of Doubt," *Forum Italicum* 13.2 (Summer, 1979): 147-68; *Eugenio Montale: Poet on the Edge* (Cambridge, MA: Harvard Univ. Press, 1981); "The Poetics of Plenitude: Malerba's *Diario di un Sognatore*," *Italica* 62.3 (1985): 201-12; "Lo Spazio in Celati's *Narratori delle Pianure*," *Nuova Corrente* 97 (1986): 65-74; "L'Identità americana di Calvino," *Nuova Corrente* 99 (1987): 363-74; "Tonino Guerra and the Space of the Screenwriter," *Annali d'Italianistica* 6 (1988): 162-78; ed., with Dino S. Cervigni, *Women's Voices in Italian Literature*, Annali d'Italianistica 7 (1989); "Montale's *Care Ombre*: Identity and its Dissolution," *Forum Italicum* 23.1-2 (1989): 212-26; "A Note on the Sense of Touch in the *Divine Comedy*," *Lectura Dantis* 5 (1989): 46-58; "Before, Beneath and Around the Text: The Genesis and Construction of Some Postmodern Prose Fictions," *Annali d'Italianistica* 9 (1991): 272-92; "Scorsese's *Who's That Knocking At My Door?*," *Romance Languages Annual* 3 (1991): 331-38; "*Pudore*: The Theory and Practice of Modesty," *Differentia* 5 (1991): 175-88; "Purgatorio X," in *Dante's "Divine Comedy": Introductory Readings: "Purgatorio*," ed. T. Wlassics (Univ. of Virginia, 1993), 142-57; "Women in Italian," in *Italian Studies in North America*, ed. M. Ciavolella & A. Iannucci (Toronto: Dovehouse, 1994), 195-214. **Bio-Bibliography:** *Directory of American Scholars*. **Business Address:** Dept. of Romance Language & Literatures, Univ. of Chicago, 1050 E. 59 St., Chicago, IL 60637.

WESTERMANN, WILLIAM L. ■ AAR Trustee 1921-32; School of Classical Studies, Prof.-in-Charge 1926-27; Historian.

WESTON, ARTHUR HAROLD ■ FASCSR 12. b. Sept. 8, 1886, Mount Vernon, ME. d. Feb. 10, 1966. BA 08, Yale Univ.; MA 09, Yale Univ.; PhD 11, Yale Univ. **Other Study:** Göttingen 1912-13. **Research/Artistic Interests:** Latin poetry, esp. Catullus & Virgil. **Career & Employment:** Yale Univ., Instr. 1913-17; Lawrence College, Appleton WI, Prof. 1919-47; Univ. of Southern California, Assc. Prof. 1947-48, Prof. 1948-52, Prof. Emer. 1952-66. **Memberships & Offices:** APA; Classical Assn. of the Pacific States. **Publications:** *Latin Satirical Writing Subsequent to Juvenal* (Lancaster PA: New Era Printing, 1915); "On Catullus XIV, 11 ff.," *Classical Journal* 20 (1924); 237; "Some Aspects of Ancient Scientific Thought," *Classical Journal* 25 (1929): 102-18; "The Ablative Absolute," *Classical Journal* 30 (1935): 298-99; "Three Dreams of Aeneas," *Classical Journal* 30 (1937): 229-32; *Selections from Latin Prose and Verse* (Boston: Allyn & Bacon, 1938). **Bio-Bibliography:** *Directory of American Scholars*.

WHARTON, EDITH NEWBOLD JONES ■ Novelist, b. 1862. d. Aug. 11, 1937. **Honors & Awards:** Officer of Legion of Honor of France; Chevalier, Order of Leopold of Belgium; NIAL, Gold Medal. **Selected Publications:** *The House of Mirth* (1905); *The Age of Innocence* (1920); *A Backward Glance* (1934). In 1897/98 she was an influential member of a committee of distinguished American women who organized events designed to encourage support of and interest in the Academy.

WHICHER, GEORGE M. ■ AAR School of Classical Studies, Prof.-in-Charge 1921-22.

WHITE, CYNTHIA ■ FAAR Classics/Archaeology 89. m. John W. White. c. Mary. BA 76, Chestnut Hill College; MA 78, Villanova Univ.; PhD 90, Catholic Univ. of America. **Other Study:** Latin Inst., NYC 1980; AAR Summer Archaeology Program 1981; VSA Summer Study 1981; Medieval Latin Inst.,

Boston 1983; Intensive Latin with Reginald Foster, Summers 1988 & 1989. **Career & Employment:** Baldwin School, Classics, Chair 1978-83; Catholic Univ. of America, Instr. 1983-91; Washington Theological Consortium 1985-91; Johns Hopkins Univ., Instr. 1988; Univ. of Arizona, Asst. Prof. 1991-present. **Memberships & Offices:** American Classical League 1976-present; APA 1982-present, Fathers of the Church Series, Ed. Bd.; VSA 1982-present; Washington Classical Soc. 1983-present; Italian Cultural Soc. 1985-91; Classical Assn. of the Atlantic States 1986-present; CAMWS 1991-present; Societas Classica Arizonensis 1994-present. **Fellowships, Honors & Awards:** Fulbright Summer Grant 1981, Fellowship 1988-89; NEH Fellowship 1982, 1983; American Classical League, McKinley Scholarship 1988; Univ. of Arizona Research Grant 1992. **Publications:** "Roman Baths," *Speculum Romanum* (1984): 36-53. **Business Address:** Classics Dept., Univ. of Arizona, ML 371, Tucson, AZ 85721.

WHITE, HELEN ELIZABETH RUSSELL ■ FAAR Classics/Archaeology 52. b. Dec. 8, 1919, Manchester, NH. d. 1984. m. Robert White. BA 41, Mt. Holyoke College; MA 42, Bryn Mawr College; PhD, Bryn Mawr College. **Research/Artistic Interests:** Latin, epigraphy, "ornamenta," inscriptions. **Career & Employment:** St. Margaret's School, Tappahannock, VA, Teacher 1942-44; Dana Hall School, Wellesley, MA, Teacher 1944-47; Mt. Holyoke College, Instr.-Asst. Prof. 1947-56. **Memberships & Offices:** APA, ArIA. **Fellowships, Honors & Awards:** Fulbright Fellowship 1952; Mt. Holyoke, Frances Mary Hazen Fellowship.

WHITE, HENRY ■ AAR Charter Mem., Diplomat.

WHITE, LAWRENCE GRANT ■ AAR Visitor 1943-51, Architect.

WHITE, ROBERT W. ■ FAAR Sculpture 55, RAAR Sculpture 69. b. Sept. 19, 1921, NYC. m. Claire Nicolas White. c. Sebastian N., Stephanie M., Christian S., Natalie L. **Study:** Portsmouth Priory, NH 1935-39; RISD 1939-42, 1945-46. **Research/Artistic Interests:** Bronze, stone, wood, terracotta, etc. **Career**

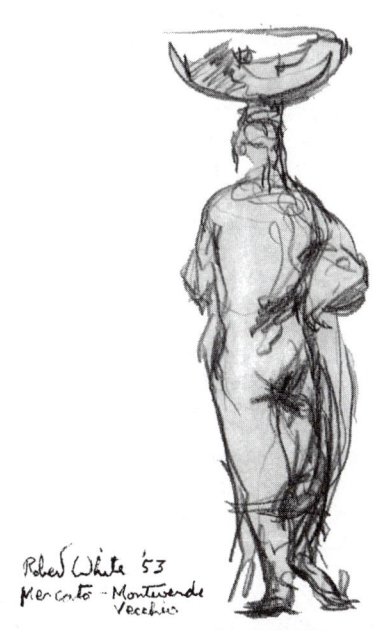

Robert W. White

& Employment: Parsons School of Design, Instr. 1949-52, 1955-56; SUNY, Stony Brook, Assc. Prof.-Prof. Emer. 1962-87. **Memberships & Offices:** NAD, Recording Sec., 2d VP, 1st VP, many juries, mem. of council; plus many other societies & many exhibition & competition juries. **Fellowships, Honors & Awards:** NAD, Assc. 1979, Academician 1982. **Exhibitions/ Performances:** Solo: Suffolk Museum, Stony Brook, NY 1948, 1956; Artists Gallery, NYC 1950; Davis Gallery, NYC 1957, 1959, 1962, 1967; Vera Lazuk Gallery, Cold Spring Harbor, NY 1957; SUNY, Stony Brook 1962; Graham Gallery, NYC 1970; Benson Gallery, Bridgehampton, NY 1971, 1979; Gallery North, Setauket, NY 1974, 1976; Graham Modern, NYC 1975, 1980, 1986, 1987, 1992; Boston Athenaeum 1976; Hartwick College, Oneonta, NY 1977; Art Dept. Gallery, Community College, Suffolk, NY 1983; Staller Center Gallery, SUNY Stony Brook 1988. **Home Address:** RFD 1, 5 Moriches Rd., St. James, NY 11780. **Business Address:** Graham Modern, 1014 Madison Ave., NYC 10021.

WHITE, STANFORD ■ AAR Charter Mem., Architect.

WHITEHEAD, PHILIP BARROWS ■ FASCSR 11-13. b. Jan. 29, 1884, Janesville, WI. d. July 3, 1965. BA 06, Beloit College; PhD 14. **Other Study:** Berlin 1910. **Research/Artistic Interests:** Early Christian archaeology, Latin poetry. **Career & Employment:** Yale Univ., Instr. 1919-23; Univ. of Vermont, Asst. Prof. 1925-27; Beloit College, Prof. 1929-49, Prof. Emer. 1949-65. **Publications:** "Degli antichi edifici componenti la chiesa dei SS. Cosma e Damiano al foro romano," *Nuovo Bullettino di Archeologia Cristiana* 19 (1913): 143-65; with G. Biasiotti, "La Chiesa dei SS. Cosma e Damiano al foro romano e gli edifici preesistenti," *Rendiconti della Pontificia Accademia Romana di Archeologia* 3 (1925): 83-122; "Church of SS. Cosma e Damiano in Rome," *AJA* 31 (1927): 1-18; "Church of S. Anastasia in Rome," *AJA* 31 (1927): 405-20; "Acts of the Council of 499," *Speculum* 3 (1928): 152-65; "A New Method of Investigating the Caesura in Latin Hexameter and Pentameter," *American Journal of Philology* 51 (1930): 358-71; "Greek Vases at Beloit," *Parnassus* 3 (May 1931): 15. **Bio-Bibliography:** Beloit College Archives; *Directory of American Scholars*.

WHITEHOUSE, DAVID ■ AAR Visitor 1980-81; British School, Dir.; Corning Museum, Dir.

WHITESIDE, EMILY MCNEELY ■ FAAR Design Arts 82. b. Sept. 27, 1926, Natchez, MS. c. Amy Whiteside Chote. BFA 48, Univ. of Texas, Austin. **Career & Employment:** Univ. of Texas, Austin, Development Asst. to Dean 1966-69; Texas Arts Comm., Assc. Dir. 1969-71; Galveston Co. Arts Council, Inc., Exec. Dir. 1971-80. **Memberships & Offices:** Victorian Soc. of America; Nat. Trust for Historic Preservation; American Council for the Arts, NYC, Consultant; NEA Expansion Arts Program Division, Panel Mem.; Galveston County Historical Comm., BoD.

WHITESIDE, MORRIS ■ Stewardson Memorial Scholar 1911-12, 1913.

WHITTENBERG, CHARLES ■ FAAR Musical Composition 66. b. July 6, 1927, St. Louis, MO. d. Aug. 22, 1984. m. Mary Whittenberg. BMus 48, Eastman School of Music. **Career & Employment:** Private Teacher, NYC 1949-63; Greenwich House Music School, NYC, Faculty 1961-63; Bennington College, Faculty 1962-84; Columbia-Princeton Electronic Music Center 1962-; American Univ., Composer in Residence 1965-66; Univ. of Connecticut, Asst. Prof., 1967-77. **Memberships & Offices:**

ACA, Ed. Bd. 1961-65; WNYC, American Music Festival, Concert Organizer 1961-63; *American Composers Alliance Bulletin*, Ed. 1962-. **Fellowships, Honors & Awards:** Guggenheim Fellowships, 1963-64, 1964-65. **Important Works:** *Dialogue and Aria*, for flute & piano 1956; *Three Songs on Texts of Rainer Maria Rilke* 1957-62; *Serenade on a Twelfth Night Carol* 1960; *Study*, for cello & tape 1960; *Structure with Chorale* 1961; *Structures*, for 2 pianos 1961; *Fantasy*, for wind quintet 1961; *Electronic Study II*, for double bass & tape 1962; *Triptych*, for brass quintet 1962; *Three Pieces for Clarinet Alone* 1963; *Identities and Variations for Piano* 1963; *Duo-Divertimento*, for flute & double bass 1963; *Chamber Concerto*, for violin & 7 instrumentalists 1963; *Event*, for chamber orchestra & tape 1963; *Trio Divertimento* 1964; *Nonet* 1964-65; *Variations*, for 9 players 1964-70; *Polyphony*, for trumpet 1965; *Games of Five*, for wind quintet 1968; *Iambi*, for 2 oboes 1968; *Concerto for Brass Quintet* 1968-69; *In Memoriam Benjamin Britten*, for percussion 1977. **Bio-Bibliography:** *Baker's Biographical Dictionary of American Musicians*.

WIGGINTON, BROOKS E. ■ FAAR Landscape Architecture 50. b. Feb. 22, 1912, Marietta, OH. m. Sally Frances Cornell. c. B. Eliot Wigginton. BA 34, Marietta College; BFA 37, Ohio State Univ.; MLA 39, Cornell Univ. **Career & Employment:** Cleveland Dept. of Parks, Landscape Arch. 1939-40; Wheeling Park Comm., WV, Landscape Arch. 1940-85; Univ. of Georgia, Prof. 1945-58; Independent Practice, Wheeling, WV 1958-85. **Fellowships, Honors & Awards:** ASLA, Fellow 1958; Marietta College, Doctor of Arts 1959; Dumbarton Oaks Library, Senior Fellow in Garden Design 1960-61. **Publications:** *Trees and Shrubs for the Southeast* (Athens, GA: Univ. of Georgia Press, 1941). **Important Works:** Oglebay Park, Wheeling, WV; M/M Gordon Hanes Garden, Winston-Salem, NC; Marietta College Campus, Marietta, OH; Dromoland Castle, Co. Clare, Ireland. **Home Address:** 2013-a Pats Pl., Tallahassee, FL 32308.

WIGGLESWORTH, FRANK ■ FAAR Musical Composition 54, RAAR Musical Composition 70. b. Mar. 3, 1918, Boston, MA. m. Anne Parker Wigglesworth. c. Philio, Henry. BA 40, Bard College; MusM 42, Converse College. **Other Study:** Composition with Otto Luening, Henry Cowell & Edgar Varese. **Research/Artistic Interests:** Concert music, ethnic music. **Career & Employment:** Columbia Univ., Instr. 1946-51; New School for Social Research 1948-89, Chair 1968-89; CUNY: Queens College, Asst. Prof. 1954-55; Bronx Community College, Assc. Prof. 1969-80. **Home Address:** 19 Downing St., NYC 10014.

WIGODSKY, MICHAEL MASHE ■ FAAR Classics/Archaeology 61. b. May 23, 1935, Houston, TX. BA 57, Univ. of Texas, Austin; MA 59, Princeton Univ.; PhD 64, Princeton Univ. **Career & Employment:** Florida State Univ., Instr. 1961-62; Stanford Univ., Instr. 1962-64, Asst. Prof. 1964-69, Assc. Prof. 1969-present. **Fellowships, Honors & Awards:** Univ. of Texas, Will Rogers Scholarship 1953-57; Princeton Nat. Fellowship 1957-58; Owen D. Young Fellowship 1958-59; Fulbright Grant 1959-60. **Publications:** "The Salvation of Ajax," *Hermes* 90 (1962): 149-58; "Anacreon & the Girl from Lesbos," *Classical Philology* 57 (1962): 109; "The Arming of Aeneas," *Classica & Medievalia* 26 (1967): 192-221; *Vergil and Early Latin Poetry*, Hermer Einzelschriften 24 (Weisbaden: Steiner Verlag, 1972); "A Pattern of Argument in Lucretius," *Pacific Coast Philology* 9 (1974): 73-78; "Nacqui sub Iulio (Inf. I, 70)," *Dante Studies* 93 (1975): 177-83; "Horace's Miser (S. 1 1 108) and Aristotelian Self-Love," *Symbolae Osloenses* 55 (1980): 33-58; "Lucretius II 20 ff.," *American Journal of Philology* 107 (1986): 402-4; "The Alleged Impossibility of Philosophical Poetry," in *Philodernus & Poetry*, ed. D. Obbink (Oxford: Oxford Univ. Press, forthcoming). **Business Address:** Dept. of Classics, Stanford Univ., Bldg. 20, Stanford, CA 94305.

WILBUR, RICHARD P. ■ FAAR Literature 55. b. Mar. 1, 1921, NYC. m. Charlotte W. Wilbur. c. Ellen, Christopher, Nathan, Aaron. **Fellowships, Honors & Awards:** Chevalier, Ordre des Plames Academique; Oscar Blumenthal Prize 1940; *Poetry Magazine,* Harris Monroe Prize 1948; Guggenheim Fellow 1952-53, 1963; Edna St. Vincent Millay Memorial Award 1957; Nat. Book Award 1957; Pulitzer Prize 1957, 1989; Ford Fellow 1960-61; Bollingen Prize 1971; US Poet Laureate 1987; AAAL 1991; MLA, Hon. Fellow; AAAS. **Publications:** *The Beautiful Changes* (1947); *Ceremony* (1950); *A Bestiary* (1955); *Things of This World* (1956); *Poems 1943-56* (1957); *Advice to a Prophet* (1961); *Poems of Richard Wilbur* (1963); *Walking to Sleep* (1969); *The Mind-Reader* (1976); *Seven Poems* (1981): *The Whale* (1982); *New and Collected Poems* (1988). **Bio-Bibliography:** Donald Hill, *Richard Wilbur* (Twayne, 1967); Wendy Salinger, *Richard Wilbur's Creation* (Ann Arbor: Univ. of Michigan Press, 1983); Bruce Michelson, *Wilbur's Poetry* (Amherst: Univ. of Massachusetts Press, 1991); Rodney Stenning Edgecombe, *A Reader's Guide to the Poetry of Richard Wilbur* (Univ. of Alabama Press, forthcoming); *Who's Who in the World.* **Home Address:** RR 1, Box 82, 87 Dodwells Rd., Cummington, MA 01026; 715R Windsor Ln., Key West, FL 33040. **Business Address:** Gilbert Parker, William Morris Agency, 1350 Ave. of the Americas, NYC 10019.

A Baroque Wall-Fountain in the Villa Sciarra

Under the bronze crown
Too big for the head of the stone cherub whose feet
A serpent has begun to eat,
Sweet water brims a cockle and braids down

Past spattered mosses, breaks
On the tipped edge of a second shell, and fills
The massive third below. It spills
In threads then from the scalloped rim, and makes

A scrim or summery tent
For a faun-ménage and their familiar goose.
Happy in all that ragged, loose
Collapse of water, its effortless descent

And flatteries of spray . . .

Richard Wilbur 8/2/92

Richard P. Wilbur

WILDER, THORNTON NIVEN ■ AAR Visiting student 1920-21. Writer. b. Apr. 17, 1897. d. Dec. 7, 1975. Dedicated *The Cabala* (1925) to the Fellows and Residents of the Academy, 1920-21. **Honors & Awards:** Pulitzer Prize 1938; Nat. Book Award 1968.

WILEY, CHARLES D. ■ FAAR Architecture 48. b. Feb. 2, 1916, St. Paul, MN. m. Alicia Wiley. c. Peter, Heather. BArch 40, Univ. of Minnesota; MArch 41, Harvard Univ. **Career & Employment:** Saarinen & Swanson 1944-45; Skidmore, Owings & Merrill 1945-56, Chicago Chief of Design 1952-56, San Fran-

cisco Chief of Design 1956-59; John Carl Warnecke & Asscs. 1959-65, 1968-72; UC, Berkeley, Lect. 1960-69; Neill Smith & Asscs. 1965-68; Stone, Marraccini & Patterson 1972-82. **Fellowships, Honors & Awards:** Harvard Univ., Julia Amory Appleton Traveling Fellowship 1941; *Architecture Magazine* Awards (3), 1st Prize 1944; Art & Architecture, Small House Competition, 1st Prize 1944; *Modern Hospital Magazine,* Hon. Mention 1944; Junior Chamber of Commerce HQ Award, 4th Prize 1950. **Important Works:** Lake Meadows Housing Development, New York Life Insurance Co., Chicago 1950s; Lever House, Original Design; General Mills Home Office Bldg., Golden Valley, MN 1956; Portland Memorial Coliseum, OR 1958; Dean McHenry Library, UC, Santa Cruz 1965; Briss Hall Laboratory Bldg., UC, Davis 1968; Halidie Plaza, San Francisco 1970; Five Out-Patient Clinics, Kaiser Permanente Health Care, Northern California 1978. **Home Address:** 126 Sixth Ave., San Francisco, CA 94118.

WILL, ELIZABETH LYDING ■ AAR Visitor 1973-74, Educator, Archaeologist. b. Apr. 27, 1924. **Research Interests:** Roman amphoras & Roman economic & social history. **Career & Employment:** Univ. of Massachusetts, Amherst, Prof.; AAR excavations at Cosa.

WILLIAMS, CHARLES KAUFMANN, II ■ AAR Visitor 1976-77; Contributor to the AAR summer archaeology training program; Archaeologist, Educator. **Career & Employment:** ASCSA, Corinth Excavations, Dir. **Honors & Awards:** ArIA, Gold Medal 1993.

WILLIAMS, EDGAR IRVING ■ FAAR Architecture 12; AAR Trustee 1919-37. b. Oct. 5, 1884, Rutherford, NJ. d. Jan. 1, 1974. m. Hulda Gustafva Olsen. c. Ingrid Helen Wackernagel; Hulda Palamona Ferris; Edith Maria Horn; Christina Nilsson Koegel. BS 08, MIT; MS 09, MIT. **Other Study:** Chateau de Lancy, Geneva 1898-99. **Research/Artistic Interests:** Pompeii restoration, Verona, library design. **Career & Employment:** Wells, Bosworth, Architectural Designer 1912-15; MIT, Instr. 1912-13, Assc. Prof. 1913-14; Guy Lowell, Architectural Designer 1915-16; E.P. Mellon, Architectural Designer 1916-37; American Red Cross, Genoa, Dir. 1917-19; Williams & Barrett, Part. 1920-28; Columbia Univ., Faculty 1921-29, 1937-46; Private Practice 1928-66; New York Public Library, Consulting Architect. **Memberships & Offices:** Fine Arts Federation, NYC, VP 1942; NAD, Pres. 1962-66; ALNY, Pres. 1939-41; Municipal Art Soc., NYC, Pres. 1950-51; AIA, Regional Dir. 1942-45; AIA College of Fellows, Vice Chancellor 1954, Chancellor 1956; Bergen County Park Comm. 1947-49; American Scenic & Historic Preservation Soc., BoT; American Architectural Found., BoT; American Fine Arts Soc., BoT 1938-40; MMA, BoT; Fine Arts Federation of New York, VP 1941-43; NSS, VP 1945-47; US State Department Adv. Comm. 1950s. **Fellowships, Honors & Awards:** Royal Soc. of the Arts, Benjamin Franklin Fellow; Royal Order of Vasa, Sweden, 1st Class, Knight 1941; AIA, Fellow 1942. **Publications:** "To Teach Housing May Also Be to Teach Architecture," *The Octagon* 11.10, (Oct. 1939). **Important Works:** Donnell Library Center, NY Public Library; Central Circulation Branch, NY Public Library; Woodridge War Memorial Public Library, NJ 1953; Manton B. Metcalf Memorial, Orange, NJ; K.D. Pierson Residence. **Exhibitions/Performances:** NYC Municipal Bldg. Art Gallery 1941. **Bio-Bibliography:** *Who Was Who in America.*

WILLIAMS, LOIS VIRGINIA ■ FAAR Classics/Archaeology 48. b. June 29, 1913, Philadelphia, PA. BA 35, Beaver College; MA 39, Univ. of Pennsylvania; PhD 46, Johns Hopkins Univ. **Career & Employment:** Montrose School for Girls, Faculty 1942-43; Juniata College, Instr. 1943-47; SUNY, Albany, Prof. 1947-79, Prof. Emer. 79-. **Fellowships, Honors & Awards:** Johns Hopkins Univ., Edmund Law Rogers Fellowship 1945-46.

WILLIAMS, MARY T. ■ AAR – New York, Exec. Sec. 1946-70s.

WILLIAMS, MILLER ■ FAAR Literature 77; School of Classical Studies, Adv. Council 1984-91. b. Apr. 8, 1930, Hoxie, AR. m. Jordan Hall. c. Lucinda Williams, Robert Williams, Karyn Williams. BS 50, Arkansas State College; MS 52, Univ. of Arkansas. **Career & Employment:** Louisiana State Univ., Instr. 1962-63, Asst. Prof. 1964-66; Univ. of Chile, Visiting Prof. 1963-64; Loyola Univ., New Orleans, Assc. Prof. 1966-69; Nat. Univ. of Mexico, Fulbright Prof. 1970; Univ. of Arkansas, Assc. Prof. 1971-73, Prof. 1973-87, Univ. Prof. 1987-present. **Memberships & Offices:** Pan American Conference, University Artists & Writers, Chile, 1st US Delegate 1964; Bread Loaf Writers' Conference, Lect. 1967-72; *New Orleans Review*, Loyola Univ., Founding Ed. 1968-70; Arkansas Poetry Circuit, Exec. Dir. 1974-80; Poetry-in-the-Prisons Program, AR, Founding Dir. 1974-76; *Translation Review*, Contributing Ed. 1978-; American Literary Translators Assn., VP 1978-79, Pres. 1979-81; *Poetry Miscellany*, Translation Ed. 1979-85; Univ. of Arkansas Press, Founding Dir. 1980-present. **Fellowships, Honors & Awards:** Henry Bellman Poetry Award 1957; Bread Loaf Fellowship 1961; Amy Lowell Traveling Scholarship 1963-64; New York Arts Fund Award 1970; Univ. of Arkansas Distinguished Research Award 1979, Distinguished Alumnus Award 1980; Lander College, SC, DHum 1983; The Poets' Prize 1990; Charity Randall Citation 1993; John William Corrington Award 1994; Socio Benemerito dell'Associazione, Centro Romanesco Trilussa, Roma 1994. **Publications:** *A Circle of Stone* (LSU Press, 1964); trans., *Recital* (Oceano De Chile, 1966); *19 Poetas de Hoy en los Estados Unidos* (USIS/Chile, 1966); with J.W. Corrington, *Southern Writing in the Sixties: Poetry* (LSU Press, 1966); with J.W. Corrington, *Southern Writing in the Sixties: Fiction* (LSU Press, 1966); trans., Nicanor Parra, *Poems & Antipoems* (New Directions, 1967); *So*

Evening: A Studio in Rome

The window here is hung in the west wall.
It lays on the opposite wall a square of light.
Sliced by the lopsided slats of the broken blind,
the light hangs like a painting. Now, and now,
the shadow of a swallow shoots across it.

I turn around to see the birds themselves,
scores of birds, hundreds, a thousand swallows.
I try to keep a single bird. I lose it.
In all that spinning not one bird spins loose.

I turn away from the window and back to work.
My eyes are caught again by the square of light.
I lean back in my chair and watch the picture
moving up the wall, the single birds
living out their lives in a frame of light,
until it touches the ceiling and fades out.
I turn around again and the swallows are gone.
The sun is gone. This minute Rome is dark
as only Rome is dark, as if somebody
could go out reaching toward it, and find no Rome.

Miller Williams
8.15.92

Miller Williams

Long at the Fair (E.P. Dutton, 1968); *Chile: An Anthology of New Writing* (Kent State Press, 1968); *The Achievement of John Ciardi* (Scott, Foresman, 1968); *The Only World There Is* (E. P. Dutton, 1971); *The Poetry of John Crow Ramson* (Rutgers Univ. Press, 1971); trans., Nicanor Parra, *Emergency Poems* (New Directions, 1972); *Contemporary Poetry in America* (Random House, 1972); *Halfway from Hoxie: New & Selected Poems* (LSU Press, 1973); with John Ciardi, *How Does a Poem Mean?* (Houghton Mifflin, 1974); with James Alan McPherson, *Railroad* (Random House, 1976); *Why God Permits Evil* (LSU Press, 1977); *A Roman Collection* (Missouri, 1980); trans., *Sonnets of Giuseppe Belli* (LSU Press, 1981); *Distractions* (LSU Press, 1981); *Ozark, Ozark: A Hillside Reader* (Missouri, 1992); *The Boys on Their Bony Mules* (LSU Press, 1983); *Patterns of Poetry: An Encyclopedia of Forms* (LSU Press, 1986); *Imperfect Love* (LSU Press, 1986); *Living on the Surface: New and Selected Poems*; (LSU Press, 1989); *Adjusting to the Light* (Missouri, 1992); Recording: *Poems of Miller Williams* (Spoken Arts). **Bio-Bibliography:** John DuVal, "Translating the Dialect: Miller Williams' 'Romanesco,'" *Translation Review* 32-33(1990): 27-31; Leon Stokesbury, "Miller Williams," in *Dictionary of Literary Biography Year Book* (Detroit: Gale Research Co., 1991), 263-74; ed., Michael Burns, *Miller Williams and the Poetry of the Particular* (Missouri, 1991); Robert Morgan, "Never Confuse a Fact with Truth: The Poetry of Miller Williams," *Mississippi Quarterly* (Winter 1992-93); *Who's Who in America; Who's Who in the World.* **Business Address:** University of Arkansas Press, Fayetteville, AR 72701.

WILLIAMS, RANDOLPH A. ■ FAAR Design Arts 82. b. Apr. 30, 1937. BFA, NYU; MFA, Sir George Williams Univ. **Important Works:** "Art on the Beach," Creative Times Comm. 1980; Sculpture Installation, Burnham Dance Co. Comm. 1981; Grand Central Project - Remy Martin Comm. 1980; "Printed Art, A View of Two Decades," MOMA Comm. 1980; "Art Across the Park," Central Park Comm. 1980.

WILLIAMS, ROBERT J. ■ FAAR History of Art 91. b. Nov. 8, 1955, Trenton, NJ. m. Carole Paul, FAAR 86. BA 76, Univ. of Pennsylvania; MA 79, Univ. of Pennsylvania; PhD 88, Princeton Univ. **Career & Employment:** UC, Santa Barbara, Asst. Prof. 1988-. **Fellowships, Honors & Awards:** Fulbright-Hays Grant 1977-78; Warburg Inst., Dame Frances Yates Fellowship 1986. **Publications:** "Notes by Vincenzo Borghini on Works of Art in San Gimignano and Volterra: A Source for Vasari's Lives," *Burlington Magazine* 127 (Jan. 1985): 17-21.

WILLIAMS, TOD CULPAN ■ FAAR Design Arts 83. b. May 11, 1943, Detroit, MI. m. Billie Tsien. c. Rachael, Kip. BA 65, Princeton Univ.; MFA 67, Princeton Univ. **Other Studies:** Cambridge Univ. 1965-66. **Career & Employment:** Richard Meier & Asscs., Architects, Assc. 1967-73; Cooper Union, Assc. Adj. Prof. 1972-; Potters & Williams 1973-76; Tod Williams & Asscs., Architects, Prin. 1973-; Inst. for Arch. & Urban Studies, Visiting Lect. 1976-77. **Fellowships, Honors & Awards:** AIA, Nat. Award 1988, 1989. **Exhibitions/Performances:** Walker Art Center, Minneapolis 1989; Whitney Museum, NYC 1990. **Bio-Bibliography:** "The Baby Boom Architects," *Metropolitan Home* (July 1983); Paul Goldberger, "Rekindling the Fires of Utopian Modernism," *NY Times* (May 6, 1990).

WILLIS, RICHARD M. ■ FAAR Musical Composition 57. b. Apr. 21, 1929, Mobile, AL. m. Carolyn Brown. c. Beverly, Richard. BMus 50, Univ. of Alabama; MusM 51, Eastman School of Music; PhD 64, Eastman School of Music. **Career & Employment:** Shorter College, Rome, GA, Prof. 1953-63; Baylor

Univ., Prof. & Composer-in-Residence 1964-present. **Memberships & Offices:** ASCAP; American Music Center; Texas Composers Forum. **Fellowships, Honors & Awards:** Sigma Alpha Iota, American Music Award 1953, 1962; Joseph Bearns Prize 1955; Howard Hanson Prize 1964; Pedro Paz Award 1965; Soc. for the Publication of American Music, Publication Award 1968; Ostvald Award 1969; Volkwein-ASBDA Award 1973; Baylor Univ., Citation 1976; Oriana Trio Competition Award; Texas Federation of Music Clubs, Citation. **Important Works:** *Symphony No. 1* 1953; *Sonatina for Violin and Piano* 1957; *String Quartet No. 2* 1961; *Evocation,* for orchestra 1967; *Three Songs from Blake,* American Inst. for Musical Studies Comm. 1970; *Petition and Thanks,* for chorus, narrator, wind ensemble, Univ. of Kentucky, Lexington Comm. 1976; *Trio for Violin, Cello, and Piano* 1982; *Five Dialogues,* for violin & piano 1983; *String Quartet No. 3* 1985; *Metamorphoses,* for alto saxophone & orchestra 1989; *Sun Circles,* for wind ensemble 1991; *Variants,* piano quartet, Quadriga Comm. 1992. Recordings: Golden Crest Records, Mark Records, Musical Heritage Soc. **Bio-Bibliography:** *Contemporary American Composers: Biographical Dictionary.* **Business Address:** School of Music, Baylor Univ., Waco, TX 76798.

WILSON, GEORGE BALCH, JR ■ FAAR Musical Composition 61. b. Jan. 28, 1927, Grand Island, NE. m. Lois Wilson. c. Brian Louis Wilson. BMus 51, Univ. of Michigan; MMus 53, Univ. of Michigan. **Other Studies:** Berkshire Music Center 1955; School of Fine Arts, Fontainebleau 1956. **Career & Employment:** Univ. of Michigan, Faculty 1961-. **Fellowships, Honors & Awards:** AAAL Citation; Univ. of Michigan Scholarship 1950-52; Presser Found. Scholarship 1951; ASCAP Publication Award 1952; Fulbright Fellowship 1953-54. **Important Works:** *String Quartet in G,* Soc. for the Publication of American Music Comm. 1952; *String Trio* 1956; *Fantasy,* for violin & piano 1958.

WILTON-ELY, JOHN ■ AAR Visitor 1990-91, Architectural Historian.

WIND, EDGAR ■ RAAR History of Art 50. b. May 14, 1900, Berlin, Germany. d. Sept. 11, 1971. m. Margaret Kellner. PhD 22, Univ. of Hamburg. **Other Studies:** Univ. of Berlin, Univ. of Freiburg, Univ. of Vienna. **Research/Artistic Interests:** The classical tradition, Renaissance art & architecture. **Career & Employment:** UNC, Instr.-Asst. Prof. 1925-27; Biblilothek Warburg, Hamburg, Research Asst. 1927-33; Univ. Hamburg, Privatdozent 1930-33; Warburg Inst., Dept. Dir. 1934-42; Univ. College, London, Hon. Lect. 1934-42; Pierpont Morgan Library & IFA, Visiting Lect. 1940-42; Univ. of Chicago, Prof. 1942-44; William Allan Neilson Research Prof. 1944-48; Smith College, Prof. 1948-55; Oxford Univ., Chichele Lect. 1954; Oxford Univ., Prof. 1955-67, Prof. Emer. 1967-71; Trinity College, Oxford, Fellow 1955-67, Hon. Fellow 1967-71; Cambridge Univ., Rede Lect. 1960; BBC, Reith Lect. 1960. **Memberships & Offices:** Aristotelian Soc.; *Journal of the Warburg Institute,* Ed. 1937-42. **Fellowships, Honors & Awards:** Guggenheim Fellow 1950; West German Republic, Order of Merit; British Acad., Serena Medal 1967; AAAS, Fellow. **Publications:** *A Bibliography of the Survival of the Classics,* 2 vols. (London: Warburg Inst., 1934-38); *Bellini's Feast of the God's* (Oxford: Oxford Univ. Press, 1948); *Pagan Mysteries of the Renaissance* (New Haven: Yale Univ. Press, 1958, 1967); *Art and Anarchy* (London: Faber & Faber, 1963, 3d ed. 1969); *Michelangelo's Prophets and Sibyls* (Oxford: Clarendon Press, 1967); *Giorgione's Tempesta* (Oxford: Clarendon Press, 1969); *Hans Memling,* ed. K.B. MacFarlane (Oxford: Clarendon Press, 1971); *The Eloquence of Symbols,* ed. Jaynie Anderson (New York: Oxford Univ. Press, 1988, rev. ed. 1993); *Hume and the*

Heroic Portrait, ed. Jaynie Anderson (Oxford; Clarendon & New York: Oxford Univ. Press, 1986). **Bio-Bibliography:** *NY Times,* Obit. (Sept. 18, 1971); Hugh Lloyd Jones, "Biographical Memoir," in Edgar Wind, *The Eloquence of Symbols,* ed. Jaynie Anderson, rev. ed. (New York: Oxford Univ. Press 1993), xiii-xxxvi, 115-30; *Contemporary Authors; Who Was Who; Who Was Who in America.*

WINES, JAMES N. ■ FAAR Sculpture 56. b. June 27, 1932, Oak Park, IL. c. Suzan. BA 56, Syracuse Univ. **Other Study:** Extensive travel to study architectural works. **Research/Artistic Interests:** Since 1985, architecture & public space design based on the fusion of buildings & context; studies in green architecture internationally, presently researching a book, tentatively titled, *The Art of Architecture in the Age of Ecology;* current built works focused on waterfront development, public spaces, landscape design, green shelter. **Career & Employment:** NYU, Prof. 1967-74; Cornell Univ., Artist-in-Residence 1969; SITE Projects, Pres. 1970-present; Dartmouth College, Artist-in-Residence 1974; Parsons School of Design, Environmental Design & Architecture, Chair 1984-91; New School, Dist. Prof. 1991-present. **Fellowships, Honors & Awards:** Pulitzer Prize Award 1958; Guggenheim Found. Fellowship 1962; Ford Found. Grant 1964; Philadelphia Museum, Nat. Sculpture Exb., 1st Award 1966; Everson Museum, Syracuse, NY, 1st Award 1971; Iron & Steel Inst., Design Award 1971; National Endowment for the Design Arts Grant 1974, 1975, 1992; Graham Found. Grant 1975, 1991; NYSCA Grant 1975; *Progressive Architecture* Magazine Annual Award 1980; American Soc. of Interior Designers Annual Award 1980, Intl. Design Award 1980; NEA Senior Sabbatical Grant 1982, Distinguished Designer Award 1983; *Interiors Magazine* Annual Award 1983, 1985, 1988; Kress Found. Grant 1984, 1991; Here and Now Pavilion, Vancouver World Expo, Design Competition, 1st Award 1984; City of Frankfurt, New Museum of Modem Art, Design Competition, Hon. Men. 1984; Ansel Adams Center for Photography, Carmel, CA, Design Competition, 1st Award 1985; Pershing Sq., Los Angeles, Design Competition, 1st Award 1986; *Architectural Record* Award for Excellence 1986; West Hollywood City Hall, Design Competition, Hon. Men. 1987;

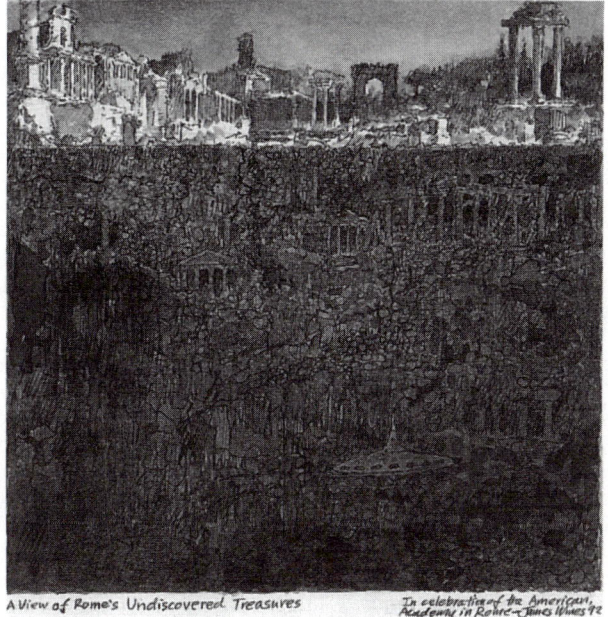

A View of Rome's Undiscovered Treasures   In celebration of the American Academy in Rome—James Wines 92

James N. Wines

Civic Center & Restoration, Old City, Le Puy-en-Velay, France, Design Competition, 1st Award 1992. **Publications:** Foreword, *On Energy* (New York: Charles Scribner's Sons, 1974), 6-10; *De-Architecture* (New York: Rizzoli, 1982); *The Highrise of Homes* (New York: Rizzoli, 1982), 95-102. **Important Works:** Indeterminate Facade, Best Products Co., Houston 1974; Notch Bldg., Best Products Co., Sacramento 1975; Ghost Parking Lot, Nat. Shopping Centers, Hamden, CT 1977; Forest Bldg., Best Products Co., Richmond, VA 1980; WilliWear Women's Showroom, NYC 1982; Inside/Outside Showroom, Best Products Co., Milwaukee 1984; McDonald's Restaurant, Chicago 1984; New York Brickwork Design Center, Glen-Gery Corp., NYC 1984; Museum of the Borough of Brooklyn 1985; Mallet Residence, NYC 1985; Highway 86, Expo 86 Assn., Vancouver, Canada 1986; Swatch Retail Store, NYC 1987; Allsteel Showroom, Long Island City, NY 1988; Four Continents Bridge, Country Communications, Hiroshima 1989; Saudi Arabian Pavilion, Seville, Spain 1992; Avenue V, Expo 92 Assn., Sevilla, Spain 1992; Horoscope Ring, Toyama, Japan Exb. Assn., 1992; Ross's Landing Park & Plaza, River City Co., Chattanooga, TN 1992. **Exhibitions/Performances:** Columbia Univ. 1973; Whitney Museum, NYC 1974; MOMA 1975; Centre Pompidou, Paris 1975; Louvre, Paris 1975; Venice Biennale 1975; Cayc Museum, Buenos Aires 1976. **Bio-Bibliography:** Bruno Zevi & James Wines, *De-Architetturizazione: Progetti e Teorie 1969-1978* (Bari: Dedalo Libri, 1978); Bruno Zevi, Piene Restany & James Wines, *SITE: Architecture as Art* (London: Academy Editions, New York: St. Martins Press, 1980); Ray Smith, *SITE: Building and Spaces*, exb. cat. (Richmond: Virginia Museum of Fine Arts, 1980); Olivier Boissiere, *Gehry, SITE, Tigerman: Trois Portraits de l'artiste en Architecte* (Paris: Editions du Moniteur, 1981); Herbert Muschamp, Toshio Nakamura, Itsuo Sakane, "SITE," *A+U* (1986): 197-225; "SITE," *Du Magazine* (Jan. 1988); Cristiano Toraldo di Francia, Aldo Frangione, Luca Ridone & Maria Grazia Chiappinelli, *SITE: Architecture 1971-1988*, exb. cat. (Rome: Onicina Edizione, 1988); Herbert Muschamp, *SITE* (New York: Rizzoli, 1989); *James Wines: Dessins d'architecture* (Paris: Le Éditions du Demi-Circle, 1989); *SITE* (New York: Rizzoli, 1989); "SITE, Green Architecture," *Architecture + Urbanism* (Dec. 1990): 68-128; "SITE," in *American Visions* (New York: Champion Paper, 1989); Barbara Radice & James Wines, "SITE/Isosak," *Terazzo* (Spring 1992): 49-79. **Home Address:** 60 Greene St., NYC 10012. **Business Address:** SITE, 632 Broadway, NYC 10012.

WINLOCK, HERBERT E. ■ AAR Trustee 1934-40, Archaeologist.

WINSLOW, WALTER K. ■ FAAR Musical Composition 90. b. Sept. 16, 1947, Salem, OR. Patricia Fortini Brown, FAAR 90. BA 70, Oberlin College; BMus 70, Oberlin Conservatory; MA 72, UC, Berkeley; PhD 75, UC, Berkeley. **Other Study:** Banff School of Fine Arts 1965-67. **Research/Artistic Interests:** Music composition, piano performance. **Career & Employment:** UC, Berkeley, Asst. Prof. 1975-82; Oberlin Conservatory, Visiting Asst. Prof. 1983-84; Reed College, Visiting Asst. Prof. 1985-86; Columbia Univ., Asst. Prof. 1987-89; Lawrenceville School, Instr. 1990-present. **Memberships & Offices:** Soc. of Composers, Region 9, Co-Chair 1979-83; ACA; Composers Guild of New Jersey; Minnesota Composers Forum; American Music Center. **Fellowships, Honors & Awards:** AAAL, Goddard Lieberson Fellowship 1983; Guggenheim Fellowship 1986; New Jersey State Council on the Arts, Composer Fellowship 1991; Rockefeller Found., Bellagio Study Center 1992. **Important Works:** *Piano Concerto* 1974; *Nahua Songs,* for soprano & piano

(CRI) 1975; *String Quartet* 1978; *Unified Field* 1979; *19 Madrigals for Five Voices* (Cori descrittivi di stato d'animo di Didone, Opus One Records) 1980; *Canzone* 1981; *Palinurus* 1982; *Himene* 1985; *Six Songs on Poems of William Stafford,* for soprano & piano 1986; *Vai Po* 1989; *The Piper of the Sacred Grove* 1990; *Locus Amoenus* 1992. Publisher: American Composers Edition. **Bio-Bibliography:** *International Who's Who in Music.* **Home Address:** 54 Humbert St., Princeton, NJ 08542. **Business Address:** Dept. of Music, Lawrenceville School, Lawrenceville, NJ 08648.

WINSOR, JACKIE ■ AAR Visitor 1986-87, Artist. b. 1941. **Fellowships, Honors & Awards:** NEA Grant 1974, 1977, 1984; Louis Comfort Tiffany Found. Grant 1977; Guggenheim Found. Grant 1978. **Exhibitions/Performances:** Solo: Paula Cooper Gallery, NYC; San Francisco Museum of Modern Art; MOMA; Art Gallery Ontario, Toronto; Fort Worth Art Museum; Milwaukee Art Museum; North Carolina Museum of Art, Raleigh.

WINSOR, PHILIP G. ■ FAAR Musical Composition 67. b. May 10, 1938, Morris, IL. m. Michele-Louise Winsor. c. Pamela, Paul, Lauren, Brondon, Bethany. BMus 60, Illinois Wesleyan Univ.; MA 63, San Francisco State Univ. **Other Study:** UC, Berkeley 1961; San Francisco Tape Music Center 1961-65; Italy Conservatory of Music, Milan 1964; Univ. of Illinois 1965-66. **Career & Employment:** San Francisco Music & Arts Inst., Instr. 1964-65; Montana State Univ., Moorhead, Asst. Prof. 1967-68; De Paul Univ., Asst. Prof. 1968-78, Assc. Prof. 1979-82; Univ. of N. Texas, Prof. 1988-present; Computer Music Studio Research Programs, Dir. 1990-present; Center for Experimental Music & Intermedia, Dir.; Univ. Center for Interdisciplinary Research, Co-Dir.; Nat. Chiao Tung Univ., Taiwan, Adj. Prof. **Memberships & Offices:** Contemporary Concerts, Inc., BoD 1972-74; Chicago Contemporary Dance Theatre, BoD 1973-77; ACA 1974-present; BMI 1969-present; Chicago Soc. of Composers, BoD 1978-82; ASUC, Regional Chair 1980; New Music Alliance, Adv. Com. 1981-82; American Music Center 1982-present; Pi Kappa Lambda Honor Soc. 1983-present; Meet the Composer, Texas, BoD 1983-85. **Fellowships, Honors & Awards:** Pacifica Found. Radio Directors Award 1961; Fulbright Fellowship 1963-64; Tanglewood Fellowship 1966; Darmstadt, Germany Music Inst. Fellowship 1966; Bennington Composers Conference Fellowship 1969; Oregon College of Education, Summer Arts Festival Award 1970; Shell Found. Faculty Development Award 1973; Ford Found. Fellowship 1973; NEA Fellowship 1977, 1979; Amherst College, New Choral Music Contest, Grand Prize 1979; Illinois Arts Council Fellowship 1980, 1981; Univ. of N. Texas Faculty Research Grants for Intermedia Composition 1982, 1983, 1984, 1986, 1987; Great Lakes Arts Alliance, Meet-the-Composer Grant 1983-84; NEA Comm. 1984; Bowdoin College, Festival of Contemporary Choral Music in America, 1st Prize 1988; National Science Council Research Grants 1989, 1990-92. **Publications:** *Computer-Assisted Music Composition: A Primer in Basic* (Princeton, NJ: Petrocelli Books, 1987); *The Computer Composer's Toolbox* (Blue Ridge, PA: Windcrest Books, 1990); *Computer Music in C: Compositional Algorithms* (New York: McGraw-Hill, 1990); *Composition by Computer: Using MIDI Synthesizers* (Taipei, Taiwan: Third Wave Publishing Group, 1990). **Important Works:** *Nothing is the Thing to Fear,* for electronic music, dancers & projections, Chicago Contemporary Dance Theatre Comm. 1971; *Flos Harmonicus III,* for one, two or three woodwind quintets, Univ. of Redlands New Music Woodwind Quintet Comm. (Pembroke Music Co.) 1972; *Stations,* for electronic music, slides & four dancers, Chicago Contemporary Dance Theatre Comm. 1973; *Actions,* for tape, tuba, trombone, actor, dancers, projections, Chicago Contemporary Dance Theatre Comm. 1973; *Honeycomb,* for orchestra, electronic music & jazz combo, De Paul Univ. Symphony Orchestra Comm. (Carl Fischer) 1974; *City,* for environmental sound components, dancers, tape, Chicago Contemporary Dance Theatre Comm. 1975; *Jamboree,* for instruments, dancers, tape, electronics, projections, Chicago Contemporary Dance Theatre Comm. 1976; *Sequence I,* for electronic music, dancers, projections, Chicago Contemporary Dance Theatre Comm. 1977; *Do Not Go Gentle into that Good Night...,* for large or small orchestra, Roosevelt Univ., Contemporary Music Ensemble 1978; *Cindy 633,* for multiple amplified pianos, Univ. of Redlands New Music Ensemble Comm. 1979; *Planesong,* for instrumental octet, Northwestern Univ. Contemporary Music Ensemble (American Composers Edition, ACA) 1980; *Anamorphoses,* for 16 instruments, Univ. of N. Texas Trumpet Ensemble Comm. 1988. **Home Address:** 2100 Colonial Dr., Denton, TX 76207.

WINTER, DAVID ■ FAAR Sculpture 90. b. 1955, Seattle, WA. BA 78, Bennington College; MFA 80, Yale Univ. **Other Study:** Whitney Museum Independent Study Program 1976. **Fellowships, Honors & Awards:** NEA Award 1988; Penny McCall Found. Grant 1989; Pollock-Krasner Found. Grant 1991. **Exhibitions/Performances:** Solo: Malinda Wyatt Gallery, NYC 1985; Barbara Toll Fine Arts, NYC 1990; The Drawing Room, Tucson 1991; Galerie Christiane Chassay, Montreal 1992; Group Shows: San Francisco Art Inst. 1977; Drawing Center, NYC 1981, 1982; PS 1, NYC 1985; Artist's Space, NYC 1986; Luhring, Augustine & Hodes Gallery, NYC 1987; John Good Gallery, NYC 1988; Barbara Toll Fine Arts, NYC 1989; Artpark, Lewiston, NY 1989; Whitney Museum at Phillip Morris, NJ 1990; Jan Turner Gallery, Los Angeles 1991; E.M. Donohue Gallery, NYC 1992. **Home Address:** 167 N 9th St., Brooklyn, NY 11211.

WINTER, EZRA AUGUSTUS ■ FAAR Painting 14. b. Mar. 10, 1886, Manistee, MI. d. Apr. 7, 1949. m. Patricia Murphy. c. Mrs. Albert Moss, Renata Hunter, Mrs. Donald Whelan. **Other Studies:** Olivet College 1906-7; Chicago Acad. of Fine Arts 1908-9. **Career & Employment:** US Shipping Bd., World War I. **Memberships & Offices:** Nat. Soc. of Mural Painters; ALNY; NIAL; NAD 1928. **Fellowships, Honors & Awards:** ALNY Gold Medal 1922; New York Soc. of Architects, Gold Medal 1923; Olivet College, Hon. LLD 1924. **Important Works:** Radio City Music Hall, NYC; Reading Rooms, Library of Congress, Washington, DC; Union Trust Bldg., Detroit; New York Cotton Exchange; Cunard Bldg., NYC; Eastman Theater, Rochester; Willard Straight Memorial, Cornell Univ.; Birmingham Public Library, AL; Rochester Savings Bank, NY; George Rogers Clark Memorial, Vincennes, IN; Monroe HS Auditorium, Rochester, NY; Federal Reserve Bldg., Washington, DC; Strauss Bank, Chicago; New York Life Bldg.; Bank of Manhattan Trust Company. **Bio-Bibliography:** *Who Was Who in America, Who Was Who in American Art.*

WINTHROP, EGERTON L. ■ AAR Charter Mem.

WIRTH, TIMOTHY ■ AAR Visitor 1991-92, US Senator.

WITKE, CHARLES ■ FAAR Classics/Archaeology 62; AAR Archaeological Summer School, Dir. 1967. b. Sept. 22, 1931, Los Angeles, CA. m. Aileen Gatten. BA 53, UCLA; MA 57, Harvard Univ.; PhD 62, Harvard Univ. **Other Study:** Independent theological study leading to ordination as an Episcopal priest 1989. **Research/Artistic Interests:** Classical & medieval Latin literature. **Career & Employment:** Univ. of Chicago, Asst. Prof. 1962-63; UC, Berkeley, Asst. Prof. 1963-67; Assc. Prof. 1967-70; SUNY,

Binghamton, Prof. 1970-71; Univ. of Michigan, Prof. 1971-present; St. Luke's Church, Ypsilanti, MI, Curate 1989-93. **Memberships & Offices:** Soc. for the Promotion of Roman Studies; MAA, Councillor 1970-72; APA, Refereee; Erasmus of Rotterdam Soc. **Fellowships, Honors & Awards:** Fulbright Fellow 1960-61; NEA Grant 1985, 1986; Warburg Inst., London, Erasmus of Rotterdam Soc., Bainton Lect. 1994. **Publications:** *Enarratio Catulliana* (Leiden: Brill, 1968); *Latin Satire: The Structure of Persuasion* (Leiden: Brill, 1970); Numen Litterarum: *The Old and the New in Latin Poetry from Constantine to Gregory the Great* (Leiden, Cologne: Brill, 1971); *Horace's Roman Odes: A Critical Examination* (Leiden: Brill, 1983); as ed. & trans., Erasmus, *Hyperaspistes,* Collected Works of Erasmus (Toronto: Univ. of Toronto Press, forthcoming); plus numerous articles & reviews in professional journals. **Bio-Bibliography:** *Who's Who in America.* **Business Address:** Dept. of Classical Studies, Univ. of Michigan, Ann Arbor, MI 48109.

WITTKOWER, RUDOLF ■ RAAR History of Art 62. b. June 22, 1901, Berlin, Germany. d. Oct. 11, 1971. m. Margot Holzmann. c. Mario Max. PhD 23, Univ. of Berlin. **Career & Employment:** Bibliotheca Hertziana, Rome, Asst. Research Fellow 1923-32; Cologne Univ., Lect. 1932-33; Warburg Inst., Staff Mem. 1934-56; Univ. of London, Reader 1945, Prof. 1949; Columbia Univ., Prof.-Chair 1956-69, Avalon Found., Prof. Emer. 1969-71; NGA, Caress Prof. 1969-71; Cambridge Univ., Slade Prof. 1970-71. **Memberships & Offices:** IAS 1971; MMA, Hon. Trustee; Warburg Inst.; AAAS; APS; Royal Inst. of British Architects; Archaeological Inst. of Great Britian & Ireland; RSA; SAH; CAA; Accademia Olimpica, Vicenza; Accademia dei Lincei, Rome; Accademia di Belle Arti, Venice; Accademia delle Scienze, Turin; Phi Beta Kappa; Max Plank Gesellschaft, Göttingen, Corresponding Mem. **Fellowships, Honors & Awards:** British Acad., Serena Medal 1957, Fellow 1958-71; Banister Fletcher Prize 1960; Guggenheim Fellow 1960-62; Duke Univ., Hon. DFA 1969; Columbia Univ., Hon. DFA 1969; Leeds Univ., England, Hon. DFA 1971. **Publications:** with Fritz Saxl, *British Art and the Mediterranean* (New York: Oxford Univ. Press, 1948); *Architectural Principles in the Age of Humanism* (London: Phaidon, 1949, 4th ed. 1971); *Bernini's Bust of Louis XIV* (London: Oxford Univ. Press, 1951); *The Drawings of the Carracci in the Royal Collection at Windsor Castle* (London: Phaidon, 1952); *Gian Lorenzo Bernini* (London: Phaidon, 1955; 3d ed., Ithaca, NY: Cornell Univ. Press, 1981); *Art and Architecture in Italy, 1600-1750* (1958; 3rd ed. Harmondsworth, England: Penguin, 1973); with Margot Wittkower, *Born under Saturn: The Character and Conduct of Artists* (New York: Random House, 1963); ed. with Irma B. Jaffee, *Baroque Art: The Jesuit Contribution* (New York: Fordham Univ. Press, 1972); *The Sculptor's Workshop: Tradition & Theory from the Renaissance to the Present* (Glasgow: Univ. of Glasgow Press, 1974); *Palladio and English Palladiansim,* ed. Margot Wittkower (London: Thames & Hudson, 1974); *Gothic vs Classic: Architectural Projects in Seventeenth-Century Italy* (New York: Brazillier, 1974); *Studies in the Italian Baroque* (Boulder, CO: Westview Press, 1975); *Allegory and the Migration of Symbols* (Boulder, CO: Westview Press, 1977); *Sculpture: Processes and Principles* (London: Allen Lane, 1977); *Ideas and Images: Studies in the Italian Renaissance* (London: Thames & Hudson, 1978); *Selected Lectures of Rudolf Wittkower: The Impact of Non-European Civilization of the Art of the West,* ed. D.M. Reynolds (New York: Cambridge Univ. Press, 1989). **Bio-Bibliography:** "Bibliography," in *Essays in the History of Architecture Presented to Rudolf Wittkower,* ed. D. Fraser, H. Hibbert, & M.J. Lewine (London: Phaidon, 1967), 377-81; *NY Times,* Obit. (Oct. 12, 1971); "Rudolf Wittkower: A Bibliography," *Burlington Magazine* 114

(1972): 173-77; *JSAH* 31 (1972): 83-91; *Contemporary Authors; Dictionary of National Biography; Who Was Who; Who Was Who in America.*

WITTON, FREDERICK ROY ■ Rotch Scholar 1915.

WOHL, BRIGITTA LINDROS ■ NEH Summer Seminar Co.-Dir. 1993.

WOHL, HELLMUT ■ RAAR History of Art 84. b. Sept. 17, 1928, Berlin, Germany. m. Alice Sedgwick. Wohl. BA 48, Harvard College; MA 52, IFA; PhD 58, IFA. **Career & Employment:** Yale Univ., Instr. 1955-59, Asst. Prof. 1960-63; Cooper Union, Asst. Prof. 1963-66; New School for Social Research, Lect. 1964-65; Boston Univ., Assc. Prof. 1966-80, Prof. 1980-present. **Fellowships, Honors & Awards:** Fulbright Grant 1952; Yale Univ., Morse Fellowship 1959; Villa I Tatti, Harvard Univ., Fellow 1988. **Publications:** "Carlos Mardel and His Lisbon Architecture," *Apollo* 97 (1973): 350-59; "Recent Studies in Portuguese Post-Medieval Architecture," *JSAH* 34 (1975): 67-73; "Beyond the Large Glass: Notes on a Landscape Drawing by Marcel Duchamp," *Burlington Magazine* 119 (1977): 763-72; *The Paintings of Domenico Veneziano, ca. 1410-1461: A Study in Florentine Art of the Early Renaissance* (New York: NYU Press, London: Phaidon Press, 1980); *Dada: Berlin, Cologne, Hanover* (Boston: Inst. of Contemporary Art, 1980); "The Revival of the Arts in Rome under Martin V," in *Rome in the Renaissance: Medieval and Renaissance Texts and Studies,* ed. P.A. Ramsey (Binghamton: SUNY Press, 1983), 171-83; "Papal Patronage and the Language of Art: The Pontificates of Martin V, Eugene IV and Nicholas V," in *Umanesimo a Roma nel Quattrocento,* ed. P. Brezzi & M. Lorch (Rome: Istituto di Studi Romani, 1984), 235-46; "The Eye of Vasari," *Mitteilungen des Kunsthistorischen Institutes in Florenz* 22 (1987): 537ff.; "Talking of Michelangelo," *Psychoanalysis and Contemporary Thought* 11 (1988): 447-81; "Duchamp's Etchings of the Large Glass and the Lovers," in *Marcel Duchamp, Artist of the Century,* ed. R.E. Kuenzli & F.M. Naumann (Cambridge: MIT Press, 1989), 168-83; "New Light on the Artistic Patronage of Sixtus V," *Arte cristiana* 80 (1992): 123-34; "'Puro senza ornato': Masaccio, Cristoforo Landino and Leonardo da Vinci," *Journal of the Warburg & Courtauld Institutes* 56 (1993): 256-60. **Home Address:** PO Box 1315, Stockbridge, MA 01262. **Business Address:** Art History Dept., Boston Univ., Boston, MA 02215.

WOLF, CHARLES ■ NIAE, John Dinkeloo Traveling Fellow 1986-87.

WOLFE, HENRY LAWRENCE ■ FAAR Painting 11. dec.

WOLOHOJIAN, STEPHAN S. ■ FAAR History of Art 90. b. Mar. 30, 1962, NYC. BA 84, Rutgers Univ.; MA 86, Harvard Univ. **Other Studies:** Ludwig-Maximillians-Universitat, Institut für Kunstgeschichte, Munich 1987-88. **Career & Employment:** *Worldwide Books,* Italian Book Reviewer 1985-87. **Fellowships, Honors & Awards:** Rutgers Univ., Scholar-Athlete Award 1982-84; Harvard Univ., Bernard Berenson Fellowship 1984; Henry Rutgers Scholar 1984; Lemmermann Found., Rome, Fellowship 1988.

WOLTMANN, FREDERICK ■ FAAR Musical Composition 39. b. May 13, 1908, Flushing, NY. dec. BMus, Eastman School of Music. **Other Studies:** Brooklyn Polytechnic Inst.; Columbia Univ. **Career & Employment:** Congregational Church of the Pelhams, Pelham, NY, Dir. of Music & Composer-in-Resi-

dence. **Fellowships, Honors & Awards:** MacDowell Colony, Fellowship 1936; NIAL, Outstanding American Composer 1941. **Important Works:** *Dance of the Torch Bearers* 1932; *Poem,* for flute & orchestra 1935; *Rhapsody,* for horn & orchestra 1935; *Legend* 1936; *Songs from a Chinese Lute,* for voice & 33 instruments 1936; *Scherzo,* for 8 winds 1937; *Songs for Autumn,* for soprano, baritone & orchestra 1937; *Piano Concerto* 1937; *The Pool of Pegasus* 1937; *From Dover Beach* 1938; *The Coliseum at Night* 1939; *Solitude* 1942; *From Leaves of Grass* 1946. **Bio-Bibliography:** *Contemporary American Composers.*

WONG, JOHN L. ■ FAAR Landscape Architecture 81; AAR Juror 1994. b. Oct. 10, 1951, Hong Kong. m. Mildred Sum-Wong. c. Alyson Taylor Wong, Nicole Kelley Wong. AA 72, City College of San Francisco; BA 74, UC, Berkeley; MLU 78, Harvard GSD. **Other Study:** Sasaki Walker Asscs., Summer-Work Study Pgm. 1973. **Career & Employment:** Leo Tscharner, Landscape Architect, Designer 1972-73; Ribera & Sue, Project Designer 1973-74; Sasaki Walker Asscs., Project Designer 1973-74; POD, Project Landscape Architect 1974-76; SWA Group: East, Project Dir. 1976-80, Boston, Prin. 1980-84, Sausalito, Prin. 1984-90, Managing Prin. 1990-present; Visiting Positions: Harvard GSD, Critic 1978-82, 1989; UC, Berkeley, Lect. 1986, 1987, 1988, 1990. **Memberships & Offices:** ASLA 1982-present; Inst. for Urban Design 1982-present; Headland Centers for the Arts 1990-present; Juror: NEA Design Arts Pgm. 1985, 1986; Artists Found. Inc., Massachusetts Artists Fellowship 1986; Davis, CA, Arboretum Nat. Design Competition 1988. **Fellowships, Honors & Awards:** UC, Berkeley, Fred B. Barlow Jr. Memorial Award 1974; ASLA Merit Award 1976, 1985, 1988, 1990, Southern California Chap. Honor Award 1984, 1986, Florida Chap. Award of Excellence; California Landscape Contractors Assn., 1st Prize 1977, 1988; Pin Oak Competition, Houston, 1st Prize 1979; Home for Better Living, 1st Honor Award 1979; Nat. Assn. of Home Builders, Project of the Year 1983; Boston Soc. of Landscape Architects Honor Award 1984, 1985; California Council of Landscape Architects Merit Award 1987; City of Los Angeles Merit Award 1988; Harbor Island Hotel Competition, San Diego, 1st Prize 1990. **Important Works:** Boca Beach Club, Boca

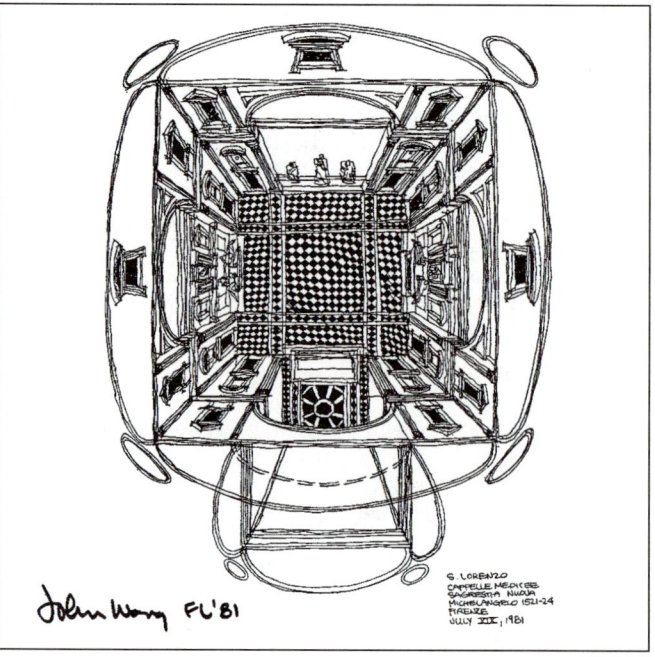

John L. Wong

Raton 1986; Disney World Master Plan, Orlando 1987; Citicorp Plaza & 7th St. Market Place, Los Angeles 1988; Kezar Corner Master Plan, San Francisco 1989; Stanford Univ., Liliore Green Rains Single Graduate Student Housing 1990; Burnaby Metropolitan Resources Library & Civic Sq., British Columbia, Canada 1991; NEXT, Inc. HQ, Redwood City, CA 1991; Ronald Regan Presidential Library & Center for Public Affairs, Simi Valley 1991; Lawrence Livermore Nat. Laboratory, DPRF/NTTC 1992; Nasu Highland Resort Master Plan, Japan 1992; G-G Roppongi Urban Development Project, Tokyo 1994; Athletics Quad, Arrillaga Sports Center & Iris & B. Gerald Cantor Center for the Visual Arts, Stanford Univ. 1995. **Exhibitions/Performances:** Harold Reed Gallery, NYC 1979; Federal Triangle Nat. Design Competition Exb., Washington, DC 1979; Copley Sq. Nat. Design Competition Exb., Boston 1984; Columbus Carspace Competition Exb., Columbus, IN 1984; Pershing Sq. Nat. Design Competition Exb., Los Angeles 1986; Todos Santos Plaza Design Competition Exb., Concord, CA 1987; Napa County Museum Design Competition Exb. 1990; Il Giardino Italiano, Memphis, TN 1992. **Business Address:** The SWA Group, 2200 Bridgeway Blvd., Sausalito, CA 94966.

WOOBY, PHILIP FRANCIS ■ FAAR Classics/Archaeology 53. b. Aug. 10, 1922, Philadelphia, PA. BA 45, St. John's Univ., Collegeville; MA 48, Univ. of Pennsylvania. **Other Studies:** Harvard Univ., 1949-. **Career & Employment:** St. Charles School, Philadelphia, Faculty 1946-48; Williston HS, Wilmington, NC, Faculty 1948-49; Howard Univ., Faculty; Cansius College, Faculty. **Publications:** *Nude to the Meaning of Tomorrow* (New York: Exposition Press Inc, 1959).

WOOD, SUSAN E. ■ FAAR Classics/Archaeology 78. b. Nov. 13, 1951, Mt. Holly, NJ. BA 73, Bryn Mawr College; MA 75, Columbia Univ.; PhD 79, Columbia Univ. **Other Study:** Cornell summer field program in archaeological drawing 1982; ANS Summer Seminar 1976. **Research/Artistic Interests:** Roman art & archaeology. **Career & Employment:** Case-Western Reserve Univ. 1979-81; Harvard Univ. 1981-87; Oakland Univ. 1987-present. **Memberships & Offices:** ArIA 1974-present; CAA 1979-present; Midwest Art History Assn. 1987-present; Detroit Classical Soc. 1991-present. **Fellowships, Honors & Awards:** Columbia Univ. President's Fellowships 1974-75, 1975-76; ANS Grant-in-Aid 1976; Whiting Fellowship 1976-77. **Publications:** *Roman Portrait Sculpture, A.D. 217-260: The Transformation of an Artistic Tradition*, CSCT 12 (1981); "Alcestis on Roman Sarcophagi," *AJA* 82 (1978): 499-510; "Subject & Artist: Studies in Roman Portraiture of the Third Century," *AJA* 85 (1981): 59-68; "Child Emperors and Heirs to Power in Third-Century Roman Portraiture," *Ancient Portraits in the J. Paul Getty Museum I: Occasional Papers on Antiquity* 4, ed. J. Frel, M. True & A. Houghton (Malibu: J. Paul Getty Museum, 1984), 115-36; "*Memoriae Agrippinae*: Agrippina the Elder in Julio-Claudian Art and Propaganda," *AJA* 92 (1988): 409-26; "Isis, Eggheads and Roman Portraiture," *Journal of the American Research Center in Egypt* 24 (1988): 219-34; "Messalina, the Wife of Claudius: Propaganda Successes and Failures of His Reign," *Journal of Roman Archaeology* 5 (1992): 219-34; "Diva Drusilla Panthea and the Sisters of Caligula," *AJA* 99 (1995). **Home Address:** 1695 Riverside Dr., Apt. 11, Rochester Hills, MI 48309. **Business Address:** Dept. of Art & Art History, Oakland Univ., Rochester, MI 48309.

WOODBRIDGE, FREDERICK J. ■ FAAR Architecture 23, Columbia Scholar, RAAR Architecture 52. b. May 18, 1900, Minneapolis, MN. d. Jan 17, 1974. m. Catherine Baldwin. c. John M., Jane. BA 21, Amherst College; BArch 23, Columbia

Univ. **Other Study:** Research fellow, Univ. of Michigan in classical archaeology; architect for excavations in Antioch of Pisidia, Turkey & Carthage, Tunisia. **Career & Employment:** McKim, Mead & White 1921-22, 1925-29; Evans, Moore & Woodbridge 1929-42; Columbia Univ., Columbia School of Architecture, Faculty 1934-42, Consulting Architect 1947-70, Teachers College, Lect. 1938-42; US Military Service, WWII; Adams & Woodbridge 1945-74. **Memberships & Offices:** NAD; ALNY, Pres. 1941-43, 1948-49; NIAE; Municipal Arts Soc. of New York, Dir.; Fine Arts Federation of NY, Pres. 1965; School Art League, NYC Pres. 1955-65. **Fellowships, Honors & Awards:** AIA, Fellow, NY Chap., Pres. 1961-62; Phi Beta Kappa. **Important Works:** House Libraries, Amherst College 1940; Alumnae House, Smith College 1940; Mission Church, Liberia, Africa 1945; Manufacturers Assn. of NJ Bldg., Trenton; Brick Presbyterian Church, Chapel & Parish House, NYC 1952; All Saints Chapel, Princeton 1960; St. Andrew's Episcopal Church, NYC 1961; St. Mark's Tower, Hobart College, Geneva, NY 1961; Girl Scouts of America HQ 1964; Trinity Parish House, NYC 1965; Episcopal Church Center, NYC 1968; Adirondack Museum, Blue Mountain Lake, NY 1965-73. **Bio-Bibliography:** *National Cyclopedia of American Biography; Who Was Who in America.*

WOODRUFF, HELEN M. ■ AAR Student Visitor 1927-28, Archaeologist. Left a bequest to the Academy through the ArIA which currently supports a fellowship in archaeology.

WOODS-MARSDEN, JOANNA ■ FAAR History of Art 87. b. Mar. 21, 1936, Dublin, Ireland. BA 57, Trinity College, Dublin; MA 65, Trinity College, Dublin; PhD 78, Harvard Univ. **Other Study:** Courtauld Inst., London 1958-59. **Career & Employment:** Montreal Museum of Fine Arts, Asst. Registrar & Curatorial Asst. 1960-64; EXPO 67, Intl. Fine Arts Exb., Asst. to Dir. 1967; Nat. Gallery of Canada, Coordinator of Intl. Exbs. 1967-72; Harvard Univ., Summer School, Asst. Prof. 1979; Univ. of British Columbia, Asst. Prof. 1980-84; UCLA, Asst.-Assc. Prof. 1984-present. **Fellowships, Honors & Awards:** Canada Council, Doctoral Fellowship 1972-76; Harvard Univ., Traveling Fellowship 1976-77; Whiting Fellow 1977-78; RSA Fellowship 1978; Villa I Tatti Fellow 1979-80; Univ. of British Columbia, Humanities Research Council Grant 1981, 1982, 1983, 1984; SSHSCC, Research Grant 1983-84, 1984-87; UCLA Award 1986-87, 1988-89, 1989-90, 1994-present; Center for the Study of Women Grant 1989-90; Center for Medieval & Renaissance Studies 1988-93; Andrew Mellon Fellowship 1986-87; APS Grant 1988; ACLS Grant 1988-89; NEH Stipend 1990-91; CASVA Fellow 1993. **Publications:** "French Chivalric Myth and Mantuan Political Reality in the *Sala del Pisanello*," *Art History* 8 (1985): 397-412; "Pictorial Legitimation of Territorial Gains in Emilia: The Iconography of the *camera peregrina aurea* in the Castle of Torchiara," in *Renaissance Studies in Honor of Craig Hugh Smyth* (Florence, 1985), 2:553-68; "Preparatory Drawings for Frescoes in the Early Quattrocento: the Practice of Pisanello," in *Drawings Defined*, ed. W. Strauss & T. Felker (New York: Abaris, 1987), 49-62; "*Ritratto al naturale*: Some Questions of Realism and Idealism in Early Renaissance Portraits," *Art Journal* 46 (1987): 209-16; *The Gonzaga of Mantua and Pisanello's Arthurian Frescoes* (Princeton: Princeton Univ. Press, 1988); "Images of Castles in Fifteenth-Century Italy: Symbols of Signoria/Symbols of Tyranny," *Art Journal* 48 (1989): 130-37; "How Quattrocento Princes Used Art: Sigismondo Pandolfo Malatesta and *Cose Militari*," *Renaissance Studies* 3.4 (1989): 387-414; "Art and Political Identity in Fifteenth-Century Naples: Pisanello, Cristoforo di Geremia and King Alfonso's Imperial Fantasies," in *Art and Politics in Late Medieval and Early Renaissance Italy,*

1250-1500, ed. Charles M. Rosenberg (Notre Dame, IN: Univ of Notre Dame Press, 1990), 11-37; "'Draw the Irrational Animals as Often as You Can from Life': Cennino Cennini, Giovannino de' Grassi, and Antonio Pisanello," *Studi di Storia dell'arte* 3 (1992): 67-78; "Verso una tipologia del ritratto di stato nel Rinascimento Italiano," in *Il Ritratto e la Memoria Materiali* 3, ed. A. Gentili, P. Morel & C. Ceri Via, Acts of the Conference Organized by Academie de France and Europa delle Corti, Rome, 1989 (Rome: Bulzoni, 1993), 31-62; "Toward a History of Art Patronage in the Renaissance: The Case of Pietro Aretino," Acts of the Symposium on Renaissance Patronage in Honor of John R. Spencer, Duke Univ., April 3, 1993, *Journal of Medieval & Renaissance Studies* 24 (1994): 275-99; "*In la Persia e nella India il mio ritratto si pregia*: Pietro Aretino e la costruzione visuale dell'intellettuale nel Rinascimento," *Acts of the Symposium on the Quincentenary of the Birth of Pietro Aretino, Arezzo, Toronto, Los Angeles, Oct. 1992*, ed. Enrico Malato (Rome, forthcoming). **Business Address:** Art History Dept., 3209 Dickson, UCLA, Los Angeles, CA 90024,.

WOOL, CHRISTOPHER ■ FAAR Painting 90. b. Sept. 16, 1955, Chicago, IL. **Study:** NYU Film School. **Fellowships, Honors & Awards:** DAAD Fellowship 1992. **Publications:** *93 Drawings of Beer on The Wall*, limited ed. (Christopher Wool, 1984); *Empire of the Goat*, limited ed. (Christopher Wool, 1985); untitled artist book, exb. cat. (Cologne: Galerie Gisela Capitain, 1988); *Black Book*, limited ed. (Cologne: Galerie Gisela Capitain & Thea Westreich Asscs., 1989); *Cats in Bag, Bags in River*, exb. cat. (Rotterdam: Boymans-van Beuningen, 1991); *Low and Slow*, artist book, limited ed. (Rome: Christopher Wool, 1991); *Away Without Leave* (Berlin: DAAD, 1993). **Important Works:** MOMA; San Francisco Museum of Modern Art; Carnegie Museum of Art, Pittsburgh; Whitney Museum, NYC; Dannheisser Found., NYC; Museum Boymans-van Beuningen, Rotterdam; Art Gallery of Ontario, Toronto; Baltimore Museum of Art; Milwaukee Art Museum; Museum of Contemporary Art, Los Angeles; Museum Moderner Kunst, Vienna; Dallas Museum of Art; AIC. **Exhibitions/Performances:** Selected: San Francisco Museum of Modern Art 1989; Stedelijk Museum, Amsterdam 1989; Whitney Museum, NYC, Biennial 1989; Martin-Gropius-Bau, Berlin 1991; Carnegie Museum of Art, Pittsburgh, 51st Carnegie Intl. 1991; Boymans-van Beuningen, Rotterdam 1991; Kolnischer Kunstverein, Cologne 1991; Kunsthalle, Bern 1991; Eli Broad Family Found., Los Angeles 1992; Documenta IX, Kassel, Germany 1992. **Home Address:** 735 E. 9 St., NYC 10009.

WORLEY, KENNETH R. ■ FAAR Painting 70. b. Jan. 19, 1942, St. Louis, MO. BFA 65, Washington Univ.; MFA 67, San Francisco Art Inst. **Other Study:** Illinois State Univ., Normal-Bloomington, color lithography 1978-80. **Research/Artistic Interests:** Painting: oil, acrylic & oil paint sticks; printmaking: relief & color lithography. **Career & Employment:** Part-time teaching: St. Louis Community College, Forest Park 1975-77, 1981-82, 1987, 1990; Univ. of Missouri, St. Louis 1976-77, 1982, 1984, 1986-91; Belleville Area College 1977-80; Washington Univ. 1978, 1981-82, 1988-93; Maryville College 1979, 1982-83, 1985-89, 1990-95; St. Louis Community College, Florissant Valley 1981-87, 1989-95; Fontbonne College 1986-88; Southern Illinois Univ., Edwardsville 1986, 1992. **Memberships & Offices:** Art St. Louis, Program Comm. 1989-95. **Fellowships, Honors & Awards:** Chaloner Found. Prize 1968-69. **Important Works:** St. Louis Community College at Florissant Valley, MO; Park Davis, St. Louis, MO; Boatmen's Bank, St. Louis, MO; Mercantile Bank, Clayton, MO; McCarthy Brothers Construction Co., St. Louis, MO; General Steel Industries, St. Louis, MO; First

Financial Bank, St. Louis, MO; 7-UP Corp., St. Louis, MO; Illinois State Univ., Normal-Bloomington; Bryn Mawr College, Providence, RI; San Francisco Art Inst. **Exhibitions/Performances:** Solo: Maine Coast Artist Gallery, Rockport, ME 1972; Messing Gallery, St. Louis, MO 1973; Emden Gallery, St. Louis, MO 1975; Bonsack Gallery, St. Louis, MO 1980; Elliot Smith, St. Louis, MO 1985, 1987, 1991; Retrospective, Forest Park Community College, St. Louis, MO 1972; and numerous group shows. **Bio-Bibliography:** Enzo Bilardello, "Pittori Americani a Roma," *Il Margritta, Periodico d'Arte Contemporanea* (1969), 6-7. **Home Address:** 5221 College Ave., St. Louis, MO 63136. **Business Address:** Elliot Smith Contemporary Art, 4727 McPherson Ave., St. Louis, MO 63108.

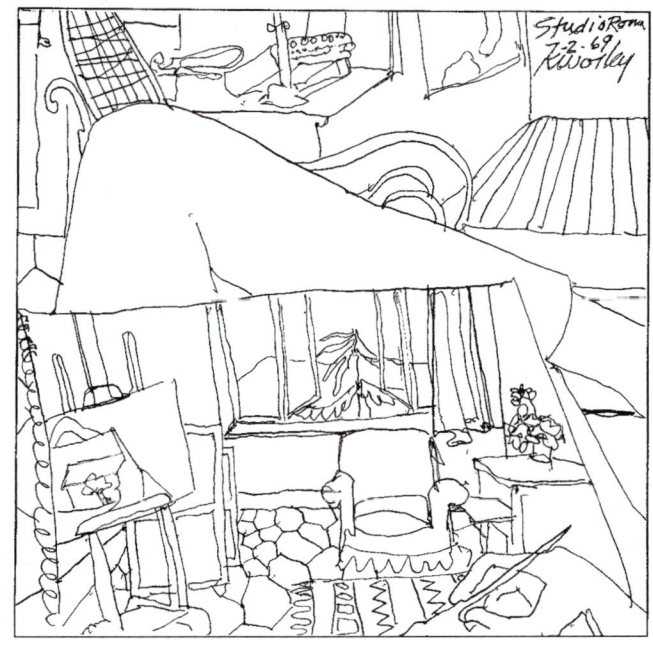

Kenneth R. Worley

WRAY, CHRISTOPHER JOHN ■ FAAR Painting 69. b. Aug. 1, 1943, NYC. m. Susan Wray. **Study:** ASL 1965-67; NYU. **Research/Artistic Interests:** Mural painting.

WRIGHT, DAVID H. ■ RAAR History of Art 91; NEH Summer Seminar Dir. 1987. b. July 11, 1929, Boston, MA. m. Georgia Sommers. c. Elizabeth S. Wright. BA 50, Harvard College; MA 51, Harvard Univ.; PhD 57, Harvard Univ. **Other Study:** Basic design with Josef Albers 1950; Univ. of Munich, archaeology, art history & Latin palaeography 1951-52; Warburg Inst., Univ. of London 1953-54. **Research/Artistic Interests:** Art & archaeology of late antiquity & the Dark Ages; codicology of early Latin manuscripts; photography (history & practice); art criticism. **Career & Employment:** Harvard College, TF & Resident Tutor 1952-53, 1955-56, Instr. & Resident Tutor 1956-60; UCLA, Lect. 1961-62; UC, Berkeley, Lect.-Prof. 1963-present. **Fellowships, Honors & Awards:** Harvard, Phi Beta Kappa 1950, Traveling Fellowship 1954-55, 1958-59; Fulbright Fellow 1953-54; IAS, Herodotus Fellow 1960-61; Dumbarton Oaks Center for Byzantine Studies, Visiting Fellow 1962-63, 1976-77, 1984, 1993-94; Assn. Intl. des Critiques d'Art 1986; Soc. of Antiquities, London, Fellow 1989; Comité Intl. de Paléographie Latine 1990. **Publications:** *The Vespasian Psalter*, Early English Manuscripts in Facsimile 14 (Copenhagen, 1967); *Vergilius Vaticanus, Commetarium*, Codices e Vaticanis Selecti 40 (Graz,

David H. Wright

1984); *Codicological Notes on the Vergilius Romanus*, Studi e testi 345 (Vatican City, 1992); *The Vatican Vergil, A Masterpiece of Late Antique Art* (Berkeley: UC Press, 1993); plus specialized articles in *The British Library Journal, Dumbarton Oaks Papers, Münchner Jahrbuch für Kunstgeschichte*, various congress volumes & festschriften, plus reviews in *Art Week* & various Bay Area journals. **Home Address:** 105 Vicente Rd., Berkeley, CA 94705. **Business Address:** UC, 405 Doe Library, Berkeley, CA 94720.

WRIGHT, HORACE WETHERILL ■ FAAR Classics/Archaeology 16. b. Aug. 5, 1884, Philadelphia, PA. d. Dec. 2, 1965. BA 08, Univ. of Wisconsin; PhD 17, Univ. of Pennsylvania. **Research/Artistic Interests:** Latin, Latin literature, Ovid, topography. **Career & Employment:** Galahad Boys School, Hudson, WI, Faculty 1908-10; St. Croix Falls HS, WI, Teacher 1910; Univ. of Missouri, Instr. 1917-18; Oberlin College, Asst. Prof. 1918-19; Bryn Mawr College, Assc. Prof. 1919-21; Lehigh Univ., Prof.-Dept. Head 1921-50. **Memberships & Offices:** Classical Assn. of the Atlantic States, VP; ArIA, Recording Sec.; APA; American Classical League; Classical Assn. of the Lehigh Valley, Founder. **Fellowships, Honors & Awards:** Univ. of Pennsylvania, Harrison Fellowship 1912-13. **Publications:** *The Sacra Idulia in Ovid's Fasti* (Newark, NJ: Essex Press, 1917); "The Age of Roman Sacrificial Victims," in *Classical Studies in Honor of John C. Rolfe*, ed. G.D. Hadzsits (Philadelphia: Univ. of Pennsylvania Press, 1931). **Bio-Bibliography:** *Who Was Who in America.*

WRIGHT, JOHN H. ■ FAAR Classics/Archaeology 68. b. Mar. 9, 1941, NYC. m. Ellen F. Wright. c. Jennifer, Emily. BA 62, Swarthmore College; MA 64, Indiana Univ.; PhD 71, Indiana Univ. **Research/Artistic Interests:** Roman comedy, Homer, traditional mountain music. **Career & Employment:** Univ. of Rochester, Instr. 1968-72, Asst. Prof. 1972-75; Northwestern Univ., Assc. Prof. 1975-77, Prof. 1977-83, John Evans Prof. 1983-present. **Memberships & Offices:** APA 1968-present; Intl. Bluegrass Music Assn. 1989-present. **Fellowships, Honors & Awards:** NEH Younger Humanist Fellowship 1973-74; Honorable Order of Kentucky Colonels 1990. **Publications:** "*Lacrimae rerum* and the Thankless Task," *Classical Journal* 62 (1966-67): 365-67; trans. with intro., *The Play of Antichrist* (Toronto: Pontifical Inst. of Mediaeval Studies, 1967); "Plautus, *Bacchides,* 525," *Classical Quarterly* ns 21 (1971): 440-41; "Naevius, *Tarentilla* Fr. I (72-74 R3)," *Rheinisches Museum für Philologie* 115 (1972): 239-42; "Homer and Elementary Greek," *Classical Journal* 68 (1972-73): 50-52; *Dancing in Chains: The Stylistic Unity of the Comoedia Palliata*, AAR Papers and Monographs 15 (Rome: AAR, 1974); trans. with intro., *The Life of Cola di Rienzo* (Toronto: Pontifical Inst. of Mediaeval Studies, 1975); "The Transformations of Pseudolus," *TAPA* 105 (1975): 403-16; "Disintegrated Assurances: The Contemporary American Response to the *Satyricon*," *Greece & Rome* 23 (1976): 32-39;

trans., "Provvisioni of the Commune of Florence," in *Giotto and Florentine Painting,* ed. Bruce Cole (New York: Harper & Row, 1976); "Publishing in North American Classical Periodicals: A Survey," *Classical Journal* 73 (1977-78): 69-73; ed., *Essays on the* Iliad: *Selected Modern Criticism* (Bloomington: Indiana Univ. Press, 1978); "*La Commedia è finita*: An Examination of Leoncavallo's Pagliacci," *Italica* 55 (1978): 167-78; "The CAS Faculty and the Summer Game," *Arts & Sciences* 1.2 (1978): 12-13; "The Language of the Masters Freshman Seminars," in *Colleges and High Schools: A New Latin League*, ed. Richard LaFleur & Gilbert Lawall (Amherst: NECN Publications, 1979), 50-54; "Giancarlo del Re: Hard Times in Rome," *La Fusta: Journal of Literature and Culture* 4.1.2 (1979): 86-98; "'Natica Jackson' and the *Medea*," *John O'Hara Journal* 2.2 (1980): 64-68; *Plautus:* Curculio, *Introduction and Notes*, APA Classical Text Series 6 (Chico, CA: Scholars Press, 1981); "Plautus (254-184 B.C.)," *Ancient Writers: Greece and Rome,* ed. T. James Luce (New York: Charles Scribner's Sons, 1982), 1:501-23; revised, Clyde Pharr, *Homeric Greek: A Book for Beginners* (Norman: Univ. of Oklahoma Press, 1985); *Traveling the High Way Home: Ralph Stanley and the World of Traditional Bluegrass Music* (Champaign: Univ. of Illinois Press, 1993). Recording: *Everything She Asks For* (River Tracks, 1993). **Bio-Bibliography:** *Who's Who in America.* **Home Address:** 1137 Noyes St., Evanston, IL 60201. **Business Address:** Dept. of Classics, Northwestern Univ., Evanston, IL 60208.

WRIGHT, WYLLIS E. ■ AAR Librarian 1930-33.

WUORINEN, CHARLES ■ RAAR Musical Composition 90. b. June 9, 1938, NYC. BA 61, Columbia Univ.; MA 63, Columbia Univ. **Career & Employment:** Columbia Univ., Instr. 1964-69, Asst. Prof. 1969-71; Manhattanville Music Curriculum Project, US Office of Education, Consultant 1967; New England Conservatory 1968-71; Princeton Univ., Visiting Lect. 1969-71; Univ. of Iowa 1970; Manhattan School of Music 1971-79; Univ. of South Florida, Visiting Composer-in-Residence 1971; Yale Univ., Visiting Prof. 1983, 1991; Rutgers Univ., Prof. 1984-present; SUNY, Buffalo, Distinguished Visiting Prof. 1989-94; NYU, Visiting Prof. 1990; Composer-in Residence: Ojai Festival 1975; Chamber Music Northwest 1978; Grand Teton Music Festival 1979, 1980; Louisville Orchestra 1984; Cabrillio Music Festival 1985; Wellesley Composers Conference 1985; San Francisco Symphony, New Music Adv. to Music Dir. 1985-89; Santa Fe Chamber Music Festival 1993. **Memberships & Offices:** American Music Soc., Great Britain, Adv. Bd.; Group for Contemporary Music, Co-Artistic Dir. 1962-present; CRI, BoD 1962-89; Bennington Composers Conference, BoT 1962-66; ISCM, BoD 1967-69; Independent Electronic Music Center, Adv. Council 1967; *Perspectives of New Music*, Ed. Bd. 1968-72; American Music Center, Dir. 1971; Meet-the-Composer, Adv. Bd. 1983, BoD 1993-preseent; New York Philharmonic, Computer Music Festival, Co-Artistic Dir. 1984; American Composers Orchestra, Pres. 1984-86; AAAS 1985; New Jersey Composers Guild, BoD 1988-present; Center for Contemporary Opera, BoD 1989-present. **Fellowships, Honors & Awards:** New York Philharmonic's Young Composers Award 1954; Bennington Composers Conference Scholarship 1956-60; Bearns Prize 1958, 1959, 1961; Alice M. Ditson Fellowship 1959; BMI-SCA Award 1959, 1961, 1962, 1963; MacDowell Colony Fellowship 1960; Phi Beta Kappa 1960; Regents College Teaching Fellowship 1961-62; Lili Boulanger Memorial Award 1961, 1962; Evans Traveling Fellowship 1961; World's Fair of Music & Sound 1962; AAAL Award 1967; Guggenheim Fellowship 1968, 1972; Ingram Merrill Fellowship 1969; Koussevitzky Intl. Recording Award 1970; Brandeis Univ., Creative Arts Awards Citation 1970; Pulitzer Prize 1970; Phoebe Ketchum Thorne Hon.

Award 1973; Finlandia Found., Arts & Letters Award 1976; Creative Artists Public Service Award 1976; Rockefeller Found. Fellowship 1979, 1981, 1982; MacArthur Found. Fellowship 1986-91. **Publications:** *Simple Composition* (London: Longman, 1979; rpt. New York: Schirmer, 1984, C.F. Peters, 1995). **Important Works:** *Chamber Concerto,* for cello & 10 instruments (Music & Art) 1963; *String Trio* (Music & Art) 1968-69; *A Reliquary for Igor Stravinsky,* for orchestra (Deutsche Grammophon) 1975; *Tashi* (Koch Intl.) 1975; *Percussion Symphony* (Nonesuch) 1976; *Fast Fantasy,* for cello & piano (New World) 1977; *New York Notes,* chamber music (Koch Intl.) 1982; *Third Piano Concerto* (Nonesuch) 1983; *Movers & Shakers,* for orchestra, Cleveland Orchestra Comm. 1984; *Bamboula Beach,* for orchestra, New World Symphony Comm. 1984; *Rhapsody for Violin and Orchestra,* San Francisco Symphony Comm. 1984; *The Golden Dance,* for orchestra (Nonesuch) 1986; *Third Piano Sonata* (Koch Intl.) 1986; *FIVE,* concerto for amplified cello & orchestra (Koch Intl.) 1987; *Third String Quartet* (New World) 1987; *Sonata for Violin & Piano* (New World), 1988; *String Sextet* (Koch Intl.) 1989; *Genesis,* San Francisco Symphony-Minnesota Orchestra Comm. 1989; *Delight of the Muses,* for orchestra, New York City Ballet Comm. 1991; *A Winter's Tale,* vocal-chamber (Koch Intl.) 1991; *Microsymphony,* Philadelphia Orchestra Comm. 1993; *Concerto for Saxophone and Orchestra* 1993; *The Celestial Sphere,* an oratorio, Handel Oratorio Soc. Comm. All works published by C.F. Peters, London; recordings available on numerous labels. **Bio-Bibliography:** Richard Burbank, *Charles Wuorinen: A Bio-Bibliography* (Westport, CT: Greenwood Press, 1992); *Baker's Biographical Dictionary; Grove Dictionary of Music; International Who's Who; Who's Who in America.* **Home Address:** 870 W. End Ave., NYC 10025. **Business Address:** Howard Stokar Mgmt., 870 W. End Ave., NYC 10025.

WURTZBURGER, JANET E.C. ■ AAR Trustee 1973.

WYNER, YEHUDI ■ FAAR Musical Composition 56, RAAR Musical Composition 91. b. June 1, 1929, Calgary, ALB, Canada. m. Nancy Braverman, Susan Davenny. c. Isaiah, Adam Z., Cassia. BA 50, Yale College; BMus 51, Yale Univ. School of Music; MA 52, Harvard Univ.; MusM 53, Yale Univ. **Career & Employment:** Queens College, CUNY, Lect. 1959-60; Turnau Opera Co., Music Dir. 1960-63; Yale Univ. School of Music, Assc. Prof. 1963-77; New Haven Opera, Music Dir. 1968-78; SUNY, Purchase, Dean of Music 1978-82, Prof. 1982-89; Brandeis Univ., Naumburg Prof. 1989-present; Visiting Prof.: Cornell Univ. 1987, Brandeis Univ. 1987-88, Harvard Univ. 1991-93. **Memberships & Offices:** ISCM, BoD; ACA; American Composers Orchestra. **Fellowships, Honors & Awards:** UC, Berkeley, A.E. Hertz Fellowship 1953; Guggenheim Fellowship 1960, 1976; NIAL Grant 1961; Brandeis Univ., Creative Arts Award 1963; NEA Grant 1976. **Important Works:** *Concert Duo,* for violin & piano (CRI) 1955-57; *Friday Evening Service,* for cantor, chorus, orchestra 1963; *Intermedio,* for soprano & string orchestra (CRI) 1974; *Fragments from Antiquity,* for soprano & orchestra 1981; *On this Most Voluptuous Night,* for soprano & chamber ensemble 1982; *String Quartet* 1985; *Toward the Center,* for piano 1988; *Sweet Consort,* for flute & piano 1988; *Dragon Choruses,* for women's voices & piano 1989; *Trapunto Junction,* for 3 brass & percussion 1991; *Prologue and Narrative,* for cello & orchestra 1994; *Lyric Harmony,* for orchestra 1995; all compositions published by American Composers Edition, NYC. **Bio-Bibliography:** *Baker's Biographical Dictionary; International Who's Who in Music; New Grove Dictionary of Music; Who's Who in America; Who's Who in Entertainment.* **Home Address:** 49 Brooks St., Medford, MA 02155.

■ ■ ■

YATES, SHARON D. ■ FAAR Painting 74. b. Apr. 3, 1942, Rochester, NY. BFA 64, Syracuse Univ.; MFA 66, Tulane Univ. **Other Study:** Syracuse Univ., Florence 1963. **Career & Employment:** Newcomb School of Art, Tulane Univ. 1964-66; Univ of Louisville 1966-68; Maryland Inst., College of Art 1968-72, 1974-present; Glasgow School of Art, Scotland 1986; Univ. of Maine, Machias 1986-90; Sunbury Shores Arts & Nature Centre, Inc., St. Andrews, NB, Canada 1987-92. **Fellowships, Honors & Awards:** Oklahoma Art Center, Oklahoma City, Purchase Award 1968; Grover M. Hermann Fine Arts Center, Marietta, OH, Grand Prize 1970-71; Union of Independent Colleges of Art Research Grant 1975; Ingram Merrill Found. Fellowship 1977-78; Maryland Inst., Ford Found. Grant 1979; Mellon Found. Grant 1984; Alliance of Independent Colleges of Art, Faculty Grant 1986; Blanch E. Colman Trust Award 1993; Maryland Inst., Trustee Award 1994. **Important Works:** Univ. Art Gallery & Museum, Univ. of Alberta, Edmonton, Canada; Oklahoma Art Center, Oklahoma City; Inner Space Design, NYC; Holt Gallery, Fine Arts Center, Towson State Univ., Towson, MD; Bates College Museum of Art, Lewiston, ME. **Exhibitions/Performances:** Solo: Univ. of Louisville, Louisville, KY 1967; Van Bokkelen Gallery, Towson State Univ., Baltimore 1970; Fine Arts Gallery, Univ. of Missouri, Columbia 1975; Fischbach Gallery, NYC 1976; Sunbury Shores Arts & Nature Centre, St. Andrews, NB, Canada 1988; Art Galleries, Univ. of Maine, Machias 1991; Maine Coast Artists, Rockport. **Bio-Bibliography:** Alan Gussow, *A Sense of Place: The Artist and the American Land* (New York: Saturday Review Press & Friends of the Earth, 1971), 50-52; Carl Little, "Sharon Yates Sees Maine at its Summer Best," *Maine Times* (Dec. 1991); Philip Isaacson, "Audience," *Maine Telegram* (Aug. 1993); Alan Gussow, *The Artist as Native: Reinventing Regionalism* (Pomegranate Art Books), 20-21. **Home Address:** RR 2, Box 4150, Lubec, ME 04652.

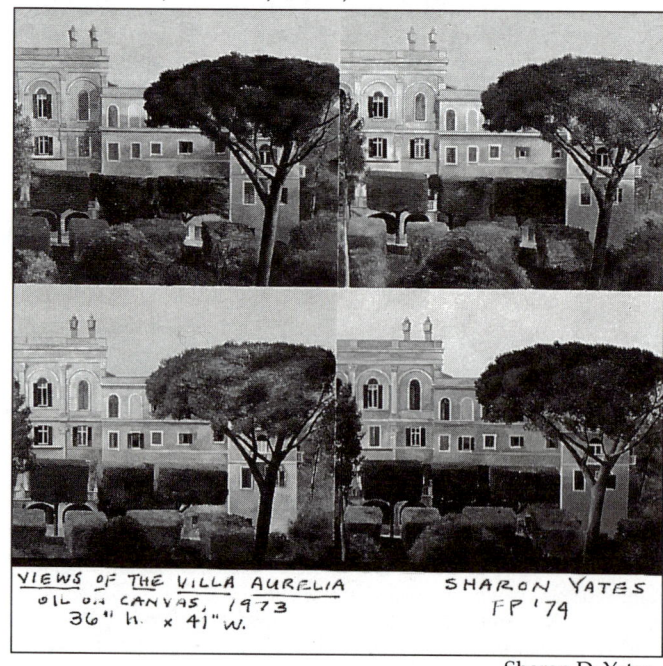

VIEWS OF THE VILLA AURELIA OIL ON CANVAS, 1973 36" h. x 41" w.   SHARON YATES FP '74

Sharon D. Yates

YEGUL, FIKRET K. ■ AAR Cosa Archaeological Team 1968. b. Oct. 27, 1942, Turkey. m. Diane G. Favro. BArch 64, Middle

East Technical Univ., Ankara; BArch 65, Yale Univ.; MArch 66, Univ. of Pennsylvania; PhD 75, Harvard Univ. **Research/Artistic Interests:** History of architecture, classical architecture, Roman architecture. **Career & Employment:** Wellesley College, Asst. Prof. 1975-76; UC, Santa Barbara, Asst. Prof. 1976-82, Assc. Prof. 1983-88, Prof. 1989-present, Chair 1988-93. **Home Address:** 2825 Puesta del Sol, Santa Barbara, CA 93105. **Business Address:** Art History Dept., UC, Santa Barbara, CA 93106.

Over the years the American Academy in Rome has provided me with invaluable opportunities to conduct research in Roman architecture. My tribute to this remarkable institution of humanistic scope is embodied in the book I have written to illuminate an aspect of its architectural and intellectual history: Gentlemen of Instinct and Breeding: Architecture at the American Academy in Rome, 1894-1940 (1991).

Fikret K. Yegul

YOUNG, ARTHUR M. ■ AAR Classical Soc., Pres. 1966.

YOUNG, HEATHER ■ NIAE, John Dinkeloo Traveling Fellow 1988-89.

Z

ZAJAC, JACK S. ■ FAAR Painting 58, RAAR Painting 68. b. Dec. 13, 1929, Youngstown, OH. m. Corda L. Eby. c. Aaron, Christian. **Study:** Scripps College, Claremont, CA 1949-52. **Career & Employment:** Pomona College, Lect. 1959-60; Artist-in-Residence: Univ. of Colorado 1963, UCLA 1969, Dartmouth College 1970; UC, Santa Cruz 1974-92. **Fellowships, Honors & Awards:** AAAL Grant 1959; Guggenheim Fellowship 1960; NAD 1990. **Important Works:** MOMA; Dartmouth College; Israel Museum, Jerusalem; Hirshhorn Museum & Sculpture Garden, Washington, DC; PAFA; Walker Art Center, Minneapolis; Butler Museum of American Art., Youngstown, OH; Honolulu Acad. of Fine Art; Los Angeles County Museum of Art; Whitney Museum, NYC; Oakland Museum, CA; UCLA. **Exhibitions/Performances:** São Paulo, Brazil Biennale 1955; Festival of Two Worlds, Spoleto, Italy 1958; AIC 1959; MOMA 1959, 1962; Guggenheim Museum, NYC 1962; Whitney Museum, NYC 1962; Pittsburgh Intl. 1965; Biennale di Roma 1968; Solo: Civic Center Plaza, Irvine, CA 1989; Fortezza di Albornoz, Orvieto 1976; Oakland Museum, CA 1990. **Home Address:** 1316 W. Cliff Dr., Santa Cruz, CA 95060.

ZAMPONI, LUCA ■ AAR – Rome, Gate Reception.

ZANKER, PAUL ■ RAAR Classics/Archaeology 89. b. Feb. 7, 1937, Konstanz, Germany. m. Dorothea von Meyer. c. Benedikt, Franziska, Peter-Paul. PhD 62, Universität Freiburg. **Other Study:** Univ. of Rome. **Research/Artistic Interests:** Greek & Roman archaeology. **Career & Employment:** Habilitation 1967; Ordinarius Klass. Arch., Göttingen 1972-76; Ordinarius Klass. Arch., Munich 1976-present. **Memberships & Offices:** Bayerische Akademie d. Wiss. 1979-present; Deutsches Archaeol. Inst., Zentraldirektion; British Acad. 1990; Accademia

Europea, London. **Publications:** *Forum Augustum: Das Bildprogramm* (Tübingen: Wasmuth, 1968); *Studien zu den Augustus-Porträts: Der Actium-Typus,* Abhandlung der Akademie der Wissenschaften Göttingen 3.85 (1973); *Klassizistische Statuen: Studien zur Veränderung des Kunstgeschmacks in der römischen Kaiserzeit* (Mainz: P. Von Zabern, 1974); "Hellenismus und Mittelitalien," *Abhandlung der Akademie der Wissenschaften Göttingen* 3.97 (1976); with K. Fittschen, *Katalog der rom. Porträts in den Capitolinischen Museen,* Vol. 3, *Kaiserinnen- und Prinzessinnenbildnisse, Frauenporträts* (Mainz: P. Von Zabern, 1983); with K. Fittschen, *Katalog der rom. Portrats in den Capitolinischen Museen.* Vol. 1, *Kaiser- und Prinzenbildnisse* I (Mainz: P. Von Zabern, 1985); with H. v. Herberg, "Römische Gräberstrassen: Selbst-darstellung, Status, Standard," *Bayerische Akademie der Wissenschaften Abhandlung* (1987); *Augustus und die Macht der Bilder* (Munich: C.H. Beck, 1987); *Pompeji: Stadtbild und Wohngeschmack* (Mainz: : P. Von Zabern, 1995); *Die Maske des Socrates* (Munich: Beck, 1995). **Home Address:** Orffstr. 23, Munich 19, D 8000 Germany.

ZAPATKA, CHRISTIAN M. ■ FAAR Architecture 91. b. Mar. 18, 1960, Washington, DC. BA 82, Georgetown Univ.; MArch 88, Princeton Univ. **Other Study:** Inst. for Architecture & Urban Studies, NYC, Intern 1983-84; Agrest & Gandelsonas, NYC, Intern 1983-85. **Research/Artistic Interests:** Architectural & urban design on many levels; research on American landscape design & urbanism. **Career & Employment:** Michael Graves, Architect, Architectural Designer 1988-90; Syracuse Univ. in Florence, Adj. Instr. 1991-92; Univ. of Michigan, Visiting. Asst. Prof. 1993; Juror & Lect. at schools in US & Italy. **Fellowships, Honors & Awards:** Princeton Univ., Univ. Fellowship 1985-88, William Norton Prize Travelling Fellowship 1988; Chicago Inst. for Architecture & Urbanism, Fellow-in-Residence 1992. **Publications:** "The American Parkways," *Lotus International* 56 (1988): 96-128; "Greenbelt, Maryland: A Report," in *The Architecture of Western Gardens* (Milan: Electa, Cambridge, MA: MIT Press, 1990); "The Edison Effect: A History of Lighting in the American City," *Lotus International* 75 (1993): 60-78; "Chicago's Monadnock Block: The Developer's Dream," *Dimensions* 8 (1994): 84-93; "Expansive Urbanism: Suturing Boston's North End," *Dimensions* 9 (1995); *The Architecture of the American Landscape*, Lotus Document 21 (Milan: Elemond Periodici & Mondadori, 1995); "Robert Moses and the Modernization/ Suburbanization of a Metropolis," *Lotus International* (forthcoming). **Exhibitions/Performances:** Paine-Webber Gallery, NYC 1987; Graham Found. for Advanced Studies in the Fine Arts 1993. **Home Address:** 330 Kingsley St., Apt. 2, Ann Arbor, MI 48104. **Business Address:** College of Achitecture & Urban Planning, Univ. of Michigan, Ann Arbor, MI 48109.

ZARINA, ASTRA ■ FAAR Architecture 63. b. Riga, Latvia. m. Anthony Costa Heywood. BArch 54, Univ. of Washington; MArch 55, MIT. **Other Study:** Technische Universitaet, Karlsruhe 1947; Intl. Centre for the Study of the Preservation & Restoration of Cultural Property (ICCROM). **Research/Artistic Interests:** History & transformations of the Theater of Pompey & environs; Città di Bagnoregio: continuity & change. Both studies include iconographic, archival, & philological material, original measured drawings, typological analysis & restoration proposals. **Career & Employment:** Astra Zarina, Architect 1962-present; Univ. of Washington, College of Architecture & Urban Planning, Prof. 1970-present, Rome Center, Dir. 1984-93; Studio La Rocca, Architects, Engineers & Planners, Part. 1978-87. **Memberships & Offices:** Univ. of Washington Medieval Colloquium 1976-present; Amici dell'ICCROM

1990-present; Assn. of American College & Univ. Programs in Italy. **Fellowships, Honors & Awards:** Univ. of Washington, Faculty Award 1953, Distinguished Teaching Award 1979; MIT, Graduate Fellowship 1954-55; MIT, Chamberlain Award 1955; Fulbright Grant 1960-61; AIA Michigan Chap., 25 Year Design Award 1987; Graham Found. Grant 1988. **Publications:** *SAAL Planungsgruppe e Astra Zarina a Berlino* (Rome: Nat. Inst. of Italian Architects, 1969); "Città di Bagnoregio: Restoration in a 2,300 Year Old Town," *House and Garden* (Spring 1974): 114-22, 214-19; *I Tetti di Roma* (Rome: Carlo Bestetti, Edizioni d'Arte, 1976); *Rome's Modern Quarters*, 5 vols. (Rome: Univ. of Washington Architecture in Rome Program, 1978-83); "Seattle Anni Settanta e lo Spirito dei Tempi" in *Ambienti Storici: La Progettazione e il Problema del Recupero della Qualità,"* Cattedra di Urbanistica II (Rome: Istituto di Architettura Edilizia e Urbanistica, Università degli Studi di Roma & the Univ. of Washington, 1978); "Freeway Park, Un Esempio per il Recupero della Città Attuale," in *Programma e Progetto per il Recupero della Città Esistente,"* Cattedra di Urbanistica II (Rome: Istituto di Architettura Edilizia e Urbanistica, Università degli Studi di Roma & the Univ. of Washington, 1979): 39-59; *Rome According to Rioni* (Rome: Univ. of Washington Architecture in Rome Program, 1980); *Pliny's Laurentine Villa Revisited* (Seattle: Univ. of Washington, 1988); *The Pio Block and Environs* (Rome: Rome & American Schools of Architecture, Univ. of Washington, 1988); *Metamorfosi* 24: 21-29, Quaderni di Architettura (1994). **Important Works:** USA Project Architect with Minoru Yamasaki & Asscs., Birmingham, MI 1956-60: Warren Methodist Church 1956; Art School for Detroit Arts & Crafts 1957; Whiting Asscs., Europe, Senior Architect & Consultant; Nat. School of Law & Administration, Leopoldville, Congo 1963; Staff housing, auditorium, recreation hall, & school for Seventh-Day Adventist Hospital, Benghazi, Libya 1963-64; Independent Practice: New Town "Maerkisches Viertel," Berlin 1965-70; McGaughy, Marshall, McMillan & Lucas, Rome, Consulting Architect: Saudi Arabian Airlines, HQ Bldg. 1966; US Officers Club, Vicenza, Italy 1967; Residential & commercial center, Kuwait 1967; Città di Bagnoregio Restoration, Italy 1967-present; Univ. of Washington, Italian Studies Programs 1970-present; Palazzo Pio Restoration, Rome 1984-89. **Home Address:** Palazzo Pio, Piazza del Biscone 95, Rome 00186, Italy. **Business Address:** Univ. of Washington, Rome Center, Palazzo Pio, Piazza del Biscone 95, Rome 00186, Italy.

ZARKER, JOHN W. ■ FAAR Classics/Archaeology 60. b. Oct. 25, 1928, Lancaster, PA. m. Katherine L. Zarker. c. Leslie Morgan, Jean Frisbee, Jeff Zarker, Carol Zarker, Sarah Hand. BA 50, Franklin & Marshall College; MA 52, UNC, Chapel Hill; PhD 58, Princeton Univ. **Other Study:** Augustan Age Rome, Vergil, Ovid. **Career & Employment:** Univ. of Texas, Instr. 1958-59; Dartmouth College, Asst.-Assc. Prof. 1961-66; Vanderbilt Univ., Assc. Prof. 1966-71; Tufts Univ., Prof. 1971-89; Duke Univ., Senior Lect. 1989-present. **Memberships & Offices:** CANE, Exec. Comm. 1978-91, Pres. 1985. **Publications:** "A Vergilian Verse in the *Carmina Epigraphica Latina,*" *Classical Journal* 57 (1961-62): 112-16; "Catullus 18-20," *TAPA* 93 (1962): 197-204; "King Eetion and Thebe as Symbols in the Iliad" *Classical Journal* 61 (1965): 110-14; "Acrostic *Carmina Latina Epigraphica,*" *Orpheus* 13 (1966): 125-51; "Aeneas and Theseus in Aeneid VI," *Classical Journal* 62 (1967): 220-26; "Amata: Vergil's Other Tragic Queen," *Vergilius* 15 (1969): 2-24; "*Mule, nihil sentis*: Catullus *Carmina* 88 and 17," *Classical Journal* 64 (1969): 172-77; "A Possible Parody of the *Carmina Latina Epigraphica,*" *Helikon* 9 (1970): 392-98; "The Hercules Theme in the *Aeneid,*" *Vergilius* 18 (1972): 34-68; "Lesbia's Charms," *Classical Journal* 68 (1973): 107-15;

"Vergil's Trojan and Italian Matres," *Vergilius* 24 (1978): 15-24; "Augustan Art and Architecture in Vergil's *Aeneid,*" in *The Age of Augustus,* ed. R. Winkes, Archaeologia Transatlantica 5:197-208; "The Tufts University-Classical Association of New England Workshop and Institute," in *The Teaching of Latin in American Schools: A Profession in Crisis,* ed. R.A. LaFleur (Scholars Press, 1987), 71-82. **Home Address:** 115 Silo Dr., Chapel Hill, NC 27514. **Business Address:** Duke Univ., Durham, NC 27708.

ZEVI, BRUNO ■ AAR Visitor 1980-81, Architect.

ZIOLKOWSKI, ADAM S. ■ Mellon East-Central European Visiting Scholar 1994.

ZIOLKOWSKI, JAN M. ■ FAAR Post-Classical/Humanistic Studies 81. b. Nov. 17, 1956, New Haven, CT. m. Elizabeth A. Ziolkowski. c. Saskia Elizabeth, Ada Margaret, Yetta Joy. BA 77, Princeton Univ.; PhD 82, Cambridge Univ. **Other Study:** Center for Arabic Studies Abroad, Cairo 1976; Univ. of Vienna 1974. **Research/Artistic Interests:** Medieval literature, esp. Latin. **Career & Employment:** Harvard Univ., Asst Prof. 1981-84, John L. Loeb Assc. Prof. of Humanities 1984-87, Prof. 1987-present. **Fellowships, Honors & Awards:** Nat. Merit Scholar 1974; Princeton Univ., Stinnecke Prize for Classics 1975, Class of 1870 Old English Prize 1976; Center for Arabic Studies Abroad Scholar 1976; Phi Beta Kappa 1977; Marshall Scholar 1977-80; NEH Summer Stipend 1983; Phi Beta Kappa Teaching Prize 1986; ACLS Fellowship 1986; Guggenheim Fellowship 1987, 1988. **Publications:** "Folklore and Learned Lore in Letaldus's Whale Poem," *Viator* 15 (1984): 107-18; *Alan of Lille's Grammar of Sex: The Meaning of Grammar to a Twelfth-Century Intellectual,* Speculum Anniversary Monographs 10 (Cambridge, MA: MAA, 1985); ed., Nigel of Canterbury, *Miracles of the Virgin Mary, in Verse: Miracula sancte Dei genitricis Marie, uersifice,* Toronto Medieval Latin Texts 17 (Toronto: Pontifical Inst. of Mediaeval Studies, 1986); "Saints in Invocations and Oaths in Medieval Literature," *Journal of English and Germanic Philology* 87 (1988): 179-92; *Jezebel: A Norman Latin Poem of the Early Eleventh Century,* Humana Civilitas: Studies and Sources Relating to the Middle Ages and the Renaissance 10 (New York: Peter Lang, 1989); ed., *On Philology* (Univ. Park, PA: Penn State Press, 1990); "The Nature of Prophecy in Geoffrey of Monmouth's *Vita Merlini,*" in *Poetry and Prophecy: The Beginnings of a Literary Tradition,* ed. James L. Kugel (Ithaca & London: Cornell Univ. Press, 1990), 151-62, 240-44; "Classical Influences on Medieval Latin Views of Poetic Inspiration," in *Latin Poetry and the Classical Tradition: Essays in Medieval and Renaissance Literature,* ed. Peter Godman & Oswyn Murray (Oxford: Clarendon Press, 1990), 15-38; "Cultural Diglossia and the Nature of Medieval Latin Literature," in *The Ballad and Oral Literature,* Harvard English Studies 16, ed. Joseph Harris (Cambridge, MA: Harvard Univ. Press, 1991), 193-213; "The Eupolemius," *Journal of Medieval Latin* 1 (1991) 1-45; "A Fairy Tale from before Fairy Tales: Egbert of Liege's '*De puellis a lupellis seruata*' and the Medieval Background of 'Little Red Riding Hood,'" *Speculum* 67 (1992): 549-75; *Talking Animals: Medieval Latin Beast Poetry* (Philadelphia: Univ. of Pennsylvania Press, 1993); preface, in Erich Auerbach, *Literary Language and Its Public* (Princeton: Princeton Univ. Press, 1993); ed. & trans., Nigel of Canterbury, *The Passion of St. Lawrence, Epigrams and Marginal Poems,* Mittellateinische Studien und Texte (Leiden: Brill, 1994); ed. & trans., *The Cambridge Songs (Carmina cantabrigiensia)* Garland Library of Medieval Literature 66, ser. A (New York: Garland, 1994). **Business Address:** Widener Library 771, Harvard Univ., Cambridge, MA 02138.

ZUBE, ERVIN H. ■ FAAR Landscape Architecture 61. b. Apr. 24, 1931, Milwaukee, WI. m. Margaret J. Zube. c. Eric C. BS 54, Univ. of Wisconsin; MLA 59, Harvard GSD; PhD 73, Clark Univ. **Other Study:** England 1977. **Research/Artistic Interests:** Landscape perceptions & values, landscape history – designed & vernacular, national parks & protected landscapes. **Career & Employment:** Univ. of Wisconsin, Asst. Prof. 1961-64; Zube & Dega Asscs. 1961-64; UC, Berkeley, Asst. Prof. 1964-65; Univ. of Massachusetts, Amherst, Prof., Dept. Head 1965-72; Research Planning & Design Asscs., Pres. 1966-70; Inst. for Man & the Environment, Dir. 1972-77; Univ. of Arizona, Tucson, Prof. 1977-present; School of Renewable Natural Resources, Dir. 1977-82. **Memberships & Offices:** Hubbard Educational Trust, BoD 1969-present; US Man & Biosphere Pgm., Directorate on Perception of Environmental Quality 1977-88, Chair 1980-86; Nat. Architectural Accrediting Bd., Dir. 1978-80; Arizona-Sonora Desert Museum, BoT 1981-90, Pres. 1989-90; Environmental Design Research Assn., BoD 1982-85, Chair 1984-85; Southwest

The Academy: people, experiences, and place-- all together:

* Along with Elizabeth Bowen, Alexie Haieff, and the "class of 61", being introduced to Italian cities, monuments, and landscapes by Laurance and Isabell Roberts.

* Visiting Italian gardens with Tommy Church, and the Porta Portese market with Jack and June Massey on Sunday mornings.

* "Living" in the Academy library for nearly six months, studying Italian garden history, discovering Byzantine architecture, and catching up on all (at least a lot) of the reading that I didn't have time to do in graduate school.

* Arguing, collaborating, being stimulated by, and playing bottle-pool with Alan Harris, Aldo Casanova, Jack Massey, George Wilson and those who didn't play, John Eaton, Ted Musho, and Jack Zajac.

* With Jack Zajac, entering a design competition for an urban plaza in Portland, Oregon -- didn't win, but the experience was great.

* Travelling and camping throughout Greece, Turkey, Yugoslavia (a Byzantine odyssey), and most of Western Europe (in search of old gardens and landscapes) with Margaret and son Eric (who was just learning to walk) -- a great experience until we encountered rain and a mud-baby on 27 consecutive days in England, Germany, France, and Holland.

* Discovering a deep interest in landscape history, designed and vernacular, an interest that has prevailed for more than three decades.

Ervin H. Zube

Ervin H. Zube

Parks & Monuments Assn., BoD 1984-94, Chair 1989-92. **Fellowships, Honors & Awards:** *Progressive Architecture* Research Citation 1977; NATO Senior Fellowship 1977; ASLA, Bradford Williams Medal 1981, Research Honor Award 1982, Fellow 1984; NEA Fellowship 1983-84; Landscape Architecture Found., LaGasse Medal 1992; Udall Center for Studies in Public Policy, Fellow 1993. **Publications:** *Landscapes: Selected Writings of J.B. Jackson* (Amherst: Univ. of Massachusetts Press, 1970); "Scenery as a Natural Resource: Implications of Public Policy and Problems of Definition, Description and Evaluation," *Landscape Architecture* 63.2 (1973): 126-32; "The Natural History of Urban Trees," *Natural History* (Nov. 1973): 48-51; with R.O. Bursh & J. Gy. Fabos, *Landscape Assessment, Values, Perceptions and Resources* (Stroudsburg, PA: Douden Hutchison & Ross, 1975); with K. Craik, *Perceiving Environmental Quality: Research and Applications* (New York: Plenum, 1976); with J.F. Palmer & J. Crystal, "Design Quality in the National Parks," *Design and Environment* 7.3 (1976): 34-37; with A. Friedman & C. Zimring, *Environmental Design Evaluation* (New York: Plenum, 1978); "The Roots of Future Innovation: Research and Theory," *Land-*

scape Architecture 70.6 (1980): 614-17; "An Exploration of Southwestern Landscape Images," *Landscape Journal* 1 (1982): 31-40; *Environmental Evaluation: Perception and Public Policy* (New York: Cambridge Univ. Press, 1984); "Themes in Landscape Assessment Theory," *Landscape Journal* 3.2 (1984): 104-11; "Landscape Planning Education: Retrospect & Prospect," *Landscape and Urban Planning* 13.5-6 (1986): 367-78; with G. Moore, *Advances in Environment, Behavior and Design*, 3 vols. (New York: Plenum, 1987, 1989, 1991); "Environmental Psychology, Global Issues and Local Landscape Research," *Journal of Environmental Psychology* 11 (1992): 321-34. **Bio-Bibliography:** *Who's Who in America; Who's Who in the East; Who's Who in the West.* **Home Address:** 7045 Camino de Fosforo, Tuscon, AZ 85718.

ZWEIG, JANET ■ FAAR Design Arts 92. b. Apr. 4, 1950, Milwaukee, WI. BA 71, Cornell Univ.; MFA 81, SUNY, Rochester. **Career & Employment:** RISD, Faculty 1982-present; Yale Univ., Visiting Critic 1991-present. **Fellowships, Honors & Awards:** Massachusetts Council on the Arts Grant 1984; Massachusetts Artists Found. Fellowship 1985; MacDowell Colony Residency 1989, 1990, 1991, 1993, 1994; Nat. Studio Program, PS 1 Museum, NYC 1990-91; Engelhard Award 1991; New York Dept. of Cultural Affairs Comm. 1993; NEA Fellowship 1994. **Important Works: Collections:** MOMA; Whitney Museum, NYC; MFA; Intl. Center of Photography, NYC; California Inst. for the Arts; Houghton Library, Harvard Univ; Cleveland Art Inst.; Wellesley College Library; Visual Studies Workshop; Museum of Contemporary Art, Chicago; AIC; Walker Art Center; Pompidou Centre, Paris; RISD. **Exhibitions/Performances:** Elvejem Museum of Art, Univ. of Wisconsin 1983; Camerawork Gallery, San Francisco 1984; Cleveland Art Inst. 1984; New England Found. for the Arts, traveling exb. 1984; UC, traveling exb. 1986; Walker Art Center, Minneapolis 1989; List Visual Art Center, MIT 1989; Univ. of Maryland, College Park 1990; PS 1 Museum, Inst. of Contemporary Art, NYC 1990, 1991; Wallace Gallery, SUNY, Old Westbury 1991; Diverse Works, Houston 1992; Sala 1, Rome 1993; Huntington Gallery, Massachusetts College of Art 1993. **Home Address:** 443 Greenwich St., Apt. 2B, NYC 10013.

ZWILICH, ELLEN TAAFFE ■ RAAR Musical Composition 90. b. Miami, FL. m. Erik Lamont. PhD, Juilliard School. **Other Studies:** Florida State Univ. **Fellowships, Honors & Awards:** Boston Musica Viva Comm.; Chamber Music Soc. of Lincoln Center Comm.; Chicago Symphony Orchestra Comm.; NY Philharmonic, Comm.; Pulitzer Prize 1983; Elizabeth Sprague Coolidge Chamber Music Prize; Guggenheim Fellowship; Ernst von Dohnanyi Citation; AAAL Award; Arturo Toscanini Music Critics Award; Oberlin College, Hon. PhD. **Important Works:** *Double Quartet for Strings* 1984; *Prologue and Variations* (New World Recording); *Cello Symphony,* Symphony No. 2 1985; *Concerto Grosso* (New World Recording) 1985, 1989; *Celebration,* for orchestra (New World Recording) 1986; *Trio,* for piano, violin & cello 1987; *Tanzspiel,* a ballet, NYC Ballet Comm. 1987; *Praeludium* 1988; *Symbolon* (New World Recording) 1989; *Concerto,* for bass trombone, strings, timpani & cymbals, c. 1990. **Bio-Bibliography:** Andrew L. Pincus, "Writing Music About Life and Living," *Berkshire Eagle* (Apr. 21, 1991); K. Robert Schwarz, "When Anything Goes, Composers Go Every Which Way," *NY Times* (June 9, 1991).

■ ■ ■

INDICES

FELLOWS OF THE AMERICAN ACADEMY
BY DISCIPLINE

ARCHITECTURE
Anthony M. Ames 84
Joseph Amisano 52
Amy Christie Anderson 81
Thomas Angotti 90
Richard W. Ayers 38
Clarence Dale Badgeley 29
Gregory S. Baldwin 71
Marc Ira Balet 75
Richard E. Baringer 53
Richard W. Bartholomew 72
Frederick C. Biehle 87
James L. Bodnar 80
Thomas L. Bosworth 81
Charles G. Brickbauer 57
Cecil Clair Briggs 31
H. Turner Brooks 84
Andrea Clark Brown 80
Theodore L. Brown 88
William P. Bruder 87
Marvin Harry Buchanan 76
Dale Claude Byrd 51
Walker Oscar Cain 48
Peter William Carl 75
Kenneth Earl Carpenter 15
John J. Casbarian 86
Judith Chafee 77
James Henry Chillman 22
Caroline B. Constant 79
Frederic Shurtleff Coolidge 48
Roger A. Crowley 85
Edwin (Teddy) Cruz 92
Wellington Willson Cummer 77
Thomas V. Czarnowski 67
Royston Tuttle Daley 62
Spero Daltas 51
Douglas Darden 89
Robert S. Davis 91
Thomas Laughead Dawson, Jr. 52
Arthur F. Deam 26
Kathryn A. Dean 87
Joseph A. De Pace 85
Judith DiMaio 78
Ron Dirsmith 60
William Douglas 28
Robert W. Evans 73
James B. Favaro 86
Ronald C. Filson 70
Mark M. Foster 84
George Fraser 28
Robert Morris Golder 63
Alexander C. Gorlin 84
Michael Graves 60
James A. Gresham 56
Brand N. Griffin 74

Olindo Grossi 36
Michael Guran 71
George E. Hartman 78
Richard Gardner Hartshorne 39
John D. Heimbaugh 70
George A. Hinds 84
William J.H. Hough 17
Sanda D. Iliescu 94
Franklin D. Israel 75
Erling F. Iverson 40
David J. Jacob 58
Allan B. Jacobs 86
James R. Jarrett 59
Robert Earl Jensen 76
Burton Kenneth Johnstone 32
E. Fay Jones 81
Wesley C. Jones 86
Wendy Evans Joseph 84
Henri V. Jova 51
Robert Kahn 82
Spence R. Kass 81
Raymond McCormick Kennedy 19
Stephen J. Kieran 81
J. Michael Kirkland 70
Grace Ricako Kobayashi 90
Peter Kommers 76
George Simpson Koyl 14
Eugene Kupper 83
James R. Lamantia, Jr. 49
James L. Lambeth 79
Gary H. Larson 83
Thomas Norman Larson 64
John Q. Lawson 81
David L. Leavitt 51
Celia Margaret Ledbetter 83
Diane Hermione Lewis 77
Ernest Farnum Lewis 11
Roy W. Lewis 86
George Tibbits Licht 37
Theodore Liebman 66
Robert S. Livesey 75
John H. MacFadyen 54
Robert Emerson Mangurian 77
Henri Gabriel Marceau 25
Tallie Burton Maule 52
Arthur May 75
David T. Mayernik 89
John J. McDonald, Jr. 83
William Gene McMinn 81
Cameron C. McNall 92
D.B. Middleton 82
Henry D. Mirick 33
Robert J. Mittelstadt 64
Grover E. Mouton III 73
Vincent Joseph Mulcahy 77

Theodore J. Musho 61
Robert L. Myers 54
John R. Naughton 85
George Harold Nelson 34
Stanley H. Pansky 53
William Pedersen 67
Charles O. Perry 66
Warren A. Peterson 55
Homer Fay Pfeiffer 30
Warren Platner 55
John Russell Pope 1897
Antoine Predock 85
George L. Queral 88
Patrick J. Quinn 80
Jason H. Ramos 91
William Reed 68
Walter Louis Reichart 33
Jesse Reiser 85
Danny M. Samuels 86
Peter Miller Schmitt 72
Thomas L. Schumacher 69
Jon Michael Schwarting 70
Frederic D. Schwartz 86
Daniel V. Scully 70
Werner Seligmann 81
Stuart Maclaren Shaw 28
Philip Trammell Shutze 20
Thomas P. Silva 89
Jorge Silvetti 86
James Kellum Smith 23
Peter F. Smith 69
Thomas Gordon Smith 80
Richard Haviland Smythe 13
Barbara Stauffacher Solomon 83
Bernard Norman Steinberg 63
Dan Robert Stewart 57
Friedrich St. Florian 85
Charles Thomas Stifter 63
James S. Stokoe 79
John T. Stonehill 60
Wayne Taylor 62
Milo H. Thompson 65
Duane Thorbeck 64
James Harrison Timberlake 83
Robert H. Timme 86
Fred Travisano 82
William Turnbull, Jr. 80
Robert Venturi 56
William K. Vinyard 90
Austris J. Vitols 65
Craig H. Walton 82
Harry Edward Warren 09
Robert A. Weppner, Jr. 36
Charles D. Wiley 48
Edgar Irving Williams 12
Frederick J. Woodbridge 23
Christian M. Zapatka 91
Astra Zarina 63

CLASSICS/ARCHAEOLOGY

Freeman William Adams 51
George Henry Allen 02
Hubert Lee Allen III 67
Albert J. Ammerman 88
Rebecca Miller Ammerman 91
James C. Anderson, jr 79
William S. Anderson 55
Henry Herbert Armstrong 03
James I. Armstrong 56
William Ayres Arrowsmith 57
Henry Ess Askew 32
William T. Avery 39
Eric C. Baade 57
Charles L. Babcock 55
Mary Taylor Babcock 54
Susan Helen Ballou 06
Barbara A. Barletta 90
Claude W. Barlow 38
Malcolm Bell III 70
Bettina A. Bergmann 82
Bertram Berman 49
Dorris Taylor Bishop 49
William Warner Bishop 1898
Marion Elizabeth Blake 25
Frances G. Blank 40
John P. Bodel 83
Smith Palmer Bovie 49
Aline Abaecherli Boyce 35
George Kenneth Boyce 35
Joseph Granger Brandt 12
Otto J. Brendel 51
T. Corey Brennan 88
Richard Brilliant 62
Dericksen M. Brinkerhoff 61
Donald Frederick Brown 41
Donald Freeman Brown 53
Frank Edward Brown 33
Virginia Brown 68
Walter Reid Bryan 22
Gregory S. Bucher 95
Paul Frederic Burke, Jr. 80
Anne Pippin Burnett 59
Howard Crosby Butler 1898
Joseph Coleman Carter 71
Saul Michael Cheilik 64
Glenn F. Chesnut 79
Ethel Leigh Chubb 21
Charles Upson Clark 01
Wendell V. Clausen 53
Emily Wadsworth Cleland 21
Jacquelyn C. Clinton 69
Guy Blandin Colburn 10
Howard Comfort 29
Diane Atnally Conlin 91
Kate Cooper 91
Jane W. Crawford 82
John Raymond Crawford 14
John S. Creaghan, SJ 48

James Joseph Mark Curry 63
Charles Densmore Curtis 15
John Day 27
Mario A. Del Chiaro 60
Willian Kendall Denison 1896
Walter Dennison 1897
Norman Wentworth De Witt 04
Susan B. Downey 65
Miriam F. Drabkin 40
Margaret Houston DuBois 72
Albert F. Earnshaw 1896-97
George H. Edgell 12
Ingrid E.M. Edlund-Berry 84
Frank Ray Elder 12
Elizabeth Cornelia Evans 32
Harry B. Evans 73
Herbert Edward Everett 06
Kenneth Sawyer Falk 53
J. Clayton Fant 92
Jesse Rufus Fears 71
Andrew M. Feldherr 90
Marleen Boudreau Flory 86
Joseph Fontenrose 52
Bettie Lucille Forte 60
Richard I. Frank 64
James L. Franklin, Jr. 75
Alfred Knox Frazer 61
Bruce W. Frier 68
Bernard D. Frischer 76
Mary-Kay Gamel Orlandi 69
Mildred McConnell Gardner 28
Katherine A. Geffcken 55
Alfred Gelstharp 33
Philip J. Gentner 07
Catherine Spotswood Gibbes 76
Judith R. Ginsburg 76
Kathryn L. Gleason 87
Robert F. Goheen 53
Charlotte Elizabeth Goodfellow 32
Arthur Ernest Gordon 24
Harold C. Gotoff 59
Chester Carr Greene 34
Richard Eugene Grimm 56
David Frederick Grose 74
Thomas D. Groves 84
Martha Leeb Hadzi 54
Anne E. Haeckl 78
David Martin Halperin 77
John Arthur Hanson 55
Austin Morris Harmon 07
Raymond Davis Harriman 16
Robert E. Hecht, Jr. 49
Guy M. Hedreen 94
Ursula M. Heibges 66
James A. Higginbotham 89
Herbert Hoffmann 58
Martha W. Hoffman 53
Richard J. Hoffman 72
Louise Adams Holland 23

R. Ross Holloway 60
Eric R. Hostetter 83
Lester Clarence Houck 39
George W. Houston 69
Michael Hamilton Jameson 59
Sheree A. Jaros 90
Dora Johnson 11
Franklin Weeks Jones 31
Laurence H. Kant 87
George Dwight Kellogg 1900
John Fawcett Kenfield III 77
Dawson Kiang 71
Adele Jeanne Kibre 32
E. Christian Kopff 79
Gretchen Kromer 73
Anne Laidlaw 61
Gordon Jennings Laing 1897
Clark D. Lamberton 08
Richmond Lattimore 35
Lillian Beatrice Lawler 26
Gregory Vincent Leftwich 91
John O. Lenaghan 59
Lydia Lenaghan 59
Ernestine Franklin Leon 23
William Levitan 88
Brooks Emmons Levy 56
Naphtali Lewis 36
Dean Putnam Lockwood 09
Elaine Pembroke Loeffler 53
Herbert S. Long 41
Elias Avery Lowe 11
Walter Lowrie 1900
Michael R. Maas 81
William L. MacDonald 56
Ralph Van Deman Magoffin 07
Martha A. Malamud 88
Berthe M. Marti 45
Susan D. Martin 81
Anna Marguerite McCann 66
Eugene Stock McCartney 16
George Englert McCracken 31
Thomas A.J. McGinn 85
William T. McKibben 51
Clarence Linton Meader 1898
Lucy Shoe Meritt 37, 50
William Stuart Messer 22
Agnes Kirsopp Lake Michels 33
Margaret M. Miles 88
Maria T. Marabini Moevs 64
Anna M. Moore 90
Floyd Leonard Moreland 69
Charles Rufus Morey 03
Christopher Frederick Moss 80
Glenn W. Most 83
Charles Theophilus Murphy 54
Helen Nagy 86
Chester F. Natunewicz 59
Norman Neuerburg 57
Richard Offner 13

Raymond Theodore Ohl 30
George N. Olcott 1899
James Henry Oliver 30
Erling C. Olsen 39
David Gerlad Orr 73
Steven E. Ostrow 75
James E. Packer 63
Thalia Alexandra Pandiri 67
Christopher C. Parslow 88
Paul Pascal 52
Carole Paul 86
Bernard Mann Peebles 34
J. Theodore Peña 85
Collice Henry Portnoff 30
Thomas Jex Preston Jr. 09
Michael C.J. Putnam 64
John T. Reardon 17
Homer Franklin Rebert 24
Mabel Douglas Reid 01
Meyer Reinhold 35
Emeline H. Richardson 52
Lawrence Richardson, jr 50
Dorothy M. Robathan 49
Charles Alexander Robinson, Jr. 26
Robert Samuel Rogers 24
Ruskin R. Rosborough 24
C. Brian Rose 92
Irene Rosenzweig 30
David O. Ross 66
Linda W. Rutland Gillison 81
Inez Scott Ryberg 26
Michele Renee Salzman 87
Frederick LaMotte Santee 27
Susan May Savage 38
Gareth L. Schmeling 78
Dorothy May Schullian 34
Ann R. Scott 67
Russell T. Scott, Jr. 66
Charles P. Segal 63
John Shapley 13
George A. Sheets 85
Rose Mary Sheldon 81
Grant Showerman 1900
George Joseph Siefert 36
Edmund Taite Silk 31
William G. Sinnigen 54
Walter Fifield Snyder 38
Joseph B. Solodow 81
Philip O. Spann 78
Edward Washburn Spofford 64
Joanne Marie Spurza 88
Gregory A. Staley 84
Chester G. Starr, Jr. 40
Lillian Starr 27
Arthur Richard Steinberg 64
Gilbert Hawthorne Taylor 20
Lily Ross Taylor 18
Susan L. TePaske-King 92
Clara Louise Thompson 09

William Richard Tongue 38
Carl R. Trahman 42
William N. Turpin 90
Myra L. Uhlfelder 50
Roger B. Ulrich 82
Albert William Van Buren 06
Esther Boise Van Deman 09
Hanry Bartlett Van Hoesen 08
Ann C. Vasaly 83
John William Vaughn 74
Anthony Pelzer Wagener 11
Margaret C. Waites 13
Rex E. Wallace 85
Joseph J. Walsh 86
Francis Redding Walton 37
Harriett Anne Weis 80
Katherine E. Welch 94
Arthur Harold Weston 12
Cynthia White 89
Helen Russell White 52
Philip Barrows Whitehead 13
Michael Mashe Wigodsky 61
Lois Virginia Williams 48
Charles Witke 62
Philip Francis Wooby 53
Susan E. Wood 78
Horace Wetherill Wright 16
John H. Wright 68
John W. Zarker 60

CONSERVATION
Margaret Holben Ellis 94
Bettina A. Raphael 94

DESIGN ARTS
Stanley Abercrombie 83
William B. Adair 92
Gerald D. Adams 68
Ross S. Anderson 90
J.H. Aronson 74
Morley Baer 80
Gordon C. Baldwin 78
Phillip R. Baldwin 94
Ellen Beasley 89
Anna Campbell Bliss 84
Robert W. Braunschweiger 74
Steven Brooke 91
Adele Chatfield-Taylor 84
Walter F. Chatham 89
Morison S. Cousins 85
Russell R. Culp 80
Robert De Fuccio 76
Andrea O. Dean 80
Joseph P. D'Urso 88
Robert (Raffaello) Regis Dvořák 72
Hsin-Ming Fung 92
Jeanne M. Giordano 87
Peter Hoppner 77
Miller Horns 90

Elizabeth Humstone 86
June M. Jordan 71
Robert E. Kramer 72
George Krause 77
Norman Krumholz 87
Michael Lax 78
Debra A. McCall 89
R. Alan Melting 70
Donald Lee Peting 78
William Lansing Plumb 86
Julie M. Riefler 87
Paul D. Schwartzman 77
Will V. Shaw 68
Alison Sky 78
Paul L. Steinberg 82
Joel Sternfeld 91
Michelle Stone 78
James A. Velleco 77
Emily McNeely Whiteside 82
Randolph A. Williams 82
Tod Culpan Williams 83
Janet Zweig 92
William Reed 67

HISTORY OF ART
James S. Ackerman 52
Nicholas Adams 88
Joseph D. Alchermes 80
Glenn M. Andres 69
Larry M. Ayres 84
Larry F. Ball 89
Susan J. Barnes 82
Elizabeth Bartman 83
Janis C. Bell 90
Miroslava Maria Beneš 84
Robert P. Bergman 80
Jeffrey Blanchard 78
Albert Boime 80
Virginia A. Bonito 80
Patricia Fortini Brown
Caroline A. Bruzelius 86
Virginia L. Bush 77
Carmen Bambach Cappel 94
Eugene A. Carroll 61
Jill E. Caskey 93
Sharon L. Cather 82
Anthony D. Colantuono 85
Maria Ann Conelli 88
Michael Conforti 76
Hereward Lester Cooke 54
Nicola Courtright 83
Brian Curran 94
Eve D'Ambra 86
Horst de la Croix 63
Charles G. Dempsey 65
Gail Feigenbaum 80
Eric Marshall Frank 82
Isabelle S. Frank 87
Jack Freiberg 77

David H. Friedman 89
Catherine E. Fruhan 89
Joachim Ernest Gaehde 57
Diane Y. Ghirado 87
David M. Gillerman 88
Dorothy F. Glass 86
Samuel D. Gruber 87
Benjamin Howard Hibbard 58
William Eatherley Hood, Jr. 74
Susan G. Hunt 84
Alice G. Jarrard 89
Christopher M.S. Johns 84
J. Richard Judson 82
Patrick Joseph Kelleher 49
Barbara A. Kellum 80
Herbert L. Kessler 85
Dale Kinney 72
Susan Elizabeth Klaiber 90
Margaret A. Kuntz 91
Laetitia Amelia La Follette 84
David A. Levine 78
Evonne A. Levy 90
Milton Joseph Lewine 61
Douglas Lewis 66
Richard B.K. McLanathan 49
Sarah C. McPhee 92
Sheila McTighe 90
Michael P. Mezzatesta 79
Margaret Koons Miller 51
William Blackall Miller 51
Henry A. Millon 60
Charles I. Minott 64
Derek A.R. Moore 84
John E. Moore 85
Jeffrey M. Muller 79
Amy L. Neff 76
Charlotte F. Nichols 83
Loren W. Partridge 68
Linda A. Pellecchia 92
Maria A. Phillips 83
John A. Pinto 75
Donald Posner 61
Catherine R. Puglisi 80
Gary M. Radke 84
Louise Rice 86
Eileen L. Roberts 81
Carol A. Rusche 94
Donna Marie Salzer 88
Susan Virginia Saward 71
Melinda Wilcox Schlitt 86
John Beldon Scott 81
Ellen R. Shapiro 78
Innis Howe Shoemaker 73
Richard W. Stapleford 67
Deborah Stott 81
William Tronzo 79
Mary Vaccaro 92
William R. Valerio 91
Patricia A. Waddy 70

Bonna D. Wescoat 92
Robert J. Williams 91
Stephan S. Wolohojian 90
Joanna Woods-Marsden 87

LANDSCAPE ARCHITECTURE
Eric Armstrong 61
Edward Bruce Baetjer 54
Julie Bargmann 90
Richard C. Bell 53
Stephen Frederick Bochkor 57
Robert Thomas Buchanan 59
Richard C. Burck 82
Vincent Charles Cerasi 50
Henri Emile Chabanne 34
Thomas Dolliver Church 60
Linda J. Cook 89
Charles Amos Currier 48
Phoebe Cutler 89
Joanna Dougherty 86
Frederick William Edmondson, Jr. 48
Jon S. Emerson 67
Eric R. Fulford 91
Ralph Esty Griswold 23
Ed C. Haag 79
Robert M. Hanna 76
Stephen C. Haus 79
Dale Harper Hawkins 52
Elizabeth Dean Hermann 87
Gary R. Hilderbrand 94
Alden Hopkins 36
Frank Dexter James 68
Dean A. Johnson 66
John F. Kirkpatrick 39
Robert Sieber Kitchen 38
Albert R. Lamb III 70
Edward Godfrey Lawson 20
James MacKenzie Lister 37
Roger B. Martin 64
Stuart M. Mertz 40
Stacy T. Moriarty 84
Richard Coolidge Murdock 33
Norman T. Newton 26
Laurie D. Olin 74
Don H. Olson 62
Thomas R. Oslund 92
Neil Hamill Park 33
George Erwin Patton 51
Paul R.V. Pawlowski 69
Peter M. Pollack 71
Thomas Drees Price 32
Charles A. Rapp 72
Michael Rapuano 30
Peter G. Rolland 78
Peter Lindsay Schaudt 91
R. Terry Schnadelbach 66
Seth H. Seablom 68
John B. Sullivan 83
Chip Sullivan 85

Charles Reuel Sutton 32
Erik Albin Svenson 58
L. Azeo Torre 76
Marc Treib 85
Morris Early Trotter 35
James R. Turner 76
Dan Tuttle 88
Michael R. Van Valkenburgh 88
E. Michael Vergason 80
Richard K. Webel 29
Brooks E. Wigginton 50
John L. Wong 81
Ervin H. Zube 61

LITERATURE
Robert E. Bagg 58
Thomas Bolt 94
Harold Brodkey 61
Joseph K. Caldwell 80
Mary Caponegro 92
John Ciardi 57
Walter Clemons, Jr. 62
Sigrid de Lima 54
Alan Dugan 63
Ralph Waldo Ellison 57
Daniel M. Epstein 78
Edward Field 82
Robert Francis 58
George P. Garrett 59
Anthony E. Hecht 51
Mark Helprin 83
Oscar Hijuelos 86
Edward Hirsch 88
Edmund L. Keeley 60
Richard L. Kenney 87
Jeanne R. Lowe 70
Mary Morris 80
John F. Peck 79
Padgett Powell 88
Gjertrud C. Schnackenberg 84
Robert G. Shacochis 90
Louis M. Simpson 58
David St. John 85
George E. Starbuck 63
William C. Styron 53
Richard P. Wilbur 55
Miller Williams 77

MUSICAL COMPOSITION
Stephen Joel Albert 67
Kathryn J. Alexander 89
Samuel Barber 37
Leslie (R.) Bassett 63
David Snow Bates 75
Robert H. Beaser 78
Jack Beeson 50
Larry Thomas Bell 83
Chester Biscardi 77

Martin I. Bresnick 76
Todd Brief 82
Elliott Carter 54
Morris M. Cotel 68
Sebastian Currier 94
William Douglas Denny 41
David Diamond 42
Tamar Diesendruck 84
John Eaton 62
Dennis J. Eberhard 79
George H. Edwards 75
Michelle L. Ekizian 89
George Herbert Elwell 27
Jack R. Fortner 68
Lucas Foss 52
Vincent S. Frohne 66
Jay Anthony Gach 83
Vittorio Giannini 36
Alexei Haieff 49
Howard Harold Hanson 24
Higo Hugo Harada 60
Stephen P. Hartke 92
John Heineman 69
James Lawrence Heinke 72
Walter Helfer 28
William D. Hellermann 74
Stanley Walker Hollingsworth 58
Lee J. Hyla 91
Andrew W. Imbrie 49
Kamran Ince 88
Herbert Reynolds Inch 34
Stephen Jaffe 81
Werner Janssen 33
Hunter Johnson 35
Jeffrey Jones 74
Ulysses Kay 52
Kent W. Kennan 39
Aaron Jay Kernis 85
Barbara Anne Kolb 71
Arthur V. Kreiger 80
Arthur Rudolf Kreutz 42
Gail Thompson Kubik 52
Ezra Laderman 64
Bun-Ching Lam 92
David A. Lang 91
Billy Jim Layton 57
Thomas Oboe Lee 87
John Anthony Lennon 81
Marvin David Levy 64
Scott A. Lindroth 86
Normand Lockwood 32
Salvatore Martirano 59
James C. Mobberley 90
Robert W. Moevs 55
Paul Moravec 85
Charles Naginski 40
William Neil 83
Paul Nelson 60
Eugene J. O'Brien 73

Daniel J. Perlongo 72
Gerald H. Plain 76
George Rochberg 51
Steve Rouse 88
Loren Rush 71
Robert Levine Sanders 29
Roger Huntington Sessions 31
Allen R. Shearer 80
Sheila J. Silver 79
William O. Smith 58
Leo Sowerby 24
Rand P. Steiger 86
Alexander Lang Steinert 30
(Curry) Tison Street 74
Randall Thompson 25
Nicholas C.K. Thorne 82
John H. Thow 78
Richard A. Trythall 67
Wintter Watts 25
Henry Weinberg 70
Louis Smith Weingarden 70
Charles Whittenberg 66
Frank Wigglesworth 54
Richard M. Willis 57
George Balch Wilson, Jr. 61
Walter K. Winslow 90
Philip G. Winsor 67
Frederick Woltmann 39
Yehudi Wyner 56

PAINTING
Harry Gregory Ackerman 34
Lennart Anderson 61
John Augustus Annus 60
Donald Aquilino 60
Jack L. Bailey 72
Gilbert Banever 36
Wulf E. Barsch 76
Dunbar Dyson Beck 30
Wayne Edison Begley 61
Ronald C. Binks 60
A. Robert Birmelin 64
Al H. Blaustein 57
Nicholas D. Blosser 85
Matthew William Boyhan 38
Daniel Boza 35
Francis Scott Bradford 27
George William Breck 1899
T.E. Breitenbach 73
Maria Eugenia Burgaleta 75
Caren R. Canier 78
Jo Anne Carson 83
Paul Chalfin 09
Frank Tolles Chamberlin 11
Carlo A. Ciampaglia 23
John Patrick Civitello 70
Dennis E. Congdon 84
Russell Cowles 20
Allyn Cox 20

Thomas H. Dahill, Jr. 57
George Davidson 16
Harry A. Davis 41
Salvatore De Maio 33
Peter B. Devries 67
Simon A. Dinnerstein 78
Joe Draegert 79
Seymour Drumlevitch 52
Charles M. Dwyer 79
Frank Perley Fairbanks 12
Barry Faulkner 10
Alan E. Feltus 72
Augustus Clemens Finley 28
Loren Russell Fisher 42
Alfred Ernst Floegel 25
Stephen S. Geldman 80
Gregory J. Gillespie 67
Leon H. Goldin 58
Robert Berkeley Green 38
Stephen Greene 54
Mark A. Greenwold 88
Alan Gussow 55
Philip Guston 49
Walter Humphrey Hahn 57
James Hanes 53
Bunny Harvey 76
Christian de Suremain Haub 84
John Edward Heliker 49
Jack Henderson 65
James J. Hennessey 64
James Joseph Hoffman 56
Frank B. Holmes 75
Walter K. Hood 55
Robert. T. Hooper 79
Robert J. Jergens 63
Richard A. Johnson 68
Clifford Edgar Jones 39
Zubel Kachadoorian 59
Deane Keller 29
Michael C. Kessler 90
Marjorie E. Kreilick 63
Benedict C. LaRico 85
Salvatore Lascari 22
Joseph L. Lasker 51
John C. Leavey 70
Kenneth Richard Lithgow 71
Bert L. Long, Jr. 91
James Owen Mahoney 35
John L. Massey 61
Eugene E. Matthews 60
Donald Magnus Mattison 31
Robert McCloskey 49
Ann McCoy 90
Melissa Meyer 81
James R. Muehlemann 82
Kathy Muehlemann 88
Michael Joseph Mueller 28
Laura M. Newman 80
John F. Obuck 89

Arthur Osver 54
William Ouellette 65
Charles A. Owens 48
Franc D. Palaia 86
William J. Patterson 67
Bernard Perlin 51
Gabor Peterdi 30
Steve Raffo 55
Roger R. Ricco 65
Norman Joseph Rubington 53
Robert Knight Ryland 06
Karen Saler 68
Raymond Saunders 66
Eugene Francis Savage 15
Edward W. Schmidt 83
Andrew Thomas Schwartz 02
Frank Henry Schwarz 24
Ronald J. Schwerin 64
David S. Shapiro 73
Philip L. Sherrod 86
Rochelle M. Shicoff 81
Donald Carl Shields 80
Judy Silver 78
Shelley A. Simpson 88
Mitchell Siporin 50
John Melza Sitton 32
Michael C. Spafford 69
Frederick Charles Stahr 15
Earl V. Staley 82
Harry I. Stickroth 17
Gilbert Leonard Stone 67
Wendy Sussman 87
Warren Saul Tanner 83
William E. Thon 48
Joan Thorne 87
John H. Wenger 72
Ezra Augustus Winter 14
Henry Lawrence Wolfe 11
Christopher Wool 90
Kenneth R. Worley 70
Christopher John Wray 69
Sharon D. Yates 74
Jack S. Zajac 58

POST-CLASSICAL/HUMANISTIC STUDIES
David Anderson 89
P. Renee Baernstein 91
Martha R. Baldwin 88
Robert Anthony Blazis 65
Denis John Bradley 72
Margaret A. Brucia 92
James Edward Bullard 75
Melissa M. Bullard 84
Anthony L. Cardoza 77
Christopher S. Celenza 94
Thomas Cerbu 83
Paul M. Clogan 67
Thomas V. Cohen 92
Thomas Culley, SJ 67

Frank Anthony D'Accone 64
Pellegrino A. D'Acierno 89
John Francis D'Amico 76
Jeffrey J. Dean 81
Victoria de Grazia 78
Richard A. Etlin 81
Richard J. Ferraro 79
Arthur M. Field 80
Linda Fowler-Magerl 65
Carmela Vircillo Franklin 85
Ann Freeman 58
Paul Francis Gehl 78
Katherine J. Gill 88
Frank D. Gilliard 65
Frederick F. Hammond 66
James Hankins 82
Gary J. Ianziti 87
Daniel Javitch 90
Beverly L. Kahn 85
Julius Kirshner 69
Thomas Forrest Kelly 86
Richard G. Kenworthy 70
Deeana C. Klepper 90
Benjamin Kohl 71
Ingrid Rowland Lacy 82
Robert E. Lerner 84
Daniel R. Lesnick 91
Mark Lilla 87
Janet Blow Long 81
Anne MacNeil 92
David R. Marsh 83
Janet M. Martin 72
Frederick J. McGinness 78
James H.S. McGregor 82
John M. McManamon, SJ 83
Nelson H. Minnich 80
John Monfasani 71
Robert Moynihan 86
Ronald G. Musto 79
Susan V. Nicassio 94
Laurie Nussdorfer 81
John W. O'Malley, SJ 65
Duane J. Osheim 76
John Francis Petruccione 91
Emil J. Polak 63
Kenneth James Pratt 63
Cynthia M. Pyle 78
Charles M. Radding 86
Diana Robin 88
Eyvind C. Ronquist 70
Alice L. Rubinstein 78
Earl George Schreiber 77
Daniel Joseph Sheerin 80
Gerald D. Silk 82
Sarah Spence 82
Carolyn E. Springer 84
Pamela F. Starr 84
Gordon Dawley Tonner 74
Pauline M. Watts 77

Rebecca J. West 79
Jan M. Ziolkowski 81

SCULPTURE
Peter Paul Abate 51
Vito Acconci 87
Edmond Romulus Amateis 24
Robert Amendola 35
John Amore 40
Suzanne H. Bocanegra 91
Brit Bunkley 86
Harry Poole Camden 27
Aldo J. Casanova 61
Gaetano Cecere 23
Lewis C. Cohen 70
Houston Conwill 85
Michael J. Cooper 80
Stephen J. Daly 75
C. (Clarence) Percival Dietsch 09
Robert G. Dodge 76
Linda Dauw Dries 69
Edward Emil Dron 70
Richard H. Ellis 65
Geraldine Erman 91
Lawrence Fane 63
Gilbert A. Franklin 49
Leo Friedlander 16
Evangelos Frudakis 52
Sherry E. Fry 11
(Theodore) Harrison Gibbs 38
Philip Grausman 65
John Clements Gregory 15
John Gulias 49
David Hammons 90
Walker K. Hancock 28
Pritchett Allen Harris 61
Charles Harvey 10
Milton E. Hebald 59
George Herms 83
Michael Scott Hrabak 74
Alexander I. Hunenko 68
Carl Paul Jennewein 20
Thomas Hudson Jones 22
Luise Kaish 72
Herbert L. Kammerer 51
Jerry B. Kearns 70
Charles Keck 04
Pamela Keech 82
Paul Joseph Kirchmer 58
Joseph Kiselewski 29
George Matthew Koren 41
Reuben R. Kramer 36
Paul A. Kubic 79
David Lapalombara 82
Pat Lasch 83
Barry Ledoux 87
Steven Allen Linn 76
Philip Rush Livingston 81
Hermon Atkins MacNeil 1899

Paul Howard Manship 12
Lizabeth Marano 86
John A. Matt 72
Ira Matteson 55
Robert J. McKnight 35
Ana Maria Mendieta 84
Alvin Meyer 26
Warren Towle Mosman 34
Gwynn Murrill 80
Berthold Nebel 17
Carlton Newton 81
Anthony J. Padovano 62
John Nick Pappas 67
Marsha S. Pels 85
Robert Pippenger 42
Albin Polasek 13
Reeva B. Potoff 81
Gordon Powell 88
Pamela "Pike" Powers 88
Gifford MacGregor Proctor 35
Lewis E. Rakosky 79
Joseph Emile Renier 20
John Walter Rhoden 54
Henry Clifford Rollins 66
David Kresz Rubins 31
Glen Sacks 91
Margo L. Sawyer 87
Concetta Scaravaglione 50
Jeffrey A. Schiff 77

William Marks Simpson 33
Susan V. Smyly 67
George Holburn Snowden 30
Dan Snyder 75
Lawrence Tenney Stevens 25
Robert Louis Strini 72
Patrick Strzelec 89
Paul Suttman 68
Carol Szymanski 89
Harry D. Thrasher 14
Thomas John Walsh 74
Sidney Biehler Waugh 32
Albert W. Wein 49
Elbert Weinberg 53
Charles Arthur Wells, Jr. 66
Stephen G. Werlick 64
Robert W. White 55
James N. Wines 56
David Winter 90

VISUAL ARTS
Matthew Geller 92
Andrew H. Ginzel 94
Kristin A. Jones 94
Rita K. McBride 92
Cliffton S. Peacock 94
Rebecca Quaytman 92
Stuart Sherman 92

FELLOWS OF THE AMERICAN ACADEMY
CHRONOLOGICALLY BY DISCIPLINE

ARCHITECTURE
John Russell Pope 1897
Harry Edward Warren 09
Ernest Farnum Lewis 11
Edgar Irving Williams 12
Richard Haviland Smythe 13
George Simpson Koyl 14
Kenneth Earl Carpenter 15
William J.H. Hough 17
Raymond McCormick Kennedy 19
Philip Trammell Shutze 20
James Henry Chillman 22
James Kellum Smith 23
Frederick J. Woodbridge 23
Henri Gabriel Marceau 25
Arthur F. Deam 26
William Douglas 28
George Fraser 28
Stuart Maclaren Shaw 28
Clarence Dale Badgeley 29
Homer Fay Pfeiffer 30
Cecil Clair Briggs 31
Burton Kenneth Johnstone 32
Henry D. Mirick 33
Walter Louis Reichart 33
George Harold Nelson 34
Olindo Grossi 36
Robert A. Weppner, Jr. 36
George Tibbits Licht 37
Richard W. Ayers 38
Richard Gardner Hartshorne 39
Erling F. Iverson 40
Walker Oscar Cain 48
Frederic Shurtleff Coolidge 48
Charles D. Wiley 48
James R. Lamantia, Jr. 49
Dale Claude Byrd 51
Spero Daltas 51
Henri V. Jova 51
David L. Leavitt 51
Joseph Amisano 52
Thomas Laughead Dawson, Jr. 52
Tallie Burton Maule 52
Richard E. Baringer 53
Stanley H. Pansky 53
John H. MacFadyen 54
Robert L. Myers 54
Warren A. Peterson 55
Warren Platner 55
James A. Gresham 56
Robert Venturi 56
Charles G. Brickbauer 57
Dan Robert Stewart 57
David J. Jacob 58
James R. Jarrett 59

Ron Dirsmith 60
Michael Graves 60
John T. Stonehill 60
Theodore J. Musho 61
Royston Tuttle Daley 62
Wayne Taylor 62
Robert Morris Golder 63
Bernard Norman Steinberg 63
Charles Thomas Stifter 63
Astra Zarina 63
Thomas Norman Larson 64
Robert J. Mittelstadt 64
Duane Thorbeck 64
Milo H. Thompson 65
Austris J. Vitols 65
Theodore Liebman 66
Charles O. Perry 66
Thomas V. Czarnowski 67
William Pedersen 67
William Reed 68
Thomas L. Schumacher 69
Peter F. Smith 69
Ronald C. Filson 70
John D. Heimbaugh 70
J. Michael Kirkland 70
Jon Michael Schwarting 70
Daniel V. Scully 70
Gregory S. Baldwin 71
Michael Guran 71
Richard W. Bartholomew 72
Peter Miller Schmitt 72
Robert W. Evans 73
Grover E. Mouton III 73
Brand N. Griffin 74
Marc Ira Balet 75
Peter William Carl 75
Franklin D. Israel 75
Robert S. Livesey 75
Arthur May 75
Marvin Harry Buchanan 76
Robert Earl Jensen 76
Peter Kommers 76
Judith Chafee 77
Wellington Willson Cummer 77
Diane Hermione Lewis 77
Robert Emerson Mangurian 77
Vincent Joseph Mulcahy 77
Judith DiMaio 78
George E. Hartman 78
Caroline B. Constant 79
James L. Lambeth 79
James S. Stokoe 79
James L. Bodnar 80
Andrea Clark Brown 80
Patrick J. Quinn 80

Thomas Gordon Smith 80
William Turnbull, Jr. 80
Amy Christie Anderson 81
Thomas L. Bosworth 81
E. Fay Jones 81
Spence R. Kass 81
Stephen J. Kieran 81
John Q. Lawson 81
William Gene McMinn 81
Werner Seligmann 81
Robert Kahn 82
D.B. Middleton 82
Fred Travisano 82
Craig H. Walton 82
Eugene Kupper 83
Gary H. Larson 83
Celia Margaret Ledbetter 83
John J. McDonald, Jr. 83
Barbara Stauffacher Solomon 83
James Harrison Timberlake 83
Anthony M. Ames 84
H. Turner Brooks 84
Mark M. Foster 84
Alexander C. Gorlin 84
George A. Hinds 84
Wendy Evans Joseph 84
Roger A. Crowley 85
Joseph A. De Pace 85
John R. Naughton 85
Antoine Predock 85
Jesse Reiser 85
Friedrich St. Florian 85
John J. Casbarian 86
James B. Favaro 86
Allan B. Jacobs 86
Wesley C. Jones 86
Roy W. Lewis 86
Danny M. Samuels 86
Frederic D. Schwartz 86
Jorge Silvetti 86
Robert H. Timme 86
Frederick C. Biehle 87
William P. Bruder 87
Kathryn A. Dean 87
Theodore L. Brown 88
George L. Queral 88
Douglas Darden 89
David T. Mayernik 89
Thomas P. Silva 89
Thomas Angotti 90
Grace Ricako Kobayashi 90
William K. Vinyard 90
Robert S. Davis 91
Jason H. Ramos 91
Christian M. Zapatka 91
Edwin (Teddy) Cruz 92
Cameron C. McNall 92
Sanda D. Iliescu 94

CLASSICS/ARCHAEOLOGY

Willian Kendall Denison 1896
Albert F. Earnshaw 1897
Walter Dennison 1897
Gordon Jennings Laing 1897
William Warner Bishop 1898
Howard Crosby Butler 1898
Clarence Linton Meader 1898
George N. Olcott 1899
George Dwight Kellogg 1900
Walter Lowrie 1900
Grant Showerman 1900
Charles Upson Clark 01
Mabel Douglas Reid 01
George Henry Allen 02
Henry Herbert Armstrong 03
Charles Rufus Morey 03
Norman Wentworth De Witt 04
Susan Helen Ballou 06
Herbert Edward Everett 06
Albert William Van Buren 06
Philip J. Gentner 07
Austin Morris Harmon 07
Ralph Van Deman Magoffin 07
Clark D. Lamberton 08
Hanry Bartlett Van Hoesen 08
Dean Putnam Lockwood 09
Thomas Jex Preston, Jr. 09
Clara Louise Thompson 09
Esther Boise Van Deman 09
Guy Blandin Colburn 10
Dora Johnson 11
Elias Avery Lowe 11
Anthony Pelzer Wagener 11
Joseph Granger Brandt 12
George H. Edgell 12
Frank Ray Elder 12
Arthur Harold Weston 12
Richard Offner 13
John Shapley 13
Margaret C. Waites 13
Philip Barrows Whitehead 13
John Raymond Crawford 14
Charles Densmore Curtis 15
Raymond Davis Harriman 16
Eugene Stock McCartney 16
Horace Wetherill Wright 16
John T. Reardon 17
Lily Ross Taylor 18
Gilbert Hawthorne Taylor 20
Ethel Leigh Chubb 21
Emily Wadsworth Cleland 21
Walter Reid Bryan 22
William Stuart Messer 22
Louise Adams Holland 23
Ernestine Franklin Leon 23
Arthur Ernest Gordon 24
Homer Franklin Rebert 24
Robert Samuel Rogers 24

Ruskin R. Rosborough 24
Marion Elizabeth Blake 25
Lillian Beatrice Lawler 26
Charles Alexander Robinson, Jr. 26
Inez Scott Ryberg 26
John Day 27
Frederick LaMotte Santee 27
Lillian Starr 27
Mildred McConnell Gardner 28
Howard Comfort 29
Raymond Theodore Ohl 30
James Henry Oliver 30
Collice Henry Portnoff 30
Irene Rosenzweig 30
Franklin Weeks Jones 31
George Englert McCracken 31
Edmund Taite Silk 31
Henry Ess Askew 32
Elizabeth Cornelia Evans 32
Charlotte Elizabeth Goodfellow 32
Adele Jeanne Kibre 32
Frank Edward Brown 33
Alfred Gelstharp 33
Agnes Kirsopp Lake Michels 33
Chester Carr Greene 34
Bernard Mann Peebles 34
Dorothy May Schullian 34
Aline Abaecherli Boyce 35
George Kenneth Boyce 35
Richmond Lattimore 35
Meyer Reinhold 35
Naphtali Lewis 36
George Joseph Siefert 36
Lucy Shoe Meritt 37
Francis Redding Walton 37
Claude W. Barlow 38
Susan May Savage 38
Walter Fifield Snyder 38
William Richard Tongue 38
William T. Avery 39
Lester Clarence Houck 39
Erling C. Olsen 39
Frances G. Blank 40
Chester G. Starr, Jr. 40
Miriam F. Drabkin 40
Donald Frederick Brown 41
Herbert S. Long 41
Carl R. Trahman 42
Berthe M. Marti 45
John S. Creaghan, SJ 48
Lois Virginia Williams 48
Bertram Berman 49
Dorris Taylor Bishop 49
Smith Palmer Bovie 49
Robert E. Hecht, Jr. 49
Dorothy M. Robathan 49
Lucy Shoe Meritt 50
Lawrence Richardson, jr 50
Myra L. Uhlfelder 50

Freeman William Adams 51
Otto J. Brendel 51
William T. McKibben 51
Joseph Fontenrose 52
Paul Pascal 52
Emeline H. Richardson 52
Helen Russell White 52
Donald Freeman Brown 53
Wendell V. Clausen 53
Kenneth Sawyer Falk 53
Robert F. Goheen 53
Martha W. Hoffman 53
Elaine Pembroke Loeffler 53
Philip Francis Wooby 53
Mary Taylor Babcock 54
Martha Leeb Hadzi 54
Charles Theophilus Murphy 54
William G. Sinnigen 54
William S. Anderson 55
Charles L. Babcock 55
Katherine A. Geffcken 55
John Arthur Hanson 55
James I. Armstrong 56
Richard Eugene Grimm 56
Brooks Emmons Levy 56
William L. MacDonald 56
William Ayres Arrowsmith 57
Eric C. Baade 57
Norman Neuerburg 57
Herbert Hoffmann 58
Anne Pippin Burnett 59
Harold C. Gotoff 59
Michael Hamilton Jameson 59
John O. Lenaghan 59
Lydia Lenaghan 59
Chester F. Natunewicz 59
Mario A. Del Chiaro 60
Bettie Lucille Forte 60
R. Ross Holloway 60
John W. Zarker 60
Dericksen M. Brinkerhoff 61
Alfred Knox Frazer 61
Anne Laidlaw 61
Michael Mashe Wigodsky 61
Richard Brilliant 62
Charles Witke 62
James Joseph Mark Curry 63
James E. Packer 63
Charles P. Segal 63
Saul Michael Cheilik 64
Richard I. Frank 64
Maria T. Marabini Moevs 64
Michael C.J. Putnam 64
Edward Washburn Spofford 64
Arthur Richard Steinberg 64
Susan B. Downey 65
Ursula M. Heibges 66
Anna Marguerite McCann 66
David O. Ross 66

Russell T. Scott, Jr. 66
Hubert Lee Allen III 67
Thalia Alexandra Pandiri 67
Ann R. Scott 67
Virginia Brown 68
Bruce W. Frier 68
John H. Wright 68
Jacquelyn C. Clinton 69
Mary-Kay Gamel Orlandi 69
George W. Houston 69
Floyd Leonard Moreland 69
Malcolm Bell III 70
Joseph Coleman Carter 71
Jesse Rufus Fears 71
Dawson Kiang 71
Margaret Houston DuBois 72
Richard J. Hoffman 72
Harry B. Evans 73
Gretchen Kromer 73
David Gerlad Orr 73
David Frederick Grose 74
John William Vaughn 74
James L. Franklin, Jr. 75
Steven E. Ostrow 75
Bernard D. Frischer 76
Catherine Spotswood Gibbes 76
Judith R. Ginsburg 76
David Martin Halperin 77
John Fawcett Kenfield III 77
Anne E. Haeckl 78
Gareth L. Schmeling 78
Philip O. Spann 78
Susan E. Wood 78
James C. Anderson, jr 79
Glenn F. Chesnut 79
E. Christian Kopff 79
Paul Frederic Burke, Jr. 80
Christopher Frederick Moss 80
Harriett Anne Weis 80
Michael R. Maas 81
Susan D. Martin 81
Linda W. Rutland Gillison 81
Rose Mary Sheldon 81
Joseph B. Solodow 81
Bettina A. Bergmann 82
Jane W. Crawford 82
Roger B. Ulrich 82
John P. Bodel 83
Eric R. Hostetter 83
Glenn W. Most 83
Ann C. Vasaly 83
Ingrid E.M. Edlund-Berry 84
Thomas D. Groves 84
Gregory A. Staley 84
Thomas A.J. McGinn 85
J. Theodore Peña 85
George A. Sheets 85
Rex E. Wallace 85
Marleen Boudreau Flory 86

Helen Nagy 86
Carole Paul 86
Joseph J. Walsh 86
Kathryn L. Gleason 87
Laurence H. Kant 87
Michele Renee Salzman 87
Albert J. Ammerman 88
T. Corey Brennan 88
William Levitan 88
Martha A. Malamud 88
Margaret M. Miles 88
Christopher C. Parslow 88
Joanne Marie Spurza 88
James A. Higginbotham 89
Cynthia White 89
Barbara A. Barletta 90
Andrew M. Feldherr 90
Sheree A. Jaros 90
Anna M. Moore 90
William N. Turpin 90
Rebecca Miller Ammerman 91
Diane Atnally Conlin 91
Kate Cooper 91
Gregory Vincent Leftwich 91
J. Clayton Fant 92
C. Brian Rose 92
Susan L. Te-Paske-King 92
Guy M. Hedreen 94
Katherine E. Welch 94
Gregory S. Bucher 95

CONSERVATION
Margaret Holben Ellis 94
Bettina A. Raphael 94

DESIGN ARTS
William Reed 67
Gerald D. Adams 68
Will V. Shaw 68
R. Alan Melting 70
June M. Jordan 71
Robert (Raffaello) Regis Dvořák 72
Robert E. Kramer 72
J.H. Aronson 74
Robert W. Braunschweiger 74
Robert De Fuccio 76
Peter Hoppner 77
George Krause 77
Paul D. Schwartzman 77
James A. Velleco 77
Gordon C. Baldwin 78
Michael Lax 78
Donald Lee Peting 78
Alison Sky 78
Michelle Stone 78
Morley Baer 80
Russell R. Culp 80
Andrea O. Dean 80
Paul L. Steinberg 82

Emily McNeely Whiteside 82
Randolph A. Williams 82
Stanley Abercrombie 83
Tod Culpan Williams 83
Anna Campbell Bliss 84
Adele Chatfield-Taylor 84
Morison S. Cousins 85
Elizabeth Humstone 86
William Lansing Plumb 86
Jeanne M. Giordano 87
Norman Krumholz 87
Julie M. Riefler 87
Joseph P. D'Urso 88
Ellen Beasley 89
Walter F. Chatham 89
Debra A. McCall 89
Ross S. Anderson 90
Miller Horns 90
Steven Brooke 91
Joel Sternfeld 91
William B. Adair 92
Hsin-Ming Fung 92
Janet Zweig 92
Phillip R. Baldwin 94

HISTORY OF ART
Patrick Joseph Kelleher 49
Richard B.K. McLanathan 49
Margaret Koons Miller 51
William Blackall Miller 51
James S. Ackerman 52
Hereward Lester Cooke 54
Joachim Ernest Gaehde 57
Benjamin Howard Hibbard 58
Henry A. Millon 60
Eugene A. Carroll 61
Milton Joeseph Lewine 61
Donald Posner 61
Horst de la Croix 63
Charles I. Minott 64
Charles G. Dempsey 65
Douglas Lewis 66
Richard W. Stapleford 67
Loren W. Partridge 68
Glenn M. Andres 69
Patricia A. Waddy 70
Susan Virginia Saward 71
Dale Kinney 72
Innis Howe Shoemaker 73
William Eatherley Hood, Jr. 74
John A. Pinto 75
Michael Conforti 76
Amy L. Neff 76
Virginia L. Bush 77
Jack Freiberg 77
Jeffrey Blanchard 78
David A. Levine 78
Ellen R. Shapiro 78
Michael P. Mezzatesta 79

Jeffrey M. Muller 79
William Tronzo 79
Joseph D. Alchermes 80
Robert P. Bergman 80
Albert Boime 80
Virginia A. Bonito 80
Gail Feigenbaum 80
Barbara A. Kellum 80
Catherine R. Puglisi 80
Eileen L. Roberts 81
John Beldon Scott 81
Deborah Stott 81
Susan J. Barnes 82
Sharon L. Cather 82
Eric Marshall Frank 82
J. Richard Judson 82
Elizabeth Bartman 83
Nicola Courtright 83
Charlotte F. Nichols 83
Maria A. Phillips 83
Larry M. Ayres 84
Miroslava Maria Beneš 84
Susan G. Hunt 84
Christopher M.S. Johns 84
Laetitia Amelia La Follette 84
Derek A.R. Moore 84
Gary M. Radke 84
Anthony D. Colantuono 85
Herbert L. Kessler 85
John E. Moore 85
Caroline A. Bruzelius 86
Eve D'Ambra 86
Dorothy F. Glass 86
Louise Rice 86
Melinda Wilcox Schlitt 86
Isabelle S. Frank 87
Diane Y. Ghirado 87
Samuel D. Gruber 87
Joanna Woods-Marsden 87
Nicholas Adams 88
Maria Ann Conelli 88
David M. Gillerman 88
Donna Marie Salzer 88
Larry F. Ball 89
David H. Friedman 89
Catherine E. Fruhan 89
Alice G. Jarrard 89
Janis C. Bell 90
Patricia Fortini Brown 90
Susan Elizabeth Klaiber 90
Evonne A. Levy 90
Sheila McTighe 90
Stephan S. Wolohojian 90
Margaret A. Kuntz 91
William R. Valerio 91
Robert J. Williams 91
Sarah C. McPhee 92
Linda A. Pellecchia 92
Mary Vaccaro 92

Bonna D. Wescoat 92
Jill E. Caskey 93
Carmen Bambach Cappel 94
Brian Curran 94
Carol A. Rusche 94

LANDSCAPE ARCHITECTURE
Edward Godfrey Lawson 20
Ralph Esty Griswold 23
Norman T. Newton 26
Richard K. Webel 29
Michael Rapuano 30
Thomas Drees Price 32
Charles Reuel Sutton 32
Richard Coolidge Murdock 33
Neil Hamill Park 33
Henri Emile Chabanne 34
Morris Early Trotter 35
Alden Hopkins 36
James MacKenzie Lister 37
Robert Sieber Kitchen 38
John F. Kirkpatrick 39
Stuart M. Mertz 40
Charles Amos Currier 48
Frederick William Edmondson, Jr. 48
Vincent Charles Cerasi 50
Brooks E. Wigginton 50
George Erwin Patton 51
Dale Harper Hawkins 52
Richard C. Bell 53
Edward Bruce Baetjer 54
Stephen Frederick Bochkor 57
Erik Albin Svenson 58
Robert Thomas Buchanan 59
Thomas Dolliver Church 60
Eric Armstrong 61
Ervin H. Zube 61
Don H. Olson 62
Roger B. Martin 64
Dean A. Johnson 66
R. Terry Schnadelbach 66
Jon S. Emerson 67
Frank Dexter James 68
Seth H. Seablom 68
Paul R.V. Pawlowski 69
Albert R. Lamb III 70
Peter M. Pollack 71
Charles A. Rapp 72
Laurie D. Olin 74
Robert M. Hanna 76
L. Azeo Torre 76
James R. Turner 76
Peter G. Rolland 78
Ed C. Haag 79
Stephen C. Haus 79
E. Michael Vergason 80
John L. Wong 81
Richard C. Burck 82
John B. Sullivan 83

Stacy T. Moriarty 84
Chip Sullivan 85
Marc Treib 85
Joanna Dougherty 86
Elizabeth Dean Hermann 87
Dan Tuttle 88
Michael R. Van Valkenburgh 88
Linda J. Cook 89
Phoebe Cutler 89
Julie Bargmann 90
Eric R. Fulford 91
Peter Lindsay Schaudt 91
Thomas R. Oslund 92
Gary R. Hilderbrand 94

LITERATURE
Anthony E. Hecht 51
William C. Styron 53
Sigrid de Lima 54
Richard P. Wilbur 55
John Ciardi 57
Ralph Waldo Ellison 57
Robert E. Bagg 58
Robert Francis 58
Louis M. Simpson 58
George P. Garrett 59
Edmund L. Keeley 60
Harold Brodkey 61
Walter Clemons, Jr. 62
Alan Dugan 63
George E. Starbuck 63
Jeanne R. Lowe 70
Miller Williams 77
Daniel M. Epstein 78
John F. Peck 79
Joseph K. Caldwell 80
Mary Morris 80
Edward Field 82
Mark Helprin 83
Gjertrud C. Schnackenberg 84
David St. John 85
Oscar Hijuelos 86
Richard L. Kenney 87
Edward Hirsch 88
Padgett Powell 88
Robert G. Shacochis 90
Mary Caponegro 92
Thomas Bolt 94

MUSICAL COMPOSITION
Howard Harold Hanson 24
Leo Sowerby 24
Randall Thompson 25
Wintter Watts 25
George Herbert Elwell 27
Walter Helfer 28
Robert Levine Sanders 29
Alexander Lang Steinert 30
Roger Huntington Sessions 31

Normand Lockwood 32
Werner Janssen 33
Herbert Reynolds Inch 34
Hunter Johnson 35
Vittorio Giannini 36
Samuel Barber 37
Kent W. Kennan 39
Frederick Woltmann 39
Charles Naginski 40
William Douglas Denny 41
David Diamond 42
Arthur Rudolf Kreutz 42
Alexei Haieff 49
Andrew W. Imbrie 49
Jack Beeson 50
George Rochberg 51
Lucas Foss 52
Ulysses Kay 52
Gail Thompson Kubik 52
Elliott Carter 54
Frank Wigglesworth 54
Robert W. Moevs 55
Yehudi Wyner 56
Billy Jim Layton 57
Richard M. Willis 57
Stanley Walker Hollingsworth 58
William O. Smith 58
Salvatore Martirano 59
Higo Hugo Harada 60
Paul Nelson 60
George Balch Wilson, Jr. 61
John Eaton 62
Leslie (R.) Bassett 63
Ezra Laderman 64
Marvin David Levy 64
Vincent S. Frohne 66
Charles Whittenberg 66
Stephen Joel Albert 67
Richard A. Trythall 67
Philip G. Winsor 67
Morris M. Cotel 68
Jack R. Fortner 68
John Heineman 69
Henry Weinberg 70
Louis Smith Weingarden 70
Barbara Anne Kolb 71
Loren Rush 71
James Lawrence Heinke 72
Daniel J. Perlongo 72
Eugene J. O'Brien 73
William D. Hellermann 74
Jeffrey Jones 74
(Curry) Tison Street 74
David Snow Bates 75
George H. Edwards 75
Martin I. Bresnick 76
Gerald H. Plain 76
Chester Biscardi 77
Robert H. Beaser 78

John H. Thow 78
Dennis J. Eberhard 79
Sheila J. Silver 79
Arthur V. Kreiger 80
Allen R. Shearer 80
Stephen Jaffe 81
John Anthony Lennon 81
Todd Brief 82
Nicholas C.K. Thorne 82
Larry Thomas Bell 83
Jay Anthony Gach 83
William Neil 83
Tamar Diesendruck 84
Aaron Jay Kernis 85
Paul Moravec 85
Scott A. Lindroth 86
Rand P. Steiger 86
Thomas Oboe Lee 87
Kamran Ince 88
Steve Rouse 88
Kathryn J. Alexander 89
Michelle L. Ekizian 89
James C. Mobberley 90
Walter K. Winslow 90
Lee J. Hyla 91
David A. Lang 91
Stephen P. Hartke 92
Bun-Ching Lam 92
Sebastian Currier 94

PAINTING
George William Breck 1899
Andrew Thomas Schwartz 02
Robert Knight Ryland 06
Paul Chalfin 09
Barry Faulkner 10
Frank Tolles Chamberlin 11
Henry Lawrence Wolfe 11
Frank Perley Fairbanks 12
Ezra Augustus Winter 14
Eugene Francis Savage 15
Frederick Charles Stahr 15
George Davidson 16
Harry I. Stickroth 17
Russell Cowles 20
Allyn Cox 20
Salvatore Lascari 22
Carlo A. Ciampaglia 23
Frank Henry Schwarz 24
Alfred Ernst Floegel 25
Francis Scott Bradford 27
Augustus Clemens Finley 28
Michael Joseph Mueller 28
Deane Keller 29
Dunbar Dyson Beck 30
Gabor Peterdi 30
Donald Magnus Mattison 31
John Melza Sitton 32
Salvatore De Maio 33

Harry Gregory Ackerman 34
Daniel Boza 35
James Owen Mahoney 35
Gilbert Banever 36
Matthew William Boyhan 38
Robert Berkeley Green 38
Clifford Edgar Jones 39
Harry A. Davis 41
Loren Russell Fisher 42
Charles A. Owens 48
William E. Thon 48
Philip Guston 49
John Edward Heliker 49
Robert McCloskey 49
Mitchell Siporin 50
Joseph L. Lasker 51
Bernard Perlin 51
Seymour Drumlevitch 52
James Hanes 53
Norman Joseph Rubington 53
Stephen Greene 54
Arthur Osver 54
Alan Gussow 55
Walter K. Hood 55
Steve Raffo 55
James Joseph Hoffman 56
Al H. Blaustein 57
Thomas H. Dahill, Jr. 57
Walter Humphrey Hahn 57
Leon H. Goldin 58
Jack S. Zajac 58
Zubel Kachadoorian 59
John Augustus Annus 60
Donald Aquilino 60
Ronald C. Binks 60
Eugene E. Matthews 60
Lennart Anderson 61
Wayne Edison Begley 61
John L. Massey 61
Robert J. Jergens 63
Marjorie E. Kreilick 63
A. Robert Birmelin 64
James J. Hennessey 64
Ronald J. Schwerin 64
Jack Henderson 65
William Ouellette 65
Roger R. Ricco 65
Raymond Saunders 66
Peter B. Devries 67
Gregory J. Gillespie 67
William J. Patterson 67
Gilbert Leonard Stone 67
Richard A. Johnson 68
Karen Saler 68
Michael C. Spafford 69
Christopher John Wray 69
John Patrick Civitello 70
John C. Leavey 70
Kenneth R. Worley 70

Kenneth Richard Lithgow 71
Jack L. Bailey 72
Alan E. Feltus 72
John H. Wenger 72
T. E. Breitenbach 73
David S. Shapiro 73
Sharon D. Yates 74
Maria Eugenia Burgaleta 75
Frank B. Holmes 75
Wulf E. Barsch 76
Bunny Harvey 76
Caren R. Canier 78
Simon A. Dinnerstein 78
Judy Silver 78
Joe Draegert 79
Charles M. Dwyer 79
Robert. T. Hooper 79
Stephen S. Geldman 80
Laura M. Newman 80
Donald Carl Shields 80
Melissa Meyer 81
Rochelle M. Shicoff 81
James R. Muehlemann 82
Earl V. Staley 82
Jo Anne Carson 83
Edward W. Schmidt 83
Warren Saul Tanner 83
Dennis E. Congdon 84
Christian de Suremain Haub 84
Nicholas D. Blosser 85
Benedict C. LaRico 85
Franc D. Palaia 86
Philip L. Sherrod 86
Wendy Sussman 87
Joan Thorne 87
Mark A. Greenwold 88
Kathy Muehlemann 88
Shelley A. Simpson 88
John F. Obuck 89
Michael C. Kessler 90
Ann McCoy 90
Christopher Wool 90
Bert L. Long, Jr. 91

POST-CLASSICAL/HUMANISTIC STUDIES
Ann Freeman 58
Emil J. Polak 63
Kenneth James Pratt 63
Frank Anthony D'Accone 64
Robert Anthony Blazis 65
Linda Fowler-Magerl 65
Frank D. Gilliard 65
John W. O'Malley, SJ 65
Frederick F. Hammond 66
Paul M. Clogan 67
Thomas Culley, SJ 67
Julius Kirshner 69
Richard G. Kenworthy 70
Eyvind C. Ronquist 70

Benjamin Kohl 71
John Monfasani 71
Denis John Bradley 72
Janet M. Martin 72
Gordon Dawley Tonner 74
James Edward Bullard 75
John Francis D'Amico 76
Duane J. Osheim 76
Anthony L. Cardoza 77
Earl George Schreiber 77
Pauline M. Watts 77
Victoria de Grazia 78
Paul Francis Gehl 78
Frederick J. McGinness 78
Cynthia M. Pyle 78
Alice L. Rubinstein 78
Richard J. Ferraro 79
Ronald G. Musto 79
Rebecca J. West 79
Arthur M. Field 80
Nelson H. Minnich 80
Daniel Joseph Sheerin 80
Jeffrey J. Dean 81
Richard A. Etlin 81
Janet Blow Long 81
Laurie Nussdorfer 81
Jan M. Ziolkowski 81
James Hankins 82
James H.S. McGregor 82
Ingrid Rowland Lacy 82
Gerald D. Silk 82
Sarah Spence 82
Thomas Cerbu 83
David R. Marsh 83
John M. McManamon, SJ 83
Melissa M. Bullard 84
Robert E. Lerner 84
Carolyn E. Springer 84
Pamela F. Starr 84
Carmela Vircillo Franklin 85
Beverly L. Kahn 85
Thomas Forrest Kelly 86
Robert Moynihan 86
Charles M. Radding 86
Gary J. Ianziti 87
Mark Lilla 87
Martha R. Baldwin 88
Katherine J. Gill 88
Diana Robin 88
David Anderson 89
Pellegrino A. D'Acierno 89
Daniel Javitch 90
Deeana C. Klepper 90
P. Renee Baernstein 91
Daniel R. Lesnick 91
John Francis Petruccione 91
Margaret A. Brucia 92
Thomas V. Cohen 92
Anne MacNeil 92

Christopher S. Celenza 94
Susan V. Nicassio 94

SCULPTURE
Hermon Atkins MacNeil 1899
Charles Keck 04
C. (Clarence) Percival Dietsch 09
Charles Harvey 10
Sherry E. Fry 11
Paul Howard Manship 12
Albin Polasek 13
Harry D. Thrasher 14
John Clements Gregory 15
Leo Friedlander 16
Berthold Nebel 17
Carl Paul Jennewein 20
Joseph Emile Renier 20
Thomas Hudson Jones 22
Gaetano Cecere 23
Edmond Romulus Amateis 24
Lawrence Tenney Stevens 25
Alvin Meyer 26
Harry Poole Camden 27
Walker K. Hancock 28
Joseph Kiselewski 29
George Holburn Snowden 30
David Kresz Rubins 31
Sidney Biehler Waugh 32
William Marks Simpson 33
Warren Towle Mosman 34
Robert Amendola 35
Robert J. McKnight 35
Gifford MacGregor Proctor 35
Reuben R. Kramer 36
(Theodore) Harrison Gibbs 38
John Amore 40
George Matthew Koren 41
Robert Pippenger 42
Gilbert A. Franklin 49
John Gulias 49
Albert W. Wein 49
Concetta Scaravaglione 50
Peter Paul Abate 51
Herbert L. Kammerer 51
Evangelos Frudakis 52
Elbert Weinberg 53
John Walter Rhoden 54
Ira Matteson 55
Robert W. White 55
James N. Wines 56
Paul Joseph Kirchmer 58
Milton E. Hebald 59
Aldo J. Casanova 61
Pritchett Allen Harris 61
Anthony J. Padovano 62
Lawrence Fane 63
Stephen G. Werlick 64
Richard H. Ellis 65
Philip Grausman 65

Henry Clifford Rollins 66
Charles Arthur Wells, Jr. 66
John Nick Pappas 67
Susan V. Smyly 67
Alexander I. Hunenko 68
Paul Suttman 68
Linda Dauw Dries 69
Lewis C. Cohen 70
Edward Emil Dron 70
Jerry B. Kearns 70
Luise Kaish 72
John A. Matt 72
Robert Louis Strini 72
Michael Scott Hrabak 74
Thomas John Walsh 74
Stephen J. Daly 75
Dan Snyder 75
Robert G. Dodge 76
Steven Allen Linn 76
Jeffrey A. Schiff 77
Paul A. Kubic 79
Lewis E. Rakosky 79
Michael J. Cooper 80
Gwynn Murrill 80
Philip Rush Livingston 81
Carlton Newton 81
Reeva B. Potoff 81
Pamela Keech 82
David Lapalombara 82

George Herms 83
Pat Lasch 83
Ana Maria Mendieta 84
Houston Conwill 85
Marsha S. Pels 85
Brit Bunkley 86
Lizabeth Marano 86
Vito Acconci 87
Barry Ledoux 87
Margo L. Sawyer 87
Gordon Powell 88
Pamela "Pike" Powers 88
Patrick Strzelec 89
Carol Szymanski 89
David Hammons 90
David Winter 90
Suzanne H. Bocanegra 91
Geraldine Erman 91
Glen Sacks 91

VISUAL ARTS
Matthew Geller 92
Rita K. McBride 92
Rebecca Quaytman 92
Stuart Sherman 92
Andrew H. Ginzel 94
Kristin A. Jones 94
Cliffton S. Peacock 94

RESIDENTS OF THE AMERICAN ACADEMY
BY DISCIPLINE

ARCHITECTURE
Max Abramovitz 61
Nelson W. Aldrich 69
Jacob Berend Bakema 69
Edward Larrabee Barnes 67, 78
Edward Charles Bassett 70
Herbert Bayer 78
Pietro Belluschi 54
Richard Bender 80
Gunnar Birkerts 76
Jean Paul Carlhian 75
Henry N. Cobb 92
Alan H. Colquhoun 85
Francis F.A. Comstock 58, 60
Romaldo Giurgola 78
Michael Graves 79
George Howe 47-50
James M. Hunter 63
David J. Jacob 70
John M. Johansen 75
Louis I. Kahn 51
Gerhard M. Kallmann 84
Leon Krier 86
Jean Labatut 53, 59, 65, 68
Frank Roy Larson 62
Donlyn Lyndon 78, 87
Noel Michael McKinnell 89
Louis A. McMillen 69
Richard Meier 73
Mary M. Miss 89
Charles W. Moore 75, 81
Nathaniel Alexander Owings 59
William Leonard Pereira 71
Elizabeth M. Plater-Zyberk 88
Colin Rowe 70
Thomas L. Schumacher 92
James Frazer Stirling 83
Edward Durell Stone 60
Paul Thiry 69
Stanley Tigerman 80
Aldo Van Eyck 66
Robert Venturi 66
Thomas R. Vreeland 74
Harry M. Weese 73
Frederick J. Woodbridge 52

CLASSICS/ARCHAEOLOGY
William S. Anderson 72
Charles L. Babcock 86
Helen H. Bacon 69
Malcolm Bell III 89
Herbert Bloch 87
Robert Brentano 79
Thomas Robert Shannon Broughton 60, 61
Frank Edward Brown 54, 55

Edward Champlin 94
John Francis D'Amico 88
John H. D'Arms 72, 84
Jean M. Davison 82
Robert H. Drews 81
Harry B. Evans 91
Karl Galinsky 73
Arthur Ernest Gordon 49
Erich S. Gruen 90
Mason Hammond 52, 63
John Arthur Hanson 71
William V. Harris 79, 83
Louise Adams Holland 60
R. Ross Holloway 70, 92
Roger A. Hornsby 83
Harry Hubbell 51
Michael Hamilton Jameson 89
Georg N. Knauer 85
Gerhard M. Koeppel 75
Anne Laidlaw 76
Eleanor Winsor Leach 83
Milton E. Lord 72
Paul L. MacKendrick 58
Ramsay MacMullen 80
Berthe M. Marti 51
Clarence Whittlesley Mendell 50
Helen F. North 80
Robert E.A. Palmer 79
John C. Pedley 90
Kyle M. Phillips, Jr. 77
Michael C.J. Putnam 70
Philip Rhinelander 64
Emeline H. Richardson 79
Lawrence Richardson, jr 79
Henry Thompson Rowell 67
Russell T. Scott, Jr. 80
Charles P. Segal 86
H. Alan Shapiro 79, 87, 92
Edmund Taite Silk 56
Erik Sjöqvist 63
Noel M. Swerdlow 91
Richard J. A. Talbert 91
William Richard Tongue 48
Paul Zanker 89

DESIGN ARTS
Donald Appleyard 75
Stephen M. Carr 75
George Krause 80
Donald Mitchell Oenslager 54

HISTORY OF ART
James S. Ackerman 75
Rudolf Arnheim 78
Henry C. Boren 68

Kathleen W.-G. Brandt 76, 82
Caroline A. Bruzelius 89
Anthony M. Clark 77
Joseph J. Connors 87
Anthony Cutler 92
Bernice F. Davidson 83
Diane M. DeGrazia 91
Philipp Fehl 67
Alfred Knox Frazer 87
Margaret Frazer 87
Siegfried Giedion 66
Anne C. Hanson 74
Francis Haskell 90
Bartlett H. Hayes 65
Phillip Hofer 57
Woldemar Horst Janson 60
Clarence Kennedy 61
Ruth Wedgewood Kennedy 61
Ernst Kitzinger 89
Richard Krautheimer 56
Irving Lavin 72, 79
Marilyn Aronberg Lavin 79
Rensselaer W. Lee 55
Milton Joeseph Lewine 73
Henry P. McIlhenny 47, 48
Henry A. Millon 66
Charles Mitchell 66
Alfred Moir 70, 80
Agnes Mongan 50, 51
Loren W. Partridge 85
Donald Posner 69
Olga Raggio 84
Peter H. Selz 72
Craig Hugh Smyth 59
Richard E. Spear 88
Leo Steinberg 76
Cecil L. Striker 71
Mark S. Weil 85
Edgar Wind 50
Rudolf Wittkower 62
Hellmut Wohl 84
David H. Wright 91

LANDSCAPE ARCHITECTURE
Richard C. Bell 75
Stuart O. Dawson 76
M. Paul Friedberg 84
J.B. Jackson 83
Daniel U. Kiley 76
Norman T. Newton 67
Martha Schwartz 92
Peter Walker 92
Richard K. Webel 63

LITERATURE
Elizabeth D. Bowen 60
Joseph A. Brodsky 81
Van Wyck Brooks 56

John D. Casey 91
Clark Coolidge 85
Malcolm Cowley 58
Nadine Gordimer 84
Francine du Plessix Gray 80
Anthony E. Hecht 69
John Hersey 70
Matthew Josephson 60
Alfred Kazin 75
Galway Kinnell 87
Archibald MacLeish 57
Frank MacShane 82
Mary McCarthy 79
Wallace E. Stegner 60
Mark Strand 83
Allen J. Tate 54
Robert Penn Warren 57

MUSICAL COMPOSITION
Claus Adam 76
John C. Adams 88
William H. Albright 79
Samuel Barber 47
Jack Beeson 66
Earle Brown 87
Elliott Carter 68
Aaron Copland 51
David Del Tredici 85
David Diamond 72
Jacob Druckman 82
John Eaton 75
Donald J. Erb 92
Ross Lee Finney 60
Lucas Foss 78
Alexei Haieff 53, 58
John H. Harbison 81
Andrew W. Imbrie 68
Leon Kirchner 74
Barbara Anne Kolb 76
Ezra Laderman 83
John La Montaine 62
Fred Lerdahl 87
Robert Hall Lewis 81
Otto Luening 58
Bohuslav (Jan) Martinů 57
Robert W. Moevs 61
Douglas Stuart Moore 47
Nicolas (Nikolai) Nabokov 54, 68
Goffredo Petrassi 56
Harold S. Shapero 71
Leo Smit 73
William O. Smith 80
Harvey D. Sollberger 89
Randall Thompson 52
Francis Thorne 94
Richard A. Trythall 70
Hugo David Weisgall 67
Frank Wigglesworth 70

Charles Wuorinen 90
Yehudi Wyner 91
Ellen Taaffe Zwilich 90

PAINTING
Mark Adams 63
William Bailey 76
Eugene Berman 59
George Biddle 52
Peter Blume 57
Louis Bouche 61
James D. Brooks 63
Gardner Cox 61
Susan Crile 90
Seymour Drumlevitch 66
Andrew Forge 85
Nancy Graves 79
Cleve Gray 80
Alan Gussow 87
Philip Guston 71
Robert G. Hamilton 74
Al Held 81
Bill Jensen 89
Alex Katz 84
Gyorgy Kepes 75
Rico Lebrun 60
Julian Levi 68
Roy F. Lichtenstein 89
Leo Manso 80
Conrad Marca-Relli 76
John L. Massey 79
Elizabeth Murray 91
Arthur Osver 58
Philip Pearlstein 82
Gabor Peterdi 77
Henry Varnum Poor III 50, 51
Gregorio Prestopino 72
Jesse Reichek 72

Dorothea Rockburne 91
Mitchell Siporin 67
Frank Stella 83
William E. Thon 56, 65
Jack Tworkov 73
Jack S. Zajac 68

POST-CLASSICAL/HUMANISTIC STUDIES
Diane Owen Hughes 92
John W. O'Malley, SJ 83
Eugene F. Rice, Jr. 75
Charles Trinkaus 77

SCULPTURE
Varujan Y. Boghosian 67, 75
Aldo J. Casanova 75
Gilbert A. Franklin 66
Frank Gillette 85
Dimitri Hadzi 74
Walker K. Hancock 57, 63
Adlai S. Hardin 62
Robert Laurent 55
Ezio Martinelli 65
Bruce Nauman 87
Constantino Nivola 72, 77
Beverly Pepper 86
Charles O. Perry 71
Judy Pfaff 88
Sidney Simon 70
Charles F. Simonds 86
Sylvia Stone 81
Harold Tovish 66
Robert W. White 69

VISUAL ARTS
Mel Bochner 92

RESIDENTS OF THE AMERICAN ACADEMY
CHRONOLOGICALLY BY DISCIPLINE

ARCHITECTURE
George Howe 47-50
Louis I. Kahn 51
Frederick J. Woodbridge 52
Jean Labatut 53
Pietro Belluschi 54
Francis F.A. Comstock 58
Jean Labatut 59
Nathaniel Alexander Owings 59
Francis F.A. Comstock 60
Edward Durell Stone 60
Max Abramovitz 61
Frank Roy Larson 62
James M. Hunter 63
Jean Labatut 65
Aldo Van Eyck 66
Robert Venturi 66
Edward Larrabee Barnes 67
Jean Labatut 68
Nelson W. Aldrich 69
Jacob Berend Bakema 69
Louis A. McMillen 69
Paul Thiry 69
Edward Charles Bassett 70
David J. Jacob 70
Colin Rowe 70
William Leonard Pereira 71
Richard Meier 73
Harry M. Weese 73
Thomas R. Vreeland 74
Jean Paul Carlhian 75
John M. Johansen 75
Charles W. Moore 75
Gunnar Birkerts 76
Edward Larrabee Barnes 78
Herbert Bayer 78
Romaldo Giurgola 78
Donlyn Lyndon 87
Michael Graves 79
Richard Bender 80
Stanley Tigerman 80
Charles W. Moore 81
James Frazer Stirling 83
Gerhard M. Kallmann 84
Alan H. Colquhoun 85
Leon Krier 86
Donlyn Lyndon 87
Elizabeth M. Plater-Zyberk 88
Noel Michael McKinnell 89
Mary M. Miss 89
Henry N. Cobb 92
Thomas L. Schumacher 92

CLASSICS/ARCHAEOLOGY
William Richard Tongue 48

Arthur Ernest Gordon 49
Clarence Whittlesley Mendell 50
Harry Hubbell 51
Berthe M. Marti 51
Mason Hammond 52
Frank Edward Brown 54
Frank Edward Brown 55
Edmund Taite Silk 56
Paul L. MacKendrick 58
Thomas Robert Shannon Broughton 60
Louise Adams Holland 60
Thomas Robert Shannon Broughton 61
Mason Hammond 63
Erik Sjöqvist 63
Philip Rhinelander 64
Henry Thompson Rowell 67
Helen H. Bacon 69
R. Ross Holloway 70
Michael C.J. Putnam 70
John Arthur Hanson 71
William S. Anderson 72
John H. D'Arms 72
Milton E. Lord 72
Karl Galinsky 73
Gerhard M. Koeppel 75
Anne Laidlaw 76
Kyle M. Phillips, Jr. 77
Robert Brentano 79
William V. Harris 79
Robert E.A. Palmer 79
Emeline H. Richardson 79
Lawrence Richardson, jr 79
H. Alan Shapiro 79
Ramsay MacMullen 80
Helen F. North 80
Russell T. Scott, Jr. 80
Robert H. Drews 81
Jean M. Davison 82
William V. Harris 83
Roger A. Hornsby 83
Eleanor Winsor Leach 83
John H. D'Arms 84
Georg N. Knauer 85
Charles L. Babcock 86
Charles P. Segal 86
Herbert Bloch 87
Alfred Knox Frazer 87
H. Alan Shapiro 87
John Francis D'Amico 88
Malcolm Bell III 89
Michael Hamilton Jameson 89
Paul Zanker 89
Erich S. Gruen 90
John C. Pedley 90
Harry B. Evans 91

Richard J.A. Talbert 91
Noel M. Swerdlow 91
R. Ross Holloway 92
H. Alan Shapiro 92
Edward Champlin 94

DESIGN ARTS
Donald Mitchell Oenslager 54
Donald Appleyard 75
Stephen M. Carr 75
George Krause 80

HISTORY OF ART
Henry P. McIlhenny 47
Henry P. McIlhenny 48
Agnes Mongan 50
Edgar Wind 50
Agnes Mongan 51
Rensselaer W. Lee 55
Richard Krautheimer 56
Phillip Hofer 57
Craig Hugh Smyth 59
Woldemar Horst Janson 60
Clarence Kennedy 61
Ruth Wedgewood Kennedy 61
Rudolf Wittkower 62
Bartlett H. Hayes 65
Siegfried Giedion 66
Henry A. Millon 66
Charles Mitchell 66
Philipp Fehl 67
Henry C. Boren 68
Donald Posner 69
Alfred Moir 70
Cecil L. Striker 71
Irving Lavin 72
Peter H. Selz 72
Milton Joeseph Lewine 73
Anne C. Hanson 74
James S. Ackerman 75
Kathleen W.-G. Brandt 76
Leo Steinberg 76
Anthony M. Clark 77
Rudolf Arnheim 78
Irving Lavin 79
Marilyn Aronberg Lavin 79
Alfred Moir 80
Kathleen W.-G. Brandt 82
Bernice F. Davidson 83
Olga Raggio 84
Hellmut Wohl 84
Loren W. Partridge 85
Mark S. Weil 85
Joseph J. Connors 87
Alfred Knox Frazer 87
Margaret Frazer 87
Richard E. Spear 88
Caroline A. Bruzelius 89
Ernst Kitzinger 89

Francis Haskell 90
Diane M. DeGrazia 91
David H. Wright 91
Anthony Cutler 92

LANDSCAPE ARCHITECTURE
Richard K. Webel 63
Norman T. Newton 67
Richard C. Bell 75
Stuart O. Dawson 76
Daniel U. Kiley 76
J.B. Jackson 83
M. Paul Friedberg 84
Martha Schwartz 92
Peter Walker 92

LITERATURE
Allen J. Tate 54
Van Wyck Brooks 56
Archibald MacLeish 57
Robert Penn Warren 57
Malcolm Cowley 58
Elizabeth D. Bowen 60
Matthew Josephson 60
Wallace E. Stegner 60
Anthony E. Hecht 69
John Hersey 70
Alfred Kazin 75
Mary McCarthy 79
Francine du Plessix Gray 80
Joseph A. Brodsky 81
Frank MacShane 82
Mark Strand 83
Nadine Gordimer 84
Clark Coolidge 85
Galway Kinnell 87
John D. Casey 91

MUSICAL COMPOSITION
Samuel Barber 47
Douglas Stuart Moore 47
Aaron Copland 51
Randall Thompson 52
Alexei Haieff 53
Nicolas (Nikolai) Nabokov 54
Goffredo Petrassi 56
Bohuslav (Jan) Martinů 57
Alexei Haieff 58
Otto Luening 58
Ross Lee Finney 60
Robert W. Moevs 61
John La Montaine 62
Jack Beeson 66
Hugo David Weisgall 67
Elliott Carter 68
Andrew W. Imbrie 68
Nicolas (Nikolai) Nabokov 68
Richard A. Trythall 70
Frank Wigglesworth 70

Harold S. Shapero 71
David Diamond 72
Leo Smit 73
Leon Kirchner 74
John Eaton 75
Claus Adam 76
Barbara Anne Kolb 76
Lucas Foss 78
William H. Albright 79
William O. Smith 80
John H. Harbison 81
Robert Hall Lewis 81
Jacob Druckman 82
Ezra Laderman 83
David Del Tredici 85
Earle Brown 87
Fred Lerdahl 87
John C. Adams 88
Harvey D. Sollberger 89
Charles Wuorinen 90
Ellen Taaffe Zwilich 90
Yehudi Wyner 91
Donald J. Erb 92
Francis Thorne 94

PAINTING
Henry Varnum Poor III 50-51
George Biddle 52
William E. Thon 56
Peter Blume 57
Arthur Osver 58
Eugene Berman 59
Rico Lebrun 60
Louis Bouche 61
Gardner Cox 61
Mark Adams 63
James D. Brooks 63
William E. Thon 65
Seymour Drumlevitch 66
Mitchell Siporin 67
Julian Levi 68
Jack S. Zajac 68
Philip Guston 71
Gregorio Prestopino 72
Jesse Reichek 72
Jack Tworkov 73
Robert G. Hamilton 74
Gyorgy Kepes 75
William Bailey 76
Conrad Marca-Relli 76

Gabor Peterdi 77
Nancy Graves 79
John L. Massey 79
Cleve Gray 80
Leo Manso 80
Al Held 81
Philip Pearlstein 82
Frank Stella 83
Alex Katz 84
Andrew Forge 85
Alan Gussow 87
Bill Jensen 89
Roy F. Lichtenstein 89
Susan Crile 90
Elizabeth Murray 91
Dorothea Rockburne 91

POST-CLASSICAL/HUMANISTIC STUDIES
Eugene F. Rice, Jr. 75
Charles Trinkaus 77
John W. O'Malley, SJ 83
Diane Owen Hughes 92

SCULPTURE
Robert Laurent 55
Walker K. Hancock 57
Adlai S. Hardin 62
Walker K. Hancock 63
Ezio Martinelli 65
Gilbert A. Franklin 66
Harold Tovish 66
Varujan Y. Boghosian 67
Robert W. White 69
Sidney Simon 70
Charles O. Perry 71
Constantino Nivola 72
Dimitri Hadzi 74
Aldo J. Casanova 75
Varujan Y. Boghosian 75
Constantino Nivola 77
Sylvia Stone 81
Frank Gillette 85
Beverly Pepper 86
Charles F. Simonds 86
Bruce Nauman 87
Judy Pfaff 88

VISUAL ARTS
Mel Bochner 92

AMERICAN ACADEMY IN ROME
WORLD WAR II SCHOLARSHIPS AND PRIZES

From 1941 until 1945 the Trustees awarded a number of scholarships for graduate study in classics and cash prizes to be used for artistic work or travel in other parts of the world.

1941
Robert A. Brooks
Walker O. Cain
Nicholas Carone
Donald L. Grieb
Herbert S. Long
Harold S. Shapero
William Talbot
Carl R. Trahman
Albert R. Tryon

1942
Warren D. Anderson
Elmore Cave
David Diamond
Albert Gould
Eleanor Harz
Andrew E. Kuby, Jr.
Elsie Lewis
Dorothy B. Muskat
Helen F. North
Laura B. Voelkel

1943
Betty Nye Hedberg
Mary-Barbara Kauffman
Ann Ruth King
Jeanette Ruth Mueller

Ellen McQuilkin Oldham
Hazel Palmer
Jethro Robinson
Laura B. Voelkel

1944
Elizabeth Hussel
Juanita Elizabeth Lacey

1945
Joseph M. Duffy, Jr.
Beatrice Gottleib
Pauline M. Morris
Robert R. Raymo
Myra Uhlfelder

From 1945 until 1947, when the Academy re-opened, a number of former G.I.s were given room and board at the Academy to enable them to remain in Italy and study.

Edwin Edwinn
Frank Gavin
John Myhers
Salvatore Scarpitta
Michael Tor
Paul Valentino

AFFILIATED FELLOWSHIPS

Affiliated fellowship holders have been an integral part of the Academy community since the founding of the Academy in 1894. Affiliated fellowship holders are the recipients of fellowships awarded by institutions such as colleges and universities, governments agencies, and arts and humanities organizations. They range in length from six weeks to a year or more.

APPLETON SCHOLARSHIP
HARVARD UNIVERSITY
(ARCHITECTURE)

Harry E. Warren 1911-12, 1913
Ralph W. Varney 1911-12, 1913
Morris Feather 1913
Morton M. Mann 1913
L.M. Hendrick, Jr. 1919-20
P.C. Knowlton 1917, 1919-20
W.G. O'Toole 1920-21, 1921-22
W.S. Vaughn 1923-24, 1924-25
O.J. Teegen 1925-26

OSCAR BRONEER FELLOWSHIP
(CLASSICS)

Funded by the Luther I. Replogle Foundation, the Oscar Broneer Fellowship is awarded in the field of Classical Studies to Fellows of the American Academy in Rome
or the American School of Classical Studies at Athens. The Broneer Fellowship recipient spends one year at the Academy and one year at the American School of Classical Studies at Athens.

Thomas D. Groves 1983-84
Rex Wallace 1984-85

Aileen Ajootian 1987-88
James Higginbotham 1988-89
Kenneth Shapiro Lapatin 1989-90
Barbette Spaeth 1990-91
Katherine E. Welch 1992-93
Ellen Perry 1993-94
Gregory S. Bucher 1994-95

BURNHAM PRIZE OF THE CHICAGO ARCHITECTURAL CLUB (ARCHITECTURE)

Pierre Blouke 1919-20
Ferdinand Eiseman 1924-25, 1925-26
Joseph F. Balis 1939-40
Tannys Langdon 1984-85
Thomas N. Rajkovich 1985-86
Leslie Ventsch 1986-87
Gilbert Gorski 1987-88
Alan Armbrust 1988-89
Jerry Johnson 1989-90
Melany Telleen 1990-91
Edward Webb 1991-92
Joseph Barden 1992-93

CRESSON SCHOLARSHIP ACADEMY OF FINE ARTS, PHILADELPHIA (ARCHITECTURE)

Thomas H. Ellett 1911-12, 1913
Phineas Paist 1911-12, 1913
W.H. Fenton 1911-12, 1913
Robert R. McGoodwin 1913
C.O. Jenny 1917, 1919-20
B. Gordon 1919-20
Alvin Meyer 1920-21, 1921-22

THE JOHN DINKELOO TRAVELING FELLOWSHIP OF THE NATIONAL INSTITUTE FOR ARCHITECTURAL EDUCATION

(Prior to 1956 the Institute was known as the Beaux Arts Society.)

Harry Sternfeld 1916, 1919-20
H.K. Bieg 1926-27
Steven Forman 1978
Julia Morgan Smyth 1979
Elizabeth Diller 1980-81
Elizabeth Masters 1981-82
Brian Healy 1982-83
Thomas K. Davis 1983-84
Mark J. O'Bryan 1984-85
John Philip Trautmann 1985-86
Tom Buresh 1986-87
Mark Motl 1986-87
Charles Wolf 1986-87

Alicia Imperiale 1987-88
Madeline Schwartzman 1987-88
John Coyne 1988-89
Margaret Griffin 1988-89
Heather Young 1988-89
Geoffrey Campbell Warner 1989-90
Roberto De Alba 1989-90
Paul Harney 1989-90
Caleb Crawford 1990-91
Johannes Marinus Knoops 1990-91
Laurie Perriello-Sharon 1990-91
Marius Mihail Calin 1991-92
Mark H. Cottle 1991-92
Janet Lynn Simon 1991-92
Joel A. Shifflet 1993-94

ITALIAN FULBRIGHT FELLOWS

Ferdinando Castagnoli 1951-52
Maria Teresa Marabini Moevs 1951-52
Maria Santangelo 1951-52
Emilio Gabba 1954-1955
Giancarlo Susini 1954-55
Giuseppe Vecchi 1954-55
Girolamo Arnaldi 1955-56
Augusto Campana 1955-56
Giovanni D'Anna 1955-56
Lelia Ruggini Cracco 1956-57
Lucia Rosa Gualdo 1956-57
Werner Johannowsky 1956-57
Piera Bocci Pacini 1956-57
Silvana Casartelli Novelli 1957-58
Silvio Panciera 1958-59
Paolo Siniscalco 1957-58
Claudio Leonardi 1958-59
Mara Bonfioli Panciera 1958-59
Giovanni Scichilone 1958-59
Rino Avesani 1959-60
Giovanni Forni 1959-60
Giovanna Vallauri Galluppi 1959-60
Lidio Gasperini 1959-60
Guido Barbieri 1960-61
Lucia Angela Ciapponi 1960-61
Mara Francesca Montana Sicari 1960-61
Franca Perusino 1961-62
Francesca Paola Palange Porten 1961-62
Sandro Stucchi 1961-62
Giovanni Colonna 1962-63
Antonino Di Vita 1962-63
Leandro Polverini 1962-63
Maria Pia Billanovich 1963-64
Giorgio Flaccavento 1963-64
Maurizio Calvesi 1964-65
Carla Sisto Canali 1964-65
Andrea Carandini 1964-65
Carla Fayer 1965-66
Gloria Ferrari Pinney 1965-66
Lorenzo Quilici 1965-66
Giovanni Uggeri 1965-66

Matilde Mazzolani 1966-67
Giosue Musca 1966-67
Franca Badoni Parise 1966-67
Fulvio Cairoli Giuliani 1967-68
Luigi Salerno 1967-68
Salvatore Settis 1967-68
Vincenzo Bilardello 1968-69
Giovanni Maria de Rossi 1968-69
Gabrielle De Vita De Angelis 1968-69
Dario Durbé 1968-69
Gabriella Capecchi 1972-73
Marcello Guaitoli 1972-73
Angelo Bartolo Russi 1973-74
Antonella Romualdi 1974-75
Ida Caruso 1975-76
Paolo Fancelli 1976-77
Stefania Jorio 1976-77
Lucrezia Campus 1977-78
Lucia Criscuolo 1978-79
Alessandra Baldini 1979-80
Maria Letizia Gualandi 1979-80
Marina Moretti 1980-81
Simonetta Segenni 1981-82
Giusto Traina 1983-84
Giuseppina Di Mores Manca 1984-85
Amalia Faustoferri 1985-86
Donatella De Grassi 1986-87
Elena Calandra 1989-90
Maria Losito 1990-91
Elisabetta Poddighe 1990-91
Giuseppe Dardanello 1991-92
Annapaola Mosca 1991-92

McKIM SCHOLARSHIP
COLUMBIA UNIVERSITY
(ARCHITECTURE)

Seth Justin Temple 1911-12, 1913
William K. Fellows 1911-12, 1913
Harry Allen Jacobs 1911-12, 1913
W.O. Raymond 1911-12, 1913
F. Livingston Pell 1911-12, 1913
Lucian Smith 1911-12, 1913
W. Lawrence Bottomley 1911-12, 1913
Joseph H. Clark 1911-12
Charles T.E. Dieterlen 1913
Wm. C. Francis 1913
Joe H. Mc Donnell 1918-19
S. Oxhandler 1920-21, 1921-22
R.M. Krob 1926-27

COLUMBIA SCHOLARSHIP

Wm. C. Francis 1911
Joseph H. Clark 1913
E. Gugler 1913
E.J. Robin 1915
F.J. Woodbridge 1923-24

MELLON EAST-CENTRAL EUROPEAN
VISITING SCHOLARS AWARD

Funded by the Andrew W. Mellon Foundation , this program was established in 1994 to serve Czech, Hungarian, Polish, and Slovak scholars who have already obtained the PhD or equivalent experience and wish to undertake a specific research project in Rome for three months.

Jan Bazant (Czech Rep.) 1994
Zygmunt M. Szweykowski (Poland) 1994
Adam S. Ziolkowski (Poland) 1994

OBERLIN FELLOWSHIP
(CLASSICS)

Dorothy V. Quayle 1928-29

PLYM FELLOWSHIP
UNIVERSITY OF ILLINOIS
(ARCHITECTURE)

C.B. McGrew 1921-22, 1922-23
E.L. Hubbell 1923-24
J.D. Tuttle 1924-25, 1925-26

PHILADELPHIA REGIONAL
VISITING ARTISTS PROGRAM AWARD

A two-year program supported by the Pew Charitable Trusts, open to Philadelphia-based artists, designers and composers. The artists are sent to Rome for two-month periods.

Donald Camp 1994
James Primosch 1994
Wesley Wei 1994

PULITZER FELLOWSHIP
NATIONAL ACADEMY OF DESIGN
(VISUAL ARTS)

Philip Bower 1924-25
Renwick Taylor 1925-26

ROTCH SCHOLARSHIP
(ARCHITECTURE)

Harold Van Buren Magonigle, 1894
Will S. Aldrich, 1895
Louis H. Boynton, 1896
Henry B. Pennell, 1897
Harry Pulsifer, 1899
Frederic Charles Hirons 1904
Chas Leroy Pearl Burnham 1906

Israel Pierre Lord 1908
Joseph McGinniss 1910
Niels Hjalmar Larsen 1911
Chas Cameron Clark 1912
William Leo Smith 1913
Ralph Johnson Batchelder 1914
Frederick Roy Witton 1915
Ralph Thomas Walker 1916
James Newhall Holden 1917
Robert Murray Blackall 1920
Wallace Kirkman Harrison 1922
Isidor Richmond 1923
Eugene Francis Kennedy, Jr. 1924
Walter F. Bogner 1925

SHELDON FELLOWSHIP
HARVARD UNIVERSITY
(COMPARATIVE LITERATURE)

A. Philip MacMahon 1915-16, 1916-17
Lester Marsh Prindle 1918-19
C.L. Sherman 1919
A.H. Alexander 1919-20
M.R. Rogers 1919-20
H.J. Leon 1919-20, 1921-22
John Bridge 1921-22, 1922-23
F.M. Carey 1923-24
Eliot Bailen 1926-27
T.D. Church 1926-27
Henry Hoover 1926-27

STEEDMAN FELLOW
WASHINGTON UNIVERSITY
(ARCHITECTURE)

The Steedman Fellowship in architecture was awarded through a competition sponsored by Washington University in St. Louis, Missouri. Prior to 1989 the Steedman Fellows were considered Fellows of the Academy.

Michael Stanton 1990

STEWARDSON MEMORIAL SCHOLARSHIP
UNIVERSITY OF PENNSYLVANIA
(ARCHITECTURE)

Percy Ash 1911-12, 1913
Arthur H. Brockie 1911-12, 1913
Herman C. Buhring 1911-12, 1913
H. Louis Duhring 1911-12, 1913
A.M. Githens 1911-12, 1913
Wm. C. Hays 1911-12, 1913
Ira W. Hoover 1911-12, 1913
W.W. Sharpley 1911-12, 1913
C.G. Spoerl 1911-12, 1913
Morris Whiteside 1911-12, 1913
Harvey Schwab 1913
Carl Howells 1913
H.L. Rubin 1919-20
R.S. Simpson 1920-21, 1921-22
O.M. Olsen 1923-24
J.F. Booton 1924-25, 1925-26
J.L. Evans 1925-26
Warren Hoak 1926-27

WHITNEY FELLOWSHIP
RADCLIFFE COLLEGE
(CLASSICS)

Eva M. Sanford 1923-24

WINCHESTER FELLOWSHIP
YALE UNIVERSITY
(PAINTING)

D.W. Orr 1919-20
Lorenzo Hamilton 1920-21, 1921-22
T.L. Johnson 1923-24
E.A. Tollefson 1924-25
P.M. Duncan 1925-26
Richard Everett, Jr. 1926-27

NOTABLE VISITORS TO THE
AMERICAN ACADEMY IN ROME

*Indicates that the specific year (or years) of visit(s) is not clear from annual reports.

1913
Lewis Einstein
Edith Wharton
George Bispham Page
Raymond Hood
William Bottomley
Percy Ash

1920-1921
Thornton Wilder

1922-1923
Wallace K. Harrison

1927-1928
Helen M. Woodruff

1932-1934
Mary A. Sollmann

1939-1940
Bernard Berenson
Axel Boethius
William C. Bullitt
David Gray
Ezra Pound

1943-1951*
Sir Leigh Ashton
Balthus
Alfred H. Barr, Jr.
Leonard Bernstein
John Cage
David E. Finley
Paul Hindemith
G.E. Kidder-Smith
Ralph Kirkpatrick
Oscar Kokoschka
Serge Koussevitzky
Paul L. MacKendrick
Marino Marini
GianCarlo Menotti
Yehudi Menuhin
Isamu Noguchi
Gisela M.A. Richter
Mark Rothko
Paul Rudolph
Stephen Spender
Oliver Strunk
Ralph E. Walker
Lawrence Grant White

1951-1955*
Alfred H. Barr, Jr.
Carl W. Blegen
William Burden
Hortense Calisher
Rene d'Harnancourt
Arthur Fizdale
Robert Gold
Lillian Hellman
William H. Jordy
Kevin Lynch
Allen Mandelbaum
Peppino Mangravite
John O. Merrill
Henry Moore
Perry Rathbone
Sir Herbert Read
Theodore Roethke
Eero Saarinen
Vincent Scully
Virgil Thomson

1955-1959*
Jonathan Barnett
Glen W. Bowersock
Serge Chermayeff
Henry Steele Commager
Milton Lewine
Martin Ostwald

1959-1964*
Winthrop Aldrich
John Mason Brown
Herbert Brownell
Prescott S. Bush
Cass Canfield
John Cheever
Robert Coates
Frederick Eaton
Eldon Elder
Osborn Elliott
Everett P. Fahy, Jr.
Richard Gardner
Arthur Goldberg
A. Whitney Griswold
Peggy Guggenheim
Guy Fraser Harrison
Henry Russell Hitchcock
Edward G. Janeway
Walter Kerr
Seymour Knox

Walter Lippmann
Leo Macaulay
John J. McCloy
Elizabeth Blair MacDougall
Paul Mellon
Sibyl Moholy-Nagy
Robert Moses
Edward R. Murrow
Mrs. Charles S. Payson
Francis T. P. Plimpton
Vincent Price
Joseph Verner Reed
Richard Rodgers
William Shirer
Adlai E. Stevenson
Louise J. Talma
Christopher Tunnard
Alan Valentine
Lucia Valentine

1964-1968*
J. Russell Lynes, Jr.
Lewis Mumford
James D. Prendergast

1964-1965
Daniel P. Moynihan

1965-1966
Robert Katz

1967-1968
Henry Smith-Miller
Paul Thek

1968-1973*
J. Russell Lynes, Jr.

1968-1969
Bernice Davidson

1969-1970
Buckminster Fuller
Henry Allen Moe
Richard Tucker

1970-1971
Margaret Alexander
Herbert J. Gans
Robbins Landon

1971-1972
Harold Clurman
Luigi Dallapiccola

1973-1974
Elisabeth Will
Lorin Hollander

1974-1975
Cleo Rickman Fitch*
Spiro Kostof

1975-1976
Peter Eisenman
James Marston Fitch
Michael Mewshaw

1976-1977
Giulio Carlo Argan
Anthony Clark
Charles Eames
George Izenour
Thomas Sokolowski
John H. Stubbs

1977-1978
Ed Bace
Marvin Eisenberg
Italo Faldi
Kenneth Koch
Georgina Masson
Joan Adams Mondale
Alberto Moravia
Franklin Murphy
Egidio Ortona
Paolo Portoghesi
Massimo Pradella
Piero Sartogo
Martin Scorsese
Gore Vidal*
Roman Vlad

1980-1981
Michelangelo Antonioni
John Brademas
Giorgio Bassani
Joseph A. Califano, Jr.
Elizabeth Gebhard
Milton Gendel
Adriano La Regina
Denis Mack Smith
Franco Muzzi
Ruggero Orlando
George Sadek
Cy Twombly
Bruno Zevi
David Whitehouse

1981-1982
Alberto Arbasino
Denise Scott Brown
Anthony Burgess
Italo Calvino
Norma Goldman
Shirley Hazzard
Paul Oskar Kristeller

Pr.ssa Elvina Pallavicini
Marilyn Perry
Maxwell Rabb
Rosamond Bernier Russell
Susan Sontag
Francis Steegmuller
Claire Stirling
Gay Talese
Frederick Vreeland

1982-1983
Giorgio Ciucci
Annie Dillard
Neil Levine
Frank MacShane
Roberto Olivetti
John Sawyer

1983-1984
Susanna Agnelli*
Enzo Crea
Enrico D'Assia
Leon Edel
Millicent Fenwick

1984-1985
Carl Andre
William Bernoudy
Mario Buotta
Pr. Giovanni del Drago*
Lawrence Ferlinghetti
Ida Panicelli
Joel Shapiro
Alan Shestak
Gioacchino Lanza Tomasi
Charles K. Williams II

1985-1986
Pietro Dorazio
Kenneth Frampton
Sol LeWitt
Curtis Bill Pepper
William Weaver

1986-1987
Daniel Boorstin
Phyllis Lambert
Eugenio LaRocca*
Jackie Winsor

1987-1988
Charles Michener
Diana Michener
Russell Oberlin

1988-1989
Donald Barthelme
James Billington
Joel Conarroe
Robert Hughes
Jannis Kounellis
Harrison Salisbury

1989-1990
William Bowen
Malcolm Campbell
Matilda Cuomo
Robert Gutman
Walter Kaiser
Jose Serebrier
George Steiner
Manfredo Tafuri
Marco Tirelli

1990-1991
Cecilia Bartoli
Anthony Grafton
Joseph Kosuth
Stephen Lash
Ting Pei
George Ranalli
Carole Rifkind
Marchese & Marchesa Sanfelice di Monteforte
Peter F. Secchia
John Wilton-Ely

1991-1992
Lidia Bastianich
Ezra Stoller
Richard Weinstein
Timothy Wirth

1992-1993
Robert Campbell
Lisa Fentress
Hugh Hardy
Henry Hopkins
Richard Mason
Michelangelo Pistoletto
Jules D. Prown
James Reston
Richard Sennett
Benno Schmidt, Jr.
Pier Luigi Tazzi
Frederick R. Weisman

1994
Reginald Bartholomew
Hillary Rodham Clinton
Henry Kissinger
Francesco Rutelli
Oscar Luigi Scalfero

CONTRIBUTING INSTITUTIONS
OF THE AMERICAN ACADEMY IN ROME
1894-1994

Founding Members are in bold.

Agnes Scott College
American Numismatic Society
Amherst College
Austin College
Barnard College
Boston University
Brandeis University
Brooklyn College
Brown University
Bryn Mawr College
Bucknell University
Carleton College
Case Western Reserve University
Catholic University of America
City College, CUNY
City University of New York
Colby College
Colgate University
College of New Rochelle
College of the Holy Cross
College of William and Mary
College of Wooster
Columbia University
Connecticut College
Cornell University
Council of American Overseas Research Centers
Dartmouth College
Dickinson College
Duke University
Emory University
Florida State University
Fordham University
Georgetown University
Hamilton College
Hartwick College
Harvard University
Haverford College
Herbert H. Lehman College
Hollins College
Howard University
Hunter College
Indiana University
Institute for Advanced Study
Institute of Mediterranean Studies
Johns Hopkins University
Kent State University
Louisiana State University
Loyola Marymount University
Loyola University
Macalaster College
Manhattan College

Manhattanville College of the Sacred Heart
Massachusetts Institute of Technology
Metropolitan Museum of Art
Michigan State University
Mt. Holyoke College
New York University, Institute of Fine Arts
North Texas State University
Northwestern University
Oberlin College
Ohio State University
Pennsylvania State University
Pontifical Institute of Mediaeval Studies
Princeton University
Queens College, CUNY
Rice University
Rosary College
Rutgers University
Saint Bonaventure University
San Francisco State University
Smith College
Smithsonian Institution
Leland Stanford Jr. University
State University of New York, Buffalo
Swarthmore College
Sweet Briar College
Syracuse University
Temple University
Texas A&M University
Trinity College
Tufts University
Tulane University
Union College
University of Akron
University of Alabama
University of Arkansas
University of California
University of California, Berkeley
University of California, Los Angeles
University of California, Santa Barbara
University of Chicago
University of Cincinnati
University of Colorado
University of Connecticut
University of Delaware
University of Florida
University of Georgia
University of Houston
University of Illinois
University of Iowa
University of Kansas
University of Kentucky

University of Maine
University of Maryland
University of Maryland, Baltimore County
University of Massachusetts
University of Michigan
University of Minnesota
University of Mississippi
University of Missouri
University of Nebraska
University of North Carolina
University of Notre Dame
University of Oklahoma
University of Oregon
University of Pennsylvania
University of Pittsburgh
University of Puget Sound
University of Rochester
University of Saint Thomas
University of South Carolina

University of South Florida
University of Southern California
University of Tennessee
University of Texas, Arlington
University of Texas, Austin
University of the South
University of Utah
University of Vermont
University of Virginia
University of Washington
University of Wisconsin, Madison
Vanderbilt University
Vassar College
Washington University
Wellesley College
Wesleyan University
Western Reserve University
Wheaton College
Williams College
Yale University

CLASSICAL SOCIETY OF THE AMERICAN ACADEMY IN ROME
OFFICERS

The Classical Society of the American Academy in Rome, open to all friends and alumni of the Academy, has traditionally provided the means by which members of the Summer School and Visiting Scholars have coordinated their efforts to support the Academy. It has been especially generous in supporting the Library and funding scholarships for the Summer School, and it plays an essential role in maintaining contacts with the regional classical societies.

PRESIDENTS
Elizabeth Haight 1939
B.L. Ullman 1940
E.H. Brewster 1941
Mary Braginton 1942
Fred M. Carey 1943
W.C. Greene 1944
Louis Lord 1945
Karl Harrington 1946
Walter Agard 1947
Henry T. Rowell 1949
E.C. Evans 1950
Arthur Gordon 1951
Lucy Shoe Meritt 1952
Philip Harsh 1953
Paul MacKendrick 1954
Joseph Fontenrose 1955
Revilo P. Oliver 1956
Charles L. Babcock 1957
Edmund Taite Silk 1958
W.T. McKibben 1959
Harry J. Leon 1960
Helen North 1961
S. Palmer Bovie 1962
William S. Anderson 1963
J. Arthur Hanson 1964
Herbert W. Benario 1965

Arthur M. Young 1966
Marian A. Schmit 1967
Richard E. Grimm/Ernestine Leon 1968
Janice M. Benario 1969
Katherine A. Geffcken 1970
Stephen Dyson 1971, 1972
Hubert Allen 1973, 1974
Anna Marguerite McCann 1975, 1976
Miranda Marvin 1977, 1978
Malcolm Bell 1979, 1980
John Van Sickle 1981, 1982
Larissa Bonfante 1983, 1984
Jacquelyn Collins Clinton 1985, 1986
Nancy T. deGrummond 1987, 1988
Elaine Gazda 1989
Gerhard Koeppel 1991
Norma Goldman 1992, 1993, 1994

CURRENT OFFICERS:
Harry Rutledge, Pres.
Kim Hartswick, VP
Ray Den Adel, Sec.
Susan Martin, Treas.
Ingrid Edlund-Berry, Former Treas.
C. Brian Rose, Newsletter Ed.
Elaine Gazda, Exec. Com.
Gerhard Koeppel , Exec. Com.

Kevin Roche
Anne Rorimer
Angelica Rudenstine
Gareth Schmeling*
J. Michael Schwarting*
George Segal
J. Kellum Smith, Jr.

Frank Stella
Josephine R. Stubbs
Robert Venturi
John Walker, III
James M. Walton
William Weed
George Weissman

AMERICAN ACADEMY IN ROME
FORMER TRUSTEES

Frank Frost Abbott
Edward Dean Adams
Frederick B. Adams, Jr.
Herbert Adams
Chester H. Aldrich
John W. Alexander
Hoyt Ammidon
Allison V. Armour
Geo. Allison Armour
Louis D. Ayres
Walter C. Baker
Sherman Baldwin
Charles T. Barney
Philip Bastedo
Dwight S. Beebe
Edwin H. Blashfield
Peter Blume
William Boring
Louis Bouché
Francis S. Bradford
Lindsay Bradford
Walter S. Brewster
Frank E. Brown
Charles E. Burchfield
Nicholas Murray Butler
John L. Cadwalader
Walker O. Cain
Vincent A. Carrozza
Newcomb Carlton
John M. Carrère
Vincent C. Cerasi
Francis Ward Chandler
Donald Chapin
Gilmore D. Clarke
Charles A. Coolidge
Harvey W. Corbett
Dean Cornwell
Royal Cortissoz
Allyn Cox
Gardner Cox
Frederic Crowninshield
Stephen Currier
Walter Damrosch
Frank Miles Day
Robert W. de Forest

William B. Dinsmoor
George E. Duckworth
James C. Egbert
Theodore N. Ely
Max Farrand
Barry Faulkner
James Earle Fraser
Leon Fraser
Daniel Chester French
Henry Clay Frick
A.M. Friend, Jr.
Cass Gilbert
Richard Watson Gilder
Phyllis W.G. Gordan
Jerome D. Greene
John Gregory
Eric Gugler
Philip Guston
Alfred E. Hamill
Charles B. Harding
David T. Harris
Fairfax Harrison
Wallace K. Harrison
Barklie McKee Henry
James Monroe Hewlett
Henry Lee Higginson
Gilbert Highet
Susan Morse Hilles
Arthur A. Houghton, Jr.
George Howe
Henry V. Hubbard
Lewis Iselin
Ellery S. James
Henry James
Pierre Jay
Allan C. Johnson
Harold F. Johnson
William H. Johnstone
Francis C. Jones
Francis Willey Kelsey
William Mitchell Kendall
George S. Koyl
C. Grant LaFarge
John LaFarge
Rensselaer W. Lee

J. Russell Lynes
Edward A. MacDowell
Clarence H. Mackay
Hermon Atkins MacNeil
James O. Mahoney
Oronzio Maldarelli
Peppino Mangravite
Paul Manship
Ezio Martinelli
George B. McClellan
Charles Follen McKim
William Rutherford Mead
Everett V. Meeks
Edward P. Mellon
Clarence W. Mendell
J. Irwin Miller
Francis D. Millet
Henry Allen Moe
Charles Moore
Douglas Stuart Moore
Edward C. Moore, Jr.
J. Pierpont Morgan
Robert Motherwell
H. Siddons Mowbray
Charles D. Norton
Irving S. Olds
Nathaniel A. Owings
John B. Pine
Charles A. Platt
William Platt
John Russell Pope
Chandler R. Post
Frederic B. Pratt
Richardson Pratt
James Sturgis Pray
Edward K. Rand
Michael Rapuano
Daniel Catton Rich
Edward Robinson

John C. Rolfe
Elihu Root
Theodore J. Roszak
Henry T. Rowell
Martin A. Ryerson
Augustus Saint-Gaudens
Eugene F. Savage
F. Augustus Schermerhorn
William T. Semple
Whitney H. Shepardson
Henry R. Shepley
Langdon S. Simons, Jr.
James Kellum Smith
Leo Sowerby
Walter P. Spalding
Eugene Speicher
Anson Phelps Stokes, Jr.
James Johnson Sweeney
Deems Taylor
Francis Henry Taylor
Myron C. Taylor
Randall Thompson
Landon K. Thorne, Jr.
William Thon
Jack Tworkov
Samuel Breck Parkman Trowbridge
Ferruccio Vitale
Peter Von Blanckenhagen
Henry Walters
H. Langford Warren
R. Gordon Wasson
Franklin C. Watkins
Sidney Waugh
Andrew F. West
William L. Westermann
Edgar I. Williams
Herbert E. Winlock
Janet E.C. Wurtzburger

AMERICAN ACADEMY IN ROME
CHARTER MEMBERS

Edwin A. Abbey
Samuel A.B. Abbott
Charles Francis Adams
John J. Albright
Edwin A. Alderman
James W. Alexander
James B. Angell
Charles T. Barney
Edward J. Berwind
Robert S. Brookings
Glenn Brown
Nicholas Murray Butler
John L. Cadwalader
Frank W. Chandler
Edward H. Coates

Thomas Jefferson Coolidge
Albert Dean Currier
Frank Miles Day
William E. Dodge
William F. Draper
William S. Eames
Charles W. Eliot
Theodore N. Ely
Marshall Field
Charles L. Freer
W.M.R. French
Lyman J. Gage
Elmer Ellsworth Garnsey
Richard Watson Gilder
Cass Gilbert

Daniel Coit Gilman
Arthur T. Hadley
Charles C. Harrison
Thomas Hastings
William H. Herriman
Charles L. Hutchinson
William M. Kendall
Charles Lanier
Frederick Layton
Austin W. Lord
George B. McClellan
Clarence H. Mackay
William C. McMillan
Frederic MacMonnies
S. Weir Mitchell
Charles Moore
Edwin D. Morgan
H. Siddons Mowbray
Frederick Law Olmsted
Francis L. Patton
Robert Swain Peabody

Henry Kirke Porter
George B. Post
Henry S. Pritchett
Frederick W. Rhinelander
James D. Richardson
Edward Robinson
Elihu Root
F. Augustus Schermerhorn
J.G. Schurman
Carl Schurz
James Speyer
James Stillman
Waldo Story
H.A.C. Taylor
Breck Trowbridge
J.Q.A. Ward
S.D. Warren
Henry White
Stanford White
Egerton L. Winthrop

AMERICAN ACADEMY IN ROME
ITALIAN COMMITTEE, 1994

Giorgio Armani
Luciano Berio
Boris Biancheri
Ilaria Borletti
Benedetta Craveri D'Aboville
Masolino d'Amico
Alessandro d'Urso
Giuseppe Galasso
Paolo Marzotto

Benedetta Origo
Piero Ottone
Carlo Perrone
Renzo Piano
Sergio Romano
Giulio and Giovanna Sacchett
Victor Uckmar
Paolo Viti

AMERICAN SCHOOL OF ARCHITECTURE IN ROME DIRECTORS

The American Academy in Rome was founded as the American School of Architecture in Rome in 1894. It assumed its present name in 1897 and, eight years later, merged with the American School of Classical Studies, which was established in Rome in 1895.

Austin W. Lord 1884-96
Will S. Aldrich 1896-97 (interim)
Samuel A.P. Abbott 1897-1903

H. Siddons Mowbray 1903-6
George W. Beck 1906-9
Frederic Crowninshield 1909-12

AMERICAN SCHOOL OF CLASSICAL STUDIES IN ROME DIRECTORS

William Gardner Hale 1895-96
Minton Warren 1896-98
Clement Lawrence Smith 1897-98

Tracy Peck 1898-99
Richard Norton 1899-1907
Jesse Benedict Carter 1907-13

AMERICAN ACADEMY IN ROME DIRECTORS

Jesse Benedict Carter 1913-17
Gorham Phillips Stevens 1917-32
James Monroe Hewlett 1932-34
Chester Holmes Aldrich 1935-40
William B. Dinsmoor 1944
    (acting, but unable to take up post)
Charles Rufus Morey 1945-46 (acting)
Laurance P. Roberts 1946-60
Richard Arthur Kimball 1960-65
Frank E. Brown 1965-69

Reginald Allen 1969-70 (acting)
Bartlett H. Hayes, Jr. 1970-73
Frank E. Brown 1973-74 (acting)
Henry A. Millon 1974-77
John D'Arms 1977-80
Sophie Consagra 1980-84
James Melchert 1984-88
Joseph Connors 1988-92
Caroline A. Bruzelius 1994-present

AMERICAN ACADEMY IN ROME
SCHOOL OF CLASSICAL STUDIES
PROFESSORS-IN-CHARGE

When the Academy merged with the American School of Classical Studies in 1913, it was organized into two schools, Fine Arts and Classical Studies, each under the supervision of a Professor-in-Charge, who was responsible for the school's program in consultation with the Director of the Academy.

This administrative arrangement continued until 1932, when the Director of the Academy began to assume the functions previously carried out by the Professor-in-Charge of the School of Fine Arts. Until 1940, when normal operations at the Academy were suspended because of the outbreak of World War II, the Professor-in-Charge of the School of Classical Studies was an annual appointment filled by an American classicist on sabbatical leave from another institution.

The Academy resumed its normal operations in 1947, and this period coincided with the beginning of the Academy's long association with excavations at Cosa in southern Etruria, where Professor Frank E. Brown had received permission from Italian authorities for an annual archaeological campaign. Brown was appointed the first post-war Professor-in-Charge that year. When he left the Academy in the fall of 1952 for a professorship at Yale University, Lily Ross Taylor of Bryn Mawr College, a Latinist and the only woman to be Professor-in-Charge, was appointed for a two-year period.

In 1971, the professorship was renamed the Andrew W. Mellon Professor-in-Charge of the School of Classical Studies. A list of Mellon appointments is supplied separately.

George L. Hendrickson 1913-14
Kirby Flower Smith 1914-15 (acting)
Henry Arthur Sanders 1915-16
Charles Upson Clark 1916-19
George L. Hendrickson 1919-20
Ralph Van Deman Magoffin 1920-21
George M. Whicher 1921-22
Tenney Frank 1922-25
Charles Rufus Morey 1925-26
William L. Westermann 1926-27
Dean Putnam Lockwood 1927-28
Henry Arthur Sanders 1928-31

Marbury Bladen Ogle 1931-34
Lily Ross Taylor 1934-35
Rodney Potter Robinson 1935-37
Mason Hammond 1937-39
Rhys Carpenter 1939-40
Frank E. Brown 1947-52
Lily Ross Taylor 1952-55
Mason Hammond 1955-57
Herbert Bloch 1957-59
T. Robert S. Broughton 1959-61
Henry Thompson Rowell 1961-63
Frank E. Brown 1963-76

AMERICAN ACADEMY IN ROME
SCHOOL OF CLASSICAL STUDIES
ANDREW W. MELLON PROFESSORS-IN-CHARGE

In 1919-20 the first Professor-in-Charge of the School of Classical Studies was appointed.
In 1974, the Andrew W. Mellon Foundation endowed the post.
Professor Frank E. Brown held the post when the name was changed to the
Andrew W. Mellon Professor-in-Charge of the School of Classical Studies in 1974.
Since that time, seven distinguished scholars have served as the Mellon Professor-in-Charge.
No appointment was made in 1976-77,1982-83 or 1992-93.

Frank E. Brown 1963-76
John D'Arms 1977-80
Lawrence Richardson, jr 1980-81
Lionel Casson 1981-82

Russell T. Scott 1984-88
Charles Babcock 1988-89
Michael C.J. Putnam 1989-91
Malcolm Bell III 1991-92, 1993-present

AMERICAN ACADEMY IN ROME
NATIONAL ENDOWMENT FOR THE HUMANITIES
SUMMER SEMINAR DIRECTORS

The National Endowment for the Humanities Summer Seminar provides college teachers
with an opportunity to meet with colleagues,
renew research interests, and prepare material for publication.
Seminars are held for six- to eight-week periods in Rome.

Lawrence T. Richardson, jr 1977
Lionel Casson 1978
Emeline Hill Richardson 1979
Frank E. Brown 1980
Robert Brentano 1983
Eleanor Windsor Leach 1986
David H. Wright 1987
Larissa Bonfante 1988
Eleanor Windsor Leach 1989

Phyllis Pray Bober 1990
Julia Haig Gaisser 1990
Richard Saller 1991
John Bodel 1991
John Pinto 1992
Dale Kinney 1993
Brigitta Lindros Wohl 1993
Elaine Gazda 1994
Miranda Marvin 1994

AMERICAN ACADEMY IN ROME
LIBRARIANS

Albert Van Buren 1908-25
Milton E. Lord 1926-30
Wyllis E. Wright 1930-33
Mahlon K. Schnacke 1933-38
Colonel Peter De Daehn 1938-39 (acting)
George Kenneth Boyce 1939-40

Colonel Peter De Daehn 1940-48, 1948-61 (acting)
Inez Longobardi 1961-75
Milton E. Lord 1971-72 (Librarian-in-Residence), 1975-76
Rogers Scudder 1977-83 (Dir. of the Library,
    a part-time post)
Lucilla Marino 1977-92
Christina Huemer 1992-present

AMERICAN ACADEMY IN ROME
STAFF, NEW YORK

Adele Chatfield-Taylor, Pres.
Wayne A. Linker, Exec.VP
Ludmila Schwarzenberg, Dir. of Development
Abraham Barretto, Receptionist-Administrative Asst.
Anibal Carrion, Finance Asst.
Karen Rose Gonon, Fellowships Coordinator
Buff Suzanne Kavelman, Dir. of Programs

Daniel Keefe, Assc. Dir. of Development
Lisa Kressbach, Centennial Coordinator
Jerry Max, Board Liaison-Public Information Officer
Marina Rodriguez, Program Asst.
Jeffery Rudell, Asst. to the Pres.
Curt Sharp, Dir. of Finance & Administration
Lily Shen, Development Asst.

AMERICAN ACADEMY IN ROME
STAFF, ROME

Caroline A. Bruzelius, Dir.
Malcolm Bell III, Andrew W. Mellon Prof.-in-Charge
Pina Pasquantonio, Asst. Dir. for Operations
Cristina Puglisi, Asst. Dir. for Properties
Caroline Howard, Events Coordinator
Marina Lella, Administrative Asst.
Daniela Prestandrea, Sec.
Karin Einaudi, Dir., *Fototeca Unione**
Richard Trythall, Music Liaison
Martha Boyden, Visual Arts Liaison

FINANCE OFFICE
Ulderico Imperatori, Dir. of Administration
Paola Amici, Cashier
Roberto La Gioia, Bookkeeper

LIBRARY STAFF
Christina Huemer, Librarian
Antonella Bucci, Assc. Librarian
Tina Mirra, Library Asst.
Antonio Palladino, Library Asst.
Paolo Imperatori, Library Asst.

GATE RECEPTION
Maurizio Alfano
Renzo Carissimi
Norman Roberson

BUILDINGS & MAINTENANCE
Giovanni Cimoroni, Superintendent
Mauro Abbatelli
Christoph dell'Ospedale

HOUSEKEEPING STAFF
Alfredo Cianfrocca
Rita Cherli
Claudia Tonetti
Mario Carboni
Fabrizio Lambiti

GROUNDS
Alessandra Vinciguerra, Superintendent of Grounds
Francesco Federici
Ciro Caponera
Luigi Cocozza
Marco Cusani
Tommaso Musa

*Fototeca Unione operates under a cooperative program sponsored by the *Unione Internazionale degli Istituti.*

THIS BOOK WAS DESIGNED AND TYPESET
AT ITALICA PRESS, NEW YORK, NY & WAS
SET IN ADOBE TRAJAN AND PALATINO.
TYPESETTING WAS COMPLETED ON
APRIL 10, 1995. IT WAS PRINTED
ON ACID-FREE GLADFELTER
PAPER BY MCNAUGHTON &
GUNN, LITHOGRAPHERS
ANN ARBOR, MI, USA.
DEO GRATIAS.

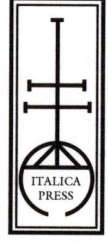